Jan. 31–Feb. 6, 2015
Shanghai, China

Association for Computing Machinery

Advancing Computing as a Science & Profession

WSDM'15

Proceedings of the Eighth ACM International Conference on Web Search and Data Mining

Sponsored by:
ACM SIGIR, ACM SIGKDD, ACM SIGMOD, and ACM SIGWEB

Supported by:
Fudan University, Shanghai Jiaotong University, Institute of Computing Technology, Baidu, Google, Microsoft, Huawei, Alibaba Group, Sogou, IBM Research, SpeechOcean, A9, Yahoo Labs, Yandex, Tencent, and Facebook

Association for
Computing Machinery

Advancing Computing as a Science & Profession

The Association for Computing Machinery
2 Penn Plaza, Suite 701
New York, New York 10121-0701

Notice to Past Authors of ACM-Published Articles
ACM intends to create a complete electronic archive of all articles and/or other material previously published by ACM. If you have written a work that has been previously published by ACM in any journal or conference proceedings prior to 1978, or any SIG Newsletter at any time, and you do NOT want this work to appear in the ACM Digital Library, please inform permissions@acm.org, stating the title of the work, the author(s), and where and when published.

ISBN: 978-1-4503-3317-7 (Digital)

ISBN: 978-1-4503-3509-6 (Print)

Additional copies may be ordered prepaid from:

ACM Order Department
PO Box 30777
New York, NY 10087-0777, USA

Phone: 1-800-342-6626 (USA and Canada)
+1-212-626-0500 (Global)
Fax: +1-212-944-1318
E-mail: acmhelp@acm.org
Hours of Operation: 8:30 am – 4:30 pm ET

Printed in the USA

Preface from General Chairs

On behalf of the organizing committee, we warmly welcome you to the 8th ACM International Conference on Web Search and Data Mining (WSDM 2015), held in Shanghai, China, from Jan. 31 to Feb. 6, 2015.

WSDM is one of the premier conferences covering research on search and data mining on the web. WSDM publishes original and high-quality papers related to search and data mining on the web, with an emphasis on practical yet principled novel approaches.

This is the first time WSDM is held in China, which has more than 500 million internet users and many internet companies, and more importantly, a very large number of researchers and engineers working in the field. We believe that WSDM 2015 in Shanghai, the largest city in China, will forge stronger ties between the local community and the international community of web search and data mining.

The technical program of WSDM 2015 includes 3 keynote speeches, 5 practice and experience talks, 39 technical papers, 4 workshops, 6 tutorials, a panel discussion, doctorial consortium, and a winter school. The 8th edition of WSDM continues the traditional activities of the conference and it also adds a new line-up to the conference, namely winter school. The goal of the winter school is to promote research on web search and data mining and introduce the fundamentals as well as recent advance of the field to people interested in it, particularly students.

We would like to express our sincere gratitude to the PC co-chairs, Evgeniy Gabrilovich and Jie Tang, who did a great job in selecting high quality papers, together with 28 senior program committee members, 220 program committee members, and 41 additional reviewers. We are also very grateful to all the other organizing committee members, including honorary chairs Guojie Li and Hong Mei, co-organizer Xuanjing Huang, advisor Irwin King, local chair Qi Zhang, winter school chairs Minyi Guo and Maosong Sun, best paper award committee chair Qiang Yang, workshop chairs Jiafeng Guo and Yoelle Maarek, tutorial chairs Eytan Adar and Min Zhang, doctorial consortium chairs Tie-Yan Liu and Cheng Xiang Zhai, Practice and Experience Track chairs Vanja Josifovski and Ying Li, finance chair Xiaolong Jin, sponsor chairs Pavel Serdyukov and Dou Shen, publication chair Jing Zhang, publicity chairs Chia Jung Lee and Xipeng Qiu, web master Junming Huang, and winter school organizer Long Zheng, whose effective work made all the events of the conference organize properly and smoothly. We would also like to thank the local organizing team members and the student volunteers from Fudan University, Shanghai Jiaotong University, and Institute of Computing Technology, who worked effectively to make the conference run smoothly and superbly.

We gratefully acknowledge the sponsorships from a number of companies, including Baidu, Google, Mcrosoft, Huawei, Alibaba, Sogou, IBM Research, SpeechOcean, A9, Tencent, Yahoo!, Yandex, Tencent, and Facebook. Special thanks also go to Fudan University, Shanghai Jiaotong University, and Institute of Computing Technology for their generous support.

Finally, we thank all the authors, presenters, and participants of the conference, and hope that you will enjoy the conference as well as the visit to Shanghai.

Xueqi Cheng
Chinese Academy of Sciences

Hang Li
Huawei Technologies

Preface by the Program Chairs

We are delighted to welcome you to the 8th ACM International Conference on Web Search and Data Mining (WSDM 2015), held in Shanghai, China, from Jan. 31 to Feb. 6, 2015. As in the previous years, WSDM continues to be a leading forum for reporting the latest research developments in the field. We are pleased to present here the proceedings of the conference.

We received a total of 238 submissions, out of which 39 were accepted for publication in the proceedings, thus reaching an acceptance rate of 16.4% (compared to 18% last year). The accepted papers are from 44 institutions in 16 countries, making WSDM a truly international forum. This year, oral presentation slots were allocated to all papers. Yet, in order to maintain the single track model that most attendees prefer, we introduced this year short 10-minute presentations. Out of the 39 accepted papers, 18 were assigned such shorter slots, while 21 were assigned longer 20-minute slots. The type of slot was chosen by the Senior PC members and Program Chairs, based on whether the topic and the content of the paper would appeal to a broad group of conference attendees. In addition to oral presentations, authors of all accepted papers were invited to present their work in an interactive poster session.

We would like to acknowledge the tremendous work of the 28 Senior Program Committee members, 220 Program Committee members, and 41 additional reviewers. The credit for creating a high quality technical program goes to them. To recognize the hard work of the best reviewers, which rarely makes it to the public limelight, this year we created Outstanding Reviewer Awards. 3 members of the Senior Program Committee and 27 members of the Program Committee received these awards.

The technical program this year featured keynotes by prominent researchers from the industry and academia, Lada Adamic (Facebook), Michael Franklin (UC Berkeley), and Thorsten Joachims (Cornell University). We thank the keynote speakers for their illuminating talks and for sharing their insights and wisdom with the conference attendees. The program also featured 5 Practice & Experience talks, which were introduced for the first time at WSDM'14. These were presented by Tushar Chandra (Google), Rong Jin (Baidu), Jure Leskovec (Stanford), Kaihua Zhu (Baidu), and Juchao Zhuo (Tencent). We thank the P&E speakers for taking the time off their busy schedules to attend the conference and share their experience in applying recent research results in industrial settings.

We would also like to thank the general chairs, Xueqi Cheng and Hang Li, who were wonderful partners in putting the conference program together, and provided us insightful guidance and advice all along the way.

Finally, we are grateful to the authors and attendees, who are the ones who make this conference possible, and have allowed WSDM to become a wonderful forum to advance Web research and become the premier ACM conference in the field.

We hope that you will find this program interesting and thought-provoking. Our goal was not only to give you the opportunity to share ideas with other researchers and practitioners from around the world, but also to foster new research and innovation in this fascinating Web era.

Evgeniy Gabrilovich
Google

Jie Tang
Tsinghua University

Table of Contents

Keynote Address 3

Session Chair: Jie Tang *(Tsinghua University)*

Session 7: User Modeling, Mobility, and Recommendations

Session Chair: Grace Hui Yang *(Georgetown University)*

Session 8: Practice & Experience Talks

Session Chair: Xuanjing Huang *(Fudan University)*

Session 9: Web Mining (2)

Session Chair: Fabrizio Silvestri *(Yahoo!)*

Tutorials

Workshop Summaries

Doctoral Consortium

WSDM 2015 Organization

Honorary Chairs: Guojie Li *(ICT, Chinese Academy of Sciences, China)*
Hong Mei *(Shanghai Jiaotong University, China)*

General Co-Chairs: Xueqi Cheng *(ICT, Chinese Academy of Sciences, China)*
Hang Li *(Huawei Technologies, China)*

Co-Organizer: Xuanjing Huang *(Fudan University, China)*

Advisor: Irwin King *(Chinese University of Hong Kong, China)*

Program Co-Chairs: Evgeniy Gabrilovich *(Google, USA)*
Jie Tang *(Tsinghua University, China)*

Local Chair: Qi Zhang *(Fudan University, China)*

Winter School Co-Chairs: Minyi Guo *(Shanghai Jiao Tong University, China)*
Maosong Sun *(Tsinghua University, China)*

Best Paper Award Committee Chair: Qiang Yang *(Hong Kong University of Science and Technology, China)*

Best Paper Committee Members: Hongyuan Zha *(Georgia Institute of Technology, USA)*
Yaron Singer *(Harvard University, USA)*
Dou Shen *(Baidu, China)*

Workshop Co-Chairs: Jiafeng Guo *(ICT, Chinese Academy of Sciences, China)*
Yoelle Maarek *(Yahoo, Israel)*

Tutorial Co-Chairs: Eytan Adar *(University of Michigan, USA)*
Min Zhang *(Tsinghua University, China)*

Doctorial Consortium Co-Chairs: Tie-Yan Liu *(Microsoft Research Asia, China)*
Cheng Xiang Zhai *(UIUC, USA)*

Practice and Experience Track Co-Chairs: Vanja Josifovski *(Google, USA)*
Ying Li *(EV Analysis Corporation, USA)*

Finance Chair: Xiaolong Jin *(ICT, Chinese Academy of Sciences, China)*

Sponsorship Co-Chairs: Pavel Serdyukov *(Yandex, Russian Federation)*
Dou Shen *(Baidu, China)*

Publicity Chairs: Chia-Jung Lee *(University of Massachusetts, USA)*
Xipeng Qiu *(Fudan University, China)*

Proceedings Chair: Jing Zhang *(Tsinghua University, China)*

Web Master: Junming Huang *(ICT, Chinese Academy of Sciences, China)*

Winter School Organizer Long Zheng *(Shanghai Jiaotong University, China)*

Steering Committee:
Ricardo Baeza-Yates *(Yahoo Labs, USA)*
Paolo Boldi *(University of Milano, Italy)*
Andrei Broder *(Google, USA)*
Brian D. Davison *(Lehigh University, USA)*
Nick Koudas *(University of Toronto, Canada)*
Hang Li *(Huawei Technologies, China)*
Bing Liu *(University of Illinois at Chicago, USA)*
Marc Najork *(Google, USA)*

Senior Program Committee:
Eytan Adar *(University of Michigan)*
Eugene Agichtein *(Emory University)*
Amr Ahmed *(Google Research)*
Wei Chen *(Microsoft Research Asia)*
Charles Clarke *(University of Waterloo)*
Nick Craswell *(Microsoft)*
Fernando Diaz *(Microsoft Research)*
Sreenivas Gollapudi *(Microsoft Research)*
Panos Ipeirotis *(New York University)*
Yehuda Koren *(Google)*
Oren Kurland *(Technion, Israel Institute of Technology)*
Wai Lam *(The Chinese University of Hong Kong)*
Ronny Lempel *(Outbrain)*
Ee-Peng Lim *(Singapore Management University)*
Huan Liu *(Arizona State University)*
Marc Najork *(Google)*
Alice Oh *(KAIST)*
Bo Pang *(Google)*
Jian Pei *(Simon Fraser University)*
Filip Radlinski *(Microsoft)*
Sunita Sarawagi *(IIT Bombay)*
Yaron Singer *(Harvard)*
Jimeng Sun *(IBM TJ Watson Research Center)*
Gerhard Weikum *(Max Planck Institute for Informatics)*
Ji-Rong Wen *(Renmin University of China)*
Xing Xie *(Microsoft Research Asia)*
Hui Xiong *(Rutgers University)*
Hongyuan Zha *(Georgia Institute of Technology)*

WSDM 2015 Program Committee & Additional Reviewers

Program Committee

Aris Anagnostopoulos
Jaime Arguello
Azin Ashkan
Javed Aslam
Yoram Bachrach
Ricardo Baeza-Yates
Sugato Basu
Luca Becchetti
Ron Bekkerman
Kedar Bellare
Andras A. Benczur
Michael Bendersky
Fabricio Benevenuto
Paul Bennett
Klaus Berberich
Bettina Berendt
Mikhail Bilenko
Roi Blanco
Paolo Boldi
Francesco Bonchi
Antoine Bordes
Alessandro Bozzon
Ulf Brefeld
Marc Bron
Rui Cai
Longbing Cao
David Carmel
Ben Carterette
Carlos Castillo
Ciro Cattuto
James Caverlee
Stefano Ceri
Raman Chandrasekar
Kevin Chang
Yi Chang
Duen Horng Polo Chau
Ling Chen
Kuan-Ta Chen
Roger Chiang
Freddy Chong
Tat Chua
Tat-Seng Chua
Kevyn Collins-Thompson
Peng Cui
Ido Dagan
Jeff Dalton
Cristian Danescu-Niculescu-Mizil
Van Dang
Dipanjan Das
Abhimanyu Das
Atish Das Sarma
Anirban Dasgupta
Brian Davison
Munmun de Choudhury
Gerard de Melo
Maarten de Rijke
Hongbo Deng
Danny Dickson
Ying Ding
Zhicheng Dou
Doug Downey
Gregory Druck
Alex Fabrikant
Paolo Ferragina
Dennis Fetterly
Norbert Fuhr
Ariel Fuxman
Wei Gao
Bin Gao
Yong Ge
Rayid Ghani
Aristides Gionis
Shantanu Godbole
Rahul Gupta
Maxim Gurevich
Ahmed Hassan
Qi He
Jingrui He
Djoerd Hiemstra
Jake Hofman
Katja Hofmann
Vagelis Hristidis
Xiaohua Tony Hu
Jimmy Huang
Xuanjing Huang
Bert Huang
Grace Hui Yang
Alejandro Jaimes
Adam Jatowt
Adam Kalai
Jaap Kamps
U Kang
Anitha Kannan
Tapas Kanungo
Yaron Kanza
Jussi Karlgren
Krishnaram Kenthapadi
Emre Kiciman
Aleksander Kolcz
Arnd Christian König
Donald Kossmann
Patty Kostkova
Alex Kotov
Dmitry Lagun
Mounia Lalmas
Silvio Lattanzi
Wang-Chien Lee
Joonseok Lee
Kristina Lerman
Cane Wing-Ki Leung
Juanzi Li
Lei Li
Tao Li
Ping Li
Edo Liberty
Chin-Yew Lin
Shou-De Lin
Jimmy Lin
Yiqun Liu
Qi Liu
Bing Liu
Yan Liu
Wei Liu
Lu Liu
Claudio Lucchese
Michael Lyu
Hao Ma
Craig Macdonald
Mark Manasse
Giovanni Manzini
Mausam
Julian Mcauley
Edgar Meij
Gabor Melli
Peter Mika
Vahab Mirrokni
Nina Mishra

Prasenjit Mitra
Marie-Francine Moens
Vincent Ng
Zaiqing Nie
Iadh Ounis
Andreas Paepcke
Themis Palpanas
Weike Pan
Alessandro Panconesi
Spiros Papadimitriou
Aditya Parameswaran
Dmitry Pechyony
Dan Pelleg
Fuchun Peng
Raffaele Perego
Benjamin Piwowarski
Simone Ponzetto
B. Aditya Prakash
Guo-Jun Qi
Tao Qin
Kira Radinsky
Karthik Raman
Justin Rao
Louiqa Raschid
Rajeev Rastogi
Sujith Ravi
Steffen Rendle
Tamas Sarlos
Lars Schmidt-Thieme
Hinrich Schuetze
John C. Shafer
James G. Shanahan
Huawei Shen
Dou Shen
Lei Shi
Stefan Siersdorfer
Fabrizio Silvestri
Yaron Singer
Sameer Singh
Ian Soboroff
Ruihua Song
Le Song
Ramakrishnan Srikant
Julia Stoyanovich
Zhong Su
Fabian M. Suchanek
Aixin Sun
Yizhou Sun
Jian-Tao Sun
Neel Sundaresan
Marcin Sydow
Idan Szpektor
Partha Talukdar
Katsumi Tanaka
Lu-An Tang
Evimaria Terzi
Hanghang Tong
Volker Tresp
Oren Tsur
Kuniaki Uehara
Sergei Vassilvitskii
Andrea Vattani
Liaoruo Wang
Chi Wang
Hongning Wang
Jun Wang
Ke Wang
Ingmar Weber
Wouter Weerkamp
Raymond Chi-Wing Wong
Lexing Xie
Tao Yang
Emine Yilmaz
Elad Yom-Tov
Nicholas Jing Yuan
Yisong Yue
Georgios Zervas
Peng Zhang
Xiangliang Zhang
Elena Zheleva
Vincent W. Zheng
Wenjun Zhou
Feida Zhu
Jiayu Zhu

Additional reviewers

Nima Anari
Yucheng Chen
Alessandro Epasto
Dora Erdos
Xuhui Fan
Esther Galbrun
Scott Gilpin
Behzad Golshan
Bo Han
Adam Jatowt
Chen Jin
Xin Jin
Jeon-Hyung Kang
Johannes Knopp
Rui Li
Zhen Liao
Ruoqian Liu
Ilya Markov
Charalampos Mavroforakis
Swapnil Mishra
Hua Ouyang
Makoto P.
André Panisson
Wen Pu
Marian-Andrei Rizoiu
Natali Ruchansky
Warren Schudy
Michael Schuhmacher
Suvash Sedhain
Mohit Sharma
Gyanit Singh
Greg Stoddard
Gabriele Tolomei
Manos Tsagkias
Lydia Weiland
Jianpeng Xu
Kunpeng Zhang
Yongfeng Zhang
Bolong Zheng
Mianwei Zhou
Yin Zhou

WSDM 2015 Sponsors & Supporters

Sponsors:

Supporters:

Platinum Supporters:

Gold Supporters:

HUAWEI

Alibaba Group 阿里巴巴集团

Silver Supporters:

Sogou 搜狗

IBM Research

speechocean 海天瑞声

Bronze Supporters:

A9

YAHOO! LABS

Yandex

Tencent 腾讯

facebook

Making Sense of Big Data with the Berkeley Data Analytics Stack

Michael Franklin
UC Berkeley
franklin@cs.berkeley.edu

ABSTRACT

The Berkeley AMPLab is creating a new approach to data analytics. Launching in early 2011, the lab aims to seamlessly integrate the three main resources available for making sense of data at scale: Algorithms (machine learning and statistical techniques), Machines (in the form of scalable clusters and elastic cloud computing), and People (both individually as analysts and in crowds). The lab is realizing its ideas through the development of a freely-available Open Source software stack called BDAS: the Berkeley Data Analytics Stack. In the four years the lab has been in operation, we've released major components of BDAS. Several of these components have gained significant traction in industry and elsewhere: the Mesos cluster resource manager, the Spark in-memory computation framework, and the Shark query processing system. BDAS features prominently in many industry discussions of the future of the Big Data analytics ecosystem – a rare degree of impact for an ongoing academic project.

Given this initial success, the lab is continuing on its research path, moving "up the stack" to better integrate and support advanced analytics and to make people a full-fledged resource for making sense of data. In this talk, I'll first outline the motivation and insights behind our research approach and describe how we have organized to address the cross-disciplinary nature of Big Data challenges. I will then describe the current state of BDAS with an emphasis on our newest efforts, including some or all of: the GraphX graph processing system, the Velox and MLBase machine learning platforms, and the SampleClean framework for hybrid human/computer data cleaning. Finally I will present our current views of how all the pieces will fit together to form a system that can adaptively bring the right resources to bear on a given data-driven question to meet time, cost and quality requirements throughout the analytics lifecycle.

Categories and Subject Descriptors

E.0 [General]

Keyword

Big Data

WSDM'15, February 2–6, 2015, Shanghai, China.
ACM 978-1-4503-3317-7/15/02.
http://dx.doi.org/10.1145/2684822.2685326

BIO

Michael Franklin is the Thomas M. Siebel Professor of Computer Science and Chair of the Computer Science Division at the University of California, Berkeley. He has over 30 years of experience in the database, data analytics, and data management fields as a researcher, lab director, faculty member, entrepreneur, and software developer. Prof. Franklin is also the Director of the Algorithms, Machines, and People Laboratory (AMPLab) at UC Berkeley. The AMPLab currently works with 23 industrial sponsors including founding sponsors Amazon Web Services, Google, and SAP, and received a National Science Foundation CISE "Expeditions in Computing" award, announced as part of the White House Big Data research initiative in March 2012. AMPLab is well-known for creating a number of popular systems in the Open Source Big Data ecosystem including Spark, Mesos, Shark, GraphX and MLlib, all parts of the Berkeley Data Analytics Stack (BDAS). Prof. Franklin is also a co-PI and Executive Committee member for the Berkeley Institute for Data Science, part of a multi-campus initiative to advance Data Science Environments. He is an ACM Fellow, a two-time winner of the ACM SIGMOD "Test of Time" award, and recipient of the outstanding Advisor Award from the Computer Science Graduate Student Association at Berkeley..

New Directions in Recommender Systems

Jure Leskovec
Stanford Unversity
jure@cs.stanford.edu

ABSTRACT

Recommender systems are an integral part of how we experience the Web today and they have become so ubiquitous that we do not even notice them anymore. However, today's recommender systems mostly treat items they recommend as black boxes and primarily focus on extracting correlations and co-counts from user behavior data. In this talk I argue that next generation recommender systems will require deep understanding of items being recommended as well as modeling the relationships between those items. I will present examples how auxiliary data about items (descriptions, reviews, product specifications) can be used to improve recommendations.

Categories and Subject Descriptors

H.4.0 Information Systems, INFORMATION SYSTEMS APPLICATIONS: General

Keyword

Recommendation system

WSDM'15, February 2–6, 2015, Shanghai, China.
ACM 978-1-4503-3317-7/15/02.
http://dx.doi.org/10.1145/2684822.2697044

Big Data: New Paradigm or "Sound and Fury, Signifying Nothing"?

Panel Organizer: Andrei Broder*
Google

Michael Franklin
University of California, Berkeley

Eric Xing
Carnegie Mellon University

Lada Adamic
Facebook

Maarten de Rijke
University of Amsterdam

Kai Yu
Baidu

PANEL OVERVIEW

The Gartner's 2014 Hype Cycle released last August moves Big Data technology from the Peak of Inflated Expectations to the beginning of the Trough of Disillusionment when interest starts to wane as reality does not live up to previous promises. As the hype is starting to dissipate it is worth asking what Big Data (however defined) means from a scientific perspective: Did the emergence of gigantic corpora exposed the limits of classical information retrieval and data mining and led to new concepts and challenges, the way say, the study of electromagnetism showed the limits of Newtonian mechanics and led to Relativity Theory, or is it all just "sound and fury, signifying nothing", simply a matter of scaling up well understood technologies? To answer this question, we have assembled a distinguished panel of eminent scientists, from both Industry and Academia: Lada Adamic (Facebook), Michael Franklin (University of California at Berkeley), Maarten de Rijke (University of Amsterdam), Eric Xing (Carnegie Mellon University), and Kai Yu (Baidu) will share their point of view and take questions from the moderator and the audience.

Categories and Subject Descriptors

A.0 General Literature, GENERAL: Conference proceedings; E.0 Data, GENERAL

Keyword: big data

Moderator's email: broder@google.com

WSDM'15, February 2–6, 2015, Shanghai, China.
ACM 978-1-4503-3317-7/15/02.
http://dx.doi.org/10.1145/2684822.2697027

Andrei Broder is a Google Distinguished Scientist. From 2005 to 2012 he was a Fellow and VP for Computational Advertising at Yahoo!. Previous positions include Distinguished Engineer at IBM and VP for Research and Chief Scientist at AltaVista. Broder has authored more than a hundred papers and was awarded more than forty US patents. His current research interests are centered on personalization, computational advertising, web search, context-driven information supply, and randomized algorithms. He is a member of the US National Academy of Engineering and a Fellow of ACM and of IEEE. Other honors include the ACM Paris Kanellakis Theory and Practice Award and a PhD Honoris Causa from the Technion.

Lada Adamic leads the Product Science group within Facebook's Data Science Team. She is also an adjunct associate professor at the University of Michigan's School of Information and Center for the Study of Complex Systems. Her research interests center on information dynamics in networks: how information diffuses, how it can be found, and how it influences the evolution of a network's structure. Her projects have included identifying expertise in online question and answer forums, studying the dynamics of viral marketing, and characterizing the structural and communication patterns in online social media. She has received an NSF CAREER award, a University of Michigan Henry Russell award, the 2012 Lagrange Prize in Complex Systems.

Michael Franklin is the Thomas M. Siebel Professor of Computer Science and Chair of the Computer Science Division at the University of California, Berkeley. He has over 30 years of experience in the database, data analytics, and data management fields as a researcher, lab director, faculty member, entrepreneur, and software developer. Prof. Franklin is also the Director of the Algorithms, Machines, and People

Laboratory (AMPLab) at UC Berkeley. The AMPLab currently works with 23 industrial sponsors including founding sponsors Amazon Web Services, Google, and SAP, and received a National Science Foundation CISE "Expeditions in Computing" award, announced as part of the White House Big Data research initiative in March 2012. AMPLab is well-known for creating a number of popular systems in the Open Source Big Data ecosystem including Spark, Mesos, Shark, GraphX and MLlib, all parts of the Berkeley Data Analytics Stack (BDAS). Prof. Franklin is also a co-PI and Executive Committee member for the Berkeley Institute for Data Science, part of a multi-campus initiative to advance Data Science Environments. He is an ACM Fellow, a two-time winner of the ACM SIGMOD "Test of Time" award, and recipient of the outstanding Advisor Award from the Computer Science Graduate Student Association at Berkeley.

Maarten de Rijke is full professor of Information Processing and Internet in the Informatics Institute at the University of Amsterdam. He holds MSc degrees in Philosophy and Mathematics (both cum laude), and a PhD in Theoretical Computer Science. He worked as a postdoc at CWI, before becoming a Warwick Research Fellow at the University of Warwick, UK. He joined the University of Amsterdam in 1998, and was appointed full professor in 2004. De Rijke leads the Information and Language Processing Systems group, one of the world's leading academic research groups in information retrieval. During the most recent computer science research assessment exercise, the group achieved maximal scores on all dimensions. His research focus is on intelligent information access, with projects on self-learning search engines, semantic search, and social media analytics.

Dr. Eric Xing is a professor in the School of Computer Science at Carnegie Mellon University. His principal research interests lie in the development of machine learning and statistical methodology, and large-scale computational system and architecture, for solving problems involving automated learning, reasoning, and decision-making in high-dimensional, multimodal, and dynamic possible worlds in complex systems. Professor Xing received a Ph.D. in Molecular Biology from Rutgers University, and another Ph.D. in Computer Science from UC Berkeley. His current work involves, 1) foundations of statistical learning, including theory and algorithms for estimating time/space varying-coefficient models, sparse structured input/output models, and nonparametric Bayesian models; 2) framework for parallel machine learning on big data with big model in distributed systems or in the cloud; 3) computational and statistical analysis of gene regulation, genetic variation, and disease associations; and 4) application of statistical learning in social networks, data mining, and vision. Professor Xing has published over 200 peer-reviewed papers, and is an associate editor of the Journal of the American Statistical Association, Annals of Applied Statistics, the IEEE Transactions of Pattern Analysis and Machine Intelligence, the PLoS Journal of Computational Biology, and an Action Editor of the Machine Learning journal, and the Journal of Machine Learning Research. He is a member of the DARPA Information Science and Technology (ISAT) Advisory Group, a recipient of the NSF Career Award, the Alfred P. Sloan Research Fellowship, the United States Air Force Young Investigator Award, and the IBM Open Collaborative Research Faculty Award.

Dr. Kai Yu is Head of Institute of Deep Learning (IDL) at Baidu , and also Senior Engineering Director , in charge of Baidu Image Search. Dr. Yu has published a number of papers with over 7000 citations. He received many awards including the Best Paper Runner-up Award of ICML-2013, the first prize of PASCAL VOC 2009, and the first prize of ImageNet competition 2010. In 2013 and 2014, his team has won three Baidu Highest Achievement Awards, for having made significant contributions to speech recognition, computer vision, online ads, and web search ranking. Since 2014, he has led a series of high-impact projects, including Baidu Brain, BaiduEye, Autonomous Driving, DuBike etc. Dr. Yu is elected to China "Top 1000 Talents", a prestigious group of technology leaders of the country. He is an Adjunct Professor of Nanjing University, Beijing University of Posts and Telecommunications, and Institute of Computing Technology, Chinese Academy of Sciences. Before joining Baidu, he worked at Microsoft, Siemens, NEC and was an Adjunct Faculty at Department of Computer Sciences at Stanford University. He received his B.Sc and M.Sc degree from Nanjing University and his Ph.D. degree from University of Munich.

Delayed-Dynamic-Selective (DDS) Prediction for Reducing Extreme Tail Latency in Web Search

Saehoon Kim*
POSTECH

Yuxiong He
Microsoft Research

Seung-won Hwang
POSTECH

Sameh Elnikety
Microsoft Research

Seungjin Choi
POSTECH

ABSTRACT

A commercial web search engine shards its index among many servers, and therefore the response time of a search query is dominated by the slowest server that processes the query. Prior approaches target improving responsiveness by reducing the tail latency of an individual search server. They predict query execution time, and if a query is predicted to be long-running, it runs in parallel, otherwise it runs sequentially. These approaches are, however, not accurate enough for reducing a high tail latency when responses are aggregated from many servers because this requires each server to reduce a substantially higher tail latency (e.g., the 99.99th-percentile), which we call extreme tail latency.

We propose a prediction framework to reduce the extreme tail latency of search servers. The framework has a unique set of characteristics to predict long-running queries with high recall and improved precision. Specifically, prediction is delayed by a short duration to allow many short-running queries to complete without parallelization, and to allow the predictor to collect a set of dynamic features using runtime information. These features estimate query execution time with high accuracy. We also use them to estimate the prediction errors to override an uncertain prediction by selectively accelerating the query for a higher recall.

We evaluate the proposed prediction framework to improve search engine performance in two scenarios using a simulation study: (1) query parallelization on a multicore processor, and (2) query scheduling on a heterogeneous processor. The results show that, for both scenarios, the proposed framework is effective in reducing the extreme tail latency compared to a start-of-the-art predictor because of its higher recall, and it improves server throughput by more than 70% because of its improved precision.

Categories and Subject Descriptors

H.3.3 [**Information Search and Retrieval**]: Search process

*This work was done during Microsoft Research internship.

WSDM'15, February 2–6, 2015, Shanghai, China.

http://dx.doi.org/10.1145/2684822.2685289.

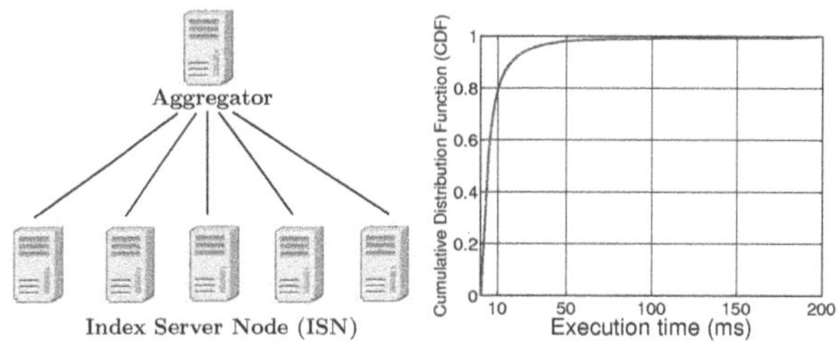

(a) Search architecture (b) Execution time CDF

Figure 1: (a) Web search engine architecture. (b) Execution time distribution on Bing ISN.

Keywords

Tail Latency; Prediction; Parallelization; Search Engine

1. INTRODUCTION

The primary objective for a web search engine is to deliver relevant web documents to its users with consistently low response times. A long response time degrades user satisfaction and reduces revenues [26]. In particular, commercial search engines optimize for reducing the high-percentile (*e.g.,* the 99th-percentile) response time, which is called the tail latency. A short tail latency offers consistently fast responses to users, which is more important than the mean response time in this context [9].

A web search engine partitions its large index across many index server nodes (ISN). A search query runs concurrently on the ISNs: Each ISN searches for best matches on its local partition, and the results are aggregated, forming the query results. In such a partition-aggregate scheme as depicted in Figure 1(a), the response time at the aggregator is determined by the slowest ISN machine: A long latency at any ISN manifests as a slow query response [9].

To reduce the aggregator tail latency, we need to reduce a much higher tail at each ISN. For example, assuming the aggregator has 40 ISNs, if we want to process 99% of user queries within 120 ms, then each ISN needs to reply within 120 ms with probability around 0.9999. In other words, for the aggregator to have 120 ms at the 99th-percentile response time, the response time of each ISN must be at most 120 ms at the 99.99th-percentile. This motivates our goal of taming the extreme tail latency, namely very high-percentile (e.g., 99.99th-percentile) latency, at ISNs.

Reducing the extreme tail latency is challenging because the workload exhibits high variability. In Figure 1(b), we measure query execution time using a production log of user queries played on an ISN running a commercial web search engine, Microsoft Bing. We find that most queries are short-running: More than 80% take less than 10 ms. However, few queries are long-running taking more than 200 ms. In particular, the average execution time is 9.1 ms while the 99.99th-percentile execution time is 202 ms, which is 22 times the average. Therefore, to reduce extreme tail latency, it is important to accelerate almost all long-running queries. A long-running query that is not accelerated appears in that tail latency. For a target of 120 ms at the 99.99th-percentile response time, for every 10,000 queries we can miss only one long-running query!

There are a few proposals to accelerate query processing by parallelization [15]. However, it is too expensive to parallelize all queries: Executing a query in parallel consumes more resources than sequential execution, motivating the need to predict the long-running queries. Recent approaches [16, 20] predict query execution time using query and index features. The prediction is used to process long-running queries in parallel and to run short-running queries sequentially [16]. However, these approaches cannot meet our target accuracy — according to our workload, to reduce the 99.99th-percentile latency, we need a predictor with target recall of 98.9% to correctly identify most of the long-running queries, and with good precision to reduce the overhead of accelerating the short-running queries misidentified as long-running.

In this paper we develop and evaluate a prediction framework for reducing the extreme tail latency. The prediction framework identifies the long-running queries, and achieves high recall with good precision by delaying prediction to exploit runtime information. First, since most queries are short-running, delaying prediction (e.g., by 10 ms) enables many short-running queries complete without ineffective acceleration. Second, and more importantly, as the query executes during this short duration, we observe the runtime behavior and identify a new set of features, which we call dynamic features, to improve prediction accuracy of estimated time. Finally, we predict estimated prediction error [4] to override an uncertain prediction by selectively accelerating the query for a higher recall.

We call our predictor *DDS*, which stands for **D**elayed, **D**ynamic, and **S**elective prediction. The framework has three characteristics: (1) Delaying the prediction, (2) exploiting Dynamic features, and (3) Selectively accelerating a query based on its predicted execution time and estimated prediction error. DDS achieves our target recall of 98.9%, while improving precision by 957% compared to a state-of-the-art predictor [16] that uses static features only.

We evaluate *DDS* in two scenarios and use simulation to assess its benefits:

- *Query parallelization on a multicore server.* We parallelize long-running queries to reduce tail latency and run short-running queries sequentially to avoid their parallelization overhead.

- *Query scheduling on a heterogeneous server.* We exploit the emerging heterogeneous processor design which combines energy efficient slow cores with high-performance fast cores. We execute the long-running queries on fast cores to reduce the tail latency and execute short-running queries on slow cores to improve throughput.

Our experiments compare *DDS* with two baselines: (1) a no-prediction baseline, which accelerates all queries in order to meet the desired latency, and (2) a state-of-the-art predictor, which we call *S*, that uses static features [16].

Our results show that, for both scenarios, *DDS* reduces tail latency for a wide range of load at the ISN and at the aggregator, while the baselines fail to meet the latency target at moderate and heavy load. To meet the desired 99.99th-percentile response time of 120 ms, the no-prediction approach needs to accelerate all queries, and *S* accelerates 83.5% of queries. In contrast, *DDS* accelerates only 7.9% of all queries because of its improved precision. As *DDS* significantly reduces the number of queries to accelerate, sparing their corresponding overhead, it increases system throughput by 74% from less than 390 QPS (queries per second) of baselines to more than 680 QPS, potentially saving more than 43% of servers required to process the same workload. As commercial search engines use thousands of servers, *DDS* presents an opportunity for significant server cost savings.

The main contributions of this paper are the following:

- We propose *DDS*, a prediction framework that exploits delayed prediction, dynamic query features, and selective acceleration (Section 3).

- We train and evaluate *DDS* using production query log and web index. At the target 98.9% recall, it shows 957% improvement in precision compared with the prior work using static features (Section 4).

- We assess the benefits of using *DDS* in a simulation study of two query acceleration techniques: query parallelization on a multicore server and query scheduling on a heterogeneous server. *DDS* effectively reduces extreme tail latency at moderate and heavy server load, and significantly increases throughput by 74% compared to prior work (Section 5).

2. BACKGROUND

In this section, we briefly describe the architecture and query processing of a web search engine.

Modern search engines, including Bing, consist of aggregators and multiple index server nodes (ISNs) as shown in Figure 1(a). Billions of documents are partitioned into hundreds of disjoint subsets, each of which is served by a single ISN. For higher efficiency, the subset of documents are constructed as an inverted index, where documents are sorted using a static score such as PageRank. When query is received, an aggregator broadcasts it to multiple ISNs if the results are not cached. A query traverses posting lists of each ISN to match documents, and computes the relevance scores of the matched documents. The aggregator collects the top-k documents for each ISN, and re-ranks the returned documents for the final list [6]. For the entire query processing, the main index of Bing follows a Document-at-a-time (DAAT) [5] strategy, where all posting lists are intersected for a multi-term query and a matched document is scored before exploring the next matched document.

The ISN is a multi-threaded server, capable of processing several queries concurrently for higher efficiency. Queries sent from the aggregator first join the waiting queue of the

Table 1: Static features in previous work [16].

Category	Feature	Description
term feature	IDF	inverse document frequency
query feature	English	Query in English or not (binary)
	NumAugTerm	# augmented requirements
	Complexity	Degree of query complexity
	RelaxCount	Relax count applied or not (binary)
	NumBefore	# terms in the original query
	NumAfter	# terms after query rewriting

Table 2: Dynamic features.

Feature name	Short Description
MaxDynScore	Maximum of dynamic scores
MinDynScore	Minimum of dynamic scores
SumDynScore	Summation of dynamic scores
AvgDynScore	Average of dynamic scores
VarDynScore	Variance of dynamic scores
NumCurrentMatchDoc	# matched documents
NumEstMatchDoc	Estimated # matched documents
FirstMatchingTime	First match time
AvgMatchingTime	Averaging match time

ISN. When a worker thread becomes available, it starts executing a query from the head of the waiting queue. The query response time consists of waiting time and execution time. The waiting time is the amount of time a query spends in the waiting queue before query processing, which is highly related to system load (i.e., the number of queries per seconds). Execution time is the amount of time to find the top-k relevant documents for a query, which is a major portion of response time unless system load is very high.

Dynamic pruning strategies [5, 29] have been proposed to reduce query processing time. While traversing the posting lists, the matched documents are dynamically scored by a complex scoring function with inputs such as the document static score, the number of query terms occurred in a document, location of query, among others. Since this score is obtainable only when a query is executed, we call it *dynamic score*. To terminate query processing, the dynamic score of future matches is estimated. If the estimated dynamic score is sufficiently low compared to the current best documents, the future matches are unlikely to supersede the current matches. Query processing is early-terminated and the top-k matched documents are sent to the aggregator.

3. PREDICTION FRAMEWORK

This section develops a prediction framework, designed to accurately identify long-running queries to reduce tail latency. To meet the goal, we first derive the accuracy requirements of the predictor. We next introduce the *DDS* prediction framework, with delayed, dynamic, and selective prediction, and discuss the design choices.

3.1 Requirements

We derive the accuracy and performance requirements to meet the 99.99th target percentile response time, in terms of precision and recall defined as follows:

$$\text{precision} = \frac{|A \cap P|}{|P|} \quad \text{recall} = \frac{|A \cap P|}{|A|}, \qquad (1)$$

where A is a set of true long-running queries, P is a set of predicted long-running queries. Precision means how many queries are predicted as long-running and recall means how many long-running queries are correctly identified. We define a query as true long-running if its execution time is greater than a given value T (e.g., $T = 100$ ms), which is determined by SLA of the web search engine. To meet a tail latency of 120 ms, we choose $T = 100$ ms, i.e., we want to accelerate queries with execution time greater than 100 ms. We do not choose $T = 120$ ms because queries can incur waiting times, which also increase query latency.

We illustrate how to compute the recall target by analyzing the query workload. Using Bing query log, we find that 0.92% of queries are long-running (their execution time is greater than $T = 100$). Therefore, recall should be at least 98.9%, because the number of the remaining long-running queries (misidentified as short-running) is $0.0092 * (1 - 0.989) = 0.0001$ of all queries, which is acceptable to optimize the 99.99th target percentile latency.

At this recall target, precision should stay high because the falsely predicted long-running queries consume unnecessary resources for acceleration. Improving precision is important: We show that under heavy load, we cannot reduce the tail latency without improved precision in Section 4.2.3 and 5.

Finally, the overhead involved in performing prediction must be small. Prediction adds additional work to query execution, increasing query response time. Since the average execution time of queries whose execution time is larger than 10 ms is 28 ms, adding 5% of it for prediction is a relatively small cost for the potential benefits. Here, we set the goal of less than 1.4 ms to predict query execution time.

3.2 Prior Work and its Limitation

We first review state-of-the-art predictor [16], which we call S as it uses **S**tatic features for prediction.

Static features are essentially statistics on terms and queries, based on which we can estimate the number of documents to be matched while applying early termination algorithms [5, 29]. Table 1 lists "memory-efficient" features (called "cheap features") to meet accuracy requirement without requiring a large memory footprint. Specifically, term feature, such as IDF score, is computed per query term, which is then combined into a single feature. Query features represent the complexity of queries, incurred from query personalization, relaxation, and rewriting.

We argue that S cannot meet the desired accuracy of reducing the extreme tail latency. In particular, S achieves a recall of 69.5% and precision of 80.3%. This recall is not high enough to reduce the 99.99th-percentile latency, which demands a recall of 98.9%.

It is possible for S to trade precision for higher recall. More precisely, S can predict a query as long-running if its predicted time is larger than a time threshold α. Lowering the time threshold α allows more queries to be identified as long-running queries, improving recall but reducing precision. When the time threshold is small enough (i.e., $\alpha = 2.5$ ms) for S to meet a recall of 98.9%, its precision drops to 1.1% only, which means we need to accelerate 83.5% of total queries, introducing significant overhead with much higher query latencies.

Our work investigates three techniques to improve the accuracy of the predictor significantly to reduce the 99.99th-percentile latency.

3.3 Delayed Prediction

We first propose *delayed prediction*, in which a query is executed for a short period of time D (which we call D delay threshold), then the prediction is made.

Delayed prediction exploits the workload characteristics and introduces three advantages: (1) The majority of the short-running queries are terminated within a very short time. From our query log, 80% of queries take less than 10 ms. These short-running queries would not be falsely identified as long-running queries, avoiding the overhead of accelerating them. (2) It reduces the runtime overhead of predicting those short-running queries, since these queries would terminate before making prediction. (3) With the short execution period, we can extract important runtime information on query processing, allowing us to employ dynamic features.

We determine the delay threshold D empirically. Longer delay allows most of the short-running queries to complete without prediction overhead and permits more time to collect dynamic signals, but prevents accelerating long-running queries early on. We evaluate several choices for D in a sensitivity study (Section 5.1.5), and choose $D = 10$ ms, which gives the best performance.

3.4 Dynamic Features

As for the second technique, we propose *DD* (for **D**elayed **D**ynamic prediction), employing dynamic features to enhance prediction accuracy. These dynamic features represent the runtime information of a query, which are collected after we run a query for a little while.

These dynamic features capture the following crucial information for prediction, unavailable from static features.

- First, some information is unknown at indexing time but affects query execution. Examples include the dynamic context of queries, including dynamic scores for pruning, location or language preference.

- Second, some information is too large to be indexed and stored in main memory. For example, "French fries recipe" appear frequently together such that aggregating the individual term features is inaccurate. Indexing such correlation using a trigram index would improve accuracy, their size is larger by orders of magnitude than individual term index and typically remains unindexed. Such correlation can be captured at runtime after processing the query for a short duration.

We focus on two categories of runtime information: matched documents and dynamic scores. Intuitively, when the number of matched documents is high on an early segment of the inverted index, we expect many matches in the entire index, indicating a long query. However, this indicator alone is not sufficient because a query with potentially many matches may terminate early without ranking all matches [5, 29] (or the queries without many matches may run long without such termination). We thus employ the information on dynamic scores: if scoring distribution shows high dynamic scores and small variance, the query is likely to terminate early, leading to shorter execution time. Inspired by these two complementary factors, we identify the following nine novel dynamic features as shown in Table 2.

- *DynScore*: statistics of the dynamic score distribution observed runtime (e.g., minimum, maximum, average, variance, and summation.) For example, *MaxDynScore* is the maximum of scores of the ranked documents at duration D.

- *NumCurrentMatchDoc*: the number of matched documents after D.

- *NumEstMatchDoc*: the estimation of total number of the matched documents when query processing is done. We adopt a simple linear estimate using:

$$\frac{\#\text{current matched documents}}{\#\text{processed documents}} \times \#\text{ total documents},$$

  where *# total documents* is the total number of documents managed by the ISN, which is in the scale of hundreds of million in our evaluation.

- *MatchingTime*: the time to find the next matched document. We use two features *FirstMatchingTime* and *AvgMatchingTime* to represent *MatchingTime* of the first document and its average respectively.

While dynamic features bring significant accuracy improvements, they are also inexpensive to obtain. Unlike some static features that may increase server memory footprint and index size, the dynamic features are byproducts of query processing and do not require main memory, which is scarce resource at index servers.

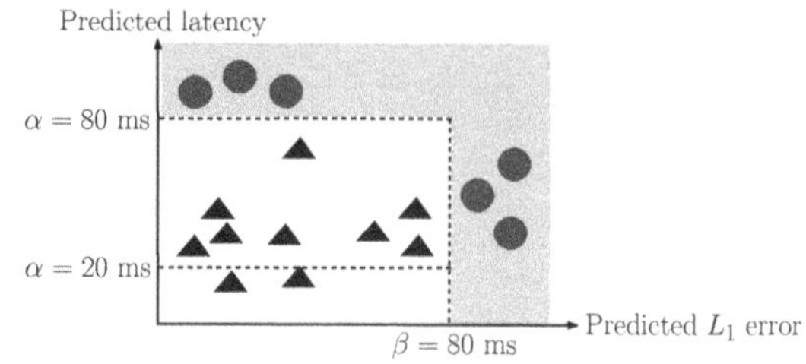

Figure 2: Illustration of selective prediction, where a red circle means a long-running query and a black triangle means a short-running query.

3.5 Selective Prediction

As for the third technique, we propose *DDS* (for **D**elayed, **D**ynamic, and **S**elective prediction), which exploits both execution time prediction and error estimation to selectively accelerate queries.

To motivate selective prediction, Figure 2 illustrates the problem of existing prediction. In this figure, existing approach estimates predicted latency (y-axis) then accelerates queries predicted to take longer than time threshold α. To identify all long-running queries (marked by circles), α should be set to 20 ms, which mis-predicts many short-running queries (marked by triangles) as long-running, causing low precision. In particular, for the queries with small prediction error, reducing time threshold can effectively improve recall with little trade-off on precision. However, we find that some mispredicted true long-running queries (with large prediction error) compromise precision by introducing many false positives.

For this reason, we extend our prediction framework to estimate not only latency but prediction error. More precisely, we introduce an error threshold β and accelerate the queries with predicted error greater than β. Back in our running example in Figure 2, this enables us to accelerate two types of queries: (1) the queries with estimated latency greater than time threshold $\alpha = 80$ ms and (2) the queries with estimated error greater than error threshold $\beta = 80$ ms. The insight of selective prediction is that we keep time threshold high based on prediction with low error, and accelerate the queries with high predicted errors, so we will not miss those long-running queries with large uncertainty on its predicted execution time.

More specifically, we build two regressors, one of which is for predicting latency and another for regression error. The training set for the first regressor, f_1, is constructed as $D = \{\boldsymbol{x}_i, y_i\}_{i=1}^n$, where $\boldsymbol{x}_i$ is the i-th covariate and y_i is the i-th response variable. We use the covariate as static with dynamic features, and the response variable as execution time. The training set for the second regressor, f_2, is constructed by a validation set consisting of $V = \{\boldsymbol{x}_i, y_i^{err} = |f_1(\boldsymbol{x}_i) - y_i|\}_{i=1}^m$.

A query is determined as a long-running query if the predicted execution time is larger than α or the predicted L_1 error is larger than β. As shown in Figure 2, a query is decided as long-running if it is in the blue shaded region.

Note that we adopt boosted regressor tree [12] to identify long-running queries instead of a classifier (such as boosted classification tree [12] or SVM), because the time threshold T of defining long-running queries can be varied and the accuracy of classifier is similar with the one of regressor.

3.6 Summary

To reduce 99.99th-percentile response time of web queries, the predictor needs to achieve very high recall of 98.9% with good precision. To meet these requirements, we propose three important techniques: (1) delayed prediction to remove unnecessary short-running queries, (2) dynamic features to achieve higher accuracy, and (3) selective prediction that combines predicted execution time with the estimated prediction error. We empirically evaluate our framework in Section 4, and we show how to leverage the framework to accelerate long-running queries in Section 5.

4. EXPERIMENTS

This section presents experimental results to validate the accuracy and effectiveness of the proposed framework. We conduct our evaluation using production index and query log. Our results show the benefits of delayed prediction, dynamic features and selective prediction. We observe 957% improvement in precision at the desired 98.9% recall compared with the prior work.

4.1 Experimental Setup

We first describe the setting for evaluation. We play 69,010 queries from a production query log at 100 QPS (queries per second) and measure their execution time. We extract static and dynamic features of these queries to construct a training and test set. In particular, we instrument the code of query processing to log all dynamic scores of the ranked documents, which we use to extract dynamic features. For the static features, we follow the same procedure introduced in [16]. To eliminate outliers, we execute the same query three times and plot its minimum. We compare *DDS* with *S*:

- *S* implements a predictor [16] using the static features discussed in Section 3.2. This is our baseline.

Table 3: Top-10 feature importance of static + dynamic features.

Feature	Importance
NumEstMatchDoc	1
MinDynScore	0.7075
MinIDF	0.2767
VarIDF	0.2730
MaxDynScore	0.2662
SumIDF	0.2076
VarDynScore	0.1982
AvgDynScore	0.1831
Complexity	0.1791
NumBefore	0.1762

- *Dynamic-Delayed-Selective (DDS)* accelerates a query when either its predicted latency $\geq$ the time threshold α or its predicted L_1 error $\geq$ the error threshold β.

We also introduce two intermediate steps from *S* to *DDS*, which are used to illustrate the individual contribution of each technique: delayed prediction, dynamic features, and selective prediction.

- *Static-Delayed (SD)* uses the same static features as in *S*, but makes a decision after $D = 10$ ms.
- *Dynamic-Delayed (DD)* delays prediction and uses both static features and dynamic features that we proposed in Section 3.2.

We use all 69,010 queries to evaluate *S*, and use 14,546 queries to evaluate delayed prediction frameworks including *DDS, SD*, and DD, because only 14,546 queries are not terminated after 10 ms. We use 10-fold cross validation (10 folds are randomly selected from a dataset) and repeat this procedure 5 times and report the average number to prevent biased results. We use boosted regression tree to predict the execution time and regression errors, where we use 100 regression trees.

4.2 Experimental Results

In this section, we identify which dynamic features are important to predict execution time, and compare *DDS* to *S*, showing the contribution of each technique: delayed prediction, dynamic features, and selective prediction.

4.2.1 Importance of Dynamic Features

Table 3 shows the top-10 feature selection results, where the importance is normalized by the highest value. The importance of a feature is evaluated by per-feature gain from the boosted tree, proportional to the total error reduction per split in the tree. The results show that dynamic features provide critical information on predicting query execution time: two dynamic features (NumEstMatchDoc and MinDynScore) outrank most of static features in terms of effectiveness. NumEstMatchDoc is most effective, being a simple but powerful estimator for the number of documents to be matched, which is highly correlated with the query execution time. However, this alone cannot predict time, as the query may terminate early depending on scoring distribution for the query. Various summary of such distribution (min, max, avg, and variance) thus play important and complementary roles in prediction.

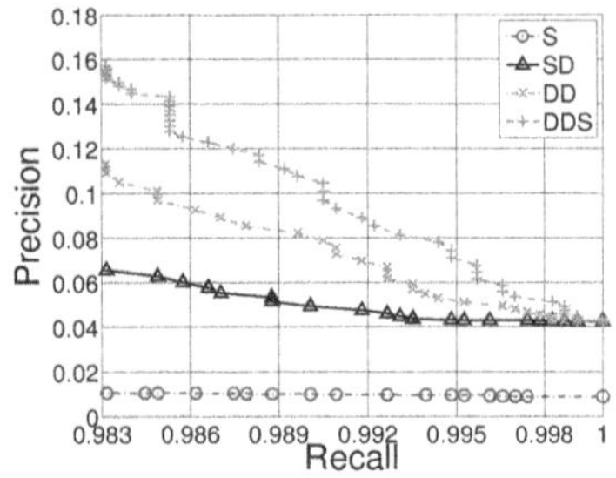

Figure 3: Precision and recall curves of four approaches by varying the time threshold α.

4.2.2 Low Prediction Overhead

As *DDS* delays prediction until a query runs for 10 ms, 80% of queries complete before that, and only 20% of queries use the predictor to estimate their execution time. In addition, the runtime overhead of prediction is less than 1 ms, which is less than 5% of the average execution time of these queries that use prediction.

4.2.3 Improved Precision

Figure 3 compares precision recall curves for *S*, *SD*, *DD* and *DDS*. All curves are obtained by varying the time threshold α (smaller α trades precision for higher recall). We set the error threshold of *DDS* to be $\beta = 10$ ms, which we empirically find to be effective. For the target 98.9% recall (to reduce 99.99th-percentile latency), Figure 3 shows, precision of *S* is about 1.1%, and *DDS* improves the precision to 11.63%, representing a 957% improvement over *S*. The detailed contributions of delayed prediction, dynamic features, and selection prediction are described next.

Contribution of delayed prediction (*S* versus *SD*): Figure 3 shows that *SD* (Static-Delayed) improves the precision from 1.1% to 5.25% compared with *S*. *SD* consistently outperforms *S* because 80% of queries terminate within 10 ms — SD saves prediction time and avoids prediction errors for those queries.

Contribution of dynamic features (*SD* versus *DD*): Figure 3 shows that *DD* (Dynamic-Delayed) improves the precision from 5.25% to 9.46%, which confirms the usefulness of dynamic features. To evaluate the effectiveness of dynamic features further, Table 4 shows the precision and recall of *SD* and *DD* while varying α. We observe that dynamic features consistently improve both precision and recall in all settings. In addition, our target recall of 98.9% is reached by *DD* when $\alpha = 20$ ms, while not by SD in the same setting.

Contribution of selective prediction (*DD* versus *DDS*): Figure 3 shows that *DDS* improves the precision from 9.46% to 11.63%, which validates the usefulness of selective prediction. In other words, selective prediction in *DDS* helps to identify long-running queries with large prediction error, and produces less false positives than *DD*.

At the recall target of 98.9%, the difference in precision between *DDS* and *S* is significant with attendant performance impact. For the query workload, we find that there are 0.92% of truly long-running queries. A precision of 11.63% indicates that *DDS* identifies 7.9% (= 0.92%/11.63%) of all queries as long-running, which is an affordable number to accelerate. In comparison, to meet the same high recall, using the state-of-the-art prior work *S* has precision of 1.1%, and thus identifies 83.5% of all queries as long-running, incurring a large cost — 9.57 times higher than *DDS* — in order to accelerate them. We discuss implications of these results in the next section.

Table 4: Precision and recall comparison between SD and DD with respect to varying α. We report each accuracy value as 'average (standard deviation)'.

Category	SD	DD
Precision ($\alpha = 100$ ms)	80.3%(0.44%)	**87.6%**(0.84%)
Recall ($\alpha = 100$ ms)	69.5%(0.44%)	**78.4%**(0.33%)
Precision ($\alpha = 60$ ms)	59.6%(0.57%)	**63.1%**(0.45%)
Recall ($\alpha = 60$ ms)	82.2%(0.33%)	**88.9%**(0.44%)
Precision ($\alpha = 40$ ms)	35.7%(0.3%)	**36.3%**(0.36%)
Recall ($\alpha = 40$ ms)	88.2%(0.3%)	**93.7%**(0.5%)
Precision ($\alpha = 20$ ms)	8.3%(0.05%)	**9.3%**(0.03%)
Recall ($\alpha = 20$ ms)	97.2%(0.4%)	**98.9%**(0.1%)

5. USING DDS TO REDUCE TAIL LATENCY

This section demonstrates how to use the proposed prediction framework *DDS* to reduce the extreme tail latency. The key idea is that *DDS* enables us to accurately accelerate only the long-running queries to reduce tail latency with affordable cost. We simulate the Bing search engine on two scenarios: (1) to parallelize long-running queries on multicore servers and (2) to schedule long-running queries on fast cores of heterogeneous servers. We evaluate the tail latency of each index server node (ISN) as well as at the aggregator for a cluster of ISNs. The simulation results show that, for both scenarios, *DDS* effectively reduces tail latency for a wide range of load, while the existing solutions fail to meet the latency target at medium and high load. At the desired tail latency, *DDS* improves the server throughput by more than 70%, potentially saving 44% search servers.

5.1 Query Parallelization

Parallelizing query processing on a search server is a potential solution to reduce query execution time [27, 15]. This is motivated by current hardware trends. A modern server has several cores, and therefore, parallelization allows multiple threads to execute a query concurrently using the available cores to reduce query execution time.

Choosing a parallelization strategy is challenging. When servers are lightly loaded and there is sufficient number of available cores, parallelizing the execution of all queries reduces their execution time, thereby reducing the response time. However, parallelizing all queries is ineffective under medium and high load because it comes with an overhead that varies among queries. Long-running queries achieve better speedup with lower overhead and higher parallelization efficiency. In contrast, parallelizing short-running queries is ineffective, giving no performance benefit while consuming additional resources taken away from long-running queries.

Figure 4 presents the measurement results on the parallelization speedup of Bing queries with different execution time (Figure 3 of [16]). The implementation details on how to execute a web search query using multiple threads and what causes the speedup/parallelism overhead are beyond the scope of this paper. Interested readers may refer to [16, 15]. The results show the queries that run longer than

80 ms achieve more than 4 times speedup by using 6 threads. In contrast, using 6 threads, the short-running queries that complete within 30 ms just achieve about 1.15 times of speedup because their execution time is dominated by the sequential part (*i.e.*, non-parallelized part) of the query processing. As the load increases, spare processor resources become limited and we can no longer afford to parallelize all queries. We thus parallelize long-running queries to reduce the high-percentile response time, and execute short-running queries sequentially to reduce parallelization overhead. We use *DDS* to decide if a query shall be parallelized.

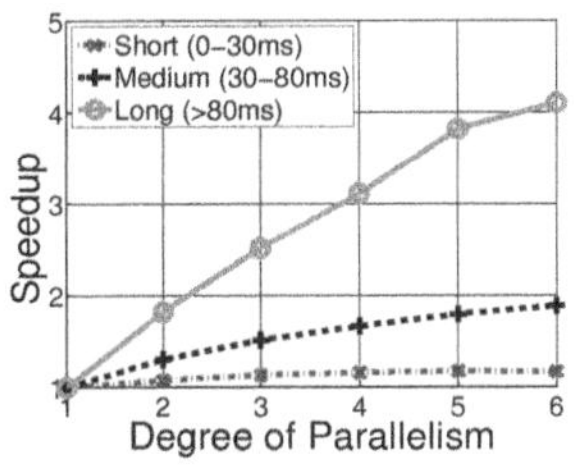

Figure 4: Parallelization efficiency of short, medium and long-running queries.

5.1.1 Experimental setup

Our experiments compare two techniques *DDS* and *S*. *S* uses static features from prior work [16] to predict query execution time before running the query and parallelizes the predicted long-running queries with 4-way parallelism. *DDS* runs a query for 10 ms sequentially and, if the query has not completed by then, it uses dynamic features of the query to predict query execution time and the prediction error. *DDS* parallelizes the query with 4-way parallelism if it is predicted as long running or if the prediction error of the query is larger than the error threshold (as in Section 4.1). Changing parallelism degree of a web search query at runtime is supported by using fine-grained parallelism [10]. In addition, we add the results of two more techniques as references: sequential execution that runs each query sequentially, and no-prediction that parallelizes all queries with 4-way parallelism.

We model a web search engine based on the architecture described in Section 2 and simulate it using a Java-based discrete-event simulator called DESMO-J [23]. The simulation models an aggregator and its 40 ISNs; each ISN has 12 cores. We drive the simulation using production query log, execution time profile (Figure 1(b)) and speedup profile (Figure 4). Queries arrive following a Poisson process, and we vary system load by changing the average arrival rate. We report the average number of 5 runs and use error bars to represent their standard deviation in the figures.

The proposed techniques target reducing the tail latency at medium and high load, rather than across all load regions. Notice that we operate Bing servers only at medium to high loads: Light load means that the system is over provisioned and load can be consolidated to use fewer server clusters; Extremely high load means that system is under provisioned and cannot meet the response time SLA for the tail latency, and load should be balanced among more server clusters.

5.1.2 Response time reduction at ISN

Figure 5 compares *DDS* with sequential execution results and two other parallelization approaches on (a) 99.99th-percentile, (b) 99.9th-percentile, and (c) mean response time. From the results we make three observations. First, parallelization significantly reduces the tail latency. Specifically, at light load (up to 350 QPS), all parallelization approaches reduce the 99.99th-percentile response time from 200 ms using sequential execution to 120 ms. Second, at medium to high load (350–700 QPS), *DDS* still achieves the same level of reduction, reducing the tail latency by 40% over sequential execution. In contrast, no-prediction and *S* have very high tail latency. Third, at extremely high load (>830 QPS), sequential execution has lower response time than the parallelized approaches as there is no free core available to run queries in parallel. However, we do not operate our servers at such very high load which leads to violating the response time SLA of 120 ms at 99.99th-percentile. The results of 99.9th-percentile show similar trend. We also include the mean response time results for completeness.

Insights behind performance improvements. We explain why *DDS* outperforms *S* at medium to high load: *DDS* enables judicious utilization of cores to long-running queries because of its higher precision.

In order to reduce 99.99th-percentile response time, we have shown in Section 3.1 that a prediction algorithm needs to achieve high recall of 98.9%. To obtain this recall, different prediction algorithms have different precision, which implies the number of queries the algorithms identify as long running (including both true long-running queries and false positive ones). *S* has precision of 1.1%. As there are 0.92% of truly long-running queries, a precision of 1.1% indicates that *S* identifies about 83.6% (= 0.92%/1.1%) of all queries as long-running, among which, majority are false positives. At light load, the parallelization overhead to accelerate the false positive queries is tolerable as there are available cores. However, when the load increases, these false positive queries take away resources from real long-running queries and their parallelization overhead prolongs the waiting time of all queries, resulting in higher response time. In comparison, *DDS* achieves the precision of 11.63%, parallelizing only 7.93% (= 0.92%/11.63%) of queries, which significantly reduces the number of queries to accelerate and their corresponding overhead. Therefore, even at high load, *DDS* still effectively reduces tail latency.

5.1.3 Contribution of three techniques of DDS

The performance improvement of *DDS* comes from its three techniques — delayed prediction, dynamic features, and selective prediction, and Figure 6 quantifies their individual contributions. In particular, we add two intermediate steps from *S* to *DDS*: *Static-Delayed (SD)*, which delays prediction but only uses static features, and *Dynamic-Delayed (DD)*, which delays prediction and uses both static and dynamic features, but without estimating prediction error.

To meet 120 ms SLA on the 99.99th-percentile response time, Figure 6 shows the following: (1) *SD* outperforms *S*, increasing throughput from 390 QPS to 600 QPS. The reason is that 80% short-running queries complete within 10 ms, and the delayed prediction executes all of these short-running queries sequentially without incurring unnecessary overhead. (2) *DD* increases the throughput further to 650 QPS. The improvement comes from the improved prediction accuracy: dynamic features increase precision to 9.46%, and thus only 9.7% of the total queries need to be parallelized. (3) *DDS* achieves the precision of 11.63% and offers a final

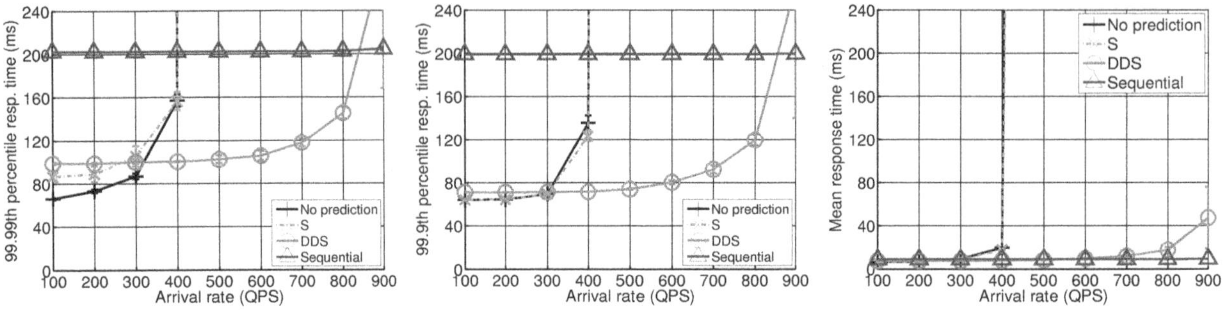

(a) 99.99th-percentile response time (b) 99.9th-percentile response time (c) mean response time

Figure 5: Response time of sequential and three parallel query execution approaches at ISN.

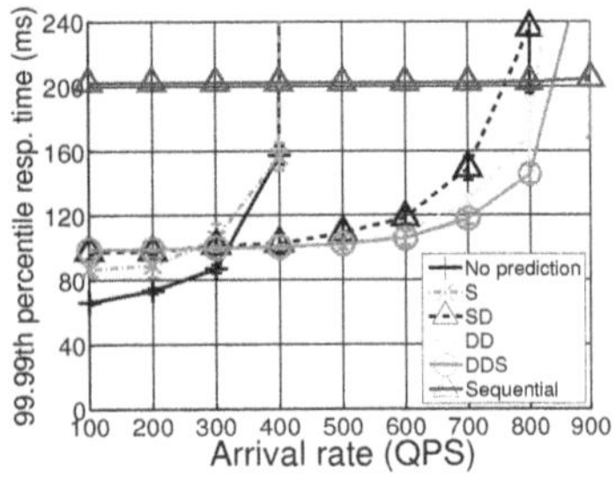

Figure 6: 99.99th-percentile response time for *S*, *SD*, *DD* and *DDS* at ISN.

boost of throughput to 700 QPS by accelerating only 7.9% of queries. It demonstrates the effectiveness of delaying the prediction, using dynamic features, and estimating the prediction error.

5.1.4 Sensitivity to different target percentiles

Figure 7(a) shows two observations when we vary the target response percentile: (1) For any given algorithm, in order to optimize for higher percentile, the ratio of the predicted long-running queries increases: trading precision for higher recall. (2) *DDS* consistently outperforms the other schemes for various target percentiles: for any given target, it requires to parallelize the smallest number of queries as it achieves the highest precision.

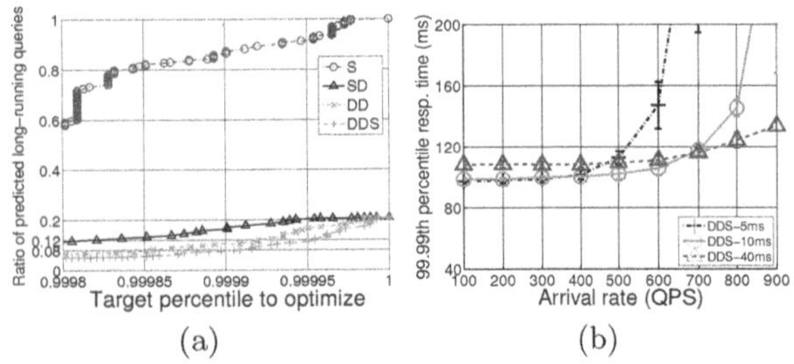

(a) (b)

Figure 7: Sensitivity study: (a) Ratio of the predicted long-running queries with varying target percentile latency; (b) Response time of *DDS* with various delay thresholds: $D = 5, 10, 40$ ms.

5.1.5 Sensitivity to delay threshold D

Figure 7(b) shows 99.99th response time for *DDS* with various delay threshold D where *DDS-5ms* means that the prediction is done after 5 ms of sequential execution. We observe that 10 ms is a practically sufficient choice. The 99.99th response time for 40 ms is consistently larger than 10 ms for small-to-mid loads, because the true long-running queries are delayed longer to be accelerated. The 99.99th response time for 5 ms is larger than 10 ms at high load, because earlier prediction does not collect sufficiently accurate dynamic information to achieve precision.

5.2 Latency Reduction at Aggregator

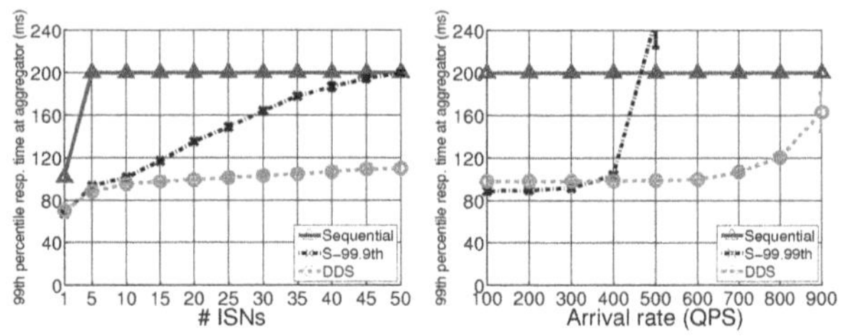

(a) Vary #ISNs, 700 QPS (b) Vary load, 40 ISNs

Figure 8: 99th-percentile latency at an aggregator.

While previous results focus on latency reduction of each ISN, this section evaluates the benefits of *DDS* on reducing aggregator-level latency. An aggregator collects results from all of its ISNs, and thus its latency is determined by the slowest ISN. To reduce tail latency at the aggregator, we need to reduce a much higher tail at each ISN. For example, if the desired x = 99th-percentile latency is $Q = 120$ for an aggregator with $k = 40$ ISNs, then each ISN needs to have $\sqrt[k]{x/100} \times 100 = 99.975 \approx 99.99$ percentage of queries with latency Q or lower, i.e., the individual ISN should have a 99.99th-percentile latency of $Q = 120$ ms or lower.[1]

We vary the number of ISNs and measure the 99th-percentile response time at the aggregator. We evaluate two approaches at 700 QPS, labelled *DDS* and *S*-99.9th. First we employ *DDS* to reduce the 99.99th-percentile latency at each ISN. Next, we introduce *S*-99.9th, which uses static features to reduce 99.9th-percentile latency at each ISN. Notice that we do not use *S*-99.99th, the default scheme with static features, which has higher recall but lower precision.

[1] We assume that ISNs operate independently since each ISN works on a random hashed partition of web documents.

At 700 QPS, S-99.99th produces very high parallelism overhead, and its latency substantially exceeds 200 ms (Figure 5). Finally, we plot the sequential results for reference.

Figure 8(a) shows how the aggregator latency of the three schemes rises with increasing number of ISNs. We set the target 99th-percentile of aggregator latency to be 120 ms. At the extreme case of only one ISN for the aggregator, we need to reduce 99th-percentile of that ISN, and the two approaches meet the goal. When the aggregator has 40 ISNs, we need to reduce around 99.99th-percentile at each ISN — S-99.9th cannot meet the goal any more. The results are consistent with our analysis. Since in practice each aggregators has many ISNs, this experiment highlights the importance of reducing the extreme tail at each ISN server.

Figure 8(b) compares the aggregator 99th-percentile latency for *DDS* and S-99.9th with varying load and with $k = 40$ ISNs. The results show *DDS* outperforms the other approaches, reducing the aggregator-level tail latency for moderate and heavy load by 40% from 200 to 120 ms.

Throughput improvement. Using *DDS* to select which queries to parallelize improves system throughput. Figure 8(b) shows that, to meet 120 ms 99th-percentile latency at the aggregator, *DDS* sustains arrival rates up to 700 QPS while the other schemes support up to around 390 QPS. *DDS* improves throughput by more than 70%.

Assume the search engine has a total workload of X QPS, and each aggregator has k ISNs. Using *DDS* requires $X/700 \times k$ servers while using fixed parallelization needs $X/390 \times k$ servers: Here, *DDS* saves $(X/390 - X/700)/(X/390) = 44\%$ of the servers to serve the same workload. As commercial search engine uses thousands of production servers, these savings are significant.

5.3 Scheduling on Heterogenous Server

A heterogeneous multicore processor is an emerging hardware composed of cores with differentiated power and performance characteristics, typically combining energy-efficient slow cores with high-performance fast cores. All cores execute the same instruction set, but they run at different speeds — the faster the core, the more power it consumes. Since power consumption increases faster than speed, a fast core executes a request in less time than a slow core, but consumes more energy. There are several proposals for heterogeneous processors [18, 2, 7], e.g., ARM recently announced their big.LITTLE processor for production [13].

We exploit the prediction results of *DDS* to improve search engine performance on the emerging heterogeneous hardware. Prior work [14] shows that, as ISNs of web search have CPU-intensive workload, a high-performance (fast) core completes a query with less time than an energy-efficient (slow) core but consumes more energy. We accelerate the predicted long-running queries using fast cores and execute short-running queries on slow cores. The high recall achieved by DDS allows us to correctly predict the majority of the long-running queries and execute them using fast cores to reduce tail latency. Good precision is also important here: although faster cores provide higher performance and complete queries faster, they have lower energy efficiency, i.e., to complete the same amount of work, they consume more energy than using slower and energy-efficient cores [24]. The good precision of DDS allows us to execute most of the short-running queries on slow cores to reduce energy consumption and improve system throughput.

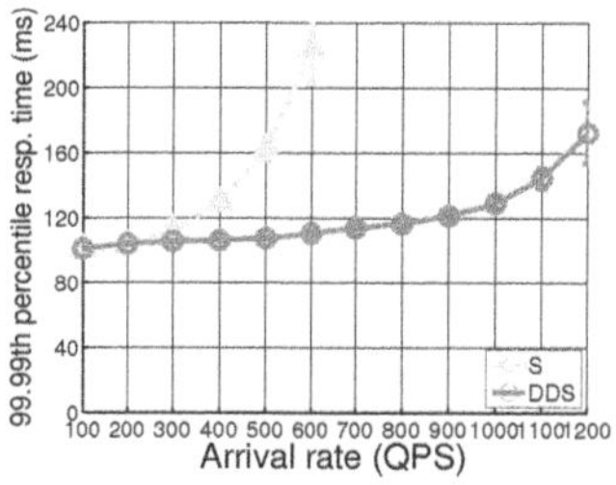

Figure 9: 99.99th-percentile response time on the heterogeneous server.

We simulate a heterogeneous server composed of 3 fast cores (i7 Sandy bridge cores) and 6 slow cores (AtomD cores). We compare DDS with S in our evaluation using the same workload as Section 5.1. Due to space limit, we only summarize the key results. As shown in Figure 9, at moderate to high load, comparing with S, DDS reduces 99.99th-percentile latency of ISN from 200 ms to 120 ms. To meet 99.99th-percentile latency target of 120 ms, *DDS* supports up to 800 QPS, while S only obtains 330 QPS. *DDS* more than doubles the server throughput. In order words, to process the same amount of query workloads, *DDS* saves more than half of the servers.

6. RELATED WORK

Execution time prediction on search queries. Prediction of search query performance can be categorized into quality and execution time prediction. Examples of quality prediction include the prediction of user satisfaction [17], and clicks to mobile advertisements [22].

In contrast, this work focuses on predicting the execution time of web search queries. Moffat *et al.* [21] show that the execution time of a query is related to the posting list lengths of its constituent query terms. However, under dynamic pruning strategies, only a limited portion of such listing is scored [1]. Macdonald *et al.* [20] incorporate term-level statistics to predict the effect of dynamic pruning. In particular, various term-level statistics (static features) are computed for each term offline. When a query arrives, the term-level features are aggregated into query-level statistics, which are used as inputs to a regression model. Meanwhile, [16] proposes query features modelling the complexity from query relaxation, rewriting and personalization, and identifies an effective subset outperforming existing predictors in terms of accuracy with lower memory footprint.

However, these predictors, relying solely on static features, could not achieve our accuracy requirements. We thus propose the use of dynamic features and error prediction for execution time prediction. We empirically show that this combination greatly improves prediction accuracy over state-of-the-art predictors that use only static features. Prediction accuracy gains can be used to optimize search systems in many ways: Macdonald *et al.* [20] uses the predicted execution time for query scheduling, [16] for parallelization, [28] for query pruning, and [11] for reducing power consumption. We use parallelization and scheduling on heterogeneous hardware as our scenarios for demonstration.

Search query parallelization. Parallelizing the processing of search queries is proposed to reduce query execution time [27, 15]. However, the prior studies do not consider the prediction of query execution time, thus they parallelize all queries, which wastes resources. Recently, a prediction-based parallelization scheme [16] predicts query execution time to parallelize long-running queries. This work improves over prior work by employing delayed, dynamic, and selective prediction. Frachtenberg [10] can be viewed as a simplistic delayed and dynamic prediction using a single feature, which is an estimation on the number of matched documents. This single feature without trained regression model does not capture other important factors contributing to the query execution time such as query complexity and pruning, and it cannot accurately predict query execution time.

Scheduling on heterogeneous servers. Prior work shows that a heterogeneous server is more suitable for applications consisting of tasks of diverse demands to improve performance or save energy [13, 8, 19, 7, 25]. For example, users run delay-sensitive tasks using fast cores, while background services use slow cores [13]. Lakshminarayana et al. schedule the thread in a parallel job with a larger remaining execution time on a fast core [19]. They predict the remaining time of jobs at PARSEC benchmark [3] based on dynamic profiling. Since these applications are not directly related to search engines, the proposed features for predicting job execution time are not appropriate for our purpose. Our work exploits the diversity (short-running versus long-running jobs) in the demand of search queries and shows how to use the predicted execution time to improve search engine performance using heterogeneous hardware.

7. CONCLUSIONS

This paper studies reducing the extreme tail latency of web search server by predicting and accelerating long-running queries. We first show that the predictor must offer high recall and good precision as our prediction requirements. We propose a novel prediction framework, *DDS*, combining delayed prediction, dynamic features and prediction error estimation. In particular, *DDS* delays the prediction until we collect dynamic signals, which are highly effective on improving prediction accuracy. Moreover, *DDS* estimates both latency and error to selectively accelerate queries, achieving high recall target with good precision. Our simulation results show that *DDS* effectively reduces the tail latency and significantly improves server throughput.

Acknowledgements: This work was partially supported by the IT R&D Program of MSIP/IITP (14-824-09-014, Machine Learning Center), National Research Foundation (NRF) of Korea (NRF-2013R1A2A2A01067464), and MSIP/Microsoft Research under ICT/SW Creative research program (NIPA-2014-H0510-14-1018). We appreciate the constructive comments provided by Myeongjae Jeon.

8. REFERENCES

[1] R. Baeza-Yates, A. Gionis, F. P. Junqueira, V. Murdock, V. Plachouras, and F. Silvestri. Design trade-offs for search engine caching. *ACM Transactions on Web*, 2008.

[2] M. Becchi and P. Crowley. Dynamic thread assignment on heterogeneous multiprocessor architectures. *ACM Computing Frontiers*, 2006.

[3] C. Bienia, S. Kumar, J. P. Singh, and K. Li. The parsec benchmark suite: Characterization and architectural implications. *Technical Report*, 2008.

[4] S. Briesemeister, J. Rahnenfuhrer, and O. Kohlbacher. No longer confidential: Estimating the confidence of individual regression predictions. *PLos ONE*, 2012.

[5] A. Z. Broder, D. Carmel, M. Herscovici, A. Soffer, and J. Zien. Efficient query evaluation using a two-level retrieval process. In *CIKM*, 2003.

[6] C. J. Burges, R. Ragno, and Q. V. Le. Learning to rank with nonsmooth cost functions. In *NIPS*, 2006.

[7] J. Chen and L. K. John. Efficient program scheduling for heterogeneous multi-core processors. In *DAC*, 2009.

[8] K. V. Craeynest, A. Jalelle, L. Eeckhout, P. Narvaez, and J. Emer. Scheduling heterogeneous multi-cores through performance impact estimation (pie). In *ISCA*, 2012.

[9] J. Dean and L. A. Barroso. The tail at scale. In *Communications of the ACM*, 2013.

[10] E. Frachtenberg. Reducing query latencies in web search using fine-grained parallelism. *World Wide Web*, 2009.

[11] A. Freire, C. Macdonald, N. Tonellotto, I. Ounis, and F. Cacheda. A self-adapting latency/power tradeoff model for replicated search engines. In *WSDM*, 2014.

[12] J. Friedman. Greedy function approximation: a gradient boosting machine. In *Annals of Statistics*, 2001.

[13] P. Greenhalgh. Big.little processing with arm cortex-a15 & cortex-a7. *ARM Whitepaper*, 2011.

[14] V. Janapa Reddi, B. C. Lee, T. Chilimbi, and K. Vaid. Web search using mobile cores: quantifying and mitigating the price of efficiency. In *ISCA*, 2010.

[15] M. Jeon, Y. He, S. Elnikety, A. L. Cox, and S. Rixner. Adaptive parallelism for web search. In *EuroSys*, 2013.

[16] M. Jeon, S. Kim, S. Hwang, Y. He, S. Elnikety, A. L. Cox, and S. Rixner. Predictive parallelization: Taming tail latencies in web search. In *SIGIR*, 2014.

[17] Y. Kim, A. Hassan, R. W. White, and Y.-M. Wang. Playing by the rules: Mining query associations to predict search performance. In *WSDM*, 2013.

[18] R. Kumar, K. I. Farkas, N. P. Jouppi, P. Ranganathan, and D. M. Tullsen. Single-isa heterogeneous multicore architectures: The potential for processor power reduction. In *MICRO*, 2003.

[19] N. B. Lakshminarayana, J. Lee, and H. Kim. Age based scheduling for asymmetric multiprocessors. In *SC*, 2009.

[20] C. Macdonald, N. Tonellotto, and I. Ounis. Learning to predict response times for online query scheduling. In *SIGIR*, 2012.

[21] A. Moffat, W. Webber, J. Zobel, and R. Baeza-Yates. A pipelined architecture for distributed text query evaluation. *Information Retrieval*, 2007.

[22] R. J. Oentaryo, E. P. Lim, D. J. W. Low, D. Lo, and M. Finegold. Predicting response in mobile advertising with hierarchical importance-aware factorization machine. In *WSDM*, 2014.

[23] B. Page and T. Lechler. Desmo-J. `http://desmoj.sourceforge.net/overview.html`.

[24] S. Ren, Y. He, S. Elnikety, and K. S. McKinley. Exploiting processor heterogeneity for interactive services. In *ICAC*, 2013.

[25] J. C. Saez, D. Shelepov, A. Fedorova, and M. Prieto. Leveraging workload diversity through os scheduling to maximize performance on single-isa heterogeneous multicore systems. *JPDC*, 2011.

[26] E. Schurman and J. Brutlag. Performance related changes and their user impact. *Velocity*, 2009.

[27] S. Tatikonda, B. B. Cambazoglu, and F. P. Junqueira. Posting list intersection on multicore architectures. In *SIGIR*, 2011.

[28] N. Tonellotto, C. Macdonald, and I. Ounis. Efficient and effective retrieval using selective pruning. In *WSDM*, 2013.

[29] H. Turtle and J. Flood. Query evaluation: strategies and optimizations. *Information Processing and Management*, 1995.

MergeRUCB: A Method for Large-Scale Online Ranker Evaluation

Masrour Zoghi Shimon Whiteson Maarten de Rijke
University of Amsterdam, Amsterdam, The Netherlands
{m.zoghi, s.a.whiteson, derijke}@uva.nl

ABSTRACT

A key challenge in information retrieval is that of *on-line ranker evaluation*: determining which one of a finite set of rankers performs the best in expectation on the basis of user clicks on presented document lists. When the presented lists are constructed using *interleaved comparison methods*, which interleave lists proposed by two different candidate rankers, then the problem of minimizing the total *regret* accumulated while evaluating the rankers can be formalized as a *K-armed dueling bandit problem*. In the setting of web search, the number of rankers under consideration may be large. Scaling effectively in the presence of so many rankers is a key challenge not adequately addressed by existing algorithms.

We propose a new method, which we call *mergeRUCB*, that uses "localized" comparisons to provide the first provably scalable K-armed dueling bandit algorithm. Empirical comparisons on several large learning to rank datasets show that mergeRUCB can substantially outperform the state of the art K-armed dueling bandit algorithms when many rankers must be compared. Moreover, we provide theoretical guarantees demonstrating the soundness of our algorithm.

Categories and Subject Descriptors

H.3.3 [**Information Storage and Retrieval**]: Information Search and Retrieval

Keywords

Evaluation; implicit feedback; on-line learning

1. INTRODUCTION

An important challenge in information retrieval is that of *ranker evaluation*: determining which of a finite set of rankers performs best in expectation. In *off-line* ranker evaluation, which goes back to the early Cranfield experiments [9], rankers are assessed based on a fixed set of queries and documents manually judged by human assessors. Unfortunately, obtaining such judgments is expensive and error prone. Furthermore, because the assessors typically did not formulate the queries on which they judge documents, their assessments may not accurately reflect how well those documents meet the needs of real users.

These difficulties can be addressed by *on-line* ranker evaluation, in which rankers are assessed using click feedback from actual users. A common approach is to use *interleaved comparison methods* [7, 8, 13, 15, 18, 23, 25], in which the document lists proposed by two candidate rankers for a given query are interleaved and the resulting list presented to the user, whose clicks are used to infer a noisy preference for one ranker over the other. Interleaving methods have been successfully applied in large-scale settings [7, 8].

The use of interleaved comparison methods gives rise to a key challenge in ranker evaluation: how to efficiently determine the best ranker from a set using only pairwise comparisons. This challenge can be formalized as a *K-armed dueling bandit* problem [32], wherein the best ranker is defined as the one that in expectation wins an interleaved comparison against every other ranker. Several algorithms have been proposed for this problem, including *interleaved filter* (IF) [32], *beat the mean* (BTM) [31], *sensitivity analysis of variables for generic exploration* (SAVAGE) [28], *relative upper confidence bound* (RUCB) [34] and *relative confidence sampling* (RCS) [33].

One challenge that such algorithms face is that the number of parameters that must be learned grows quadratically with K, the number of rankers. This in turn results in excessive exploration. The challenge is especially relevant in the case of web search, where a large number of rankers may be under consideration.[1] Some algorithms, such as SAVAGE, RUCB and RCS have difficulty scaling to large K. Other algorithms such as IF and BTM avoid this problem by making more restrictive assumptions, such as a total ordering of the rankers, that make it possible to identify the best ranker without explicitly considering all parameters. However, this approach is problematic because the required assumptions often do not hold in web search settings.

In this paper, we remedy these shortcomings by bridging the gap between these two approaches. Specifically, we propose and evaluate a new method for evaluating rankers, called *mergeRUCB*, that makes only weak assumptions about the K-armed dueling bandit problem, but provably requires only $\mathcal{O}(K)$ comparisons and therefore performs well when many rankers must be compared, as is typically the case in web search. As the name suggests, mergeRUCB uses a divide and conquer strategy to reduce the number of exploratory comparisons carried out by the evaluation process. It proceeds by grouping rankers into small batches so that fewer comparisons are needed before rankers can be eliminated.

To validate mergeRUCB, we evaluate its performance on large

[1]Kohavi et al. [21] report that on any given day over 200 concurrent experiments are being run at Bing, with users ending up in one of billions of possible variants of the site.

WSDM'15, February 2–6, 2015, Shanghai, China.

ACM 978-1-4503-3317-7/15/02 ...$15.00.
http://dx.doi.org/10.1145/2684822.2685290.

Microsoft, Yandex and Yahoo! learning to rank datasets. Our results show that mergeRUCB significantly and substantially outperforms multiple state of the art K-armed dueling bandit algorithms. Moreover, we provide theoretical performance guarantees that bound how much regret can be accumulated by mergeRUCB.

The main contributions of this paper are thus:

1. Proposing a new K-armed dueling bandit algorithm that scales well with the number of rankers (cf. §4).
2. Experimentally comparing its performance against existing K-armed dueling bandit algorithms (cf. §5 and §6).
3. Providing theoretical results guaranteeing the proper functioning of the algorithm (cf. §7); moreover, our regret bounds are the first that are completely linear in K, without imposing impractical assumptions.

2. PROBLEM SETTING

One approach to ranker evaluation is to use manual expert annotations in a TREC-like setting [29]. However, collecting the necessary annotations is expensive and, because they are not based on real users, such annotations may not reflect real users' actual information needs. An attractive alternative is thus to evaluate rankers *on-line* using feedback from real users. One way to obtain such feedback is to measure the *click-through rate* [17]. However, such feedback is often unreliable, since click-through rates can have substantial variance, particularly across users and topics [19, 20, 25, 26].

Fortunately, on-line feedback can also be obtained using *interleaved comparison methods*, which give *relative* feedback about how one ranker compares to another and have been shown to be more reliable [7, 23]. To compare two rankers on a given query, an interleaved comparison constructs a ranking that is an amalgamation of the rankings proposed by the two rankers for that query. Schemes for constructing the amalgamation include *balanced interleave* [18], *team draft* [25], *document constraints* [13], *probabilistic interleave* [15], and *optimized interleave* [24].

However, since interleaved comparison methods require feedback from real users, each comparison has significant real-world costs, i.e., if either of the compared rankers is poor, the interleaved ranking may also be poor, leaving the user dissatisfied. An important question is thus how to find the best ranker in a way that minimizes these costs.

This problem can be formalized as a K-armed dueling bandit problem [32], which is itself an extension of the *K-armed bandit* problem [3]. In the K-armed bandit problem, there are K rankers, $\{\rho_1, \ldots, \rho_K\}$. At each *time-step*, a ranker ρ_i can be tried, generating a *reward* drawn from an unknown stationary distribution with expected value μ_i, which might be a quantity like click-through rate [6].

The K-armed *dueling* bandit problem is a variation that models the relative feedback available in settings like ranker evaluation with interleaved comparison methods. The problem is defined by a matrix $\mathbf{P} = [p_{ij}]$ of *preference probabilities*. At each *time-step*, two rankers (ρ_i, ρ_j) are compared, e.g., using an interleaved comparison method, and with probability p_{ij} ranker ρ_i beats ρ_j. In this paper, we assume that there exists a *Condorcet winner* [28]: a ranker, which without loss of generality we label ρ_1, such that $p_{1i} > \frac{1}{2}$ for all $i > 1$. In other words, when interleaved with any other ranker, the Condorcet winner is expected to win.

The goal of a K-armed dueling bandit algorithm is to minimize the total *regret* it accumulates. Regret is a measure of the lost opportunity incurred by performing interleaved comparisons between suboptimal rankers. More specifically, the regret resulting from a comparison between rankers ρ_i and ρ_j is defined to be $\frac{p_{1i}+p_{1j}}{2} - 0.5$, i.e., the average suboptimality of the two rankers with respect to the Condorcet winner. Furthermore, *cumulative regret at time T*, R_T, is the sum of regret accumulated in the first T time-steps. In the context of online ranker evaluation for web search, we are interested in algorithms that minimize cumulative regret, since that means that fewer poor-quality rankings are shown to the users, hence lowering the risk of user frustration.

3. RELATED WORK

To our knowledge, the earliest method for the K-armed dueling bandit problem is *interleaved filter* (IF) [32], which proceeds as follows: a ranker $\hat{\rho}$ is randomly chosen to be compared against all other rankers; these comparisons are repeated until another ranker ρ' either loses to or beats $\hat{\rho}$ by a wide margin, i.e., the winner scores so many more wins over the loser that one can conclude with high confidence that the loser can be eliminated. If $\hat{\rho}$ is the winner, ρ' is eliminated from the pool of rankers and not compared against any other rankers. If $\hat{\rho}$ is the loser, it is eliminated from the pool of rankers and ρ' becomes the new $\hat{\rho}$. This process continues until all but one of the rankers is eliminated.

More recently, the *beat the mean* (BTM) algorithm has been shown to outperform IF [31]. BTM works by focusing exploration on the rankers that have been involved in the fewest comparisons. When it determines that a ranker fares on average too poorly in comparison to the remaining rankers, it removes it from consideration. More precisely, BTM considers the performance of each ranker against the *mean ranker* by averaging the ranker's scores against all other rankers and uses these estimates to decide which ranker should be eliminated. BTM is currently the state of the art for K-armed dueling bandit problems for the web search setting in which we are interested, that is, with large numbers of rankers K. However, so far, the performance of BTM has not been evaluated on large-scale online evaluation tasks using large learning to rank datasets. In this paper, we demonstrate that our proposed algorithm outperforms BTM on such datasets.

IF and BTM require the comparison probabilities p_{ij} to satisfy conditions that are difficult to verify without specific knowledge about the dueling bandit problem at hand. Specifically, IF and BTM require a *total ordering* $\{\rho_1, \ldots, \rho_K\}$ of the rankers to exist such that $p_{ij} > \frac{1}{2}$ for all $i < j$. In [33, 34], the authors show that, in the case of the LETOR and MSLR datasets, the probability of a total ordering existing decreases quickly as the number of rankers increases, due to the presence of cyclical relationships among rankers other than the Condorcet winner.

Sensitivity analysis of variables for generic exploration (SAVAGE) [28] is a more recent algorithm that outperforms both IF and BTM by a wide margin when the number of rankers is small. However, in cases with large numbers of rankers, SAVAGE was significantly outperformed by BTM. One version of SAVAGE, which we call *Condorcet SAVAGE*, assumes only the existence of a Condorcet winner and performed the best experimentally [28]. Condorcet SAVAGE compares pairs of rankers uniformly randomly until there exists a pair for which one of the rankers beats the other by a wide margin, in which case the loser is removed from the pool of rankers under consideration.

Relative upper confidence bound (RUCB) [34] and *relative confidence sampling* (RCS) [33] are two related algorithms that select rankers to compare by first choosing a ranker that is believed to be a good candidate for the Condorcet winner, and then choosing a second ranker that has the best chance of disproving the hypothesis that the first ranker is indeed the Condorcet winner. RUCB uses confidence intervals to carry this out, while RCS uses sampling.

RUCB has strong theoretical guarantees, while RCS currently has none. However, RCS was shown to outperform RUCB on small-scale ranker evaluation problems. So far, neither algorithm has been tested on large-scale evaluation problems. Our extensive experimentation shows that, when there are few rankers, RCS tends to perform better than RUCB but, for the case with many rankers, RUCB performs better. However, for the case with many rankers, our proposed algorithm mergeRUCB outperforms both of them. Moreover, the regret bounds proven for RUCB take the form

$$\mathcal{O}(K^2) + \mathcal{O}(K \log T),$$

while our bound is linear in K, taking the form $\mathcal{O}(K \log T)$.

However, these bounds are not directly comparable because RUCB does not require δ, the probability of failure, to be passed to the algorithm explicitly. Instead, we let the user of the algorithm specify how risk averse they want the algorithm to be, which is not an option with RUCB or RCS.

4. METHOD

In this paper, we propose mergeRUCB, shown in Algorithm 1, to deal with online ranker evaluation problems involving many rankers. As with sorting algorithms, most naive approaches to the K-armed dueling bandit problem suffer from quadratic dependence on K because they require every ranker to be compared against every other ranker. However, this quadratic dependence can be avoided by a mergesort-style algorithm that carries out comparisons only "locally," i.e., items are placed in small batches that are processed separately and then merged together.

The same principle underlies mergeRUCB. The crucial difference is that, unlike in sorting, one comparison is not sufficient to determine which of a pair of rankers is better, since feedback is stochastic. Furthermore, the number of times two rankers must be compared is larger if the rankers are more similar. In the worst case, we have $p_{ij} = 0.5$ and the two rankers cannot be distinguished. This case is problematic because ρ_i and ρ_j might be weak rankers overall (i.e., lose badly to other rankers), in which case comparing them to each other many times will incur large regret. MergeRUCB deals with this difficulty by using the best ranker in the batch to eliminate the rest. If a batch contains only similar rankers and is thus too slow in eliminating rankers, it is combined with other batches that have more variety.

In the following, we explain the components of mergeRUCB, which proceeds in *stages* (Line 4). Before the first stage, the algorithm groups rankers into small batches $\mathcal{B}_i$ (Line 2). Then, within each stage, mergeRUCB carries out interleaved comparisons among rankers that reside in the same batch. At any given time, the choice of rankers to compare against each other inside a given batch is guided by a matrix $\mathbf{U}$ of upper confidence bounds (Line 7), which is obtained by optimistically estimating the preference probabilities p_{ij}: the optimism is included to ensure sufficient exploration among the rankers. The matrix $\mathbf{U}$ is used both to eliminate rankers if they lose to other rankers by a wide margin (Line 8) and to choose the ranker ρ_d (Line 10) that is selected so as to hasten the elimination of ρ_c, which is chosen randomly. The algorithm proceeds in this fashion until the number of remaining rankers becomes small (Line 12), at which point the stage is concluded by merging pairs of batches together to form bigger batches (Line 13). This initiates the next stage, and the process repeats until a single ranker remains. Our theoretical results state that the probability that this remaining ranker is the Condorcet winner is greater than $1 - \delta$.

Algorithm 1 mergeRUCB(δ)

Input: A set of rankers $\rho_1, \ldots, \rho_K$;
an oracle that can take a pair of rankers and return one as the winner (e.g., an interleaved comparison method);
the size of each partition, $p \geq 4$;
the maximum probability of failure, δ;
$\alpha > \frac{1}{2}$.

1: $\mathbf{W} \leftarrow \mathbf{0}_{K \times K}$ *// 2D array of wins:* $\mathbf{W}_{ij}$ *is the number of times* ρ_i *has beaten* ρ_j

2: $\mathcal{B}_1 = \Big\{ \underbrace{\{\rho_1, \ldots, \rho_p\}}_{B_1}, \ldots, \underbrace{\{\rho_{(b_1-1)p+1}, \ldots, \rho_K\}}_{B_{b_1}} \Big\}$, a set of disjoint batches of rankers, with $b_1 = \lfloor \frac{K}{p} \rfloor$

3: $C(\delta) = \left\lceil \left(\frac{(4\alpha-1)K^2}{(2\alpha-1)\delta} \right)^{\frac{1}{2\alpha-1}} \right\rceil$

4: $S = 1$ *// The stage that the algorithm is in.*

5: **for** $t = 1, 2, \ldots$ **do**

6: $\quad i = t \mod b_S$

7: $\quad \mathbf{U} = \frac{\mathbf{W}}{\mathbf{W}+\mathbf{W}^T} + \sqrt{\frac{\alpha \ln(t+C(\delta))}{\mathbf{W}+\mathbf{W}^T}}$, where all operations are element-wise.

8: $\quad$ For any $\rho_k \in B_i$ if $\mathbf{U}_{kl} < \frac{1}{2}$ for any $\rho_l \in B_i$, remove ρ_k from B_i.

9: $\quad$ Select $\rho_c \in B_i$ randomly.

10: $\quad$ Set $d := \underset{\{l | \rho_l \in B_i \setminus \{\rho_c\}\}}{\arg\max} \mathbf{U}_{lc}$.

11: $\quad$ Compare ρ_c against ρ_d and increment $\mathbf{W}_{cd}$ if c won and $\mathbf{W}_{dc}$ otherwise.

12: $\quad$ **if** $\sum_i |B_i| \leq \frac{K}{2^I}$ **then**

13: $\quad\quad$ Combine pairs of batches of rankers so that each new batch has between $p/2$ and $3p/2$ rankers in it, pairing the smallest batches with the largest ones, making sure that each batch contains at least two rankers. Update the sets B_i, putting them all in the set $\mathcal{B}_S$, and define $b_S := |\mathcal{B}_S|$.

14: $\quad\quad S = S + 1$

15: $\quad$ **end if**

16: **end for**

---

5. EXPERIMENTAL SETUP

Our experiments address the following research questions:

RQ1 Does mergeRUCB outperform BTM, the state of the art online ranker evaluation algorithm for large-scale evaluation problems?

RQ2 How does mergeRUCB scale as the number of rankers increases in comparison to existing algorithms?

RQ3 How does the click model affect the scalability of the various algorithms?

RQ4 How does the performance of mergeRUCB depend on the parameters α and p? In particular, how do our default parameters perform?

We conduct experiments on four large-scale learning to rank datasets, namely the Microsoft Learning to Rank dataset (MSLR), the Yandex Internet Mathematics 2009 dataset and the Yahoo! Learning to Rank (YLR) Challenge datasets 1 and 2. Basic information about these datasets is included in Table 1.

Using these datasets, we create a finite set of rankers, each of which corresponds to a ranking feature provided in the dataset, e.g. PageRank or BM25. From this set of rankers, we choose subsets on which we test our algorithms. Therefore, in the experiments carried out here, the ranker evaluation task corresponds to determining which single feature constitutes the best ranker. From one

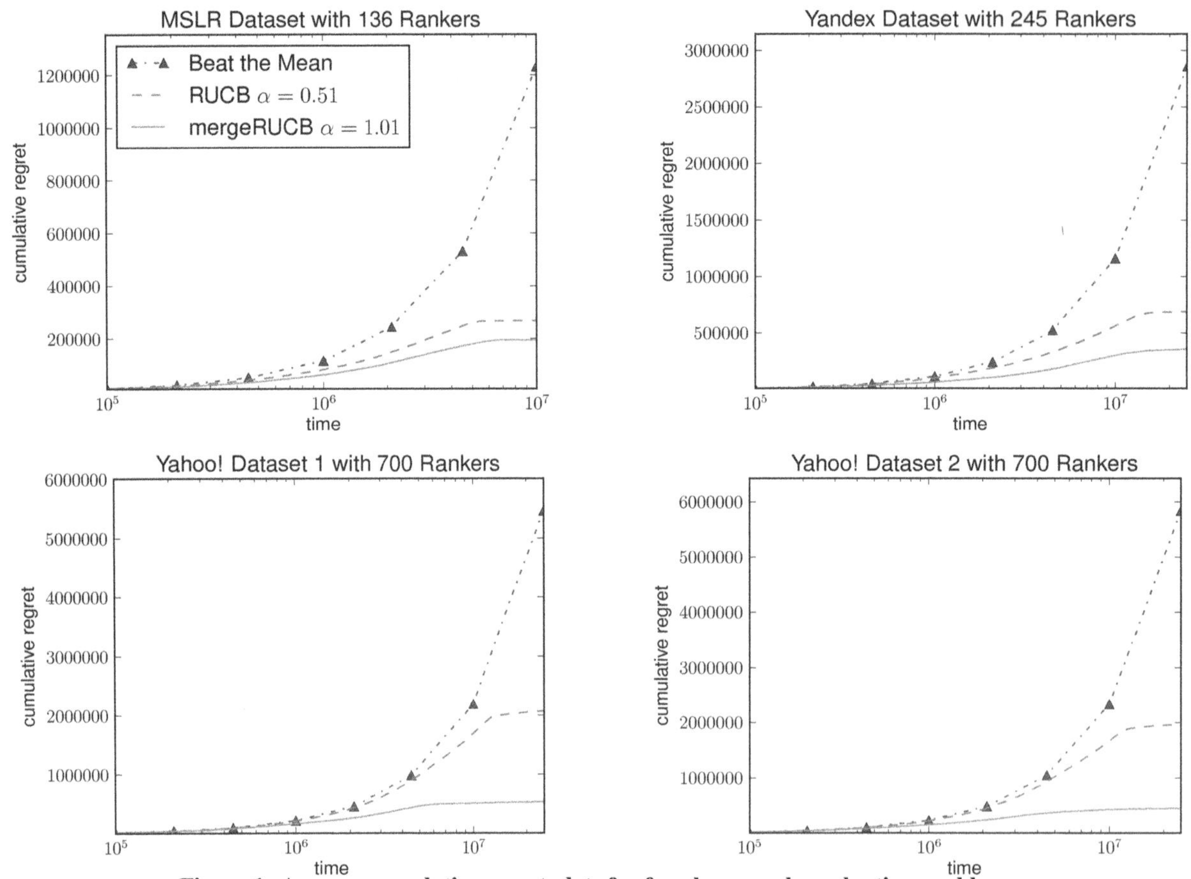

Figure 1: Average cumulative regret plots for four large-scale evaluation problems.

Table 1: The specifics of the datasets used.

Datasets	Queries	URLs	Features	Reference
MSLR-WEB30K	31,531	3,771,125	136	[22]
Yandex	9,124	97,290	245	[30]
YLR Set 1	19,944	473,134	700	[5]
YLR Set 2	1,266	34,815	700	[5]

point of view, this is a rather artificial setup because when optimizing a search engine one is rarely (if ever) interested in determining which single feature performs the best; instead, what is often of greater interest is comparing different rankers that were produced as the outcome of different learning to rank algorithms. However, what determines the difficulty of a dueling bandit problem is not the quality of the individual rankers but rather the difference in quality between pairs of rankers. So, for instance, evaluating K rankers that are very small modifications on the random ranker is as difficult as, say, evaluating K rankers that are small variations on LambdaMART [4]. More precisely, given a preference matrix $\mathbf{P}$, what determines the difficulty it poses for the dueling bandit algorithm is how close to 0.5 its entries are, and indeed, from our experience, the preference matrices of the feature rankers of the datasets listed in Table 1 does contains many entries that are very close to 0.5.

Given the above observation, we opted to use feature rankers in our experiments rather than, for instance, rankers produced by different learning to rank algorithms in order to both facilitate the reproducibility of our experimental results and to avoid having our results depend upon arbitrary choices made in the process of training such rankers. Nonetheless, comparing various dueling bandit algorithm on better performing rankers is an important research question that we postpone to future work.

To compare a pair of rankers, we use *probabilistic interleave* (PI) [14], though any other interleaved comparison method could be used instead. To model the user's click behavior on the resulting interleaved lists, we employ a probabilistic user model [10, 14] that uses as input the manual labels (classifying documents as relevant or not for given queries) provided with both datasets. Queries are sampled randomly and clicks are generated probabilistically by conditioning on these assessments using a user model that resembles the behavior of an actual user [12]. This approach follows an experimental paradigm that has previously been used for assessing the performance of rankers [13–16]. We used a software package called Lerot [27] to carry out these comparisons.[2]

For the large-scale experiments in §6.1, aimed at answering RQ1, we use all of the feature rankers available in these datasets and perform the comparisons between rankers by directly using Lerot to simulate interleaved comparisons. In this case, our assumption that there exists a Condorcet winner happens to be satisfied in the case of all four datasets. For all other experiments, for each value of K tested, we choose 10 subsets of rankers of size K and apply each algorithm to each subset: this choice is made by sampling subsets of size K at random and keeping the first 10 that have Condorcet winners. As illustrated in [33], the probability that a subset has a Condorcet winner depends on K, but is generally very high. In addition, since the Lerot-based experiments for RQ1 took three months to complete,[3] we use a faster proxy setup for

[2]The interested reader can find the repository at the following URL: `https://bitbucket.org/ilps/lerot`

[3]This was primarily due to shortcomings of the competing algo-

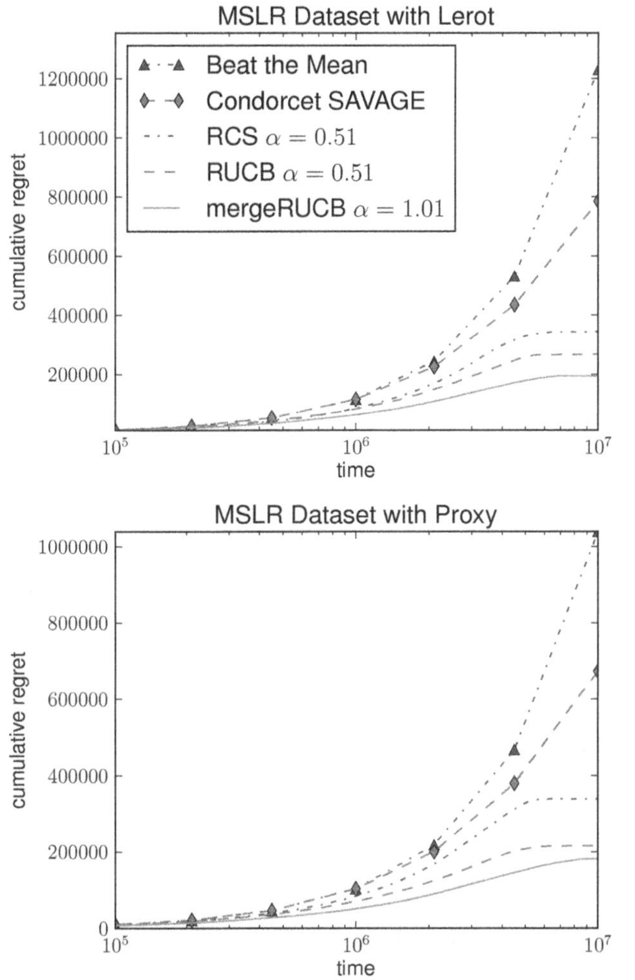

Figure 2: Average cumulative regret on the 136-ranker evaluation problem arising from the MSLR dataset using Lerot (top) or the proxy approach (bottom).

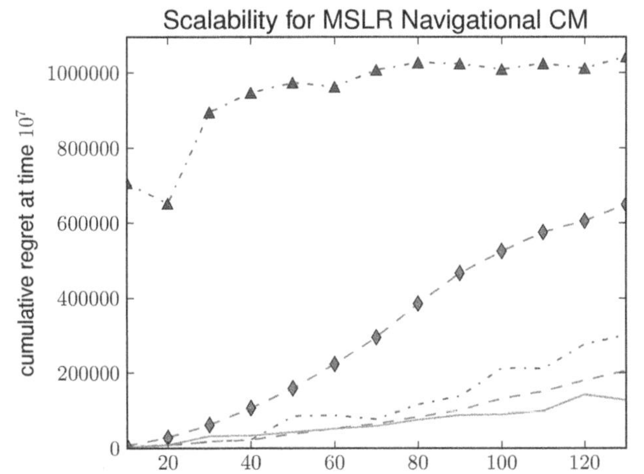

Figure 3: Average cumulative regret after 10^7 iterations on K-ranker evaluation problems with K ranging from 10 to 130.

the other experiments: for each pair of feature rankers ρ_i, ρ_j in the MSLR dataset, we estimate the probability p_{ij} that ρ_i beats ρ_j by simulating 400,000 interleaved comparisons between the two using Lerot.[4] Given these numbers p_{ij}, in the remaining experiments, we perform comparisons between rankers ρ_i and ρ_j for each pair (i, j) by drawing a sample from the Bernoulli distribution with mean p_{ij}, i.e., by flipping a biased coin. This is a standard approach to evaluating dueling bandit algorithms (cf. [31, 32, 34]). We verify the accuracy of the proxy approach in §6.2.

In principle, the proxy approach could also be used for the Yandex and the Yahoo! datasets. However, given the higher number of feature rankers in those datasets, obtaining the same level of precision on the preference probabilities p_{ij} would require orders of magnitude more computational resources. Indeed, it is more efficient to use Lerot directly for those experiments. Given this constraint, our experiments using the proxy method cannot go beyond 136 rankers.

In all experiments other than those in §6.5, we use the following parameter settings: $\alpha = 1.01$ and $p = 4$. In fact, the only constraint on α is that it should be greater than 0.5 in order for $C(\delta)$ (cf. Line 3 in Algorithm 1) to be well-defined and for our theoretical results in §7 to hold. However, as α approaches 0.5, the expression for $C(\delta)$ grows super-exponentially as a function of α, and so the benefits of having more slowly growing confidence intervals (cf. Line 7 of Algorithm 1) are outweighed by the added exploration caused by starting with larger confidence intervals. Indeed, as demonstrated in §6.5, there is little or no gain from changing these parameters from the above values. Moreover, for all of our experiments, we chose the probability of failure, δ to be 0.01. Finally, all experiments other than those in §6.4 used the navigational click model (cf. Table II of [15]) to simulate user click behavior.

6. RESULTS AND DISCUSSION

In this section, we present our experimental results.

6.1 Large scale experiments

We first address our main research question, **RQ1**. We tested mergeRUCB on the full set of feature vectors of the four large learning to rank datasets described in Table 1, directly using Lerot instead of the proxy approach. The MSLR results, shown in Fig. 1 (top-left), were carried out for 10 million time-steps, since two of the three algorithms converge to the Condorcet winner within that time frame. For the remaining datasets, we extended the horizon to 25 million time-steps, again to make sure two of the three algorithms converge. These results are shown in the remaining plots in Fig. 1. Note that, in these plots and those that follow, the time axis uses a log scale, while the vertical axis uses a linear scale.

For these experiments, we tested three algorithms: mergeRUCB and RUCB, which had the best performance in the scalability experiments in §6.3, together with BTM, which is the state of the art K-armed dueling bandit algorithm for large K, according to [28, 31]. These plots show that, as the number of rankers increases (going from 136 to 245 to 700), so does the difference between the performance of mergeRUCB and the remaining algorithms.

6.2 Lerot simulation vs Bernoulli samples

The remaining results presented in this work use the proxy approach described in §5. So, before proceeding further, we validate the proxy approach by showing that it provides qualitatively similar results to those generated with Lerot. To do so, we compare the performances of five K-armed dueling bandit algorithms on

rithms, which need to be run sequentially. By contrast, mergeRUCB can easily be parallelized across different batches.

[4]The resulting matrices can be found here (as Numpy matrices): `http://ilps.science.uva.nl/sites/ilps.science.uva.nl/files/PrefMats.zip`

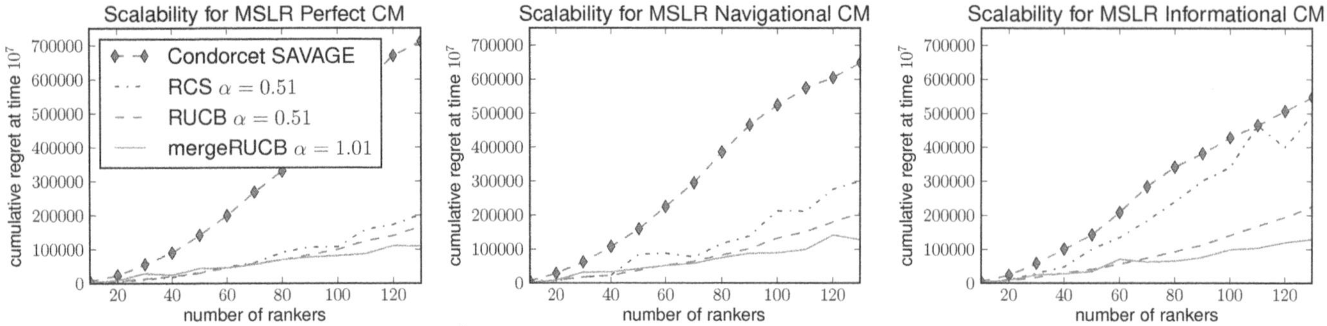

Figure 5: Average cumulative regret after 10^7 iterations on K-ranker evaluation problems with K ranging from 10 to 130 for the perfect (left), navigational (middle), and informational (right) click models.

the MSLR dataset using both approaches. The results for Lerot are shown in Fig. 2 (top), while those of the proxy approach are shown in Fig. 2 (bottom). Comparing the two plots shows that there is no qualitative difference in the relative performance of the various dueling bandit algorithms under consideration here. Consequently, we use the proxy method to conduct the experiments described in the rest of this section.

6.3 Dependence on K

To address **RQ2**, we compare 5 dueling-bandit algorithms on K-ranker evaluation experiments with K ranging from 10 to 130 in increments of 10 with the K rankers chosen randomly from the 136 feature rankers in the MSLR dataset.

Fig. 3 shows the results: the horizontal axis measures K, the number of rankers, while the vertical axis shows the regret accumulated after 10^7 iterations. As this plot demonstrates, for $K \geq 70$, mergeRUCB outperforms all other dueling bandit algorithms.

Of course, while Fig. 3 shows performance across different values of K, it does so for only one moment in time: after 10^7 iterations. However, comparing Fig. 3 to Fig. 2 confirms that, for $K = 136$, the regret accumulated by the algorithm after 10^7 time-steps is a good indication of the overall performance of the algorithm over time. Fig. 4 confirms that the same is true when $K = 70$.

6.4 Effect of click models

To address **RQ3**, we conducted the same scalability test as in §6.3, using three different click models proposed in [15], namely the *perfect*, *navigational* and *informational* click models. The perfect click model represents the behavior of a persistent user, who inspects every single document in the retrieved list and clicks on each document with a probability proportional to the document's relevance to the given query. The navigational click model simulates the behavior of a user who is trying to satisfy a specific information need and is likely to stop inspecting the items in the list upon viewing a relevant document. Finally, the informational click model mimics the behavior of a user whose information need is not satisfied by a single document and is trying to gather information about a general topic. Accordingly, the informational click model is more likely to continue inspecting the items retrieved by the ranker even after encountering a relevant document.

The results, shown in Fig. 5, demonstrate that RCS is affected more severely by the click model than either mergeRUCB or RUCB. This is because, in our experience, RCS tends to be sensitive to the margins by which the Condorcet winner beats the remaining rankers: as these gaps shrink, the performance of RCS degrades dramatically. This is precisely what takes place when one replaces the perfect click model with the navigational one and the latter with the informational click model, since doing so increases the number of clicks in interleaved comparisons, making them noisier.

6.5 Parameter dependence

To address **RQ4**, we repeated the experiments in §6.3, using the following grid of parameters:

$$(p, \alpha) \in \{4, 6, 8, 10\} \times \{0.71, 0.81, 0.91, 1.01, 1.11, 1.21\}.$$

Fig. 6 shows, for each number of rankers, the minimum and maximum cumulative regrets accumulated by mergeRUCB across the above set of parameters, as well as the regret for the default parameters used in the other experiments. Note that the vertical axis uses a log scale, which is chosen to facilitate comparing the three curves for small values of K, since in a linear plot they would be too close to distinguish from each other. As can be seen from the plots, the

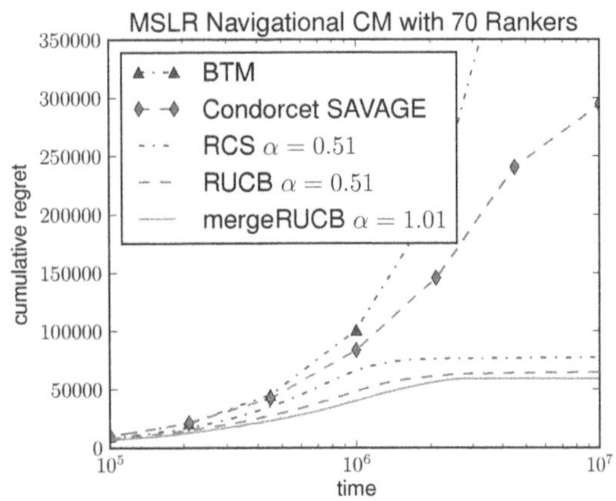

Figure 4: Average cumulative regret on the 70-ranker evaluation problem arising from MSLR.

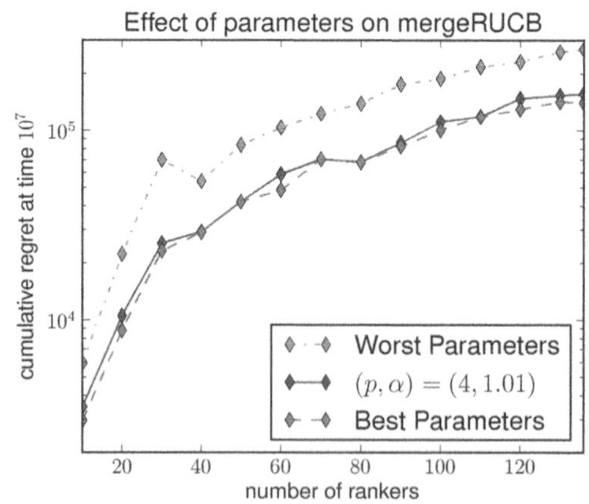

Figure 6: Effect of parameters on mergeRUCB's with MSLR dataset and navigational click model.

regret accumulated by mergeRUCB, using the default parameters $(p, \alpha) = (4, 1.01)$, is consistently close, if not equal, to the regret accumulated by the best choice of parameters, which validates our intuition that the default parameters are sensible.

7. PERFORMANCE GUARANTEES

In this section, we provide theoretical guarantees for the proper functioning and scalability of mergeRUCB. We begin by listing a number of reasonable assumptions that we impose upon the problem in order to guarantee the proper functioning of the algorithm:

A1. We assume that there is no repetition of rankers, i.e., any pair of rankers ρ_i and ρ_j are different and thus $p_{ij} \neq 0.5$, unless both rankers are *uninformative*: they provide no useful information and so lose to all other rankers, i.e., $p_{ki} \geq 0.5$ and $p_{kj} \geq 0.5$ for all k.

A2. We assume that at most a third of the rankers are uninformative.

In online ranker evaluation in web search settings, assumption **A1** is reasonable because the rankers ρ_i under evaluation are typically the result of substantial deliberation and research and so the chances of the same informative ranker appearing twice are slim. The second assumption is motivated by the Yahoo! Learning to Rank challenge dataset, in which either 104 or 181 (depending on the dataset) out of 700 feature rankers always return zero. More generally, it is plausible that some uninformative rankers are inadvertently included in the evaluation process. However, if there are too many of them, the evaluation task will be lengthened.

Here, we provide a high probability bound on the regret accumulated by mergeRUCB; Table 2 lists our notation.

THEOREM 1. *Given a K-armed dueling bandit problem with rankers $\rho_1, \dots, \rho_K$ with ρ_1 the Condorcet winner, then if we apply mergeRUCB(δ), with probability $1-\delta$ we have the following bound on cumulative regret at time T:*

$$R_T \leq \frac{16\alpha pK \ln(T + C(\delta)) \max_j \Delta_{1j}}{\min_{S=1,\dots,\lceil \log_2 K\rceil} \widehat{\Delta}_S^2} \leq \frac{8\alpha pK \ln(T + C(\delta))}{\min_{\{(i,j)\,|\,p_{ij}\neq 0.5\}} \Delta_{ij}^2}.$$

This theorem says that if mergeRUCB is run for T time-steps with probability of failure set to δ, then with probability $1 - \delta$, the total regret accumulated by the algorithm is bounded by an expression that is logarithmic in T and linear in K. This in turn tells us that the number of suboptimal interleaved comparisons grows linearly in K, since accumulating non-zero regret corresponds to suboptimal comparisons. Unlike existing results in the literature, the strongest of which take the form $\mathcal{O}(K^2) + \mathcal{O}(K \log T)$, Theorem 1 is the first regret bound that is completely linear in K.

Furthermore, even though as stated the above theorem is a high probability bound, by setting $\delta = 1/T$, we obtain a bound on the expected regret of mergeRUCB at time T as follows: since the maximum amount of regret that the algorithm can accumulate in the first T time-steps is bounded by T, we have

$$\begin{aligned}\mathbf{E}R_T &\leq \delta T + (1-\delta)\frac{8\alpha pK \ln(T + C(\delta))}{\Delta_{\min}^2}\\ &\leq 1 + \frac{8\alpha pK \ln T}{\Delta_{\min}^2} + \frac{8\alpha pKC(1/T)}{T\Delta_{\min}^2},\\ &\leq 1 + \frac{8\alpha pK \ln T}{\Delta_{\min}^2} + \frac{8\alpha pK\left(\frac{T(4\alpha-1)K^2}{(2\alpha-1)}\right)^{\frac{1}{2\alpha-1}}}{T\Delta_{\min}^2},\end{aligned}$$

Table 2: List of notation used in Section 7.

Symbol	Definition
K	Number of rankers
α	Exploration parameter in Algorithm 1
δ	Probability of failure
p	Initial size of the batches
S	Stage of the algorithm
$\mathcal{B}_S$	Set of batches in stage S
b_S	Number of batches in stage S
R_T	Cumulative regret at time T
$w_{ij}(t)$	Number of times ρ_i beat ρ_j in the first t time-steps
$N_{ij}(t)$	$w_{ij}(t) + w_{ji}(t)$
$u_{ij}(t)$	$\mathbf{U}_{ij} := \frac{w_{ij}(t)}{N_{ij}(t)} + \sqrt{\frac{\alpha \ln t}{N_{ij}(t)}}$
$l_{ij}(t)$	$1 - u_{ji}(t)$
$C(\delta)$	$\left\lceil \left(\frac{(4\alpha-1)K^2}{(2\alpha-1)\delta}\right)^{\frac{1}{2\alpha-1}} \right\rceil$
Δ_{ij}	$p_{ij} - 0.5$
$\Delta_{B,\min}$	$\min_{i,j\in B} \Delta_{ij}$
T_B	$\frac{4\alpha\binom{q-1}{2}\log(T + C(\delta))}{\Delta_{B,\min}^2}$
T_i	T_{B_i}
$\widehat{\Delta}_S$	$\left(\frac{2b_S}{3}+1\right)^{th}$ largest element of $\{\Delta_{B,\min} \mid B \in \mathcal{B}_S\}$
$\widehat{T}_S$	$\frac{8\alpha pK \ln(T + C(\delta))}{\widehat{\Delta}_S^2}$
$\ln t$	Natural logarithm of t

where $\Delta_{\min} = \min_{\{(i,j)\,|\,p_{ij}\neq 0.5\}} \Delta_{ij}^2$ and the second inequality is obtained by using a Taylor expansion of $\ln t$ at $t = T$. Now, if $\alpha \geq 1$, the last summand in the right-hand side of the above inequality is in $\mathcal{O}(1)$, and so we have a finite-horizon expected regret bound of the form $\mathcal{O}(K \ln T)$. Moreover, this finite horizon bound can be turned into an infinite horizon one (up to $\ln \ln T$ factors) using the 'squaring trick' [2]. We would like to emphasize that these results hold under very general assumptions that do not preclude the existence of cyclical relationships among the rankers.

The proof of Theorem 1 relies on the following lemma.

LEMMA 2. *In mergeRUCB(δ), consider a batch B of size q, at least one of whose rankers is informative. Let $\Delta_{B,\min}$ denote the smallest nonzero gap $\Delta_{kl} := |p_{kl} - \frac{1}{2}| \neq 0$, with $\rho_k, \rho_l \in B$. Then, the number of comparisons N_B that could have happened between pairs of rankers in B before it is merged with another batch is bounded with probability $1-\delta$ as follows:*

$$N_B < T_B := \frac{4\alpha\binom{q-1}{2}\ln(T + C(\delta))}{\Delta_{B,\min}^2}.$$

The proof of this lemma follows directly from the fact that the number of comparisons between any pair of rankers in the batch is at most $\frac{4\alpha \ln(T+C(\delta))}{\Delta_{B,\min}^2}$, as proven in Lemma 3 below, since there are $\binom{q-1}{2}$ distinct pairs of rankers in B.

LEMMA 3. *Given any pair of distinct rankers $\rho_i, \rho_j \in B$, the maximum number of comparisons that could have been carried out between these two rankers in the first T time-steps of Algorithm 1 before a merger between B and another batch occurs, is bounded by $\frac{4\alpha \ln(T+C(\delta))}{\Delta_{B,\min}^2}$.*

The proof of Lemma 3 considers the two possible cases: either at least one of the rankers under consideration is informative or both are uninformative. In the first case, if the two rankers have been compared more times than the above number, we show that one of the two must have eliminated the other, while in the second case, if the two rankers have been compared too many times, then a third, informative ranker (whose existence is guaranteed by the assumption of the lemma) must have eliminated one of them.

The proof of the above lemma relies on the following result, which we repeat here for the reader's convenience:

LEMMA 4 (LEMMA 1 IN [34]). *Let $\mathbf{P} := [p_{ij}]$ be the preference matrix of a K-armed dueling bandit problem with arms $\{a_1, \ldots, a_K\}$. Then, for any dueling bandit algorithm and any $\alpha > \frac{1}{2}$ and $\delta > 0$, we have*

$$P\Big(\forall t > C(\delta), i, j,\ p_{ij} \in [l_{ij}(t), u_{ij}(t)]\Big) > 1 - \delta.$$

PROOF OF LEMMA 3. Let us begin by assuming that the number of comparisons between ρ_i and ρ_j is greater than $\frac{4\alpha \ln(T+C(\delta))}{\Delta^2_{B,\min}}$, and let us distinguish between two cases:

1. *At least one of ρ_i and ρ_j is informative*: in this case, by assumption **A1**, we know that $p_{ij} \neq 0.5$, and moreover by Lemma 4, we know that with probability $1-\delta$ we have $p_{ij} \in [l_{ij}(t), u_{ij}(t)]$, with t being the last time that ρ_i was compared against ρ_j and $l_{ij} := 1 - u_{ji}$. However, this tells us that one of the two rankers should have been eliminated already, since we have

$$u_{ij}(t) - l_{ij}(t) = 2\sqrt{\frac{\alpha \ln(t + C(\delta))}{N_{ij}(t)}} \leq 2\sqrt{\frac{\alpha \ln(T + C(\delta))}{N_{ij}(t)}}$$
$$< 2\sqrt{\frac{\alpha \ln(t + C(\delta))}{\frac{4\alpha \ln(T + C(\delta))}{\Delta^2_{B,\min}}}} = \Delta_{B,\min} \leq \Delta_{ij}, \qquad (1)$$

where the last inequality is due to our assumption that $N_{ij}(t) > \frac{4\alpha \ln(T+C(\delta))}{\Delta^2_{B,\min}}$. Therefore, the confidence interval $[l_{ij}(t), u_{ij}(t)]$ does not contain 0.5, which is the criterion used by Algorithm 1 to eliminate rankers.

2. *Rankers ρ_i and ρ_j are both uninformative*: by assumption **A1** and Lemma 4, uninformative rankers cannot eliminate informative rankers, so no matter how many rankers have been eliminated from B, there must be an uneliminated third ranker ρ_k that is informative in the batch together with ρ_i and ρ_j, and by assumption **A1**, we have $p_{ki} > 0.5$ and $p_{kj} > 0.5$. Again, applying Lemma 4 as in the previous case, we know that with probability $1 - \delta$ we have $0.5 = p_{ij} \in [l_{ij}(t), u_{ij}(t)]$; on the other hand, using the same chain of inequalities as in (1), we can deduce that

$$u_{ij}(t) - l_{ij}(t) < \Delta_{B,\min} \leq \min\{\Delta_{ki}, \Delta_{kj}\}. \qquad (2)$$

Now, in order for ρ_i to have been compared to ρ_j at time t, we must have had one of the following two scenarios:

(a) mergeRUCB chose $c = i$ and $d = j$ at time t: this requires the satisfaction of the following two conditions:

- $u_{ij}(t) \geq 0.5$, by Line 8 of Algorithm 1.
- $l_{ij}(t) \leq p_{ik}$: this is because in order to have $d = j$, we must have $u_{ji}(t) \geq u_{ki}(t)$ and by Lemma 4, we have $u_{ki}(t) \geq p_{ki}$, and so $l_{ij}(t) := 1 - u_{ji}(t) \leq 1 - p_{ki} = p_{ik}$.

This means that we have $u_{ij}(t) - l_{ij}(t) \geq \Delta_{ki}$. However, this contradicts inequality (2), so we could not have had $(c, d) = (i, j)$.

(b) mergeRUCB chose $c = j$ and $d = i$ at time t: repeating the same argument as in the previous case with i and j swapped, we get $u_{ji}(t) - l_{ji}(t) \geq \Delta_{kj}$, which also contradicts inequality (2).

Therefore, our assumption that the number of comparisons between ρ_i and ρ_j is greater than $\frac{4\alpha \ln(T+C(\delta))}{\Delta^2_{B,\min}}$ cannot hold in either scenario. □

Next, we prove Theorem 1, the main idea of which is as follows. The central difficulty in the proof is that there may exist batches that consist entirely of uninformative rankers. This is problematic because in these batches no rankers are eliminated, since for each pair of rankers ρ_i, ρ_j in such a batch, we have $p_{ij} = 0.5$ and so with high probability we have neither $u_{ij} < 0.5$ nor $u_{ji} < 0.5$. The proof overcomes this difficulty by showing that such fully uninformative batches all disappear at the end of the first stage of the algorithm. This occurs because of how the batches are merged at the end of each stage (cf. Line 13 of Algorithm 1): the largest batches are combined with the smallest ones. Since uninformative batches inevitably fail to eliminate any rankers, they have the largest number of rankers, while the smallest batches are guaranteed to contain informative rankers. Therefore, from the second stage onwards, mergeRUCB is guaranteed not to compare rankers in a batch, none of whose elements will be eliminated.

PROOF OF THEOREM 1. We begin by considering the first stage of the algorithm:

$S = 1$ During the first stage, we have two types of batches: those that consist solely of uninformative rankers and those that contain at least one informative ranker. Assumption **A2** implies that at least two thirds of the batches have at least one informative ranker, so we can apply Lemma 2 to them.

To estimate number of time-steps mergeRUCB spends in its first stage, we introduce the following notation: recall from Algorithm 1 that b_1 is the number of partitions in the first stage of the algorithm and let $\widehat{\Delta}_1$ denote the $\left(\frac{2b_1}{3} + 1\right)^{th}$ largest number in the set $\{\Delta_{B,\min} | B \in \mathcal{B}_1\}$. Now, once all but one of the rankers in every batch B with $\Delta_{B,\min} \geq \widehat{\Delta}_1$ have been eliminated, the algorithm moves to the next stage. This occurs because at least half of the rankers have been eliminated, since there are $\frac{2b_1}{3} + 1$ batches, inside which $p - 1$ rankers are eliminated, and so the total number of eliminated rankers is at least

$$\left(\frac{2b_1}{3} + 1\right)(p-1) \geq \frac{2(b_1+1)}{3}(p-1) \geq \frac{2K}{3p}(p-1)$$
$$\geq \frac{2K}{3}\frac{3}{4} \geq \frac{K}{2}. \qquad \text{(since } p \geq 4\text{)}$$

Therefore, Line 12 of Algorithm 1 forces the next stage to begin. Now, applying Lemma 2 to the $\frac{2b_1}{3}$ batches B with $\Delta_{B,\min} \geq \widehat{\Delta}_1$, and using the fact that the size of the batches is at most $2p$ (cf. Line 2 of Algorithm 1), we can conclude that with probability $1 - \delta$ the number of time-steps in the first stage of mergeRUCB could not have been more than

$$\frac{K}{p} \times \frac{4\alpha\binom{2p}{2}\ln(T + C(\delta))}{\widehat{\Delta}_1^2} \leq \frac{8\alpha p K \ln(T + C(\delta))}{\widehat{\Delta}_1^2} =: \widehat{T}_1.$$

$S \geq 2$ At the end of the first stage of the algorithm, we combine the largest remaining batches with the smallest ones. The fact that exactly half of the rankers were eliminated in the first stage implies that this policy for combining batches forces every fully uninformative batch to acquire an informative ranker, since by

Assumption **A1** and Lemma 4, the probability of an uninformative ranker eliminating an informative ranker is less than δ. Hence, from this point on, we can apply Lemma 2 to every batch.

We can use a similar argument as with the first stage of the algorithm to bound the number of time-steps that mergeRUCB would spend in the Sth stage. To that end, let $\widehat{\Delta}_S$ denote the $\left(\frac{2b_S}{3}+1\right)^{th}$ largest number in the set $\{\Delta_{B,\min} | B \in \mathcal{B}_S\}$. Now, applying the same argument as above and using the fact that in stage S we have $K/2^{S-1}$ rankers, we get that the number of comparisons in stage S of mergeRUCB is bounded by $\frac{8\alpha p K \ln(T+C(\delta))}{2^{S-1}\widehat{\Delta}_S^2} =: \widehat{T}_S$.

After $\lceil \log_2 K \rceil$ stages, only a single ranker remains, beyond which point mergeRUCB goes on interleaving that ranker with itself. This ranker is the Condorcet winner with probability $1-\delta$ because the probability of the Condorcet winner being eliminated by another ranker is at most δ. Therefore, in order to estimate the total regret accumulated by mergeRUCB we can sum the $\widehat{T}_S$ for $S = 1, \ldots, \lceil \log_2 K \rceil$ and multiply the result by the maximum regret any comparison can result in, which is $\max_j \Delta_{1j}$. This gives the bound in the statement of Theorem 1 once we notice that

$$\sum_{S=1}^{\lceil \log_2 K \rceil} \frac{1}{2^{S-1}\widehat{\Delta}_S} \leq \frac{2}{\min\limits_{S=1,\ldots,\lceil \log_2 K \rceil} \widehat{\Delta}_S^2}$$

This concludes the proof of Theorem 1. □

A tighter result could be obtained by bounding the regret for comparisons inside batch B during the Sth stage of mergeRUCB with $\max_{i,j \in B} \Delta_{ij}$ rather than $\max_j \Delta_{1j}$. This would make the statement of the theorem more difficult to understand and the proof longer, so we opted for this simpler, slightly weaker bound for the sake of readability and brevity.

8. RECENT DEVELOPMENTS

Recently, three new dueling bandit algorithms were proposed: Doubler, MultiSBM and Sparring [1]. While Doubler and MultiSBM have performance guarantees, these hold only under the stringent assumption that each ranker has an underlying absolute utility, from which the preference matrix **P** is generated. This precludes the presence of cyclical preference relationships among the rankers and, as demonstrated in [33, 34], such a total ordering assumption is often violated in practice. Sparring has no performance guarantees but outperforms Doubler and MultiSBM in the experiments presented in [1].

Because of the recency of their publication, a comprehensive experimental comparison involving these new methods was not feasible, since large-scale experiments with Lerot would require months to complete and the proxy method cannot go beyond 136 rankers, as discussed in §5. However, we do offer some preliminary small-scale results here. We excluded Doubler from these results since in the experiments performed in [1], it was outperformed by all other algorithms in every single experiment. Our results, shown in Fig. 7, suggest that MultiSBM is consistently outperformed by most existing state-of-the-art algorithms, while the situation is more complicated for Sparring.

Sparring performs well in some cases, as shown in Fig. 7 (top). The fact that Sparring outperforms mergeRUCB in this setting with few rankers is not surprising, since mergeRUCB is designed to excel given many rankers and is already outperformed by both RUCB and RCS when there are only few rankers. However, even given only few rankers, there are settings in which Sparring does poorly, as shown in Fig. 7 (bottom). In our preliminary experiments, Sparring's performance degrades dramatically as the top *Borda scores* become closer to each other, where the Borda score for ranker ρ_i is defined to be $\sum_j p_{ij}$ [28]. This phenomenon occurs because Sparring chooses rankers to interleave based on its estimate of their Borda scores. Given the potential of Sparring to fail in this way, its practical utility in online ranker evaluation may be limited. More extensive empirical comparisons, especially in settings with many rankers, as well as a theoretical analysis of Sparring, are needed.

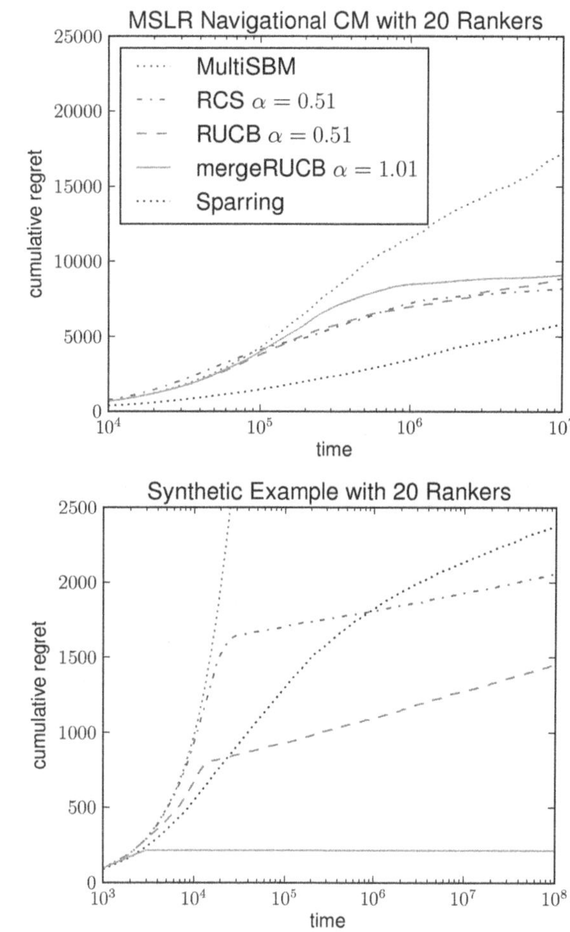

Figure 7: Comparisons against Sparring.

9. CONCLUSION

In this paper, we proposed a new algorithm, called mergeRUCB, for the online ranker evaluation problem in situations that are of particular interest for web search, i.e., with large numbers of rankers. We conducted extensive experimentation to understand the behavior of this algorithm in comparison to other online evaluations algorithms. The results of these experiments demonstrate that mergeRUCB can significantly outperform existing state of the art algorithms on large-scale evaluation problems. Moreover, we provided theoretical guarantees proving the proper functioning of mergeRUCB.

The algorithm presented in this paper makes it feasible for search engines to perform large-scale online ranker evaluation experiments that might be too costly if other K-armed dueling bandit algorithms were used. Furthermore, our theoretical results provide the necessary assurance for undertaking such large-scale evaluation tasks.

Since we care more about the worst-case performance of ranker evaluation algorithms than their average performance, our regret bounds are high probability rather than in expectation, unlike previous work such as [32, 34].

In future work, we intend to conduct more thorough comparisons with the recently proposed Sparring algorithm, whose behavior is not as well understood and whose performance can vary substantially, as we have briefly seen, depending on the online ranker evaluation at hand. Another possible direction for future research is to use the "locality" ideas in this paper together with continuous armed bandit algorithms like Branch and Bound [11] to extend online ranker evaluation to an infinite number of rankers, for instance if the rankers are defined in terms of continuous parameters.

Acknowledgments. We would like to thank the reviewers for their many helpful comments on this manuscript.

This research was partially supported by the European Community's Seventh Framework Programme (FP7/2007-2013) under grant agreement nr 312827 (VOX-Pol), the Netherlands Organisation for Scientific Research (NWO) under project nrs 727.011.005, 612.001.116, HOR-11-10, 640.-006.013, 612.066.930, the Center for Creation, Content and Technology (CCCT), the Dutch national program COMMIT, the ESF Research Network Program ELIAS, the Elite Network Shifts project funded by the Royal Dutch Academy of Sciences (KNAW), the Netherlands eScience Center under project number 027.012.105, the Yahoo! Faculty Research and Engagement Program, the Microsoft Research PhD program, and the HPC Fund.

REFERENCES

[1] N. Ailon, Z. Karnin, and T. Joachims. Reducing dueling bandits to cardinal bandits. In *ICML*, 2014.

[2] K. Amin, M. Kearns, and U. Syed. Bandits, query learning, and the haystack dimension. In *COLT 2011 - The 24th Annual Conference on Learning Theory, June 9-11, 2011, Budapest, Hungary*, pages 87–106, 2011.

[3] P. Auer, N. Cesa-Bianchi, and P. Fischer. Finite-time analysis of the multiarmed bandit problem. *Machine Learning*, 47 (2-3):235–256, 2002.

[4] C. J. Burges. From ranknet to lambdarank to lambdamart: An overview. Techn. Report MSR-TR-2010-82, Microsoft Research, June 2010.

[5] O. Chapelle and Y. Chang. Yahoo! learning to rank challenge overview. *Journal of Machine Learning Research-Proceedings Track*, 14:1–24, 2011.

[6] O. Chapelle and L. Li. An empirical evaluation of Thompson sampling. In *NIPS*, 2011.

[7] O. Chapelle, T. Joachims, F. Radlinski, and Y. Yue. Large-scale validation and analysis of interleaved search evaluation. *ACM Trans. Inf. Syst.*, 30:1–41, 2012.

[8] A. Chuklin, A. Schuth, K. Hofmann, P. Serdyukov, and M. de Rijke. Evaluating aggregated search using interleaving. In *CIKM 2013*. ACM, 2013.

[9] C. W. Cleverdon, J. Mills, and M. Keen. Factors determining the performance of indexing systems. In *ASLIB Cranfield project*. 1966.

[10] N. Craswell, O. Zoeter, M. Taylor, and B. Ramsey. An experimental comparison of click position-bias models. In *WSDM '08*, pages 87–94, 2008.

[11] N. de Freitas, A. Smola, and M. Zoghi. Exponential regret bounds for Gaussian process bandits with deterministic observations. In *ICML '12*, 2012.

[12] F. Guo, C. Liu, and Y. M. Wang. Efficient multiple-click models in web search. In *WSDM '09*, pages 124–131, New York, NY, USA, 2009. ACM.

[13] J. He, C. Zhai, and X. Li. Evaluation of methods for relative comparison of retrieval systems based on clickthroughs. In *CIKM '09*, pages 2029–2032, 2009.

[14] K. Hofmann, S. Whiteson, and M. de Rijke. A probabilistic method for inferring preferences from clicks. In *CIKM '11*, pages 249–258, USA, 2011.

[15] K. Hofmann, S. Whiteson, and M. de Rijke. Fidelity, soundness, and efficiency of interleaved comparison methods. *ACM Trans. Inf. Syst.*, 31(4), 2013.

[16] K. Hofmann, S. Whiteson, and M. de Rijke. Balancing exploration and exploitation in listwise and pairwise online learning to rank for information retrieval. *Information Retrieval*, 16(1):63–90, 2013.

[17] S. Ji, K. Zhou, C. Liao, Z. Zheng, G.-R. Xue, O. Chapelle, G. Sun, and H. Zha. Global ranking by exploiting user clicks. In *SIGIR '09*, 2009.

[18] T. Joachims. Evaluating retrieval performance using clickthrough data. In J. Franke, G. Nakhaeizadeh, and I. Renz, editors, *Text Mining*, pages 79–96. 2003.

[19] S. Jung, J. L. Herlocker, and J. Webster. Click data as implicit relevance feedback in web search. *Information Processing & Management*, 43(3):791–807, 2007.

[20] J. Kamps, M. Koolen, and A. Trotman. Comparative analysis of clicks and judgments for IR evaluation. In *WSCD'09*, pages 80–87, 2009.

[21] R. Kohavi, A. Deng, B. Frasca, T. Walker, Y. Xu, and N. Pohlmann. Online controlled experiments at large scale. In *KDD '13*, pages 1168–1176. ACM, 2013.

[22] Microsoft Learning to Rank Datasets, 2012. `http://research.microsoft.com/en-us/proj\-ects/mslr/default.aspx`.

[23] F. Radlinski and N. Craswell. Comparing the sensitivity of information retrieval metrics. In *SIGIR '10*, pages 667–674, 2010.

[24] F. Radlinski and N. Craswell. Optimized interleaving for online retrieval evaluation. In *WSDM '13*, 2013.

[25] F. Radlinski, M. Kurup, and T. Joachims. How does clickthrough data reflect retrieval quality? In *CIKM '08*, pages 43–52, 2008.

[26] F. Scholer, M. Shokouhi, B. Billerbeck, and A. Turpin. Using clicks as implicit judgments: expectations versus observations. In *ECIR'08*, pages 28–39, 2008.

[27] A. Schuth, K. Hofmann, S. Whiteson, and M. de Rijke. Lerot: an online learning to rank framework. In *Living Labs '13*, 2013.

[28] T. Urvoy, F. Clerot, R. Féraud, and S. Naamane. Generic exploration and k-armed voting bandits. In *ICML*, 2013.

[29] E. M. Voorhees and D. K. Harman. *TREC: Experiment and Evaluation in Information Retrieval*. MIT Press, 2005.

[30] Yandex Internet Mathematics 2009 Dataset, 2009. `http://imat2009.yandex.ru/en/datasets`.

[31] Y. Yue and T. Joachims. Beat the mean bandit. In *ICML*, 2011.

[32] Y. Yue, J. Broder, R. Kleinberg, and T. Joachims. The K-armed dueling bandits problem. *J. Comp. Syst. Sciences*, 78(5):1538–1556, 2009.

[33] M. Zoghi, S. Whiteson, M. de Rijke, and R. Munos. Relative confidence sampling for efficient on-line ranker evaluation. In *WSDM '14*, 2014.

[34] M. Zoghi, S. Whiteson, R. Munos, and M. de Rijke. Relative upper confidence bound for the k-armed dueling bandits problem. In *ICML*, 2014.

Engagement Periodicity in Search Engine Usage: Analysis and its Application to Search Quality Evaluation

Alexey Drutsa
Yandex
Moscow, Russia
adrutsa@yandex.ru

Gleb Gusev
Yandex
Moscow, Russia
gleb57@yandex-team.ru

Pavel Serdyukov
Yandex
Moscow, Russia
pavser@yandex-team.ru

ABSTRACT

Nowadays, billions of people use the Web in connection with their daily needs. A significant part of the needs are constituted by search tasks that are usually addressed by search engines. Thus, daily search needs result in regular user engagement with a search engine. User engagement with web sites and services was studied in various aspects, but there appear to be no studies of its regularity and periodicity. In this paper, we studied periodicity of the user engagement with a popular search engine through applying spectrum analysis to temporal sequences of different engagement metrics. We found periodicity patterns of user engagement and revealed classes of users whose periodicity patterns do not change over a long period of time. In addition, we used the spectrum series as metrics to evaluate search quality.

Categories and Subject Descriptions:

H.1.2 [User/Machine Systems]: Human information processing; H.5.2 [User interface]: Evaluation/methodology.

General Terms: Measurement, Experimentation

Keywords: User engagement; periodicity; DFT; spectrum analysis; quality metrics

1. INTRODUCTION

Some aims of users navigating the Web arise extremely rarely, some others arise repeatedly and make users access certain web services on a regular basis. The permanent usage of a particular service usually refers to a *user engagement* with it. The engagement is one of the major aspects [18] of user behavior that affects the profit and the popularity for majority of web sites. Thus, it is highly important for a web service to know and understand how its users are engaged. In order to describe and quantify user engagement, a series of metrics are developed. They could reflect different aspects of user engagement, from loyalty (e.g., the number of sessions per user per day [21]) to activity (e.g., the number of visited web pages [15]).

WSDM'15, February 2–6, 2015, Shanghai, China.

http://dx.doi.org/10.1145/2684822.2685318.

Web service usage is closely related to the individual life cycles of users (work, entertainment, holidays, etc.) that should result in periodicity of user engagement metrics. However, to the best of our knowledge, the effects of repetition and periodicity in user engagement are largely understudied in the existing research on user engagement (see Section 2).

In the current paper, we focus on periodicity in search behavior of users engaged by a search engine. On the one hand, one week and one year periodicity of behavioral metrics averaged over all users is well known[1]. On the other hand, the periodicity patterns for each individual user could vary significantly and may not match with the average periodicity [14]. For instance, an office worker uses a search engine for her work-related purposes at her work place. Therefore, her engagement with the search engine will be observed only within working days with different intensity which depends on the worker's schedule. On the other hand, a student may intensify her search engine usage during preparations for a test that could be held once every two or more weeks. Thus her search periodicity pattern differs from the pattern of the office worker. This motivates us to develop a methodology that detects periodicity phenomena in user engagement, and, in our work, we study and apply a technique that extracts individual periodic patterns of search engine users.

In order to catch periodicity in user engagement variance, we apply *spectrum analysis*[2]. Namely, we regard basic engagement metrics of a user (obtained from internal logs of a popular search engine) as time series within 4-week periods. Then, we translate them into sequences of Fourier amplitudes in a *frequency domain* by means of *the discrete Fourier transform* (*DFT*). We perform a detailed analysis of the obtained data and we show that there are identifiable patterns of user periodic behavior. Then we study the changes of these patterns over a period of five months. Further, we find stable groups of users that do not change their 4-week periodicity pattern during the long time period. We also show that the user engagement metrics extracted from the frequency domain are more consistent over the five-month period than the ones extracted from the source time domain. All these results justify the positive effect of applying the DFT for extracting periodicity from the user behavior data and *represent the first major contribution of this study.*

We reinforce the results of our analysis by applying the proposed method to evaluation of changes in a search sys-

[1]It is noted both in related work [14, 16, 20, 22, 24, 17] and observed in our study (see Section 5).

[2]Spectrum analysis is commonly used for identification of periodic phenomena in temporal sequences [23, 22, 24].

tem. Development of a search engine is based on ongoing updates, which are shipped permanently. In order to validate the positive effect of a change or at least to prevent its negative consequences, the development team compares the updated version of the service with respect to the previous one. The comparison is made in terms of quality, which needs to be quantified. This motivates to develop and study new search engine *quality metrics*. Variations in the ranking algorithm or the user interface (UI) may significantly change the habitual ways of interaction with the service and, therefore, may affect user periodicity behavior, which could serve as an indicator of these changes. In order to examine this assumption, we apply our periodicity patterns as new quality metrics (56 in total) and we validate them on a series of experiments that show (a) their insensitivity to changes, where updated version coincide with the previous one and (b) their sensitivity to artificial deterioration of the quality of different components of the search engine (such as the ranking algorithm, the UI, and the engine efficiency). In our experiments, we show that frequency domain approach for extracting periodicity patterns can be effectively used to provide more sensitive quality metrics for search engine evaluation. *We regard this as the second major contribution of our study.*

The rest of the paper is organized as follows. In Section 2, the related work is presented. In Section 3, the periodicity patterns of individual user behavior are introduced and the research questions are stated. In Section 4, we describe our user engagement data. In Section 5, the basic analysis of the periodicity patterns is presented. In Section 6, the long-term changes of user periodicity behavior are studied. In Section 7, the periodicity patterns are applied as metrics for search quality evaluation. In Section 8, the study's conclusions and future work are presented.

2. RELATED WORK

We compare our research with other studies in three aspects. The first one relates to search engine usage studies. The second one concerns periodicity in user behavior. The third aspect refers to analysis of user engagement with web services in general.

Search engine usage studies. On the one hand, the search engine usage studies on a high level could be divided with respect to short-term (within a search task or a search session) and long-term (across a series of such tasks and sessions) usage. On the other hand, they could be regarded both with respect to user interaction with the service and with respect to user's profit from usage of the service[3]. All these aspects are closely interrelated. For example, user dissatisfaction with a particular attempt to solve a search task may lead to a switch [25, 7, 4, 19] to another search engine on the short-term level. Simultaneously, a series of satisfied interactions with the service lead to the notion of user happiness [6, 9, 8, 10] on the long-term level. In our work, we study user engagement which is the long term user interaction component of the described classification.

Existing studies of user engagement with a search engine are three-fold. First, the studies [26, 11] discovered the relationship between search success and search engine reuse with respect to three search engines of different popularity. The authors of [26] also identified three groups of behavior patterns of simultaneous usage of the search engines within 6-month period (users who use only one search engine, who change search engines periodically, and who switch to another search engine and do not return back). In our work, we study 4-week behavior patterns, and their tendency to be stable during 5-month period is identified.

Second, some studies focused on the prediction of future changes in some user engagement metrics. Prediction of user switching type (no switch, persistent switch, or oscillating switch) between search engines during 26 weeks was studied in [26]. The authors of [21] developed a binary classifier to predict user engagement increase/decrease in the future week. They utilized the average number of sessions as the primary engagement metric on a par with some non-engagement measures (query types, user satisfaction, etc.) from the last three weeks.

Third, user engagement is used as service quality metrics for search engine evaluation. The search engine quality can be evaluated on different levels: the quality of a particular service component (e.g., a ranking algorithm, the user interface, etc.) and the quality of the web service as a whole either on short-term interactions (e.g., by evaluating search task satisfaction, switching, etc.) or on long-term usage (e.g., changes in happiness and engagement). The authors of [21] evaluated different changes in search relevance of a popular search engine by means of the A/B testing methodology with respect to the average number of sessions and several non-engagement measures reflecting query types and user satisfaction. The absence time (the time between two user visits) on a par with other engagement metrics was applied [5] to compare different ranking algorithms used at Yahoo! Answers by means of survival analysis. This methodology was applied in the recent study [2] to evaluate a web search engine changes in its ranking algorithm and its user interface. In our study, we utilize 56 new features resulted from the DFT of 4 engagement measures in order to evaluate, by means of A/B tests, different changes of the search engine ranking algorithm, changes of the user interface, and changes of the engine efficiency (see Section 7).

Periodicity in user behavior. To the best of our knowledge, no existing study investigated periodicity of individual user engagement. The existing works refered to the periodicity problem as seasonal factor (i.e., between years [20, 14]) or as weekday specific factor (i.e., between weeks [16, 17]). In both cases the term "periodicity" was mentioned either as a component of trend models (seasonal-trend decomposition methods [20, 16] or autocorrelation techniques [27, 17]) or as a variability of user behavior within a week (which was taken into account by introducing the day of the week as additional variable of models [5] and by providing different models for weekdays and weekends separately [16, 14]). In our work, we apply the DFT [23] to user engagement time series in order to encode the periodic behavior of an *individual user*[4]. Then, deep short-term and long-term analysis of user engagement periodicity are provided (see Sections 5 and 6 respectively).

User engagement with web services. The user engagement was studied not only for search engines, but also

[3]Actually, these classifications could be applied to any user need and to any product or service satisfying the need (not necessarily a search need).

[4]The DFT was applied to time series of query popularity (*aggregated over all users*) [22, 17, 24] and was used to detect dominant periods of the popularity variation over time.

for a wide range of web sites. The time between two successive user visits was used to understand differences in behavioral, content, and structural characteristics of web sites [1]. The authors of [16] compared different web sites with respect to user engagement metrics of popularity, activity, and loyalty that are aggregated over users for each web site. Using these metrics they obtained some engagement patterns (models) of the studied web sites. The research described in [15] is also devoted to comparison of a web site group with respect to multitasking user behavior, which analysis takes into account backpaging and tab switching during a browsing session. They used the number of page views and the dwell time (the presence time on a web site), both on visit and session levels, as the main engagement metrics of user activity. In our work, we study individual periodic behavior patterns of users (not web sites) based on both loyalty and activity aspects of their engagement.

3. FRAMEWORK AND NOTATIONS

In this section, we introduce methods of spectrum analysis [23] (also known as Fourier analysis) whose main component is the *discrete Fourier transform (DFT)*. We remind the key points of the DFT in the next subsection. After that we motivate and discuss its application to the problem of extracting patterns of user engagement periodicity.

3.1 Discrete Fourier transform

Let $\mathbf{x} = (x_0, x_1, .., x_{N-1})$ be a sequence of N complex numbers, i.e., a vector in the space $\mathbb{C}^N$. Let $\{\mathbf{f}^k\}_{k=0}^{N-1}$ be the basis, where each basis vector $\mathbf{f}^k$ is the harmonic (sine wave) with coordinates $f_n^k = e^{\mathbf{i}\omega_k n}/N$, $n \in \mathbb{Z}_N$[5]. The values $\omega_k = 2\pi k/N$, $k \in \mathbb{Z}_N$, are called the *Fourier frequencies* (angular frequencies). Then, the *discrete Fourier transform (DFT)* of the sequence $\mathbf{x}$ is the sequence of its coordinates in the harmonic basis $\{\mathbf{f}^k\}_{k=0}^{N-1}$, that is, the series of complex numbers

$$X_k = \sum_{n=0}^{N-1} x_n e^{-\mathbf{i}\omega_k n}, \quad \omega_k = \frac{2\pi k}{N}, \quad k \in \mathbb{Z}_N. \tag{1}$$

So, the DFT is a bijective map from *the source domain* into *the frequency domain* $\mathcal{F}(\mathbf{x}) = (X_0, .., X_{N-1})$, $\mathcal{F} : \mathbb{C}^N \leftrightarrow \mathbb{C}^N$.

Each complex number X_k could be represented in the form $X_k = |X_k|e^{\mathbf{i}\varphi_k}, k \in \mathbb{Z}_N$, where $|X_k|$ is the absolute value of the complex number and φ_k is its argument. The sequence of the absolute values normalized by N

$$\mathcal{A}(\mathbf{x}) = \Big(\frac{|X_0|}{N}, .., \frac{|X_{N-1}|}{N}\Big), \quad \mathcal{A} : \mathbb{C}^N \to \mathbb{R}_+^N, \tag{2}$$

is called *the amplitude series* (the amplitude vector or periodogram w.r.t. ω_k [23]). The sequence of the arguments $\Phi(\mathbf{x}) = (\varphi_0, .., \varphi_{N-1})$, $\Phi : \mathbb{C}^N \to [0, 2\pi)^N$, is called *the phase vector*. The amplitude $\mathcal{A}(\mathbf{x})_k$ represents the magnitude of the sine wave with the frequency ω_k presented in the series $\mathbf{x}$, whereas the phase $\Phi(\mathbf{x})_k$ represents how this wave is shifted.

If $\mathbf{x} \in \mathbb{R}^N$, then $X_0 \in \mathbb{R}$, and the DFT of $\mathbf{x} \in \mathbb{R}^N$ possesses the symmetry property: $X_k = \overline{X}_{N-k}$, $k = 1, .., [N/2]$[6]. If $\mathbf{x} \in \mathbb{R_+}^N$ (the case of our study), then $X_0 \geq 0$ and $|X_k| \leq X_0$, $k \in \mathbb{Z}_N$. Thus, without loss of generality, from here on in the paper the investigation of the amplitude series $\mathcal{A}(\mathbf{x})$ is replaced by investigation of its truncated part $\mathcal{A}(\mathbf{x}) = (\mathcal{A}(\mathbf{x})_0, .., \mathcal{A}(\mathbf{x})_{[N/2]})$ (using the same notation).

[5]We remind that $e^{\mathbf{i}\varphi} = \cos\varphi + \mathbf{i}\sin\varphi$, $\mathbf{i}$ is imaginary unit, and $\mathbb{Z}_N = \{0, 1, .., N-1\}$.

[6]$\overline{z} = a - \mathbf{i}b$ is the complex conjugate of $z = a + \mathbf{i}b$.

3.2 Periodicity patterns

Further we discuss some useful properties of the studied transformation. Let us consider some examples. Suppose that the time series $(0, .., 0, x_n, 0, .., 0)$, $n \in \mathbb{Z}_N$, has only one non-zero element (e.g., it represents a single user activity), then its amplitude vector is constant $(|x_n|/N, ..., |x_n|/N)$ independently of the position n of the non-zero value x_n in the series (e.g., see Fig. 2, col. "cS6"). In other words, the time information (position) of the single activity is accommodated in the phase component, whereas the activity type is bear by the amplitude component. The second example is provided by a time series, which is nearly constant (e.g., it represents a permanent constant user activity), i.e., $\mathbf{x} = (a + \varepsilon_0, .., a + \varepsilon_{N-1})$, $|\varepsilon_n| \ll |a|$, $n \in \mathbb{Z}_N$. In this case, the amplitude vector is of the form $(|a| + \delta_0, \delta_1, ..., \delta_{N-1})$ with small components $|\delta_k| \ll |a|$, $k \in \mathbb{Z}_N$ (e.g., see Fig. 2, col. "A1"). So, the amplitude vector carries the proportions between the magnitudes of the sine waves of different periodicity and disregards their shifts encoded by phases. Thus, the amplitude vector is the main component of the DFT for our study of user periodicity[7].

The main goal of our study is to catch patterns of user engagement periodicity. In order to separate this periodicity from the total amount of user engagement, we normalize the amplitude series by its zeroth component and obtain the normalized amplitude series $\mathcal{A}_{\mathcal{N}}(\mathbf{x}) = \mathcal{A}(\mathbf{x})/\mathcal{A}(\mathbf{x})_0$, which we refer to as *the periodicity pattern*[8]. Note that the normalized amplitudes are equal to the amplitudes of the normalized source series, i.e., the equality $\mathcal{A}_{\mathcal{N}}(\mathbf{x}) = \mathcal{A}(\mathbf{x}/\|\mathbf{x}\|_1)$ holds, where $\|\mathbf{x}\|_1 = \sum_{n=0}^{N-1} |x_n|/N$ is the l_1-norm of $\mathbf{x}$. Thus, we have $\mathcal{A}_{\mathcal{N}}(\mathbf{x}) = \mathcal{A}_{\mathcal{N}}(\mathbf{y})$, if $\mathbf{x} = \lambda\mathbf{y}$. It means that the normalized amplitude $\mathcal{A}_{\mathcal{N}}(\mathbf{x})$ captures periodicity of $\mathbf{x}$ with respect to its scale and does not distinguish between two source series that differ by a multiplicative constant only.

Series under study. In our work, we study time series of different user engagement features and their transformations. Given a user's engagement feature, under our study are the following series: (a) $\mathbf{x}$ is *the source time series* of the feature of length N; (b) $\mathcal{A}(\mathbf{x})$ is *its amplitude series* of length $[N/2]+1$; and (c) $\mathcal{A}_{\mathcal{N}}(\mathbf{x})$ is *its periodicity pattern* (or normalized amplitude series) of length $[N/2]$.

3.3 Research questions

The main goal of our study is to identify the benefit of spectrum analysis methodology for analysis of user engagement (and particularly its periodicity). Thereupon, we translate this objective into the following research questions:

- **[RQ1]** Could clusters of users with common periodicity behavior be identified?
- **[RQ2]** Could users with stable periodicity be identified?
- **[RQ3]** Could the features of spectrum analysis be used with profit in a practical problem faced by a search engine?

[7]A study of phases is left for future work.

[8]Since we always have $\mathcal{A}_{\mathcal{N}}(\mathbf{x})_0 = 1$, we assume that the series $\mathcal{A}_{\mathcal{N}}(\mathbf{x})$ begins with $\mathcal{A}_{\mathcal{N}}(\mathbf{x})_1$ from here on in the paper.

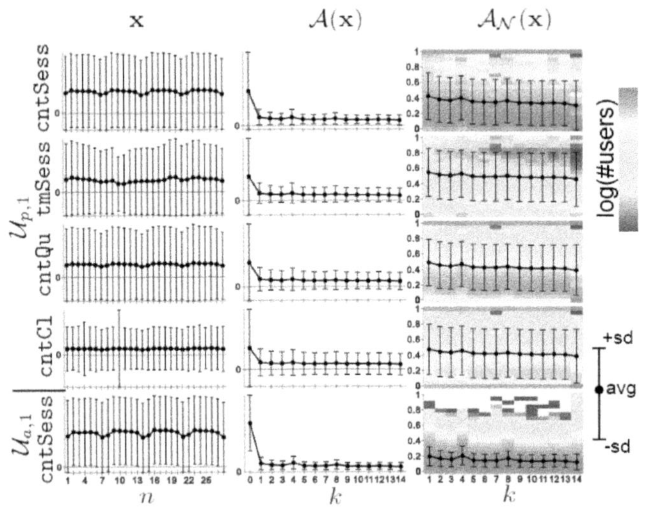

Figure 1: The distribution (*avg*, *sd*, and the heat map) of users from the sets $\mathcal{U}_{p,1}$ and $\mathcal{U}_{a,1}$ w.r.t. each component of the source time series x, the amplitude series $\mathcal{A}(\mathbf{x})$, and the periodicity pattern $\mathcal{A}_{\mathcal{N}}(\mathbf{x})$ for each engagement measure.

4. THE DATA

Engagement measures. For each user, we study 4 basic additive measures, which represent both loyalty and activity aspects of user engagement. They are (aggregated over a day):

- the number of sessions (`cntSess`);
- the presence time (sum of session times, `tmSess`);
- the number of queries (`cntQu`);
- the number of clicks (`cntCl`).

The measure `cntSess` corresponds to the loyalty aspect of user engagement, whereas the measures `tmSess`, `cntQu` and `cntClick` correspond to user activity [5, 18, 21].

Time periods. We take the logs of Yandex[9], one of the most popular search engines, from the 1st September, 2013 to 15th March, 2014 (196 days). For each user, we split her actions (i.e., interactions with all web services of Yandex) to sessions[10]. Using this data, for each day in the time period and for each user, we calculate number of sessions, presence time, number of queries, and number of clicks that she produced in that day. Then we define 28-day period (4 weeks) as the basic time length of the source sequences under study (i.e., $N = 28$)[11]. We split the data sequences to 7 consecutive 28-day periods $\{\mathbb{T}_i\}_{i=0}^{6}$, $|\mathbb{T}_i| = 28$.

Sets of users[12]. Then, for each $i = 1,..,5$, we build the set $\mathcal{U}_{p,i}$ consisting of users that have at least one action during each of the time periods $\mathbb{T}_{i-1}$, $\mathbb{T}_i$, and $\mathbb{T}_{i+1}$[13]. For a deeper study on periodicity, we also consider the *set of active users* $\mathcal{U}_{a,i} \subset \mathcal{U}_{p,i}$ $(i = 1,..,5)$ formed by those users that have actions at 14 days of the period $\mathbb{T}_i$ at least. The user set $\mathcal{U}_{a,i}$ consists of around 33-39% of the users from the set $\mathcal{U}_{p,i}$, but it makes 72-79% of their sessions, 74-83% of their presence time, 73-81% of their queries, and 74-82% of their clicks (depending on i). We use the intersection of the user sets $\mathcal{U}_p = \bigcap_{i=1}^{5} \mathcal{U}_{p,i}$ (a user is presented in each time period) and $\mathcal{U}_a = \bigcap_{i=1}^{5} \mathcal{U}_{a,i}$ (a user is active in all time periods) for long-term studies. Each of the studied user sets contains several millions of users.

Thus, for each engagement measure (`cntSess`, `tmSess`, `cntQu`, and `cntCl`), for each time period $\mathbb{T}_i, i = 1,..,5$, and for each user belonging to the set $\mathcal{U}_{p,i}$, we have the 28-length source time series of the engagement measure. So, each user may possess up to 20 source time series, each of them is processed through the DFT providing the 15-length amplitude series and 14-length periodicity patterns.

5. SPECTRUM ANALYSIS

In this section, we provide the analysis of the periodicity patterns within one time period. First, we provide basic analysis of the studied series for our data sets. Second, we identify groups of users that represent similar periodicity behavior. The results are presented for the time period $\mathbb{T}_1$, the ones for the other periods are analogous. The relationships among the periods are studied in the next section.

5.1 Basic distributions of the series

In Fig. 1, we present[14] the distribution (the average value *avg*, the standard deviation *sd*, and the heat map) of users from the set $\mathcal{U}_{p,1}$ with respect to each component of the source time series $\mathbf{x}$, the amplitude series $\mathcal{A}(\mathbf{x})$, and the periodicity pattern $\mathcal{A}_{\mathcal{N}}(\mathbf{x})$ for each of the 4 engagement measures. We see that the components of the source time series $\mathbf{x}$ vary considerably among users. The loyalty user engagement measure is less oscillating than the activity ones: the average values of normalized amplitudes $\mathcal{A}_{\mathcal{N}}(\mathbf{x})$ are greater than 0.4 for (`tmSess`, `cntQu`, and `cntCl`) and are lower than 0.4 for `cntSess`. However, the distributions' shapes do not differ noticeably among engagement measures. Therefore, due to the space constraints, several results discussed further are reported only for one engagement measure (usually for `cntSess`), when they are similar for the others.

The same results are presented at the bottom of Fig. 1 for the active users $\mathcal{U}_{a,1}$ (they interact with the search engine at least 14 days in the time period) only for the number of sessions (`cntSess`). The main difference from the set $\mathcal{U}_{p,1}$ is seen at the top of its heat map: the periodicity patterns are noticeably lower 1. Hence, some other observations made for the set $\mathcal{U}_{p,1}$ are more clearly visible for the active users: the distributions of the normalized amplitudes $\mathcal{A}_{\mathcal{N}}(\mathbf{x})$ are shifted closer to 0 and smoother (see also Fig. 3), the peaks at frequencies $k \in \{4, 8\}$ are more dominating among others.

The peaks in the distributions of the $\mathcal{A}_{\mathcal{N}}(\mathbf{x})_k$ for the set $\mathcal{U}_{p,1}$ (see Fig. 3(p)) correspond to the clusters of periodicity patterns (further in our study) whose centroids are presented in Fig. 4. As well, we observe analogous steps on the dis-

[9] yandex.com

[10] A session is commonly defined as a sequence of actions whose dwell times are less than 30 minutes [2, 5, 12, 21].

[11] This length allows to catch periodicity between weeks and, meanwhile, study its long-term changes as we further describe.

[12] In this paper, we use cookie IDs to identify users as done in other studies on user engagement [5, 15, 21].

[13] Thus, we eliminate the impact on our periodicity patterns from the effects, when a user can start for the first time or finish at all using the search engine in the studied time period $\mathbb{T}_i$ (e.g., a user clears its browser cookies). It is about 24-27% of all users depending on i.

[14] From here on in the paper we hide all absolute values for confidentiality reasons.

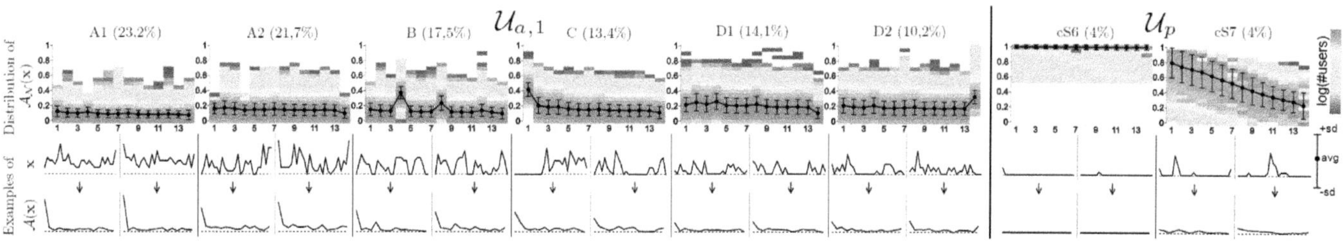

Figure 2: The distribution and examples of users from several periodicity models (A1, A2, B, C, D1, D2, cS6, and cS7) w.r.t. the number of sessions cntSess (see Section 5.2 for details).

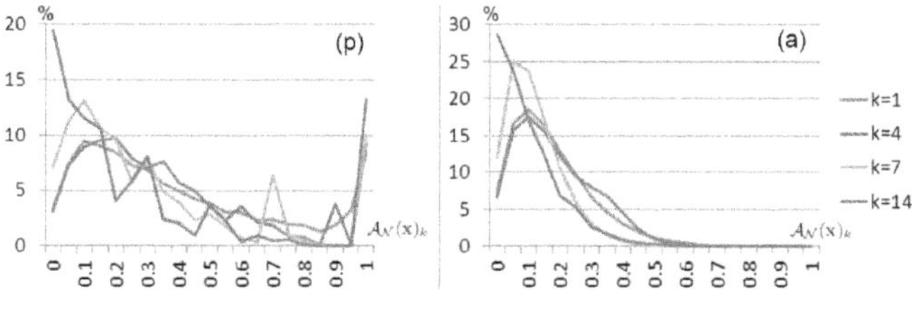

Figure 3: Density of distribution of users $\mathcal{U}_{p,1}$ (p) and $\mathcal{U}_{a,1}$ (a) w.r.t. the value $\mathcal{A}_{\mathcal{N}}(\texttt{cntSess})_k, k = 1, 4, 7, 14$.

tributions of the active users $\mathcal{U}_{a,1}$ (e.g., see Fig. 3(a) for the freq. $k = 4$ near the value 0.36 and $k = 14$ near 0.25), they are also detected further in our study (see Fig. 2).

The weekly periodicity is clearly observed on the values of the source time series averaged over users. This periodicity is also detected by the periodicity patterns and is expressed by the peaks on the amplitude series at frequencies $k = 4$ and 8[15]. These frequencies are responsible for the weekly periodicity, as it is seen for users whose activity drops at weekends (see Fig. 2, col. "B"). A single day interaction type with the web service (as examples in Fig. 2, col. "cS6") could not be detected by the average values of the series, while the heat maps of periodicity patterns detect such type of activity (Fig. 1, $\mathcal{A}_{\mathcal{N}}(\mathbf{x})$ are near 1) and show a considerable amount of such users (see also several slices of distribution in Fig. 3(p)). Thus, our periodicity patterns are able to catch and encode basic periodicity types. Further in our paper, we show how the periodicity patterns detect more complicated activity types, which are difficult to find in the source time series with the naked eye.

5.2 User engagement periodicity models

In this subsection, we identify groups of users which have similar periodicity behavior. They are referred to as *the periodicity models* of user engagement. We utilize standard k-means clustering algorithm with respect to the periodicity patterns $\mathcal{A}_{\mathcal{N}}(\mathbf{x})$ that were treated as vectors of 14-dimensional space of normalized amplitudes. We run it 10 times with random seed means for different numbers of clusters K (from 2 to 30). Further we report the most interesting results only. We find that the most sensible and stable clusters are detected for $K = 7$ (for all users) and for $K = 6$ (for active users)[16].

We present the results of the clustering for the active users $\mathcal{U}_{a,1}$ in Fig. 2 with respect to the number of sessions cntSess

[15]From the DFT properties, it follows that the amplitudes $\mathcal{A}(\mathbf{x})_k = 0$ for k not divisible by 4, if the series $\mathbf{x}$ is periodical with period 7 ($N = 4 \cdot 7$).

[16]For these K, all 10 runs converges to the same centroids. Greater K results in different centroids for different seed means.

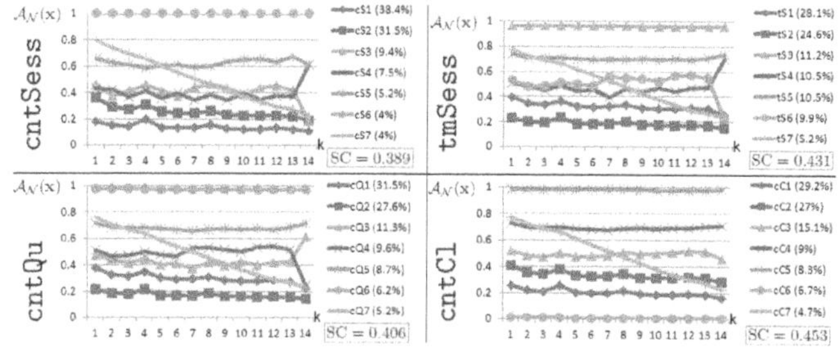

Figure 4: The 7 cluster centroids for each engagement measure across users $\mathcal{U}_p$.

(the silhouette coefficient[17] SC = 0.322): there are the periodicity models **A1** (23.2%), **A2** (21.7%), **B** (17.5%), **C** (13.4%), **D1** (14.1%), and **D2** (10.2%). Each group is supplied by the heat map of its periodicity pattern distribution and two example users with its source time and amplitude series which are close to the centroids. The periodicity models **A1**, **A2**, **B**, and **C** have strong and coherent interpretations. The users from **A1** (*the permanent model*) interact with the search engine permanently and, thus, their periodicity patterns are small (i.e., all sine waves are smaller than a constant). The users of **A2** behave similarly (together with **A1** they form 44.9% of all users), but their variation in interaction activity is higher. The users from **B** (*the office worker model*) interact with the web service with week-periodicity, which strongly reflects in the domination of the 4-th and 8-th components of their periodicity patterns (i.e., the sine waves with the periods multiple of 7 days dominate among others). The users from **C** (*the holiday model*) have up to 10-day drop in search engine usage[18], which is reflected in the domination of the 1-st component of the periodicity patterns (i.e., the sine wave with the period of 28 days dominates others). The activities of users from **D1** and **D2** have both large variation and have no sensible periodic interpretation. The relationship between all these periodicity models during the 20-week time period is studied in Section 6.

We present the centroids and the silhouette coefficients (SC) of 7-clustering of all users $\mathcal{U}_p$ (not only active, as before) with respect to periodicity patterns of different user engagement measures in Fig. 4. First, we see that the obtained periodicity models are of similar form in vast majority of the cases. The only one exception is the group **cC6**, which represents the users that have no clicks at all (i.e., the source time series of the number of clicks consists of zero values). The other user engagement measures cannot have zero time-

[17]en.wikipedia.org/wiki/Silhouette_(clustering)

[18]We remind that the absence of a user activity at the start or at the end is not caused by their start or end of usage of the search engine (see Section 4)

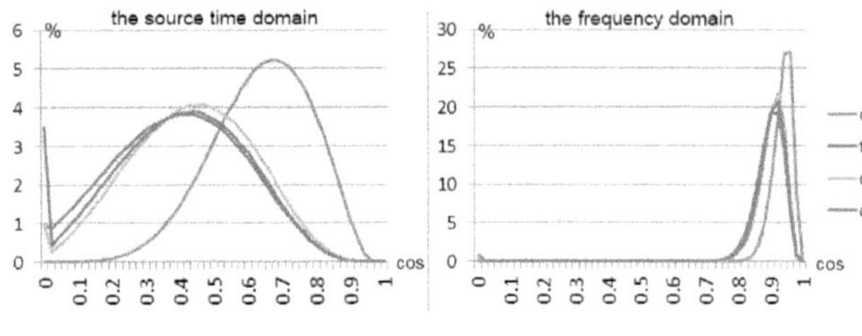

Figure 5: Density of distribution of users $\mathcal{U}_a$ w.r.t. theirs correlation coefficients between the time periods $\mathbb{T}_1$ and $\mathbb{T}_2$ for the source time series and for the amplitude series.

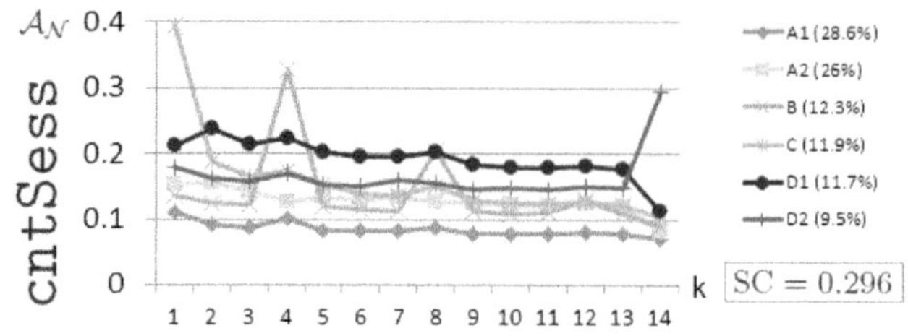

Figure 6: The 6 cluster centroids for active users $\mathcal{U}_a$.

series, thus the analogous cluster is not detected for them. Second, comparing the models of all users (w.r.t. the number of sessions `cntSess`) and the ones of the active users $\mathcal{U}_{a,1}$ (Fig. 2), we see that the latter ones do not include the clusters **cS5**, **cS6**, and **cS7**, due to the latter clusters represent the users with very low activity model. For instance, the periodicity models **cS6** and **cS7** are presented in Fig. 2, where the examples demonstrate which periodicity behavior are encoded by each model.

The basic and cluster analyses of user periodicity behavior, described in this section, allow us to conclude, that *the periodicity patterns provide strong identification of several large user clusters with common coherent periodicity behavior*. It is the answer to the **RQ1**.

6. LONG-TERM PERIODICITY CHANGES

In the previous section, we provided a deep analysis of the source time series and their periodicity patterns of individual users within a 4-week period. Now we study how the periodicity patterns change across a sequence of such periods, namely within a 20-week period.

6.1 Correlation between the series

First of all, we investigate how the user series (both the source time series and the periodicity patterns) are similar across periods $\{\mathbb{T}_i\}_{i=1}^5$ for the same user. We measure the series similarity in terms of correlation of series, i.e., the cosine of the angle between the series: $\cos(\mathbf{x},\mathbf{y}) = (\mathbf{x},\mathbf{y})/(\|\mathbf{x}\|\|\mathbf{y}\|)$ for any non-zero series $\mathbf{x},\mathbf{y}$, $(\mathbf{x},\mathbf{y}) = \sum_n x_n y_n$ and $\|\mathbf{x}\|^2 = (\mathbf{x},\mathbf{x})$. Thus, given a user, the engagement measure, the series type (the source time series or the periodicity pattern), and time periods $\mathbb{T}_i$ and $\mathbb{T}_j$, one has a correlation coefficient whose distribution over a set of users is investigated.

The distributions of users $\mathcal{U}_a$ w.r.t. their correlation coefficients between the time periods $\mathbb{T}_1$ and $\mathbb{T}_2$ for the source time series and for the amplitude series are presented in Fig. 5. The average values of the correlation coefficients for the source time series are equal to $0.65_{\text{sd}0.15}$ for `cntSess`, $0.41_{\text{sd}0.19}$ for `tmSess`, $0.44_{\text{sd}0.18}$ for `cntQu`, and $0.41_{\text{sd}0.19}$ for `cntCl`, whereas the ones for the amplitude series are $0.95_{\text{sd}0.03}$ for `cntSess`, $0.91_{\text{sd}0.04}$ for `tmSess`, $0.91_{\text{sd}0.07}$ for `cntQu`, and $0.90_{\text{sd}0.1}$ for `cntCl`. The results for all users $\mathcal{U}_p$ are less dramatic, but analogous. For instance, for the number of sessions `cntSess`, the average values are $0.39_{\text{sd}0.26}$ (the time domain) and $0.89_{\text{sd}0.06}$ (the frequency domain). Meanwhile, the distributions for the same series types (both in the time domain and the frequency domain) do not vary noticeably over the distance between the time periods. For instance, the average values among active users $\mathcal{U}_a$ for `cntSess` in the frequency domain are $0.945_{\text{sd}0.03}$ for the pair $\mathbb{T}_1 - \mathbb{T}_3$, $0.939_{\text{sd}0.03}$ for $\mathbb{T}_1 - \mathbb{T}_4$, $0.943_{\text{sd}0.03}$ for $\mathbb{T}_1 - \mathbb{T}_5$.

These results show that the same time series data have significantly better correlation across months in the frequency domains (processed through the DFT) than in the time domain (in the source form) both for all users and for its active subset. In other words, the periodicity patterns catch those individual user behavior traits that do not change during a long time period.

6.2 Transitions between periodicity models

In order to investigate, how user's periodicity models change over a long time period, we apply the clustering algorithm (as in the previous section) to the active users $\mathcal{U}_a$[19]. The resulting cluster centroids are presented in Fig. 6. We see that the obtained periodicity models are of the same form as for $\mathcal{U}_{a,1}$ in Fig. 2, but differ in their sizes due to differences in the time periods (see further).

The transition map of users $\mathcal{U}_a$ between the six periodicity models (user groups) during 20-week time period ($\mathbb{T}_i, i = 1,..,5$) is represented in Fig. 7. The nodes' radii are proportional to the sizes of the groups at each time period $\mathbb{T}_i, i = 1,..,5$. The thickness of the lines between the nodes are proportional to the amount of users that switch between the models. Each transition $\mathbb{T}_i \to \mathbb{T}_{i+1}, i = 1,..,4$, is supplied by a diagram of switching between the models (the bar graphs represent the percent of users that stay in the same cluster or switch to another one w.r.t. the number of all users). From Fig. 7, one could learn that there are 3 stable periodicity models (**A1**, **A2**, and **B**) across all periods except $\mathbb{T}_4$. At the time period $\mathbb{T}_4$, *the holiday model* **C** grows by significantly accumulating users from other groups and especially from the clusters **A1**, **A2**, and **B**. And further, at the time period $\mathbb{T}_5$, the usual distribution of users restores.

What happens at the time period $\mathbb{T}_4$? One could see that the periodicity model **C** corresponds to the periodicity pattern, where the frequency ω_1 dominates others (see Fig. 2, col. "C"). It corresponds to the users whose activity is absent at a continuous half of the time period (see Section 5.2). The time period $\mathbb{T}_4$ contains the Christmas and New Year holidays. So, we suppose that the transitions $\mathbb{T}_3 \to \mathbb{T}_4$ and $\mathbb{T}_4 \to \mathbb{T}_5$ catch users vacancies (holidays). While the groups **A1** (*the permanent model*) and **A2** lose about 12% and 17%, respectively, of their users at $\mathbb{T}_4$ for benefit of **C** (usually, they lose 7% and 11%, resp.), the outflow of users from *the office worker model* **B** to the cluster **C** raises up to 32%, being usually at 8.5% at different periods $\mathbb{T}_i$. The periodic structure of **B** corresponds to the weekly periodical activity (e.g., as of an office worker, see Fig. 2, col. "B"), that is, the users whose activity is weekly periodical and occurs mostly

[19]Each user from $\mathcal{U}_a$ possesses 5 periodicity patterns (one per each 4-week time period $\mathbb{T}_i, i = 1,..,5$), each of these patterns is utilized in the k-means algorithm.

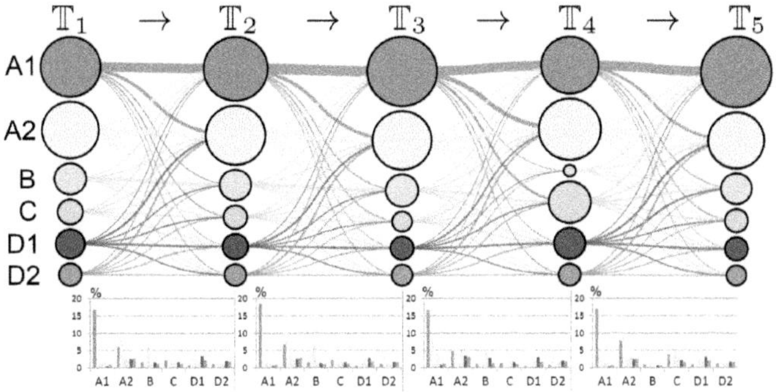

Figure 7: The transition map of the users $\mathcal{U}_a$ between the 6 periodicity clusters during the 20-week period ($\{\mathbb{T}_i\}_{i=1}^5$) and the diagrams for each transition $\mathbb{T}_i \to \mathbb{T}_{i+1}, i = 1, .., 4$ (see Section 6.2 for details).

within working days, are significantly subjected to vacation seasons. It is the second argument, which supports our supposition. So, people take a holiday during a year and the vast majority of them are taken near the Christmas, which is identified by the observed long-term changes of *the holiday model* **C**.

In order to identify users who do not change their periodicity models, we present in Table 1 col. **(I)** the proportions of users that have the same periodicity model across all 4-week time periods w.r.t. the size of the periodicity model group at the first 4-week period $\mathbb{T}_1$. We see that only *the permanent model* **A1** of the search engine usage has a significant fraction (28.6%) of users with stable periodicity model, the second one (by a large margin) is *the office worker model* **B**. Further, we join the periodicity models into sets of models and, for each set, we calculate the proportions of users whose periodicity model holds in the set across all 4-week time periods (i.e., users *oscillate between models* in the set) w.r.t. the sum of the sizes of the set's periodicity model groups at the first 4-week period $\mathbb{T}_1$. These proportions of users who oscillate between 2, 4, and 5 models across the 20-week period are presented in Table 1 at the bottom triangle under the diagonal of col. **(II)**, at the top triangle above the diagonal of col. **(II)**, and at col. **(III)** respectively. A cell in raw **X** and column **Y** of the upper triangle of col. **(II)** corresponds to the set of 4 models, which does not contain models **X**, **Y**. A cell in raw **X** from col. **(III)** corresponds to the set of 5 models, which does not contain model **X**. For instance, the cell (**B**, **D1**) reports that 56.4% of users who have periodicity models **A1**, **A2**, **C**, or **D2** (a set of models) at the first period $\mathbb{T}_1$ do not leave these 4 models in the next 4 periods. We see that the oscillation between **A1** and **A2** models is most stable among all 2-model oscillations. Meanwhile, we see that the best stable 5-model oscillation is the one which does not include *the office worker model* **B**, which represents weekly periodicity. Thus, we identified the following stable user behaviors: (a) *a user is likely to use search engine permanently if she has the same usage at the initial time period*; (b) *it is unlikely that user will behave as an office worker if she did not do it at the initial time period.*

Summarizing the results, first, we found that the periodicity behavior encoded in the periodicity patterns is significantly more stable in long-term perspective than the user behavior data presented in the time domain. Second, we found that the users with definitive models of periodicity behavior stick to one periodicity model across months and

Table 1: Fraction of users that have stable periodicity model across 20 weeks (I) and that oscillate between 2 (the bottom triangle of (II)), 4 (the top triangle of (II)), and 5 (III) models.

	(I)	(II)						(III)
		A1	A2	B	C	D1	D2	
A1	28.6%	—	26.1%	35.6%	27.7%	22.2%	30.1%	52.3%
A2	1.9%	36.6%	—	27.6%	24.5%	30.4%	32.8%	40.3%
B	3.3%	22.9%	5.5%	—	47.9%	56.4%	53.6%	74.4%
C	0.2%	27.7%	5.4%	11.8%	—	45%	45%	59.3%
D1	0.9%	20.2%	6.1%	7.9%	3.1%	—	55.2%	66.2%
D2	0.8%	22.7%	6%	3.4%	1.3%	4.5%	—	68.4%

the changes in their models are mostly become caused by changes in their life style (e.g., taking Christmas holidays). Finally, we conclude that *the periodicity patterns catch individual user traits that are mostly stable during a long time period.* It is the answer to the **RQ2**.

7. SEARCH ENGINE QUALITY METRICS

In this section we show how the periodicity patterns of user engagement could be used as evaluation metrics of the search engine quality.

Quality evaluation problem. The quality could be measured at different stages of the search engine development processes and for changes in different components of the system. User engagement metrics are believed to be the most relevant to the company profit and they are able to quantify the quality of changes in any service component on the same measurement scale. Therefore, these metrics are the most universal and are used to qualify the appropriateness of lower-level quality metrics developed for more specific development tasks. A measure claimed to be used as a quality metric should be validated in a series of experiments. These experiments should show that (a) the deviation of the measure from zero is not significant in a comparison of two identical versions of the service and (b) the metric indicates a significant difference of two versions of the system (usually, the current production version and another one with some artificial deterioration).

In order to compare two states of the service, we apply the technique of *A/B experiments* (*A/B tests*) [3, 21, 13], which is widely used in search engine evaluation. The essence of the method consists in sampling of two groups of users (A and B) from the whole flow of users of the service. The users from the group A (*the control group*) and B (*the treatment group*) are exposed during some time period to the old service version and to the new one, respectively. After the experimentation time period, the quality metric is calculated for these users, and the relative difference of the average values [21] over the user groups is calculated:

$$\text{Diff} = \chi \cdot (\text{avg}_B(m) - \text{avg}_A(m))/\text{avg}_A(m)^{20}.$$

Nonetheless, the quantity Diff could not serve itself as an indicator of positive or negative consequences of the evaluated update of the search engine. The relative difference of the averaged values should be controlled by a statistical significance test. In our study, we apply two-sample t-test (as in [3, 21]) to decide weather the metric aggregated over users from the treatment group is significantly larger or smaller

[20]The factor χ is randomly chosen once in our study in order to hide real values for confidentiality reasons.

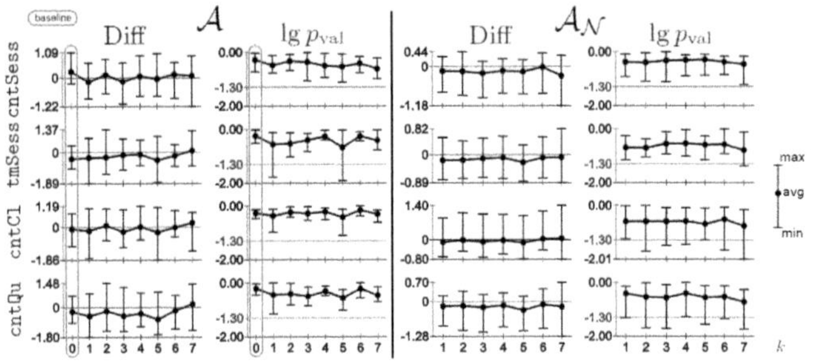

Figure 8: Results of 5 control experiments (A/A tests) for 4 user engagement features, for $\mathcal{A}$ and $\mathcal{A}_{\mathcal{N}}$ transformations (avg/max/min of Diff and $\lg p_{\text{val}}$).

than that aggregated over users from control one. We considered a commonly used threshold $p_{\text{val}} = 0.05$ for the p-value of the test. We also use decimal logarithm $\lg p_{\text{val}}$ in our figures whose threshold is $\lg p_{\text{val}} = \lg 0.05 \approx -1.3$.

Experiment setup. In our work, we conduct 25 A/B experiments in total: 3 for different changes in the ranking algorithm, 5 for the engine response time increase, 12 for different changes in the user interface, and 5 control experiments (so-called A/A tests [3]), where old and new versions of the system coincide. Each experimentation has 14-day time period, which is motivated by the following arguments. On the one hand, the experiment duration directly affects the speed of the decision to ship the service update, and, therefore, it should be as short as possible. On the other hand, the difference in behavior of control and treatment groups should be obtained on the desirable level of statistical significance, which also depends on the length of the period. The study [21] of user engagement metrics (`cntSess`) w.r.t. A/B tests shows that the metric aggregated over one day of experiment has poor significance level, and it is recommended [13] to accumulate metric values at 2-week period.

Our periodicity patterns and amplitudes of user engagement are believed to be a good extension of existing quality metrics based on user engagement, because they are alternative approaches of metric accumulation (besides the summation and averaging), and we rely on the following intuition. The periodicity pattern encodes variation of a user behavior over time. It tends to 0, if the variation is low, and tends to 1 otherwise (as it observed in Sections 5 and 6). Hence, a negative or positive change in a search engine component influences user behavior in *some of her search tasks*[21], thus, it changes user behavior variation and, therefore, her periodicity pattern. So, in this section (unlike the remainder of the paper), we use the DFT for the time series with the length $N = 14$ and, therefore, the truncated amplitude vector has the length $[N/2] + 1 = 8$. So, we investigate 56 *new scalar user engagement metrics*: for each user engagement feature $\{\texttt{cntSess}, \texttt{tmSess}, \texttt{cntQu}, \texttt{cntCl}\}$ (see Section 4) with the time series $\mathbf{x}$, we study the amplitudes $\mathcal{A}(\mathbf{x})_k$ and their normalized values $\mathcal{A}_{\mathcal{N}}(\mathbf{x})_k, k = 1, .., 7$ (the periodicity pattern). The amplitude $\mathcal{A}(\mathbf{x})_0$ is the average value of the time series $\mathbf{x}$, therefore, it serves as the baseline metric[22].

Experimental results. First of all, we present the results for 5 control experiments (A/A tests) in Fig. 8 (the average and the max/min values of Diff and $\lg p_{\text{val}}$ w.r.t. 5

[21]Usually a search engine update is noticeable in very small number of scenarios of interaction with the web service.

[22]The average value of `cntSess` was studied in [21].

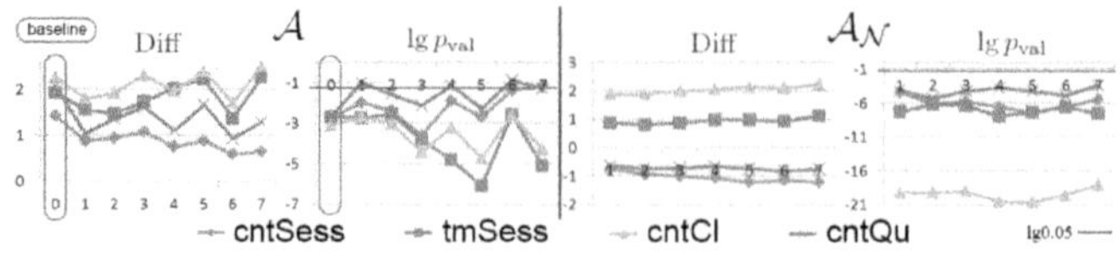

Figure 9: Results of the swap-2 ranking deterioration (A/B tests) for $\mathcal{A}$ and $\mathcal{A}_{\mathcal{N}}$ transformations.

obtained values). We see that, for almost all metrics, the average value of Diff is near zero. Expectedly, the significance levels of A/A tests averaged over each metric are very low ($p_{\text{val}} > 10^{-0.72}$). Meanwhile, some metrics catch a significant difference (the p-value < 0.05 or $\lg p_{\text{val}} < -1.3$) between equal versions of the web service on one control experiment among 5: two amplitudes ($\{\mathcal{A}(\texttt{tmSess})_k\}_{k=1,5}$) and some normalized ones ($\mathcal{A}_{\mathcal{N}}(\texttt{tmSess})_7$, $\{\mathcal{A}_{\mathcal{N}}(\texttt{cntCl})_k\}_{k\neq 1,5}$, and $\{\mathcal{A}_{\mathcal{N}}(\texttt{cntQu})_k\}_{k\neq 4}$). The number of passed control experiments by each metrics is reported as the *first number* in the cells of Table 2.

Ranking quality evaluation. Now we apply our metrics to evaluate the search engine changes. We start from the ranking algorithm that is the main component of the service. In the first experiment, we swap two random results from the first quintuple with two random ones from the second quintuple in all results presented for the treatment group B (the "swap-2" experiment). The results of the experiment are presented in Fig. 9. One could see that all normalized amplitudes $\mathcal{A}_{\mathcal{N}}$ of all user engagement measures provide a very high significance level ($p_{\text{val}} < 10^{-3.77}$) and strongly outperform the corresponding baseline average values $\mathcal{A}(\,\cdot\,)_0$ w.r.t. the significance level. Moreover, we learn that amplitudes $\mathcal{A}$ of the presence time `tmSess` and the number of clicks `cntCl` have also a high significance level ($p_{\text{val}} < 10^{-2.56}$) and almost all of them outperform the baseline average values $\mathcal{A}(\,\cdot\,)_0$ by the significance level. The number of queries `cntQu` has some significant amplitudes, but all of them are outperformed by the average value. The same is valid for the number of sessions `cntSess`, but the amplitude $\mathcal{A}(\texttt{cntSess})_3$ outperforms the baseline metric.

We conduct two other experiments whose ranking deterioration are weaker than the one of the "swap-2" experiment. They are personalization switch off ("PersOff") and the swap of the second and the fourth results ("2-4-swap"). Unfortunately, only a few metrics catch significant differences in these experiments: they are the amplitudes $\mathcal{A}(\texttt{cntSess})_{k=3,7}$ and $\mathcal{A}(\texttt{cntQu})_7$ ($p_{\text{val}} < 10^{-1.75}$), the normalized amplitudes $\mathcal{A}_{\mathcal{N}}(\texttt{cntSess})_{k=1,3}$, and $\mathcal{A}_{\mathcal{N}}(\texttt{cntQu})_1$ ($p_{\text{val}} < 10^{-1.36}$) for "PersOff", and the amplitude $\mathcal{A}(\texttt{cntSess})_5$ ($p_{\text{val}} < 10^{-1.303}$) for "2-4-swap". For the baseline average values $\mathcal{A}(\,\cdot\,)_0$, p-values do not pass the threshold of 0.05. Finally, we report the number of ranking experiments passed by each metric as the *first digit* of the *superscript* in the cells of Table 2.

Evaluation of UI changes. The second main component of any web service is the user interface (UI). In Fig. 10 and Fig. 11 we demonstrate the results for 7 A/B experiments on *heavy UI changes* and 5 A/B experiments on *light UI changes* correspondingly (the average and the max/min values of Diff and $\lg p_{\text{val}}$). The heavy UI changes include deterioration of link colors, margins, opacity, and fonts of the search results, whereas the light changes include neutral variations of the UI. We see that a part of the heavy UI changes is caught by almost all metrics, however, amplitudes of the presence time `tmSess` and the number of clicks

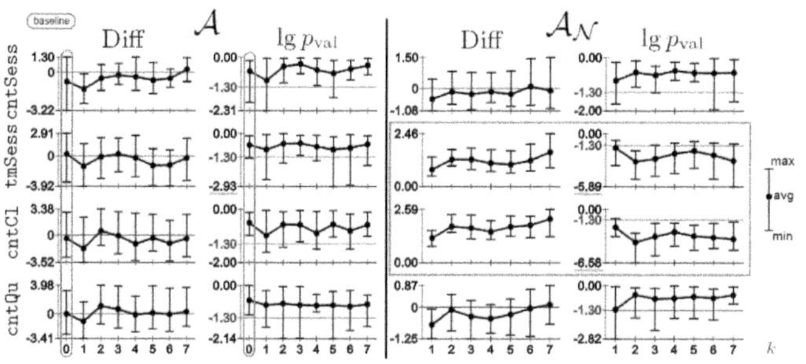

Figure 10: Results of 7 UI change experiments for 4 user engagement metrics, $\mathcal{A}$ and $\mathcal{A}_{\mathcal{N}}$ transformations (avg/max/min of Diff and $\lg p_{\text{val}}$).

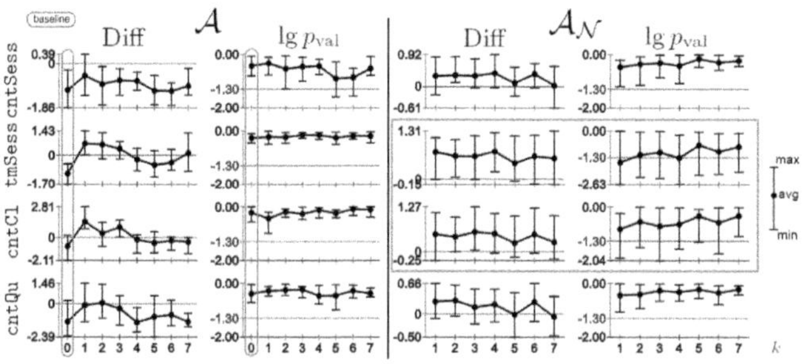

Figure 11: Results of 5 light UI change experiments for 4 user engagement features, $\mathcal{A}$ and $\mathcal{A}_{\mathcal{N}}$ transformations (avg/max/min values of Diff and $\lg p_{\text{val}}$).

cntCl have p-value higher than 0.1 at average. On the contrary, their normalized amplitudes catch all the changes in the UI on a highly significant level (outlined by red boxes in both figures) and outperform the baseline average metrics $\mathcal{A}(\cdot)_0$. As well, these 14 metrics detect light UI changes as significant, whereas the other metrics detect no significant differences (see Fig. 11). We conclude that the periodicity patterns of the presence time `tmSess` and the number of clicks `cntCl` could be effectively applied to evaluate changes of the UI. We report the number of UI experiments passed by each metric by the *first* and the *second* digits of the *subscript* in the cells of Table 2.

Evaluation of server slowdown. We conduct 5 A/B experiments, where the server response time is artificially increased by $m\tau$ seconds[23], $m = 1, .., 5$. We find that only the normalized amplitudes $\mathcal{A}_{\mathcal{N}}$ of the presence time `tmSess` detected both of the two largest response time increments as significant changes (almost all $p_{\text{val}} < 10^{-2}$). These metrics outperform the baseline, see Fig. 12. We report the number of response time experiments passed by other metrics by the *second digit* of the *superscript* in the cells of Table 2.

Discussion. The results of all 25 A/B experiments for all 60 studied quality metrics are summarized in Table 2: the first number in a cell is the number of passed ($p_{\text{val}} > 0.05$) control experiments (5 in total) and the second one is the number of passed ($p_{\text{val}} \leq 0.05$) deterioration experiments (20 in total). The latter one is detailed by indexes in the cell: the digits in the superscripts report the numbers of passed ranking (3 in total) and response time (5 in total) experiments; the ones in the subscripts report the number of passed UI (7 in total) and light UI (5 in total) experiments.

In each row of Table 2 we chose the best metrics in the following way. Among quality metrics that pass all 5 control

[23]The factor τ is hidden for confidentiality reasons.

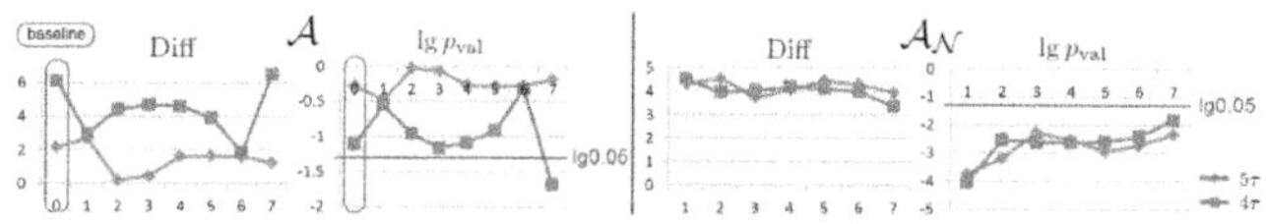

Figure 12: Results of 2 experiments with response time increasing for the presence time metric, for $\mathcal{A}$ and $\mathcal{A}_{\mathcal{N}}$ transformations.

experiments, we highlighted in **boldface** the ones with the highest number of passed deterioration experiments. Among quality metrics that pass 4 control experiments, we also chose those with the highest number of passed deterioration experiments. In the cases, when this number exceeds that of the best metrics without fails on control experiments, we highlight the metric in blue color. The first column contains 4 baseline metrics (BS).

The significant deterioration of the main web service component leads to strong changes in all metrics (all normalized amplitudes $\mathcal{A}_{\mathcal{N}}$ and almost all amplitudes $\mathcal{A}$ for the "swap-2" experiment, Fig. 9). But, when a change becomes less noticeable, different metrics show different sensitivity levels. Some studied metrics are sensitive to all changes in any component of the search engine (e.g., metrics derived from the presence time `tmSess`), the others specialize on catching differences in only one component (e.g., some metrics derived from the number of queries `cntQu` for "PersOff" experiment). If we allow using metrics that fail one of the control experiment, we obtain several quality metrics based on `cntQu`, which are more sensitive than the `cntQu`-based metrics without such fails (the last row in Table 2).

All metrics derived form the session count `cntSess` well pass the control A/A experiments and some of them catch both the ranking changes ($\mathcal{A}$ tend to grow, whereas $\mathcal{A}_{\mathcal{N}}$ tend to drop) and some UI changes (both $\mathcal{A}$ and $\mathcal{A}_{\mathcal{N}}$ tend to drop). The metrics derived from the presence time `tmSess` are most sensitive and almost all of them catch all types of studied changes with very high statistical significance level. The values Diff of the normalized amplitudes $\mathcal{A}_{\mathcal{N}}$(`tmSess`) for the response time changes are 5 times larger than the ones for the ranking changes. The metrics derived from the click count `cntCl` show the results similar to those for the presence time `tmSess` (except for the response time changes). This is naturally enough, since additional clicks lead to additional presence time. This assumption is supported by the results for the response time changes, where the changes in the presence time are caused by the engine efficiency and not by the user behavior. The metrics derived from the query count `cntQu` show their advantage on the experiment with personalization switching off, where one of its amplitudes and one of its normalized amplitudes outperform the baseline quality metrics. The users exposed to non-personalized results tend to submit more queries for some search tasks, what causes the changes in the periodicity amplitudes.

Finally, we conclude that *the baseline quality metrics are significantly outperformed by vast majority of the new periodicity metrics both in terms of significance level (p-value) and sensitivity to different search engine changes.* It is the answer to the **RQ3**.

8. CONCLUSIONS AND FUTURE WORK

In our work, we introduced *the periodicity pattern* (by means of the DFT) as an unified form for representation of user behavior periodicity. Namely, for a user, for 4-week pe-

Table 2: The number of passed A/B experiments by each of the 60 quality metrics (see Section 7 for details).

x	BS $\mathcal{A}(\mathtt{x})_0$	$\mathcal{A}(\mathtt{x})_1$	$\mathcal{A}(\mathtt{x})_2$	$\mathcal{A}(\mathtt{x})_3$	$\mathcal{A}(\mathtt{x})_4$	$\mathcal{A}(\mathtt{x})_5$	$\mathcal{A}(\mathtt{x})_6$	$\mathcal{A}(\mathtt{x})_7$	$\mathcal{A}_{\mathcal{N}}(\mathtt{x})_1$	$\mathcal{A}_{\mathcal{N}}(\mathtt{x})_2$	$\mathcal{A}_{\mathcal{N}}(\mathtt{x})_3$	$\mathcal{A}_{\mathcal{N}}(\mathtt{x})_4$	$\mathcal{A}_{\mathcal{N}}(\mathtt{x})_5$	$\mathcal{A}_{\mathcal{N}}(\mathtt{x})_6$	$\mathcal{A}_{\mathcal{N}}(\mathtt{x})_7$
cntSess	$5 \mid 3 \left[\begin{smallmatrix}11\\10\end{smallmatrix}\right]$	$5 \mid 3 \left[\begin{smallmatrix}10\\20\end{smallmatrix}\right]$	$5 \mid 1 \left[\begin{smallmatrix}10\\00\end{smallmatrix}\right]$	$5 \mid 2 \left[\begin{smallmatrix}20\\00\end{smallmatrix}\right]$	$5 \mid 1 \left[\begin{smallmatrix}10\\00\end{smallmatrix}\right]$	$\mathbf{5 \mid 4} \left[\begin{smallmatrix}20\\11\end{smallmatrix}\right]$	$5 \mid 3 \left[\begin{smallmatrix}11\\01\end{smallmatrix}\right]$	$5 \mid 1 \left[\begin{smallmatrix}10\\00\end{smallmatrix}\right]$	$\mathbf{5 \mid 4} \left[\begin{smallmatrix}20\\20\end{smallmatrix}\right]$	$5 \mid 2 \left[\begin{smallmatrix}20\\00\end{smallmatrix}\right]$	$5 \mid 3 \left[\begin{smallmatrix}11\\10\end{smallmatrix}\right]$	$5 \mid 2 \left[\begin{smallmatrix}11\\00\end{smallmatrix}\right]$	$5 \mid 1 \left[\begin{smallmatrix}10\\00\end{smallmatrix}\right]$	$5 \mid 2 \left[\begin{smallmatrix}10\\10\end{smallmatrix}\right]$	$5 \mid 2 \left[\begin{smallmatrix}10\\10\end{smallmatrix}\right]$
tmSess	$5 \mid 3 \left[\begin{smallmatrix}11\\10\end{smallmatrix}\right]$	$4 \mid 3 \left[\begin{smallmatrix}10\\20\end{smallmatrix}\right]$	$5 \mid 2 \left[\begin{smallmatrix}10\\10\end{smallmatrix}\right]$	$5 \mid 1 \left[\begin{smallmatrix}10\\00\end{smallmatrix}\right]$	$5 \mid 4 \left[\begin{smallmatrix}10\\30\end{smallmatrix}\right]$	$4 \mid 3 \left[\begin{smallmatrix}10\\20\end{smallmatrix}\right]$	$5 \mid 3 \left[\begin{smallmatrix}10\\20\end{smallmatrix}\right]$	$5 \mid 3 \left[\begin{smallmatrix}11\\10\end{smallmatrix}\right]$	$5 \mid 10 \left[\begin{smallmatrix}12\\34\end{smallmatrix}\right]$	$\mathbf{5 \mid 12} \left[\begin{smallmatrix}12\\72\end{smallmatrix}\right]$	$5 \mid 11 \left[\begin{smallmatrix}12\\62\end{smallmatrix}\right]$	$5 \mid 10 \left[\begin{smallmatrix}12\\52\end{smallmatrix}\right]$	$5 \mid 7 \left[\begin{smallmatrix}12\\31\end{smallmatrix}\right]$	$5 \mid 10 \left[\begin{smallmatrix}12\\52\end{smallmatrix}\right]$	$4 \mid 10 \left[\begin{smallmatrix}12\\61\end{smallmatrix}\right]$
cntCl	$5 \mid 2 \left[\begin{smallmatrix}11\\00\end{smallmatrix}\right]$	$5 \mid 4 \left[\begin{smallmatrix}10\\30\end{smallmatrix}\right]$	$5 \mid 2 \left[\begin{smallmatrix}10\\10\end{smallmatrix}\right]$	$5 \mid 1 \left[\begin{smallmatrix}10\\00\end{smallmatrix}\right]$	$5 \mid 2 \left[\begin{smallmatrix}10\\10\end{smallmatrix}\right]$	$5 \mid 1 \left[\begin{smallmatrix}10\\00\end{smallmatrix}\right]$	$5 \mid 2 \left[\begin{smallmatrix}10\\10\end{smallmatrix}\right]$	$5 \mid 1 \left[\begin{smallmatrix}10\\00\end{smallmatrix}\right]$	$5 \mid 8 \left[\begin{smallmatrix}10\\61\end{smallmatrix}\right]$	$4 \mid 10 \left[\begin{smallmatrix}11\\71\end{smallmatrix}\right]$	$4 \mid 10 \left[\begin{smallmatrix}11\\71\end{smallmatrix}\right]$	$4 \mid 10 \left[\begin{smallmatrix}11\\71\end{smallmatrix}\right]$	$\mathbf{5 \mid 10} \left[\begin{smallmatrix}11\\71\end{smallmatrix}\right]$	$4 \mid 10 \left[\begin{smallmatrix}11\\71\end{smallmatrix}\right]$	$4 \mid 9 \left[\begin{smallmatrix}11\\70\end{smallmatrix}\right]$
cntQu	$5 \mid 1 \left[\begin{smallmatrix}10\\00\end{smallmatrix}\right]$	$5 \mid 2 \left[\begin{smallmatrix}00\\20\end{smallmatrix}\right]$	$\mathbf{5 \mid 3} \left[\begin{smallmatrix}10\\20\end{smallmatrix}\right]$	$\mathbf{5 \mid 3} \left[\begin{smallmatrix}10\\20\end{smallmatrix}\right]$	$5 \mid 0 \left[\begin{smallmatrix}00\\00\end{smallmatrix}\right]$	$5 \mid 2 \left[\begin{smallmatrix}10\\10\end{smallmatrix}\right]$	$5 \mid 1 \left[\begin{smallmatrix}00\\10\end{smallmatrix}\right]$	$\mathbf{5 \mid 3} \left[\begin{smallmatrix}10\\20\end{smallmatrix}\right]$	$4 \mid 4 \left[\begin{smallmatrix}20\\20\end{smallmatrix}\right]$	$4 \mid 3 \left[\begin{smallmatrix}11\\10\end{smallmatrix}\right]$	$4 \mid 2 \left[\begin{smallmatrix}10\\10\end{smallmatrix}\right]$	$\mathbf{5 \mid 3} \left[\begin{smallmatrix}11\\10\end{smallmatrix}\right]$	$4 \mid 3 \left[\begin{smallmatrix}11\\10\end{smallmatrix}\right]$	$4 \mid 3 \left[\begin{smallmatrix}11\\10\end{smallmatrix}\right]$	$4 \mid 1 \left[\begin{smallmatrix}10\\00\end{smallmatrix}\right]$

riod, for 4 time series (the number of sessions, the presence time, the number queries and the number of clicks) we studied the amplitudes of the sine waves which compose the time series w.r.t. the DFT. Our basic and cluster analyses of user periodicity behavior show, that the periodicity patterns provide strong identification of several large user clusters with common coherent periodicity behavior.

Then, we studied how the periodicity patterns describe a long-term user behavior (during 20-week period). We found that the periodicity behavior, encoded in the periodicity patterns, is significantly more stable in long-term perspective than the user behavior data ranged by time. We find also that the users with definitive models of periodicity behavior stick to one periodicity model across months and the changes in their models are mostly caused by the changes in their life style (e.g., taking Christmas holidays). Thus, the periodicity patterns catch individual user traits that are mostly stable during a long time period.

We applied our periodicity patterns to a practical problem. We used the periodicity patterns as quality metrics (56 new scalar metrics in total) of search engine changes (such as the ranking algorithm, the UI, and the engine efficiency changes) by means of A/B tests. We found that the baseline quality metrics are significantly outperformed by vast majority of the new periodicity metrics both in terms of significance level (p-value) and sensitivity to different search engine changes.

Future work. We believe that our periodicity patterns will be of interest to researchers to be used in many practical problems. Our work is the first touch in this area, and in the future we can, first, extend the set of user engagement measures by investigating more sophisticated ones. Second, we can study the periodicity of user behavior across several web services. Third, we can also experiment with the size of the time window, e.g., study the periodicity patterns within a day. Finally, we can study the relationships between the periodicity user engagement metrics and other search engine quality metrics such as satisfaction, switching, etc.

9. REFERENCES

[1] E. Adar, J. Teevan, and S. T. Dumais. Large scale analysis of web revisitation patterns. In *CHI'2008*, pages 1197–1206, 2008.

[2] S. Chakraborty, F. Radlinski, M. Shokouhi, and P. Baecke. On correlation of absence time and search effectiveness. In *SIGIR'2014*, pages 1163–1166, 2014.

[3] A. Deng, Y. Xu, R. Kohavi, and T. Walker. Improving the sensitivity of online controlled experiments by utilizing pre-experiment data. In *WSDM'2013*, pages 123–132, 2013.

[4] A. Diriye, R. White, G. Buscher, and S. Dumais. Leaving so soon?: understanding and predicting web search abandonment rationales. In *CIKM'2012*, pages 1025–1034, 2012.

[5] G. Dupret and M. Lalmas. Absence time and user engagement: evaluating ranking functions. In *WSDM'2013*, pages 173–182, 2013.

[6] H. A. Feild, J. Allan, and R. Jones. Predicting searcher frustration. In *SIGIR'2010*, pages 34–41, 2010.

[7] Q. Guo, R. W. White, Y. Zhang, B. Anderson, and S. T. Dumais. Why searchers switch: understanding and predicting engine switching rationales. In *SIGIR'2011*, pages 335–344, 2011.

[8] A. Hassan, X. Shi, N. Craswell, and B. Ramsey. Beyond clicks: query reformulation as a predictor of search satisfaction. In *CIKM'2013*, pages 2019–2028, 2013.

[9] A. Hassan, Y. Song, and L.-w. He. A task level metric for measuring web search satisfaction and its application on improving relevance estimation. In *CIKM'2011*, pages 125–134, 2011.

[10] A. Hassan and R. W. White. Personalized models of search satisfaction. In *CIKM'2013*, pages 2009–2018, 2013.

[11] V. Hu, M. Stone, J. Pedersen, and R. W. White. Effects of search success on search engine re-use. In *CIKM'2011*, pages 1841–1846. ACM, 2011.

[12] B. J. Jansen, A. Spink, and V. Kathuria. How to define searching sessions on web search engines. In *Advances in Web Mining and Web Usage Analysis*, pages 92–109. Springer, 2007.

[13] R. Kohavi, A. Deng, R. Longbotham, and Y. Xu. Seven rules of thumb for web site experimenters. In *KDD'2014*, 2014.

[14] T. Kramár and M. Bieliková. Context of seasonality in web search. In *Advances in Information Retrieval*, pages 644–649. Springer, 2014.

[15] J. Lehmann, M. Lalmas, G. Dupret, and R. Baeza-Yates. Online multitasking and user engagement. In *CIKM'2013*, pages 519–528, 2013.

[16] J. Lehmann, M. Lalmas, E. Yom-Tov, and G. Dupret. Models of user engagement. In *User Modeling, Adaptation, and Personalization*, pages 164–175. Springer, 2012.

[17] K. Radinsky, K. Svore, S. Dumais, J. Teevan, A. Bocharov, and E. Horvitz. Modeling and predicting behavioral dynamics on the web. In *WWW*, 2012.

[18] K. Rodden, H. Hutchinson, and X. Fu. Measuring the user experience on a large scale: user-centered metrics for web applications. In *SIGCHI'2010*, pages 2395–2398, 2010.

[19] D. Savenkov, D. Lagun, and Q. Liu. Search engine switching detection based on user personal preferences and behavior patterns. In *SIGIR'2013*, pages 33–42, 2013.

[20] M. Shokouhi. Detecting seasonal queries by time-series analysis. In *SIGIR'2011*, pages 1171–1172, 2011.

[21] Y. Song, X. Shi, and X. Fu. Evaluating and predicting user engagement change with degraded search relevance. In *WWW'2013*, pages 1213–1224, 2013.

[22] M. Vlachos, C. Meek, Z. Vagena, and D. Gunopulos. Identifying similarities, periodicities and bursts for online search queries. In *SIGMOD'2004*, pages 131–142, 2004.

[23] W. W.-S. Wei. *Time series analysis.* Addison-Wesley Redwood City, California, 1994.

[24] R. West, R. W. White, and E. Horvitz. From cookies to cooks: Insights on dietary patterns via analysis of web usage logs. In *WWW'2013*, pages 1399–1410, 2013.

[25] R. W. White and S. T. Dumais. Characterizing and predicting search engine switching behavior. In *CIKM'2009*, pages 87–96, 2009.

[26] R. W. White, A. Kapoor, and S. T. Dumais. Modeling long-term search engine usage. In *User Modeling, Adaptation, and Personalization*, pages 28–39. Springer, 2010.

[27] Y. Zhang, B. J. Jansen, and A. Spink. Time series analysis of a web search engine transaction log. *Information Processing & Management*, 45(2):230–245, 2009.

Toward Predicting the Outcome of an A/B Experiment for Search Relevance

Lihong Li *
Microsoft Corp
One Microsoft Way
Redmond, WA 98052
lihongli@microsoft.com

Jin Young Kim †
Microsoft Corp
One Microsoft Way
Redmond, WA 98052
jink@microsoft.com

Imed Zitouni
Microsoft Corp
One Microsoft Way
Redmond, WA 98052
izitouni@microsoft.com

ABSTRACT

A standard approach to estimating online click-based metrics of a ranking function is to run it in a controlled experiment on live users. While reliable and popular in practice, configuring and running an online experiment is cumbersome and time-intensive. In this work, inspired by recent successes of offline evaluation techniques for recommender systems, we study an alternative that uses historical search log to reliably predict online click-based metrics of a *new* ranking function, without actually running it on live users.

To tackle novel challenges encountered in Web search, variations of the basic techniques are proposed. The first is to take advantage of diversified behavior of a search engine over a long period of time to simulate randomized data collection, so that our approach can be used at very low cost. The second is to replace exact matching (of recommended items in previous work) by *fuzzy* matching (of search result pages) to increase data efficiency, via a better trade-off of bias and variance. Extensive experimental results based on large-scale real search data from a major commercial search engine in the US market demonstrate our approach is promising and has potential for wide use in Web search.

Categories and Subject Descriptors

H.4 [**Information Systems Applications**]: Miscellaneous

General Terms

Experimentation; Performance

Keywords

Web search; information retrieval; experimentation; evaluation; contextual bandits

*Joint first authorship

†Joint first authorship

WSDM'15, February 2–6, 2015, Shanghai, China.
Copyright 2015 ACM 978-1-4503-3317-7/15/02 ...$15.00.
http://dx.doi.org/10.1145/2684822.2685311.

1. INTRODUCTION

Many Web-based services are by nature systems that interact with users. A search engine, for example, starts with a query issued by a user, returns a ranked list of documents, and observes user feedback often in the form of clicks and document consumption. Other examples are advertising and recommender systems that suggest one or multiple items to a user and in return receive feedback such as whether the user adopts/purchases the item(s) or not. Very often, such user feedback strongly indicates quality of the system. In advertising and recommender systems, for instance, it is natural to prefer a system with high adoption/conversion rate and possibly the revenue associated with it (*e.g.*, [7, 20]).

In Web search ranking, the problem we focus on in this work, useful signals can be extracted from user (click) feedback to infer whether a search event is successful or not. Commonly used examples include click-through rate (CTR), time to click on the search result page (SERP), and mean reciprocal of click positions, *etc.* In this paper, we consider the problem of estimating the average value of such pre-defined *online* signals across user visits.

Although human judgment labels are commonly used in practice to optimize such Web-based systems, they are inherently approximations to the quality of end user experience. This limitation suggests the need and importance to measure and optimize online metrics, even though label-based optimization can be a very useful starting point.

Often the metric of interest depends on user feedback, and hence on system output as well.[1] Therefore, one usually does not know what the user feedback *would have been* if the system output changes, unless a highly accurate user model is available. Such an observation leads to a fundamental challenge when estimating a metric of a search engine: based on search log collected by running a version of the engine on users in the past, it is often difficult or even impossible to reliably estimate a metric of a *modified* engine.

The standard approach to this problem is to run an A/B experiment(*e.g.*, [16]), also known as a randomized controlled experiment: incoming users are randomly split into two groups, where the *control* group is served by a baseline system and the *treatment* group by a variant. After running the experiment for a period of time (often ranging from one week to a few weeks), online metrics of the two systems are compared, and the one with higher metric values wins. While A/B experiments are highly valuable for making data-

[1]In this paper, we focus on metrics that depend on user feedback. Metrics that do *not* depend on user feedback are typically easy to estimate from historical data.

driven decisions to improve Web-based services, they are expensive for a few reasons. First, the turn-around time is long: it usually takes days or even weeks before comparisons of the control and treatment engines start to be statistically significant. Second, the engineering efforts are nontrivial to run a flight: as the new ranker will serve live users, substantial care has to be taken to ensure the ranker does not lead to catastrophic results. Third, search traffic is a limited resource. Quite often, multiple experiments compete for search traffic, and it is challenging to run several experiments at the same time.

Offline evaluation is therefore of great, practical interest. It aims to predict online metrics of a search engine *without* actually running it on live users, thus addressing all three difficulties above and substantially improving experimentation agility and quality. Offline evaluation has been studied and successfully applied to recommendation and advertising (*e.g.*, [3, 7, 17, 21, 27]), using statistical tools from causal inference. The key of these techniques is to first collect randomized data and then properly correcting sampling bias when evaluating a new system.

In the context of Web search ranking, however, the problem is even more challenging due to the exponentially large number of possible SERPs for any given query. First, data collection is very expensive since all possible SERPs will need to be shown with nonzero probability, a condition often required by reliable offline evaluation methods [3, 21]. Second, offline evaluation results' variance roughly depends reciprocally on the number of possible SEPRs (*c.f.*, Section 5) and can be too large in practice to be useful.

Our contributions are three-fold. First, to the best of our knowledge, our work is the first to apply causal inference techniques to offline-evaluate metrics of a Web search ranker. Second, in order to address novel challenges encountered in Web search, two variations of the basic offline evaluation technique are proposed and studied, making the method realistic for this application domain. Third, we demonstrate the proposed solution is promising through extensive experiments using large-scale real search log from a commercial search engine.

2. PRELIMINARIES

This section provides notation, setup, and related work.

2.1 Notation

Here, we formulate the ranking problem as a contextual bandit, a popular model in machine learning and statistics, for capturing interaction between user and the search ranker. In a contextual bandit [18], the system repeatedly observes contextual information that is independent and identically distributed (IID). For each observation, it takes an *action* and receives a possibly randomized *reward*. The reward depends on contextual information and the selected action, and rewards for other (not selected) actions are not observed.

In the context of Web search ranking, we denote the set of contextual information by $\mathcal{Q}$—the set of distinct queries, and for any $q \in \mathcal{Q}$, let $\mathcal{A}_q$ be the set of actions—the set of possible SERPs for query q. A ranker, denoted π, selects a SERP $a \in \mathcal{A}_q$. For convenience in this paper, we consider the general case where π is stochastic. That is, for each q, it computes a multinomial distribution $\pi(\cdot|q)$ over $\mathcal{A}_q$, so that $a \in \mathcal{A}_q$ is chosen with probability $\pi(a|q)$. In practice, π is often a deterministic function [4, 29]. For this important special case, we abuse notation a bit using $\pi(q)$ to denote the unique action π selects for query q. In the contextual bandit literature, π is often considered as a *policy*. In the rest of the paper, the pairs policy/ranker, context/query, and action/SERP are used interchangeably.

The interaction between ranker and user proceeds in a round-by-round fashion as follows: at round t,

1. A user visits the search engine and submits a query $q \in \mathcal{Q}$, drawn IID from some unknown distribution D.
2. The ranker selects the action $a = \pi(q) \in \mathcal{A}_q$; that is, it shows the SERP a to the user.
3. The user consumes the SERP and based on her feedback a numerical reward signal $r \in \mathbb{R}$ is computed.

A few notes are in place. First, we assume $r \in [0, R]$ for some known constant $R > 0$, since any bounded reward signal can be easily shifted and rescaled to lie within this range. Second, the distribution that q is drawn from can be time-dependent, to reflect daily and weekly population changes of queries encountered by a search engine. Our approach (and its associated guarantees) is not affected when the distribution becomes time-dependent.

The possibly stochastic reward signal measures how successful the system meets the user's need in that round. Its distribution depends on both the query and the action, and is not known (and usually difficult to model accurately). Examples of rewards are found in the next subsection. Our goal in this work is to estimate the average value of a *pre-defined* reward function when serving users with a *new* ranker π:

$$v(\pi) := \mathbb{E}_{q \sim D, a \sim \pi(\cdot|q)}[r] = \mathbb{E}_q \left[\sum_{a \in \mathcal{A}_q} \pi(a|q) \mathbb{E}[r|q,a] \right] . \quad (1)$$

In words, the metric is the average reward obtained by running the (possibly stochastic) policy on queries encountered by a search engine over a long period of time. If π is deterministic, the definition may be simplified as

$$v(\pi) := \mathbb{E}_{q \sim D}[r|q, \pi(q)] . \quad (2)$$

2.2 Example Metrics

Many important metrics used in practice can be obtained by defining appropriate rewards. For example, if we define r to be 1 if there is a click on the SERP and 0 otherwise, then $v(\pi)$ is the per-impression click-through rate (CTR) of the ranker. One can also easily define similar metrics for clicks that satisfy certain desired conditions, or incorporate monetary information to measure revenue.

Another popular type of metrics attempts to quantify how soon a user finds the information she needs. An example is the amount of time it takes for a user to click (or take any other pre-defined user action) after she submits a query. A related one is the reciprocal rank of the document that the user clicks on the SERP.

In our experiment, we focus on estimating the fraction of successful search activities of a ranking function. This requires defining what it means by a success in a Web search scenario, which typically depends on user clicks on the documents, amount of time spent on clicked documents (e.g., [5]), positions of clicked documents, and perhaps other information. For sensitivity reasons, the precise definition of success cannot be revealed, but it suffices to note that this metric is nothing but a concrete way to define the reward signal in the contextual bandit framework. A reader can simply interpret it as CTR of the whole SERP (not individual documents on the SERP), without sacrificing understanding of the technical details of this work.

2.3 Related Work

A lot of work has been done to evaluate rankers in information retrieval and Web search [25]. The dominant approach is to collect relevance labels from human judges for a collection of query-document pairs, which are then used to compute *offline* metrics like mean average precision [1] and normalized discounted cumulative gains [14]. For these metrics, the label information used to compute them is independent of user feedback, unlike the online metrics we focus on here. Such a non-interactive nature makes the judgment-based approach a relatively inexpensive and easy-to-use solution for ranking function evaluation.

However, the non-interactive nature also causes limitations, as pointed out by several authors [2, 28], as they are approximations of the quality of end user experience. Consequently, in industry, people have also measured various online metrics that indicate whether a search activity is successful or not. These metrics are the ones we try to estimate in this paper, since they depend on user feedback. The standard way is to run an A/B experiment (*e.g.*, [1, 16]) to directly measure online metrics, or to run an interleaving experiment that gives directional evaluation results [6, 24]. In contrast to existing methodology, we aim to rely on historical data to perform *offline* estimates of them.

Recent, some authors applied offline evaluation techniques to estimate online metrics for a specific type of experiments, namely interleaving [12, 13]. Such interesting work assumes availability of properly randomized, interleaved SERPs, and uses such data to predict outcomes of interleaving experiments for a new pair of rankers. In contrast, our focus here is for more general online experiments and can be directly applied to a wider range of online metrics (such as those involving revenue), with minimal need for data collection.

An alternative to A/B testing is to build a user click model and then use it to simulate user clicks on results produced by a new ranker. Much progress has been made in the past that led to refined models that deepen our understanding of user engagement (*e.g.*, [8, 10, 11]). Furthermore, some of these click models can be used to define useful offline metrics that have positive correlations with certain online metrics [9]. Here, we aim to estimate the online metrics themselves, instead of finding an proxy metric.

As explained in Section 3, the approach we take here is closely related to previous offline evaluation work for recommender and advertising systems based on contextual bandits [18, 21], and to causal inference in statistics [17] as well. Our work is along the same line, although we make two critical adjustments to enable it to work for Web search. The first is the idea of using "natural exploration" to replace active exploration [26], taking advantage of inherent diversity of a search engine. The second is to use approximate action matching for a better bias/variance trade-off.

3. BASIC TECHNIQUES WHEN RANDOMIZATION DATA ARE AVAILABLE

If one is able to run the policy on live users (that is, *online* evaluation), as in an A/B experiment, it is straightforward to estimate the policy value: we can simply run the policy to serve users, observe user feedback, compute the reward for each impression, and then average the reward. By the law of large numbers, this empirical average will converge to the true metric value with probability one.

However, the fundamental challenge in offline evaluation lies in the following *counterfactual* nature: for a particular query, if the ranker produces a different ranking than the one by the data-collection ranker, it is difficult, if not impossible at all, to reliably predict user feedback in response to the new ranking result. One therefore simply does not have the reward information for evaluating a new ranker.

As studied in previous work [21, 3], the key to reliable offline evaluation is to use randomization during data collection. Specifically, we may run an experiment on a small fraction of users that is dedicated to randomized data collection: when a user issues a query q, instead of always following production ranker π_0 to return a SERP $\pi_0(q)$, we add some pre-defined noise to π_0 so that a random SERP is shown to the user, with reward observed and recorded. Note that such randomization occurs on the impression level, so if the same user issues the same query a second time, she may see a different SERP. The process can be adapted if one is interested in user-level or search-session-level metrics.

When the data-collection experiment finishes, we will have a set of "exploration" data $\mathcal{D} = \{\langle q_i, a_i, p_i, r_i \rangle\}_{1 \le i \le n}$, where i indexes a distinct impression, q_i is the query issued by user in that impression, a_i is a ranking list (say, top 10 document list), $p_i = p(a_i|q_i)$ is the probability of showing a_i for q_i in the data-collection flight, and r_i is the resulting click-based metric (say, search-success-or-not, time to click). In the literature, p_i is also known as the *propensity score*.

Now, given *any* new, possibly randomized ranker π, we can estimate its value by the following estimator [3, 26]:

$$\widehat{v}_1(\pi) := \frac{1}{n} \sum_{i=1}^{n} \frac{\pi(a_i|q_i)}{p_i} r_i \,.$$

The intuition behind the estimator is that, for any given query q, some actions have higher selection probability during data collection, so they are over-represented in the data. The division by propensity scores is to correct such a sampling bias. In fact, it can be easily shown that the estimator is unbiased in the following sense:

$$\mathbb{E}[\widehat{v}_1(\pi)] = v(\pi) \,.$$

In other words, on average $\widehat{v}_1$ is identical to the true policy value that we try to estimate. Therefore, as long as variance is controlled, one can estimate the policy value to within a certain confidence level; further details and discussions can be found in [3, 19, 26].

4. SIMULATE RANDOMIZATION WITH PRODUCTION RANKER DIVERSITY

The approach above assume availability of randomized exploration data, a large amount of which may not be easy to collect, due to various practical restrictions like user dissatisfaction concerns. In contrast, the production ranker already produces a large amount of search log at almost no cost. It would be desirable to extract the most use of such data.

One idea that we pursue here is to use inherent diversity in ranker behavior (for the same query, in different flights and/or over different time periods) to *simulate* randomization, even if the individual rankings were computed deterministically in each impression. Such diversity is usually caused by factors such as continuous updates of the ranking function, changing features of query–document pairs, constant updates of the engine's indexes, etc. Such diversity leads to "natural exploration" behavior of the system that we will try to take advantage of. Since such data will play the same role as the (randomized) exploration data described previously, we use the same notation $\mathcal{D} = \{\langle q_i, a_i, p_i, r_i \rangle\}_{1 \le i \le n}$ for it and also refer it to as the exploration data. No confusion should be raised, as it is the only data we use for the following discussions and experiments. Furthermore, the ranker we try to evaluate is in general different from past rankers that were used to generate exploration data.

To be precise, let us define by

$$n(q) := \sum_{i=1}^{n} \mathbb{I}\{q_i = q\}$$
$$n(q,a) := \sum_{i=1}^{n} \mathbb{I}\{q_i = q, a_i = a\}$$

the counts of query q and of the query-SERP pair (q, a), respectively, observed in the exploration data, where $\mathbb{I}\{C\}$ is 1 if condition C holds true and 0 otherwise. The probability of the simulated randomization becomes

$$p_i = p(a_i|q_i) := \frac{n(q_i, a_i)}{n(q_i)},$$

and the previous unbiased estimator becomes

$$\widehat{v}_1(\pi) = \frac{1}{n} \sum_i \frac{\pi(a_i|q)n(q_i)}{n(q_i, a_i)} r_i .$$

By grouping the terms in the summation by distinct query-action pairs, we obtain the following offline metric estimator for a new ranker:

$$\begin{aligned} \widehat{v}_1(\pi) &= \frac{1}{n} \sum_q n(q) \sum_{a \in \mathcal{A}_q} \pi(a|q) \widehat{r}(q,a) \\ &= \sum_q \widehat{\mu}(q) \sum_{a \in \mathcal{A}_q} \pi(a|q) \widehat{r}(q,a) , \end{aligned} \quad (3)$$

where $\widehat{\mu}(q) := n(q)/n$ is the relative frequency of q in data $\mathcal{D}$, and

$$\widehat{r}(q,a) := \frac{1}{n(q,a)} \sum_i \mathbb{I}\{q_i = q, a_i = a\} r_i$$

is the average of reward for (q, a) in $\mathcal{D}$. We adopt the convention that $\widehat{r}(q, a) = 0$ when $n(q, a) = 0$. In other words, the estimator $\widehat{v}_1$ is like first building a regressor $\widehat{r}$ to predict $\mathbb{E}[r(q, a)]$ for every observed (q, a) pairs, and then plugging it in the definition of $v(\pi)$. For this reason, it is also called a *regression estimator* and is near-optimal in a strong statistical sense: for reasonable sample size n, the regression estimator's mean square error is always within constant factor of the optimal estimator's mean square error, and is asymptotically optimal as the sample size goes to infinity. [22]

4.1 A Variant with Target Query Distribution

In our experiment, we will use data collected in the past (the exploration data) to estimate online metrics for flights that occurred later (the test data). It is a reasonable assumption that query distributions in exploration and test data are similar. But for certain segments of queries, this assumption is likely to be violated. For example, time-sensitive queries may have a highly varying distribution over a short period of time, so queries that are common six months ago may not be popular any more now, and vice versa. Such a gap makes it hard to *validate* the evaluation approach we propose here.

To remove this gap, we can replace $\widehat{v}_1$ above by summing over queries in test data, although the reward estimates $\widehat{r}$ are still estimated using exploration data. This yields a slightly different estimator, denoted $\widehat{v}_2$:

$$\begin{aligned} \widehat{v}_2(\pi) &:= \frac{1}{n_*} \sum_q n_*(q) \sum_{a \in \mathcal{A}_q} \pi(q,a) \widehat{r}(q,a) \\ &= \frac{1}{n_*} \sum_q \sum_{a \in \mathcal{A}_q} n_*(q,a) \widehat{r}(q,a) , \end{aligned} \quad (4)$$

where n_*, $n_*(q)$, and $n_*(q, a)$ are the corresponding counts in test data, and the second equality is due to the observation that the ranker to be evaluated is defined through test data by $\pi(a|q) = n_*(q, a)/n_*(q)$.

It should be emphasized that $\widehat{v}_2$ is given to remove query distribution mismatch between exploration and test data for the purpose of our experiments in the paper. What it tries to validate empirically is whether metrics are similar between exploration and treatment data, when query distributions match perfectly. But when building an experiment success predictor in reality, test data are not available, since frequent online experiments with new rankers is what we try to avoid in the first place. On the other hand, there is a reason to use as many search log as possible to get better estimate of $\widehat{r}$ and to increase coverage of (q, a), implying pretty outdated data have to be used. So, query frequencies $n(q)$ observed *in the past* (used in $\widehat{v}_1$) may be quite different from what would be observed if π is flighted *now*. An easy fix is to use recent search log to obtain query frequencies $n(q)$ and plug them in $\widehat{v}_1$.

4.2 Special Case for Deterministic π

In most practical situations, we are interested in evaluating a deterministic ranker, in which case the estimator can be simplified from the more general form presented earlier. We provide the formula here due to the importance of such a special case. Recall from Section 2 that, when π is deterministic, $\pi(q)$ refers to the unique action it selects for query q. The two estimators can be expressed as:

$$\widehat{v}_1(\pi) = \frac{1}{n} \sum_q n(q) \widehat{r}(q, \pi(q)) ,$$
$$\widehat{v}_2(\pi) = \frac{1}{n_*} \sum_q n_*(q) \widehat{r}(q, \pi(q)) .$$

4.3 Variance Estimation

In addition to the *point* estimates given above, variance information is also needed to evaluate whether a difference between estimates of two policies' values is statistically significant. Here, we give a simple-to-compute *approximation* for variance.

First of all, recall that $r_i \in [0, R]$ for some constant R. If r_i corresponds to binary events like click-or-not or success-or-not, then $R = 1$. Under the boundedness condition, the variance of r_i can be bounded by $\mathbb{V}(r_i) \le R^2/4$, which is tight when r_i is a Bernoulli random variable (taking values in $\{0, R\}$) with parameter $1/2$. Since $\widehat{r}(q,a)$ is the average of $n(q,a)$ such IID random variables, we immediately have

$$\mathbb{V}(\widehat{r}(q,a)) \le \frac{R^2}{4n(q,a)}. \tag{5}$$

Consequently, the variance of the two estimators follows immediately:

$$\begin{aligned}
\mathbb{V}(\widehat{v}_1(\pi)) &= \frac{1}{n^2}\sum_q \sum_{a\in\mathcal{A}_q} \frac{\pi(a|q)^2 n(q,a)^2}{p(a|q)^2}\mathbb{V}(\widehat{r}(q,a)) \\
&\le \frac{R^2}{4n^2}\sum_q \frac{n(q)^2}{n_*(q)^2}\sum_{a\in\mathcal{A}_q}\frac{n_*(q,a)^2}{n(q,a)}, \\
\mathbb{V}(\widehat{v}_2(\pi)) &= \frac{1}{n_*^2}\sum_q\sum_{a\in\mathcal{A}_q} n_*(q,a)^2\mathbb{V}(\widehat{r}(q,a)) \\
&\le \frac{R^2}{4n_*^2}\sum_q\sum_{a\in\mathcal{A}_q}\frac{n_*(q,a)^2}{n(q,a)}.
\end{aligned}$$

For the important special case when π is deterministic, the above formula may be simplified as

$$\begin{aligned}
\mathbb{V}(\widehat{v}_1(\pi)) &= \frac{1}{n^2}\sum_q n(q)^2\mathbb{V}(\widehat{r}(q,\pi(q))) \\
&\le \frac{R^2}{4n^2}\sum_q \frac{n(q)^2}{n(q,\pi(q))} \\
\mathbb{V}(\widehat{v}_2(\pi)) &= \frac{1}{n_*^2}\sum_q n_*(q)^2\mathbb{V}(\widehat{r}(q,\pi(q))) \\
&\le \frac{R^2}{4n^2}\sum_q \frac{n_*(q)^2}{n(q,\pi(q))}.
\end{aligned}$$

Given a variance estimate, confidence intervals can be estimated. For example, 95% confidence interval is $1.96 \times \sqrt{\mathbb{V}(\widehat{v}_i(\pi))}$.

Note that the above variance estimation formula works for both continuous and discrete-valued metrics, as long as the metrics have a bounded range inside $[0, R]$. While being very general, the variance upper bound given in Equation 5 may not be most tight. An empirically better alternative, as discussed in previous work [3, 19], is to estimate $\mathbb{V}(\widehat{r}(q,a))$ from data, using classic normal approximation techniques or recent statistics results [23].

4.4 Limitations

Although the proposal here is inspired by the unbiased estimator reviewed in Section 3 and shares many similarities, the estimator obtained from *simulated* exploration data loses the nice unbiasedness guarantee in general. One key problem is that, the search log is not exploratory enough to cover *all* possible rankings for any query. Consequently, if for some query q the target policy π selects a ranking that has no occurrence in data (meaning $n(q,\pi(q)) = 0$), there will be no information to predict what the online metric would be if ranking $\pi(q)$ is displayed to the user.

Another source of bias of our approach is introduced by potential confounding in the data [3] — for example, when selection of SERPs in exploration data depends on both the query and additional information (such as user location).

Randomized data collection can remove these two biases, hence should be attempted whenever possible.

5. FUZZY MATCHING

A major difficulty common to the approaches in Sections 3 and 4 is that $\mathcal{A}_q$ can be large for many queries q, leading to two consequences:

- The larger $\mathcal{A}_q$ is, the smaller $n(q,a)$ tends to be for every a, and a larger variance is expected from our estimators (*c.f.*, Equation 5). To understand the influence, consider the special situation when π is deterministic, all $n(q)$ are identical and equals n/Q (Q is the number of distinct queries found in D), and $|\mathcal{A}_q| = K$. Then, the variance estimation for $\widehat{v}_1$, as given in the previous section, becomes $R^2K/(4n)$. So the variance roughly grows linearly with the size of average size of $\mathcal{A}_q$.
- The larger $\mathcal{A}_q$ is, the less likely metric information can be extracted from data to estimate $v(\pi)$. In fact, as observed empirically, queries that share common SERPs between exploration and test data tend to be more head-ish ones. It follows that $\mathcal{A}_q$ tends to be larger when q is tail, and so have lower chances to be included in the offline estimation formula.

The idea of *fuzzy matching* is to relax the condition of *exact* matching between two rankings, so that two rankings a and a' are considered identical when they are "close" enough. By doing so, we can effectively reduce the size of $\mathcal{A}_q$, since many rankings collapse into one, and can alleviate the difficulty described above.

Here, we consider a special case of fuzzy matching that focus on top-ranked URLs in a ranking. For example, if we only focus on the top $L = 4$ URLs on the SERP, two rankings that only differ in positions below L will be treated as the same ranking. Such fuzzy matching will inevitably introduce bias in the evaluation results (since URLs below top L do have influence on metrics), but hopefully we will be able to find a good trade-off by choosing L properly.

Some notation is in place. For any query q, let $\mathcal{A}_q$ be all rankings observed in data. We say $a \sim a'$ if a and a' are considered the same. With the binary equivalence relation $\sim$, $\mathcal{A}_q$ can be partitioned into a collection of distinct subsets, $\mathcal{A}_{q,1}, \mathcal{A}_{q,2}, \ldots$, so that each $\mathcal{A}_{q,j}$ contains rankings that are considered identical. Now, we just need to treat $\mathcal{A}_{q,i}$ as new actions and apply the same techniques as before, to compute an estimate and confidence intervals. Similar to the exact-match case, define the following quantities:

$$\begin{aligned}
n(q,\mathcal{A}_{q,j}) &:= \sum_{a\in\mathcal{A}_{q,j}} n(q,a) \\
\tilde{r}(q,\mathcal{A}_{q,j}) &:= \frac{\sum_i \mathbb{I}\{q_i = q, a_i \in \mathcal{A}_{q,j}\} r_i}{\sum_i \mathbb{I}\{q_i = q, a_i \in \mathcal{A}_{q,j}\}} \\
&= \frac{1}{n(q,\mathcal{A}_{q,j})}\sum_i \mathbb{I}\{q_i = q, a_i \in \mathcal{A}_{q,j}\} r_i
\end{aligned}$$

Finally, given q and a, let $j(q,a)$ be the (inverted) index such that $a \in \mathcal{A}_{q,j(q,a)}$.

For fuzzy matching with binary relation $\sim$, the previous estimators can be adapted using the quantities above:

PROPOSITION 1. *The estimator in Equation 3 becomes the following with fuzzy matching:*

$$\tilde{v}_1(\pi) = \sum_q \widehat{\mu}(q) \sum_{a\in\mathcal{A}_q} \frac{\sum_{a'\sim a}\pi(a'|q)n(q,a)\widehat{r}(q,a)}{\sum_{a'\sim a} n(q,a')}$$

The extension to $\widehat{v}_2$ is similar.

6. EXPERIMENTS

In this section, we describe the experiments to evaluate the performance of the prediction method. Our experiment has several objectives. First, we would like to know how accurate the predictions for individual flights are. Also, since the goal of online experiment is to determine the relative performance of each flight, we would like to know how accurately the relative performance between two ranking methods are predicted.

For this paper, our method is to use the existing experimentation data to evaluate the prediction technique. In other words, we collected experimentation data for a year, and split the data into two periods to generate the exploration and test data, respectively. Finally, we can see to what extent the metric value estimates based on exploration data approximate the metric values in test data.

6.1 Data Collection

For our experiment, we used large-scale log data from the random sample of ranking-related online experiments for a major search engine in US market. Each record in the data takes the form of (Query, Top-8 results, Metric Values, Impression Count). Our data contains the log data of one year period, where the first 6 months are used as exploration-set and the following months are used as test set. Our data set contains 190 ranking algorithms (rankers) within 44 ranking experiments.

We created two types of data sets for our experiments which are then used to estimate and evaluate the model, respectively. First, we used the data in Period I to generate the exploration data set described in Section 4. That is, we aggregated the data by query, action, the (simulated) probability of action and reward values. Second, we used the data in Period II to generate the test data set. That is, we aggregated the data by *ranker*, query, action, the (simulated) probability of action and reward values.

Given the two data sets, our experiment is to estimate the metric value for each ranker in the test data using reward signals from the exploration data. We achieve this by joining the exploration and test data using (query, action) as key. And the fuzzy matching introduced in Section 5 is used to control the definition of action used for the experiments using both estimators $\tilde{v}_1$ and $\tilde{v}_2$.

6.2 Results

6.2.1 *Metric Value Prediction*

We present the results for predicting absolute metric values, where we plotted the predicted metric values against actual metric values. The results in Figure 1 and Figure 2 shows that the correlation is strongest when defining action based on Top 3 web results, followed by Top 5 web results. In fact, there seems to be virtually no correlation when using Top 8 web results (i.e., exact match) to define action.

Table 1 shows the same trends, where the level of correlation (Cor(.)) gets lower as we define action in a more fine-grained manner. As a possible explanation, you can see that the number of (Query,Action) matches decreases sharply when we use the exact match. Between the 1st and the 2nd estimator, we find that the 2nd estimator provides slightly better correlation, which implies that the mismatch in query count does have some impact.

Table 1: Results for predicting absolute metric values.

TopK	Cor($\widehat{v}_1$)	Cor($\widehat{v}_2$)	#(Query,Action)
3	0.549	0.596	645,749,791
5	0.431	0.438	244,046,777
8	-0.271	-0.254	63,646,334

Table 2: Results for predicting the delta in metric values between two rankers.

TopK	Accuracy	Correlation
3	58.5%	0.450
5	56.1%	0.396
8	50.7%	0.370

6.2.2 *Metric Delta Prediction*

We present the results for predicting the delta in metric values between two rankers. Each experiment in our test data contains two rankers: one is a baseline ranker ("control") and the other is a proposed new ranker ("treatment"). The experiment was used to discover whether the proposed ranker is superior to the baseline ranker. Such pairs of rankers are therefore ideal pairs for our purpose to predict metric deltas.

In particular, for each experiment, we calculated the difference in the metric value between the two rankers. The results in Figure 3 shows the distribution of predicted delta between two rankers within each experiment for varying level of approximate match, against the true metric differences based solely on test data. It can be seen that the correlation is quite strong for Top-3 (fuzzy) match, and worst for Top-8 (exact) match.

While the scatterplot shows the general trend, what really matters are the decisions based on the values. In other words, each comparison between two rankers can be determined to be WIN (proposed ranker significantly better than the baseline), LOSS (proposed ranker significantly worse than the baseline), or TIE (otherwise). We want to see whether our offline evaluation method gives good predictions of online flight successes or not.

In order to make decisions based on the metric values, we used the two-sample t-test with p-value threshold of 0.05 on both predicted and actual delta values. Then we calculated the accuracy as the sum of diagonal divided by the total number of pairs being compared. Table 2 presents the accuracy values as well as the correlation between the predicted and actual delta. Note that if we make random decisions among WIN/LOSS/TIE, the accuracy is 33.3%, and our improvement is statistically significant. If we predict the majority outcome, the prediction is TIE which is not useful at all.

Table 3 presents the confusion table between predicted outcome and the actual outcome of experiments, as well as the accuracy/recall of predictions for each outcome. Again, there seems to be a clear bias in the prediction results. That is, there are many cases where predicted outcome was positive (a WIN case) while actual outcome was TIE (or even LOSS), but very few cases in the opposite direction. We can call it an "optimistic" bias in that the prediction results are more positive than actual experimental outcome. We delve

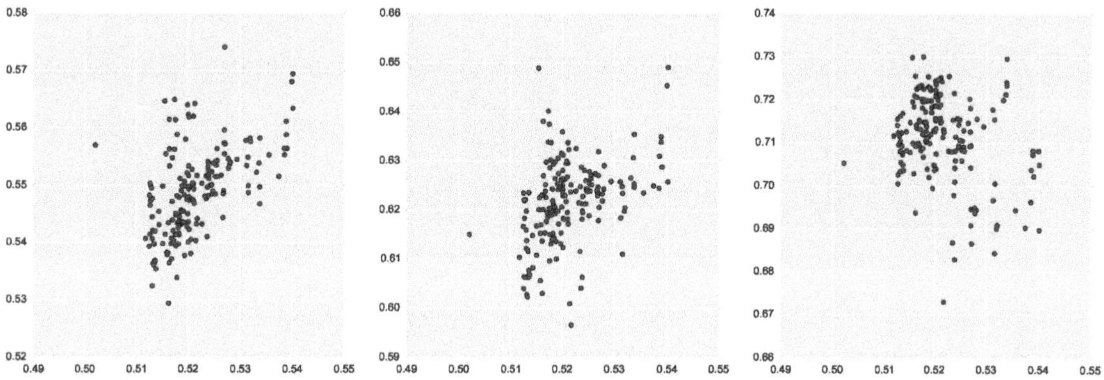

Figure 1: **Scatterplot for actual (X) vs. predicted (Y) click ratio based on the 1st estimator ($\widehat{v}_1$), where the action is defined by Top 3, 5 and 8 web results, respectively.**

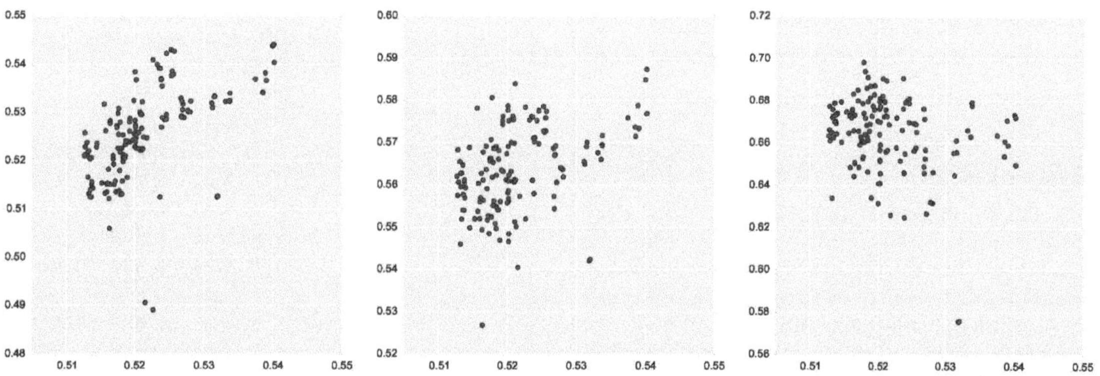

Figure 2: **Scatterplot for actual (X) vs. predicted (Y) click ratio based on the 2nd estimator ($\widehat{v}_2$), where the action is defined by Top 3, 5 and 8 web results, respectively.**

into why that is the case in the following sections. Such a bias is also reflected by the relatively high accuracy of LOSS predictions

It should be noted that, for our purpose, an optimistic bias is relatively easy to handle: if a proposed ranker is predicted to be a WIN, one can run it in a real experiment on users to find out whether it is really the case. On the other hand, if a LOSS prediction is made, it is a strong indication that the ranker is not worth running a real experiment. Therefore, our technique can be used to weed out unpromising techniques early on without going through with an online experiment.

Finally, we examine how often the offline prediction gives results opposite to the actual outcomes. A *disagreement* happens when a WIN is predicted for a LOSS flight or when a LOSS is predicted for a WIN flight. The *disagreement ratio* is the ratio between number of disagreements and number of WIN/LOSS flights. As shown in Table 4, the disagreement ratio is reasonably low across various K values.

Table 3: WIN/TIE/LOSS confusion table between actual outcomes (columns) and predicted outcomes (rows) for different K values of topK fuzzy matching. Accuracy/recall are also included for each outcome.

K=3	LOSS	TIE	WIN	Accuracy	Recall
WIN	3.4%	19.0%	13.7%	37.8%	65.1%
TIE	8.8%	38.0%	6.8%	70.9%	63.4%
LOSS	6.8%	2.9%	0.5%	66.7%	35.9%
K=5	LOSS	TIE	WIN	Accuracy	Recall
WIN	3.9%	11.7%	5.9%	27.3%	27.9%
TIE	12.2%	47.3%	15.1%	63.4%	78.9%
LOSS	2.9%	1.0%	0.0%	75.0%	15.4%
K=8	LOSS	TIE	WIN	Accuracy	Recall
WIN	4.4%	18.5%	7.3%	24.2%	34.9%
TIE	12.7%	41.5%	13.7%	61.2%	69.1%
LOSS	2.0%	0.0%	0.0%	100%	10.3%

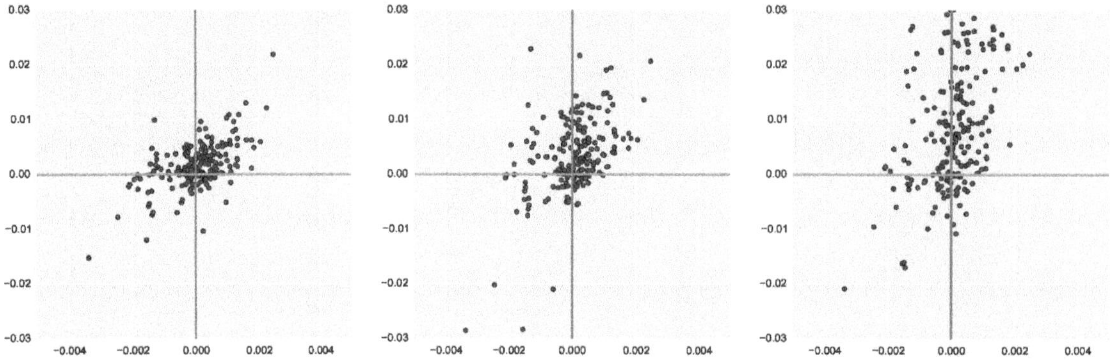

Figure 3: Scatterplot for actual (X) vs. predicted (Y) delta in click ratio between two rankers in the same experiment where the action is defined by Top 3, 5 and 8 web results, respectively.

K	3	5	8
Disagreement ratio	9.8%	9.8%	11.0%

Table 4: Disagreement ratio for different K values.

6.3 Analysis of Bias

In Section 6.2.2, we observed that the metric delta prediction results are more optimistic than actual experimental outcome. This means that the predicted metric value for experimental ranker tends to be higher than the control ranker. Among many possible explanations, one clear difference between two rankers is the coverage of exploration data. That is, experimental rankers should produce more results that are not found in the exploration data set than the control rankers, which is mostly the rankers already in production.

In order to verify the hypothesis, we investigated the relationship between the degree of optimistic bias measured by the ratio of predicted metric value against actual metric value, and the coverage of exploration data in terms of the percentage of matching records. Figure 4 shows the results, where the negative correlation is clear in the rightmost plot, which employs the exact matching strategy.

The result indicates that the increase in coverage means reduced bias, and the trend is most conspicuous for the case of exact match. This trend is consistent with what we observed in Figure 3 and Table 3, where the results were most concentrated in the upper left corner for exact match case.

6.4 Segment-level Results

Our prediction method relies on the assumptions that there is no confounding in the exploration data (*c.f.*, Section 4.4), that there are sufficient amount of exploration data (i.e., metric values for different set of results) for each query, and that we have enough observations for each (Query, Action) pair. The other requirement is that the users' click behavoir would be consistent between exploration and exploration data for the same query.

Since these assumptions may not hold for certain type of queries, we can hypothesize that the performance of prediction method should vary across different query segments. We classified queries into different segments, and then calculated the predicted and actual metric values as before, to see how the correlation between predicted and actual metric values changes for different segments.

Table 5: Correlation between predicted and actual metric values for different segments with different K values in fuzzy matching.

TopK	Segment	Cor	Count
3	Head	0.916	364,757
	Body	0.962	553,892,081
	Tail	0.722	90,867,404
	Local	0.342	60,448,865
	Navigational	0.642	120,343,701
	Overall	0.934	645,124,406
5	Head	0.875	345,640
	Body	0.894	229,862,589
	Tail	0.860	13,636,733
	Local	0.413	24,049,649
	Navigational	0.648	58,680,950
	Overall	0.885	243,845,041
8	Head	0.563	304,142
	Body	0.962	61,433,473
	Tail	0.993	1,809,956
	Local	0.453	6,369,383
	Navigational	0.575	23,107,195
	Overall	0.872	63,547,643

The results in Figure 5 shows the level of correlation for different segments. It is clear that the correlation for the body segment is strongest in overall in Top 3 and 5 matching, and that the Local segment has lowest correlation, followed by Navigational. Table 5 presents the same results with the number of matching records. Note that the number of tail queries in Top 8 match is much smaller than Top 3 and 5 matches. We hypothesize that this have led to exceptionally higher correlation on that segment.

Between Head/Body/Tail, the Body segment shows the highest correlation in overall, which is reasonable in that there would be sufficient variety of per-query results shown to the user, with enough sample size for each result. In Head segment where there are many signals for ranking, we

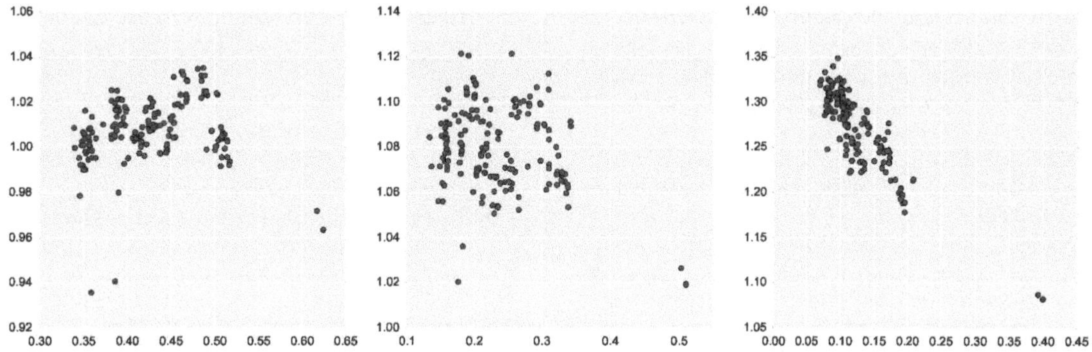

Figure 4: Scatterplot for the ratio of predicted metric value against actual metric value, plotted against % of matching records, where the action is defined by Top 3, 5 and 8 web results, respectively.

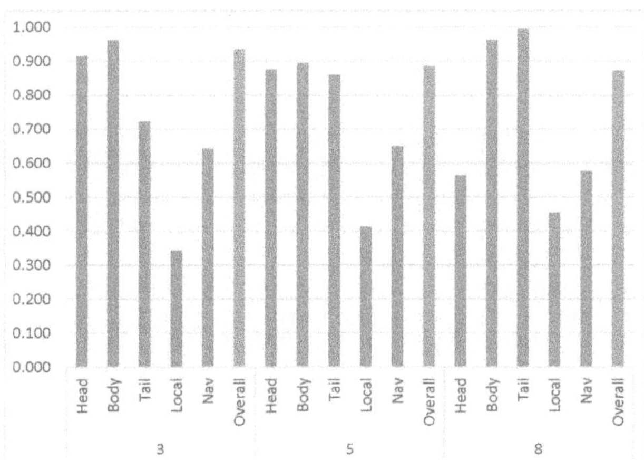

Figure 5: Correlation between predicted and actual metric values for different segments with varying K values in fuzzy matching.

are unlikely to observe lots of variation in Top-k results. For tail, while the variety might exist, there should be very few data points for each alternative ranking.

Low correlation for local segment can be explained if we note that the click pattern is likely to vary across different locations even for the same query, creating confounding that leads to a bias. For navigational queries, where the clicks would be heavily skewed toward the top few results, we hypothesized that there may not be enough exploration data that can allow effective prediction.

7. CONCLUSIONS

In this work, we proposed an offline approach to estimating online metrics of a new ranker that typically depend on user feedback. This approach does not require running every such new ranker on live users and is therefore less expensive than standard A/B experiments. Compared to previous work with the same motivation in recommender and advertising systems, we proposed two variations to address novel challenges encountered in Web search.

Our approach shows promise based on extensive experiments on large-scale data collected from a major search engine. The fuzzy matching technique based on Top-3 results can predict actual metric values closely (Pearson correlation 0.6), and the prediction of experimental results between control and treatment ranking techniques shows reasonably high accuracy upto 58.5% – significantly higher than chance results (33.3%).

The promising results lead to a few directions for future work. First, while there is no conceptual difficulty, we would like to apply the same technique to estimate session-level and user-level metrics. Second, we conjecture that our evaluation method can benefit from more flexible fuzzy matching criterion, in which the similarity between two SERPs of the same query can be measured by a real number (*e.g.*, [15]), as opposed to the binary same-or-different SERP matching outcomes considered in this paper.

Acknowledgement

We thank Dongwoo Kim for help in our experiments, and the anonymous reviewers for numerous suggestions that improved the presentation of the paper.

8. REFERENCES

[1] Ricardo Baeza-Yates and Berthier Ribeiro-Neto. *Modern Information Retrieval: The Concepts and Technology behind Search.* ACM Press Books. Addison-Wesley Professional, 2nd edition, 2011.

[2] Nicholas J. Belkin. Some(what) grand challenges for information retrieval. *ACM SIGIR Forum*, 42(1):47–54, 2008.

[3] Léon Bottou, Jonas Peters, Joaquin Quiñonero Candela, Denis Xavier Charles, D. Max Chickering, Elon Portugaly, Dipankar Ray, Patrice Simard, and Ed Snelson. Counterfactual reasoning and learning systems: The example of computational advertising. *Journal of Machine Learning Research*, 14:3207–3260, 2013.

[4] Christopher J. C. Burges, Tal Shaked, Erin Renshaw, Ari Lazier, Matt Deeds, Nicole Hamilton, and

Gregory N. Hullender. Learning to rank using gradient descent. In *Proceedings of the 22nd International Conference on Machine Learning*, pages 89–96, 2005.

[5] Georg Buscher, Ludger van Elst, and Andreas Dengel. Segment-level display time as implicit feedback: A comparison to eye tracking. In *Proceedings of the 32nd Annual International ACM SIGIR Conference on Research and Development in Information Retrieval*, pages 67–74, 2009.

[6] Olivier Chapelle, Thorsten Joachims, Filip Radlinski, and Yisong Yue. Large scale validation and analysis of interleaved search evaluation. *ACM Transactions on Information Science*, 30(1), 2012.

[7] Olivier Chapelle, Eren Manavoglu, and Romer Rosales. Simple and scalable response prediction for display advertising. *ACM Transactions on Intelligent Systems and Technology*. To appear.

[8] Olivier Chapelle and Ya Zhang. A dynamic Bayesian network click model for Web search ranking. In *Proceedings of the 18th International Conference on World Wide Web*, pages 1–10, 2009.

[9] Aleksandr Chuklin, Pavel Serdyukov, and Maarten de Rijke. Click model-based information retrieval metrics. In *Proceedings of the 36th International ACM SIGIR Conference on Research and Development in Information Retrieval*, pages 493–502, 2013.

[10] Georges Dupret and Benjamin Piwowarski. A user browsing model to predict search engine click data from past observations. In *Proceedings of the 31st Annual International ACM SIGIR Conference on Research and Development in Information Retrieval*, pages 331–338, 2008.

[11] Fan Guo, Chao Liu, Anitha Kannan, Tom Minka, Michael J. Taylor, Yi-Min Wang, and Christos Faloutsos. Click chain model in Web search. In *Proceedings of the 18th International Conference on World Wide Web*, pages 11–20, 2009.

[12] Katja Hofmann, Anne Schuth, Shimon Whiteson, and Maarten de Rijke. Reusing historical interaction data for faster online learning to rank for IR. In *Proceedings of the 6th ACM International Conference on Web Search and Data Mining*, pages 183–192, 2013.

[13] Katja Hofmann, Shimon Whiteson, and Maarten de Rijke. Estimating interleaved comparison outcomes from historical click data. In *Proceedings of the 21st ACM International Conference on Information and Knowledge Management*, pages 1779–1783, 2012.

[14] Kalervo Järvelin and Jaana Kekäläinen. Cumulated gain-based evaluation of IR techniques. *ACM Transactions on Information Systems*, 20(4):422–446, 2002.

[15] Gabriella Kazai and Homer Sung. Dissimilarity based query selection for efficient preference based IR evaluation. In *Proceedings of the European Conference on Information Retrieval*, pages 172–183, 2014.

[16] Ron Kohavi, Roger Longbotham, Dan Sommerfield, and Randal M. Henne. Controlled experiments on the web: Survey and practical guide. *Data Minining and Knowledge Discovery*, 18:140–181, 2009.

[17] Diane Lambert and Daryl Pregibon. More bang for their bucks: Assessing new features for online advertisers. *SIGKDD Explorations*, 9(2):100–107, 2007.

[18] John Langford, Alexander L. Strehl, and Jennifer Wortman. Exploration scavenging. In *Proceedings of the 25th International Conference on Machine Learning*, pages 528–535, 2008.

[19] Lihong Li, Shunbao Chen, Ankur Gupta, and Jim Kleban. Counterfactual analysis of click metrics for search engine optimization. Technical Report MSR-TR-2014-32, Microsoft Research, 2014.

[20] Lihong Li, Wei Chu, John Langford, and Robert E. Schapire. A contextual-bandit approach to personalized news article recommendation. In *Proceedings of the 19th International Conference on World Wide Web*, pages 661–670, 2010.

[21] Lihong Li, Wei Chu, John Langford, and Xuanhui Wang. Unbiased offline evaluation of contextual-bandit-based news article recommendation algorithms. In *Proceedings of the 4th International Conference on Web Search and Data Mining*, pages 297–306, 2011.

[22] Lihong Li, Remi Munos, and Csaba Szepesvári. On minimax optimal off-policy policy evaluation. Technical report, Microsoft Research, 2014.

[23] Andreas Maurer and Massimiliano Pontil. Empirical Bernstein bounds and sample-variance penalization. In *Proceedings of the Twenty-Second Conference on Learning Theory*, pages 247–254, 2009.

[24] Filip Radlinski and Nick Craswell. Optimized interleaving for online retrieval evaluation. In *Proceedings of the 6th ACM International Conference on Web Search and Data Mining*, pages 245–254, 2013.

[25] Stephen Robertson. On the history of evaluation in IR. *Journal of Information Science*, 34(4):439–456, 2008.

[26] Alexander L. Strehl, John Langford, Lihong Li, and Sham M. Kakade. Learning from logged implicit exploration data. In *Advances in Neural Information Processing Systems 23*, pages 2217–2225, 2011.

[27] Liang Tang, Romer Rosales, Ajit Singh, and Deepak Agarwal. Automatic ad format selection via contextual bandits. In *Proceedings of the 22nd ACM International Conference on Information & Knowledge Management*, pages 1587–1594, 2013.

[28] Andrew H. Turpin and William Hersh. Why batch and user evaluations do not give the same results. In *Proceedings of the 24th ACM SIGIR Conference on Research and Development in Information Retrieval*, pages 225–231, 2001.

[29] Zhaohui Zheng, Hongyuan Zha, Tong Zhang, Olivier Chapelle, Keke Chen, and Gordon Sun. A general boosting method and its application to learning ranking functions for web search. In *Advances in Neural Information Processing Systems 20*, pages 1000–1007, 2008.

Optimal Space-time Tradeoffs for Inverted Indexes

Giuseppe Ottaviano[1], Nicola Tonellotto[1], Rossano Venturini[1,2]
[1] National Research Council of Italy, Pisa, Italy
[2] Department of Computer Science, University of Pisa, Pisa, Italy
giuseppe.ottaviano@isti.cnr.it, nicola.tonellotto@isti.cnr.it, rossano.venturini@unipi.it

ABSTRACT

Inverted indexes are usually represented by dividing posting lists into constant-sized blocks and representing them with an encoder for sequences of integers. Different encoders yield a different point in the space-time trade-off curve, with the fastest being several times larger than the most space-efficient. An important design decision for an index is thus the choice of the fastest encoding method such that the index fits in the available memory.

However, a better usage of the space budget could be obtained by using faster encoders for frequently accessed blocks, and more space-efficient ones those that are rarely accessed. To perform this choice optimally, we introduce a linear time algorithm that, given a query distribution and a set of encoders, selects the best encoder for each index block to obtain the lowest expected query processing time respecting a given space constraint.

To demonstrate the effectiveness of this approach we perform an extensive experimental analysis, which shows that our algorithm produces indexes which are significantly faster than single-encoder indexes under several query processing strategies, while respecting the same space constraints.

Categories and Subject Descriptors

H.3.2 [**Information Storage and Retrieval**]: Information Storage; E.4 [**Coding and Information Theory**]: Data Compaction and Compression

Keywords

Compression; Knapsack Problems; Inverted Indexes

1. INTRODUCTION

Web search engines need to carefully organize billions of documents into efficient data structures to timely answer queries submitted by their users. The most central of such data structures is the inverted index, which, in its most basic and popular form, is a collection of sorted sequences of integers [5, 16, 28, 32]. An inverted index has to fulfill two goals: it must be able to efficiently process users' queries, and it must be able to compactly store large collections of documents, in order to fit in the available memory.

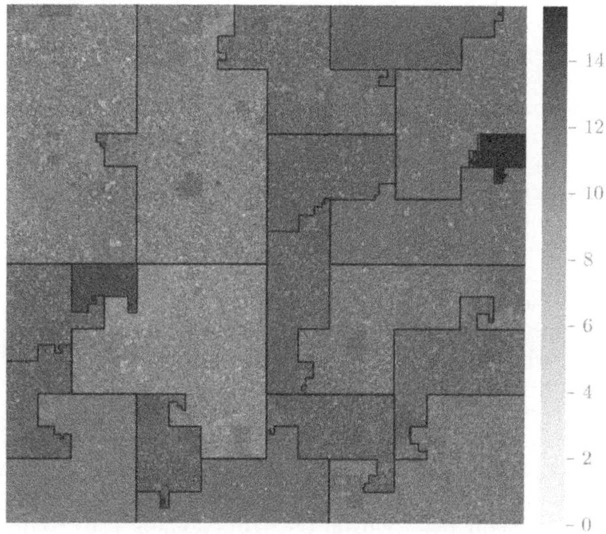

Figure 1: Access counts of 20 of the top 30 most accessed lists, plotted along a Hilbert curve (log scale).

The main ingredient to achieve the second goal is the compression of the sequences of integers that constitute the index. This is however at odds with the first goal, since more space-efficient sequence encoders have usually more complex, and hence slower, decoding. For this reason, a large amount of literature has focused on devising fast and space-efficient compression techniques, producing a multitude of encoders with different characteristics [15, 17, 19, 21, 25, 30].

While state-of-the-art encoders obtain very good space-time tradeoffs, we argue that using a single encoder for the entire index is wasteful: with typical query distributions some terms are more frequent than others, and even within the same posting list the skipping performed by most query processing algorithms produces regions of the list that are rarely accessed. We can visualize this effect in Figure 1, which shows the number of accesses for each posting in the 30 most accessed lists in an index, mapped to a square through a Hilbert curve so that list intervals are mapped to areas; the noisy appearance and the presence of darker spots indicate

WSDM'15, February 2–6, 2015, Shanghai, China.

ACM 978-1-4503-3317-7/15/02 ...$15.00.
http://dx.doi.org/10.1145/2684822.2685297.

a large variability in access frequencies (details on how this statistics were computed can be found in Section 6).

In this scenario, it is clear that we can improve the efficiency of an index by compressing frequently accessed regions with faster but less space-efficient encoders, and rarely accessed regions with a compact but slow encoder. This can be done without incurring any overhead with the popular representation of posting lists which divides each list into constant-sized blocks (e.g., 128 postings) and encodes them independently, since we can just choose a different encoder for each block.

However, it is not obvious how to perform this choice, as it depends on the space-time characteristics of the encoders and on the distribution of the values in the block. This issue is even more severe for encoders that offer a space-time tradeoff parameter, such as PForDelta, because choosing the parameter independently for each block could be suboptimal in global sense. For these reasons, we introduce the *Space-Constrained Expected Time Minimization* problem: given a query distribution and a set of encoders, our goal is to select an encoder for each block of the index to minimize the expected query processing time, subject to a given space constraint. To perform this choice optimally we describe a linear time greedy algorithm that is guaranteed to find a solution which is at least as fast as the optimal one but may exceed the space budget by no more than few bytes, which is a negligible overhead for a typical index of several gigabytes.

An early version of this problem has been proposed in [30], where the authors describe an hybrid index organization applying different encoders to different posting lists. Our result has three fundamental differences. First, we select the best encoders for each block inside posting lists while they work at a posting list granularity, thus failing to exploit the skew in access frequencies within the same posting list. Second, we use a radically different technique to assess the decoding time for each decoder, which reduces the measurement time while improving accuracy. Finally, they describe a heuristic algorithm with no approximation guarantees; the algorithm is only sketched and lacks many important details that would allow to analyze its complexity, which is at least quadratic in the number of encoders. On the other hand, our optimization algorithm is provably optimal modulo a negligible space overhead, and its complexity is linear in both the number of blocks and encoders.

Our Contributions. We list here our main contributions.

1. We define the Space-Constrained Expected Time Minimization problem, a refined and formalized version of a problem introduced in [30]. We then propose an algorithm which produces an exact solution for this problem in $\Theta(m^2 \log m)$ time, where m is the total number of postings, thus disproving the NP-Hardness claim stated in [30].

2. Since the quadratic nature of the above algorithm makes it unfeasible in any practical scenario, we design a linear time solution derived from a greedy algorithm presented in [24] with additive approximation guarantees: it finds a solution with expected query time at least as low as the optimal one which may exceed the space budget by no more than the size of a single block. Thus, the introduced additive approximation is completely negligible in practice: a typical budget of several billions of bytes is exceeded only by a few hundreds of bytes.

3. We introduce a technique to obtain fast and accurate estimates of the expected decoding time of a block for each decoder, based on their features, circumventing the limitations in resolution and noise of CPU timers. We obtain that the overall predicted query processing times are within 4% of the actual ones.

4. We test the effectiveness of our approach on realistic datasets and queries with an extensive experimental analysis. We obtain indexes that follow a smooth space-time curve, dominating state-of-the-art methods such as OptPFD and Partitioned Elias-Fano on almost all query processing strategies. For instance, we are able to obtain indexes that are up to 2.16 times smaller than those obtained with the fastest encoder, while being no more than 14% slower.

2. BACKGROUND AND RELATED WORK

Index Organization. Given a collection $\mathcal{D}$ of documents, the *inverted index* of $\mathcal{D}$ is a collection of *posting list*, one for each term t appearing at least once in any document of the collection. Each document in $\mathcal{D}$ is represented by a natural number called document identifier, or *docid*. A posting list is the list of all the docids of documents that contain the term t. The set of such terms is usually called the *dictionary* or the *lexicon*. Posting lists often includes additional information about each document, so each docid appearing in a posting list may include, for example, the number of occurrences of the term in the document (the *term frequency* in the document), and/or the set of positions where the term occurs in the document (the *term positions* in the document) [5, 16, 32].

In this work, we consider document-sorted inverted indices, as used by at least one major search engine [8]; this enables fast query processing and efficient compression. Other efficient retrieval techniques such as frequency-sorted [26] or impact-sorted indices [1] are possible. However, there is no evidence of such index layouts in common use within commercial search engines [18].

In our experiments we focus our attention on posting lists storing docids and frequencies; we do not store positions or other additional data, since they have different nature and often require specialized compression techniques [29], thus they are outside of the scope of this paper. We also ignore additional per-document or per-term information, such as the mappings between docids and URLs, or between term identifiers and actual terms, as their space is negligible compared to the index size.

Index Compression. Inverted indexes resort to compression to reduce their space occupancy. Index compression ultimately reduces to the problem of representing sequences of integers for both docids and frequencies, specifically strictly monotone sequences for docids, and positive sequences for the frequencies. The two are equivalent: a strictly monotone sequence can be turned into a positive sequence by subtracting from each element the one that precedes it (also known as *delta encoding*), the other direction can be achieved by computing prefix sums. For this reason most of the work assumes that the posting lists are delta-encoded and focuses on the representation of sequences of positive integers.

Representing such sequences of integers in compressed space is a crucial problem, studied since the 1950s with applications going beyond inverted indexes. A classical solution is to assign to each integer an uniquely-decodable variable length binary code code; examples are *unary codes*, *Elias Gamma/Delta codes*, and *Golomb/Rice codes* [21].

Bit-aligned codes can be inefficient to decode as they require several bitwise operations, so byte-aligned or word-aligned codes are usually preferred if speed is a main concern. *Variable byte* [21] or *VByte* is the most popular byte-aligned code. In VByte the binary representation of a non-negative integer x is split into groups of bytes, whose length depends on the value of the integer to be encoded. Stepanov *et al.* [25] present a variant of variable byte (called *Varint-G8IU*) which exploits SIMD operations of modern CPUs to further speed up decoding.

A different approach is to encode simultaneously *blocks* of integers in order to improve both compression ratio and decoding speed. The underlying idea is to partition the sequence of integers into blocks of fixed or variable length and to encode each block separately. The integers in each block are all encoded with the same number of bits h, which must be large enough to accommodate all the values in the block. This technique, also called binary packing or packed binary [3, 15], is usually applied with blocks of constant size (e.g., $b = 128$ integers). There are several variants of this approach which differentiate themselves for their encoding or partitioning strategies [9, 15, 23]. For example, *Simple-9* and *Simple-16* [2, 3, 30] are two popular variants of this approach.

A major space inefficiency of binary packing is the fact that the presence of few large values in the block forces the algorithm to encode all its integers with a large h, thus affecting the overall compression performance. To address this issue, *PForDelta* (PFD) [33] introduces the concept of *patching*. In PFD, h is an arbitrary parameter; all the values that fit in h bits are binary packed, while those that do not fit are called *exceptions*, and encoded separately with a different encoder; we refer to PFD as the family of encoders $\mathsf{PFD}(h)$ depending on the value width h. Variants of PFD use different strategies to encode the exceptions and their positions; we use the variant described in Yan *et al.* [30], using Simple-16 for both. They also describe two strategies, namely NewPFD and OptPFD, to select the value of h for a given block. In particular, OptPFD chooses the one that minimizes the space occupancy.

A completely different approach is taken by *Binary Interpolative Coding* [17], which skips the delta-encoding step and directly encodes monotone sequences. This method recursively splits the sequence of integers in two halves, encoding at each split the middle element and recursively the two halves. At each recursive step the range that encloses the middle element is reduced, and so is the number of bits needed to encode it. Experiments [19, 23, 28, 30] have shown that Binary Interpolative Coding is the best encoding method for highly clustered sequence of integers. However, this space efficiency is paid at the cost of a very slow decoding algorithm.

The *Elias-Fano* representation of monotone sequences [11, 12] has been recently applied to the compression of inverted indexes [27], showing excellent query performance thanks to its efficient random access and search operations. Its space occupancy is competitive with some state-of-the-art methods such as γ-δ-Golomb codes and PForDelta. However, it fails to exploit the local clustering that inverted lists usually exhibit, namely the presence of long subsequences of close identifiers. Recently, Ottaviano and Venturini [19] describe a new representation based on partitioning the list into chunks and encoding both the chunks and their endpoints with Elias-Fano, hence forming a two-level data structure. This partitioning enables the encoding to better adapt to the local statistics of the chunk, thus exploiting clustering and improving compression. They also show how to minimize the space occupancy of this representation by setting up the partitioning as an instance of an optimization problem, for which they present a linear time algorithm that is guaranteed to find a solution at most $(1+\epsilon)$ times larger than the optimal one, for any given $\epsilon \in (0, 1)$.

Query Processing. Given a term query as a (multi-)set of terms, the basic query operations are the boolean conjunctive (AND) and disjunctive (OR) queries, retrieving the documents that contain respectively all the terms or at least one of them. In many scenarios the query-document pairs can be associated with a *relevance score* which is usually a function of the term frequencies in the query and in the document, and other global statistics. Instead of the full set of matches, for scored queries it is often sufficient to retrieve the k highest scored documents for a given k. A widely used relevance score is BM25 [20], which we will use in our experiments.

The classical query processing strategies to match documents to a query fall in two categories: in a term-at-a-time (TAAT) strategy, the posting lists of query terms are processed and scored sequentially to build the result set, while, in a document-at-a-time (DAAT) strategy, the query term postings lists are processed in parallel, keeping them aligned them by docid. We will focus on the DAAT strategy as it is the most natural for docid-sorted indexes.

The alignment of the posting lists during DAAT processing can be achieved by means of the $\mathsf{NextGEQ}(d)$ operator, which returns the smallest docid in the posting list that is greater than or equal to d. A efficient implementation of the function $\mathsf{NextGEQ}(d)$ is crucial to obtain the typical subsecond response times of Web search engines. The trivial implementation that scans and checks sequentially the whole posting lists is usually too slow; typically, *skipping* strategies are employed. The basic idea is to divide the lists in small blocks that are compressed independently, and to store additional information about each block, in particular the maximum docid present in the block. This allows to find and decode only the block that may contain the sought docid by scanning the list of maximum docids, thus skipping a potentially large number of useless blocks. This basic approach can be improved also by exploiting query log information [7].

Solving scored disjunctive queries with DAAT can be very inefficient. Various techniques to enhance retrieval efficiency have been proposed, by dynamically pruning docids that are unlikely to be retrieved. Among them, the most popular are MaxScore [26] and WAND [4]. Both strategies augments the index by storing for each term its maximum score contribution, thus allowing to skip large segments of posting lists if they only contain terms whose sum of maximum impacts is smaller than the scores of the top-k documents found up to that point.

3. PROBLEM DEFINITION

In this section we introduce the Space-Constrained Expected Time Minimization problem as follows: given a query distribution $\mathcal{Q}$ and an arbitrary set $\mathcal{E}$ of k encoders, select an encoder for each index block to minimize the expected time to process queries drawn according to the distribution, subject to a given space constraint B. The problem is more formally defined in the following.

We assume that each posting list is split into blocks of size b, except the last block of each list which may contain fewer than b postings. We use n to denote the total number of blocks in the inverted index. Since each block can be encoded with any encoder in $\mathcal{E}$, an assignment of encoders to blocks can be modeled as a assignment φ from the n blocks to encoders in $\mathcal{E}$, hence $\varphi \in \mathcal{E}^n$. Given an assignment φ, φ_i is thus the encoder assigned to the ith block. We denote with $s_{i,j}$ the size of the encoding of the ith block with the jth encoder, and with $t_{i,j}$ its decoding time.

We aim at finding an assignment φ that minimizes the expected processing time of queries drawn from a probability distribution $\mathcal{Q}$, subject to a total space budget B, as follows:

$$\begin{aligned} \underset{\varphi \in \mathcal{E}^n}{\text{minimize}} \quad & \mathop{\mathbb{E}}_{q \sim \mathcal{Q}} [T(q, \varphi)] \\ \text{subject to} \quad & \sum_{i=1}^{n} s_{i,\varphi_i} \leq B, \end{aligned} \tag{1}$$

where we denote with $T(q, \varphi)$ the time to process the query q with a predetermined query processing strategy, such as Ranked AND or WAND. We assume that the processing time can be decomposed into a component T_p independent from the assignment φ, plus a component T_d which only accounts for the decoding time of the blocks, and thus depends only on the set of the blocks that the processing algorithm needs to decode, which we denote with $A(q)$. The processing time can thus be written as $T(q, \varphi) = T_p(q) + T_d(A(q), \varphi)$. Since $T_p(q)$ does not depend on the encoders choice, we can safely ignore it in the optimization.

We assume that we do not have access to the query distribution, but we can obtain a sample from it, namely a query log Q. The expected decompression time can thus be estimated with the empirical mean over Q; since $T_d(A(q), \varphi)$ is just the sum of the decoding times for all the blocks decoded during the query q, by linearity we can reformulate the problem as follows:

$$\begin{aligned} \underset{\varphi \in \mathcal{E}^n}{\text{minimize}} \quad & \sum_{i=1}^{n} f_i t_{i,\varphi_i} = \sum_{i=1}^{n} \hat{t}_{i,\varphi_i} \\ \text{subject to} \quad & \sum_{i=1}^{n} s_{i,\varphi_i} \leq B, \end{aligned} \tag{2}$$

where f_i is the number of times the block the ith block was decoded while processing the query log Q, and $\hat{t}_{i,j} = f_i t_{i,j}$ represents the overall decoding time of the ith block when encoded with the jth encoder. The counts f_i can be computed exactly just by processing all the queries in the query log and counting the number of decodings of each block. We defer to Section 5 the description of how to obtain the numbers $s_{i,j}$ and $t_{i,j}$.

4. LINEAR TIME ALGORITHM

In the following we describe a linear-time algorithm that finds an additive approximation to the solution of the Space-Constrained Expected Time Minimization problem defined in the previous section. The solution adopts a greedy strategy, which is guaranteed to find an assignment which is at least as good as the optimal one with respect to its expected processing time but exceeds the space budget constraint by no more than $S_{\max}$ bits, where $S_{\max}$ denotes the size in bits of the largest encoding of a block. Since a block can be always encoded plain within $b \log d$ bits, we have $S_{\max} \leq b \log d$ bits, where d denotes the number of documents in $\mathcal{D}$. In a typical instance, the block size b is 128 postings and $\log d \leq 32$ bits, so that $S_{\max}$ is at most 4,096 bits. Thus, the introduced additive approximation is completely negligible in practice: the budget B of several billions of bits is exceeded only by a few thousands of bits. This approximated solution is computed in linear time, namely, $\Theta(nk)$, which is linear in the number of blocks in the index.

We start by reducing our problem to the so-called *Multiple-Choice Knapsack Problem* (MCKP) [24]. In this problem, we are given a set of n classes of items. Each class contains at most k different items. Each item has its own weight and penalty. The goal is that of choosing *exactly* one item for each class so that the sum of the penalties is minimized, subject to a given knapsack capacity B.

In our setting, the classes correspond to the blocks to be encoded: each item in class i corresponds to a possible encoder j for the block i, so that the item's weight is the space occupancy $s_{i,j}$ and item's penalty is the expected decoding time $\hat{t}_{i,j}$. The goal is to minimize the expected query processing time subject to the space budget B. The integer linear programming formulation of the problem is as follows.

$$\begin{aligned} \text{minimize} \quad & \sum_{i=1}^{n} \sum_{j=1}^{k} x_{i,j} \hat{t}_{i,j} \\ \text{subject to} \quad & \sum_{i=1}^{n} \sum_{j=1}^{k} x_{i,j} s_{i,j} \leq B, \\ & \sum_{j=1}^{k} x_{i,j} = 1, \quad i \in \{1, \ldots, n\} \\ & x_{i,j} \in \{0, 1\}, \quad i \in \{1, \ldots, n\}, \; j \in \{1, \ldots, k\} \end{aligned} \tag{3}$$

The optimization variable $x_{i,j}$ represents the choice of the encoder for block i, and is 1 if the chosen encoder is j and 0 otherwise (in our notation, $x_{i,j} = 1$ if and only if $\varphi_i = j$).

In its general formulation the Multiple-Choice Knapsack Problem is NP-Hard [24]. There exists, however, a pseudo-polynomial time algorithm based on a standard Dynamic Programming approach, which requires $\Theta(nB)$ time and space. Thus, this immediately implies the existence of a polynomial time algorithm that finds an optimal assignment for any instance in our index compression scenario. Indeed, the complexity of this algorithm becomes $O(m^2 \log m)$ time and space, where m is the total number of postings, since $n \leq m$ and B is at most $m \log m + O(m)$ bits, since at worst each posting can be represented with $\log m + O(1)$ bits. Due to its quadratic nature, this solution is clearly unfeasible in any practical scenario, and only serves to disprove the NP-Hardness claim stated in Yan *et al.* [29].

Our linear-time approximated algorithm proceeds by finding the exact solution of the *Continuous Multiple-Choice Knapsack Problem* (CMCKP). This is the relaxation of the original problem in which any variable $x_{i,j}$ can take any real value in $[0, 1]$ instead of being forced to be either 0 or 1. Obviously, since CMCKP is less restrictive than MCKP, an optimal solution for the former is at least as good as an optimal solution for the latter, whenever both are subject to the same space budget. It is known that an optimal solution for CMCKP has the following important property [24]. There exists an optimal solution for CMCKP in which the assignment of the variables $x_{i,j}$ is such that there are either n or $n+1$ non-zero variables. If there are n non-zero variables, then there is a non-zero variable for each of the n possible classes and these are all set to 1. Thus, this is also a feasible and optimal solution for MCKP. If there are $n+1$ non-zero variables, then $n-1$ classes have their non-zero variables set to 1. The remaining class, say i, has exactly two fractional non-zero variables, say $x_{i,p}$ and $x_{i,q}$. Thus, this solution is *almost* a feasible solution for MCKP. This can be turned into an approximated solution for MCKP by setting one of these variables to 1 and the other to 0. If we set to 1 the variable of the item with the smallest decode time, say p, the obtained solution is such that (1) it is at least as good as the original one; (2) its space budget B may be exceeded, but, in any case, by no more than $s_{i,p} \leq S_{\max}$ bits.

Interestingly, an optimal solution for CMCKP can be found with a greedy strategy which works in two phases. In the first phase, the algorithm applies two fundamental *dominance criteria* in order to discard items that are not necessary to find an optimal solution. In the second phase, the algorithm starts choosing items according to a criterion that favors items introducing a larger marginal improvement of the penalty/weight tradeoff.

The first phase discards all the items dominated by other items according to the following two dominance criteria.

Dominance criterion 1 Let p and q be two items in same class i. Item q is dominated by item p if and only if $s_{i,p} \leq s_{i,q}$ and $\hat{t}_{i,p} < \hat{t}_{i,q}$.

Dominance criterion 2 Let p, q and r be three items in the same class i such that $s_{i,p} < s_{i,q} < s_{i,r}$ and $\hat{t}_{i,p} \geq \hat{t}_{i,q} \geq \hat{t}_{i,r}$. Item q is dominated by items p and q if and only if the following condition holds $\frac{\hat{t}_{i,p}-\hat{t}_{i,q}}{s_{i,p}-s_{i,q}} \geq \frac{\hat{t}_{i,q}-\hat{t}_{i,r}}{s_{i,q}-s_{i,r}}$.

If item q in class i is dominated according to at least one of the above criteria, then there exists an optimal solution for CMCKP which does not select item q (i.e., $x_{i,q} = 0$) [24]. This implies that the algorithm can safely discard all these dominated items without affecting the optimality result. This phase is essential for the correctness of the next phase.

Once the dominated items have been discarded, the algorithm sorts items within each class increasingly by their weights. With a little abuse of notation, from now on we refer to item j in class i as the jth smallest item within this ordered sequence. By the absence of dominated items, the penalties give a non increasing sequence. Thus, if there are $\ell \leq k$ items in class i, we have $s_{i,1} < s_{i,2} < \ldots < s_{i,\ell}$ and $\hat{t}_{i,1} \geq \hat{t}_{i,2} \geq \ldots \geq \hat{t}_{i,\ell}$.

The algorithm starts the next phase by constructing a base solution which contains the first item of each class. Observe that this solution is the one with the smallest possible space occupancy. This base solution is subsequently refined in order to improve the processing time by exploiting the available space budget. This is done by employing a greedy strategy that selects items in non increasing order of the ratio $\lambda_{i,j} = \frac{\hat{t}_{i,j}-\hat{t}_{i,j-1}}{s_{i,j-1}-s_{i,j}}$. This ratio measures the marginal penalty decrease per unit weight that we can obtain by replacing item $j-1$ with item j in class i. This is done by sorting all the items according to their ratio and by scanning this sorted sequence of items. When the algorithm processes the item j in class i, it replaces item $j-1$ with j in class i within the current solution (i.e., it sets $x_{i,j-1}$ to 0 and $x_{i,j}$ to 1). The algorithm stops as soon as the space budget is exceeded. The last two modified variables $x_{i,j-1}$ and $x_{i,j}$ can be adjusted and made fractional to match the budget. This is guaranteed to be an optimal solution for CMCKP [24].

Note that a single run of this algorithm is able to find all the optimal solutions for any possible budget constraint. Indeed, any step of the algorithm finds a solution which is optimal for its space occupancy. Moreover, all the possible space budgets are found in this way.

The time complexity of the algorithm is dominated by the time required to sort the items (i.e., $\Theta(nk \log(nk))$ time). This time complexity can be improved to $\Theta(nk)$ by replacing the sorting step with a (modified) linear time median selection algorithm [31]. Due to space limitations, we omit the details of this faster solution; furthermore, in practice we can use off-the-shelf optimized sorting implementations, so the sorting step does not dominate the running time. Hence, the last improvement is only of theoretical interest.

5. DECODING TIME PREDICTION

The optimization algorithm requires the knowledge of the space occupancy $s_{i,j}$ and of the decoding time $t_{i,j}$, for each block i and each encoder j. While the space occupancy can be computed deterministically and exactly just by encoding the block, the decoding times span from tens to hundreds of nanoseconds, hence it is hard to assess them reliably, due to the low resolution and high noise of CPU timers. In order to quantify these times with sufficient accuracy, a direct solution could be to measure the time to decode the block several times and divide by the number of runs; however this would make the measuring algorithm prohibitively slow. Moreover, any attempt to make the measurements faster by running several threads in parallel would further increase the noise.

We propose to quantify the decoding times by splitting the measurement in two steps. First, a *profiling step* running in a controlled single-threaded environment is carried out, by averaging several runs of decoding on a large random sample of the index blocks, in order to cover accurately the distribution of different blocks. Second, from these measurements we learn predictors that use features extracted from the block values to predict the decoding time for each decoder. Then, the each predictor is used in the optimization algorithm to estimate $t_{i,j}$ for each block and decoder.

We model the predictor as a linear combination of features of the values in the block with non-negative weights. Being non-negative, the weight of a feature can be interpreted as the contribution of that feature to the decoding time. Given a block i we call $\mathbf{x_i}$ its feature vector; the predictor is thus $t_{i,j} = \mathbf{x_i}^T \mathbf{w_j} + b_j$ where $\mathbf{w_j}$ is the weights vector and b_j the bias learned for the decoder j.

To obtain a robust learned model we use an L_1 loss function rather than the more popular L_2 loss, and we add an L_1 regularization component which is known to make the solutions sparse [13]. Given a multiset set $\mathcal{T}_j = \{(\mathbf{x}, t)\}$ of block features and their respective measured decoding times with decoder j we thus compute $\mathbf{w_j}, b_j$ as the solution of the minimization problem:

$$\min_{\mathbf{w_j}, b_j \geq 0} \sum_{(\mathbf{x},t)\in\mathcal{T}_j} |\mathbf{x}^T\mathbf{w_j} + b_j - t| + \mu|\mathcal{T}_j|\|\mathbf{w}\|_1$$

where μ is the regularization parameter. The problem can be written as a linear program and solved with standard convex optimization algorithms; however, we found that it is faster to use a smooth approximation of the absolute value, namely the Huber loss function [14], and use a quasi-Newton solver, specifically L-BFGS [6], without compromising the accuracy of the solution.

6. EXPERIMENTAL ANALYSIS

The effectiveness of our approach in a practical setting relies on several hypotheses. First, that the different space-time characteristics of different encoders can be exploited successfully, and that their decoding times can be accurately estimated. Second, that our query processing time model fits the measured data. Finally, that block access statistics induced by a typical query log exhibit a skew that makes it convenient to use different encoders for different blocks.

In this section we validate our hypotheses with an extensive experimental evaluation in a realistic and reproducible setting, using state-of-the-art encoders, standard benchmark text collections and a large query log.

6.1 Experimental setup

Encoders. In our experiments the set $\mathcal{E}$ of encoders is composed as follows. First, we use PFD(h) for all the values of h as different encoders; this way the assignment of h to each block is optimized globally rather than on a per-block basis as in strategies like OptPFD. We then add two encoders which represent the best space occupancy and the best decoding time. For the former we choose Binary Interpolative Coding, which consistently outperforms every other encoder both in the literature and in our own experiments. For the latter we adopt Varint-G8IU, which according to the experiments in [15] is the fastest among those that support small block sizes and unaligned reads, which are needed because blocks with different alignments are concatenated together.

The encoder type chosen for each block is written by prepending one byte to the encoding of the block, which adds a negligible overhead to the overall space. The last block of each list may have fewer than b postings, in which case we call it a *partial* block and always compress it with Interpolative. Since it is accessed at most once per query, its decoding time is negligible, and the vast majority of partial blocks belongs to the single-block lists of rare terms. For these reasons we also focus our analysis only on blocks with exactly b postings, which we call *full*.

We compare the indexes obtained with our algorithm, which we call *hybrid*, against single-encoder indexes using Interpolative, OptPFD, and Varint-G8IU; again, we always compress partial blocks with Interpolative. We also compare against the recently introduced Partitioned Elias-Fano indexes [19]. We remark that Elias-Fano is not included in the set of encoders $\mathcal{E}$ because its characteristics are not suitable for our model. Indeed, Elias-Fano is faster than other encoders to decode single postings but slower to decode an entire block. However, the latter is the key operation at the basis of our model.

Datasets. We performed our experiments on the following datasets.

- ClueWeb09 is the ClueWeb 2009 TREC Category B collection, consisting of 50 million English web pages crawled between January and February 2009.
- Gov2 is the TREC 2004 Terabyte Track test collection, consisting of 25 million `.gov` sites crawled in early 2004; the documents are truncated to 256 kB.

	ClueWeb09	Gov2
Documents	50,131,015	24,622,347
Terms	92,094,694	35,636,425
Postings	15,857,983,641	5,742,630,292

Table 1: Basic statistics for the test collections

For each document in the collection the body text was extracted using Apache Tika.[1], and the words lowercased and stemmed using the Porter2 stemmer; no stopwords were removed. The docids were assigned according to the lexicographic order of their URLs [22] Table 1 reports the basic statistics for the two collections.

The results on Gov2 and ClueWeb09 are very similar, hence in the following we focus most of our analysis on the larger dataset ClueWeb09.

Queries. The queries used in our experiments are taken from the MSN Search query log from 2006,[2] comprising 15 million queries sampled over the month of May and submitted from the US. We filter out all the queries which contain terms not present in the index, and all single-term queries, as their results can be precomputed separately.

We select the first million queries in chronological order as a training set to compute the counts f_i, and measure the query times on a sample of 5000 queries taken from the remaining queries, to simulate a realistic scenario where the index is optimized based on past queries.

Processing strategies. To test the performance on query strategies that make use of both the docids and the occurrence frequencies we perform BM25 top-10 queries using 3 different algorithms: Ranked AND, which scores the results of a conjunctive query, WAND [4], and MaxScore [26].

Estimation of the access counts. The block access counts f_i must be computed using the query processing strategies that will be used at query time; rather than building different index optimized for each query processing strategy we test, we assume a realistic scenario in which the index is optimized once and queried with different query strategies. For this reason we process each query in the training set with all the three processing strategies, and add up the counts. Figure 1 in the introduction shows the result of this counting on the

[1] `http://tika.apache.org/`

[2] `http://research.microsoft.com/en-us/um/people/nickcr/wscd09/`

ClueWeb09 dataset using the query training set for 20 of the top 30 most accessed posting lists.

Blocks never accessed with the training set would have zero overall time $\hat{t}_{i,j} = f_i t_{i,j}$, thus the algorithm would force them to be compressed with Interpolative regardless of the budget; to avoid this we use Laplace smoothing when estimating the counts f_i, i.e., we add 1 to each access count. In our model this is equivalent to estimating the block access probability with maximum a posteriori with a Dirichlet prior, rather than with maximum likelihood. This does not make a measurable difference in practice, since our training set is large enough to access the vast majority of the index: the fraction of unseen full blocks is less than 9%.

Testing details. All the algorithms are implemented in C++11 and compiled with GCC 4.9 with the highest optimization settings. The tests are performed on a machine with 8 Intel Core i7-4770K Haswell cores clocked at 3.50GHz, with 32GiB RAM, running Linux 3.13.0. The indexes are saved to disk after construction, and memory-mapped to be queried, so that there are no hidden space costs due to loading of additional data structures in memory. Before timing the queries we ensure that the required posting lists are fully loaded in memory.

The source code is available at `https://github.com/ot/ds2i/tree/WSDM15` for the reader interested in further implementation details or in replicating the experiments.

6.2 Results

Decoding time prediction. To predict the decoding time we use the following features: size of the compressed block (`size`), bit length of the largest integer (`max_h`), number of non-zero values (`nonzeros`), and sum of the logarithms of the values (`sum_of_logs`). For PFD(h) we also add the number of exceptions (`pfor_exceptions`). We found that the decoding time of PFD is fairly insensitive on the value width h, so we use the same predictor for all the PFD decoders.

To evaluate the performance of the predictors we perform an usual 80-20 split of the data into a training set and a test set, and measure the average absolute error. As a baseline, we compare against a constant predictor which returns the median of the decoding times regardless of the features.

Decoder	Time	C. Err	L. Err	HWF
Interpolative	640.8	73.3	20.0	`nonzeros`
PFD	97.8	66.6	7.7	`pfor_exceptions`
Varint-G8IU	42.4	3.5	1.8	`size`

Table 2: Median time (Time), average absolute error for the constant (C. Err) and linear (L. Err) predictors, and highest weighted feature in the linear model (HWF). All the numbers are in nanoseconds.

As shown in Table 2, we find that the linear predictor significantly reduces the error with respect to the median predictor, bringing it down to less than 8% of the median time in all cases. The highest improvement occurs with PFD, which exhibits a large variability in decoding time, as it is highly affected by the number of exceptions.

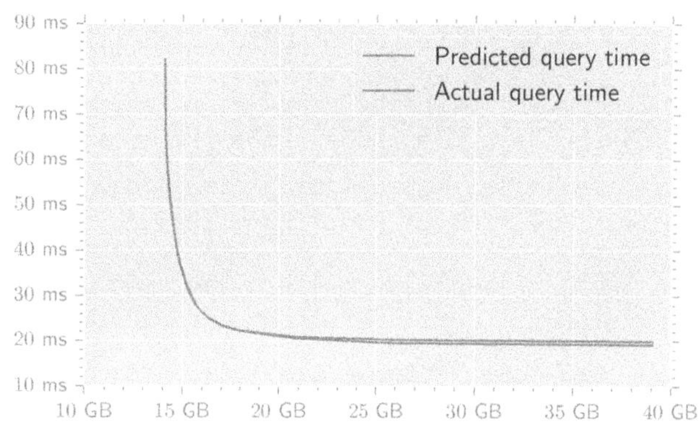

Figure 2: Predicted and actual average query times for different index spaces on the ClueWeb09 dataset.

Model validation. To test the validity of our query processing time model we compare the predicted average query time, that is $\tilde{T} = \sum_{i=1}^{n} f_i t_{i,\varphi_i}$, where the f_is are computed on the test set, with the actual average query time T using all the query processing strategies. Recall that $T = \tilde{T} + T_p(q)$, where $T_p(q)$ is assumed independent from the choice of the encoders and thus constant along the space-time curve.

We estimate $T_p(q)$ by taking the average of the differences between T and $\tilde{T}$ with different index spaces, and plot the predicted and actual query times in Figure 2. Note that the two curves are very close; in fact, the predicted times are within 4% of the actual times. Taken into account the additive factor $T_p(q)$, this error is very close to the prediction error on the single blocks, thus suggesting that an improvement on the decoding time prediction would further reduce this already small gap.

Construction time. Almost all the phases of hybrid index construction can be trivially parallelized, since each list can be handled independently. The only phase that is inherently sequential is the greedy one, which is just a scan of the sorted $\lambda_{i,j}$s and it is extremely fast. We report here the times for the ClueWeb09 dataset, using 8 threads.

The most time-consuming task is the computation of the ratios $\lambda_{i,j}$, since it involves compressing each block with each encoder to measure the space and estimate the decoding time, taking about 14 minutes. We then store the $(i, j, \lambda_{i,j}, s_{i,j}, t_{i,j})$ tuples in a file and use an external algorithm to sort them by $\lambda_{i,j}$, specifically the implementation in STXXL [10]. The reason is twofold: first, the tuples may be so many that they do not fit in memory; second, this way we can reuse the vector of sorted tuples to build indexes on several points of the space-time curve. Besides, going through disk does not affect seriously this step, taking about 6 minutes.

The next phase is the greedy algorithm that finds the space-time tradeoff by scanning the sorted vector of tuples. While this phase must be run on a single thread, it takes just a little more than a minute. The last step is using the assignments found by the greedy algorithm to construct the actual index, which takes from 5 to 8 minutes, depending on the percentages of the various chosen encoders. Note that this is roughly the same time needed to construct a single-encoder index; the overall algorithm is thus about 4 times slower than the construction of a single-encoder index. However, it can be

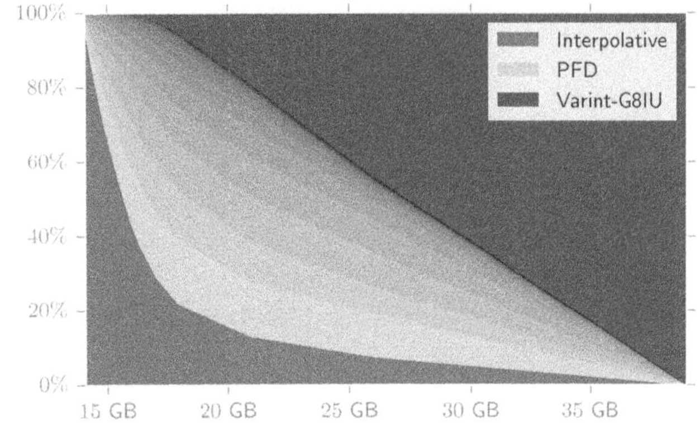

Figure 3: Percentage of full blocks compressed with each encoder for different index spaces. For PFD different shades denote different values of h.

made faster by increasing the parallelism in the first phases, while the final index construction is dominated by I/O in all cases.

Index spaces and query times. We report in Figure 4 the space-time tradeoff curves of our Hybrid and the single-encoder indexes on ClueWeb09. The different plots show the overall index size in gigabytes and the average query time, in milliseconds per query, for the three different processing strategies, namely Ranked AND, WAND and MaxScore. Interpolative and Varint-G8IU are on the extremes of the curve, being respectively the smallest and the fastest. Note that all Hybrid tradeoff curves are smooth, as they can achieve any point within their space-time tradeoff curve; any of these points is an optimal solution within a space margin of at most 512 bytes. The convexity of the curves shows no dominated points, according to both dominance criteria 1 and 2.

Partitioned EF index confirms its excellent performance with strategies that perform a large number of skips, namely Ranked AND and WAND. Conversely, its performance worsens on MaxScore, which depends on enumerating the *union* of the so-called *essential* lists, thus the decoding speed for such lists plays an important role in the overall processing time.

To get some insight on the choices made by the optimization algorithm, we show in Figure 3 the percentages of blocks that are compressed with each encoder by varying the available space budget. Not surprisingly, Hybrid chooses Interpolative for a vast majority of the blocks with a very small budget, and Varint-G8IU with a very large budget. Perhaps surprisingly, instead, the algorithm assigns PFD to about 10% of the blocks even at the smallest space budget, showing that Interpolative is dominated by PFD on those blocks. However, it is interesting to observe how the choices change in the regime where PFD becomes more prevalent. As we mention above, the value of h in PFD(h) influences both the encoding size and the decoding time. In general, a small value of h implies a small encoding size but the presence of several exceptions slows down the decoding speed. This is apparent in Figure 3: initially Hybrid prefers small values of h to favor space efficiency, and then it starts to increase h as the available budget increases to favor time efficiency.

Table 3 reports the index space, both as overall size in gigabytes, and broken down in bits per integers for docids

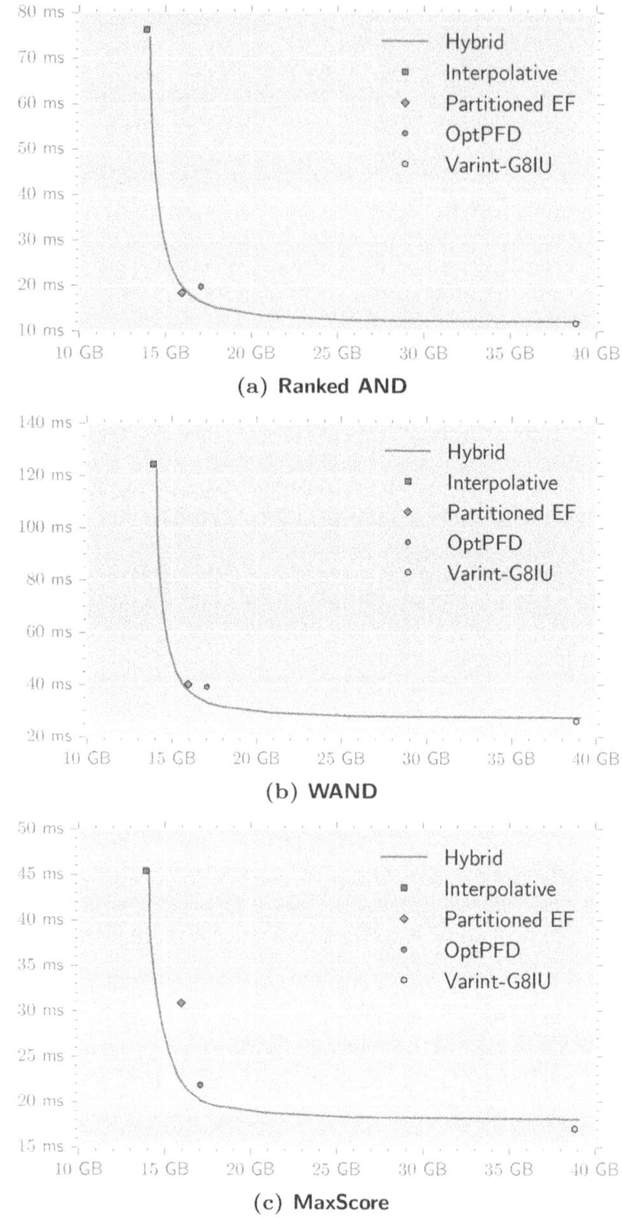

Figure 4: Average query times for different index spaces and strategies on the ClueWeb09 dataset.

and frequencies, as well as the average query time, in milliseconds per query, for the three processing strategies, for both datasets. For our Hybrid index, we select a few points from its space-time tradeoff curve, which help to more accurately compare its results to the closer single-encoder index.

On the extreme of the space-time tradeoff curve, which favors space occupancy disregarding query processing time, Hybrid@1 achieves almost the same space of Interpolative. On ClueWeb09, Hybrid@1 produces a slightly larger index (about 1%) than Interpolative. Even if in this case Hybrid@1 minimizes its space occupancy by compressing almost all the blocks with Interpolative code, it has a space overhead of 0.0625 bits per posting due to extra byte per block to write the encoder type. Interestingly, on Gov2 a large number of

	Space GB	Docids bpi	Freqs bpi	Ranked AND ms	WAND ms	MaxScore ms
			ClueWeb09			
Hybrid@1	14.08	5.21	1.90	74.7	122.4	45.5
Hybrid@2	14.58	5.35	2.01	38.4	62.9	31.4
Hybrid@Partitioned EF	15.94	5.77	2.27	19.8	37.7	22.3
Hybrid@OptPFD	17.04	6.13	2.47	16.4	33.1	20.1
Hybrid@3	20.92	7.33	3.22	13.3	29.2	18.8
Hybrid@4	26.00	8.56	4.55	12.3	27.9	18.3
Hybrid@5	39.05	10.81	8.89	12.1	27.5	18.1
Interpolative	13.90	5.15	1.87	76.3	124.4	45.4
Partitioned EF	15.94	5.85	2.20	18.4	40.2	30.9
OptPFD	17.04	6.18	2.41	19.7	39.2	21.9
Varint-G8IU	38.82	10.75	8.83	11.8	26.1	17.0
			Gov2			
Hybrid@1	4.21	3.85	2.01	14.1	26.2	11.4
Hybrid@2	4.54	4.12	2.21	4.2	8.7	5.9
Hybrid@Partitioned EF	4.65	4.21	2.27	3.7	7.8	5.5
Hybrid@OptPFD	4.92	4.44	2.42	3.1	6.9	5.1
Hybrid@3	6.36	5.52	3.34	2.5	5.9	4.8
Hybrid@4	8.07	6.62	4.63	2.5	5.8	4.7
Hybrid@5	13.83	10.40	8.87	2.4	5.8	4.7
Interpolative	4.26	3.80	2.14	14.5	27.0	11.5
Partitioned EF	4.65	4.10	2.38	4.0	8.6	8.0
OptPFD	4.92	4.48	2.38	3.8	8.2	5.5
Varint-G8IU	13.75	10.35	8.81	2.3	5.5	4.4

Table 3: Index spaces, both overall space in gigabytes and broken down into docids and frequencies in bits per integer, along with average query times in milliseconds for the query strategies considered.

blocks is better compressed with PFD than with Interpolative; this is exploited by Hybrid@1 which is able to improve the space of Interpolative by roughly 1%.

The ability of Hybrid to achieve any point in the tradeoff curve can be exploited to remain close to the best possible space occupancy but significantly improve the query time. For example, Hybrid@2 is obtained by imposing a space budget which is within $5-7\%$ the space occupancy of Interpolative. This gives an index faster than Interpolative by factors that range, depending on the query processing strategy, between 1.45 and 1.99 on ClueWeb09, and 1.95 and 3.45 on Gov2.

With Hybrid@Partitioned EF we set the budget to the space occupancy of Partitioned EF. Hybrid@Partitioned EF is faster than Partitioned EF on all the strategies but Ranked AND on ClueWeb09, where Partitioned EF is 7% faster. With WAND, Hybrid@Partitioned EFis faster by 6% on ClueWeb09 and 9% on Gov2. As expected, these percentages increase with MaxScore where they become 28% on ClueWeb09 and 31% on Gov2.

Similarly, Hybrid@OptPFD is obtained by setting the budget to the space of OptPFD. On the same conditions, Hybrid@OptPFD is always faster than OptPFD. The largest improvement is 18% on Gov2 and 17% on ClueWeb09, both with the Ranked AND strategy.

On the other extreme of the space-time tradeoff curve, which favors query processing time, Varint-G8IU index is slightly faster than Hybrid@5. Even if Hybrid@5 encodes all the blocks with the Varint-G8IU encoder, there is a small time overhead due to the dispatching of the block decoding code, which is most noticeable on MaxScore. However, if we renounce to at most 8% of Varint-G8IU overall time efficiency, we obtain an index, see Hybrid@4, which significantly reduces the space occupancy by a factor 1.49 on ClueWeb09 and 1.7 on Gov2. Finally, Hybrid@3 is slower than Varint-G8IU by no more than 14% and reduces the space occupancy by a factor 1.86 on ClueWeb09 and 2.16 on Gov2.

7. CONCLUSIONS & FUTURE WORK

In this paper we introduced and motivated the study of the Space-Constrained Expected Time Minimization problem. We presented a linear-time algorithm that computes optimal solutions with a negligible additive approximation. An extensive experimental analysis in a realistic and reproducible setting validates all the hypotheses at the basis of our model and shows that the obtained indexes dominate state-of-the-art single-encoder methods such as OptPFD and Partitioned Elias-Fano with most query processing strategies.

Since our solution takes the set of encoders to be optimized as a parameter, future experiments will investigate the consequences of optimizing with other encoders. Elias-Fano representation is one of the few encoders which cannot benefit from this approach. Indeed, compared to the other encoders, Elias-Fano is faster in providing random access to single postings but it is slower in decoding large chunks of consecutive postings (see e.g., [19] and references therein). An interesting open problem would be thus to design a solution which is able to model and to optimize the index using encoders that have these characteristics.

Finally, our solution optimizes by assuming that the posting lists are split into constant-size blocks. Allowing blocks of variable sizes relaxes the range of the achievable space-time tradeoffs, and, thus, may further improve the overall results. However, this increases the difficulty of the optimization problem, since the access statistics must be taken at the posting level. The design of an efficient algorithm in this setting is left as an interesting open problem.

Acknowledgements

This work was supported by EC-funded projects InGeoClouds (FP7-297300), MIDAS (FP7-318786) and eCloud EU Project (CIP-325091), by Italy's MIUR-funded project PRIN ARS Technomedia 2012.

8. REFERENCES

[1] V. N. Anh, O. de Kretser, and A. Moffat. Vector-space ranking with effective early termination. In *SIGIR*, pages 35–42, 2001.

[2] V. N. Anh and A. Moffat. Inverted index compression using word-aligned binary codes. *Inf. Retr.*, 8(1), 2005.

[3] V. N. Anh and A. Moffat. Index compression using 64-bit words. *Softw., Pract. Exper.*, 40(2):131–147, 2010.

[4] A. Z. Broder, D. Carmel, M. Herscovici, A. Soffer, and J. Y. Zien. Efficient query evaluation using a two-level retrieval process. In *CIKM*, pages 426–434, 2003.

[5] S. Büttcher, C. L. A. Clarke, and G. V. Cormack. *Information retrieval: implementing and evaluating search engines.* MIT Press, Cambridge, Mass., 2010.

[6] R. H. Byrd, J. Nocedal, and R. B. Schnabel. Representations of quasi-newton matrices and their use in limited memory methods. *Mathematical Programming*, 63(1-3):129–156, 1994.

[7] F. Chierichetti, S. Lattanzi, F. Mari, and A. Panconesi. On placing skips optimally in expectation. In *WSDM*, pages 15–24, 2008.

[8] J. Dean. Challenges in building large-scale information retrieval systems: invited talk. In *WSDM*, 2009.

[9] R. Delbru, S. Campinas, and G. Tummarello. Searching web data: An entity retrieval and high-performance indexing model. *J. Web Sem.*, 10:33–58, 2012.

[10] R. Dementiev, L. Kettner, and P. Sanders. Stxxl: standard template library for xxl data sets. *Software: Practice and Experience*, 38(6):589–637, 2008.

[11] P. Elias. Efficient storage and retrieval by content and address of static files. *J. ACM*, 21(2):246–260, 1974.

[12] R. M. Fano. On the number of bits required to implement an associative memory. *Memorandum 61, Computer Structures Group, MIT, Cambridge, MA*, 1971.

[13] T. Hastie, R. Tibshirani, and J. H. Friedman. *The Elements of Statistical Learning.* Springer, 2001.

[14] P. J. Huber et al. Robust estimation of a location parameter. *The Annals of Mathematical Statistics*, 35(1):73–101, 1964.

[15] D. Lemire and L. Boytsov. Decoding billions of integers per second through vectorization. *Software: Practice & Experience*, 2013.

[16] C. D. Manning, P. Raghavan, and H. Schülze. *Introduction to Information Retrieval.* Cambridge University Press, 2008.

[17] A. Moffat and L. Stuiver. Binary interpolative coding for effective index compression. *Inf. Retr.*, 3(1), 2000.

[18] A. Moffat, W. Webber, J. Zobel, and R. Baeza-Yates. A pipelined architecture for distributed text query evaluation. *Inf. Retr.*, 10:205–231, June 2007.

[19] G. Ottaviano and R. Venturini. Partitioned Elias-Fano indexes. In *SIGIR*, pages 273–282, 2014.

[20] S. E. Robertson and K. S. Jones. Relevance weighting of search terms. *Journal of the American Society for Information science*, 27(3):129–146, 1976.

[21] D. Salomon. *Variable-length Codes for Data Compression.* Springer, 2007.

[22] F. Silvestri. Sorting out the document identifier assignment problem. In *ECIR*, pages 101–112, 2007.

[23] F. Silvestri and R. Venturini. VSEncoding: Efficient coding and fast decoding of integer lists via dynamic programming. In *CIKM*, pages 1219–1228, 2010.

[24] P. Sinha and A. A. Zoltners. The multiple-choice knapsack problem. *Operations Research*, 27(3):503–515, 1979.

[25] A. A. Stepanov, A. R. Gangolli, D. E. Rose, R. J. Ernst, and P. S. Oberoi. Simd-based decoding of posting lists. In *CIKM*, pages 317–326, 2011.

[26] H. Turtle and J. Flood. Query evaluation: Strategies and optimizations. *Information Processing & Management*, 31(6):831 – 850, 1995.

[27] S. Vigna. Quasi-succinct indices. In *WSDM*, 2013.

[28] I. H. Witten, A. Moffat, and T. C. Bell. *Managing gigabytes (2nd ed.): compressing and indexing documents and images.* Morgan Kaufmann Publishers Inc., 1999.

[29] H. Yan, S. Ding, and T. Suel. Compressing term positions in web indexes. In *SIGIR*, pages 147–154, 2009.

[30] H. Yan, S. Ding, and T. Suel. Inverted index compression and query processing with optimized document ordering. In *WWW*, pages 401–410, 2009.

[31] E. Zemel. An O(n) algorithm for the linear multiple choice knapsack problem and related problems. *Inf. Process. Lett.*, 18(3):123–128, 1984.

[32] J. Zobel and A. Moffat. Inverted files for text search engines. *ACM Comput. Surv.*, 38(2), 2006.

[33] M. Zukowski, S. Heman, N. Nes, and P. Boncz. Super-scalar RAM-CPU cache compression. In *ICDE*, 2006.

Understanding and Predicting Graded Search Satisfaction

Jiepu Jiang[1], Ahmed Hassan Awadallah[2], Xiaolin Shi[2], and Ryen W. White[2]

[1] School of Computer Science, University of Massachusetts Amherst

[2] Microsoft Research Redmond

jpjiang@cs.umass.edu, {hassanam, xishi, ryenw}@microsoft.com

ABSTRACT

Understanding and estimating satisfaction with search engines is an important aspect of evaluating retrieval performance. Research to date has modeled and predicted search satisfaction on a binary scale, i.e., the searchers are either satisfied or dissatisfied with their search outcome. However, users' search experience is a complex construct and there are different degrees of satisfaction. As such, binary classification of satisfaction may be limiting. To the best of our knowledge, we are the first to study the problem of understanding and predicting graded (multi-level) search satisfaction. We examine sessions mined from search engine logs, where searcher satisfaction was also assessed on multi-point scale by human annotators. Leveraging these search log data, we observe rich and non-monotonous changes in search behavior in sessions with different degrees of satisfaction. The findings suggest that we should predict finer-grained satisfaction levels. To address this issue, we model search satisfaction using features indicating search outcome, search effort, and changes in both outcome and effort during a session. We show that our approach can predict subtle changes in search satisfaction more accurately than state-of-the-art methods, affording greater insight into search satisfaction. The strong performance of our models has implications for search providers seeking to accurately measure satisfaction with their services.

Categories and Subject Descriptors

H.3.4 [**Information Storage and Retrieval**]: Systems and Software – *performance evaluation (efficiency and effectiveness)*. H.1.2 [**Models and Principles**]: User/Machine Systems – *human factors*.

Keywords

Search satisfaction; evaluation; utility; effort; session.

1. INTRODUCTION

The evaluation of search systems can be performed on the basis of result relevance, or alternative measures of the search experience (e.g., satisfaction, usability). When the focus is on relevance, *metrics* such as average precision or nDCG [17] are often computed using human relevance judgments from third-party assessors. Once relevance judgments are gathered, they are reusable and metrics can be computed across systems, allowing direct comparisons of system performance. However, studies indicate there are imperfect correlations between these evaluation metrics and searchers' actual ratings of their search experience (usually considered as the gold standard) [2, 15]. Methods to elicit searcher feedback on the search experience have been proposed in [9, 10]. However, this feedback is difficult to collect (e.g., it can require costly laboratory studies).

An emerging approach for evaluating Web search engines is to predict the quality of the search experience from search interaction data [1, 8, 10, 11, 14]. Search interactions can be studied at scale using retrospective analysis of existing search engine log data or intentional manipulations of the search experience (e.g., in controlled experiments [25]). For example, Hassan et al. used search logs to predict search success [13], searcher satisfaction [11], and whether searchers are struggling or exploring during search episodes [14]. Feild et al. [8] focused on searcher frustration, Ageev et al. [1] on search success, Guo et al. [10] on search engine switching, and Liu et al. [26, 27] and Arguello et al. [3] on search task difficulty. The evaluation approach epitomized by these studies combines aspects of evaluation metrics and asking searchers directly for feedback. It relies on signals from searchers' behavior in natural settings, but requires neither relevance judgments nor explicit feedback. These advantages make it a useful evaluation technique for search providers, who have abundant search logs comprising query and click behavior on which to perform such analysis.

Despite the strong progress, we believe current methods and accompanying studies have the following two important limitations:

First, existing research did not advance our understanding of the searchers' experience during searching. They are mostly black box techniques that receive search interaction data as input and return predictions of outcomes such as satisfaction, frustration, and success. Despite the availability of these predictions, we still do not understand why searchers are satisfied, frustrated, or successful.

Second, in existing studies, the quality of searchers' experience in using the system is estimated on a binary scale. For example, searcher satisfaction is predicted as either satisfied (SAT) or dissatisfied (DSAT) in previous studies [11, 13, 35]. In these studies, datasets of randomly sampled search sessions extracted from search engine query logs had only about 20% of the sessions as DSAT. Important unanswered questions include: Are the 80% SAT search sessions equivalent? What are the differences among SAT sessions? Can we predict subtle differences in satisfaction from features such as observable behavior?

To the best of our knowledge, this paper makes the first attempt to address these two shortcomings in the specific case of satisfaction prediction. In doing so, we make the following contributions:

First, we perform an in-depth analysis characterizing differences in searcher interaction per graded levels of search satisfaction. We show the value of search outcome compared with search effort best explains and most strongly correlates with search satisfaction. In addition, there are rich and non-monotonous differences in search behavior in sessions with different satisfaction levels. Our study extends the current understanding by disclosing the effects of search outcome, effort, and their dynamics over the course of a session on levels of search satisfaction.

Second, we identify effective sets of features related to search outcome, effort, and their changes. Each group of features makes a unique contribution in satisfaction prediction. We divide the sessions into four satisfaction levels. For example, effort features are

WSDM'15, February 2–6, 2015, Shanghai, China.

http://dx.doi.org/10.1145/2684822.2685319

critical in distinguishing between sessions with very high and high satisfaction levels, while features associated with changes in effort and outcomes are most effective in discriminating dissatisfied and moderately satisfied sessions.

Third, our prediction methods are effective and significantly outperform prior methods. Our regression model predicts continuous satisfaction values with moderate correlation to annotators' satisfaction ratings. Additionally, our approach outperforms prior methods in classifying sessions between adjacent satisfaction levels.

The remainder of the article describes our methods and findings.

2. RELATED WORK

In this section, we review related work in the following two areas. First, we summarize previous work on the measurement of satisfaction, both within search settings and beyond. Second, we review approaches to predicting the quality of the search experience and the relevance of search results based on search interaction data.

2.1 Satisfaction

Satisfaction is widely adopted as a subjective measure of search experience. Kelly ([23], p. 117) reviewed a definition: "satisfaction can be understood as the fulfillment of a specified desire or goal." When evaluating search systems, satisfaction can be determined regarding not only the holistic search experience but also some specific aspects [34], e.g., result completeness, result relevance, system response time, caption formatting, and general appearance of the user interface. Although the concept is widely used in retrieval settings, we did not find any literature in information retrieval defining and explaining searcher satisfaction in a principled way.

In contrast, user satisfaction with generic information systems has been studied extensively in the context of management information systems. These studies focused on developing valid instruments (schemes of designing questionnaires) for measuring satisfaction. They usually adopted a factorized approach. For example, Bailey et al. [6] and Ives et al. [16] developed and validated an instrument involving 39 factors. McKinney et al. [31] developed an instrument for customer satisfaction in eCommerce with 34 factors related to information and system quality. These studies provide exhaustive enumerations of the factors that contribute to user satisfaction, but still do not explain satisfaction in a principled way.

We further seek the explanation of satisfaction outside the scope of information and computer science. In economics, there is a close relationship between satisfaction and utility. For example, Mankiw ([29], p. 285) introduced utility as "a person's subjective measure of well-being or satisfaction." Marshall ([30], p. 94) equates both the utility of products and consumer's satisfaction with product purchases to the price that the consumer is willing to pay for the product. This motivates us to explain satisfaction in terms of utility. For example, Su [34] defined utility as a measure of worth of search results versus time, physical effort, and mental effort expended. This suggests that we can consider searcher satisfaction as a compound measure of multiple factors, including search outcome and search effort. In a recent study, Yilmaz et al. [37] also confirmed the impact of searcher effort on document relevance and utility.

Another line of previous work that motivates our explanation of search satisfaction is the study of consumer psychology. Oliver et al. [32] verified that post-purchase consumer satisfaction is a function of pre-purchase consumer expectation and the disconfirmation after purchase (the discrepancy between perceived and expected utility of the product). The disconfirmation factor suggests that we can explain searcher satisfaction by comparing actual search outcomes to expected search outcome. As we will demonstrate in Section 4, with certain assumptions, this explanation is equivalent to the comparison of search outcomes and search effort.

2.2 Predicting Satisfaction and Others

Large-scale search engine logs contain massive amounts of search interaction data that can be useful as implicit searcher feedback. Such implicit feedback data can be employed to predict the quality of the search experience (e.g., searcher satisfaction) as well as other useful information such as result relevance and searcher preferences. In this subsection, we review related studies and approaches.

Hassan et al. [11, 13], Ageev et al. [1], and Wang et al. [35] modeled search success and satisfaction based on the structure of searchers' action sequences. They make the assumption that in successful and unsuccessful, or satisfied and dissatisfied sessions, searchers may perform different types of actions. Hassan et al. [11, 13] represented action sequences using Markov models. Ageev et al. [1] and Wang et al. [35] enhanced these models using conditional random fields and structured learning.

Feature-oriented approaches were also widely used in modeling aspects of the search experience. Researchers focused more on the types of features and adopted general classifiers in prediction. For example, Feild et al. [8] combined search interaction features as well as information from other sensors to predict frustration. Hassan et al. [12, 14] incorporated query reformulation features to further improve satisfaction prediction and identify struggling sessions. Guo et al. [10] predicted search engine switching, and Liu et al. [26, 27] and Arguello et al. [3] predicted search task difficulty.

Our work is different from previous research in that we move beyond binary satisfaction to predict graded search satisfaction. In addition, we model searcher satisfaction based on a combination of search outcome and searcher effort, which is well-grounded in theory, including previous work on consumer psychology.

3. DATA

In order to study graded search satisfaction, we sampled and annotated search tasks from the search logs of consenting users of the Microsoft Bing search engine in April, 2014. These logs were collected through a widely-distributed browser toolbar. These log entries included a unique identifier for each searcher, a timestamp for each page view, a unique browser window identifier, and the URL of the Web page visited. Intranet and secure (https) URL visits were excluded at the source. In order to reduce variability in search behavior caused by geographic and linguistic differences, we only include entries generated in the English speaking United States locale. From these logs we extracted raw search sessions. Every raw session began with a search query and could contain further queries and visits to clicked search results. A session ended if the searcher was idle for more than 30 minutes. These raw sessions were later segmented into search tasks (where a task resolves to a single information need) using Jones et al.'s methodology [21]. Jones et al. [21] showed that many raw search sessions consist of multiple tasks and may result in one or more queries. We use the term *search session* to refer to queries and other search activity belonging to the same search task throughout the paper. To remove navigational and simple informational tasks, we excluded single-query sessions.

The search sessions in our dataset were annotated with session search satisfaction and query result quality by crowd workers. For each session, we showed the annotators: 1) queries in the search session and search engine result page (SERP) dwell time; 2) links to search result pages for these queries; 3) the URLs of any clicked results and associated dwell times. We enforced that annotators visit the SERPs for all queries and visit the clicked result webpages before they can submit their judgments. Since they were third-party annotators, requiring these steps was meant to help annotators maximally restore the original searchers' experience. We paid annotators 10 cents for each of the sessions that they annotated.

Employing third-party crowd workers to annotate logged search sessions is inexpensive and also feasible for search engines, who are unable to contact searchers directly given privacy considerations. One limitation is that this method is less reliable than searchers' own ratings, and thus may introduce some biases. However, in spite of the inaccuracy introduced by the third-party judgment, many previous studies [11, 13, 35] have reached solid conclusions by adopting similar data collection methods. Moreover, collecting searchers' own ratings in a laboratory study could introduce another type of bias. For example, with user studies (e.g., [1]) it is difficult to simulate real search scenarios.

After assessor quality verification, we retained judgments for 476 search sessions. Each session includes three annotators' ratings on 1) search satisfaction of the whole session, and 2) result quality of each individual query in the session. The annotators rated session satisfaction using a 5-point Likert scale ranging from 1 (*very unsatisfied*) to 5 (*very satisfied*). They rated query result quality at three scales: *very useful* (2), *somewhat useful* (1), and *not useful* (0). We use the average score of the three annotators as the gold standard in our study. As will be analyzed in Section 6, individual annotators' ratings strongly correlate with average rating ($r = 0.68$). Krippendorf's alpha coefficient was 0.62, signifying both reasonable agreement between annotators and the subjectivity of the annotation task.

We assign sessions into four satisfaction levels as follows: *very high* ($4.33 < s \leq 5$, 11.1% of the sessions); *high* ($4.0 \leq s \leq 4.33$, 39.7%); *medium* ($3.33 \leq s \leq 3.67$, 33.4%); *low* ($s \leq 3$, 15.8%). The grouping strategy ensures that there are sufficient sessions at each of the four satisfaction levels to perform statistical analysis. Despite this grouping, most instances are grouped into *high* and *medium* levels; only 27% are in the two extreme groups (*low* and *very high*).

4. GRADED SEARCH SATISFACTION

As reviewed in Section 2.1, we first consider satisfaction as the searcher's subjective measure on the utility of search systems and results. Since utility is usually considered as the value of search results compared to the effort spent on searching, we also examine satisfaction on these two aspects. Considering the notion of utility and satisfaction are not consistently defined, we define our own notion of the constructs to avoid confusion.

Satisfaction. Satisfaction is the searcher's subjective preference on the utility of search systems and their search results. The higher the system utility is for the searcher, the more satisfied the searcher would be. In our analysis and experiments, satisfaction is measured as the average rating of three annotators on session satisfaction.

Search outcome (gain). Search outcome is the value of search results to the searcher, i.e., the quantity of useful information found.

Search effort (cost). Search effort is the cost of acquiring information from the search engine, e.g., issuing queries, examining result snippets on SERPs, reading clicked results, etc.

In the remainder of this section, we present findings showing that: 1) Annotators' satisfaction ratings are strongly correlated with the search outcome compared with searcher effort. This verifies our assumption on the notion of searcher satisfaction. 2) Search outcome and effort have complex and non-monotonous changes within sessions with different satisfaction levels, which suggests novel ways of modeling searcher satisfaction.

4.1 Satisfaction, Search Outcome, and Effort

To verify our assumption that satisfaction is the value of search outcome compared with search effort, we begin by examining the relationship between satisfaction and search outcome and effort. We directly measure satisfaction using annotators' average ratings. We use the following methods to approximate outcome and effort.

We use session cumulated gain (sCG) [18] as a measure of the search outcome in a session, which is the sum of each query's gain as in Equation (1). We do not discount later queries' search gains (i.e., sDCG) as suggested by Järvelin et al. [18], because their reason for discounting is to normalize the value of results by effort. We hope to measure the value of results without considering effort.

Table 1. Correlation of several measures with satisfaction.

Measure	Correlation w/ Satisfaction	
	Pearson	**Kendall**
Search Outcome (sCG)	0.27	0.22
Search Effort (# queries)	-0.24	-0.23
Search Outcome / Effort (sCG / #queries)	**0.77**	**0.59**
sDCG (Järvelin et al [18])	0.41	0.29
nsCG	**0.77**	**0.59**
nsDCG (Kanoulas et al. [22])	0.75	0.57

All the correlation values are statistically significant ($p < 0.01$).

In Equation (1), a query q's gain is originally calculated by summing the gains across q's relevant results. Due to the lack of document relevance judgments, we use annotators' query quality ratings as to represent the query's gain. That is, here sCG is calculated as the sum of all queries' quality ratings in the session.

$$outcome = sCG = \sum_{i=1}^{n} gain(q_i) \quad (1)$$

For search effort, we follow the economic model of search interactions [5] and measure search effort in a session by Equation (2), which is proportional to the number of queries issued in a session. In Equation (2), Q is the number of queries. The total search effort is the sum of four components. $c_q \cdot Q$ is the effort of querying; $c_v \cdot V \cdot Q$ is the effort of viewing pages; $c_s \cdot S \cdot Q$ is the effort of inspecting snippets; $c_a \cdot A \cdot Q$ is the effort of assessing results. All of the four parts are proportional to the number of queries. In this research we simply adopt the number of queries as a rough measure of effort.

$$effort = c_q \cdot Q + c_v \cdot V \cdot Q + c_s \cdot S \cdot Q + c_a \cdot A \cdot Q \propto Q \quad (2)$$

Table 1 shows the correlations between satisfaction and search outcome (sCG), effort (# queries), and average search outcome per effort (sCG / # queries). Results show that satisfaction has a weak positive correlation with search outcome (Pearson's $r = 0.27$) and a weak negative correlation with search effort ($r = -0.24$). In comparison, we observed a strong correlation ($r = 0.77$) between satisfaction and average search outcome per effort (sCG / # queries). Such a strong correlation verifies our assumption that it is appropriate to explain satisfaction as a relative measure of outcome versus effort.

Our findings also shed light on the validity of search session evaluation metrics. Järvelin et al.'s sDCG [18] only has a moderate correlation with satisfaction ($r = 0.41$), while its normalized version (nsDCG) has a strong correlation ($r = 0.75$), which is adopted as the evaluation metric in the TREC session track 2010. The version of nsDCG that we adopted is the same as that used in Kanoulas et al.'s studies [22] ($bq = 4$). We found that the normalized version of sCG without discounting (nsCG), as in Equation (3), has the strongest correlation with satisfaction ($r = 0.77$). When calculating sDCG, nsDCG, and nsCG, we use the sCG defined in Equation (1).

We found that under certain assumptions, nsCG is equivalent to our explanation of satisfaction (sCG / # queries). As in Equation (3), nsCG is the ratio between the actual search outcome (sCG) and the ideal search outcome (sCG_{ideal}). We assume that the ideal search outcome can be achieved via the maximum gain in each query, i.e., $gain_{\max}(q)$. If we further assume the maximum gain on each query is a constant, i.e., $gain_{\max}(q)$ is the same for different q, nsCG is proportional to sCG/Q, which is exactly our explanation of satisfaction. This explains why nsCG is also strongly correlated with searcher satisfaction ratings in our dataset.

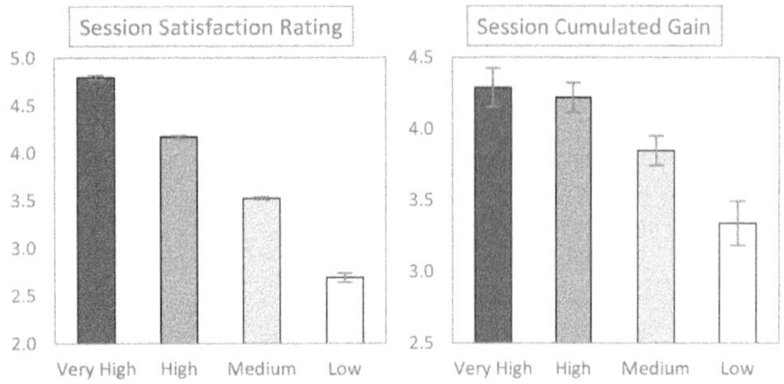

(a) (b)

Figure 1. Average human rating and session cumulated gain (sCG) in sessions of different satisfaction levels.

Note that with a different assumption, Equation (3) also offers the second explanation of satisfaction we reviewed in Section 2.1. Although originally introduced as a normalization factor for *sCG*, it seems reasonable to equate sCG_{ideal} to the searcher's expected outcome of the session, i.e., assuming they expect to obtain maximum search gain for each issued search query. Under such a premise, *nsCG* and Equation (3) is exactly a measure for the discrepancy between actual search outcome and expected search outcome.

$$nsCG = \frac{sCG}{sCG_{ideal}} = \frac{\sum_q gain(q)}{\sum_q gain_{\max}(q)} = \frac{\sum_q gain(q)}{Q \cdot gain_{\max}(q)} \propto \frac{sCG}{Q} \quad (3)$$

To sum up, findings in this section show that it is appropriate to explain satisfaction as search outcome compared with search effort, or equivalently, the difference between the actual and the expected search outcome. Here we focus on the first explanation given the lack of searcher expectation annotation. In the remainder of the section, we will analyze the differences in search outcome, effort, and related behavior in sessions with different satisfaction levels.

4.2 Tradeoff between Outcome and Effort

Figure 1 shows annotators' average satisfaction ratings and sCG (measuring search outcome) in sessions of four satisfaction levels. The error bars show standard error of each measure. Figure 1(a) shows that less satisfied sessions always have significantly lower ratings from the assessors ($p < 0.01$). However, Figure 1(b) shows that less satisfied sessions do not always have less search outcome. The sCG of sessions with *very high* and *high* satisfaction are 4.29 and 4.22 respectively (no significant difference at $p < 0.05$). But there are significantly less search outcomes in sessions with *medium* and *low* satisfaction (3.85 and 3.34, $p < 0.01$). This shows that low search outcome is indicative of low satisfaction, but high search outcome does not always mean complete satisfaction.

Figure 2 further explains how search outcome is accumulated in a session by showing the number of queries and the average gain of the queries in the session (measured by the assessors' average query quality rating). Figure 2(b) shows that in less satisfied sessions, searchers issue less effective queries (with significantly less gain per query, $p < 0.01$). Here we measure a query's gain using the average of annotators' query quality ratings (ranges from 0 to 2). In order to accomplish the search goal, searchers tend to issue more queries to compensate for the limited useful information gained in a session. As shown in Figure 2(a), searchers issue significantly more search queries in less satisfying sessions ($p < 0.01$). Table 1 also shows that the number of queries has a significant negative correlation with satisfaction.

Our results show adaptive searchers behaviors similar to those reported in a study by Smith and Kantor [33]. They assigned participants to search on systems with different performance and found that searchers will adapt their search strategy to ineffective search systems, by issuing more queries. Our results differ in that all searchers used the same system, but similar adaptive behavior is observed when query performance of the system is different. This suggests that it is common for searchers to issue more queries to compensate for the limited search effectiveness, regardless of the cause, e.g., ineffective systems, novice searchers, or tasks.

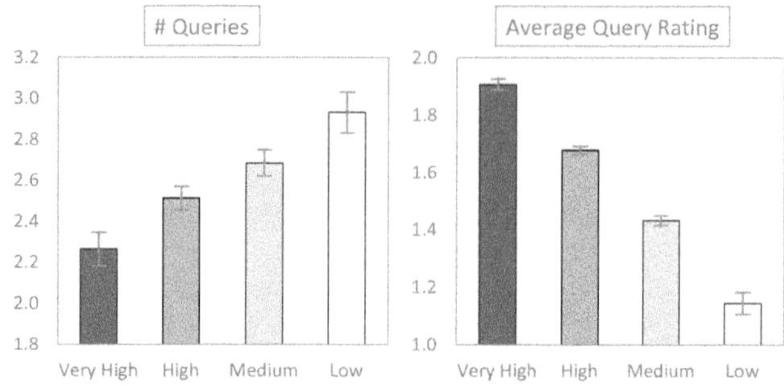

(a) (b)

Figure 2. Number of issued queries and average query rating in sessions of different satisfaction levels.

However, we note that searchers do not always expend additional effort to the extent of achieving the same amount of search outcome as they can accomplish when queries are effective. As shown in Figure 2(b), searchers issue more queries in *high* satisfaction sessions and achieve comparable search outcomes as others do in the *very high* satisfaction sessions. But in the *medium* and *low* satisfaction sessions, searchers do not expend sufficient extra effort (issue a sufficient number of additional queries) to accomplish the similar amount of search outcome as they could in *very high* and *high* satisfaction sessions.

Findings reported in this section suggest we can distinguish sessions with different satisfaction levels from search behavior related to search outcome, query effectiveness, and effort (e.g., the number of search queries issued). In less satisfying sessions, searchers issue fewer effective queries and reformulate more queries to compensate for the loss. In our dataset, the total search outcome does not differ greatly in sessions with *very high* and *high* satisfaction, but is significantly lower in sessions with *medium* and *low* satisfaction.

4.3 Different Types of Search Effort

In the previous section we used the number of queries as an estimate of search effort. In this section, we further examine different types of effort in sessions with different satisfaction levels. We adhere to the effort function in the economic model of search interaction [5] (Equation 2) and consider three types of effort: 1) issuing queries, 2) examining result snippets, and 3) assessing clicked results. We ignore the cost of reading multiple SERPs for a query ($c_V \cdot V \cdot Q$) because SERP pagination is rare in Web search scenarios.

We first examine the cost of issuing queries by considering query length. We assume that longer queries incur higher cost because they require more effort to type into the query box. We also examine the frequencies of using query suggestions, which is less expensive than formulating a query statement directly [4].

Figure 3 shows that in less satisfied sessions, searchers have higher cost of issuing queries and are more likely to switch to alternative query mechanisms such as query suggestions. As shown in Figure 3(a), in sessions with *very high* and *high* satisfaction, searchers issue significantly shorter queries than others do in sessions with *medium* and *low* satisfaction ($p < 0.05$). The trends are the same regardless of whether we remove stop words. Figure 3(b) shows that searchers adopt significantly more query suggestions in sessions with *medium* and *low* satisfaction than others do in ses-

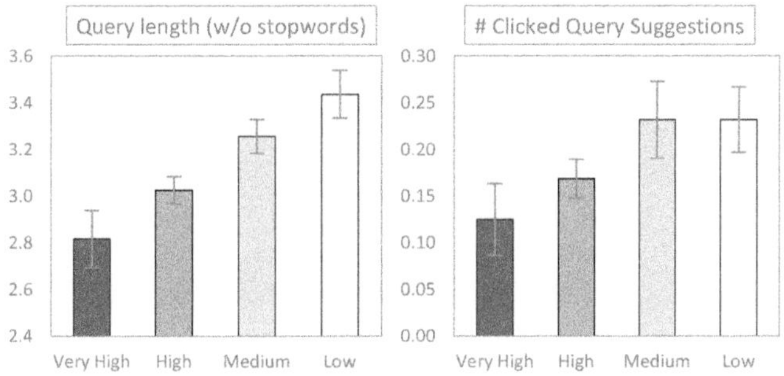

(a) (b)

Figure 3. The cost of formulating queries (in terms of query length) and the frequencies of using query suggestions.

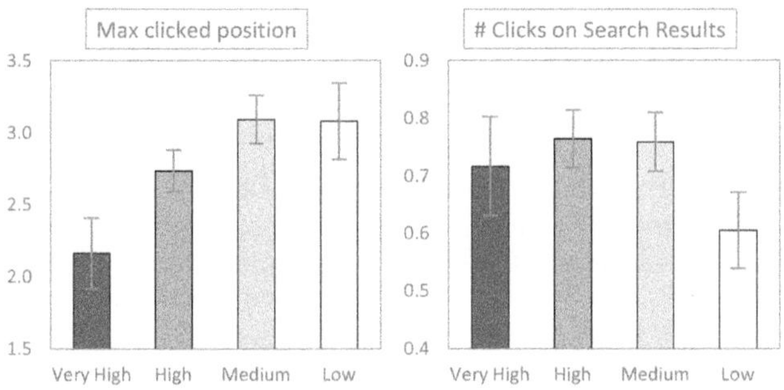

(a) (b)

Figure 4. The number and the average rank of the clicked results in session of different satisfaction levels.

sions with *very high* and *high* satisfaction ($p < 0.05$). In both figures, the differences are not significant between the *very high* and *high* satisfaction sessions, and between the *medium* and *low* satisfaction sessions. Note that due to some data limitations, we lacked sufficient information to normalize the frequencies of using query suggestions by whether the SERP showed query suggestions to the searcher or not. Therefore, the chances of using query suggestions in Figure 3(b) is underestimated.

We further measure the effort involved in examining result snippets using the ranks of the clicked results, i.e., deeper examination of the result lists equates to higher cost. Many user studies [19, 20, 28] have suggested that in general searchers examine search results from top to bottom, with a decreasing likelihood of clicking on results as a function of rank position, and terminate their review of the search results at a certain position. Therefore, the depth of examining result snippets is equal to or deeper than the ranks of the clicked result snippets, because searchers are likely to have examined these result snippets before clicking on a particular result. The effort of assessing results is measured in terms of the average number of clicks per query. In addition to the click depth, there are also costs associated with reading the text on the landing pages. For simplicity, we ignore these reading effects in our study.

Figure 4 illustrates the effort of examining snippets and assessing results in sessions with different satisfaction levels. Figure 4(a) shows that the maximum clicked rank (as the lower bound of the position of examined snippets) in sessions with *very high* satisfaction is significantly fewer than those in other three sessions ($p < 0.01$). However, we did not observe significant difference among sessions with *high*, *medium*, and *low* satisfaction levels. Figure 4(b) shows that searchers clicked significantly fewer results in sessions with *low* satisfaction compared with the other outcomes ($p < 0.05$), but there is no significant difference between sessions with *very high*, *high*, and *medium* satisfaction.

Table 2. Correlation of effort measures with satisfaction.

Search Cost	Correlation with Satisfaction	
	Pearson's r	Kendall's tau-b
Query length (w/ stop words)	-0.10**	-0.10**
Query length (w/o stop words)	-0.14**	-0.11**
Maximum click position	-0.14**	-0.12**
Average click position	-0.16**	-0.12**
Minimum click position	-0.16**	-0.10*
# clicks / query	0.05	0.04
# total clicks in a session	-0.02	0.00
# queries	-0.24**	-0.23**
# adopted query suggestions	-0.16**	-0.13**

* and ** denote correlation values that are significant at $p < 0.05$ and $p < 0.01$.

One important question is: how do different types of search effort affect satisfaction? Table 2 provides some insight by showing correlations between different types of effort and searcher satisfaction. The effort of issuing queries (measured by query length) and examining result snippets (measured by maximum click position) negatively affect search satisfaction. However, we did not observe significant correlation between search satisfaction and the effort of assessing the search results (i.e., the number of result clicks).

The findings in this section show that we can further incorporate different types of search effort into satisfaction modeling. In general, the effort of issuing queries and examining result snippets have overall negative correlations with searcher satisfaction. In addition, some of the related search behavior does not change consistently as a function of search satisfaction level. For example, the maximum click rank may only be able to distinguish sessions with *very high* satisfaction from others, but cannot further discriminate among sessions with *high*, *moderate*, and *low* satisfaction. Conversely, the effort of assessing result webpages seems only indicative of *low* satisfaction sessions but does not differ a lot in other sessions. The complexity of search effort in sessions with different degrees of satisfaction further confirms that it is over-simplified to classify session satisfaction into a binary scale.

4.4 Changes of Gain and Cost in a Session

Since previous user studies have identified changes in search behavior within a session over time [19], we sought to understand whether search outcome and effort also change over time. If so, are some changes indicative of searcher satisfaction? In this section, we examine changes in search outcome and effort at the beginning and the end of the session, and their relationship with satisfaction.

Figure 5 shows that both search outcome and assessing effort will increase over time in sessions with *high* or *medium* satisfaction levels, but not in the *very high* or *low* satisfaction sessions. This suggests that we may further predict satisfaction via changes of search outcome and effort. The figures show the comparison of query rating (measuring per-query search outcome) and the number of clicks (measuring the effort of assessing results) between the first query and the last query of the sessions. The changes in both measures are significant in sessions with *high* and *medium* satisfaction levels ($p < 0.01$), but insignificant in the *very high* and *low* satisfaction sessions. For sessions with a *very high* degree of satisfaction, we suspect that this is because the first query is already very successful (the average quality rating is 1.87, with a maximum value of 2) and there is little room for improvement. For sessions with *low* satisfaction, searcher may be unable to reformulate better queries.

From Figure 5, we can observe that query reformulation success and failure may affect search satisfaction. We further tested this hypothesis in sessions with *high*, *medium*, and *low* levels of satisfaction. We excluded the sessions with *very high* satisfaction level since there is little chance of the searcher reformulating better que-

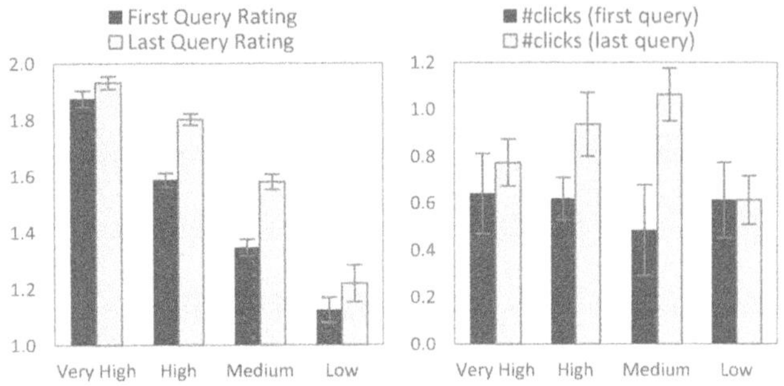

(a) (b)

Figure 5. Changes of query search gain and clicking effort.

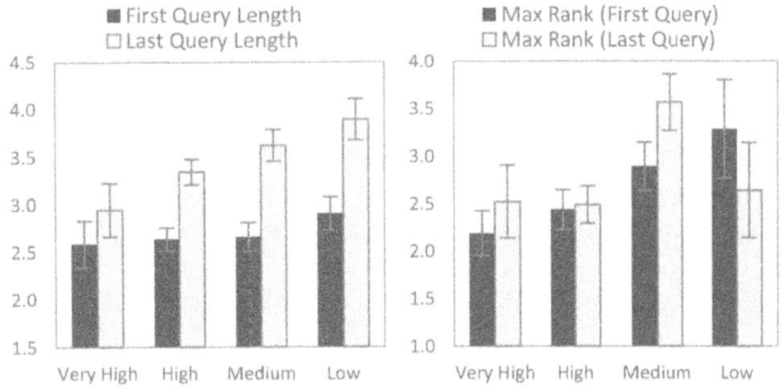

(a) (b)

Figure 6. Changes of cost in querying and examining snippets.

Table 3. Correlation of query reformulation with satisfaction in sessions other than *very high* satisfaction.

Search Cost	Correlation with Satisfaction	
	Pearson's r	Kendall's tau-b
Last - First Query Rating	0.20 **	0.13 *
% reform better	0.11	0.09
% reform equal	0.10	0.07
% reform worse	-0.22 **	-0.20 **

* and ** denote correlation values that are significant at $p < 0.05$ and $p < 0.01$.

ries. Table 3 shows the results. We found a positive correlation between the change of query quality rating and satisfaction, and a negative correlation for the likelihood of query reformulation failure.

Figure 6 shows the comparison of query length (cost of formulating queries) and maximum click rank (cost of examining snippets) at the beginning and the end of the session. We can observe overall significant increase of query length in sessions, but the magnitude of increase in the *very high* satisfaction sessions are significantly smaller ($p < 0.05$) than those in other sessions. For the effort of examining snippets (Figure 6(b)), we did not observe significant change in the maximum click rank of results in sessions with *very high* and *high* satisfaction. However, there are significant increases in the maximum click rank in sessions with *medium* satisfaction, but significant decreases in maximum click rank in dissatisfied sessions. As we will show in Section 5.3, the former helps distinguish between *very high* and *high* satisfaction, while the latter can help distinguish *medium* from *low* satisfaction.

4.5 Summary of Findings

To conclude, in this section we first verify that satisfaction can be best explained as the value of the search outcome compared with the degree of search effort. After further examination, we found from our analysis that sessions with different satisfaction levels vary greatly but non-monotonously in search outcome, effort, and changes in these measures. This suggests that we can leverage the search behaviors that are related to search outcome and effort to better model search satisfaction. Conversely, the non-monotonous changes suggest that it is non-trivial and necessary to understand

Table 4. Search outcome features and correlations. Values that are not significant at $p < 0.05$ are omitted ("-").

Features	Correlation w/ SAT				Correlation w/ sCG			
	All	VH/H	H/M	M/L	All	VH/H	H/M	M/L
ClickDwell	0.16	-	-	-	0.17	0.19	0.14	-
QSumClickDwell	0.13	-	-	-	0.10	-	-	-
SSumClickDwell	0.11	-	-	-	0.23	0.26	0.20	0.18
QueryInterval	0.22	0.18	-	0.13	-	-	-	-
SSumQueryInterval	0.18	0.15	-	-	0.18	-	0.15	0.21
SessionDuration	0.14	-	-	-	0.15	0.15	0.14	-
Q#Click T<5	-0.12	-0.13	-0.14	-	-	-	-	-
Q#Click T<15	-0.12	-	-0.15	-	-	-	-	-
Q#Click T≥60	0.16	-	-	0.15	0.14	-	-	0.17
S#Click	-	-0.13	-	-	0.24	0.27	0.22	0.26
S#Click T<10	-0.18	-0.14	-0.15	-	0.13	0.22	0.15	0.16
S#Click T≥185	0.16	-	-	0.18	0.23	0.18	0.19	0.24

and predict the subtle differences between graded satisfaction levels. In the next section, we will describe features for predicting search outcome, effort, and their changes over a search session.

5. FEATURES FOR PREDICTION

We now introduce our methods of predicting search satisfaction. In doing so, we adopt a feature-oriented approach. In accordance with our findings from Section 4, we select features related to search outcome, effort, and their changes in a search session. We examine the predictive power of features by their correlations (Pearson's r) with search satisfaction, search outcome (sCG), and the changes in query quality in a session. We suspected that some features may only be indicative of satisfaction within a particular range. Therefore, correlations are examined in all sessions (ALL) and three ranges: 1) sessions with *very high* and *high* satisfaction (VH/H); 2) sessions with *high* and *medium* satisfaction (H/M), and; 3) sessions with *medium* and *low* satisfaction (M/L). The results in the remainder of this section confirm our suspicions about satisfaction ranges.

5.1 Search Outcome Features

Previous studies (e.g., [24]) have found that SERP and click dwell time can indicate the quality of a SERP and clicked result. Thus, we include features related to SERP and click dwell time as search outcome features. Table 4 shows some representative features and their correlations with satisfaction and search outcome (sCG).

Click Dwell Time. We include the average dwell time of a click (ClickDwell) and the sum of click dwell time in a query and in a session (QSumClickDwell and SSumClickDwell). We consider the average, maximum, and minimum values of QSumClickDwell in multiple queries of a session (Table 4 shows the average value). We found that ClickDwell and SSumClickDwell have significant correlations with sCG in nearly all the ranges, but they do not significantly correlate with satisfaction in VH/H, H/M, and M/L.

Query Dwell Time. We measure query dwell time by the difference of the time that two adjacent queries were submitted (QueryInterval). We ignore this measure for the last query of each session. We compared this measure with the server-side query dwell time measure and found it has stronger correlation with satisfaction and sCG. We also consider the average, maximum, and minimum values of QueryInterval and the sum of the value in a session (SSumQueryInterval). Table 4 shows that query dwell time measures have significant correlations with satisfaction in the VH/H range, but no significant correlations in H/M and M/L ranges. The sum of query dwell times in a session also correlates with search outcome (sCG).

SAT and DSAT Clicks. We follow previous studies and divide clicks into satisfactory (SAT) clicks and dissatisfactory (DSAT) clicks by dwell time. SAT clicks are those with dwell time $\geq T_{sat}$ and DSAT clicks $< T_{dsat}$. We consider the number of SAT and DSAT clicks in a query (Q#Click) as well as its total number in a session (S#Click). Previous studies [11] adopted T_{sat}=30s and T_{dsat}=15s. However, we noticed that there is no universal threshold that can obtain the best correlations with sessions in three ranges simultaneously. Thus, for each of the three ranges, we select T_{sat} and T_{dsat} with the strongest correlations with satisfaction. For example, T_{dsat}=5s has the strongest correlation in the VH/H range, but T_{dsat}=15s has a stronger one in H/M. Table 4 shows that the number of DSAT clicks have significant correlations with satisfaction in VH/H and H/M ranges (e.g. Q#Click T<5, T<15, and S#Click T<10), but the number of SAT clicks has stronger correlations in the M/L range (e.g. Q#Click T≥60 and S#Click T≥185). The total number of clicks in a session (even the DSAT clicks) have a significant strong correlation with the search outcome (sCG).

Table 4 shows that most of our search outcome features do correlate with the actual search outcome (sCG) and satisfaction in general (for all sessions). However, many features do not have consistent significant correlation with satisfaction in all three ranges of satisfaction. This confirms our suspicion expressed at the beginning of the section, and suggests that different measure may contribute differently and predict satisfaction within a certain range.

5.2 Search Effort Features

Search effort features include the effort metrics that we analyzed in Section 4.3 and their variants. The variants include: the number of queries without clicks (#Queries w/o Click), the average, MAX, and MIN rank of clicks in a query (QAvgClickPos), the longest and shortest query length in a session (SMaxQLength), and the total number of unique query terms in a session (#UniqQTerms).

Query Similarity. We also include query similarity in the search effort measures. Hassan et al. [14] discovered that a high similarity between queries may indicate that the searcher is "struggling" in a search session. Struggling inevitably increases searcher effort. Table 5 shows the correlations between satisfaction and some of the query similarity features. QEditDistanceBin is a binary feature with value 1 if the edit distance between two queries ≤ 2. QJaccardSim is the Jaccard similarity between two queries' term sets. Q#CommonCharLeft is the longest subsequence of characters in common between two queries starting from the left side of the query strings. We calculate these measures between each adjacent query pair in a session and adopt the average, MAX, and MIN values in a session as search effort features (Table 5 shows only the average values). Results show that query similarity measures have negative correlations with satisfaction in general. The effectiveness of these features is also different across the three satisfaction ranges, e.g., query similarity cannot distinguish satisfaction in M/L sessions.

The results in Table 5 validate our search effort features in that they do negatively correlate with search satisfaction. In addition, the results also suggest that for each adjacent satisfaction level, we may need to use different sets of effort features in prediction.

5.3 Outcome and Effort Change Features

Many of the features in Section 5.1 and 5.2 are based on query-level measures that indicate a query's search outcome or effort. For these measures, we calculate the difference of value in the last query of a session versus that of the first query. We include these measures as those indicating changes in search outcome and effort during the course of a search session. Table 6 shows some representative features and their correlations with satisfaction and the actual change of search outcome in a session (measured by the difference of query quality ratings between the first and last query).

Table 6 shows that the search outcome change features are usually correlated with the actual changes in search outcome, e.g. the sum of click dwell time in a query (Δ QSumClickDwell) and the number of SAT clicks (Δ Q#Click T≥60). However, these features do not always correlate well with satisfaction. For example, changes in the number of SAT clicks (Δ Q#Click T≥60) can only distinguish between the *medium* and *low* satisfaction sessions (M/L), and changes in the number of DSAT clicks (Δ Q#Click T<50) only weakly correlate with the *high* and *medium* satisfaction sessions (H/M).

Table 5. Search effort features and correlations. Values that are not significant at $p < 0.05$ are omitted ("-").

Features	Correlation w/ SAT			
	All	VH/H	H/M	M/L
#Queries	-0.24	-	-0.11	-0.18
#Queries w/o Click	-0.25	-	-0.14	-0.18
QAvgClickPos	-	-0.20	-	-
QMaxClickPos	-	-0.19	-	-
QMinClickPos	-0.09	-0.18	-	-
SMaxQLength	-0.21	-0.15	-	-
#UniqQTerms	-0.16	-	-	-0.13
QEditDistanceBin	-0.22	-	-0.16	-
QJaccardSim	-0.14	-0.18	-	-
Q#CommonCharLeft	-0.14	-	-0.11	-

Table 6. Outcome and effort change features and correlations. Values that are not significant at $p < 0.05$ are omitted ("-").

Feature	Correlation w/ SAT				Correlation w/ Q Rating Change			
	All	VH/H	H/M	M/L	All	VH/H	H/M	M/L
Δ QSumClickDwell	-	-	-	-	0.15	0.16	0.16	0.15
Δ Q#Click T≥60	-	-	-	0.15	0.25	0.24	0.26	0.27
Δ Q#Click T<50	-	-	-0.11	-	-	-	-	-
EndClick	0.23	-	-	0.26	0.16	0.19	0.18	0.15
Δ QEditDistanceBin	-0.10	-	-	-0.16	-	-	-	-
Δ QJaccardSim	-	-	-0.11	-	-	-	-	-
Δ Q#CommonWord	-	-	-0.13	-	-	-	-	-
Δ QLength	-0.11	-0.14	-	-	-	-	-	-
Δ QMaxClickPos	-	-	-	0.16	-	-	-	-

To conclude, results in this section show that the discriminative power of features is not consistent in all sessions. For many of the features, it may only be able to indicate changes in search satisfaction within certain ranges. As we will show in the next section, different features have different degrees of effectiveness in predicting search satisfaction of sessions at different satisfaction ranges.

5.4 Incorporating Action Transition Features

To capitalize on successful prior methods for satisfaction modeling, we include action transition features into our model. These transitions come from the Markov model approach [11], which takes advantage of the occurrence of action transitions. To leverage this approach in our predictive model, we use the count of each action transition in the Markov model as a part of our feature set.

6. EVALUATION

In this section, we describe the evaluation of our model. We consider the following two scenarios. First, we evaluate how well we can predict the actual session satisfaction through regression analysis (Section 6.1). Second, we examine how well we can distinguish between sessions of two adjacent satisfaction levels (Section 6.2). Results in this section help answer the following questions:

RQ1: How well can we predict searchers' satisfaction in a continuous interval and between adjacent satisfaction levels?

RQ2: How much does each category of features contribute to the prediction of search satisfaction?

RQ3: Where are the difficulties in predicting search satisfaction?

6.1 Prediction in a Continuous Interval

We experimented with different regression models including linear regression, Poisson regression, and boosted tree regression. We found that Poisson regression yielded the best results and report its results in this section. We evaluate regression using Normalized

Table 7. Regression of average session satisfaction ratings.

Features	NRMSE (0-1, the lower the better)	Correlation w/ SAT
Outcome	0.171	0.283
Effort	0.167	0.352
Change	0.165	0.374
All	**0.161**	**0.431**
All + MML	0.162	0.429
Individual Annotator	-	**0.687**

The darker and lighter shadings indicate differences with "All" that are significant at $p < 0.01$ and 0.05. All the correlations are statistically significant at $p < 0.01$.

Root Mean Square Error (NRMSE, smaller value means better prediction) and the Pearson's correlation (r) between the predicted and actual satisfaction values. For each group of features, we generate 10 runs and evaluate each run using 10-fold cross validation. This results in NRMSE values on 100 folds in total. We report the average value of NRMSE and test statistical significance using a Welch t-test. Due to the variability of correlation value in small samples, we report the overall correlation value in 100 folds.

Table 7 shows the results. Among the three groups of features, outcome features are the least predictive and resulted in the largest prediction error and the lowest correlation with the actual values. Whereas, the correlation of all outcome features is still stronger than those of any single outcome features shown in Table 4. The effort and change features have comparable predictive power. Unsurprisingly, using all three groups of features (All) results in better prediction of satisfaction than any of them alone. The predicted satisfaction values also have a moderate correlation with the actual satisfaction value ($r = 0.431$). However, little performance is gained by further combining with action transition features (All + MML).

A moderate correlation with the actual satisfaction values indicates a reasonably effective prediction. However, since we are the first to predict search satisfaction in a continuous interval, there is no accepted baseline method. To further study the effectiveness of our prediction, we examine how well an individual annotator can assess satisfaction (the average value of three annotators). As shown in Table 7, the correlation between an individual annotators' ratings and the average ratings is 0.687. This indicates the subjectivity of the task itself and can be considered as an upper bound for automatic methods. In comparing against individual annotators' assessments (with also an imperfect correlation), our prediction is reasonably effective, yet there is still some room for improvement.

6.2 Predicting Adjacent Satisfaction Levels

6.2.1 Experiment Settings

Given the prediction task in Section 6.1, it is difficult to make comparisons with previous approaches which predicted satisfaction as binary states. In addition, the overall effectiveness of regression in all sessions masks some details of the strengths and weaknesses of features in predicting satisfaction at different ranges. Therefore, we further evaluate how well our approaches can classify sessions with two adjacent satisfaction levels, e.g., between sessions with *very high* and *high* satisfaction levels (Section 6.2.2), between *high* and *medium* levels (Section 6.2.3), and between *medium* and *low* levels (Section 6.2.4). We begin by applying the features separately. Then we combine them (All) and further combine them with the Markov action transition features (All + MML). We tested logistic regression, SVM, and FastRank and report results using logistic regression since it has best performance in our dataset.

This evaluation scenario enables us to compare our methods and those described in previous work. We adopt the Markov model (MML) [13] as a baseline. The set of actions for MML is the same as those used by Hassan [13]. Ageev et al. [1], Hassan [11] and Wang et al. [35] modeled similar set of actions using Conditional Random Fields (CRF), Generative Models and Structured Learning (AcTS). According [11] and [35], the CRF, the generative model and AcTS approaches improved average F_1 score of MML by about 4%, 4% and 8% respectively on their dataset. Here we did not implement CRF, the generative model and AcTS for comparison, but we will compare the relative improvements of our method with the scale of improvements reported in their papers as an indirect comparison with them.

In a similar way to the dataset employed in previous studies [1, 11, 13, 35], the satisfaction labels in our dataset are unevenly distributed. Therefore, we evaluate classification mainly by the F_1 scores of the two classes and the macro-average F_1 score. For each approach, we generate 10 runs, each using 10-fold cross validation. We report the average value on the 100 folds and test set, and compute the statistical significance of any observed differences.

Table 8. Classification of *very high* and *high* sessions.

	F_1			Accuracy
	Average	*Very high*	*High*	
Outcome	0.507	0.138	0.876	0.784
Effort	**0.567**	**0.263**	0.872	0.783
Change	0.474	0.072	0.877	0.782
All	0.558	0.235	**0.880**	**0.794**
All + MML	0.556	0.234	0.879	0.791
MML	0.470	0.076	0.864	0.767
All *high*	0.438	-	0.877	0.781

Darker and lighter shadings indicate sig. diffs with MML (at $p < 0.01$ and 0.05).

6.2.2 Classify Very High and High Satisfaction

Table 8 shows results of classification between sessions with the *very high* and *high* degree of satisfaction. Among the three groups of features, effort features are the most predictive. The differences in F_1 scores between effort features and other two groups are significant at $p < 0.01$. This is consistent with our observations in Section 4.2, i.e. *very high* and *high* satisfaction sessions mainly differ in terms of the search effort instead of the search outcome. We did not observe any improvements from combining the three features. Using effort features alone has the highest F_1 in classifying sessions with *very high* satisfaction levels, but combining features results in significantly lower F_1 on sessions with this grading ($p < 0.05$).

Our approach (All) significantly outperforms the Markov model in both average F_1 score (+18.7%) and accuracy (+3.5%). The magnitude of the gain sis also greater in comparison with that of CRF and AcTS in studies by Wang et al. [35]. In fact, using outcome or effort features alone results in significantly better F_1 than MML. The main reason is the poor effectiveness of MML in classifying sessions with *very high* satisfaction levels. Due to the limited effectiveness of MML in distinguishing VH/H sessions, little is gained from combining our features with those derived from the action transitions (All + MML).

It is worth noting that even our best approach (using effort features alone) also did not perform all that effectively in recognizing the *very high* satisfaction sessions (the F_1 score is only 0.263). This indicates that it is more challenging to classify adjacent satisfaction levels, whose sessions may only have very subtle differences.

6.2.3 Classify High and Medium Satisfaction

Table 9 shows the evaluation results of classification between *high* and *medium* satisfaction levels. All of our approaches significantly outperform MML in both F_1 score and accuracy ($p < 0.01$). This further demonstrates the difficulty of the MML method in recognizing subtle differences of adjacent satisfaction levels.

We observe that the effort and change features are more effective than the outcome features (the difference between outcome and change in average F_1 score is significant at $p < 0.05$). In comparing

Table 9. Classification of the *high* and *medium* sessions. All the methods are significantly better than MML at p<0.01.

	F_1			Accuracy
	Average	*High*	*Medium*	
Outcome	0.546	0.661	0.431	0.579
Effort	0.578	0.705	0.451	0.618
Change	0.583	0.681	0.485	0.609
All	0.601	0.714	0.488	0.636
All + MML	**0.612**	**0.724**	**0.500**	**0.647**
MML	0.489	0.599	0.379	0.519
All *high*	0.352	0.704	-	0.543

The darker and lighter shadings indicate differences with "All" that are significant at $p < 0.01$ and 0.05.

Table 10. Classification of the *medium* and *low* sessions.

	F_1			Accuracy
	Average	*Medium*	*Low*	
Outcome	0.407	0.810	0.004	0.680
Effort	0.498	0.806	0.190	0.688
Change	0.644	0.810	**0.478**	0.724
All	0.623	0.813	0.433	0.721
All + MML	**0.649**	**0.821**	0.477	**0.736**
MML	0.577	0.797	0.356	0.699
All *high*	0.405	0.809	-	0.680

The darker and lighter shadings indicate differences with MML that are significant at $p < 0.01$ and 0.05.

the performance of the effort and change features, it appears that effort features can better recognize sessions with *high* level of satisfaction, but change features can better classify sessions in *medium* satisfaction level (with higher F_1 scores in each class). We also observed significant improvements after combining three groups of features. This shows that the three groups of features are effectively modeling different aspects of the differences between the sessions with *high* and *medium* satisfaction levels. There is also a small but insignificant improvement by further combining with action transition features (All + MML).

We achieved better performance in distinguishing between the *high* and *medium* satisfaction sessions, than between *very high* and *high* satisfaction levels. Table 8 shows that the best average F_1 score for *high*/*medium* is 0.612 versus 0.567 for *very high* / *high*. It may be relatively easier to classify the *high* and *medium* satisfaction levels. Due to the limited discriminative power of MML in this task scenario, our approach also achieved remarkable improvements in both average F_1 score (+25%) and accuracy (+24.6%).

6.2.4 Classify Medium and Low Satisfaction

We further evaluate classification between *medium* and *low* satisfaction levels. Sessions with *low* level of satisfaction have dissatisfactory ratings ($s \leq 3$, ranging from 1 to 5), which is similar to the DSAT class in binary satisfaction classification in previous studies. We observed that the Markov model performs effectively in this scenario, with an average F_1 score 0.577 compared with 0.470 and 0.489 in previous two satisfaction ranges (Tables 8 and 9).

Among the three groups of features, change features are the most effective. Outcome and effort features have limited effectiveness in recognizing dissatisfied sessions (F_1 scores < 0.2). Change features also achieved the highest F_1 score in classifying the dissatisfied sessions compared with those that combine all features. We achieved even higher average F_1 score and accuracy from combining with the action transition features (All + MML). One explanation is the strength of the MML model for this particular task.

In comparison with the baseline approach (MML), our best approach (All + MML) still achieved significant improvements in average F_1 (+12.5%) and accuracy (+5.3%). The high performance of the Markov model shows that the strength of our method probably lies in classifying sessions with *medium* and *low* satisfaction. That is, instead of recognizing highly satisfactory sessions, MML is more likely to be a strong classifier for DSAT sessions.

6.2.5 Summary of Results

To sum up, our results answer our three research questions:

First (regarding RQ1 and RQ3), we found limited effectiveness of a well-established previous method (the Markov model) in identifying the subtle differences among *very high*, *high*, and *medium* satisfaction levels. Results indicate that our approach can identify such minor differences of satisfaction more effectively. We also found that the true strength of the Markov model may lie in recognizing DSAT sessions. In this scenario, our approach still achieved significantly better performance. The regression analysis in Section 6.1 also shows that our model can predict satisfaction scores with moderate correlation with the actual scores from judges ($r = 0.43$).

Second (for RQ2), as we suspected, different groups of features contribute diversely in different scenarios. For example, effort features contribute remarkably in distinguishing *very high* and *high* satisfaction sessions. The change features distinguish *medium* and *low* satisfaction sessions. All three feature groups contribute substantially to discriminating *high* and *medium* satisfaction sessions.

7. DISCUSSION AND IMPLICATIONS

We have studied the important issue of graded search satisfaction. Although degrees of satisfaction may be captured during laboratory studies, in many settings, including retrospective analysis of large-scale log data collected by search engines, satisfaction is modeled as a binary variable. We suspected that this may be insufficient to accurately assess and compare the performance of these search systems. Our findings clearly show that satisfaction is sufficiently nuanced that it needs to be modeled at greater granularity than has been done traditionally. Rich and non-monotonous differences in behavior are noted at all satisfaction levels studied, suggesting that there may be subtle distinctions between the levels of search satisfaction and a non-binary assessment may be justified. In addition, we show that by considering both the amount of information gained during a session (the outcome) and the effort involved in obtaining that information, we can accurately model search satisfaction. Leveraging information about outcome and effort let us develop a predictive model to accurately predict *graded* search satisfaction.

Despite the promise of our methods, we also acknowledge some limitations. The satisfaction judgments collected as part of this study were provided by third-party judges. Ideally the judgments of search satisfaction would be sourced from searchers in-situ at search time. This creates significant additional overhead for searchers, especially if we are asking them to provide both quality ratings for the results for each query and an overall multi-level rating for the session. We were concerned that such overhead would dissuade searchers from providing feedback both in our experiment, or more generally in natural settings as part of a broader deployment of satisfaction elicitation methods (limiting the impact of our conclusions). More research is needed into methods to incentivize searchers to provide ratings, to streamline the rating process, or to intelligently sample sessions so that we do not need to probe searchers at every session. In addition, search satisfaction in previous studies as well as in this paper is measured using extremely simple instruments (e.g., simply asking searchers or annotators whether they are satisfied). As we reviewed in Section 2.1, in many other fields researchers have developed complex and factorized instruments for measuring user satisfaction in other systems. This suggests we may also need more robust instruments for measuring searcher satisfaction. We also focused on gain and effort in this study. However, there are other factors that can influence the types of search behavior observed, including the nature of the search task and the tenacity of the searcher. Further studies are required to understand the role of these and other factors on behavior and search satisfaction.

The strong performance of our models has implications for search providers who aim to accurately measure satisfaction with their services. Typically, satisfaction with online services is evaluated on a binary scale in automatic evaluation approaches. However, modeling *degrees* of satisfaction allows for a more complete understanding of the performance of systems, and the more accurate prioritization of cases where potentially-negative experiences are identified. Moving forward, we must develop and evaluate our predictive models in large-scale settings to understand whether they can yield richer insights about aggregated search experiences than their binary equivalents in practice. In addition, search satisfaction estimates are used in a number of settings beyond system measurement, including evaluating short- and long-term personalization [7], as labels for implicit feedback [9], and in learning about biases in search behavior [36]. The satisfaction judgments in these settings have traditionally been binary, but understanding the impact of graded search satisfaction is also an important future direction.

8. CONCLUSION

Search satisfaction is a complex construct. Despite the complexity, to our knowledge it has hitherto been modeled as a binary variable in the measurement of satisfaction with search systems. In this paper, we performed a detailed study of graded search satisfaction in the context of Web search. We used logged search session data mined from users of the Microsoft Bing search engine and detailed judgments about session satisfaction on a multi-point scale from human annotators. Through our analysis we observe clear differences in search behavior in sessions with different satisfaction levels. Given the presence of these differences, we developed a predictive model that can more accurately estimate graded search satisfaction than existing satisfaction modeling methods by considering search outcomes and searcher effort, both independently and in combination. Our findings are of critical importance to search providers as they attempt to measure system performance based only on implicit signals in log data. Future work involves improving the performance of our model, additional testing against binary equivalents, and experimenting with applying graded satisfaction in different settings, especially surrounding the richer analysis of search engine performance that our graded satisfaction modeling enables.

REFERENCES

[1] M. Ageev et al. 2011. Find it if you can: A game for modeling different types of web search success using interaction data. In *SIGIR'11*: 345–354.

[2] A. Al-Maskari et al. 2007. The relationship between IR effectiveness measures and user satisfaction. In *SIGIR'07*: 773–774.

[3] J. Arguello. 2014. Predicting search task difficulty. In *ECIR'14*: 88–99.

[4] L. Azzopardi et al. 2013. How query cost affects search behavior. In *SIGIR'13*: 23–32.

[5] L. Azzopardi. 2014. Modelling interaction with economic models of search. In *SIGIR'14*: 3–12.

[6] J. E. Bailey and S. W. Pearson. 1983. Development of a tool for measuring and analyzing computer user satisfaction. *Management Science*, 29(5): 530–545.

[7] P. N. Bennett et al. 2012. Modeling the impact of short- and long-term behavior on search personalization. In *SIGIR'12*: 185-194.

[8] H. Feild et al. 2010. Predicting searcher frustration. In *SIGIR'10*: 34–41.

[9] S. Fox et al. 2005. Evaluating implicit measures to improve web search. *ACM TOIS*, 23(2): 147–168.

[10] Q. Guo et al. 2011. Why searchers switch: understanding and predicting engine switching rationales. In *SIGIR'11*: 335-344.

[11] A. Hassan. 2012. A semi-supervised approach to modeling web search satisfaction. In *SIGIR'12*: 275–284.

[12] A. Hassan et al. 2013. Beyond clicks: Query reformulation as a predictor of search satisfaction. In *CIKM'13*: 2019–2028.

[13] A. Hassan et al. 2010. Beyond DCG: User behavior as a predictor of a successful search. In *WSDM'10*: 221–230.

[14] A. Hassan et al. 2014. Struggling or exploring? Disambiguating long search sessions? In *WSDM'14*: 53–62.

[15] S. B. Huffman and M. Hochster. 2007. How well does result relevance predict session satisfaction? In *SIGIR'07*: 567-574.

[16] B. Ives et al. 1983. The measurement of user information satisfaction. *CACM*, 26(10): 785–793.

[17] K. Järvelin and J. Kekäläinen. 2000. IR evaluation methods for retrieving highly relevant documents. In *SIGIR'00*: 41–48.

[18] K. Järvelin et al. 2008. Discounted cumulated gain based evaluation of multiple-query IR sessions. In *ECIR'08*: 4–15.

[19] J. Jiang et al. Searching, browsing, and clicking in a search session: changes in user behavior by task and over time. In *SIGIR'14*: 607–616.

[20] T. Joachims et al. 2005. Accurately interpreting clickthrough data as implicit feedback. In *SIGIR'05*: 154–161.

[21] R. Jones and K. Klinkner. 2008. Beyond the session timeout: automatic hierarchical segmentation of search topics in query logs. In *CIKM'08*: 699–708.

[22] E. Kanoulas et al. 2011. Evaluating multi-query sessions. In *SIGIR'11*: 1053–1062.

[23] D. Kelly. 2009. Methods for evaluating interactive information retrieval systems with users. *Foundation and Trends in Information Retrieval*, 3(1-2): 1–224.

[24] Y. Kim et al. 2014. Modeling dwell time to predict click-level satisfaction. In *WSDM'14*: 193–202.

[25] R. Kohavi et al. 2009. Controlled experiments on the web: survey and practical guide. *Data Mining and Knowledge Discovery*. 18(1): 140–181.

[26] J. Liu et al. 2012. Exploring and predicting search task difficulty. In *CIKM'12*: 1313–1322.

[27] J. Liu and N. J. Belkin. 2010. Personalizing information retrieval for multi-session tasks. In *SIGIR'10*: 26–33.

[28] L. Lorigo et al. 2006. The influence of task and gender on search and evaluation behavior using Google. *IP&M*, 42(4): 1123–1131.

[29] G. Mankiw. 2010. *Principles of Macroeconomics*. South-Western Cengage Learning.

[30] A. Marshall. 2009. *Principles of Economics: Abridged Edition*. Cosimo Classics.

[31] V. McKinney et al. 2002. The measurement of Web-customer satisfaction: an expectation and disconfirmation approach. *Information Systems Research*, 13(3): 296–315.

[32] R. L. Oliver. 1980. A cognitive model of the antecedents and consequences of satisfaction decisions. *Journal of Marketing Research*. 17(4): 460–470.

[33] C. L. Smith and P. B. Kantor. 2008. User adaptation: Good results from poor systems. In *SIGIR'08*: 147–154.

[34] L. T. Su. 2003. A comprehensive and systematic model of user evaluation of Web search engines. *JASIST*, 54(13): 1175–1192.

[35] H. Wang et al. 2014. Modeling action-level satisfaction for search task satisfaction prediction. In *SIGIR'14*: 123–132.

[36] R. W. White. 2013. Beliefs and biases in web search. In *SIGIR'13*: 3–12.

[37] E. Yilmaz et al. 2014. Relevance and effort: an analysis of document utility. In *CIKM'14*: 91–100.

Robust Tree-based Causal Inference for Complex Ad Effectiveness Analysis

Pengyuan Wang[†] Wei Sun[§] Dawei Yin[†] Jian Yang[†] Yi Chang[†]
[†]Yahoo Labs, Sunnyvale, CA, USA
[§]Purdue University, West Lafayette, IN,USA
[†]{pengyuan, daweiy, jianyang,yichang}@yahoo-inc.com [§]sun244@purdue.edu

ABSTRACT

As the online advertising industry has evolved into an age of diverse ad formats and delivery channels, users are exposed to complex ad treatments involving various ad characteristics. The diversity and generality of ad treatments call for accurate and causal measurement of ad effectiveness, i.e., how the ad treatment *causes* the changes in outcomes without the confounding effect by user characteristics. Various causal inference approaches have been proposed to measure the causal effect of ad treatments. However, most existing causal inference methods focus on univariate and binary treatment and are not well suited for complex ad treatments. Moreover, to be practical in the data-rich online environment, the measurement needs to be highly general and efficient, which is not addressed in conventional causal inference approaches.

In this paper we propose a novel causal inference framework for assessing the impact of general advertising treatments. Our new framework enables analysis on uni- or multi-dimensional ad treatments, where each dimension (ad treatment factor) could be discrete or continuous. We prove that our approach is able to provide an unbiased estimation of the ad effectiveness by controlling the confounding effect of user characteristics. The framework is computationally efficient by employing a tree structure that specifies the relationship between user characteristics and the corresponding ad treatment. This tree-based framework is robust to model misspecification and highly flexible with minimal manual tuning. To demonstrate the efficacy of our approach, we apply it to two advertising campaigns. In the first campaign we evaluate the impact of different ad frequencies, and in the second one we consider the synthetic ad effectiveness across TV and online platforms. Our framework successfully provides the causal impact of ads with different frequencies in both campaigns. Moreover, it shows that the ad frequency usually has a treatment effect cap, which is usually over-estimated by naive estimation.

Categories and Subject Descriptors

G.3 [**PROBABILITY AND STATISTICS**]: Statistical Computing; J.1 [**ADMINISTRATIVE DATA PROCESSING**]: Business, Marketing

WSDM'15, February 2–6, 2015, Shanghai, China.

http://dx.doi.org/10.1145/2684822.2685294.

Keywords

Causal Inference; Advertising; Online Strategy Measurement

1. INTRODUCTION

In the current online advertising ecosystem, user are exposed to ads with diverse formats and channels, and user's behaviors are caused by complex ad treatments combining of various factors. The online ad delivery channels include search, display, mail, mobile and so on. Besides the multi-channel exposure, ad creative characteristics and context may also affect ad effectiveness [33]. Hence the ad treatments are becoming a combination of various factors mentioned above. The complexity of ad treatments calls for accurate and causal measurement of ad effectiveness, i.e., how the ad treatment *causes* the changes in outcomes [1].

Ideally, the gold standard of accurate ad effectiveness measurement is the experiment-based approach, such as A/B test, where different ad treatments are randomly assigned to users. However, the cost of fully randomized experiments is usually very high [10, 25, 35] and in some rich ad treatment circumstances, such fully randomized experiments are even infeasible. The major obstacles to achieve fully randomized experiments are as follows. 1) Implementing a platform for supporting ideal experiments, i.e., perfect randomization, often involves the change of system architecture, which might cause much prohibited engineering effort. 2) When the treatments are a combination of various factors, one might not be able to fully explore all possible combinations of treatments due to the lack of population. 3) The treatment may not be feasible for large-scale experiments, such as the number of ad impressions. In online advertising, it is easy to randomly assign users to see or not see the ad impression, but it is difficult to fully control the number of impressions, except utilizing field experiment [2], which is costly and usually can be conducted only on a relatively small scale. 4) Even if the experiments are perfectly randomized and the ad treatments can fit into an experiment framework, one still should be cautious due to the fact that the randomized experiments may hurt both user experience and ad revenue. Hence it is critical and necessary to provide statistical approaches to estimate the ad effectiveness directly from observational data rather than experimental data.

Previous studies based on observational data try to establish direct relationship between the ad treatment and a success signal, e.g., purchase, brand keyword searching [1], and etc. However, in obser-

[1]An outcome is the user's response in the ad campaigns, such as whether or not the user clicks a link, searches for the brand or visits websites. A success is an action favored by the advertiser, such as click, search or site visitation.

[2]A field experiment is a research study conducted in a natural setting in which the experimenter manipulates one or more independent variables under carefully controlled conditions [17].

vational data, typically the user characteristics may affect both the exposed ad treatment and the success tendency. Such confounding effects of user characteristics are called 'selection biases' [32], and ignoring the confounding effects may lead to biased estimation of the treatment effect [32]. For example, assume in an auto campaign all of exposed users are males and all of the non-exposed users are females. If the males generally have a larger success rate than females, the effectiveness of the campaign could be overestimated because of the confounding effects of the user characteristics—in this case, gender: It might just be that males are more likely to be exposed and perform success actions. Therefore, the relationship between the ad treatments and the success is not causal without eliminating the selection bias. A straightforward approach attempting to eliminate the selection biases is to adjust the outcome with the user characteristics using supervised learning. However the user characteristics may have complex relationships, e.g., nonlinearity, with the treatments and the outcome, and it is not trivial to estimate the causal effect of the treatment by adjusting the outcome with the user characteristics directly.

To address the aforementioned problems, the causal inference has started to attract attention in the online advertising field [10, 13, 35, 38] . Causal inference aims to infer unbiased causality effect of the ad treatment from observational data on chosen outcome metric, e.g., the effect of ads on success rates, by eliminating the impact of the confounding factors such as user characteristics. However, measuring general/complex ad treatment effectiveness is still facing three major challenges. First, the general ad treatment can be much more complex than binary ad treatment. It could be a discrete or continuous, single- or multi-dimensional treatment. To design an analytics framework encompassing so many ad factors is not trivial. Second, the online observational dataset typically has huge volume of records and user characteristics, which demands the methodology to be highly efficient. Traditional statistical causal inference approaches usually cannot reach efficiency required by the advertising industry. Third, when the treatments become more complex, existing methods are usually sensitive to parameter settings (more details in Section 5). To overcome the sensitivity, a robust causal inference approach is also wanted.

In this paper, we propose a computationally efficient tree-based causal inference framework to tackle the general ad effectiveness measurement problem. Our model is well suited for the online advertising datasets which consist of complex treatments, huge volume of users, and high-dimensional features. The novelty and advantages of the proposed method can be summarized as follows:

- Our causal inference is fully general, where the treatment can be single- or multi-dimensional, and it can be binary, categorical, continuous, or a mixture of them. We prove that this framework offers an unbiased estimation of the treatment effect under standard assumptions.
- Compared to previous causal inference work, the proposed approach is more robust and highly flexible with minimal manual tuning. Our tree-based approach automatically determines the important tuning parameters that were chosen arbitrarily in the traditional causal inference methods in a nonparametric way. In addition, it is easy to implement and computationally efficient for large scale online data.
- The tree-based framework is further wrapped in a bagging (boostrapping) procedure to enhance the stability and improve the performance of the final estimator. More importantly, our bagged strategy provides with statistical inference of the obtained point estimators, where the confidence intervals of the estimated treatment effects could be established for hypothesis testing purpose.

We apply the framework to an online advertising campaign and a cross-platform campaign that involves both TV and online platforms, and provide practical guideline to assess advertising strategy on one or more platforms. Our extensive experiments provide the causal impact of ad with different frequencies from one or more platforms, and further show that the ad frequency usually has a treatment effect cap that could have been over-estimated by naive estimations. Hence it is important for the ad providers to make appropriate adjustment for the number of the ads delivered to the users.

Our framework is not limited to online advertising, but is also applicable to other tasks (e.g., social science, and user engagement studies) where causal impact of general treatments (e.g., UI design, content format, ad context, and etc.) needs to be measured with observational data.

2. METHODOLOGY

In this section we briefly review the causal inference theory [21], and then propose our tree-based causal inference framework.

We define the set of potential treatment values to be $\mathcal{T}$, and hence each value $\mathbf{t} \in \mathcal{T}$ indicates a specific treatment, which can be uni- or multi-dimentional. For a specific user, the treatment is a random variable $\mathbf{T}$, which is supported on $\mathcal{T}$. Similarly we define the potential outcome associated with a specific treatment $\mathbf{t}$ as $Y(\mathbf{t})$, which is the random variable mapping the given treatment $\mathbf{t}$ to a potential outcome supported on the set of potential outcomes $\mathcal{Y}$. Since the treatment can be uni- or multi-dimensional, we use the boldface $\mathbf{T}$ and $\mathbf{t}$ to indicate a multivariate treatment variable and T and t to indicate a univariate treatment variable. In this paper, all the methodologies designed for multivariate treatment $\mathbf{T}$ may also be applied to univariate treatment T. In the binary treatment case, $\mathcal{T} = \{0, 1\}$ with 1 indicates, for example, ad exposure and 0 indicates no ad exposure. In general, $\mathcal{T}$ could be multivariate and of a mixture of categorical and continuous variables. Typically, one would like to evaluate the effect of treatment $\mathbf{t}$ on the outcome Y, removing the confounding effect of $\mathbf{X}$.

For each user, indexed by $i = 1, 2, ..., N$, we observe a vector of pretreatment covariates (i.e., user characteristics) $\mathbf{X}_i$ of length p, a treatment $\mathbf{T}_i$, and an univariate outcome Y_i (e.g., purchase indicator) corresponding to the treatment received.

2.1 Primer for Causal Inference

In the causal inference framework for treatment impact measurement, two standard assumptions are usually made in order to unbiasedly evaluate the effect of the treatment [21, 30].

Assumption 1: Stable unit treatment value assumption. "The potential outcome for one unit should be unaffected by the particular assignment of treatments to the other units" [12]. This assumption allows us to model the outcome of one subject independent of another subject's treatment status, given the covariates.

Assumption 2: Strong ignorability of treatment assignment (also called 'Unconfoundedness'). Given the covariates $\mathbf{X}$, the distribution of treatment assignment $\mathbf{T}$ is independent of the potential outcome $Y(\mathbf{t})$ for all $\mathbf{t} \in \mathcal{T}$. This assumption allows us to model the treatment with respect to the covariates, independent of the outcome. It means all the user characteristics that are related to both the treatment assignment and the outcome have been collected.

When making causal inference, the primary interest is the distribution $p(Y(\mathbf{t})|\mathbf{X})$ for each $\mathbf{t} \in \mathcal{T}$ and fixed $\mathbf{X}$, or its average over the population $p(Y(\mathbf{t})) = \int_X p(Y(\mathbf{t})|\mathbf{X})p(\mathbf{X})d\mathbf{X}$. Due to the fact that in observational studies we observe only one of the potential outcome $Y(\mathbf{T} = \mathbf{t}) \in \mathcal{Y}$ for each $\mathbf{t} \in \mathcal{T}$, we must condition on the observed treatment assignment in order to obtain $p(Y(\mathbf{t}))$. As pointed out in [21], a solution is to condition on the observed covariates. According to Assumption 2, we have $p(Y(\mathbf{t})|\mathbf{T}=\mathbf{t},\mathbf{X}) = p(\mathbf{T}=\mathbf{t}|Y(\mathbf{t}),\mathbf{X})p(Y(\mathbf{t})|\mathbf{X})/p(\mathbf{T}=\mathbf{t}|\mathbf{X}) = p(Y(\mathbf{t})|\mathbf{X})$, and hence

$$p(Y(\mathbf{t})) = \int_{\mathbf{X}} p(Y(\mathbf{t})|\mathbf{T}=\mathbf{t},\mathbf{X})p(\mathbf{X})d\mathbf{X}. \quad (1)$$

In principle, one can model $p(Y(\mathbf{t})|\mathbf{T}=\mathbf{t},\mathbf{X})$ directly, but experience shows that the result can be strongly biased if the relationship between $\mathbf{T}$ and $\mathbf{X}$ is omitted or mis-specified [21]. When the observed covariates $\mathbf{X}$ is low-dimensional, one way to avoid this bias is to classify subjects according to $\mathbf{X}$ and estimate (1) via the weighted average over $\mathbf{X}$. However as the dimension of $\mathbf{X}$ increases, exact sub-classification according to covariates becomes computationally infeasible.

To address the high-dimensionality issue of $\mathbf{X}$, Rosenbaum and Rubin [30] introduced the balancing score to summarize the information required to balance the distribution of covariates and proposed the propensity score method for the binary treatment problem. The balancing score is the random variable such that conditioned on it, the observed covariates and the treatment assignment are independent. By sub-classifying the balancing score, we can obtain a valid causal inference of the treatment effect. The basic algorithm is summarized in Table 1. Later on, Imai and van Dyk [21] introduced the propensity function to generalize the propensity score method to general treatments. Specifically, the propensity function $e(\mathbf{X})$ is defined as the conditional density of the treatment given the observed covariates, i.e., $e(\mathbf{X}) = p(\mathbf{T}|\mathbf{X})$. It was shown that this propensity function is a balancing score, that is, $p(\mathbf{T}|\mathbf{X}) = p(\mathbf{T}|e(\mathbf{X}))$. Hence we can obtain $p(Y(\mathbf{t}))$ in (1) as

$$p(Y(\mathbf{t})) = \int_{e(\mathbf{X})} p(Y(\mathbf{t})|\mathbf{T}=\mathbf{t},e(\mathbf{X}))p(e(\mathbf{X}))de(\mathbf{X}). \quad (2)$$

To compute the integral in (2), Imai and van Dyk [21] assumed that there existed a unique finite-dimensional parameter θ such that the propensity function $e(\mathbf{X})$ depended on $\mathbf{X}$ only through $\theta(\mathbf{X})$. For example, when the conditional distribution of $\mathbf{T}|\mathbf{X} \sim \mathrm{N}(\mathbf{X}^T\beta,\Sigma)$ with some parameter β, the propensity function $e(\mathbf{X})$ is the Gaussian density function which can be fully characterized by $\theta(\mathbf{X}) = \mathbf{X}^T\beta$. In this case, θ is also a balancing score, and hence we can obtain $p(Y(\mathbf{t}))$ in (2) as

$$p(Y(\mathbf{t})) = \int_{\theta} p(Y(\mathbf{t})|\mathbf{T}=\mathbf{t},\theta)p(\theta)d\theta. \quad (3)$$

This integral can be approximated by classifying the subjects into several sub-classes with similar value of θ, estimate the treatment effect within each sub-class, and then average the estimators from each sub-class. Usually θ has a much smaller dimension than X, hence this strategy tackles the high dimensionality issue of the covariates in (1) [21].

Table 1: Algorithm of Propensity Score Method with Sub-classification

Input:	Y_i, $\mathbf{X}_i$, treatment T_i for $i = 1,2,...N$.
Output:	Estimated treatment effect for t.
Step 1:	Find a balancing score B_i for each subject such that $T_i \perp \mathbf{X}_i|B_i$.
Step 2:	Sub-classify the subjects with similar balance score B_i into S sub-classes.
Step 3:	Within each sub-class s, calculate the number of subjects N_s and estimate the treatment effect $R_s(t)$ for each treatment t.
Step 4:	Estimate the population treatment effect as a weighted average of $R_s(t)$, where the weight is proportional to N_s.

2.2 Robust Tree-Based Causal Inference

The approach in (3) is vulnerable to the model misspecification when assuming the parametric form of $\mathbf{T}|\mathbf{X}$, and the final treatment effect estimation is sensitive to the number of sub-classes and the strategy of sub-classification [19]. A larger number of sub-classes leads to a more accurate estimation of the integral in (3) but inevitably implies a less accurate estimation of the inner conditional distribution $p(Y(\mathbf{t})|\mathbf{T}=\mathbf{t},\theta)$ due to limited observations in each sub-class. Furthermore, although equal-frequency strategy is generally used to form the sub-classes [21, 32], experiments showed that this strategy often leads to highly unable estimators for the extreme sub-classes [19]. Therefore, it is in great demand to introduce a model free method which can avoid the choice of the number of sub-classes and the strategy of sub-classification. To overcome the aforementioned issues, we propose a tree-based causal inference method for general treatment problem.

Recall that we can obtain the unbiased estimation of treatment effect by (2). Naturally we can approximate this integral by classifying the subjects into several sub-classes with similar value of $e(\mathbf{X})$, and then average the estimators from each sub-class. We utilize the tree structure to model $e(\mathbf{X})$ nonparametrically and classify the users automatically (Section 2.2.2). The number of sub-classes is also determined by the tree model, and hence we avoid arbitrary selection of the number of sub-classes. Compared to the previous methods, the tree-based model is a nonparametric approach, which requires fewer assumptions. We also propose a bootstrapping aggregated approach to further boost the performance (Section 2.2.2).

2.2.1 *Tree-Based Causal Inference*

As discussed above, the unbiased treatment estimation $p(Y(\mathbf{t})) = \int_{e(\mathbf{X})} p(Y(\mathbf{t})|\mathbf{T}=\mathbf{t},e(\mathbf{X}))p(e(\mathbf{X}))de(\mathbf{X})$ can be approximated by classifying users with similar $e(X)$, and then one can obtain unbiased estimation of the treatment effect with each sub-class. The tree-based structure naturally partitions the given predictor space into disjoint groups, and hence is ideal to automize the classification and the rest of the causal inference calculation.

Specifically, we hereby adopt a tree-structure on modeling $p(\mathbf{T}|\mathbf{X})$ with the treatment $\mathbf{T}$ as the dependent variable and the covariates $\mathbf{X}$ as the independent variables, which builds the tree in the way that the distribution of treatment becomes homogeneous within each partitioned sub-class. In other words, through tree-based method, we automatically obtain the benefit of the two-step sub-classification method (Table 1), which first models $\mathbf{T}|\mathbf{X}$ to find a balancing score and then partitions the subjects based on the value of the balancing score.

We then estimate the treatment effect within each leaf node, and take the weighted average across all the leaf nodes as the final estimation. The detailed algorithm is described in Table 2. In Figure 8 and Table 7 of Section 4.2, we employ an example to illustrate each step of this algorithm.

Table 2: Algorithm of (Single) Tree-Based Model

Input:	Y_i, $\mathbf{X}_i$, treatment $\mathbf{T}_i$ for $i = 1,2,...N$.
Output:	Estimated treatment effect for $\mathbf{t}$.
Step 1:	Fit a tree-based model with dependent variable $\mathbf{T}_i$ and independent variable $\mathbf{X}_i$.
Step 2:	Within each leaf node s, calculate the number of subjects N_s and estimate the treatment effect $R_s(\mathbf{t})$ for each treatment $\mathbf{t}$.
Step 3:	Calculate the final treatment effect as in (4).

Note that the method to estimate the treatment effect R_s in step 2 may vary with great flexibility. For example, when the treatment $\mathbf{T}$ is discrete, a straightforward nonparametric way to estimate the treatment effect in each node s is to compute the average of outcome Y corresponding to various treatments $\mathbf{T}$, and then subtract the averaged outcome of a baseline treatment. For instance, for a bivariate and binary treatment $\mathbf{T} = (T_1, T_2)^T$ with $(T_1, T_2) \in \{0, 1\}^2$, within each node s, we can estimate the effect of treatment $\mathbf{t}$ as $R_s(\mathbf{t}) = \bar{Y}(\mathbf{t}) - \bar{Y}(\mathbf{t}_0)$ with $\mathbf{t}_0 = (0, 0)^T$ as the baseline treatment, where $\bar{Y}(\cdot)$ refers to the averaged outcome. When the treatment $\mathbf{T}$ is continuous, one could choose to fit any proper nonparametric or parametric model for $Y|(\mathbf{T}, \mathbf{X})$ within each sub-class s. The choice of the specific model to fit within leaf node s is not the focus of this paper, but our algorithm is flexible that any proper model can be utilized.

Under the two standard assumptions as in Section 2.1, we prove that the proposed tree-based causal inference estimation is unbiased.

THEOREM 1. *Under Assumptions 1-2 and the condition that the subjects in each leaf node have a homogeneous density of* $\mathbf{T}$, *the effect of treatment* $\mathbf{t}$ *is equal to the expected outcome corresponding to treatment* $\mathbf{t}$ *averaged over the leaf node in the proposed tree-based method.*

Proof of Theorem 1: The condition that in each leaf node the subjects have a homogeneous density of $\mathbf{T}$ implies that conditioning on the leaf node is equivalent to conditioning on $e(\mathbf{X}) = p(\mathbf{T}|\mathbf{X})$. Therefore, the treatment effect induced from the proposed algorithm is $E_{e(\mathbf{X})}\{E[Y(\mathbf{t})|\mathbf{T} = \mathbf{t}, e(\mathbf{X})]\}$ for any given treatment $\mathbf{t}$. Next we will show that this equals $E[Y(\mathbf{t})]$. According to the assumptions 1-2 and the fact that $e(\mathbf{X})$ is a balancing score, we have

$$p(Y(\mathbf{t}), \mathbf{T}, \mathbf{X}|e(\mathbf{X})) = p(Y(\mathbf{t}), \mathbf{X}|e(\mathbf{X}))p(\mathbf{T}|e(\mathbf{X})).$$

Integrating both sides with respect to $\mathbf{X}$ leads to the conclusion that $Y(\mathbf{t}) \perp\!\!\!\perp \mathbf{T}|e(\mathbf{X})$. Therefore, for any $\mathbf{t} \in \mathcal{T}$, we have $E[Y(\mathbf{t})] = E_{e(\mathbf{X})}\{E[Y(\mathbf{t})|e(\mathbf{X})]\} = E_{e(\mathbf{X})}\{E[Y(\mathbf{t})|\mathbf{T} = \mathbf{t}, e(\mathbf{X})]\}$. This ends the proof of Theorem 1. ∎

We comment that the assumption of a homogeneous density of $\mathbf{T}$ within each leaf node is standard. Similar condition has also been imposed in Theorem 5 of [36]. An intuitive explanation is that the tree automatically seeks the partition such that the predictor space is the most separable and hence the distribution of $\mathbf{T}$ gets more and more homogeneous within each leaf node as the tree grows [36].

In our algorithm, we follow the CART [7] guideline to construct the single tree in Step 1 of Table 2. The tuning parameters are chosen based on a 10-fold cross validation. After the tree construction, within each leaf node s, we estimate $R_s(\mathbf{t})$ and then estimate the final averaged treatment effect (ATE) as

$$\widehat{\text{ATE}} = \sum_s \frac{N_s}{N}\{R_s(\mathbf{t}) - R_s(\mathbf{t}_0)\}, \tag{4}$$

where $\mathbf{t}_0$ is the baseline treatment.

2.2.2 Bagged Tree-Based Causal Inference

A single tree suffers from the instability issue since a small perturbation to the samples may lead to tremendous changes in the constructed tree [7]. The bootstrap aggregating (bagging) introduced by Breiman [6] is frequently applied to enhance the performance of non-robust methods by reducing the variance of a predictor . We here adopt the bagging strategy to improve the robustness of our framework.

In the bagged tree-based causal inference, we repeatedly generate bootstrap samples (i.e., a set of random samples drawn with replacement from the dataset), estimate the treatment effect based on the samples, and calculate the final results by averaging the results from the bootstrap sample sets at the end. The detailed implementation is in Table 3. The theoretical justification of this bagged tree-based causal inference model is due to the unbiased estimation of single tree-based method in Theorem 1 and the consistency of the bagging method for CART shown by Bühlmann and Yu [8].

Table 3: Algorithm of Bagged Tree-Based Model

Input:	Y_i, $\mathbf{X}_i$, treatment $\mathbf{T}_i$ for $i = 1, 2, ...N$.
Output:	Estimated treatment effect for $\mathbf{t}$.
Step 1:	Construct a bootstrap sample $\mathcal{D}^*$ according to the empirical distribution of the observations.
Step 2:	Compute the bootstrapped treatment effect estimator $\widehat{\text{ATE}}^*$ based on $\mathcal{D}^*$ via Table 2.
Step 3:	Repeat Steps 1-2 B times and output the final estimator $\widehat{\text{ATE}}_\text{B}$ in (5) and SD in (6).

Note that our bagged causal inference model is able to establish the confidence interval of the estimated treatment effect. In Step 3 of Table 3, we can calculate the bootstrapped mean $\widehat{\text{ATE}}_\text{B}$ and standard deviation SD of $\widehat{\text{ATE}}_\text{B}$ according to B bootstrapped treatment effect estimators in Step 2. Specifically,

$$\widehat{\text{ATE}}_\text{B} = \frac{1}{B}\sum_{b=1}^{B} \widehat{\text{ATE}}^{*(b)}, \tag{5}$$

$$\text{SD} = \frac{1}{\sqrt{B}}\left(\frac{1}{B-1}\sum_{b=1}^{B}\left(\widehat{\text{ATE}}^{*(b)} - \widehat{\text{ATE}}_\text{B}\right)^2\right)^{1/2}, \tag{6}$$

where b is the bootstrap sample set index. If the bootstrapped estimators follow a normal distribution, we can obtain the 95% confidence interval of ATE as $(\widehat{\text{ATE}}_\text{B} - 1.96 * \text{SD}, \widehat{\text{ATE}}_\text{B} + 1.96 * \text{SD})$. Otherwise, the middle 95% quantile of $\widehat{\text{ATE}}^{*(1)}, \ldots, \widehat{\text{ATE}}^{*(B)}$ could be used.

Another advantage of the bagged model is that flexible subsampling strategies can be incorporated into robust causal inference framework, which is useful, even necessary when addressing some practical problems. For instance, modern online ad datasets typically suffer from the severely imbalanced outcome, e.g., most users are not exposed to any ad. Our robust causal inference framework is able to employ the subsampling and backscaling strategy as described in [38]. Specifically, in the subsampling step, we sample the exposed users with a higher probability than the non-exposed users and estimate the treatment effect via our framework based on the sample dataset. The success rates calculated from the subsamples are then back-scaled to the whole population level according to the sampling rates. This method has been examined carefully in [38] and shown to achieve substantial improvement of out-of-sample predictions.

2.2.3 Summary

The utilization of the tree-based structures fully automizes the causal inference pipeline in a nonparametric way without prespecified assumptions for outcome or treatment models, and the bagging further improves the robustness. To sum up, we visualize the approach with the following roadmap:

1. In order to obtain a valid causal inference of the treatment, we need to account for the confounding impact of user features (Figure 1).
2. Employ a tree model to estimate the propensity function (Figure 2). The tree model automatically classifies the users into groups within which the distribution of treatment is homogeneous.
3. Conditioned on each propensity function, the treatment and user features are independent. Therefore, within each tree leaf node, the impact of the treatment on the outcome is the real treatment effect (Figure 3). We then estimate the population-level treatment effect by a weighted average of the estimators from each leaf node.

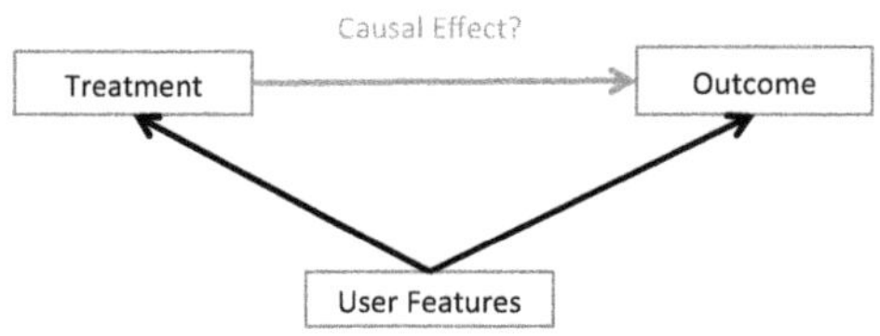

Figure 1: Confounding effect of user features.

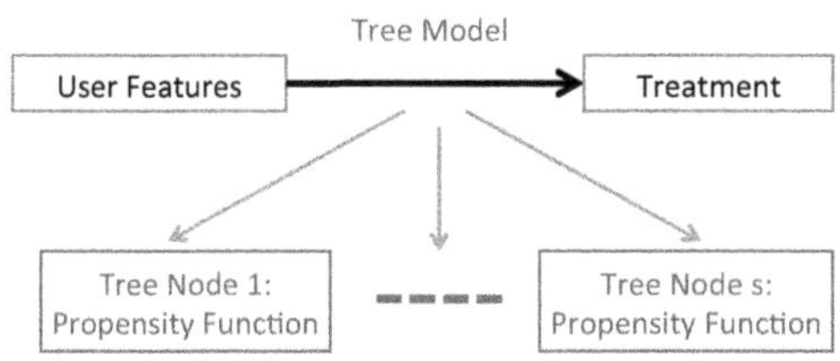

Figure 2: Estimate the propensity function via the proposed tree model.

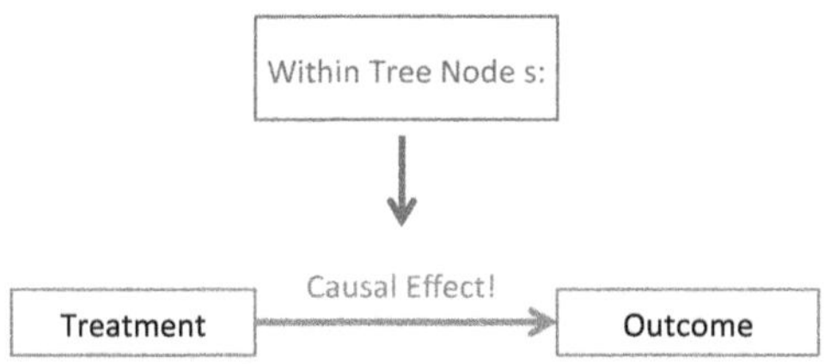

Figure 3: Obtain causal effect by conditioning on the propensity function estimated from each tree leaf node.

3. SIMULATION STUDY

To better understand our framework, we use two simulated examples to asses our tree-based causal inference framework and compare it with direct modeling methods. The simulation results show that, when there are confounding covariates contributed to both treatment assignments and outcome, which is common in observational studies, direct modeling methods without propensity function adjustment lead to severe biases, while our tree-based framework shows no significant biases and significantly improves the accuracy and robustness of the treatment impact measurement.

3.1 Without Treatment Effect

In the first simulation, the treatments have no causal effect on the outcome and the superficial correlation between treatments and outcome is due to the confounding effects of the covariates.

We set the 5-dimensional covariate $\mathbf{X}$ as the exponential values of five randomly generated standard normal variables. This generation mimics our real data where the covariates are all nonnegative. We then generate two binary treatments T_1, T_2 and a binary outcome Y. This process is summarized as follows.

$$\mathbf{Z} = (Z_1, \ldots, Z_5)^T \sim N_5(0, \mathrm{I});$$
$$\mathbf{X} = \exp(\mathbf{Z});$$
$$T_j \sim \text{Bernoulli}(\pi_j) \text{ with } \text{logit}(\pi_j) = \beta_j^T \mathbf{X} \text{ for } j = 1, 2;$$
$$Y \sim \text{Bernoulli}(\pi_y) \text{ with } \text{logit}(\pi_y) = \beta_y^T \mathbf{X}.$$

We set the coefficients $\beta_1 = (1, -1, -1, -1, 1)$, $\beta_2 = (1, 0, -1, -1, 1)$, and $\beta_y = (1, -1, -1, -1, 0)$. We choose these coefficients to ensure that the outcome is roughly balanced. In the above simulation, the treatment $\mathbf{T}$ is not involved in the generation of Y and there is no treatment effect. The sample size is fixed as $n = 1000$.

Table 4: Percentages of mistakenly considering the coefficients of treatments to be different than 0. "T1" and "T2" refer to the treatment T_1 and treatment T_2, respectively, and "either" means either the effect of treatment T_1 or that of treatment T_2 is overestimated.

Model A			Model B		
T1	T2	Either	T1	T2	Either
11%	9%	20 %	0	0	0

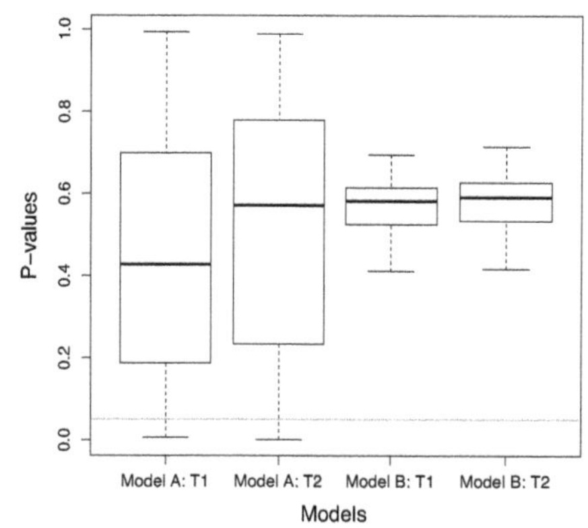

Figure 4: P-values for the coefficients of treatments. "Model A: T1" ("Model A: T2") corresponds to the effect of treatment T_1 (T_2) in Model A. Similar meanings are used for Model B. When the p-value is less than 0.05 (red line), the corresponding estimated treatment effect is significantly different from 0.

We compare the direct modeling method and the proposed tree-based method in fitting the simulation dataset.

1) **Model A: Direct Modeling.** A linear logistic regression with dependent variable Y and independent variables $(\mathbf{T}, \mathbf{X})$. The treatment impact is measured as the fitted coefficient of $\mathbf{T}$.

2) **Model B: Our Proposed Model.** The proposed tree-based method in Table 2. In step 3 of Table 2, within each mode s, we fit a linear logistic regression for Y with independent variables $(\mathbf{T}, \mathbf{X})$. The treatment impact is captured by the averaged coefficients of $\mathbf{T}$ over all nodes.

We repeat the above generation and inference process 100 times, and record the number of times that these two methods mistakenly consider the coefficients of $\mathbf{T}$ to be significantly different than 0 under the 95% confidence level. Recall that the true causal impacts of both treatments are 0. However, as shown in Table 4, the direct modeling approach (Model A) incorrectly discovers the causal impact of either treatment 20% of the times. On the other hand, our approach (Model A) always correctly finds that the treatment impact is not significantly different than 0. This illustrates the advantage of our model.

Next we plot the p-values of the fitted coefficients for treatments T_1 and T_2 in Figure 4. Note that the true coefficients for both treatments are not significantly different from 0 and ideally the p-values should be larger than 0.05. As shown in Figure 4, Model A overestimates the treatment effect as some of their p-values are very small. Furthermore, it produces a very unstable p-values over the 100 replicates, which hinders its applicability in practice. In contrast, Model B delivers very stable and accurate inference results.

Finally, we demonstrate the covariance balance performance of our tree-based algorithm. Figure 5 plots the absolute values of the correlations between each treatment and each of the covariates in Model A and Model B. Due to the propensity function adjustment, our Model B shows a considerable reduction in the correlation over Model A. This illustrates why our causal inference model improves the performance over the directly modeling methods.

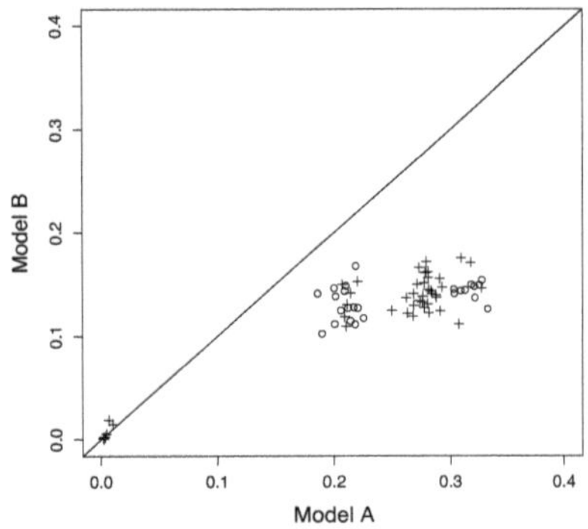

Figure 5: Correlations between two treatments and the covariates in Model A and Model B. The circle (cross) indicates the correlation with treatment T_1 (T_2). Results are from 5 replications.

3.2 With Treatment Effect

In the second simulation, both treatments have real causal effects on the outcome. Specifically, we generate data as follows.

$$X_1, X_2, X_3, X_4, X_5 \overset{iid}{\sim} U[0,1];$$
$$T_1 \sim \text{Bernoulli}(\pi_1) \text{ with } \text{logit}(\pi_1) = 1 - X_1 - X_2;$$
$$T_2 \sim \text{Bernoulli}(\pi_2) \text{ with } \text{logit}(\pi_2) = 1 - 2X_2 - 2X_3;$$
$$Y \sim \text{Bernoulli}(\pi_y) \text{ with } \text{logit}(\pi_y) =$$
$$-2 + 2T_1 - 2T_2 + 2X_1 - 2X_2 + 2X_3 - 2T_1X_3 + 2T_2X_4.$$

In this example, covariates X_1, X_2, X_3 are confounders that affect both treatment $\mathbf{T}$ and outcome Y, covariate X_4 is an causal effect modifier, and X_5 is a totally irrelevant feature.

In this 2-dimensional treatment example, the true effect of treatment T_j is $\text{E}[Y(\mathbf{t}_j)] - \text{E}[Y(\mathbf{t}_0)]$ with $\mathbf{t}_1 = (1,0)^T$, $\mathbf{t}_2 = (0,1)^T$, and $\mathbf{t}_0 = (0,0)^T$. Simple calculation implies that the true treatment effects of T_1 and T_2 are 0.196 and -0.138, respectively.

We compare two direct modeling methods (Models 1-2 below) and the proposed tree-based methods (Models 3-4 below) as well as their bagged versions (Models 5-6 below).

1) **Model 1**: a naive approach which estimates the treatment effect of T_j as $\bar{Y}(\mathbf{t}_j) - \bar{Y}(\mathbf{t}_0)$ for $j = 1,2$.

2) **Model 2**: a linear logistic regression with dependent variable Y and independent variables $(\mathbf{T}, \mathbf{X})$.

3) **Model 3**: the proposed tree-based method in Table 2. In step 3 of Table 2, within each leaf node s, we estimate the treatment effect of T_j as $\bar{Y}(\mathbf{t}_j) - \bar{Y}(\mathbf{t}_0)$ for $j = 1,2$.

4) **Model 4**: the proposed tree-based method in Table 2. In step 3 of Table 2, within each leaf node s, we fit a linear logistic regression for Y with independent variables $(\mathbf{T}, \mathbf{X})$.

5) **Model 5**: the bagged version of **Model 3**.

6) **Model 6**: the bagged version of **Model 4**.

To measure the accuracy of the treatment effect estimators, we compute the absolute difference of the true treatment effect and the estimated treatment effect of above models. In Figure 6, we report the sum of errors of both treatments for each model over 100 replications. The standard deviation bar of the errors are also shown. As demonstrated in Figure 6, our Model 6 achieves the minimal error and our tree-based models outperform their counterparts without propensity function adjustment. Specifically, for the naive treatment estimation methods, Model 1 has the largest error. After tree-based propensity function adjustment, Model 3 improves the estimation accuracy and Model 5 further improves the accuracy via bagging. For the logistic modeling method, Model 6 outperforms the tree-based logistic method Model 4, while the latter greatly improves the direct logistic method Model 2. To sum up, the tree-based methods significantly reduce the errors in treatment effect estimation of the direct methods, and the bagged versions help to further enhance the performance.

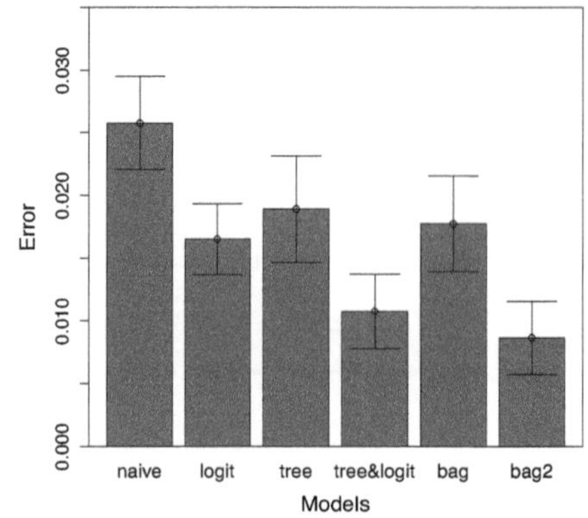

Figure 6: Errors of treatment effect estimation in Section 3.2. In the X-axis, "naive", "logit", "tree", "tree&logit", "bag", and "bag2" refer to Models 1-6, respectively.

4. REAL APPLICATIONS

In this section we apply the proposed framework on two real campaigns. The first campaign is from a major telecommunication company, where we measure the impact of ads with different frequencies. Hence the treatment is a one-dimensional scalar (Section 4.1). The second campaign is from a major auto insurance company and involves multiple ad exposure across TV and online platforms (Section 4.2). We measure the frequency impact of the ads from both platforms, as well as the synthetic impact of the two platforms. In both campaigns, the success action is defined as an online quote.

Note that our framework applies to general ad treatments. The two applications serve as examples to show the efficacy of the methodology, and there is not obvious obstacle to apply the framework to measure treatments including other factors of ad strategies.

4.1 Single Treatment Study

This dataset contains about 0.7 millions users (0.5 million non-exposed users and 0.2 million exposed users) collected during a 3-day campaign[3]. The overall success rate, i.e., the percentage of users making a success action, is about 2.4%. In this example, the ad treatment is the frequency of ad exposures, which is continuous and one-dimensional. The maximal number of ad frequency is 331, while 95% of the frequency are less than 17. This data contains 1010 user features, including the demographic information, online activities, and ad exposure information. Among these features, some are potential confounding variables related to both treatment and outcome. For example, a user with more active online behaviors tends to see more ads and simultaneously has a larger chance to make a success action. In this application, we aim to measure the causal impact of ad exposure frequency, removing the bias due to user characteristics.

To illustrate how our tree model builds a homogeneous treatment density within each node, we compare the variance of the treatment

[3]The reported dataset and results are deliberately incomplete and subject to anonymization, and thus do not necessarily reflect the real portfolio at any particular time.

before and after the tree adjustment. In the original dataset, the variance of the treatment is 110.14. After utilizing our tree model, the weighted variance reduces to 79.08, which has a 28% improvement over the original variance.

We next illustrate the frequency impact on the success rates. According to the algorithm in Section 2, within each leaf node, there could be various ways to estimate the treatment impact via controlling the confounding effect of the covariates on treatments. This choice of modeling method within each node is not the focus of this paper. In this section, for illustration purpose, we utilized a straight-forward estimation method. Specifically, we compare 1) a naive approach which computes the plain success rates corresponding to the various ad frequencies and 2) an adjusted approach via our tree-based causal inference model where the corresponding success rates are computed within each node and then averaged with weights proportional to the node sizes as in (4).

The naive and adjusted estimators of the treatment impact are shown in Figure 7. The general trend of the naive estimation indicates that success rate increases as the number of ad exposure increases. However, interestingly, our method suggests that the success rate increases at the beginning, then decreases, and finally stabilizes. Specifically, the maximal success rate (0.055) is obtained when the users are shown 12 ads, and then success rate stabilizes around 0.045. This agrees with the findings in [24] that ad frequency has nearly linear increasing effect at the beginning and has nearly constant effect for users eligible to see more ads. The one standard deviation bar shows that the maximal success rate at 12 ads is significant larger than others, where the standard deviations get larger as the ad frequency increases due to less samples. To sum up, our result advises that 12 ads are sufficient to maximize the success rate in this campaign and there is little demand for this telecommunication company to deliver more than 12 ads to the eligible users.

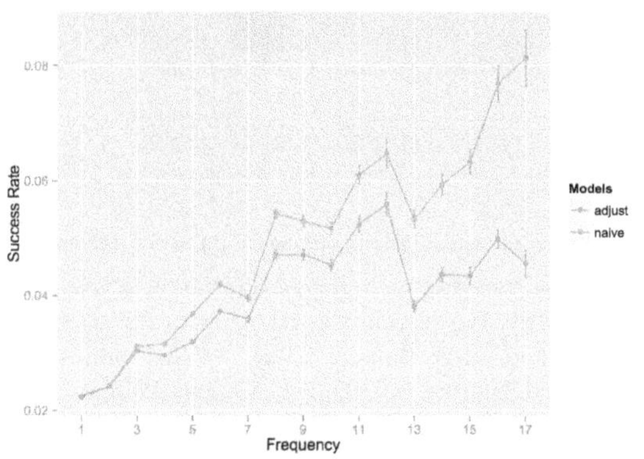

Figure 7: Success rates and their corresponding one standard deviation bars of the naive and adjusted models. X-axis is the frequency of ad exposure.

4.2 Cross-Platform Study

In the cross-platform study from an auto insurance company, the treatment is a two-dimensional vector, containing the numbers of ad exposures from TV and online platform, separately. We measure the impact of TV and online ads together, and hence address the synthetic impact of ad exposure from both platforms.

The dataset contains about 37 million users with 23 million non-exposed users and 14 million exposed users during a 30-day campaign. The original data are extremely imbalanced since the success rates are only 0.204% in the non-exposed group and 0.336% in the exposed group. To deal with this imbalance issue, we employ the subsampling and backscaling proposal in Section 2.2.2, based on which the success rates of non-exposed group and exposed group in the sample increase to 16.9% and 16.7%, respectively. The summary statistics of the original dataset and one sample are shown in Tables 5.

Table 5: Sizes of all online-tv data and one of its sample. "success" or "no success" refers to the size of users who make or do not make a success action, respectively. "M" refers to million.

	Non-exposed		Exposed		Total
	Success	No Success	Success	No Success	
All	46472	23 M	48082	14 M	37 M
Sample	1784	8757	1189	3270	15000

The features include the demographic information, personal interest, and online and TV activities. A sample of the features and their corresponding values are shown in Table 6 for illustration. Specifically, the demographic information consists of the user's gender, age, etc.; the personal interest measures how a user is interested in a specific category, e.g., auto; the online activity captures how often a user visits a particular website and the ad exposures to other companies; and the TV activity collects the TV watching information and the TV ad exposures. In this campaign, there are 2542 features in total.

Table 6: Sample features in the cross-platform study

Feature	Value
Demographic Info and Interest	
Demographic | Gender I Male	0
Demographic | Gender I Female	1
Demographic| Age	27
...	
Interest | Celebrities	0.01
Interest | Auto I New	0.23
Interest | Auto I Used	0.65
...	
Online Network Activities	
Site Visitation | Finance	67.4
Site Visitation | Movies	1.3
Site Visitation | Sports	0.0
...	
Ad Impression | Auto I Company 1	7.24
Ad Impression | Insurance I Company 2	9.43
...	
TV Activities	
TV Program Viewership | Movies	2.5
TV Program Viewership | Sports	53.1
...	
TV Ad Impression	132.7
...	

To demonstrate each step of our algorithm in Table 2, we show a single tree fitted by treating the two-dimensional treatment as the dependent variable and the covariates as the independent variables in Figure 8. In this single tree, nodes 4, 5, 8, 9, 10, and 11 are the leaf nodes.

Within each leaf node in Figure 8, we calculate the success rates of non-exposed group and the exposed group for a given treatment, and hence the treatment effect is estimated as the difference of the two success rates. Then the population level treatment effect is estimated as the weighted average of the results from each node with weight proportional to the node sizes. We take the treatment with 1 tv ad exposure and 2 online ad exposures as an example to illustrate the estimation process. Table 7 shows the results in estimating its treatment effect.

To compare the results from naive estimation without propensity adjustment and the causal inference estimation with the proposed framework, we first show the naive estimator for the ad frequency impact by simply computing the averaged outcomes corresponding

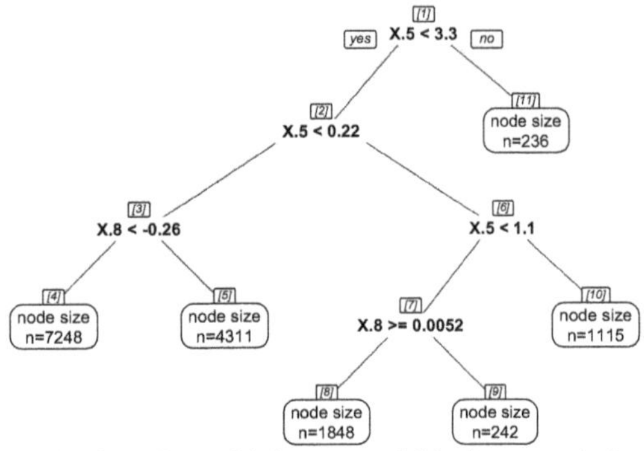

Figure 8: Tree of causal inference model in the cross-platform study.

Table 7: Treatment effect of the case with 1 tv ad exposure and 2 online ad exposure in the cross-platform study. The success rates, treatment effects (TE), and averaged treatment effect (ATE) are given in 10^{-3}.

Node Index	Size	Non-exposed Success Rate	Treatment Success Rate	TE	ATE
[4]	7248	1.14	3.84	2.70	
[5]	4311	0.85	1.45	0.60	
[8]	1848	0.56	0.66	0.10	1.86
[9]	242	0.42	0	−0.42	
[10]	1115	0.92	6.70	5.78	
[11]	236	3.32	0	−3.32	

to various treatments. We group both TV and online ad frequencies as 0, 1, 2, 3 ,4, 5, 6-10, and 11-15 buckets. We employ this grouping scheme since the frequency decreases sharply when it is larger than 5 and most of the frequency is less than 15. As shown in Figure 9, the naive estimator implies that the highest success rate is obtained when the users are shown 11-15 TV ads and 11-15 online ads. In addition, it shows that generally the ad effects get larger as the number of ad exposures increases for both TV and online platforms. However, we will show that this plausible conclusion is biased and the superficial treatment effect is affected by the confounding effect of the user features.

By controlling the confounding effects of the covariates, our tree-based casual inference estimator is able to generate an unbiased estimator. We employed our bagging tree-based algorithm with B=100 according to Table 3. As illustrated in Figure 10, the largest success rate is obtained when the users are shown 5 online ads and 5 TV ads. Furthermore, we find that the online ad effect is marginally larger than the TV ad by comparing the success rate of 0 TV ad exposure (first column in Figure 10) with that of 0 online ad exposure (first row in Figure 10). This suggests that users generally has a larger chance to conduct quotes on the insurance company website when they are shown online ads instead of the TV ads. Finally, similar to the discovery in Section 4.1, both the online and TV ad effects will increase to a maximal value and then decrease as the users are shown more ads. Therefore, it is crucial for the ad providers to make appropriate adjustment based on the number and type of the ads the users have been exposed to.

Furthermore, we employ the bootstrapping approach to estimate the standard deviation of the ATE estimator based on (6). Figure 11 shows the top five highest success rates as well as their corresponding one standard deviation bars. Clearly, the combination of 5 online ads and 5 TV ads is shown to achieve a significantly larger success rate than other combinations.

In order to illustrate the flexibility of our tree-based causal inference algorithm, in contrast to the above nonparametric method applied within each leaf node of the constructed tree, we fit a sparse logistic regression [18] with the success as the binary outcome, and the ad exposures from the two platforms and their interaction term as well as the user features as the independent variables. The tuning

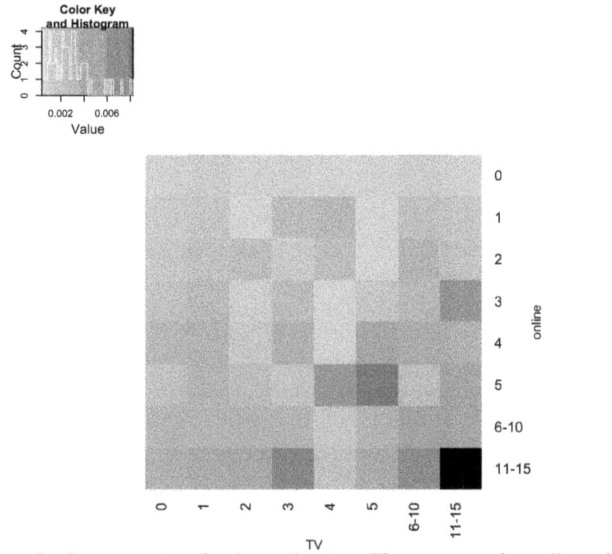

Figure 9: Success rates of naive estimator. The rows are the online ad frequency and the columns are the TV ad frequency

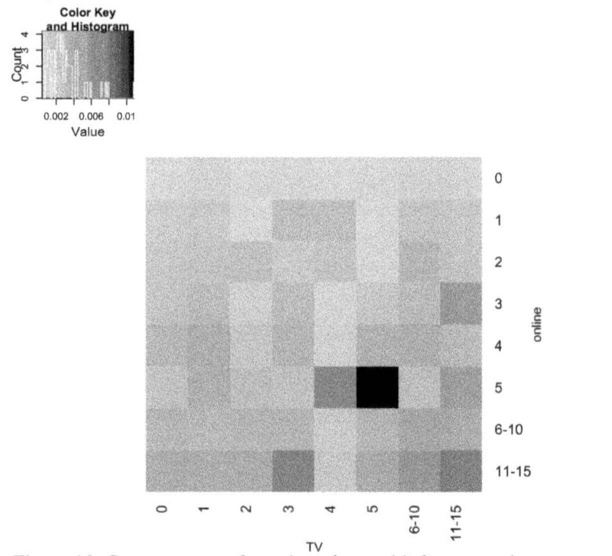

Figure 10: Success rates of tree-based causal inference estimator.

parameter λ in the sparse logistic regression model is selected via cross validation [16]. The causality coefficients of the ad exposure from online, TV and interaction are 0.066, −0.001, and −0.0001 with the standard deviations 0.0393, 0.0183, and 0.0005. This ensures that online ad exposure has relatively positive effect on the success rate while the TV ad exposure has no significant effect. Hence the treatment effect is dominated by the online ad exposures, which is consistent with our findings with the above nonparametric method.

4.3 Model Validation

We have proved that the proposed causal inference framework provides an unbiased estimation of the treatment effect in Section 2, and verified it with several simulations in Section 3. Here we further validate our tree-based causal inference model with the cross-platform analysis in Section 4.2 by showing the covariate balancing effect in real data. Following [21] we first normalized each covariate and then regress it on both the online and TV treatments via the Gaussian linear regression. We record the p-values corresponding to the t-statistics for the coefficients of the treatments in each regression. As shown in Figure 12, the lack of balance is evident in the original data since most of the coefficients of the TV

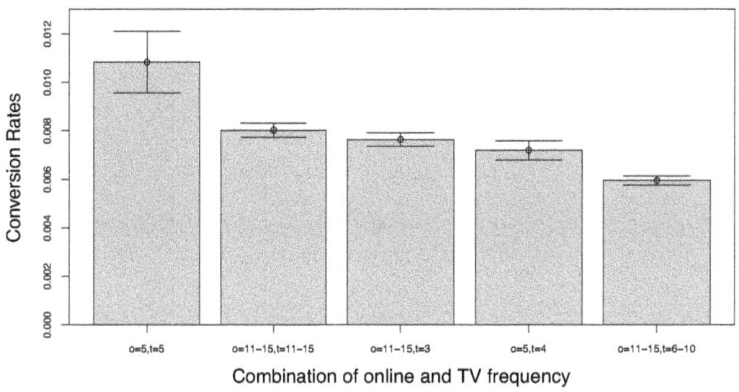

Figure 11: Top 5 success rates and their one standard deviation bars according to our tree-based causal inference estimator. In the X-axis, label "o=5,t=5" refers to the combination of 5 online ad exposures and 5 TV ad exposures. Similar meanings for other labels.

treatment (before: T_2) are significantly different from 0. Therefore, without controlling the balance of the covariates the direct modeling approaches may lead to severe biases in the treatment effect estimations [30]. After adjusting the propensity function via our tree-based method, the percentages of nonzero coefficients of the online and TV treatments reduce from 13.3%, 86.7% to 0 and 6.2%, respectively. Hence our approach successfully balances the covariates and leads to more accurate estimations.

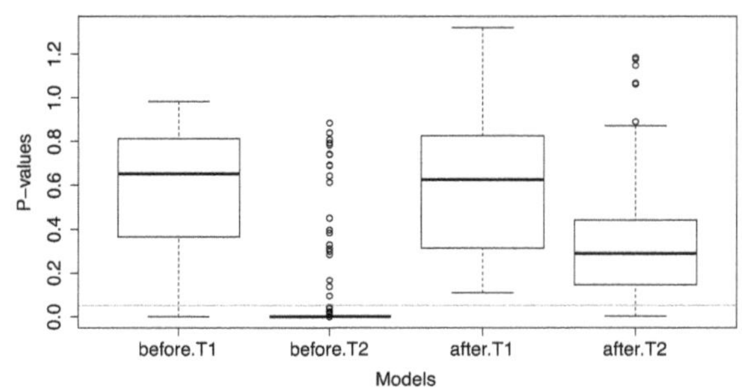

Figure 12: P-values of coefficients by regressing **X** on **T**. The red line is the baseline 0.05. "before.T1" ("before.T2") is the box plot of the p-values for the coefficient of online (TV) treatment before adjustment; "after.T1" ("after.T2") is the corresponding p-values after applying our tree-based model.

5. RELATED WORK

In this section we briefly review three folds of related work: 1) the experiment-based measurement, 2) the propensity-based causal inference that focuses on binary treatments, and 3) general treatment causal inference. The first line of work serves as the gold standard, but meets challenges in practice. We link the second and third lines of literatures with our work and reveal the novelty of our framework.

The experimental approach is the gold standard to estimate treatment effect. When the randomized experiments are available, various regression approaches by regressing the outcome on the treatments can be employed to compute the ad effectiveness from causality perspective (i.e., how the ad treatment causes changes in the outcomes) [3, 27]. However, in reality, the cost and difficulty of successfully performing fully randomized experiments are very high [10, 35], and some experiments may not even be feasible for complex treatments. To avoid the difficulties in experimental approaches, direct comparison and regression-based approaches have been utilized in observational studies. However, direct comparison of the outcomes from different treatment groups in the observational data can lead to severe overestimation of the effects of advertising [1, 27], and the regression-based approaches rely on the pre-specified functional form of the model and are vulnerable to model misspecification [29, 32, 34]. In addition, when the outcome is binary, prior research suggested that at least 8 events should be observed for every covariate in the regression model [9], which prevents its application in practice [2]. Therefore, an unbiased and flexible model is in demand in the observational study.

The causal inference methodologies are able to offer an unbiased estimation of the ad treatment effect from observational data and hence fundamentally overcome the disadvantages of experiments and direct observational studies. Most of the previous causal inference methodologies focus on binary or categorial treatments. The causal inference framework for the observational studies with a binary treatment was original proposed by Rosenbaum and Rubin [30]. They first introduced the concept of propensity score and the inverse propensity score weighting estimation method. This method is also generalized to multi-category treatments [31] and ordinal treatments [23, 28], which have been widespread in various fields, including health care [4], social science [26], politics [20], online behavior study [14]. In online advertising market, causal inference methods have been developed to estimate the causal effects of a binary treatment. For example, [10] applied the causal analysis to industrial advertising data of moderate size, [35] explored the benefits of estimating several other parameters of interest via the targeted maximum likelihood estimation, and [13] used causal inference for a multi-attribution problem. Yet, these methods were typically applied to single treatment case with small to medium user group and moderate success rates. Recently, [38] applied the inverse propensity weighting causal inference method for the large scale online advertising data. Nevertheless, their work mainly focused on the univariate treatment scenarios and was not well suited for general and complex treatment measurements. Besides propensity-based causal inference methodologies, structural equation model [5], inference based on decomposition of the joint distribution of the treatment and response variables [22, 11], and before-and-after studies [39] are also used for causal inference from different points of view.

To expand the scope of causal inference from a binary treatment to a general treatment, a propensity function-based framework is proposed [21]. However, in practice, it is a non-trivial task to estimate this propensity function and there is few investigation on how to choose the number of sub-classes in grouping the users with similar propensity functions. In reality, the treatment effect estimation could be sensitive to the choice of the sub-class size. Another causal inference framework is the causal inference tree (CIT) in the machine learning community [36]. It models both the treatment and outcome simultaneously with respect to the user characteristics by imposing a parametric assumption on the joint density of treatment and outcome.

Our tree-based causal inference framework is substantially different with all the previous work. Our framework is a nonparametric approach that does not require specific assumptions of the joint or separated density functions of ad treatment and outcome as in [36]. Furthermore, it automatically groups subjects (i.e., users in online advertising cases) within the same leaf node of the tree, and hence avoid the arbitrary specification of number of classes as in [21]. It is fully general and flexible that the treatment can be multi-dimensional combining discrete and/or continuous treatment factors, and it is computationally more efficient than regression-based propensity score methods. Most importantly, we prove that our treatment effect estimation is unbiased under weak assumptions.

6. CONCLUSION AND DISCUSSION

This paper proposes a robust tree-based causal inference framework for complex treatment measurement. Our framework utilizes the tree-based structure embedded in a bagging procedure to achieve efficient computation, flexible modeling, unbiased estimation and robust inference. It is able to provide practical guideline to assess advertising strategy. To show the efficacy of our framework, we apply it to two real world applications—an online advertising campaign and a cross-platform campaign. Our framework successfully provides the causal impact of ads with different frequencies and further shows that the ad frequency has a treatment effect cap, which is usually over-estimated by naive estimation. Hence it is important for the ad providers to make appropriate adjustment for ad frequency to reach optimal results.

In this paper, the proposed methodology solves the problem of general treatment measurement. However, in some extreme cases that the treatments and confounding features are both high-dimensional and sparse, and direct application of the methodology is computationally infeasible. For the future work, we would like to design a more sophisticated way for modeling $p(\mathbf{T}|\mathbf{X})$. Another interesting direction is to use the causal inference framework to online media layout optimization problem [37] and effectiveness measurement of user engagement strategies [15].

7. REFERENCES

[1] M. Abraham. The off-line impact of online ads. *Harvard Business Review*, 86(4): 28, 2008.

[2] P. Austin. An introduction to propensity score methods for reducing the effects of confounding in observational studies. *Multivariate Behavioral Research*, 46:399–424, 2011.

[3] J. Barajas, J. Kwon, R. Akella, A. Flores, M. Holtan, and V. Andrei. Marketing campaign evaluation in targeted display advertising. In *Proceedings of the Sixth International Workshop on Data Mining for Online Advertising and Internet Economy*, page 5. ACM, 2012.

[4] A. Basu, D. Polsky, and W. G. Manning. Use of propensity scores in non-linear response models: the case for health care expenditures. Technical report, National Bureau of Economic Research, 2008.

[5] L. Bottou, J. Peters, J. Quiñonero-Candela, D. X. Charles, D. M. Chickering, E. Portugaly, D. Ray, P. Simard, and E. Snelson. Counterfactual reasoning and learning systems: the example of computational advertising. *The Journal of Machine Learning Research*, 14(1):3207–3260, 2013.

[6] L. Breiman. Bagging predictors. *Machine Learning*, 24(2):123–140, 1996.

[7] L. Breiman, J. Friedman, C. J. Stone, and R. A. Olshen. *Classification and Regression Trees*. Chapman & Hall/CRC, 1984.

[8] P. Bühlmann and B. Yu. Analyzing bagging. *The Annals of Statistics*, 30(4):927–961, 2002.

[9] M. Cepeda, R. Boston, J. Farrar, and B. Strom. Comparison of logistic regression versus propensity score when the number of events is low and there are multiple confounders. *American Journal of Epidemiology*, 158:280–287, 2003.

[10] D. Chan, R. Ge, O. Gershony, T. Hesterberg, and D. Lambert. Evaluating online ad campaigns in a pipeline: causal models at scale. In *Proceedings of SIGKDD*, pages 7–16. ACM, 2010.

[11] Z. Chen, K. Zhang, L. Chan, and B. Schölkopf. Causal discovery via reproducing kernel hilbert space embeddings. *Neural computation*, pages 1–34, 2014.

[12] D. R. Cox. *Planning of experiments*. Wiley, 1958.

[13] B. Dalessandro, C. Perlich, O. Stitelman, and F. Provost. Causally motivated attribution for online advertising. In *Proceedings of the Sixth International Workshop on Data Mining for Online Advertising and Internet Economy*, page 7. ACM, 2012.

[14] A. Dasgupta, K. Punera, J. M. Rao, X. Wang, J. Rao, and X.-J. Wang. Impact of spam exposure on user engagement. In *USENIX Security*, 2012.

[15] G. Dupret and M. Lalmas. Absence time and user engagement: evaluating ranking functions. In *Proceedings of WSDM*. ACM, 2013.

[16] J. Friedman, T. Hastie, and R. Tibshirani. glmnet: Lasso and elastic-net regularized generalized linear models. *R package version 1.4.*, 2009.

[17] G. Harrison and J. A. List. Field experiments. *Journal of Economic Literature*, 27:1013–1059, 2004.

[18] T. Hastie, R. Tibshirani, and J. Friedman. *The Elements of Statistical Learning*. Springer, 2009.

[19] K. Hullsiek and T. Louis. Propensity score modeling strategies for the causal analysis of observational data. *Biostatistics*, 2:179–193, 2002.

[20] K. Imai. Do get-out-the-vote calls reduce turnout? the importance of statistical methods for field experiments. *American Political Science Review*, 99(2):283–300, 2005.

[21] K. Imai and D. A. Van Dyk. Causal inference with general treatment regimes. *Journal of the American Statistical Association*, 99(467), 2004.

[22] D. Janzing, J. Mooij, K. Zhang, J. Lemeire, J. Zscheischler, P. Daniušis, B. Steudel, and B. Schölkopf. Information-geometric approach to inferring causal directions. *Artificial Intelligence*, 182:1–31, 2012.

[23] M. M. Joffe and P. R. Rosenbaum. Invited commentary: propensity scores. *American Journal of Epidemiology*, 150(4):327–333, 1999.

[24] G. A. Johnson, R. A. Lewis, and D. H. Reiley. Add more ads? experimentally measuring incremental purchases due to increased frequency of online display advertising. *Working Paper*, 2013.

[25] R. Kohav and R. Longbotham. Unexpected results in online controlled experiments. *SIGKDD Explorations*, 12(2), 2010.

[26] M. Lechner. Earnings and employment effects of continuous gff-the-job training in east germany after unification. *Journal of Business & Economic Statistics*, 17(1):74–90, 1999.

[27] R. A. Lewis, J. M. Rao, and D. H. Reiley. Here, there, and everywhere: correlated online behaviors can lead to overestimates of the effects of advertising. In *Proceedings of WWW*, pages 157–166. ACM, 2011.

[28] B. Lu, E. Zanutto, R. Hornik, and P. R. Rosenbaum. Matching with doses in an observational study of a media campaign against drug abuse. *Journal of the American Statistical Association*, 96(456):1245–1253, 2001.

[29] S. Perkins, W. Tu, M. Underhill, X. Zhou, and M. Murray. The use of propensity scores in pharmacoepidemiologic research. *Pharmacoepidemiology and Drug Safety*, 9:93–101, 2000.

[30] P. R. Rosenbaum and D. B. Rubin. The central role of the propensity score in observational studies for causal effects. *Biometrika*, 70(1):41–55, 1983.

[31] P. R. Rosenbaum and D. B. Rubin. The central role of the propensity score in observational studies for causal effects. *Biometrika*, 70(1):41–55, 1983.

[32] P. R. Rosenbaum and D. B. Rubin. Reducing bias in observational studies using subclassification on the propensity score. *Journal of the American Statistical Association*, 79(387):516–524, 1984.

[33] G. Rosenkrans. The creativeness & effectiveness of online interactive rich media advertising. *Journal of Interactive Advertising*, 9(2):18–31, 2009.

[34] D. Rubin. Estimating causal effects from large data sets using propensity scores. *Annals of Internal Medicine*, 127:757–763, 1997.

[35] O. Stitelman, B. Dalessandro, C. Perlich, and F. Provost. Estimating the effect of online display advertising on browser conversion. *Data Mining and Audience Intelligence for Advertising*, 8, 2011.

[36] X. Su, J. Kang, J. Fan, R. A. Levine, and X. Yan. Facilitating score and causal inference trees for large observational studies. *The Journal of Machine Learning Research*, 13(1):2955–2994, 2012.

[37] L. Tang, R. Rosales, A. Singh, and D. Agarwal. Automatic ad format selection via contextual bandits. In *Proceedings of CIKM*, pages 1587–1594. ACM, 2013.

[38] P. Wang, Y. Liu, M. Meytlis, H.-Y. Tsao, J. Yang, and P. Huang. An efficient framework for online advertising effectiveness measurement and comparison. *Proceedings of WSDM*, 2014.

[39] P. Wang, M. Traskin, and D. S. Small. Robust inferences from a before-and-after study with multiple unaffected control groups. *Journal of Causal Inference*, pages 1–26, 2013.

The Power of Random Neighbors in Social Networks

Silvio Lattanzi
Google, Inc.
New York, NY 10011
silviol@google.com

Yaron Singer
Harvard University
Cambridge, MA 02138
yaron@seas.harvard.edu

ABSTRACT

The friendship paradox is a sociological phenomenon first discovered by Feld which states that individuals are likely to have fewer friends than their friends do, on average. This phenomenon has become common knowledge, has several interesting applications, and has also been observed in various data sets. In his seminal paper Feld provides an intuitive explanation by showing that in any graph the average degree of edges in the graph is an upper bound on the average degree of nodes. Despite the appeal of this argument, it does not prove the existence of the friendship paradox. In fact, it is easy to construct networks – even with power law degree distributions – where the ratio between the average degree of neighbors and the average degree of nodes is high, but all nodes have the *exact same degree* as their neighbors. Which models, then, explain the friendship paradox?

In this paper we give a strong characterization that provides a formal understanding of the friendship paradox. We show that for any power law graph with exponential parameter in (1,3), when every edge is rewired with constant probability, the friendship paradox holds, i.e. there is an asymptotic gap between the average degree of the sample of polylogarithmic size and the average degree of a random set of its neighbors of equal size. To examine this characterization on real data, we performed several experiments on social network data sets that complement our theoretical analysis. We also discuss the applications of our result to influence maximization.

1. INTRODUCTION

In popular culture, the *friendship paradox* is known as the somewhat discouraging statement that our friends have more friends than we do. This statement is an interpretation of a result discovered by Feld [10] which states that individuals are likely to have fewer friends than the mean number of friends their friends have. Superficially, since the number of friends a person has often translates to social status, the friendship paradox receives considerable attention. Beyond this interpretation, the idea that the degree of a random neighbor may be substantially larger than that of a random node has interesting applications for immunization [5, 19] and influence maximization [28], and it has also been verified experimentally in large online social networks [13, 30].

Despite everything we know about it, our mathematical understanding of the friendship paradox is still limited. In his seminal paper, Feld provides an intuitive explanation for the friendship paradox by showing that in *any* graph the average degree of edges in the graph is an upper bound on the average degree of nodes. This however, is far from proving the friendship paradox – that a node is likely to have a smaller degree than the average degree of her friends. In fact, as we will later show, it is easy to construct networks – *even with power law degree distributions* – where the ratio between the average degree of neighbors and the average degree of nodes is high, but all nodes have the *exact same degree* as their neighbors. In other words, not all graphs exhibit the friendship paradox, degree distribution does not explain it, and other structural properties need to be considered. Given the evidence in social network data sets, the question is why the friendship paradox exists.

Which models explain the friendship paradox?

The inception of network science is largely due to seminal mathematical models that explain phenomenon such as small-worlds [17, 31] and power-law degree distributions [?]. In these models we have a mathematical definition for the phenomenon exhibited: short distances in the network are defined as polylogarithmic in its size, heavy tail degree distribution as a power-law. But how should we mathematically define existence of the friendship paradox in a network? A possible definition of the friendship paradox is the existence of an asymptotic gap between a random node and its random neighbor. In a regular network, where all nodes have the same degree, there is no difference between the degree of any node and that of its neighbors, so the friendship paradox does not holds. In a star network on the other hand, where a randomly selected node is likely to be an endpoint with its only neighbor being the center, the ratio between a node and its neighbor is linear in the size of the network, and the friendship paradox holds. So what lies between these extremes that can serve as good model for social networks?

Algorithmic implications. The massive adoption of online social networking technologies in recent years is drawing substantial interest to the study of information diffusion in social networks. In particular, a problem which received

WSDM'15, February 2–6, 2015, Shanghai, China.

http://dx.doi.org/10.1145/2684822.2685293.

significant attention by the data mining community is that of influence maximization. First posed by Domingos and Richardson [8, 26] and further formulated by Kempe, Kleinberg, and Tardos [16], influence maximization is the algorithmic challenge of selecting individuals who can serve as early adopters of a new product or technology in a manner that will trigger a large cascade in the social network.

Although there has been substantial progress on the problem throughout the past decade, naive application of state-of-the-art algorithms is often ineffective. In many applications, one only has access to a small *sample* of the network in which individuals have low influence potential, and algorithms that select their users from such samples have a limited effect. In marketing applications for example, merchants often reward influential users who visit their online store, or who have engaged in other ways (subscribe to a mailing list, follow the brand, install an application etc.). If we think of users who arrive at a store or follow a brand as being randomly sampled from the network, it follows that observing high-degree users is a rare event simply because the degree distributions of social networks are heavy-tailed.

Two- stage approaches. As an alternative to spending the entire budget on nodes in the sample, recent work advocates for a two-stage approach called *Adaptive Seeding* [28]: In the first stage, a fraction of the budget is spent on nodes in the sample for the purpose of attracting their neighbors to join the set of potential influencers (e.g. attract neighbors to visit the website, follow the brand, register their email, etc.). In the second stage, after some neighbors have joined, the remainder of the budget is used to select an influential set of individuals from the (hopefully larger) set of accessible nodes. Intuitively, a good strategy is one which selects nodes in the first stage s.t. in expectation over all the possible arrivals of neighbors in the second stage, influence can then be maximized with the remaining budget. The main result in [28] is a constant factor approximation algorithm for a class of influence models that includes the well-studied independent cascade and linear threshold influence models [16].

Showing that the friendship paradox exists in social networks implies that adaptive seeding algorithms can indeed enable dramatic improvements for information dissemination.We illustrate how the friendship paradox translates to potential influence of two-stage approaches in Figure 1.

1.1 The friendship paradox

The rationale behind a two-stage approach is that while samples of a graph will likely have low degree nodes, they may have high degree *neighbors*. Intuitively, since high degree nodes have many neighbors (by definition), one would hope such nodes will be connected to the sample. In simple terms, we are guided by the following question:

Are random nodes likely to have high degree neighbors in a social network?

One central contribution in this paper is to explore this question at depth and provide analytical and empirical evidence to show that this is the case. For a given graph described through a mathematical model of a social network, we are interested in understanding whether with *constant probability* a random node has a neighbor which has an asymptotically higher degree, i.e. whether the ratio between the degree of a node and its neighbor asymptotically grows with the size of the graph. We refer to the phenomenon of a random node having an asymptotically higher-degree neighbor with constant probability as the *friendship paradox*. Stated in these terms, our objective is understand whether the friendship paradox exists in social networks.

Figure 2: An illustration of two power law networks. The network on the right (B) is created using the network on the left (A) and is a set of disjoint cliques. Thus despite being power law every node has exactly the same degree as its neighbor.

1.2 The friendship paradox

As mentioned before the friendship paradox in social network has been first observed by Feld [10] which states that in any graph, the average degree of neighbors is an upper bound on the average degree of nodes in the graph. Before we describe our results, it would be useful to discuss how the friendship paradox and our goals differ from the implications of Feld's result.

- **Size matters.** To identify asymptotic ratios, we must be able to quantify how many more neighbors a neighbor has.
- **Averages do not imply likelihood.** Perhaps the most critical distinction is that the friendship paradox is a statement about averages, and does not imply that a node is likely to have a lower degree than her neighbor. So, for the purpose of designing algorithms the friendship paradox is inapplicable.
- **Random neighbor vs. random node's neighbor** It is important to emphasize that our result is not a constant probability version of Feld's result. The constant probability version of Feld's result is the ratio between the degree of a randomly selected node v and the degree of a *random neighbor* y *in the graph.* Note that y is not necessary a neighbor of x. To see that these are two different random variables consider the star of N nodes: the expected degree of friends of a random node is $N-1/N$, while a constant probability version of Feld gives $N/2$.

1.3 The structure of social networks

Perhaps the most common assumption about the structure of social networks and complex systems in general, is that their degree distribution is heavy tailed. In this paper we focus on the most commonly cited heavy tail distribution, the power law distribution: the likelihood of observing a node with degree i in the network is proportional to $i^{-\beta}$, where β is a constant that depends on the network. [1]

[1]There is an interesting debate on the degree distribution of social network graphs [24]. Different papers support different heavy tail distributions: power law, log normal, double Pareto, etc. Here we focus on power law distributions for simplicity.

Figure 1: An illustration of the friendship paradox in different networks. The two networks above are of the same size in terms of nodes and edges but with different topologies. The graph on the left has edges connected between nodes uniformly at random, and the graph on the right is a random graph with degree distribution close to a power law, i.e. the probability of observing a node of degree i is proportional to $i^{-\beta}$ for some constant β. In the first network the friendship paradox does not hold while in the second one it does. In each network we performed the following experiment: we selected five random nodes to represent the sample S, which are depicted in yellow, their neighbors $\mathcal{N}(S)$ are depicted in orange and their neighbors which is the potential influence of $\mathcal{N}(S)$ are depicted in red. The rest of the nodes are represented in pink.

In Figure 2 we illustrate an example showing that the power law property does not suffice to show that a node is likely to have less their friends than her friend. Essentially, one can take any power law network (illustrated as network A) and turn it into a power law network where each node of degree d in the original network is represented as an isolated clique of size $d+1$. A series of such graphs has a power law degree distribution. In Section 3 we show such a construction which formally holds for networks with finite degree distributions. This example is obviously contrived, but nevertheless it proves an important point: power law degree distributions alone do contain enough information about the network to study the likelihood of a node to have a high degree neighbor. If we wish to *prove* properties on social networks we will need to consider some form of a model. An important property to consider is the presence of long-range edges. Long-range links were first observed by Granovetter [12] and are often modeled as random edges [17, 31].

A general model for social networks. Following the above discussion and inspired by the work of Watts and Strogatz [31], we analyze the following family of graphs: we start from *any*(potentially adversarial) power law network and then we "re-wire" each edge in the network with some fixed probability. The implication is that one can take *any model of a social network* as long as its degree distribution follows a power law, allow every edge to have some fixed probability to be connected at random, and our results will hold. Thus even the most contrived examples of power law networks can be slightly perturbed and succumb to our analysis.

Additional models. It is important to emphasize that the results we show here also hold for other well-studied models of social networks[2]. In particular, our results also hold for the *configuration model* [4] with power law degree distributions for finite graphs [1](this is a special case of our model) and preferential attachment model [3], both widely used in social network analysis (see e.g. [1, 27, 25]).

[2]We omit the proofs for these models here due to lack of space, though the techniques we show here can be extended to these models as well.

1.4 Our results

Informally, our main result is that small samples suffice to observe the friendship paradox in social networks. More formally, for any power law graphs with parameter $\beta \in (1,3)$, allowing every edge to be rewired with constant probability, we show there is an asymptotic gap between the average degree of the sample of polylogarithmic size and the average degree of a random set of its neighbors of equal size. The algorithmic implication being that, for example, influence maximization strategies can be dramatically improved by being applied on neighbors.

To show the importance of random edges, we first show a construction of a finite power law network where the friendship paradox does not hold – every node has almost the same degree as its neighbor. We then analyze the case where only a single node is sampled from the network. We show that the question of whether an asymptotic gap exists between a set of randomly drawn nodes and their neighbors depends on the parameters of the graph. Our result show a threshold phenomenon: for graphs whose degree distribution is a power law with $\beta \in (1,2]$ an asymptotic gap exists, while for $\beta \in (2,3)$ it does not. Using this analysis we develop our main result for polylogarithmic samples.

To examine how these results relate to real data, we performed several experiments on social network data sets.

1.5 Related Work

The friendship paradox is directly related to Feld's friendship paradox [10, 11]. Feld gives an explicit characterization of the average degree of a neighbor in terms of the expected degree and variance of the degree distribution in the network and observes that the average degree of neighbors will be strictly greater than the average degree of nodes when the variance is greater than 0. In addition, Feld provides experimental evidence strengthening his thesis. Based on these intuitions, several heuristics for detecting contagions and designing immunization strategies have been suggested [5, 6], and our results here provide provable guarantees for these techniques.

Recently, large scale experiments showed that individuals are indeed likely to have less friends than the average number of friends their friends have in the Facebook [30] and Twitter networks [13]. Our work is somewhat complementary to these works and provides rigorous analysis of the phenomena observed in their experiments.

From a technical perspective, a related research direction recently explored is social sampling. In this context the goal is usually to sample a subgraph and maintain properties of the original graph [20], compute some statistics in sublinear time [7, 14, 15], or find a subset of the nodes with a certain property [2]. Despite some similarities, our work is different as we focus on finding high degree nodes in a network using an existing sample and we only consider the the node's immediate neighbors.

2. PRELIMINARIES

Power law graphs. We use the same definition of a power law network that is used in [1]. A graph has a power law distribution if the number of nodes of degree i is $\lfloor \frac{e^\alpha}{i^\beta} \rfloor$. Since the sum of the degrees in a network has to be even, the number of nodes of degree 1 should either be $\lfloor e^\alpha \rfloor$ or $\lfloor e^\alpha + 1 \rfloor$ depending on the parity of the sum of the higher degree nodes in the graph. For simplicity, throughout the rest of the paper we assume that the the number of nodes of degree 1 is e^α, and note that all the results naturally extend to the general definition. For brevity we set $C = e^\alpha$ and use N and M to denote the number of nodes and edges in the graph, respectively. We denote the average degree of a set B as $d(B)$.

Social network model. We will analyze the following random graph model, which is inspired by the small-world model of Watts and Strogatz [31]. We start from an arbitrary (potentially adversarial) graph with a power law distribution and then "rewire" each edge in the graph with constant probability $p > 0$. Rewiring is done by first selecting all the edges that have to be rewired and then by applying the technique used in the configuration model [4]: every edge selected to be rewired is split into two stubs attached to the nodes corresponding with the endpoints of that edge, and the set of all stubs are then connected uniformly at random. The importance of this model is that it shows that even when starting from an adversarial structure (**potentially with a strong community structure or even a disconnected network**) a small fraction of randomness suffices to observe an asymptotic gap between the degree of a sampled set of nodes and their neighbors. In case of self-loops, we count a node as a neighbor of itself (in most of the setting the number of self loops is extremely small).

3. MISBEHAVED POWER LAWS

In this section we show that there exists a family of power law graphs such that the ratio between the degree of a node and the degree of its neighbor is constant for every node in the graph.[3]

[3]We note that for simplicity we prove a result for $\beta = 2$, although similar counter-examples can be constructed for other values of β. We also note that it is easy to modify our construction to obtain a connected graph.

PROPOSITION 3.1. *There exist a family of power law graphs with $\beta = 2$ such the ratio between the degree of any node and the degree of any of its neighbor is at most a constant.*

PROOF. First we order the nodes in an increasing degree order. We begin by generating the stubs, initializing each node with unassigned stubs. For all nodes of degree smaller than $\frac{\sqrt{N}}{400}$,[4] starting from the first node we sequentially match each unassigned stub of a node v with an unassigned stub of the minimum ranked node with an available unassigned stub which is not already connected to v.

An interesting property of this ordering is that for every node v of degree smaller than $\frac{\sqrt{N}}{400}$ it is always possible to connect it with the subsequent $d(v)$ nodes. This is true because we consider nodes in an increasing degree order. Note that in this way every node of degree smaller $\frac{\sqrt{N}}{400}$ is connected with nodes that have a degree that is at least half of its degree, and at most double its degree. In fact, every node v connects with at most $d(v)$ subsequent nodes and $\frac{d(v)}{2}$ preceding nodes.

Now we have to assign the edges between all the nodes of degree larger than $\frac{\sqrt{N}}{400}$. But this can be done by assigning edges arbitrarily (for example using the configuration model on the remaining stubs) since the maximum degree node has degree $\sqrt{N}$ and so the ratio between the degree of any two nodes with degree larger than $\frac{\sqrt{N}}{400}$ is at most constant. □

4. SINGLE SAMPLES

As a preliminary to the main results in Section 5, we investigate the case in which the sample is of a constant size. As we will now show, when we consider small samples the question of whether neighbors yield better results largely depends on the parameters of the graph. While an interesting result in of itself, the lemmas for establishing this will also be instrumental for proving the main result in Section 5.

Throughout the rest of this paper we use $G(\beta, p)$ to denote the family of graphs with power law degree distributions with exponent β in which every edge has some small, constant probability $p > 0$ to be rewired at random.

LEMMA 4.1. *Let u be a node sampled from $G(\beta, p)$ with $\beta \in (1, 2)$ and let v be a neighbor of u drawn u.a.r.. Then, for any constant $\epsilon > 0$, with constant probability the ratio between the degree of u and v is $\Omega\left(N^{\frac{\beta-1}{\beta}-\epsilon}\right)$.*

PROOF. We first compute the average degree of a node in $G(\beta, p)$. Using the fact that the generalized harmonic sum converges to a constant when $\beta > 1$, i.e. $\sum_{i=1}^{\infty} \frac{1}{i^\beta} \in O(1)$, we can conclude that the number of nodes in a power law graph with $\beta \in (1, 3)$ is:

$$N = \sum_{i=1}^{\Delta} \left\lfloor \frac{C}{i^\beta} \right\rfloor = \sum_{i=1}^{\lceil C^{1/\beta} \rceil} \left\lfloor \frac{C}{i^\beta} \right\rfloor \in \Theta(C)$$

where Δ is used to denote the largest degree in the graph. The number of edges is:

$$M = \sum_{i=1}^{\lceil C^{1/\beta} \rceil} i \left\lfloor \frac{C}{i^\beta} \right\rfloor = O\left(\sum_{i=1}^{\lceil C^{1/\beta} \rceil} \left\lfloor \frac{C}{i^{\beta-1}} \right\rfloor \right) \in \Theta\left(C^{\frac{2}{\beta}}\right)$$

[4]In the proof we use 400 for simplicity, the proof can be extended to hold for every large constant C instead of 400.

where we use the fact that that the generalized harmonic sum for $0 < \alpha < 1$ is equal to $\sum_{i=1}^{t} i^{-\alpha} \in \Theta\left(t^{1-\alpha}\right)$. The average degree of a node in $G(\beta, p)$ is therefore in $\Theta\left(C^{\frac{2}{\beta}-1}\right)$. So, by Markov's inequality, we know that when we select a random node with probability $\frac{1}{2}$ its degree is at most twice its expected degree. Thus, with probability $\frac{1}{2}$ we sample a node of degree $O\left(C^{\frac{2}{\beta}-1}\right)$.

To lower bound the degree of a random neighbor, we show that with constant probability an edge is incident to a high degree node. To show this we calculate the number of endpoints of edges incident to nodes of degree at least K, denoted $A_{d>K}$:

$$A_{d>K} = \sum_{i=\lceil K \rceil}^{\lceil C^{1/\beta} \rceil} i \left\lfloor \frac{C}{i^\beta} \right\rfloor = \Theta\left(C\left(C^{\frac{2}{\beta}-1} - K^{2-\beta}\right)\right)$$

since that for $\alpha < 1$, $\sum_{i=k}^{n} \frac{1}{i^\alpha} = \Theta(n^{1-\alpha} - k^{1-\alpha})$.

Therefore the number of endpoints of edges incident to nodes with degree greater or equal to $K = C^{1/\beta-\epsilon}$ is $\Theta(M)$. If we restrict our attention to endpoints of *rewired* edges incident to nodes with degree greater or equal to $K = C^{1/\beta-\epsilon}$, denoted by $R_{d>K}$, then by linearity of expectation we have that $E[R_{d>K}] = pA_{d>K} \in \Theta(M)$. Unfortunately the probability that the endpoints are rewired is not independent. In fact, two endpoints incident to the same edge are either both rewired or both not. So to obtain a concentration result we cannot apply the Chernoff bound. Fortunately in this case we can use the method of bounded difference [23] which tells us that the fact that an edge is rewired changes the value of $R_{d>K}$ by an additive factor of 2 at most, and we have that $R_{d>K} \in \Theta(M)$.

So with constant probability a random neighbor of a random node would be connected to the node by a *rewired* edges and this edge with constant probability will point to a node in $R_{d>K} \in \Theta(M)$.

Thus, for $\beta \in (1,2)$ with constant probability the ratio between a node a random neighbor is at least:

$$K\left(\frac{M}{N}\right)^{-1} = \Omega\left(C^{\frac{\beta-1}{\beta}-\epsilon}\right) = \Omega\left(N^{\frac{\beta-1}{\beta}-\epsilon}\right). \quad \square$$

The case when $\beta = 2$: we can apply the same technique as above for $\beta = 2$. In this case as in the above proof the number of nodes is $N \in \Theta(C)$ and the number of edges is:

$$M = \sum_{i=1}^{\lceil C^{1/\beta} \rceil} i \left\lfloor \frac{C}{i^2} \right\rfloor = O\left(\sum_{i=1}^{\lceil C^{1/\beta} \rceil} \left\lfloor \frac{C}{i} \right\rfloor\right) \in \Theta\left(C \log C\right)$$

where this time we use the fact that that the harmonic sum is equal to $\sum_{i=1}^{t} i^{-1} \in \Theta(\log t)$. When $\beta = 2$ the number of endpoints of edges incident to nodes of degree at least K is:

$$A_{d>K} = \sum_{i=\lceil K \rceil}^{\lceil C^{1/\beta} \rceil} i \left\lfloor \frac{C}{i^\beta} \right\rfloor = \Theta\left(C\left(\log C - \log K\right)\right)$$

where we use the fact that $\sum_{i=k}^{n} \frac{1}{i} = \Theta(\log n - \log k)$. Using the same technique one can show that with constant probability the ratio between the degree of u and v is $\Omega\left(\log^\alpha N\right)$, for any constant $\alpha > 0$.

Corollary 4.2. *Let u be a randomly selected node from $G(\beta, p)$ with $1 < \beta \le 2$, and let v a randomly selected neighbor of u. Then with constant probability we have:*

$$\frac{d(v)}{d(u)} \in \omega(1).$$

4.1 Phase transition for $\beta > 2$

Somewhat surprisingly, we now show that when $\beta > 2$ the friendship paradox does not hold for a single node – and not even for a sample of a constant size, and even when all edges are rewired at random. In other words, when $\beta > 2$ a constant number of nodes do not suffice to observe asymptotic gaps between degrees of the sample and their neighbors, even in a random graph model.

Lemma 4.3. *Let u be a node sampled from $G(\beta, 1)$ with $\beta \in (2,3)$, and let v be a random neighbor of u. Then, w.h.p. the ratio between the degree of u and that of v is $\Theta(1)$.*

Proof. First, note that in this case we also have that the number of nodes is $N \in \Theta(C)$. The number of edges when $2 < \beta < 3$ is:

$$M = \sum_{i=1}^{\lceil C^{1/\beta} \rceil} i \left\lfloor \frac{C}{i^\beta} \right\rfloor = O\left(\sum_{i=1}^{\lceil C^{1/\beta} \rceil} \left\lfloor \frac{C}{i^{\beta-1}} \right\rfloor\right) = \Theta(C)$$

because in this setting $\beta - 1 > 1$. Thus the number of nodes of degree greater or equal to K in the graph is $O\left(\frac{C}{K}\right)$. So for any function $f(N) \in \omega(1)$, the probability of randomly picking a node of degree at least $f(N)$ is $o(1)$. Thus when we sample a node u.a.r, w.h.p. it will have a constant degree.

We will now show that when sampling a single node, w.h.p. also a randomly selected neighbor has degree smaller than $f(N)$, for any function $f(N)$ strictly increasing with N and such that $f(N) \in \omega(1)$ implying that w.h.p. the degree of a random neighbor is also constant. For $2 < \beta < 3$, the number of endpoints of nodes with degree larger than K is:

$$A_{d>K} = \sum_{i=\lceil K \rceil}^{\lceil C^{1/\beta} \rceil} i \left\lfloor \frac{C}{i^\beta} \right\rfloor = \Theta\left(C\left(K^{2-\beta} - C^{\frac{2}{\beta}-1}\right)\right)$$

Here for $\alpha > 1$, $\sum_{i=k}^{n} \frac{1}{i^\alpha} = \Theta(k^{1-\alpha} - n^{1-\alpha})$. The endpoints of edges incident to nodes of degree at least $\lceil f(N) \rceil$ is therefore $A_{d>\lceil f(N) \rceil} \in o(N)$. The number of edges of degree greater than $f(N)$ is therefore sublinear in the number of the nodes and so all but an $o(1)$-fraction of the nodes will have no incident edge of degree at least $f(N)$. $\square$

5. POLY-LOGARITHMIC SAMPLES

In this section we show our main result, namely that for any $\beta \in (1,3)$ polylogarithmic-sized samples suffice to see asymptotic ratios between the degree of a sample and its set of friends. Intuitively, this implies that as long as we have access to a relatively small size of the social network it is possible to reach nodes of relatively high-degree. The results here hold for any set of poly-logarithmic size, but we discuss sizes of $\log N$ for simplicity.

LEMMA 5.1. *Let S be a set of $\Theta(\log N)$ nodes sampled uniformly at random from $G(\beta, p)$, for $\beta \in (2,3)$. Then, w.h.p. the average degree in S is $\Theta(1)$.*

PROOF. From lemma 4.3, we know that the expected degree of a sampled node is $O(1)$. Thus, by linearity of expectation, the expected total degree of the sample is $O(\log N)$. By applying Markov's inequality we get that the probability that the total degree is in $\omega(\log N)$ is $o(1)$. □

PROPOSITION 5.2. *Let S be a set of $\Theta(\log N)$ nodes sampled uniformly at random from $G(\beta, p)$ for $\beta \in (2,3)$, and let T_S be a set obtained by selecting a single neighbor u.a.r. from every node in S. Then, w.h.p.*

$$\frac{d(T_S)}{d(S)} \in \omega(1)$$

PROOF. The main idea behind is to show that w.h.p. T_S contains $\omega(1)$ nodes of degree $O(\log N)$ when we have a sample of size $\log N$. We will first lower-bound the probability of sampling one of these nodes and then show the result holds w.h.p. when we sample $\log N$ elements. From the proof of Lemma 4.3 we know that the number of endpoints of edges incident to nodes with degree at least $\lceil c \log N \rceil$, $A_{d > c\log N} \in \Theta\left(\frac{C}{\lceil c\log N\rceil^{\beta-2}}\right)$. Recall that $R_{d>c\log N}$ is the number of rewired edges incident to nodes of degree bigger than $\log N$. Also in this case by linearity of expectation we have $E[R_{d>c\log N}] = pA_{d>c\log N}$. Applying the method of bounded difference with lipschitz condition 2 we have that $R_{d>c\log N}$ is strongly concentrated around its mean. Thus, the probability that a random edge of a node in S points to a neighbor with degree at least $c \log N$ is at least:

$$\frac{R_{d>c\log N} - 1}{M} = \frac{\Theta\left(\frac{C}{\lceil c\log N\rceil^{\beta-2}}\right)}{\Theta(C)} = \Theta\left(\frac{1}{\lceil c\log N\rceil^{\beta-2}}\right).$$

Now, let Y_i be the random variable which equals 1 if the randomly selected neighbor of the node i in S has degree at least $c \log N$ and 0 otherwise. We have that:

$$\begin{aligned}\mathbb{E}\left[\sum_{i\in S} Y_i\right] &= \log N \cdot \mathbb{E}[Y_i] = \log N\left(\frac{E_{d>c\log N}}{M}\right)\\ &= \Theta\left(\log N^{3-\beta}\right).\end{aligned}$$

Unfortunately the random variables Y_i are neither independent nor nicely correlated so we cannot use a Chernoff bound to get a high probability result directly. To overcome this difficulty, we show that the probability the sum of the Y_is is bigger than a value D dominates the probability that the sum of a random variable X_i that counts the number of heads of a coin that gives heads with probability $\frac{(E_{d>c\log N}) - \log N}{M}$ and tails otherwise is bigger than a value D. Note that we are sampling only $\log N$ edges, thus for every i the number of edges of degree bigger than $c \log N$ that we still have not used is bigger or equal than $E_{d>c\log N} - \log N$ for all i. Thus the probability that Y_i is equal 1 is higher than the probability of the same event for X_i for all i, hence the sum of the random variables Y_i dominates the sum of the random variables X_i. But $\mathbb{E}[\sum_{i\in S} X_i] = \Theta\left(\log N^{3-\beta}\right)$. Furthermore the X_i are independent so by Chernoff we get that $\sum_{i\in S} X_i \in \Omega\left(\log N^{3-\beta}\right)$ with probability $1 - o(1)$. Thus using stochastic domination, we have that w.h.p. at least $\Omega\left(\log N^{3-\beta}\right)$ sampled neighbors have degree bigger than $c \log N$.

Now in order to conclude the proof we have to show that those $\Omega\left(\log N^{3-\beta}\right)$ selected neighbors of high degree are different nodes. To this end we will show that any node in the graph is selected at most a constant number of times with high probability, which will imply the result.

The node of maximum degree is the most likely to be selected and it has degree $C^{\frac{1}{\beta}} = \Theta\left(C^{\frac{1}{\beta}}\right)$ so the probability of sampling it in one sample is $\Theta(C^{-1+\frac{1}{\beta}}) \in O(C^{-\frac{1}{2}})$. Thus the probability of sampling the highest degree node three times in $\log N$ samples is smaller than $\binom{\log N}{3}\Theta(C^{-\frac{3}{2}}) = o(C^{-1})$. Thus, using the union bound, no node is sampled more than twice with high probability. So the set of neighbors with high probability contains $\Omega\left(\log N^{3-\beta}\right)$ distinct nodes that have degree bigger or equal to $c \log N$, thus the average degree is w.h.p. at least $\Omega\left(\log N^{3-\beta}\right)$. □

The case when $\beta \in (1,2]$: The proof requires a different approach when $1 < \beta \leq 2$. Roughly, the core idea is to amplify the results of the single sample case to show that w.h.p. we get at least one high degree node.

PROPOSITION 5.3. *Let S be a set of $\log N$ nodes sampled uniformly at random from $G(\beta)$ where $1 < \beta \leq 2$, and let $N(S)$ be a set obtained by selecting a single neighbor u.a.r. from every node in S. Then, w.h.p. the ratio between the sum of degrees of S and that of $N(S)$ is $\omega(1)$.*

In order to prove the proposition we first bound the average degree of the set of sample nodes:

LEMMA 5.4. *Let S be a set of $\Theta(\log N)$ nodes sampled uniformly at random from $G(\beta)$, for $1 < \beta < 2$. Then, w.h.p. the average degree in S is $\Theta\left(C^{\frac{2}{\beta}-1}\right)$.*

The proof uses the same Markov inequality argument as in Lemma 5.1 and is omitted. To conclude the main proof we show that with high probability we pick at least one very high degree node.

LEMMA 5.5. *Let S be a set of $\Theta(\log N)$ nodes sampled uniformly at random from $G(\beta, p)$ for $\beta \in (1,2)$, and let T_S be a set obtained by selecting a single neighbor u.a.r. from every node in S. Then, w.h.p. $d(T_S) \in \Omega\left(N^{\frac{\beta-1}{\beta}-\epsilon}\right)$, for any constant $\epsilon > 0$.*

PROOF. The results follow directly from the previous lemma and by the fact that we can amplify the probability of getting a high degree node using $\Theta(\log N)$ samples. □

Using similar technique we can prove for $\beta = 2$ that the ratio is in $\Omega(\log^{\alpha}(N))$, for any constant $\alpha > 0$.

THEOREM 5.6. *For any $\beta \in (1,3)$, let S be a set of $\Theta(\log N)$ nodes sampled uniformly at random from $G(\beta, p)$, and let T_S be a set obtained by selecting a single neighbor u.a.r. from every node in S. Then, w.h.p. there is ratio between $d(T_S)$ and $d(S)$ is in $\in \omega(1)$.*

6. EXPERIMENTS

We conducted several experiments to evaluate and further study the friendship paradox in different online communities and social networks. Since analytical results only hold

Network	*# of Nodes*	*# of Edges*	β	C
Orkut	3,072,441	117,185,083	0.7470	223,989
LiveJournal	3,997,962	34,681,189	1.0322	520,041
Wikipedia	2,394,385	5,021,410	1.9548	80,033
YouTube	1,134,890	2,987,624	1.4212	160,927
DBLP	317,080	1,049,866	1.2048	64,983
SlashDot	82,168	948,464	1.2146	13,805
Enron	36,692	367,662	1.1636	11,322

Table 1: Networks' statistics.

on stylized models, our primary motivation was to witness the existence of the phenomenon in the data. We used 8 different publicly available data sets: the Orkut social network [32], the Live Journal blogging community [32], the Wikipedia author network [21], the YouTube social network [32], the DBLP author network [32], the Slashdot user community network [22], and the Enron email communication network [18]. These networks vary in size and degree distribution and provide insight on the effect network parameters have on the friendship paradox.

We began by characterizing the networks according to their degree distribution. We fitted each network to a power law graph with different parameters of β and $C = e^{\alpha}$, using methods that optimize over final sum of squares of residuals. We summarize the main network statistics in Table 1. Note that for almost all the networks $1 < \beta < 3$. We first considered the effects of the sample size and network topology on the friendship paradox, as we now describe.

The effects of sample size. To experimentally observe the way in which the sample size affects the friendship paradox, we compared the degree distributions of sampled sets and those of their neighbors as a function of the sample size. For each network, for every $j \in \{10, 20, 30, \ldots, 500\}$ we sampled j nodes u.a.r. and computed the degree distribution of the sampled nodes and the average degree distribution of all their neighbors. Note that the average degree distribution of all their neighbors is the average of selecting a neighbor at random from each node in the sample. Each such iteration is a snapshot of the friendship paradox for a set of size j. For each sample size j, we repeated this experiment 5 times. We then computed the ratio between the average degree of neighbors and the average degree in the sample. We plot the results in Figure 3.

As the figure shows, the friendship paradox varies across the different networks. The lowest gap we observed experimentally was in the DBLP network where the ratio averaged over all sample size iterations was 2.5 and the largest was 150 in the YouTube network. In all networks we see a large gap in the first iteration when the sample size is 10 and the neighbors' average degree distribution is large.

In all networks there is a trend of decrease in the friendship paradox as the sample size increases. This trend can be intuitively explained using the analysis from the previous sections: Since we showed that the friendship paradox is large at already the small sample size of $\log N$, this implies that when the sample S is of size $\log N$, the high degree nodes of the graph are in the neighborhood S. As the sample size increases we are more likely to sample high degree nodes in S while the degree distribution of S will becomes smaller as the high degree nodes are exhausted early.

Recall that in Section 4 we showed that with parameter $\beta \in (1, 2]$ the friendship paradox occurs even when the sample sizes are small. Interestingly, this phenomenon can also be observed on the data sets we examined, all of which were found to have parameters in this range, with the exception of the Orkut network for which $\beta < 1$.

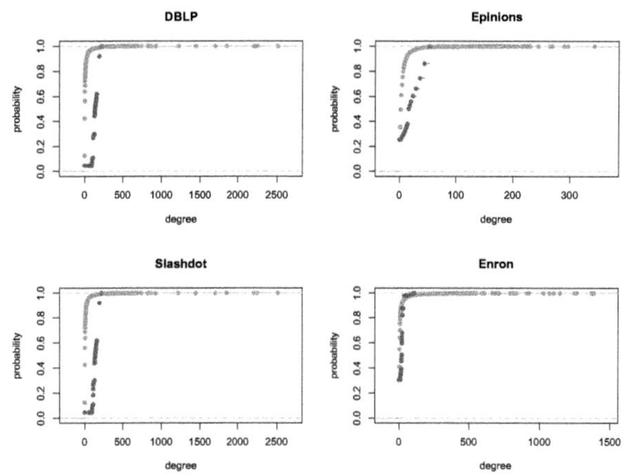

Figure 6: The CDFs of the degrees of nodes and the average degree of the neighbors in the network.

One hypothesis is that the friendship paradox occurs due to the fact that in social networks neighbors indeed are more likely to have a high degree. An alternative hypothesis however could be that when considering neighbors, the size of the sample is larger. That is, a set of S nodes sampled at random generates a neighborhood of size $n = |\bigcup_{u \text{ is neighbor of } S} \{u\}|$ and it may be that a set of size n sampled uniformly at random from the graph could have a similar effect. To test this hypothesis, we conducted the following experiment. For each $j = 1, \ldots, 100$ we sampled j nodes u.a.r. from the network which gave us a set of neighbors N_j. We then sampled $|N_j|$ nodes u.a.r. from the network, and compared the ratios between their average degree distribution. We depict the results in Figure 4 which supports our hypothesis.

To further investigate the effect of the sample size on the friendship paradox, we computed the degree distribution of *all* the nodes in the networks and for each node we averaged its' neighbors' degree distribution. In Figure 6 we plot the CDF of these distributions for the DBLP, Epinions, Slashdot, and the Enron networks. In the figure, the nodes' degree distribution is depicted in red and the average neighbors' degree distribution in blue. The expansion is the right shift between the distributions. The CDF shows that the majority of nodes' degree distribution is well below the average of their neighbors; however for nodes in top percentiles, this is no longer true. As the sample size increases these nodes are more likely to appear in the sample and diminish the expansion effect.

The effects of network topology. It is easy to see analytically that the friendship paradox cannot occur in regular graphs, where every node has the same degree. To view this experimentally, for each network $G = (V, E)$ in our data sets we also generated a random graph by running a process which assigns $|E|$ edges uniformly at random between $|V|$ nodes. We used the same process as above to observe the gap under different sample sizes. As expected, for these

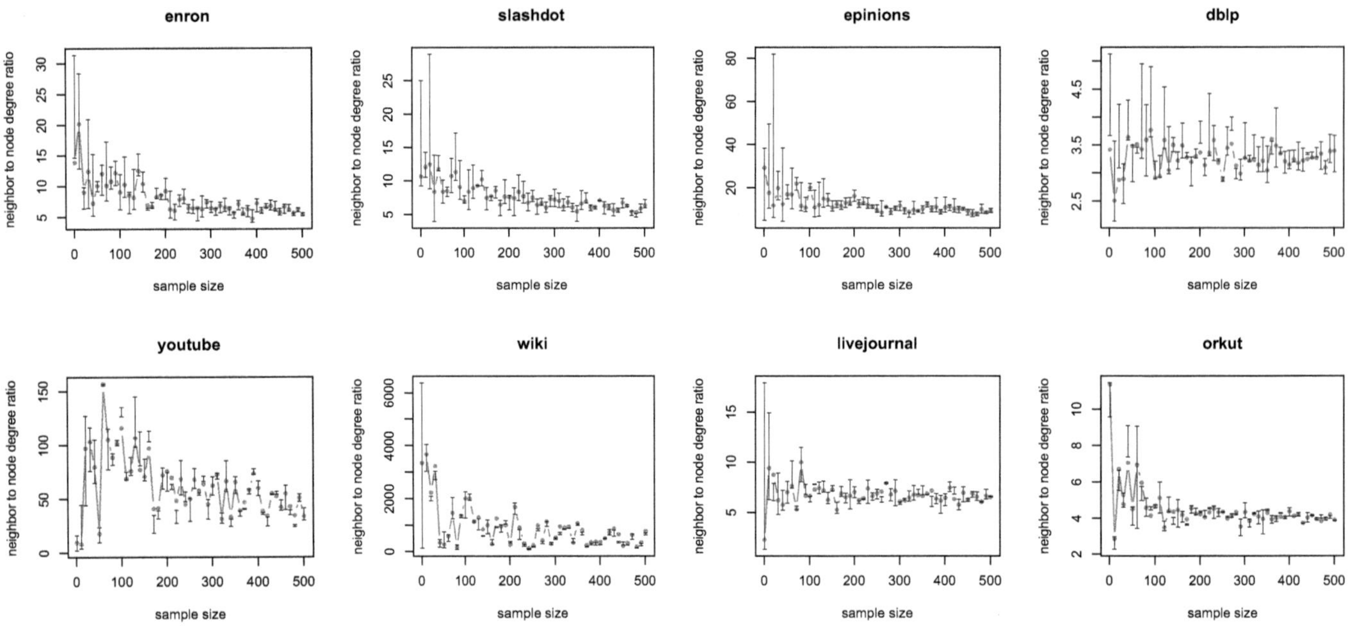

Figure 3: The ratio between average degrees of a sampled set and its neighbors.

graphs, regardless of sample size, the average degree of the sample and that of their neighbors were nearly identical.

High degree nodes in neighbors vs. in sample. To strengthen our results, we compared the average degree of the top 1% and 10% of neighbors and degrees from the sample. We plot the results in Figure 5 which show a clear dominance of selecting from the set of neighbors.

Beyond the first circle. It seems natural to ask whether the results extend beyond the immediate circle of friends. The first question is whether nodes which are two hops away from a randomly sampled node have a higher degree on average as well. The second question is whether the average degree grows as we further explore the graph. For a given set S, we use $\mathcal{N}_i(S)$ to denote the neighbors who are exactly i hops away from S in the graph. To observe the change in the degree distribution as a function of distance from a node, we conducted the following experiment. For each network, we sampled 5 nodes uniformly at random(u.a.r.), and conducted a BFS crawl of 4 levels from all nodes in the set. In each level we measured the degree distribution of all nodes in the level, and computed its average. In Figure 7 we plot the average degree as a function of the level, as well as the percentage of increase in average degree between levels.

Figure 7 gives experimental evidence that suggests that the friendship paradox would be most dramatic between the sampled set and its immediate neighborhood. In the Slashdot and Epinions networks depicted in red and black, respectively, the degree distribution is maximized in $\mathcal{N}_1(S)$, and in the Enron and DBLP networks the maximum is achieved in $\mathcal{N}_2(S)$. In all networks the largest increase in percentage is between S and $\mathcal{N}_1(S)$. This phenomenon also seems to be a derivative of the fact that in power law graphs high degree nodes are likely to be found in the immediate neighborhoods of many nodes.

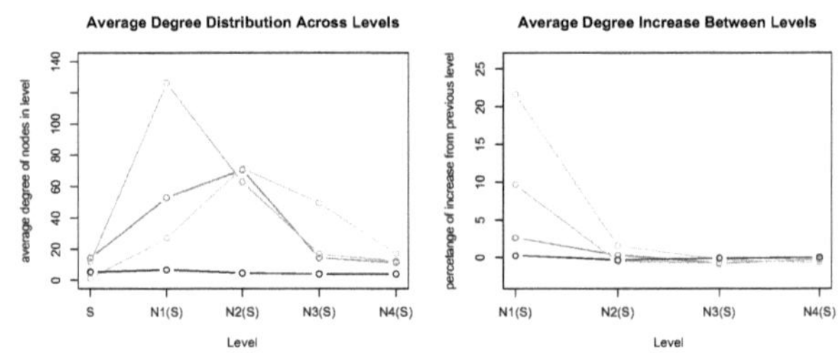

Figure 7: The degree distribution of a sampled set and its neighborhoods. Enron, Slashdot, Epinions, and DBLP correspond to the blue,red, green,black lines, respectively.

Applications. Besides being a fundamental sociological phenomena the friendship paradox has also practical applications. For example, it has already been used successfully to design immunization strategy [5, 6]. In this section we study an application of the friendship paradox to viral marketing. Recall that in our setting we do not have complete knowledge of the network and so we cannot use the classic efficient algorithms for influence maximization.

In particular we consider the case where a node can seed a cascade from only a random set of node or using their random neighbor. From our experimental results in the previous setting it is clear that using random neighbors would be the best choice in the well-studied *voter model* [8, 9, 26, 29]. To strengthen our results we consider the classic *independent cascade* and *linear threshold* [16] and we study experimentally the effect of seeding a cascade in a random set or in random set of neighbors. As shown in the results in figure 8 also in this more challenging setting using a set of

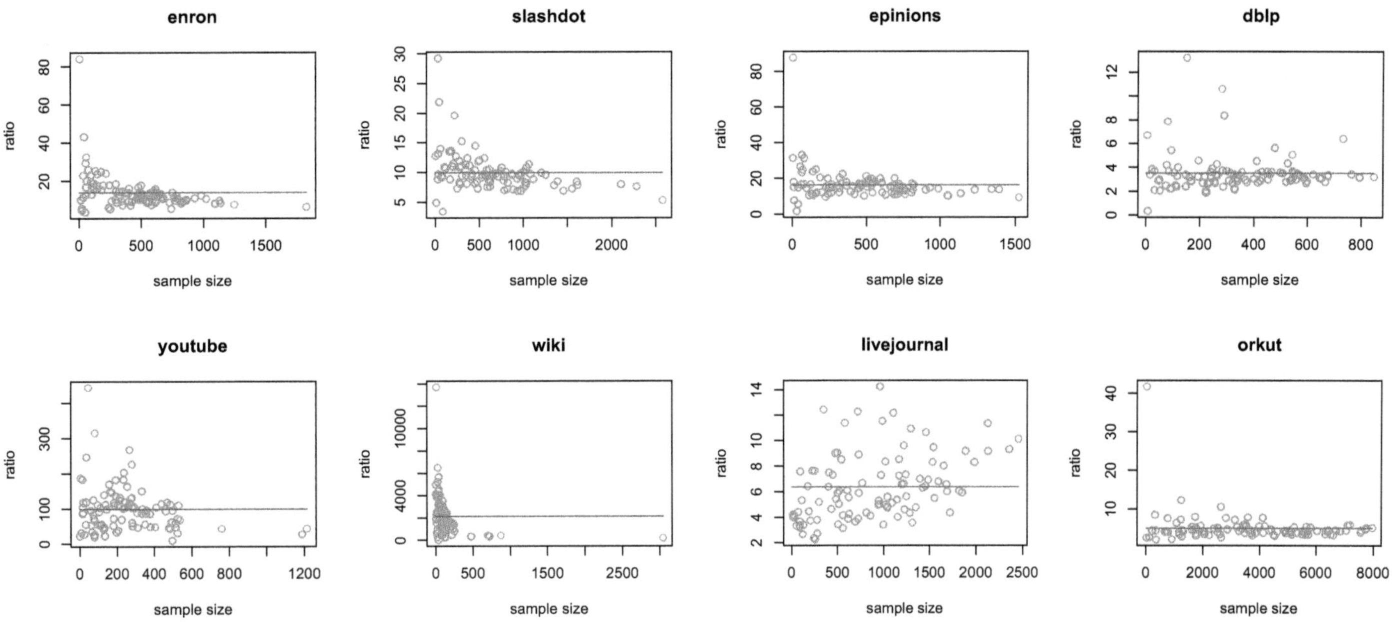

Figure 4: The ratio between average degree of a set of neighbors and a set of randomly sampled nodes from the graph of equal size.

random neighbors clearly outperform using a set of random nodes.

7. CONCLUSIONS

The friendship paradox is a fundamental phenomena in social networks, in this paper we strengthen the understanding of this phenomena by showing that in a very large family of random graph there is an asymptotic gap between the average degree of a set of random nodes and their neighbors. Furthermore we complement our theoretical results with a rich experimental analysis that show the relevance of the phenomena. Finally we also describe a possible viral marketing application of the friendship paradox.

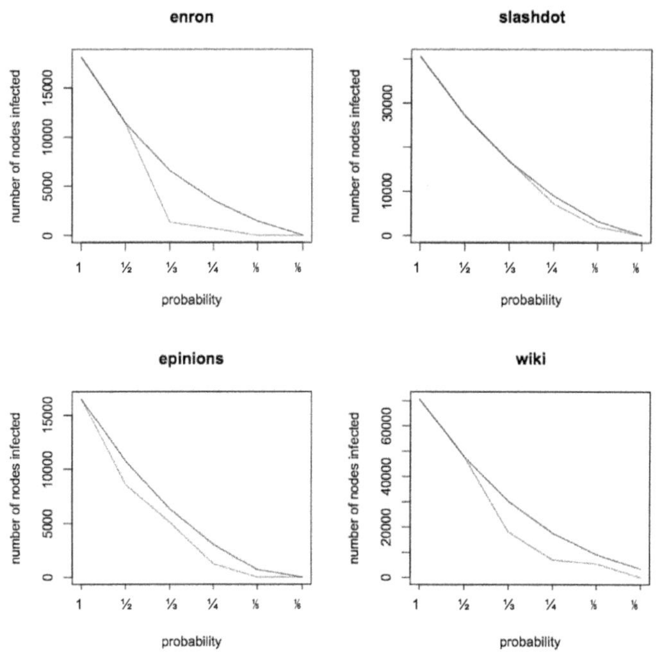

Figure 8: Number of the nodes influenced when a random set of node of size 10 is seeded(red line) as source of a cascade and when 10 random neighbors are seeded(blue line) as a function of the infection probability. Clearly the friendship paradox plays an important role also in this setting.

8. REFERENCES

[1] W. Aiello, F. Chung, and L. Lu. A random graph model for power law graphs. In *STOC*, 2000.

[2] L. Backstrom and J. M. Kleinberg. Network bucket testing. In *WWW*, 2011.

[3] A.-L. Barabási and R. Albert. Emergence of scaling in random networks. *Science*, 1999.

[4] B. Bollobás. A probabilistic proof of an asymptotic formula for the number of labelled regular graphs. *European J. Combin.*, 1980.

[5] N. A. Christakis and J. H. Fowler. Social Network Sensors for Early Detection of Contagious Outbreaks. . In *PLoS ONE*, 2010.

[6] R. Cohen, S. Havlin, and D. Ben-Avraham. Efficient immunization strategies for computer networks and populations. *Physical Review Letters*, 2003.

[7] A. Dasgupta, R. Kumar, and D. Sivakumar. Network bucket testing. In *KDD*, 2012.

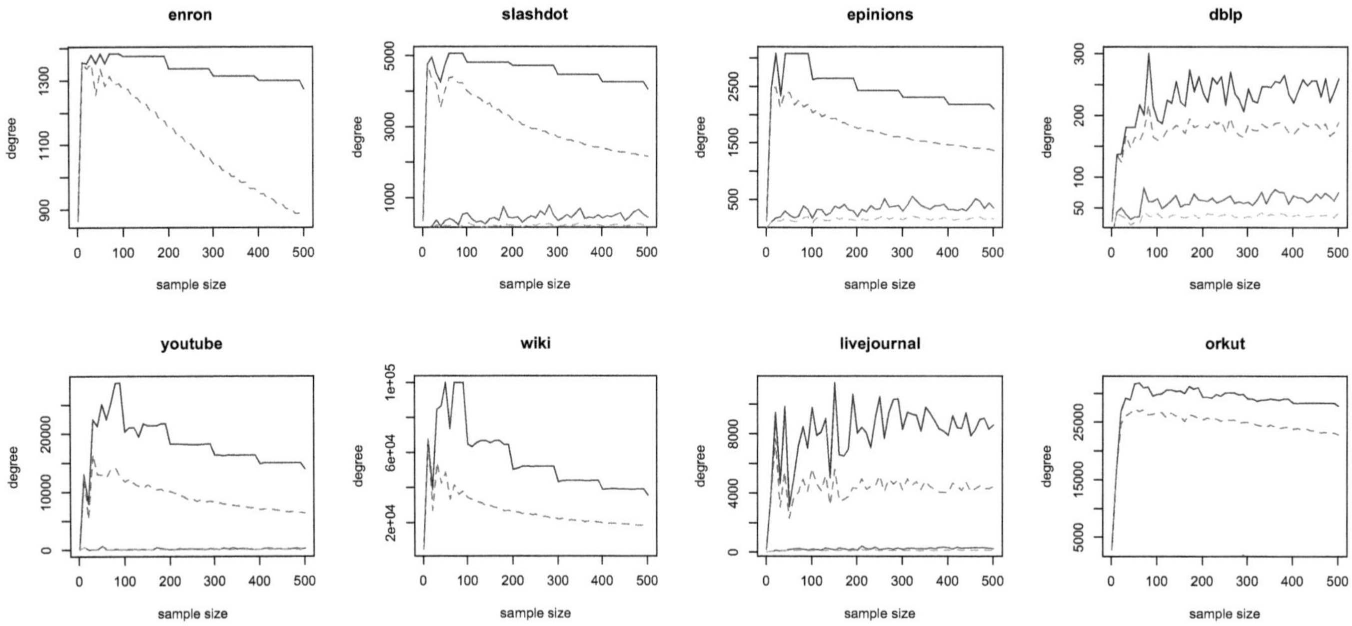

Figure 5: High degree nodes via neighbors vs. via sample. Blue lines depict top 1% and top10% (dotted) of neighbors; Red lines depict op 1% and top10% (dotted) of nodes from the sample.

[8] P. Domingos and M. Richardson. Mining the network value of customers. In *KDD*, pages 57–66, 2001.

[9] E. Even-Dar and A. Shapira. A note on maximizing the spread of influence in social networks. *Inf. Process. Lett.*, 111(4):184–187, 2011.

[10] S. Feld. Why your friends have more friends than you do. *American Journal of Sociology*, 1991.

[11] S. L. Feld and B. Grofman. Variation in class size, the class size paradox, and some consequences for students. *Research in Higher Education*, 6, 1977.

[12] M. Granovetter. The strength of weak ties: A network theory revisited. *Sociological Theory*, 1, 1983.

[13] N. O. Hodas, F. Kooti, and K. Lerman. Friendship paradox redux: Your friends are more interesting than you. *CoRR*, abs/1304.3480, 2013.

[14] L. Katzir, E. Liberty, and O. Somekh. Estimating sizes of social networks via biased sampling. . In *WWW*, 2011.

[15] L. Katzir, E. Liberty, and O. Somekh. Framework and algorithms for network bucket testing. . In *WWW*, 2012.

[16] D. Kempe, J. Kleinberg, and É. Tardos. Maximizing the spread of influence through a social network. In *KDD*.

[17] J. Kleinberg. Navigation in a small world. *Nature*, 406:257–275, 2000.

[18] B. Klimt and Y. Yang. In *First Conference on Email and Anti-Spam (CEAS)*, Mountain View, CA.

[19] M. Lelarge. Efficient Control of Epidemics over Random Networks. In *SIGMETRICS*, 2009.

[20] J. Leskovec and C. Faloutsos. Sampling from large graphs. In *KDD*, 2006.

[21] J. Leskovec, D. Huttenlocher, and J. Kleinberg. Predicting Positive and Negative Links in Online Social Networks. In *WWW*, 2010.

[22] J. Leskovec, K. Lang, A. Dasgupta, and M. Mahoney. Community structure in large networks: Natural cluster sizes and the absence of large well-defined clusters. *Internet Mathematics*, 6, 2009.

[23] C. McDiarmid. On the method of bounded di?erences. *Surveys in Combinatorics*, 1989.

[24] M. Mitzenmacher. A brief history of generative models for power law and lognormal distributions. *Internet mathematics 1 (2)*, 2004.

[25] M. Newman. The structure and function of complex networks. *SIAM review*, 45(2):167–256, 2003.

[26] M. Richardson and P. Domingos. Mining knowledge-sharing sites for viral marketing. In *KDD*, pages 61–70, 2002.

[27] F. Santos and J. P. T. Lenaerts. Evolutionary dynamics of social dilemmas in structured heterogeneous populations. *PNAS*, 2006.

[28] L. Seeman and Y. Singer. Adaptive seeding in social networks. In *FOCS*, 2013.

[29] Y. Singer. How to win friends and influence people, truthfully: influence maximization mechanisms for social networks. In *WSDM*, pages 733–742, 2012.

[30] J. Ugander, B. Karrer, L. Backstrom, and C. Marlow. The anatomy of the facebook social graph. *CoRR*, abs/1111.4503, 2011.

[31] D. Watts and S. Strogatz. Collective dynamics of 'small-world' networks. *Nature*, 393, 409-410.

[32] J. Yang and J. Leskovec. Defining and Evaluating Network Communities based on Ground-truth. In *ICDM*, 2012.

Negative Link Prediction in Social Media

Jiliang Tang[‡], Shiyu Chang[♯], Charu Aggarwal[†] and Huan Liu[‡]
[‡]Computer Science & Engineering, Arizona State University
[♯] Beckman Institute, University of Illinois at Urbana-Champaign
[†] IBM T.J. Watson Research Center
{Jiliang.Tang,Huan.Liu}@asu.edu[‡],{chang87}@illinois.edu[♯],{charu}@us.ibm.com[†]

ABSTRACT

Signed network analysis has attracted increasing attention in recent years. This is in part because research on signed network analysis suggests that negative links have added value in the analytical process. A major impediment in their effective use is that most social media sites do not enable users to specify them explicitly. In other words, a gap exists between the importance of negative links and their availability in real data sets. Therefore, it is natural to explore whether one can predict negative links automatically from the commonly available social network data. In this paper, we investigate the novel problem of negative link prediction with only positive links and content-centric interactions in social media. We make a number of important observations about negative links, and propose a principled framework NeLP, which can exploit positive links and content-centric interactions to predict negative links. Our experimental results on real-world social networks demonstrate that the proposed NeLP framework can accurately predict negative links with positive links and content-centric interactions. Our detailed experiments also illustrate the relative importance of various factors to the effectiveness of the proposed framework.

Categories and Subject Descriptors

H3.3 [**Information Storage and Retrieval**]: Information Search and Retrieval—*Information filtering*

General Terms

Algorithms; Design; Experimentation

Keywords

Negative Links; Negative Link Prediction; Signed Social Networks; Social Media

WSDM'15, February 2–6, 2015, Shanghai, China.
Copyright 2015 ACM 978-1-4503-3317-7/15/02 ...$15.00.
http://dx.doi.org/10.1145/2684822.2685295.

1. INTRODUCTION

Social networks have enabled a vast diversity of relations between users such as friendships in Facebook[1], follower relations in Twitter[2] and trust relations in Epinions[3]. The increasing availability of large-scale online social network data is useful not only for various tasks in social network analysis such as community detection [20] and link prediction [15], but it is also leveraged for various traditional data mining tasks such as feature selection [22] and recommendations [21]. The vast majority of existing research has overwhelmingly focused on social networks with only positive links. However, social networks can contain both positive and negative links. Examples of signed social networks include Epinions with trust and distrust links, and Slashdot[4] with friend and foe links. The recent availability of signed social networks in social media sites such as Epinions and Slashdot has motivated increasing research on signed network analysis [11, 13, 3].

It is evident from recent work that negative links have significant added value over positive links in various analytical tasks. For example, a small number of negative links can significantly improve positive link prediction [7, 13], and they can also improve the performance of recommender systems in social media [24, 18]. Similarly, trust and distrust relations in Epinions can help users find high-quality and reliable reviews [7]. Furthermore, the specification of negative links is interesting in its own right. On the other hand, it is generally not very desirable for online social networks to explicitly collect negative links [8, 12]. As a consequence, most social media sites such as Facebook and Twitter do not enable users to explicitly specify negative links. Therefore, it is natural to question whether one can predict negative links automatically from the available data in social networks. A key assumption is that while *explicit* data is often not available about negative links, the combination of content-centric and structural data in social networks may contain implicit information about negative linkages. While this problem is very challenging [3], the results of such an approach have the potential to improve the quality of the results of a vast array of applications.

To preserve the generality of our approach, it is important to use social network data which is pervasively available across social networks in various forms. First, an obvious source of useful data are the positive linkages which

[1]https://www.facebook.com/
[2]https://twitter.com/
[3]http://www.epinions.com/
[4]http://slashdot.org/

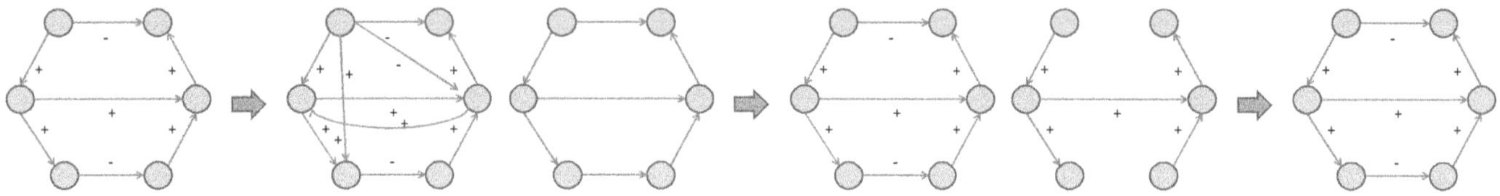

(a) Positive and Negative Link Prediction (b) Sign Prediction (c) Negative Link Prediction

Figure 1: An Illustration of the Differences of Positive and Negative Link Prediction, Sign Prediction and Negative Link Prediction.

are commonly available in most social networks. Second, in most social media sites, users can create or post content[5] and other users can comment, like/dislike and rate such content. In fact, such user interactions form the dominant social media activities[6], today. For example, users can comment, like, or dislike content such posts and videos. Another example is the case of Epinions, where users can rate the helpfulness of reviews written by others. In this paper, we study the novel problem of negative link prediction from these two pervasive sources in social media. However, we do not assume that examples of negative links are available. To achieve this goal, we need (a) theories explaining the relevance of positive links and content-centric user interactions for negative link prediction, and (b) combining these theories with mathematical models to predict negative links. These goals are achieved by our novel framework for the negative link prediction problem (NeLP). Our main contributions are summarized below,

- We provide a principled way to exploit positive links and content-centric user interactions for the problem of negative link prediction;
- We propose a novel framework NeLP to predict negative links by incorporating positive links and content-centric user interactions mathematically; and
- We evaluate the proposed NeLP framework in real-world social media datasets to understand the effectiveness and mechanisms of the proposed framework.

The rest of paper is organized as follows. In Section 2, we formally define the negative link prediction problem. We perform preliminary analysis on these datasets in Section 3 to study the interaction between existing social theories and negative link presence. In Section 4, we combine these theories with a mathematical formulation for negative link prediction. This is referred to as the NeLP framework. Section 5 presents experimental results with discussions. Section 6 briefly reviews related work. Finally, Section 7 concludes with future work.

2. PROBLEM STATEMENT

Let $\mathcal{U} = \{u_1, u_2, \ldots, u_m\}$ be the set of m users in the social network. A signed network can be decomposed into a positive network component $\mathcal{G}_p(\mathcal{U}, E_p)$ and a negative network component $\mathcal{G}_n(\mathcal{U}, E_n)$ where E_p and E_n are the sets of positive and negative links, respectively. Let $\mathcal{P} = \{p_1, p_2, \ldots, p_M\}$ be the set of M pieces of content such as posts. We use $\mathbf{A} \in \mathbb{R}^{m \times M}$ to denote the user-content relationships where $\mathbf{A}_{ij} = 1$ if p_j is created by u_i, and $\mathbf{A}_{ij} = 0$ otherwise. Users can express opinions on content via comments, likes/dislikes, and ratings. Some social media sites provide explicit ways of enabling user feedback on content. Examples include likes/dislikes in Youtube, and "very helpful"/"not helpful" ratings in Epinions. Other more common forms of feedback in large-scale social networks such as Facebook and Twitter allow users to express their opinions in the form of textual comments and replies. In such cases, we adapt off-the-shelf opinion mining tools to extract user opinions from such texts. We use $\mathbf{O} \in \mathbb{R}^{m \times M}$ to represent the user-post opinion relations where $\mathbf{O}_{ij} = 1$, $\mathbf{O}_{ij} = -1$ and $\mathbf{O}_{ij} = 0$, if u_i expresses positive, negative and neutral (or no) opinions, respectively, on p_j.

With the aforementioned notations and definitions, the problem of negative link prediction in social media is formally defined as follows:

Given the positive network $\mathcal{G}_p$, and content-centric user interactions $\mathbf{A}$ and $\mathbf{O}$, we aim to develop a predictor f to predict the negative network $\mathcal{G}_n$ with $\mathcal{G}_p$, $\mathbf{A}$ and $\mathbf{O}$ as,

$$f: \{\mathcal{G}_p, \mathbf{A}, \mathbf{O}\} \rightarrow \mathcal{G}_n \quad (1)$$

The negative link prediction problem in this paper is quite different and much more challenging than the existing frameworks for positive/negative link prediction [13], and the sign prediction problem [26]. An illustration of their differences for the existing variations of the problem is demonstrated in Figure 1 as follows:

- One of the existing variations predicts positive and negative links from existing positive and negative links. On the other hand, as illustrated in Figure 1(c), we do not assume the existence of negative links.
- The second variation (Figure 1(b)) predicts signs of *already existing* links. On the other hand, the negative link prediction problem needs to identify the pairs of nodes between which negative links *are predicted to* exist.

3. DATA ANALYSIS

Because positive link prediction is dependent on "typical" behavior of social networks such as triadic closure, it is natural to explore similar properties of negative links with respect to other positive links, and content-centric interactions. Such an understanding lays the groundwork for a meaningful negative link-prediction model. For the purpose of this study, we collected two datasets from Epinions and Slashdot, that explicitly allow users to express both positive

[5]The term "content" may be manifested in diverse ways such as statuses, tweets, images, or videos.

[6]`http://www.marketingprofs.com/charts/2010/4101/social-media-brand-followers-hunting-for-deals`

Table 1: Statistics of the Epinions and Slashdot Datasets.

	Epinions	Slashdot
# of Users	14,765	7,275
# of Positive Links	272,513	67,705
# of Negative Links	52,704	20,851
# of Posts	612,321	300,932
# of Positive Opinions	6,937,986	1,742,763
# of Negative Opinions	163,502	42,260

and negative links. Note that the negative links in these two datasets only serve as a ground-truth about typical properties and the underlying social theories. However, they are not explicitly used in the proposed framework for the problem of negative link prediction.

Epinions is a popular product review site. Users can create both positive (trust) and negative (distrust) links to other users. They can write reviews for various products and other users can express opinions on these reviews with the use of "helpfulness" ratings from 1 to 6. In this work, we view ratings larger than 3 as positive, and those lower than 3 as negative. This assumption is used to populate the user-content opinion matrix $\mathbf{O}$ of the Epinions dataset.

Slashdot is a technology news platform in which users can create friend (positive) and foe (negative) links to other users. They can also post news articles. Other users may annotate these articles with their comments and opinions. In this case, we computed the sentiment polarities of comments based on an off-the-shelf manually labeled sentiment lexicon, i.e., MPQA Subjectivity Lexicon [7]. These sentiment polarities are used to populate the user-content opinion matrix.

Some additional preprocessing was performed on these two datasets by filtering users without any positive and negative links. A number of key statistics of these datasets are illustrated in Table 1[8]. It is evident from these statistics that users are more likely to express positive opinions than negative opinions in social media.

3.1 Where Are our "Enemies"?

Our first analytical task is to examine the typical structural relationships of "enemies" within the positive network. In other words, if u_i has a negative link to u_j in the negative network $\mathcal{G}_n$, we investigate the typical position of u_j with respect to u_i in the positive network $\mathcal{G}_p$. In the following sections, we will use u_i+u_j, u_i-u_j and u_i?u_j to denote positive, negative and missing links between u_i to u_j, respectively.

For each negative link u_i-u_j in $\mathcal{G}_n$, we use breadth-first search to compute the shortest path from u_i to u_j in $\mathcal{G}_p$. If paths exist from u_i to u_j, we report the length of the shortest path. Otherwise we report the length as "inf" to indicate there is no path from u_i to u_j in $\mathcal{G}_p$. The ratio distributions of the lengths of the shortest paths for all negative links are demonstrated in Figures 2(a) and 2(b) for Epinions and Slashdot, respectively. In both datasets, more than 45% of negative links u_i-u_j have shortest path lengths less than 3, and more than 80% of them have shortest path lengths less than 4. These results suggest that our "enemies" are often close to us in the positive network $\mathcal{G}_p$. For example, about 82.64% and 87.86% of enemy-pairs are within 3-hops of each

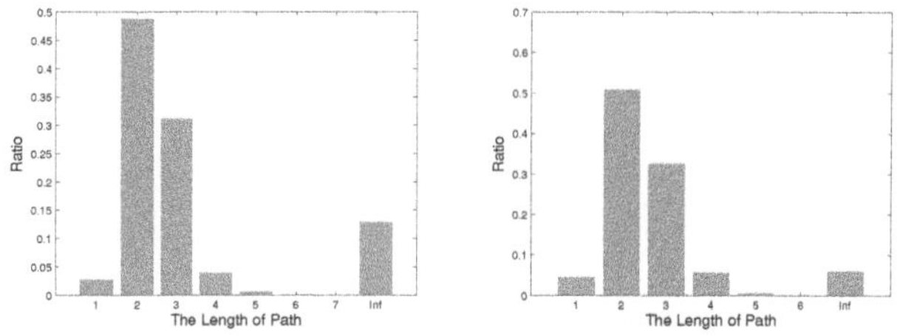

(a) Epinions (b) Slashdot

Figure 2: Ratio Distributions of the Length of Shortest Path for Pairs with Negative Links in the Positive Networks.

other in the positive networks of Epinions and Slashdot, respectively.

3.2 Social Theories in Signed Networks

In this subsection, we investigate two of the most important social theories for signed networks, i.e., balance theory [9, 2] and status theory [14].

In general, balance theory is based on the intuition that "the friend of my friend is my friend" and "the enemy of my enemy is my friend" [9]. This theory relates the balance of signs on a triad involving three users in a social network with positive and negative links. We use s_{ij} to denote the sign of the link between u_i and u_j where $s_{ij} = 1$ (or $s_{ij} = -1$) if there is a positive link (or a negative link) between u_i and u_j. Balance theory suggests that a triad $\langle u_i, u_j, u_k \rangle$ is balanced if the following is true - (a) $s_{ij} = 1$ and $s_{jk} = 1$, then $s_{ik} = 1$; or (b) $s_{ij} = -1$ and $s_{jk} = -1$, then $s_{ik} = 1$.

For a triad $\langle u_i, u_j, u_k \rangle$, there are four possible signed combinations (+,+,+), (+,+,-), (+,-,-) and (-,-,-), while only (+,+,+) and (+,-,-) are balanced. Based on the discussion in [13], the directions of links are ignored in the study of balance theory because balance theory is designed for undirected networks. We computed the relative presence of these four possible combinations and find that 92.31% and 93.01% of triads in Epinions and Slashdot are balanced, respectively.

In status theory, a positive link from u_i to u_j indicates that u_i has a higher status than u_j; while a negative link from u_i to u_j indicates that u_i has a lower status than u_j. For a triad, status theory suggests that if we take each negative link, reverse its direction, and flip its sign to positive, then the resulting triangle (with all positive link) should be acyclic. We first obtain all triads and then follow the above way to examine whether these triads satisfy status theory or not. We find that 94.73% and 93.38% of triads in Epnions and Slashdot satisfy status theory, respectively.

3.3 Negative Links and Content-centric Interactions

Content-centric interactions relate the opinion of user u_i on the content posted by user u_j. The user u_i can express negative opinions on content posted by another user u_j by disliking, giving negative comments, or negative ratings. Such types of content-centric interactions may be viewed as negative interactions between u_i and u_j. A negative interaction from u_i to u_j is often a manifestation of user u_i's disagreement and antagonism toward u_j. It is therefore reasonable to surmise that negative interactions might be correlated with negative links. In this subsection, we study the correlation between negative interactions and negative links.

[7]http://mpqa.cs.pitt.edu/lexicons/subj$_$lexicon

[8]Datasets and code will be available at http://www.public.asu.edu/~jtang20/SignedNetwork.htm

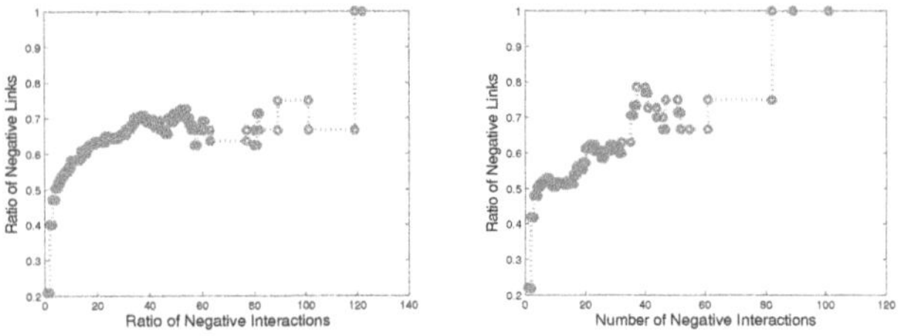

(a) Epinions (b) Slashdot

Figure 3: The Ratios of Negative Links with respect to the Number of Negative Interactions.

Let $\mathbf{N} \in \mathbb{R}^{m \times m}$ be a user-user negative interaction matrix where $\mathbf{N}_{ij}$ denotes the number of negative interactions from u_i to u_j. We can obtain $\mathbf{N}$ from the user-content authorship matrix $\mathbf{A}$ and the user-content opinion matrix $\mathbf{O}$ as $\mathbf{N} = -\mathbf{A}(\mathbf{O}^-)^\top$ where $\mathbf{O}^- = \frac{\mathbf{O}-|\mathbf{O}|}{2}$ is the negative part of $\mathbf{O}$. To verify the correlation between negative interactions and negative links, we aim to answer the following question: Are pairs of users with negative interactions more likely to have negative links than those without negative interactions?

For each pair $\langle u_i, u_j \rangle$ with negative interactions (or $\mathbf{N}_{ij} \neq 0$), we first randomly select a user u_k that u_i does not have negative interactions with (or $\mathbf{N}_{ij} = 0$), and then use S (or R) to indicate whether $\langle u_i, u_j \rangle$ (or $\langle u_i, u_k \rangle$) has a negative link where $S = 1$ (or $R = 1$) if u_i has a negative link to u_j (or u_i has a negative link to u_k), otherwise $S = 0$ (or $R = 0$). Let $\mathbf{s}$ be a vector of Ss over all pairs of users with negative interactions and $\mathbf{r}$ be the corresponding vector of Rs. We conduct a two-sample t-test on $\mathbf{s}$ and $\mathbf{r}$. The null hypothesis and the alternative hypothesis are defined as $H_0 : \mathbf{s} \leq \mathbf{r}$, $H_1 : \mathbf{s} > \mathbf{r}$. The null hypothesis is rejected at significance level $\alpha = 0.01$ with p-values of 5.72e-89 and 1.93e-109 for Epinions and Slashdot, respectively. Evidence from the t-test suggests a positive answer to the question: *there is a strong correlation between negative interactions and negative links, and users with negative interactions are likely to have negative links.*

We further investigate the direct impact of negative interactions on negative links. For a given value of K, we calculated the ratio of pairs with both negative links and at least K negative interactions over all pairs with at least K negative interactions. The ratio distributions with respect to the number of negative interactions are demonstrated in Figures 3(a) and 3(b), respectively. Note that the ratios of randomly selected pairs with negative links among all $n(n-1)$ pairs of users are 2.4177e-04 and 3.9402e-04 in Epinions and Slashdot, respectively. From the figures, we note that the ratios are much higher than the random ones even when K is very small. This observation further supports the existence of the correlation between negative interactions and negative links. Furthermore with increase of K, the ratios tend to increase. Therefore, an increase in the number of negative interactions increases the likelihood of negative links between users.

3.4 Discussion

We summarize the insights obtained in the aforementioned discussion as follows:

- Most of our "enemies" are close to us within a few (e.g., 2 or 3) hops in the positive network.
- Most of triads in signed networks satisfy balance theory and status theory.
- Pairs of users with negative interactions are more likely to have negative links than those without them.
- Negative interactions between users increase the propensity of negative links.

These observations provide the groundwork for our proposed framework for negative link prediction.

4. THE PROPOSED FRAMEWORK - NeLP

Algorithms for all variations of the link prediction problem are either unsupervised methods [15, 10] or supervised methods [17, 13]. Supervised methods consider the link prediction problem as a classification problem by using the existence of links as labels and have several advantages over unsupervised methods such as superior performance, adaptability to different data domains, and variance reduction [17]. Similar to traditional supervised link prediction, we can consider the negative link prediction problem as a classification problem where we need to construct labels and extract features. Different from traditional link prediction, there are unique challenges in preparing training data in the negative link prediction problem. For example, existing links are given in traditional link prediction such as positive links in positive link prediction, and positive and negative links in positive and negative link prediction, while existing negative links are not given in the negative link prediction problem. Next we will first give details about label construction and feature extraction for the negative link prediction problem. Finally, the optimization formulation and solution will be discussed.

4.1 Label Construction

Let E_o denote pairs of users with missing links. In most previous formulations of link prediction, including the signed version, label construction is trivial because the presence of links is specified. However, we study the scenario where no negative links are provided, and therefore the labels for E_n are really an unspecified subset of $E_o \cup E_n$. What is worse, the sizes of E_n and E_o are extremely imbalanced. For example, the imbalance ratios $E_n : E_o$ are 1:4131 and 1:2534 in Epinions and Slashdot respectively. We treat missing links as positive samples and negative links as negative samples. Label construction is to construct positive and negative samples from $E_o \cup E_n$. Since the ratio of E_o in $E_n \cup E_o$ are often bigger than 99.9%, we can randomly select a subset of samples from $E_n \cup E_o$ as positive samples PS. Next we introduce a way to select samples from $E_n \cup E_o$ as negative samples based on previous observations. The process is shown in Algorithm 1.

Next, we describe Algorithm 1 for negative sample construction. The strong correlation between negative interactions and negative links suggests that users with negative interactions are likely to have negative links. Therefore from line 2 to line 4 in Algorithm 1, we construct negative sample candidates based on this observation. With the positive links from $\mathcal{G}_p$ and negative links u_i-u_j from NS, we construct a signed network $\mathcal{G}$ in line 5. Most of the triads in signed networks satisfy status theory. Therefore we refine NS by (a) excluding $\langle u_i, u_j \rangle$ from NS if u_i-u_j is in any triads of $\mathcal{G}$ that does not satisfy status theory in line 6; and (b)

Algorithm 1: Negative Sample Construction

Input : The positive network $\mathcal{G}_p$ and user-user negative interaction matrix $\mathbf{N}$

Output : Negative sample set NS and the reliability weight matrix $\mathbf{W}$

1: Initialize $NS = \emptyset$
2: **for all** $\mathbf{N}_{ij} \neq 0$ **do**
3: $NS = NS \cup \{\langle u_i, u_j \rangle\}$
4: **end for**
5: Construct $\mathcal{G}$ as a signed network with positive links from $\mathbf{G}_p$ and negative links u_i-u_j from NS
6: Remove samples $\langle u_i, u_j \rangle$ from NS if u_i-u_j is in any triads of $\mathcal{G}$ that does not satisfy status theory
7: Add samples $\langle u_i, u_k \rangle$ into NS if u_i-u_k can make all triads that involve u_i and u_k in $\mathcal{G}$ satisfying status theory
8: **for all** $\langle u_i, u_j \rangle \in NS$ **do**
9: Calculate a reliability weight $\mathbf{W}_{ij}$
10: **end for**

adding samples $\langle u_i, u_k \rangle$ into NS if u_i-u_k can make all triads that involve u_i and u_k in $\mathcal{G}$ satisfying status theory in line 7. The reliability of these negative samples may vary. For example, observations from data analysis indicate that negative sample candidates with more negative interactions are more likely to have negative links, and are therefore more likely to be reliable. Therefore, we associate each $\langle u_i, u_j \rangle$ with a reliability weight $\mathbf{W}_{ij}$, which is defined as follows:

$$\mathbf{W}_{ij} = \begin{cases} f(\mathbf{N}_{ij}) & \text{if } \mathbf{N}_{ij} \neq 0 \\ r & \text{otherwise} \end{cases}. \tag{2}$$

if the pair $\langle u_i, u_j \rangle \in NS$ has negative interactions, we define the reliability weight as a function f of the number of negative interactions $\mathbf{N}_{ij}$ where $f(x) \in [0, 1]$ is a non-decreasing function of x. This is because the more negative interactions two users have, the more likely it is that a negative link exists between them. Otherwise, the pair $\langle u_i, u_j \rangle \in NS$ is added by line 7 in Algorithm 1 and we set the reliability weight to a constant r.

4.2 Feature Extraction

We extract three types of features corresponding to user features, pair features and sign features. User features and pair features are extracted from two given sources, such as positive links and content-centric interactions, as follows:

- User features are extracted for each user u_i including u_i's indegree (or outdegree) in terms of positive links, the number of triads that u_i involved in, the number of content-centric items (e.g., posts) that u_i creates, the number of u_i's posts that obtain positive (or negative) opinions, and the number of positive (or negative) opinions u_i expresses; and

- Pair features are extracted for a pair of users $\langle u_i, u_j \rangle$ including the number of positive (or negative) interactions from u_i to u_j, the number of positive (or negative) interactions from u_j to u_i, Jaccard coefficients of indegree (or outdegree) of u_i and u_j in terms of positive links, and the length of the shortest path between u_i and u_j.

We construct a weighted signed network with the given positive links and negative links from NS where the weights of positive links are 1 and the weights of negative links are their reliability weights. For a pair $\langle u_i, u_j \rangle$, signed features include weighted indegree (or outdegee) in terms of negative links of u_i, weighted indegree (and outdegee) in terms of negative links of u_j, Jaccard coefficients of indegree (or outdegree) of u_i and u_j in terms of negative links and 16 weighted triads suggested by [13].

With definitions of user features, pair features and sign features, we extract 45 features in total for each pair $\langle u_i, u_j \rangle$ including 8 user features of u_i, 8 user features of u_j, 7 pair features, and 22 signed features.

4.3 The NeLP Optimization Framework

Through label construction and feature extraction, we prepare training data to learn classifiers for the negative link prediction problem. However, the labels of the training data are noisy, and especially so for negative samples. Therefore, it is necessary for the base classifier to be tolerant to training data noise. In this paper, we choose a soft-margin version of support vector machines as our basic classifier because it has been proven to be highly noise-tolerant [5].

Let $\mathcal{X} = \{x_1, x_2, \ldots, x_N\}$ be the set of user pairs in $E_o \cup E_n$ and $\mathbf{x}_i$ be the feature vector representation of the pair x_i. The standard soft-margin support vector machine for the negative link prediction problem is as follows:

$$\begin{aligned} \min_{\mathbf{w}, b, \epsilon} \quad & \frac{1}{2}\|\mathbf{w}\|_2^2 + C \sum_{x_i \in PS \cup NS} \epsilon_i \\ s.t. \quad & y_i(\mathbf{w}^\top \mathbf{x}_i + b) \geq 1 - \epsilon_i, \; x_i \in PS \cup NS \\ & \epsilon_i \geq 0 \;\; x_i \in PS \cup NS \end{aligned} \tag{3}$$

Eq. (3) introduces the term ϵ_i for the soft-margin slack variable of x_i, which can be viewed as the allowance for the noise in this training sample. The parameter C controls the degree of impact of this term. In the negative link-prediction problem, the noise-levels of positive and negative samples are different because positive samples PS are generally more robust than the (indirectly derived) negative samples. As discussed earlier, the reliability of negative samples is explicitly quantified with their weights. These intuitions suggest that we should allow more errors in negative samples especially when their weights suggest unreliability. This yields the following formulation:

$$\begin{aligned} \min_{\mathbf{w}, b, \epsilon} \quad & \frac{1}{2}\|\mathbf{w}\|_2^2 + C_p \sum_{x_i \in PS} \epsilon_i + C_n \sum_{x_j \in NS} c_j \epsilon_j \\ s.t. \quad & y_i(\mathbf{w}^\top \mathbf{x}_i + b) \geq 1 - \epsilon_i, \quad x_i \in PS \\ & y_j(\mathbf{w}^\top \mathbf{x}_j + b) \geq 1 - \epsilon_j, \quad x_j \in NS \\ & \epsilon_i \geq 0, \; \epsilon_j \geq 0 \end{aligned} \tag{4}$$

In Eq. (4), we use two parameters C_p and C_n to weight the positive and negative errors differently. We use a larger value for C_p compared to C_n to reflect the differential behavior of the positive and negative samples. For a negative sample x_j, we introduce a weight c_j to further control its error based on its quantified reliability weight. For the negative sample x_j corresponding to the pair $\langle u_i, u_k \rangle$, we set $c_j = \mathbf{W}_{ik}$ where $\mathbf{W}_{ik}$ is the reliability weight for $\langle u_i, u_k \rangle$. This additional term allows differential control of the noise in negative samples of varying reliability.

Balance theory suggests that triads in signed networks are likely to be balanced. Therefore, if there is a positive link between u_i and u_j, and both u_i and u_j do not have positive links with another user u_k, the types of (u_i, u_k) and (u_j, u_k) in the negative graph $\mathcal{G}_n$ are likely to be the same. In other words, to ensure the structural balance, it is likely that both are negative links where $\langle u_i, u_j, u_k \rangle$ forms a balanced triad or both are missing links where there is no triad among $\langle u_i, u_j, u_k \rangle$. With this intuition, we introduce a matrix $\mathbf{B}$ where $\mathbf{B}_{h\ell} = 1$ if there is a positive link between u_i and u_j where we assume that x_h and x_ℓ denote pairs $\langle u_i, u_k \rangle$ and $\langle u_j, u_k \rangle$ respectively. Otherwise, we assume that $\mathbf{B}_{h\ell} = 0$. Then, we force x_h and x_ℓ to have the same types of links if $\mathbf{B}_{h\ell} = 1$ by introducing a balance-theory regularization:

$$\min \quad \frac{1}{2}\sum_{h,\ell} \mathbf{B}_{h\ell}(\mathbf{w}^\top \mathbf{x}_h - \mathbf{w}^\top \mathbf{x}_\ell)_2^2 = \mathbf{w}^\top \mathbf{X}\mathcal{L}\mathbf{X}^\top \mathbf{w} \qquad (5)$$

Here, $\mathcal{L}$ is the Laplacian matrix based on $\mathbf{B}$. The number of pairs in $E_n \cup E_o$ is usually very large, which leads to a large number of terms in the balance theory regularization. The observation from data analysis suggests that our "enemies" are usually close to us in the positive network. Hence, in this work, we only consider pairs whose shortest path lengths are 2, and pairs in NS and PS in the balance theory regularization. We assume that there are $l + \mu$ samples in $\mathbf{X}$ where the first l ones are from $PS \cup NS$. The significance of the introduction of the balance theory regularization is two-fold. First, it allows us to model balance theory. Second, it allows us to include more samples during the learning process in addition to NS and PS. A similar function is achieved by this approach, as achieved by unlabeled samples in semi-supervised learning [28]. With these components, the proposed NeLP framework is able to solve the following optimization problem:

$$\begin{aligned}
\min_{\mathbf{w},b,\epsilon} \quad & \frac{1}{2}\|\mathbf{w}\|_2^2 + C_p \sum_{x_i \in PS} \epsilon_i + C_n \sum_{x_j \in NS} c_j \epsilon_j \\
& + \frac{C_b}{2}\mathbf{w}^\top \mathbf{X}\mathcal{L}\mathbf{X}^\top \mathbf{w} \\
s.t. \quad & y_i(\mathbf{w}^\top \mathbf{x}_i + b) \geq 1 - \epsilon_i, \quad x_i \in PS \\
& y_j(\mathbf{w}^\top \mathbf{x}_j + b) \geq 1 - \epsilon_j, \quad x_j \in NS \\
& \epsilon_i \geq 0, \ \epsilon_j \geq 0
\end{aligned} \qquad (6)$$

We solve the optimization problem in Eq. (6) based on the dual form [1]. The classical representer theorem states that the solution to this minimization problem of Eq.(6) exists in $\mathcal{H}_K$ and can be written as follows:

$$\mathbf{w}^* = \sum_i \alpha_i K(\mathbf{x}_i, \mathbf{x}) \qquad (7)$$

Eq.(6) can be rewritten as follows:

$$\begin{aligned}
\min_{\alpha,b,\epsilon} \quad & \frac{1}{2}\alpha^\top \mathbf{K}\alpha + C_p \sum_{u_i \in PS} \epsilon_i + C_n \sum_{u_j \in NS} c_j \epsilon_j + \frac{C_b}{2}\alpha^\top \mathbf{K}\mathcal{L}\mathbf{K}\alpha \\
s.t. \quad & y_i(\sum_k \alpha_k K(\mathbf{x}_k, \mathbf{x}_i) + b) \geq 1 - \epsilon_i, \quad u_i \in PS \\
& y_j(\sum_k \alpha_k K(\mathbf{x}_k, \mathbf{x}_j) + b) \geq 1 - \epsilon_j, \quad u_j \in NS \\
& \epsilon_i \geq 0, \ \epsilon_j \geq 0
\end{aligned} \qquad (8)$$

where $\mathbf{K}$ is the Gram matrix over all samples.

We define s_i for x_i as follows:

$$s_i = \begin{cases} C_p & \text{for } x_i \in PS, \\ C_n c_i & \text{for } x_i \in NS. \end{cases} \qquad (9)$$

After the introduction of two sets of multipliers β and γ, the Lagrangian function of Eq.(8) is as follows:

$$\begin{aligned}
L(\mathbf{w}, b, \epsilon, \alpha, \gamma) = & \frac{1}{2}\alpha^\top(\mathbf{K} + C_b \mathbf{K}\mathcal{L}\mathbf{K})\alpha + \sum_{i=1}^{l} s_i \epsilon_i \\
& - \sum_{i=1}^{l} \beta_i [y_i(\sum_k \alpha_k K(\mathbf{x}_k, \mathbf{x}_i) + b) - 1 + \epsilon_i] - \sum_{i=1}^{l} \gamma_i \epsilon_i
\end{aligned} \qquad (10)$$

where β and γ are Lagrange multipliers.

To obtain the dual representation, we set

$$\begin{aligned}
\frac{\partial L}{\partial b} &= 0 \Rightarrow \sum_{i=1}^{l} \beta_i y_i = 0 \\
\frac{\partial L}{\partial \epsilon_i} &= 0 \Rightarrow s_i - \beta_i - \gamma_i = 0 \Rightarrow 0 \leq \beta_i \leq s_i
\end{aligned} \qquad (11)$$

With Eq. (11), we can rewrite the Lagrangian as a function of only α and β as follows:

$$L(\alpha, \beta) = \frac{1}{2}\alpha^\top(\mathbf{K} + C_b \mathbf{K}\mathcal{L}\mathbf{K})\alpha - \alpha^\top \mathbf{K}\mathbf{J}^\top \mathbf{Y}\beta + \sum_{i=1}^{l} \beta_i \qquad (12)$$

in Eq. (12), $\mathbf{J} = [\mathbf{I}\ \mathbf{0}]$ where $\mathbf{I}$ is an $l \times l$ identity matrix and $\mathbf{0}$ is a $l \times \mu$ rectangular matrix with all zeros, and $\mathbf{Y}$ is a $l \times l$ diagonal matrix composed by labels of samples in PS and NS.

By setting $\frac{\partial L}{\partial \alpha} = 0$, we obtain

$$\alpha = (\mathbf{I} + C_b \mathbf{K}\mathcal{L})^{-1}\mathbf{J}^\top \mathbf{Y}\beta \qquad (13)$$

After substituting back in the Lagrangian function, we obtain the dual problem as a quadratic programming problem:

$$\begin{aligned}
\max_{\beta} \quad & \sum_{i=1}^{l} \beta_i - \frac{1}{2}\beta^\top \mathbf{Q}\beta \\
s.t. \quad & \sum_{i=1}^{l} \beta_i y_i = 0 \\
& 0 \leq \beta_i \leq s_i
\end{aligned} \qquad (14)$$

where $\mathbf{Q}$ is defined as follows:

$$\mathbf{Q} = \mathbf{Y}\mathbf{J}\mathbf{K}(\mathbf{I} + C_b \mathbf{K}\mathcal{L})^{-1}\mathbf{J}^\top \mathbf{Y} \qquad (15)$$

5. EXPERIMENTS

In this section, we present experiments which (a) quantify the performance of the proposed NeLP framework in predicting negative links, and (b) evaluate the contribution of various model components to the performance. We begin by introducing performance evaluation metrics, which are useful in both contexts.

5.1 Evaluation Metrics

All forms of link prediction can be viewed as highly imbalanced classification problems. In such cases, straightforward accuracy measures are well known to be misleading [25]. For example, in a sparse network, the trivial classifier that labels all samples as missing links can have a 99.99% accuracy. In negative link prediction, we aim to achieve high

Table 2: Confusion Matrix of a Binary Classifier.

	True class = -1	True class = 1
Predicted class = -1	true pos. (tp)	false pos. (fp)
Predicted class = 1	false neg. (fn)	true neg. (tn)

precision and recall over negative links, defined in terms of the confusion matrix of a classifier as shown in Table 2: $precision = \frac{tp}{tp+fp}$ and $recall = \frac{tp}{tp+fn}$. Usually precision and recall are combined into their harmonic mean, the F-measure. Therefore we will adopt F1-measure as one metric for the performance evaluation. As suggested in [25], in some scenarios, we put more emphasis on precision because the most challenging task is to seek some negative links with high probability, even at the price of increasing false negatives. Hence, we also report the precision performance.

5.2 Performance of Negative Link prediction

In this subsection, we assess the proposed framework in terms of (a) the performance of NeLP with respect to baseline methods; and (b) the generalization of the proposed framework across social media sites. For the first evaluation, we define the following baseline methods:

- *Random*: This predictor randomly guesses the labels of samples. As suggested in positive link prediction [16], a random predictor should be used as a baseline method to meaningfully demonstrate the performance significance of other predictors;
- *sPath*: Observations in data analysis suggest that our "enemies" are always close to us in the positive network and *sPath* assigns negative links to pairs whose shortest path lengths is L;
- *negIn*: Given the strong correlation between negative interactions and negative links, *negIn* suggests negative links to these pairs with negative interactions;
- *negInS*: after obtaining negative link candidates via *negIn*, *negInS* further refines these candidates by performing a removing step and an adding step as shown in Algorithm 1; and
- *NeLP-negIn*: NeLP-negIn is a variant of the proposed NeLP framework. Instead of using negative links suggested by *negInS* as NeLP, NeLP-negIn uses negative links found by *negIn*.

For parameterized methods, we report the best performance of each baseline method. For NeLP, we set its parameters as $\{C_p = 1, C_n = 0.5, C_b = 0.1\}$ and $\{C_p = 1, C_n = 0.7, C_b = 0.01\}$ in Epinions and Slashdot, respectively. We empirically find that $f(x) = 1 - \frac{1}{\log(1+x)}$ works well for the proposed framework. More details about parameter sensitivity of NeLP will be discussed in later subsections. The comparison results are demonstrated in Table 3.

We make the following observations:

- *sPath* obtains much better performance than random guessing, which further supports the hypothesis that our "enemies" are close to us in the positive network;
- *negIn* improves the performance significantly in both datasets. These results suggest the existence of correlation between negative interactions and negative links;

Table 3: Performance Comparison of Negative Link Prediction in Epinions and Slashdot.

Algorithms	Epinions		Slashdot	
	F1	Precision	F1	Precision
random	0.0005	0.0002	0.0008	0.0004
sPath	0.0040	0.0075	0.0090	0.0172
negIn	0.2826	0.2097	0.1986	0.1483
negInS	0.2893	0.2124	0.2072	0.1524
NeLP-negIn	0.3206	0.2812	0.2394	0.2083
NeLP	0.3242	0.2861	0.2441	0.2139

- by removing candidates suggested by *negIn* that do not satisfy status theory and adding candidates to make open triads closure to satisfy status theory, *negInS* outperforms *negIn*. For example, *negInS* gains 2.37% and 1.45% relative improvement in terms of F1-measure in Epinions and Slashdot, respectively. These results indicate that status theory can help us remove some noisy samples and add some useful samples for training. These observations can also be used to explain the reason why the performance of NeLP based on negative links suggested by *negInS* is better than that based on *negIn*; and
- the proposed framework always obtains the best performance. There are three important components of NeLP. First, NeLP introduces C_n to control errors in negative samples. Second, NeLP introduces c_j to control the error in the sample x_j, which is related to the number of negative interactions based on our observations from data analysis. Third, NeLP introduces balance theory regularization to model balance theory, which also allows us to include more samples in the classifier learning process. More details about the effects of these components will be discussed in a later subsection.

Because the classifier learned by the proposed framework is based on the same set of features extracted from pervasively available sources for most social media sites, it is possible to generalize the classifier learned in one site to other sites and we further investigate how well the learned classifier generalizes across social media sites. In particular, we evaluate the performance of the classifier on Epinions (or Slashdot), which is learned from Slashdot (or Epinions). The results are shown in Figure 4. Note that in the figure $x \rightarrow y$ denotes training on x and evaluating on y. These results show that there is very good generalization of the classifier learned by NeLP although there is remarkably little decrease in performance regardless of which dataset is used for training. In summary, compared to baseline methods, the proposed framework obtains significant performance improvement, and it also has very good generalization across social media sites.

5.3 Component Analysis of NeLP

In this subsection, we investigate the effects of various NeLP components on its performance. In NeLP, we introduce C_n, c_j and C_b to control three components of NeLP. In particular, C_n controls errors from negative samples, c_j controls the error from the negative sample x_j and C_b controls the contribution from the balance theory regularization. By setting $C_p = 1$ and varying different values of C_n, c_j and C_b, we can examine the impact of these components on the

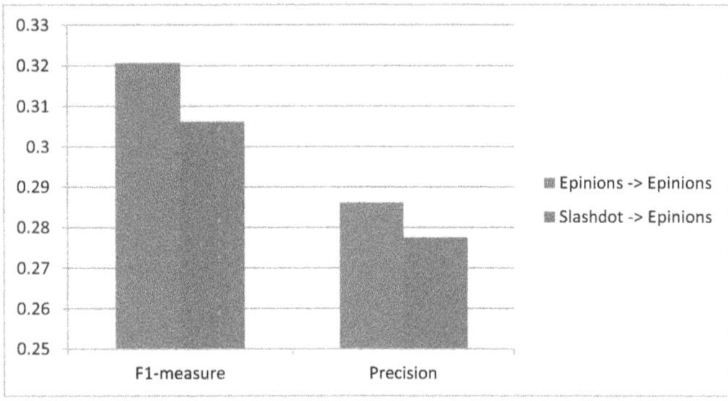

(a) Epinions

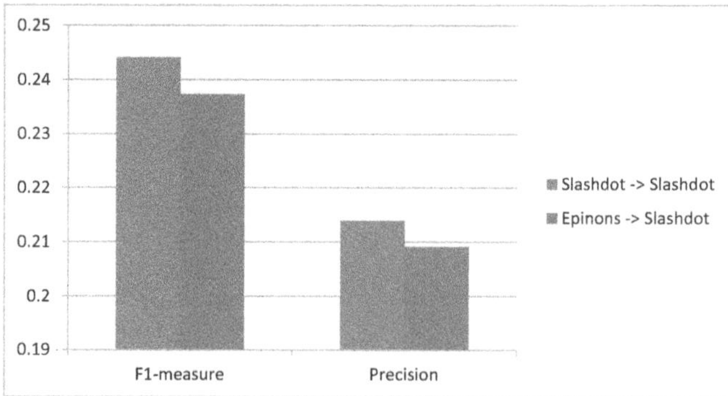

(b) Slashdot

Figure 4: The Negative Link Prediction Performance across Epinions and Slashdot where $x \to y$ denotes training on x and evaluating on y.

Table 4: Component analysis for NeLP in Epinions.

C_n	c_j	C_b	F1-measure	Precision
0.5	$f(x) = 1 - \frac{1}{\log(1+x)}$	0.1	0.3242	0.2861
1	$f(x) = 1 - \frac{1}{\log(1+x)}$	0.1	0.3188	0.2793
0.5	f(x) = 1	0.1	0.3067	0.2612
0.5	$f(x) = 1 - \frac{1}{\log(1+x)}$	0	0.3084	0.2686
1	f(x) = 1	0	0.2992	0.2342

Table 5: Component Analysis of NeLP in Slashdot.

C_n	c_j	C_b	F1-measure	Precision
0.7	$f(x) = 1 - \frac{1}{\log(1+x)}$	0.01	0.2441	0.2139
1	$f(x) = 1 - \frac{1}{\log(1+x)}$	0.01	0.2403	0.2094
0.7	f(x) = 1	0.01	0.2287	0.1902
0.7	$f(x) = 1 - \frac{1}{\log(1+x)}$	0	0.2347	0.1972
1	f(x) = 1	0	0.2213	0.1722

performance of NeLP. The results of component analysis are shown in Tables 4 and 5 for Epinions and Slashdot, respectively.

The first row in each table represents the performance of NeLP with all three components. We make the following observations about different variations of NeLP in other rows of the table:

- in the second row, we set $C_n = 1$, which gives equal weights to positive and negative samples. This approach effectively eliminates the *differential* importance given to errors from negative samples. The performance degrades, which suggests that the errors of negative and positive samples should be treated differently;
- in the third row, we set $c_j = 1$ instead of the reliability weight related to the number of negative interactions to eliminate the component controlling the error in the negative sample x_j. The performance reduces a lot. For example, the precision reduces by 8.70% and 11.08% in Epinions and Slashdot, respectively. These results support the importance of the number of negative interactions to indicate the reliability of negative samples;
- in the fourth row, we set $C_b = 0$ to eliminate the contribution from the balance theory regularization. and the performance is consistently worse than that with the balance theory regularization. This illustrates the importance of the balance theory regularization in the proposed NeLP framework; and
- in the fifth row, we eliminate all these three components and the performance further degrades. These results suggest that the three components contain complementary information.

5.4 Impact of Balance Theory Regularization

The analysis of the previous subsection shows the importance of balance theory regularization. In this subsection, we perform a more detailed analysis of the impact of the balance theory regularization on NeLP by showing how the performance varies with the changes in the value of C_b. This parameter controls the contribution from the balance theory regularization. We vary the values of C_b as $\{0, 0.001, 0.01, 0.05, 0.1, 0.5, 1\}$ and the results are shown in Figures 5(a) and 5(b) for Epinions and Slashdot, respectively. In general, with increase in C_b, the performance first improves, peaks, and then drops dramatically.

In particular, with the increase of C_b, we make the following observations:

- By increasing the value of C_b from 0 to 0.001, the performance increases significantly. For example, NeLP gains 4.02% and 4.41% in terms of precision in Epinions and Slashdot, respectively. These results further support the importance of the balance theory regularization in the NeLP framework;
- Within certain parameter ranges, such as from 0.001 to 0.1 in Epinions, the performance is relatively stable. This property is practically useful because it makes it easier to set C_b; and
- After certain values such as 0.05 in Slashdot, the performance decreases dramatically. A large value C_b results in balance theory regularization dominating the learning process at the expense of other factors.

In summary, the parameter analysis on C_b suggests that balance theory regularization is important for the NeLP framework.

6. RELATED WORK

In this section, we briefly review work which is related to different variants of the link prediction problem.

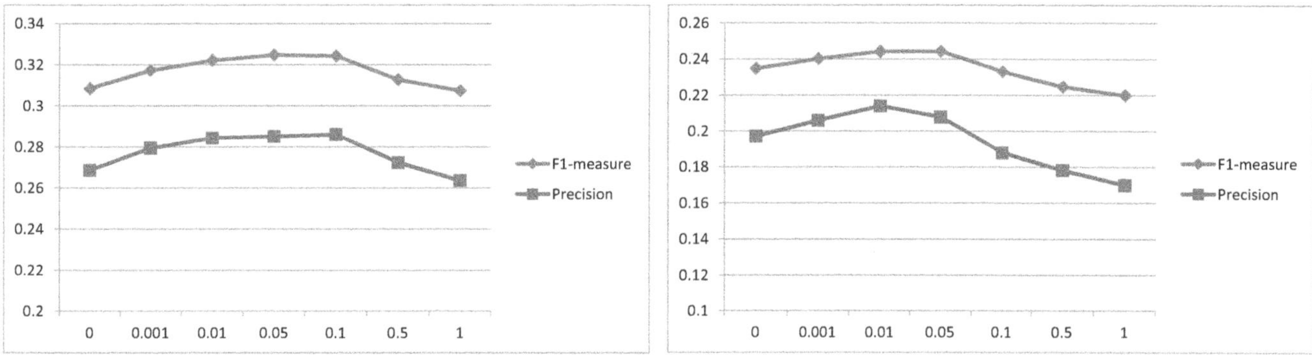

(a) Epinions (b) Slashdot

Figure 5: The Impact of the Balance Theory Regularization on NeLP

6.1 Positive Link Prediction

Positive link prediction infers new positive links in the near future based on a snapshot of a positive network. Existing methods can be roughly divided into unsupervised methods and supervised methods. Unsupervised methods are usually based on the topological structure of the given positive network. In [15], several unsupervised link prediction algorithms are proposed, such as Katz, Jaccard's coefficient and Adamic/Adar. In [19], several unsupervised algorithms based on low-rank matrix factorization are proposed. There are usually two steps for supervised methods. First, they extract features from available sources to represent each pair of users and consider the existence of positive links as labels. Second, they train a binary classifier based on the representation with extracted features and labels. In [17], the authors show several advantages of supervised link prediction algorithms such as superior performance, adaptation to different domains and variance reduction. In [25], the features extracted from human mobility have very strong predictive power and can significantly improve the positive link prediction performance.

6.2 Positive and Negative Link Prediction

Positive and negative link prediction infers new positive and negative links by giving a snapshot of a signed network, which has attracted increasing attention in recent years [?]. In [7], an algorithm based on trust and distrust propagation is proposed to predict trust and distrust relations. In [13], local-topology-based features based on balance theory are extracted to improve the performance of a logistic regression classifier in signed relation prediction. Features derived from longer cycles in signed networks can be used to improve the positive and negative link prediction performance [4]. In [10], a low-rank matrix factorization approach with generalized loss functions is proposed to predict trust and distrust relations.

6.3 Sign Prediction

Sign prediction infers the sign of a given link. In [26], user behavior of decision making can be used to predict signs of a given unsigned network accurately. The authors also show the importance of modeling balance theory and status theory in the sign prediction problem. Tang et al. proposed a framework to incorporate social theories such as status theory into a machine learning model and infer the signs of links in a target network by borrowing knowledge from a different source network [23]. In [27], the authors use the transfer learning approach to leverage sign information from an existing and mature signed network to predict signs for a newly formed signed social network.

7. CONCLUSION

Research in signed network analysis suggests that negative links have added value over positive links and they can potentially help various social media services such as recommender systems. However, most social media sites do not enable their users to specify negative links. This makes the problem of negative link prediction more challenging. In this paper, we investigate the problem of negative link prediction. To preserve the generality of our approach, we use positive links and content-centric interactions as sources to predict negative links because these two sources are pervasively available in social media. We first analyze the impact of various social theories, such as balance theory and status theory, on negative links. Then we leverage these insights to provide a principled way to exploit positive links and content-centric interactions. Finally, we propose the NeLP framework for negative link prediction. Experimental results on two real-world social media datasets demonstrate the effectiveness and generalization of the proposed framework. Further experiments illustrate the impact of various model components.

There are several interesting directions needing further investigation. First, negative links predicted by the proposed framework may benefit various social media applications such as positive link prediction and recommender systems. Therefore, we plan to investigate how to incorporate the proposed framework into these applications to improve their performance. Second, in addition to positive links and content-centric interactions, the user-generated content is also pervasively available in social media. We would like to investigate whether user generated content is useful and how to exploit it for the negative link prediction problem. Finally the constructed labels in the studied problem may be noisy; hence we choose a noise-tolerant support vector machine as the basic algorithm for the proposed framework. Learning with noisy labels has been extensively studied in the machine learning community [6] and we will experiment with the use of other noise-tolerant algorithms as basic algorithms for the problem of negative link prediction.

Acknowledgments

This material is based upon work supported by, or in part by, the U.S. Army Research Office (ARO) under contract/grant number 025071, the Office of Naval Research(ONR) under grant number N000141010091, and the Army Research Laboratory and was accomplished under Cooperative Agreement Number W911NF-09-2-0053. The views and conclusions contained in this document are those of the authors and should not be interpreted as representing the official policies, either expressed or implied, of the Army Research Laboratory or the U.S. Government. The U.S. Government is authorized to reproduce and distribute reprints for Government purposes notwithstanding any copyright notation here on.

8. REFERENCES

[1] M. Belkin, P. Niyogi, and V. Sindhwani. On manifold regularization. In *Proceedings of the Tenth International Workshop on Artificial Intelligence and Statistics (AISTAT 2005)*, pages 17–24, 2005.

[2] D. Cartwright and F. Harary. Structural balance: a generalization of heider's theory. *Psychological Review*, 63(5):277, 1956.

[3] K.-Y. Chiang, C.-J. Hsieh, N. Natarajan, A. Tewari, and I. S. Dhillon. Prediction and clustering in signed networks: A local to global perspective. *arXiv preprint arXiv:1302.5145*, 2013.

[4] K.-Y. Chiang, N. Natarajan, A. Tewari, and I. S. Dhillon. Exploiting longer cycles for link prediction in signed networks. In *Proceedings of the 20th ACM international conference on Information and knowledge management*, pages 1157–1162. ACM, 2011.

[5] N. Cristianini and J. Shawe-Taylor. *An introduction to support vector machines and other kernel-based learning methods.* Cambridge university press, 2000.

[6] B. Frénay, M. Verleysen, et al. Classification in the presence of label noise: a survey. *IEEE Transactions on Neural Networks and Learning Systems*, pages 25–17, 2013.

[7] R. Guha, R. Kumar, P. Raghavan, and A. Tomkins. Propagation of trust and distrust. In *Proceedings of the 13th international conference on World Wide Web*, pages 403–412. ACM, 2004.

[8] R. Hardin. Distrust: Manifestations and management. *Distrust*, 8:3–33, 2004.

[9] F. Heider. Attitudes and cognitive organization. *The Journal of psychology*, 21(1):107–112, 1946.

[10] C.-J. Hsieh, K.-Y. Chiang, and I. S. Dhillon. Low rank modeling of signed networks. In *Proceedings of the 18th ACM SIGKDD international conference on Knowledge discovery and data mining*, pages 507–515. ACM, 2012.

[11] J. Kunegis, A. Lommatzsch, and C. Bauckhage. The slashdot zoo: mining a social network with negative edges. In *Proceedings of the 18th international conference on World wide web*, pages 741–750. ACM, 2009.

[12] J. Kunegis, J. Preusse, and F. Schwagereit. What is the added value of negative links in online social networks? In *Proceedings of the 22nd international conference on World Wide Web*, pages 727–736. International World Wide Web Conferences Steering Committee, 2013.

[13] J. Leskovec, D. Huttenlocher, and J. Kleinberg. Predicting positive and negative links in online social networks. In *Proceedings of the 19th international conference on World wide web*, 2010.

[14] J. Leskovec, D. Huttenlocher, and J. Kleinberg. Signed networks in social media. In *Proceedings of the 28th international conference on Human factors in computing systems*, pages 1361–1370. ACM, 2010.

[15] D. Liben-Nowell and J. Kleinberg. The link prediction problem for social networks. In *Proceedings of 12th International Conference on Information and Knowledge Management*, 2003.

[16] D. Liben-Nowell and J. Kleinberg. The link-prediction problem for social networks. *Journal of the American society for information science and technology*, 58(7):1019–1031, 2007.

[17] R. N. Lichtenwalter, J. T. Lussier, and N. V. Chawla. New perspectives and methods in link prediction. In *Proceedings of the 16th ACM SIGKDD international conference on Knowledge discovery and data mining*, pages 243–252. ACM, 2010.

[18] H. Ma, M. R. Lyu, and I. King. Learning to recommend with trust and distrust relationships. In *Proceedings of the third ACM conference on Recommender systems*, pages 189–196. ACM, 2009.

[19] A. K. Menon and C. Elkan. Link prediction via matrix factorization. In *Machine Learning and Knowledge Discovery in Databases*, pages 437–452. Springer, 2011.

[20] S. Papadopoulos, Y. Kompatsiaris, A. Vakali, and P. Spyridonos. Community detection in social media. *Data Mining and Knowledge Discovery*, 24(3):515–554, 2012.

[21] J. Tang, X. Hu, and H. Liu. Social recommendation: a review. *Social Network Analysis and Mining*, 3(4):1113–1133, 2013.

[22] J. Tang and H. Liu. Feature selection with linked data in social media. In *SDM*, pages 118–128. SIAM, 2012.

[23] J. Tang, T. Lou, and J. Kleinberg. Inferring social ties across heterogenous networks. In *Proceedings of the fifth ACM international conference on Web search and data mining*, pages 743–752. ACM, 2012.

[24] P. Victor, C. Cornelis, M. De Cock, and A. Teredesai. Trust-and distrust-based recommendations for controversial reviews. In *Web Science Conference (WebSci'09: Society On-Line)*, number 161, 2009.

[25] D. Wang, D. Pedreschi, C. Song, F. Giannotti, and A. Barabási. Human mobility, social ties, and link prediction. In *KDD*, pages 1100–1108. ACM, 2011.

[26] S.-H. Yang, A. J. Smola, B. Long, H. Zha, and Y. Chang. Friend or frenemy?: predicting signed ties in social networks. In *SIGIR*, pages 555–564. ACM, 2012.

[27] J. Ye, H. Cheng, Z. Zhu, and M. Chen. Predicting positive and negative links in signed social networks by transfer learning. In *WWW*, pages 1477–1488, 2013.

[28] X. Zhu, Z. Ghahramani, J. Lafferty, et al. Semi-supervised learning using gaussian fields and harmonic functions. In *ICML*, volume 3, pages 912–919, 2003.

Sarcasm Detection on Twitter: A Behavioral Modeling Approach

Ashwin Rajadesingan, Reza Zafarani, and Huan Liu
Computer Science and Engineering
Arizona State University
{arajades, reza, huan.liu}@asu.edu

ABSTRACT

Sarcasm is a nuanced form of language in which individuals state the opposite of what is implied. With this intentional ambiguity, sarcasm detection has always been a challenging task, even for humans. Current approaches to automatic sarcasm detection rely primarily on lexical and linguistic cues. This paper aims to address the difficult task of sarcasm detection on Twitter by leveraging behavioral traits intrinsic to users expressing sarcasm. We identify such traits using the user's past tweets. We employ theories from behavioral and psychological studies to construct a behavioral modeling framework tuned for detecting sarcasm. We evaluate our framework and demonstrate its efficiency in identifying sarcastic tweets.

Categories and Subject Descriptors

H.2.8 [**Database Management**]: Database Applications—*Data mining*

Keywords

Sarcasm Detection; Behavioral Modeling; Social Media

1. INTRODUCTION

In recent years, social media sites such as Twitter have gained immense popularity and importance. These sites have evolved into large ecosystems where users express their ideas and opinions uninhibitedly. Companies leverage this unique ecosystem to tap into public opinion on their products or services and to provide real-time customer assistance. Not surprisingly, most large companies have a social media presence and a dedicated team for marketing, after-sales service, and consumer assistance through social media.

With the high velocity and volume of social media data, companies rely on tools such as HootSuite[1], to analyze data and to provide customer service. These tools perform tasks such as content management, sentiment analysis, and extraction of relevant messages for the company's customer service representatives to respond to. However, these tools lack the sophistication to decipher more nuanced forms of language such as sarcasm or humor, in which the meaning of a message is not always obvious and explicit. This imposes an extra burden on the social media team — already inundated with customer messages — to identify these messages and respond appropriately. Table 1 provides two examples where the customer service representatives fail to detect sarcasm. Such public gaffes not only upset the already disgruntled customers but also ruin the public images of companies.

Our goal in this study is to tackle the difficult problem of sarcasm detection on Twitter. While sarcasm detection is inherently challenging, the style and nature of content on Twitter further complicate the process. Compared to other, more conventional sources such as news articles and novels, Twitter is (1) more informal in nature with an evolving vocabulary of slang words and abbreviations and (2) has a limit of 140 characters per tweet which provides fewer word-level cues and adds more ambiguity.

Current research on sarcasm detection on Twitter [38, 10, 20, 29] has primarily focused on obtaining information from the text of the tweets. These techniques treat sarcasm as a linguistic phenomenon, with limited emphasis on the psychological aspects of sarcasm. However, sarcasm has been extensively studied in psychological and behavioral sciences and theories explaining when, why, and how sarcasm is expressed have been established. These theories can be extended and employed to automatically detect sarcasm on Twitter. For example, Rockwell [32] identified a positive correlation between cognitive complexity and the ability to produce sarcasm. A high cognitive complexity of an individual can be manifested on Twitter in terms of the language complexity of the tweets.

Hence, to follow a systematic approach, we first theorize the core forms of sarcasm using existing psychological and behavioral studies. Next, we develop computational features to capture these forms of sarcasm using user's current and past tweets. Finally, we combine these features to train a learning algorithm to detect sarcasm. We make the following contributions in this paper:

1. We identify different forms of sarcasm and demonstrate how these forms are manifested on Twitter.

2. We introduce behavioral modeling as a new, effective approach for detecting sarcasm on Twitter; we pro-

[1] https://hootsuite.com/

WSDM'15, February 2–6, 2015, Shanghai, China.

ACM 978-1-4503-3317-7/15/02 ...$15.00.
http://dx.doi.org/10.1145/2684822.2685316.

Table 1: Examples of Misinterpreted Sarcastic Tweets.

Example	Users	Tweets
1	User 1	you are doing great! Who could predict heavy travel between #Thanksgiving and #NewYearsEve. And bad cold weather in Dec! Crazy!
	Major U.S Airline	We #love the kind words! Thanks so much.
	User 1	wow, just wow, I guess I should have #sarcasm
2	User 2	Ahhh..**** reps. Just had a stellar experience w them at Westchester, NY last week. #CustomerSvcFail
	Major U.S Airline	Thanks for the shout-out Bonnie. We're happy to hear you had a #stellar experience flying with us. Have a great day.
	User 2	You misinterpreted my dripping sarcasm. My experience at Westchester was 1 of the worst I've had with ****. And there are many.

pose and evaluate the **SCUBA** framework — **S**arcasm **C**lassification **U**sing a **B**ehavioral modeling **A**pproach.

3. We investigate and demonstrate the importance of historical information available from past tweets for sarcasm detection.

In section 2, we review related sarcasm detection research. In section 3, we formally define sarcasm detection on Twitter. In section 4, we discuss different forms of sarcasm and outline SCUBA, our behavioral modeling framework for detecting sarcasm. In section 5, we demonstrate how different forms of sarcasm can be identified within Twitter. In section 6, we detail our experiments. Section 7 concludes this research with directions for future work.

2. RELATED WORK

Sarcasm has been widely studied by psychologists, behavioral scientists and linguists for many years. Theories explaining the cognitive processes behind sarcasm usage such as the echoic reminder theory [18], allusional pretense theory [19], and implicit display theory [39] have been extensively researched. However, automatic detection of sarcasm is a relatively unexplored research topic and a challenging problem [25]. While studies on automatic detection of sarcasm in speech [35] utilizes prosodic, spectral and contextual features, sarcasm detection in text has relied on identifying text patterns [4] and lexical features [10, 17].

Davidov et al. [4] devised a semi-supervised technique to detect sarcasm in Amazon product reviews and tweets. They used interesting pattern-based (high frequency words and content words) and punctuation-based features to build a weighted k-nearest neighbor classification model to perform sarcasm detection. Reyes et al. [28] focused on developing classifiers to detect verbal irony based on ambiguity, polarity, unexpectedness and emotional cues derived from text. González-Ibáñez et al. [10] introduced a sarcasm detection technique using numerous lexical features (derived from LWIC [27] and Wordnet Affect [34]) and pragmatic features such as emoticons and replies. Liebrecht et al. [20] used unigrams, bigrams and trigrams as features to detect sarcastic Dutch tweets using a balanced winnow classifier. More recently, Riloff et al. [29], used a well-constructed lexicon-based approach to detect sarcasm based on an assumption that sarcastic tweets are a contrast between a positive sentiment and a negative situation.

As described, past studies on sarcasm detection have primarily focused on linguistic aspects of sarcasm and used only the text of the tweet. We introduce a systematic approach for effective sarcasm detection by not only analyzing the content of the tweets but by also exploiting the behavioral traits of users derived from their past activities. We map research on (1) *what causes people to use sarcasm?*, (2) *when is sarcasm used?* and (3) *how is sarcasm used?*, to observable user behavioral patterns on Twitter that can help build a comprehensive supervised framework to detect sarcasm.

3. PROBLEM STATEMENT

Sarcasm, while similar to irony, differs in that it is usually viewed as being caustic and derisive. Some researchers even consider it to be aggressive humor [1] and a form of verbal aggression [37]. While researchers in linguistics and psychology debate about what exactly constitutes sarcasm, for the sake of clarity, we use the Oxford dictionary's definition of sarcasm[2] as "*a way of using words that are the opposite of what you mean in order to be unpleasant to somebody or to make fun of them.*" We formally define the sarcasm detection problem on Twitter as follows:

Definition. ***Sarcasm Detection on Twitter.*** *Given an unlabeled tweet* $\boldsymbol{t}$ *from user* $\mathbf{U}$ *along with a set of* $\mathbf{U}$*'s past tweets* $\mathbf{T}$*, a solution to sarcasm detection aims to automatically detect if* $\boldsymbol{t}$ *is sarcastic or not.*

In addition to following a behavioral modeling approach, our problem is different from past sarcasm detection research which use only text information from $\boldsymbol{t}$ and do not consider the user's past tweets $\mathbf{T}$ that are available on Twitter.

4. SCUBA: BEHAVIORAL MODELING FRAMEWORK

Sarcastic tweets are not always created in isolation. When posting sarcastic tweets, users make conscious efforts to express their thoughts through sarcasm. They may decide to use sarcasm as a behavioral response to a certain situation, observation, or emotion. These situations, observations, or emotions may be observed and analyzed on Twitter.

It is observed that some individuals have more difficulty in creating or recognizing sarcasm than others due to cul-

[2]www.oxfordlearnersdictionaries.com/definition/english/sarcasm

tural differences, language barriers, and the like. In contrast, some individuals have a higher propensity to use sarcasm than others. Hence, SCUBA also considers the user's likelihood of being a *sarcastic person*. This can be achieved on Twitter by analyzing the user's past tweets. Using existing research on sarcasm and our observations on Twitter, we find that sarcasm generation can be characterized as one (or a combination) of the following:

Sarcasm as a contrast of sentiments

A popular perception of sarcasm among researchers is that sarcasm is a contrast of sentiments. A classical view of sarcasm, based on the traditional pragmatic model [11], argues that sarcastic utterances are first processed in the literal sense and if the literal sense is found incompatible with the present context, only then is the sentence processed in its opposite (ironic) form. This perceived contrast may be expressed with respect to mood, affect or sentiment.

Sarcasm as a complex form of expression

Rockwell [32] showed that there is a small but significant correlation between cognitive complexity and the ability to produce sarcasm. A high cognitive complexity involves understanding and taking into account, multiple perspectives to make cogent decisions. Furthermore, expressing sarcasm requires determining if the environment is suitable for sarcasm, creating an appropriate sarcastic phrase and assessing if the receiver would be capable of recognizing sarcasm. Therefore, sarcasm is a complex form of expression needing more effort than usual from the user.

Sarcasm as a means of conveying emotion

Sarcasm is primarily a form of conveying one's emotions. While sarcasm is sometime interpreted as aggressive humor [1] or verbal aggression [37], it also functions as a tool for self expression. Past studies [12], recognize that sarcasm is usually expressed in situations with negative emotions and attitudes.

Sarcasm as a possible function of familiarity

Friends and relatives are found to be better at recognizing sarcasm than strangers [31]. Further, it has been demonstrated that the knowledge of language [3] and culture [33] also play an important role in the recognition and usage of sarcasm.

Sarcasm as a form of written expression

Sarcasm in psychology has been studied primarily as a spoken form of expression. However, sarcasm is quite prevalent in written form as well, especially with the advent of online social networking sites. Through time, users have become more adept at conveying sarcasm in writing by including subtle markers that indicate to the unassuming reader, that the phrase might be sarcastic. For example, while "*you're so smart*" does not hint at sarcasm, "*Woowwww you are SOOOO cool*"[3] elicits some doubts about the statement's sincerity.

[3]An original tweet collected.

We believe that when expressing sarcasm, the user would invariably exhibit one or more of these forms. Therefore, SCUBA incorporates a behavioral modeling approach [42] for sarcasm detection that utilizes features which capture the different forms of sarcasm. These extracted features are utilized in a supervised learning framework along with some labeled data to determine if the tweet is sarcastic or not. In our setting, labeled data is a set of tweets, among which sarcastic tweets are known. As the novelty of the approach lies in the behavioral modeling and not the actual classifier, we explain in detail how sarcasm can be modeled and incorporated into SCUBA in the following section.

5. SCUBA: REPRESENTING FORMS OF SARCASM

Users' efforts in generating sarcasm are manifested in many ways on Twitter. In this section, we describe how the aforementioned forms are realized on Twitter and how one can construct relevant features to capture these form in the context of Twitter.

5.1 Sarcasm as a contrast of sentiments

5.1.1 Contrasting connotations

A common means of expressing sarcasm is to use words with contrasting connotations within the same tweet. For example, in *I love getting spam emails!*, *spam* obviously has a negative connotation while *love* is overwhelmingly positive. To model such occurrences, we construct features based on (1) affect and (2) sentiment scores.

We obtain affect score of **words** from a dataset compiled by Warriner et al. [41]. This dataset contains affect (valence) scores for 13,915 English lemmas which are on a 9-point scale, with 1 being the least pleasant.

The sentiment score is calculated using SentiStrength [36]. SentiStrength is a lexicon-based tool optimized for tweet sentiment detection based on sentiments of individual words in the tweet. Apart from providing a ternary sentiment result {positive, negative, neutral} for the whole tweet, SentiStrength outputs two scores for each word. A negative sentiment score from -1 to -5 (not-negative to extremely-negative) and a positive sentiment score from 1 to 5 (not-positive to extremely-positive). Here, we use SentiStrength's lexicon to obtain **word** sentiment scores. From these sentiment and affect scores, we compute the following:

$$A = \{\,\text{affect}(w) \mid w \in t\}, \tag{1}$$

$$S = \{\,\text{sentiment}(w) \mid w \in t\}, \tag{2}$$

$$\Delta_{\text{affect}} = \max(A) - \min(A), \tag{3}$$

$$\Delta_{\text{sentiment}} = \max(S) - \min(S), \tag{4}$$

where t is the tweet and w is a word in t. The affect(w) outputs the affect score of word w. The sentiment(w) outputs the sentiment score of word w. Δ_{affect} and $\Delta_{\text{sentiment}}$ indicate the level of contrast in terms of affect and sentiment infused into the tweet by the user. We use Δ_{affect} and $\Delta_{\text{sentiment}}$ as features (2 features).

SentiStrength and the dataset provided by Warriner et al. [41] can only provide sentiment and affect scores for unigrams. Hence, we construct a lexicon of positive and negative sentiment bigrams and trigrams used on Twitter following an approach similar to Kouloumpis et al. [16] as follows:

1. We collect about 400,000 tweets with positive sentiment hashtags such as **#love**, **#happy**, **#amazing**, etc., and 400,000 tweets with negative sentiment hashtags such as **#sad**, **#depressed**, **#hate**, among others.

2. From these tweets, we extracted the bigrams and trigrams along with their respective frequencies. We filter out bigrams and trigrams with frequencies less than 10.

3. For each bigram or trigram b, we find its associated sentiment score, $\frac{POS(b) - NEG(b)}{POS(b) + NEG(b)}$, where $POS(b)$ is the number of occurrences of b in the positive tweets dataset and $NEG(b)$ is the number of occurrences of b in the negative tweets dataset. We filter out bigrams or trigrams with sentiment scores $\in (-0.1, 0.1)$. This sentiment measure is similar to association scores given by Liu et al. [21].

Using the generated lexicon, we include as features, the number of n-grams with positive sentiment scores, the number of n-grams with negative sentiment scores, the summation of scores for positive n-grams, and the summation of scores for negative n-grams (4 features).

5.1.2 *Contrasting present with the past*

Sometimes, the user may set up a contrasting context in her previous tweet and then, choose to use a sarcastic remark in her current tweet. To model such behavior, we obtain the sentiment expressed by the user (i.e., positive, negative, neutral) in the previous tweet and the current tweet using SentiStrength. Then, we include the type of sentiment transition taking place from the past tweet to the current tweet (for example, *positive* $\rightarrow$ *negative*, *negative* $\rightarrow$ *positive*) as a feature (1 feature). In total, there are nine such transitions involving the combinations of positive, negative and neutral sentiments. To provide a historical perspective on the user's likelihood for such sentiment transitions, we compute the probability for all nine transitions using the user's past tweets. The transition probabilities along with the probability of the current transition are included as features in our framework (10 features).

5.2 Sarcasm as a complex form of expression

5.2.1 *Readability*

As sarcasm is widely acknowledged to be hard to read and understand, we adapt standardized readability tests to measure the degree of complexity and understandability of the tweet. We use as features: number of words, number of syllables, number of syllables per word in the tweet derived from the Flesch-Kincaid Grade Level Formula [8], number of polysyllables[4] and the number of polysyllables per word in the tweet derived from SMOG [22] (6 features).

Inspired by the average word length feature used in the Automated Readability Index [15], we formulate a more comprehensive set of features using the word length distribution $L = \{l_i\}_{i=1}^{19}$ constructed from tweet t as follows:

1. For each word w in t, we compute its character length $|w|$. For convenience, we ignore words of length 20 or more. We construct a word length distribution $L = \{l_i\}_{i=1}^{19}$ for t, where l_i denotes the number of words in the tweet with character length i.

2. L may be represented succinctly using the following 6-tuple presentation:

$$< \mathbb{E}[l_w], med[l_w], mode[l_w], \sigma[l_w], \min_{w \in t} l_w, \max_{w \in t} l_w >, \quad (5)$$

where $\mathbb{E}$ is the mean, *med* is the median, *mode* is the mode and σ is the standard deviation.

We include the 6-tuple representation as features in our framework (6 features).

Further, given the availability of the user's past tweets, we examine if there is a noticeable difference in the word length distribution between the user's current tweet and her past tweets. It must be noted that while sarcastic tweets may also be present in the user's past tweets, because of their relative rarity, the past tweets when taken in entirety, would 'average out' any influence possibly introduced by a few past sarcastic tweets. Therefore, any difference from the norm in the word length distribution of the current tweet can be captured. To capture differences in word length distribution, we perform the following steps:

1. From the user's current tweet, we construct a probability distribution D_1 over length of words in the tweet.

2. From the user's past tweets, we construct a probability distribution D_2 over length of words in all the past tweets.

3. To calculate the difference between the world length distribution of the current tweet and the past tweets, we calculate the Jensen-Shannon (JS) divergence between D_1 and D_2:

$$JS(D_1||D_2) = \tfrac{1}{2}KL(D_1||M) + \tfrac{1}{2}KL(D_2||M), \quad (6)$$

where $M = \frac{D_1+D_2}{2}$ and KL is the KL-divergence: $KL(T_1||T_2) = \sum_i \ln(\frac{T_1(i)}{T_2(i)})T_1(i)$.

We include the JS-divergence value as a feature (1 feature).

5.3 Sarcasm as a means of conveying emotion

5.3.1 *Mood*

Mood represents the user's state of emotion. Intuitively, the mood of the user may be indicative of her propensity to use sarcasm; if the user is in a bad (negative) mood, she may choose to express it in the form of a sarcastic tweet. Therefore, we gauge the user's mood using sentiment expressed in her past tweets. However, we cannot assume that the user's mood is encapsulated in her last n tweets. Therefore, we capture the mood using her past tweets as follows:

1. For each past tweet t, we compute its positive sentiment score pos(t) and its absolute negative sentiment score neg(t) using SentiStrength.

2. We divide the user's past tweets into overlapping buckets based on the number of tweets posted prior to the current tweet.

3. Each bucket b_n consists of the previous n tweets posted by the user. We select $n \in \{1, 2, 5, 10, 20, 40, 80\}$.

[4]Polysyllables are words containing three or more syllables.

4. In each b_n, we capture the user's perceived mood using two tuples. The first tuple consists of four features:

$$<\sum^{+}, \sum^{-}, P, \max(\sum^{+}, \sum^{-})>, \quad (7)$$

where $\sum^+$ and $\sum^-$ are the total positive and negative sentiments in b_n: $\sum^+ = \sum_{t \in b_n} \text{pos}(t)$, $\sum^- = \sum_{t \in b_n} \text{neg}(t)$. P is either $+$ or $-$. $P = +$, when $\sum^+ > \sum^-$, and $P = -$, otherwise. The second tuple consists of six features:

$$< n_+, n_-, n_0, n, Q, \max(n_+, n_-, n_0) >, \quad (8)$$

where n_+ is the number of positive tweets, n_- is the number of negative tweets, and n_0 is the number of neutral tweets present in b_n(found using SentiStrength). n is the total tweets present in b_n and Q indicates what the majority of tweets are, i.e., $Q \in \{+, -, 0\}$. For example, $Q = +$, when $n_+ = max(n_+, n_-, n_0)$. We include both tuples for each b_n as features in SCUBA ($7 \times (4 + 6) = 70$ features).

As one's mood remains constant for a limited amount of time, we also gauge the user's mood within a specific time window. However, we cannot assume that the user's mood is encapsulated within t minutes. Therefore, we divide the user's past tweets into buckets b_t, which consists of all the tweets posted by the user within t minutes from the current tweet. Here, $t \in \{1, 2, 5, 10, 20, 60, 720, 1440\}$ minutes (1440 minutes = 1 day). For each bucket b_t, we include the tuples in (7) and (8) also as features ($8 \times 10 = 80$ features).

5.3.2 *Affect and sentiment*

As sarcasm is a combination of affect and sentiment expression, we examine how affect and sentiment are expressed in sarcastic tweets. To this end, we construct a sentiment score distribution SD. SD consists of 11 values, each value being the number of words in the tweet with sentiment score i, where $i \in [-5, 5]$. We also construct an affect score distribution AD. AD contains 9 values. Each value is the number of words in the tweet with an affect score j, where $j \in [1, 9]$. We normalize counts in SD and AD. We include both distributions as features (11+9=20 features). Similar to Eq. (5), we represent these distributions as 6-tuples and include them as features (12 features). We also include the number of affect words, number of sentiment words, and the tweet's overall sentiment (positive, negative, or neutral) as features in SCUBA (3 features).

To capture differences in sentiment expression in sarcastic tweets versus non-sarcastic ones, we compare the sentiment score distribution of the user's past tweets to that of her current tweet. Following a procedure similar to that of Section 5.2.1, we calculate the JS-divergence value between the past and current sentiment score distributions and include it as a feature (1 feature).

Finally, to gain insights into how a user employs Twitter to express emotion, we determine the range of sentiments expressed by the user in the past. To perform this, for all sentiment scores $i \in [-5, 5]$, we compute the number of tweets with sentiment score i in all past tweets of the user. By normalizing these counts, we obtain a probability distribution over sentiment scores in past tweets. We include this probability distribution as a feature (11 features).

5.3.3 *Frustration*

When individuals experience unjust situations, they sometimes turn to social media as an effective outlet for their complaints and frustrations [2]. These frustrations are often expressed in the form of sarcasm [9] (see example tweets in Table 1). We hypothesize that as users encounter unpleasant situations in real life, they react spontaneously by posting tweets to vent out their frustration. Therefore, they diverge from their regular tweeting patterns.

To capture this behavioral pattern, using the user's past tweets, we construct an expected tweet posting time probability distribution. From each of the user's past tweets, we extract the tweet creation time, using which, we build a normalized 24 bin distribution TD (one for each hour). TD approximates the probability of the user tweeting at each hour. For each tweet, using the TD for the user posting it, we find the likelihood of the user posting the tweet at that hour. The lower the likelihood, the more divergent the tweet is from the user's usual tweeting patterns. Low likelihood scores indicate that the user is not expected to tweet at that particular time and that the user has gone out of her way to tweet at that time, therefore, in some sense, the tweet is spontaneous in nature. We include the likelihood of the user tweeting at that particular hour as a feature (1 feature).

We also observe that users tend to post successive tweets in short quick bursts when they vent out their frustrations; therefore, we include the time difference between the examined tweet and the previous tweet posted by the user as a feature (1 feature). Finally, a common way to express frustration is by using swear words. Using the list of most common swear words provided by Wang et al. [40], we check for the presence of such words in the tweet and include their presence using a boolean feature (1 feature).

5.4 Sarcasm as a possible function of familiarity

5.4.1 *Familiarity of language*

Intuitively, one would expect a user who uses a form of language as complex as sarcasm to have good command over the language. Therefore, we measure the user's language skills with features that are inspired by standardized language proficiency cloze tests. In cloze tests, proficiency is evaluated based on vocabulary, grammar, dictation, and reading levels [23]. As dictation and reading levels pertain to the oratory and reading skills of the user that cannot be measured from written text, we focus on constructing features that best represent the vocabulary and grammar skills.

Vocabulary Skills. We determine the size of user's vocabulary from user's past tweets. We include as features, the total number of words, total number of distinct words used and the ratio of distinct words to total words used to measure the user's redundancy in word usage (3 features).

Grammar Skills. To measure grammar skills, we investigate how the user employs different parts-of-speech (POS). The POS tags for words in the tweets are generated using TweetNLP's [24] POS tagger. TweetNLP generates 25 possible tags such as *interjections* or *emoticons*. We obtain the POS tag for every word in the tweet and build a corresponding POS probability distribution and include it as features (25 features). As English grammar is intricate and nuanced, it is difficult to extensively measure a user's grammar expertise. However, one can check for correct grammatical usage for commonly used words. We check the correct grammatical usage for "your" and "its", both frequently used. We observe that users often mistakenly use words such as "your" instead of "you're' and "its" instead of "it's". Using all past tweets of a user, we obtain the POS of the word used immediately after "your" and "its". If the word has been used in the correct grammatical sense, the POS of the succeeding word should not be a verb (example, "your doing great!" is incorrect), adverb (example, "its freakin' amazing" is incorrect) or a determiner (such as "a" or "the"). We include as features, the fraction of times the two words were used in incorrect grammatical form by the user (2 features). There are other POS that can render the usage of "your" or "its" incorrect; however, for correctness, we adopt a conservative strategy by checking only for verbs, adverbs, and determiners.

Sarcastic users, in addition to their vocabulary and grammar skills, are familiar with sarcasm as an expression form.

Familiarity with Sarcasm. For measuring user's familiarity with sarcasm, we include the number of past occurrences of `#not` or `#sarcasm` hashtags as a feature (1 feature). Further, it has been shown that people in different regions perceive and use sarcasm differently (see Dress et al.'s study [5]). Thus, we try to infer the location of the user. However, the user provided location on Twitter is often noisy as it is a *free-text* field in which any text may be inputted. Therefore, we approximate the user's location with her time zone and include it as a feature (1 feature).

5.4.2 Familiarity of environment

Users express sarcasm better when they are well acquainted with their environment. Just as people are less likely to use sarcasm at a new, unfamiliar setting, users take time to get familiar with Twitter before posting sarcastic tweets. We measure a user's familiarity with Twitter in terms of her usage familiarity, parlance familiarity, and social activity.

Usage Familiarity. We measure usage familiarity using the number of tweets posted, number of days on Twitter (i.e., Twitter age), and the average number of daily tweets and include all as features (3 features). These features provide indications of the duration and the intensity at which the user has been using Twitter. We also measure familiarity in terms of the user's frequency of Twitter usage. From the user's past tweets, we compute the time differences between all pairs of successive tweets. We represent the distribution of these time differences as a 6-tuple similar to Eq. (5), and include them as features (6 features).

Twitter Parlance Familiarity. To capture user familiarity with *Twitter parlance*, we include the number of retweets, mentions and hashtags used in past tweets as features (3 features). Experienced Twitter users often use shortened words (by removing vowels, using numbers, etc.) to circumvent the 140 character limit. Hence, we include the presence of alphanumeric words (boolean), presence of words without vowels (boolean), as well as the percentage of dictionary words present in the tweet as features (3 features).

Social Familiarity. We measure social familiarity by identifying how embedded a user is in Twitter's social graph. Hence, we include the number of friends and followers as features (2 features). To adjust for longevity, we divide the numbers of friends and followers by the user's Twitter age and include them as features (2 features).

5.5 Sarcasm as a form of written expression

While low pitch, high intensity and a slow tempo [30] are vocal indicators of sarcasm, users attempting to express sarcasm in writing are devoid of such devices. Therefore, users may be forced to use certain writing styles to compensate for the lack of visual or verbal cues. We categorize such behavior into prosodic and structural variations.

5.5.1 Prosodic variations

Users often repeat letters in words to stress and over-emphasize certain parts of the tweet (for example, *sooooo*, *awesomeeee*) to indicate that they mean the opposite of what is written. We capture such usage by including as boolean features, the presence of repeated characters (3 or more) and the presence of repeated characters (3 or more) in sentiment-loaded words (such as, loveeee) (2 features). We also include the number of characters used, and the ratio of the number of distinct characters to the total characters used in the tweet as features (2 features).

We also observe that users often capitalize certain words to emphasize changes in tone (if the tweet were to be read out loud). We account for such changes by including the number of capitalized words in the tweet as a feature (1 feature). Other users capitalize certain parts-of-speech (POS) to exaggerate or to vent their frustration. Using TweetNLP, we obtain the POS tag for each capitalized word in the tweet. Then, we compute the probability distribution of POS tags for capitalized words and include it as features (25 features).

Users also use certain punctuations to express non-verbal cues that are crucial for sarcasm deliverance in speech. For example, users use "*" to indicate emphasis, "..." to indicate pause, "!!!" for exclamations (sometimes over-done to indicate sarcasm). Thus, we include as features, the normalized distribution of common punctuation marks (.,!?'*") (7 features). To compare the user's current usage of punctuations to her past usage, similar to Eq. (6), we calculate the JS-divergence value between the current and past punctuation distribution and include it as a feature (1 feature).

5.5.2 Structural variations

We observe that sarcastic tweets sometimes have a certain structure wherein the user's views are expressed in the first few words of the tweet, while in the later parts, a description of a particular scenario is put forth, e.g., *I love it when my friends ignore me.* To capture possible syntactic idiosyncrasies arising from such tweet construction, we use as features, the POS tags of the first three words and the last three words in the tweet (6 features). We also include the position of the first sentiment-loaded word (0 if not present) and the first affect-loaded word (0 if not present) as a feature (2 features). Given the structure followed in constructing sarcastic tweets, we also check for positional variations in the hashtags present in the tweet. We trisect the tweet based on the number of words present and include as features the number of hashtags present in the each of the three parts of the tweet (3 features).

To capture differences in syntactic structures, we examine parts of speech tags present in the tweet. Similar to Eq. (6), we construct a probability distribution over the POS tags present in the current tweet as well as POS tags in past tweets and include the Jensen-Shannon divergence value between the two distribution as a feature (1 feature).

Past studies on quantifying linguistic style [14] have used lexical density, intensifiers, and personal pronouns as important measures to gauge the writing style of the user. Lexical density is the fraction of information carrying words present in the tweet (nouns, verbs, adjectives, and adverbs). Intensifiers are words that maximize the effect of adverbs or adjectives (for example, so, or very). Personal pronouns are pronouns denoting a person or group (for example, me, our, or her). We include as features the lexical density, the number of intensifiers used, the number of first-person singular, first-person plural, second-person, and third-person pronouns present in the tweet (6 features).

In total, we construct 335 features based on the behavioral aspects of sarcasm.

6. EXPERIMENTS

In this section, the SCUBA framework is systematically evaluated through a series of experiments. First, we detail the data collection process and our dataset. Next, we train SCUBA and compare its performance to baselines. Then, we determine the contribution of different feature sets to SCUBA's performance. We conduct feature importance analysis to determine a small set of features that are most beneficial for sarcasm detection. Finally, we examine the robustness of our framework under different scenarios.

6.1 Data collection

We validate our framework using a dataset[5] of tweets from Twitter. To obtain a set of sarcastic tweets, we query the Streaming API using keywords `#sarcasm` and `#not` filtering out non-English tweets and retweets. We also remove tweets containing mentions and URLs as obtaining information from media and URLs is computationally expensive. We limit our analysis to tweets which contain more than three words as we found that tweets with fewer words were very noisy or clichéd (e.g., *yeah, right! #sarcasm*). Davidov et al. [4] noted that some tweets containing the `#sarcasm` hashtag were *about* sarcasm and that the tweets themselves were not sarcastic. To limit such occurrences, we include only tweets that have either of the two hashtags as its last word; this reduces the chance of obtaining tweets that are not sarcastic. After preprocessing, we obtained about 9104 sarcastic tweets which were self described by users as being sarcastic using the appropriate hashtags. We remove the `#sarcasm` and `#not` hashtags from the tweets before proceeding with the evaluation.

To collect a set of general tweets (not sarcastic), we used Twitter's Sample API which provides a random sample of tweets. These tweets were subjected to the same aforementioned preprocessing technique. Finally, for each tweet in the collected dataset, we extract the user who posted the tweet and then, we obtained that user's past tweets (we obtain the past 80 tweets for each user).

Some examples of tweets in the dataset are:

1. *This paper is coming along... #not*
2. *Finding out your friends' lives through tweets is really the greatest feeling. #sarcasm*

The above examples illustrate the difficulty of the task at hand. The first tweet may or may not be sarcastic purely depending on the context (which is not available in the tweet). Even if some background is provided, as in the case of the second tweet, clearly, it is still a complicated task to map that information to sarcasm.

It must also be noted that, to avoid confusion and ambiguity when expressing sarcasm in writing, the users choose to explicitly mark the sarcastic tweets with appropriate hashtags. The expectation is that these tweets, if devoid of these hashtags, might be difficult to comprehend as sarcasm even for humans. Therefore, our dataset might be biased towards the hardest forms of sarcasm. Using this dataset, we evaluate our framework and compare it with existing baselines.

6.2 Performance evaluation

Naturally, the class distribution over tweets is skewed towards the non-sarcastic tweets. Therefore, we evaluate the SCUBA framework using different class distributions (1:1, 10:90, 20:80, where 1:1 means for every sarcastic tweet in the dataset, we introduce 1 tweet that is not sarcastic.). We include AUC (Area under the ROC Curve) apart from accuracy as a performance measure as AUC is robust to class imbalances [7]. This analysis gives an insight into how well SCUBA performs under varied distributions. We compare SCUBA to the following baselines.

6.2.1 Baselines

We compare our framework against 6 baselines. The first two are based on a state-of-the-art lexicon-based technique by Riloff et al. [29]. The basic premise of their method is that sarcasm can be viewed as a contrast between a positive sentiment and a negative situation. They construct three phrase lists (positive verb phrases, positive predicative expressions, and negative situations) from 175,000 tweets using a parts-of-speech aware bootstrapping technique that extracts relevant phrases. Different combinations of these phrase lists were used to decide if a tweet is sarcastic or not. Using their phrase lists, we re-implement two of their approaches:

[1] **Contrast Approach**. The method marks a tweet as sarcastic if it contains a positive verb phrase or positive predicative expression along with a negative situation phrase.

[2] **Hybrid Approach**. The method marks a tweet as sarcastic if it is marked sarcastic either by the bootstrapped-lexicon approach or by a bag-of-words classifier trained on unigrams, bigrams, and trigrams. To provide a comparable framework to the Hybrid Approach, we include the prediction of the discussed n-gram classifier into SCUBA as a feature. We call our n-gram augmented framework, SCUBA++.

[3] **SCUBA - `#sarcasm`**. To quell doubts that SCUBA merely labels all tweets from users who have previously used `#sarcasm` or `#not` as sarcastic, we completely remove that particular feature and perform the same classification task.

[4] **Random Classifier**. The baseline classifies the tweets randomly into sarcastic and non-sarcastic.

[5] **Majority Classifier**. It classifies all tweets into the majority class (known from the class distribution).

[6] **n-gram Classifier**. The same n-gram model used in the hybrid approach that classifies tweets into sarcastic and non-sarcastic based on their unigrams, bi-grams, and tri-grams.

[5]The dataset can be obtained by contacting the first author.

Table 2: Performance Evaluation using 10-fold Cross-Validation.

Technique	Dataset Distribution					
	1:1		20:80		10:90	
	Acc.	AUC	Acc.	AUC	Acc.	AUC
SCUBA	83.46	0.83	88.10	0.76	92.24	0.60
Contrast Approach	56.50	0.56	78.98	0.57	86.59	0.57
SCUBA++	86.08	0.86	89.81	0.80	92.94	0.70
Hybrid Approach	77.26	0.77	78.40	0.75	83.87	0.67
SCUBA - `#sarcasm`	83.41	0.83	87.53	0.74	91.87	0.63
n-gram Classifier	78.56	0.78	81.63	0.76	87.89	0.65
Majority Classifier	50.00	0.50	80.00	0.50	90.00	0.50
Random Classifier	49.17	0.50	50.41	0.50	49.78	0.50

Table 3: Feature Set Analysis.

Features	Accuracy
All features	83.46 %
– Complexity-based features	73.00 %
– Contrast-based features	57.34 %
– Emotion expression-based features	71.52 %
– Familiarity-based features	73.67 %
– Text expression-based features	76.72 %

6.2.2 Training the Framework

Before training, we select a suitable classifier for SCUBA. We evaluate SCUBA's performance using multiple supervised learning algorithms on our collected dataset (with class distribution 1:1). We evaluate using a J48 decision tree, ℓ_1-regularized logistic regression, and ℓ_1-regularized ℓ_2-loss SVM[6] to obtain an accuracy of 78.06%, 83.46%, and 83.05%, respectively. We choose ℓ_1-regularized logistic regression for comparison with the baselines.

We use 10-fold cross-validation technique to evaluate the framework's performance, the results of which are given in Table 2. From the results, we observe that SCUBA++ clearly outperforms all other techniques for every class distribution and for both accuracy and AUC. Note that only SCUBA and SCUBA++ perform better than the majority classifier for highly skewed distributions (90:10). We also observe that while the Hybrid Approach performs much better than the Contrast Approach, it is still not very effective for skewed distributions. Also, we notice that when the past sarcasm feature is removed from SCUBA, we obtain similar performance outcomes indicating the minimal effect of using this feature on the framework's performance. Both random classifier and the majority classifier obtain an AUC score of 0.5, which is the minimum possible AUC score attainable. To evaluate the benefit of using different feature sets, we perform the following feature set analysis. This analysis allows us to make informed decisions about which feature sets to consider if computationally constrained.

6.3 Feature set analysis

We divide the list features into sets depending on the different forms of sarcasm from which they were derived - features based on complexity, based on contrast, based on expression of emotion, based on familiarity, and based on expression in text form.

[6]We use Weka [13], LIBLINEAR [6], and Scikit-learn [26].

Table 3 shows the performance of SCUBA using each of the feature sets individually. While all feature sets contribute to SCUBA's performance, they do so unequally. Clearly, all feature sets perform much better than contrast-based features. This further shows the need to view sarcasm through its varied facets and not a particular form of expression (such as contrast seeking).

To gain deeper insights into which specific features are most important for detecting sarcasm, we perform the following feature importance analysis.

6.4 Feature importance analysis

As observed, different feature sets have different effects on the performance. While we may use many features to detect sarcasm, clearly, some features are more important than others. Therefore, we perform a thorough analysis of features to determine the features that contribute the most to detecting sarcasm. This analysis can be done with any feature selection algorithm. We use the odds-ratio (coefficients from ℓ_1-regularized logistic regression) for the importance analysis. The top 10 features in decreasing order of importance for sarcasm detection are the following:

1. Percentage of emoticons in the tweet.
2. Percentage of adjectives in the tweet.
3. Percentage of past words with sentiment score 3.
4. Number of polysyllables per word in the tweet.
5. Lexical density of the tweet.
6. Percentage of past words with sentiment score 2.
7. Percentage of past words with sentiment score -3.
8. Number of past sarcastic tweets posted.
9. Percentage of positive to negative sentiment transitions made by the user.
10. Percentage of capitalized hashtags in the tweet.

Interestingly, we observe that features derived from all forms of sarcasm: text expression-based features (1, 2, 5, 10), emotion-based features (3, 6, 7), familiarity based features (8), contrast-based features (9) and complexity-based features (4) rank high in terms of discriminative power.

6.5 Evaluating effectiveness of historical information

In our framework for detecting sarcastic tweets, we have included the user's historical information on Twitter in the form of past tweets. However, it might be computationally expensive to process and use all the past tweets for classification. Furthermore, it is unrealistic to assume access to so many past tweets for each user will be always available. Therefore, it is imperative that we identify the optimum number of past tweets to be used to detect sarcasm. To do this, we measure SCUBA's performance by executing the sarcasm classification multiple times while varying the number of past tweets available to us.

Figure 1 shows the performance obtained with varied past tweets (smoothened using a moving-average model). We observe that with no historical information, we obtain an accuracy of 79.38%, which still outperforms all baselines. Interestingly, using only the user's past 30 tweets, we obtain a considerable gain (+4.14%) in performance. However, as we add even more historical tweets, the performance does not significantly improve. Therefore, if computationally constrained, one can use only the past 30 tweets and expect a comparable performance.

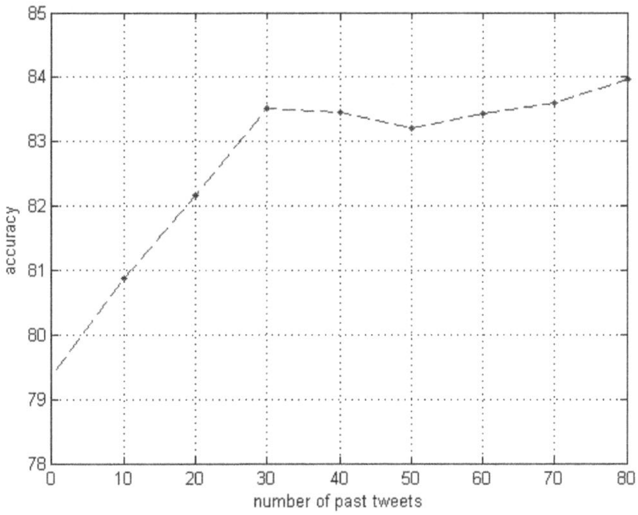

Figure 1: Effect of Historical Information on Sarcasm Detection Performance.

7. CONCLUSIONS AND FUTURE WORK

In this paper, we introduce SCUBA, a behavioral modeling framework for sarcasm detection. We discuss different forms that sarcasm can take, namely: (1) as a contrast of sentiments, (2) as a complex form of expression, (3) as a means of conveying emotion, (4) as a possible function of familiarity and (5) as a form of written expression. We construct relevant features to represent these forms on Twitter. We train a supervised learning algorithm using the constructed features to detect sarcastic tweets. Through multiple experiments, we demonstrate that SCUBA is effective in detecting sarcastic tweets. SCUBA's main two advantages are considering psychological and behavioral aspects of sarcasm and leveraging users' historical information to decide whether tweets are sarcastic or not.

Importantly, we have demonstrated that even limited historical information may greatly help improve the efficiency of sarcasm detection. This makes SCUBA a good fit for real-world, real-time applications which have high computational constraints. It is important to note that while we perform our evaluation and experiments on a Twitter dataset, SCUBA can be generalized to other social media sites. It can be easily expanded by including other site-specific features. This further widens the scope of applicability of SCUBA to different social media sites.

With nearly all major companies having a social media presence, SCUBA can complement existing sentiment analysis technologies to better serve the needs of consumer assistance teams online. With consumer assistance teams aiming for a zero-waiting time response to customer queries through social media, undetected sarcasm can result in embarrassing gaffes and potential PR disasters. Using SCUBA, social media teams can better detect sarcasm and deliver appropriate responses to sarcastic tweets.

In the future, we wish to expand SCUBA to also factor in users' social networks and their current and past interactions for sarcasm detection. This bodes well with existing research [31] which suggests that users are more likely to use sarcasm with friends than with strangers. Further, we wish to apply our behavioral modeling framework to detect other non-literal forms of language such as humor.

ACKNOWLEDGMENTS

This work was supported, in part, by the Office of Naval Research grants N000141410095 and N000141310835. We would also like to thank Dr. Heather Pon-Barry and Dr. Subbarao Kambhampati for their constructive criticisms and suggestions that helped improve this work.

8. REFERENCES

[1] M. Basavanna. *Dictionary of psychology*. Allied Publishers, 2000.

[2] F. Bi and J. A. Konstan. Customer service 2.0: Where social computing meets customer relations. *IEEE Computer*, 45(11):93–95, 2012.

[3] H. S. Cheang and M. D. Pell. Recognizing sarcasm without language: A cross-linguistic study of english and cantonese. *Pragmatics & Cognition*, 19(2), 2011.

[4] D. Davidov, O. Tsur, and A. Rappoport. Semi-supervised recognition of sarcastic sentences in twitter and amazon. In *Proceedings of the Fourteenth Conference on Computational Natural Language Learning*, pages 107–116. Association for Computational Linguistics, 2010.

[5] M. L. Dress, R. J. Kreuz, K. E. Link, and G. M. Caucci. Regional variation in the use of sarcasm. *Journal of Language and Social Psychology*, 27(1):71–85, 2008.

[6] R.-E. Fan, K.-W. Chang, C.-J. Hsieh, X.-R. Wang, and C.-J. Lin. Liblinear: A library for large linear classification. *The Journal of Machine Learning Research*, 9:1871–1874, 2008.

[7] T. Fawcett. An introduction to {ROC} analysis. *Pattern Recognition Letters*, 27(8):861 – 874, 2006. {ROC} Analysis in Pattern Recognition.

[8] R. Flesch. A new readability yardstick. *Journal of applied psychology*, 32(3):221, 1948.

[9] R. W. Gibbs. Irony in talk among friends. *Metaphor and symbol*, 15(1-2):5–27, 2000.

[10] R. González-Ibáñez, S. Muresan, and N. Wacholder. Identifying sarcasm in twitter: A closer look. In *ACL (Short Papers)*, pages 581–586. Citeseer, 2011.

[11] H. P. Grice. Logic and conversation. In P. Cole and J. L. Morgan, editors, *Syntax and semantics*, volume 3. New York: Academic Press, 1975.

[12] H. P. Grice. Some further notes on logic and conversation. In P. Cole, editor, *Syntax and Semantics 9: Pragmatics*, pages 113–127. 1978.

[13] M. Hall, E. Frank, G. Holmes, B. Pfahringer, P. Reutemann, and I. H. Witten. The weka data mining software: an update. *ACM SIGKDD explorations newsletter*, 11(1):10–18, 2009.

[14] Y. Hu, K. Talamadupula, S. Kambhampati, et al. Dude, srsly?: The surprisingly formal nature of twitter's language. In *ICWSM*, 2013.

[15] J. P. Kincaid, R. P. Fishburne Jr, R. L. Rogers, and B. S. Chissom. Derivation of new readability formulas (automated readability index, fog count and flesch reading ease formula) for navy enlisted personnel. Technical report, DTIC Document, 1975.

[16] E. Kouloumpis, T. Wilson, and J. Moore. Twitter sentiment analysis: The good the bad and the omg! *ICWSM*, 11:538–541, 2011.

[17] R. J. Kreuz and G. M. Caucci. Lexical influences on the perception of sarcasm. In *Proceedings of the Workshop on computational approaches to Figurative Language*, pages 1–4. Association for Computational Linguistics, 2007.

[18] R. J. Kreuz and S. Glucksberg. How to be sarcastic: The echoic reminder theory of verbal irony. *Journal of Experimental Psychology: General*, 118(4):374, 1989.

[19] S. Kumon-Nakamura, S. Glucksberg, and M. Brown. How about another piece of pie: The allusional pretense theory of discourse irony. *Journal of Experimental Psychology: General*, 124(1):3, 1995.

[20] C. Liebrecht, F. Kunneman, and A. van den Bosch. The perfect solution for detecting sarcasm in tweets# not. *WASSA 2013*, page 29, 2013.

[21] W. Liu and D. Ruths. What's in a name? using first names as features for gender inference in twitter. In *Analyzing Microtext: 2013 AAAI Spring Symposium*, 2013.

[22] G. H. McLaughlin. Smog grading: A new readability formula. *Journal of reading*, 12(8):639–646, 1969.

[23] J. Oller, John W. Scoring methods and difficulty levels for cloze tests of proficiency in english as a second language. *The Modern Language Journal*, 56(3):pp. 151–158, 1972.

[24] O. Owoputi, B. O'Connor, C. Dyer, K. Gimpel, N. Schneider, and N. A. Smith. Improved part-of-speech tagging for online conversational text with word clusters. In *Proceedings of NAACL-HLT*, pages 380–390, 2013.

[25] B. Pang and L. Lee. Opinion mining and sentiment analysis. *Foundations and trends in information retrieval*, 2(1-2):1–135, 2008.

[26] F. Pedregosa, G. Varoquaux, A. Gramfort, V. Michel, B. Thirion, O. Grisel, M. Blondel, P. Prettenhofer, R. Weiss, V. Dubourg, et al. Scikit-learn: Machine learning in python. *The Journal of Machine Learning Research*, 12:2825–2830, 2011.

[27] J. W. Pennebaker, M. E. Francis, and R. J. Booth. Linguistic inquiry and word count: Liwc 2001. *Mahway: Lawrence Erlbaum Associates*, page 71, 2001.

[28] A. Reyes, P. Rosso, and D. Buscaldi. From humor recognition to irony detection: The figurative language of social media. *Data & Knowledge Engineering*, 74:1–12, 2012.

[29] E. Riloff, A. Qadir, P. Surve, and Silva. Sarcasm as contrast between a positive sentiment and negative situation. In *EMNLP*, pages 704–714. ACL, 2013.

[30] P. Rockwell. Lower, slower, louder: Vocal cues of sarcasm. *Journal of Psycholinguistic Research*, 29(5):483–495, 2000.

[31] P. Rockwell. Empathy and the expression and recognition of sarcasm by close relations or strangers. *Perceptual and motor skills*, 97(1):251–256, 2003.

[32] P. Rockwell. The effects of cognitive complexity and communication apprehension on the expression and recognition of sarcasm. *Hauppauge, NY: Nova Science Publishers*, 2007.

[33] P. Rockwell and E. M. Theriot. Culture, gender, and gender mix in encoders of sarcasm: A self-assessment analysis. *Communication Research Reports*, 18(1):44 – 52, 2001.

[34] C. Strapparava and A. Valitutti. Wordnet affect: an affective extension of wordnet. In *LREC*, volume 4, pages 1083–1086, 2004.

[35] J. Tepperman, D. R. Traum, and S. Narayanan. " yeah right": sarcasm recognition for spoken dialogue systems. In *INTERSPEECH*, 2006.

[36] M. Thelwall, K. Buckley, G. Paltoglou, D. Cai, and A. Kappas. Sentiment strength detection in short informal text. *Journal of the American Society for Information Science and Technology*, 61(12):2544–2558, 2010.

[37] M. Toplak and A. N. Katz. On the uses of sarcastic irony. *Journal of Pragmatics*, 32(10):1467–1488, 2000.

[38] O. Tsur, D. Davidov, and A. Rappoport. Icwsm-a great catchy name: Semi-supervised recognition of sarcastic sentences in online product reviews. In *ICWSM*, 2010.

[39] A. Utsumi. Verbal irony as implicit display of ironic environment: Distinguishing ironic utterances from nonirony. *Journal of Pragmatics*, 32(12):1777–1806.

[40] W. Wang, L. Chen, K. Thirunarayan, and A. P. Sheth. Cursing in english on twitter. In *Proceedings of the 17th ACM conference on Computer supported cooperative work & social computing*, pages 415–425. ACM, 2014.

[41] A. B. Warriner, V. Kuperman, and M. Brysbaert. Norms of valence, arousal, and dominance for 13,915 english lemmas. *Behavior research methods*, pages 1–17, 2013.

[42] R. Zafarani and H. Liu. Connecting users across social media sites: a behavioral-modeling approach. In *Proceedings of the 19th ACM SIGKDD international conference on Knowledge discovery and data mining*, pages 41–49. ACM, 2013.

Modeling and Predicting Retweeting Dynamics on Microblogging Platforms

Shuai Gao
gao_shuai@mail.sdu.edu.cn

Jun Ma
majun@sdu.edu.cn

Zhumin Chen
chenzhumin@sdu.edu.cn

School of Computer Science and Technology, Shandong University

ABSTRACT

Popularity prediction on microblogging platforms aims to predict the future popularity of a message based on its retweeting dynamics in the early stages. Existing works mainly focus on exploring effective features for prediction, while ignoring the underlying arrival process of retweets. Also, the effect of user activity variation on the retweeting dynamics in the early stages has been neglected. In this paper, we propose an extended reinforced Poisson process model with time mapping process to model the retweeting dynamics and predict the future popularity. The proposed model explicitly characterizes the process through which a message gain its retweets, by capturing a power-law temporal relaxation function corresponding to the aging in the ability of the message to attract new retweets and an exponential reinforcement mechanism characterizing the "richer-get-richer" phenomenon. Further, we introduce the notation of weibo time and integrate a time mapping process into the proposed model to eliminate the effect of user activity variation. Extensive experiments on two Weibo datasets, with 10K and 18K messages respectively, well demonstrate the effectiveness of our proposed model in popularity prediction.

Categories and Subject Descriptors

H.3.3 [**Information Storage and Retrieval**]: Online Information Services—*Web-based services*

General Terms

Algorithm, Measurement

Keywords

Popularity Prediction; Reinforced Poisson Process; Retweeting Dynamics; Microblogging Platforms

1. INTRODUCTION

In recent years, online social networks (OSNs) such as Facebook, Twitter, YouTube etc., have become increasingly popular for their important roles in information sharing and interpersonal communication. The prevalence of OSNs has brought along an enormous and ever growing amount of user generated content (e.g., blogs, videos, photos and messages etc.). Recently, the study of predicting the popularity of user generated content has drawn much attention for its remarkable practical value in numerous applications, including trend forecasting [7, 10, 17, 32], understanding the collective human behavior [6, 19, 31], election prediction [28, 30], movie revenue estimation [2] and media advertising [1, 15] etc. Future popularity of user generated content indicates the intensity with which people would react and hence has the potential to influence the policy decisions.

On microblogging platforms, such as Twitter[1] and Weibo[2], messages gain their popularity as being retweeted [13]. Generally, the popularity prediction problem on microblogging platforms is defined as follows: given a message, predicting its future popularity based on its retweeting dynamics in the early stages, where the popularity of a message is represented by the number of its retweets. To address this problem, considerable efforts have been invested in the past years. In general, current methods fall into the following two main paradigms. One treats the prediction problem as a regression or classification task, making predictions by exploring relevant factors and applying standard regression or classification methods [4, 8, 11, 18]. These methods have been successful in revealing many explicable and effective factors for prediction. However, there are still numerous factors to be considered and these methods are always based on some assumptions or simplification of major factors. The other one treats the retweeting dynamics as time series, making predictions by fitting these time series into certain class of functions [9, 19, 31]. The drawback of these methods is that they model the retweeting dynamics in a mean-field way by focusing on the average amount of retweets received in a fixed time window, ignoring the underlying arrival process of retweets.

Recently, Shen et al. [23] proposed a generative probabilistic model using a *reinforced Poisson process* (RPP) to model explicitly the process through which individual items gain their popularity. The model captures three key ingredients of popularity dynamics: (i) fitness of an item, characterizing its inherent competitiveness against other items; (ii) a general temporal relaxation function corresponding to the aging in the ability to attract new attention; (iii) a reinforcement mechanism characterizing the well-known "richer-get-richer" phenomenon. Despite

[1]http://twitter.com
[2]http://weibo.com

WSDM'15, February 2–6, 2015, Shanghai, China.

http://dx.doi.org/10.1145/2684822.2685303.

its remarkable success in modeling the citation dynamics as reported in [23], there remains some limitations when applied to model the retweeting dynamics. Firstly, unlike the temporal relaxation function which can be adjusted with respect to specific domain, the reinforcement mechanism in RPP model is fixed to be a linear function of received popularity. However, in this paper, we show that this may not hold true for retweeting dynamics. Moreover, the original RPP model does not consider the effect of user activity variation on the popularity dynamics. Generally, users are more active during the daytime than in the midnight. Hence, considering the number of retweets that a message receives in the first hour after been posted, a message posted during daytime will on average receive more retweets than messages posted during midnight. Neglecting the effect of user activity variation may cause the misinterpretation of the relative interestingness of a given message.

In this paper, we extended the general reinforced Poisson process model and addressed the above deficiencies by introducing a power-law temporal relaxation function, an exponential reinforcement function and a time mapping process. Specifically, through analyzing the real data, we found that the temporal relaxation in retweeting dynamics follows a power-law distribution instead of a log-normal distribution as in [23]. Further, observing that the reinforcement effect becomes weaker when the popularity of message grows larger, we proposed a reinforcement function with an exponential decay to capture this phenomenon. Moreover, to eliminate the effect of user variation on the retweeting dynamics, we introduced the notation of *weibo time* and applied a time mapping process to transform the time moments in the retweeting dynamics into weibo time. Putting all these together, we named the proposed model PETM (a reinforced Poisson process model with **P**ower-law relaxation, **E**xponential reinforcement and **T**ime **M**apping process). Finally, we provided a detailed description for the modeling, learning and prediction process of the proposed model.

To evaluate the performance of our proposed model, focusing on the popularity prediction task, we conducted extensive experiments on two Weibo datasets, with 10K and 18K messages respectively. The experimental results show that our proposed model outperforms two baseline models, i.e., SH model [25] and ML model [21], and achieves a remarkable improvement over the original RPP model with a log-normal relaxation function and a linear reinforcement function. Moreover, we show that the prediction performance of a series of RPP models can be significantly improved by integrating the time mapping process. Additionally, we also investigate the inherent characteristics of the parameters of our proposed model.

The novelties and main contributions of this paper are summarized as follows:

- By analyzing real datasets, we reveal that the temporal relaxation which characterizes the aging of a message in retweeting dynamics follows a power-law distribution, and the reinforcement effect declines as the popularity grows which can be captured by a reinforcement function with an exponential decay.
- We introduce the notation of weibo time and propose a time mapping process to eliminate the effect of user activity variation on the retweeting dynamics.
- We present an extended reinforced Poisson process model, namely PETM, by integrating a power-law temporal relaxation function, an exponential reinforcement function and a time mapping process with the original RPP model. Extensive experiments on two Weibo datasets validate the effectiveness of the proposed model in popularity prediction task.

The rest of this paper is organized as follows. We present a review of related work in Section 2. The preliminaries including the formal definition of popularity prediction problem and the description of general reinforced Poisson process model are provided in Section 3. We give a detailed description for the modeling, learning and prediction process of the proposed model in Section 4. In Section 5, we describe the datasets, comparison methods and evaluation metrics used in our experiments. The experimental results and discussion are presented in Section 6. We conclude our paper in Section 7.

2. RELATED WORK

Popularity prediction of user generated content has been widely studied in the literature. Recent studies on microblogging platforms include popularity prediction for hashtag (or trend) and individual message. Typical solutions include the regression models [4, 12, 27], classification models [8, 10, 11, 18, 16] and time series models [19, 31, 32]. For regression or classification models, previous works mainly focus on exploring effective features for prediction. As an initial effort, Bongwon et al. [24] examined a number of features that might affect retweetability of tweets and found that content features such as URLs and hashtags have strong relationship with retweetability. Tsur et al. [27] employed a regression model to predict hashtag frequency on a weekly basis based on 25-week Twitter data. The features used in their experiments are mainly extracted from the hashtag itself. Hong et al. [11] treated the prediction problem as a classification task and investigated a wide spectrum of features including content features derived from the message, context features (structural features) extracted from the underlying user network and temporal features obtained from the observed popularity dynamics. Similar features have also been investigated in [18] and [8]. Generally speaking, the context features are more effective than content features, while the prediction performance can be further improved when combing the temporal features. For time series models, Matsubara et al. [19] proposed SpikeM, which used the self-excited Hawkes conditional Poisson process to model the power-law relaxation of popularity dynamics. Despite of its promising predictive power, the dependence on exogenous factors and the fixed power-law relaxation function limit its generalization ability.

Recently, there have been pioneering data-driven analysis of popularity prediction on different kinds of user generated content, e.g., news articles [3, 26], YouTube videos [1, 7, 15, 21, 25], diggs in Digg [1, 14, 25], posts in Facebook [5] and papers [23, 29] etc. Focusing on diggs in Digg and videos in YouTube, Szabo et al. [25] found a high log-linear correlation existed between the popularity on early days and later days, and presented three regression models for prediction. Following [25], Pinto et al. [21] proposed a multivariate linear regression model which split the training period into several equal intervals, and predicted the future popularity of a video as a linear function of views count in every interval.

The most close research to ours was conducted by Shen et al. [23]. They proposed the general framework of reinforced Poisson process model and applied the model to predict the future citations of a given paper. Inspired by this study, in this paper, we proposed a extended reinforced Poisson process model to characterize the retweeting dynamics.

3. PRELIMINARIES

3.1 Problem Statement

In this work, we aim to model the retweeting dynamics of a single message in the early stages and use the model to predict its popularity in the future. For a given message m, we use the number of "retweets" to measure its popularity. Then, we sort all its retweets according to their post time in ascending order, forming a chain of messages. The post time for the kth retweet is denoted by $\mathcal{T}_k^m$. Specially, we use $\mathcal{T}_0^m$ to denote the post time of the original message. The post time $\mathcal{T}$ is measured in Unix timestamp which is a number indicating the seconds which have elapsed since 1970-01-01 00:00:00, UTC. Further, we define the *age* of kth retweet t_k^m as the elapsed time from $\mathcal{T}_0^m$, which can be calculated by $t_k^m = \mathcal{T}_k^m - \mathcal{T}_0^m$. The number of retweets at age t is denoted by $N(t)$. During the modeling and prediction process, following the definition in [25], we call *reference time* T_r the time when we intend to predict the popularity of a message whose age with respect to the post time is T_r. Also, by *indicator time* T_i we refer to the age the message when we perform the prediction, namely that how long we can observe the retweeting history in order to extrapolate. Generally, we have $T_i < T_r$. Intuitively, T_i measures the length of the training period for the model. The retweeting dynamics of message m up to T_i is characterized by a set of time moments $\{t_k^m\}(1 \le k \le n_m)$ when each retweet arrives, where n_m is the total number of retweets in this training period. Formally, the prediction problem can be described as: for a message m, given its retweeting dynamics $\{t_k^m\}$ up to the indicator time T_i, predicting its popularity at the reference time T_r.

3.2 Reinforced Poisson Process Model

The reinforced Poisson process (RPP) model was first proposed in [29, 23] to model the stochastic popularity dynamics for items in a complex evolving system. The model captures three key ingredients simultaneously: (i) fitness of an item, characterizing its inherent competitiveness against other items; (ii) a general temporal relaxation function corresponding to the aging in the ability to attract new attention; (iii) a reinforcement mechanism characterizing the well-known "richer-get-richer" phenomenon. In the following, with respect to the retweeting dynamics on microblogging platforms, we give a more general definition of RPP model.

Given a message m, its retweeting dynamics $\{t_k^m\}$ up to T_i can be modeled as reinforced Poisson process which is characterized by the rate function $\lambda_m(t,k)$ as

$$\lambda_m(t,k) = c_m f_m(t) r_m(k) \tag{1}$$

where c_m is intrinsic attractiveness of the message, $f_m(t)$ is the general temporal relaxation function which characterizes the aging effect, and $r_m(k)$ is the general reinforcement function depicting the "richer-get-richer phenomenon". Instead of defining $r_m(k)$ to be the number of retweets as in [29, 23], we generalize the reinforcement function to be any piecewise constant function which is defined on number of retweets k, i.e., during the time interval between kth and $(k+1)$th retweet, $r_m(k)$ stays unchanged.

Next, we describe the modeling process of general RPP model. Given the $(k-1)$th retweet arrives at t_{k-1}^m, the probability that the kth retweet arrives at t_k^m follows

$$p_1(t_k^m | t_{k-1}^m) = c_m f_m(t_k^m) r_m(k-1) e^{-\int_{t_{k-1}^m}^{t_k^m} c_m f_m(s) r_m(k-1) \mathrm{d}s} \tag{2}$$

while the probability that no retweet arrives between $t_{n_m}^m$ and T_i is

$$p_0(T_i | t_{n_m}^m) = e^{-\int_{t_{n_m}^m}^{T_i} c_m f_m(s) r_m(n_m) \mathrm{d}s} \tag{3}$$

The RPP model assumes that retweets from different time intervals are statistically independent. Hence by incorporating Equation 2 and Equation 3, the likelihood of the observing retweeting dynamics $\{t_k^m\}$ up to T_i follows

$$\mathcal{L} = p_0(T_i | t_{n_m}^m) \prod_{k=1}^{n_m} p_1(t_k^m | t_{k-1}^m) \tag{4}$$

By taking logarithm, we can get the log-likelihood function ℓ as

$$\begin{aligned} \ell = \ln \mathcal{L} &= \ln \Big(p_0(T_i | t_{n_m}^m) \prod_{k=1}^{n_m} p_1(t_k^m | t_{k-1}^m) \Big) \\ &= n_m \ln c_m + \sum_{k=1}^{n_m} \Big(\ln f_m(t_k^m) + \ln r_m(k-1) \Big) - c_m X_m \end{aligned} \tag{5}$$

where

$$X_m = \sum_{k=1}^{n_m} \int_{t_{k-1}^m}^{t_k^m} f_m(s) r_m(k-1) \mathrm{d}s + \int_{t_{n_m}^m}^{T_i} f_m(s) r_m(n_m) \mathrm{d}s \tag{6}$$

4. MODEL

In this section, we first give the specific forms for temporal relaxation function and reinforcement function with respect to retweeting dynamics. Then we describe the hourly variation of user activity and the proposed time mapping process. Lastly, we give a detailed description for the proposed model, including the modeling, learning and prediction process.

4.1 Temporal Relaxation Function

As shown in the rate function (Equation 1), the retweeting dynamics of a message is controlled by three independent forces, which are difficult to separate from each other. Hence to determine the specific form of temporal relaxation function, we need to control the other factors, isolating the temporal decay. Specifically, we group messages with same fitness c and same reinforcement $r(k)$, and look at the time when they were retweeted again. Since we do not know c beforehand, we roughly consider messages which are posted in a fixed time period and receive the same number of retweets in one hour after being posted as having the same fitness. Note that the reinforcement $r(k)$ is a function of the number of retweets k, by selecting messages with

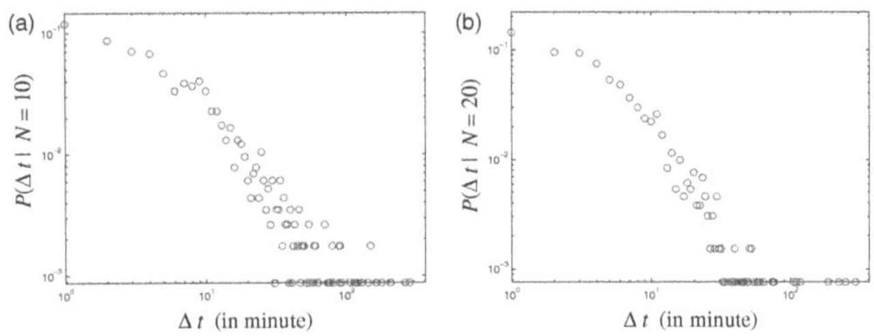

Figure 1: Empirical validation of power-law decay

same retweet number, the reinforcement is also controlled. Therefore we selected messages posted between 10am and 11am with fixed cumulative retweet number N in the first hour after being posted, and tracked the moment when their retweets number changed from N to $N+1$. Then we measured Δt in minutes, i.e., minutes passed when $N \to N+1$ took place. Note that all values of Δt are greater than 60 since the messages have been posted for more than 1 hour before the $(N+1)$th retweet happens. Hence, to illustrate the distribution of Δt more clearly, we subtract 60 from Δt given that subtracting a constant from a random variable will not change its distribution. Then we show $P(\Delta t|N)$ when N is 10 and 20 in Figure 1. We can easily find that the temporal relaxation function is best approximated by a power-law function

$$f_m(t_k) = t_k^{-\gamma_m} \quad (\gamma > 0) \tag{7}$$

The power-law decay of influence has also been reported in blogs [20] and videos [6].

4.2 Reinforcement Function

In this section, we study the reinforcement mechanism in retweeting dynamics and address the following issues: (1) whether the reinforcement mechanism exists in retweeting dynamics, i.e., whether the previously retweets can trigger more subsequent retweets? (2) if the reinforcement mechanism does exist, how to model it? To answer the first question, we follow the similar method as proposed in [22], which is to measure the preferential attachment mechanism from the empirical data, one keeps a constant time window and looks at the growth of degrees as a function of existing degree. Similarly, here in the analysis of retweeting dynamics, we first fix a constant time window, and then measure the number of retweets that a message received before and within this time window. Specifically, given a fixed time window, we use Φ to denote the number of retweets that each message received before this time window, and use ϕ to measure the average number of retweets for each message with Φ retweets received in this time window. In Figure 2, we show how ϕ varies with Φ when the time window is fixed to be 10:30am–10:45am (Figure 2(a)) and 10:45am–11:00am (Figure 2(b)). Generally speaking, for both examined time window, ϕ is linearly proportional to Φ, i.e., $\phi \propto \Phi$. The dashed lines correspond to the best linear fitting. This is reasonable since this linearity can lead to a power-law message popularity distribution as shown in Figure 4. In previous literature [23, 29], a simple linear function is used to capture this linear reinforcement

$$r_m(k) = k + 1 + \epsilon \tag{8}$$

where $k \geq 0$ and ϵ denotes the effective number of retweets which plays the role of prior belief. The linearly

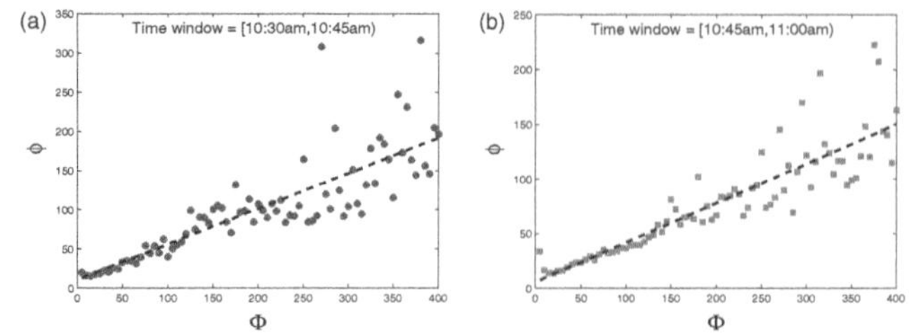

Figure 2: Empirical validation of reinforcement mechanism

reinforcement function is defined based on the assumption that all retweets (including the original message) are created equally. Therefore, we can rewrite Equation 8 as $r_m(k) = \sum_{j=0}^{k} 1 + \epsilon$, where in the summation $\sum_{j=0}^{k} 1$ each retweet contributes 1 to the reinforcement function as assumed. However, by further examining Figure 2, we can find that when Φ grows larger, a large amount of ϕ fall below the dashed line, indicating that ϕ grows slower than linearly with Φ. One possible reason for this phenomenon is that the retweets are not created equally and with the number of retweets grows larger, the contribution of the subsequent retweets to the reinforcement function become smaller. Hence, to capture the decay of contribution for each retweet, we assume that the contribution decay follows an exponential distribution, i.e., for the jth retweet, the contribution to the reinforcement function $r_m(k)$ is $e^{-\alpha_m j}$, where $\alpha_m > 0$. By adding the contribution of all retweets together, we get the modified reinforcement function as follows

$$r_m(k) = \sum_{j=0}^{j=k} e^{-\alpha_m j} + \epsilon = \frac{\varepsilon - e^{-\alpha_m (k+1)}}{1 - e^{-\alpha_m}} \quad (\alpha_m > 0) \tag{9}$$

where $\varepsilon = 1 + \epsilon - \epsilon e^{-\alpha_m}$. Henceforth, we call Equation 9 the exponential reinforcement function.

4.3 User Activity and Time Mapping

In this section, we examine another important factor, user activity, which is not considered by the original RPP model. To investigate the hourly variation of user activity, we randomly selected about 10 thousand users from Weibo and crawled all their messages posted between 2013-07-01 00:00:00 and 2013-07-31 23:59:59, which results in 1.6 millon messages. We first show the average number of messages posted during a given hour as a function of time in Figure 3(a). Clearly, we can see that user activity varies over time, namely that users are highly active during daytime and inactive in midnight. Hence, depending on the time of day when messages are posted, the number of initial retweets that messages get will differ greatly, as illustrated in Figure 3(b), where we show the average number of retweets that a message receives in the first hour after being posted (blue curve). As can be expected, messages posted at higher active periods of a day will on average receive more retweets in the first hour than messages posted at less active periods. For example, a message posted at 11am can on average get 25 retweets in the first hour, while it will only get 5 retweets if it is posted at 4am. Therefore, if we do not eliminate the effect of user activity variation, we may misinterpret the relative interestingness of a message only based on the observation made in a few hours after it has been posted.

To eliminate the effect of user activity variation, we introduce the notation of *weibo time*, where we measure time not by wall time (seconds), but by the number of messages that users post on Weibo. To map the wall time into weibo time, we first use τ and $\hat{\tau}$ to denote the second in a day, which are measured by wall time and weibo time respectively. Both τ and $\hat{\tau}$ take values in $[0, 86400)$ where 86400 is the number of seconds in a day. The difference between them is that τ can only be integer while $\hat{\tau}$ can be decimal. Then through analyzing the dataset, we get the average number of messages posted per second M^* and in each second M_τ. M^* is a constant number while M_τ varies with τ. To be clear, we show M_τ as a function of τ in Figure 3(c). Obviously, M_τ takes larger value in daytime than in midnight, which can further illustrate the hourly variation of user activity. Now, we can define the mapping function g as

$$\hat{\tau} = g(\tau) = \sum_{j=0}^{\tau} M_j / M^* \tag{10}$$

The image of mapping function $g(\tau)$ is shown in Figure 3(d) (blue curve). Next, for each original timestamp $\mathcal{T}$ in dataset, we denote the corresponding mapped timestamp as $\hat{\mathcal{T}}$. To map from $\mathcal{T}$ to $\hat{\mathcal{T}}$, we first need to transform $\mathcal{T}$ into the corresponding second of day τ_* by

$$\tau_* = \text{mod}(\mathcal{T} + 8 * 3600, 86400) \tag{11}$$

where $\text{mod}(a, b)$ returns the modulus after division of a by b and 3600 is the number of seconds in an hour. Since Weibo locates in China, UTC+8 time zone, we need to add $8 * 3600$ to each $\mathcal{T}$ before the modulo operation. Lastly, by incorporating Equation 11 and Equation 10, we can get the mapped timestamp $\hat{\mathcal{T}}$ by

$$\hat{\mathcal{T}} = \mathcal{T} - \tau_* + \hat{\tau}_* = \mathcal{T} - \tau_* + g(\tau_*) \tag{12}$$

After timestamp mapping, we show the average number of retweets that a message receives in the first weibo hour after being post in Figure 3(b) (red curve). As can be seen, the average retweets number slightly changes over the post time, indicating that the mapping from wall time to weibo time can largely mitigate the impact of message's post time on its early-stage popularity and eliminate the effect of user activity variation.

4.4 Modeling Learning and Prediction

In this section, we describe in detail how to model the retweeting dynamics for a given message under the reinforced Poisson process framework with power-law temporal relaxation function (Section 4.1) and exponential reinforcement function (Section 4.2). Also, we show how to integrate the time mapping process (Section 4.3) into the reinforced Poisson process framework. In the following, we describe the model learning and prediction process step by step, and we start with the input of the model.

Input time moments. As defined in Section 3.1, for a given message m, its retweeting dynamics can be characterized by a set of non-decreasing time moments $\{t_k^m\}$, where t_k^m denotes the age of the kth retweet and t_0^m is the age of the original message which is 0. The drawback of this definition is that since the temporal relaxation function $t^{-\gamma_m}$ takes a power-law form, it will be infinity when $t = t_0^m = 0$. To avoid this, we manually add a constant value t^* to all t_k^m.

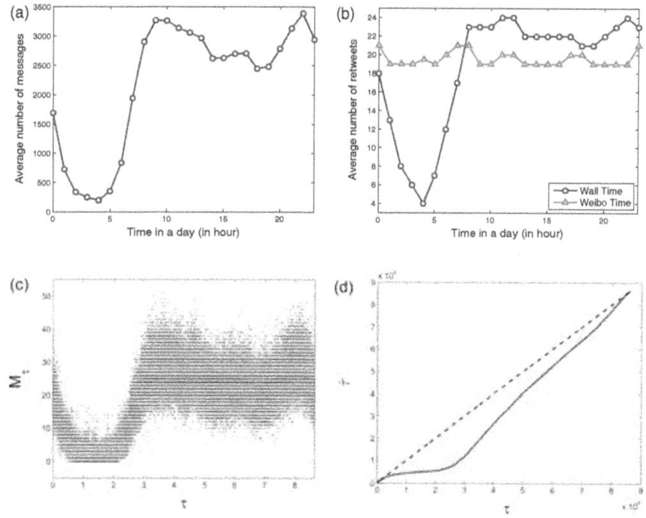

Figure 3: User activity variation and Time mapping

Formally, we redefine t_k^m as

$$t_k^m = \mathcal{T}_k^m - \mathcal{T}_0^m + t^* \tag{13}$$

Also, henceforth in the modeling and prediction process, when we refer to indicator time T_i and reference time T_r, their values are $T_i + t^*$ and $T_r + t^*$ respectively.

Further, to integrate the time mapping function into the RPP model, we first need to map the original timestamps $\{\mathcal{T}_k^m\}$ into $\{\hat{\mathcal{T}}_k^m\}$ using Equation 12, and then get t_k^m as

$$t_k^m = \hat{\mathcal{T}}_k^m - \hat{\mathcal{T}}_0^m + t^* \tag{14}$$

Here, we use time series $\{t_i^m\}$ up to T_i as the input of the modeling process. For ease of calculation of the power-law temporal relaxation function, we measure t_k^m in hours and set $t^* = 1$ for all the messages. For simplicity and clarity, henceforth we will omit the superscript m which is used to represent message m.

Model Formulation. By substituting the power-law temporal relaxation function Equation 7 and the exponential reinforcement function Equation 9 into the general rate function Equation 1, we can get the specific form of rate function for retweeting dynamics as

$$\lambda(t_k, k) = \frac{c t_k^{-\gamma}(\varepsilon - e^{-\alpha(k+1)})}{1 - e^{-\alpha}} \tag{15}$$

Then, by substituting Equations 7 and 9 into the general log-likelihood function Equation 5, we can get the log-likelihood for the retweeting dynamics $\{t_k\}$ up to T_i as

$$\begin{aligned} \ell &= n \ln c + \sum_{k=1}^{n} \Big(\ln f(t_k) + \ln r(k-1) \Big) - cX \\ &= n \ln \frac{c}{1 - e^{-\alpha}} + \sum_{k=1}^{n} \Big(\ln(\varepsilon - e^{-\alpha k}) - \gamma \ln t_k \Big) - cX \end{aligned} \tag{16}$$

where

$$X = \sum_{k=1}^{n+1} \frac{(t_k^{1-\gamma} - t_{k-1}^{1-\gamma})(\varepsilon - e^{-\alpha k})}{(1-\gamma)(1 - e^{-\alpha})} \tag{17}$$

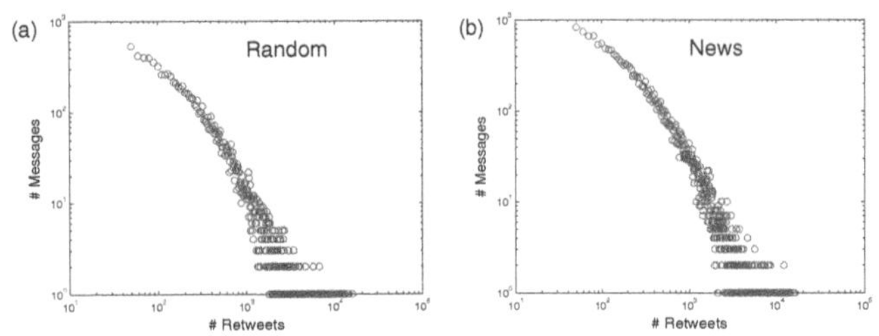

Figure 4: Popularity distribution

Note that we manually set $t_{n+1} = T_i$ for the sake of simplification. It does not mean that the $(n+1)$th retweets arrives at T_i.

Parameter Estimation. Here, we denote the optimal values for parameters $\{c, \gamma, \alpha\}$ as $\{c^*, \gamma^*, \alpha^*\}$. For the fitness parameter c, we can get its optimal value c^* in closed form by maximizing the log-likelihood function in Equation 16 as

$$c^* = \arg\max_c \ell = n/X \tag{18}$$

For parameters γ and α, the optimal values can be found by maximizing the log-likelihood ℓ using the gradient ascent method. The gradients for each parameter are

$$\frac{\partial \ell}{\partial \gamma} = -\sum_{k=1}^{n} \ln t_k - c\frac{\partial X}{\partial \gamma} \tag{19}$$

$$\frac{\partial \ell}{\partial \alpha} = -\frac{ne^{-\alpha}}{1-e^{-\alpha}} + \sum_{k=1}^{n} \frac{\epsilon e^{-\alpha} + ke^{-\alpha k}}{\varepsilon - e^{-\alpha k}} - c\frac{\partial X}{\partial \alpha} \tag{20}$$

where

$$\frac{\partial X}{\partial \gamma} = \sum_{k=1}^{n+1} \frac{\varepsilon - e^{-\alpha k}}{1-e^{-\alpha}} \left(\frac{t_{k-1}^{1-\gamma} \ln t_{k-1} - t_k^{1-\gamma} \ln t_k}{1-\gamma} + \frac{t_k^{1-\gamma} - t_{k-1}^{1-\gamma}}{(1-\gamma)^2} \right) \tag{21}$$

$$\frac{\partial X}{\partial \alpha} = \sum_{k=1}^{n+1} \frac{(t_k^{1-\gamma} - t_{k-1}^{1-\gamma})(ke^{-\alpha k} - (k-1)e^{-\alpha(k+1)} - e^{-\alpha})}{(1-\gamma)(1-e^{-\alpha})^2} \tag{22}$$

Following the standard gradient ascent method, update rules at the jth iteration are shown in the following equations.

$$\gamma^{(j+1)} = \gamma^{(j)} + \beta_1 \cdot \frac{\partial \ell}{\partial \gamma} \tag{23}$$

$$\alpha^{(j+1)} = \alpha^{(j)} + \beta_2 \cdot \frac{\partial \ell}{\partial \alpha} \tag{24}$$

where β_1 and β_2 are the learning rate at each iteration. The algorithm stops when the change in an iteration is small enough.

Prediction. With the obtained optimal parameters, i.e., c^*, γ^* and α^*, we can use the model to predict the expected number of retweets $N(t)$ at any given time moment t. Incorporating with the rate function of retweeting dynamics in Equation 15, we treat the prediction task as the following differential equation

$$\frac{\mathrm{d}N(t)}{\mathrm{d}t} = c^* t^{-\gamma^*} \frac{\varepsilon - e^{-\alpha^*(N(t)+1)}}{1-e^{-\alpha^*}} \tag{25}$$

with the boundary condition $N(T_i) = n$. By solving this differential equation, we get the prediction function

$$N(t) = \left(\ln(1+e^Y) - Y - \ln\varepsilon - \alpha^*\right)/\alpha^* \tag{26}$$

where

$$Y = \frac{\varepsilon c^* \alpha^* (T_i^{1-\gamma^*} - t^{1-\gamma^*})}{(1-\gamma^*)(1-e^{-\alpha^*})} - (n+1)\alpha^* - \ln(\varepsilon - e^{-\alpha^*(n+1)}) \tag{27}$$

5. EXPERIMENTAL SETUP

5.1 Datasets

Since this paper focuses on modeling the retweeting dynamics and predicting the future popularity of a given message on microblogging platforms, we conducted extensive experiments on two datasets of Weibo messages. Each dataset contains a set of original messages posted during July 1–31, 2013. For each message, we recorded the post timestamps for it and all its retweets in one month after been posted. We adopted two different crawling strategies and obtained the following two datasets.

- *Random*: To construct the random dataset, we first randomly selected 10,000 seed users and crawled all their original messages posted during July 1–31 2013. The crawling process produced in total 0.8 million original messages. Then we manually removed messages with more than 20,000 retweets since the crawling process for their retweets is too time consuming. Also, messages with less than 50 retweets are removed since they usually stop receiving more retweets in the first few hours. Thus we randomly selected 10K messages from the rest of the crawled messages to construct the random dataset. In this dataset, the mean and median values for message popularity are 450 and 210 respectively.

- *News*: In this dataset, we concentrated on a specific type of message—news. To begin with, we manually selected 25 prestigious news accounts and crawled all their original posts during July 1–31, 2013. Similarly with Random dataset, messages with retweets number larger than 20,000 or less than 50 are neglected. The resulting dataset contains in total 18K original messages and its statistics is shown in Table 1. As can be seen, since the number of followers for all these news account are larger than 1 million, their posted messages on average gain more retweets than these in Random dataset. For News dataset, the mean and median values for message popularity are 529 and 238 respectively.

Since few messages can receive more retweets after been posted for one month, we use the number of retweets that a message gets in the first month since posted to measure its final popularity. We show the distribution of the message final popularity for both datasets in Figure 4. As can be seen, both distributions follow power-law.

5.2 Comparison Methods

To examine the efficiency of our modified RPP models, two variations of RPP model and two widely used regression models were introduced for comparison. Specifically, the comparison methods in our experiments are listed as follows:

- **SH** [25]: the linear regression method for logarithmic popularity, which is proposed by Szabo and Huber-

Table 1: Statistics of News Dataset

Account Name	A1	A2	A3	A4	A5	A6	A7	A8	A9	A10	A11	A12	A13
# Follower[1]	3.8	9.2	10.8	3.3	11.1	5.1	4.2	9.2	7.2	9.4	5.9	6.0	6.3
# Message	1062	232	1164	77	1373	239	301	1246	1519	672	318	922	577
Avg. # Retweet	113.3	653.8	741.1	170.0	331.4	453.8	339.4	797.6	315.8	234.7	323.3	380.4	751.7
Account Name	A14	A15	A16	A17	A18	A19	A20	A21	A22	A23	A24	A25	
# Follower	3.7	9.4	3.8	9.6	0.7	4.8	5.9	16.0	1.4	20.8	22.2	5.6	
# Message	1843	1922	158	178	693	1685	1103	1143	383	1381	972	830	
Avg. # Retweet	118.1	143.1	772.3	1479.5	42.0	410.1	362.1	378.9	499.8	1543.3	1887.4	168.7	

[1] # Follower is measured in million.

man. The SH model is represented by

$$\ln N(T_r) = a_1 \ln N(T_i) + a_0 \tag{28}$$

- **ML** [21]: the multivariate linear regression model. The training period $[0, T_i]$ is split equally into p intervals and the number of retweets received in each interval is seen as popularity *deltas*. The ML model predicts the popularity of a message at T_r as a linear function of p popularity deltas. Here, we set $p = 6$.
- **LL** [23]: RPP model with a log-normal relaxation function as in Equation 29 and a linear reinforcement function as in Equation 8. This model has been used to modeling the citation dynamics.

$$f_m(t; \mu_m, \sigma_m) = \frac{1}{\sqrt{2\pi}\sigma_m t} e^{-\frac{(\ln t - \mu_m)^2}{2\sigma_m^2}} \tag{29}$$

- **PL**: RPP model with a power-law relaxation function as in Equation 7 and a linear reinforcement function as in Equation 8.
- **PE**: RPP model with a power-law relaxation function as in Equation 7 and an exponential reinforcement function as in Equation 9.

Note that we do not employ the LE model, i.e. RPP model with a log-normal relaxation function and an exponential reinforcement function, for comparison since the modeling and prediction process for it is far too complicated to be implemented. Moreover, the input for the RPP models can be with or without the time mapping as in Equation 12. In order to distinguish them, we add **TM** to each RPP models' name. The time mapping version of RPP models applied for comparison consist of LLTM, PLTM and PETM.

5.3 Evaluation Metrics

The same as in [23], we use Mean Absolute Percentage Error (*MAPE*) and *Accuracy* to evaluate the performance of all the prediction models. Let $N_m(t)$ be the real number of retweets for message m up to time t, and $\hat{N}_m(t)$ be the predicted number of retweets. The MAPE measures the average deviation between predicted and real popularity over an aggregation of messages. For a dataset of M messages, the MAPE is defined as

$$MAPE = \frac{1}{M} \sum_{m=1}^{M} \left| \frac{\hat{N}_m(t) - N_m(t)}{N_m(t)} \right| \tag{30}$$

The Accuracy measures the fraction of messages correctly predicted for a given error tolerance ζ. It is defined as

$$Accuracy = \frac{1}{M} \sum_{m=1}^{M} \mathrm{I}\left[\left| \frac{\hat{N}_m(t) - N_m(t)}{N_m(t)} \right| \leq \zeta \right] \tag{31}$$

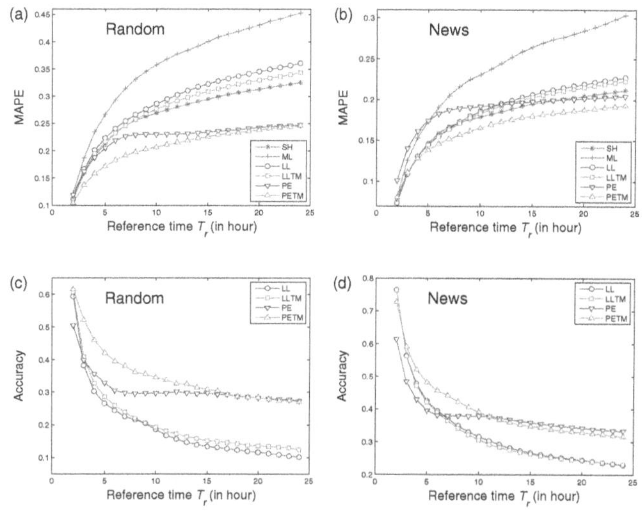

Figure 5: Prediction results for different models

where $\mathrm{I}[X]$ is an indicator function which returns 1 if the statement X is true and 0 otherwise. Here, we set the threshold $\zeta = 0.1$ in this paper.

6. EXPERIMENTAL RESULTS

In this section, we first report extensive experimental results on both Random and News datasets to validate the effectiveness of our proposed PE and PETM models. Then we give detailed analysis of the model parameters.

6.1 Prediction Results

We begin our analysis by comparing the prediction performance of different models on Random and News datasets. Specifically, by fixing the indicator time T_i to be 1, we evaluate the prediction performance of our proposed PE and PETM models as well as four comparison models including SH, ML, LL and LLTM, with reference time T_r varying from 2 to 24. The parameter ϵ is set to be 10 for all RPP models. Figure 5 shows the comparison results. Generally speaking, the proposed PETM model can always achieve the best prediction performance for each T_r on both datasets. When removing the time mapping process, the PE model can also show better performance than the other four models on Random dataset as shown in Figure 5(a) and 5(c). However, on News dataset in Figure 5(b) and 5(d), the PE model shows worse performance than the other models except ML model in terms of MAPE when T_r is smaller than 10, and it begins to show better performance when T_r grows larger. That indicates the PE model can well predict the long-term popularity of a given message but it

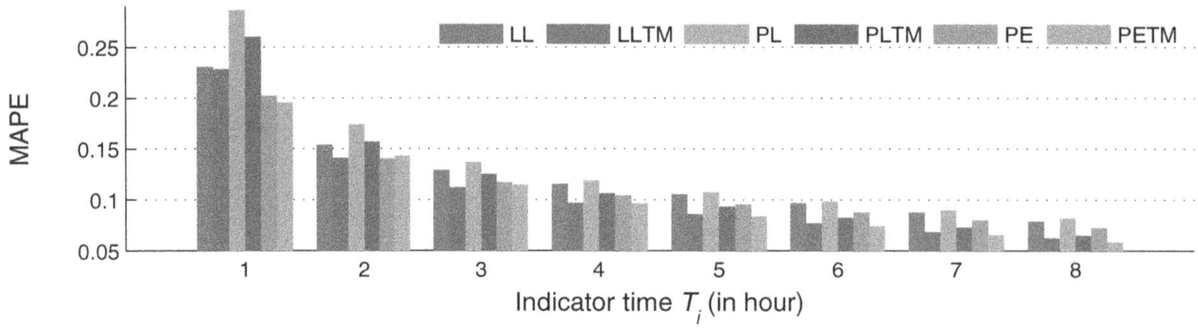

Figure 6: The performance comparison for different RPP models on News dataset with the variation of T_i

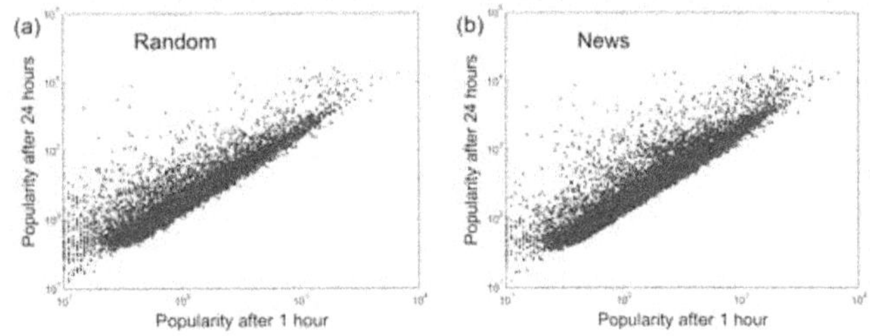

Figure 7: Popularity Correlation

cannot well capture the early evolution of the retweeting dynamics. Also, by comparing LL and LLTM models with PE and PETM models, we find that the performance of PE models are better than LL models in terms of both measurements on both datasets and the superiority increases with T_r, which means the proposed PE models are more appropriate to model the retweeting dynamics on microblogging platforms. For the other two baseline methods, SH model performs better than LL models in terms of MAPE and ML model shows the worst performance on both datasets. Both of them are regression method and try to capture the correlation between the early popularity and future popularity. The ML model works linearly and the SH model works in a logarithmic manner. As can be seen from Figure 7, the early popularity and future popularity is logarithmically correlated. That explains why the SH model can yield a moderate MAPE value while the ML model cannot achieve a better prediction performance. However, both of them show poor performance in terms of Accuracy. We do not show the accuracy for these two method since they are all equal to zero when $T_i \geq 2$.

Further, we carried out extensive experiments on News dataset to examine the following issues: (i) the prediction performance of different RPP models when T_i varies; (ii) the effect of T_i on the prediction performance of RPP models; (iii) the effect of time mapping process on the prediction performance of RPP models. To be specific, we apply a series of RPP models, including LL, PL and PE models, with and without the time mapping process, on News dataset with the indicator time T_i varying from 1 to 8. Since most messages in dataset stop receiving more retweets after being posted for 24 hours, we fix the reference time T_r to be 24 to check the ability for different models in predicting the popularity of a message. We use MAPE to measure the prediction performance and set the parameter ϵ again to be 10. The experimental results are shown in Figure 6.

First, we examine the prediction performance of different RPP models when T_i varies. For fair comparison, we compare the performance of RPP models with and without the time mapping process separately. As can be seen from Figure 6, for models without time mapping process, the PE model performs the best on the entire range of T_i, and the PL model shows the worst performance. The same observation can be made for models with time mapping process, except that when $T_i = 2$ and 3, the performance of PETM is slightly worse than LLTM. Generally speaking, the superior predictive power of PE models indicates that the retweeting dynamics can be better characterized by integrating the power-law temporal decay function with the exponential reinforcement function. Also, we can find that the exponential reinforcement function plays a very important role in PE models since when the reinforcement function is replaced by a linear function, as in PL models, the prediction performance drops significantly.

Then, we examine the effect of T_i on the prediction performance of RPP models. Intuitively, T_i is the length of training period. As shown in Figure 6, for all RPP models, the MAPE decreases as T_i increases, indicating that increasing the training period can improve the prediction performance for all the models. However, we can also see that the rate at which MAPE declines slows down quickly, e.g., the rate of decline for PETM model drops from 26.9% at $T_i = 1$ to 10.7% at $T_i = 8$. This means the marginal gain for performance improvement diminishes with the increasing of the training period. This is caused by that the amount of training data added to the model decreases as T_i increases, namely that, when T_i becomes larger, the number of retweets that a message receives in the T_ith hour is generally smaller than it receives in the $(T_i - 1)$th hour. Though T_i is increased by one hour at each time, the amount of training data does not grow proportionally.

Finally, we examine the effect of time mapping process on the prediction performance of all models. As we can see from Figure 6, for a fixed T_i, comparing with models without the time mapping, the MAPE drops significantly when adding the time mapping process to each model. This result confirms that the use activity variation can affect the retweeting dynamics and harm the performance of prediction models. By integrating the time mapping process to each prediction model, we can eliminate the effect of use activity variation and improve the prediction performance. Moreover, we observe that when T_i grows larger, the decrease in MAPE becomes more evident for

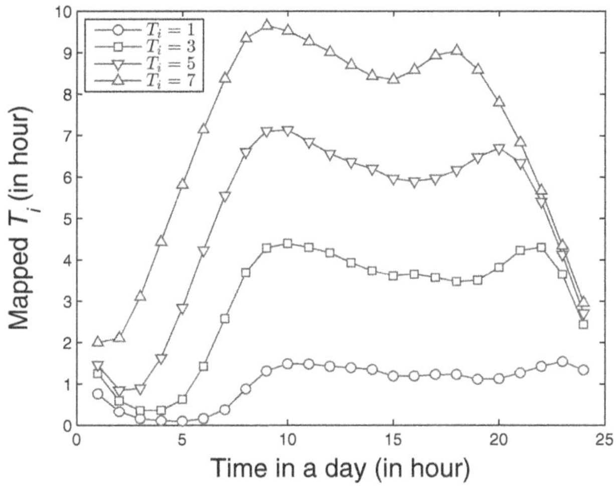

Figure 8: Variation of mapped indicator time T_i

all models. The reason for this result is that the effect of user activity variation becomes more obvious with the increasing of T_i. To be more clear, in Figure 8 we show the variation of mapped T_i with the posted time of message varying from 1h to 24h. As we can see, the magnitude of change for the mapped T_i becomes larger when T_i increases. For example, the minimum value and maximum value of the mapped T_i are 0.09 and 1.54 when $T_i = 1$, while they are 2.00 and 9.65 when $T_i = 7$. That means, with the length of training period grows larger, the effect of user activity variation becomes more evident. Hence, the improvement in prediction performance by integrating the time mapping process becomes more obvious. To sum up, the experimental results certify the effectiveness of the proposed time mapping process.

6.2 Analysis of Model Parameters

In our proposed PE and PETM models, there are in total four parameters $\{\epsilon, c, \gamma, \alpha\}$, where ϵ is set manually and the others are derived from the model learning process. In this section, we first examine the effect of parameter ϵ on the prediction performance of the proposed models, and then investigate the inherent characteristics of the learned parameters.

As defined in Section 4.2, the parameter ϵ is the effective number of retweets which plays the role of prior belief. Here, to examine the effect of ϵ, by fixing $T_i = 1$ and $T_r = 24$, we conducted experiments on News dataset to check the prediction performance of LL, LLTM, PE and PETM models with $\epsilon = 5, 10, 15, 20$. The results are shown in Table 2. As can be seen, we can draw the similar conclusion as in [23] that decreasing ϵ can reduce MAPE for all four models. Since a larger ϵ implies a weaker role of the reinforcement mechanism in RPP models, this result indicates the disparity in retweet numbers is appropriately captured by the reinforcement mechanism. Moreover, we find that if ϵ is too small, e.g. $\epsilon = 5$, the MAPE becomes larger again. This result implies that ϵ should not be set too small since it balances the strength in the reinforcement mechanism. Overall speaking, the experimental results certify the importance of reinforcement mechanism in modeling the retweeting dynamics.

Further, taking PETM model on News dataset as an example, we show the distribution of the learned parameters.

Table 2: Effect of prior number of retweets ϵ

Parameter	Methods[1]			
	LL	LLTM	PE	PETM
$\epsilon = 5$	0.2324	0.2286	0.2109	0.1944
$\epsilon = 10$	0.2274	0.2230	0.2046	0.1928
$\epsilon = 15$	0.2848	0.2557	0.2285	0.2168
$\epsilon = 20$	0.2928	0.2860	0.2510	0.2399

[1] The performance is measured in MAPE.

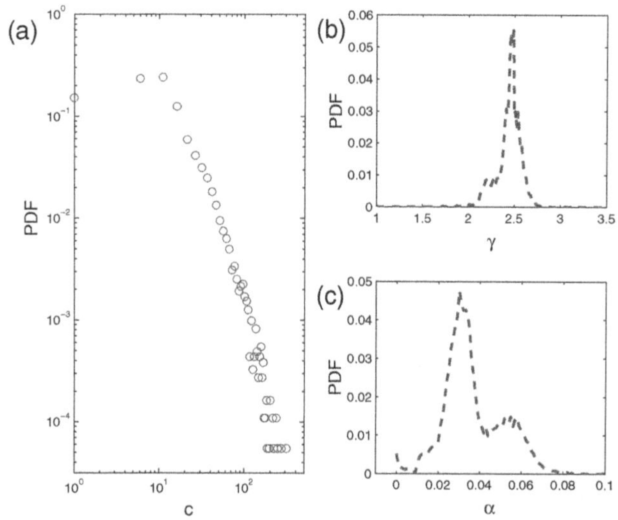

Figure 9: Distributions of model parameters

Figure 9(a) illustrates the distribution of fitness parameter c. Clearly we can see that c follows roughly a power-law distribution, indicating that most of messages share the similar small fitness value, while only a small portion of messages are created to be stronger competitive than others. For the exponent of power-law temporal relaxation function, parameter γ, as shown in Figure 9(b), most values of γ lie between 2 and 3. Moreover, we show the distribution of decay factor α in exponential reinforcement function in Figure 9(c). Note that, a smaller α indicates a weaker decay in the reinforcement function. When $\alpha = 0$, the exponential reinforcement function degenerates into the linear reinforcement function. From Figure 9(c) we can find that the value of α ranges from 0 to 0.1, indicating that the decay parameter α takes effect in the reinforcement function.

7. CONCLUSIONS AND FUTURE WORK

In this paper, we proposed an extended reinforced Poisson process model with time mapping process to model the retweeting dynamics and predict the future popularity for messages on microblogging platforms. The proposed model captures a power-law temporal relaxation function which corresponds to the aging in the ability of a message to attract new retweets and an exponential reinforcement function which characterizes the "richer-get-richer" phenomenon. Both the temporal relaxation function and the reinforcement function are derived from real data. Further, observing that the hourly variation of user activity can affect the retweeting dynamics in the early stages, we introduced the notation of weibo time and applied a time mapping process to transform the time moments in the retweeting dynamics into weibo time. To evaluate the effectiveness of our proposed model, we conducted extensive experiments on two Weibo datasets, with 10K and 18K messages respectively. The experimental results show that our proposed model outperforms existing prediction models in popularity prediction problem.

In the future, we will focus on enriching the proposed model by incorporating more relevant factors, e.g., structural factors derived from the underlying user network and the content factors extracted from the message itself.

Acknowledgements

This work is supported by the National Natural Science Foundation of China (61272240, 61103151), the Doctoral Fund of Ministry of Education of China (20110131110028), the Excellent Middle-Aged and Youth Scientists of Shandong Province (BS2012DX017) and the Natural Science Foundation of Shandong Province (ZR2012FM037).

8. REFERENCES

[1] M. Ahmed, S. Spagna, F. Huici, and S. Niccolini. A peek into the future: predicting the evolution of popularity in user generated content. In *WSDM*, pages 607–616, 2013.

[2] S. Asur and B. A. Huberman. Predicting the future with social media. In *WI-IAT*, volume 1, pages 492–499, 2010.

[3] R. Bandari, S. Asur, and B. A. Huberman. The pulse of news in social media: Forecasting popularity. In *ICWSM*, 2012.

[4] P. Bao, H.-W. Shen, J. Huang, and X.-Q. Cheng. Popularity prediction in microblogging network: a case study on sina weibo. In *WWW*, pages 177–178, 2013.

[5] J. Cheng, L. Adamic, P. A. Dow, J. M. Kleinberg, and J. Leskovec. Can cascades be predicted? In *WWW*, pages 925–936, 2014.

[6] R. Crane and D. Sornette. Robust dynamic classes revealed by measuring the response function of a social system. *PNAS*, 105(41):15649–15653, 2008.

[7] F. Figueiredo. On the prediction of popularity of trends and hits for user generated videos. In *WSDM*, pages 741–746, 2013.

[8] S. Gao, J. Ma, and Z. Chen. Effective and effortless features for popularity prediction in microblogging network. In *WWW*, pages 269–270, 2014.

[9] M. Gomez-Rodriguez, J. Leskovec, et al. Modeling information propagation with survival theory. In *ICML*, pages 666–674, 2013.

[10] M. Gupta, J. Gao, C. Zhai, and J. Han. Predicting future popularity trend of events in microblogging platforms. *ASIST*, 49(1):1–10, 2012.

[11] L. Hong, O. Dan, and B. D. Davison. Predicting popular messages in twitter. In *WWW*, pages 57–58, 2011.

[12] A. Kupavskii, L. Ostroumova, A. Umnov, S. Usachev, P. Serdyukov, G. Gusev, and A. Kustarev. Prediction of retweet cascade size over time. In *CIKM*, pages 2335–2338, 2012.

[13] H. Kwak, C. Lee, H. Park, and S. Moon. What is twitter, a social network or a news media? In *WWW*, pages 591–600, 2010.

[14] K. Lerman and T. Hogg. Using a model of social dynamics to predict popularity of news. In *WWW*, pages 621–630, 2010.

[15] H. Li, X. Ma, F. Wang, J. Liu, and K. Xu. On popularity prediction of videos shared in online social networks. In *CIKM*, pages 169–178, 2013.

[16] F. M. Lilian Weng and Y.-Y. Ahn. Virality prediction and community structure in social networks. *Scientific reports*, 3, 2013.

[17] S. Lin, X. Kong, and P. S. Yu. Predicting trends in social networks via dynamic activeness model. In *CIKM*, pages 1661–1666, 2013.

[18] Z. Ma, A. Sun, and G. Cong. On predicting the popularity of newly emerging hashtags in twitter. *JASIST*, 2013.

[19] Y. Matsubara, Y. Sakurai, B. A. Prakash, L. Li, and C. Faloutsos. Rise and fall patterns of information diffusion: Model and implications. In *KDD*, pages 6–14, 2012.

[20] M. McGlohon, J. Leskovec, C. Faloutsos, M. Hurst, and N. Glance. Finding patterns in blog shapes and blog evolution. In *ICWSM*, 2007.

[21] H. Pinto, J. M. Almeida, and M. A. Gonçalves. Using early view patterns to predict the popularity of youtube videos. In *WSDM*, pages 365–374, 2013.

[22] S. Redner. Citation statistics from 110 years of physical review. *PHYSICS TODAY*, 58(6):49–54, 2005.

[23] H.-W. Shen, D. Wang, C. Song, and A.-L. Barabási. Modeling and predicting popularity dynamics via reinforced poisson processes. In *AAAI*, 2014.

[24] B. Suh, L. Hong, P. Pirolli, and E. H. Chi. Want to be retweeted? large scale analytics on factors impacting retweet in twitter network. In *Socialcom*, pages 177–184, 2010.

[25] G. Szabo and B. A. Huberman. Predicting the popularity of online content. *Commun. ACM*, 53:80–88, 2010.

[26] M. Tsagkias, W. Weerkamp, and M. De Rijke. Predicting the volume of comments on online news stories. In *CIKM*, pages 1765–1768, 2009.

[27] O. Tsur and A. Rappoport. What's in a hashtag?: content based prediction of the spread of ideas in microblogging communities. In *WSDM*, pages 643–652, 2012.

[28] A. Tumasjan, T. O. Sprenger, P. G. Sandner, and I. M. Welpe. Predicting elections with twitter: What 140 characters reveal about political sentiment. *ICWSM*, 10:178–185, 2010.

[29] D. Wang, C. Song, and A.-L. Barabási. Quantifying long-term scientific impact. *Science*, 342(6154):127–132, 2013.

[30] C. Williams and G. Gulati. What is a social network worth? facebook and vote share in the 2008 presidential primaries. American Political Science Association, 2008.

[31] J. Yang and J. Leskovec. Patterns of temporal variation in online media. In *WSDM*, pages 177–186, 2011.

[32] P. Zhang, X. Wang, and B. Li. On predicting twitter trend: Factors and models. In *ASONAM*, 2013.

On Integrating Network and Community Discovery

Jialu Liu
University of Illinois at Urbana-Champaign
Urbana, IL, USA
jliu64@illinois.edu

Charu Aggarwal
IBM T. J. Watson Research Center
Yorktown, NY, USA
charu@us.ibm.com

Jiawei Han
University of Illinois at Urbana-Champaign
Urbana, IL, USA
hanj@illinois.edu

ABSTRACT

The problem of community detection has recently been studied widely in the context of the web and social media networks. Most algorithms for community detection assume that the entire network is available for online analysis. In practice, this is not really true, because only restricted portions of the network may be available at any given time for analysis. Many social networks such as *Facebook* have privacy constraints, which do not allow the discovery of the entire structure of the social network. Even in the case of more open networks such as *Twitter*, it may often be challenging to crawl the entire network from a practical perspective. For many other scenarios such as adversarial networks, the discovery of the entire network may itself be a costly task, and only a small portion of the network may be discovered at any given time. Therefore, it can be useful to investigate whether network mining algorithms can integrate the network discovery process tightly into the mining process, so that the best results are achieved for particular constraints on discovery costs. In this context, we will discuss algorithms for integrating community detection with network discovery. We will tightly integrate with the cost of actually discovering a network with the community detection process, so that the two processes can support each other and are performed in a mutually cohesive way. We present experimental results illustrating the advantages of the approach.

Categories and Subject Descriptors

H.4 [**Information Systems Applications**]: Miscellaneous

Keywords

Community Detection; Network Discovery

1. INTRODUCTION

Most network mining methods such as community detection usually assume that the entire network is available for analysis. In practice, social networks are extremely hard to fully discover because of their size and privacy concerns. Some examples of cases where the network is not fully discoverable are as follows:

- Many adversarial networks (such as terrorist networks) are challenging to discover completely. Usually, the linkage structures of the most important targets in the network are extremely costly to discover. On the other hand, the local regions within the proximity of some of less important nodes may be more easily discovered.
- In many information networks, an effort is required in order to determine the relationships for a given node. This imposes a cost on the community discovery process, which needs to be explicitly modeled in the analysis. For example, in protein interaction-networks, the relationship analysis of a protein node to other nodes in the network is often a data-driven and computationally intensive affair in its own right.
- Many social networks have privacy constraints which restrict the discovery of its linkage structure. For example, *Facebook* prevents the discovery of the linkage structure of participants with a private profile.
- Many online social networks impose limits on the data volume that can be crawled in any given period of time. In addition, bandwidth and space constraints naturally limit the size of the network that can be reasonably crawled in such scenarios. This limits the size of the network which can be available for any knowledge discovery task. For example, while the *Facebook* network contains over 800 million nodes, it may require about 2 weeks to discover the linkage structure of 1 million users in the network [12]. The integration of community and network discovery enables the fast discovery of a much smaller, but more representative network along with its underlying communities, in cases where exhaustive discovery is not practical.

In practice, network mining algorithms such as community detection are often applied to incomplete snapshots of the underlying networks. Since the quality of any mining process is highly dependent on the completeness of the underlying data, this implies that the network discovery phase critically impacts the final results available to the community detection process. Therefore, it is interesting to investigate whether the integration of the network discovery and mining process can provide higher quality results than a separation of these phases which are inherently inter-dependent.

An important observation in the context of many community detection applications is that, in many cases, we may wish to cluster a particular *target set of nodes of interest* from the known parts of the network. Most of the nodes in

WSDM'15, February 2–6, 2015, Shanghai, China.
Copyright 2015 ACM 978-1-4503-3317-7/15/02 ...$15.00.
http://dx.doi.org/10.1145/2684822.2685323 .

the network (and their linkage structure) outside this target may not be known in advance, and in many cases, their community structure may even be impossible to discover because of the privacy constraints in many real social networks such as *Facebook*.

The integration of the specifics of an analytical task into the network discovery process is likely to lead to a more focused approach which is well optimized for that task. In applications where the entire network is not available cleanly at a given time, the process of community discovery is *myopic*, in that it proceeds with partial information about the network at any given time. Furthermore, if the target set of nodes belongs to a particular local region of the network, it would seem wasteful to even attempt to discover irrelevant regions of the entire network from an analytical perspective. Since the discovery of links in the network comes at a cost, it is therefore important to direct the discovery process judiciously in order to obtain the best results. Furthermore, in many practical applications, it may not be possible to discover a very large network exhaustively within a modest amount of time; therefore it is critical to use community detection as an approach to balance the network discovery process effectively over the portions of the network relevant to the target nodes. Thus, network discovery and community discovery are two mutually dependent processes which enhance one another.

In this paper, we will present a method to tightly integrate community and network discovery, by alternating these phases in a mutually enhancing and cost-sensitive process. In order to achieve this goal, we will interweave an incremental community maintenance algorithm with an algorithm which queries carefully selected nodes in the network for further exploration of their locality. It is clear that the direction of this mutually enhancing process will be highly influenced by the target node set.

An important observation is that not all nodes are equally important from the perspective of community discovery, and therefore the node selection approach is critically important to the process. For example, consider the case illustrated in Fig. 1, in which the known parts of the network (in terms of nodes and edges) are illustrated in black, whereas the unknown parts of the network are illustrated in gray. We note that the existence of an unlabeled gray node is essentially unknown. This means that all of its incident edges (dashed lines) must also be unknown, since none of its neighbors have ever been queried. In the Fig. 1, we have shown four possibilities for nodes being queried, which are denoted by 1, 2, 3 and 4 respectively. It is clear that node 2 and 4 have smaller degree in the known network compared to nodes 1 and 3. In many cases, this is a direct result of the fact that the corresponding node also has low degree in the overall network, as a result of which it is often a poor choice to query. However, the degree alone tells us very little about the choice of node to query, especially when we are trying to discover all the communities in the network in a balanced and easy way. For examples, nodes 1 and 3 have similar degree, with the main difference that node 3 has known incident edges all from community A while node 1 is connected to different communities in the network. As a result, it is more likely that by querying node 3, we may be able to learn more about community A and increase its density. If we query node 1 instead, two communities then will merge together and render it difficult to partition them later. It is clear that the

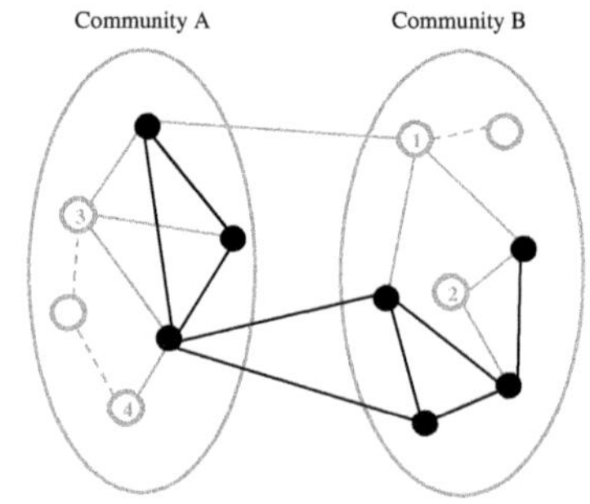

Figure 1: An illustrative example: selection of node interacts with the community discovery process.

known linkages in the discovered network provide us with interesting hints about the portions of the network to query, especially when we can relate them to the communities in the underlying network. This motivates the integration of the community and network discovery problem in a unified framework.

This paper is organized as follows. The remainder of this section discusses related work. In Section 2, we present the integrated model for network and community discovery. In Section 3, we present algorithms for integrating network and community discovery. Section 4 contains the experimental results. Section 5 contains the conclusions and summary.

1.1 Related work

The problem of community detection is related to that of finding dense regions in the underlying graph [11, 26]. Community detection is generally defined in the form of a clustering/partition of the underling network [8, 9, 15, 10, 2]. Surveys of a number of important algorithms for community detection are provided in [22, 10]. Evolutionary characteristics of dynamic communities are studied in [1, 7, 8]. The problem of community detection has also been studied in the context of combining node and edge content in order to improve its effectiveness [20, 24, 27]. Some work has been done [17] on community detection with incomplete information networks with the use of available content. This work is however not designed for dynamic network discovery in conjunction with community detection.

On the network discovery and sampling side, significant work has been done on sampling large graphs [16, 21], though these methods assume knowledge of the structure of the entire network for the sampling process. Some work has been done on sampling web documents [3, 14], though these methods use simple random walk methods in conjunction with web page content. This is often not suited to community discovery, especially in scenarios where significant content is not available. Some recent methods [12, 13, 25] have extended these random walk methods to social networks, though these methods are not necessarily focused on determining the best communities in the underlying network, especially where the costs of exploring different nodes may be quite different.

2. INTEGRATED MODEL FOR COMMUNITY AND NETWORK DISCOVERY

In this section, we will discuss the integrated model for network and community discovery. We assume that the social network in which the communities need to be discovered are denoted by $G = (N, A)$, where the set of nodes is denoted by N and the set of edges by A. We note that the set of nodes N and edges A are not known in advance, but can only be discovered at a cost. Initially, only the portion $G_s = (N_s, A_s, Q_s)$ is known, and it is assumed that the communities need to be discovered over a target set of nodes $N_t \subseteq N_s$. Therefore, we have $N_t \subseteq N_s \subseteq N$. The set Q_s contains the costs for the corresponding nodes in N_s, and this set has one entry for each node in N_s. In many real applications, very little about the linkage structure of the nodes in N_t may be known, and it is critical to discover those portions of the network, which are best related to the different target nodes. In the most extreme case, we may know nothing about the network at all beyond the target set we wish to cluster. In this case, the edge set A_s is empty, the set N_s and N_t are identical.

Our model assumes that incrementally larger portions of the network will be discovered by this process, which will help in further improving our knowledge of the community structure of the target set N_t. This will in turn provide us with better hints about further directions of exploration. During this process, we assume that the *currently known portions* of the network are denoted by $G_c = (N_c, A_c, Q_c)$, where $N_c \subseteq N$ and $A_c \subseteq A$. It is not necessary that all the edges incident on any particular node in N_c are included in A_c. The currently known portion of the network at the point of initialization is $G_c = G_s = (N_s, A_s, Q_s)$, though the size of the network G_c increases as more portions of it are discovered over time. We assume that the user has the ability to query any node $i \in N_c$ in order to determine all the (observable) nodes which are incident on it, and cost of doing so is given by $q_i \in Q_c$. For simplicity, we assume that the network G is binary and undirected. We note that the case, where the linkage structure of a node i cannot be discovered at all (eg. a private nodes in *Facebook*) can be easily modeled by setting $q_i = B + 1$ for that node where B represents budget. Furthermore, in some applications, the value of q_i may be the same, whereas in other more complex biological or adversarial networks, the value of q_i may vary across different nodes, depending upon the importance of the target. In cases where q_i cannot be estimated effectively, the default a-priori assumption is that the costs of querying different nodes are identical. In many practical applications such as *Facebook*, this cost may be estimated from the binary set $\{1, B+1\}$, depending upon whether or not that node is a private node. We assume that a quick estimate q_i on the cost of discovering the locality of a node can be determined, once that node has been revealed during the network discovery process. In some applications, where no a-priori information is available, the budget constraint may be expressed in terms of the maximum number of nodes, which are allowed to be queried.

The integrated problem of community and network discovery is to effectively determine the communities in the underlying social network within a given budget B on the costs. We further note that soft variations of this problem are possible, in which a hard budget may not be specified, but any-time (or any-budget) algorithms can be designed for progressively enhancing the community structure over time. By querying nodes in the network for their adjacent locality, we also discover many neighbors of nodes in the network which have not been queried so far. The communities in the network are constructed simultaneously with the network discovery process, and the current structure of communities is used as one of the inputs for deciding the order of querying the nodes. It is critical to discover the link structure of nodes in an order which best enables a robust discovery of the underlying communities at a low cost but high coverage. We will formulate the problem of integrated network and community discovery as follows:

Definition 1 (Network and Community Discovery). *Given a starting network $G_s = (N_s, A_s, Q_s)$, a target node set $N_t \subseteq N_s$, and an ability to query any node i from the currently discovered set of nodes for their adjacent links at cost c_i, cluster the target node set N_t into the set of k most tightly linked communities in the network within a total query budget B.*

2.1 Desiderata for Network and Community Discovery

We note that the network and community discovery problems are two tightly integrated problems, whose solutions mutually enhance one another. In most real world situations, the entire network can never be discovered in practice. Nevertheless, a robust discovery of the underlying network and the underlying communities has a number of goals which happen to be common in practice. These goals are as follows:

- It is desirable to discover as many nodes of the network in the locality of the target set N_t as possible within the given budget constraints. This would be a common goal of any network discovery method, which attempts to discover the locality of the target nodes of interest, in order to determine their relationships with one another.
- The discovered portions of the network should be as well balanced over the different portions of the network (relevant to the target nodes) as possible. In terms of the communities in the underlying network, this implies that the different communities in the network (containing the target nodes) should have a similar percentage of discovered nodes. This requirement tends to suggest that the community and network discovery problems are tightly integrated problems which need to be solved in unison.
- It is desirable to discover communities which are highly clustered and the corresponding nodes are densely linked together. This would be a common goal of any community discovery method.

We note that some of the afore-mentioned goals are unique to community detection, and others are unique to network discovery, and yet others are common goals of community and network discovery. Therefore, it makes sense to design algorithms for network and community discovery in a single unified framework in the context of a target node set.

3. NETWORK AND COMMUNITY DISCOVERY ALGORITHMS

We will design an incremental algorithm for community as well as network discovery which maintains a current network $G_c = (N_c, A_c, Q_c)$, in which the network N_c is always dynamically partitioned into a current set of K communities denoted by $\mathcal{C}^c = \mathcal{C}_c^1, \ldots, \mathcal{C}_c^K$. It is assumed that we initially know nothing about the network beyond the target set we wish to cluster. The algorithm proceeds in a set of alternating steps of *discovering localities of specific nodes* and then

Algorithm *NetDiscover*(Initial Network: G_s, Budget: B, Number of Communities: K, Target Node set: N_t)

$G_c = G_s = (N_s, A_s, Q_s)$
Initialize current cost $q = 0$
Query target nodes N_t, update G_c, q
Initialize sampled nodes set $S = N_t$
$\mathcal{C}_c$ = Initial clustering on subgraph of G_c induced by S
while *budget B is not exhausted* **do**
  $i = ChooseNode(G_c, \mathcal{C}_c, S, q, B)$
  $S = S \cup \{i\}$
  $q = q + q_i$
  $G_i = (N_i, A_i, Q_i) = DiscoverLocality(i)$
  $G_c = G_c \cup G_i = (N_c \cup N_i, A_c \cup A_i, Q_c \cup Q_i)$
  $\mathcal{C}_c = UpdateCommunity(G_c, i, S, \mathcal{C}_c)$
end

Algorithm 1: Integrating Network and Community Discovery

updating the communities with this discovered locality. Each step of the algorithm proceeds through successive querying of a node in the network followed by the re-adjustment of the current communities in the network. The overall framework of the integrated algorithm is presented in Alg. 1.

This re-adjustment of the communities is performed on the induced subgraph of G_c based on sampled nodes set S, which have already been discovered so far. An induced subgraph is defined as follows.

Definition 2 (Induced Subgraph). *$G' = (N', A')$ is the induced subgraph of $G = (N, A)$ based on the node set N' if $N' \subseteq N$ and $A' = (N' \times N') \cap A$.*

Clearly, the effectiveness of the approach depends critically upon the order of nodes discovered in the network. The choice of node discovery also depends upon the current community structure of the network, and therefore it is critical to maintain a high quality clustering of the network during the querying process. It is worth noting that we query all the target nodes as the first step in order to ensure the connectivity of G_c for initial clustering. Furthermore, it is important to discover the linkage structures in the network, as they relate to the target nodes.

The overall framework of the algorithm in Alg. 1 critically depends upon the process used for discovering the nodes, and updating the community structure. These are respectively denoted by *ChooseNode* and *UpdateCommunity* in Alg. 1. We will discuss these components subsequently in the following subsections.

3.1 Network Discovery

Each iteration of the algorithm in Alg. 1 needs to decide the choice of the node to query. The discovery of the appropriate node to query in order to further explore the best locality is critical in the context of the current community structure $\mathcal{C}_c$. Since the goal of our approach is community detection, we focus on the selection of node from the current set of candidates in $N_c - S$, which better helps in partitioning the target nodes. There are several key criteria for designing an effective network discovery module.

Before introducing them, we will first examine the overall algorithmic framework for choosing the node (denoted by the *ChooseNode* function in Function 1. This function first computes a score based on a certain measure for each candidate node in G_c and then adjusts the score depending upon its cost. In the end, the node with the lowest score is returned by the function. This is added to S, the set of nodes which have been queried so far.

Function *ChooseNode*(Current Network: G_c, Clustering: $\mathcal{C}_c$, Sampled nodes set: S, Current cost: q, Budget: B)

Initialize dictionary D (key: candidate nodes, value: score)
for *each node i in $N_c - S$* **do**
  if $q + q_i \leq B$ **then**
    $D[i] = ComputeScore(G_c, S, \mathcal{C}_c, i)$
  end
end
$AdjustScore(D, Q_c)$
if *D is empty* **then**
  Send Message: Budget B is exausted
else
  return node with lowest score in D
end

Function 1: Network Discovery

From our practical study, we discovered three main criteria for the design of the *ComputeScore* function:

- **High Purity:** It is better for the neighborhood of a node belonging to the same partition. This tends to help that community to be more dense and push the center of that community far apart from other communities.
- **Large Observed Degree:** We note that the successive querying of nodes increases our partial information about the link structure of other nodes in the network (*i.e.* nodes not already in S) for future querying. Nodes with more *observed* links are preferred. Because it is assumed that the unobservable links of a node are proportional to the already discovered links. By choosing such nodes, we can help expand G_c quickly and render the network denser.
- **Balanced Communities:** It is critical to keep different partitions balanced through the process of node and edge addition into G_c. Unbalanced partitions are usually detrimental both for the qualitative results found by the community detection approach, and for the stability of the incremental community discovery algorithm, which is used in the approach.

These criteria provide the insights needed for the effective design of the function for network discovery. We propose two simple measures for the *ComputeScore* function inspired from *Normalized Cut* and *Modularity* following the criteria.

3.1.1 Normalized Cut

The normalized cut criterion measures the total dissimilarity between the different communities in the context of the total similarity within the same communities [23]. It was originally proposed for the graph segmentation problem, and is defined as follows:

$$\sum_{k=1}^{K} \frac{cut(\mathcal{C}_c^k, S - \mathcal{C}_c^k)}{assoc(\mathcal{C}_c^k, S)}$$

Here, $cut(\mathcal{C}_c^i, \mathcal{C}_c^j)$ is the count of the edges between two groups of nodes: $\mathcal{C}_c^i$ and $\mathcal{C}_c^j$. The notation $assoc(\mathcal{C}_c^i, S)$ denotes the total degrees of nodes in C_c^i within the subgraph of G_c induced by S. The minimization of the $Ncut$ measure, tends to minimize the similarity across a cut, while simultaneously maximizing the similarity within the same community. The balance among different communities is directly incorporated through dividing the cut by total edge count for each community.

While the $Ncut$ measure was originally designed for image segmentation in the context of static graphs, our goal here is to greedily select a node which can minimize the $Ncut$ measure after adding it into the graph. Hence, the new measure considering the added new node i is defined as follows:

$$\min_{k'} \sum_{k=1,k\neq k'}^{K} \frac{cut(C_c^k, S\cup\{i\} - C_c^k)}{assoc(C_c^k, S\cup\{i\})} + \frac{cut(C_c^{k'}\cup\{i\}, S - C_c^{k'})}{assoc(C_c^{k'}\cup\{i\}, S\cup\{i\})} \tag{1}$$

Under the assumption that the community membership of the old nodes in the graph do not change after adding new nodes, we try different possibilities for membership for the new node, and return the minimum value.

3.1.2 Modularity

Modularity is another well-known measure to evaluate the strength of partitioning a network into communities [9]. It is the *additional* fraction of the edges that fall within the given communities over the expected fraction, if the edges were distributed at random:

$$\sum_{k=1}^{K}\left(e(C_c^k, S) - a(C_c^k, S)^2\right)$$

Here, $e(C_c^k, S)$ is the fraction of edges for which both end points are in the same community C_c^k on the induced subgraph of G_c by S. And $a(C_c^k, S)$ is the fraction of edges with at least one of the end node lie in communities C_c^k on the induced subgraph of G_c by S.

Different from the Normalized Cut, networks with high modularity have dense connections between the nodes within the same community and sparse connections between nodes in different communities. It is reported in [28], that the modularity measure works well when the communities in the network have comparable size. The well-known resolution limit of modularity [29] reflects its preference over large communities, which is not a problem in our setting because communities are maintained to be balanced. Therefore, when a new node is added into the induced graph of G_c by S, we iteratively set different labels to the new node and recompute modularity in order to find the choice that results in the largest value. Since the previous measure ($Ncut$) was a minimization problem, and modularity is a maximization function, we use the negative of the score for consistency in implementation. Therefore, the score function is defined as follows:

$$-\max_{k'} \sum_{k=1,k\neq k'}^{K}\left(e(C_c^k, S\cup\{i\}) - a(C_c^k, S\cup\{i\})^2\right) + \left(e(C_c^{k'}\cup\{i\}, S\cup\{i\}) - a(C_c^{k'}\cup\{i\}, S\cup\{i\})^2\right) \tag{2}$$

3.1.3 Incorporating Costs

In the previous discussion, we mainly focus on two measures satisfying the three criteria: high purity, large degree and balanced communities, while overlooking the trade off between the computed score of the node according to Eq. 1 or 2 and its cost.

```
Function AdjustScore(Score Dictionary D, Cost Set Q_c)
Sort D by ascending values to determine rank()
for each node i in D.keys do
  | D[i] = rank(i) × q_i^μ
end
```

Function 2: Adjust Score

Instead of directly balancing between the scores computed through Eq. 1 or 2 and the cost Q_c, the ranking among different nodes is preferred since they present a relatively stable choice over unknown and possibly widely varying distributions of $Ncut$ and $Modularity$. A general and simple method to handle the trade off is preferable. Specifically, we use the following function:

$$D[i] = rank(i) \times q_i^{\mu} \tag{3}$$

The parameter μ in the function is set for adjusting the relative importance between the node's query cost and its contribution for network discovery. For high values of μ, the cost portion weights more in the function and low-cost nodes are preferred. When $\mu = 0$, the selection of node is only dependent on the *ComputeScore* function. Our implementation of the approach is described in Function 2. We will study the selection of appropriate μ in the experimental section.

3.2 Community Discovery

As described in Alg. 1, the *UpdateCommunity* function is executed during each iteration together with locality discovery process. We would like to be able to perform this process incrementally in an efficient way. Another characteristic of our scenario is that when new nodes and edges are gradually merged into the existing network, it is naturally required that the community detection algorithm can be incrementally updated and the new partition must be consistent with the last update. The third requirement is related to the fixed number of communities. We adopt a generative model [2], which has a fast and closed-form EM solution and propose an incremental and efficient update process.

As in all EM methods, the algorithm proceeds with the use of parametric learning. For each node i in the network, a set of parameters θ_{ik} define the propensity of node i to have edges of community k. Therefore, under the independence assumption, the value $\theta_{ik}\cdot\theta_{jk}$ represents the expected number of edges of community k that lie between nodes i and j. And the exact number A_{ij} is Poisson distributed around this expected value. Thus the probability of generating a graph $G = (N, A)$ is:

$$P(G|\theta) = \prod_{i\leq j} \frac{(\sum_k \theta_{ik}\theta_{jk})^{A_{ij}}}{A_{ij}!} \exp(-\sum_k \theta_{ik}\theta_{jk})$$

By using the EM framework to maximize the likelihood, we can show that the following update equations can be derived for the expectation and maximization steps respectively:

$$q_{ij}(k) = \frac{\theta_{ik}\theta_{jk}}{\sum_k \theta_{ik}\theta_{jk}} \quad (4)$$

$$\theta_{ik} = \frac{\sum_j A_{ij} q_{ij}(k)}{\sqrt{\sum_{ij} A_{ij} q_{ij}(k)}} \quad (5)$$

The cluster membership (or label) of a node may be obtained based on the maximum likelihood principle:

$$Label_i = \text{argmax}_k\, \theta_{ik}$$

Function 3 shows the afore-mentioned details of the *UpdateCommunity* function, with the corresponding E- and M-steps. A key point to keep in mind is that the incremental nature of the algorithm can be leveraged for efficient parameter learning. In particular, since the *UpdateCommunity* function is called repeatedly, on a continuously incremented network, there is no need to learn the parameters of all the edges during each call. Only those edges, which are linked to the newly added node are initialized, and the parameters from previous iterations provide a good starting point for the other edges. It is evident that the time complexity of *UpdateCommunity* function is $O(|(S \times S) \cap A_c|K + |S|K)$. This is still quite high. Therefore, we design an efficient strategy called *local updating* in order to improve the underlying efficiency.

Function *UpdateCommunity*(Network: G_c, New node: i, Sampled nodes set: S, Clustering: $\mathcal{C}_c$)

```
Initialize q_ij(k) for edges linked to it
while not convergent and #iterations not exceeded do
    for each community k do
        for each node in induced subgraph of G_c by S do
            Update θ_ik according to Eq. 4
        end
        for each edge in induced subgraph of G_c by S do
            Update q_ij(k) according to Eq. 5
        end
    end
end
```

Function 3: Community Discovery

During each run of *UpdateCommunity*, after *ChooseNode* and *DiscoverLocality*, it is expected that the cluster membership of some nodes are changed, and the parameters in the generative community detection model, e.g., q_{ij} and θ_i, are updated. However, with the expansion of the size of the crawled network, the cluster membership and EM parameters become more and more stable without significant changes with increase in network size. Under such conditions, a global update process, which works with all nodes and edges, would seem to be rather wasteful, considering its limited improvement of the partition result. On the other hand, a local update process, focuses on the locality of the new node added to the network.

In the local update process, the locality is first defined to be the induced subgraph of G_c by the chosen node i and its neighborhood. Similar to the global update process described in Function 3, the edges linked to i need to be initialized. After this, both θ_i and q_{ij} within the locality can be updated according Eqs. 4 and 5. It is worth noting that in the local update version of Eq. 5, the denominator $\sqrt{\sum_{ij} A_{ij} q_{ij}(k)}$ should still refer to all edges between sampled nodes set S instead of just the locality. Fortunately, this value can be easily computed based on the last update when node i was not in S. Moreover, as θ_i changes over time, and it is affected by the M-step computation for other nodes, all nodes in S should be updated as well. Therefore, the overall time complexity of the local update is $O(|S|K)$.

The idea in the local update process is to allow small errors in nodes which are not significantly affected by the increase in the network size. However, it is also important to ensure that such errors do not become cumulative over time, and affect the algorithm significantly. Therefore, we combine local and global updates by periodically running a global update. In our case, we set the condition that the global update is run, only when the network size (in terms of the number of edges) increases by at least 10%. We further note that as the network size increases, the global update process is run less and less frequently on a relative basis.

4. EXPERIMENTAL RESULTS

In this section, we will show that the integration of community and network discovery provides significantly more effective results over other methods which do not treat the two as an integrated process.

4.1 Effectiveness Measures

The effectiveness was measured with the help of externally available class labels. These class labels were not used in the clustering process, and therefore they provide an intuitive validation measure for the quality of the clustering process. Let there be m different class label values on the nodes. We further note that the effectiveness was measured only in terms of the target nodes, since the goal of the community detection process is to determine the clusters on this target set of nodes in the network. Let $r_1 \ldots r_k$ be the number of (labeled) target nodes in the k different clusters found by the algorithm. We note that the value of k may not necessarily be the same as the number of classes m. Let p_{ij} be the fraction of the labeled target nodes in the i_{th} cluster, which belong to the j_{th} class. Then, the dominant class label fraction for the i_{th} cluster is given by:

$$E_i = \max_{j \in [1,\ldots m]} p_{ij} \quad (6)$$

We note that E_i is always in $(0, 1]$, and in the ideal case, where all nodes of the cluster belong to the same class, the value of E_i is 1. Then, the average cluster purity ACP is defined as follows:

$$ACP = \frac{\sum_{i=1}^{k} r_i \cdot E_i}{\sum_{i=1}^{k} r_i} \quad (7)$$

A high value of cluster purity will indicate good quality of clustering. Of course, by increasing the granularity of clustering (i.e. increasing k), the average cluster purity is likely to increase over a constant number of class labels m. In the limiting case, when each labeled target node is placed in its own cluster, the average cluster purity will be 1.

The afore-mentioned measure is defined only on the basis of the *dominant* label of each cluster and tends to ignore the behavior of the other less dominant labels. In order to incorporate those labels into the measure, it is possible to define a measure known as the average cluster entropy

(ACE) of a cluster by analogously defining the entropy F_i of cluster i as follows:

$$F_i = 1 - \sum_{j=1}^{m} p_{ij}^2 \quad (8)$$

The entropy is closely related to the gini-index. Lower values of entropy are synonymous with better purity. For example, a cluster which contains all nodes of the same label will have an entropy of 0. A cluster whose nodes are evenly distributed among the m different classes will have a rather large entropy value of $1 - 1/m$. Correspondingly, we define the average cluster entropy as follows:

$$ACE = \frac{\sum_{i=1}^{k} r_i \cdot F_i}{\sum_{i=1}^{k} r_i} \quad (9)$$

The value of ACE lies in $[0, 1-1/m]$. However, unlike ACP, the value of ACE is lower for a better clustering.

4.2 Data Set Descriptions

Table 1: Statistics of the three data sets

Dataset	Nodes	Edges	#Target	Clusters
Synthetic	36,000	199,654	500	10
DBLP	28,702	66,832	115	4
IMDB	153,369	1,631,604	1,000	5

We used one synthetic and two real data sets for testing our approach. Important statistics of them are summarized in Table 1. We describe these data sets below:

Synthetic dataset: Among the 36,000 nodes of the network, one sixth are generated from 5 clusters as "meaningful" nodes according to [4] where each node has 3 out-cluster and 8 within-cluster neighbors. The left 30,000 nodes are acting as "noisy" nodes because their links to neighbors are randomly generated. Target nodes are sampled from the 6,000 "meaningful" candidates with the expectation that as the network expands, new discovered "meaningful" nodes can help improve the community detection performance.

DBLP dataset: It is a collection of bibliographic information on major computer science journals and proceedings.[1] In this experiment, we view the authors as the nodes in the network and link any pair of authors if they have co-authored papers. 115 authors from four real research groups led by Prof. Christos Faloutsos, Prof. Dan Roth, Prof. Jiawei Han and Prof. Michael Jordan respectively are selected as target nodes.

IMDB dataset: The Internet Movie Database (IMDB)[2] is an international organization whose objective is to provide useful and up to date movie information freely available on-line. We create the network based on the co-actor and co-director relationship among different movies. The genre information is considered as the clustering label and from which we pick family, thriller, romance, comedy and adventure as the genres for generating target nodes.

4.3 Compared Algorithms

As the effectiveness of the approach depends critically upon the order of nodes discovered in the network, and the network discovery part is our main focus, we maintain the same community detection algorithm discussed in Section 3.2 while testing different network discovery strategies. Specifically, we compared the following strategies, some of which are ours, and the others are baselines:

- *Random Sampling approach (Baseline):* This strategy randomly picks one node from $N_c - S$ as the candidate to discover its locality. This approach is blind to the community structure, though it represents the most commonly used strategy for network discovery.
- *Greedy approach (Baseline):* Unlike the random sampling approach, which achieves a uniform distribution over nodes in $N_c - S$, the largest degree node from the current discovered subgraph is selected. This has the virtue of discovering as much of the network as possible. In some cases, this can help the community detection process, since it provides a greater amount of information about the underlying network.
- *Degree + Entropy approach (Baseline):* This approach covers the first two criteria mentioned for the design of the *ComputeScore* function: purity and large observed degree. The particular measure computed for each node is *entropy/degree* where *entropy* is computed based on the clustering distribution of the node's one-hop neigbhourhood. Node with the smallest value is selected.
- *Ncut-based Search (Ours):* As described in an earlier section, this approach uses a canonical normalized cut measure for providing best results in terms of the criteria described earlier.
- *Modularity-based Search (Ours):* This is the modularity-based approach for node se selection, which was described earlier in the paper.

To simulate real world scenario, we must assign cost to nodes in the network. Due to the fact that many types of data studied in the physical and social sciences can be approximated with the Zipf distribution, we decided to use it to generate the cost. At the beginning, we shuffle all the nodes and assign each node its index in the shuffled list from 1 to $|S|$. Then we compute the cost of node i as follows:

$$cost_i = \frac{1/index(i)^{\lambda}}{\sum_{n}^{|S|}(1/n^{\lambda})} \quad (10)$$

Here λ is the value of the exponent characterizing the distribution. Larger values of λ correspond to greater skew. In this paper, we conducted two sets of experiments, in the first of which λ is set to 0, corresponding to the case where costs are constant. In the second case, the value of λ was set to 0.8.

4.4 Practical Details

In order to randomize the experiments, 20 test runs with different random initializations were conducted and the average performance is reported. For the sake of comparison, even though both random sampling and greedy approach do not depend on the community detection results, we still run the *UpdateCommunity* function after each run of network discovery module. This provides a temporally uninterrupted insight about how the different methods perform at each step.

Since generative models are prone to get trapped in local optimum because of the large solution space, we use spectral clustering [19] to obtain the partition and then incorporate

[1] http://www.informatik.uni-trier.de/ ley/db/
[2] http://www.imdb.com/

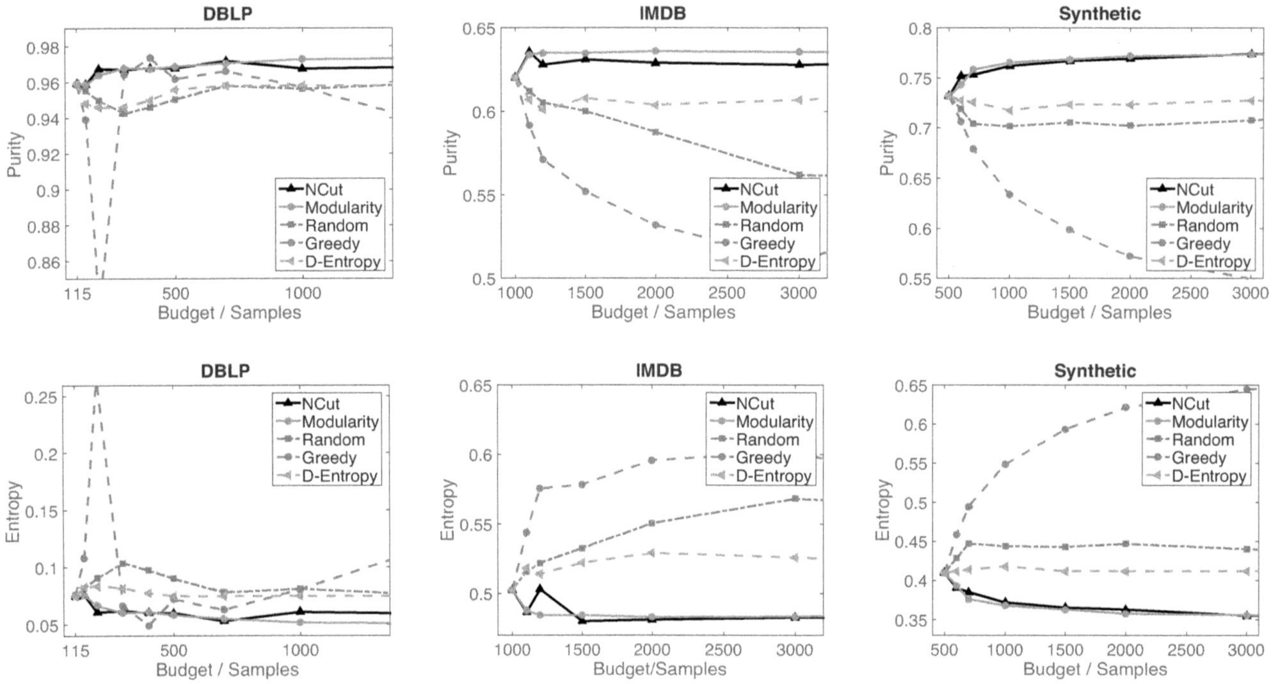

Figure 2: Performance of *NetDiscover* on different network discovery strategy on three datasets.

this into the generative model as prior. For each edge (i, j) in the network, as q_{ij} can be viewed as the probabilities that one edge belongs to certain clusters [2], we first initialize it randomly, and after this add a small value to the corresponding clusters according to the linked nodes' labels from spectral clustering. This way of initialization is also applied to the incremental "local update" function for new nodes merged into G_c based on existing nodes' community memberships. Multiple trials are done to find the maximum likelihood. To further accelerate the EM updates, we select multiple nodes at one time, saving the time cost on *ComputeScore* function.

4.5 Effectiveness Results

The program was implemented in Python and all the experiments are conducted on a desktop running Windows 7 Professional, with an Intel Core I7 2600, 16GB memory and Python 2.7 installed. We conducted three sets of experiments. In the first set, each node's cost is equal to 1, and the budget is expressed in terms on the number of nodes. The second set of experiments take cost into consideration, and the last set contains sensitivity experiments.

4.5.1 Results with constant costs

In this set of experiments, the cost of each node is set to 1, and therefore the budget is a limit on the number of nodes in S. Fig. 2 shows the clustering performance (purity / entropy) of different network discovery algorithms on all the three data sets. In each case, we have shown the incremental performance of the algorithm with increasing value of the budget (number of nodes) on the X-axis. For each data set, we have alternately shown the purity and entropy measures on the Y-axis. It is evident that the schemes which are sensitive to the underlying community structure outperform the baselines significantly.

One interesting aspect of the results was that the performance of the baselines *actually worsen* with increasing budget. This is a result which is counter-intuitive; after all, more knowledge about the network should enhance the quality of the community discovery. It turns out that this is not really true– when we are trying to perform community detection in the context of a specific set of target nodes, *a network discovery process which is blind to the underlying community structure is likely to add noisy and irrelevant nodes and links for understanding the community structure in that target set.* In fact, even though the greedy baseline discovers the largest knowledge about the link structure, it performs worse than even the random sampling baseline, as it adds a lot of noisy information to the network structure. Furthermore, the greedy baseline is the least stable among all algorithms. For the case of our two integrated algorithms, it is evident that the quality of the results generally improve with increasing budget. In particular, the improvement over small ranges of the budget is quite significant. However, this improvement tapers off after a while, when all the *relevant* link structure for the particular set of target nodes has been discovered, and it does not necessarily help to add further structural information to the community detection process.

In terms of the relative behavior of our two algorithms, it is evident from the charts that the average behavior of the modularity-based algorithm was slightly superior over the data sets. At the same time, the modularity-based approach was more stable than the Ncut-based method in terms of providing more consistent results.

Specifically, Fig. 4 gives two snapshots of experiments on DBLP data set about the neighborhood of Prof. Christos Faloutsos from two different network discovery strategies. Clearly our proposed one incorporates more knowledge from the network into the induced subgraph.

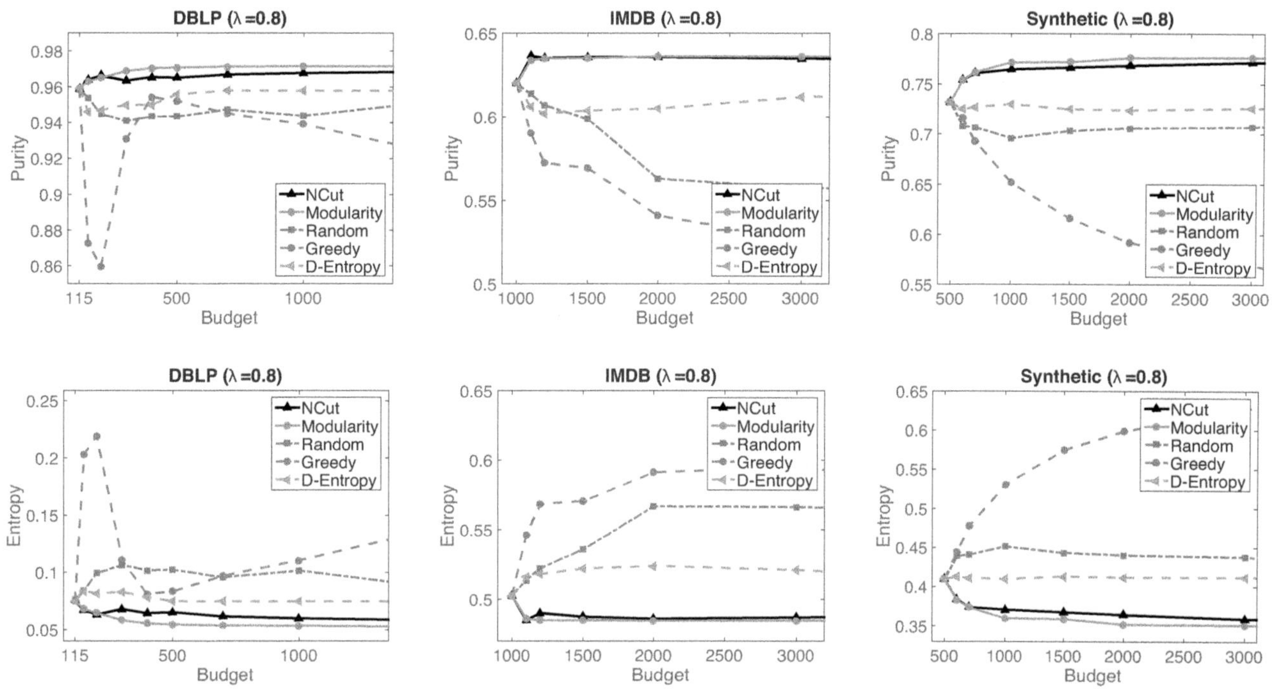

Figure 3: Performance of *NetDiscover* on different network discovery strategy on three datasets.

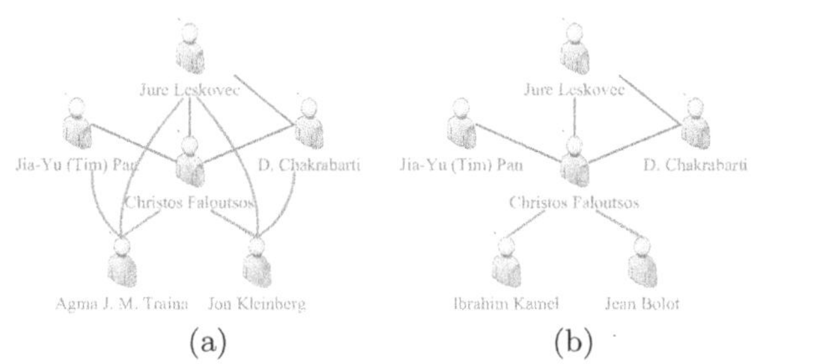

Figure 4: (a) Neighborhood of Prof. Christos Faloutsos using Ncut-based Search (b) using random sampling approach

4.5.2 *Results with variable node costs*

We test our algorithms on the simulated skewed-cost scenario which is generated according to the Zipf distribution. The results with increasing budget are illustrated in Fig. 3. The costs were normalized to the same average value of 1 as the previous case for convenience of comparisons.

When the cost is involved in the decision of choosing new nodes, the small-cost and good-quality nodes are preferred. Therefore, more nodes can be crawled within the same budget. So within the same budget, more nodes are discovered. This helps the discovery process. It is evident that even in this case, both our community detection schemes were superior the baselines. While the curves of our proposed strategies were shifted somewhat because of the incorporation of costs, the overall trends remained the same in this case as well. Thus, our approach is superior to the baselines in both the scenarios.

4.5.3 *Parameter study*

It is evident from the previous section that the algorithm is able to achieve effective results even in the cost-centric case. We note that the choice of the parameter μ regulates the impact of costs in the network discovery process. Therefore, this section will test the impact of this parameter.

Due to the space limitation, we show the result only for modularity-based algorithm on the synthetic data set, since we found the sensitivity behavior to be similar across our two algorithms on the different data sets. We study the performance with respect to different values of μ in the first figure in Fig. 5. The figure next to it depicts the number of nodes involved in the incremental network.

For larger values of μ, nodes with smaller cost are more easily chosen. This helps the network expand more quickly. Therefore, with larger values of μ, the community detection performance improves more when budget is relatively small. At the same time, the performance curve flattens more quickly as the "useful" nodes are exhausted. As mentioned before, some good-quality but high-cost nodes could be missed when μ is large, and this tends to impact the performance. Among all the curves, the best one is with μ set to 0.05. Such a small parameter helps the algorithm to choose a small-cost node when there exist multiple candidates with the same quality (rank). The experiments seem to suggest that when the budget is limited, it is more important to focus on lower cost nodes and set μ to a large value. On the other hand, when the budget is large, it is more rewarding to focus to high-quality nodes, and therefore μ may be set to a lower value.

5. CONCLUSIONS

Social and information networks are often massive, and it is not possible to discover the entire network for problems such as community discovery. In many real-life situations, the network may not be fully discoverable in practice. The results of this paper suggest that it can be fruitful to integrate the community detection and network discovery

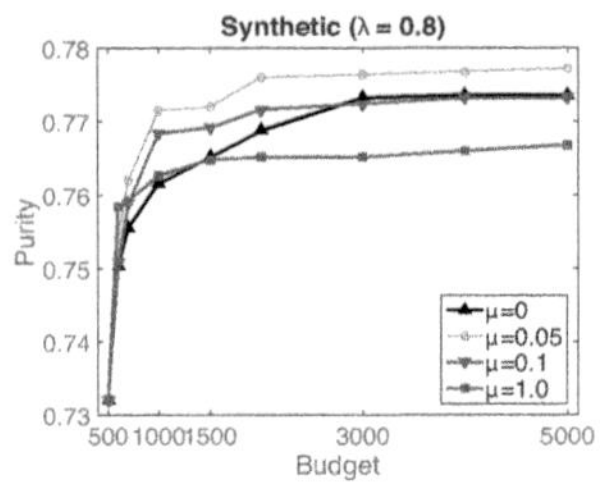

(a)

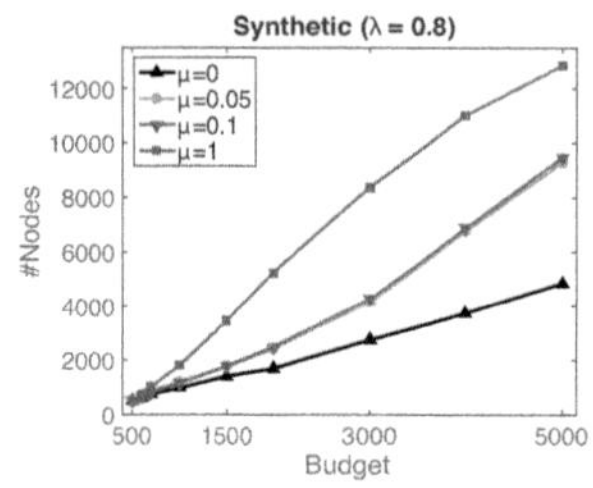

(b)

Figure 5: (a) Performance of *NetDiscover* with respect to budget (different μ) (b) Total discovery wrt budget (different μ)

processes into a unified framework. This can provide much more effective results than an approach which tries to blindly discover the network for a variety of mining algorithms.

6. ACKNOWLEDGEMENTS

Research was sponsored in part by the Army Research Lab. under Cooperative Agreement No. W911NF-09-2-0053, the Army Research Office under Cooperative Agreement No. W911NF-13-1-0193, National Science Foundation IIS-1017362, IIS-1320617, and IIS-1354329, HDTRA1-10-1-0120, and MIAS, a DHS-IDS Center for Multimodal Information Access and Synthesis at UIUC.

7. REFERENCES

[1] L. Backstrom, D. P. Huttenlocher, J. M. Kleinberg, and X. Lan, Group formation in large social networks: membership, growth, and evolution, *ACM KDD Conference*, pp. 44–54, 2006.

[2] B. Ball, B. Karrer and M. E. J. Newman, An efficient and principled method for detecting communities in networks, Physical Review, E 84(3), 036103, 2011.

[3] E. Baykan, M. Henzinger, S. Keller, S. De Castelberg, and M. Kinzler, A comparison of techniques for sampling web pages, *CoRR*, abs/0902.1604, 2009. `http://arxiv.org/abs/0902.1604`

[4] U. Brandes, M. Gaertler and D. Wagner, Experiments on graph clustering algorithms, *European Symposium on Algorithms*, pp. 568–579, 2003.

[5] C. Aggarwal and H. Wang, *Managing and Mining Graph Data*, Springer, 2010.

[6] C. Aggarwal, *Social Network Data Analytics*, Springer, 2011.

[7] D. Chakrabarti, R. Kumar, and A. Tomkins, Evolutionary clustering, *ACM KDD Conference*, pp. 554–560, 2006.

[8] Y. Chi, X. Song, D. Zhou, K. Hino, and B. L. Tseng, Evolutionary spectral clustering by incorporating temporal smoothness, *ACM KDD Conference*, pp. 153–162, 2007.

[9] A. Clauset, M. E. J. Newman, and C. Moore, Finding community structure in very large networks, *Physical Review*, E 70(6), 066111, 2004.

[10] S. Fortunato, Community detection in graphs, *Physics Reports*, 486(3), pp. 75–174, 2010.

[11] D. Gibson, R. Kumar, and A. Tomkins, Discovering large dense subgraphs in massive graphs, *VLDB Conference*, pp. 721–732, 2005.

[12] M. Gjoka, M. Kurant, C. T. Butts, and A. Markopoulou, Walking in Facebook: A Case Study of Unbiased Sampling of OSNs, *IEEE INFOCOM Conference*, pp. 1–9, 2010.

[13] M. Gjoka, C. T. Butts, M. Kurant, and A. Markopoulou, Multigraph Sampling of Online Social Networks, *IEEE Journal on Measurement of Internet Topologies*, 29(9), pp. 1893–1905, October 2011.

[14] M. R. Henzinger, A. Heydon, M. Mitzenmacher, and M. Najork, On near-uniform URL sampling, *WWW Conference*, pp. 295–308, 2000.

[15] R. Kumar, P. Raghavan, S. Rajagopalan, and A. Tomkins, Trawling the web for emerging cyber-communities, *WWW Conference*, pp. 1481–1493, 1999.

[16] J. Leskovec and C. Faloutsos, Sampling from large graphs, *ACM KDD Conference*, pp. 631–636, 2006.

[17] W. Lin, X. Kong, P. Yu, Q. Wu, Y. Jia, and C. Li, Community detection in incomplete information networks, *WWW Conference*, pp. 341–350, 2012.

[18] Y.-R. Lin, J. Sun, P. Castro, R. B. Konuru, H. Sundaram, and A. Kelliher, Extracting community structure through relational hypergraphs, *WWW Conference*, pp. 1213–1214, 2009.

[19] A. Y. Ng, M. Jordan, and Y. Weiss, On spectral clustering: Analysis and an algorithm, *NIPS Conference*, pp. 849–856, 2001.

[20] G. Qi, C. Aggarwal, and T. Huang, Community detection with edge content in social media networks, *IEEE ICDE Conference*, pp. 534–545, 2012.

[21] B. Ribeiro and D. Towsley, Estimating and sampling graphs with multidimensional random walks, *ACM SIGCOMM Conference*, pp. 390–403, 2010.

[22] S. Schaeffer, Graph Clustering, *Computer Science Review*, 1(1), pp. 27–64, 2007.

[23] J. Shi and J. Malik, *Normalized Cuts and Image Segmentation*, *IEEE Transactions on Pattern Analysis and Intelligence*, 22(8), pp. 888–905, 2000.

[24] T. Yang, R. Jin, Y. Chi, and S. Zhu, Combining link and content for community detection: a discriminative approach, *ACM KDD Conference*, pp. 927–936, 2009.

[25] S. Ye, J. Lang, and F. Wu, Crawling online social graphs, *Asia-Pacific Web Conference*, pp. 236–242, 2010.

[26] Z. Zeng, J. Wang, L. Zhou, and G. Karypis, Out-of-core coherent closed quasi-clique mining from large dense graph databases, *ACM TODS Journal*, 31(2), 2007.

[27] Y. Zhou, H. Cheng, and J. X. Yu, Graph clustering based on structural/attribute similarities, *VLDB Conference*, pp. 718–729, 2009.

[28] S. Zhang and H. Zhao, Community identification in networks with unbalanced structure, *Physical Review*, E 85(6), 066114, 2012.

[29] S. Fortunato and M. Barthelemy, Resolution limit in community detection, *Proceedings of the National Academy of Sciences* , 104(1), pp. 36–41, 2007.

On the Accuracy of Hyper-local Geotagging of Social Media Content

David Flatow[1,2], Mor Naaman[1], Ke Eddie Xie[1,3], Yana Volkovich[1,4], Yaron Kanza[1,5]
[1] Jacobs Institute, Cornell Tech, 111 8th Ave New York, NY 10011, USA
[2] Stanford University, 450 Serra Mall, Stanford, CA 94305, USA
[3] Twitter Inc., 1355 Market Street, San Francisco, CA 94103, USA
[4] Barcelona Media, Av. Diagonal 177, 08018 Barcelona, Spain
[5] Technion – Israel Institute of Technology, Haifa 36000, Israel
dflatow@stanford.edu, {mor, kanza, yana}@jacobs.cornell.edu, exie@twitter.com

ABSTRACT

Social media users share billions of items per year, only a small fraction of which is geotagged. We present a data-driven approach for identifying non-geotagged content items that can be associated with a *hyper-local* geographic area by modeling the location distributions of n-grams that appear in the text. We explore the trade-off between accuracy and coverage of this method. Further, we explore differences across content received from multiple platforms and devices, and show, for example, that content shared via different sources and applications produces significantly different geographic distributions, and that it is preferred to model and predict location for items according to their source. Our findings show the potential and the bounds of a data-driven approach to assigning location data to short social media texts, and offer implications for all applications that use data-driven approaches to locate content.

Categories and Subject Descriptors

H.3.5 [**Information Storage and Retrieval**]: On-line Information Services—*Web-based services*

Keywords

Geotagging; Social Media; Location-based Services

1. INTRODUCTION

The vast amounts of data shared on social media reflect people's attitudes, attention, activities and interests, thus offering unique opportunities to analyze and reason about our world and our society. With associated geographic information, these social-media items allow us to understand, for the first time, what geographic areas people are paying attention *to*, and where they pay attention *from*. Mining this dataset can prove hugely valuable to a diverse set of applications, including improving city management [34], journalism [18], tourism [5, 22, 21], health [24] and more.

We call a social media item *geotagged* when it is associated with geographic coordinates, usually indicating where the item was created. However, only a minor portion of the content posted on social media sites such as Twitter, Instagram and Flickr is geotagged. Reported and estimated numbers range from 2% of the items for Twitter[1], to 25% on Instagram[2].

Nevertheless, many of the items that are *not* geotagged may still provide valuable geographic information if they can be associated correctly with the location where they were created. In this work, we are interested in associating non-geotagged social media items with *hyper-local* geographic locations. Such a process will increase the amount of data associated with a location (e.g., a park, a venue) and allow for more robust search and data mining applications. For example, increasing the amount of content available for Madison Square Park in New York may allow park administrators to more robustly model and monitor activities using public social media data.

Most recent work on locating non-geotagged content in social media focuses on inferring locations of users [2, 3, 12] rather than of individual content items. A common approach to the problem is identifying spatial aspects of phrases in unstructured texts (e.g., text in items posted by the user, or the text in the user's profile). While attempting to improve geographic coverage, these systems, for the most part, do not consider accuracy bounds, and instead emphasize the extraction of a general "user location". For example, posting about the Steelers (a Pittsburgh football team) could increase a user's probability of being located in Pittsburgh, but would not be able to expose where in Pittsburgh the user may be. Conversely, our goal here is to identify individual social media items that can be located with high precision inside a *small (hyper-local) geographic region*. In particular, this paper investigates a data-driven approach for hyper-localization of content, and explores the bounds and trade-offs of such a method.

Our approach to localizing social media items involves: (1) identifying phrases that can be accurately (based on data) associated with a specific location, and (2) identifying items that contain these phrases. In an approach inspired by

WSDM'15, February 2–6, 2015, Shanghai, China.
Copyright 2015 ACM 978-1-4503-3317-7/15/02 ...$15.00.
http://dx.doi.org/10.1145/2684822.2685296.

[1] http://blog.gnip.com/twitter-geo-data-enrichment/

[2] http://bits.blogs.nytimes.com/2012/08/16/instagram-refreshes-app-include-photo-maps/

Priedhorsky et al. [19], we train a model on text contained in geotagged items with the goal of identifying n-grams that are geo-specific: a *large* portion of the items containing the n-gram are posted from a *small* area (the portion of items and the area size are configurable parameters).Our model generates an iterative Gaussian model for each n-gram in order to discover hyper-local phrases that can be used to predict locations for non-geotagged content.

Indeed, localizing social media items is not an easy task for several reasons [8]. First, it is a priori unknown which areas will be associated with textual terms and which will not. Second, it is a priori unknown which n-grams will be associated with hyper-local regions. Thus, a naive search by examining areas or n-grams does not work well. More importantly, there are many terms that can be roughly associated with areas, but are not localized enough to be associated with a hyper-local region, and erroneously using such terms may lead to errors or inaccurate results. Thus, it is important to provide an accurate localization method but also understand the limitation of the proposed method.

We explore the bounds, properties and trade-offs of such a hyper-local geotagging solution, on (and across) different data sources. An important question this paper addresses is whether these geographic models are specific to the type or source of content. For example, are location models discovered based on posts of iPhone users also relevant for localizing posts of Android users? Can Twitter tweets be used for localizing Instagram photos or vice versa? Answering these questions could be critical for data mining applications that perform and build on geotagged data.

We collected more than 14 million Twitter posts that were geotagged by users within the area of New York City. The Twitter posts in the dataset were created using different devices (iPhone, Android) and originated from different applications (Instagram, Foursquare). We use these data for our training and test sets. New York is one of the most georeferenced cities in the world (it covers around 2.5% of the total geotagged Twitter content [14]), and serves as an excellent testing ground for our methods. Of course, the framework would be effective in other geographical regions as well.

The contributions of this work include:

- Introducing a data-driven approach to identify phrases (n-grams) associated with hyper-local regions;
- Investigating and evaluating the approach across multiple social media data types and data sources;
- Exposing the limitations and properties of models from different sources and at different scales;

2. RELATED WORK

The problem of geotagging social Web data has received significant attention recently. Related studies can be divided into three broad (and overlapping) areas: geotagging of social media content, understanding characteristics of geographical areas from social media data, and modeling textual location references in social media.

2.1 Geotagging Social Content

Most recent studies on automatic text-based geolocation of social media content aimed to identify location(s) of a social media *user*. While localizing users or posts are related problems, they have distinct properties and biases. Knowing users' overall location is, perhaps, a first step to predicting location for individual posts. For Twitter, research has shown that *home*, or primary, location for each user can be learned by analyzing content of tweets. These predictions usually do not go below city-level [2, 3, 4, 12, 17]. A few recent works incorporated additional features such as time zones [17] or friends locations [4] to find correctly the location of the home city, for roughly 80% of Twitter users, with median error of 6.33km. Schulz et al. [25] proposed multi-indicator approach that combines various spatial indicators from the user's profile and the tweet's message for estimating the location of a tweet as well as the user's home location. Here, in contrast, we are not interested in a user's overall location. Our goal is identifying content items that were posted from specific geographic areas, with finer granularity than city-level.

Some studies applied traditional language models to geotagging, e.g. Hong et al. [10] used k-means clustering, Eisenstein et al. [7] used Dirichlet Process mixture, and Kling et al. [13] used multi-Dirichlet process. Our work, however, is related to the methods introduced in [19] and [32]. Priedhorsky et al. [19], for example, used a Gaussian Mixture Model (GMM) to estimate a tweet's location based on the distribution of n-grams that appear in the tweet and associated content to it (e.g. user profile information). In particular, they generated geographic density estimates for all n-grams, and used density information to provide a final location estimate for content, regardless of the geographic scope. In contrast, we attempt to identify n-grams that can predict the location of a tweet with high precision.

Mapping social media content to geographical locations typically implies some discretization of the spatial area. For example, geographical locations might be clustered as a grid [26, 33]. However, the fixed-grid based representations have a limitation of not capturing variability in shapes and sizes of geographical regions. One of the possible ways to overpass such limitation is to define an alternative grid construction, for example by using k-d trees [23]. A different way of representing geographic areas is to use a continuous function over the space [19], an approach we take in this work as well.

2.2 Characterizing Geographic Areas

A related set of studies used information about geographic regions in geotagged social media to extract information and characterize geographic areas [1, 5, 6, 16, 20, 29].

Ahern et al. [1] proposed a model that aggregates knowledge in the form of "representative tags" for arbitrary areas in the world by analyzing tags associated with the georeferenced Flickr images. Crandell et al. [5] used Flickr to find relations between photos and popular places in which the photos were taken and showed how to find representative images for popular landmarks. Similarly, Kennedy et al. [11] generate representative sets of images for landmarks using Flickr data. Quercia et al. [20] proposed applying sentiment analysis to geo-referenced tweets in London in order to find the areas of the city characterized by "well being". A recent review by Tasse [28] listed other possible applications of social media for understanding urban areas.

2.3 Characterizing Location References

Efforts were made to characterize location references (in text) within social media content. Rattenbury et al. [22] used an approach similar to the one presented in this paper, when trying to identify Flickr tags that refer to specific geographic places or specific events based on the spatiotemporal distribution of geotagged photos carrying that tag. However, the authors did not apply their models to geocoding new items, did not explore hyper-local content, and did not extract phrases from free-form text like we do here. Further, Thomee and Morales [30] find that different language variants of toponyms can be mapped to each other by exploiting the geographic distribution of tagged media.

Recent work by Shaw et al. [27] mapped users noisy checkins on Foursquare to semantically extract meaningful suggestions from a database of known points of interest. In particular, by aggregating locations from geotagged checkins, the authors were able to create geographic models for different venues using multi-dimensional Gaussian models. Earlier work from Flickr, Alpha Shapes[3], modeled information available from geotagged images on Flickr to create geographic models for places like neighborhoods, towns, etc. Finally, Li et al. [15] not only explored point-of-interest mentions on Twitter but also connected them to the relative temporal values of the visits.

3. GEOTAGGING FRAMEWORK

Our framework for associating geographic locations with social media items uses *training data* to identify n-grams that are *geo-specific* — n-grams whose associated items' locations have little geographic variance. The process also results in location estimates for the n-grams that are deemed geo-specific. The discovered n-grams are used for geotagging items from the *test set*, where items are associated with a location based on the n-grams they contain. For example, if "Madison Square Park" is detected as a geo-specific n-gram, a tweet in the test set that includes such n-gram will be associated with the location assigned to this n-gram.

Note that the method we use does not aim to produce a general "best guess" for the location of an item; nor does it aim to identify an approximate location of a user, given a set of items. Instead, we are interested in identifying individual items that, with certain (high) accuracy, can be associated with a hyper-local location, such as a neighborhood, landmark or street corner. Note that multi-item and user-level information may very well be useful even in this scenario. We discuss this opportunity in more depth below.

Next, we describe the statistical process of identifying a geo-specific n-gram and the procedure for modeling its location. We detail the procedure for assigning locations to tweets in the test set (Section 3.2). Finally, we discuss and propose metrics (Section 3.3) to evaluate the performance, accuracy and bounds of this approach.

3.1 Localizing n-grams

We start by finding frequent n-grams, i.e. n-grams that appear in many posts within the training dataset. Next, we associate each n-gram with the geographic locations of the posts containing it. The main task is to use this data to (1) decide whether a given n-gram is geo-specific, and (2) model the location for a given geo-specific n-gram. We use a data-driven approach, inspired by Priedhorsky et al. [19] and Chang et al. [32]. In brief, we apply an iterative procedure of discovering the location model for a given n-gram, by removing outliers and recomputing a Gaussian model for the remaining locations in each step. For each n-gram w_j, this process determines whether locations of tweets associated with w_j are describing a hyper-local area, and if so, computes the parameters of the area.

For convenience, we refer to social media content items as tweets, i.e. posts on Twitter, in the definitions below. However, the methods we propose could be applied to other types of social media items, e.g. Instagram photos. We denote as T the set of tweets in the training set and each tweet from this set as $t_i \in T$. The geographic location of t_i is denoted l_i. An n-gram is a consecutive sequence of n terms. A tweet contains an n-gram if the n terms appear contiguously in the tweet.

Let T_{w_j} be the set of all tweets containing the n-gram w_j. Let $\bar{T}_{w_j}$ be some subset of T_{w_j} and let $\bar{L}_{w_j}$ be the set of locations for tweets $t_i \in \bar{T}_{w_j}$. Further, we can fit a two dimensional Gaussian $\mathcal{N}_j$ to the set of locations $\bar{L}_{w_j}$ and define, based on the Gaussian, an ellipse $E_{2,\mathcal{N}_j}$. We construct $E_{2,\mathcal{N}_j}$ to have orientation, shape, and center defined by $\mathcal{N}_j$. Specifically, $E_{2,\mathcal{N}_j}$ is scaled so that its major and minor axes have lengths $2\sigma_1$ and $2\sigma_2$, where σ_1^2 and σ_2^2 are the first and second eigenvalues of Σ respectively. We decide that w_j is geo-specific if we find a subset $\bar{T}_{w_j} \subseteq T_{w_j}$, for adjustable parameters s and τ, such that:

- The fraction of tweets $\frac{|\bar{T}_{w_j}|}{|T_{w_j}|}$ is greater than a ratio parameter τ, and
- The area of the ellipse $E_{2,\mathcal{N}_j}$ is smaller than an area parameter s

We define a characteristic function $\mathcal{X}(s, \tau, w_j)$ such that $\mathcal{X}(s, \tau, w_j) = 1$ if the algorithm decides that w_j is geo-specific under parameters (s, τ). If $\mathcal{X}(s, \tau, w_j) = 1$, we output $\mathcal{N}_j$. Using this final Gaussian, $\mathcal{N}_j$, we can compute the ellipse $E_{2,\mathcal{N}_j}$ that approximates the area represented by w_j.

To find whether a subset $\bar{T}_{w_j}$ that matches this criteria exist, we apply and iterative modeling procedure, described in more detail in Algorithm 1. The procedure includes the following steps, starting with $\bar{T}_{w_j} = T_{w_j}$ (the full set of tweets):

1. If $\frac{|\bar{T}_{w_j}|}{|T_{w_j}|} < \tau$, set $\mathcal{X}(s, \tau, w_j) = 0$ and break.
2. Fit the two dimensional Gaussian $\mathcal{N}_j$ to the set of locations $\bar{L}_{w_j}$ and compute $E_{2,\mathcal{N}_j}$.
3. If area$(E_{2,\mathcal{N}_j}) \leq s$, set $\mathcal{X}(s, \tau, w_j) = 1$ and break.
4. Remove all the tweets outside of $E_{2,\mathcal{N}_j}$ (i.e. are more than two standard deviations from the center of $\mathcal{N}_j$).

We repeat this process until some $\bar{L}_{w_j}$ is deemed *geo-specific*, the proportion of tweets goes below τ, or an iteration limit is met. We say that n-gram w_j is *geo-specific* if at any point in an iterative outlier removal procedure both parameters s and τ are satisfied. For example, if $s = 4km^2$ and $\tau = 0.8$, w_j is geo-specific if at least 80% of the posts in T_{w_j} are contained in some $E_{2,\mathcal{N}_j}$ with an area smaller than $4km^2$ at any step in the iterative outlier removal process.

3.2 Assigning a Location to a Tweet

When associating locations for a tweet t_i in the test set, we follow these simple rules. We first identify all n-grams w_j such that w_j is contained in t_i, $\mathcal{X}(s, \tau, w_j) = 1$ and w_j is not contained in any other n-gram w_k that satisfies the

[3]code.flickr.net/2008/10/30/the-shape-of-alpha

Algorithm 1: Iterative Modeling Procedure

```
Data: L(w_j), MaxArea: s, Ratio threshold: τ, Iteration
      Limit: k
Result: Boolean: GeoSpecific_j; Gaussian: N_j
GeoSpecific_j ← false;
iteration ← 0;
L̄_{w_j} ← L_{w_j};
while iteration ≤ k do
    if |L̄_{w_j}| / |L_{w_j}| < τ then
        break;
    end
    μ ← mean(L̄_{w_j});
    Σ ← cov(L̄_{w_j});
    N_j ← {μ, Σ};
    if Area(E_{2,N_j}) ≤ s then
        GeoSpecific_j ← true;
        break;
    end
    L^{temp}_{w_j} ← ∅;
    for i in L̄_{w_j} do
        if i is in E_{2,N_j} then
            L^{temp}_{w_j}.add(i);
        end
    end
    L̄_{w_j} ← L^{temp}_{w_j};
    iteration ← iteration + 1;
end
return GeoSpecific_j, N_j;
```

requirement. In other words, we find the longest possible n-grams in t_i that are geo-specific.

In our analysis, we associate a tweet with a location $\hat{l}_i$ according to the center of the Gaussian model for an n-gram it contains. If a tweet $t_i \in T_{test}$ contains a single geo-specific n-gram w_j, we associate the tweet with μ_j from $\mathcal{N}(\mu_j, \Sigma_j)$. If a tweet contains more than one geo-specific n-gram whose centers are all pairwise within $0.5km$ of each other, we use the parameters of the most common of these n-grams. Setting the minimum ratio τ at 0.8 and the maximum allowed area s fixed at $4km^2$, less than one percent of tweets with at least one geo-specific n-gram in the iPhone or Android test set contained multiple geo-specific n-grams. For the Instagram test sets, while roughly 27% of the tweets in the test set contained multiple geo-specific n-grams, 73% of these instances could be explained by multiple geo-specific n-grams that were nearby each other and of these, 42% were simply cases where the n-grams were subsets of a longer phrase. For example, "New York Public" and "York Public Library" are subsets of the longer phrase "New York Public Library". Other approaches to handling multiple geo-specific n-grams include choosing the most accurate n-gram (the one with the smallest error) as the n-gram predicting the location of the tweet, using language processing to extract more information, or explicitly modeling the co-occurrence of such n-grams (we discuss such approaches in Section 7).

Finally, and naturally, a tweet t_i that does not contain any geo-specific n-gram w_j is not associated with a location.

3.3 Metrics

We use three key metrics to evaluate the performance of our hyper-local geotagging framework on different datasets and with different parameters: error, precision, and coverage. In all cases, we have a training set of tweets with known locations, and a test set of tweets, with locations hidden, for which the algorithm decides whether or not to assign an estimated location. In this setup, the *error* captures the geographic distance between an assigned location and a true location of a tweet from the set of test tweets. *Precision* is the proportion of tweets whose true location is within the core ellipse of the tweet's assigned Gaussian. *Coverage* refers to the portion of tweets in the test dataset for which the algorithm is able to assign a location.

Next, we formalize these metrics. Note that we do not directly evaluate the n-gram information that is produced by the algorithm. One option would be to manually code the n-gram that the algorithm determines as geo-specific, e.g. by a human judge. Another option would be to evaluate the modeled locations associated with each n-gram, again, by a human. However, since we are taking a data-driven approach here, we do not need to directly evaluate the n-grams. In fact, the data may expose trends that would be non-obvious to a person. For example, the n-gram Nintendo turns out to be location-sensitive in some New York datasets [8], due to the Nintendo store at Rockefeller Plaza.

3.3.1 Error

We define the error for tweet $t_i \in T_{test}$ as the geographic distance between the true (hidden) location of the tweet l_i and the tweet's estimated location $\hat{l}_i$. We use the center of the Gaussian associated with the tweet, as described in Section 3.2, as the estimated location. We use the Haversine distance $d(l_i, \hat{l}_i)$ to compute the error. Another option to define the error would be computing the distance from the ellipse $E_{2,\mathcal{N}_j}$ (not from the center) defined by the Gaussian model assigned to the tweet. We do not use this type of error measurement in this work, for simplicity. The *accuracy* is the inverse of the error. We consider it with respect to a given accuracy parameter δ. The accuracy is equal to 1 when $d(l_i, \hat{l}_i) \leq \delta$, and it is $d(l_i, \hat{l}_i)^{-1}$ otherwise. Thus, when the error is small the accuracy is high (near 1) and when the error much larger than δ, the accuracy is low.

3.3.2 Precision

We define precision as the fraction of tweets whose true locations fall within the core ellipse $E_{2,\mathcal{N}_j}$ computed for the n-gram w_j. In other words, the precision for a test set T_{test} of size n is $\frac{\sum_{i=1}^{n} R(t_i)}{n}$, where $R(t_i) = 1$ if l_i is in $E_{2,\mathcal{N}_j}$, and 0 otherwise. This method has the property that the criterion for a precise prediction is a function of parameter choices s and τ. For example, a prediction that is deemed precise in a model with large area s (a model with a loose definition of hyper-locality) may not be precise in a model with a small area s (stricter definition of hyper-locality).

3.3.3 Covearge

Coverage is defined as the fraction of tweets in the test set for which we can predict a location given a set of model parameters. More specifically, it is the fraction of tweets in the test set with a single geo-specific n-gram or multiple adjacent n-grams. Maximizing coverage is a conflicting goal to maximizing accuracy and precision. Setting the parameters such that only n-grams with highly accurate models are used (e.g. by setting a small area s and high minimum ratio τ) can result in a small number of n-grams that are geo-specific, and by extension, a small number of tweets that contain these n-grams.

4. EXPERIMENTS

We explore the trade-offs and properties of the n-gram based geocoding approach in a series of experiments with a number of Twitter datasets. As mentioned above, even within Twitter, there are multiple sources and types of data shared by different users. For example, tweets can include photos or contain text-only; the source of the tweets can be another application, like the photo-sharing application Instagram or the location-check-in application Foursquare; or tweets can be generated by different types of devices, such as the Andriod phone or the iPhone. Research so far had not considered the source or type of content when creating location and geographic models. Here we explore that issue in more depth as we expect the source will have a significant effect on the geographic distribution of content.

We describe the datasets and provide more detail on extracting candidate n-grams in Section 4.1. In Section 4.2 we examine the performance of the method in respect to the metrics defined above, using the different datasets, and with different parameter settings. In Section 4.3 we examine the performance across datasets, or rather, what happens when we mix content from different sources in our training and testing datasets.

4.1 Datasets

We collected geotagged tweets shared from the New York City area spanning two years from July, 2012 to July, 2014. This core dataset of 14.5 million geotagged tweets is the basis for the derived datasets we use in all experiments. We extract from the dataset four mutually exclusive sets of tweets according to each tweet's original source application: Foursquare, Instagram, Twitter for iPhone, and Twitter for Android (the source information is available for each tweet retrieved using the Twitter API). For all experiments, we use the first 651 days of tweets (July 21st, 2012 to May 3rd, 2014) as training data, and the remaining 80 days (May 4th to July 23rd, 2014) as test data with a one day gap in-between to simulate a real-world case where you build models on extant data before applying to incoming information. The rate at which content is generated is different for each source. For example, roughly four times as many tweets with location information in the New York City area are shared from iPhones as there are from Android phones. In order to evaluate performance on a per training item basis we sample random tweets from each data source so that all training sets and all testing sets, respectively, contain the same number of items (training: 1,014,574, testing: 257,083). Finally, we created a TW-All dataset, where we randomly sampled from the entire set of Tweets to create a dataset that mimics the properties of the full dataset but is comparable in size to the others. The different datasets and distinct number of users in each of the sampled datasets we used for our experiments are listed in Table 1.

The source applications are different on many — sometimes interleaving — dimensions, including their function, the device they are running on, and even the demographics of their users. Instagram is a photo-sharing application

Name	% of Total In dataset	% Used For train/test	Users In train/test
TW-iPhone	60%	15%	151,431
TW-Android	16%	57%	72,692
TW-Instagram	9%	97%	166,965
TW-Foursquare	9%	100%	78,598
TW-ALL	100%	9%	222,608
Other (not used)	6%	0%	N.A.

Table 1: The datasets used in the experiments

whose users can choose to post their photos to Twitter, often with a caption much shorter than a "normal" tweet. Foursquare is a location check-in app where users can choose to share their check-in ("I'm at Cornell Tech") on Twitter, often with just the check-in default text. Finally, Twitter for iPhone and Twitter for Android are two Twitter mobile applications, that, while similar in nature and design, differ in the type of mobile device they run on, which subsequently also results in a different user population (note that we do not have device information for posts from Foursquare or Instagram). Given these differences, we expect the different sources to produce different types of information, and, therefore, different models of location.

The items in our test data, extracted from the same source as the modeling/training data, conveniently have associated location information. As a result, we can robustly evaluate our methods through experimentation. However, we do note that using this test data may also introduce bias. Of particular concern is that the distribution of text and locations in the global Twitter dataset are different than those in the geotagged tweets. However, we believe our approach is useful enough to create a baseline understanding of the potential (and challenges) of these types of methods.

To generate candidate n-grams, we tokenized the message text and location description into n-grams of length $n = 1, 2, 3$ by splitting words delimited by whitespace and removing English stop words. In order to mitigate spam (often one user sharing hundreds of similar spam messages) n-grams used by fewer than 5 unique users or appearing in fewer than 20 unique tweets were removed.

4.2 Exploring the Parameter Space

For each parameter setting in each dataset we examine the impact on various measures of performance. In particular, we vary the minimum ratio parameter τ and the area s, defined in Section 3.1, and examine the effect on accuracy, precision and coverage as defined in Section 3.3. Recall that the minimum ratio parameter τ controls the precision of the model, i.e. how much content we allow in the model that is outside the core ellipse,. The parameter s controls the maximum size of the core ellipse for each model. Higher minimum ratios and smaller maximum areas correspond to stricter standards for classifying a given n-gram as geo-specific and generally lead to higher accuracy and lower coverage. To capture the balance between accuracy/precision and coverage we also include the F-score, $2\frac{Precision*Coverage}{Precision+Coverage}$, in the figures.

The results are shown in Figures 1 and 2. Figure 1 shows results for varying the minimum ratio τ with maximum allowed area s fixed at $4km^2$. Figure 2 varies s with the minimum ratio τ fixed at 0.8. The curves shown are for all the different datasets, where each curve represents the results for

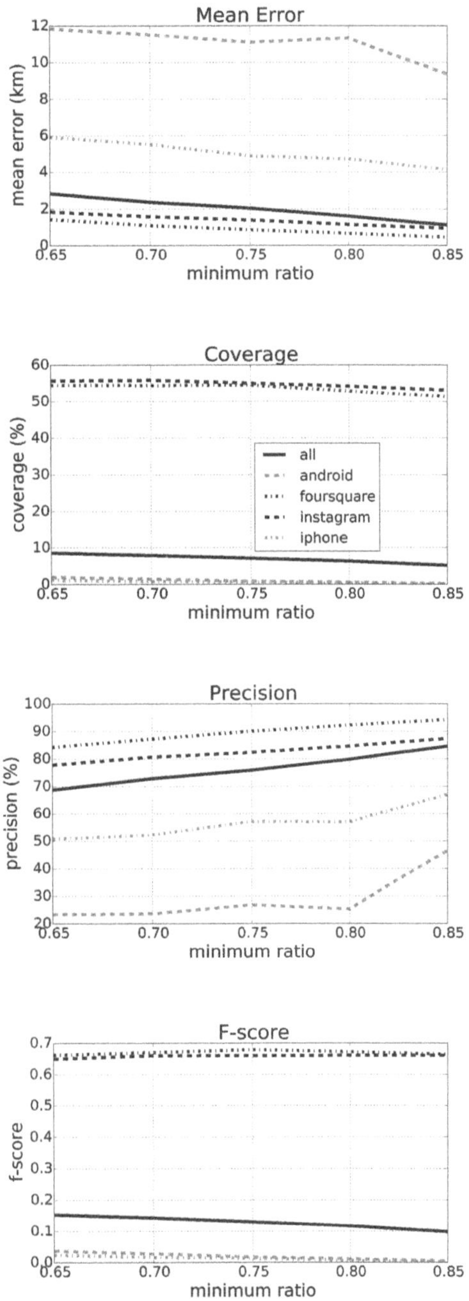

Figure 1: Effects of varying τ (minimum ratio) on performance for different datasets fixing $s = 4km^2$

training and testing on the same source. For example, the solid black lines in Figure 1 show that when using TW-All for training (using the training sample) and testing (on the test data), when the minimum ratio is set to 0.8, the mean error is 1.6, the coverage is 6.3% (6.3% of tweets in the test set can be assigned a location), the precision is 79.8%, and the F-score is 0.12 (dragged down by the low coverage).

While the results seem promising, there is significant variation in performance between the datasets. In particular, the performance for geotagging content from Instagram and Foursquare demonstrates high accuracy, precision and coverage. At the same time, results for predicting locations for the iPhone or Android datasets are low in all these metrics, and especially in terms of coverage. For the TW-All dataset, as a random sample from the content (and with a heavy representation of iPhone data), results are in between.

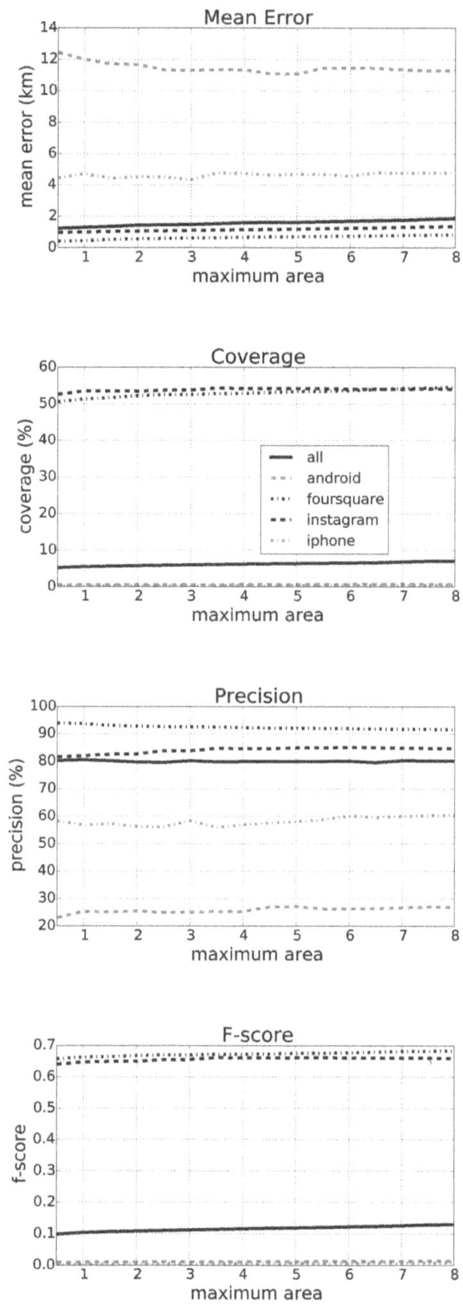

Figure 2: Effects of varying s (maximum area) on performance for different datasets fixing $\tau = 0.8$

In reality, we can have the most impact for real-world applications by geotagging Android/iPhone and Instagram content. Content originating from Foursquare is already geotagged: if not associated with location on the Twitter platform, it includes a link to a Foursquare venue that pinpoints the content by identifying the venue. Instagram content, however, may be more interesting to fill locations for — we provide some preliminary numbers below in Section 6. Most important, though, are tweets from Android and iPhone, as (1) they represent a much larger portion of Twitter data, (2) they are less likely to be geotagged (see Section 6), and (3) they are most similar in characteristics to other sources of Twitter items (e.g. the Twitter web site [19]).

Figure 2 also demonstrates that the results are not very sensitive to s, the maximum area size parameter. In other words, when an n-gram demonstrates strong geo-specific tendencies, the model correctly captures and represents that information regardless of area size.

Next, we explore the performance based on specific test sets, focusing on TW-iPhone and TW-Instagram, while experimenting with different *training* sets.

4.3 Cross-Model Performance

Figure 3(a) shows the performance when training on different datasets, while testing on the key TW-iPhone data set (i.e., on tweets posted from the Twitter for iPhone application). The n-gram extraction and modeling was performed on multiple training sets with parameters $s = 4km, \tau = 0.8$. One can see in Figure 3(a) that when using the TW-All dataset for training, roughly half of the geotagged tweets in the TW-iPhone test data set are geotagged within a $1.0km$ radius of their true location. Somewhat surprisingly, the accuracy of the results increases when using TW-All compared to using TW-iPhone for training (recall that TW-All is a sample of all tweets, with roughly 60% of tweets emerging from iPhone). We believe that the reason for the improved accuracy is the additional coverage provided by n-grams that are detected as location-specific with support from Foursquare and Instagram.

There are significant differences in coverage between the training sets. Using the TW-iPhone training set results in much lower coverage (0.3%) than TW-All (1.3%), TW-Foursquare (6.4%) and TW-Instagram (5.1%), when testing on TW-iPhone. One possible explanation for this low coverage, which we discuss more in Section 7, is the weak *aboutness* of TW-iPhone content and lower rate of location references, relative to other datasets such as TW-Foursquare or TW-Instagram. Our experiments support this hypothesis due to the fact that the low coverage is driven not by the failure to locate geo-specific n-grams but rather by the failure to identify a large number of geo-specific n-grams.

Figure 3(b) shows the same analysis when testing on the TW-Instagram dataset. Clearly, the results are significantly better than testing on TW-iPhone with more than 80% of the items geotagged within $1.0km$ of their true location when using datasets other than TW-Android for training. The coverage is also much better across the board: 38.1% for training on TW-All, 47.2% for TW-Foursquare, 54.2% for TW-Instagram, 3.8% for TW-Android, and 4.6% for TW-iPhone.

In summary, the results of our cross-model experimentation show that when geotagging hyper-local content for search and data mining apps, not all data is created equal. Considering the source of the training data, as well as the source of the test data could prove critical to the performance and accuracy of the solution. Next, we explore the differences in location models that are created based on different sources of data.

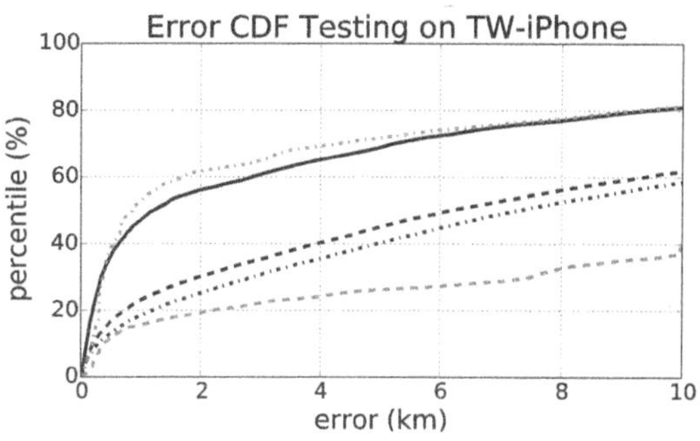

(a) test set = TW-iPhone

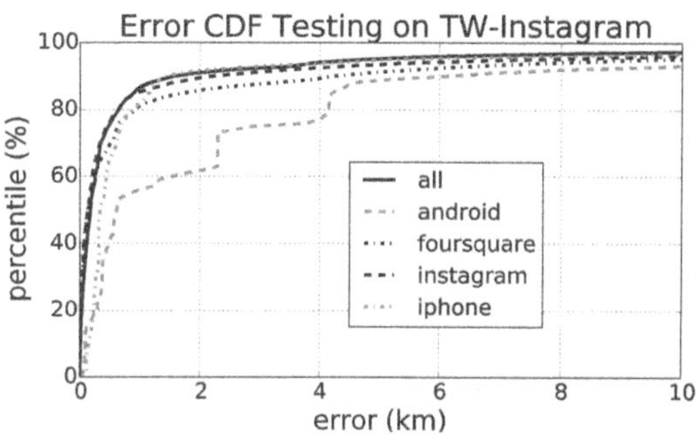

(b) test set = TW-Instagram

Figure 3: Performance when training with different datasets and testing on TW-iPhone and TW-Instagram

5. N-GRAM "GRAVITY"

As we have seen in previous sections, the performance in terms of accuracy and precision varies greatly between the different sources. Are there significant differences between location models for n-grams that are geo-specific across different sources, or are the differences only due to different n-grams are extracted from each training dataset? In this section we touch on the differences in "gravity", our colloquial term referencing the dispersion of tweet locations, for n-grams that are detected as geo-specific across three different training datasets: TW-iPhone, TW-Instagram and TW-Foursquare. Figure 4 shows that there are significant differences in the dispersion of locations for the three datasets, even for the same n-grams. The figure shows, for the top thirteen n-grams that were identified as geo-specific in each of the three sources, the average distance between the location l_i of tweet in the *training* set, to the center of the final Gaussian model $\mathcal{N}_j$. For example, for the n-gram "NYCC New York", in the TW-iPhone dataset, the average distance between the n-gram tweets in the training set to the center of the model was $1.14km$. The same distance computed on the TW-Instagram training set was $0.015km$.

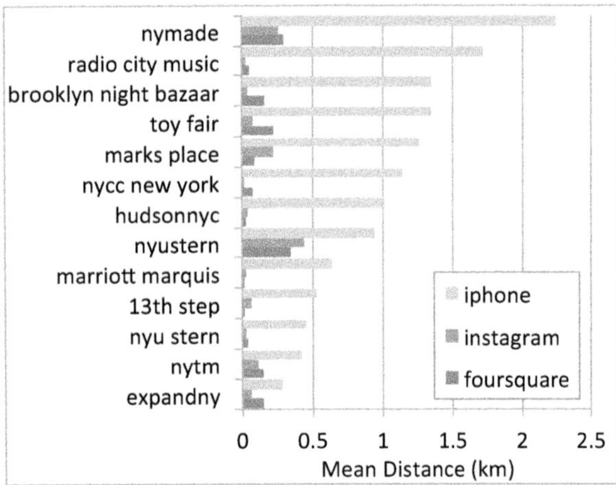

Figure 4: N-Gram gravity for multiple sources

There are multiple potential contributors to the fact that the iPhone data is more dispersed, including the "aboutnesss" of content, the accuracy of location provided by the application, and the semantics of posts from the different sources. We discuss these in more length in Section 7. Regardless of the reason for the differences in dispersion, it is clear that the phenomena has a direct effect on the results for the different datasets.

6. POTENTIAL GAINS

We have seen in Section 5 that we can achieve a significant gain in items that are associated with a precise location, at least for certain types of data and items. Under these assumptions, what are the patterns and scale of these gains?

We measure the relative frequency of posts geotagged in the New York area coming from different application sources in Table 1. Ideally we would like to geotag every post that has hyper-local geographic relevance. But what fraction of posts, in the best case scenario, can be geotagged? Twitter is reported to have about 2% geotagged content, but there are no reported numbers of portions of geotagged for individual sources. We performed a preliminary study where we track a sample set of keywords on the Twitter stream to estimate the portion of geotagged items posted to Twitter by the different applications. For example, between 1% and 10% of the tweets posted from Twitter for iPhone for the keywords we tracked where geotagged (3% for the keyword "New York", 4% for the common word "at"). Foursquare showed a much higher ratio, anywhere from 22% to 72% (26% for "New York", 71% for "at"). Posts made from Twitter for Android ranged between 2% and 17% for the different terms (2% for "New York", 4% for "at") and Instagram posts to Twitter were, for the phrases we tracked, between 10% and 42% geotagged ("New York": 42%, "at": 14%).

These numbers, with our results above, indicate an opportunity for significant gains in the amount of content associated with hyper-local data. For example, for content from Instagram, we report 60% coverage for our default parameter settings (see Figure 1). In other words, if just 20% of the Instagram content posted to Twitter is geotagged, we can get a further lift of $0.6 \times 0.8 = 0.48$ of the items posted from Instagram, more than tripling the amount of available data. This potential boost is performed with precision close to 90% (Figure 1).

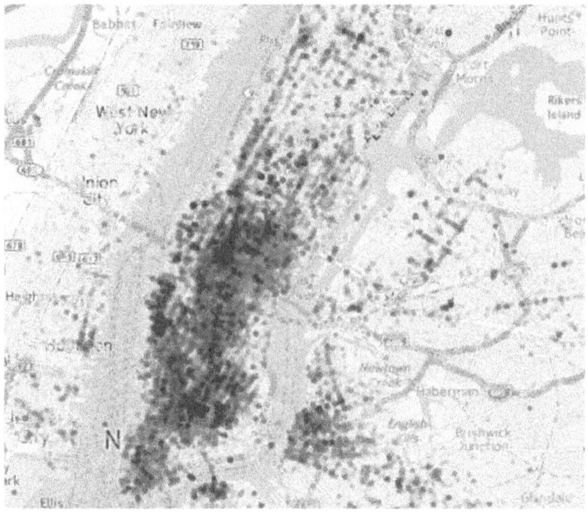

(a) training data locations

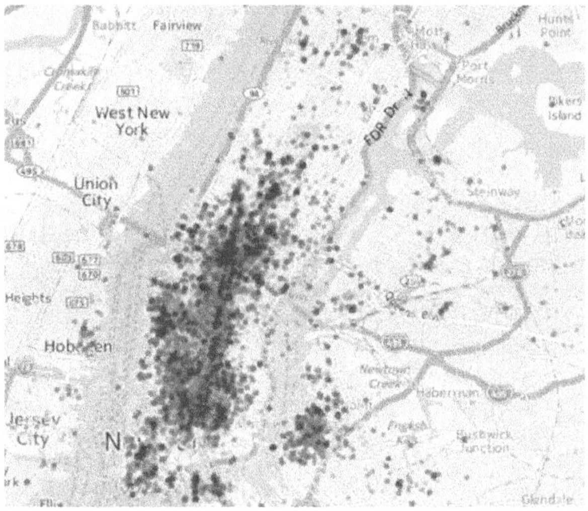

(b) predicted locations (gain)

Figure 5: Heatmaps of training and predicted tweets from TW-Instagram dataset, sampled to use same number of observations

How is this gain distributed? Figure 5 shows the geographic distribution of content items in the TW-Instagram training set (Figure 5(a)) and the locations of items associated with predicted location from the test set (Figure 5(b)) (we randomly sub-sampled from the training set so both figures show the same number of items). We used the default settings for the analysis in this figure ($s = 4.0km, \tau = 0.8$), and show only a portion of the geographic area we covered in our analysis. Points that are colored red indicate a higher concentration for that area. As is evident in the figure, most of the gain occurs in the already-popular areas where most content is posted (i.e., midtown and downtown Manhattan). Indeed, the methods we propose above bring a "rich get richer" phenomena, where the models are most robust, and allow for associating content with additional social media items, in the areas that are already covered.

7. DISCUSSION AND CONCLUSIONS

A data-driven approach for geocoding individual social media items at a hyper-local scale has the potential to extend the geographic coverage of social media data, but its performance may depend on the distribution of the data according to its source. We used Twitter data to identify and model geo-specific n-grams, based on the location distribution of tweets associated with them. We then predicted locations for individual tweets based on a given tweet's geo-specific n-gram's locations (if any). The performance of this method was highly contingent on the source of the data. Data from the check-in application Foursquare and the photo sharing application Instagram were highly location-specific in general, and as a result, the method produced location estimates with high accuracy. Conversely, tweets from "regular" Twitter clients, like Twitter for iPhone, demonstrated low accuracy, and even when geo-specific n-grams were detected from these sources, the breadth of the location model for these n-grams was much larger than the same model in data posted to Twitter through Instagram or Foursquare.

There are a number of possible reasons for the differences between sources, chief among them the *aboutness* of the content and the density of location-based references. We regard the aboutness of posts in social media as the likelihood of the posts to be about a geo-specific feature. Foursquare has clear and strong aboutness as posts are often of the format "I am at...". Instagram, as a photo sharing service, also has strong aboutness: when a photo is taken, the text is very likely to reference to object that is in it, and that object is likely to be nearby (although it may not be, e.g. in the case of the Empire State Building). For a regular Twitter client, aboutness could be more dispersed, as people are more likely to make comments like "I am headed to Central Park" or "I hear the Empire State Building was lit in blue and white today" — both comments that are quite unlikely on Foursquare and Instagram. Related, the density of location references is lower in non-Foursquare and non-Instagram content, as people may converse on any topic.

Nevertheless, we have shown that significant reach can be achieved for certain applications under certain conditions with a potential to more than triple the amount of available, geotagged content for Instagram, for example. However, the lift that is gained demonstrates the "rich get richer" phenomena, where places that were already significantly covered are more likely to gain new content than other areas. This phenomena is likely to bias the distribution of social media geotagged content even more significantly. Hecht and Stephens describe the implications of such bias in respect to urban and rural communities [9].

It is important to note that the results described here are somewhat over-optimistic because they are based on data from a single locale (i.e. New York City). For instance, an n-gram like "city hall" may be geo-specific when examining a New York-only dataset, but in a world-wide dataset there would be many different city halls. However, the concern can be somewhat mitigated by additional information a system may have, e.g. the user profile information or the IP address.

Another key limitation in our approach is the bias introduced by building models based on geotagged data. In fact, Twitter had recently reported (see footnote 1) that 1% of the users produce 66% of the geotagged items. It is entirely possible that the data we trained and tested on is significantly biased, e.g., the type of content that is posted may be different between users that geotag their content versus others. Of course, bias can also result from the fact that most geotagged content is posted from specific Twitter applications. These concerns are also significant, but can be mitigated by a couple of factors. First, as we show above, we can achieve significant lift even when training and testing with the data from the same source, somewhat limiting the bias. Second, as reported by Priedhorsky et al. [19], the difference between geotagged and non-geotagged tweets is limited; the authors report a correlation of 0.85 between the unigram frequency vectors for each set. On the other hand, there are a number of avenues for future work that could further improve the results reported here. First, using language analysis and, in particular, extracting tense and time references [15] could help improve the models for TW-iPhone data where people are likely to post plans and reviews with their location references. A more refined approach to combining multiple n-grams that appear in tweets could take into account their likelihood and co-variation models. Additionally, using user level information, e.g. profile or historic data, has the potential to greatly improve performance. Further, our model could be refined to not only rely on geographic information, but include temporal information as well [22]. Note, however, that a photo's geographic and temporal metadata may not always be accurate [31]. Nonetheless, modeling by space, time and source may allow more gains in geolocating content in hyper-local areas.

Ultimately, the gain in content associated with hyper-local geographic areas can help create better models, and understand better the activities in different geographic areas. For example, we can use these data to provide more robust information to people interested in monitoring the activities, say, in Central Park. Such gains will provide for new ways to reflect the activities in the park, detect outliers and unusual activities, and help users with specific search and data mining tasks.

8. ACKNOWLEDGEMENTS

This work is supported in part by the National Science Foundation grant numbers 1446374 and 1444493. Any opinions, findings, and conclusions or recommendations expressed in this material are those of the author(s) and do not necessarily reflect the views of the National Science Foundation. The work of Yaron Kanza was supported in part by ISF grant 1467/13. Yana Volkovich was supported by the People Programme (Marie Curie Actions, from the FP7/2007-2013) under grant agreement no.600388 managed by REA and ACCIÓ.

9. REFERENCES

[1] S. Ahern, M. Naaman, R. Nair, and J. H.-I. Yang. World explorer. In *Proc. of the Joint Conf. on Digital Libraries* (JCDL), 2007.

[2] S. Chandra, L. Khan, and F. B. Muhaya. Estimating twitter user location using social interactions–a content based approach. In *Proc. of the IEEE Conf. on Privacy Security, Risk and Trust* (PASSAT) and *IEEE Conf. on Social Computing* (SocialCom), 2011.

[3] Z. Cheng, J. Caverlee, and K. Lee. You are where you tweet. In *Proc. of the ACM Conf. on Information and Knowledge Management* (CIKM), 2010.

[4] R. Compton, D. Jurgens, and D. Allen. Geotagging one hundred million Twitter accounts with total variation minimization. Available From *CoRR*, abs/1404.7152, 2014.

[5] D. J. Crandall, L. Backstrom, D. Huttenlocher, and J. Kleinberg. Mapping the world's photos. In *Proc. of the International Conf. on World Wide Web* (WWW), 2009.

[6] N. Dalvi, R. Kumar, and B. Pang. Object matching in tweets with spatial models. In *Proc. of the ACM Conf. on Web Search and Data Mining* (WSDM), 2012.

[7] J. Eisenstein, A. Ahmed, and E. P. Xing. Sparse additive generative models of text. In *Proc. of the International Conf. on Machine Learning*, (ICML), 2011.

[8] I. Grabovitch-Zuyev, Y. Kanza, E. Kravi, and B. Pat. On the correlation between textual content and geospatial locations in microblogs. In *Proc. of the ACM Workshop on Managing and Mining Enriched Geo-Spatial Data* (GeoRich), 2014.

[9] B. Hecht and M. Stephens. A tale of cities: Urban biases in volunteered geographic information. In *Proc. of the AAAI Conf. on Weblogs and Social Media* (ICWSM), 2014.

[10] L. Hong, A. Ahmed, S. Gurumurthy, A. J. Smola, and K. Tsioutsiouliklis. Discovering geographical topics in the twitter stream. In *Proc. of the International Conf. on World Wide Web* (WWW), 2012.

[11] L. S. Kennedy and M. Naaman. Generating diverse and representative image search results for landmarks. In *Proc. of the International Conf. on World Wide Web* (WWW) ,2008.

[12] S. Kinsella, V. Murdock, and N. O'Hare. I'm eating a sandwich in Glasgow. In *Proc. of the ACM International Workshop on Search and Mining User-Generated Contents* (SMUC), 2011.

[13] C. C. Kling, J. Kunegis, S. Sizov, and S. Staab. Detecting non-gaussian geographical topics in tagged photo collections. In *Proc. of the 7th ACM International Conf. on Web Search and Data Mining* (WSDM), 2014.

[14] K. Leetaru, S. Wang, A. Padmanabhan, and E. Shook. Mapping the global Twitter heartbeat: The geography of Twitter. *First Monday*, 18(5), May 2013.

[15] C. Li and A. Sun. Fine-grained location extraction from tweets with temporal awareness. In *Proc. of the ACM Conf. on Research & Development in Information Retrieval* (SIGIR), 2014.

[16] D. Lian and X. Xie. Mining check-in history for personalized location naming. *ACM Transactions on Intelligent Systems and Technology* (TIST), 5(2):32, 2014.

[17] J. Mahmud, J. Nichols, and C. Drews. Home location identification of Twitter users. Available from *CoRR*, abs/1403.2345, 2014.

[18] J. N. Matias and A. Monroy-Hernandez. NewsPad: Designing for collaborative storytelling in neighborhoods. In *CHI'14 Extended Abstracts on Human Factors in Computing Systems*, 2014.

[19] R. Priedhorsky, A. Culotta, and S. Y. Del Valle. Inferring the origin locations of tweets with quantitative confidence. In *Proc. of the ACM Conf. on Computer Supported Cooperative Work* (CSCW), 2014.

[20] D. Quercia, J. Ellis, L. Capra, and J. Crowcroft. Tracking gross community happiness from tweets. In *Proc. of the ACM Conf. on Computer Supported Cooperative Work* (CSCW), 2012.

[21] D. Quercia, R. Schifanella, and L. M. Aiello. The shortest path to happiness: Recommending beautiful, quiet, and happy routes in the city. In *Proc. of the ACM Conf. on Hypertext and Social Media*, 2014.

[22] T. Rattenbury, N. Good, and M. Naaman. Towards automatic extraction of event and place semantics from Flickr tags. In *Proc. of the ACM Conf. on Research and Development in Information Retrieval* (SIGIR), 2007.

[23] S. Roller, M. Speriosu, S. Rallapalli, B. Wing, and J. Baldridge. Supervised text-based geolocation using language models on an adaptive grid. In *Proc. of the Joint Conf. on Empirical Methods in Natural Language Processing and Computational Natural Language Learning* (EMNLP-CoNLL), 2012.

[24] A. Sadilek, H. A. Kautz, and V. Silenzio. Modeling spread of disease from social interactions. In *AAAI Conf. on Weblogs and Social Media* (ICWSM), 2012.

[25] A. Schulz, A. Hadjakos, H. Paulheim, J. Nachtwey, and M. Mühlhäuser. A multi-indicator approach for geolocalization of tweets. In *AAAI Conf. on Weblogs and Social Media* (ICWSM), 2013.

[26] P. Serdyukov, V. Murdock, and R. van Zwol. Placing Flickr photos on a map. In *Proc. of the ACM Conf. on Research and Development in Information Retrieval* (SIGIR), 2009.

[27] B. Shaw, J. Shea, S. Sinha, and A. Hogue. Learning to rank for spatistemporal search. In *Proc. of the ACM Conf. on Web Search and Data Mining* (WSDM) 2013.

[28] D. Tasse and J. I. Hong. Using social media data to understand cities. Technical report, Carnegie Mellon University, 2014.

[29] B. Thomee and A. Rae. Uncovering locally characterizing regions within geotagged data. In *Proc. of the International Conf. on World Wide Web* (WWW), 2013.

[30] B. Thomee, G. De Francisci Morales. Automatic discovery of global and local equivalence relationships in labeled geo-spatial data In *Proc. of the ACM Conf. on Hypertext and Social Media*, 2014.

[31] B. Thomee, J.G. Moreno, D.A. Shamma. Who's time is it anyway?: investigating the accuracy of camera timestamps In *Proc. of the ACM Conf. on Multimedia*, 2014.

[32] H. wen Chang, D. Lee, M. Eltaher, and J. Lee. @Phillies Tweeting from Philly? Predicting Twitter user locations with spatial word usage. In *IEEE/ACM International Conf. on Advances in Social Networks Analysis and Mining* (ASONAM), 2012.

[33] B. P. Wing and J. Baldridge. Simple supervised document geolocation with geodesic grids. In *Proc. of the Annual Meeting of the Assoc. for Computational Linguistics: Human Language Technologies* (HLT), 2011.

[34] C. Xia, R. Schwartz, K. Xie, A. Krebs, A. Langdon, J. Ting, and M. Naaman. CityBeat: Real-time social media visualization of hyper-local city data. In *Companion Publication of the 23rd International Conf. on World Wide Web* (WWW), 2014.

Learning from User Interactions

Thorsten Joachims
Department of Computer Science
Department of Information Science
Cornell University
Ithaca, NY, USA
tj@cs.cornell.edu

ABSTRACT

The ability to learn from user interactions can give systems access to unprecedented amounts of world knowledge. This is already evident in search engines, recommender systems, and electronic commerce, and other applications are likely to follow in the near future (e.g., education, smart homes). More generally, the ability to learn from user interactions promises pathways for solving knowledge-intensive tasks ranging from natural language understanding to autonomous robotics.

Learning from user interactions, however, means learning from data that does not necessarily fit the assumptions of the standard machine learning models. Since interaction data consists of the choices that humans make, it has to be interpreted with respect to how humans make decisions, which is influenced by the decision context and constraints like human motivation and human abilities.

In this talk, I argue that we need learning approaches that explicitly model user-interaction data as the result of human decision making. To this effect, the talk explores how integrating microeconomic models of human behavior into the learning process leads to new learning algorithms that have provable guarantees under verifiable assumptions and to learning systems that perform robustly in practice. These findings imply that the design space of such human-interactive learning systems encompasses not only the machine learning algorithm itself, but also the design of the interaction under an appropriate model of user behavior.

Categories and Subject Descriptors

I.2.6 [Learning]; H.1.2 [User/Machine Systems]; H.3.5 [Online Information Services]

General Terms

Algorithms, Experimentation, Theory

Keyword

Machine Learning, Implicit Feedback, Explicit Feedback, User Models

WSDM'15, February 2–6, 2015, Shanghai, China.
ACM 978-1-4503-3317-7/15/02.
http://dx.doi.org/10.1145/2684822.2685326

BIO

Thorsten Joachims is a Professor in the Department of Computer Science and in the Department of Information Science at Cornell University. His research interests center on a synthesis of theory and system building in machine learning, with applications in information access, language technology, and recommendation. His past research focused on support vector machines, text classification, structured output prediction, convex optimization, learning to rank, learning with preferences, and learning from implicit feedback. In 2001, he finished his dissertation advised by Prof. Katharina Morik at the University of Dortmund. From there he also received his Diplom in Computer Science in 1997. Between 2000 and 2001 he worked as a PostDoc at the GMD Institute for Autonomous Intelligent Systems. From 1994 to 1996 he was a visiting scholar with Prof. Tom Mitchell at Carnegie Mellon University.

ACKNOWLEDGMENTS

This work was funded in part through NSF Awards IIS-1217686, IIS-1247696, IIS-1247637, a Google PhD Fellowship, a JTCII CornellNYC Award, and a gift from Bloomberg.

Learning to Recommend Related Entities to Search Users

Bin Bi*
UCLA
bbi@cs.ucla.edu

Hao Ma
Microsoft Research
haoma@microsoft.com

Bo-June (Paul) Hsu
Microsoft Research
paulhsu@microsoft.com

Wei Chu
Microsoft
chu.wei@microsoft.com

Kuansan Wang
Microsoft Research
kuansan.wang@microsoft.com

Junghoo Cho
UCLA
cho@cs.ucla.edu

ABSTRACT

Over the past few years, major web search engines have introduced *knowledge bases* to offer popular facts about people, places, and things on the entity pane next to regular search results. In addition to information about the entity searched by the user, the entity pane often provides a ranked list of related entities. To keep users engaged, it is important to develop a recommendation model that tailors the related entities to individual user interests.

We propose a probabilistic Three-way Entity Model (TEM) that provides personalized recommendation of related entities using three data sources: *knowledge base*, *search click log*, and *entity pane log*. Specifically, TEM is capable of extracting hidden structures and capturing underlying correlations among *users*, *main entities*, and *related entities*. Moreover, the TEM model can also exploit the click signals derived from the entity pane log. We further provide an inference technique to learn the parameters in TEM, and propose a principled preference learning method specifically designed for ranking related entities. Extensive experiments with two real-world datasets show that TEM with our probabilistic framework significantly outperforms a state of the art baseline, confirming the effectiveness of TEM and our probabilistic framework in related entity recommendation.

Categories and Subject Descriptors: H.3.3 [Information Search and Retrieval]

General Terms: Algorithm, Experimentation

1. INTRODUCTION

Traditionally, web search engines have led users toward web pages chosen by lexical matches against the search string. However with the introduction of *knowledge bases* over the past few years, commercial search engines are moving towards retrieval based on a semantic understanding of the user query. The knowledge base is being used to provide popular facts about people, places, and things alongside traditional search results. It allows search to evolve from returning pages that match query terms to finding *entities* that the words describe.

A knowledge base is a centralized repository of content about entities, their attributes and mutual relationships. Well-known examples of knowledge bases include Freebase, YAGO, Microsoft Satori, and Google Knowledge Graph. For instance, Freebase consists of a large set of metadata about movies, music, books, well-known people, and things. A subset of the entities and their relations in Freebase is depicted in Figure 1. It includes entities corresponding to four people, two movies and their genres. The links between the entities represent their relationships, such as "*Adam McKay* is the director of *Anchorman*" and "*Kristen Wiig* is an actor appearing in *Anchorman 2*". In this example, "director", "actor" and "genre" are attributes of the entity *Anchorman*.

With the introduction of a knowledge base, a web search engine enables users to search for things – movies, celebrities, landmarks and more – and instantly get rich information relevant to the queries. Figure 2 shows an example search result for the query "pacific rim" together with its entity pane provided by a commercial search engine. The search engine recognizes that "pacific rim" is the title of a movie corresponding to an entity in the knowledge base. We refer to the entity a user searches for as the *main entity*. An entity pane that presents information about the main entity shows up to the right of the regular search results. On the entity pane, in addition to the description of the movie *Pacific Rim*, a list of movies related to *Pacific Rim* is also visually presented below. We refer to an entity related to the search as a *related entity*. The provided related entities allow users to quickly access other relevant entities and offer the ability to explore more information within the same search session. In order to keep users engaged, it is important to develop a recommendation model that generates related entities closely matched with their interests.

Currently, major search engines recommend related entities based on their similarities to the main entity that the user searched for. There are various measures of the similarity between a main entity and an entity to recommend. A common measure is the frequency of the two entities being co-clicked in the same session across all search users. A related entity is recommended if and only if it is frequently co-clicked with the main entity. This co-click based approach essentially maximizes the likelihood that people agree on the relatedness irrespective of any individual user. Such a global

*This work was done when the first author was on a summer internship at Microsoft Research.

WSDM'15, February 2–6, 2015, Shanghai, China.

http://dx.doi.org/10.1145/2684822.2685304.

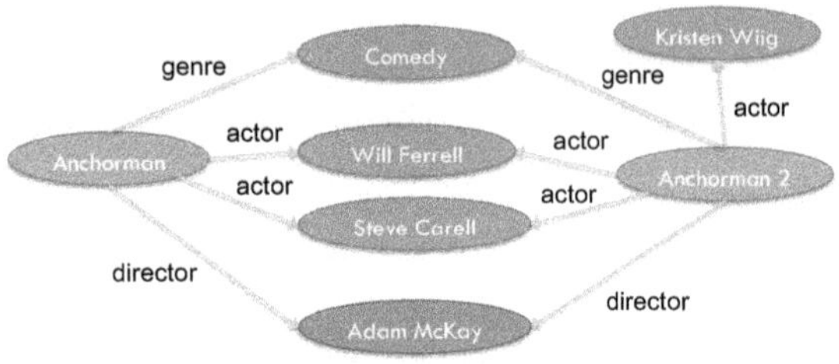

Figure 1: Example of the entities and their relations taken from Freebase

recommendation method brings the same list of related entities to every user who searches for the same main entity, as user-specific information is completely ignored. But the same recommendation cannot satisfy users with distinct interests. For example, given a movie as the main entity, one user may be interested in viewing the other movie entities with the same director, while another user may want to view the movie entities from the same genre.

To the best of our knowledge, no work has been done on developing a recommendation model for a search engine to tailor related entities to an individual user's unique taste and preference. To personalize recommendations, we need to build user-specific profiles from their interactions with the search engine. In this paper, the users' interactions are collected in the *search click log* and the *entity pane log*. The search click log stores history of user clicks on URLs, while the entity pane log stores clicks on the entity pane. In this work, we aim to build a probabilistic recommendation model that can customize the suggested entities, which are related to a given main entity, based on the user's past history stored in the usage logs.

Despite considerable research on the *search click log* over the last decade, little is known about the emerging *entity pane log*. This work also represents the first study exploiting the entity pane's implicit user feedback for entity recommendation. Our empirical studies find that the entity pane click-through rates (CTR) play important roles in enhancing recommendation quality of related entities. Therefore, we include these strong CTR signals in the recommendation model.

In addition to CTRs, our recommendation model involves three important dimensions: *user*, *main entity*, and *related entity*. Without the user dimension, the model would degenerate to a global recommendation method which fails to personalize suggested entities, as discussed above. On the other hand, if recommendations were based purely on the user dimension, while totally ignoring main entities, then the suggested entities would be utterly unrelated to the searches. The interactive feedback in the usage logs reveals the three-way correlations among these three dimensions. The recommendation model aims to discover and exploit their ternary relationships. We refer to our probabilistic recommendation model as Three-way Entity Model, abbreviated as TEM.

To determine the parameters in TEM, we propose learning their optimal values from a training set of observations constructed from the entity pane log. As mentioned above, this log contains user feedback on the relatedness of recommended entities. Positive observations can be readily derived from click feedback by interpreting a user click as a vote in favor of relatedness. Nevertheless, it is nontrivial to derive negative observations, since a non-click may not indicate the absence of relatedness. We propose a principled

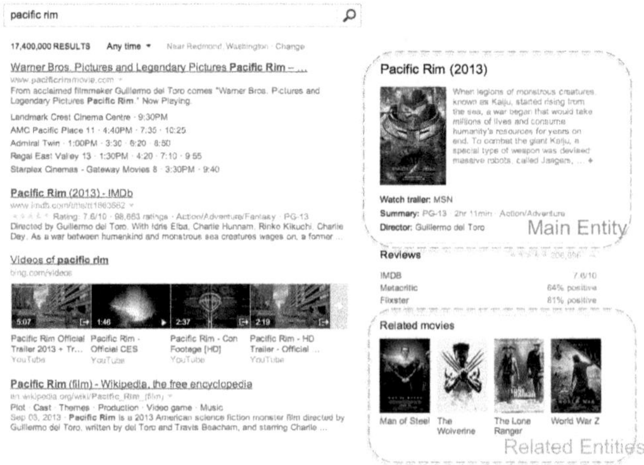

Figure 2: Example of search results with the entity pane taken from a commercial web search engine

solution to this issue, specialized for the problem of ranking related entities.

The major contributions of our work are summarized as follows:

1. This paper presents the first solution – the probabilistic model TEM– for a search engine to personalize its recommendation of related entities. The recommended entities are customized to be not only related to the given main entity, but also tailored to the user's interest and preference.

2. The TEM model leverages three data sources: *knowledge base*, *search click log*, and *entity pane log*. This is the first work to utilize the entity pane log to recommend related entities. Specifically, the CTRs derived from the entity pane log turn out to be strong signals for entity recommendation.

3. The TEM model uncovers the underlying three-way relationships among *user*, *main entity*, and *related entity*. Jointly modeling all three dimensions prevents TEM from making static or irrelevant recommendations. An inference technique is introduced to learn the parameters of TEM.

4. We propose a principled method for training set construction to work around the problem of missing negative samples. The proposed method is specifically designed for ranking related entities.

5. We conducted extensive experiments with two real-world datasets of different domains collected from a commercial web search engine. The experimental results demonstrate that TEM with our probabilistic framework significantly outperforms the state of the art used by a commercial search engine. It confirms the effectiveness of TEM and our probabilistic framework in entity recommendation and the efficacy of personalization.

The rest of this paper is organized as follows. In Section 2, we describe the prior work related to ours. The problem statement is given in Section 3. Section 4 introduces our TEM model. In Section 5, we present the experimental results. Finally, we conclude the paper in Section 6.

	User ID	Time	Main entity	Related entity	Rank	Click
Instance; Page impression 1	32	7/9/2013 10:32:26	Pacific Rim	Man of Steel	1	0
Page impression 1	32	7/9/2013 10:32:26	Pacific Rim	The Wolverine	2	0
Page impression 1	32	7/9/2013 10:32:26	Pacific Rim	The Lone Ranger	3	1
Page impression 1	32	7/9/2013 10:32:26	Pacific Rim	World War Z	4	0
Page impression 2	498	6/16/2013 15:16:41	Leonardo DiCaprio	Kate Winslet	1	0
Page impression 2	498	6/16/2013 15:16:41	Leonardo DiCaprio	Baz Luhrmann	2	0
Page impression 2	498	6/16/2013 15:16:41	Leonardo DiCaprio	Johnny Depp	3	1

Figure 3: Sample records taken from an entity pane log

2. RELATED WORK

A research topic related to our work is personalized web services, including web search and entity/news recommendation, although the tasks are quite different. Micarelli et al. [12] provided a summary of research works on this topic. Personalized search exploits user search histories to deliver more relevant results than those provided by traditional search engines [15]. Unlike the task addressed in this paper, Blanco et al. [4] worked on a fundamentally different entity recommendation task. The goal of their work was to recommend possible future queries related to the user's current search query based on a knowledge base. In their paper, the future queries were referred as to related entities, as opposed to the related entities in our context. Chu and Park [6] proposed a feature-based bilinear regression framework for personalized recommendation on news content. This approach greatly alleviated the cold-start issue of recommending for new users by leveraging interest patterns in user profiles recognized from regression over historical interactive feedback. Sun et al. [16] introduced CubeSVD to perform three-way data analysis for personalized search. Similar to personalized search, our work exploits prior user actions to model their interests for personalized recommendation on related entities.

Over recent decades, a few studies have been conducted on three-way data analysis. Acar and Yener [1] gave an overview of multiway models, algorithms as well as their applications in diverse disciplines. These studies commonly represented observational data as a third-order tensor, which is a higher-order generalization of a vector and a matrix. A three-way model was then constructed for extracting hidden structures and capturing underlying correlations between variables in the third-order tensor. A well-known three-way model, called Tucker3, was introduced by Tucker [17, 7]. It is an extension of singular value decomposition to third-order tensors. Tucker3 has been successful in many applications [16, 18].

Three-way data analysis has been widely performed in the context of multiverse recommendation. Karatzoglou et al. [10] introduced a collaborative filtering method based on third-order tensor decomposition to provide context-aware recommendations. Rendle and Schmidt-Thieme [14] used the tensor decomposition technique in recommending to users tags for annotating specific items in social tagging systems. Despite its success in recommender systems, tensor decomposition does not apply to related entity recommendation. In particular, tensor decomposition suffers from the cold-start problem, as it represents each object in the system with a unique ID. Given the knowledge base and the usage logs, tensor decomposition cannot utilize the valuable information derived from the various nature of data sources. In order to do so, we developed TEM, a new probabilistic model for three-way data analysis.

Table 1: Notations used throughout this paper

Notation	Description
X	Feature matrix for users
Y	Feature matrix for main entities
Z	Feature matrix for related entities
u	User identity
m	Main entity
r	Related entity
$\mathbf{x}_u$	Feature vector for user u
$\mathbf{y}_m$	Feature vector for main entity m
$\mathbf{z}_r$	Feature vector for related entity r
U	Number of unique users
M	Number of main entities
R	Number of related entities
I	Number of features for each user
J	Number of features for each main entity
K	Number of features for each related entity
Θ	Model parameter
η, β	Weight coefficients
o	Preference relation

3. PROBLEM STATEMENT

In a nutshell, the objective of this paper is to recommend to the user a ranked list of entities relevant to the main entity by leveraging three pieces of information: *knowledge base*, *search click log*, and *entity pane log*.

Figure 3 presents a few sample records from the entity pane click log of a real search engine. Each row represents an *instance* indicating whether user u clicked related entity r given main entity m. There are two *page impressions* in the table, each of which indicates the list of related entities recommended for a given (u, m) pair. The *Rank* column gives the rank of each related entity in recommendation lists, and the *Click* column indicates whether related entities were clicked or not (1 for click, 0 for no click).

For notational convenience, let U denote the total number of unique users in the log, M denote the total number of main entities, and R denote the total number of related entities. The notations used throughout this paper are given in Table 1. Some of the notations will be explained in later sections.

As discussed above, a click event is naturally associated with three salient dimensions: $User \times Main\ entity \times Related\ entity$.

[User dimension]

The user dimension targets user interest patterns, building search profiles by logging user interactions with the search engine. In this paper, a user profile maps a user to a vector of entities and attributes representing the user's interests. In order to model user interest as accurately as possible, we collect click history from two sources: *search click log* and *entity pane log*. The former records user click history on URLs, while the latter reflects user click history on entities.

Since the *search click log* reports user clicks on URLs, but we are looking for user interest in entities, we need a mapping from URLs to entities. Fortunately, with the help of the open source Freebase[1] knowledge base, it is easy to map users to the entities they are interested in. An illustration is shown in Figure 4.

Each entity in Freebase is linked to some URLs that are related to this entity. For example, for the movie *Avatar*[2], by utilizing the relationships "/common/topic/official_website"

[1] `http://www.freebase.com/`

[2] `http://www.freebase.com/m/0bth54`

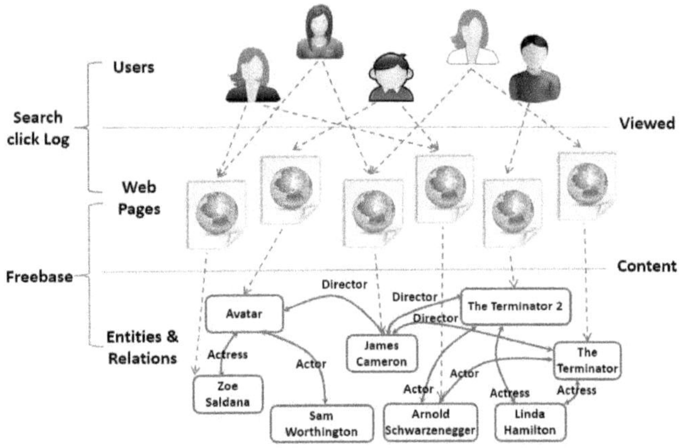

Figure 4: Illustration on joining search click log with Freebase knowledge base

and "/common/topic/topic_equivalent_webpage", we can obtain this movie's official site, IMDb pages as well as Wikipedia pages, etc. Moreover, other information related to this movie is available to us, including actors, directors, genres, producers, etc. With the help of this data, user-clicked URLs in *search click log* can be mapped to corresponding entities in Freebase, as demonstrated in Figure 4. The attributes of these entities can also be obtained from the Freebase knowledge base.

For the *entity pane log*, as shown in Figure 3, the clicked entities are already known, so we can simply extract corresponding attributes from Freebase to represent user interests. By combining the above signals, entities and their attributes can be used to model users in a naturally way. For instance, a group of users may often view entities about action movies, while another group may prefer basketball players. If users are modeled appropriately through their usage patterns, these preferences and interests should help the search engine recommend related entities more accurately. Some sample features we extract for users are shown in Table 3 in Section 5.

Formally, each user is represented as a vector of features, denoted by $\mathbf{x}$, where $\mathbf{x} \in \mathbb{R}^I$ and I is the number of user features.

[Main entity]

In nature, the main entity reflects the search user's current search interest. In addition to user profiling by modeling his or her interest pattern based on the usage log, it is important to capture a user's current search intent expressed by the main entity, which provides valuable context. Ignoring main entities will compromise the performance of a recommendation model. In particular, if related entities are obtained based purely on the user's past preferences, while neglecting to model his or her current interest, then the recommended entities will be completely independent of what the user is searching for, leading to dissatisfaction.

The feature space for main entities is spanned by their attributes extracted from the knowledge base. Each main entity is represented as a vector of features, denoted by $\mathbf{y}$, where $\mathbf{y} \in \mathbb{R}^J$ and J is the dimensionality of the feature space for main entities.

[Related entity]

A user may click a related entity when it is aligned with both the user's interest pattern and current intent. User clicks on related entities are the interactive feedback used to relate patterns in user features to main entities. For example, suppose there is a fan of the film director *Steven Spielberg*. (Such a user can be identified from his or her past usage pattern.) Given a movie as a main entity, a good recommender should recommend the other movies related not just to the given entity, but also directed by *Steven Spielberg*, instead of recommending movies related in other ways, such as sharing the same actors.

Each related entity is represented as a column vector of features, denoted by $\mathbf{z}$, where $\mathbf{z} \in \mathbb{R}^K$ and K is the number of features for each related entity.

As we have argued, all three dimensions, $User \times Main\ entity \times Related\ entity$, can improve entity recommendation, which motivates our joint modeling of these factors. The joint model is intended to capture structural dependencies of the three dimensions, revealing the underlying ternary relations.

Problem Statement *Given the feature representations for users* $\mathbf{x}$, *main entities* $\mathbf{y}$ *and related entities* $\mathbf{z}$, *we aim to develop a recommendation model that uncovers the three-way correlations among them to recommend a ranked list of entities related to a given main entity for any user.*

4. THREE-WAY ENTITY MODEL

In this section, we present a three-way probabilistic model, TEM, designed to uncover the pattern correlations among $\mathbf{x}$, $\mathbf{y}$ and $\mathbf{z}$ for recommending related entities. More specifically, we first define a real-valued function $\Psi_{umr}(\Theta)$ of the model parameter Θ which captures the ternary relationship among the three dimensions. A likelihood function is then employed to relate the values of $\Psi_{umr}(\Theta)$ to observed actions on related entities. Finally, the parameter Θ is obtained by performing inference on TEM. The effect of the three-way interactions will be analyzed in this section.

4.1 Trilinear function

To jointly model users, main entities, and related entities, we define a trilinear function Φ_{umr} of $\mathbf{x}_u$, $\mathbf{y}_m$, and $\mathbf{z}_r$ as follows:

$$\Phi_{umr}(\eta) = \sum_{i=0}^{I}\sum_{j=0}^{J}\sum_{k=0}^{K} \eta_{ijk} \cdot x_{ui} \cdot y_{mj} \cdot z_{rk}, \quad (1)$$

where $\mathbf{x}_u$ denotes the feature vector for user u, $\mathbf{y}_m$ denotes the feature vector for main entity m, and $\mathbf{z}_r$ denotes the feature vector for related entity r. x_{ui} is the i-th feature of $\mathbf{x}_u$, y_{mj} is the j-th feature of $\mathbf{y}_m$, and z_{rk} is the k-th feature of $\mathbf{z}_r$. η consists of a set of weight coefficients, which is introduced to capture the associations among the three objects $\mathbf{x}_u$, $\mathbf{y}_m$, and $\mathbf{z}_r$. The weight η_{ijk} quantifies the affinity of three features x_{ui}, y_{mj}, and z_{rk}. Note that η can be represented as a third-order tensor, where the value of each entry η_{ijk} will be learned from historical logs.

In order for the trilinear function to capture the pairwise associations between the three dimensions, we prepend a 1 at the beginning of each feature vector. As a result, the users, main entities, and related entities are represented as:

$$\begin{aligned}\mathbf{x}_u &= [1, x_{u1}, x_{u2}, \cdots, x_{uI}]^T,\\ \mathbf{y}_m &= [1, y_{m1}, y_{m2}, \cdots, y_{mJ}]^T,\\ \mathbf{z}_r &= [1, z_{r1}, z_{r2}, \cdots, z_{rK}]^T.\end{aligned}$$

Notice that when there is a large number of features for each dimension, $\eta \in \mathbb{R}^{(I+1)\times(J+1)\times(K+1)}$ becomes a huge tensor for which inference is intractable. To overcome this problem, we need to reduce the dimensionality of each feature vector. Given massive training data, we resort to random projections [9] for dimensionality reduction. Random projections essentially project each feature space onto a random lower-dimensional subspace, which yield results comparable to conventional dimensionality reduction approaches such as Principal Component Analysis (PCA). However, random projections are significantly less computationally expensive than PCA. We study the effect of random projections on entity recommendation in the experiment section.

4.2 CTR incorporation

The three-way associations, which are systematically modeled by the trilinear function $\Phi_{umr}(\eta)$, contribute an important indicator to entity recommendation, especially for the rare/new entities for which we have zero or insufficient click data. To further enhance the recommendation quality of popular entities, we derive CTR features from the interactive feedback collected in the entity pane log. The CTRs have been shown to be strong signals for various recommendation tasks [11, 8]. CTR is defined as the ratio of the number of clicks on a certain related entity and the number of page impressions in which the related entity is presented. We extract three sets of CTRs from the entity pane log:

1. $CTR(r)$: CTRs on related entities
2. $CTR(m,r)$: CTRs on main entities and related entities
3. $CTR(u,m,r)$: CTRs on users, main entities, and related entities

Following hybrid approaches proposed for personalized search and recommendation [5, 2, 6], we integrate the trilinear function $\Phi_{umr}(\eta)$ with the CTR features, and define a real-valued function $\Psi_{umr}(\Theta)$ as:

$$\begin{aligned}\Psi_{umr}(\Theta) &= \Phi_{umr}(\eta) + \beta^T \mathbf{c}^{umr} \\ &= \sum_{i=0}^{I}\sum_{j=0}^{J}\sum_{k=0}^{K} \eta_{ijk} \cdot x_{ui} \cdot y_{mj} \cdot z_{rk} + \beta^T \mathbf{c}^{umr}, \quad (2)\end{aligned}$$

where $\mathbf{c}^{umr}$ is a vector of CTR features specific to user u, main entity m and related entity r. β is a vector of weight coefficients. $\Theta = (\eta, \beta)$ consists of all the parameters to be learned from historical logs.

4.3 Likelihood function

In this subsection, we introduce a likelihood function to relate the values of $\Psi_{umr}(\Theta)$ to the click log collected from the entity pane. The click log provides user preferences for related entities by keeping track of clicks as implicit feedback. One important fact about the click log is that only positive observations are available - each click can be considered as positive feedback for the corresponding triple (u, m, r) indicating that user u is interested in viewing entity r, which is related to main entity m. However, the non-clicked triples (u, m, r) (i.e., given main entity m, user u did not click recommended entity r on the entity pane), do not provide such clear conclusions. There are at least two different interpretations for any non-clicked triple. One possibility is negative feedback, meaning that the user was not interested in the recommended entity. Another possibility is that the user did not even see the entity, in which case the user's interested in the entity is unknown.

User ID	Time	Main entity	Related entity	Rank	Click
32	7/9/2013 10:32:26	Pacific Rim	Man of Steel	1	0
32	7/9/2013 10:32:26	Pacific Rim	The Wolverine	2	0
32	7/9/2013 10:32:26	Pacific Rim	The Lone Ranger	3	1
32	7/9/2013 10:32:26	Pacific Rim	World War Z	4	0
498	6/16/2013 15:16:41	Leonardo DiCaprio	Kate Winslet	1	0
498	6/16/2013 15:16:41	Leonardo DiCaprio	Baz Luhrmann	2	0
498	6/16/2013 15:16:41	Leonardo DiCaprio	Johnny Depp	3	1

Figure 5: Preference relations induced by the click feedback in the entity pane log

If we simply ignore all non-clicked triples, typical machine learning algorithms are not able to learn anything from the positive observations alone. One may opt to consider the non-clicked triples as negative feedback. More specifically, training data is created by assigning positive class labels to clicked triples, and negative class labels to non-clicked triples. The problem with this approach is that all non-clicked triples the algorithm predicts in the future are presented to the learning algorithm as negative observations. This approach misinterprets non-clicked triples, which are actually missing values.

To address this problem, we use triple pairs as training data instead of individual triples. As opposed to replacing non-clicked triples with negative observations, we assume that users prefer the related entities they clicked over all other non-clicked ones on the same page impression. More specifically, given two triples (u, m, r_i) and (u, m, r_j) in the same page impression, user u prefers entity r_i over entity r_j if and only if r_i was clicked by u while r_j was not, which is denoted by $r_i^{u,m} \succ r_j^{u,m}$. Note that this assumption reasonably disregards click position bias, given the fact that only several related entities are presented in each page impression. This is different from the long lists of web search results, in which users are prone to click top ranked pages.

We create training data $\mathcal{D}$ by including all preference relations induced, as follows:

$$\mathcal{D} = \{(u, m, r_i, r_j) | r_i^{u,m} \succ r_j^{u,m} \vee r_j^{u,m} \succ r_i^{u,m}\}, \quad (3)$$

where each preference relation $o = (u, m, r_i, r_j)$ is considered as a training sample. For the entities that are both clicked by a user, we cannot infer any preference. The same is true for two entities either of which a user did not click. The running example in Figure 5 shows the preference relations induced by the click feedback in the entity pane log. In the first page impression, as the user clicked the related entity *The Lone Ranger*, we infer that he or she prefers *The Lone Ranger* over the other three recommended movies, indicated by the arrows in the figure. Similarly, it can be inferred that, for the second page impression, the user is more interested in *Johnny Depp* than the others.

A logistic function $\mathcal{F}(\cdot)$ as the likelihood function is then employed to relate the values of $\Psi_{umr}(\Theta)$ to the pairwise preference, as follows:

$$\begin{aligned} & p(r_i^{u,m} \succ r_j^{u,m} | \Psi_{umr_i}(\Theta), \Psi_{umr_j}(\Theta)) \\ = & \frac{1}{1 + e^{-g_{r_i,r_j}^{u,m}(\Psi_{umr_i}(\Theta) - \Psi_{umr_j}(\Theta))}} \\ = & \mathcal{F}(g_{r_i,r_j}^{u,m}(\Psi_{umr_i}(\Theta) - \Psi_{umr_j}(\Theta))), \quad (4)\end{aligned}$$

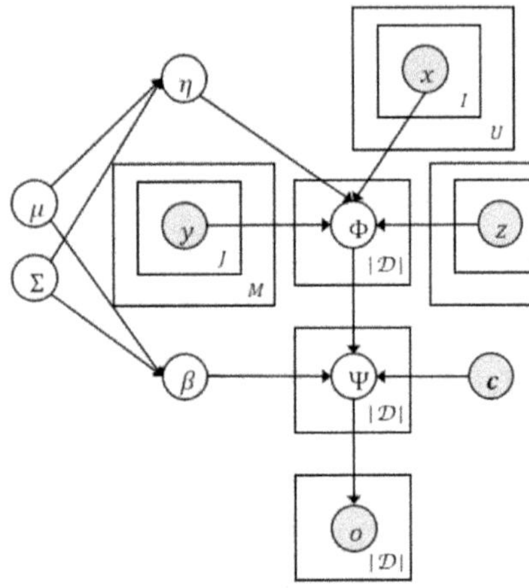

Figure 6: Graphical representation of Three-way Entity Model

where $g^{u,m}_{r_i,r_j} \in \{-1, 1\}$ denotes whether user u clicks r_i or r_j for main entity m:

$$g^{u,m}_{r_i,r_j} = \begin{cases} 1 & \text{if } u \text{ clicks } r_i \text{ given } m, \\ -1 & \text{if } u \text{ clicks } r_j \text{ given } m. \end{cases}$$

The probability $p(r_i^{u,m} \succ r_j^{u,m} | \Psi_{umr_i}(\Theta), \Psi_{umr_j}(\Theta))$ gives the likelihood that user u prefers entity r_i over entity r_j, both related to main entity m. Given the inferred parameter Θ, the likelihood of observing all preference relations in training data is then given by:

$$\begin{aligned} p(\mathcal{D}|\Theta) &= \prod_{(u,m,r_i,r_j)\in\mathcal{D}} p(r_i^{u,m} \succ r_j^{u,m} | \Psi_{umr_i}(\Theta), \Psi_{umr_j}(\Theta)) \\ &= \prod_{(u,m,r_i,r_j)\in\mathcal{D}} \frac{1}{1 + e^{-g^{u,m}_{r_i,r_j}(\Psi_{umr_i}(\Theta) - \Psi_{umr_j}(\Theta))}} \\ &= \prod_{(u,m,r_i,r_j)\in\mathcal{D}} \mathcal{F}(g^{u,m}_{r_i,r_j}(\Psi_{umr_i}(\Theta) - \Psi_{umr_j}(\Theta))). \end{aligned} \tag{5}$$

4.4 TEM & Inference

As discussed above, we need to learn the parameter Θ (i.e., η and β) from observed preference relations induced by user clicks on the entity pane, so that related entities can be recommended in the future.

For notational clarity, we define $\bar{\Theta}$ as a vector concatenating all the entries in η and β. The $\bar{\Theta}$ is considered as a random variable, and assumed to follow a Gaussian distribution:

$$\bar{\Theta} \sim \text{Gaussian}(\mu, \Sigma). \tag{6}$$

We impose a zero-mean isotropic Gaussian prior on the variable $\bar{\Theta}$, i.e.,

$$p(\bar{\Theta}) = \frac{1}{\sqrt{2\pi}\sigma} e^{-\frac{\sum_i \bar{\theta}_i^2}{2\sigma^2}}. \tag{7}$$

The graphical representation of the probabilistic model TEM is given in Figure 6. First, η is sampled from a Gaussian distribution. Given the η as well as features $\mathbf{x}_u$, $\mathbf{y}_m$, and $\mathbf{z}_r$, by Equation (1) we obtain the value of function $\Phi_{umr}(\eta)$ for each triple (u, m, r) in the training data $\mathcal{D}$. Incorporating $\Phi_{umr}(\eta)$ into the features of click-through rates weighted by β, which is drawn from a Gaussian distribution, gives the value of function $\Psi_{umr}(\Theta)$, using Equation (2). With the value of $\Psi_{umr}(\Theta)$, each preference relation o in $\mathcal{D}$ can be obtained by the likelihood function defined as in Equation (4).

We learn the parameter $\bar{\Theta}$, consisting of η and β by fitting the probabilistic model TEM to the training data $\mathcal{D}$. Specifically, we obtain the posterior distribution of the parameter Θ given all observations in training data $\mathcal{D}$, according to the Bayes' Rule:

$$p(\bar{\Theta}|\mathcal{D}) = \frac{p(\bar{\Theta})p(\mathcal{D}|\bar{\Theta})}{p(\mathcal{D})} \propto p(\bar{\Theta})p(\mathcal{D}|\bar{\Theta}), \tag{8}$$

where $p(\bar{\Theta})$ is the prior distribution defined as in Equation (7), and $p(\mathcal{D}|\bar{\Theta})$ is the likelihood of observing all preference relations defined as in Equation (5). *Maximum a posteriori* (MAP) estimation is then conducted to infer the parameter $\bar{\Theta}$. That is, we find a $\bar{\Theta}$ such that the posterior probability $p(\bar{\Theta}|\mathcal{D})$ is maximized, i.e.,

$$\begin{aligned} &\arg\max_{\Theta} p(\bar{\Theta}|\mathcal{D}) \\ &= \arg\max_{\Theta} p(\bar{\Theta})p(\mathcal{D}|\bar{\Theta}) \\ &= \arg\max_{\Theta}\{\frac{1}{\sqrt{2\pi}\sigma} e^{-\frac{\sum_i \bar{\theta}_i^2}{2\sigma^2}} \\ &\times \prod_{(u,m,r_i,r_j)\in\mathcal{D}} \frac{1}{1 + e^{-g^{u,m}_{r_i,r_j}(\Psi_{umr_i}(\Theta) - \Psi_{umr_j}(\Theta))}}\}. \end{aligned} \tag{9}$$

We can equivalently transform this optimization problem into maximizing the logarithm of the posterior probability $p(\bar{\Theta}|\mathcal{D})$ as follows:

$$\begin{aligned} &\arg\max_{\Theta} \mathcal{L}(\bar{\Theta}) \\ &= \arg\max_{\Theta} \log p(\bar{\Theta}|\mathcal{D}) \\ &= \arg\max_{\Theta}\{-\frac{\sum_i \bar{\theta}_i^2}{2\sigma^2} \\ &+ \sum_{(u,m,r_i,r_j)\in\mathcal{D}} \log \frac{1}{1 + e^{-g^{u,m}_{r_i,r_j}(\Psi_{umr_i}(\Theta) - \Psi_{umr_j}(\Theta))}}\}. \end{aligned} \tag{10}$$

Equation (10) is an unconstrained convex optimization problem, which has a unique maximum. We use the *Limited-memory BFGS* algorithm [13] to solve the optimization problem and to estimate the parameters η and β. This involves computation of the gradients $\nabla_\eta \mathcal{L}(\bar{\Theta})$ and $\nabla_\beta \mathcal{L}(\bar{\Theta})$, i.e.:

$$\begin{aligned} \frac{\partial \mathcal{L}(\bar{\Theta})}{\partial \eta_{ijk}} &= \sum_{(u,m,r_a,r_b)\in\mathcal{D}} \{\frac{g^{u,m}_{r_a,r_b}}{1 + e^{g^{u,m}_{r_a,r_b}(\Psi_{umr_a}(\Theta) - \Psi_{umr_b}(\Theta))}} \\ &\times x_{ui} y_{mj} (z_{r_a k} - z_{r_b k}) - \frac{\eta_{ijk}}{\sigma^2}\}, \end{aligned} \tag{11}$$

$$\begin{aligned} \frac{\partial \mathcal{L}(\bar{\Theta})}{\partial \beta_i} &= \sum_{(u,m,r_a,r_b)\in\mathcal{D}} \{\frac{g^{u,m}_{r_a,r_b}}{1 + e^{g^{u,m}_{r_a,r_b}(\Psi_{umr_a}(\Theta) - \Psi_{umr_b}(\Theta))}} \\ &\times (c_i^{umr_a} - c_i^{umr_b}) - \frac{\beta_i}{\sigma^2}\}. \end{aligned} \tag{12}$$

With the parameter estimate $\hat{\Theta} = (\hat{\eta}, \hat{\beta})$, we can recommend a ranked list of entities r related to the main entity m searched by any user u. More specifically, given any triple (u, m, r), we compute the value of function $\Psi_{umr}(\hat{\Theta})$ by:

$$\Psi_{umr}(\hat{\Theta}) = \sum_{i=0}^{I} \sum_{j=0}^{J} \sum_{k=0}^{K} \hat{\eta}_{ijk} \cdot x_{ui} \cdot y_{mj} \cdot z_{rk} + \hat{\beta}^T \mathbf{c}^{umr}. \tag{13}$$

Table 2: Statistics of experimental datasets

Dataset	# users	# entities	# instances
Movie	36,641	15,409	224,567
Celebrity	26,371	2,016	1,450,609

Related entities are then ranked in descending order of the $\Psi_{umr}(\hat{\Theta})$ scores. Entities with the highest scores will be recommended to the user u.

4.5 Three-way Interaction Effect

The TEM model raises the important question: How significant is the effect of the three-way correlations to modeling user clicks? To answer this question, one may test the statistical significance of the interaction effect with a t-test on the weights η which quantify the correlations among $\mathbf{x}_u$, $\mathbf{y}_m$, and $\mathbf{z}_r$. This practice, however, misinterprets the weight coefficients η in the nonlinear TEM model [3]. The correct measure of the three-way interaction effect for TEM should be a third partial derivative of the likelihood function $\mathcal{F}(\cdot)$ instead.

Let Δ denote either the derivative or the difference operator, depending on whether the corresponding feature values are discrete or continuous. The three-way interaction effect is then estimated by $\hat{\mu}_{xyz} = \frac{\Delta^3\mathcal{F}}{\Delta x\Delta y\Delta z}$. When x, y and z are discrete features, the interaction effect can be derived as:

$$\begin{aligned}\hat{\mu}_{xyz} &= \frac{\Delta^3\mathcal{F}}{\Delta x\Delta y\Delta z}\\ &= \mathcal{F}(\eta_x+\eta_y+\eta_z+\eta_{xy}+\eta_{xz}+\eta_{yz}+\eta_{xyz}+\tilde{\mathbf{c}})\\ &\quad -\mathcal{F}(\eta_x+\eta_y+\eta_{xy}+\tilde{\mathbf{c}})-\mathcal{F}(\eta_x+\eta_z+\eta_{xz}+\tilde{\mathbf{c}})\\ &\quad -\mathcal{F}(\eta_y+\eta_z+\eta_{yz}+\tilde{\mathbf{c}})+\mathcal{F}(\eta_z+\tilde{\mathbf{c}})\\ &\quad +\mathcal{F}(\eta_y+\tilde{\mathbf{c}})+\mathcal{F}(\eta_x+\tilde{\mathbf{c}})-\mathcal{F}(\tilde{\mathbf{c}}) \qquad (14)\end{aligned}$$

where the η terms denote the weights of the features specified by the respective subscripts, and $\tilde{\mathbf{c}}$ represents the linear combination of all remaining features and weight coefficients. When some or all of x, y and z are continuous features, we can derive similar equations for the interaction effect, which are omitted due to the lack of space.

The standard error of the interaction effect estimate $\hat{\mu}_{xyz}$ is obtained by the Delta method:

$$\hat{\mu}_{xyz} \sim \text{Gaussian}\left(\mu_{xyz}, \frac{\partial}{\partial\eta}\left[\frac{\Delta^3\mathcal{F}}{\Delta x\Delta y\Delta z}\right]\Omega_\eta\frac{\partial}{\partial\eta}\left[\frac{\Delta^3\mathcal{F}}{\Delta x\Delta y\Delta z}\right]\right), \qquad (15)$$

which gives the estimate of the asymptotic variance of $\hat{\mu}_{xyz}$:

$$\hat{\sigma}^2_{xyz} = \frac{\partial}{\partial\eta}\left[\frac{\Delta^3\mathcal{F}}{\Delta x\Delta y\Delta z}\right]\hat{\Omega}_\eta\frac{\partial}{\partial\eta}\left[\frac{\Delta^3\mathcal{F}}{\Delta x\Delta y\Delta z}\right], \qquad (16)$$

where $\hat{\Omega}_\eta$ is a consistent covariance estimator of η.

For the t-test, we define the t statistic as $t = \frac{\hat{\mu}_{xyz}}{\hat{\sigma}_{xyz}}$. With the statistic, we test the null hypothesis that the overall effects of the three-way interactions equal zero for given training data, which gives p-value < 0.05. So we reject the null hypothesis, which indicates the fact that the three-way interaction effect is statistically significant to modeling user clicks on related entities.

5. EMPIRICAL EVALUATION

In this section, we report the experimental results of TEM on real-world data collected by a commercial search engine.

Table 3: Features for movie & celebrity recommendation

Movie recommendation	
User dimension	*Main & related movie*
Viewed entities	
Types of viewed entities	Actors
Viewed movie's actors	Directors
Viewed movie's directors	Genres
Viewed movie's genres	Country of origin
Viewed movie's country	Language
Viewed movie's language	Producers
Viewed movie's producers	Series
Viewed movie's series	Story
Viewed movie's story	Subject
Viewed movie's subject	Music
Viewed movie's music	......
......	

Celebrity recommendation	
User dimension	*Main & related celebrity*
	Profession
Viewed entities	Movie acted
Types of viewed entities	Movie directed
Attributes of viewed entities	Book written
Viewed pop singers	Music genre
Viewed business leaders	Organization
Viewed writers	Spouse
Viewed musicians	Nationality
Viewed actors	Language
Viewed film directors	Types
......	......

We compare the results of TEM against those of several competitors. Analysis and discussion of the experimental results are presented in this section.

5.1 Data

Although TEM is a generic probabilistic model which is applicable to recommending various kinds of entities, we take two specific types of recommendation tasks as case studies for empirical evaluation: *movie recommendation* and *celebrity recommendation*. The movie recommendation task is to recommend a ranked list of movies that are related to the movie searched by the user. For celebrity recommendation, we aim to present to the user other celebrities related to the one he or she searched for.

We collected the entity pane log data for March 2013 through July 2013 from a commercial search engine. For the two recommendation tasks, movies and celebrities were extracted by aligning the entities in the log with those in Freebase. Freebase is a collaborative knowledge base of more than twenty million entities, including well-known people, places, movies and things. The basic statistics of the movie dataset and the celebrity dataset are given in Table 2.

Table 3 lists some features we used for the two recommendation tasks (Due to the space limitation, we do not list all the features in this paper). Specifically, to develop user profiles, by joining *search click log*, *entity pane log* and the Freebase *knowledge base* (See Section 3 for details), we collected the popular entities the users had viewed together with their attributes/types as features, such as popular movies, pop stars and well-known writers. Each of the features was represented as the frequency of its occurrence in the logs for each user. In addition, for movie recommendation, with the help of the knowledge base we included the attributes (i.e., genres, countries, languages, etc.) of the movies viewed into the user dimension. This enables the model to learn user characteristics from the various aspects of their viewed

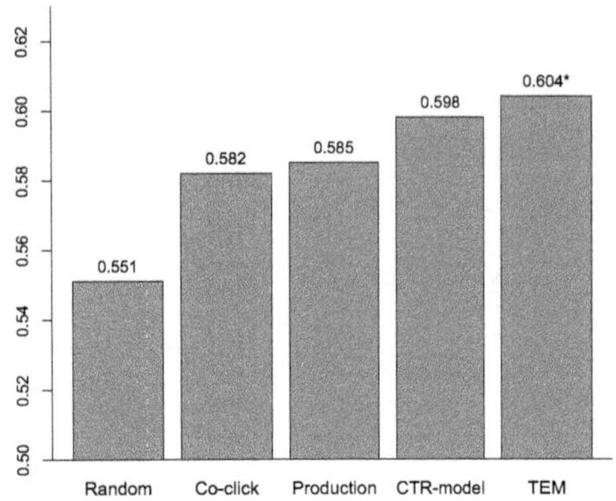

Figure 7: MRR for movie recommendation

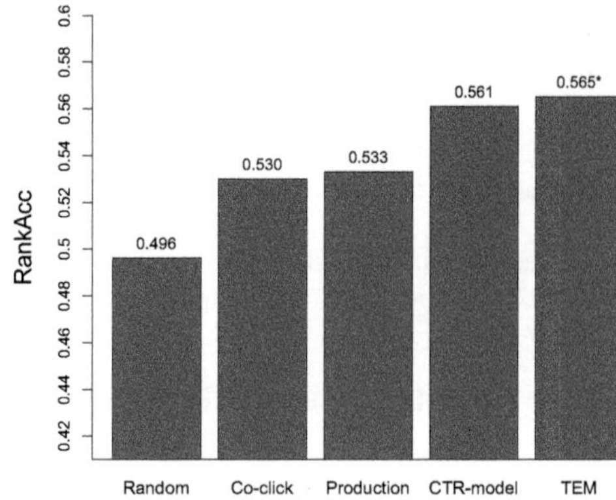

Figure 8: RankAcc for movie recommendation

movies, and thus to recommend related movies based on their preferences. As for celebrity recommendation, we included popular celebrities the users had viewed in the user-specific feature vectors, such as business leaders, musicians, actors and directors. For main entities and related entities, we constructed two different feature sets for the movie task and the celebrity task. For movie recommendation, we extracted the attributes of the movies as features, such as actors, directors, genres, languages, and subjects, whereas the celebrity recommendation model selected the celebrity-related features, such as the movies directed by the directors, the books written by the writers, and their spouses. With the domain-specific feature sets, TEM is able to discover the correlations among the three dimensions for recommending related entities.

In addition to the features listed in Table 3, we obtained the features of click-through rates (CTR) which are considered very strong signals for recommendation. More specifically, based on the entity pane log, we collected r-specific CTRs: $CTR(r)$, (m, r)-specific CTRs: $CTR(m, r)$, and (u, m, r)-specific CTRs: $CTR(u, m, r)$. We also collected from the search log the frequency of entities viewed in the same session. As a result, for movie recommendation there were a total of 1653 features for each user, and 419 features for each main entity and related entity. For celebrity recommendation, there were a total of 1938 features for each user, and 562 features for each main entity and related entity.

5.2 Evaluation strategy

To evaluate the quality of entity recommendation, we split both the movie dataset and the celebrity dataset into a training set and a test set. The test set consisted of the latest page impression for each user, and the training set contained the rest. That is, TEM was used to rank a list of entities related to the last main entity searched by each user.

Let Q be a set of tuples (u, m). For each tuple $(u, m) \in Q$, a recommendation algorithm returns a ranked list of related entities with respect to user u and main entity m. To analyze the recommendation results, we used two evaluation metrics. The first metric was the standard Mean Reciprocal Rank (MRR). The Reciprocal Rank of a ranked list is the multiplicative inverse of the rank of the first hit in the list. The MRR score of a recommendation algorithm is the average reciprocal rank obtained by the ranked lists given by the algorithm with respect to the set Q. Formally,

$$MRR = \frac{1}{|Q|} \sum_{n=1}^{|Q|} \frac{1}{rank^{(n)}}, \quad (17)$$

where $rank^{(n)}$ is the rank of the first clicked entity in the ranked list for the n-th tuple. The other metric used for evaluation was called RankAcc. RankAcc was introduced to measure what fraction of preference orders $r_i \succ r_j$ is captured by a ranked list of recommended entities. Formally, we define RankAcc of a recommendation algorithm as:

$$RankAcc = \frac{1}{|Q|} \sum_{n=1}^{|Q|} \frac{|\{(r_i^{(n)}, r_j^{(n)}) | i < j \wedge r_i^{(n)} \succ r_j^{(n)}\}|}{|\{(r_i^{(n)}, r_j^{(n)}) | i < j\}|}, \quad (18)$$

where i and j are the ranks of related entities r_i and r_j in the ranked list, respectively. So $i < j$ suggests that entity r_i is ranked higher than entity r_j. Therefore, the fraction in Equation (18) gives the number of preference orders $r_i \succ r_j$ consistent with the rank orders out of the total number of pairs (r_i, r_j) induced by the rank.

5.3 Recommendation accuracy

We first evaluated the recommendation quality of the compared algorithms, *Random*, *Co-click*, *Production*, *CTR-model*, and *TEM* on the two real-world datasets. The *Random* approach is a naive algorithm which randomly ranks the related entities in each page impression[3]. *Co-click* exploits the valuable signal that an entity should be recommended for another given entity if and only if the two entities are frequently co-clicked. Specifically, given a main entity m, *Co-click* estimates $p(r|m)$, the conditional probability of recommending related entity r, based on the number of their co-occurrences in the click log. *Co-click* then ranks the entities r by the conditional probabilities $p(r|m)$. The co-click signal by itself has been shown to be very effective and the strongest baseline method for entity recommendation [19]. *Production* represents the recommendation approach currently employed by a commercial search engine. It reflects the state of the art in the specific application by major search engines. *CTR-model* is a simplified version of *TEM*. It builds up the recommendation model in a way similar to *TEM*, except that *CTR-model* only utilizes the CTR features without incorporating the trilinear function $\Phi_{umr}(\eta)$. In essence, *CTR-model* and *TEM* build upon the same probabilistic framework, while different in feature sets used for training. We introduced the *CTR-model* in the interests of investigating the power of the CTR features derived from the entity pane log as well as the power of our probabilistic

[3]The number of related entities presented in each page impression is greatly limited by a user's screen size. It is normally ranging from 3 to 5. As a result, an algorithm which always provides the worst rankings would produce the MRR score approximately 0.25.

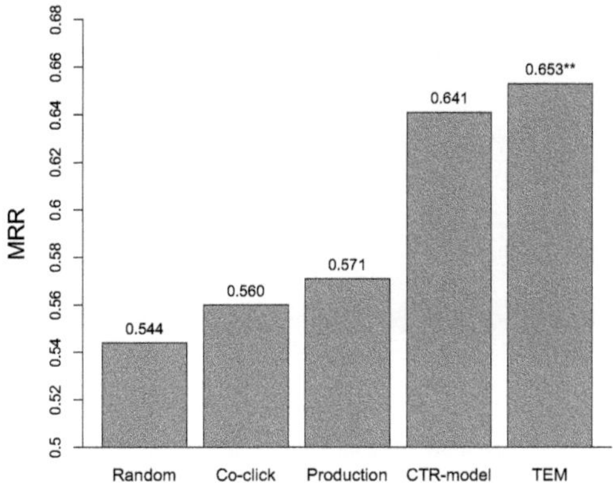

Figure 9: MRR for celebrity recommendation

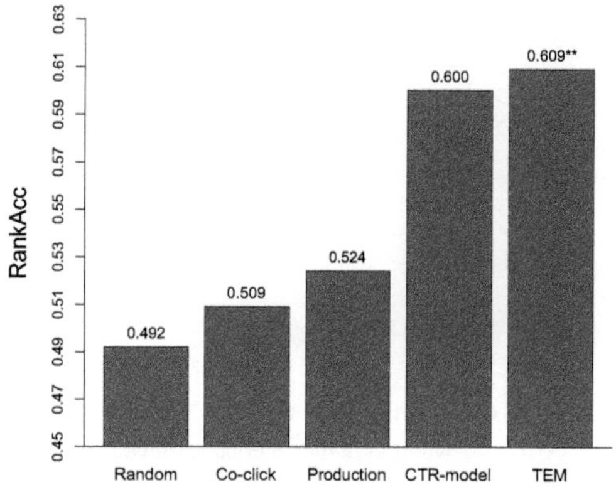

Figure 10: RankAcc for celebrity recommendation

framework. We set $\sigma^2 = 5$ for the Gaussian prior in the probabilistic framework. For the *TEM* model, we set the number of random projection dimensions as 20, since that produced the best recommendations.

Figure 7 shows the MRR score of each algorithm for movie recommendation. From this figure, we observe that the other four methods are clearly superior to the *Random* approach. *Co-click* and *Production* give similar MRR results, as current search engines recommend related entities based on the co-click signal. It is interesting to see that *CTR-model* produces a high MRR result, even better than the state-of-the-art baseline *Production*. This shows the great potential of the click feedback in the entity pane log. Also, it suggests the ability of our probabilistic framework to leverage CTR signals for entity recommendation. To further compare *CTR-model* and *TEM*, we performed a paired t-test which had p-value < 0.05, denoted by $*$. It indicated that the improvement of *TEM* over *CTR-model* is statistically significant. Figure 8 depicts the RankAcc scores of all compared algorithms for movie recommendation. From this figure, we observe the pattern similar to that of Figure 7.

For celebrity recommendation, the MRR and the RankAcc are shown in Figure 9 and Figure 10, respectively. Again, it is observed that *CTR-model* produces much higher MRR and RankAcc than those of both baselines *Co-click* and *Production*, and that *TEM* consistently outperforms all the other methods. To further measure the improvement of *TEM* over *CTR-model*, we performed a paired t-test between the two approaches. The $**$ in both figures indicate p-value < 0.01, which show that *TEM* significantly improves over *CTR-model*.

5.4 Efficacy of personalization

Our *TEM* model personalizes recommendation results by taking the user dimension into consideration. The user dimension captures a user's past interactions with the search engine, such as the various types of entities he or she has viewed and their characteristics. *TEM* analyzes the underlying associations between induced user profiles and their actions on the entity pane to recommend the related entities tailored to their interests.

We took movie recommendation as a case study to investigate the personalization efficacy of *TEM*. Table 4 depicts an example of ranking the movie entities related to the movie *The Great Gatsby* by the four approaches *Co-click*, *Production*, *CTR-model*, and *TEM*. The particular search user was a fan of actor *Leonardo DiCaprio*, who starred in *The Great Gatsby*. Among the four related movies, the user jumped

Table 4: Related movies recommended for a fan of actor Leonardo DiCaprio by *Co-click*, *Production*, *CTR-model*, and *TEM*

User		
A fan of actor Leonardo DiCaprio		
Main movie entity		
The Great Gatsby		
Related movie entities		
Co-click / Production	*CTR-model*	*TEM*
Iron Man 3	Iron Man 3	Django Unchained
Man of Steel	Star Trek (2013)	Iron Man 3
Star Trek (2013)	Django Unchained	Star Trek (2013)
Django Unchained	Man of Steel	Man of Steel

to *Django Unchained* to explore, which is the only movie starring *Leonardo DiCaprio*. Since the user had viewed the entity of *Leonardo DiCaprio*, by analyzing her historical logs *TEM* recognized her interest and thus put *Django Unchained* at the top of the ranked list. On the other hand, the other three approaches failed to customize the ranking of the related movies based on the user's interest.

To further study the personalization efficacy of *TEM*, we conducted a quantitative evaluation. In particular, we first split the movie test set into five subsets based on the numbers of movie entities viewed by the users in the past. The number of users in each test subset is given in Figure 11. It is seen that 42% of users have viewed at least one movie entity in our log. The methods *Co-click*, *Production*, *CTR-model*, and *TEM* were used to recommend related movies for the users in each test set to evaluate their efficacy of personalization. Figure 12 shows the MRR scores of each algorithm on each test set. From this figure, it is observed that the three methods *Co-click*, *Production* and *CTR-model* produce consistent MRR results across the different test sets in spite of the drop for the "7∼9" set[4]. This suggests that the unique preference of an individual user has little effect on the three methods for customizing the recommendation results. Our *TEM* model, however, increases the MRR as users have viewed an increasing number of movie entities. This confirms *TEM*'s ability to personalize recommended entities. Enriching user profiles will potentially improve the quality of recommendation of *TEM* for users.

5.5 Effect of random projections

In this section, we investigate the effect of random projections on the quality of recommendation for *TEM*. In par-

[4]The MRR for the test set "7∼9" is not statistically reliable given the small number of users in the set.

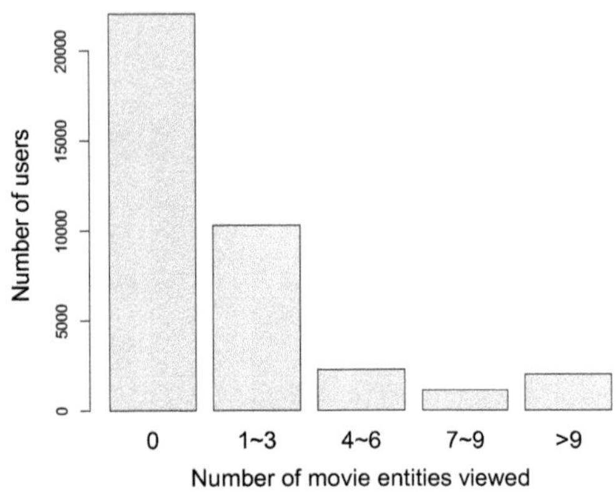

Figure 11: User distribution over the numbers of movie entities viewed in the past

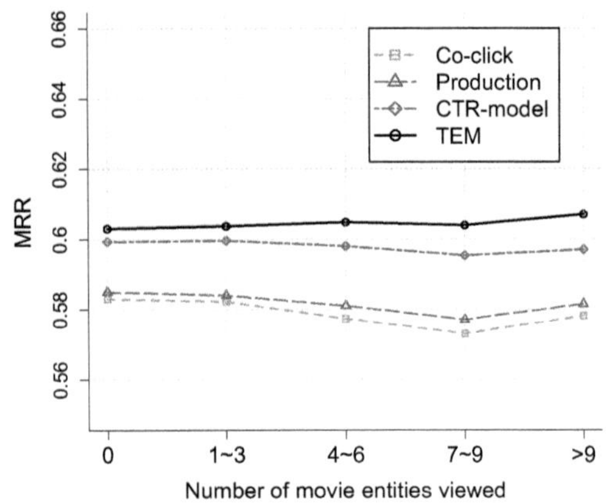

Figure 12: MRR for varying numbers of movie entities viewed in the past

ticular, we applied *TEM* to the training data of varying-dimensional feature space produced by random projections, and computed MRR for each random projection dimension. Figure 13 plots the MRR scores of the two recommendation tasks for different random projection dimensions. We observe that as more dimensions were used, *TEM* produced better recommendation results for both tasks. This is not surprising because increasing the number of random projection dimensions increases the capacity of the *TEM* model by giving it more tunable parameters, and also preserves more information about the original data.

6. CONCLUSION

This paper addresses the problem of recommending entities related to the main entity returned to a user by a web search engine. We propose the probabilistic model TEM, which leverages the three data sources, *knowledge base*, *search click log*, and *entity pane log*, for personalized recommendation of related entities. The TEM model not only utilizes the CTR signals derived from the entity pane log, but also exploits the three-way relationships among *user*, *main entity*, and *related entity*. Experimental results on movie recommendation and celebrity recommendation show that TEM with our probabilistic framework significantly improves over the state of the art technique employed by a major search engine. This confirms the effectiveness of TEM and the probabilistic framework on related entity recommendation.

7. REFERENCES

[1] E. Acar and B. Yener. Unsupervised multiway data analysis: A literature survey. *IEEE TKDE*, 2009.

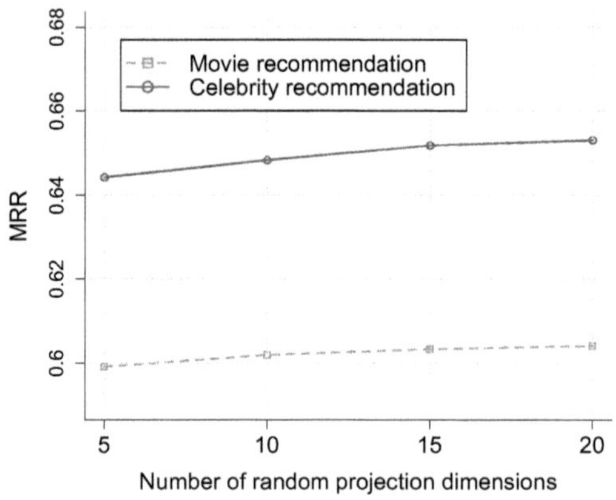

Figure 13: MRR for varying random projection dimensions

[2] J.-w. Ahn, P. Brusilovsky, J. Grady, D. He, and S. Y. Syn. Open user profiles for adaptive news systems: Help or harm? In *Proc. of WWW '07*, pages 11–20, Canada, 2007.

[3] C. Ai and E. C. Norton. Interaction terms in logit and probit models. *Economics Letters*, 80(1):123 – 129, 2003.

[4] R. Blanco, B. B. Cambazoglu, P. Mika, and N. Torzec. Entity recommendations in web search. In *International Semantic Web Conference (2)*, pages 33–48. Springer, 2013.

[5] R. Burke. Hybrid systems for personalized recommendations. In *Proc. of ITWP '03*, pages 133–152, Acapulco, Mexico, 2005.

[6] W. Chu and S.-T. Park. Personalized recommendation on dynamic content using predictive bilinear models. In *Pro. of WWW '09*, pages 691–700, Madrid, Spain, 2009.

[7] R. Coppi and S. Bolasco, editors. *Multiway data analysis.* North-Holland Publishing Co., Amsterdam, 1989.

[8] Y. Inagaki, N. Sadagopan, G. Dupret, A. Dong, C. Liao, Y. Chang, and Z. Zheng. Session based click features for recency ranking. In *Proc. of AAAI '10.* AAAI Press.

[9] P. Indyk and R. Motwani. Approximate nearest neighbors: Towards removing the curse of dimensionality. In *Proc. of STOC '98*, pages 604–613, Dallas, Texas, USA, 1998.

[10] A. Karatzoglou, X. Amatriain, L. Baltrunas, and N. Oliver. Multiverse recommendation: N-dimensional tensor factorization for context-aware collaborative filtering. In *Proc. of RecSys '10*, pages 79–86, Barcelona, Spain, 2010.

[11] A. Mehta, A. Saberi, U. Vazirani, and V. Vazirani. Adwords and generalized online matching. *Journal of the ACM*, 54(5), Oct. 2007.

[12] A. Micarelli, F. Gasparetti, F. Sciarrone, and S. Gauch. The adaptive web. chapter Personalized Search on the World Wide Web, pages 195–230. Berlin, Heidelberg, 2007.

[13] J. Nocedal and S. Wright. *Numerical Optimization.* Springer series in operations research and financial engineering. Springer, New York, NY, 2nd edition, 2006.

[14] S. Rendle and L. Schmidt-Thieme. Pairwise interaction tensor factorization for personalized tag recommendation. In *Proc. of WSDM '10*, pages 81–90, New York, USA, 2010.

[15] M. Speretta and S. Gauch. Personalized search based on user search histories. In *Proc. of WI '05*, pages 622–628, Washington, DC, USA, 2005.

[16] J.-T. Sun, H.-J. Zeng, H. Liu, Y. Lu, and Z. Chen. Cubesvd: A novel approach to personalized web search. In *Proc. of WWW '05*, pages 382–390, Chiba, Japan, 2005.

[17] L. R. Tucker. The extension of factor analysis to three-dimensional matrices. In *Contributions to mathematical psychology.*, pages 110–127. New York, 1964.

[18] M. A. O. Vasilescu and D. Terzopoulos. Multilinear image analysis for facial recognition. In *Proc. of ICPR '02*, pages 511–514, 2002.

[19] X. Yu, H. Ma, B.-J. P. Hsu, and J. Han. On building entity recommender systems using user click log and freebase knowledge. In *Proc. of WSDM '14*, pages 263–272, New York, NY, USA, 2014.

Will This Paper Increase Your h-index? Scientific Impact Prediction

Yuxiao Dong
Dept. of Computer Science and Engineering, and iCeNSA
University of Notre Dame
Notre Dame, IN 46556
ydong1@nd.edu

Reid A. Johnson
Dept. of Computer Science and Engineering, and iCeNSA
University of Notre Dame
Notre Dame, IN 46556
rjohns15@nd.edu

Nitesh V. Chawla
Dept. of Computer Science and Engineering, and iCeNSA
University of Notre Dame
Notre Dame, IN 46556
nchawla@nd.edu

ABSTRACT

Scientific impact plays a central role in the evaluation of the output of scholars, departments, and institutions. A widely used measure of scientific impact is citations, with a growing body of literature focused on predicting the number of citations obtained by any given publication. The effectiveness of such predictions, however, is fundamentally limited by the power-law distribution of citations, whereby publications with few citations are extremely common and publications with many citations are relatively rare. Given this limitation, in this work we instead address a related question asked by many academic researchers in the course of writing a paper, namely: "Will this paper increase my h-index?" Using a real academic dataset with over 1.7 million authors, 2 million papers, and 8 million citation relationships from the premier online academic service ArnetMiner, we formalize a novel scientific impact prediction problem to examine several factors that can drive a paper to increase the primary author's h-index. We find that the researcher's authority on the publication topic and the venue in which the paper is published are crucial factors to the increase of the primary author's h-index, while the topic popularity and the co-authors' h-indices are of surprisingly little relevance. By leveraging relevant factors, we find a greater than 87.5% potential predictability for whether a paper will contribute to an author's h-index within five years. As a further experiment, we generate a self-prediction for *this* paper, estimating that there is a 76% probability that it will contribute to the h-index of the co-author with the highest current h-index in five years. We conclude that our findings on the quantification of scientific impact can help researchers to expand their influence and more effectively leverage their position of "standing on the shoulders of giants."

Categories and Subject Descriptors

H.2.8 [**Database Management**]: Database Applications—*Data Mining*; H.3.7 [**Information Search and Retrieval**]: Digital Libraries

Keywords

Scientific impact; Science of science; Citation prediction; Popularity prediction

WSDM 2015, February 02 - 06 2015, Shanghai, China

http://dx.doi.org/10.1145/2684822.2685314.

1. INTRODUCTION

Integral to the success of scientific research is the publication and dissemination of impactful work and findings.

Every scientific researcher leaves his or her own indelible mark on an ever-expanding body of literature through a personal track-record of academic publications. The impact of each of these publications—both to a field of research and, by extension, to the reputation of the author—can be influenced by a variety of factors. For example, significant research work may start from a small number of exploratory papers that builds up to pioneering work within a field, resulting in a series of less impactful papers that serve as stepping-stones to those of greater impact. Or a researcher may publish in different fields each with differing audiences and levels of popularity, resulting in publications on some topics receiving more attention than those on others. Or, along with many publications that incrementally advance a field, a researcher may produce a groundbreaking work that transforms the field or even stimulates a new research area. As a result of such factors, a researcher's body of work is likely to be comprised of publications of varying impact. Accordingly, the impact of any particular publication can be difficult to predict.

Yet while the impact of individual publications may vary, a researcher's influence and productivity is measured by his or her body of work as a whole. Often, the researcher's total number of citations is used as a measure of impact, while the researcher's total number of publications is used as a measure of productivity. However, while these simple measures can be useful, they can also have drawbacks. For example, the total number of citations can be skewed by the impact of a solitary well-cited, impactful paper. Similarly, the total number of publications can be increased by a large number of poorly cited papers. Moreover, as citations demonstrate a power law distribution, with the vast majority of publications receiving few citations, these simple measures are difficult to estimate using traditional regression analysis [15, 5]. Thus, answering the question of how many citations a given paper will receive is often ineffective for practical purposes.

In light of these difficulties and limitations, we instead address an analogous question asked by many academic researchers in the course of writing a paper: "Will *this* paper increase my h-index?"

The h-index is an index that attempts to measure both the productivity and impact of the published work of a scientist or scholar. The index was suggested in 2005 by Jorge E. Hirsch as a tool for determining theoretical physicists' relative quality, and is based on the distribution of citations received by a given researcher's publications. As described by Hirsch: "A scientist has index h if h of his/her N_p papers have at least h citations each, and the other $(N_p - h)$ papers have no more than h citations each" [8]. In other words, a scholar with an index of h has published h papers, each of which has been cited in other papers at least h times. Thus, the h-index is a function of both the number of publications and the number of citations per publication.

The index is designed to improve upon simpler measures such as the total number of citations or publications. Moreover, because only the most highly cited articles contribute to the h-index, its determination is a relatively simpler process. Hirsch has demonstrated that h has high predictive value for whether a scientist has won honors like National Academy membership or the Nobel Prize [8]. As a result of its simplicity and predictive value, the h-index has become a *de facto* standard for measuring academic performance and scientific impact.

Contributions. In this work, we formalize the question of whether a paper will influence an author's h-index as a novel scientific impact prediction problem. Our prediction task is to determine whether a given paper will, within a pre-defined timeframe, increase the h-index of its primary author (i.e., the researcher with the maximum h-index among the paper's author list). Factors such as the researcher's current influence, the publication topic, and the publication venue may, among many other factors, play a role in determining the degree to which the publication contributes to the researcher's influence. A resulting challenge is the interplay of such factors, which can confound attempts to generate effective predictions. Considerations such as the variability of the h-index according to the "academic age" of a researcher, the widely differing citation conventions among different fields, and the co-authorship of researchers with differing h-indices can make it difficult to isolate the nature and degree to which a given researcher's h-index is influenced by any particular factor. Our work focuses on addressing and overcoming these issues to generate novel, effective scientific impact predictions and to investigate precisely what role a variety of factors play in these predictions.

Given the task of predicting whether a publication will contribute to an author's h-index, we find surprisingly strong performance for the problem of scientific impact prediction. Our results demonstrate that we can predict whether a paper will contribute to an author's h-index within five years with an F_1 score of 0.776 as shown in Figure 1. Our study further finds that the most telling factors for determining whether a given paper will contribute to the primary author's h-index are the author's authority on the publication topic and the venue in which the paper is published (see Figure 1 blue bars). In contrast, we find that the popularity of the publication topic and the co-authors' h-indices are surprisingly inconsequential for determining whether the paper will contribute to the primary author's h-index (see Figure 1 orange and red bars). We also find that (1) the contribution of papers to researchers with higher h-indices is more difficult to predict than it is for researcher's with lower h-indices (cf. Figure 1 a vs. b and c vs. d); and (2) the task is more predictable given a long timeframe than a short one (cf. Figure 1 a vs. c and b vs. d). Overall, our findings unveil mechanisms for quantifying scientific impact and provide concrete suggestions to researchers for better expanding their scientific influence and, ultimately, for more effectively "standing on the shoulders of giants."

A potential concern with this work is that by targeting the h-index, our findings may result in unintended side effects by a principle referred to by economists as Goodhart's Law. The law essentially says that once a measure is chosen as a performance indicator it begins to lose value, as measurement can distort the practice being measured. Restated more succinctly by [19], it means that "when a measure becomes a target, it ceases to be a good measure." Be that as it may, we believe that understanding the characteristics of scientific impact measures is imperative to their informed use,

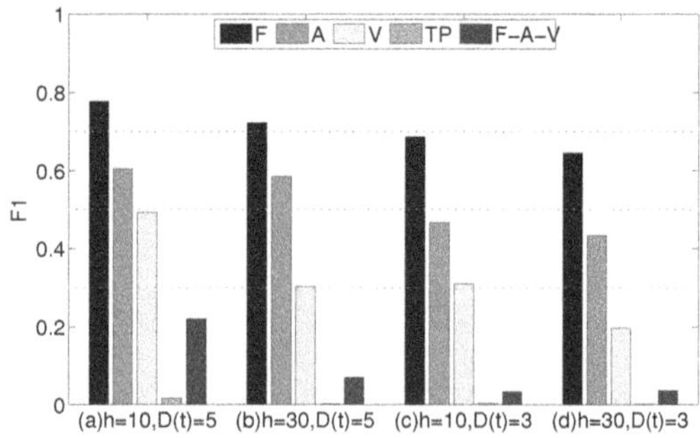

Figure 1: Predictability of whether one paper will increase the h-index ($\geq h$) of its primary author within $D(t)$ years. F: full factor set; A: only authority factors; V: only venue factors; TP: only topic popularity factors; F-A-V: full factors without authority and venue factors.

and *in no way should our research be construed as advocating the use of the h-index as a deciding factor in one's research pursuits.*

2. DATA AND PROBLEM

In this section, we first describe the academic data we use, then characterize the h-index from the data, and finally formalize our predictive task—that is, scientific impact prediction.

2.1 Data Description

In this paper, we use the real-world academic dataset[1] from ArnetMiner [23], which is the world-leading free online service for academic social network analysis and mining. The dataset contains 1,712,433 authors with 2,092,356 papers from computer science venues held between 1960 and 2012. Each paper includes information on the title, abstract, authorship, references, and publication venue and year. In total, the dataset represents 4,258,615 collaboration relationships and 8,024,869 citation relationships.

Next, we briefly explore and report the data characteristics of the author-paper-citation data. Figure 2 shows the distributions of the number of citations for each paper and the h-index of each author. In our dataset, both metrics follow heavy-tailed distributions (i.e., distributions with a "tail" that is "heavier" than that of an exponential). Moreover, only 6.91% (154,985) of the papers have more than 50 citations, while 0.0125% (159) of the researchers have an h-index over 60.

Characterizations of the h-index. The h-index is defined as the number of papers with citation number $\geq h$, which is a useful index to characterize the scientific output of a researcher [8]. Figure 3 presents the basic characteristics of scientific impact in terms of h-index. Positive linear relationships are clearly observed between the h-index and the number of papers, average number of citations, and number of co-authors in Figures 3(a), 3(b), and 3(c), respectively. Figure 3(b) shows that the average number of citations for each author is larger than her/his h-index. Figure 3(d) illustrates the ratio between one's h-index and the number of papers conditioned on her/his h-index. This ratio initially decreases, stabilizing after an h-index of about 20. From Figure 3(e), we see that the h-indices of one's co-authors increase as her/his h-index grows. The reversion point between author and co-author h-indices occurs when one's h-index reaches about 8 or 9, a typical point at which

[1]The dataset is publicly available at `http://arnetminer.org/citation` and `http://arnetminer.org/AMinerNetwork`.

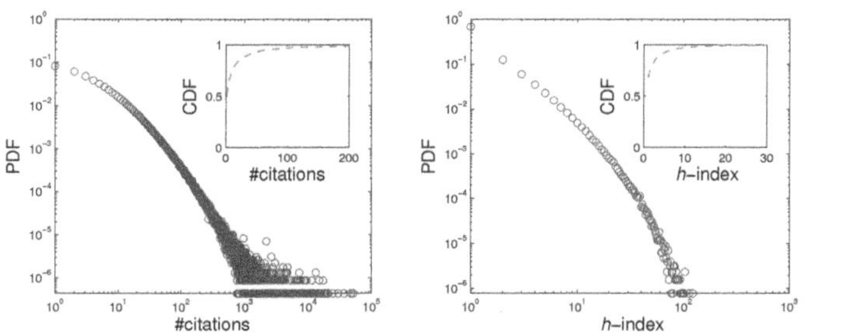

(a) Distribution of citations counts (b) h-index distribution

Figure 2: Distributions of the citation counts of papers and the h-indices of authors. The heavy-tailed distributions indicate that the prediction of both metrics is not fit for regression problems. In this dataset, 6.91% (154,985) of the papers obtain more than 50 citations and 0.0125% (159) of the researchers have h-indices greater than 60.

Ph.D. students graduate. Finally, in Figure 3(f), we examine the interplay between authors' h-index and the length of time they spend in academia (the date difference between one's first and last publications). Clearly, we see that the increase of h-index is initially slow upon first entering academia. As the h-index increases, the accumulations of influence, resources, connections, and previous papers further drive one's h-index and scientific impact expands at an increasingly rapid rate. In other words, the aphorism that "the rich get richer" is demonstrated in academia, whereby the influence of individuals who have already accumulated a great deal of influence increases at a disproportionally quick rate. All characteristics are observed at a 95% confidence interval.

2.2 Problem Definition

Traditionally, the task of scientific impact prediction is formulated as a regression problem for predicting citation counts [28]. However, the intrinsically heavy tailed distribution of citation counts, demonstrated in Figure 2(a), make such predictions necessarily skewed [5]. Alternatively, given a threshold c for the citation count, the task can be formulated as a classification problem—that is, a problem of inferring whether the number of citations for a given paper will reach c. Even with this formulation, the way in which citation counts are distributed presents inherent challenges, including how to determine the threshold c and how to avoid the overrepresentation or underrepresentation of different papers. Similar issues also arise for predicting the h-index of each author.

Our approach is inspired by the work of [5], where the authors consider the problem of Facebook cascade growth prediction. They formulate the problem as a binary classification task where, given the first k reshares of content within a cascade, they are tasked with predicting whether the cascade will reach $2k$. For our work, we formulate an analogous task: Given a paper, we predict whether that paper will increase the h-index of the authors in the future. We formalize the problem of scientific impact prediction next.

Problem 1. **Scientific Impact Prediction:** Given the publication corpus C before timestamp t, each paper (document) $d \in C$ published in timestamp t, and the primary author's h-index (max-h-index) among the authors of d, the task is to predict whether the number of citations for each paper d will reach max-h-index after a given time period Δt.

The primary author is defined as the author of the given paper with the highest h-index. We address the issues noted above by using a local threshold max-h-index for each paper's future citation count. For example, according to Google Scholar, as of Nov. 25th, 2014, Dr. Yizhou Sun and Dr. Jiawei Han's h-indices are 19 and 125, respectively. By setting $t = 2014$ and $\Delta t = 3$ years, we aim to predict whether each of Dr. Sun's papers (assuming her h-index is larger than each of her co-authors') published in 2014 will get more than 19 citations by 2017. But if one paper is co-authored by Dr. Sun and Dr. Han, the task becomes to infer whether this paper's citation count will reach 125 by 2017. Realistically, the authors' h-indices may increase during the duration Δt, but it is intractable to capture this evolution in detail. In this sense, we consider the objective of collecting citations for each paper as static and leave the evolving case for future work.

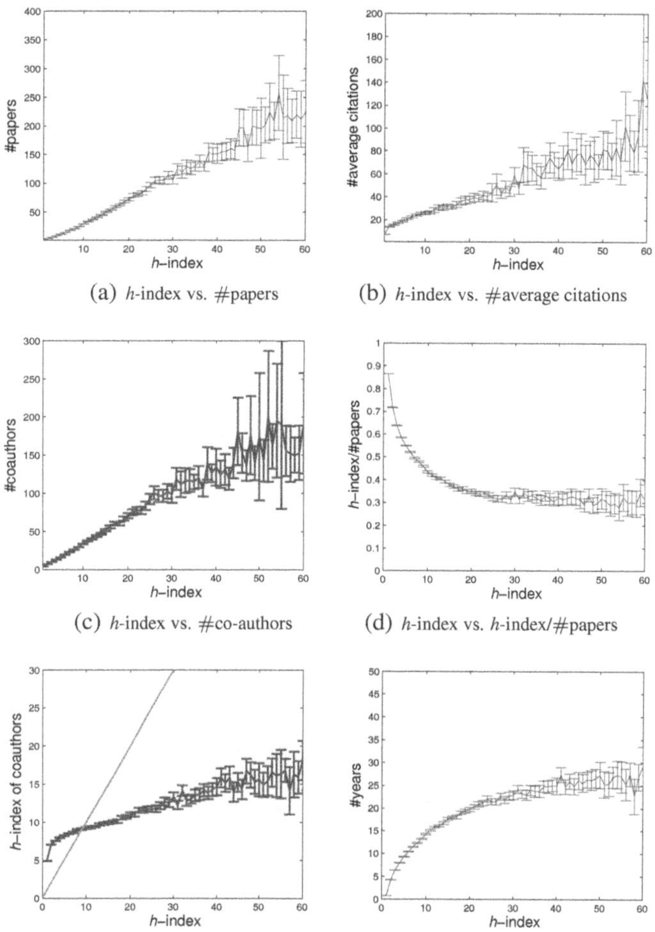

(a) h-index vs. #papers (b) h-index vs. #average citations (c) h-index vs. #co-authors (d) h-index vs. h-index/#papers (e) h-index vs. co-authors' h-index (f) h-index vs. #years

Figure 3: Characterizations of the h-index. (b) The average number of citations for each author is larger than her/his h-index. (d) The ratio between one's h-index (≥ 20) and her/his number of papers stabilize at 0.3. (e) Typically, the author's h-index becomes larger than the co-authors' h-indices at the expected point of the author's Ph.D. graduation. (f) The rate at which the h-index increases itself increases as the length of time spent in academia becomes longer (*i.e., the rich get richer*).

This proposed problem of scientific impact prediction is completely different from the cascade growth prediction problem [5], which needs the observation of the first k reshares (citations), and further predicts the future reshare counts. Our problem is also fundamentally different from the traditional citation count prediction problem [28], which focuses on the regression task to predict scientific impact. In contrast, our problem is to predict each paper's future impact conditioned on the authors. The chief advantage of this proposed formulation is that it can be leveraged for a variety of real-world applications, such as author h-index and popularity prediction [18], expert finding [31], and credit allocation [17, 11].

3. SCIENTIFIC IMPACT FACTORS

To quantify scientific impact, it is natural to use the number of citations obtained by each paper and its authors. Recall that given a paper d, our objective is to predict whether the number of citations c_d obtained within a given time period Δt will be larger than its primary author's h-index (denoted as max-h-index). We investigate the factors that drive a paper's citation count to become greater than its primary author's h-index, including the paper's author(s), content, published venue, and references, as well as social and temporal effects related to its author(s). Table 1 lists the six different groups of factors investigated. Figures 4 and 5 show the importance of different factors as evaluated by correlation coefficients. In Figure 4, we present the changes of factor importance as predicted for scholars with different h-indices. In Figure 5, the changes of factor correlation are plotted as the time period Δt is varied.

3.1 Author Factors

The predictive task for each paper naturally depends on the authors themselves, including both the primary author and his or her co-authors. Prior work has been devoted to examining the interplay between scientific impact (number of citations) and the average values of authors' attributes [28, 4]. Given our problem formulation, we also investigate the attributes of the primary author of each paper, such as the ratio of the author's previous papers contributing to his or her h-index. Additionally, as the first author usually leads the collaboration, the spread of a paper's scientific impact also relies highly on the impact of the first author. We thus consider the probability that the number of citations obtained by the first author's previous publications is greater than the primary author's h-index. Further, the overall impact of all co-authors should have the potential to influence a paper's quality and popularity. Thus the sum of all authors' h-indices is used to simulate their overall impact. Since each paper has a unique local threshold (max-h-index) in our classification problem, we calculate the relative value of each factor by dividing it by the max-h-index. For example, the first author's h-index divided by the max-h-index is designed to model the author's effect on the success of the paper. Moreover, the author's productivity, i.e., the number of his or her previous publications, has a positive effect on the future citation counts of the paper due to self-citation behavior [2].

Significance. Figure 4(a) and 5(a) clearly show that *A-max-ratio* of one paper—i.e., the ratio between the max-h-index and the number of papers attributed to its primary author—has the highest correlation with the probability that it will collect at least max-h-index citations among all seven author factors. We also observe that the author factor correlations are not sensitive to the two parameters, illustrated by the lower thresholds for the primary author's h-index and Δt.

3.2 Content Factors

Aside from the attributes of its authors, another intuitive factor affecting a paper's success is its content. Topic modeling is a widely used method for extracting and mining the content of literature and can be used to extract "topics" that occur in a collection of documents. One of the most popular topic modeling methods is known as Latent Dirichlet Allocation (LDA), a generative probabilistic approach that views each document as a mixture of various topics [3]. Similar to previous work on modeling citation counts [28], we run a 100-topic LDA model on the title and abstract of the corpus C published before time t and the target papers published at time t, which returns the probability distribution $p(z|d)$ over topics $z \in Z$ assigned for each paper d. We define the following features based on each paper's topic distribution, including popularity, novelty, diversity, and authority.

First, we consider that as popular topics attract more attention, it is relatively easy for papers related to such topics to accrue citations. To capture this effect, we quantify the popularity of each topic z across the overall corpus by

$$popularity(z) = \sum_{d \in C} p(z|d) \times c_d,$$

where $p(z|d)$ is the probability that paper d distributes on topic z and c_d is the number of citations d collects until the timestamp t. Given one target paper d_t at time t, its popularity is defined as

$$\textit{C-popularity}(d_t) = \sum_{z \in Z} popularity(z) \times p(z|d_t). \quad (1)$$

Second, the novelty of a paper is considered an essential factor in assessing its contribution to the scientific community. Previous work assumes that the novelty of an article can be determined by measuring the difference between its content and that of its references [28]. We utilize the Kullback-Leibler divergence [12] to capture the sum of the difference between d_t's topic distribution and the topic distribution of each of its references. Specifically,

$$\textit{C-novelty}(d_t) = \frac{\sum_{d_r \in R} KL(p(Z|d_t), p(Z|d_r))}{|R|} \quad (2)$$

$$KL(p(Z|d_t), p(Z|d_r)) = \sum_{z \in Z} \log \frac{p(z|d_t)}{p(z|d_r)} p(z|d_t),$$

where R is the set of d_t's references.

Third, the topic diversity of a paper, defined as the breadth of its topic distribution, is able to distinguish between different types of papers, such as between surveys and technical work. We follow the definition of diversity in [28] as calculated by Shannon entropy:

$$\textit{C-diversity}(d_t) = \sum_{z \in Z} -p(z|d_t) \log p(z|d_t). \quad (3)$$

Fourth, Kleinberg has pointed out that, in a hyperlinked web environment, a good authority represents a page that is linked by many hubs [10]. Similarly, authority in academia is denoted by being highly cited by others in a specific domain of expertise. To measure the authority of researcher a on topic z, we propose the following definition:

$$authority(a, z) = \sum_{d \in C_a} p(z|d) \times c_d,$$

where C_a is the researcher a's previous publications. Therefore, given the target paper d_t, the author's authority is distributed over the topic distribution of d_t, i.e.,

$$\textit{C-authority}(d_t, a) = \sum_{z \in Z} p(z|d_t) \times authority(a, z). \quad (4)$$

This definition of authority comes from the intuition that the correspondence between the paper's topic distribution and its authors' expertise help assure its quality.

Table 1: Factor Definition. We employ six categories of factors, comprised of author, topic, reference, social, venue, and temporal attributes. max-*h*-index denotes the *h*-index of the primary author (i.e., the author with the maximum *h*-index) of a given paper.

	Factor	Description
Author	*A-first-max*	The first author's h-index divided by the max-h-index.
	A-ave-max	The average h-index of all authors divided by the max-h-index.
	A-sum-max	The sum of h-indices divided by the max-h-index.
	A-first-ratio	The ratio between max-h-index and the number of papers attributed to the first author.
	A-max-ratio	The ratio between max-h-index and the number of papers attributed to the primary author.
	A-num-authors	The number of authors of the given paper.
	A-num-first	The number of papers by the first author.
Content	*C-popularity*	The average number of citations over different topics (see Eq. 1).
	C-popularity-ratio	The average number of citations over different topics divided by the max-h-index.
	C-novelty	The topic novelty of this paper (see Eq. 2).
	C-diversity	The topic diversity of this paper (see Eq. 3).
	C-authority-first	The consistence between the first author's authority and this paper (see Eq. 4).
	C-authority-max	The consistence between the primary author's authority and this paper.
	C-authority-ave	The average consistence between each author's authority and this paper.
Venue	*V-ratio-max*	The ratio between the number of papers $\geq$max-h-index citations divided by the max-h-index.
	V-citation	The average number of citations of all references divided by the max-h-index.
Social	*S-degree*	The number of co-authors of the paper's authors.
	S-pagerank	The PageRank values of the paper's authors in the weighted collaboration network.
	S-h-co-author	The average h-index of co-authors of the paper's authors divided by the max-h-index.
	S-h-weight	The weighted average h-index of co-authors of the paper's authors divided by the max-h-index.
Reference	*R-ratio-max*	The ratio between the number of references $\geq$max-h-index and the total number of references.
	R-citation	The average number of citations divided by the maximum h-index.
Temporal	*T-ave-h*	The average Δh-indices of the authors between now and three years ago.
	T-max-h	The maximum Δh-index between now and three years ago.
	T-h-first	The Δh-index of the first author between now and three years ago.
	T-h-max	The Δh-index of the max-h-index author between now and three years ago.

Significance. From Figures 4(b) and 5(b), we find that there is a strong correlation between a paper's probability of contributing to its primary author's h-index and the authority-based content factors from that paper. Perhaps surprisingly, the current topic popularity and the diversity or novelty of the paper's content have much lower correlations than its authors' expertise. This observation suggests that, when authoring a paper, rather than following the current trend or hot topic, it is more important to instead focus on what one is good at. Finally, the increase of the primary author's h-index is accompanied by a corresponding rise in the importance of several authority factors, indicating that highly influential scholars are more easily recognized as the experts and authorities in their respective fields.

3.3 Venue Factors

Top venues attract high-quality submissions, and high-quality submissions elevate the reputation of their respective venues. Google Scholar metrics show that different venues have large differences in their $h5$-indices[2], which is defined as the h-index when only considering articles published within the last 5 complete years. For example, in the field of data mining and analysis, the top three venues are ACM SIGKDD, IEEE TKDE, and ACM WSDM, with $h5$-indices of 69, 57, and 54, respectively. In contrast, most other venues in this field typically have $h5$-indices between 10 and 20. In light of these differences, we engage in the investigation of how different venues influence the probability that a paper contributes to the author's h-index. Two heuristic metrics are examined, namely (1) the average number of citations each paper in the venue collects and (2) the ratio between the number of papers in the venue with at least max-h-index citations to the venue's total number of papers. Every researcher aims to publish scientific results in well-respected journals and conferences, so our intuition is that top venues help researchers spread their scientific impact and, more specifically, to increase the citation counts of their papers, which further offers a large potential to increase their h-indices.

3.4 Social Factors

Previous studies show that researchers have the tendency to cite their co-authors' work [2]. As shown in Figure 3(c), our preliminary results show that a researcher's h-index is also positively correlated with his or her total number of collaborators/co-authors. To explore this trend, we extract a weighted collaboration network from the dataset, where each author is denoted as a node, and each link between two nodes is connected if the researchers have col-

[2] `http://scholar.google.com/citations?view_op=top_venues&hl=en`. Accessed on Nov. 25th, 2014.

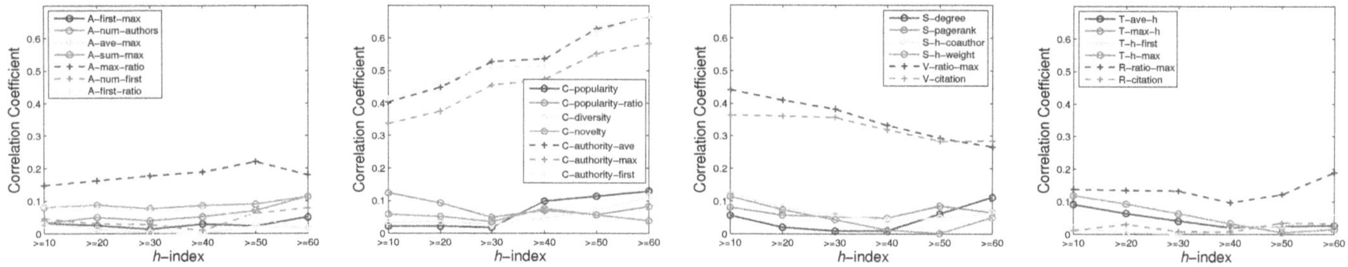

(a) Author factors (b) Content factors (c) Social and venue factors (d) Reference and temporal factors

Figure 4: Factor correlation analysis when predicting for scholars with different h-indices. t=2007 and Δt=5 years. Author's authority on a subject and published venue are the most highly correlated factors.

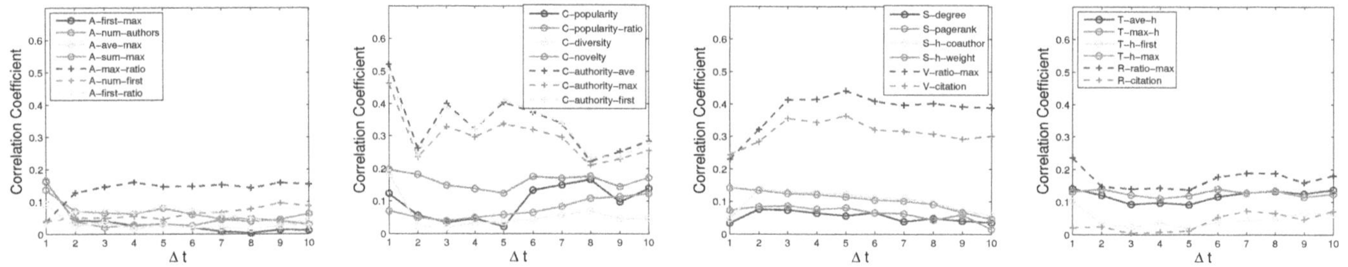

(a) Author factors (b) Content factors (c) Social and venue factors (d) Reference and temporal factors

Figure 5: Factor correlation analysis as the time period Δt is varied. Note that t=2007 and a minimum threshold for the primary author's h-index is set to 10.

laborated with each other. The weight of each link is defined as the frequency of collaborations. We then extract four attributes for each node (author) from the collaboration network, including the number of co-authors (degree), the PageRank score, the average h-index of co-authors, and the weighted average h-index of co-authors. For a given paper, the highest values among its authors for these four metrics are used as social factors.

Significance. The factor correlations of social and venue factors are shown in Figures 4(c) and 5(c). Both subfigures demonstrate the prominently positive correlation of venue factors. This discovery coincides with the fact that the scientific researchers have the highly motivated tendency to publish results in top venues. Perhaps more interestingly, the correlation between several venue factors and researchers' h-indices decreases as the researchers' h-indices increase. This indicates that gathering into leading venues can help to initially elevate researchers' reputations, but it is the researchers' growing peer-influence itself, rather than the venue, that further increases their prominence. Nevertheless, compared to venue factors, social factors have only a limited correlation with whether a paper will increase its primary author's h-index.

3.5 Reference Factors

The scientific impact of a scholarly work is often quantified by its respective citation count. In this way, the more times a publication is cited by others, the larger its assumed impact. Conversely, as most scientific research is undertaken by "standing on the shoulder of giants," we ask whether highly cited papers actually tend to acknowledge the previous "giants" upon whom they stand. Two intuitive factors are used to evaluate this question, namely (1) the ratio of a paper references that have at least max-h-index citations to the paper's total number of references and (2) the average number of citations accumulated by the paper's references.

3.6 Temporal Factors

As fast-rising phenomena typically attract the attention of crowds more easily, a "rising star" in academia can attract publicity. Previous work has found that temporal information can be a powerful factor in modeling scientific impact [2, 28], so it seems straightforward that the speed at which an author's h-index grows should affect the rate at which her/his papers contribute to her/his h-index. To capture this effect, we examine the increase of authors' h-indices within the past three years. Specifically, we consider four temporal factors, including the h-index changes of the first author, the max-h-index author, and the average change and maximum change among all authors. The specific definitions are shown in Table 1.

Significance. From Figures 4(d) and 5(d), we can see that among the reference and temporal factors, *R-ratio-max*, i.e., the ratio between the number of references that have accumulated at least max-h-index citations and the total number of references, demonstrates the most influence on the success of h-index contribution. Other important factors are illustrated by the rising trends of both the primary author's h-index and all authors' average h-index. However, their effects are more pronounced for the young "rising star" (low h-index) than for the established, highly influential "giants" (high h-index).

3.7 Summary

According to the correlation analysis above, we provide the following intuitions relating to academia:

- A scientific researcher's authority on a topic is the most decisive factor in facilitating an increase in his or her h-index. This coincides with the fact that the society fellows (e.g., ACM/IEEE fellow or membership of NAS/NAE) or lifetime honors (e.g., Turing award) are typically awarded for contributions to a topic or domain.

- The level of the venue in which a given paper is published is another crucial factor in determining the probability that it will contribute to its authors' h-indices. Top venues make one outstanding and expand one's scientific impact; gradually, one's impact further helps to increase the venue's prestige. The suggestion here lies in the every scholar's aim: *Target and publish influential scientific results in top venues.*

- People in social society often follow vogue trends. However, publishing on an academically "hot" but unfamiliar topic is unlikely to further one's scientific impact, at least as measured by an increase in one's h-index. This reminds us that *one should not turn to follow the vogue topics that are beyond his or her expertise.*

4. EXPERIMENTS

In this section, we demonstrate the predictability of whether a paper will contribute to its primary author's h-index within a given timeframe.

4.1 Experimental Setup

The task is to predict whether the papers published in time t will contribute to the h-indices of the authors (the max-h-index author for each paper) within a given time period Δt. For example, by setting $t = 2007$, $\Delta t = 5$ years, and the minimum max-h-index to 10, we collect all the papers published in 2007, extract the features from the corpus before 2007, and observe whether the number of citations for each paper in 2007 is larger than or equal to the maximum h-index of its authors in 2012 (the last year represented in our dataset).

Methods. As our problem is formulated as a classification task, we use a series of different classifiers, including logistic regression (LRC), random forest (RF), and bagged decision trees (BAG). While we also generated experiments using support vector machines, naïve Bayes models, and neural networks, we found that their performance was very poor compared to the other three methods; thus their results have been omitted. Due to its predictive ability, ease of implementation, and interpretability, we primarily use logistic regression to analyze factor contributions and parameter settings.

Evaluation. We employ half of the instances for training and the remaining half for validation. To quantitatively evaluate the predictability of the problem, we report the performance in terms of precision, recall, F_1 score, area under the receiver operating characteristic (AUC), and accuracy. Furthermore, our problem can be viewed as a ranking task, namely ranking all papers of one scholar in the reverse order of probability that each paper will increase his or her h-index. Therefore, the precision at the top 3 results (Pre@3) and mean average precision (MAP) are also used to evaluate the performance.

4.2 Prediction Results

We present the predictability of whether a paper published in 2007 will contribute to the primary author's h-index within five years. The prediction is applied on the papers whose primary author's h-index is at least 10 in 2007. The resulting set of papers contains 21,519 instances, of which 30.46% successfully contributed to their primary author's h-indices. Table 2 lists the predictive performance of different methods.

Table 2: Predictive results generated by different methods. t=2007, Δt=5 years, and h-index threshold is set to 10. LRC — Logistic Regression; RF — Random Forest; BAG — Bagged decision trees; R—Random guess with half predicted positive and half negative. The results of support vector machine, naïve Bayes, and neural network models are omitted due to their poor performance on this task.

Method	Pre.	Rec.	F_1	AUC	Accu.	Pre@3	MAP
R	0.305	0.500	0.375	0.500	0.500	0.674	0.522
LRC	0.854	0.711	0.776	0.938	0.875	0.925	0.965
RF	0.785	0.815	0.800	0.939	0.876	0.957	0.979
BAG	0.802	0.821	0.811	0.951	0.884	0.950	0.978

Overall, the random guessing would achieve an F_1 score of 0.375 and an accuracy of 0.5. However, by our methodology, the predictive power significantly outperforms random guessing with an F_1 score of over 0.776 (+107% increase) and an accuracy of more than 0.875 (+75% increase). In terms of precision, recall, and AUC score, the performance is still promising. As the three selected methods achieve similar results, logistic regression is chosen as the primary classifier to examine the remaining experiments

4.3 Factor Contribution

To predict whether a paper will increase its primary author's h-index, we devise six groups of different factors (see §3) that may drive the growth of scientific impact. To explore the contributions of each group to the prediction task, we employ two methods: (1) we remove each group of factors and keep the remaining five to evaluate the predictive performance; and (2) we add or use only one group of factors to evaluate the predictive performance. Figure 6 shows the F_1 scores for the two cases. The contributions of different groups of factors show a high degree of variability. When removing factor groups, the 30% drop in F_1 score by removing the content factors indicates that they are significantly importance to this prediction task. By contrast, the marginal decreases in performance demonstrated by all other factors imply they provide only limited contributions. When using only one factor group, the content factors still play the most important role (0.70 F_1 score) in predicting the growth of scientific impact. Venue factors also achieve a reasonable performance. The contribution analyses are consistent with the factor correlation results elaborated upon in the previous section.

We further examine the contributions of each individual factor. We choose the information gain ratio (IGR) to determine which of the factors are the most important. The information gain for a factor x_k is the expected reduction in entropy—that is, uncertainty—achieved by learning the state of that factor. For each factor x_k, then, the IGR of x_k, denoted $IGR(x_k)$, is simply defined as the information gain $IG(x_k)$ divided by the intrinsic value $IV(x_k)$ of x_k, i.e., $IGR(x_k) = IG(x_k)/IV(x_k)$. The higher the $IGR(x_k)$ for factor x_k, the greater its importance.

Table 3 lists the information gain ratio and corresponding ranking of each single factor. Clearly, the topic authority of the primary author matters the most (*C-authority-max*), followed by the authorities of the other co-authors (*C-authority-ave* and *C-authority-first*). The following positions, from the 4th to the 7th, are held by the two venue factors and the two reference factors. The IGR of the remaining factors decrease to the next lowest order of magnitude, which indicates that they provide relatively limited contributions to the prediction task.

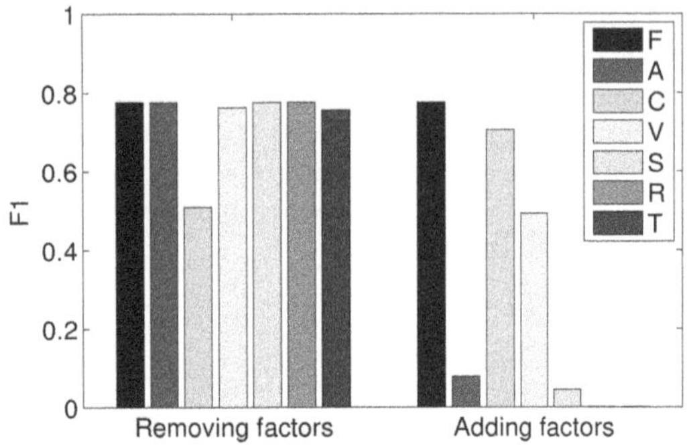

Figure 6: Factor contribution analysis. F denotes training a logistic regression model with a full feature set. A—Author factors; C—Content factors; V—Venue factors; S—Social factors; R—Reference factors; T—Temporal factors. The left side of the figure illustrates the effects of removing each group of factors, while the right side illustrates the effects of using only each group of factors for training.

4.4 Predictability of Papers with Different Constraints

Our experimental results provide evidence of the predictability of whether one paper will contribute to the h-index of it primary author within five years. Two intuitive questions naturally arise: First, is a primary author with a high or a low h-index more predictable? Second, is a paper more predictable given a long or short timeframe? To answer these questions, we investigate the predictability of papers conditioned on the primary author's h-index and the length of the given timeframe Δt.

Figure 7 shows the predictive performance with different constraints. On one hand, it suggests that our prediction task is more difficult for papers with a high h-index primary author. Recall that the higher the primary author's h-index, the higher the local threshold for this paper during classification. Intuitively, then, as we consider authors with higher h-indices, it becomes increasingly difficult for any particular paper to reach the defined local threshold, which makes the corresponding prediction task increasingly nontrivial. On the other hand, the rising lines as the increase of Δt imply that our prediction task is easier when given a longer timeframe. Intuitively, papers can accrue more citations as time goes on, during which time the authors' influence may increase, which may further compound the rate at which citations accrue. In this way, it becomes quite likely that the papers will contribute to their respective authors' h-indices if simply given a long enough timeframe.

Overall, the task of determining which papers will increase one' h-index is more predictable when conducted over a relatively long timeframe for those who have relatively low h-indices.

4.5 Case Studies

We illustrate several case studies to demonstrate the effectiveness of our methodology for quantifying scientific impact. Our case studies include two researchers and two data mining conferences, and conclude with the self-prediction of *this* paper.

Two anonymous scholars. We choose two anonymous scholars, A_{86} and A_{33}, who in 2007 had substantially different h-indices (86 and 33, respectively). We examine the difference in the predictability of whether the papers published by each author in 2007 would contribute to his or her respective h-index by 2012. From

Table 3: Information Gain Ratio (IGR) of each factor. IGR is used to decide the relevant extent of features. Here, IGR is between 0 and 1, with higher values indicating greater relevance.

	Factor	IGR	Ranking
Author	*A-first-max*	0.0028	21
	A-num-authors	0.0021	25
	A-ave-max	0.0021	24
	A-sum-max	0.0044	17
	A-max-ratio	0.0085	9
	A-num-first	0.0031	19
	A-first-ratio	0.0049	16
Content	*C-popularity*	0.0026	22
	C-popularity-ratio	0.0077	10
	C-diversity	0.0013	26
	C-novelty	0.0089	8
	C-authority-ave	0.0873	2
	C-authority-first	0.0637	3
	C-authority-max	0.0963	1
Venue	*V-ratio-max*	0.0473	4
	V-citation	0.0463	5
Social	*S-degree*	0.0022	23
	S-pagerank	0.0051	15
	S-h-coauthor	0.0073	11
	S-h-weight	0.0052	14
Reference	*R-ratio-max*	0.0127	6
	R-citation	0.0105	7
Temporal	*T-ave-h*	0.0039	18
	T-max-h	0.0056	13
	T-h-first	0.0028	20
	T-h-max	0.0056	12

Figure 8(a), we can observe the skewed heavy-tailed distributions for the number of citations their papers published in 2007 have obtained by 2012. Back in 2007, A_{86}'s and A_{33}'s h-indices were 86 and 33, respectively. In 2012, 8 of A_{86}'s 48 publications published in 2007 have obtained at least 86 citations and 9 of A_{33}'s 26 publications have obtained at least 33. In other words, while the ratio of the papers that have contributed to A_{86}'s h-index is relatively low (8/48), this is actually a result of the researcher's high h-index, which corresponds to a large scientific impact. In contrast, A_{33}'s relatively low h-index compared to A_{86} makes the ratio of papers that contribute to A_{33}'s h-index higher than those that contribute to A_{86}'s. Table 4 shows the predictive results of whether their papers in 2007 would contribute to their h-indices in 2012, from which we make two observations. First, the performance of the model for both researchers is much higher than random guessing with respect to F_1 score, AUC, and accuracy. Second, the overall performance for A_{33} is significantly higher than that for A_{86}, which suggests a greater predictability for researchers with relatively lower h-indices.

KDD and ICDM. Using ACM SIGKDD and IEEE ICDM as examples, we present the effects that different conferences have on spreading scientific impact and contributing to authors' h-indices. Currently, KDD and ICDM are considered two of the world's premier research conferences in data mining. Back in 2007, ICDM was in its seventh year, while KDD was in its thirteenth year. Fig-

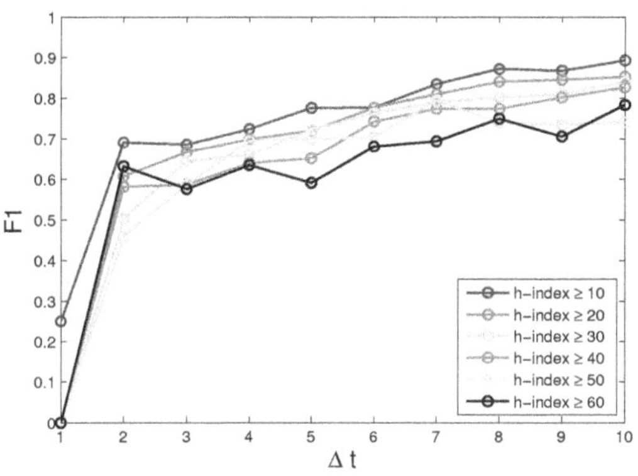

Figure 7: Predictive performance by varying the constraints.

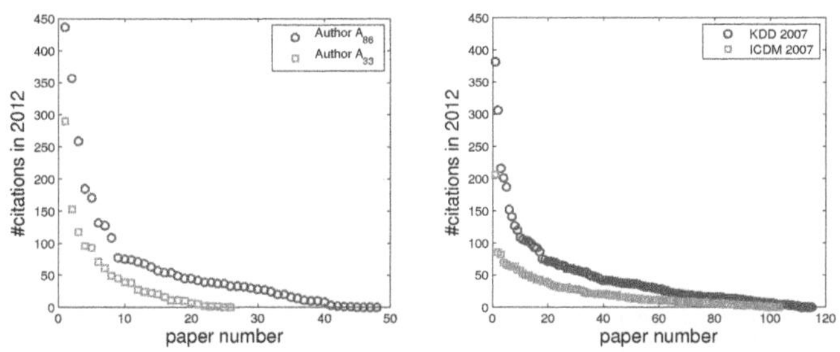

(a) #citations of two authors' papers. (b) #citations of two venues' papers.

Figure 8: Case studies of citation counts in 2012 for papers published in 2007. In 2012, 8 of A_{86}'s 48 papers and 9 of A_{33}'s 26 papers published in 2007 obtained #citations over 86 and 33 (A_{86}'s and A_{33}'s h-indices in 2007), respectively.

ure 8(b) plots the number of citations in 2012 for all papers published in these two venues in 2007. In our dataset, we observe that KDD'07 and ICDM'07 papers contribute to their primary authors' h-indices in different proportions. We further examine which conference has papers that are, in terms of their contribution to the h-indices of their respective authors, more predictable. This comparison is illustrated by Table 5. The prediction results for KDD'07 papers are generally better than ICDM'07 in terms of recall and and F_1 score, and are competitive with ICDM'07 in terms of precision, AUC, and accuracy. Overall, both venues demonstrate promising predictability in the spread of the scientific impact of their respective publications.

Self-prediction for *this* paper. Finally, we perform a self-prediction on whether *this* paper will contribute to its primary author's h-index by 2019. Keeping in mind that using the methodology employed in this paper would technically require unavailable training data (i.e., data composed of publications from 2014 and their citation counts in 2019), we instead revert to using the logistic regression model trained on the data from 2007 to generate this prediction. To generate features for this paper, we insert this paper into the 2012 data and make the assumption that it was accepted by the venue to which we have submitted at that time. The author factors, for example, are extracted from their respective author profiles circa 2012. With the approximate model and features, we estimate that the probability that this paper will contribute to the h-index of the author with highest h-index within five years is around 76%. With a pinch of optimism, we leave the evaluation of the fidelity of this prediction as an exercise for future readers.

Table 4: Predictive results for two anonymous authors. t=2007 and Δt=5 years. Pre@k: k=8 (A_{86}); k=9 (A_{33}).

Authors	Pre.	Rec.	F_1	AUC	Accu.	Pre@k	MAP
A_{86}	0.500	0.375	0.429	0.584	0.833	0.375	0.346
A_{33}	1.000	0.667	0.800	0.856	0.885	0.667	0.849

Table 5: Predictive results for KDD'07 and ICDM'07 papers. t=2007, Δt=5 years and logistic regression is used. In our dataset, KDD'07 and ICDM'07 papers contribute to their primary authors' h-indices in different proportions.

Venues	Pre.	Rec.	F_1	AUC	Accu.
KDD'07	0.800	0.889	0.842	0.884	0.818
ICDM'07	0.842	0.593	0.696	0.886	0.825

5. RELATED WORK

Scientific impact modeling is being extensively explored and has become an important and popular research topic, particularly since the rise of two recent, successive *Science* papers in 2013 [24, 27]. The study of scientific impact by scholarly researchers offers the potential to help scholars more effectively disseminate their work and expand their scientific influence.

Traditionally, the number of citations has been widely used as a measurement of scientific impact for both individual papers and solitary scientific researchers. Several practical metrics are designed based on the number of citations to reflect scientific impacts. Garfield proposed the idea of impact factor for indexing and evaluating the quality of journals [6]. Recently, Hirsch proposed the h-index, which is able to measure both the productivity and popularity of researchers [8]. In this setting, on the one hand scholars aim to publish results in high-impact journals to collect more citations and increase their h-indices, while on the other hand the journals attempt to accept solid and potentially influential work to improve their impact factors. Accordingly, both impact factor and h-index successfully characterize the motivation and behaviors of the scientific community.

Besides measuring scientific impact, a large body of work has been focused on the prediction of scientific impact. The 2003 ACM SIGKDD Cup introduced a competition focused around citation count prediction [7], with the task of estimating the number of citations of one paper given its previous number of citations. Following this, many efforts have been made to predict the number of future citations for scholarly work. Castillo et al. studied the correlation between author reputation and citations [4]. Yan et al. examined a series of features important to future citations [28, 29]. Wang et al. uncovered basic mechanisms that govern scientific impact, which has the power to quantify and predict citation counts [27, 18]. However, the effectiveness of such predictions is fundamentally limited by the power law distribution of citations. Herein we (re)define the impact prediction problem by addressing a question of interest to many academic researchers, namely: "will this paper increase my h-index?" The major difference between our work and previous work lies in that, rather than solving a regression task in a highly skewed environment, we address the problem by generating a local threshold (the author's h-index) for each paper's future citation count.

Our work is also related to other mining tasks in academic data such as citation recommendation [16, 22, 30], topic influence [13, 21], collaboration prediction [20, 26], and analysis of citation networks [25] and academic social networks [23]. Furthermore, as the formalization of our predictive task is partly inspired by the cascade growth prediction problem [5], the prediction of scientific impact has relations with predicting the popularity [9, 14, 1] of online "paper" (e.g., tweet, video, photo) in social media.

6. CONCLUSION

In this paper, we examine scientific impact by formalizing a novel problem that can be reduced to the following question: will a paper contribute to its primary author's h-index within a given timeframe? Previous, rich work on predicting the number of citations of individual papers is fundamentally limited by the heavy-tailed distribution of citation counts. Our problem definition differs by offering a great potential to quantify scientific impact on the interplay between scientific researchers and publications. We examine six groups of factors from different perspectives that may drive a paper to obtain enough citations to contribute to its primary author's h-index.

By experimenting on a large-scale public academic dataset, we find that two factors—(1) the authors' authority on the publication topic and (2) the publication venue—play the most decisive roles in determining whether a paper will contribute to its primary author's h-index. Surprisingly, we notice that the popularity of the publication topic and the co-authors' influence are not correlated to the prediction target. Our study also demonstrates a greater than 87.5% potential predictability for whether a paper will contribute to its primary author's h-index within five years. Overall, our findings unveil mechanisms for quantifying scientific impact and provide concrete suggestions to researchers for better expanding their scientific influence and, ultimately, for more effectively "standing on the shoulders of giants."

Notwithstanding the extensive and promising results of the present work, there is still much room left for future work. First, while this work is conducted only on literature from computer science, it is necessary to examine the observed patterns in other scientific disciplines, such as physics, mathematics, biology, and so on. Second, since authors' h-indices evolve within the prediction timeframe, it would be natural to design methodologies that could capture the co-evolution of authors' h-indices and citation counts.

Acknowledgments. This work is supported by the Army Research Laboratory under Cooperative Agreement Number W911NF-09-2-0053, the U.S. Air Force Office of Scientific Research (AFOSR) and the Defense Advanced Research Projects Agency (DARPA) grant #FA9550-12-1-0405, and the National Science Foundation (NSF) Grant OCI-1029584.

7. REFERENCES

[1] M. Ahmed, S. Spagna, F. Huici, and S. Niccolini. A peek into the future: Predicting the evolution of popularity in user generated content. In *WSDM '13*, pages 607–616. ACM, 2013.

[2] S. Bethard and D. Jurafsky. Who should I cite: Learning literature search models from citation behavior. In *CIKM '10*, pages 609–618. ACM, 2010.

[3] D. M. Blei, A. Y. Ng, and M. I. Jordan. Latent Dirichlet allocation. *JMLR*, 3:993–1022, 2003.

[4] C. Castillo, D. Donato, and A. Gionis. Estimating the number of citations using author reputation. In *SPIRE '07*, pages 107–117. Springer, 2007.

[5] J. Cheng, L. Adamic, P. A. Dow, J. M. Kleinberg, and J. Leskovec. Can cascades be predicted? In *WWW '14*, pages 925–936, 2014.

[6] E. Garfield. Citation indexes for science: A new dimension in documentation through association of ideas. *Science*, 122(3159):108–111, 1955.

[7] J. Gehrke, P. Ginsparg, and J. M. Kleinberg. Overview of the 2003 kdd cup. *SIGKDD Explorations*, 5(2):149–151, 2003.

[8] J. E. Hirsch. An index to quantify an individual's scientific research output. *Proceedings of the National Academy of Sciences*, 102(46):16569–16572, 2005.

[9] L. Hong, A. S. Doumith, and B. D. Davison. Co-factorization machines: Modeling user interests and predicting individual decisions in Twitter. In *WSDM '13*, pages 557–566. ACM, 2013.

[10] J. M. Kleinberg. Authoritative sources in a hyperlinked environment. *Journal of the ACM*, 46(5):604–632, 1999.

[11] J. M. Kleinberg and S. Oren. Mechanisms for (mis)allocating scientific credit. In *STOC '11*, pages 529–538. ACM, 2011.

[12] S. Kullback and R. A. Leibler. On information and sufficiency. *Annals of Machematical Statistics*, 22(1):79–86, 1951.

[13] L. Liu, J. Tang, J. Han, M. Jiang, and S. Yang. Mining topic-level influence in heterogeneous networks. In *CIKM '10*, pages 199–208. ACM, 2010.

[14] H. Pinto, J. M. Almeida, and M. A. Gonçalves. Using early view patterns to predict the popularity of youtube videos. In *WSDM '13*, pages 365–374. ACM, 2013.

[15] F. Radicchi, S. Fortunato, and C. Castellano. Universality of citation distributions: Toward an objective measure of scientific impact. *PNAS*, 2008.

[16] X. Ren, J. Liu, X. Yu, U. Khandelwal, Q. Gu, L. Wang, and J. Han. ClusCite: Effective citation recommendation by information network-based clustering. In *KDD '14*, 2014.

[17] H.-W. Shen and A.-L. Barabási. Collective credit allocation in science. *PNAS*, 2014.

[18] H.-W. Shen, D. Wang, C. Song, and A.-L. Barabási. Modeling and predicting popularity dynamics via reinforced poisson processes. In *AAAI '14*, 2014.

[19] M. Strathern. Improving ratings: audit in the British university system. *European Review*, 5(03):305–321, 1997.

[20] Y. Sun, J. Han, C. C. Aggarwal, and N. V. Chawla. When will it happen?: Relationship prediction in heterogeneous information networks. In *WSDM '12*, pages 663–672. ACM, 2012.

[21] J. Tang, J. Sun, C. Wang, and Z. Yang. Social influence analysis in large-scale networks. In *KDD '09*, pages 807–816, 2009.

[22] J. Tang and J. Zhang. A discriminative approach to topic-based citation recommendation. *Advances in Knowledge Discovery and Data Mining*, pages 572–579, 2009.

[23] J. Tang, J. Zhang, L. Yao, J. Li, L. Zhang, and Z. Su. Arnetminer: Extraction and mining of academic social networks. In *KDD '08*, pages 990–998, 2008.

[24] B. Uzzi, S. Mukherjee, M. Stringer, and B. Jones. Atypical combinations and scientific impact. *Science*, 342(6157):468–472, 2013.

[25] D. Vu, A. Asuncion, D. Hunter, and P. Smyth. Dynamic egocentric models for citation networks. In *ICML '11*, pages 857–864, 2011.

[26] C. Wang, J. Han, Y. Jia, J. Tang, D. Zhang, Y. Yu, and J. Guo. Mining advisor-advisee relationships from research publication networks. In *KDD '10*, pages 203–212, 2010.

[27] D. Wang, C. Song, and A.-L. Barabási. Quantifying long-term scientific impact. *Science*, 342(6154):127–132, 2013.

[28] R. Yan, C. Huang, J. Tang, Y. Zhang, and X. Li. To better stand on the shoulder of giants. In *JCDL '12*, pages 51–60. ACM, 2012.

[29] R. Yan, J. Tang, X. Liu, D. Shan, and X. Li. Citation count prediction: Learning to estimate future citations for literature. In *CIKM '11*, pages 1247–1252. ACM, 2011.

[30] X. Yu, Q. Gu, M. Zhou, and J. Han. Citation prediction in heterogeneous bibliographic networks. In *SDM '12*, pages 1119–1130, 2012.

[31] J. Zhang, J. Tang, and J. Li. Expert finding in a social network. In *DASFAA '07*, pages 1066–1069, 2007.

Concept Graph Learning from Educational Data

Yiming Yang, Hanxiao Liu, Jaime Carbonell, Wanli Ma
Carnegie Mellon University
{yiming, hanxiaol, jgc, mawanli}@cs.cmu.edu

ABSTRACT

This paper addresses an open challenge in educational data mining, i.e., the problem of using observed prerequisite relations among courses to learn a directed universal concept graph, and using the induced graph to predict unobserved prerequisite relations among a broader range of courses. This is particularly useful to induce prerequisite relations among courses from different providers (universities, MOOCs, etc.). We propose a new framework for inference within and across two graphs—at the course level and at the induced concept level—which we call Concept Graph Learning (CGL). In the training phase, our system projects the course-level links onto the concept space to induce directed concept links; in the testing phase, the concept links are used to predict (unobserved) prerequisite links for test-set courses within the same institution or across institutions. The dual mappings enable our system to perform an interlingua-style transfer learning, e.g. treating the concept graph as the interlingua, and inducing prerequisite links in a transferable manner across different universities. Experiments on our newly collected data sets of courses from MIT, Caltech, Princeton and CMU show promising results, including the viability of CGL for transfer learning.

Categories and Subject Descriptors

I.2.6 [**Learning**]: Concept learning; Induction; Parameter learning; I.5.2 [**Design Methodology**]: Pattern analysis; Classifier design and evaluation

General Terms

Algorithms; Performance; Design; Experimentation; Theory

Keywords

Multi-scale directed graph learning; online education; transfer learning; new inference algorithms

WSDM'15, February 2–6, 2015, Shanghai, China.

ACM 978-1-4503-3317-7/15/02 ...$15.00.
http://dx.doi.org/10.1145/2684822.2685292.

1. INTRODUCTION

The large and growing amounts of online education data present both open challenges and significant opportunities for machine learning research to enrich educational offerings. One of the most important challenges is to automatically detect the prerequisite dependencies among massive quantities of online courses, and to support decision making such as curricula planning for students, and to support course and curriculum design by teachers based on existing course offerings. One example is to find a coherent sequence of courses among MOOC offerings from different providers that respect implicit prerequisite relations. A more specific example would be a new student who just enters a university for a MS or PhD degree. She is interested in machine learning and data mining courses, but finds it difficult to choose among many courses which look similar or with ambiguous course titles to her, such as *Machine Learning, Statistical Machine Learning, Applied Machine Learning, Machine Learning with Large Datasets, Scalable Analytics, Advanced Data Analysis, Statistics: Data Mining, Intermediate Statistics, Statistical Computing*, and so on. Taking all the courses would imply taking forever to graduate, and possibly waste a big portion of her time due to the overlapping content. Alternately, if she wants to choose a small subset, which courses should she include? How should she order the courses without sufficient understanding about the prerequisite dependencies? Often prerequisites are explicit within an academic department but implicit across departments. Moreover, if she already took several courses in machine learning or data mining through Coursera or in her undergraduate education, how much do those courses overlap with the new ones? Without an accurate representation about how course contents overlap with each other, and how course ordering would affect the efficiency or difficulty of learning by students, it is difficult to answer her questions. Universities solve this problem in the old-fashioned way, via academic advisors, but it is not clear how to solve it in MOOC environments or cross-university offerings where courses do not have unique ID's and not described in a universally controlled vocabulary. Ideally, we would like to have a universal graph whose nodes are canonical and discriminant concepts (e.g. "*convexity*" or "*eigenvalues*") being taught in a broad range of courses, and whose links indicate pairwise preferences in sequencing the teaching of these concepts. For example, to learn the concepts of *PageRank* and *HITS*, students should have already learned the concepts of *eigenvectors, Markov matrices* and *irreducibility of matrices*. This means directed links from *eigenvectors, Markov*

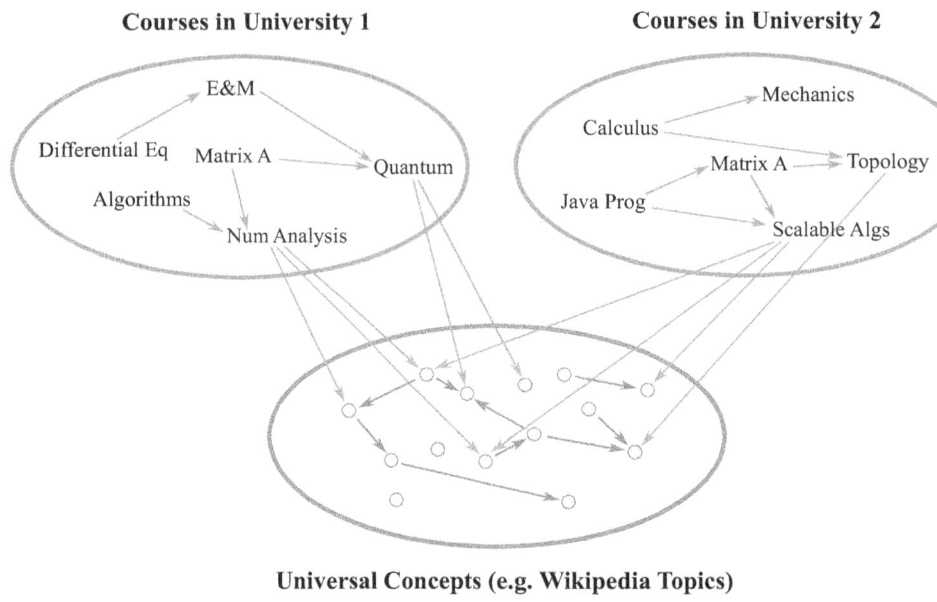

Figure 1: The framework of two-scale directed graphs: The higher-level graphs have courses (nodes) with perquisite relations (links). The lower-level graph consists of universal concepts (nodes) and pairwise preference in learning or teaching concepts. The links between the two levels are system-assigned weights of concepts to each course.

matrices and *irreducibility* to *PageRank* and *HITS* in the concept graph. To generalize this further, if there are many directed links from the concepts in one course (say *Matrix Algebra*) to the concepts in another course (say *Web Mining* with *Link Analysis* as a sub-topic), we may infer a prerequisite relation between the two courses. Clearly, having a directed graph with a broad coverage of universal concepts is crucial for reasoning about course content overlap and prerequisite relationship, and hence important for educational decision making, such as curriculum planning by students and modularization in course syllabus design by instructors.

How can we obtain such a knowledge-rich concept graph? Manual specification is obviously not scalable when the number of concepts reaches tens of thousands or larger. Using machine learning to automatically induce such a graph based on massive online course materials is an attractive alternative; however, no statistical learning techniques have been developed for this problem, to our knowledge. Addressing this open challenge with principled algorithmic solutions is the novel contribution we aim to accomplish in this paper. We call our new method Concept Graph Learning (CGL). Specifically, we propose a multi-scale inference framework as illustrated in Figure 1, which consists of two levels of graphs and cross-level links. Generally, a course would cover multiple concepts, and a concept may be covered by more than one course. Notice that the course-level graphs do not overlap because different universities do not have universal course IDs. However, the semantic concepts taught in different universities do overlap, and we want to learn the mappings between the non-universal courses and the universal concept space based on online course materials.

In this paper we investigate the problem of concept graph learning (CGL) with our new collections of syllabi (including course names, descriptions, listed lectures, prerequisite relations, etc.) from the Massachusetts Institute of Technology (MIT), the California Institute of Technology (Caltech), the Carnegie Mellon University (CMU) and Princeton. The syllabus data allow us to construct an initial course-level graph for each university, which may be further enriched by discovering latent pre-requisite links. As for representing the universal concept space, we study four representation schemes (Section 2.2), including 1) using the English words in course descriptions, 2) using sparse coding of English words, 3) using distributed word embedding of English words, and 4) using a large subset of Wikipedia categories. For each of these representation schemes, we provide algorithmic solutions to establish a mapping from courses to concepts, and to learn the concept-level dependencies based on observed prerequisite relations at the course level. The second part, i.e., the explicit learning of the directed graph for universal concepts, is the most unique part of our proposed framework. Once the concept graph is learned, we can predict *unobserved* prerequisite relations among any courses, including those not in the training set and by different universities. In other words, CGL enables an interlingua-style transfer learning as to train the models on the course materials of some universities and to predict the prerequisite relations for the courses in other universities. The universal transferability is particularly desirable in MOOC environments where courses are offered by different instructors in many universities. Since universities do not have unified course IDs, the course-level sub-graphs of different universities do not overlap with each other, and the prerequisite links are only local within each sub-graph. Thus to enable cross-university transfer, it is crucial to project course-level prerequisite links in different universities onto the directed links among universal concepts.

The bi-directional inference between the two directed graphs makes our CGL framework fundamentally different from existing approaches in graph-based link detection [16, 19,

20], matrix completion [4, 9, 13] and collaborative filtering [24]. That is, our approach requires explicit learning of the concept-level directed graph and optimal mapping between the two levels of links while other methods do not (see Section 4 for more discussion).

Our main contributions in this paper can be summarized as:

1. A novel framework for within- and cross-level inference of prerequisite relations at the course-level and the concept-level directed graphs;
2. New algorithmic solutions for scalable graph learning;
3. New data collections from multiple universities with syllabus descriptions, prerequisite links and lecture materials;
4. The first evaluation for prerequisite link prediction in within- and cross-university settings.

The rest of the paper is organized as follows: Section 2 introduces the formal definitions of our framework and inference algorithms; Section 3 describes the new data sets we collected for this study and future benchmark evaluations, and reports our empirical findings; Section 4 discusses related work; and Section 5 summarizes the main findings in this study.

2. FRAMEWORK & ALGORITHMS

2.1 Notation

Let us formally define our methods with the following notation.

- n is the number of courses in a training set;
- p is the dimension of the universal concept space (Section 2.2;
- $x_i \in \mathbb{R}^p$ for $i = 1, 2, \ldots, n$ are the bag-of-concepts representation of a course in the training set;
- X is an n-by-p matrix where each row is $x_i^\top$;
- Y is an n-by-n matrix where each cell is the binary indicator of the prerequisite relation between two courses, i.e., $y_{ij} = 1$ means that course j is a prerequisite of course i, and $y_{ij} = -1$ otherwise.
- A is a p-by-p matrix, whose elements are the weights of directed links among concepts. That is, A is the matrix of model parameters we want to optimize given the training data in X and Y.

2.2 Representation Schemes

What is the best way to represent the contents of courses to learn the universal concept space? We explore different answers with four alternate choices as follows:

1. ***Word-based Representation (Word)***: This method uses the vocabulary of course descriptions plus any listed keywords by the course providers (MIT, Caltech, CMU and Princeton) as the entire concept (feature) space. We applied standard procedures for text preprocessing, including stop-word removal, term-frequency (TF) based term weighting, and the removal of the rare words whose training-set frequency is one. We did not use TF-IDF weighting because the relative small number of "documents" (courses) in our data sets do not allow reliable estimates of the IDF part.
2. ***Sparse Coding of Words (SCW)***: This method projects the original n-dimensional vector representations of words (the columns in the course-by-word matrix) onto sparse vectors in a smaller k-dimensional space using Non-negative Matrix Factorization [18], where k is much smaller than n. One can view the lower dimensional components as the system-discovered latent concepts. Intrigued by the successful application of sparse coding in image processing [11], we explored its application to our graph-based inference problem. By applying the algorithm in [14] to our training sets we obtained a k-dimensional vector for each word; by taking the average of word vectors in each course we obtained the bag-of-concept representation of the course. This resulted in an n-by-k matrix X, representing all the training-set courses in the k-dimensional space of latent concepts. We set $k = 100$ in our experiments based on cross validation.
3. ***Distributed Word Embedding (DWE)***: This method also uses dimension-reduced vectors to represent both words and courses, similar to SCW. However, the lower dimensional vectors for words are discovered by multilayer neural networks through deep learning, based on word usage w.r.t contextual, syntactic and semantic information [17, 21]. Intrigued by the popularity of DWE in recent research in Natural Language Processing and other domains [6, 5], we explored its application to our graph-based inference problem. Specifically, we deploy DWE trained on Wikipedia articles by Rami et al. [1], in a domain which is semantically close to that of academic courses.
4. ***Category-based Representation (Cat)***: This method used a large subset of Wikipedia categories as the concept space. We selected the subset via a pooling strategy as follows: We used the words in our training-set courses to form 3509 queries (one query per course), and retrieved the top 100 documents per query based on cosine similarity. We then took the union of the Wikipedia category labels of these retrieved documents, and removed the categories which were retrieved by only three queries or less. This process resulted in a total of 10,051 categories in the concept space. The categorization of courses was based on the earlier highly scalable very-large category space work reported in [10]: the classifiers were trained on labeled Wikipedia articles and then applied to the word-based vector representation of each course for (weighted) category assignments.

Each of the above representation schemes may have its own strengths and weaknesses. *Word* is simple and natural but rather noisy, because semantically equivalent lexical variants are not unified into canonical concepts and there could be systematic vocabulary variation across universities. Also, this scheme will not work in cross-language settings, e.g., if courses descriptions are in English and Chinese. *Cat* would be less noisy and better in cross-language settings, but the automated classification step will unavoidably introduce errors in category assignments. *SCW* (sparse coding of words) reduces the total number of model parameters via dimensionality reduction, which may lead to robust training (avoiding overfitting) and efficient computation, but at the risk of losing useful information in the projection from the original high-dimensional space to a lower dimensional space. *DWE* (distributed word embedding) deploys recent advances in deep learning of word meanings in context. However, reliable word embedding require the availability of large volumes of training text (e.g., Wikipedia articles); the potential mismatch between the training domain (for which large volumes of data can be obtained easily) and the test domain (for which large volumes of data are hard or costly to obtain) could be a serious issue. Yet another distinction among these representation schemes is that Word and Cat produce human-understandable concepts and links, while *SCW* and *DWE* produce latent factors which are harder to interpret by humans.

By exploring all the four representation schemes in our unified framework for two-level graph based inference, and by examining their effectiveness in the task of link prediction of prerequisite relations among courses, we aim to obtain a deeper understanding of the strengths and weaknesses of those representational choices.

2.3 The Optimization Methods

We define the problem of concept graph learning as a key part of learning-to-predict prerequisite relations among courses, i.e., for the two-layer statistical inference we introduced in Section 1 with Figure 1. Given a training set of courses with a bag-of-concepts representation per course as a row in matrix X, and a list of known prerequisite links per course as a row in matrix Y, we optimize matrix A whose elements specify both the direction (sign) and the strength (magnitudes) of each link between concepts. We propose two new approaches to this problem: a classification approach and a learning-to-rank approach. Both approaches deploy the same extended versions of SVM algorithms with squared hinge loss, but the objective functions for optimization are different. We also propose a nearest-neighbor approach for comparison, which predicts the course-level links (prerequisites) without learning the concept-level links.

2.3.1 The Classification Approach (CGL.Class)

In this method, we predict the score of the prerequisite link from course i to course j as:

$$\hat{y}_{ij} = f_A(x_i, x_j) = x_i^\top A x_j \tag{1}$$

The intuition behind this formula is shown in Figure 2. It can be easily verified that the quantity $x_i^\top A x_j$ is the summation of the weights of all the paths from node i to node j in this graph, where each path is weighted using the product of the corresponding x_{ik}, $A_{kk'}$ and $x_{jk'}$.

The criterion for optimizing matrix A given training data x_i for $i = 1, 2, \ldots, n$ and true labels y_{ij} for all course pairs is defined as:

$$\min_A \sum_{i,j} \left(1 - y_{ij}\left(x_i^\top A x_j\right)\right)_+^2 + \frac{\lambda}{2}\|A\|_F^2 \tag{2}$$

where $(1 - v)_+ = \max(0, 1 - v)$ denotes the hinge function, and $\|\cdot\|_F$ is the matrix Frobenius norm. The 1st term in

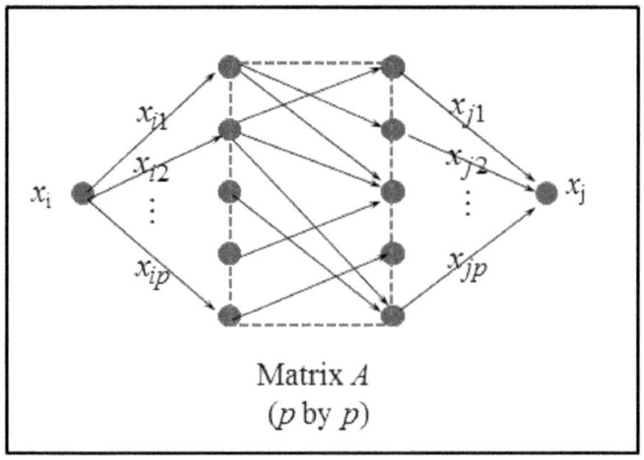

Figure 2: The weighted connections from course i to course j via matrix A which encodes the directed links between concepts

formula 2 is the empirical loss; the 2nd term is the regularization term, controlling the model complexity based on the large margin principle. We choose to use the squared hinge loss $(1 - v)_+^2$ the first term to gain first-order continuity of our objective function, enabling efficient computation using accelerated gradient descent [22, 23]. This efficiency improvement is crucial because we operate on pairs of courses, and thus have a much larger space than in normal classification (e.g. classifying individual courses).

2.3.2 The Learning-to-Rank Approach (CGL.Rank)

Inspired by the learning-to-rank literature [12], we explored going beyond the binary classifier in the previous approach to one that essentially learns to rank prerequisite preferences. Let Ω_i be the set of course pairs with the true labels $y_{ij} = 1$ for different j's, and $\bar{\Omega}_i$ the pairs of courses with the true labels $y_{ij} = -1$ for different k's, we want our system to give all the pairs in Ω_i higher score than that of any pair in $\bar{\Omega}_i$. We call this the partial-order preference over links conditioned on course i. Let T be the union of tuple sets $\{(i, j, k) | (i, j) \in \Omega_i, (i, k) \in \bar{\Omega}_i\}$ for all i in $1, 2, \ldots, n$. We formulate our optimization problem as:

$$\min_A \sum_{(i,j,k)\in T} \left(1 - \left(x_i^\top A x_j - x_i^\top A x_k\right)\right)_+^2 + \frac{\lambda}{2}\|A\|_F^2$$

Or equivalently, we can rewrite the objective as:

$$\min_A \sum_{(i,j,k)\in T} \left(1 - \left(\left(XAX^\top\right)_{ij} - \left(XAX^\top\right)_{ik}\right)\right)_+^2 + \frac{\lambda}{2}\|A\|_F^2$$

Solving this optimization problem requires us to extend standard packages of SVM algorithms in order to improve computational efficiency because the number of model parameters (p^2) in our formulation is very large. For example, with the vocabulary size of 15,396 words in the MIT dataset, the number of model parameters is over 237 million. When p (the number of concepts) is much larger than n (the number of courses), one may consider solving this optimization problem in the dual space instead in the primal space. However, even in the dual space, the number of variables is still $O(n^3)$, corresponding to all the tuples of $i, j, k \in \{1, 2, \ldots, n\}$, and the kernel matrix is on the order of of $O(n^6)$. We address these computational challenges in Section 2.4.

2.3.3 The Nearest-Neighbor Approach (kNN)

Different from the two approaches above where matrix A plays a central role, as a different baseline, we propose to predict the prerequisite relationship for any pair of courses based on matrix X and Y but not A. Let (u, v) be a new pair of courses in the test set, and x_u and x_v be the bag-of-concept representations of u and v, respectively. We score each pair (i, j) in the training set as:

$$\hat{y}_{ij} = \left(x_u^\top x_i\right) \times \left(x_v^\top x_j\right) \quad \forall i, j = 1, 2, \ldots, n$$

By taking the top pairs in the training set and by assigning the corresponding $y_{i,j}$ to the new pairs, we perform the k-nearest neighbor computation. If we normalize the vectors, the dot-products in the above formula become the cosine similarity. This approach requires nearest-neighbor search on-demand; when the number of course pairs in the test set is large, the online computation would be substantial.

Via cross validation, we found that k = 1 (1NN) works best for this problem on the current data sets.

2.4 Scalable Algorithms

As we have pointed out in Section 2.3.2 , the p^2 model parameters in matrix A and the n^3 constraints make the optimization of CGL.Rank computationally challenging. No standard optimization packages can be applied for large p and n. We address this problem by reformulating the objective in a way that the true number of model parameters reduces to $O(n^2)$.

Recall that our original objective (Section 2.3.2) is:

$$\min_{A \in \mathbb{R}^{p \times p}} \sum_{(i,j,k) \in T} \ell\left(\hat{Y}_{ij} - \hat{Y}_{ik}\right) + \frac{\lambda}{2} \|A\|_F^2 \quad \text{s.t. } \hat{Y} = XAX^\top \tag{3}$$

where $\hat{Y}$ is n-by-n, the matrix of the predicted course-level links. A is a p-by-p matrix of the induced concept-level links (weighted). $\ell(v) = (1-v)_+^2$ is the squared hinge loss. Denote the optimal solution of (3) by A^*, we are going to show that this solution can always be written as $A^* = X^\top BX$ some n-by-n ($n \ll p$) matrix B.

We argue that A^* must be identical to the optimal solution of the following problem:

$$\min_{A \in \mathbb{R}^{p \times p}} \|A\|_F^2 \quad \text{s.t.} \quad XAX^\top = XA^*X^\top := \hat{Y}^* \tag{4}$$

Otherwise, the solution for (4) will lead to the same loss as A^* in (3) but a smaller regularization penalty, which is contradictory to our assumption that A^* is the optimal solution for (3). Notice that (4) is just the matrix version of the *minimum norm problem for an underdetermined linear system* (because $p^2 > n^2$), which has a closed-form solution [2, 3, 8] as below:

$$A^* = X^\top K^{-1} \hat{Y}^* K^{-1} X \tag{5}$$

where $K = XX^\top$. By defining $B := K^{-1}\hat{Y}^*K^{-1}$, we have $\hat{Y}^* = KBK$ and $A^* = X^\top BX$. Hence the regularization in (3) becomes

$$\|A\|_F^2 = \text{tr}\left(AA^\top\right) = \text{tr}\left(X^\top BXX^\top B^\top X\right) = \text{tr}\left(XX^\top BXX^\top B^\top\right) = \text{tr}\left(\hat{Y}B^\top\right)$$

and (3) can be rewritten as an optimization w.r.t B which only involves $O\left(n^2\right)$ variables:

$$\min_{B \in \mathbb{R}^{n \times n}} \sum_{(i,j,k) \in T} \ell\left(\hat{Y}_{ij} - \hat{Y}_{ik}\right) + \frac{\lambda}{2} \text{tr}\left(\hat{Y}B^\top\right) \quad \text{s.t. } \hat{Y} = KBK \tag{6}$$

The substantially reduced number of parameters in (6) allows us to efficiently compute the gradient even for extremely large p^2 (by reducing the per-iteration cost). Moreover, the smoothness of our objective function enables us to deploy Nestrerov's accelerated gradient descent [22, 23], ensuring a convergence rate in the order of t^{-2} where t is the number of steps, i.e., the reduced number of iterations.

2.5 Algorithm Implementation

The gradient for (6) w.r.t B is given by

$$-2K \left(\sum_{(i,j,k) \in T : \delta_{ijk} > 0} e_i \left(e_j - e_k\right)^\top \delta_{ijk} \right) K + \lambda \hat{Y}$$

here $\delta_{ijk} = 1 - \left(\hat{Y}_{ij} - \hat{Y}_{ik}\right)$, $\hat{Y} = KBK$ and e_i, e_j, e_k are all unit vectors. The detailed implementation of the accelerated gradient descent is summarized in Alg. 1.

Algorithm 1 Concept Graph Learning

```
procedure CGL.RANK(X, T, λ, η)
    K ← XX^T
    t ← 1, B ← 0, Q ← 0
    while not converge do
        Δ ← 0
        Ŷ ← KBK
        for (i, j, k) in T do
            δ_ijk ← 1 − (Ŷ_ij − Ŷ_ik)
            if δ_ijk > 0 then
                Δ_ij ← Δ_ij + δ_ijk
                Δ_ik ← Δ_ik − δ_ijk
        P ← B − η (λŶ − 2KΔK)
        B ← P + (t−1)/(t+2) (P − Q)
        Q ← P
        t ← t + 1
    A ← X^T BX
    return Ŷ, A
```

3. EXPERIMENTS

3.1 Data and Metrics

We collected course listings, including course descriptions and available pre-requisite structure from MIT, Caltech, CMU and Princeton[1]. The first two were complete course catalogs, and the latter two required spidering and scraping, and hence we collected only Computer Science and Statistics for CMU, and Mathematics for Princeton. This implies that we can test within-university prerequisite discovery for all four—though MIT and Caltech will be most comprehensive—and cross university only pairs where the training university contains the disciplines in the test university.

Table 1 summarizes the datasets statistics.

[1]The datasets are available at
`http://nyc.lti.cs.cmu.edu/teacher/dataset/`

Table 1: Datasets Statistics

University	# Courses	# Prerequisites	# Words
MIT	2322	1173	15396
Caltech	1048	761	5617
CMU	83	150	1955
Princeton	56	90	454

Table 2: Results of within-university prerequisite prediction

Algorithm	Data	AUC	MAP
CGL.Rank	MIT	0.96	0.46
CGL.Class	MIT	0.86	0.34
1NN	MIT	0.76	0.30
CGL.Rank	Caltech	0.95	0.33
CGL.Class	Caltech	0.86	0.27
1NN	Caltech	0.60	0.16
CGL.Rank	CMU	0.79	0.55
CGL.Class	CMU	0.70	0.38
1NN	CMU	0.75	0.43
CGL.Rank	Princeton	0.92	0.69
CGL.Class	Princeton	0.89	0.61
1NN	Princeton	0.82	0.58

To evaluate performance, we use the *Mean Average Precision* (MAP) which has been the preferred metric for in information retrieval for evaluating ranked lists, and the Area Under the Curve of ROC (ROC/AUC or simply AUC) which in popular in link detection evaluations.

3.2 Within-university Prerequisite Prediction

We tested all the methods on the dataset from each university. We used one third of the data for testing, and the remaining two thirds for training and validation. We conducted 5-fold cross validation on the training two-thirds, i.e., trained the model on 80% of the training/validation data set, and tuned extra parameters on the remaining 20%. We repeated this process 5 times with a different 80-20% spit in each run. The results of the 5 runs were averaged in reporting results. Figure 3 and Table 2 summarize the results of CGL.Rank, CGL.Class and 1NN. All the methods used the English words as the representation scheme in this first set of experiments. Notice that the AUC scores for all methods are much higher than the MAP scores. The high AUC scores derive in large part from the fact that AUC gives an equal weight to the system-predicted true positives, regardless of their positions in system-produced ranked lists. On the other hand, MAP weighs more heavily the true positives in higher positions of ranked lists. In other words, MAP measures the performance of a system in a harder task: Not only the system needs to find the true positives (along with false positives), it also needs to rank them higher than false positives as possible in order to obtain a high MAP score. Using a more concrete example, a totally useless system which makes positive or negative predictions at random with 50% of the chances will have an AUC score of 50%. But this system will have an extremely low score in MAP because the change for a true positive to randomly appear in the top of a ranked list will be low when true negatives dominate in the domain. Our data sets are from such a domain because each course only requires a very small number of other courses as prerequisites. Back to our original point, regardless the popularity of AUC in link detection evaluations, its limitation should be recognized: the relative performance among methods is more informative than the absolute values of AUC.

Table 3: CGL.Rank with four representations

Concept	Data	AUC	MAP
Word	MIT	0.96	0.46
Cat.	MIT	0.93	0.36
SCW	MIT	0.93	0.33
DWE	MIT	0.83	0.09
Word	Caltech	0.95	0.33
Cat.	Caltech	0.93	0.32
SCW	Caltech	0.91	0.22
DWE	Caltech	0.76	0.12
Word	CMU	0.79	0.55
Cat.	CMU	0.77	0.55
SCW	CMU	0.73	0.43
DWE	CMU	0.67	0.35
Word	Princeton	0.92	0.69
Cat.	Princeton	0.84	0.68
SCW	Princeton	0.82	0.60
DWE	Princeton	0.77	0.50

As we can see in Figure 3, the relative ordering of the methods in AUC and MAP are indeed highly correlated across all the data sets. MAP emphasizes positive instances in the top portion of each ranked list, and hence is more sensible for measuring the usefulness of the system where the user interacts with system-recommended prerequisite lists. Comparing the results on all the methods, we see that CGL.Rank dominates the others in both AUC and MAP on most data sets.

3.3 Effects of Representation Schemes

Figure 4 and Table 3 summarize the results of CGL.Rank with the four representation schemes, i.e., Word, Cat, SCW (sparse coding of words) and DWE (distributed word embedding), respectively. Again the scores of AUC and MAP are not on the same scale, but the relative performance suggest that Word and Cat are competitive with each other (or Word is slightly better one some data sets), followed by SCW and then DWE. In the rest of the empirical results reported in this paper, we focus more on the performance of CGL.Rank with Word as the representation scheme because they perform better, and the space limit does not allow us to present all the results for every possible permutation of method, scheme, dataset and metric.

3.4 Cross-university Prerequisite Prediction

In this set of experiments, we fixed the same test sets which were used in within-university evaluations, but we alter the training sets across universities, yielding transfer learning results where the models were trained with the data from a different university than those where they were tested. By fixing the test sets in both within- and cross-university evaluations we can compare the results on a common basis. The competitive performance of Cat in comparison with Word is encouraging, given that Wikipedia categories are defined as general knowledge, and the classifiers (SVM's) we used for category assignment to courses were

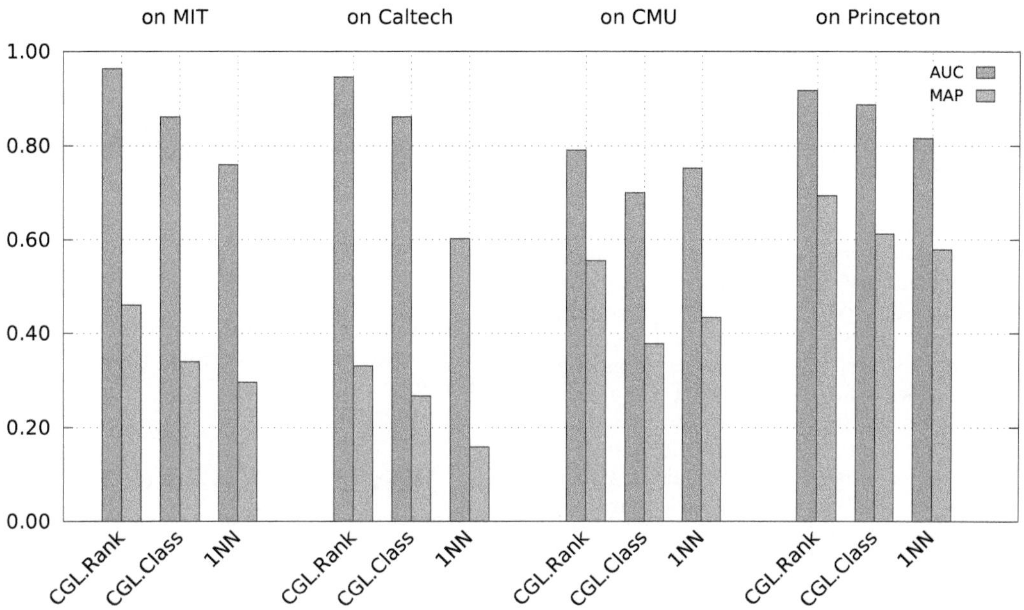

Figure 3: Different methods in within-university prerequisite prediction: All the methods used words as concepts.

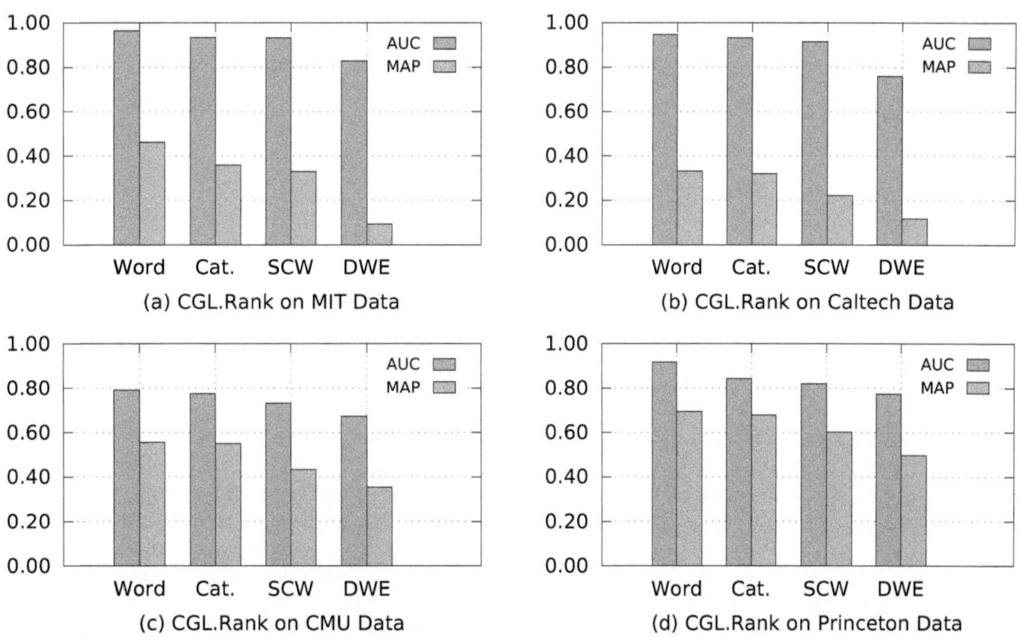

Figure 4: CGL.Rank with different representation schemes in within-university prerequisite prediction

trained on Wikipedia articles instead of the course materials (because we do not have human assigned Wikipedia category labels for courses). This means that the Wikipedia categories indeed have a good coverage on the concepts being taught in universities (and probably MOOC courses), and that our pooling strategy for selecting a relevant subset of Wikipedia categories is reasonably successful.

Table 4 and Figure 5 show the results of CGL.Rank (using words as concepts). Recall that the MIT and Caltech data cover the complete course catalogs, while the CMU data only cover the Computer Science and Statistics, and the Princeton data only over the Mathematics. This implies that we can only measure transfer learning on pairs where the training university contains the disciplines in the test university. By comparing the red bars (when the training university and the test university is the same) and the blue bars (when the training university is not the same as the test university), we see some performance loss in the transfer learning, which is expected. Nevertheless, we do get transfer, and this is the first report on successful transfer learning of educational knowledge, especially the prerequisite structures in disjoint graphs, across different universities through a unified concept graph. The results are therefore highly encouraging and suggest continued efforts to improve. Those results also suggest some interesting points, e.g., MIT might have a better coverage of the topics taught in Caltech, compared to the inverse. And, MIT courses seem to be closer to those in Princeton (Math) compared with those of CMU.

Table 4: CGL.Rank in within-university and cross-university settings

Training	Test	MAP	AUC
MIT	MIT	0.46	0.96
Caltech	MIT	0.13	0.88
Caltech	Caltech	0.33	0.95
MIT	Caltech	0.25	0.86
CMU	CMU	0.55	0.79
MIT	CMU	0.34	0.70
Caltech	CMU	0.28	0.62
Princeton	Princeton	0.69	0.92
MIT	Princeton	0.46	0.72
Caltech	Princeton	0.43	0.58

3.5 Experiment Details

We tested the efficiency of our proposed algorithms on a single machine with an Intel i7 8-core processor and 32GB RAM. On the largest MIT dataset with 981,009 training tuples and 490,505 test tuples, it took 3.08 minutes for CGL.Rank to reach a convergence rate of 1e-3 at 103 iterations with only 401MB memory. We also tested the effectiveness of using an accelerated version of gradient descent. Without the acceleration, that is, when using the ordinary gradient descent instead, it took 37.3 minutes and 1490 iterations to reach the same objective value. CGL.Class is equally efficient as CGL.Rank in terms of run time, though the latter is superior in terms of result quality. As for our 1NN baseline, it took 2.88 hours since a huge number ($2 \times 981,009 \times 490,505$) of dot-products need to be computed on the fly.

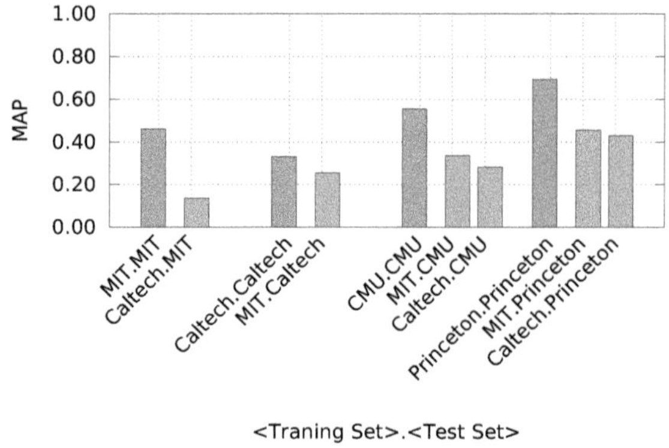

Figure 5: CGL.Rank results in within-university (red) and cross-university (blue) prerequisite prediction

4. DISCUSSION AND RELATED WORK

Whereas the task of inferring prerequisite relations among courses and concepts, and the task of inferring a concept network from a course network in order to transfer learned relations are both new, as are the extensions to the SVM algorithms presented, our work was inspired by methods in related fields, primarily:

In collaborative filtering via matrix completion the literature has focused on only one graph, such as a bipartite graph of u users and m preferences (e.g. for movies or products). Given some known values in the u-by-m matrix, the task is to estimate the remaining values (e.g. which other unseen movies or products would each user like) [24]. This is done via methods such as affine rank minimization [9] that reduce to convex optimization [3].

Another line of related research is transfer learning [7, 25, 26]. We seek to transfer prerequisite relations between pairs of courses within universities to other pairs also within universities, and to pairs that span universities. This is inspired by but different from the transfer learning literature. Transfer learning traditionally seeks to transfer informative features, priors, latent structures and more recently regularization penalties [15]. Instead, we transfer shared concepts in the mappings between course-space and concept-space to induce prerequisite relations.

Although our evaluations primarily focus on detecting prerequisite relations among courses, such a task is only one direct application of the automatically induced universal concept graph. Other important applications include automated or semi-automated curriculum planning for personal education goals based on different backgrounds of students, and modularization in course syllabus design by instructors. Both tasks require interaction between humans (students or teachers) and the system-induced concept graph, and exploring options and optimal paths. How well can our system support such a need? Although we do not have a formal evaluation in that aspect in this paper, we believe that of our system-induced links among concepts would be suggestive and useful. The fact that CAT (i.e., the category-based representation scheme) performs relatively well in our evaluations gives some comfort, and visual inspection of the inferred links at the concept level also supports that conclusion, though with occasional errors, such as the one high-

Table 5: Examples of linked Wikipedia categories in our system-induced concept graph

1st Wikipedia Category	Linked Wikipedia Category
"Partial differential equations"	"Ordinary differential eqns."
"Ethnography"	"Geography"
"Extrasolar Planets"	"Chaos Theory"
"British Industrial designers"	"Graphic Design"

lighted in red in Table 5 below. The first column in the table are examples of system-assigned Wikipedia categories to courses in our data sets; the second column consists of the linked Wikipedia categories with the higher weight (assigned by our system) given each category in the first column, which means that the concept in the 2nd-column should be taught before the corresponding concept in the first column.

5. CONCLUDING REMARKS

We conducted a new investigation on automatically inferring directed graphs at both the course level and the concept level, to enable prerequisite prediction for within-university and cross-university settings.

We proposed three approaches: a classification approach (CGL.Class), a learning to rank approach (CGL.Rank), and a nearest-neighbor search approach (kNN). Both CGL.Class and CGL.Rank (deploying adapted versions of SVM algorithms) explicitly model concept-level dependencies through a directed graph, and support an interlingua-style transfer learning across universities, while kNN makes simpler prediction without learning concept dependencies. To tackle the extremely high-dimensional optimization in our problems (e.g., 2×10^8 links in the concept graph for the MIT courses), our novel reformulation CGL.Rank enables the deployment of fast numerical solutions. On our newly collected datasets from MIT, Caltech, CMU and Princeton, CGL.Rank proved best under MAP and ROC/AUC, and computationally much more efficient than kNN.

We also tested four representation schemes for document content: using the original words, using Wikipedia categories as concepts, using a distributed word representation, and using sparse word encoding. The first two: original words and Wikipedia-derived concepts proved best. Our results in both the within-university and cross-university settings are highly encouraging.

We envision that the cross-university transfer learning of our approaches is particularly important for future application to MOOCs where courses come from different providers and across institutions, and there are seldom any explicit prerequisite links. A rich suite of future work includes:

- Testing on cross-university or cross-course-provider prerequisite links. We have tested cross-university transfer learning, but the inferred links are within each target university, rather than cross-institutional links. A natural extension of the current work is to predict cross-institutional prerequisites. For this kind of evaluation we will need labeled ground truth of cross-university prerequisites.
- Cross-language transfer. Using the Wikipedia categories and Wikipedia entries in different languages, it would be an interesting challenge to infer prerequisite relations for courses in different languages by mapping to the Wikipedia category/concept interlingua.
- Extensions of the inference from single source to multiple sources, from single media (text) to multiple media (including videos), and from single granularity level (courses) to multiple levels (including lectures).
- Deploying the induced concept graph for personalized curriculum planning by students and for syllabus design and course modularization by teachers.

6. ACKNOWLEDGMENTS

This work is supported in part by the National Science Foundation (NSF) under grant IIS 1350364.

7. REFERENCES

[1] R. Al-Rfou, B. Perozzi, and S. Skiena. Polyglot: Distributed word representations for multilingual nlp. *arXiv preprint arXiv:1307.1662*, 2013.

[2] A. Ben-Israel and T. N. Greville. *Generalized inverses*, volume 13. Springer, 2003.

[3] S. Boyd and L. Vandenberghe. *Convex optimization.* Cambridge university press, 2004.

[4] E. J. Candès and B. Recht. Exact matrix completion via convex optimization. *Foundations of Computational mathematics*, 9(6):717–772, 2009.

[5] Y. Chen, B. Perozzi, R. Al-Rfou, and S. Skiena. The expressive power of word embeddings. *arXiv preprint arXiv:1301.3226*, 2013.

[6] R. Collobert, J. Weston, L. Bottou, M. Karlen, K. Kavukcuoglu, and P. Kuksa. Natural language processing (almost) from scratch. *The Journal of Machine Learning Research*, 12:2493–2537, 2011.

[7] C. Do and A. Y. Ng. Transfer learning for text classification. In *NIPS*, 2005.

[8] D. W. Fausett and C. T. Fulton. Large least squares problems involving kronecker products. *SIAM Journal on Matrix Analysis and Applications*, 15(1):219–227, 1994.

[9] M. Fazel. *Matrix rank minimization with applications.* PhD thesis, PhD thesis, Stanford University, 2002.

[10] S. Gopal and Y. Yang. Recursive regularization for large-scale classification with hierarchical and graphical dependencies. In *Proceedings of the 19th ACM SIGKDD international conference on Knowledge discovery and data mining*, pages 257–265. ACM, 2013.

[11] P. O. Hoyer. Non-negative matrix factorization with sparseness constraints. *The Journal of Machine Learning Research*, 5:1457–1469, 2004.

[12] T. Joachims, H. Li, T.-Y. Liu, and C. Zhai. Learning to rank for information retrieval (lr4ir 2007). In *SIGIR Forum*, volume 41, pages 58–62, 2007.

[13] C. R. Johnson. Matrix completion problems: a survey. In *Proceedings of Symposia in Applied Mathematics*, volume 40, pages 171–198, 1990.

[14] H. Kim and H. Park. Nonnegative matrix factorization based on alternating nonnegativity constrained least squares and active set method. *SIAM Journal on Matrix Analysis and Applications*, 30(2):713–730, 2008.

[15] M. Kshirsagar, J. Carbonell, and J. Klein-Seetharaman. Transfer learning based

methods towards the discovery of host-pathogen protein-protein interactions. In *Proc of ISMB*, volume 40, pages 171–198, 1990.

[16] J. Kunegis and A. Lommatzsch. Learning spectral graph transformations for link prediction. In *Proceedings of the 26th Annual International Conference on Machine Learning*, pages 561–568. ACM, 2009.

[17] Q. V. Le and T. Mikolov. Distributed representations of sentences and documents. *arXiv preprint arXiv:1405.4053*, 2014.

[18] D. D. Lee and H. S. Seung. Learning the parts of objects by non-negative matrix factorization. *Nature*, 401(6755):788–791, 1999.

[19] D. Liben-Nowell and J. Kleinberg. The link-prediction problem for social networks. *Journal of the American society for information science and technology*, 58(7):1019–1031, 2007.

[20] R. N. Lichtenwalter, J. T. Lussier, and N. V. Chawla. New perspectives and methods in link prediction. In *Proceedings of the 16th ACM SIGKDD international conference on Knowledge discovery and data mining*, pages 243–252. ACM, 2010.

[21] T. Mikolov, K. Chen, G. Corrado, and J. Dean. Efficient estimation of word representations in vector space. *arXiv preprint arXiv:1301.3781*, 2013.

[22] Y. Nesterov. A method of solving a convex programming problem with convergence rate o (1/k2). In *Soviet Mathematics Doklady*, volume 27, pages 372–376, 1983.

[23] Y. Nesterov. On an approach to the construction of optimal methods of minimization of smooth convex functions. *Ekonomika i Mateaticheskie Metody*, 24:509–517, 1988.

[24] X. Su and T. M. Khoshgoftaar. A survey of collaborative filtering techniques. *Advances in artificial intelligence*, 2009:4, 2009.

[25] L. Yang, S. Hanneke, and J. Carbonell. A theory of transfer learning with applications to active learning. *Machine learning*, 90(2):161–189, 2013.

[26] J. Zhang, Z. Ghahramani, and Y. Yang. Flexible latent variable models for multi-task learning. *Machine Learning*, 73(3):221–242, 2008.

Review Synthesis for Micro-Review Summarization

Thanh-Son Nguyen
School of Information Systems
Singapore Management University
tsnguyen.2013@phdis.smu.edu.sg

Hady W. Lauw
School of Information Systems
Singapore Management University
hadywlauw@smu.edu.sg

Panayiotis Tsaparas*
Dept. of Computer Science
University of Ioannina
Greece
tsap@cs.uoi.gr

ABSTRACT

Micro-reviews is a new type of user-generated content arising from the prevalence of mobile devices and social media in the past few years. Micro-reviews are bite-size reviews (usually under 200 characters), commonly posted on social media or check-in services, using a mobile device. They capture the immediate reaction of users, and they are rich in information, concise, and to the point. However, the abundance of micro-reviews, and their telegraphic nature make it increasingly difficult to go through them and extract the useful information, especially on a mobile device. In this paper, we address the problem of summarizing the micro-reviews of an entity, such that the summary is *representative*, *compact*, and *readable*. We formulate the summarization problem as that of synthesizing a new "review" using snippets of full-text reviews. To produce a summary that naturally balances compactness and representativeness, we work within the Minimum Description Length framework. We show that finding the optimal summary is NP-hard, and we consider approximation and heuristic algorithms. We perform a thorough evaluation of our methodology on real-life data collected from Foursquare and Yelp. We demonstrate that our summaries outperform individual reviews, as well as existing summarization approaches.

Categories and Subject Descriptors

H.4 [**Information Systems Applications**]: Miscellaneous; H.2.8 [**Database Applications**]: Data Mining

General Terms

Algorithms, Experimentation

Keywords

micro-review summarization; review synthesis

*This work has been supported by the Marie Curie Reintegration Grant project titled JMUGCS which has received research funding from the European Union.

WSDM'15, February 2–6, 2015, Shanghai, China.

ACM 978-1-4503-3317-7/15/02 ...$15.00.
http://dx.doi.org/10.1145/2684822.2685321.

1. INTRODUCTION

The confluence of the two fast-moving trends, the increasing penetration of mobile devices and the prevalence of social media, has given rise to a new breed of mobile social media platforms. Exemplars of such platforms include the well-known check-in services Foursquare and Facebook Places. In such services, users interact by sharing their experiences on various venues and services (restaurants, pubs, salons, etc.) with their friends and the public, providing invaluable decision aids to future customers.

A byproduct of this behavior is *micro-reviews*: concise, bite-sized reviews produced on micro-blogging platforms and location-based social networks. For instance, in Foursquare, micro-reviews, more popularly known as *tips*, are limited to 200 characters, and they are written by users when checking in at a particular point of interest. These tips serve several purposes: They may offer opinion on some aspects of the restaurant ("*Great place to stop by for a quick bite or for a good cup of coffee. Bustling atmosphere and reasonable prices.*"); They may give recommendations on what to order ("*We particularly love the coffee gelato flavor from Eataly. Light and creamy.*"); They may be actual "tips" or suggestions ("*If you live in the neighborhood shop after 8:30PM for minimal human traffic and shorter lines.*").

There are some characteristic differences between micro-reviews and regular reviews found on sites such as Yelp. Micro-reviews are concise, making a crisp point about a specific aspect, whereas reviews typically cover various aspects comprehensively. Micro-reviews tend to be spontaneous, giving a real-time reaction to the author's current experience, whereas reviews tend to be contemplative and reflective. Micro-reviews are often accompanied by check-ins, which lend them a degree of authenticity. Micro-reviews are growing faster than regular reviews. For instance, Foursquare content (micro-reviews) is growing 65% per year on a base of 35 million users, while Yelp content (reviews) is growing 41% per year, on a larger base of 108 million users[1].

Micro-reviews are thus an important source of information for users seeking information for making decisions. However, their increased popularity has led to an abundance of content. It is common for popular venues to have several hundreds of micro-reviews. While the concise and telegraphic nature of an individual micro-review makes it easy to convey a specific point, the very same property makes it difficult to go through a *collection* of micro-reviews to extract useful information, especially on a mobile device. This is because

[1]`http://www.fastcompany.com/3015168/foursquares-tips-growing-faster-than-yelps-reviews`

the collection consists of a large volume of fragmented opinions, all by different authors, expressing views that in some cases are highly repetitive. There exists useful information in the collection, but it is scattered across multiple micro-reviews, and as a result, diluted and obscure to the reader. To make the collective wisdom of micro-reviews useful, we need to piece it together into a single coherent piece of text.

We therefore consider the following problem. Given a collection of tips about an entity, produce a text summary of the information content of the tips. Ideally, this summary should capture most, if not all, of the points made by the tips in the collection, in a concise and coherent fashion that is easy to consume on a mobile device. Inspired by the highly complementary nature of micro-reviews and reviews, we propose to use review content for this task. While micro-reviews are good at identifying the salient points about an entity, a review is often a coherent, well-written piece of text, produced by an author who seeks to comprehensively describe her experience with the entity. We propose to *synthesize* a new "review", by taking the "best" parts of some reviews, and putting them together into a text summary.

Overview of our approach. We now give a high-level overview of our methodology. Given a set of tips about an entity (e.g., a restaurant), and a set of reviews about the same entity, we seek to construct a *readable*, *compact* and *representative* summary of the tips, using the review text. We assume that each review can be split into multiple coherent *snippets*, e.g., paragraphs. The summary we construct will be a collection of snippets (possibly from multiple reviews) that best capture the information content of the tips.

The representativeness and compactness objectives are often conflicting. A highly representative summary contains more and longer snippets, making it less compact. A highly compact summary may under-represent the information content of the tips. To model this trade-off holistically, in Section 3.2, we formulate our problem within the Minimum Description Length (MDL) framework, where we view the tips as being encoded by the snippets, and we seek to find a collection of snippets that produce the encoding with the minimum number of bits. We show that finding the optimal summary is NP-hard (Section 3.3). We establish a connection between our problem and the Uncapacitated Facility Location Problem, and show that there exists an algorithm with $(1 + \log n)$-approximation ratio for n tips. We also consider different heuristic algorithms for optimizing the MDL cost (Section 4). In Section 5, to investigate the efficacy of our algorithms, we compare them empirically to several baselines on real data from Foursquare and Yelp, in terms of representativeness, compactness, and readability.

Contributions. In this work, we make the following contributions. *First,* we introduce the problem of micro-review summarization, by synthesizing a summary from review snippets. We formulate constructing a compact and representative summary as a novel combinatorial optimization problem within the MDL framework. *Second,* we prove that finding the optimal summary is NP-hard. We show that our problem can be formulated algorithmically as an instance of Uncapacitated Facility Location Problem, for which there exists a $(1 + \log n)$-approximation greedy algorithm. *Third,* in addition to the greedy algorithm, we consider several heuristic algorithms. We demonstrate their efficacy on real-life datasets with respect to existing reviews, as well as summaries generated by existing techniques.

2. RELATED WORK

We now relate our work to the existing literature, broadly categorized into works that focus on summarization, mining reviews, and minimum description length.

Document Summarization. The objective of document summarization is to reduce one or more text documents into a compressed text. Broadly speaking, there are two categories of approaches. The first consists of *extractive methods*, which select text snippets (e.g., sentences, paragraphs) from the documents to be summarized. This selection may be based on clustering [20], or ranking [17]. The second consists of *abstractive methods*, which build some form of semantic representation, and then generate new or edited pieces of text to express that representation [5, 4].

If we consider micro-reviews simply as text, our problem can be seen as an instance of document summarization. Our work is related to extractive summarization, but with a key difference that we select text snippets, not from the corpus to be summarized (i.e., tips), but from an independent corpus of a different type (i.e., reviews). To validate our approach, we will compare against exemplars of both extractive (i.e., MEAD [20]) and abstractive (i.e., OPINOSIS [5]) methods in our experiments (see Section 5).

There are also other forms of summaries. For instance, reviews may be summarized in terms of the statistical distributions of sentiments for various features or aspects [9, 27], or by listing just the "key phrases" [6, 16]. These are orthogonal directions to our goal of producing a flowing text as a summary.

Review Mining. Our work is related to several lines of work in mining reviews. While we synthesize a "review" to create a summary of micro-reviews, there is a previous effort to create a synthetic review [23] to simulate a *fake review*. *Review ranking* seeks to rank reviews based on some notion of "quality" [14]. *Review selection* [12] seeks to select a specified number K of reviews based on some criteria, and it is commonly formulated as a variation of the maximum coverage problem [24, 11].

There exists previous work on review selection for covering micro-review content [18]. The problem of review selection is fundamentally different from micro-review summarization. Review selection imposes the restriction of selecting multiple *full* reviews from the existing corpus, while summarization aims at creating a single piece of text. Furthermore, in review selection, any individual review is not necessarily representative of all the points raised by tips, while the set of reviews as a whole is not necessarily compact, since the same points may be covered in multiple reviews. By synthesizing a "review", we do not run into the above issues, as it is not necessary to select whole reviews, but instead only the snippets that best represent the micro-reviews. To validate this point, in the experiments (see Section 5), we will compare to the review selected by [18], and more generally to all existing reviews in the dataset as well.

While reviews have been studied extensively, relatively little attention has been paid to micro-reviews. Most of the previous work on Foursquare, for example, look at it as a location-based social network, paying attention to the factors of locations and social links, rather than to the textual content of the micro-reviews. For instance, the aspects that have been studied include geographic analysis [19] and location-based recommendation [25].

Minimum Description Length. Minimum description length (MDL), introduced by Rissanen [21], is a well-established principle for model selection [7]. MDL itself is a general framework. The specification of the model space, and the manner in which the model describes the data, vary across applications. For instance, [1] employs MDL to model the interaction between two types of objects (expressed as an adjacency matrix) to find cross-associations. We also employ MDL to model the "interaction" between review snippets and micro-reviews, but our objective is different in selecting review snippets that summarize micro-reviews.

The optimization problem we define within the MDL framework is an instance of the Uncapacitated Facility Location Problem (UFLP) (see Section 3.3). There are also works on metric UFLP [22, 10, 13], but the metric assumption does not apply to our case.

3. PROBLEM FORMULATION

In this section, we formulate the micro-review summarization problem as a combinatorial optimization problem within the Minimum Description Length framework.

3.1 Preliminaries

Given a specific entity of interest (e.g., a restaurant), we are given as input a set of n micro-reviews (or tips) $\mathcal{T}$ for that entity. Each tip $t \in \mathcal{T}$ is modeled as a bag of words $\{w_1, w_2, \ldots, w_{|t|}\}$, where each word is drawn from a vocabulary W. This vocabulary is the universe of all the terms that appear in any tip or review.

In addition, we are given a set of m full-text reviews $\mathcal{R}$ for the same entity. We view each review $R \in \mathcal{R}$ as a collection of *snippets* $\{r_1, r_2, \ldots, r_{|R|}\}$. Each snippet $r \in R$ is a contiguous piece of text within R. In this work, we treat each review paragraph as a snippet. Snippets of different granularity can also be defined, such as, sentences, or text windows of a pre-specified length. We opt to work with paragraphs because they correspond to thematic units of variable length defined by the author herself, which are usually self-contained and discuss a coherent atomic idea of the author. Similar to tips, each snippet r is modeled as a bag of words drawn from the vocabulary W. The union of snippets from all reviews in $\mathcal{R}$ is denoted $\mathcal{U}_{\mathcal{R}}$.

A summary S is a set of review snippets, i.e., $S \subseteq \mathcal{U}_{\mathcal{R}}$. Given $\mathcal{T}$ and $\mathcal{R}$, our objective is to find the "best" summary of $\mathcal{T}$. Customarily, a summary is good if it can represent the underlying content being summarized (representativeness), and it can do so with a significantly shorter length than the full content (compactness). The two requirements, representativeness and compactness, are inherently conflicting. A longer summary may capture the underlying content better than a shorter summary. However, a summary that is too long is no longer a "summary". The goal is to find a "sweet spot" that balances the representativeness and compactness in a holistic way so as to obtain the best possible summary.

3.2 Problem Definition

To identify this "optimal" summary, we turn to Minimum Description Length (MDL) [21], a parameter-free framework for model selection. MDL deals with the issue of how to choose a model that can describe the data as concisely as possible [7]. A very complex model may be able to describe the data concisely, but the model itself would be very expensive to describe. In contrast, a simple model is easy to describe, but then describing the data becomes expensive. Importantly, MDL is parameter-free. It automatically determines the best model that balances both the cost of the model and the cost of describing the data using that model.

In our case, the data to describe are the tips in $\mathcal{T}$. A model is a summary $\mathcal{S}$, consisting of a collection of review snippets, and an assignment of each tip to one of the selected snippets. The snippet describes, or summarizes, the tips assigned to it. Let S denote the set of snippets in the summary, and let T_r denote the set of tips assigned to a snippet $r \in S$. The summary $\mathcal{S}$ is defined as the pair $\mathcal{S} = (S, \{T_r\}_{r \in S})$.

The quality of a solution is evaluated by a cost function $cost(\mathcal{T}, \mathcal{S})$ which is the cost to describe the data in $\mathcal{T}$ using the model $\mathcal{S}$. This cost function is decomposed into two parts: the model cost $model(\mathcal{S})$ which is the cost to describe the model $\mathcal{S}$, and the data cost $data(\mathcal{T}|\mathcal{S})$ which is the cost to describe the data in $\mathcal{T}$ given the model $\mathcal{S}$. A solution with low cost balances between having a complex descriptive model (high model cost) which describes accurately the data (low data cost), and a simple model (low model cost) which yields a complex description of the data (high data cost).

MDL has a natural information-theoretic interpretation, as a lossless encoding mechanism for the underlying data. The MDL cost function can be interpreted as the cost of communicating the data between two parties. In this case, the sender sends the model to the receiver, and then the description of the data using the model. The cost is computed as the number of bits needed to transmit the data.

For our problem, we are interested in encoding documents, which are "bags of words", that is, multisets of words. Any single document, or any corpus (collection) of documents, $\mathcal{D}$, defines a *language model* $M_D = (D, P_D)$, which consists of the vocabulary D of the document, and a probability distribution P_D over the words of the vocabulary. The probability $P_D(w)$ of word $w \in D$ is (usually) defined as the fraction of times that word w appears in $\mathcal{D}$.

It is well known in information theory [2] that given a domain D and a distribution P_D over this domain, the optimal encoding of D assigns a codeword of length $-\log P_D(w)$ to every element $w \in D$. This optimal encoding can be asymptotically achieved using the Huffmann encoding. Therefore, a language model $M_D = (D, P_D)$ defines an encoding of the words in the vocabulary D, and an encoding of words defines a language model. We will use the two interchangeably. We use $\text{bits}_D(w) = -\log P_D(w)$ to denote the length of the encoding of word w in the language model M_D. We also refer to this as the *cost* of the encoding. For a bag of words s from the vocabulary D, the cost of the encoding of s is

$$\text{bits}_D(s) = -\sum_{w \in s} \log P_D(w) = \sum_{w \in s} \text{bits}_D(w)$$

where, the sum over the set s, accounts for the multiple occurrences of the words in s.

We can now describe the MDL formulation of our problem, which describes the process of encoding and transmitting the set of tips $\mathcal{T}$ using the model defined by the summary $\mathcal{S}$. First, we assume that both the sender and the recipient already share the knowledge of the global vocabulary W and the language model (code) M_W for the vocabulary W. This model may be derived from any known corpus of the English language, but in our work we assume that it is defined by the collection of reviews $\mathcal{R}$. Using this common information, we can define the model and data costs.

Model Cost. We begin by describing the summary $\mathcal{S} = (S, \{T_r\}_{r \in S})$ to the recipient, as follows.

1. First, we communicate the number of tips $n = |\mathcal{T}|$, which is the same for any model, and does not affect model selection.

2. We then communicate the number of snippets $k = |S|$ in the summary. Since $k \in [1, n]$, this can be done using $\log n$ bits.

3. We then communicate which tips are assigned to each snippet. For every snippet r, the tips in T_r will be transmitted together in sequence; therefore, we only need to communicate the transition points when we switch from one snippet to the next. For k snippets, there are $(k-1)$ transition points, and each transition is a value between 1 to n. This can be done using $(k-1) \times \log n$ bits.

4. Finally, we need to transmit the snippets $r \in S$. We use the model M_W to encode the snippets, resulting in $\sum_{r \in S} \text{bits}_W(r)$ number of bits.

Putting everything together, the cost for transmitting the model is computed as follows.

$$\begin{aligned} model(S) &= \log n + (k-1)\log n + \sum_{r \in S} \text{bits}_W(r) \\ &= \sum_{r \in S} (\log n + \text{bits}_W(r)) \end{aligned} \tag{1}$$

Data Cost. Given our model $\mathcal{S}$, we now encode the tips in $\mathcal{T}$ with the corresponding snippets. Let $r \in S$ denote one of the snippets. The snippet r is a bag of words, and defines a language model $M_r = (W, P_r)$. We will use this model to encode the set of tips in T_r associated to r by our model.

To compute the encoding cost for T_r, we need to address the following issue. Since the snippet r contains a subset of the words in W, for any word $w \notin r$ we have $P_r(w) = 0$ and thus the encoding cost is infinite. Therefore, we need to "smooth" the language model M_r, such that all terms in W would have non-zero probabilities. There are a number of smoothing methods [15]. We adopt the Laplace or additive smoothing, which adds $\alpha|W|$ number of word occurrences to r, and shares this count uniformly among all the words in the vocabulary. This method belongs to the class of Bayesian smoothing, specifically with uniform Dirichlet priors [26]. The smoothed generation probability of a word is as follows.

$$P_r(w) = \frac{\text{tf}_{r,w} + \alpha}{|r| + \alpha|W|} \tag{2}$$

In this equation, $\text{tf}_{r,w}$ is the number of occurrences of the word w in the snippet r, while α is the smoothing coefficient. Larger α tends towards a more even distribution over words. In the extremes, for $\alpha = 0$ we obtain the original probability, while for $\alpha \to \infty$ we obtain the uniform distribution.

Given the definition of $P_r(w)$ we can now define the encoding cost of tip t by snippet r as follows.

$$\text{bits}_r(t) = -\sum_{w \in t} \log P_r(w)$$

The encoding cost of the set of all tips is defined as follows.

$$data(\mathcal{T}|\mathcal{S}) = \sum_{r \in S} \sum_{t \in T_r} \text{bits}_r(t) \tag{3}$$

Given the definition for the model and data cost, the total cost for the summary $\mathcal{S}$ of the set of tips $\mathcal{T}$ is Equation 4.

$$\begin{aligned} cost(\mathcal{T}, \mathcal{S}) &= model(\mathcal{S}) + data(\mathcal{T}|\mathcal{S}) \\ &= \sum_{r \in S} \left[(\log n + \text{bits}_W(r)) + \sum_{t \in T_r} \text{bits}_r(t) \right] \end{aligned} \tag{4}$$

This equation clearly shows the trade-off between the model cost and the encoding cost. A greater number of snippets, or longer snippets, contribute to a more complex model $\mathcal{S}$ with higher model cost. However, it has the potential to decrease the encoding cost. Conversely, a very simple model may have a low model cost, but high encoding cost.

We are now ready to formally state our problem.

PROBLEM 1 (MICRO-REVIEW SUMMARIZATION (MIRS)). *Given a set of tips or micro-reviews $\mathcal{T}$, a set of reviews $\mathcal{R}$, find a summary $\mathcal{S}$, such that $cost(\mathcal{T}, \mathcal{S})$ is minimized.*

3.3 Complexity and Approximability

We now study the MIRS problem theoretically. We show that the problem is NP-hard. However, using a connection between MIRS and the Uncapacitated Facility Location Problem we can show that there exists a greedy algorithm with a $(1 + \log n)$-approximation ratio.

LEMMA 1. *The* MIRS *problem is NP-hard.*

PROOF SKETCH. The proof is based on a reduction from vertex cover (known to be NP-hard). Vertex cover seeks the minimum set of vertices in a graph, such that all edges in the graph are incident on at least one of the vertices in this set. In particular, we consider vertex cover on a regular graph [3]. In a d-regular graph, all vertices have degree exactly d.

We show that vertex cover on a d-regular graph $G(V, E)$ is a special instance of the MIRS problem with $\alpha = 0$. For each edge $e \in E$, we create a tip t_e, containing a unique word w_e for this edge (e.g., the edge ID). The size of the vocabulary $|W|$ is thus the same as the number of edges $|E|$. For each vertex $v \in V$, we create a review with one snippet r_v, containing d words corresponding to the d edges of v.

Since every vertex v has exactly d edges, correspondingly every snippet r_v contains exactly d words. Therefore, in the language model M_{r_v} we have $P_{r_v}(w_e) = 1/d$ for any word $w_e \in r_v$. This means that using any r_v to encode t_e, when e is incident on v, requires a constant number of $\text{bits}_{r_v}(t_e) = \log d$ bits. Since $\alpha = 0$, it costs infinitely high for r_v to encode t_e, when e is not incident on v.

Since every edge is incident on exactly two vertices, correspondingly every word occurs in exactly two snippets. Therefore, all words in W have the same frequency, and therefore, in the model M_W, we have that $P_W(w_e) = 1/n$ for all $w_e \in W$. In turn, this means that $\text{bits}_W(r) = d \log n$ for any r. Therefore, minimizing $cost(\mathcal{T}_E, \mathcal{S})$, where $\mathcal{T}_E$ is the set of tips corresponding to E, is equivalent to finding the set V_S with the minimum number of snippets (vertices) that collectively contain all the words (cover all the edges). □

Since the MIRS problem is NP-hard, we look for algorithms with known approximation guarantees. We can prove the following lemma.

LEMMA 2. *There exists a* $(1 + \log n)$*-approximation algorithm for the* MIRS *problem.*

PROOF. We will prove the lemma by showing that the MIRS is an instance of the UNCAPACITATED FACILITY LOCATION PROBLEM (UFLP) [8]. For UFLP, we are given a set of facilities $\mathcal{U_R}$ and a set of customers $\mathcal{T}$. We also know the cost f_r for opening each facility $r \in \mathcal{U_R}$, as well as the cost c_{rt} to serve customer $t \in \mathcal{T}$ from facility r. The goal is to determine which subset of facilities to open (i.e., $y_r = 1$ if facility r is opened, and 0 otherwise), and which customers to service from each opened facility (i.e., $x_{rt} = 1$ if customer t is serviced from facility r, and 0 otherwise), so as to minimize the total cost $\sum_{r \in \mathcal{U_R}} [f_r \cdot y_r + \sum_{t \in \mathcal{T}} c_{rt} \cdot x_{rt}]$.

It is easy to see that in the case of MIRS, the snippets are the facilities, and the tips are the customers. The cost of opening a facility r is the cost of encoding the review snippet r: $f_r = \log n + \text{bits}_W(r)$. The cost of servicing a customer t at facility r is the encoding cost of a tip t using the snippet r: $c_{rt} = \text{bits}_r(t)$. Here, $y_r = 1$ if $r \in S$, and $y_r = 0$ if $r \notin S$; $x_{rt} = 1$ if $t \in T_r$, and $x_{rt} = 0$ if $t \notin T_r$.

There is a body of work on approximation algorithms for the UFLP problem [22, 10], however most work is focused on the case where the service cost, c_{rt}, between customers and facilities defines a distance metric. This does not apply to MIRS, where $\text{bits}_r(t)$ is not metric (it is easy to see that it is not even reflexive). One known approximation algorithm for the non-metric UFLP is the greedy algorithm for MINIMUM WEIGHT SET COVER (MWSC) [8]. We describe the algorithm in Section 4.1. This algorithm has a provable approximation ratio of $1 + \log n$, where n is the number of tips, or customers. □

4. ALGORITHMS

We now propose algorithms for the MIRS problem. We assume that the encoding cost of every snippet f_r, $\forall r \in \mathcal{U_R}$, and the encoding cost of any tip using any snippet c_{rt}, $\forall r \in \mathcal{U_R}, t \in \mathcal{T}$ have been pre-computed. The output of the algorithms is a summary $\mathcal{S} = (S, \{T_r\}_{r \in S})$.

4.1 Greedy Synthesis

This is the approximation algorithm for the non-metric UFLP, which finds a solution to an instance of the MINIMUM WEIGHT SET COVER (MWSC) problem. The MIRS can be cast as an instance of MWSC, as follows. For every pair (r, T_r), consisting of a snippet $r \in \mathcal{U_R}$ and a subset of tips $T_r \subseteq \mathcal{T}$, we define a set that "covers" the elements in T_r, with weight $f_r + \sum_{t \in T_r} c_{rt}$. Solving MWSC by finding the sub-collection of all such sets that cover all the tips in $\mathcal{T}$ with the smallest total weight also provides a solution to the corresponding MIRS instance. While enumerating all possible pairs of (r, T_r) explicitly may be intractable, [8] shows that, for each r, it is sufficient to consider those pairs (r, T_r^k), for $k = 1, \ldots, |\mathcal{T}|$, where T_r^k denotes the first k tips in a linear order of non-decreasing c_{rt}.

The pseudocode of the GREEDY SYNTHESIS algorithm is shown in Algorithm 1. In each step, we pick the pair (r, T_r) that is most effective, i.e., having the lowest average cost (line 3 in the algorithm). This can be done in $O(|\mathcal{U_R}| \times |\mathcal{T}|)$ time. Once such a pair is identified, r is included in the output S, and the tips in T_r are removed from further consideration (line 4). This process is repeated until all the tips in $\mathcal{T}$ have been covered. Finally, we assign each tip to the "closest" snippet in S with the lowest encoding cost. This step is needed since the greedy selection may not have associated a tip with the lowest encoding cost snippet in S.

Algorithm 1: Greedy Synthesis

1 Initialize $S = \emptyset$; $T = \mathcal{T}$; $U = \mathcal{U_R}$
2 **while** $T \neq \emptyset$ *or* $U \neq \emptyset$ **do**
3   Find the pair (r, T_r), where $r \in U$ and $T_r \subseteq T$, which minimizes $\frac{f_r + \sum_{t \in T_r} c_{rt}}{|T_r|}$
4   Update $S = S \cup r$; $U = U \setminus r$; and $T = T \setminus T_r$
5 **return** S *and* $\forall r \in S, T_r = \{t \in \mathcal{T} | r = \arg\min_{r' \in S} c_{r't}\}$

Algorithm 2: Partitional Synthesis

1 $S_1 = \{r\}$, where $r = \arg\min_{r' \in \mathcal{U_R}} f_{r'} + \sum_{t \in \mathcal{T}} c_{r't}$.
2 $C_1 = cost(S, \mathcal{T})$
3 **for** $k = 2, \ldots, |\mathcal{T}|$ **do**
4   Let S_k be k random snippets drawn from $\mathcal{U_R}$.
5   **repeat**
6   **for** $r \in S_k$ **do**
7             $T_r = \{t \in \mathcal{T} \mid r = \arg\min_{r' \in S_k} c_{r't}\}$.
8   **for** T_r **do**
9             $r^* = \arg\min_{r' \in \mathcal{R}} f_{r^*} + \sum_{t \in T_r} c_{r^*t}$.
10   replace r with r^* in S_k.
11   **until** $C_k = cost(S_k, \{T_r\}_{r \in S_k})$ *does not change*
12   **if** $C_k > C_{k-1}$ **then**
13   break
14 **return** S_{k-1} *and* $\{T_r\}_{r \in S_{k-1}}$

4.2 Partitional Synthesis

In GREEDY SYNTHESIS, the snippets already selected affect the choice of the next snippet, but previous decisions are never reconsidered or changed. We now consider a heuristic that considers the solution that tries to identify a local minimum in the MDL cost function. The heuristic is motivated by the observation that given a summary with k snippets, the assignment of tips to the snippets defines a partition of the tips into k clusters. The intuition is to search the space of possible tip partitions and snippet selections to find one with the lowest MDL cost.

This algorithm, which we name PARTITIONAL SYNTHESIS, is described by Algorithm 2. It considers different values for k (the number of snippets), starting from $k = 1$ and going potentially up to n. We try to find the best solution with k snippets through an iterative process reminiscent of k-means clustering. Starting with a random selection of k snippets, we assign each tip to the snippet that best encodes it (lines 6–7 of the algorithm). In turn, for each collection of tips, we find the snippet that encodes this collection with the lowest cost (lines 8–10 of the algorithm). This iterative process is conducted until the total cost does not further improve, thus reaching a local optimum. To ensure that we do not select a poor solution due to bad choice of the initial snippets, for a given k we repeat the process with M random initializations, and we pick the best solution. We keep increasing the value of k as long as we obtain a solution with a lower MDL cost. If for some k there is no further improvement, we terminate the algorithm and return the current best solution. The complexity of this process is linear with respect to its variables, i.e., $O(k \times M \times |\mathcal{U}_{\mathcal{R}}| \times |\mathcal{T}|)$.

4.3 Hierarchical Synthesis

Motivated by the parallels between our summarization problem and clustering, we consider an algorithm that constructs a partition of the tips in a top-down hierarchical fashion. This algorithm, which we call HIERARCHICAL SYNTHESIS, is described in Algorithm 3. Starting from an existing number of partitions (initially 1), we split an existing partition into two. To determine which partition to split, we rank the existing partitions in decreasing order of average encoding cost. We then try to split the highest-ranked partition T_r associated with snippet r (lines 5–6 of the algorithm). The split is conducted using the PARTITIONAL SYNTHESIS as a subroutine with $k = 2$ (line 7). If the split is sucessful, resulting in a lower cost, we replace r with the two new snippets r_1 and r_2, and proceed to the next iteration (lines 8–10). Otherwise, we try to split the next highest-ranked snippet/partition that has not been tried. If none of the existing partitions can be split to improve the cost, the algorithm terminates and returns the current best solution. The complexity of this algorithm is similar to PARTITIONAL SYNTHESIS, but in practice it is faster, since when going from $k-1$ to k, we only need to split one partition into two.

Algorithm 3: Hierarchical Synthesis

1 $S_1 = \{r\}$, where $r = \arg\min_{r' \in \mathcal{U}_{\mathcal{R}}} f_{r'} + \sum_{t \in \mathcal{T}} c_{r't}$.
2 $C_1 = cost(S, \mathcal{T})$
3 **for** $k = 2, \ldots, |\mathcal{T}|$ **do**
4   **repeat**
5   Let r be the next un-tried snippet in S_{k-1} with highest $\frac{f_r + \sum_{t \in T_r} c_{rt}}{|T_r|}$.
6   Let T_r be $\{t \in \mathcal{T} | r = \arg\min_{r' \in S_{k-1}} c_{r't}\}$.
7   Find new snippets r_1 and r_2 using PARTITIONAL SYNTHESIS to split T_r into 2 partitions.
8   **if** *successful split* **then**
9       $S_k = (S_{k-1} \setminus r) \cup \{r_1, r_2\}$
10   break
11   **until** *all snippets in* S_{k-1} *have been tried*
12   **if** *no split* **then**
13   break
14 **return** S_{k-1} *and* $\{T_r\}_{r \in S_{k-1}}$

5. EXPERIMENTS

Our objective is to investigate the effectiveness of our methodology in producing summaries that are representative, compact, and readable. We note that computational efficiency is not a major concern, as this is expected to be an offline batch operation, and the proposed heuristics are efficient. GREEDY SYNTHESIS completes in seconds on a machine with Intel Xeon CPU @ 2.90GHz. PARTITIONAL SYNTHESIS and HIERARCHICAL SYNTHESIS with a hundred random initializations complete in a few minutes. If necessary, these random trials are embarrassingly parallelizable.

5.1 Dataset

As input, we require paired sources of micro-reviews and reviews concerning the same entities. For this, we turn to Foursquare and Yelp. For reviews, we crawl Yelp to collect all the reviews of the top 110 restaurants in New York City with the most number of reviews as of March 2012. For micro-reviews, we crawl Foursquare to collect all the tips of the same 110 restaurants. Because some restaurants in Foursquare have too few tips, we filter out 8 restaurants with less than 50 tips each, and retain the remaining 102 restaurants for experiments. The statistics of this dataset are shown in Table 1. On average, a restaurant has 145 tips. Meanwhile, the average number of reviews per restaurant is 947. Since each review contains multiple snippets (i.e., paragraphs), it results in an average of 3K snippets per restaurant. Each restaurant constitutes a distinct instance of the micro-review summarization problem.

	Min	Max	Average	Median
#tips	51	498	145	133
#reviews	584	3,460	947	782
#snippets	1,263	12,298	3,117	2,612

Table 1: Statistics of 102 Restaurants in the Dataset

5.2 Comparison of Proposed Algorithms

We first compare the performance of the three proposed algorithms in Section 4, both in terms of the MDL cost optimization, as well as in terms of the nature of snippets selected, for different values of the smoothing factor α.

Figure 1(a) shows the average MDL cost per restaurant (in bits) achieved by each algorithm. Fewer bits are better. PARTITIONAL SYNTHESIS and HIERARCHICAL SYNTHESIS achieve lower (better) MDL costs than GREEDY SYNTHESIS. The first two approaches are heuristics that explore the solution space by adjusting the selected snippets and tip assignments to lower the MDL cost. In contrast, GREEDY SYNTHESIS selects the snippets one at a time, each time selecting the best snippet in terms of the MDL cost. Since every snippet selection is final, GREEDY SYNTHESIS cannot lower its cost by changing a previously picked snippet. PARTITIONAL SYNTHESIS is also slightly better than HIERARCHICAL SYNTHESIS, as the former has more flexibility in exploring the space of possible partitions for finding the best one, while HIERARCHICAL SYNTHESIS is restricted to always splitting one partition into two at any one time.

We then examine the selected snippets, and we observe that there is a qualitative difference in the kinds of snippets selected by the different algorithms. Figure 1(b) shows the average number of snippets picked by each algorithm, while Figure 1(c) shows the average length of those snippets in terms of the number of words. GREEDY SYNTHESIS picks many more snippets, but those snippets tend to be shorter. At each step, GREEDY SYNTHESIS selects the snippet that can encode a number of tips with the smallest average cost. The model cost of a snippet is effectively amortized over the number of tips covered (line 3). Therefore, the tendency is to pick very short snippets, whose cost can be averaged across a small number of tips. As a result, GREEDY SYNTHESIS has to pick many of these short snippets to encode all the tips. In contrast, PARTITIONAL SYNTHESIS and HIERARCHICAL SYNTHESIS consider the cost of the summary as a whole, instead of looking at each snippet independently. This results in a solution with fewer snippets that are more substantial (longer), and can encode multiple tips.

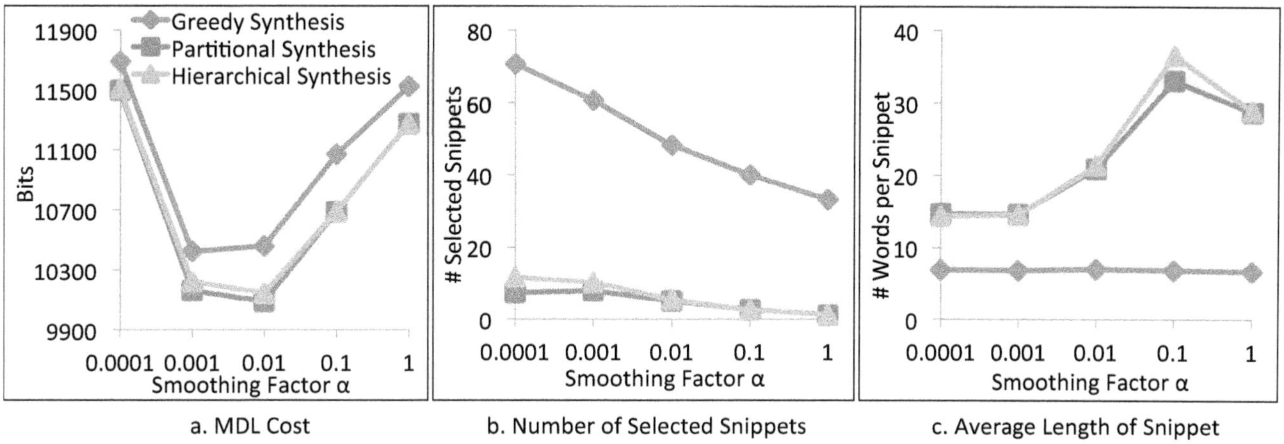

Figure 1: Comparison of Proposed Synthesis Algorithms

We observe that for all algorithms, as α increases, initially the MDL cost decreases, and then increases again. On one hand, with a smaller α, more bits are required to encode a word in a tip that is "missing" from the corresponding snippet. Therefore, the tendency is to pick more snippets, so that at least one snippet would contain some rare words that appear in a tip. With more snippets, each snippet only needs to represent a small number of tips, favoring shorter snippets that are more similar to tips. On the other hand, with a larger α, fewer bits are required to encode a "missing" word. The tendency is to pick fewer snippets that can represent more tips, which lowers the model cost, but increases the encoding cost. The trade-off between encoding and model costs as α changes causes the U-shaped trend in Figure 1(a).

The best α seems to be 0.01, where PARTITIONAL SYNTHESIS and HIERARCHICAL SYNTHESIS reach the minimum, and GREEDY SYNTHESIS is close to the minimum. Subsequently, we will use $\alpha = 0.01$ as the default value.

5.3 Comparison with Existing Reviews

To validate the utility of synthesizing a "review", instead of just selecting one of the existing reviews, we now compare the summaries produced by our algorithms against the collection of existing reviews in the dataset.

Representativeness. To evaluate representativeness, we map it to the notion of relevance in IR. Intuitively, a good summary should be a highly relevant document to any of the tips (when the latter are used as a queries). We thus propose to evaluate representativeness within a retrieval framework. We create a corpus consisting of the reviews and the summary we want to evaluate, and we use the tips as queries against this corpus. We consider our summary to be good if it is highly ranked for most of the tips. For the IR component in our evaluation, we adopt the vector space model [15]. Each document in our corpus (i.e., a review, or the summary) is represented by a $tf \cdot idf$ vector, with dimensionality equal to the vocabulary size. The tf value of a word is the count of occurrences of the word in the document. The idf is defined as $\log \frac{N}{df}$, where N is the total number of reviews, and df is the number of reviews that contain the word. Each query (i.e., a tip) is also represented by a $tf \cdot idf$ vector, where idf is derived from reviews. If a query term does not appear in any review, its idf is set to $\log N$, as if $df = 1$. The relevance of a document to a query is the cosine similarity between their $tf \cdot idf$ vectors.

For each restaurant, we issue every tip in turn as a query, and assign a rank to every document. We order the documents according to their average rank, and then compute the *representativeness score*, which is expressed as percentile rank. The best document will have 100%, which implies that it outperforms all the other reviews.

Table 2 shows the percentile rank of our summaries, as compared to all existing reviews. In this experiment we construct the corpus for each restaurant by adding the summary to be evaluated together with the reviews for this restaurant. The percentile rank is averaged across all restaurants in the dataset. Table 2 shows that our three algorithms produce summaries with very high percentile ranks, around 99.9%. The last column of the table shows the percentage of restaurants for which our summaries obtain the highest rank. Both GREEDY SYNTHESIS and PARTITIONAL SYNTHESIS have higher representativeness scores than all existing reviews for 97% of the restaurants, whereas HIERARCHICAL SYNTHESIS obtains 93%. Since our summaries are at the top most of the time, this explains why the above percentile ranks are very close to 100% (top rank).

While our summaries outperform the existing reviews for the vast majority of query tips, it is also instructive to see how other methods of selecting a review perform on the same task. The middle three rows of Table 2 are different ways to identify the "best" review. In this case the representativeness score is computed for a corpus consisting of only the reviews for a restaurant, not including the summaries.

Lowest MDL Review selects the review with the lowest MDL score. This review scores very high percentile rank of almost 93%, which is still lower than our summaries, validating the need for synthesizing a "review", instead of selecting just one review. Its very high percentile rank also validates our MDL formulation in identifying a good review.

EffMaxCover Review is the review selected by the algorithm in [18], where the goal is to select the review that covers as many tips as possible, subject to an efficiency constraint (we follow the same settings as used in [18]). While it still attains a high percentile rank of 79%, it does not perform as well as our summaries. This is expected as it is designed for a different problem (review selection) with a different concern (efficiency constraint).

Method	Representativeness (percentile rank among reviews)	Highest Rank (percentage of restaurants)
GREEDY SYNTHESIS	99.97%	97.06%
PARTITIONAL SYNTHESIS	99.99%	97.06%
HIERARCHICAL SYNTHESIS	99.89%	93.14%
Lowest MDL Review	92.94%	5.88%
EffMaxCover Review	79.36%	0.98%
Most Useful Review	60.76%	0.00%
Shortest Review	8.97%	0.00%
Median Review	51.91%	0.00%
Longest Review	84.33%	5.88%

Table 2: Comparison with Reviews: Representativeness

Method	Compactness	
	(# words)	(percentile rank among reviews)
GREEDY SYNTHESIS	337.5	8.8%
PARTITIONAL SYNTHESIS	104.8	52.9%
HIERARCHICAL SYNTHESIS	114.9	49.7%
Lowest MDL Review	66.3	51.0%
EffMaxCover Review	114.7	50.5%
Most Useful Review	327.0	19.5%
Shortest Review	1.6	100.0%
Median Review	106.3	50.3%
Longest Review	833.2	0.2%

Table 3: Comparison with Reviews: Compactness

Most Useful Review selects the review with the highest usefulness votes given by Yelp users. It has relatively low percentile rank of around 60%. There are many factors affecting how users cast their usefulness votes, which are not always correlated to the comprehensiveness of the review, which could explain the low representativeness score.

For completeness, we also include several reviews selected based on length (number of words) alone. The results are quite expected. *Shortest Review* is not representative, with low percentile rank of around 9%. Unsurprisingly, *Median Review* with median length also has percentile rank close to the median, around 52%. Helped by its length, *Longest Review* has high representativeness score of 84%, but this comes at the cost of the compactness.

Compactness. Another concern is compactness. This can be measured in a more straightforward manner, by counting the number of words. We assign each review a percentile rank, which measures the percentage of reviews are at least as long (no better) as the review at hand. The last three rows of Table 3 show that, as expected, *Shortest Review* has 100% percentile rank (most compact), with only 1.6 words on average. Some reviews contain only one or two words (e.g., "*Amazing!*"). *Longest Review* has 833 words (least compact), whereas *Median Review* has 106 words.

Our objective is not to create the shortest summary (which is trivial), but rather a representative summary of short length. A reasonable target is to create a summary of length comparable to the median length. Table 3 shows that indeed both PARTITIONAL SYNTHESIS and HIERARCHICAL SYNTHESIS produce summaries that are very close to the median length. PARTITIONAL SYNTHESIS is slightly shorter, with 104.8 words, whereas HIERARCHICAL SYNTHESIS is slightly longer, with 114.9 words. As previously explained, GREEDY SYNTHESIS generates many more snippets, resulting in a longer summary of 337.5 words. *EffMaxCover Review* is also around the median, whereas *Lowest MDL Review* is more compact, and *Most Useful* review is longer.

5.4 Comparison with Baselines

We now compare our summaries with those generated by existing text summarization methods, which summarize the tips directly without relying on reviews.

As baselines, we compare against two popular methods, for which a public implementation is available: OPINOSIS[2] [5], which is an example of abstractive summarization, and MEAD[3] [20], which is an example of extractive summarization. For both, we use their default settings. As in [5], for MEAD, we turn off the effect of sentence position in text, which is not relevant to our case. Both OPINOSIS and MEAD require as input the expected length of the summary. For a fair comparison, we use the length of the summary produced by PARTITIONAL SYNTHESIS, our best-performing technique, as an input parameter to OPINOSIS and MEAD. For MEAD, we specify the same number of words. OPINOSIS outputs a ranked set of sentences that meet some criteria, so we create a summary by selecting the top sentences until we reach the word threshold, or until we exhaust all the sentences.

For completeness, we include two versions of our algorithm based on partitional synthesis. The original PARTITIONAL SYNTHESIS uses review snippets to summarize tips. Another variant, which we call PARTITIONAL SYNTHESIS WITH TIPS, does not rely on reviews at all, and instead creates a summary using tips (as snippets) to represent tips.

Benchmarking against Reviews. First, we conduct the same experiment as in Section 5.3. Table 4 shows their representativeness scores. Evidently, the PARTITIONAL SYNTHESIS based on review snippets is the best. It is better than the tip-based variant, which suggests that using review snippets is more effective than using tips only.

Both our variants are better than the baselines. OPINOSIS has percentile rank of around 86%, and achieves the top rank only for 23% of the restaurants. MEAD has slightly better percentile rank, with 90%, but worst top rank, with 12%.

Method	Representativeness (percentile rank among reviews)	Highest Rank (percentage of restaurants)
PARTITIONAL SYNTHESIS	99.99%	97.06%
PARTITIONAL SYNTHESIS WITH TIPS	98.86%	57.84%
OPINOSIS	86.01%	23.53%
MEAD	90.78%	12.75%

Table 4: Comparison with Baselines: Representativeness (with respect to reviews)

Table 5 shows the comparison in terms of compactness. As expected, PARTITIONAL SYNTHESIS and MEAD have very similar lengths, both around 100 words. PARTITIONAL SYNTHESIS WITH TIPS produces slightly shorter summary for the same setting of $\alpha = 0.01$. OPINOSIS is much shorter, with around 42 words. This is because OPINOSIS tends to generate very short sentences. Even after we use all the output sentences, we may not attain the same length as the others. To show that OPINOSIS is not disadvantaged, we

[2] `kavita-ganesan.com/opinosis-summarizer-library`
[3] `http://www.summarization.com/mead/`

also show the average number of sentences for various methods. OPINOSIS uses the most sentences, but because they are shorter, it results in fewer words overall. The behavior and the performance of Opinosis is reasonable, since its main focus is on generating short blurbs from very similar sentences, rather than a full-fledged summary.

Method	Compactness (# words)	Compactness (percentile rank among reviews)	#sentences
PARTITIONAL SYNTHESIS	104.8	52.9%	9.2
PARTITIONAL SYNTHESIS WITH TIPS	82.8	61.6%	8.2
OPINOSIS	41.6	83.6%	10.8
MEAD	104.5	53.3%	5.4

Table 5: Comparison with Baselines: Compactness (with respect to reviews)

Head-to-head Comparison. The previous comparison is indirect, since it compares each method against all reviews, but not against each other. Here, we perform a head-to-head comparison, by repeating the same retrieval experiment for the different summarization techniques. In this case the corpus consists of only the summaries generated by PARTITIONAL SYNTHESIS, PARTITIONAL SYNTHESIS WITH TIPS, OPINOSIS, and MEAD, and for each query (tip), we rank these four summaries. Table 6 shows the comparison in terms of representativeness.

PARTITIONAL SYNTHESIS has the highest percentile rank with 93%, as compared to 69% for PARTITIONAL SYNTHESIS WITH TIPS, which in turn has higher percentile rank than the baselines OPINOSIS with 47% and MEAD with 41%. PARTITIONAL SYNTHESIS emerges at the top rank for 75% of restaurants, significantly higher than the other methods.

Method	Representativeness (percentile rank among reviews)	Highest Rank (percentage of restaurants)
PARTITIONAL SYNTHESIS	92.89%	75.49%
PARTITIONAL SYNTHESIS WITH TIPS	69.36%	18.63%
OPINOSIS	47.30%	3.92%
MEAD	40.69%	1.96%

Table 6: Comparison with Baselines: Representativeness (head-to-head)

Readability. A summary is ultimately meant for human consumption. We thus want to evaluate the readability of our summaries. Since there is no good way to assess readability automatically, we rely on a user study. For this study, we use the 20 restaurants with the highest number of tips. We use five human judges, who are not related to this work, and for each restaurant, we show each human judge the four summaries by PARTITIONAL SYNTHESIS, PARTITIONAL SYNTHESIS WITH TIPS, OPINOSIS, and MEAD respectively, in random order, without identifying the methods. Each human judge is requested to give a rating from 1 to 5 to each summary, where 1 (lowest) indicates a badly-written piece of text that is not readable, and 5 (highest) indicates a very well-written piece of text that is highly readable. We then compute the average rating given by the judges.

Table 7 shows the readability scores of the four methods. The score of 4.23 (out of 5) for PARTITIONAL SYNTHESIS indicates that the human judges find the summaries

Method	Readability Score
PARTITIONAL SYNTHESIS	4.23
PARTITIONAL SYNTHESIS WITH TIPS	3.99
OPINOSIS	2.07
MEAD	3.47

Table 7: Readability Scores

well-written and highly readable. This is also higher than the score of 3.99 obtained by PARTITIONAL SYNTHESIS WITH TIPS. Paired samples t-test shows that the difference is statistically significant at 5% level.

Both our variants score higher than the baselines. MEAD, which selects sentences from tips, has a lower readability score of 3.47. OPINOSIS has a below-average score of 2.07. This is expected since its summary consists of a collection of blurbs. In addition, OPINOSIS relies on generating new sentences, which is a hard task.

The overall ordering between methods is consistent among all the judges. We also conduct a correlation analysis on how the independent judges agree on the ratings of individual summaries. For this, we measure the Pearson's correlation coefficient between any two judges, which ranges from -1 (anti-correlated) to 1 (perfectly correlated). Across the ten pairs of judges, the correlation coefficient ranges from 0.4 to 0.7, with an average of 0.6. These correlation values are high, indicating significant agreement between the judges.

Case Study. In Figure 2, we show example summaries for the restaurant *Eataly*[4]. The summary by PARTITIONAL SYNTHESIS (Figure 2(a)) covers the various aspects of the restaurant: the grocery store, the food (pasta, cheeses), the wine, and the gelato. Overall it has consistency and continuity, and it successfully selects atomic snippets to cover specific aspects (e.g., the part about the gelato comes from a single snippet). The summary by PARTITIONAL SYNTHESIS WITH TIPS (Figure 2(b)) is compact and dense, but is not as descriptive and narrative. The summary of OPINOSIS (Figure 2(c)) contains useful information and keywords, but it is not presented in a flowing, articulate manner. In the summary of MEAD (Figure 2(d)) the individual sentences (extracted from tips) are readable, but they tend to capture peculiarities (e.g., Jimmy Fallon, Sammy Hagar), rather than things that are pertinent to the place. The gelato is described in merely two words: *Gelato Great!*.

6. CONCLUSION

We introduce the problem of summarizing micro-reviews. Our proposed approach is to synthesize a summary from review snippets. The goal is a summary that is representative of the micro-reviews, yet compact and readable. To balance the conflicting objectives of representativeness and compactness holistically, we formulate the problem within the Minimum Description Length (MDL) framework. Minimizing the MDL cost is NP-hard. Through a connection to Uncapacitated Facility Location Problem (UFLP), we establish an approximation guarantee of $1 + \log n$, where n is the number of micro-reviews. We also propose three heuristic algorithms to solve the problem. Experiments on Foursquare and Yelp datasets show that our methodology results in highly representative and compact summaries.

[4]`https://foursquare.com/v/eataly-nyc/4c5ef77bfff99c74eda954d3`

I love this place. i come here to get anything and everything Italian. Like many others have noted, this place is confusing. It's part food court, part grocery store, part coffee shop, part bookstore. Eataly tries to be a one-stop shop for all things Italian. They've got everything you'd want for a good Italian dinner - fresh meat, seafood, pasta, cheese, etc. Loved the fresh pasta in the Pizza and Pasta section. Also great place to shop for everything Italian even if a little pricey. We put our names in at the pasta place and went to have wine while we waited. Order a bottle of wine, nibble on the cheese, bread, meats, and olives. The gelato is also really good. I got the pistachio gelato, and it was some of the best I've had. When I get gelato, I want it to really taste like the flavor that it is, and this gelato did not disappoint. Amazing. The food was great! it was very crowded, but worth it.

(a) Partitional Synthesis

Try the pizza, the pasta, the wine, everything's great here 50,000 square feet of pure Italian with a rooftop beer garden, a cooking school, bakery, coffee shop, fresh pasta counter, a butcher, & any pantry item you'll need to play chef at home. disregard the duplicate venues, this is the right one! This place is great! Some of the best gelato I've ever tasted! Find one of the only American foods in this fine Italian markets.

(b) Partitional Synthesis with Tips

fresh pasta , butcher , any pantry item you 'll need to play chef at home. a better value.../: it 's a fun place to browse if your in the area. the bakery and with $ 2,80 you get the best onions focaccia you 've ever had. the pizza and the fettuccine con coda alla vaccinara are both superb. sunday april 3rd , renee and the derelicts redux performed great live music. cooking school , bakery , coffee shop , fresh pasta counter , butcher. they make the whole eataly experience even better and much more fun. fresh pasta. they will be back on the 17th. good food. great italian. the food is great. prime rib sandwich. artisanal italian food and wine marketplace. gelato is amazing. cooking school , coffee. redux performed great. great live music. new york. hard to move. authentic italian. hot chocolate. amazing food. delicious food. many people. fresh vegetables. amazing place. reasonable prices.

(c) Opinosis

send your photos of food to: posteat.ly check out beer garden 50,000 square feet of pure Italian with a rooftop beer garden, a cooking school, bakery, coffee shop, fresh pasta counter, a butcher, & any pantry item you'll need to play chef at home. Go to the pasta restaurant and get the cracked pepper pa Try the entrance on 23rd to avoid the line to get in crazy place with amazing Italian food & products. Amazing place for a seafood, charcuterie, cheeses, caviar, wine & champagne lunch Can be obez at this place I love everything about this place...panini, piazza for the cheese board, lavazza espresso bar, beer garden, the market...their homemade mozzarella is amazing! too crowded in lunch time, but it worth it. at least try the gelato for desert after having a bite at one of the food tents of the mad square park.

(d) Mead

Figure 2: Summaries for *Eataly*

7. REFERENCES

[1] D. Chakrabarti, S. Papadimitriou, D. S. Modha, and C. Faloutsos. Fully automatic cross-associations. In *KDD*, 2004.

[2] T. M. Cover and J. A. Thomas. *Elements of information theory*. John Wiley & Sons, 2012.

[3] U. Feige. Vertex cover is hardest to approximate on regular graphs. Technical report, Citeseer, 2003.

[4] K. Filippova. Multi-sentence compression: Finding shortest paths in word graphs. In *COLING*, 2010.

[5] K. Ganesan, C. Zhai, and J. Han. Opinosis: a graph-based approach to abstractive summarization of highly redundant opinions. In *COLING*, 2010.

[6] K. Ganesan, C. Zhai, and E. Viegas. Micropinion generation: an unsupervised approach to generating ultra-concise summaries of opinions. In *WWW*, 2012.

[7] P. D. Grünwald, I. J. Myung, and M. A. Pitt. *Advances in minimum description length: Theory and applications*. MIT Press, 2005.

[8] D. S. Hochbaum. Heuristics for the fixed cost median problem. *Mathematical Programming*, 1982.

[9] M. Hu and B. Liu. Mining and summarizing customer reviews. In *KDD*, 2004.

[10] K. Jain and V. V. Vazirani. Approximation algorithms for metric facility location and k-median problems using the primal-dual schema and lagrangian relaxation. *JACM*, 2001.

[11] T. Lappas, M. Crovella, and E. Terzi. Selecting a characteristic set of reviews. In *KDD*, 2012.

[12] T. Lappas and D. Gunopulos. Efficient confident search in large review corpora. In *ECML/PKDD*, 2010.

[13] N. Lazic, B. J. Frey, and P. Aarabi. Solving the uncapacitated facility location problem using message passing algorithms. In *AISTATS*, 2010.

[14] Y. Lu, P. Tsaparas, A. Ntoulas, and L. Polanyi. Exploiting social context for review quality prediction. In *WWW*, 2010.

[15] C. D. Manning, P. Raghavan, and H. Schütze. *Introduction to Information Retrieval*, volume 1. Cambridge University Press, 2008.

[16] X. Meng and H. Wang. Mining user reviews: from specification to summarization. In *ACL-IJCNLP*, 2009.

[17] R. Mihalcea and P. Tarau. TextRank: Bringing order into texts. In *ACL*, 2004.

[18] T.-S. Nguyen, H. W. Lauw, and P. Tsaparas. Using micro-reviews to select an efficient set of reviews. In *CIKM*, 2013.

[19] A. Noulas, S. Scellato, C. Mascolo, and M. Pontil. An empirical study of geographic user activity patterns in foursquare. *ICWSM*, 2011.

[20] D. R. Radev, H. Jing, M. Styś, and D. Tam. Centroid-based summarization of multiple documents. *Information Processing & Management*, 2004.

[21] J. Rissanen. Modeling by shortest data description. *Automatica*, 1978.

[22] D. B. Shmoys, É. Tardos, and K. Aardal. Approximation algorithms for facility location problems. In *ACM Symposium on Theory of Computing*, 1997.

[23] H. Sun, A. Morales, and X. Yan. Synthetic review spamming and defense. In *KDD*, 2013.

[24] P. Tsaparas, A. Ntoulas, and E. Terzi. Selecting a comprehensive set of reviews. In *KDD*, 2011.

[25] M. Ye, P. Yin, and W.-C. Lee. Location recommendation for location-based social networks. In *SIGSPATIAL*, 2010.

[26] C. Zhai and J. Lafferty. A study of smoothing methods for language models applied to information retrieval. *TOIS*, 2004.

[27] L. Zhuang, F. Jing, and X.-Y. Zhu. Movie review mining and summarization. In *CIKM*, 2006.

Fast and Space-Efficient Entity Linking in Queries

Roi Blanco
Yahoo Labs
Barcelona, Spain
roi@yahoo-inc.com

Giuseppe Ottaviano
ISTI-CNR
Pisa, Italy
giuseppe.ottaviano@isti.cnr.it

Edgar Meij
Yahoo Labs
Barcelona, Spain
emeij@yahoo-inc.com

ABSTRACT

Entity linking deals with identifying entities from a knowledge base in a given piece of text and has become a fundamental building block for web search engines, enabling numerous downstream improvements from better document ranking to enhanced search results pages. A key problem in the context of web search queries is that this process needs to run under severe time constraints as it has to be performed *before* any actual retrieval takes place, typically within milliseconds.

In this paper we propose a probabilistic model that leverages user-generated information on the web to link queries to entities in a knowledge base. There are three key ingredients that make the algorithm fast and space-efficient. First, the linking process ignores any dependencies between the different entity candidates, which allows for a $O(k^2)$ implementation in the number of query terms. Second, we leverage hashing and compression techniques to reduce the memory footprint. Finally, to equip the algorithm with contextual knowledge without sacrificing speed, we factor the distance between distributional semantics of the query words and entities into the model.

We show that our solution significantly outperforms several state-of-the-art baselines by more than 14% while being able to process queries in sub-millisecond times—at least two orders of magnitude faster than existing systems.

Categories and Subject Descriptors

H.3.1 [**Information Storage and Retrieval**]: Content Analysis and Indexing

General Terms

Experimentation, Measurement

Keywords

Entity Linking; Wikipedia; Queries; Web Search

WSDM'15, February 2–6, 2015, Shanghai, China.

ACM 978-1-4503-3317-7/15/02 ...$15.00.
http://dx.doi.org/10.1145/2684822.2685317.

1. INTRODUCTION

Commercial web search engines are presenting increasingly advanced and rich user experiences that include displays of answers, facts, entities, and other structured results. Such web search user experiences are centered around understanding and displaying information pertinent to entities present in or meant by the query, since users increasingly expect to find the actual answers and/or entities that satisfy their information need, rather than merely the documents that mention them. One critical step in this process is understanding the entities that are mentioned in queries and linking them to a reference Knowledge Base (KB). Such linking has to be performed on a very limited time and space budget as it needs to happen before any actual search process commences.

Linking free text to entities—often referred to as *entity linking*—typically comprises three steps: (i) identifying candidate mentions, i.e., which part(s) of the text to link, (ii) identifying candidate entities for each mention, and (iii) disambiguating the candidate entities based on some notion of context and coherence [14]. Recent research has made extensive use of open KBs or entity repositories such as Freebase, IMDB, Wikipedia, as well as private or proprietary ones [5]. Most linking methods from the literature, however, assume that the input text is relatively clean and grammatically correct and that it provides sufficient context [7, 11]. Queries, on the other hand, are short, noisy, and full of shorthand and other ungrammatical text, and provide very limited context for the words they contain. Hence, it is not obvious that automatic entity linking methods that have been shown to work well on news articles or web pages perform equally well on this domain. Moreover, the efficiency aspects of linking systems are not a focal point in the literature. Entity linking for web search queries poses some interesting technical challenges due to the sheer volume of the data, its dynamic nature, the creative language usage, and the required tradeoff between speed and disambiguation quality. Entity linking for queries has not received considerable attention in the literature, except for type spotting for named entity recognition [13], linking queries to semantic web concepts [19], and providing a full structured representation of the query [34].

In this paper we propose a new probabilistic model and algorithm for entity linking in web search queries that extracts a large number of candidate *aliases* for entities from click-through information and anchor text. In order to keep these large amounts of data manageable, we compress all candidates using state-of-the-art hashing and bit encoding techniques. Our algorithm is able to swiftly detect the entities in the query because we drop all the dependence assumptions from potential candidate entities. In practice, this means that the model might not able to distinguish between situations such as "brad pitt seven" and "brad pitt olympics" if they are not present in our alias set[1] However, we are able to impose contextual knowledge by introducing a new *contextual relevance model* that uses learned representations of query words and entities, and it is able to quickly compute a relevance measure between a string of text and an entity. This way, the algorithm is able to link entities with just a forward-backward scanning procedure that can be implemented efficiently using dynamic programming in $O(k^2)$, where k is the number of query terms.

The remainder of this paper is organized as follows. Section 2 reviews some works related to ours. Section 3 introduces the probabilistic model, along with the contextual model. Section 4 presents experiments and results comparing our approaches with state of the art baselines in terms of linking quality and speed. The paper concludes in Section 5.

2. RELATED WORK

Automatically generating links to a knowledge base is one way of providing semantics to digital items. Entity linking has become an ubiquitous way to add semantics to different media types, most notably in text [22, 25] and across different genres, such as news, archives, or tweets [6, 8, 20]. The comprehensiveness, popularity, and free access to Wikipedia has made it a rich source and the most popular target knowledge base for entity linking.

Many methods for entity linking are heavily inspired by those from the field of word sense disambiguation [27]. The main challenge entity linking systems have to face is ambiguity, i.e., how to distinguish among different entities with the same label and also a possible lack of specificity, in which case more generic and possibly less meaningful entities are identified. These issues are generally addressed by identifying segments, key phrases or weighting terms based on, e.g., document-frequency inspired heuristics. For instance, a simple and frequently taken approach for linking text to concepts is to perform lexical matching between (parts of the text) and the titles [9, 21], an approach related to keyword-based interfaces to databases [36].

Milne and Witten [25] introduced one of the earliest papers on linking text to Wikipedia, which uses machine learning and unambiguous candidates for disambiguation. Among those methods, "commonness" is a popular unsupervised baseline for either short or long textual fragments [11, 20]. We use it as a baseline and describe it further in Section 4.3. In this line of work, Ratinov et al. [33] propose the use of a "local" approach (e.g., commonness) to generate a disambiguation context and then apply "global" machine learning for disambiguation. Pilz and Paaß [30] extended previous bag of word approaches for disambiguation with Latent Dirichlet Allocation generated topics, comparing topic distributions of source document with candidate entities. Recent approaches make extensive use of topic modeling, for example Houlsby and Ciaramita [16] perform inference with a variant of LDA in which each topic corresponds to a Wikipedia article, i.e., an entity. Below we include the work of Cheng and Roth [7] (which is an extension of [33]) as a representative baseline of an inference-based method. This approach tries to embed context and ensure topical coherence by linking a set of semantically-related mentions to a set of semantically-related concepts simultaneously.

The first works geared specifically towards disambiguating entities in queries focus almost exclusively on Named Entity Recognition but applied to a domain different than the usual long text found news and articles [26]. For instance Guo et al. [13] propose a language model that includes weak supervision to learn relationships, e.g., `lyrics` to `music`. Moving forward, Pantel et al. [29] predict entity type distributions in Web search queries via so-called *intents* (strings that give contextual clues about the entity type) mined from query logs. We too make use of query logs for gathering evidence, although we aim at disambiguation and not type spotting. Hu et al. [17] propose a similar approach through query intent classification. Sawant and Chakrabarti [34] assume that entities have already been annotated in text and tackle the related task of extracting query target types and words that are type hints. Pound et al. [31, 32] focus on retrieving an ordered selection of attributes, taken from a static KB, and ranking syntactic relationships from queries via a collective assignment problem.

In the case of queries—especially in the context of web search—one would need to add entity annotations as quickly as possible in order to be of any use to subsequent processes such as actual retrieval. Topic modeling approaches which typically need to perform online parameter estimation are too time-consuming. Furthermore, they are of little help when there is limited context such as in the case of queries. Little work exist on entity linking methods for queries to date. Meij et al. [19] perform entity linking in the context of the semantic web and include session history-based features to provide additional context. Proof of the increasing interest from industry and academia in query entity linking in the context of web search, however, is the recent ERD challenge[2]. In this paper we use a large (~2.5K queries) test set from a commercial web search engine that is easily available for download.

Other relevant streams of work are related to query log mining [2], providing a signal orthogonal to that of textual corpora. For instance, Paşca [28] mined instances of semantic classes from query logs using information extraction and Alfonseca et al. [1] mined query logs to find attributes of entity instances. Once equipped with a reliable entity linking system, it is possible to provide deeper query analyses of user patterns and web usage [15].

None of the previous works deals with the problem of linking entities in the context of web search, i.e, operating in the shortest amount of time possible with additional storage constraints, nor they introduce richer *semantic* contexts as our approach does.

3. MODELING ENTITY LINKING

For our entity linking model we establish a connection between entities and their *aliases* (which are their textual representations, also known as *surface forms*) by leveraging anchor text or user queries leading to a click on the Web page that represents the entity. In the context of this paper we focus on using Wikipedia as KB and therefore only consider anchor text within Wikipedia and clicks from web search results on Wikipedia results—although it is general enough to

[1]Brad Pitt is the name of both a US Celebrity/Actor and a lesser known Australian boxer.

[2]`http://web-ngram.research.microsoft.com/ERD2014/`

also accommodate other sources of information. The problem we address consists of automatically segmenting the query and simultaneously selecting the right entity for each segment. Our Fast Entity Linker (FEL) tackles this problem by computing a probabilistic score for each segment-entity pair and then optimizing the score of the whole query. Note that we do not employ any supervision and let the model and data operate in a parameterless fashion; it is however possible to add an additional layer that makes use of human-labeled training data in order to enhance the performance of the model. We leave investigating such an additional step for future work. In the remainder of this section we detail our specific model, as well as how we incorporate context through a novel contextual relevance model and the efficiency optimizations we apply, including advanced compression techniques.

3.1 Fast Entity Linker

We begin by introducing our model, which we describe using the following random variables, assuming as an event space $S \times E$ where S is the set of all sequences and E the set of all entities known to the system:

s	is a sequence of terms $t \in s$
$\mathbf{s}$	represents a segmentation (sequence of sequences of terms) where $s \in \mathbf{s}$ is drawn from the set S
$\mathbf{e}$	represents a set of entities $e \in \mathbf{e}$, where each e is drawn from the set E
a_s	indicates if s is an alias
$a_{s,e}$	indicates if s is an alias pointing (linking/clicked) to e
c	indicates which collection acts as a source of information query log or Wikipedia (c_q or c_w)
$n(s,c)$	is the count of s in c
$n(e,c)$	is the count of e in c

Let q be the input query, which we represent with the set S_q of all possible segmentations of its tokens $t_1 \cdots t_k$. The algorithm will return the set of entities $\mathbf{e}$, along with their scores, that maximizes

$$\operatorname*{argmax}_{\mathbf{e} \in E} \log P(\mathbf{e}|q) = \operatorname*{argmax}_{\mathbf{e} \in E, \mathbf{s} \in S_q} \sum_{e \in \mathbf{e}, s \in \mathbf{s}} \log P(e|s) . \quad (1)$$

In Eq. 1 we assume independence of the entities given a query segment. Each individual entity/segment probability is then estimated as:

$$\begin{aligned} P(e|s) &= \sum_{c \in \{c_q, c_w\}} P(c|s) P(e|c,s) \\ &= \sum_{c \in \{c_q, c_w\}} P(c|s) \sum_{a_s = \{0,1\}} P(a_s|c,s) P(e|a_s,c,s) \\ &= \sum_{c \in \{c_q, c_w\}} P(c|s) \Big[P(a_s = 0|c,s) P(e|a_s = 0, c, s) \\ &\quad + P(a_s = 1|c,s) P(e|a_s = 1, c, s) \Big] . \end{aligned} \quad (2)$$

The maximum likelihood probabilities are the following (note that in this case $P(e|a_s = 0, c, s) = 0$ and therefore the right hand side of the summation cancels out):

$$P(c|s) = \frac{n(s,c)}{\sum_{c'} n(s,c')} \quad (3)$$

$$P(a_s = 1|c,s) = \frac{\sum_{s:a_s=1} n(s,c)}{n(s,c)} \quad (4)$$

$$P(e|a_s = 1, c, s) = \frac{\sum_{s:a_{s,e}=1} n(s,c)}{\sum_{s:a_s=1} n(s,c)} . \quad (5)$$

Those maximum likelihood probabilities can be smoothed appropriately using an entity prior. Using add-one and Dirichlet priors smoothing the probabilities results in:

$$P(e|c) = \frac{n(e,c) + 1}{|E| + \sum_{e \in E} n(e,c)} \quad (6)$$

$$P(e|a_s, c, s) = \frac{\sum_{s:a_{s,e}=1} n(s,c) + \mu_c \cdot p(e|c)}{\mu_c + \sum_{s:a_s=1} n(s,c)} . \quad (7)$$

In this case $P(e|c) = P(e|a_s = 0, c, s)$, and $P(a_s = 0|c,s) = 1 - P(a_s = 1|c,s)$. Similarly, we smooth $P(c|s)$ using Laplace smoothing (add-one smoothing).

Note that some terms might not be covered by any segment s and therefore not link to any entity. To handle these segments, we define a special entity `not_linked` and set $P(\texttt{not\_linked}|s) = \ell$ where ℓ is a global hyperparameter that can tuned to set the propensity of the algorithm to link segments.

An alternative to Eq. 1 would be to select the segmentation that optimizes the score of the top ranked entity:

$$\operatorname*{argmax}_{\mathbf{e} \in E, \mathbf{s} \in S_q} \max_{e \in \mathbf{e}, s \in \mathbf{s}} P(e|s). \quad (8)$$

Both Eq. 1 and Eq. 8 are instances of the same general segmentation problem, defined as follows. Given a sequence of terms $\mathbf{t} = t_1 \cdots t_k$, denote any segment of the sequence with

$$[t_i t_{i+1} \ldots t_{i+j-1}], \forall i, j \geq 0. \quad (9)$$

Let $\gamma(s)$ be any scoring function that maps segments to real numbers, then the maximum score of a segmentation is defined as follows:

$$\begin{aligned} & m(t_1, t_2, \ldots, t_k) = \\ & \max \Big(\phi\left(m(t_1), m(t_2, \ldots, t_k)\right), \phi\left(\gamma([t_1 t_2]), m(t_3 \ldots t_k)\right) \\ & \quad , \ldots, \phi\left(\gamma([t_1 \ldots, t_{k-1}]), m(t_k)\right), \gamma([t_1 \ldots t_k]) \Big), \end{aligned} \quad (10)$$

where $m(t_1) = \gamma([t_1])$ and $\phi(a,b)$ is an associative aggregation function, such as $\phi(a,b) = a + b$ in the case of Eq. 1 and $\phi(a,b) = \max(a,b)$ in the case of Eq. 8. Since the scoring function $s(\cdot)$ only depends on the given segment and not on the others, the segmentation with maximum score can be computed in $O(k^2)$ time using dynamic programming.

We instantiate the problem above would be the following scoring function

$$\gamma(s) = \text{HIGHESTSCORE}(s,q) = \max_{e \in E} \log P(e|s,q), \quad (11)$$

that, given a segment s of the query and a *context* q (the query itself), returns the highest score among the entities associated with the alias s; when the segment does not match any alias, and hence it has no associated entities, it returns a value that is an identity for the aggregation function $\phi(\cdot,\cdot)$; it also returns an identity if the segment is empty. In the basic FEL model the context is ignored, so $P(e|s,q)$ is just

Algorithm 1 Entity-linking algorithm

Require: A user query q, a function HIGHESTSCORE($\cdot$), and an aggregation function $\phi(\cdot, \cdot)$.

```
p ← TOKENIZE(q)
l ← LENGTH(p)
maxscore[] ← new array[l + 1]
previous[] ← new array[l + 1]
for i = 0 to l do
    for j = 0 to i do
        score ← φ(maxscore[j], HIGHESTSCORE(p[j : i], q))
        if score > maxscore[i] then
            maxscore[i] ← score
            previous[i] ← j
        end if
    end for
end for
return maxscore[l]
```

$P(e|s)$. Algorithm 1 details our full algorithm. Note that it makes $O(k^2)$ calls to the HIGHESTSCORE function, which is acceptable since the number of terms in a query is usually very small.

3.2 Modeling Context

In our algorithm above, the probability of an entity given an alias is computed independently of the other aliases that match the query or the surrounding words. As we pointed out, this is a design choice to enable a fast linking algorithm. However, the context of the alias can help to disambiguate the candidate entities. For example, a user submitting the query "Hollywood lyrics" is probably interested in the song rather than the geographical location; if the only matching alias is `Hollywood`, the algorithm will not be able to disambiguate between candidates.

To exploit the contextual information in the remainder of the query we introduce a *contextual relevance model*, that is, we estimate the probability that the entity e is relevant to the context $\mathbf{t}$, in this case the whole query. This probability can be incorporated into our model by factoring it into the HIGHESTSCORE function. To this aim, we need to compute $P(e|s,q)$ where s is the string segment and q is the context $t_1 \cdots t_k$. Then $P(e|s,q) = \frac{P(e)P(s,q|e)}{P(s,q)}$ and, assuming independence between q and s and conditional independence given e, we get $P(e|s,q) = \frac{P(e)}{P(q)P(s)} \cdot P(q|e)P(s|e)$, which is equal to $P(e|s)\frac{P(q|e)}{P(q)}$. The first factor is estimated as in Eq. 2. To estimate the second factor efficiently we again assume conditional independence on e and write it as $\prod_i \frac{P(t_i|e)}{P(q)}$. We are thus interested in estimating $P(t|e)$, i.e. the probability that the term t is relevant to the entity e.

We estimate $P(t|e)$ using a multiset $\mathcal{R}_e$ of words t that are known to be relevant to e; in our experiments, we use the words in the first section of the Wikipedia article on e. A simple approach would be to just count the number of occurrences of t, $P(t|e) = \frac{|\{t \in \mathcal{R}_e\}|}{|\mathcal{R}_e|}$, which would make the model a multi-class Naive Bayes classifier. This approach has two problems, however. First, the number of parameters (that is, the collection of multisets $\mathcal{R}_e$), is essentially as large as the collection of texts. Second, it does not take into account the semantic similarity of words, namely that if a word t_1 is relevant to an entity e and t_2 is close in meaning to t_1, it is likely that t_2 is relevant to e as well. We therefore use *continuous representations of words*, specifically the **`word2vec`** embeddings [24]. These embeddings map words to vectors of real numbers so that words that are close in meaning are mapped to vectors close in cosine distance. The vectors are computed in a completely unsupervised fashion text by exploiting the distributional semantics hypothesis. That is, words that co-occur often with the same words are close in meaning. We denote as $v_t \in \mathbb{R}^D$ the vector that represents the word t. We use these word vectors to model $P(t|e)$ as a binary logistic regression classifier, that is, we map each entity e to a vector $v_e \in \mathbb{R}^{D+1}$ and define $P(t|e) = \sigma([v_t\ 1] \cdot v_e)$, where $\sigma(x) = \frac{1}{1+e^{-x}}$. Since we need to compute the product of the probabilities $P(t_i|e)$ in order to score each entity e with a query, the overall complexity is $O(kD)$ operations. Below we refer to this method as *LR*.

Each classifier v_e is trained with L_2-regularized logistic regression to distinguish the multiset $\mathcal{R}_e$ (the positive examples) from the unigram distribution from the whole collection (the negative examples). Since this would require training on a set of examples as large as the dictionary, we use a method known as *negative sampling* [23]: we sample ρ words from the unigram distribution as negative examples, so that the overall number of examples is bounded by $O(|\mathcal{R}_e|)$. The vector v_e, then, is computed as the maximum of the function

$$\sum_{t \in \mathcal{R}_e} \log \sigma([v_t\ 1] \cdot v_e) + \sum_{t \in \mathcal{N}_e} \log \sigma(-[v_t\ 1] \cdot v_e) - \lambda \|v_e\|_2^2, \quad (12)$$

where $\mathcal{N}_e$ is the multiset of $\rho|\mathcal{R}_e|$ negative samples and λ is the regularization parameter. In Section 4.2 we detail how to tune ρ and λ in an unsupervised manner.

Note that the whole model consists of one vector of D numbers for each word in the dictionary and one vector of $D+1$ numbers for each entity in the knowledge base. Even using a 32-bit floating point number representation, the space occupancy would be $4(E(D+1) + WD)$, where E is the number of entities and W the number of words, regardless of the size of the sets $\mathcal{R}_e$. In Section 3.3.2 we describe a method to reduce this even further.

An alternative approach to model the relevance of e for a query is to define the entity vector v_e as the centroid of the vectors representing the words in $\mathcal{R}_e$, that is

$$v_e = \frac{1}{|\mathcal{R}_e|} \sum_{t \in \mathcal{R}_e} v_t, \quad (13)$$

and similarly the query vector v_q as the centroid of the vectors of the words of the query, that is $v_q = \frac{1}{k}\sum_i v_{t_i}$, and defining the relevance as the cosine $\cos(v_q, v_e)$. Aggregating the vectors of bags of words by taking their centroid is a widely used approach with continuous word representations, due to an increased efficiency [24].

The main advantage is higher efficiency when scoring a query against a set of entities; since the vector v_q is computed only once, scoring an entity requires only $O(D)$ operations, as opposed to $O(kD)$ for LR. Since the number of query terms is always small in practice, the difference is almost negligible. On the other hand, the cosine distance cannot be interpreted as a probability and it provides no measure of confidence. A simple way to verify this is to visualize the multisets $\mathcal{R}_e$ as clusters in the high-dimensional space: their centroids are a good indication of the location of the clusters, but they contain no information about their spread. For example, if a query vector is equidistant from a very broad cluster and a very tight cluster, the broad cluster should have higher confidence, but the centroid method cannot distinguish the two. In fact, as we will see below, Centroid is outperformed by LR in both a benchmark task and in the actual entity linking task.

3.3 Optimizations

In this section we detail the three types of optimizations we employ, including early stopping and two kinds of compression.

3.3.1 Early Stopping

With the added contextual scoring HIGHESTSCORE($p[i:j], q$) must now return, among all the entities that match the alias $p[i:j]$, the one that maximizes $P(e|s)\frac{P(q|e)}{P(q)}$, so the probability must be computed for each entity. First, note that we can remove the denominator $P(q)$ from the computation, since it does not depend on the entity. Then, the score to compute becomes $P(e|s)P(q|e)$. The first component is the basic FEL score, the second is the contextual relevance. The contextual relevance might take longer to compute than the FEL score, because it involves retrieving the entity vectors from the model data structure and computing several vector-vector products. However, we are only interested in retrieving the highest-scored entity. We can significantly reduce the number of score computations by early-stopping the process in a safe way. We do this by noting that $P(q|e)$ is at most 1; hence, if e_* is the top-scoring entity and e a candidate entity, if $P(e|s) < P(e_*|s)P(q|e_*)$ then a fortiori the full score of e cannot be higher than that of e_*. With this in mind, we can process the entities sorted by decreasing score $P(e|s)$ and stop computing the contextual relevance score as soon as $P(e|s)$ is smaller than the full score of the current top-scoring entity. This technique reduces the overall runtime of the algorithm by a factor of 5.

3.3.2 Compressing the Vectors

We now turn to the data structure used to store the word and entity vectors. The data structure represents a general mapping from strings to vectors, which we can split in two parts: a mapping from n strings to numeric identifiers in $[0, n)$, and the actual vectors, which is convenient to see as a matrix $V \in \mathbb{R}^{n \times D}$, whose rows are the vectors. The mapping can be easily represented with a minimal perfect hash function, which computes the identifier of a string in constant time and guarantees that no collisions can occur between strings of the key set. Such a function can however return arbitrary values on other strings; to make the collision probability negligible a constant-sized *signature* is associated to each string, so that it can be checked whether the string being looked up was present in the key set. This data structure is commonly referred to as a signed minimal perfect hash function for which we use the Sux4J implementation.[3]

To store the matrix V we adopt standard techniques from vector quantization and signal compression (for reference see [12]) and quantize the entries of the matrix with an uniform dead-zone quantizer, that is, an element x is quantized as $\mathrm{sgn}(x)\lfloor |x|/q \rfloor$ for a given quantization parameter q. We use the same q for all the elements in the matrix, and choose the largest value that yields a target error bound; specifically, we target a relative error in L_2 norm of the vectors of 0.1, which produced no measurable loss in accuracy of the vectors in our experiments. The integers obtained from quantization are then encoded with Golomb codes; since the columns of the matrix might have different statistics, we use a different Golomb modulus for each column. We concatenate the encodings of each vector into a single bit stream, and store their starting positions in an Elias-Fano monotone sequence data structure that allows to retrieve them in constant time.

To further improve the compression of the word vectors we note that transforming them with any operation that preserves the mutual cosine distances does not affect their quality. We can therefore apply the orthogonal Karhunen–Loève transform [12] to the vectors before compressing them, without having to apply the inverse transform at decoding time. The transform improves the compression by about 10% without affecting the overall accuracy. It is however not possible to apply the same technique to the entity vectors, since it would not preserve the scalar products against the word vectors unless the inverse transform is applied in decoding, which would be prohibitively slow.

Overall, the compressed vector representations take 3.44 bits per entry for the word vectors, 3.42 for the Centroid vectors, and 3.83 for the LR, which is almost 10 times smaller than using 32-bit floating points numbers.

[3]http://sux.dsi.unimi.it/

	Number	Size
Alias strings	114M	7.24 bytes/alias
Entity strings	4.6M	25.22 bytes/alias
Entity values (rows 5,6)	9.2M	3.72 bits/value
Alias values (rows 1-4, 7, 8)	912M	5.32 bits/value

Table 2: Size of compressed features and strings.

3.3.3 Compressing the Features

We also generate a compressed data structure to hold the information about aliases and entities. The numerical features required by the model are summarized in Table 1. The data structure is a hash table represented as follows. Each key of the table corresponds to a different alias and the values are split into two parts: entity-independent features (rows 1-4) stored as a monotone sequence of integers, and a sequence of N entity-dependent features (rows 5-8), one per candidate entity. For compactness, entities in the table are represented with a numerical id although we hold a separate identifier to string map stored as a front-coded list. We store integer values using Elias-Fano monotone sequences [10]. However, and given that the number of entities is several orders of magnitude smaller than the number of aliases, we store the alias-independent features (rows 5,6) in its own Elias-Fano list, indexed by entity id. The alias strings are perfectly-hashed in a similar fashion to the word vectors and we hold an additional (compressed) list of cut pointers indicating the boundaries of the per alias information in the compressed list of values. The size of the different components of the hash table is detailed in Table 2.

Note that once the scoring function is fixed it would be sufficient to store just the mapping from aliases to (entity, score) pairs; however, this would require to recompute the data structure if the score function needs to be modified. In this case we favor flexibility over space, since the savings would be very small and the time to compute the scores is negligible.

	Features included for every alias
1	Number of times the alias was submitted as a query $n(s, c_q)$
2	Number of times the alias resulted in a click $\sum_{s:a_s=1} n(s, c_q)$
3	Number of times the alias was found in Wikipedia's text $n(s, c_w)$
4	Number of times the alias was present inside anchor text $\sum_{s:a_s=1} n(s, c_w)$
	Features included for every entity
5	Number of times the entity's Wikipedia page was clicked after a query was submitted $n(e, c_q)$
6	Number of times the entity's Wikipedia page was linked $n(e, c_q)$
	Alias and entity features
7	Number of times the alias resulted in a click in the entity's Wikipedia page e, $\sum_{s:a_{s,e}=1} n(s, c_q)$.
8	Number of times the alias occurred in an anchor pointing to the entity's Wikipedia page e, $\sum_{s:a_{s,e}=1} n(s, c_w)$

Table 1: Features in the data structure.

4. RESULTS AND DISCUSSION

This section describes the experiments we performed to assess effectiveness and efficiency of our entity linking model for web search queries. Prior to that, we describe the queries and data used for evaluation and detail the baselines we compare our methods against. Additionally, we describe a procedure for automatically tuning the hyperparameters of the context model and a comparison between the performance of Centroid and LR vectors, independent of the linking task.

4.1 Data

All the experiments use Wikipedia as a knowledge base and Yahoo's Webscope[4] search query log to entities, which is a publicly available editorial set that contains annotations for 2583 queries distributed across 980 user sessions. The dataset contains manually identified links to entities in the form of Wikipedia articles and provides the means to train, test, and benchmark such systems using manually created, gold standard data. In order to build our data structures, we use Yahoo query logs spanning 18 months, and all of Wikipedia's anchor text extracted from a Wikipedia dump dated May 2014. The contextual vectors described in Section 3.2 are built using the same Wikipedia version. Note that for our current experiments all our data is using Wikipedia as a knowledge base, although it would easily be possible to extract information from user actions on other domains. The only requirement is that the entities' web pages are consolidated. One could, e.g., collect information about *actors* and *movies* by looking at clicks landing on `imdb.com` web pages. The final structure contains 4.6M entities, which comprises the set of those Wikipedia entries that correspond to articles proper, i.e., category, help, and discussion pages are discarded. After some basic normalization (punctuation stripping and case folding) the number of aliases mined from the anchor text and query logs totals 113M. It is interesting to examine the distribution of the number of entities that are potential targets for a given alias. Figure 1 displays the frequencies of the number of entities per alias for the whole entity-alias set. For instance, there are about 10^8 aliases that only point to one entity. The figure indicates a heavy-tailed distribution. However, this distribution is different if we take a look at how the number of candidate entities per alias differs across queries. Over a sample of 1M random queries the average number of entities per alias is 93.85 with a standard deviation of 335.284, which implies there is a large set of entities to disambiguate and the size of this set can vary greatly from query to query. If we break down this average and deviation by alias length (Figure 2), we observe that it drops dramatically when the length of the alias query segment referring to the entity is greater than 1. In practice this means that unigram aliases are more difficult to disambiguate even though they have a considerably higher frequency and that the linker has to somehow balance the tradeoff between longer aliases with a more precise meaning and more frequent smaller but ambiguous words. Conversely, Figure 3 plots the different number of aliases that are associated with entities, which is another heavy-tailed distribution. The majority of the aliases (86%) point to a single entity.

[4]`http://webscope.sandbox.yahoo.com/`

k	Centroid	LR
5	7.857	7.386
10	5.711	5.385
15	4.575	4.363
20	3.931	3.883

Table 3: Accuracy for the retrieval task.

The features compressed in the data structure are described in Table 1. All the features are integer values and stored in a contiguous block of memory as described in the next section. Per-entity features are also kept in contiguous blocks of memory and referenced appropriately from aliases features using the entity id, in order to avoid wasting storage unnecessarily. It is finally worth to remark that our models are almost parameter free—there is a smoothing parameter μ per input source (query logs, anchor text) and a regularization parameter for the word vectors. We self-tune the regularization parameters automatically using the method described in Section 4.2. The μ parameters have limited impact on the performance and were set to a fixed value of 10. For ranking entities we employ Eq. 1 in our linking algorithm.

4.2 Training Entity Vectors

We train the word vectors with the original `word2vec` code on a text collection of 3 billion words extracted from Wikipedia, using the standard vector dimensionality $D = 200$. To train the LR entity vectors we use the SciPy implementation of L-BFGS on the loss function Eq. 12, computing the

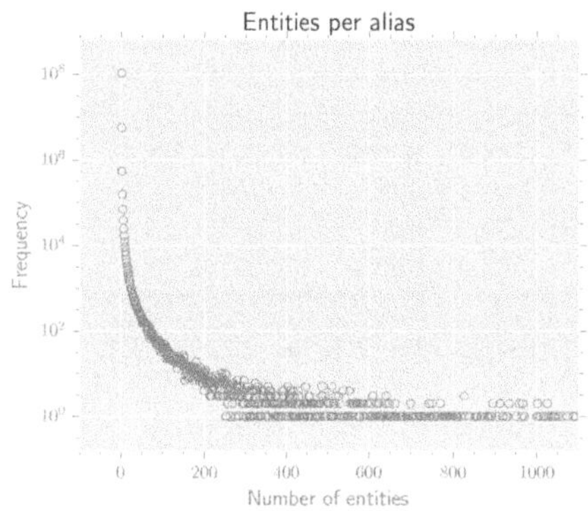

Figure 1: Distribution of the number of entities per alias (logscale).

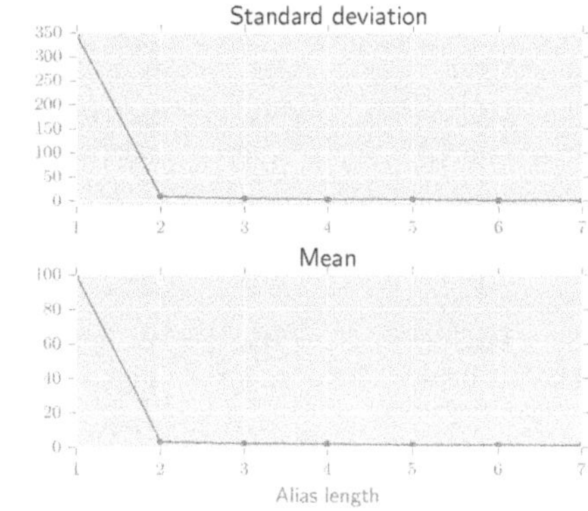

Figure 2: Standard deviation and mean of the number of entities per alias for different alias lengths.

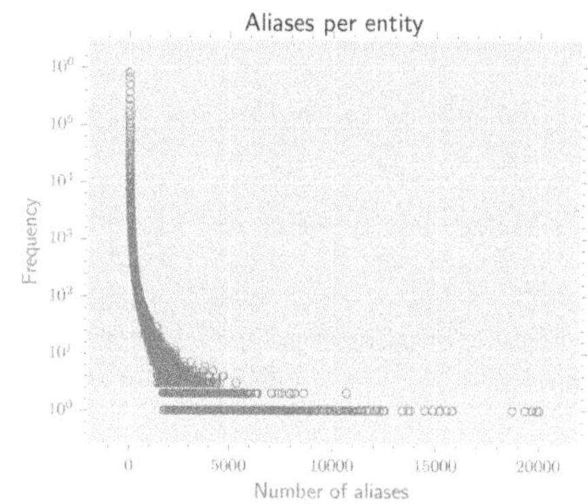

Figure 3: Distribution of the number of aliases per entity (logscale).

function and its gradients using Theano [3]. Note that the task is trivially parallelizable, as every entity vector can be computed independently. Computing vectors for all the 4.6 million entities in our knowledge base with the chosen hyperparameters takes about 12 hours on a machine with 32 cores. Given the scarcity and sparsity of labeled query examples we seek an unsupervised way to tune the hyperparameters λ and ρ (the regularization parameter and the number of negative samples). To this aim we define an artificial task which we call the *retrieval task*, and optimize the parameters on it. We define the retrieval task as follows. We sample a set of entities $\mathcal{E}_{\text{train}}$ among those whose multiset $\mathcal{R}_e$ has at least 50 words, and extract a subsample $\mathcal{E}_{\text{test}} \subset \mathcal{E}_{\text{train}}$. For each entity e in $\mathcal{E}_{\text{train}}$ we hold out k words from $\mathcal{R}_e$ and train the entity vector on the remaining words. Then, for each entity e in $\mathcal{E}_{\text{test}}$ we use the k held out words to score all the entities in $\mathcal{E}_{\text{train}}$ and compute the rank of e in the induced ranking. Then, inspired by the standard discount gains in DCG metrics, we define the accuracy as the average logarithm of the ranks.

We observe that as the number of negative samples ρ increases the accuracy improves but the training time grows linearly; we find a satisfactory trade-off at $\rho = 20$, where the accuracy reaches a plateau. With respect to the regularization parameter, instead, we find a maximum at $\lambda = 10$. In Table 3 we report the accuracy numbers for Centroid and LR trained with the above hyperparameters, for different values of k, using 50K entities for $\mathcal{E}_{\text{train}}$ and $5,000$ entities for $\mathcal{E}_{\text{test}}$. Note that LR outperforms Centroid in all cases.

4.3 Entity Linking

We now compare the performance of our FEL models against several baselines: state-of-the-art systems (Wikifier and TAGME), a retrieval approach based on language models, and *commonness*. This latter method is a popular unsupervised baseline and has been shown to perform quite well on various kinds of input texts (tweets, news items, etc.) [11, 20]. It is defined as

$$cmns(e, s) = \frac{|L_{e,s}|}{\sum_{e'} |L_{e',s}|}, \tag{14}$$

where e is an entity, s a sequence of terms and $L_{e,s}$ the set of all links within Wikipedia with anchor text s that target the page that represents e. In order to process the queries using this method, we split each query into every single term n-gram starting from the longest possible, i.e., the whole query. Then we try to match each n-gram with anchor texts as found in Wikipedia. In the case an anchor text is found we score the entities based on *cmns* and ignore the smaller, constituent n-grams. Otherwise we recurse and try to match the (n-1)-grams. Information retrieval-based approaches (denoted LM) make use of a Wikipedia index and can rank the pages using their content. We indexed each Wikipedia article using different fields (title, content, anchors, first paragraph, redirects, and categories) and implemented the method by Kim and Croft [18] for ranking the different pages. This method computes a per-field weighting term based on the query. In effect, it determines the likelihood that a term is generated by a certain document field, based on all the documents in the collection. It then uses this likelihood to create a per-field-weighted query using Dirichlet priors smoothing. We note the performance of this method on its own is quite poor. We therefore enhanced it using a query-independent feature and rerank the obtained search results by the amount of clicks on a Wikipedia page as document prior (LM-Click). The method denoted *Bing* is a reference baseline that issues the query through the Bing search API and returns the first Wikipedia page as a result. This is a strong baseline in that commercial Web search engines use supervised, machine learned ranking models incorporating a large number of features, including features derived from the text of entity pages, the hyperlink graph and user interactions (click logs).

Ferragina and Scaiella [11] propose a method called TAGME with an explicit focus on short texts. They use a voting scheme in conjunction with heavy pruning of n-grams unrelated to the input text. This results in a fast method that is especially suitable for short text. As such we include the results of querying the TAGME REST API as a baseline.

Ratinov et al. [33] propose the use of a "local" approach (e.g., commonness) to generate a disambiguation context and then apply "global" machine learning for disambiguation. Wikifier[5] is an implementation of this state-of-the-art system which combines Wikipedia pages, gazetteers, and Wordnet. We denote our Fast Entity Linker as FEL, and the

[5] `http://cogcomp.cs.illinois.edu/page/demo_view/Wikifier`

	P@1	MRR	MAP	R-Prec
LM	0.0394	0.1386	0.1053	0.0365
LM-Click	0.4882	0.5799	0.4264	0.3835
Bing	0.6349	0.7018	0.5388	0.5223
Wikifier	0.2983	0.3201	0.2030	0.2086
TAGME	0.6682	0.7043	0.5458	0.5462
Commonness	0.7336	0.7798	0.6418	0.6464
FEL	0.7669	0.8092	0.6528	0.6575
FEL+Centroid	0.8035	0.8366	0.6728	0.6765
FEL+LR	**0.8352**	**0.8684**	**0.6912**	**0.6883**

Table 4: Performance of the different linking methods on the Webscope dataset . FEL outperforms significantly all the baselines (t-test, p<0.01, P@1) except for commonness. FEL+Centroid outperforms significantly all the baselines and FEL, and FEL+LR is significantly better than the rest.

two methods that use contextual vectors are FEL+Centroid and FEL+LR to indicate the different ways the vectors are learned.

4.3.1 Results

We evaluate the different systems using early precision metrics, i.e, Precision at rank 1 (P@1), Mean Reciprocal Rank (MRR), R-Precision (R-Prec) and also Mean Average Precision (MAP). We remark that our methods return the ranked list of entities that maximize the likelihood of a query segmentation; because this segmentation potentially contains several entities, we return one entity per identified query chunk (as a ranked list). In this respect, recall oriented metrics would promote methods that return multiple interpretations for the same query span (this would be partially the case for MAP). We report on statistical significance using a two-sided t-test with $p < 0.01$.

Table 4 shows the main entity linking results. With respect to the baselines, Wikifier was designed primarily for entity linking on longer texts and underperforms heavily with respect to the rest of the methods. TAGME is specifically designed for short texts and performs better, although both commonness and FEL outperform it by a large margin. Retrieval-based approaches are not competitive on their own. Retrieving entities using the Bing search API, which presumably uses a large amount of available signals for ranking, is the first competitive baseline, along with commonness. Somehow surprisingly, in our dataset this baseline outperformed every other baseline by a large margin. FEL clearly and significantly outperforms all the baselines, except for commonness. FEL+Centroid, however, significantly outperforms all the baselines as well as FEL, and FEL+LR is in turn significantly better than all other methods.

4.4 Runtime Performance

We now turn into comparing the execution times of different systems. All the experiments were conducted on a standard MacBook Pro, with 2.7 GHz Intel Core i7 cpu and 16GB of RAM. Timings were measured on a random sample of 1M queries and each experiment was repeated 5 times; below we report the average numbers. A natural candidate for a fast baseline would be an index-based structure that can perform quick look-ups of aliases with entity candidate information. In the open source domain, arguably the fastest inverted file-based system would be MG4J,[6] which in its most recent version has an index built around the idea of quasi-succinct monotone sequences [35]. We rank entities using a standard BM25 scorer over the title and body fields. We also compare with Wikifier, which uses Lucene indexes and several gazetteers as its basic data-structures. Wikipedia MG4J's indexes occupy approximately 2GB of compressed data (over 6GB including positional information), whereas Wikifier's gazetteers and indexes add up to over 6GB.

System	Average time	Data size
Wikifier	44.32 ms	6.8G
Retrieval (And)	13.63 ms	2.5G
Retrieval (Or)	210.13 ms	2.5G
FEL	0.14 ms	1.8G
FEL+Centroid	0.27 ms	2.3G
FEL+LR	0.40 ms	2.3G

Table 5: Entity linking efficiency. For FEL and FEL+{Centroid,LR} we include the size of all the compressed data structures. For *Retrieval* we include the size of the indexes without positional information, and for Wikifier the size of the indexes and gazetteers.

The results for the efficiency experiments are shown in Table 5. FEL outperforms the Wikifier approach 300-fold. When we compare FEL and FEL+Context, we observe that factoring the contextual vectors into the ranking adds an overhead of 0.13 ms in the case of Centroid and 0.26 ms in the case of LR. MG4J in AND mode—while being remarkably fast for a stand-alone index-based system—has a very low recall and it is not a viable solution for entity linking. In contrast, MG4J in OR mode is 4 orders of magnitude slower than FEL. We highlight that the vectors decompression procedure is responsible for the biggest part of the runtime overhead. The dynamic pruning procedure described in Section 3.3.1 alleviates this problem by a factor of 5, yielding average query times below half a millisecond. Without early termination, the contextual algorithm has an overhead of about 2 ms over FEL.

4.5 Error Analysis

We now illustrate some of the caveats and advantages of the proposed methods. Our FEL model makes mistakes of different kinds. A fraction of these errors come from typos in the queries that are not accounted for in the aliases that we use. When we incorporate a proprietary query spelling corrector before linking, the performance of our methods is increased by approximately 3% (MAP increases to 0.7000, P@1 to 0.8610). Examples of other kinds of errors are illustrated in Table 6. Some of them have to do with overly popular candidates, or whenever there are two concepts that are too similar (`Crossbreed` versus `Dog_Type`) and the provided context is not enough to discriminate among them. On the other hand, too much context might promote entities that are too specific, such as in the case of the Sheraton Hotel in Kansas. Table 7 displays some queries that were improved from the context-agnostic FEL when using FEL+LR. In those cases, the semantic descriptions taken from the abstracts of the entity pages are a signal strong enough to

[6] `http://mg4j.di.unimi.it`

Query	Answer	Correct Answer	Type of Error
designer dogs types	`Dog_type`	`Crossbreed`	Parallel concept
clinton falls asleep	`Clinton_Falls_Township`	`Bill_Clinton`	Wrong segmentation
candidate killed in storm	`Storm_(Marvel_Comics)`	`Storm`	Candidate too popular
france world cup 98 reaction	`FIFA_World_Cup`	`FIFA_World_Cup_1998`	Not enough context
2005 presidential election in Egypt	`Elections_in_Egypt`	`2005_Elections_in_Egypt`	Not enough context
kansas city hotels airport	`Sheraton_Kansas_City_Hotel`	`Kansas_City`	Too much context

Table 6: Different examples of mistakes made by the context aware system along with their types, top linked entity displayed.

Query	FEL answer	FEL+Context
install roof insulation	`Insolation`	`Building_insulation`
inventor of gunpowder	`Gunpowder`	`History_of_gunpowder`
us political map	`Map`	`Red_states_and_blue_states`
dj jobs	`Jobs_(film)`	`Disc_jockey`
buy used car parts online	`Automobile`	`Used_car`
what is the longest running tv show	`Television`	`The_Simpsons`

Table 7: Example queries that were *corrected* from the base system FEL when the contextual vectors were incorporated into the model, top linked entity displayed.

boost entity candidates that are more related to the query, e.g., `History_of_gunpowder` versus `Gunpowder`.

5. CONCLUSIONS

In this paper we have described a probabilistic model for entity linking on web search queries. This task already poses numerous challenges by itself but a major limitation in the context of web search is that we are heavily constrained from a runtime perspective, imposing time and space requirements whilst maintaining accuracy. Our method leverages information from query logs and anchor texts to automatically obtain a large number of aliases for the entities in a knowledge base and uses a probabilistic model to rank entities in query segments. Our model uses dynamic programming to generate the best entity segmentation and, in order to add information about the query context into the ranking, we devise a novel way of aggregating vectors that encode word distributional semantics. This new contextual vector model significantly outperforms various state-of-the-art baselines from the literature on a public test set comprised of 2.5K queries, while being able to provide sub-millisecond response times—several orders of magnitude faster than entity linking systems from the literature.

Furthermore, all the data structures used by our system are compressed using state-of-the-art hashing, quantization, and integer encoding techniques. This yields a final data-pack storing hundreds of millions of aliases for all 4.6M Wikipedia entities using less than 2GB of storage. We also note that the size of the word vector representations can be reduced by an order of magnitude without any execution overhead.

For future work, we would like to test the scalability of the system when considering hundreds of millions of entities and billions of aliases. This might require to employ static pruning algorithms to reduce the size of the compressed data structures [4]. Additionally, we generated the contextual vectors using Wikipedia but we could expand the input sources to accommodate for other types of data, such as queries or news, which could incorporate more interesting contextual relations that fall outside of encyclopedic knowledge (e.g., trends, gossip, etc.). Another interesting line of work could involve incorporating session-level features into the entity linking process in order to make use of a richer source of contextual information. Finally, we believe that our contextual entity models are general enough to be of value in different types of applications that make use of word aggregation distributional similarities.

Acknowledgments

The authors would like to thank Sebastiano Vigna and Hugues Bouchard for their kind help in implementing the system described in the paper, and their support with uncountable useful suggestions. The second author was supported by Midas EU Project (318786), eCloud EU Project (325091) and by the Yahoo Faculty Research and Engagement Program.

References

[1] E. Alfonseca, M. Pasca, and E. Robledo-Arnuncio. Acquisition of instance attributes via labeled and related instances. In *Proceedings of the 33rd International ACM SIGIR Conference on Research and Development in Information Retrieval*, 2010.

[2] R. Baeza-Yates, C. Hurtado, and M. Mendoza. Query recommendation using query logs in search engines. In *Proceedings of the 2004 International Conference on Current Trends in Database Technology*, 2004.

[3] J. Bergstra, O. Breuleux, F. Bastien, P. Lamblin, R. Pascanu, G. Desjardins, J. Turian, D. Warde-Farley, and Y. Bengio. Theano: a CPU and GPU math expression compiler. In *Proceedings of the Python for Scientific Computing Conference (SciPy)*, June 2010. Oral Presentation.

[4] R. Blanco and A. Barreiro. Probabilistic static pruning of inverted files. *ACM Trans. Inf. Syst.*, 28(1):1:1–1:33, Jan. 2010.

[5] R. Blanco, B. B. Cambazoglu, P. Mika, and N. Torzec. Entity recommendations in web search. In *The*

Semantic Web - ISWC 2013 - 12th International Semantic Web Conference, 2013.

[6] M. Bron, B. Huurnink, and M. de Rijke. Linking archives using document enrichment and term selection. In *Proceedings of the 15th International Conference on Theory and Practice of Digital Libraries: Research and Advanced Technology for Digital Libraries*, 2011.

[7] X. Cheng and D. Roth. Relational inference for wikification. In *Proceedings of the 2013 Conference on Empirical Methods in Natural Language Processing, EMNLP 2013*, 2013.

[8] S. Cucerzan. Large-scale named entity disambiguation based on wikipedia data. In *Proceedings of EMNLP-CoNLL 2007*, 2007.

[9] S. Dill, N. Eiron, D. Gibson, D. Gruhl, R. Guha, A. Jhingran, T. Kanungo, S. Rajagopalan, A. Tomkins, J. A. Tomlin, and J. Y. Zien. Semtag and seeker: Bootstrapping the semantic web via automated semantic annotation. In *Proceedings of the 12th International Conference on World Wide Web*, 2003.

[10] P. Elias. Efficient storage and retrieval by content and address of static files. *J. ACM*, 21(2):246–260, 1974.

[11] P. Ferragina and U. Scaiella. Tagme: On-the-fly annotation of short text fragments (by wikipedia entities). In *Proceedings of the 19th ACM International Conference on Information and Knowledge Management*, 2010.

[12] A. Gersho and R. M. Gray. *Vector Quantization and Signal Compression*. Kluwer Academic Publishers, Norwell, MA, USA, 1991. ISBN 0-7923-9181-0.

[13] J. Guo, G. Xu, X. Cheng, and H. Li. Named entity recognition in query. In *Proceedings of the 32Nd International ACM SIGIR Conference on Research and Development in Information Retrieval*, 2009.

[14] B. Hachey, W. Radford, J. Nothman, M. Honnibal, and J. R. Curran. Evaluating entity linking with Wikipedia. *Artificial Intelligence*, 194(0):130 – 150, 2013.

[15] L. Hollink, P. Mika, and R. Blanco. Web usage mining with semantic analysis. In *Proceedings of the 22nd International Conference on World Wide Web*, 2013.

[16] N. Houlsby and M. Ciaramita. A scalable gibbs sampler for probabilistic entity linking. In *Advances in Information Retrieval*. Springer, 2014.

[17] J. Hu, G. Wang, F. Lochovsky, J.-t. Sun, and Z. Chen. Understanding user's query intent with wikipedia. In *Proceedings of the 18th International Conference on World Wide Web*, 2009.

[18] J. Kim and W. B. Croft. A field relevance model for structured document retrieval. In *Advances in Information Retrieval - 34th European Conference on IR Research, ECIR 2012*, 2012.

[19] E. Meij, M. Bron, L. Hollink, B. Huurnink, and M. de Rijke. Mapping queries to the Linking Open Data cloud: A case study using DBpedia. *Web Semantics: Science, Services and Agents on the World Wide Web*, 9(4):418 – 433, 2011.

[20] E. Meij, W. Weerkamp, and M. de Rijke. Adding semantics to microblog posts. In *Proceedings of the Fifth ACM International Conference on Web Search and Data Mining*, 2012.

[21] P. N. Mendes, A. Passant, P. Kapanipathi, and A. P. Sheth. Linked open social signals. In *Proceedings of the 2010 IEEE/WIC/ACM International Conference on Web Intelligence and Intelligent Agent Technology - Volume 01*, 2010.

[22] R. Mihalcea and A. Csomai. Wikify!: Linking documents to encyclopedic knowledge. In *Proceedings of the Sixteenth ACM Conference on Conference on Information and Knowledge Management*, 2007.

[23] T. Mikolov, K. Chen, G. Corrado, and J. Dean. Efficient estimation of word representations in vector space. *CoRR*, abs/1301.3781, 2013.

[24] T. Mikolov, I. Sutskever, K. Chen, G. S. Corrado, and J. Dean. Distributed representations of words and phrases and their compositionality. In *NIPS '13*, 2013.

[25] D. Milne and I. H. Witten. Learning to link with wikipedia. In *Proceedings of the 17th ACM Conference on Information and Knowledge Management*, 2008.

[26] D. Nadeau and S. Sekine. A survey of named entity recognition and classification. *Linguisticae Investigationes*, 30(1):3–26, 2007.

[27] R. Navigli. Word sense disambiguation: A survey. *ACM Comput. Surv.*, 41(2):10:1–10:69, 2009.

[28] M. Paşca. Weakly-supervised discovery of named entities using web search queries. In *Proceedings of the Sixteenth ACM Conference on Conference on Information and Knowledge Management*, 2007.

[29] P. Pantel, T. Lin, and M. Gamon. Mining entity types from query logs via user intent modeling. In *The 50th Annual Meeting of the Association for Computational Linguistics*, 2012.

[30] A. Pilz and G. Paaß. From names to entities using thematic context distance. In *Proceedings of the 20th ACM International Conference on Information and Knowledge Management*, 2011.

[31] J. Pound, I. F. Ilyas, and G. Weddell. Expressive and flexible access to web-extracted data: A keyword-based structured query language. In *Proceedings of the 2010 ACM SIGMOD International Conference on Management of Data*, 2010.

[32] J. Pound, S. Paparizos, and P. Tsaparas. Facet discovery for structured web search: A query-log mining approach. In *Proceedings of the 2011 ACM SIGMOD International Conference on Management of Data*, 2011.

[33] L. Ratinov, D. Roth, D. Downey, and M. Anderson. Local and global algorithms for disambiguation to wikipedia. In *Proceedings of the 49th Annual Meeting of the Association for Computational Linguistics*, 2011.

[34] U. Sawant and S. Chakrabarti. Learning joint query interpretation and response ranking. In *Proceedings of the 22nd International Conference on World Wide Web*, 2013.

[35] S. Vigna. Quasi-succinct indices. In *Proceedings of the Sixth ACM International Conference on Web Search and Data Mining*, 2013.

[36] J. X. Yu, L. Qin, and L. Chang. Keyword search in relational databases: A survey. *IEEE Data Eng. Bull.*, 33(1):67–78, 2010.

On Tag Recommendation for Expertise Profiling: A Case Study in the Scientific Domain

Isac S. Ribeiro, Rodrygo L. T. Santos,
Marcos A. Gonçalves, Alberto H. F. Laender
Department of Computer Science
Universidade Federal de Minas Gerais
Belo Horizonte, MG, Brazil
{isacsandin,rodrygo,mgoncalv,laender}@dcc.ufmg.br

ABSTRACT

Building expertise profiles is a crucial step towards identifying experts in different knowledge areas. However, summarizing the topics of expertise of a given individual is a challenging task, primarily due to the semi-structured and heterogeneous nature of the documentary evidence available for this task. In this paper, we investigate the suitability of tag recommendation as a mechanism to produce effective expertise profiles. In particular, we perform a large-scale user study with academic experts from different knowledge areas to assess the effectiveness of multiple supervised and unsupervised tag recommendation approaches as well as multiple sources of textual evidence. Our analysis reveals that traditional content-based tag recommenders perform well at identifying expertise-oriented tags, with article keywords being a particularly effective source of evidence across profiles in different knowledge areas and with various levels of sparsity. Moreover, by combining multiple recommenders and sources of evidence as learning signals, we further demonstrate the effectiveness of tag recommendation for expertise profiling.

Categories and Subject Descriptors

H.3.4 [**Information Storage and Retrieval**]: Systems and Software—*User profiles and alert services*

General Terms

Experimentation, Measurement

Keywords

Expertise profiling; tag recommendation; learning to rank

1. INTRODUCTION

The online possibilities for people to interconnect and share experiences and knowledge is unprecedented. One domain that can benefit tremendously from such interconnection possibilities is science. In particular, researchers from multidisciplinary scientific areas can establish new contacts, form networks, and collaborate on challenging research problems. However, the large number of researchers acting online and searching for relevant contacts and partnerships requires new tools and services for automatically finding experts in a given knowledge area. Two challenges need to be addressed for these services to work properly: (1) the construction of *profiles* that can meaningfully describe a researcher's expertise and (2) the design of algorithms capable of ranking researchers according to such expertise profiles. The latter task, denoted *expert finding*, has recently received a lot of attention from the academic community [3]. The task of *expertise profiling*, on the other hand, has received considerably less attention [27, 28] and is hence our focus.

There are several challenges related to the construction of meaningful expertise profiles, such as: (i) balancing between conciseness versus representativeness, (ii) identifying the best topics to summarize sometimes very long careers, (iii) dealing with the evolution of topics of interest over time, and (iv) extracting and aggregating several sources of expertise evidence including online curricula vitae, pages in different digital libraries, and social networks. To address some of these challenges, we approach the expertise profiling problem as a problem of *tag recommendation for people* (or *people tagging*). Although tag recommendation has been studied before for a range of different types of online media [10, 15, 18, 19, 30], people tagging is an area which has been less investigated and with opportunities for improvements.

In this paper, we investigate the suitability of tag recommendation for producing effective expertise profiles. To this end, we perform a large-scale user study involving 1,288 respondents (of 5,355 contacted) among the most prominent researchers from different areas of knowledge in Brazil to assess the effectiveness of people tagging for expertise profiling. As a source of expertise evidence, we leverage each researcher's curriculum vitae (CV) as archived in the Lattes Platform,[1] an internationally renowned initiative that manages information about science, technology, and innovation related to individual researchers and research institutions in Brazil [20]. Our investigation contrasts three representative content-based tag recommendation algorithms from the literature, exploiting three textual sources of expertise evidence from the publications listed in each researcher's Lattes CV, namely, their title, abstract, and keywords. Our experimental results demonstrate the effectiveness, completeness, and robustness of the expertise profiles built through tag recom-

[1] `http://lattes.cnpq.br`

WSDM'15, February 2–6, 2015, Shanghai, China.
Copyright 2014 ACM 978-1-4503-3317-7/15/02 ...$15.00.
http://dx.doi.org/10.1145/2684822.2685320.

mendation for researchers in different areas of knowledge and for various levels of sparsity of the available textual evidence. While keyword-based expertise profiles are shown to be particularly effective, we further investigate the suitability of multiple learning to rank (L2R) strategies for combining the considered recommendation algorithms and sources of evidence as learning features. Our results show that the best learning strategies, which are based on an ensemble of rankers, can produce results about 21.5% better than the best tag recommender baseline used in isolation. Moreover, we show that a profiling effectiveness of 80% of that attained by the most effective learned model can be achieved using only two features, which further hints on the potential applicability of tag recommendation in real deployments. To the best of our knowledge, the size of this investigation in terms of coverage (a whole country), disparate areas of knowledge, algorithms, and data source alternatives is unique.

In summary, the major contributions of this paper are:

1. A large-scale user study for expertise profiling with the most prominent Brazilian researchers in different knowledge areas and with various career lengths.
2. A thorough empirical assessment of the effectiveness of multiple unsupervised and supervised tag recommenders for automatic expertise profiling.

In the remainder of this paper, Section 2 covers related work in several areas such as expertise profiling, tag recommendation, and evaluation of tag recommenders. Section 3 details the methodology underlying our experimental evaluation, including the procedures for mining and ranking candidate tags, as well as for collecting relevance judgements in our large-scale user study. Section 4 discusses the results of our experimental evaluation. Finally, Section 5 provides our concluding remarks and directions for future work.

2. RELATED WORK

Expertise profiling is an essential component of any expert finding or expert retrieval system [3]. There has been some investigation on the theme for a while (see, for instance, [2] and [12]), but the interest remains, with very recent work dedicated to the temporal aspects of expertise [14, 27]. In this work, we approach the expertise profiling problem as one of *people tagging* [28]. This solution has several advantages, such as: (i) uniform and concise representation of the profile, (ii) existence of previous methods in other domains to suggest or rank a set of candidate tags, (iii) capability of generating different "tag clouds" for different periods in a person's career, (iv) uniform treatment of the sources of information as "bags of candidate tags", etc. These advantages can help a people-tagging approach overcome some of the challenges in expertise profiling mentioned in Section 1. However, people tagging is a problem much less investigated than tag recommendation for other types of "objects".

Tag recommendation approaches have been proposed for a wide range of media types, mainly in the so-called Web 2.0 [4, 5, 6, 10, 15, 18, 19, 30]. The state-of-the-art techniques for this task exploit co-occurrence patterns with previously assigned tags, expanding an initial set of tags I_0 for an object o with other tags that co-occur with tags in I_0, although in different objects of the collection. The most relevant tags can then be used to induce a tag cloud to represent the object o. For instance, Canuto et al. [10] compared several L2R algorithms for the task of tag recommendation, but they do assume that I_0 is not empty. When there are no tags initially available, as is the case in many scenarios for people tagging, such methods do not work properly [23]. Other works exploit connections among objects that enable the propagation of tags from a tagged object to an untagged one [21, 29, 32, 38]. This can be seen as a type of collaborative filtering approach [13]. In contrast, in this paper, we adopt a pure content-based approach, by exploiting only generally available evidence from the contents of the publications written by the researcher to be tagged.

A relevant approach to our work, yet in the context of object tagging, was proposed by Venetis et al. [33]. In particular, they defined a series of metrics that capture structural properties of a tag cloud. For instance, the coverage of a tag cloud represents the fraction of all objects that can be retrieved by the tags in the cloud. Based on the proposed metrics, they developed a satisfaction model to evaluate the quality of a tag cloud for a given search task. This model considers the probability that the tags in the cloud will fail to satisfy the information need of a user who employs them to browse or search a document collection. Using this model, they performed a quantitative analysis of several algorithms for tag selection. The best performing among these algorithms are used as alternative tag recommenders in our analysis.

The closest approach to ours is the work of Serdyukov et al. [28], who proposed a method for people tagging for expertise profiling in an enterprise domain. While our primary goal is to assess the suitability of tag recommendation for expertise profiling, there are important differences between their work and ours. First, our domain is a scientific one, meaning that the evidence we exploit is completely different. Indeed, while they leveraged features such as web documents, discussion lists and enterprise search clickthrough, we exploit features that are specific to scientific documents, such as title, abstract, and keywords. Second, in their evaluation, they contrasted the recommended tags with self-created profiles. If a recommended tag was not in the profile created by the own employees, the tag would be automatically considered as irrelevant. Such an arguably strict form of evaluation may explain the low performance figures reported in their work. In contrast, we employ a TREC-like pooling approach to gather relevance judgements for tags suggested by nine different recommenders (i.e., three tag recommendation algorithms deployed with three different sources of evidence). Finally, they approached tag recommendation as a classification task, using a logistic regression classifier to determine whether a tag was relevant or not, with the confidence of this classification used to induce an overall ranking. On the other hand, we approach this task as an explicit L2R task, and contrast nine state-of-the-art L2R algorithms to leverage the scores produced by our nine considered tag recommenders as learning features.

Finally, the evaluation of tag recommenders is a research issue by itself. Most previous works rely on an automatic evaluation procedure in which part (usually 50%) of the tags assigned to an object already in the system are used for training purposes, while the remaining ones are used as the gold standard that should be predicted by the recommender. This is mostly due to the inherent difficulties and cost associated with manual user evaluations. Moreover, it is arguably hard for an assessor to judge if a tag assigned by a different user (i.e., a user who has not uploaded the object

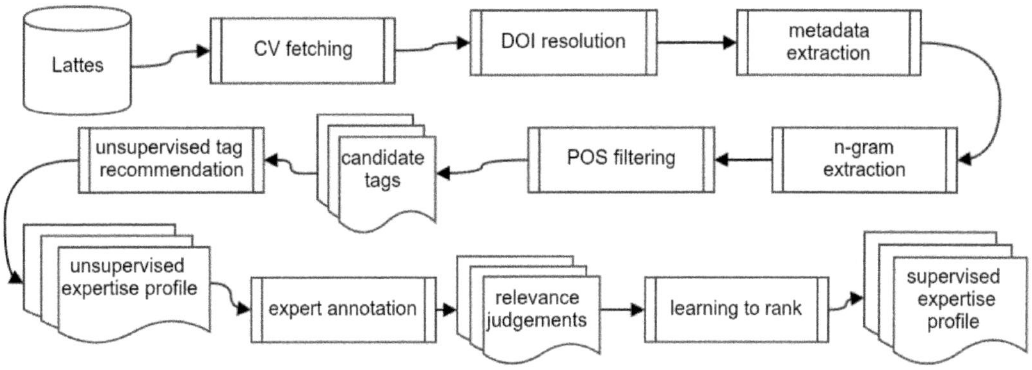

Figure 1: Overview of our experimental methodology.

or is not necessarily familiar with it) is relevant to an object whose interpretation may be subjective (e.g., an image or a video). The problem with this type of evaluation is that a possibly relevant tag for an object may be recommended but it will not be considered as relevant if it is not in the current gold standard. Due to the aforementioned difficulties, only a handful of works (e.g., [7, 25, 29, 31, 34]) assessed tag recommendations with manual user evaluations, usually performed in a very small scale. In contrast, we present a large-scale study involving 1,288 respondents (of 5,355 contacted) among the most prominent researchers in different areas of knowledge currently working in Brazil. Moreover, these assessors can be considered as ideal ones, since they are assessing representations of their own scientific production over the years. In this sense, the dataset we build is a valuable asset for other researchers working on related areas. We intend to make this dataset available soon.

3. EXPERIMENTAL METHODOLOGY

Tag recommendation approaches have been traditionally evaluated by partitioning existing sets of tags, contributed by a multitude of different users, into training and test. The evaluation of people tagging poses additional challenges, primarily because the people being tagged must agree on the relevance of the tags assigned to them. The importance of such an approval is further exacerbated when tags have an expertise orientation, which is our focus here. Despite this, carrying out large-scale user evaluations is often costly and time consuming, which may explain the scarcity of such evaluations in the literature. In this section, we describe the experimental methodology adopted in our work, which supports one such evaluation. In particular, we discuss the selection of a representative target set of experts, the acquisition of expertise evidence about them, the generation of candidate expertise profiles through tag recommendation, and the assessment of the generated profiles. Figure 1 provides an overview of the entire methodology. Statistics of the produced test collection are presented afterwards.

3.1 Data Acquisition

The first step towards producing a test collection for expertise profiling is to choose a representative set of experts. In 2008, the Brazilian National Council for Scientific and Technological Development (CNPq) introduced a funding program to foster networks of collaborative research in several areas considered strategic for the country. Together, the 123 awarded research groups, called National Institutes of Science and Technology (INCTs),[2] comprise over 6,000 of the most prominent researchers from all areas of knowledge working in Brazil. Our test collection is built around these researchers as a representative set of experts to be profiled. In particular, we believe that the breadth of their expertise and their heterogeneous career paths poses realistic challenges to evaluating expertise profiling approaches.

Having selected a set of experts for evaluation, we must collect evidence of their expertise, to be mined in order to produce effective expertise profiles. To this end, as discussed in Section 1, we resorted to the Lattes Platform, a publicly accessible repository of academic information maintained by CNPq, which archives up-to-date CVs for researchers working in both public as well private research institutions in Brazil. In particular, of over 6,000 researchers in our target group, we managed to collect the Lattes CV of 5,355 of them.[3] From each collected CV, we extracted information about all publications up to April 2014. To establish a common ground for researchers in different areas, we focused on journal publications, which are generally seen as the main venue for research dissemination in most areas, and leave the exploration of other sources of evidence for future work.

Having collected the CVs and extracted the titles of all journal publications contained in them, we started to crawl additional metadata corresponding to each publication. For the publications with no Digital Object Identifier (DOI), we performed a query using their citation data to the API of the CrossRef service.[4] With the provided and discovered DOIs, the next step was to collect the metadata using the services of the respective publishers. In particular, we restricted ourselves to the twenty most prolific publishers, which respond for more than 80% of the total number of publications to be collected, as shown in Figure 2. For each publication from these publishers, we extracted its abstract and list of keywords. In addition to the publication title already extracted from the Lattes CV, these metadata form three sources of textual evidence for expertise mining.

[2] http://goo.gl/FdjqRo

[3] The Lattes CV for the remaining researchers could not be collected due to persistent download failures.

[4] http://www.crossref.org

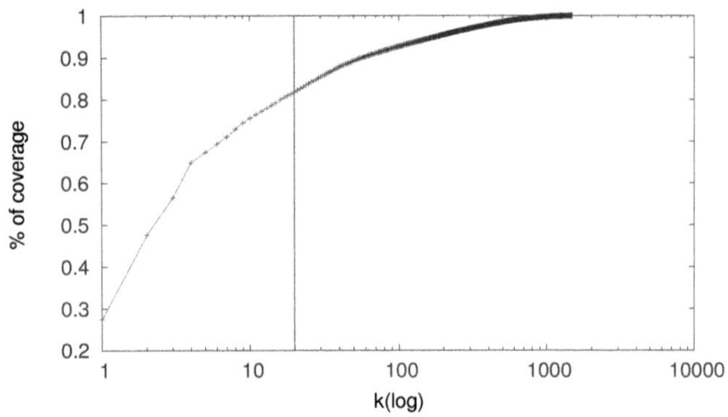

Figure 2: Publications covered by the top k publishers.

3.2 Profile Generation

After acquiring publication metadata to construct different sources of expertise evidence, namely, title, abstract, and keywords, the next step was to generate a candidate expertise profile for each researcher. To this end, we mined candidate tags from each source of evidence by extracting n-grams with varying sizes (from $n = 1$ to $n = 3$). In order to further discard tags unlikely to represent any topic of expertise, we performed a small pilot study with volunteers, including graduate students and staff from our research group. Based upon a random sample with 7,123 tags, this pilot study identified 57 part-of-speech (POS) patterns [22] commonly associated with syntactically malformed tags. In particular, we selected POS patterns with minimum confidence of 90% and minimum support of 15 tags to maximize F1 in our pilot study. Accordingly, the selected POS patterns were used to filter out potentially malformed tags from our candidate set. An example POS filter is NN-IN-VBG (i.e., noun, preposition, gerund), which removed tags such as "proposal after executing" and "testing for validating".

Finally, in order to avoid the limitations of self-created ground-truth profiles, as discussed in Section 2, we generated a pool of diverse tags to be assessed by each researcher. To this end, we chose three representative content-based tag recommendation algorithms, which are commonly used as ranking components within state-of-the-art machine-learned tag recommenders from the literature [33]:

POP: A popularity-based tag recommendation algorithm, which returns the top k tags according to the term frequency (TF) of each tag.

TFIDF: A traditional content-based tag recommendation algorithm, which chooses the top k tags according to their TF×IDF score, where IDF stands for the inverse document frequency of a tag, which is based on the number of publications where it occurs. This algorithm is similar to POP, with the exception that the IDF component further helps demote too popular tags in favor of more discriminative ones.

COV: A recommendation algorithm that seeks to maximize the coverage of a researcher's publications that can be retrieved by the top k selected tags. This algorithm uses an iterative, greedy strategy for choosing the top k tags by selecting, at each iteration, the tag that covers the most yet uncovered publications.

Each of these three algorithms was applied on top of each of the three considered sources of evidence, namely, title, abstract, and keywords, hence producing nine different recommenders. Lastly, we pooled the ranking produced by each of these recommenders to depth 50 in order to produce a final pool of tags to be assessed by each researcher.

3.3 Profile Assessment

The next step in our evaluation methodology was to gather relevance assessments for each of the tags pooled for each researcher using the nine devised recommenders. To this end, we invited the 5,355 researchers for which we could produce a candidate expertise profile to assess the relevance of the tags in this profile. Of the 5,355 contacted researchers, 1,288 responded to our invitation and participated in the assessment in a period of two weeks in July 2014. Such a high response rate of nearly 25% testifies to the relevance of the study for the community itself. Figure 3 provides a breakdown of the number of respondents per area of knowledge. From the figure, we note that the response rate was roughly consistent across areas, with Health Science—the largest community in our study—contributing most of the respondents.

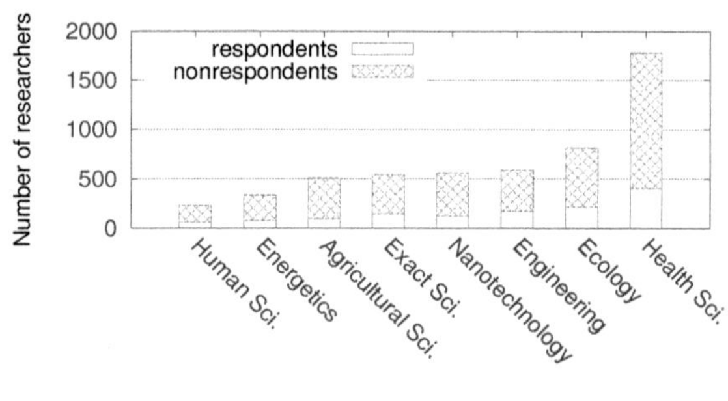

Figure 3: Number of respondents per area of knowledge.

A screenshot of the relevance assessment interface (translated from Portuguese) is presented in Figure 4. During the assessment, each researcher was presented with 60 tags in no particular order, selected in a round-robin fashion from the top 50 tags returned by each of the nine pooled recommenders. The researcher was then asked to assess the relevance of each tag according to the following four-point scale:

1. *"The tag is malformed (a spurious tag)"*
2. *"The tag is well-formed, but is not relevant to describe my work"*
3. *"The tag is well-formed, but is only partially relevant to describe my work"*
4. *"The tag is well-formed and is highly relevant to describe my work"*

Figure 5 shows a distribution of assessed tags for each of the eight areas of knowledge considered in our study. From the figure, we first note that the distribution of tags assessed according to the aforementioned four-point scale is consistent across the different areas. More importantly, we note that, for all knowledge areas, the proportion of malformed tags is lower than that of the other classes taken together. This further demonstrates the appropriateness of the chosen recommenders for identifying potentially relevant tags.

Dear Rodrygo Luis Teodoro Santos

As part of a research project of the National Institute of Science and Technology for the Web, we have developed new methods to generate a representative list of tags to describe the topics of expertise of researchers based on their scientific production. We would like to invite you to validate this list of topics for your particular case.

The tags listed below were automatically generated based on the publications available in our Lattes curriculum with the goal of describing the most representative topics of your research.

For each tag, please indicate one of the following options:

1. The tag **is malformed** (a spurious tag)
2. The tag is well-formed, but **is not relevant** to describe my work
3. The tag is well-formed, but **is only partially relevant** to describe my work
4. The tag is well-formed and **is highly relevant** to describe my work

Tag	**Classification**	**Tag**	**Classification**	**Tag**	**Classification**
learning-to-rank	○ 1 ○ 2 ○ 3 ○ 4	missing full text	○ 1 ○ 2 ○ 3 ○ 4	whens and hows	○ 1 ○ 2 ○ 3 ○ 4
web search engines	○ 1 ○ 2 ○ 3 ○ 4	query suggestions	○ 1 ○ 2 ○ 3 ○ 4	component-based software development	○ 1 ○ 2 ○ 3 ○ 4
expert search	○ 1 ○ 2 ○ 3 ○ 4	note that existing	○ 1 ○ 2 ○ 3 ○ 4	search	○ 1 ○ 2 ○ 3 ○ 4
search result diversification	○ 1 ○ 2 ○ 3 ○ 4	wizard tool	○ 1 ○ 2 ○ 3 ○ 4	query-dependent	○ 1 ○ 2 ○ 3 ○ 4
mimicking web search	○ 1 ○ 2 ○ 3 ○ 4	documents with respect	○ 1 ○ 2 ○ 3 ○ 4	web services	○ 1 ○ 2 ○ 3 ○ 4

Figure 4: Screenshot of the tag assessment system (translated from Portuguese).

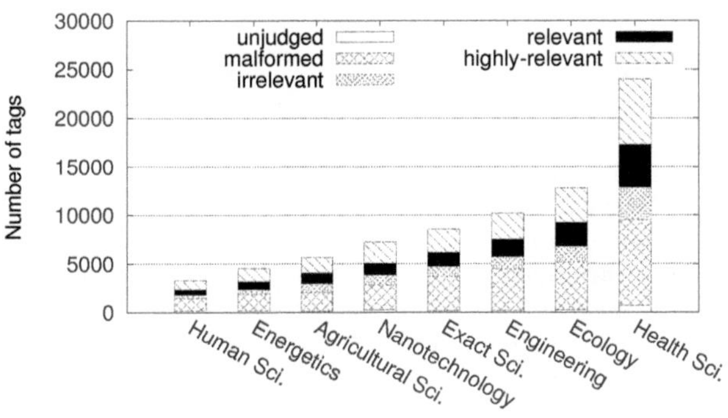

Figure 5: Distribution of assessed tags per area.

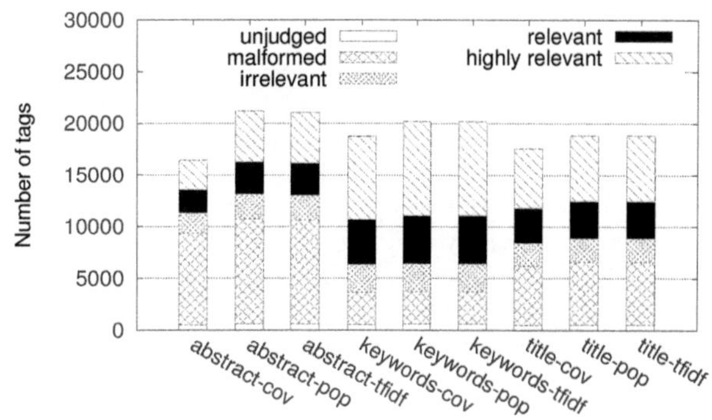

Figure 6: Distribution of assessed tags per recommender.

A similar distribution to the one shown in Figure 5 is shown in Figure 6, however across the nine tag recommenders used for pooling. From the figure, we note the higher incidence of malformed tags among abstract-based tag recommenders, despite the POS filtering step applied to remove such tags. On the other hand, titles have relatively fewer malformed tags, with keywords having the best performance in this aspect. As we will further explore in Section 4, this can be partially explained by the space constraints inherent to each of these sources of evidence and the corresponding care taken by a researcher while filling each of them.

Salient statistics of the produced test collection are summarized in Table 1. From the table, it is worth noting the representativeness of the sample data obtained with respect to the universe of INCT researchers contacted. Equally interesting are the idiosyncrasies of individual areas, particularly in terms of the average number of publications per researcher (#ppr) and the average number of tags the respondents deemed partially (#rtpr) and highly relevant (#htpr) to represent their expertise. As we will discuss in Section 4, this test collection is used to assess the suitability of tag recommendation as a mechanism to automatically generate expertise profiles. In addition, we further leverage the produced relevance assessments as labeled data for learning to rank for expertise profiling. We intend to make the produced test collection available for the benefit of the community.

	contacted		respondents			
area	#res	#ppr	#res	#ppr	#rtpr	#htpr
Agricultural Sci.	507	43.06	94	50.06	11.57	16.71
Ecology	812	25.35	216	27.00	11.20	16.45
Energetics	333	29.26	76	32.22	10.53	17.92
Engineering	588	24.26	175	21.74	10.18	15.32
Exact Sci.	542	49.95	144	56.13	9.85	16.65
Health Sci.	1,783	48.13	403	52.03	11.00	16.68
Human Sci.	229	15.31	58	15.33	8.69	16.36
Nanotechnology	561	50.32	122	58.75	9.93	17.77
Total	5,355	39.41	1,288	41.85	10.60	16.62

Table 1: Statistics of the generated test collection, including the number of researchers (#res) and of publications per researcher (#ppr) for contacted as well as respondent researchers. For the latter, we also show the number of relevant (#rtpr) and highly relevant (#htpr) tags per researcher.

4. EXPERIMENTAL EVALUATION

In this section, we thoroughly analyze the suitability of tag recommendation for expertise profiling. In particular, we aim to answer the following research questions:

Q1. How effective is tag recommendation as a mechanism for automatic expertise profiling?

Q2. How complete is tag recommendation as a mechanism for automatic expertise profiling?

Q3. How robust is tag recommendation as a mechanism for automatic expertise profiling?

Q4. Can we effectively learn to recommend expertise tags?

The results of our analysis are discussed in the subsequent sections, which address each of these questions in turn.

4.1 Profiling Effectiveness

To address question Q1, we assess three representative content-based tag recommendation algorithms from the literature, namely TFIDF, POP, and COV [33]. As discussed in Section 3, each algorithm is provided with textual evidence of a researcher's expertise, derived from the researcher's publication titles, abstracts, or keywords, and produces an expertise profile for the researcher. Figure 7 summarizes the retrieval effectiveness of the expertise profiles generated by different combinations of recommendation algorithm and textual evidence. For each combination, we report normalized discounted cumulative gain (nDCG) figures for multiple ranking cutoffs [1]. In particular, to compute nDCG, we assign partially and highly relevant tags the relevance labels 1 and 2, respectively. Malformed and irrelevant tags are both assigned a relevance label 0. For the sake of readability, error bars denoting 95% confidence intervals are omitted as they are smaller than the plotted symbols.

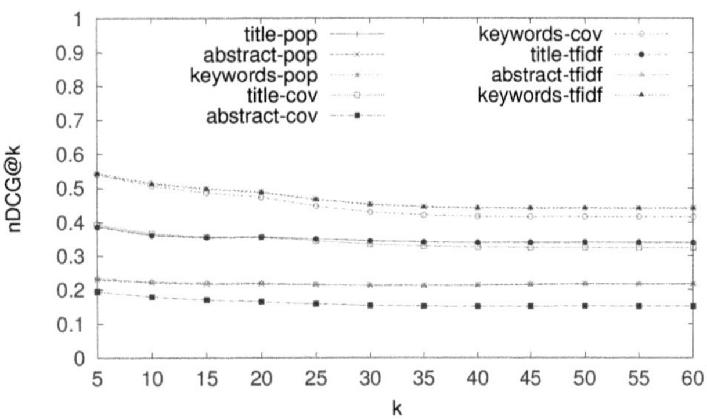

Figure 7: Profiling effectiveness in terms of nDCG at various ranking cutoffs. Error bars are ommited for readability.

Regarding the different tag recommendation algorithms considered in our investigations, from Figure 7, we first note that TFIDF performs similarly to POP, which is somewhat expected. In particular, as shown in Figure 8, nearly 80% of all tags occur only once, and over 90% occur at most twice in the entire corpus. In this scenario, with the majority of tags showing similar scarcity, the IDF component has little impact on the final ranking produced by the TFIDF algorithm. As a result, the ranking produced by TFIDF resembles a pure TF-based ranking, which is essentially equivalent to the ranking produced by the content-based POP algorithm.

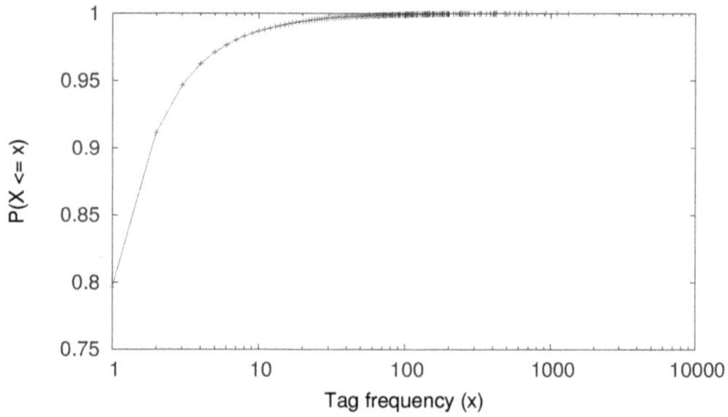

Figure 8: Cumulative distribution of tag frequencies.

From Figure 7, we also note that both TFIDF and POP outperform the COV algorithm. In order to explain this behavior, Table 2 shows the average pairwise overlap among the top 10 tags retrieved by the POP algorithm, in terms of the Jaccard coefficient obtained by comparing the publications where these tags are mentioned. From the table, we observe that the top tags returned by POP have little overlap with respect to one another in terms of the publications that they cover. Indeed, the average pairwise overlap of the tags ranked by POP is as low as 0.102805 in the best case, when considering publication abstracts as a source of expertise evidence. As a result, explicitly seeking to promote a high coverage of these publications, as proposed by the COV algorithm, has little extra benefit, and can even harm the effectiveness of the recommended tags, as is the case when using abstracts. Moreover, COV is computationally more expensive than TFIDF and POP, and hence should be eschewed in favor of these faster approaches, whenever effectiveness is the primary expertise profiling concern.

evidence	Jaccard
abstract	0.102805 ± 0.009586
keywords	0.097010 ± 0.007868
title	0.044094 ± 0.003939

Table 2: Average pairwise Jaccard coefficient for the top 10 tags generated by POP using different textual evidence.

Regarding which textual features are useful expertise indicators, keywords provide a more effective expertise evidence compared to titles, which in turn perform more effectively than abstracts. These observations are consistent across the entire range of nDCG in Figure 7 and suggest that the more constrained the source of evidence, the more useful an expertise indicator it is. Indeed, with limited room for conveying an idea, researchers must strive to ensure that this idea is carefully described. Conversely, less constrained sources of evidence, such as abstracts, provide more freedom for content generation, yet they are more prone to noise. As an illustrative example, Table 3 shows the top 5 tags generated by POP using each of the considered sources of evidence for building an expertise profile for one of the authors of this paper. Looking at the generated tags, we observe that while keyword-based tags are more likely to represent a valid topic of expertise, such as "web search" and "learning to rank", the other sources of evidence may contribute with further plausible tags, such as "search engines" and "weighting models".

keywords	title	abstract
web search	digital	weighting models
learning to rank	search result	learning to rank
relevance	learning to rank	combination
diversity	component-based	search result
digital libraries	search engines	ambiguous query

Table 3: Top 5 tags generated by POP using keywords, title, and abstract for one of the authors of this paper.

Recalling question Q1, the results in this section attest the suitability of traditional content-based tag recommendation algorithms for identifying relevant topics of expertise. In particular, a recommender based on the POP algorithm with tags extracted from the researchers' publication keywords generates the most effective expertise profiles.

4.2 Profiling Completeness

The results in Section 4.1 show that traditional content-based tag recommendation algorithms can produce effective expertise profiles. A natural question that arises in this scenario is how complete these profiles are. In particular, to address Q2, we analyze the completeness of the expertise profiles produced through tag recommendation. To assess the completeness of an expertise profile, we borrow the tag coverage metric proposed by Venetis et al. [33]. In our case, coverage@k measures the fraction of all publications from a researcher that can be retrieved by the top k tags in this researcher's expertise profile. Figures 9(a)-(c) show such coverage figures at different ranking cutoffs k for all considered combinations of recommendation algorithm and textual evidence. Once again, error bars are omitted for readability.

From Figures 9(a)-(c), we first observe that, with only a few top retrieved tags, most combinations of recommendation algorithm and textual evidence are able to cover the majority of the researchers' scientific production. In particular, abstract and keywords-based profiles have coverage@10 figures of nearly 90%. Title-based expertise profiles, on the other hand, require around 50 tags to attain the same level of coverage. Regarding the three considered recommendation algorithms, COV, which directly aims at improving coverage, is particularly effective at earlier ranking cutoffs when applied on abstracts. On titles and keywords, COV is more effective at deeper cutoffs, with statistically significant improvements compared to both TFIDF and POP.

Recalling question Q2, the results in this section attest the completeness of the expertise profiles built through tag recommendation. Indeed, all considered recommenders are able to comprehensively convey a researcher's expertise with only a few top ranked tags. The COV algorithm, which seeks to promote tags with a high coverage of a researcher's publications, can be particularly advantageous to this end.

4.3 Profiling Robustness

The results presented thus far attest the suitability of tag recommendation for expertise profiling in terms of the effectiveness and completeness of the recommended tags. In this section, we investigate two factors that may affect such an effective performance. In particular, in order to address Q3, we assess the effectiveness of tag recommendation for building expertise profiles in different areas of knowledge, as well as for expertise evidence of different levels of sparsity. Regarding the latter, Figure 10 shows the profiling effectiveness of all considered combinations of tag recommendation algorithm and textual evidence in terms of nDCG@10 for researchers with different numbers of journal publications.

From Figure 10, we first observe that all approaches perform reasonably well even for researchers with only a few publications in their curriculum. This highlights the robustness of these approaches against sparse expertise evidence. Nonetheless, we note that the larger the researcher's curriculum, the more effective the produced expertise profile. Indeed, larger curricula tend to offer both breadth for covering distinct expertise topics, as well as depth for reassuring the importance of core topics. However, larger curricula may also introduce noise in the tag recommendation process. This is particularly the case for more verbose sources of evidence, such as abstracts. In particular, besides achieving an inferior performance compared to recommenders based on titles and keywords, recommenders based on abstracts are also less influenced by the amount of available evidence.

In addition to assessing the impact of the amount of available expertise evidence, Figure 11 shows the profiling effectiveness of the aforementioned combinations of recommendation algorithm and textual evidence for the eight areas of knowledge represented in our corpus, as described in Section 3. From Figure 11, we note three clear patterns of effectiveness across the different areas of knowledge, corresponding to the three different textual evidence employed. In particular, abstracts lead to a more stable effectiveness across areas, whereas keywords and titles are more unstable. While all considered areas have roughly the same number of relevant tags per researcher, as also discussed in Section 3, some interesting results can be observed. For instance, Agricultural Science generally shows the highest performances among all areas. Health Science, which by far has the largest number of relevant tags as well as of researchers in our corpus, has an intermediate performance for all considered recommendation algorithms and textual evidence. Lastly, Human Science has one of the lowest performances with abstracts and titles, but one of the best with keywords. This suggests that different sources of evidence may provide complementary benefits, as we will discuss in the next section.

Recalling question Q3, the results in this section demonstrate the robustness of tag recommendation for expertise profiling. While the availability of larger expertise evidence improves the effectiveness of the produced profiles, the considered combinations of recommendation algorithm and textual evidence perform robustly even for sparse data. Different areas of knowledge, on the other hand, have different impact on tag recommendation, yet without noticeably compromising the attained effectiveness for any particular area.

4.4 Learning Expertise Profiles

The results in Sections 4.1 through 4.3 demonstrate the effectiveness, completeness, and robustness of tag recommendation for expertise profiling, with keyword-based tags being particularly effective. From these results, one may argue that relying on keywords alone could be sufficient for generating an effective expertise profile, given that keywords are generally carefully informed by the researchers themselves. Nevertheless, other sources of evidence could provide further relevant tags that are not mentioned among the re-

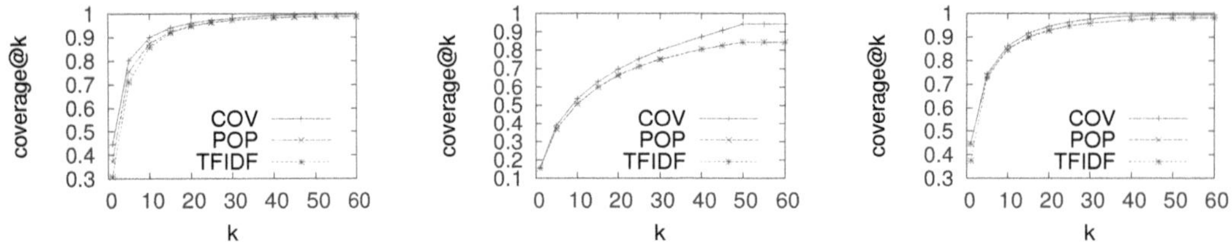

(a) Abstract (b) Title (c) Keywords

Figure 9: Coverage of publications for multiple tag recommendation algorithms and textual evidence.

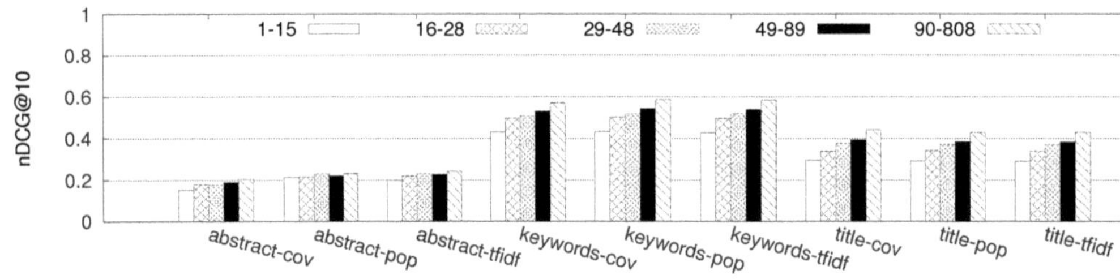

Figure 10: Profiling effectiveness for researchers with different numbers of journal publications.

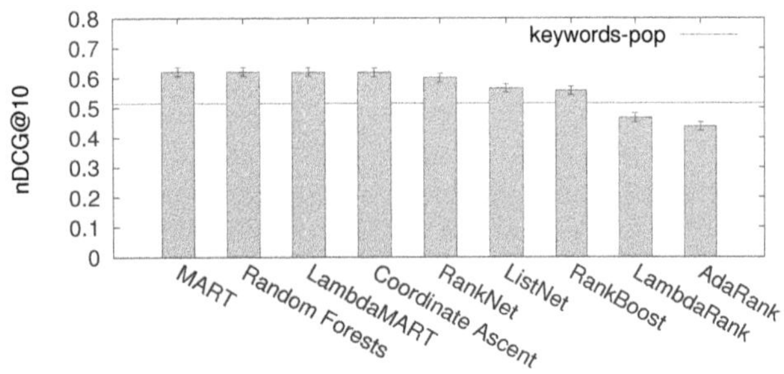

Figure 12: Profiling effectiveness of L2R algorithms.

searchers' publication keywords. In this section, we assess the complementarity of these sources of evidence combined to the TFIDF, POP, and COV recommendation algorithms. To this end, we address question Q4 by seeking to learn an effective ranking model for expertise profiling.

To address question Q4, we assess the suitability of the aforementioned tag recommenders as features for learning to rank for expertise profiling. In particular, we test nine state-of-the-art L2R algorithms from the literature, as implemented in the RankLib library:[5] MART [17], RankNet [9], RankBoost [16], AdaRank [36], Coordinate Ascent [24], LambdaMART [35], LambdaRank [26], ListNet [11], and Random Forests [8]. For each of these L2R algorithms, we perform a 5-fold cross validation in order to optimize nDCG@10, with three folds used for training, one for validation, and one for testing. Accordingly, in Figure 12, we report nDCG@10 figures averaged across the test folds for each individual L2R algorithm. Error bars indicate 95% confidence intervals for the reported means. Finally, a horizontal line indicates the performance of the single most effective feature identified in Figure 7, namely, keywords-pop.

[5] `http://sourceforge.net/p/lemur/wiki/RankLib/`

From Figure 12, we observe a statistical tie among MART, Random Forests, LambdaMART, and Cordinate Ascent. In addition, these four L2R algorithms are statistically superior to the remaining five (RankNet, Listnet, RankBoost, LambdaRank, and AdaRank). It is also worth noticing that three out of four of the best L2R algorithms are based on ensembles of learners. Compared to our baseline for this investigation, the keywords-pop recommender, most L2R algorithms improve, often significantly, with gains of up to 21.5% in terms of nDCG@10. Such an improvement demonstrates the complementarity of the various considered recommenders as features for learning effective expertise profiles.

In order to further evaluate the importance and impact of each feature on the performance of the learned models, we first sort these features by their estimated information gain [37]. Table 4 shows the results of this analysis, listing all nine considered features in increasing order of their information gain, i.e., from the least to the most informative one. From the table, we can see that the results are very consistent with the previous effectiveness results, with keyword-based recommenders having the highest information gain, which is substantially superior than that of the remaining features. In particular, the five least informative features have similarly low information gain values.

With the order imposed by the computed information gain of each feature in Table 4, we further assess their impact on the expertise profiling model learned using MART, the best performing L2R algorithm in Figure 12. In particular, starting with the MART model that uses all features, we remove one feature at a time, from the least to the most informative. At each removal step, a new MART model is learned based upon the remaining features through a 5-fold cross validation, until we have only a single feature, namely, keywords-pop. Table 5 shows the results of this experiment, in terms of nDCG@10 averaged over the test folds, along with 95% confidence intervals for the means.

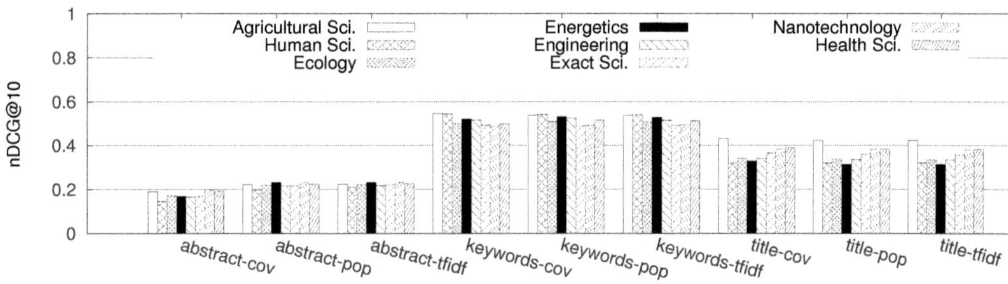

Figure 11: Profiling effectiveness for various areas of knowledge.

feature	inf. gain
title-tfidf	0.007200
title-pop	0.008010
title-cov	0.008210
abstract-tfidf	0.008900
abstract-pop	0.009730
abstract-cov	0.023060
keywords-cov	0.045410
keywords-tfidf	0.056220
keywords-pop	0.057830

Table 4: Information gain of individual features.

feature	nDCG@10
all features	0.621862 ± 0.013161
-titles-tfidf	0.621292 ± 0.013148
-title-pop	0.619677 ± 0.013174
-title-cov	0.612476 ± 0.013140
-abstract-tfidf	0.611220 ± 0.013126
-abstract-pop	0.608421 ± 0.013274
-abstract-cov	0.608024 ± 0.013301
-keywords-cov	0.605045 ± 0.013290
-keywords-tfidf	0.511833 ± 0.012279

Table 5: Profiling effectiveness after removing features.

As observed from Table 5, all features have a positive impact on the final performance of the learned model, with the least informative ones causing smaller losses when removed. This is consistent with our previous analyses. However, it is interesting to note that if we consider only the two best features for L2R, namely, keywords-pop and keywords-tfidf, the gains over the baseline are already considerable, around 18.2%, which corresponds to about 85% of the total gains obtained when using all nine features together. This result has positive impacts in terms of the trade-off "cost versus effectiveness" in the proposed L2R combination.

The results in this section demonstrate the complementarity of the aforementioned tag recommenders for identifying relevant topics of expertise. Turning back to research question Q4, these results show that an even superior expertise profiling effectiveness can be attained by leveraging these recommenders as features for a L2R algorithm. Moreover, as demonstrated through a feature removal analysis, combining a very reduced set of these features can still lead to significant gains in effectiveness, while potentially reducing the computational cost incurred by this solution.

5. CONCLUSIONS

We have investigated the suitability of tag recommendation for automatic expertise profiling, with a case study in the scientific domain. Towards this goal, we performed a large-scale user study with academic experts from all areas of knowledge working in Brazil in order to produce a comprehensive test collection for expertise profiling. With the produced test collection, we assessed the effectiveness, completeness, and robustness of the expertise profiles produced by nine different recommenders, derived from representative content-based tag recommendation algorithms from the literature applied to three different sources of expertise evidence: publication's titles, abstracts, and keywords. Our experiments demonstrate that most recommenders do satisfy such properties to a large extent, with the best ones being those based on TF or TFIDF when applied to keywords. Differently from most previous works, our analysis was conducted with a large number of real experts who can be considered as ideal evaluators for the task at hand.

The low intersection of the suggestions produced by the nine considered recommenders also motivated us to combine them by using multiple L2R strategies. To this end, we tested nine state-of-the-art L2R algorithms from the literature, with the best ones producing gains of more than 20% in effectiveness when compared to the best recommender used in isolation. Finally, we also performed an analysis of the available evidence for the rankers and found that a combination of just a couple of the best features produces most of the observed gains. As a result, the tag recommendation solutions investigated here have a potential application for real expertise profiling deployments, such as enterprises as well as academic or business-oriented social networking services.

As future work, we want to perform a historical analysis of the researchers' expertise profiles over time, using our rich dataset to better understand the evolution of topics of interest in different areas of knowledge. We also intend to further improve the effectiveness of the produced tag recommendations by using other sources of expertise evidence (e.g., coauthorship and citation networks) as well as more advanced noise filtering strategies to remove malformed tags. Finally, we plan to investigate the suitability of tag recommendation for the companion task of expert finding.

6. ACKNOWLEDGMENTS

This work is partially funded by the Brazilian National Institute of Science and Technology for the Web (grant MCT-CNPq 573871/2008-6), and by the authors' individual grants and scholarships from CAPES, CNPq, and FAPEMIG.

7. REFERENCES

[1] R. A. Baeza-Yates and B. Ribeiro-Neto. *Modern Information Retrieval.* 2 edition, 2011.

[2] K. Balog and M. de Rijke. Determining Expert Profiles (With an Application to Expert Finding). In *Proc. of JCDL*, pages 2657–2662, 2007.

[3] K. Balog, Y. Fang, M. de Rijke, P. Serdyukov, and L. Si. Expertise retrieval. *FTIR*, 6(2–3):127–256, 2012.

[4] F. Belém, E. Martins, T. Pontes, J. Almeida, and M. Gonçalves. Associative Tag Recommendation Exploiting Multiple Textual Features. In *Proc. of SIGIR*, pages 1033–1041, 2011.

[5] F. Belém, R. Santos, M. Gonçalves, and J. Almeida. Topic Diversity in Tag Recommendation. In *Proc. of RecSys*, 2013.

[6] F. M. Belém, E. F. Martins, J. M. Almeida, and M. A. Gonçalves. Personalized and object-centered tag recommendation methods for Web 2.0 applications. *Inf. Process. Manage.*, 50(4):524–553, 2014.

[7] B. Bi and J. Cho. Automatically Generating Descriptions for Resources by Tag Modeling. In *Proc. of CIKM*, 2013.

[8] L. Breiman. Random forests. *Machine learning*, 45(1):5–32, 2001.

[9] C. Burges, T. Shaked, E. Renshaw, A. Lazier, M. Deeds, N. Hamilton, and G. Hullender. Learning to Rank Using Gradient Descent. In *Proc. of the ICML*, pages 89–96. ACM, 2005.

[10] S. Canuto, F. M. Belém, J. M. Almeida, and M. A. Gonçalves. A Comparative Study of Learning-to-Rank Techniques for Tag Recommendation. *JIDM*, 4(3):453–468, 2013.

[11] Z. Cao, T. Qin, T.-Y. Liu, M.-F. Tsai, and H. Li. Learning to Rank: from Pairwise Approach to Listwise Approach. In *Proc. of ICML*, pages 129–136. ACM, 2007.

[12] M. de Rijke, K. Balog, T. Bogers, and A. van den Bosch. On the Evaluation of Entity Profiles. In *Proc. of CLEF*, pages 94–99, 2010.

[13] M. D. Ekstrand, J. T. Riedl, and J. A. Konstan. Collaborative filtering recommender systems. *Found. Trends Hum.-Comput. Interact.*, 4(2):81–173, 2011.

[14] Y. Fang and A. Godavarthy. Modeling the Dynamics of Personal Expertise. In *Proc. of SIGIR*, pages 1107–1110, 2014.

[15] F. Figueiredo, F. Belém, H. Pinto, J. Almeida, M. Gonçalves, D. Fernandes, E. Moura, and M. Cristo. Evidence of Quality of Textual Features on the Web 2.0. In *Proc. of CIKM*, pages 909–918, 2009.

[16] Y. Freund, R. Iyer, R. E. Schapire, and Y. Singer. An efficient boosting algorithm for combining preferences. *JMLR*, 4:933–969, 2003.

[17] J. H. Friedman. Greedy function approximation: a gradient boosting machine. *AOS*, pages 1189–1232, 2001.

[18] N. Garg and I. Weber. Personalized, Interactive Tag Recommendation for Flickr. In *Proc. of RecSys*, pages 67–74, 2008.

[19] P. Heymann, D. Ramage, and H. Garcia-Molina. Social Tag Prediction. In *Proc. of SIGIR*, pages 531–538, 2008.

[20] J. Lane. Let's make science metrics more scientific. *Nature*, 464(7288):488–489, 2010.

[21] Z. Lin, G. Ding, M. Hu, J. Wang, and J. Sun. Automatic Image Annotation Using Tag-Related Random Search Over Visual Neighbors. In *Proc. of CIKM*, pages 1784–1788, 2012.

[22] C. D. Manning and H. Schütze. *Foundations of Statistical Natural Language Processing.* 1999.

[23] E. F. Martins, F. M. Belém, J. M. Almeida, and M. A. Gonçalves. On cold start for associative tag recoomendation. *JASIST (accepted for publication)*, 2014.

[24] D. Metzler and W. B. Croft. Linear feature-based models for information retrieval. *Information Retrieval*, 10(3):257–274, 2007.

[25] R. Prokofyev, A. Boyarsky, O. Ruchayskiy, K. Aberer, G. Demartini, and P. Cudré-Mauroux. Tag Recommendation for Large-scale Ontology-based Information Systems. In *Proc. of ISWC*, 2012.

[26] C. Quoc and V. Le. Learning to rank with nonsmooth cost functions. *NIPS*, 19:193, 2007.

[27] J. Rybak, K. Balog, and K. Nørvåg. Temporal Expertise Profiling. In *Proc. of ECIR*, pages 540–546. 2014.

[28] P. Serdyukov, M. Taylor, V. Vinay, M. Richardson, and R. W. White. Automatic People Tagging for Expertise Profiling in the Enterprise. In *Proc. of ECIR*, pages 399–410, 2011.

[29] S. Siersdorfer, J. S. Pedro, and M. Sanderson. Automatic Video Tagging Using Content Redundancy. In *Proc. of SIGIR*, pages 395–402, 2009.

[30] B. Sigurbjörnsson and R. van Zwol. Flickr Tag Recommendation Based on Collective Knowledge. In *Proc. of WWW*, pages 327–336, 2008.

[31] B. Sigurbjörnsson and R. van Zwol. Flickr Tag Recommendation Based on Collective Knowledge. In *Proc. 17th International Conference on World Wide Web (WWW)*, pages 327–336, 2008.

[32] Y. Song, L. Zhang, and C. Giles. Automatic tag recommendation algorithms for social recommender systems. *TWEB*, 5:1–31, 2011.

[33] P. Venetis, G. Koutrika, and H. Garcia-Molina. On the Selection of Tags for Tag Clouds. In *Proc. of WSDM*, pages 835–844, 2011.

[34] L. Wu, L. Yang, N. Yu, and X.-S. Hua. Learning to Tag. In *Proc. of WWW*, pages 361–370, 2009.

[35] Q. Wu, C. J. Burges, K. M. Svore, and J. Gao. Adapting boosting for information retrieval measures. *Information Retrieval*, 13(3):254–270, 2010.

[36] J. Xu and H. Li. Adarank: a Boosting Algorithm for Information Retrieval. In *Proc. of SIGIR*, pages 391–398. ACM, 2007.

[37] Y. Yang and J. O. Pedersen. A Comparative Study on Feature Selection in Text Categorization. In *Proc. of the ICML*, pages 412–420, 1997.

[38] D. Yin, S. Guo, B. Chidlovskii, B. Davison, C. Archambeau, and G. Bouchard. Connecting Comments and Tags: Improved Modeling of Social Tagging Systems. In *Proc. of WSDM*, pages 547–556, 2013.

FLAME: A Probabilistic Model Combining Aspect Based Opinion Mining and Collaborative Filtering

Yao Wu
School of Computing Science
Simon Fraser University
Burnaby, BC, Canada
wuyaow@sfu.ca

Martin Ester
School of Computing Science
Simon Fraser University
Burnaby, BC, Canada
ester@cs.sfu.ca

ABSTRACT

Aspect-based opinion mining from online reviews has attracted a lot of attention recently. Given a set of reviews, the main task of aspect-based opinion mining is to extract major aspects of the items and to infer the latent aspect ratings from each review. However, users may have different preferences which might lead to different opinions on the same aspect of an item. Even if fine-grained aspect rating analysis is provided for each review, it is still difficult for a user to judge whether a specific aspect of an item meets his own expectation. In this paper, we study the problem of estimating personalized sentiment polarities on different aspects of the items. We propose a unified probabilistic model called Factorized Latent Aspect ModEl (FLAME), which combines the advantages of collaborative filtering and aspect based opinion mining. FLAME learns users' personalized preferences on different aspects from their past reviews, and predicts users' aspect ratings on new items by collective intelligence. Experiments on two online review datasets show that FLAME outperforms state-of-the-art methods on the tasks of aspect identification and aspect rating prediction.

Categories and Subject Descriptors

H.3.3 [**Information search and retrieval**]: Text Mining

General Terms

Algorithms, Experimentation

Keywords

Collaborative Filtering; Opinion Mining; Text Mining

1. INTRODUCTION

Nowadays, products and services offered on most online E-commerce websites are accompanied by abundant user-generated reviews, which can help users make better decision. For instance, if a user wants to know more about the battery life of a laptop, comments on the battery life of this specific laptop by other users are more reliable than those given in the official description of the product. However, the volume of reviews grows so rapidly that it gets extremely difficult for users to find useful information in short time. Thus mining useful information out of these huge amount of reviews has become an important way to improve user satisfaction of these online E-commerce websites.

Figure 1: A Sample Review On Amazon

Aspect-based opinion mining [10] has attracted a lot of attention recently. Given a collection of reviews on a set of items, aspect-based opinion mining methods extract major aspects out of every item based on how often they have been commented by users, and learn users' sentiment polarities toward each aspect based on the opinionated words they used in the reviews. Figure 1 shows a sample review from Amazon[1]. The user assigns a 5-star overall rating, and expresses his opinions on several aspects of the product. From a set of reviews like this, aspect-based opinion mining methods can automatically extract the aspects of the product, such as *performance*, *display*, *value* and *size*, as well as infer latent sentiment scores for each aspect, e.g., 5 stars on its *display*.

Much work has been proposed to help users digest and exploit large number of reviews by aspect-based opinion mining techniques, including information extraction from reviews [11], uncovering the latent aspects of the review sentences [13], inferring the latent aspect ratings and aspect weights of each review document [22, 23], aspect-based review summarization for products [11, 9], etc. These methods either focus on *review-level* analysis (extracting useful information within each review) to help users easily find what they need from a piece of review, or make *product-level* summarization (aggregating the opinions of all the users) to provide an overview of users' feedback on a product. However, an important factor is typically ignored – *preference diver-*

[1] `http://www.amazon.com`

WSDM'15, February 2–6, 2015, Shanghai, China.

http://dx.doi.org/10.1145/2684822.2685291.

sity, i.e., users have different preferences that their opinions on the same item may differ from each other. For example, the *food* of the same restaurant might be delicious for some users but terrible for others. When choosing restaurants, a user might want to know whether a restaurant meets his *own* expectation on the aspect of *food*. But when facing a large number of reviews expressing various opinions, it becomes extremely difficult for the user to make the decision: 1) it's impossible for the user to read all the reviews even if the fine-grained *review-level* analysis is provided. 2) the user has no idea of which reviews are more reliable or which reviewers share similar tastes with him. 3) *product-level* summarization is also unreliable since it is generated from reviews by users with different tastes. To help users better utilize the existing reviews, we argue that a new method is required, which can learn a user's personalized preferences on different aspects from his past reviews of other items, and predict his preferences on the aspects of a given item by mining the opinions by other users with similar preferences.

A popular method of learning user preferences is *Collaborative Filtering*, which predicts a user's interests by collaboratively collecting preferences from many other users. Typical collaborative filtering methods take the numeric overall ratings as inputs [7, 19], assuming that users with the same ratings share the same tastes. However, two users who have assigned the same 5-stars to a restaurant might have significantly different reasoning; one might like its *food* while the other likes its *service*. Text reviews provide rich information to make it possible to understand preferences of users at a finer granularity. Some recent work has shown the benefits of utilizing text reviews within the collaborative filtering methods [12, 24]. Unlike these work, we aim at collectively exploring users' preferences on different aspects of the items. A challenge here is that aspect-based sentiment scores are not *explicitly* specified by users, but *implicitly* expressed in the reviews. We propose a new model combining aspect-based opinion mining and collaborative filtering to collectively learn users' preferences on different aspects.

In this work, we introduce the problem of *Personalized Latent Aspect Rating Analysis*. Given a collection of reviews of a set of items by a set of users, the goal is to solve the following two tasks: *a*) learn the latent aspects and their word distribution over a pre-defined vocabulary, and the latent aspect ratings for each review; *b*) for any user u in the data set, predict the latent aspect ratings on the items that he has not yet reviewed. Existing aspect-based opinion mining methods such as [22, 23, 14] are able to solve task a, but are unsuitable for solving task b since they require the text of user u's review for item i as input. Task b is also different from the well-studied rating prediction problem in recommender systems, the goal of which is to predict the overall rating while we want to predict the aspect ratings.

To address the problem of Personalized Latent Aspect Rating Analysis, we propose a unified probabilistic model called Factorized Latent Aspect ModEl (FLAME), which combines the advantages of both collaborative filtering and aspect-based opinion mining so that the two methods can mutually enhance each other. The general idea of FLAME is that we can learn users' preferences based on their past reviews, so that we can collaboratively predict a user's preference of an aspect of an item from the opinions of other users with similar tastes. FLAME improves existing aspect-based opinion mining methods by being able to infer aspect ratings of users on new items[2], and enhances collaborative filtering methods by leveraging reviews to analyze users' preferences on different aspects of items.

We empirically evaluate the proposed FLAME on a hotel review data set from TripAdvisor[3] and a restaurant review data set from Yelp[4]. Experimental results show that FLAME can effectively extract meaningful aspects and predict aspect ratings of a user on new items to him.

The remainder of the paper is organized as follows. Section 2 is devoted to related work. Section 3 introduces the problem definition and useful notations. Section 4 presents the proposed model and describes the inference and parameters estimation techniques. In Section 5 & 6, we report the experimental results on two review data sets and discuss some other applications of the proposed model. Finally, Section 7 concludes the paper with a summary and discusses potential future work.

2. RELATED WORK

Our work is related to two research topics: Collaborative Filtering and Aspect-based Opinion Mining.

2.1 Collaborative Filtering

Collaborative filtering (CF) is a popular method widely used in recommender systems. The assumption behind collaborative filtering is that a given user is more likely to like items that are liked by other users with similar tastes. Various state-of-the-art CF methods are based on latent factor models [7]. Latent factor models assume that a user's rating on a particular item depends on the inner dot product of the latent user factors and the latent item factors.

Some work combining collaborative filtering with *Topic Models* has been proposed to leverage text information in recommender systems. Topic models are introduced by [1] for learning the hidden dimensions of text. The basic assumption of topic models is that documents are represented by mixtures of some latent topics where topics are associated with a multinomial distribution over words of a vocabulary. The earliest work integrating collaborative filtering with topic model is CTM [21], which is proposed for article recommendation. CTM simultaneously trains a topic model on the collection of articles and a latent rating factor model on the ratings of users on articles, while assuming that the latent factors of items depend on the latent topic distributions of their text. A recent work [12] proposes a model called HFT, which aims at improving collaborative filtering using reviews. HFT considers latent rating factors of an item as the properties that the item possesses, and assumes that if a product exhibits a certain property (higher latent rating factor value), this will correspond to a particular topic being discussed frequently (higher probability in topic distribution) [12]. HTF first aggregates all the reviews of an item into a single document, and uses a similar method as CTM to train a topic model and a latent factor model together.

Different from CTM and HTF which learn topic distributions for each item, our approach learns for each review its aspect distribution *as well as* its rating distribution on each aspect.

---

[2]Note that *new items* for a user are the items that he has not rated yet.

[3]`http://www.tripadviosr.com`

[4]`http://www.yelp.com`

2.2 Aspect-based Opinion Mining

The main task of aspect-based opinion mining is extracting the aspects and learning the aspect ratings from a collection of reviews of a given item. Most of the early works of opinion mining are frequency-based approaches [5, 11]. These approaches usually mine the aspects and sentiments by counting the frequencies of words and their co-occurrences with some pre-defined seed words. Recently, several methods based on the variants of topic models [1] have been proposed [20, 25, 6, 14, 15] to learn the aspects and sentiments automatically from the data. These work extends topic models by adding another kind of latent variables to model the latent sentiments of words, i.e., words in reviews are not only dependent on the topics they belong to, but are also related to the sentiments of the reviewers. The most related work is the Latent Aspect Rating Analysis Model (LARAM) [22, 23], which aims at inferring the latent aspect ratings of given reviews. LARAM assumes the overall rating of a review is generated by a weighted sum of the latent aspect ratings, and are generated from the words and the latent topic allocations of the words by a linear regression function. LARAM learns the latent aspect ratings for each review and aspect weights for each reviewer. It should be noted that the aspect weights in LARAM are different from the personalized aspect ratings in our problem. The weights in LARAM represent the importance of the aspects for a reviewer, but personalized tastes represent the ratings/sentiments of users on different aspects. Two reviewers may share similar aspect weights but have totally different ratings on a given aspect.

The main limitation of above aspect-based opinion mining methods is that they do not consider user preferences (across multiple reviews and items) in the learning procedures so that they are unable to predict users' opinions on other items which they have not written reviews on.

The very recently published ETF [24] also considers aspect based opinion mining and collaborative filtering simultaneously. However, ETF employs the aspect-based opinion mining as a preprocessing step, while ours is a unified model with opinion mining as a part of the model. This enables our approach to be used to analyze the aspect distributions of the reviews and latent aspect ratings expressed in the reviews as in [22, 23]. Besides, ETF can not predict users' preferences on the aspects of items.

3. PROBLEM DEFINITION

We assume as input a collection of reviews of some products from a specific category (e.g. restaurant) by a group of reviewers, and each review comes with an overall rating (e.g. 1-5 stars) to express the overall satisfaction of the reviewer.

Review: A review is a piece of text describing opinions of a reviewer towards a specific item. Formally, we use $\mathcal{D} = \{d_1, d_2, ..., d_D\}$ to denote a set of review text documents. For each $d \in \mathcal{D}$, $u_d \in \mathcal{U}$ denotes the user who writes review d and $i_d \in \mathcal{I}$ denotes the reviewed item. We use $\mathcal{D}_u$ to denote the set of reviews that user u writes and use $\mathcal{D}_i$ to denote the set of reviews for item i.

Overall Rating: The overall rating r_d of a review document d is a numerical rating indicating the overall opinion of d, i.e., $r_d \in \mathcal{R}$, where $\mathcal{R} = \{1, 2, ..., R\}$.

Aspect: An aspect is an attribute of the item that has been commented on in a review, e.g., "food", "location" and "service" for a restaurant. In this paper, we only consider the case that all the items are from a same category, i.e., they share the same set of aspects. We use a to denote an aspect, where $a \in \mathcal{A}$ and $\mathcal{A} = \{1, 2, ..., A\}$.

Table 1: Mathematical Notations

Symbol	Size	Description
$\mathcal{U}$	U	Users $\mathcal{U} = \{u \mid u = 1, ..., U\}$
$\mathcal{I}$	I	Items $\mathcal{I} = \{i \mid i = 1, ..., I\}$
$\mathcal{D}$	D	Documents $\mathcal{D} = \{d \mid d = 1, ..., D\}$
$\mathcal{A}$	A	Aspects $\mathcal{A} = \{a \mid a = 1, ..., A\}$
$\mathcal{R}$	R	Numerical ratings $\mathcal{R} = \{r \mid r = 1, ..., R\}$
ϕ_u	$\mathbb{R}^K$	latent vector of user u
ϕ_i	$\mathbb{R}^K$	latent vector of item i
$\phi_{i,a}$	$\mathbb{R}^K$	latent vector of aspect a of i
η	$\mathbb{R}^A$	background aspect distribution
η_u	$\mathbb{R}^A$	aspect distribution of user u
η_i	$\mathbb{R}^A$	aspect distribution of item i
β_a	$\mathbb{R}^V$	word distribution of aspect a
$\gamma_{a,r}$	$\mathbb{R}^V$	word distribution of aspect a and rating r
$\boldsymbol{\theta}_d$	$\mathbb{R}^A$	aspect distribution of document d
$\varphi_{d,a}$	$\mathbb{R}^R$	rating distribution of aspect a of document d
a_t	$\mathbb{R}^1$	aspect of sentence t
s_t	$\mathbb{R}^1$	aspect rating of sentence t

Aspect Rating: The aspect rating $r_{d,a}$ of a review document d is the reviewer u_d's rating towards to the aspect a of the item i_d.i It indicates the opinion of the reviewer regarding to the properties of the corresponding aspect of the item. Note that our method does not need aspect ratings as input, but instead it infers them from the data.

Personalized Latent Aspect Rating Analysis: Given a collection of reviews of a set of items by a set of users, the goal is to solve two tasks: a) learn the latent aspects, which represents each aspect as a distribution on a pre-defined vocabulary, and the latent aspect ratings for each review, which indicate the opinions of the reviewer towards the aspects of the item; b) predict the latent aspect ratings for user u on new item i that he has not reviewed.

Some important notations used in this paper are listed in Table 1. We use bold math symbols $\boldsymbol{x}_i$ to denote vectors, where the subscript i is used for indexing different vectors. The j-th element of the vector $\boldsymbol{x}_i$ is denoted by $\boldsymbol{x}_i[j]$.

4. PROPOSED MODEL

In this section, we propose the unified probabilistic model *Factorized Latent Aspect ModEl* (FLAME) to address the problem of Personalized Latent Aspect Rating Analysis.

When writing the review, the reviewer first selects a subset of aspects he wants to comment on. We assume that each review document d is associated with an aspect distribution $\boldsymbol{\theta}_d \in \mathbb{R}^A$, which represents the importances of the aspects in the review. The aspect distribution $\boldsymbol{\theta}_d$ depends on three factors: the global aspect distribution $\boldsymbol{\eta}_0$, the aspect distribution of the reviewer $\boldsymbol{\eta}_u$ and the aspect distribution of the item $\boldsymbol{\eta}_i$. $\boldsymbol{\eta}_0$ represents how much each aspect is likely to be mentioned among all the reviews. $\boldsymbol{\eta}_u$ represents reviewer u's preferences on the aspects to comment, e.g., if a user cares more on the *value* of a hotel, he prefers to mention this aspect in his reviews. $\boldsymbol{\eta}_i$ indicates which aspects of item i are more likely to be mentioned. Some aspects are more likely to be mentioned in the reviews of an item. For example, if the food of a restaurant is great, it will receive a lot of praises of the *food* in the reviews. On the other hand, if some aspects of an item are terrible, reviewers would like to criticize on these aspects in their reviews.

Based on this assumption, we define $\boldsymbol{\theta}_d$ using a additive generative methods as follows:

$$\boldsymbol{\theta}_d[a] = \frac{\exp(\boldsymbol{\eta}_0[a] + \boldsymbol{\eta}_u[a] + \boldsymbol{\eta}_i[a])}{\sum_{a'=1}^{A} \exp(\boldsymbol{\eta}_0[a'] + \boldsymbol{\eta}_u[a'] + \boldsymbol{\eta}_i[a'])} \tag{1}$$

where $\{\boldsymbol{\eta}\} = \{\boldsymbol{\eta}_0, \boldsymbol{\eta}_u, \boldsymbol{\eta}_i | u \in \mathcal{U}, i \in \mathcal{I}\}$ are A-dimensional vectors generated from zero-mean Gaussian distributions.

$$\begin{aligned} \boldsymbol{\eta}_0 &\sim \mathcal{N}(\mathbf{0}, \sigma_\eta \boldsymbol{I}) \\ \boldsymbol{\eta}_u &\sim \mathcal{N}(\mathbf{0}, \sigma_\eta \boldsymbol{I}) \\ \boldsymbol{\eta}_i &\sim \mathcal{N}(\mathbf{0}, \sigma_\eta \boldsymbol{I}) \end{aligned} \tag{2}$$

For each aspect, the reviewer has a latent sentiment polarity expressing his opinion on that aspect of the item. We extend Probabilistic Matrix Factorization (PMF) [19] to model the user-specific aspect ratings. PMF assumes that the user u has a vector of latent factors $\boldsymbol{\phi}_u \in \mathbb{R}^K$, which represents his personalized preferences that influence his opinions. Analogously, each item has a latent vector $\boldsymbol{\phi}_i \in \mathbb{R}^K$. The overall rating of u for i is generated by the dot product of the user latent factor and the item latent factor. In our model, to predict user u's opinion on a specific aspect a of item i, we assume there is a latent factor $\boldsymbol{\phi}_{i,a} \in \mathbb{R}^K$ for each aspect a of an item i, and the aspect rating $r_{d,a}$ of review document d is generated from the dot product of the user latent vector $\boldsymbol{\phi}_u$ and the item aspect latent vector $\boldsymbol{\phi}_{i,a}$[5]. The item aspect latent vector $\boldsymbol{\phi}_{i,a}$ describes the latent properties of the corresponding aspect of the item.

$$r_{d,a} \sim \mathcal{N}(\boldsymbol{\phi}_u^\top \boldsymbol{\phi}_{i,a}, \sigma_a^2) \tag{3}$$

To control the model complexity, zero-mean Gaussian priors are placed on the latent factors:

$$\begin{aligned} \boldsymbol{\phi}_u &\sim \mathcal{N}(\mathbf{0}, \sigma_u^2 \boldsymbol{I}) \\ \boldsymbol{\phi}_{i,a} &\sim \mathcal{N}(\mathbf{0}, \sigma_{i,a}^2 \boldsymbol{I}) \end{aligned} \tag{4}$$

We can not directly use the continuous value $r_{d,a}$ to model the word generative process since we need discrete ratings to define the aspect-sentiment vocabulary (see Equation 11). We introduce another latent variable $\boldsymbol{\varphi}_{d,a} \in \mathbb{R}^R$ to represent document d's rating distribution on aspect a, where $\boldsymbol{\varphi}_{d,a}[r]$ is the probability of $p(r_{d,a} = r)$ and $\sum_{r=1}^{R} \boldsymbol{\varphi}_{d,a}[r] = 1$. We define $\boldsymbol{\varphi}_{d,a}$ as follows:

$$\begin{aligned} \boldsymbol{\varphi}_{d,a}[r] &= \frac{\mathcal{N}(r | \boldsymbol{\phi}_u^\top \boldsymbol{\phi}_{i,a}, \sigma_{r,a}^2)}{\sum_{r'=1}^{R} \mathcal{N}(r' | \boldsymbol{\phi}_u^\top \boldsymbol{\phi}_{i,a}, \sigma_{r,a}^2)} \\ &= \frac{\exp\left(-\frac{(r - \boldsymbol{\phi}_u^\top \boldsymbol{\phi}_{i,a})^2}{2\sigma_{r,a}^2}\right)}{\sum_{r'=1}^{R} \exp\left(-\frac{(r' - \boldsymbol{\phi}_u^\top \boldsymbol{\phi}_{i,a})^2}{2\sigma_{r,a}^2}\right)} \end{aligned} \tag{5}$$

[5]Note that for simplicity we always assume that there is an extra constant column in user/item latent factors to model the bias effect.

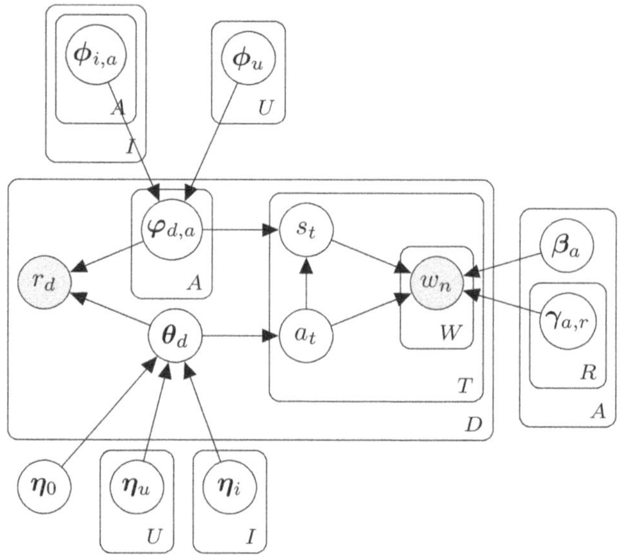

Figure 2: FLAME in graphical model notation.

We assume the overall rating of document d is generated from the weighted sum of the aspect ratings, where the aspect weights consist to the aspect distribution of the document.

$$r_d \sim \mathcal{N}(\sum_a \boldsymbol{\theta}_d[a] \mathbb{E}[r_{d,a}], \sigma_r^2) \tag{6}$$

where $\mathbb{E}[r_{d,a}] = \boldsymbol{\phi}_u^\top \boldsymbol{\phi}_{i,a}$.

For the process of generating words, we follow the assumption in [20, 13, 25] that the words in one sentence of a review refer to the same aspect. Topics learned under this assumption are *local* topics that preserve sentence-level word concurrences [20], while models like LDA [1] produce *global* topics that preserve document-level word concurrences. *Global* topic models are not suitable for aspect identification. For example, because the words *room* and *location* appear together in most reviews, *global* topic models are mostly likely to cluster them in the same topic, but *local* topic models assume they refer to different topics.

For each sentence t in the review d, we draw an aspect a_t from the aspect distribution of the review:

$$a_t \sim Multi(\boldsymbol{\theta}_d) \tag{7}$$

and a sentiment rating $s_t \in \{1, 2, ..., R\}$ on the aspect a_t from the aspect rating distribution:

$$s_t \sim Multi(\boldsymbol{\varphi}_{d,a_t}) \tag{8}$$

Then, in each sentence t, the reviewer selects a set of words $w_n \in t$ to express his opinions on the aspect a_t. We define an aspect-sentiment multinomial word distribution $\boldsymbol{\alpha}_{a,s}$ on the vocabulary, where $\boldsymbol{\alpha}_{a,s}[j]$ represents the probability of generating the j-th word from the vocabulary for aspect a and aspect rating s. w_n can be an aspect word, e.g., *battery*, or a sentiment word, e.g., *good*. So we assume that $\boldsymbol{\alpha}_{a,s}$ depends on two factors: $\boldsymbol{\beta}_a$ and $\boldsymbol{\gamma}_{a,s}$, where $\boldsymbol{\beta}_a$ represents the correlation between the words and the aspect a, and $\boldsymbol{\gamma}_{a,s}$ represents the correlation between the words and the pair of

Algorithm 1 Generative process of FLAME.

Draw $\boldsymbol{\eta} \sim \mathcal{N}(\mathbf{0}, \sigma_\eta^2 \boldsymbol{I})$
for all $u \in \mathcal{U}$ **do**
  Draw $\boldsymbol{\phi}_u \sim \mathcal{N}(\mathbf{0}, \sigma_u^2 \boldsymbol{I})$
  Draw $\boldsymbol{\eta}_u \sim \mathcal{N}(\mathbf{0}, \sigma_\eta^2 \boldsymbol{I})$
end for
for all $i \in \mathcal{I}$ **do**
  Draw $\boldsymbol{\eta}_i \sim \mathcal{N}(\mathbf{0}, \sigma_\eta^2 \boldsymbol{I})$
  for all $a \in \mathcal{A}$ **do**
    Draw $\boldsymbol{\phi}_{i,a} \sim \mathcal{N}(\mathbf{0}, \sigma_{i,a}^2 \boldsymbol{I})$
  end for
end for
for all $a \in \mathcal{A}$ **do**
  Draw $\boldsymbol{\beta}_a \sim \mathcal{N}(\mathbf{0}, \sigma_\beta^2 \boldsymbol{I})$
  for all $r \in \mathcal{R}$ **do**
    Draw $\boldsymbol{\gamma}_{a,r} \sim \mathcal{N}(\mathbf{0}, \sigma_\gamma^2 \boldsymbol{I})$
    Set $\boldsymbol{\alpha}_{a,r}$ using Equation (9)
  end for
end for
for all $d \in \mathcal{D}$ **do**
  Set $\boldsymbol{\theta}_d$ using Equation (1)
  Set $\boldsymbol{\varphi}_d$ using Equation (5)
  Draw r_d using Equation (6)
  // Generate each sentence t in document d
  for all $t \in d$ **do**
    Draw $a_t \sim \text{Multi}(\boldsymbol{\theta}_d)$
    Draw $s_t \sim \text{Multi}(\boldsymbol{\varphi}_d, \boldsymbol{a}_t)$
    // Generate each word n in sentence t
    for all $n \in t$ **do**
      Draw $w_n \sim \text{Multi}(\boldsymbol{\alpha}_{a_t,s_t})$
    end for
  end for
end for

aspect a and aspect rating s.

$$\boldsymbol{\alpha}_{a,s}[j] = \frac{\exp(\boldsymbol{\beta}_a[j] + \boldsymbol{\gamma}_{a,s}[j])}{\sum_{l=1}^{V} \exp(\boldsymbol{\beta}_a[l] + \boldsymbol{\gamma}_{a,s}[l])} \tag{9}$$

where $\boldsymbol{\beta}_a$ and $\boldsymbol{\gamma}_{a,r}$ are V-dimensional vectors generated from zero-mean Gaussian distributions.

$$\begin{aligned} \boldsymbol{\beta}_a &\sim \mathcal{N}(\mathbf{0}, \sigma_\beta \boldsymbol{I}) \\ \boldsymbol{\gamma}_{a,r} &\sim \mathcal{N}(\mathbf{0}, \sigma_\gamma \boldsymbol{I}) \end{aligned} \tag{10}$$

The word w_n is generated as follows:

$$p(w_n|a_t, s_t, \boldsymbol{\alpha}) \sim Multi(\boldsymbol{\alpha}_{a_t,s_t}) \tag{11}$$

Figure 2 shows the graphical representation of FLAME, omitting the priors $\{\sigma\}$. We summarize the generative process in Algorithm 1.

4.1 Variational Inference

In general, we use an EM-style method to learn the parameters in our model. We adopt a mixture of maximum a posteriori (MAP) point estimates and Bayesian inference as in [3]. To be specific, we use a combination of MAP estimation over $\boldsymbol{\Xi} = \{\{\boldsymbol{\eta}\}, \{\boldsymbol{\phi}\}, \boldsymbol{\beta}, \boldsymbol{\gamma}\}$ and Bayesian variational inference over the other latent variables $\boldsymbol{\Delta} = \{\boldsymbol{a}, \boldsymbol{s}\}$ to derive a lower bound of the log likelihood of the data, and maximize the bound with respect to $\boldsymbol{\Xi}$ and variational parameters. It should be noted that $\boldsymbol{\theta}$ and $\boldsymbol{\varphi}$ are not latent variables in our model. They are fixed given $\boldsymbol{\eta}$ and $\boldsymbol{\phi}$, as shown in Equation (1) and (5).

The variational distributions of the latent variables in $\boldsymbol{\Delta}$ are defined as follows:

$$q(\boldsymbol{a}, \boldsymbol{s}|\boldsymbol{\pi}, \boldsymbol{\lambda}) = \prod_d \prod_{t \in d} q(a_t|\boldsymbol{\pi}_t) q(s_t|\boldsymbol{\lambda}_t) \tag{12}$$

where $\boldsymbol{\pi}_t \in \mathbb{R}^A$ and $\boldsymbol{\lambda}_t \in \mathbb{R}^R$ are free multinomial parameters.

We get the lower bound of the log likelihood of the data as follows:

$$\begin{aligned} \mathcal{L} = &\sum_d \Big(\langle \log p(r_d|\boldsymbol{\phi}_u, \boldsymbol{\phi}_{i,a}, \boldsymbol{\theta}_d) \rangle + \sum_{t \in d} \Big(\langle \log p(a_t|\boldsymbol{\theta}_d) \rangle \\ &+ \langle \log p(s_t|\boldsymbol{\varphi}_d, a_t) \rangle + \sum_{n \in t} \langle \log p(w_n|a_t, s_t, \boldsymbol{\beta}, \boldsymbol{\gamma}) \rangle \Big) \Big) \\ &+ \sum_u \Big(\langle \log p(\boldsymbol{\phi}_u|\sigma_u) \rangle + \langle \log p(\boldsymbol{\eta}_u|\sigma_\eta) \rangle \Big) \\ &+ \sum_i \Big(\langle \log p(\boldsymbol{\phi}_i|\sigma_i) \rangle + \sum_a \langle \log p(\boldsymbol{\phi}_{i,a}|\sigma_{i,a}) \rangle \\ &+ \langle \log p(\boldsymbol{\eta}_i|\sigma_\eta) \rangle \Big) + \langle \log p(\boldsymbol{\eta}|\sigma_\eta) \rangle \\ &+ \sum_a \langle \log p(\boldsymbol{\beta}_a|\sigma_\beta) \rangle + \sum_a \sum_r \langle \log p(\boldsymbol{\gamma}_{a,r}|\sigma_\gamma) \rangle \\ &- \sum_d \sum_{t \in d} \Big(\langle \log q(\boldsymbol{a}_t|\boldsymbol{\pi}_t) \rangle + \langle \log q(\boldsymbol{s}_t|\boldsymbol{\lambda}_t) \rangle \Big) \end{aligned} \tag{13}$$

where $\langle p(\boldsymbol{\Omega}) \rangle$ denotes the expectation of the probability of p given the distribution $q(\boldsymbol{\Omega})$.

4.2 Learning the Parameters

In general, the learning procedure can be viewed as coordinate ascent in $\mathcal{L}$, i.e., alternatively optimizing one set of parameters while fixing the others.

Updating $\boldsymbol{\pi}$: We get the solution of $\boldsymbol{\pi}_t$ by setting $\frac{\partial \mathcal{L}_{[\boldsymbol{\pi}_t]}}{\partial \boldsymbol{\pi}_t} = 0$ with the constraint $\sum_a \boldsymbol{\pi}_t[a] = 1$.

$$\boldsymbol{\pi}_t[a] \propto \boldsymbol{\theta}_d[a] \prod_r \Big(\boldsymbol{\varphi}_{d,a}[r]^{\boldsymbol{\lambda}_t[r]} \prod_j \boldsymbol{\alpha}_{a,r}[j]^{c_{t,j} \boldsymbol{\lambda}_t[r]} \Big) \tag{14}$$

where $c_{t,j}$ is the frequency of the j-th word in sentence t. Since $c_{t,j}$ is sparse, the complexity of updating $\boldsymbol{\pi}_t$ is $O(c_t \cdot R \cdot A)$, where c_t is the number of words in sentence t. The total complexity for updating $\boldsymbol{\pi}$ in one EM iteration is $O(c \cdot R \cdot A)$, where c is the number of words of all the documents.

Updating $\boldsymbol{\lambda}$: The update procedure of $\boldsymbol{\lambda}$ is similar to that for $\boldsymbol{\pi}$.

$$\boldsymbol{\lambda}_t[r] \propto \prod_a \boldsymbol{\varphi}_{d,a}[r]^{\boldsymbol{\pi}_t[a]} \prod_j \boldsymbol{\alpha}_{a,r}[j]^{c_{t,j} \boldsymbol{\pi}_t[a]} \tag{15}$$

The complexity of updating $\boldsymbol{\lambda}$ in one EM iteration is also $O(c \cdot A \cdot R)$.

Updating $\boldsymbol{\phi}_u$: We can get $\mathcal{L}_{[\boldsymbol{\phi}_u]}$ by only retaining those terms in $\mathcal{L}$ that are a function of $\boldsymbol{\phi}_u$:

$$\begin{aligned} \mathcal{L}_{[\boldsymbol{\phi}_u]} = &\sum_{d \in \mathcal{D}_u} \Big(- \frac{(r_d - \sum_a \boldsymbol{\theta}_d[a] \boldsymbol{\phi}_u^\top \boldsymbol{\phi}_{i,a})^2}{2\sigma_r^2} \\ &+ \sum_t \sum_a \sum_r \boldsymbol{\pi}_t[a] \boldsymbol{\lambda}_t[r] \log \boldsymbol{\varphi}_{d,a}[r] \Big) - \frac{\boldsymbol{\phi}_u^\top \boldsymbol{\phi}_u}{2\sigma_u^2} \end{aligned} \tag{16}$$

The derivative of $\mathcal{L}_{[\phi_u]}$ with respect to ϕ_u depends on ϕ_u, so we have to use a gradient ascent based method to update ϕ_u.

Updating $\phi_{i,a}$:

$$\mathcal{L}_{[\phi_{i,a}]} = \sum_{d\in\mathcal{D}_i}\left(-\frac{(r_d-\sum_a \boldsymbol{\theta}_d[a]\phi_u^\top\phi_{i,a})^2}{2\sigma_r^2}\right.$$
$$\left.+\sum_{t\in d}\sum_a\sum_r \boldsymbol{\pi}_t[a]\boldsymbol{\lambda}_t[r]\log\varphi_{d,a}[r]\right) \quad (17)$$
$$-\frac{\phi_{i,a}^\top\phi_{i,a}}{2\sigma_{i,a}^2}$$

We also use a gradient ascent based method to update $\phi_{i,a}$.

Updating η:

$$\mathcal{L}_{[\eta_0]} = \sum_{d\in D}(-\frac{(r_d-\sum_a\boldsymbol{\theta}_d[a]\mathbb{E}[r_{d,a}])^2}{2\sigma_r^2}$$
$$+\sum_{t\in d}\sum_a\boldsymbol{\pi}_t[a]\log\boldsymbol{\theta}_d[a]) - \frac{\eta_0^\top\eta_0}{2\sigma_\eta^2}$$
$$=\boldsymbol{\pi}_D^\top\eta_0 - \frac{\eta_0^\top\eta_0}{2\sigma_\eta^2} - \sum_{d\in D}\frac{(r_d-\sum_a\boldsymbol{\theta}_d[a]\mathbb{E}[r_{d,a}])^2}{2\sigma_r^2}$$
$$-\sum_{d\in D}N_d\log\left(\sum_{a'}\exp\left(\eta_0[a']+\eta_u[a']+\eta_i[a']\right)\right) \quad (18)$$

where $\boldsymbol{\pi}_D = \sum_{d\in D}\sum_{t\in d}\boldsymbol{\pi}_t$ and $N_d = \sum_{t\in d}\sum_a\boldsymbol{\pi}_t[a] = \sum_{t\in d}1$ is the number of sentences in d.

We apply gradient ascent method to optimize η_0. The derivative with respect to $\eta_0[a]$ is :

$$g(\eta_0[a]) =\boldsymbol{\pi}_D[a] - \sum_{d\in D}N_d\boldsymbol{\theta}_d[a] - \frac{\eta_0[a]}{\sigma_\eta^2}$$
$$+\sum_{d\in D}\frac{(r_d-\sum_a\boldsymbol{\theta}_d[a]\mathbb{E}[r_{d,a}])(\boldsymbol{\theta}_d[a])(1-\boldsymbol{\theta}_d[a])}{\sigma_r^2} \quad (19)$$

The update formula of η_u and η_i is similar. The only difference is to replace $\mathcal{D}$ in Equation (19) with $\mathcal{D}_u$ and $\mathcal{D}_i$ respectively, where $\mathcal{D}_u$ is the set of reviews of user u and $\mathcal{D}_i$ is the set of reviews of item i.

Updating β and γ:

$$\mathcal{L}_{[\boldsymbol{\beta}_a]} = \boldsymbol{c}_a^\top\boldsymbol{\beta}_a - \frac{\boldsymbol{\beta}_a^\top\boldsymbol{\beta}_a}{2\sigma_\beta^2}$$
$$-\sum_d\sum_{t\in d}\boldsymbol{\pi}_t[a]c_t\sum_r\boldsymbol{\lambda}_t[r]\log\left(\sum_l\exp\left(\boldsymbol{\beta}_a[l]+\gamma_{a,r}[l]\right)\right) \quad (20)$$

where $\boldsymbol{c}_a[j] = \sum_d\sum_{t\in d}\boldsymbol{\pi}_t[a]c_{t,j}$, and $c_t = \sum_j c_{t,j}$ denotes the number of words in sentence t.

We use Newton's method to optimize $\boldsymbol{\beta}_a$. The derivative with respect to $\boldsymbol{\beta}_a$ is :

$$g(\boldsymbol{\beta}_a) =\boldsymbol{c}_a - \sum_r C_{a,r}\boldsymbol{\alpha}_{a,r} - \frac{\boldsymbol{\beta}_a}{\sigma_\beta^2} \quad (21)$$

where $C_{a,r} = \sum_d\sum_{t\in d}\boldsymbol{\pi}_t[a]c_t\boldsymbol{\lambda}_t[r]$ represents the expected word counts for each (a,r) combination. The Hessian matrix is:

$$H(\boldsymbol{\beta}_a) = \sum_r C_{a,r}\boldsymbol{\alpha}_{a,r}\boldsymbol{\alpha}_{a,r}^\top - diag(\sum_r C_{a,r}\boldsymbol{\alpha}_{a,r} + \frac{1}{\sigma_\beta}\mathbf{1}) \quad (22)$$

The update formula for $\boldsymbol{\beta}_a$ is:

$$\boldsymbol{\beta}_a^{(t+1)} = \boldsymbol{\beta}_a^{(t)} - \boldsymbol{H}^{-1}(\boldsymbol{\beta}_a^{(t)})g(\boldsymbol{\beta}_a^{(t)}) \quad (23)$$

We use a linear algorithm for the Hessian matrices with special structure [18, 1, 3], which lets the complexity of computing $\boldsymbol{H}^{-1}(\boldsymbol{\beta}_a)g(\boldsymbol{\beta}_a)$ be $O(V)$ instead of $O(V^3)$.

We can also get the derivative and Hessian of $\gamma_{a,r}$ as follows:

$$g(\gamma_{a,r}) =\boldsymbol{c}_{a,r} - C_{a,r}\boldsymbol{\alpha}_{a,r} - \frac{\gamma_{a,r}}{\sigma_\gamma^2} \quad (24)$$

where $\boldsymbol{c}_{a,r}[j] = \sum_d\sum_{t\in d}\boldsymbol{\pi}_t[a]\boldsymbol{\lambda}_t[r]c_{t,j}$.

$$H(\gamma_{a,r}) = C_{a,r}\boldsymbol{\alpha}_{a,r}\boldsymbol{\alpha}_{a,r}^\top - diag(C_{a,r}\boldsymbol{\alpha}_{a,r} + \frac{1}{\sigma_\gamma}\mathbf{1}) \quad (25)$$

The complexity of updating $\gamma_{a,r}$ is also linear in the size of the vocabulary.

Computational Complexity: To conclude, the complexity of one update iteration is $O(c\cdot A\cdot R+T\cdot A\cdot K+D\cdot K+(I+U)\cdot A+A\cdot R\cdot V)$, where c is the total number of words in the corpus, T is the number of sentences in the corpus, and D is the number of documents in the corpus. Usually K, A and R are small constants, so the complexity is linear to the size of the review dataset.

Implementation Notes: An important issue is how to initialize the model. We use the following initialization steps. Taking the TripAdvisor data set as an example, we initialize $\boldsymbol{\beta}_a$ using the names of the aspect, i.e., we set $\boldsymbol{\beta}_{room,room} = 1$ for the aspect *room*, and then learn the aspect distribution of each sentence only based on the initialized $\boldsymbol{\beta}$. Similar techniques are also used in [13]. The aspect ratings of each sentence are initialized using the overall rating of the review. The parameters $\{\sigma\}$ can also be learned using the coordinate ascent-like procedure. We set them manually in our implementation, e.g., we set $\sigma_r^2 = 1$, $\sigma_{r,a}^2 = 0.5$, $\sigma_\eta = 10$, etc. Some optimization techniques, e.g., L-BFGS [17] and backtracking line search [2], are applied to accelerate the gradient ascent updates.

5. EXPERIMENTAL EVALUATION

In this section, we first describe the data sets we used in our experiments and then discuss the experimental results on different tasks.

5.1 Data Sets and Preprocessing

We use two review data sets for our experimental evaluation: the TripAdvisor *hotel* review data[6] and Yelp review data[7]. In the TripAdvisor data, besides the overall rating, users are also asked to provide the aspect ratings on 6 pre-defined aspects: *Location*, *Sleep Quality*, *Room*, *Service*, *Value* and *Cleanliness*, on a scale from 1 star to 5 stars. We use these ground-truth aspect ratings to evaluate our model on the task of aspect rating prediction. For Yelp data set, we

[6]http://www.cs.cmu.edu/~jiweil/html/hotel-review.html
[7]http://www.yelp.com/dataset_challenge

Table 2: Dataset Statistics

	TripAdvisor	Yelp
# Users	9,419	6,944
# Items	1,904	3,315
# Reviews	66,637	115,290
Density	0.37%	0.50%
# Sentences Per Review	12.60 ± 8.64	11.67 ± 7.80
# Words Per Sentence	7.50 ± 3.76	6.47 ± 4.64

extract a subset which only contains the reviews on *restaurants*.

We use the following preprocessing procedure on both of the data sets. We first remove non-English reviews and reviews with less than 3 sentences or 20 words, and then iteratively remove users with less than 5 reviews and items with less than 5 reviews. For the text in reviews, we remove stop words and words that occur in less than 5 reviews, and stem the remaining words using the PorterStemmer[8]. After the preprocessing, we have a *hotel* review data set including 66,637 hotel reviews of 1,904 hotels and a *restaurant* review data set including 115,290 reviews of 3,315 restaurants. The detailed statistics are listed in Table 2.

We randomly split both of the data sets into training and test sets. Specifically, for each user, we randomly select 20% of his reviews as test examples (For users with less than 10 reviews, we randomly select 2 reviews as test examples) and put the rest reviews into the training sets. We train the models on the training data sets and test their performance on the test data sets. We use the model initialization method and parameters selection strategies as discussed in Section 4.

5.2 Quantitative Evaluation

5.2.1 Perplexity on Held-out Reviews

As in standard topic models, we use *perplexity* of the held-out test data sets to compare the generalization performance of FLAME with some other state-of-the-art models.

Evaluation Measure. *Perplexity* is a standard measure for topic models to measure how the model can generate future documents [1]. For review mining, a good aspect-based topic model should be able to predict what the reviewer will write in a new review, which leads to a lower perplexity. A strong correlation of the perplexity and accuracy of aspect-based topic models is shown in [15]. We use a lower bound on perplexity as in [4].

$$\text{Perplexity}(\mathcal{D}_{test}) = \exp\left(-\frac{\sum_d \langle \log p(\boldsymbol{w}_d|\Xi)\rangle - \langle p(\boldsymbol{\Delta}_d)\rangle}{\sum_d N_d}\right)$$

We compare FLAME with the basic LDA model [1] and the D-LDA model presented in [15]. D-LDA is a state-of-the-art aspect-based opinion mining model which can be seen as a generalization of several other models [20, 6]. For D-LDA, we also use the assumption that the words in one sentence refer to the same aspect as in FLAME and other models [15, 20, 6]. In the aspect-based topic models, we actually use $A \times R$ latent topics, so we compare with LDA using both A topics (LDA-A) and $A \times R$ topics (LDA-AR).

[8]`http://tartarus.org/martin/PorterStemmer/`

Table 3: Perplexity on the held-out data sets

	TripAdvisor	Yelp
LDA-A	1012.80	767.24
LDA-AR	918.07	728.00
D-LDA	771.05	621.24
FLAME	**733.12**	**590.46**

For all the models, we use the same parameter settings and stopping criteria. We set $R = 5$ for all the aspect-based topic models. We train the models using the reviews in the training sets and evaluate the perplexity on the test sets. We test various numbers of latent aspects $A = \{6, 12, 24\}$. Since the relative results are similar, we choose $A = 6$ for discussion. Table 3 shows the perplexity on test data sets of FLAME and the comparison partners. We can see that D-LDA and FLAME, which are specifically designed for aspect-based opinion mining, significantly outperform basic LDA methods. FLAME achieves the best results among all the models on both of the data sets. We believe this is because FLAME can predict personalized aspect distribution as well as aspect rating distribution, which other models do not consider.

5.2.2 Aspect Rating Prediction on Held-out Reviews

Since we need the ground-truth aspect ratings to quantitatively compare FLAME with other methods, we evaluate the aspect rating prediction only on the TripAdvisor data set. In order to align the latent aspects to the pre-defined aspects in the TripAdvisor data set, we set A to be 6 and use the initialization techniques discussed in Section 4.

We use the evaluation measures in [22, 23] to evaluate different methods:

- Root Mean Square Error (RMSE) of the predicted aspect ratings compared with the ground-truth aspect ratings.

- Pearson Correlation inside reviews (ρ_A) to measure how well the predicted aspect ratings preserve the relative order of aspects within a review.

$$\rho_A = \frac{1}{D}\sum_{d=1}^{D} \rho(\boldsymbol{s}_d, \boldsymbol{s}_d^*)$$

  where $\boldsymbol{s}_d^*$ is the ground-truth aspect ratings for document d, and $\boldsymbol{s}_d$ is predicted aspect ratings.

- Pearson Correlation between personalized ranking of items ρ_I. For each user and each aspect, we rank the items by their predicted aspect ratings, and measure how the ranked lists preserve the ground truth.

$$\rho_I = \frac{1}{U \cdot A}\sum_{u=1}^{U}\sum_{a=1}^{A} \rho(\boldsymbol{s}_{\mathcal{I}_u,a}, \boldsymbol{s}_{\mathcal{I}_u,a}^*)$$

  where $\mathcal{I}_u$ is the set of items in user u's test data, $\boldsymbol{s}_{\mathcal{I}_u,a}$ is the predicted aspect ratings on the set of items and $\boldsymbol{s}_{\mathcal{I}_u,a}$ is the ground-truth ratings.

- Zero-One Ranking loss ($L_{0/1}$) [8], which measures the percentage of mis-ordered pairs of items for each user.

Table 4: **Aspect rating prediction on test set of TripAdvisor data**

	PMF	LRR+PMF	FLAME
RMSE	**0.970**	1.000	0.980
ρ_A	N/A	0.110	**0.195**
ρ_I	0.304	0.177	**0.333**
$L_{0/1}$	0.210	0.238	**0.196**

It is computed as follows:

$$\sum_u \sum_{i,j \in \mathcal{I}_u} \frac{1}{Z_u} \sum_{a=1}^{A} \mathbf{1}[(\boldsymbol{s}_{u,i,a} - \boldsymbol{s}_{u,j,a}) \cdot (\boldsymbol{s}^*_{u,i,a} - \boldsymbol{s}^*_{u,j,a}) < 0]$$

where Z_u is the number of pairs in user u's test set, $\boldsymbol{s}_{u,i,a}$ is the predicted rating of user u of item i on aspect a, and $\boldsymbol{s}^*_{u,i,a}$ is the ground-truth aspect rating. We do not choose nDCG since each user has few samples in the test data (2.2 test samples per user), the values of nDCG tend to be very close to 1 for all comparison partners.

An intuitive solution of aspect rating prediction is just using the overall rating of the review as prediction. We use PMF [19] to predict the overall ratings of the reviews in the test set and use the predicted overall ratings as predictions for aspect ratings. To our best knowledge, [22, 23] are the only work that predict aspect ratings at review-level. However, they can only predict aspect ratings based on users' reviews. In order to predict the aspect ratings in test set, we first apply the LRR model [22] to extract aspect ratings for each review in the training set, and then use PMF [19] to train and to predict the aspect ratings in test set (we call it LRR+PMF). We use the code of LRR provided by the authors. Same training and testing strategies are applied to all the models for fair comparison. We also test the performance of with different values of the dimensions of latent factors. The relative results are similar, so we only choose $K = 10$ for discussion. Table 4 presents the results for aspect rating prediction on the test set. We also highlight the best performance in each measure in bold.

A general observation is that FLAME outperforms other baseline models on all the measures except RMSE. It has been discussed in [22] that RMSE is less important than other measures since it does not reflect how the relative order of the aspect ratings is preserved. ρ_A measures how a method preserves the relative order of aspect ratings within a review. PMF uses the same predicted ratings for all aspects, so it is not applicable for ρ_A. ρ_I and $L_{0/1}$ are the most important measures for our task where we want to rank items based on the predicted aspect ratings. PMF outputs exactly the same item ranking lists for all aspects, thus it is not suitable for real-world applications. We can see that FLAME gets the best results on the two measures. The gain is especially significant compared to LRR+PMF, where there are about 90% improvement on ρ_I and 40% improvement on $L_{0/1}$.

Note that LRR+PMF does not achieve desirable performance. The reason is that it is a two-step approach that the errors induced in the first step have significant influence on the performance of the second step.

5.3 Qualitative Evaluation

In this subsection, we evaluate FLAME on the task of aspect identification. We perform qualitative analysis of the top words obtained by FLAME to see whether FLAME can produce meaningful aspects.

Figure 3 shows the word-cloud visualization of top words (after stemming) with the highest generating probability in the aspect-rating specific word distributions. We only show 3 aspects due to space limits. The three word-cloud figures in the left column present the topic distribution $\boldsymbol{\beta}$ for the aspects *location*, *service* and *room*, respectively. In general, the top words generated by FLAME represent meaningful and interpretable topics. We observe that the top words match our intuition, e.g., words like "location", "walk", "street" have higher weights in the word distribution of aspect *location*. The middle and right columns show the top words of the 2-star ($\gamma_{a,2}$) and 5-star ($\gamma_{a,5}$) word distributions of for the three aspects,. The aspect-rating specific word distribution can automatically learn the sentiment oriented words, e.g., words like "bad", "old", "creepy" and "homeless" have high weights in the 2-star word distribution of the aspect *location*, while the words like "view", "great", "perfect", "best" have high weights in the 5-star word distribution of *location*.

One contribution of FLAME is that the aspect-rating topics have sentiment polarities, i.e., 5-star topics are more positive than 4-star, and so on. This is different from previous work [20, 14, 16] where the latent ratings in these models are rating labels which do not correspond to sentiment polarities.

6. FURTHER APPLICATIONS

The detailed analysis on personalized latent aspect ratings enables a wide range of applications. Here we discuss three sample applications.

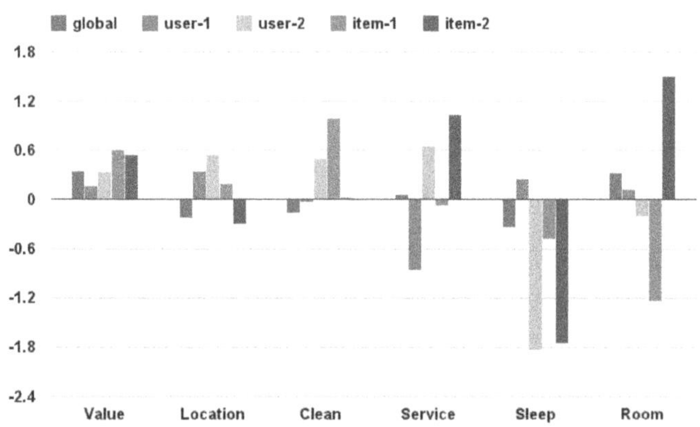

Figure 4: Aspect Weights. *Global* **represents the values of** η_0. *user-1* **and** *user-2* **are the aspect weights** η_u **of two randomly sampled users, and** *item-1* **and** *item-2* **are the values of** η_i **for two randomly sampled items.**

Aspect Distribution: Since FLAME can infer the aspect weights for users and item, we can easily use the values of η_0, η_u and η_i for the rating behavior analysis. Figure 4 shows some sample results on TripAdviosr data. From the histogram *Global* in the figure, we can see that *Value* and *Room* are the most discussed aspects, and most people rarely mention the aspect *Sleep*. Note that the values of η_u

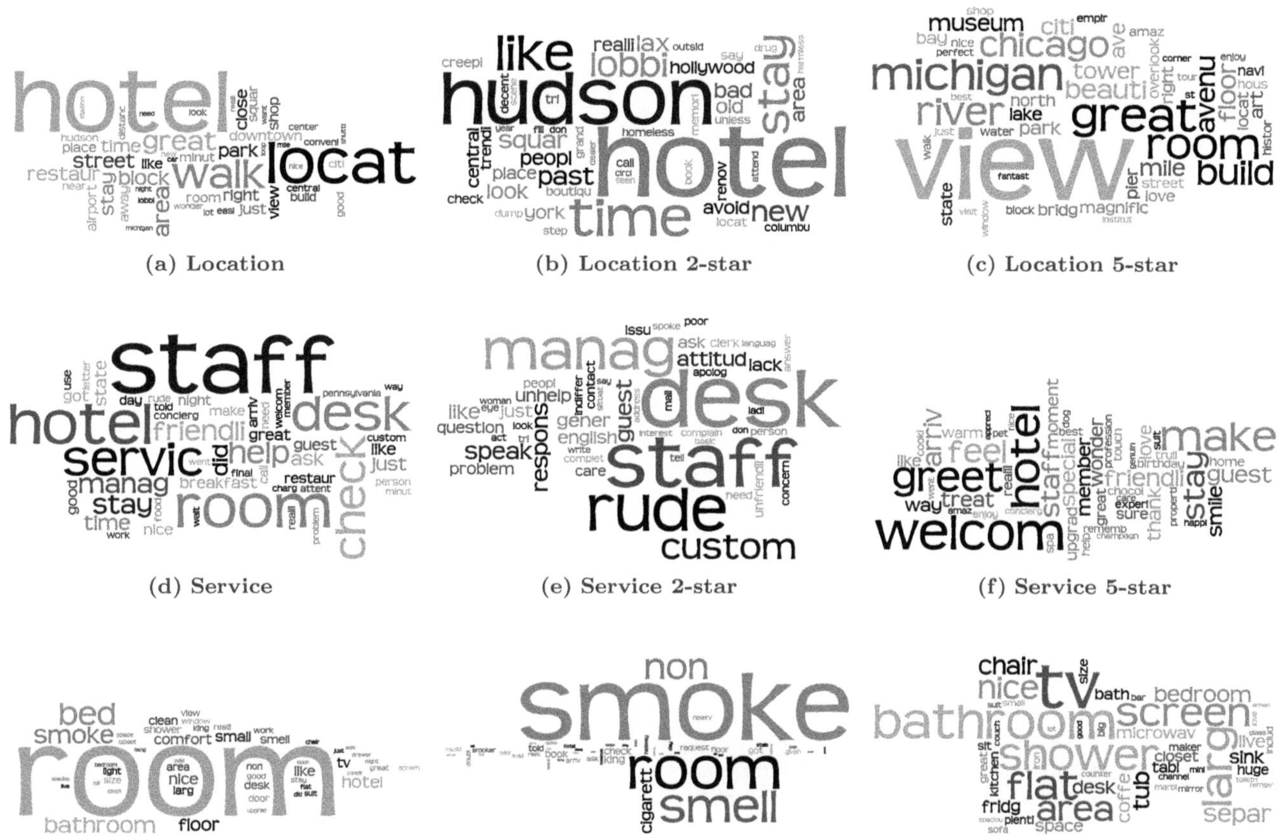

(a) Location (b) Location 2-star (c) Location 5-star

(d) Service (e) Service 2-star (f) Service 5-star

(g) Room (h) Room 2-star (i) Room 5-star

Figure 3: Word-cloud visualization of top words with highest generating probability in β and γ. The left Word size reflects the weight of each word. The three rows are the top words in the topic distributions for the aspects *location*, *service* and *room*, respectively. The left column shows the top words in the aspect-word distributions β of the three aspects. The middle and right columns show the top words in the aspect-rating-word distributions γ. The middle column shows negative ones (2-star) and the right column shows positive ones (5-star).

indicates the biases of users deviating from the global aspect weights. We can see that *user-1* likes to comment on the *Location* and *Sleep*, while *user-2* cares more about the *Service*, *Clean* and *Location*. The two users have opposite weights for the aspects *Service* and *Sleep*. Thus, when they are searching for hotels, the aspects they care about are different. It indicates that letting users choose to rank items based on aspects which they cares about is very useful. The aspect weights of items can be used to help merchants to improve their services. If a specific aspect is discussed a lot and most of the reviews are negative, the merchant should think about how to improve this aspect.

Personalized Review Recommendation: As discussed in Section 1, facing a large number of reviews expressing different opinions, a user might have no idea of which reviews are reliable. FLAME can alleviate this problem by sorting the reviews by the similarities between reviewers with current user. A simple way of computing the similarities between users is to compute the distance between their latent factors. Since personalized review recommendation is hard to evaluate, we would like to leave it as a future work on some data sets with ground-truth of user feedback on reviews.

Recommendation Explanation: Traditional collaborative filtering methods only provide predicted scores for then items, but can not produce reasonable explanations with the recommendations. A recent work [24] has shown the possibility of using the aspect weights to generate some explanations. FLAME can produce more persuasive recommendation explanations by the predicted aspect ratings and some selected reviews written by similar users.

7. CONCLUSION

In this paper, we introduce the problem of Personalized Latent Aspect Rating Analysis to model users' preferences on different aspects. We propose a unified probabilistic model FLAME which combines aspect-based opinion mining and collaborative filtering. FLAME extracts aspect ratings from the review text, and predicts aspect ratings of an item that a user has not yet reviewed based on aspect ratings within other reviews of the item by other users with similar preferences. Our experimental evaluation on a hotel review data set and a restaurant review data set shows that FLAME can effectively solve the research problem. The qualitative evaluation shows that FLAME can automatically extract meaningful aspects and sentiment-oriented aspects. We also investigate the ability of FLAME on the task of generating future review text. Most importantly, our experiments on TripAdvisor data sets show that FLAME significantly outperforms state-of-the-art methods in terms of accuracy of aspect rating prediction.

Some websites like TripAdvisor provide the option of rating some pre-defined aspects. Although these aspect ratings are typically incomplete, they may be helpful to partially guide the learning of latent aspect ratings. It is worth to explore a semi-supervised extension of FLAME. In this paper, we only consider one same type of items, e.g., hotels or restaurants. We plan to consider datasets with multiple types of items which have different aspects, where users may also have different preferences on different types of items.

8. REFERENCES

[1] D. M. Blei, A. Y. Ng, and M. I. Jordan. Latent dirichlet allocation. *J. Mach. Learn. Res.*, 3:993–1022, Mar. 2003.

[2] S. P. Boyd and L. Vandenberghe. *Convex optimization*. Cambridge university press, 2004.

[3] J. Eisenstein, A. Ahmed, and E. P. Xing. Sparse additive generative models of text. In *Proceedings of the 28th International Conference on Machine Learning (ICML-11)*, pages 1041–1048, 2011.

[4] M. Hoffman, F. R. Bach, and D. M. Blei. Online learning for latent dirichlet allocation. In *advances in neural information processing systems*, pages 856–864, 2010.

[5] M. Hu and B. Liu. Mining and summarizing customer reviews. In *Proceedings of the tenth ACM SIGKDD international conference on Knowledge discovery and data mining*, KDD '04, pages 168–177, New York, NY, USA, 2004. ACM.

[6] Y. Jo and A. H. Oh. Aspect and sentiment unification model for online review analysis. In *Proceedings of the fourth ACM international conference on Web search and data mining*, pages 815–824. ACM, 2011.

[7] Y. Koren, R. Bell, and C. Volinsky. Matrix factorization techniques for recommender systems. *Computer*, 42(8):30–37, 2009.

[8] J. Lee, S. Bengio, S. Kim, G. Lebanon, and Y. Singer. Local collaborative ranking. In *Proceedings of the 18th international conference on World wide web*, 2014.

[9] F. Li, C. Han, M. Huang, X. Zhu, Y.-J. Xia, S. Zhang, and H. Yu. Structure-aware review mining and summarization. In *Proceedings of the 23rd International Conference on Computational Linguistics*, pages 653–661. Association for Computational Linguistics, 2010.

[10] B. Liu. Opinion mining and sentiment analysis. In *Web Data Mining*, pages 459–526. Springer, 2011.

[11] B. Liu, M. Hu, and J. Cheng. Opinion observer: analyzing and comparing opinions on the web. In *Proceedings of the 14th international conference on World Wide Web*, WWW '05, pages 342–351, New York, NY, USA, 2005. ACM.

[12] J. McAuley and J. Leskovec. Hidden factors and hidden topics: understanding rating dimensions with review text. In *Recsys*, 2013.

[13] J. McAuley, J. Leskovec, and D. Jurafsky. Learning attitudes and attributes from multi-aspect reviews. In *Data Mining (ICDM), 2012 IEEE 12th International Conference on*, pages 1020–1025. IEEE, 2012.

[14] S. Moghaddam and M. Ester. Ilda: interdependent lda model for learning latent aspects and their ratings from online product reviews. In *Proceedings of the 34th international ACM SIGIR conference on Research and development in Information Retrieval*, SIGIR '11, pages 665–674, New York, NY, USA, 2011. ACM.

[15] S. Moghaddam and M. Ester. On the design of lda models for aspect-based opinion mining. In *Proceedings of the 21st ACM international conference on Information and knowledge management*, CIKM '12, pages 803–812, New York, NY, USA, 2012. ACM.

[16] S. Moghaddam and M. Ester. The flda model for aspect-based opinion mining: addressing the cold start problem. In *Proceedings of the 22nd international conference on World Wide Web*, WWW '13, pages 909–918, 2013.

[17] J. Nocedal. Updating quasi-newton matrices with limited storage. *Mathematics of computation*, 35(151):773–782, 1980.

[18] G. Ronning. Maximum likelihood estimation of dirichlet distributions. *Journal of statistical computation and simulation*, 32(4):215–221, 1989.

[19] R. Salakhutdinov and A. Mnih. Probabilistic matrix factorization. In *Advances in neural information processing systems*, pages 1257–1264, 2007.

[20] I. Titov and R. McDonald. Modeling online reviews with multi-grain topic models. In *Proceedings of the 17th international conference on World Wide Web*, pages 111–120. ACM, 2008.

[21] C. Wang and D. M. Blei. Collaborative topic modeling for recommending scientific articles. In *Proceedings of the 17th ACM SIGKDD international conference on Knowledge discovery and data mining*, KDD '11, pages 448–456, New York, NY, USA, 2011. ACM.

[22] H. Wang, Y. Lu, and C. Zhai. Latent aspect rating analysis on review text data: a rating regression approach. In *Proceedings of the 16th ACM SIGKDD international conference on Knowledge discovery and data mining*, pages 783–792. ACM, 2010.

[23] H. Wang, Y. Lu, and C. Zhai. Latent aspect rating analysis without aspect keyword supervision. In *Proceedings of the 17th ACM SIGKDD international conference on Knowledge discovery and data mining*, pages 618–626. ACM, 2011.

[24] Y. Zhang, G. Lai, M. Zhang, Y. Zhang, Y. Liu, and S. Ma. Explicit factor models for explainable recommendation based on phrase-level sentiment analysis. In *Proceedings of the 37th international ACM SIGIR conference on Research and development in Information Retrieval*, SIGIR '14, Gold Coast, Australia, 2014. ACM.

[25] W. X. Zhao, J. Jiang, H. Yan, and X. Li. Jointly modeling aspects and opinions with a maxent-lda hybrid. In *Proceedings of the 2010 Conference on Empirical Methods in Natural Language Processing*, EMNLP '10, pages 56–65, Stroudsburg, PA, USA, 2010. Association for Computational Linguistics.

Semantic Matching in APP Search

Juchao Zhuo, Zeqian Huang, Yunfeng Liu, Zhanhui Kang, Xun Cao, Mingzhi Li, Long Jin
Tencent Inc.
Netac Building, High-tech sixth south road, Nanshan District,
Shenzhen, P. R. China, 518000
{jojozhuo, bobbyhuang, glenliu, kegokang, xuncao, mingzhili, arvinjin}@tencent.com

ABSTRACT

Past years, with the growth of smart-phones and applications, APP market has become an important mobile internet portal. As an important function in application market, APP search gains lots of attentions.However, mismatch between queries and APP is the most critical problem in APP search because of less text within term matching search engine.

In this talk, we describe a semantic matching architecture in APP search, which mining topics and tags in big data. It enriches query and APP representations with topics and tags to achieve semantic matching in search.

Some challenge must be considered:

1) How to extract tag-APP relationship from large web text.

2) How to use machine learning technologies to process de-noising and computing confidence.

3) How to hybrid ranking apps retrieved by different matching method.

These will be introduced in some of our related works and as examples to describe how semantic matching is used in Tencent MyApp, an application market which serving hundreds of millions of users.

WSDM'15, February 2–6, 2015, Shanghai, China.
ACM 978-1-4503-3317-7/15/02.
http://dx.doi.org/10.1145/2684822.2697046

Categories and Subject Descriptors

H.3.3 [**Information Search and Retrieval**]: Search process; Retrieval models

Keywords

Semantic matching, app search, app store, topic mode, tag mining

Boosting Search with Deep Understanding of Contents and Users

Kaihua Zhu
Baidu
Baidu Campus, No. 10 Shangdi
10th Street, Beijing, China
zhukaihua@baidu.com

ABSTRACT

Recent years have witnessed dramatic changes in how people interact with search engines. Search engines are expected to be more intelligent in understanding users' intention and fulfilling users' needs with direct answers rather than raw information. Furthermore, search engines are expected to be equipped with recommendation and dialogue capabilities, making the interaction with users more natural and smoother. In this talk, I will introduce Baidu's work on how to make some of them come true through the deep understanding of users, queries and web pages, and discuss challenges behind these technologies.

Categories and Subject Descriptors

H.3.1 INFORMATION STORAGE AND RETRIEVAL, Content Analysis and Indexing: Linguistic

Keyword

Deep question answering, Dialogue, Recommendation

WSDM'15, February 2–6, 2015, Shanghai, China.
ACM 978-1-4503-3317-7/15/02.
http://dx.doi.org/10.1145/2684822.2697047

Driven by Food: Modeling Geographic Choice

Ravi Kumar Mohammad Mahdian Bo Pang Andrew Tomkins Sergei Vassilvitskii
Google
Mountain View, CA
{ravi.k53, mahdian, bopang42, atomkins, sergeiv}@gmail.com

ABSTRACT

In this work we study the dynamics of geographic choice, i.e., how users choose one from a set of objects in a geographic region. We postulate a model in which an object is selected from a slate of candidates with probability that depends on how far it is (*distance*) and how many closer alternatives exist (*rank*). Under a discrete choice formulation, we argue that there exists a factored form in which unknown functions of rank and distance may be combined to produce an accurate estimate of the likelihood that a user will select each alternative. We then learn these hidden functions and show that each can be closely approximated by an appropriately parameterized lognormal, even though the respective marginals look quite different. We give a theoretical justification to support the presence of lognormal distributions.

We then apply this framework to study restaurant choices in map search logs. We show that a four-parameter model based on combinations of lognormals has excellent performance at predicting restaurant choice, even compared to baseline models with access to the full (densely parameterized) marginal distribution for rank and distance. Finally, we show how this framework can be extended to simultaneously learn a per-restaurant quality score representing the residual likelihood of choice after distance and rank have been accounted for. We show that, compared to a per-place score that predicts likelihood without factoring out rank and distance, our score is a significantly better predictor of user quality judgments.

1. INTRODUCTION

We consider the problem of modeling geographic choice: how users choose one among a set of objects in a geographic region. We study this problem and postulate a general model by analyzing a large maps query log for directions to the single-largest consumer business type [38]: restaurants. More specifically, for each request for directions to a particular restaurant, we consider that restaurant as the *chosen* one among all possible alternatives in the region.

The list of important covariates on restaurant choice is long and well-studied. Restaurant choice can be affected by cuisine type, price, quality, and other venue-specific metadata. Breaking reviews or word of mouth may lead to local bursts of activity. Group social dynamics may play a significant role. These factors are similar to ones affecting people's choices over various consumer products and have been relatively well-studied. But choices over geo-entities like restaurants must also take into account the actual physical locations of the candidate restaurants under consideration. The most obvious contribution comes from the distance between the user and a particular candidate. However, the likelihood of selecting a restaurant at a particular distance must also depend critically on the nature of the *other* candidates. A restaurant 5km from the user in Tokyo is vanishingly likely to be selected, while another restaurant at the same distance in Iowa may be the overwhelmingly most likely choice.

Our goal in this paper is to study how these different factors operate, rather than to optimize prediction accuracy by incorporating as many features as possible. While we do give specific functional forms for transformations by which these factors should be incorporated into general place recommendation systems, this work is not a proposal for a place recommender.

1.1 Distance, rank, and popularity

We now describe the three key factors we study in more detail. First, we consider the absolute *distance* to the restaurant. Second, to capture a candidate's role relative to alternatives, we consider the number of these alternatives that are closer to the user; we use *rank* to denote this number. Finally, after a detailed study of rank and distance, we incorporate a per-restaurant residual *popularity* score to improve the prediction; we believe this score has value in its own right as a measure of quality. The score may be viewed as the residual likelihood of an object to be chosen after distance and rank have been accounted for.

There is a significant body of work studying the dynamics of geographic choice. Much of this work focuses on the distance to each object, and in many cases falls under the rubric of "gravity laws," in which the desirability of an object at a particular distance is proportional to an inverse polynomial function of the distance; see the book [10]. We will show that predictions of geographic choice based on distance alone is insufficient.

Alternative proposals based on rank rather than distance, dating back to Stouffer's original proposals from 1940 [34], have shown improvements in predictive power. Noulas et al. [24] have observed a good fit between the rank of a destination and the probability of its selection, showing that the log of the probability drops inversely with the log of the rank of the object. In the context of restaurants, we observe the same form as theirs roughly from rank 150 and above, but for lower ranks, the marginal likelihood drops slower than what they observed. While there may be more sophisticated approaches to predicting based on distance, our baseline measures show rank alone outperforming distance alone. Consistent with previous work, we observe that rank, as an implicit measure of the competitive landscape, provides good predictions of choice.

WSDM'15, February 2–6, 2015, Shanghai, China.

http://dx.doi.org/10.1145/2684822.2685300 .

However, the form of the rank marginal varies when we stratify by the density of restaurants in the area of the query, suggesting that predictions based solely on rank are limited in the accuracy they can attain. We provide evidence to suggest that human decision making involves an interplay of both rank and distance and that simply considering rank, either alone or bucketed by average density, will not suffice. Our proposed model captures this interplay with only four parameters, and significantly outperforms dense models based on the entire marginal distributions of rank or distance.

Thus, a natural approach to predict the likelihood of selecting a particular candidate restaurant is to use its rank, distance, or other features. One could imagine a function of rank, distance, cost, cuisine, etc., that returns the likelihood of a restaurant being selected. However, this approach is problematic, as the likelihood of selecting a restaurant depends on not just the restaurant's features but also the attractiveness of the alternatives. To address this issue, we propose a simple model based on modeling an intrinsic desirability of each option and normalizing across different alternatives via a discrete choice framework.

1.2 A discrete choice model

The appropriate formulation, therefore, is slightly more general: given a set of alternatives with their features, determine a distribution over the alternatives so as to maximize likelihood of the data. We derive such a distribution by making a simplifying assumption. R. Duncan Luce in 1959 [20] formulated the *Choice Axiom*, which states that a user's likelihood to select an object A over object B is unaffected by the nature of the other alternatives. While this axiom is likely not strictly true for geographic choice in general, it provides a good approximation that yields a valuable functional form for our analysis. Luce's Choice Axiom implies that each alternative i may be assigned a score s_i such that $\Pr[\text{user chooses } i] = s_i / \sum_j s_j$, i.e., the user's likelihood to choose i is proportional to s_i, but with a normalization factor that depends on the alternatives. Hence, an object with some set of features might be likely in one setting but unlikely in another, even though the score is unchanged, because the stronger alternatives of one setting provide a larger normalizing constant.

We must therefore determine the form of the score s_i of object i. To begin, we will express this as a function of the rank and distance of i with respect to the user; later, we will introduce the concept of i's overall quality. Consider a situation in which a user selects object i from a set of alternatives. Our challenge will lie in teasing apart the relative contribution of i's distance versus its rank, or some complex element of their interplay. We make a simplifying assumption that will be borne out by our analysis: the score s_i of object i, occurring with rank r at distance d, may be written as $s_i = f_r(r) \cdot f_d(d)$, i.e., the score of a object is the product of some unknown function f_r of its rank and some unknown function f_d of its distance. One may view this as a univariate function of rank capturing the rank-specific component of this mental process, multiplicatively modified by a univariate function of distance capturing the travel cost. This form is fairly general, though not universal.

Given this functional form, we turn to the techniques of discrete choice modeling to optimize the functions. As we have no preconceptions about the forms of f_r and f_d, we will quantize ranks and distances, then perform an optimization that will empirically estimate the value of f_r and f_d pointwise so as to optimize likelihood. We then study the form of the resulting pointwise estimates in order to model the shape and capture the aggregate behavior in a more parsimonious fashion. We detail the algorithms to perform the pointwise estimation optimally. Our approach has the pleasing property that employing the resulting functions in order to select objects will produce selections that simultaneously exactly reproduce the rank and distance marginals of the original data; it is not in general obvious how to attain this property without such a technique.[1]

1.3 Parametric forms

After our optimization, we have learned non-parametric functions of rank and distance that combine to give us a good approximation of likelihood. We fit a large number of parametric function families to the resulting data, and show that both distance and rank contributions are approximated well by lognormal univariates. Note that these functions of rank and distance are quite different from the marginal distributions in the data; these are instead hidden distributions that are not directly observable, but which emerge as the underlying factors that according to our model drive the process of selecting an object. The lognormal form for the hidden functions of both rank and distance was quite surprising to us, as the rank marginal does not have a good fit to a lognormal distribution. None of our earlier efforts to tease out the relationship between these factors led us to consider such a form. We present some discussion of the implications of this finding below.

We fit the shape parameters for the lognormal functions of rank and distance, resulting in a final likelihood model of choosing an object i with rank r_i and at distance d_i from a set C of alternatives:

$$\Pr[\text{user chooses } i \in C] = \frac{f_r(r_i) \cdot f_d(d_i)}{\sum_{j \in C} f_r(r_j) \cdot f_d(d_j)},$$

where

$$f_r(\cdot) \sim \text{LogNormal}(\mu_r, \sigma_r), \quad f_d(\cdot) \sim \text{LogNormal}(\mu_d, \sigma_d).$$

The parameters $\mu_r, \sigma_r, \mu_d, \sigma_d$ fully specify the model.

We use both the parametric and non-parametric versions of these imputed rank and distance functions, as well as a number of baselines, to compare the likelihoods generated by our model for the restaurant directions case, and show that these two functions outperform other natural alternatives. The model performs well over a variety of densities from urban to rural settings. We expand on this observation by providing some theoretical justification. Under one fairly weak assumption regarding the layout of places, and another commonly-held assumption regarding human perception of the relative cost of growing time intervals, these lognormal functions are in fact the optimal outcomes under an entropy maximization framework (see Section 6).

1.4 Residual as quality

Having established a concise understanding of aggregate choice given rank and distance, we turn to the question of incorporating a quality score for each individual object. We may expect that certain objects will be chosen more often than predicted by rank and distance alone; we would like to explain the residual (positive or negative) by a score representing "quality," or more accurately, whatever attributes of an object cause it to be visited more often than its physical location relative to its clientele would predict.

The machinery developed above applies naturally to this setting, but the optimization problem we must solve now includes a much larger number of parameters. In this new formulation, we assume that each object i is endowed with a quality w_i, and that the likelihood of selecting i is proportional to $f_r(r_i) \cdot f_d(d_i) \cdot w_i$, with

[1]Note that this result will hold in expectation if the optimizer is allowed to fit parameters for each individual rank and distance. In our experiments, we run the optimization on a quantized form, and hence recover the marginals for the quantized ranks and distances, which are less precise than the full marginals.

the usual normalization.[2] In this general case, as well as the simplified version above, the gradients of the likelihood function have a simple and easily interpretable form that we will describe later.

After the optimization, we find that for restaurants, the likelihood of selecting any individual restaurant has on average increased by 87% over the best model we had available without per-place scores. This figure is computed as the geometric mean of the increase in likelihood over all candidate places.

2. DATA

We collected a random sample of anonymized direction queries issued at Google Maps (`maps.google.com`) during a period of 170 days in 2012. Each direction query consisted of the timestamp, the query normalized to the form "from: `src` to: `dst`", and the distance of travel as computed by Google Maps. Note that `src` or `dst` can specify a location as a (`lat, lon`) pair or as an explicit address (e.g., `1600 Amphitheatre parkway, Mountain View, CA 94043`). When `src = (lat, lon)`, the direction request is more likely to have originated from a mobile device. Since it is common for users to keep updating directions en route, resulting in a series of decreasing distances for a single trip, the distance distribution in this type of request may not reflect the actual end-to-end distances people travel. Hence, unless otherwise specified, we restrict most of the analysis to directions where `src` is a piece of text (denoted `src = text`).

We obtained a database of business listings and restricted it to a large random subset of US/Canadian restaurants. We then extracted directions where `dst` is recognized (by the system) to be one of the restaurants in our subset.[3] The final dataset consists of 15,454,095 directions where `src = text`; this covered 410,488 restaurants. A small fraction of the traffic (∼5%) appeared to be "just checking" (e.g., `src` and `dst` are oceans apart). If we consider 200km to be the threshold of driving distance for the restaurant intent, 405,889 restaurants have at least one directions query within 200km, and 232,230 have at least 10 qualifying queries.

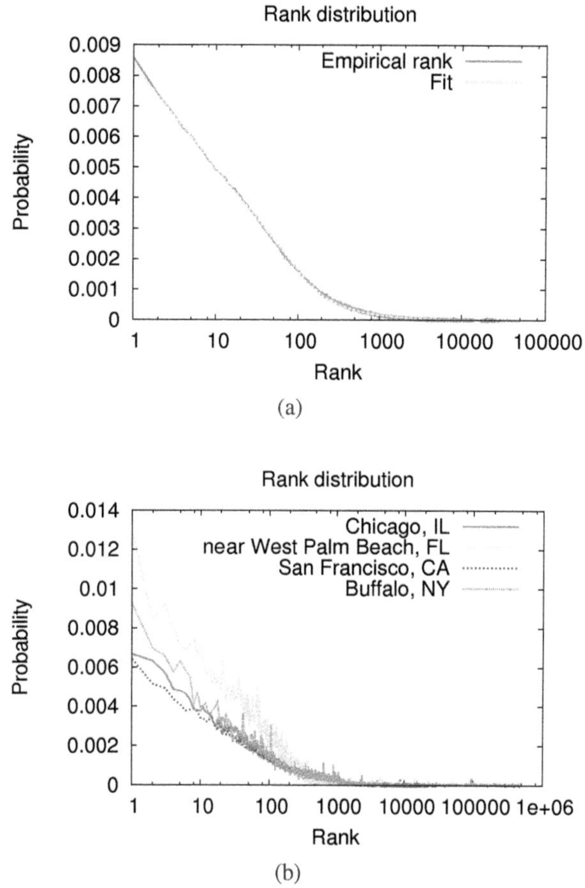

Figure 1: Overall rank distribution and rank distribution for a few urban areas.

3. RANK VS. DISTANCE

In this section we explore the roles of rank and distance in the geographic choice process, using the data described in Section 2. Intuitively, the rank, or the number of objects closer than a particular object, corresponds to the amount of competition faced by this object in the geographic area. In the context of our case study, we first study the impact of the rank of the restaurant on the decision process. We begin by showing that rank alone does not capture the richness and variability of users' actions.

In Figure 1(a) we show the global distribution of the rank of the restaurant visited by the user. Note that the empirical distribution can be approximated nearly perfectly with the decay proportional to $\log(1/\text{rank})$ for small ranks (under 150) and proportional to $1/\text{rank}$ for ranks above 150. The same phenomenon holds even as we zoom in on specific areas. Figure 1(b) shows the empirical rank distributions for four areas with different restaurant densities. Observe that the specific shapes of the curves differ for different regions; we will consider a generalization of this effect later.

3.1 The effect of density

We now refine our analysis to take into account the density of restaurants in the area of the query. We define the (restaurant) *density* (more specifically, average density at a rank) of the source location of a query as follows. For a given source location and a given rank r, we compute the distance d_r of the restaurant at rank r to the source location. The average density of the first r restaurants is r divided by the area of the circle with radius d_r, which is proportional to d_r^2; we define $\rho_r = r/d_r^2$. We compute ρ_r at $r = 100$ and use it as the measure for the density of the source location. We then bucket density values on log-scale and put each direction into the appropriate bucket according to its ρ_{100} value. For each density bucket, we can plot the empirical distribution of the rank of the restaurant visited as well as the empirical distribution of distance traveled. The results are shown in Figure 2.

Figure 2(a) shows that the empirical distributions of rank are well-separated for users originating from regions with different density values. Indeed, users in less dense regions (e.g., West Palm Beach, Florida) are much more likely to choose restaurants at lower ranks than those in denser regions (e.g., San Francisco, California). The distribution corresponding to the latter is therefore flatter when compared to that of the former. Hence rank alone, when conflated across a wide range of densities, misapprehends user choice significantly. On the other hand, Figure 2(b) shows that employing distance alone is just as bad. The distributions of distances traveled by users in dense and sparse regions are again well-separated, if not worse: users in dense regions do not need to travel long distances to have plenty of options and hence their distance distribution is correspondingly left-shifted.

[2] Note that we do not require a function $f_w(w_i)$, as w_i is inherently non-parametric—the w_i's *are* the function.

[3] The details of these recognition methods are beyond the scope of this work.

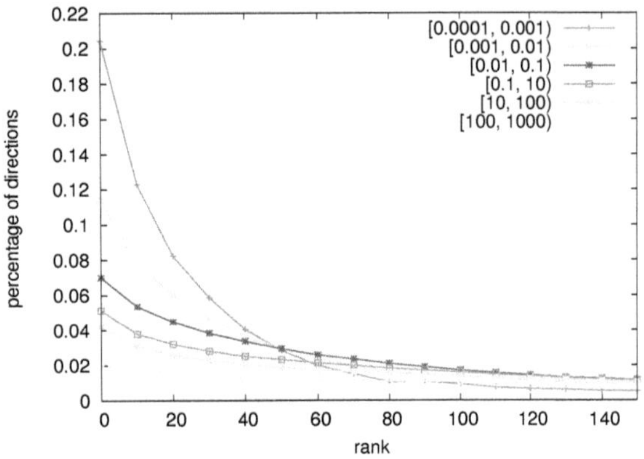

(a)

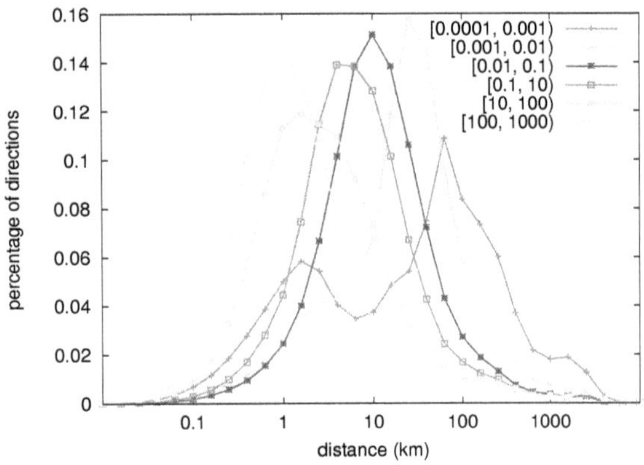

(b)

Figure 2: Distribution of rank and distance for different densities. Each curve corresponds to a set of directions from a source location whose density (ρ_{100}) is in the given range.

Note also that while most curves more or less follow the lognormal shape, the curve for the least dense region (red curve, $\rho_{100} \in [0.0001, 0.001)$) is bimodal. In comparison, the different curves in Figure 2(a) seem to correspond to functions with different parameters, but coming from the same family. This prompts us to ask the following question: can we describe the empirical observations with a set of rank distributions parameterized by density?

3.2 A closer look at density

We consider a region as *smooth* if ρ_r is a constant (relatively speaking) at least for reasonably small r (e.g., ≤ 200). More specifically, we consider a region encircling r restaurants as ϵ-smooth if for a small ϵ and a constant ρ, we have $|\rho_{r'} - \rho| \leq \epsilon$ for all $r' \leq r$. If the local neighborhood of a source is smooth, then we can capture its local density with a single parameter ρ rather than a family of ρ_r's. Hence we can model all directions originating from regions with density ρ with a single rank distribution.

Figure 3 plots ρ_{200} (y-axis) vs ρ_{100} (x-axis). If ρ_r were relatively constant for most regions encircling 200 restaurants, then most points would fall within a narrow band along the diagonal line of $y = x$. Figure 3(a) shows the heat map on a log-log scale (where the color corresponds to log of count for that cell). While this gives us the entire range, it compacts the data in a way that is hard to interpret. Figure 3(b) shows the heat map for density values between 1 and 10. Here we can clearly see that many points fall

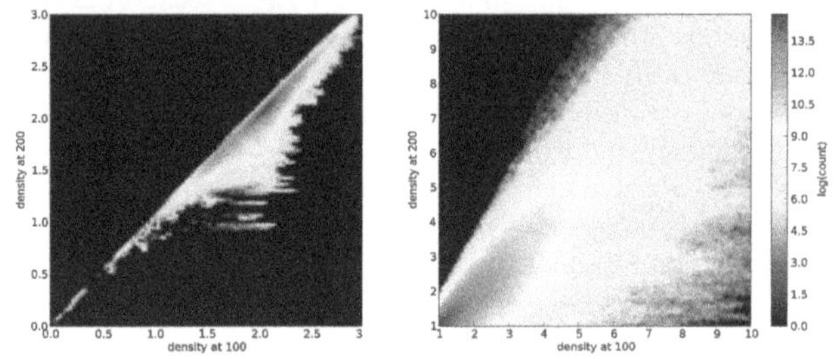

(a) log scale (b) zoom-in (linear scale)

Figure 3: ρ_{200} (y-axis) vs ρ_{100} (x-axis).

outside of a close band around $y = x$. Indeed, if we compute the CDF for $|\rho_{200} - \rho_{100}|/\rho_{100}$, we observe that ρ_{200} is within 20% of ρ_{100} for only about half of the time. This phenomenon also repeats itself at smaller r: e.g., the CDF for $|\rho_{100} - \rho_{50}|/\rho_{50}$ has a similar shape.

One might suspect that the variability in the densities observed is due to the natural tendency of many restaurants to be located in groups close together; zoning ordinances further enforce this phenomenon. However, this hypothesis is not borne out in the data—while restaurants do occur in groups, we observed that these groups are (essentially) uniformly distributed as a function of the distance from a randomly placed user. Therefore, the cumulative distribution is not affected by the natural clustering of eateries.

These observations suggest that it is hard to capture the local density of a source location with a single parameter ρ, since objects may not be uniformly distributed geographically. Indeed, for the restaurant case, we could not find a simple analytic form to capture the relationship between rank and distance; we believe this is true for other types of objects as well. Instead, we propose a unified model of user choices that depends on both rank, distance, and a per-object quality measure.

4. A GEOGRAPHIC CHOICE MODEL

We saw above that multiple factors play a role in determining the probability a user will choose a particular geographic object (i.e., driving to a specific restaurant in the context of restaurants). The rank plays a role, as one is more likely to go to a closer object; the absolute distance is also crucial, as one is not likely to drive hours for it; and it is intuitive that some inherent quality of the object also plays a role. In this section we set up a framework to model how these different factors can be combined to give a prediction of a user's choice, and how we can learn about the quality of objects by estimating the underlying model parameters.

At the heart of our model is a discrete choice model that describes how an agent chooses among a set of alternatives. For this, we use a classical model due to [20], which is based on the following axiom: the relative probability of choosing between two options a and b is independent of the presence of other options. This axiom results in the following probabilistic model. Suppose that every object i has some total score s_i; this score can be a function of many factors. In particular, we consider a model where the score is a function of the distance between the user and the object, the rank of the object among all options available to the user, as well as some inherent metric, which we will refer to as *wonderfulness*. Presented with scores for all objects in a set C of alternatives,

$$\Pr[\text{user selects object } i] = \frac{s_i}{\sum_{j \in C} s_j}.$$

Given such a simple model of user behavior, we ask for the best set of scores s_i that explain the data. Assume we are given a set Q of observations about a user's choice. For each observation, we know the set of alternatives, as well as the alternative chosen by the user. In the context of restaurant direction queries, Q is the set of direction queries to restaurants; the restaurant to which query q is directed is denoted by $r(q)$, and the set of restaurants that the user could have queried for is denoted by $C(q)$. The score of a restaurant i for the query q is denoted by $s_{i,q}$. Given these, the likelihood of these observations in our model can be written as:

$$L(Q) = \prod_{q \in Q} \frac{s_{r(q),q}}{\sum_{j \in C(q)} s_{j,q}}.$$

The log likelihood, $\mathrm{LL}(Q)$ is then:

$$\mathrm{LL}(Q) = \sum_{q \in Q} \log s_{r(q),q} - \sum_{q \in Q} \log \left(\sum_{j \in C(q)} s_{j,q} \right).$$

In order to efficiently find the best scores, we show that $\mathrm{LL}(Q)$ is a concave function in the logarithm of all variables, and therefore gradient ascent on $\mathrm{LL}(Q)$ amounts to a natural multiplicative update step on all of the scores.

LEMMA 1. *$\mathrm{LL}(Q)$ is a concave function of all of $\log s_{i,q}$'s simultaneously.*

PROOF SKETCH. We show that the second partial derivatives are always non-negative. Let $z_{i,q} = \log s_{i,q}$. Then we can rewrite the likelihood as:

$$\mathrm{LL}(Q) = \sum_{q \in Q} z_{r(q),q} - \sum_{q \in Q} \log \left(\sum_{j \in C(q)} e^{z_{j,q}} \right).$$

Computing the first partial derivative, we have:

$$\frac{\partial \mathrm{LL}}{\partial z_{i,q}} = [i = r(q)] - \frac{e^{z_{i,q}}}{\sum_{j \in C(q)} e^{z_{j,q}}}. \quad (1)$$

The second partial with respect to another variable $z_{k,q'}$ is zero if $q' \neq q$. If $q' = q$, this second partial is equal to:

$$\frac{\partial^2 \mathrm{LL}}{\partial z_{i,q} \partial z_{k,q}} = \frac{e^{z_{i,q}} e^{z_{k,q}}}{\sum_{j \in C(q)} e^{z_{j,q}}}.$$

The rest of the proof follows from the well-known properties of log-partition functions [16]. □

We note two simple, yet powerful consequences of the following concavity result: first, since LL is a concave function, it is possible to efficiently optimize it even when the variables $z_{i,q}$ are subject to additional linear constraints. For example, we can optimize the likelihood if $z_{i,q}$ is a linear combination of a rank factor, a distance factor, and a quality factor. This is precisely what we will use next.

Second, note that in Equation (1), the first term is exactly the number of times a particular object was selected. The second term is exactly the *expected* number of times the object should be selected, given the current setting of the weights. This means that the optimum can be characterized by equations that state that the expected marginal over any variable should be equal to the observed marginal.

ALGORITHM. Given the above observations, we can optimize the function using a gradient ascent algorithm. Let δ_i be the discrepancy between the expected and the observed value (i.e., the value from (1). Then the gradient update is:

$$s_i^{\text{new}} = \eta \cdot e^{\delta_i} \cdot s_i^{\text{old}},$$

where η is the learning rate. This leads to a particularly simple algorithm: at every iteration, compute the discrepancy between the expected and the actual number of times each object was selected and use that to perform a multiplicative update on the weights. Renormalize the weights to keep the maximum weight at 1 and repeat until convergence.

4.1 Decomposing the scores

We have howed that it is easy to efficiently compute the best scores associated with each object via a simple multiplicative update algorithm, even when the variables are subject to linear constraints. We already know that the distance to the object, and its rank play a large role in the decision process.

We model these three as having multiplicative effects, i.e., for a user u considering an object i, the score s_i can be decomposed as $s_i = f_d(d(i,u)) \cdot f_r(r(i,u)) \cdot w_i$, where f_d is a function of the distance $d(i,u)$ between the user and the object, f_r is a function of the rank $r(i,u)$ of the object for the user, and w_i is the inherent wonderfulness.

Let $g_d(d(i,u)) = \log f_d(d(i,u)), g_r(r(i,u)) = \log f_r(r(i,u))$, and $y_i = \log w_i$. The likelihood maximization problem can be written as a concave program:

$$\text{Maximize: } \sum_{q \in Q} z_{r(q),u(q)} - \sum_{q \in Q} \log \left(\sum_{j \in C(q)} e^{z_{i,u(q)}} \right),$$

$$\text{subject to: } z_{i,u} = g_d(d(i,u)) + g_r(r(i,u)) + y_i \qquad \forall i, u.$$

We use the gradient ascent algorithm described below to solve this problem: We proceed in phases, with each phase consisting of three gradient ascent steps. In the first step, we only compute the gradient on the coordinates related to the function f_d, which governs the influence of the distance of the object to the user. Upon updating these coordinates, we then perform a gradient ascent step only on the coordinates related to f_r, which is responsible for the influence of the rank of the object; finally, in the third step, we update the intrinsic quality parameters referred to by w_i.

Note that this simple gradient ascent algorithm is not one of the polynomial-time algorithms for solving a concave maximization problem subject to linear constraints. In fact, it is not hard to see that if we write the objective as a function of the variables f_d, f_r, and w_i, this function is a concave function of individual variables, but it is not necessarily a concave function of the vector of all these variables. This means that the gradient ascent will converge to a local maximum, but not necessarily to a global maximum.

5. ANALYZING RESTAURANT CHOICE

We have now defined a geographic choice model that learns unknown functions of rank and distance, and optionally simultaneously learns a per-place wonderfulness score. We have shown how to learn this model, and how to use it for prediction. Model in hand, we now turn to an analysis of restaurant choice via driving directions in map search logs, using the data described in Section 2.

First, to get a good understanding of the effect of both rank and distance, we perform the gradient ascent in Section 4.1 while ignoring the wonderfulness parameter for each restaurant. We factor the score for a restaurant at distance d and rank r as:

$$s(d,r) = f_d(d) \cdot f_r(r).$$

In the context of restaurants, to estimate f_d and f_r, we discretize both distance (between 1km and 300km[4]) and rank (up to 10K) into

[4]Everything below 1km is folded into 1km and distances beyond 300km are thrown out.

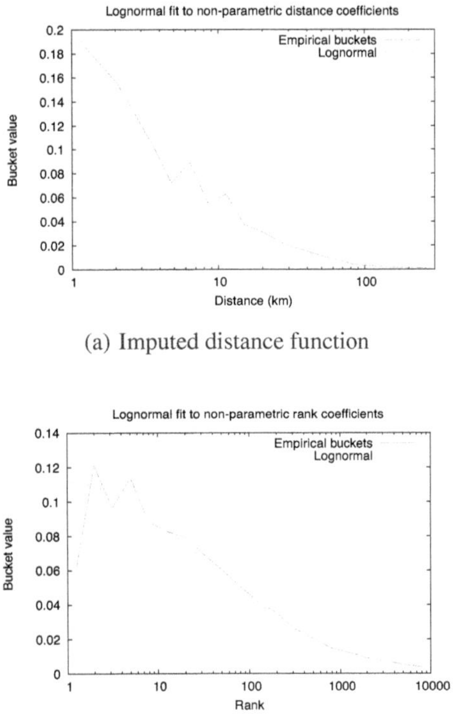

(a) Imputed distance function

(b) Imputed rank function

Figure 4: The maximum likelihood functions of impact of distance and rank on user's choice.

20 buckets each, binned on the log-scale. We can compute a non-parametric fit for f_r and f_d in the factored joint model by iteratively re-computing $f_r(r)$ and $f_d(d)$ for the 20 r values and 20 d values on a set of 100K training instances. We refer to the resulting f_d and f_r values as the *Non-Parametric Fit* (or *NPF*) coefficients, which are shown in red solid curves in Figures 4(a), 4(b) respectively.

The figures show that the distributions have a remarkably good fit to a lognormal distribution. Roughly speaking this shows three regimes that people face when deciding on a restaurant—for restaurants that lie in the head of the rank distribution (the closest half dozen establishments), there is little difference between the top few restaurants; for those that lie in the body (about top 250) there is a definite decline in probability as a function of the rank. For those in the tail, the decline is still prominent, but is much less significant. A similar explanation applies to the distance trade-off function: for the closest 20km or so, the score drops linearly with the log of the distance; however, the distance effect flattens out beyond the 20km driving range.

5.1 Comparing against baselines

Next, we examine how well these NPF coefficients (and their parametric fit) capture the data, in comparison to a number of baseline models. In what follows, all models were trained on the same set of 100K training instances as NPF, and the likelihood of each chosen destination was computed for a separate set of 100K test instances. We report the geometric means of these per-instance likelihoods for each model in Table 1.

The scoring function using the NPF coefficients provides the best performance in terms of yielding the highest likelihood over the test data. We then fit a parametric model to these NPF coefficients for $f_r(r)$ and $f_d(d)$ respectively. We experimented with both a lognormal form and a sigmoid form. While the performance is slightly worse than NPF, both yielded significant improvement over modeling rank (or distance) alone, with lognormal fit being the slightly better of the two.

Setting f_r and f_d to other forms can result in useful degenerate scoring functions. If both f_r and f_d are constants, then we get back a uniform scoring function, where each restaurant is equally likely. If we take f_r to be a constant c, then we get back a scoring function based on distance alone (i.e., a distance marginal). We estimate $\hat{f}_d$ as the ratio of the number of times d was chosen to the number of times d was an option. Similarly setting f_d to be a constant yields a rank marginal. While both are significantly better than the uniform baseline, rank marginal is much more effective.

At first glance, it might look like modeling rank alone explains unseen data better than modeling distance alone. However, there is a caveat for using the empirical distance marginal as f_d. While the rank marginal can be interpreted as the probability of observing *a* candidate restaurant at rank r being chosen, the distance marginal can only be interpreted as the probability of choosing restaurants whose distance is between d and $d + \Delta d$. That is, $P_d(d)$ needs to be shared among restaurants at distance d away (or between d and $d + \Delta d$ for a small Δd). And for larger d, $P_d(d)$ needs to be shared among more instances to yield the probability of going to *one* restaurant at distance d. If we have a function $n(d)$ that captures the number of restaurants at distance d, we could have set $f_d(d) = P_d(d)/n(d)$. By setting $f_d(d) = P_d(d)$, restaurants farther away are given more probability mass than they should.

Nonetheless, for both baselines using empirical marginal distributions, we did not (need to) bucket the data in the same coarse granularity as we did for NPF coefficient estimation. In that sense, NPF is a more parsimonious model, but it still outperforms all the baselines. Indeed, even the model using lognormal fits parameterized by only four parameters (two for f_r and two for f_d) outperforms the marginals. This validated our intuition that it is important to model the rank and distance jointly, and neither sufficiently captures geo-related aspects of restaurant choice.

5.2 Incorporating quality scores

In the above computation we did not include a parameter specific to each restaurant. We run the full optimization with per-restaurant wonderfulness scores. We restrict our attention to those restaurants in the Bay Area (those within 100km of Chez Panisse, Berkeley).

One should interpret the wonderfulness score as follows. Once rank and distance have been taken into account, wonderfulness captures the relative likelihood of a user to visit one place over another. For uniformly distributed users and places, this will exactly equal popularity, but in fact users and places are not uniformly distributed. As an example, consider Figure 5. This shows two popular restaurants: In-N-Out Burger (in Mountain View), and House of Prime Rib (in San Francisco). The figure shows the distances traveled to each. In-N-Out draws traffic from further afield, garnering more visits relative to rank and distance-based likelihood, and hence scores higher under wonderfulness.

To evaluate our approach, we compare the induced ordering of the restaurants to two different ratings: one set of well known critic ratings, which we denote by C, and a set of user-generated ratings U. As a baseline, we take a simple measure of popularity of a particular establishment, based on counts from our data. For each pair of ratings, we compute the Kendall's tau rank correlation; the results are shown in Table 2.

The orderings provided by W and P are highly correlated with each other, this is expected as the wonderfulness scores provide a residual popularity once the rank and distance effects are taken

Scoring function		Likelihood
NPF	Non-parametric factored model: red solid curves in Figures 4(a) and 4(b)	5.3
NPF-lognormal	Lognormal fit to NPF coefficients: green dotted curves in Figures 4(a) and 4(b)	5.1
NPF-sigmoid	Sigmoid fit to NPF coefficients	4.9
Rank only	$f_r(r)$ = rank marginal, $f_d(d) = \text{const}$	4.6
Distance only	$f_d(d)$ = distance marginal, $f_r(r) = \text{const}$	3.9
Uniform	Each restaurant equally likely: $s(r, d) = \text{const}$	1.1

Table 1: Likelihood (in 10^{-4}) of different estimation procedures.

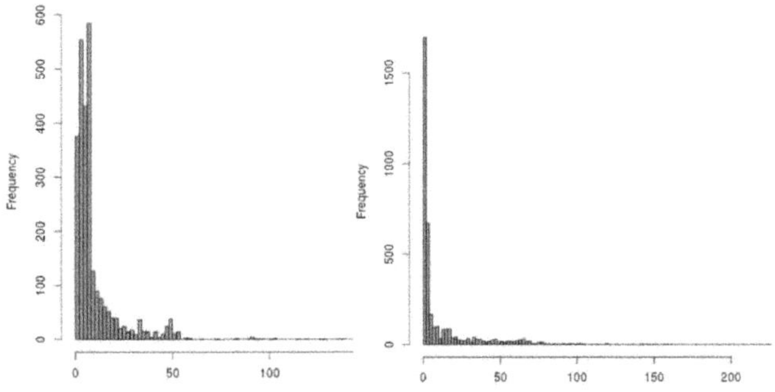

(a) In-N-Out Burger (b) House of Prime Rib

Figure 5: Distribution of distance traveled (km). Note that In-N-Out Burger will have a higher wonderfulness score since it draws a large fraction of its visits from further away.

	P	C	U
W	0.86	0.14	0.16
P	-	0.12	0.06

Table 2: Kendall tau rank correlation between rankings induced by different restaurant rating systems.

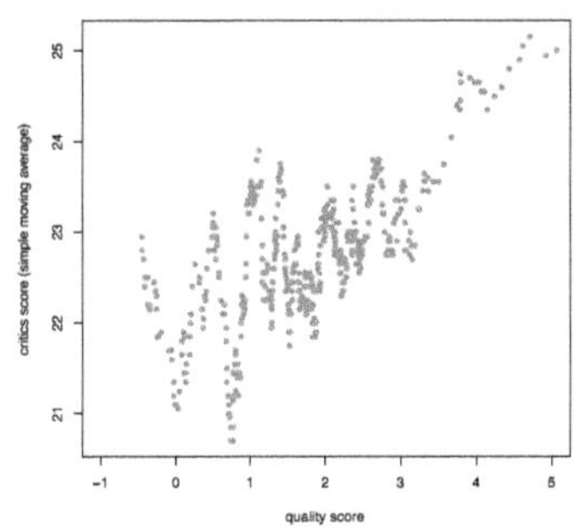

Figure 6: Scatter plot of wonderfulness versus critic score.

into consideration. In that sense W provides a refinement to P. As the correlations with U and C show this refinement significantly improves the observed correlation and wonderfulness is a better estimate of user generated scores. The result is significant with $p < 0.05$.

Figure 6 shows a scatter plot of wonderfulness versus the critic score. Kendall's tau is unforgiving, but the scatter plot shows that the score does correlate with the critics.

While it is encouraging that wonderfulness shows good correlation with both critics and users, our actual goal in introducing the measure is to improve likelihood, as this represents a baseline model for personalization and other extensions. For our Bay Area dataset, we recomputed likelihood scores of restaurant choice using our most effective model of rank and distance. We also measured the improvement in likelihood by incorporating wonderfulness scores. Recall that our empirical measurement of the rank and distance univariates require 40 parameters to fit, and are well-approximated by the four-parameter lognormal fit. Wonderfulness, on the other hand, incorporates a parameter for each restaurant, so we would expect higher likelihood. The result shows that incorporating these scores further improves the likelihood by a multiplicative factor of 1.87.

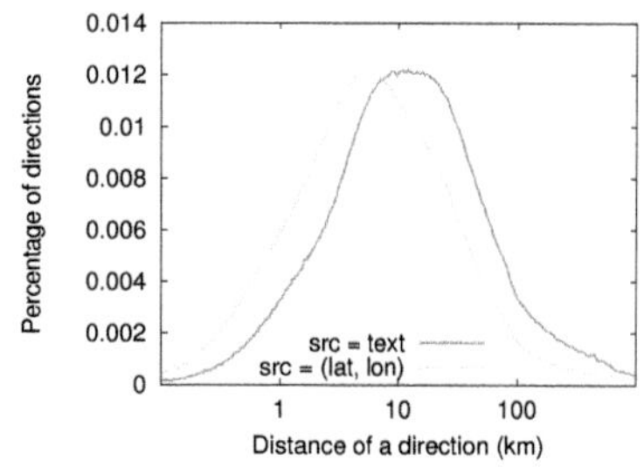

Figure 7: Distribution of individual-direction distances; $\log_{10}(\text{distance})$ is bucketed in units of 0.02.

5.3 Other trends

Before switching to a theoretical discussion of the lognormal forms we have observed for rank and distance, we close our empirical analysis with a brief exploration of the spatial, temporal, and quality trends in restaurant choice. For the analysis, in addition to `src = text`, we used a sample of the driving distances for `src = (lat, lon)` directions but with `src` information removed.

Spatial trends: 12km to food. Figure 7 shows the distribution of direction queries at varying distances plotted on a log scale. Similar to previous works on human mobility, we observe that as the distance goes up, the fraction goes down. For `src = text`, we observe that the median distance is 12km. The empirical observation over distances is symmetric along this point: the fraction of directions with distance between $(1.2, 12)$ is 42.9%, and the fraction of directions with distance between $(12, 120)$ is 42.3%. One may argue that this distribution is underestimating the actual foot traffic at smaller distances—clearly one does not need to look up for directions for a trip to the main cafe at work. More generally, our dataset may under-represent "neighborhood" traffic where people already knew how to reach a nearby venue. Nevertheless, 50% of the directions are trying to reach a destination within a small radius of 12km. For `src = (lat, lon)`, we observe higher fraction of traffic at shorter distances as expected—refreshing directions en route alone would have caused the distance distribution for `src = (lat, lon)` to shift to the left.

Temporal trends: TGIF. Figure 8(a) plots the median distance traveled on each day (relative to Monday), which clearly peaks

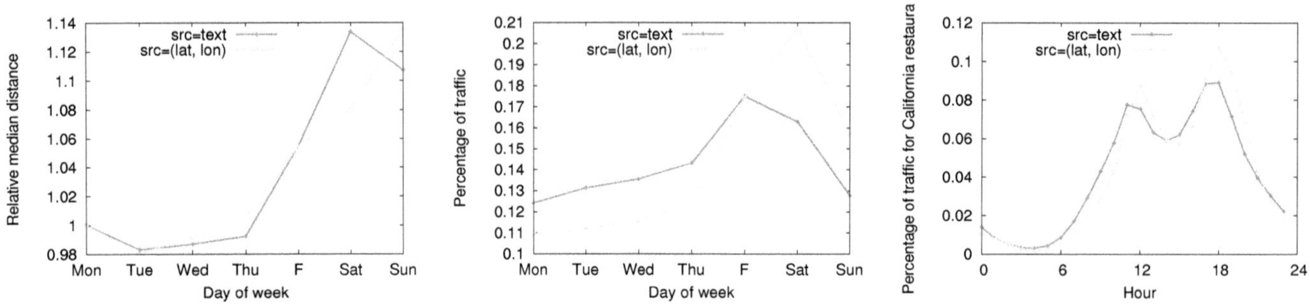

(a) Average weekly distance. (b) Average weekly direction queries. (c) Hourly direction queries to California restaurants.

Figure 8: Temporal trends.

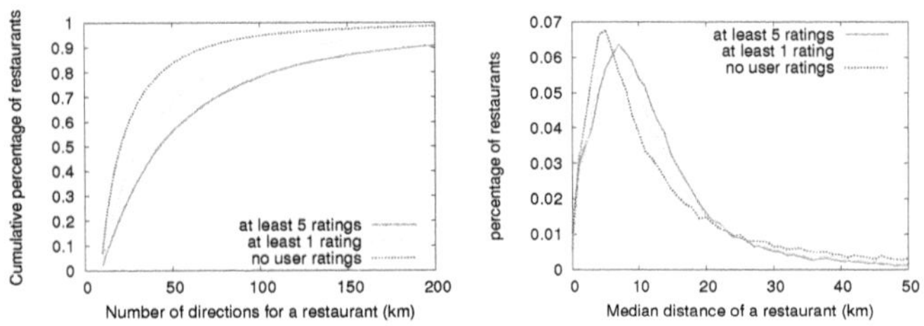

(a) #ratings vs. #directions (b) #ratings vs. median distance

Figure 9: Quality trends.

during the weekend for both `src = text` and `src = (lat, lon)`. Figure 8(b) plots the fraction of direction queries associated with different days of the week. We observe that `src = text` directions peak on Fridays, while `src = (lat, lon)` directions peak on Saturdays. One hypothesis is people are more likely to go to unfamiliar and farther away places during the weekends, for which direction queries en route are sometimes inevitable.

Lastly, we plot the hourly trend of direction queries in Figure 8(c). To avoid any complication due to timezones, we restricted to directions ending in a California restaurant. There is clearly a lunch peak and a dinner peak. Compared to the `src = text` directions, the distribution of `src = (lat, lon)` direction traffic is slightly right-shifted, reflecting a more real-time direction need.

Quality trends: Star value. We examine the relationship between a restaurant's popularity measure and the number of directions it gets as well as the median distance users are willing to drive. To this end, we aggregate `src = text` directions by their destinations and pick restaurant with at least 10 directions. We then obtain the number of user ratings associated with each restaurant (from a popular online rating service), and group the restaurants into those with no ratings at all, and those with at least one rating. We also extract a subset of the second group as restaurants with at least five ratings. Figure 9(a) plots the cumulative fraction of restaurants with different number of directions. If a restaurant has no user ratings, then it is more likely to have fewer number of directions directed at it. And a restaurant with more user ratings is more likely to receive more directions. More interestingly, as we can see from Figure 9(b), a restaurant with more ratings is also more likely to have a higher median distance than one with fewer or no ratings. In other words, restaurants with (more) ratings are more likely to attract people from further away.

6. RATIONALE FOR LOGNORMALS

There are a few instances of lognormally-decaying functions of distance in the literature. A notable example is the log-distance path loss model for radio signal strength as a function of distance [27]; this process however applies to the distribution of signal strength at fixed distance from the transmitter, which is not applicable to our situation. On the other hand, lifetime distributions of biotic (longevity analysis) and abiotic (failure analysis) entities are frequently modeled by lognormal distributions ever since the classical work of [17]. According to these models, under *multiplicative degradation* a set of small multiplicative shocks apply over the evolution of the process, which results in a lognormal distribution of total degradation at fixed time t, and also a lognormal distribution of time to failure.

We may however speculate another root cause for the lognormal shape of the hidden rank and distance functions that our model learns. We had shown that the density is non-uniform and complex. For the sake of modeling, however, let us make a weaker assumption: the number of candidates at distance d for most individual instances of choice is reasonably approximated by some polynomial of d. For uniform density, this polynomial would be a quadratic, but we will allow any polynomial. Say object i will occur at some polynomial distance $\alpha(i)$, and will hence attain score

$$f_r(i) \cdot f_d(\alpha(i)) = \frac{1}{i\alpha(i)2\pi\sigma_d\sigma_r} e^{-\frac{(\ln i-\mu_r)^2}{2\sigma_i^2}-\frac{(\ln \alpha(i)-\mu_d)^2}{2\sigma_d^2}}.$$

This function follows the general form of a lognormal in rank, as do the resulting likelihoods, as the normalizing constant is the same for all candidates. We may therefore ask why a lognormal distribution is a natural function. A possible explanation comes from work of [13] and [33], who introduce an explanation based on entropy maximization. In our domain, the explanation proceeds as follows.

First, we argue that a user selecting an object incurs two costs. First, there is a *consideration cost*: the amount of time spent deliberating about where to go. We again make a simplifying assumption that users begin by considering closer places, and then only later consider more distant alternatives. Assuming a constant cost of consideration for each object, this results in cost linear in i to consider the first i places. Second, the user incurs a *travel cost*, which is proportional to the distance.

The next step of the derivation is to appeal to a well-studied law in human behavior: the *Weber–Fechner law*, which states that for a broad range of external stimuli, human perception of the intensity of the stimulus is proportional to the logarithm of the intensity [21, 23]. The law has been observed broadly to hold for human perception of time. Thus, assuming that a user examines candidate places until finding an acceptable one, the number of distinguishable buckets of places in terms of travel and consideration time grows as $(\log r)(\log d)$, which is proportional to $\log^2 r$ according to our simplifying assumption.

Assuming the user has some upper bound on how much cost they are willing to incur in choosing an object, we may now ask for the maximum entropy distribution under this cost function. By an application of Lagrange multipliers, the resulting distribution is seen to be lognormal in distance or rank. Indeed, the problem is to

$$\text{Maximize: } \sum_i p(i) \log p(i),$$
$$\text{subject to: } \sum_i p(i) \log^2 i \leq B.$$

The resulting Lagrangian is

$$\sum_i p(i) \log p(i) + \lambda \left(\sum_i p(i) \log^2 i - B \right).$$

Taking derivatives gives

$$\log p(i) = -1 - \lambda \log^2 i,$$

which yields our lognormal:

$$p(i) \propto \exp\left(-\lambda \log^2 i\right).$$

To summarize, we began this work plotting likelihood to choose a place as a function of rank, and separately of distance. These marginal distributions showed particular forms that were not well approximated by lognormal functions. We then applied our choice model in order to factor likelihood of choice into a product of unknown functions of rank and distance. To our surprise, even though the marginals have different forms, both unknown functions are well-approximated by lognormals. In this section we have shown that under two mild assumptions, these forms are in fact predicted by an entropy maximization framework. This suggests that the surprisingly good fits we saw in Figures 4(a), 4(b) are no coincidence, but capture an underlying process with a formal justification.

7. OTHER RELATED WORK

We already discussed the past work on geographic choice in Section 1. Other related work includes the work on human mobility patterns, rank-based models, geographic data mining, and mining directions in map search logs.

Human mobility patterns have been studied for decades; we list a few recent ones. Brockmann et al. [2] study the circulation of bank notes in the United States and found that the distribution of travel distances follows a power law; they conclude that human travel is a Lévy flight (see also [28]). In contrast, by tracking the location of mobile phone users, Gonzalez et al. [12] argue that human movements exhibit high degree of spatial and temporal regularity. The gravity model has been a popular model for explaining migration patterns; see the work of Simini et al. [32] and Jung et al. [15], the book [10], and the survey on urban trip distribution [8]. Levy [18] studies the migration patterns of humans and uses that to explain the gravitational law of social interaction. Social ties have also been used to explain human movements [4]. Taplin and Qiu [35] model the tourist attractions in Australia using population, travel times, and traffic. All these works deal with studying and modeling human travel patterns. Our work, on the other hand, is focused on directions with distances at finer granularities. In addition, rather than conflating different types of human mobilities, we pick a particular and important type of human travel: to restaurants.[5]

Rank-based models have been rediscovered several times in the past. They have been proposed as a better alternative to distance-based models since they can handle regions of varying densities in a mathematically clean manner. The related notion of intervening opportunities was first proposed by [34]: "the number of persons going a given distance is directly proportional to the number of opportunities at that distance and inversely proportional to the number of intervening opportunities." It has subsequently been studied in various settings [11, 14, 22, 37]. Liben-Nowell et al. [19] use rank-based friendships to explain the small-world phenomenon in social networks. Using FourSquare checkin data, Noulas et al. [24] propose a rank-based model for explaining urban mobility. They argue that rank-distance is a much better measure than physical distance, when it comes to mobility. Our work also considers rank as an alternative measure to distance. However, our findings are far more intricate: in a geographic choice context, we argue that neither suffices by itself.

The use of geographic information in various search and data mining tasks has been a hot area of research. Backstrom et al. [1] and Crandall et al. [6] study the role of IP-based geography in queries and geotagged images. Using geographic information in tweets has also been explored in a variety of topics including linguistics, entity matching, and geolocation [9, 25, 7, 29, 5, 31]. Data mining of GPS is also a well-studied topic. Cao et al. [3] consider mining significant semantic locations from GPS data and Zheng et al. [40] use GPS data for location-based recommendation; see also [41, 26, 30, 39]. Our work does not rely on IP/tag/GPS geolocation but uses the online direction queries as a powerful intent for physical visits: a user issuing a direction query to a place is more likely to visit the place than a user merely searching for the place. Furthermore, GPS data applies to a lot of locations from a few number of users, whereas direction queries correspond to a much broader range of users.

To the best of our knowledge, there has been very little work on studying directions in map query logs. Venetis et al. [36] use map queries to determine the importance of places of interest; their work is more on the efficient indexing of direction queries and a ranking methodology based on it. Xiao et al. [38] study map search logs, but their analysis is mainly focused on its general statistical properties rather than on directions. However, they also find that restaurant is the most popular map query category.

8. CONCLUSIONS

In this work we studied the dynamics of geographic choice. We analyzed the role of the geometric distance to an object as well as the rank-distance and found intricate connections between the two notions. We used these insights to propose a model of user behavior that captures the effects of rank, distance, and quality. We applied this model to study the properties of direction queries to restaurants on Google maps. Our work opens up an array of future research directions, e.g., using these insights to improve the recommendation and studying mobility patterns via direction queries as a proxy for non-routine adventure-seeking human behavior.

Acknowledgments

We thank Bill Heavlin, Gueorgi Kossinets, Daryl Pregibon, and the Google Maps team for their help.

[5]Directions to restaurants forms the largest category among all direction queries; see [38].

9. REFERENCES

[1] L. Backstrom, J. M. Kleinberg, R. Kumar, and J. Novak. Spatial variation in search engine queries. In *WWW*, pages 357–366, 2008.

[2] D. Brockmann, L. Hufnagel, and T. Geisel. The scaling laws of human travel. *Nature*, 439(7075):462–465, 2006.

[3] X. Cao, G. Cong, and C. Jensen. Mining significant semantic locations from GPS data. *VLDB*, 3(1-2):1009–1020, 2010.

[4] E. Cho, S. Myers, and J. Leskovec. Friendship and mobility: User movement in location-based social networks. In *KDD*, pages 1082–1090, 2011.

[5] D. J. Crandall, L. Backstrom, D. Cosley, S. Suri, D. Huttenlocher, and J. Kleinberg. Inferring social ties from geographic coincidences. *PNAS*, 107(52):22436–22441, 2010.

[6] D. J. Crandall, L. Backstrom, D. P. Huttenlocher, and J. M. Kleinberg. Mapping the world's photos. In *WWW*, pages 761–770, 2009.

[7] N. Dalvi, R. Kumar, and B. Pang. Object matching in tweets with spatial models. In *WSDM*, pages 43–52, 2012.

[8] S. Easa. Urban trip distribution in practice. I: Conventional analysis. *Journal of Transportation Engineering*, 119(6):793–815, 1993.

[9] J. Eisenstein, B. O'Connor, N. A. Smith, and E. P. Xing. A latent variable model for geographic lexical variation. In *EMNLP*, pages 1277–1287, 2010.

[10] S. Erlander and N. Stewart. *The Gravity Model in Transportation Analysis: Theory and Extensions*. CRC Press, 1990.

[11] R. Freymeyer and P. Ritchey. Spatial distribution of opportunities and magnitude of migration: An investigation of Stouffer's theory. *Sociological Perspectives*, pages 419–440, 1985.

[12] M. Gonzalez, C. Hidalgo, and A. Barabasi. Understanding individual human mobility patterns. *Nature*, 453(7196):779–782, 2008.

[13] K. C. Gros and D. G. Markovic. Neuropsychological constraints to human data production on a global scale. *Eur Phys J B*, 85(28), 2012.

[14] K. Haynes, D. Poston, and P. Schnirring. Intermetropolitan migration in high and low opportunity areas: Indirect tests of the distance and intervening opportunities hypotheses. *Economic Geography*, 49(1):68–73, 1973.

[15] W. Jung, F. Wang, and H. Stanley. Gravity model in the Korean highway. *Europhysics Letters*, 81(4):48005, 2008.

[16] D. Koller and N. Friedman. *Probabilistic Graphical Models: Principles and Techniques*. MIT Press, 2009.

[17] A. Kolmogorov. On a logarithmic normal distribution law of the dimensions of particles under pulverization. *Dokl. Akad Nauk*, 31(2):99–101, 1941.

[18] M. Levy. Scale-free human migration and the geography of social networks. *Physica A: Statistical Mechanics and its Applications*, 389(21):4913–4917, 2010.

[19] D. Liben-Nowell, J. Novak, R. Kumar, P. Raghavan, and A. Tomkins. Geographic routing in social networks. *PNAS*, 102(33):11623–11628, 2005.

[20] R. D. Luce. *Individual Choice Behavior: A Theoretical Analysis*. Wiley, 1959.

[21] S. Masin, V. Zudini, and M. Antonelli. Early alternative derivations of Fechner's law. *J. History of the Behavioral Sciences*, 45:56–65, 2009.

[22] E. Miller. A note on the role of distance in migration: Costs of mobility versus intervening opportunities. *Journal of Regional Science*, 12(3):475–478, 1972.

[23] R. S. Moyer and T. K. Landauer. Time required for judgements of numerical inequality. *Nature*, 215(5109):1519–1520, 1967.

[24] A. Noulas, S. Scellato, R. Lambiotte, M. Pontil, and C. Mascolo. A tale of many cities: Universal patterns in human urban mobility. *PLoS ONE*, 7(5):e37027, 05 2012.

[25] B. O'Connor, J. Eisenstein, E. P. Xing, and N. A. Smith. Discovering demographic language variation. In *Workshop on Machine Learning for Social Computing at NIPS*, 2010.

[26] D. Quercia, N. Lathia, F. Calabrese, G. Di Lorenzo, and J. Crowcroft. Recommending social events from mobile phone location data. In *ICDM*, pages 971–976, 2010.

[27] T. Rappaport. *Wireless Communications: Principles and Practice*. Prentice Hall PTR, 2nd edition, 2001.

[28] I. Rhee, M. Shin, S. Hong, K. Lee, S. Kim, and S. Chong. On the Lévy-walk nature of human mobility. *IEEE/ACM Transactions on Networking*, 19(3):630–643, 2011.

[29] A. Sadilek, H. Kautz, and J. Bigham. Finding your friends and following them to where you are. In *WSDM*, pages 723–732, 2012.

[30] S. Scellato, C. Mascolo, M. Musolesi, and J. Crowcroft. Track globally, deliver locally: Improving content delivery networks by tracking geographic social cascades. In *WWW*, pages 457–466, 2011.

[31] S. Scellato, A. Noulas, R. Lambiotte, and C. Mascolo. Socio-spatial properties of online location-based social networks. In *ICWSM*, pages 329–336, 2011.

[32] F. Simini, M. González, A. Maritan, and A. Barabási. A universal model for mobility and migration patterns. *Nature*, 484(7392):96–100, 2012.

[33] P. Sobkowicz, M. Thelwall, K. Buckley, G. Paltoglou, and A. Sobkowicz. Lognormal distributions of user post lengths in Internet discussions - a consequence of the Weber–Fechner law? *EPJ Data Science*, 2(2), 2013.

[34] S. Stouffer. Intervening opportunities: A theory relating mobility and distance. *American Sociological Review*, pages 845–867, 1940.

[35] J. Taplin and M. Qiu. Car trip attraction and route choice in Australia. *Annals of Tourism Research*, 24(3):624–637, 1997.

[36] P. Venetis, H. Gonzalez, C. Jensen, and A. Halevy. Hyper-local, directions-based ranking of places. *VLDB*, 4(5):290–301, 2011.

[37] W. Wadycki. Stouffer's model of migration: A comparison of interstate and metropolitan flows. *Demography*, 12(1):121–128, 1975.

[38] X. Xiao, Q. Luo, Z. Li, X. Xie, and W.-Y. Ma. A large-scale study on map search logs. *TWEB*, 4(3), 2010.

[39] M. Ye, P. Yin, W. Lee, and D. Lee. Exploiting geographical influence for collaborative point-of-interest recommendation. In *SIGIR*, pages 325–334, 2011.

[40] V. W. Zheng, Y. Zheng, X. Xie, and Q. Yang. Collaborative location and activity recommendations with GPS history data. In *WWW*, pages 1029–1038, 2010.

[41] Y. Zheng, L. Zhang, X. Xie, and W.-Y. Ma. Mining interesting locations and travel sequences from GPS trajectories. In *WWW*, pages 791–800, 2009.

Hiring Behavior Models for Online Labor Markets

Marios Kokkodis
NYU Stern
mkokkodi@stern.nyu.edu

Panagiotis Papadimitriou
Elance-oDesk
papadimitriou@elance-odesk.com

Panagiotis G. Ipeirotis
NYU Stern
panos@stern.nyu.edu

ABSTRACT

In an online labor marketplace employers post jobs, receive freelancer applications and make hiring decisions. These hiring decisions are based on the freelancer's observed (*e.g.* education) and latent (*e.g.* ability) characteristics. Because of the heterogeneity that appears in the observed characteristics, and the existence of latent ones, identifying and hiring the best possible applicant is a very challenging task. In this work we study and model the employer's hiring behavior. We assume that employers are utility maximizers and make rational decisions by hiring the best possible applicant at hand. Based on this premise, we propose a series of probabilistic models that estimate the hiring probability of each applicant. We train and test our models on more than 600,000 job applications obtained by oDesk.com, and we show evidence that the proposed models outperform currently in-use baselines. To get further insights, we conduct an econometric analysis and observe that the attributes that are strongly correlated with the hiring probability are whether or not the freelancer and the employer have previously worked together, the available information on the freelancer's profile, the countries of the employer and the freelancer and the skillset of the freelancer. Finally, we find that the faster a freelancer applies to an opening, the higher is the probability to get the job.

1. INTRODUCTION

Online labor marketplaces (OLMs) such as oDesk.com, and Freelancer.com allow employers to connect with freelancers around the globe to accomplish diverse tasks including web development, writing and translation, accounting, etc. These marketplaces are growing fast and the freelancer annual earnings are expected to grow from $1 billion in 2012 to $10 billion by 2020 [2].

Although such platforms have provided the employers with a solution to the scarcity of local talent, they have not really changed the process that employers have to go through to source the ideal candidates for their tasks: an employer needs initially to describe the job opening requirements to which freelancers that are looking for opportunities can apply. Then, the employer has to (1) review all applicants by looking at their online profile information and/or by personally interviewing them, and (2) come up with a hiring decision.

To evaluate an applicant, the employer has to assess both observed and latent characteristics. The observed characteristics usually include a list of skills, the educational background, the work history and the certifications or tests that the applicant has taken. The latent characteristics include the freelancer's quality and true ability on his listed qualifications. The existence of latent characteristics, the heterogeneity that appears in the observed ones as well as the interactions between the two make the matching process a very challenging task; Hiring decisions are based on manually shaped expectations of complicated similarities between job openings, employers and freelancers. These expectations usually come with high uncertainties, since performing a task is an "experience good" [37]: for both the freelancer and the employer, it is practically infeasible to know the outcome of their collaboration in advance.

To minimize the level of uncertainty, most of the online labor marketplaces have developed reputation systems. Freelancers get rated for the tasks they accomplish and these ratings become part of their online resumes. Employers can then get a better picture of the freelancers' past performance and make better informed hiring decisions. However, in online labor markets, as well as in most of the online markets in general, reputation scores are very skewed towards high ratings (J-shape distributions, see Hu *et al.* [22]), and as a result they become almost uninformative. Since reputation systems fail to provide insightful information about the freelancers' quality, how do employers make hiring decisions? What are the characteristics that value the most?

In this work we focus on answering these questions. We propose a series of increasing complexity predictive models that describe employers' hiring decisions. We start our analysis by assuming that employers are rational utility maximizers; Their utility is straightforwardly maximized along with the probability of selecting the best possible applicant for each specific opening. Based on this assumption, we first propose a ranking aggregator that ranks candidates in all the available dimensions and then aggregates these ranks to create a global ranking. Next, we draw on empirical economics and propose a Logit model [46] and finally, we built a probabilistic graphical model (Bayesian network). We compare our models with the vanilla reputation score baseline, where each employer ranks the available applicants based on their previously collected feedback score.

We train and test all proposed approaches on a unique dataset of *real* transactional oDesk data. In particular, this

WSDM'15, February 2–6, 2015, Shanghai, China.
Copyright 2015 ACM 978-1-4503-3317-7/15/02 ...$15.00.
http://dx.doi.org/10.1145/2684822.2685299 .

dataset consists of *more than 600,000 job applications* on *more than 50,000 openings* related to four different task categories. We use different evaluation metrics and show evidence that our models significantly outperform the vanilla reputation baseline. Next, we perform an econometric analysis and observe that the attributes that are strongly correlated with the hiring probability are whether or not the freelancer and the employer have previously worked together, the available information on the freelancer's profile, the countries of the employer and the freelancer and the skillset of the contractor. Finally, our analysis shows that the faster the freelancer applies to an opening, the higher is the probability to get hired.

Our work is the first to study the association of different characteristics with hiring decisions by incorporating a massive amount of observational data. We believe that understanding how hiring decisions are made is beneficial for both the employers and the contractors, and *critical* for the marketplace. In particular, by developing approaches that estimate the applicants' hiring probabilities: (1) employers will be able to make better-informed and faster decisions based on the suggested applicants' rankings, (2) freelancers will save time by not applying to openings that have very low hiring probability and (3) the marketplace might identify weaknesses in freelancers' profiles (*e.g.* skills not reported, the profile description is not sufficient *etc.*) and suggest targeted profile improvements based on how each profile characteristic affect hiring decisions. As a result, our proposed approaches will minimize the friction in the marketplace[1] and increase both the marketplace's transaction volume as well as the overall satisfaction of the freelancers and the employers.

2. BACKGROUND

In this section, we provide background information regarding online labor markets as well as research that dealt with hiring decisions in offline workplaces. We further briefly discuss the key differences between our scenario, and the "learning to rank" framework which is usually found in information retrieval (IR) problems. Finally, we position our study and argue about its uniqueness.

2.1 Online labor markets

Current research in Online Labor Markets (*OLMs*) spans across a variety of problems. A stream of work focuses on the validity of behavioral experiments in these markets and in particular on Amazon Mechanical Turk [3,20,42]. The general consensus of these studies is that online experiments appear to be as valid (both internally and externally) as laboratory field experiments. A different group of studies focuses on incentivizing freelancers as well as finding ways to manage the quality of their outcomes [10,19,24,25,36,44,45]. These studies propose and evaluate a set of social and financial incentives and they further provide sophisticated techniques that assure a certain level of outcome quality. Finally, Kokkodis and Ipeirotis focused on how past reputation transfers to new tasks [29], and they further quantified the value of skills in *OLMs* [30].

2.2 Hiring Decisions

Previous studies dealt with several dimensions of the matching problem in offline markets. Lindeboom et. al [33] studied the effectiveness of search and recruitment channels. Audra J. Bowlus [6] focused on the extent to which the level of job mismatching varies over the business cycle and how it is dealt with by the labor market. Finally Yael S. Hadass [18] studied the impact of the spread of online recruiting on the matching of freelancers and firms.

On a different direction, a lot of work has focused on gender and attractevness biases in hiring decisions [11,12,16,16, 28,34,38]. The overall consensus of all of these studies is that gender and attractiveness have a strong effect on hiring decisions, but the type of the effect depends on the environment, the position, and the employer.

A lot of work has focused on other characteristics that affect hiring decisions. In particular, Forsythe *et al.* [14] found that female applicants' clothing is an avenue for influencing the selection decision for management positions. Rasa and Carpenter [43] found that the influence of demographics is modest and less important than other variables, such as the applicant's skills and qualifications. Hu [21] found that large firms hire younger applicants than small firms Yakubovich [52] found that a freelancer is more likely to get a job through a weak tie rather than a strong one. Recently Acquisti and Fong [1] found (1) that only a minority of US firms likely search online for candidates' information and (2) evidence of discrimination linked to political party affiliation. Finally, A. Pallais [39] studied the cold-start problem (i.e. hiring inexperienced freelancers) in *OLMs* and showed that both hiring freelancers and providing more detailed evaluations substantially improves freelancers' subsequent employment outcomes.

2.3 Learning to rank

Our problem has conceptual similarities with the "learning to rank" problem (*i.e.* the construction of ranking models), commonly found in information retrieval [47]. State of the art ranking approaches mainly use either a pairwise approach, which reduces ranking to classification on document pairs w.r.t. the same query (see [8,15,27,41,54]) or a listwise approach, which performs learning directly on document list by optimizing either some information retrieval evaluation measures or by minimizing listwise loss functions (see [9,49–51,53]).

We argue that the hiring problem we study has a strong peculiarity that doesn't allow for as-is adaptation of learning-to-rank algorithms: We lack multiple ranks: in our scenario, there is no ground truth in terms of which applicant is better than other. We only observe whether or not an applicant got hired; the rest of the applicants are then getting assigned with the same rank.

The hiring decision problem we study is very close to the "product search problem" [32]. One main difference is that job openings usually have completely independent groups of applicants with each other, while the pool of a certain product alternatives is usually the same. In their work, Li *et al.* propose a Logit model for homogenous consumers (an approach we adapt in this work as well), and a BLP model [4] for heterogeneous consumers. To train the BLP model, they use product-specific data from multiple markets, which is practically impossible to do in our case (*i.e.* acquire employers/contractors data from multiple *OLMs*).

Our work is the first one to study how a series of characteristics of both the employer and the freelancer collectively affect hiring decisions. The emergence of *OLMs* allow us for the first time to perform such a study in a large scale (hundreds of thousands of applications, tens of thousands of hiring decisions, multiple task categories). The premise of *OLMs* (remote freelancers, zero face-to-face interaction) sug-

[1]See also Brynjolfsson and Smith [7]

gests that gender/attractiveness biases should have a small (if any) effect in hiring decisions. Hence in this study we focus on features such as the freelancer's skills, reputation, education, certifications, demographics, pay rate, *etc.* We discuss these characteristics next.

3. FEATURES IN HIRING DECISIONS

In this section we describe the set of characteristics that (we believe) affect hiring decisions in *OLMs*. This set includes straightforward features (*e.g.* accumulated reputation score) as well as derived features (*e.g.* a combination of the employer's and the freelancer's countries).

3.1 Freelancer Characteristics

The first cluster of straightforward attributes we believe have an effect on employers' hiring decisions appear on the freelancer's profile; In particular we consider the average feedback score of the freelancer (*feedback*), the time of the application (*i.e.* whether the applicant applies first, second *etc.*) (*time*), the total hours that the freelancer has worked on the oDesk platform (*hours*), the number of jobs that the freelancer has completed (*jobs*), the hourly billing (mentioned on the freelancer's profile (*bill*)) and bidding (*bid*) pay rate of the freelancer, the number of tests that the freelancer has completed in the past (*tests*), the freelancer's years of experience (self-reported) (*exp*), and the freelancer's education (*edu*). We further consider a binary variable that controls whether the freelancer just joined the marketplace (*new*).

As we discussed in the introduction, hiring decisions come with high uncertainty: it is practically impossible for the employer to know beforehand the performance of a freelancer. Reputation systems usually minimize this uncertainty since they provide some information about the past performance of freelancers. As a result, it is rational to assume that employers, who have limited practical knowledge of the skills and abilities of a remote freelancer, often consult these reputation systems to better understand whether a freelancer is qualified and suitable for the task at hand.

Two other signals that contributes towards minimizing this uncertainty (and as a result we expect to have an effect on hiring decisions) is the freelancer's number of completed jobs and hours worked in the marketplace. In online marketplaces, users that receive low feedback scores usually abandon, and they either create new accounts and re-join or find an alternative marketplace to use (see Jerath *et al.* [26]). As a result, users that accumulate long history on the marketplace are ceteris paribus more trustful than users with no hirstory.

The hourly billing and pay rates of the freelancer also signal the unobserved quality of the freelancer. Intuitively, on average, a freelancer that gets paid more to complete a certain task is better than a freelancer with a lower pay rate for the same task. Similar arguments also apply for the freelancer's education[2], the number of tests that the freelancer has taken[3] as well as the freelancer's self-reported years of experience on similar tasks.

Finally, since new freelancers always join the marketplace, and because we don't want to "unfairly" penalize them for their zero values in "feedback","hours" and "jobs", we include a binary variable to control for the fact that these contractors are "new" to the marketplace.

[2]We consider five levels of education: High school, Diploma, Bachelor, Masters and PhD

[3]*OLMs* make available a list of certification tests to their users. For example, oDesk.com provides the following set of tests https://www.odesk.com/tests

Rank	Employer's Country	Freelancer's country	PMI
TOP	Nicaragua	Nicaragua	4.95
	Mexico	Sierra Leone	4.79
	Moldova	Argentina	4.66
	South Korea	South Korea	4.66
	Puerto Rico	Panama	4.14
BOTTOM	United Kingdom	India	-1.74
	Australia	India	-1.74
	United States	Bangladesh	-1.82
	United States	Pakistan	-1.85
	United States	India	-2.13

Table 1: Combination of countries that have high PMI.

3.2 Freelancer - Employer characteristics

So far we analyzed characteristics that are straightforwardly extracted from the online profile of the freelancer. Next, we describe how combined information from the freelancer's and the employer's profile might affect hiring decisions.

First, we believe that the combination of freelancer's and employer's locations has an effect on the hiring probability; For example, an employer from the United States might have a strong positive prior for freelancers from the United States, and as a result a strong hiring preference for such freelancers. To quantify and study the effect of location on hiring decisions we use the Point-wise Mutual Information (PMI) of the two countries (see Bouma [5]). PMI is a measure of how much the actual probability of a particular co-occurance of two events (in our case the freelancer's country c_w and the employer's country c_e) differs from what we would expect to see if the two events were independent. Formally:

$$PMI(c_w, c_e) = \log \frac{\Pr(c_w, c_e)}{\Pr(c_w)\Pr(c_e)} \quad (1)$$

PMI takes positive and negative values, it is zero if the two events are independent, and it maximizes when the two events are perfectly associated. To estimate the necessary probabilities we use our training sets (see section 5.1). Some of the combinations that have very high and very low PMI values are shown in Table 1. It's interesting to notice the separation between rare events (for example employers from Nicaragua) and very frequent ones (for example employers from U.S.A. and freelancers from India). In line with intuition, co-location of the freelancer and the employer also appears to have a high PMI score (for instance Korea - Korea and Nicaragua - Nicaragua).

Next, we believe that whether or not the freelancer has previously worked with the same employer (potential re-hire) must have an effect on hiring decisions. Intuitively on average, a freelancer who wants to work again with the same employer must have had an overall successful experience with that employer.

3.3 Freelancer - Opening characteristics

The last set of features we consider originate in the interaction of the freelancer and the opening at hand. Based on the belief that the set of applicant's skills in combination with the set of required skills of the specific job opening must have a strong effect on hiring decisions, we compute the inner product of the two. Intuitively, the higher the in-

	Applicant	jobs	feedback
Opening 1	Anna	3	5
	Michael	4	5
Opening 2	George	1	3
	Mary	1	3

Table 2: Opening-dependent hiring decisions.

ner product the higher is the compatibility of the applicant for the task at hand. Similarly, we further estimate the inner product between the required skills of the opening and the certifications that a freelancer has (exams). For example, let's assume that a freelancer has only one certification in Java, and that the opening requires Java and SQL. Then the inner product of this freelancer and the opening will be 1. The intuition is the same as before.

Finally, we include the percentage of shared information between the opening description and the freelancer's profile. By using a bag of words approach [35] we compute the cosine similarity between an opening description and an applicant's profile. In particular, using bigrams, we create a binary vector representation of the freelancer profile ($\mathbf{w}_w$) and the opening ($\mathbf{w}_o$). We then compute the cosine similarity (m) of the two vectors:

$$m(\mathbf{w}_w, \mathbf{w}_o) = \frac{\mathbf{w}_w \cdot \mathbf{w}_o}{||\mathbf{w}_w|| \, ||\mathbf{w}_o||},$$

where $||\cdot||$ is the $L2$ norm.

3.4 Average pairwise transformation

The introduction of these features in probabilistic models is not straightforward; Each hiring decision is opening-specific; the instances of each opening are strongly dependent and directly comparable within the opening, but not across openings. As a result, we end up having a set of non-comparable instances to build our probabilistic models on. Consider for example two different openings in the same category, and suppose that each one of these two openings has the two applicants shown in Table 2. The set of applicants of the first opening is superior to the set of applicants of the second opening: the feedback scores of all applicants in opening 1 strictly dominate the feedback scores of candidates in opening 2. The same applies to jobs. The employer of each opening however, will choose to hire one of the available applicants[4]; As a result, the hiring decisions for the two openings in Table 2, will be based on different evaluation criteria that use pairwise comparisons of the available applicants.

Since we learn a global model on hiring decisions, we overcome this inconsistency that naturally appears in our data in the following way: for every feature, we first rank all the instances within an opening in descending order. Then, we compute the average pairwise difference of each instance, with all the other instances in an opening. Specifically, for each instance i and for each feature $x_{i,k} \in \boldsymbol{X}$ we have:

$$x_{i,k}^{transformed} = \frac{1}{|o| - 1} \sum_{j \neq i} x_{i,k} - x_{j,k}, \tag{2}$$

[4]Note that this is a peculiarity of our dataset, since we only consider openings that lead to a single hiring decision. In practice, the employer could have chosen not to hire anyone. We further discuss the limitations that our dataset imposes in Section 8.1.

	$x_{i,jobs}$	$x_{i,jobs}^{transformed}$
Anna	3	$((3-1)+(3-0))/2 = 2.5$
Mary	1	$((1-3)+(1-0))/2 = -0.5$
John	0	$((0-3)+(0-1))/2 = -2$

Table 3: Example of the average pairwise transformation for feature *jobs*. We assume that these are the only three applicants in the opening at hand, hence $|o| = 3$.

where $|o|$ is the number of applications in opening o ranked in descending order of values x_k. To clarify this process, consider an example with three applicants, Mary, Anna and John. In Table 3 we show the number of completed jobs for these three applicants in decreasing order. Their transformed values are shown in the third column. Note that the proposed transformation is a variation of the pairwise transformation, which is commonly used in ranking approaches (*e.g.* [27][5]). We apply this transformation to all our features but "time". The reason is that by definition "time" compares applicants within an opening, while it takes the same values across openings.

4. PROBLEM FORMULATION

Before we describe our approaches, it is important to clearly formulate the problem we study:

Problem Definition: *Given an opening, an employer and a set of applicants with specific characteristics, we are interested in **estimating** the **hiring probability** of these applicants.*

In this section we present models that explicitly address this problem. In particular, we first describe a simple ranking model that is based on applicant's reputation; we later use this model as a baseline. Next we present three different approaches of increasing complexity: (1) a ranker aggregator, (2) a Logit Model and (3) a Bayesian Network. For the rest of this work, we assume that all dimensions discussed in section 3 form a feature vector $\boldsymbol{X}$.

4.1 Feedback Score Baseline

Based on the intuition that freelancer's reputation should have a strong effect on hiring decisions, we propose a baseline that ranks applicants based on their feedback score. Specifically in the oDesk platform, after the completion of a task, the employer supplies feedback scores (integers between 0 and 5) to the freelancer in the following six fields: "Availability" ($f1$), "Communication" ($f2$), "Cooperation" ($f3$), "Deadlines" ($f4$), "Quality" ($f5$), "Skills" ($f6$). This vanilla model ranks all available applicants based on their average feedback scores, and assumes that the top applicant for each opening is the one that gets hired. Ties are resolved by the time of application (*i.e.* the fastest applicant gets the job). Because of the simplicity of this model and our belief that hiring decisions draw on a much more complex process, we use this model as a baseline, and we tackle our problem from three different perspectives, which we discuss next.

4.2 Ranker aggregator

Based on the premise that employers take into account multiple dimensions for ranking the available applicants, and

[5]In all our experiments the proposed transformation outperform the pairwise transformation presented in [27].

Feedback	Past Jobs	Skills	Aggregator (median)
Mary	Anna	Anna	Anna (1)
Anna	Mary	Mary	Mary (2)
John	John	John	John (3)

Table 4: Example of Ranker Aggregator

not just their reputation, we propose a ranker aggregator. Our goal is to use information from all the available dimensions we discussed in section 3 and come up with a set of ranked applicants for each opening. To do so, we consider previous work on rank aggregation methods for web documents (see Dwork et al. [13]). We first create separate rankings in each available dimension of the feature vector $\boldsymbol{X}$. Then, for each application in an opening, we compute its median position across all rankings. We finally use these values (median) to rank the available applicants.

To clarify this process, assume that our feature vector consists of only three dimensions, "Feedback" , "Past Jobs" and "Skills", i.e., $\boldsymbol{X} = [$ Feedback, Past Jobs, Skills]. Now suppose that for a specific opening, we have three applicants, Mary, Anna, and John. For each of the three dimensions, we create a ranking of these applicants, shown in Table 4. The proposed aggregator function takes the median of all positions of each applicant across the three rankings, and creates an aggregated ranking, presented in the rightmost column of the table. As a result, Anna with median '1' is ranked first; Mary with median '2' is ranked second, *etc.* Note that the length of our feature vector is $|\boldsymbol{X}| = 15$, and as a result ties are very rare. If however ties occur, we resolve them chronologically, as in the feedback baseline.

4.3 Logit model

The ranker aggregator is an intuitive approach that uniformly assigns equal weights to each dimension of the feature vector $\boldsymbol{X}$. However, in practice, such a uniform assignment is an oversimplification of reality: employers have individual preferences, and as so, they value some features more than others. For example, the skills of an applicant and the number of previous completed jobs might have stronger effect on the employer's hiring decisions than the location of the applicant, or vice a versa. To study this anticipated weight variation across the different features, we draw on empirical economics and propose a Logit binary choice model [17].

In the logit model, the conditional probability of hiring an applicant i given the feature vector $\boldsymbol{X}_i$ is given by the following:

$$\Pr(Y_i = hire|\boldsymbol{X}_i) = \frac{\exp(\boldsymbol{\beta X}'_i)}{1+\exp(\boldsymbol{\beta X}'_i)}\,, \quad (3)$$

where $\boldsymbol{\beta}$ is the vector of coefficients, and $Y_i \in \{hire, nohire\}$. To estimate the vector of coefficients we use maximum likelihood. In particular, we assume that each instance (observation) in our dataset is i.i.d.[6], and we estimate the likelihood function as follows:

$$\Pr(Y_1 = y_1, ..., Y_n = y_n|\boldsymbol{X}) = \prod_{y_i=hire} \Lambda(\boldsymbol{\beta X}') \prod_{y_i=nohire} (1-\Lambda(\boldsymbol{\beta X}'))\,,$$

where$\Lambda(\ .)$ is the logistic sigmoid [17].

[6]we discussed this assumption in section 3.4.

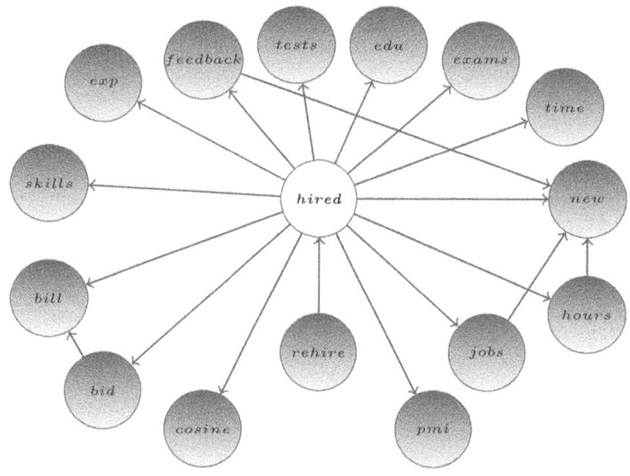

Figure 1: Structure of the proposed Bayesian network.

4.4 Bayesian Network Approach

The nature of our problem suggests that many of the features are correlated with each other. For example, the number of previously completed jobs is strongly correlated with whether or not the freelancer is new. Bayesian networks are able to capture these dependencies, and provide a probabilistic estimation of the target variable by taking into consideration the structure of the network. For our case, we propose the network presented in Figure 1. Intuitively we suggest that if an employer and a freelancer have worked together in the past, then the hiring decision is directly affected by their previous interaction (hired node has only one parent, the "rehire" node). Hiring decisions are correlated with all the other characteristics, in a father - child relationship. We further propose that the pay rate (bid) is correlated with the bill rate (bill) and that whether or not an applicant is new in the marketplace affects the applicant's reputation, hours worked and completed number of jobs[7].

The joint distribution of the proposed network is given by the following equation (see Koller and Friendman [31]):

$$\Pr(Y, \boldsymbol{X}) = \Pr(Y|rehire) \prod_{x_i \in \boldsymbol{X}} \Pr\left(x_i|Pa(x_i)\right)\,, \quad (4)$$

where $Pa(x_i)$ is the parent of the node x_i. Because we are interested in estimating the conditional probability of $\Pr(Y|\boldsymbol{X})$, we get the following:

$$\begin{aligned}\Pr(Y|\boldsymbol{X}) &= \frac{\Pr(Y,\boldsymbol{X})}{\Pr(\boldsymbol{X})} \\ &= \frac{Pr(Y|rehire)\prod_{x_i\in\boldsymbol{X}}\Pr\left(x_i|Pa(x_i)\right)}{\Pr(\boldsymbol{X})}\end{aligned}$$

Next, since all values of vector $\boldsymbol{X}$ are observed, we can simply estimate the conditional probabilities by counting the

[7]Even though we propose this network by intuition, we further experimented with learning the structure of the network through the data by using different scoring functions and learning algorithms (see also [31]). In our evaluation, the intuitive model presented here performed significantly better than all the automatically learned structures.

Opening	Top-2 ranked applications	True Label	Outcome
1	1	*nohire*	Success
	2	*hire*	
2	1	*nohire*	Failure
	2	*nohire*	
3	1	*hire*	Success
	2	*nohire*	

Table 5: Accuracy at top-n toy example.

joined appearances in our training sets:

$$\Pr\left(x_i|pa(x_i)\right) = \frac{N\left(x_i, pa(x_i)\right)}{N\left(pa(x_i)\right)},$$

where $N(e)$ is the number that evidence e appears in our training set.

5. EXPERIMENTAL SETUP

In this section we discuss the experimental setup we use to build and evaluate our approaches. We start by presenting characteristics of the oDesk transactional data we used in our analysis, and then we present and reason about the evaluation metrics we used.

5.1 oDesk Data

oDesk is a global job marketplace with a plethora of tools targeted to businesses that intend to hire and manage remote freelancers. In the past decade, the company experienced a consistent exponential growth in transaction volume. At oDesk, people from all over the world can post any type of task and hire freelancers to work and deliver a requested outcome.

In terms of contracts, there are two types of openings: Hourly and Fixed paid. In this study we present results only on Hourly openings[8]. We analyze a total of 630,000 job applications that lead to more than 50,000 hiring decisions. All this data was sampled between September 1st 2012 and December 31st 2013.

Our approaches use time sensitive features. For example, consider the number of tests taken by the freelancer and their scores. At different times, this feature is expected to take different values, since freelancers constantly try to improve their profiles. The same applies to skills, profile information *etc.* To overcome this naturally occurring transience we take snapshots of freelancers' profiles at the time of application.

Our data span across four different task categories: web development, software development, writing and translation and design and multimedia. The reason for choosing more than one task category is to study how the proposed approaches behave, given that employers might possibly follow different category-specific hiring decision processes. For instance, it is possible that the average employer who makes a hiring decision on a writing task opening, follows a completely different selection process than the average employer who hires freelancers on web programming tasks.

We split our data across these categories and we build different category-specific models. We further separate vertically (on openings) our data into training and test sets (67%-33%). To avoid overfitting, we build all our models on the training sets and evaluate them on the respective test sets. We focus on openings that have between 2 and 50 applicants, and that led to a *single hiring decision.* As a result, the distribution of our data is highly skewed towards "no-hires"; 94% of the applications we consider are "no-hires". This makes the evaluation of our models trickier, since using a metric such as the accuracy of our predictions would be naive: a classifier that would always predict "no-hire" would have an accuracy of 94%. We discuss next the established metrics we used to evaluate our models.

[8]Our approaches have been successfully tested on Fixed price openings as well.

5.2 Evaluation Metrics

The first metric we use to evaluate the predictive power of our approaches is the Area Under the Curve[9] (**AUC**). Intuitively, the AUC can be seen as the probability that our model will rank a "positive" instance (e.g. a hire) higher than a "negative" one.

The next metric we use is the **lift** (see also [48]). We define the lift as follows:

$$lift = \frac{\Pr[+|top\ x\%\ ranked]}{\Pr(+)}, \quad (5)$$

where $\Pr[+|top\ x\%\ ranked]$ is the probability of randomly selecting a positive instance (a hire) in the top $x\%$ ranked instances of the test set, and $\Pr(+)$ is the probability of randomly choosing a positive instance across the test set. Intuitively the lift shows how many times better than random our models' rankings are.

These two metrics evaluate the global performance of our models, but they don't capture the per opening performance. To study the per opening performance we define the **accuracy at top-n** (ACC-n) as the probability that our model will rank a true positive (TP) instance in the top n instances of each job opening. For clarity, we present an example on Table 5, where we consider only three openings, and we examine only the top-2 ranked applications for each one of these openings. Our model predicts a true positive (TP) instance for openings 1 and 3. We consider these two openings as successful predictions at top-2. Then, by assuming that these three openings represent our test set, we estimate the ACC-2 by applying the following formula:

$$\text{ACC-n} = \frac{\#\ successes}{\#\ openings} \quad (6)$$

In our example we get $ACC - 2 = 2/3$.

6. EXPERIMENTAL RESULTS

In this section we analyze the performance of our approaches. Following the flow presented in section 5, we first discuss the resulting AUCs and Lifts of our models, and then we present their accuracies at top-n (ACC-n).

In Table 6 we show the area under the curve for all our models and the baseline, for the task categories we study. Recall than a randomized model will give AUC = 0.5 (see Foster and Fawcett [40]). First, we notice that the resulting rankings of the feedback baseline outperforms a random ranker, with AUC values between 0.535 and 0.548. One might argue that this slightly improvement of the feedback baseline over a random classifier is counterintuitive; freelancers' reputation should play a critical role in hiring decisions. There are two observations that explain this result. First, as we discussed earlier, feedback scores in online workplaces tend to form J-shaped distributions (see also Hu et

[9]Detailed analysis about the use of AUC can be found in the work by Provost and Fawcett [40].

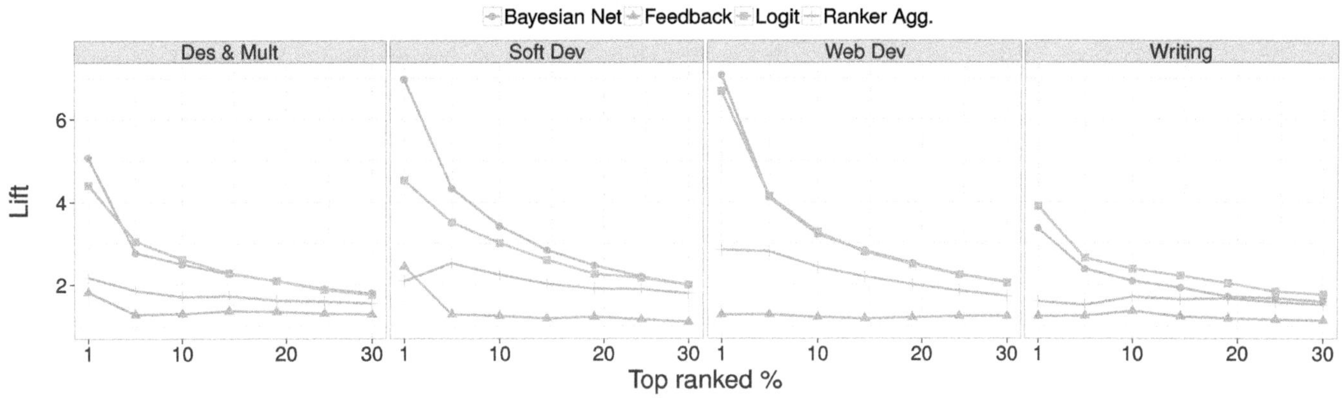

Figure 2: The lift values for all the proposed approaches and the baseline, for the four task categories we study.

al. [23]): most of the freelancers have excellent reputation (5 stars). In our training set the median is 5 and the average 4.7! Furthermore, these J-shaped feedback distributions can be explained by the user survival patterns in online communities: users that receive low feedback scores are unable to get hired again, so they leave the marketplace (or rejoin with different credentials) [26]. Another explanation why the feedback score does not perform well is the fact that amongst the applications we study, roughly 15% originate from freelancers without any previous history in the marketplace, hence no feedback score.

The AUC of the ranker aggregator and the two probabilistic models (Logit and Bayesian network) ranges between 0.628 and 0.74, significantly higher than the feedback baseline's values. Recall that intuitively, AUC is the probability of ranking a positive instance (i.e., a hire) higher than a negative one, so we can say that our models rank positive instances on top of negative instances with different probabilities up to 0.74. In the context of predicting hiring decisions, this probability is really high (recall that 94% of the applications are "nohires". If we compare the three proposed approaches, the Bayesian Network slightly outperforms the Logit Model, which in turn outperforms the ranker aggregator; as expected, increasing the algorithm complexity provided better results.

Next, in Figure 2 we present the *lifts* (see equation 5) of all the proposed approaches and the feedback baseline. The results are similar to the AUC scores. First, all three models perform significantly better than the feedback baseline. As with the AUC scores, the Bayesian Network slightly outperforms the Logit model, which in turn outperforms the ranker aggregator. For "Software Development" and "Web Development" lift reaches 7 for the top 1% ranked instances; This means that if we focus on the top-1 percent of our resulting rankings, we are 7 times more likely to randomly select a positive instance than by choosing an instance from the entire testing dataset.

Finally, we compute the $ACC\text{-}n$ (see Equation 6) for $n = 1, 2, ..., 5$ for all the proposed approaches, the feedback baseline, as well as a random ranker (based on the time of application). In Figure 3 we show the results. The Bayesian approach and the Logit model perform much better than the ranker aggregator and the feedback baseline in all categories. As expected, the Random ranker has the lowest performance. The actual probabilities of predicting a hiring decisions are impressive; In the "Software Development" category, the Bayesian approach ranks the applicants in a way that 28% of the times, the applicant who ranks first is the one who gets hired! At random, this probability is 10%. In other words, we see an improvement of 280%! In "Web Development" this probability is 20%. Similar observations can be made for the other two categories.

7. ECONOMETRIC ANALYSIS

In this section we study the association of each one of the variables on hiring decisions by analyzing the results of our Logit models from an econometric perspective. In particular we focus on the effect of each one of our variables on the hiring probability. This analysis is extremely useful since it provides insights about the behavior of the employers that is tricky (if not impossible) to capture by just looking at the coefficients of the Logit models (or the conditional probabilities of the proposed Bayesian network).

7.1 Marginal Effects Interpretation

The coefficient values of the proposed logit models do not represent the effect of each variable on the hiring probability [17]. To estimate the effect of each one of the variables, we have to calculate their marginal effects; in particular, we estimate the partial derivative of $\Pr(Y|\boldsymbol{X})$ *w.r.t.* each feature x_i:

$$\frac{\partial}{\partial x_i}\left(\frac{\exp(\boldsymbol{\beta X})}{1+\exp(\boldsymbol{\beta X})}\right) = \beta_i \frac{\exp(\boldsymbol{\beta X})}{(1+\exp(\boldsymbol{\beta X}))^2}\,. \tag{7}$$

Recall that $\boldsymbol{\beta}$ is the vector of coefficients of $\boldsymbol{X}$ (see Equation 3). To compute the marginal effects of each coefficient we evaluate the previous equation at the means of the feature distributions in our training sets [17].

Table 7 shows the marginal effects of all the variables broken down by task category. To better understand the interpretation of a marginal effect of a variable consider the following example: Suppose that we are interested on the effect of the feedback score f_i on the hiring probability of an applicant i. Recall that all our features have been transformed by equation 2. The marginal effect that f has on web development tasks is 0.004. This implies that if the transformed feedback score in an opening increases by one, all else equal,

Category	Feedback	Ranker	Logit	Bayes Net
Des & Mult	0.545	0.628	0.671	0.670
Soft Dev	0.533	0.675	0.722	0.728
Web Dev	0.548	0.660	0.730	0.738
Writing	0.537	0.634	0.664	0.646

Table 6: The per-category AUC for all the proposed approaches and the baseline.

Feature	Des & Mult	Soft Dev	Web Dev	Writing
time	-0.002***	-0.004***	-0.002***	-0.004***
bill	-0.002***	-0.002***	-0.002***	-0.003***
cosine	0.199***	0.281***	0.176***	0.318***
edu	-0.002**	-0.001	-0.002***	0.0
exams	0.002	0.004	0.001	0.003
exp	0.0	0.0	0.0	0.001***
feedback	0.004***	0.003*	0.004***	0.002
hours	0.002***	-0.002**	0.001**	0.0
jobs	0.0*	0.0***	0.0***	0.0**
new	0.012***	0.003	0.012***	0.007
tests	-0.001**	-0.001*	0.0.	0.001*
bid	0.003***	0.002***	0.002***	0.004***
pmi	0.005**	0.013***	0.009***	0.027***
rehires	0.028***	0.056***	0.041***	0.022***
skills	0.005***	0.006**	0.007***	0.009***

Table 7: Marginal Effects of the Logit Models in all categories. Significance codes: '*' 0.001,'**' 0.01, '*' 0.05, '.' 0.01**

the hiring probability of freelancer i, $\Pr(Y_i = hire|\boldsymbol{X}_i)$, will increase on average by $0.004 * 1$. In other words, the higher the positive value of a marginal effect, the stronger is the contribution to the hiring probability.

7.2 How each feature affects hiring decisions

Looking at Table 7, we observe that for all four categories, the signs of all significant coefficients agree[10], which provides an extra verification that these models explain the data well. In all categories the strongest effect comes from "cosine" and "rehires" (0.022 to 0.318). For example, in "Software Development", if an applicant is the only one within an opening who has been previously hired by the employer at hand, gets a boosts in hiring probability of 5.6%. On the other hand, in "Design & Multimedia", if an applicant's profile cosine similarity with the opening is higher than all other applicants in that opening by 0.01, then this applicant's probability will increase by 0.318 * 0.01 = 3.2%. These two observations are expected: in order for a freelancer to apply to an opening of an employer that has already collaborated with in the past, we can rationally assume that their collaboration was successful. Furthermore, given that their collaboration was successful, a risk-minimizer employer would choose to work again with this freelancer; Hence the high marginal effect. Similarly, the more coherent and informative the profile of an applicant is, and the more "similar" to the job opening, the higher is the chance that this applicant is suitable for the job.

The next two features that have a strong effect on hiring probability are the pmi score between the applicant's and the employer's countries and the skills' inner product of the contractor and the opening. For the skills, the strong effect is expected: it's the minimum requirements a freelancer must meet in order to get hired. The fact that most of the applicants satisfy these minimum requirements is the reason this effect is not stronger. For the pmi score, we notice that it has a relatively strong effect on all categories but writing. In writing, the effect is much higher (0.027). By looking in our data, we observed that the most frequent {employer-country, freelancer-country} pair that appears in "Writing" is {"USA",'Philippines"}, with a pmi score of 0.229, three times higher than the average PMI score in "Writing", 0.08. On the contrary, in "Web Development" for example, the most common {employer-country, freelancer-country} pair is {"USA","India"}, with a pmi score of 0.43, only slightly above the average pmi score of "Web Development" which is 0.42. The fact that the most frequent pair has a very high pmi score compared to the category average means that very frequently {"USA",'Philippines"} pairs will have higher transformed scores (Equation 2), which explains the strong effect of pmi scores in "Writing".

For new applicants, we observe that in "Web Development" and "Design & Multimedia" the coefficient is significant and positive. This is counterintuitive: being a new contractor shouldn't contribute at all to the hiring probability. However, recall that the reason we included this binary feature is to control for the zero "feedback", "hours" and "jobs" of a new freelancer (see also Sections 3 and 4.4). In our dataset, 10% of all new applicants' applications result in hires; since for all these hires "feedback","jobs" and "hours" were zero, the binary variable "new" balances out this "unfair" penalization by resulting to a positive effect.

As we discussed in Section 3.4, since the time of application is universal across all openings, we exclude it from the transformation of Equation 2. As a result, the negative effect we observe on table 7 is interpreted as follows: if an applicant moves up one rank in *time* (*e.g.* from 2 to 1), then the effect of this change in "Software Development" hiring probability will be (1-2)*(-0.004) = 0.4%. As a result, all else equal, the earlier a freelancer applies, the higher the hiring probability will be.

Finally "feedback" and the biding price ("bid") appear to have a small but significant positive effect, while the billing price and the level of education have small but significant negative effect.

8. DISCUSSION AND FUTURE WORK

In this work we studied hiring decisions in online labor markets. We proposed three different approaches that rank applicants based on their hiring probabilities. To build and evaluate our approaches, we used real transactional data from oDesk.com, and we showed that all our models perform significantly better over the vanilla feedback baseline. Finally we analyzed the (correlational) effect of each variable on the hiring probability of an applicant and found that the attributes that have the strongest positive effect are whether or not the freelancer and the employer have previously worked together, the available information on the freelancer's profile, the countries of the employer and the freelancer, the skillset of the contractor, as well as the time of application. In the following paragraphs we briefly discuss the limitations of our work and our future directions.

8.1 Limitations

Our first limitation comes from the fact that we built a global model under the assumption that our pool of employers is homogeneous in terms of hiring decisions. This

[10] We ignore the non-significant effects (*i.e.* those values that are not followed by at least one "*"). "hours" and "tests" are the only exceptions, but their marginal effects are really weak around 0.001)

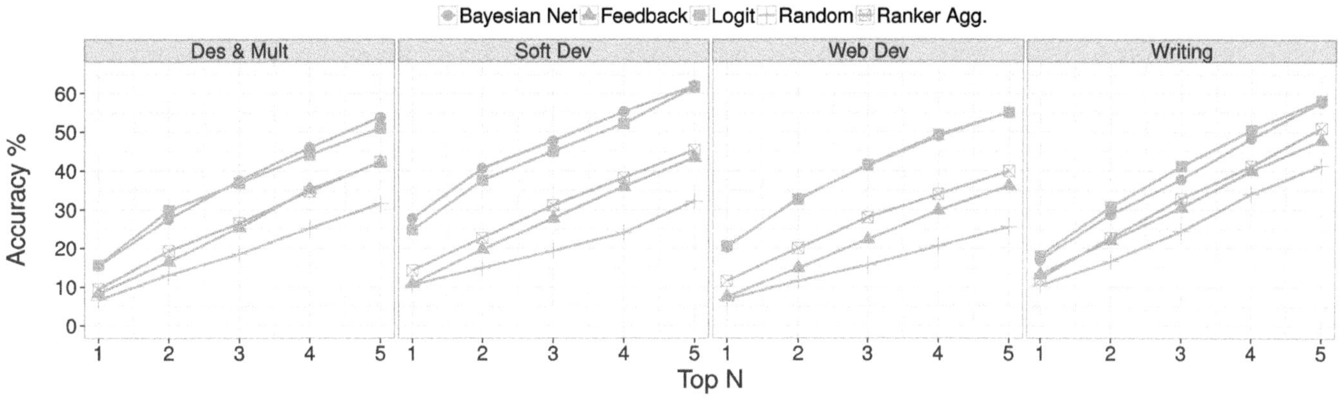

Figure 3: The accuracy at top-n (ACC-n) for all the proposed approaches, the feedback baseline and a random ranker, for all four categories we study.

is generally not true since employers' individual preferences might vary. Our analysis captures an average behavior of employers in the four task categories we examine.

The second important note is that our work does not study causality: we don't imply that the included features of our models have a causal relationship with hiring decisions. We clearly observe that those features can very well explain hiring decisions and that they are highly correlated with the probability of hiring.

The third limitation of our study derives from the dataset that we used. Since our goal was to study how employers make hiring decisions, we only considered openings that lead to a single hire. Our dataset does not capture the behavior of employers who decide (for whatever reason) not to hire anyone of the available applicants. As a result, our proposed approaches should not be used as-is to recommend potential candidates (*i.e.* freelancers that haven't applied yet) to employers. We briefly discuss in Section 8.2 how we can extend this analysis to create a suitable freelancer recommendation framework.

8.2 Future Directions

In the future, we intend to extend this study in three dimensions. First we plan to study "what attracts better applicants". At oDesk.com, at the end of each completed task, both the employer and the freelancer assign feedback to each other. By considering successful hires (positive instances) those that feedback scores were mutually high, and unsuccessful ones (negative instances) those that the pairwise feedback scores were low, we can study the job description characteristics that are correlated with the successful hires.

Second, as we discussed in the limitations section, our models are not ideal for recommending potential good candidates that haven't yet applied to an opening. We intend to extend this work by incorporating in our dataset openings that remain unfilled, and study why employers choose to not hire anyone of the available freelancers. We will then use this information to built a framework that will recommend high quality freelancers to new openings.

Finally, once we have a complete model that provides good estimates of the hiring probability of each *active freelancer* (not applicant) on each *active opening*, we can work towards maximizing the closing rate of openings in the marketplace. In particular, assume that we are given a bipartite graph, where the edges represent current applications from the available freelancers. The question we propose to study is how can we re-allocate these edges in order to maximize not just the filling rate of jobs, but also, the expected payoff (*e.g. OLM* revenue) from the available openings.

9. REFERENCES

[1] A. Acquisti and C. M. Fong. An experiment in hiring discrimination via online social networks. *Available at SSRN 2031979*, 2013.

[2] A. Agrawal, J. Horton, N. Lacetera, and E. Lyons. *Digitization and the Contract Labor Market: A Research Agenda.* University of Chicago Press, September 2013.

[3] A. J. Berinsky, G. A. Huber, and G. S. Lenz. Evaluating online labor markets for experimental research: Amazon. com's mechanical turk. *Political Analysis*, 20(3):351–368, 2012.

[4] S. Berry, J. Levinsohn, and A. Pakes. Automobile prices in market equilibrium. *Econometrica: Journal of the Econometric Society*, pages 841–890, 1995.

[5] G. Bouma. Normalized (pointwise) mutual information in collocation extraction. In *Proceedings of the Biennial GSCL Conference*, pages 31–40, 2009.

[6] A. J. Bowlus. Matching freelancers and jobs: Cyclical fluctuations in match quality. *Journal of Labor Economics*, 13(2):pp. 335–350, 1995.

[7] E. Brynjolfsson and M. D. Smith. Frictionless commerce? a comparison of internet and conventional retailers. *Management Science*, 46(4):563–585, 2000.

[8] C. Burges, T. Shaked, E. Renshaw, A. Lazier, M. Deeds, N. Hamilton, and G. Hullender. Learning to rank using gradient descent. In *Proceedings of the 22nd international conference on Machine learning*, pages 89–96. ACM, 2005.

[9] Z. Cao, T. Qin, T.-Y. Liu, M.-F. Tsai, and H. Li. Learning to rank: from pairwise approach to listwise approach. In *Proceedings of the 24th international conference on Machine learning*, pages 129–136. ACM, 2007.

[10] D. Chandler and J. Horton. Labor allocation in paid crowdsourcing: Experimental evidence on positioning, nudges and prices. In *Proceedings of the 3rd Human Computation Workshop, HCOMP*, volume 11, 2011.

[11] S. L. Cohen and K. A. Bunker. Subtle effects of sex role stereotypes on recruiters' hiring decisions. *Journal of Applied Psychology*, 60(5):566, 1975.

[12] H. K. Davison and M. J. Burke. Sex discrimination in simulated employment contexts: A meta-analytic investigation. *Journal of Vocational Behavior*, 56(2):225–248, 2000.

[13] C. Dwork, R. Kumar, M. Naor, and D. Sivakumar. Rank aggregation methods for the web. In *Proceedings of the 10th international conference on World Wide Web*, pages 613–622. ACM, 2001.

[14] S. Forsythe, M. F. Drake, and C. E. Cox. Influence of applicant's dress on interviewer's selection decisions. *Journal of Applied Psychology*, 70(2):374, 1985.

[15] Y. Freund, R. Iyer, R. E. Schapire, and Y. Singer. An efficient boosting algorithm for combining preferences. *The Journal of machine learning research*, 4:933–969, 2003.

[16] D. C. Gilmore, T. A. Beehr, and K. G. Love. Effects of applicant sex, applicant physical attractiveness, type of rater and type of job on interview decisions*. *Journal of Occupational Psychology*, 59(2):103–109, 1986.

[17] W. Greene. *Econometric Analysis*. Prentice Hall, 2012.

[18] Y. Hadass. The effect of internet recruiting on the matching of freelancers and employers. *Available at SSRN 497262*, 2004.

[19] J. J. Horton and L. B. Chilton. The labor economics of paid crowdsourcing. In *Proceedings of the 11th ACM conference on Electronic commerce*, pages 209–218. ACM, 2010.

[20] J. J. Horton, D. G. Rand, and R. J. Zeckhauser. The online laboratory: Conducting experiments in a real labor market. *Experimental Economics*, 14(3):399–425, 2011.

[21] L. Hu. The hiring decisions and compensation structures of large firms. *Industrial and Labor Relations Review*, pages 663–681, 2003.

[22] N. Hu, J. Zhang, and P. Pavlou. Overcoming the j-shaped distribution of product reviews. *Communications of the ACM*, 52(10):144–147, 2009.

[23] N. Hu, J. Zhang, and P. A. Pavlou. Overcoming the j-shaped distribution of product reviews. *Commun. ACM*, 52(10):144–147, Oct. 2009.

[24] P. G. Ipeirotis and J. J. Horton. The need for standardization in crowdsourcing. CHI, 2011.

[25] P. G. Ipeirotis, F. Provost, and J. Wang. Quality management on amazon mechanical turk. In *Proceedings of the ACM SIGKDD workshop on human computation*, pages 64–67. ACM, 2010.

[26] K. Jerath, P. S. Fader, and B. G. Hardie. New perspectives on customer "death" using a generalization of the pareto/nbd model. *Marketing Science*, 30(5):866–880, 2011.

[27] T. Joachims. Optimizing search engines using clickthrough data. In *Proceedings of the eighth ACM SIGKDD international conference on Knowledge discovery and data mining*, pages 133–142. ACM, 2002.

[28] K. Kawakami, J. F. Dovidio, and S. van Kamp. Kicking the habit: Effects of nonstereotypic association training and correction processes on hiring decisions. *Journal of Experimental Social Psychology*, 41(1):68–75, 2005.

[29] M. Kokkodis and P. G. Ipeirotis. Have you done anything like that?: predicting performance using inter-category reputation. In *Proceedings of the sixth ACM international conference on Web search and data mining*, pages 435–444. ACM, 2013.

[30] M. Kokkodis and P. G. Ipeirotis. The utility of skills in online labor markets. In *International Conference on Information Systems (ICIS)*, 2014.

[31] D. Koller and N. Friedman. *Probabilistic graphical models: principles and techniques*. MIT press, 2009.

[32] B. Li, A. Ghose, and P. G. Ipeirotis. Towards a theory model for product search. In *Proceedings of the 20th international conference on World wide web*, pages 327–336. ACM, 2011.

[33] M. Lindeboom, J. V. Ours, and G. Renes. Matching employers and freelancers: An empirical analysis on the effectiveness of search. *Oxford Economic Papers*, 46(1):pp. 45–67, 1994.

[34] K. S. Lyness and M. K. Judiesch. Are women more likely to be hired or promoted into management positions? *Journal of Vocational Behavior*, 54(1):158–173, 1999.

[35] C. Manning and H. Schütze. *Foundations of Statistical Natural Language Processing*. MIT Press, 1999.

[36] W. Mason and D. J. Watts. Financial incentives and the performance of crowds. *ACM SigKDD Explorations Newsletter*, 11(2):100–108, 2010.

[37] P. Nelson. Information and consumer behavior. *The Journal of Political Economy*, 78(2):311–329, 1970.

[38] J. D. Olian, D. P. Schwab, and Y. Haberfeld. The impact of applicant gender compared to qualifications on hiring recommendations: A meta-analysis of experimental studies. *Organizational Behavior and Human Decision Processes*, 41(2):180–195, 1988.

[39] A. Pallais. Ineffiient hiring in entry-level labor markets. *Available at SSRN 2012131*, 2012.

[40] F. Provost and T. Fawcett. Robust classification for imprecise environments. *Machine Learning*, 42(3):203–231, 2001.

[41] C. Quoc and V. Le. Learning to rank with nonsmooth cost functions. *NIPSâĂŹ07*, 19:193, 2007.

[42] D. G. Rand. The promise of mechanical turk: How online labor markets can help theorists run behavioral experiments. *Journal of theoretical biology*, 299:172–179, 2012.

[43] S. M. Raza and B. N. Carpenter. A model of hiring decisions in real employment interviews. *Journal of Applied Psychology*, 72(4):596, 1987.

[44] A. D. Shaw, J. J. Horton, and D. L. Chen. Designing incentives for inexpert human raters. In *Proceedings of the ACM 2011 conference on Computer supported cooperative work*, pages 275–284. ACM, 2011.

[45] V. S. Sheng, F. Provost, and P. G. Ipeirotis. Get another label? improving data quality and data mining using multiple, noisy labelers. In *Proceedings of the 14th ACM SIGKDD international conference on Knowledge discovery and data mining*, pages 614–622. ACM, 2008.

[46] K. Train. *Discrete choice methods with simulation*. Cambridge university press, 2009.

[47] A. Trotman. Learning to rank. *Information Retrieval*, 8(3):359–381, 2005.

[48] I. Witten and E. Frank. *Data Mining: Practical machine learning tools and techniques*. Morgan Kaufmann, 2005.

[49] F. Xia, T.-Y. Liu, J. Wang, W. Zhang, and H. Li. Listwise approach to learning to rank: theory and algorithm. In *Proceedings of the 25th international conference on Machine learning*, pages 1192–1199. ACM, 2008.

[50] J. Xu and H. Li. Adarank: a boosting algorithm for information retrieval. In *Proceedings of the 30th annual international ACM SIGIR conference on Research and development in information retrieval*, pages 391–398. ACM, 2007.

[51] J. Xu, T.-Y. Liu, M. Lu, H. Li, and W.-Y. Ma. Directly optimizing evaluation measures in learning to rank. In *Proceedings of the 31st annual international ACM SIGIR conference on Research and development in information retrieval*, pages 107–114. ACM, 2008.

[52] V. Yakubovich. Weak ties, information, and influence: How freelancers find jobs in a local russian labor market. *American sociological review*, 70(3):408–421, 2005.

[53] Y. Yue, T. Finley, F. Radlinski, and T. Joachims. A support vector method for optimizing average precision. In *Proceedings of the 30th annual international ACM SIGIR conference on Research and development in information retrieval*, pages 271–278. ACM, 2007.

[54] Z. Zheng, K. Chen, G. Sun, and H. Zha. A regression framework for learning ranking functions using relative relevance judgments. In *Proceedings of the 30th annual international ACM SIGIR conference on Research and development in information retrieval*, pages 287–294. ACM, 2007.

Just in Time Recommendations - Modeling the Dynamics of Boredom in Activity Streams

Komal Kapoor, Karthik Subbian, Jaideep Srivastava
Department of Computer Science
University of Minnesota, Minneapolis, MN 55455
{kapoor,karthik,srivasta}@cs.umn.edu

Paul Schrater
Department of Psychology & Computer Science,
University of Minnesota
Minneapolis, MN 55455
schrater@cs.umn.edu

ABSTRACT

Recommendation methods have mainly dealt with the problem of recommending new items to the user while *user visitation behavior* to the familiar items (items which have been consumed before) are little understood. In this paper, we analyze user activity streams and show that user's temporal consumption of familiar items is driven by boredom. Specifically, users move on to a different item when bored and return to the same item when their interest is restored. To model this behavior we include two latent psychological states of preference for items - sensitization and boredom. In the sensitization state the user is highly engaged with the item, while in the boredom state the user is disinterested. We model this behavior using a Hidden Semi-Markov Model for the gaps between user consumption activities. We show that our model performs much better than the state-of-the-art temporal recommendation models at predicting the revisit time to the item. Moreover, we attribute two main reasons for this: (1) recommending items that are not in the bored state for the user, (2) recommending items where user has restored her interests.

Categories and Subject Descriptors

H.3.3 [**Information Search and Retrieval**]: Information Filtering; H.2.8 [**Database Management**]: Database Applications - Data Mining

General Terms

Algorithms, Experimentation, Human Factors, Measurement

Keywords

Dynamic Preferences; Boredom; Temporal Recommender Systems; Activity Streams

1. INTRODUCTION

"Boring is the right thought at the wrong time"
- Jack Gardner, Words Are Not Things

WSDM'15, February 2–6, 2015, Shanghai, China.

http://dx.doi.org/10.1145/2684822.2685306.

Recommendation systems are portals to the world of information, as they facilitate and control users interactions with content. The success of these recommendation systems directly depends on the quality of user engagement. The existing internet platforms (such as Last.fm, Netflix.com) allow users to engage with two types of items in a session: new and familiar. For instance, in the Last.fm music dataset[1], on average 23% of a user's interactions are with the new items and the rest are with the familiar items. However, most of the existing models [27, 28, 17, 38, 16, 30, 37, 8, 32] deal only with the recommendation of new items to the user, while understanding *user consumption choices* for the familiar items remains mostly unexplored.

Changing preferences cause the user interest in familiar items to be sensitive to time. Existing temporal models [39, 26, 6, 11, 29, 24] have largely focused on predicting future rating value for a user-item pair using time dynamics. A popular approach is to use time decaying functions to characterize the rating behavior of the user over time [11]. Others estimate the temporal interest of a user for a particular item by combining the user, item and time (latent) factors [27, 17]. While these methods are time-sensitive, understanding the temporal dynamics of user behavior is not their main focus. More specifically, they do not answer the question, *"When the user would visit, revisit or engage with an item?"*, rather they answer "What is the rating of the user-item pair in future?". As a result, such methods do not adequately adapt to the temporal patterns in users engagement with items.

In this work, we model the time-gap between successive consumption activities of a user in the activity stream by specifically focusing on the psychological state of boredom. Users often get bored with a particular item they were engaging with before and move on to a different item of interest. This is similar to an user listening to a single song multiple times or watching multiple movies from a single genre and then switching to a different album or movie genre after certain period of engagement. Mostly they return to the original item of interest after a *gap period.* Such temporal patterns in item consumption significantly impact recommendation design for these systems.

The *gap-behavior* in activity streams is governed by two important content consumption characteristics: (1) user is definitely not interested in an item she is bored of (despite its popularity and her own past interest) and (2) user may revisit the item, if her interest is restored. This is an important observation in consumer research in order to understand

[1] See experiments section for more details

the changing consumer preferences [31, 14]. We extend this idea further using behavioral psychology to represent these characteristics as two important states of user behavior [12]: sensitization and boredom. In the sensitization state the user is highly engaged with the item, while in the boredom state the user is disinterested. The activity gap characterizes these two states in a most natural way. In the sensitized state the activity gaps are quite small as the user actively revisits the item and in the boredom state the gap is relatively large. The duration in each state and gap lengths may vary depending on the user and item characteristics.

Surprisingly, most of the related work assume that the popular and well rated items by the user are good choices for recommendation. These models completely ignore the fact that the *user may get bored* of these recommendations, despite her past interactions. We perform several experiments in this paper to confirm that sensitization and boredom states exist in user activity streams. Moreover, we show that such behavioral models can predict the revisit time more accurately than existing state-of-the-art techniques.

1.1 Contributions and Organization

We explicitly model user latent psychological states, *sensitization* and *boredom*, using a Hidden Semi-Markov Model (HSMM) and use the model to predict the *the gap between user activities*. The model works in an *online manner* which is well-suited for activity streams. Furthermore, our model is flexible enough to compute a preference score for items as a function of time. We use this flexibility to propose a STiC recommender that ranks familiar items based on the dynamic preference score. Our model is found to be better suited for the recommending task than several state-of-the-art baselines [25, 36, 11, 26, 9].

There are three important results shown in this work. Existing time-sensitive recommendation models are good at predicting ratings for the future, but do not perform well in predicting the revisit time of the user. We demonstrate through our model and experiments that activity streams exhibit two important psychological states of user behavior: sensitization and boredom. Moreover, to the best of our knowledge, this is the first work that talks about modeling gap between user activities using latent psychological states to understand the dynamics of user's consumption behavior.

The paper is organized as follows. In the remainder of this section we discuss the related work. In section 2, we discuss the temporal content consumption behavior using the semi-markov model. We describe the the dataset and the details of the model estimation process in section 3. We also validate our model by comparing our approach to several variants in this section. Followed in section 4 we evaluate our approach on a recommendation task and compare it against popular baselines, such as SVD++, TimeSVD++, Tensor-ALS, and Restricted Boltzmann Machine (RBM). We present the conclusion in section 5.

1.2 Related Work

The problem of recommending interesting items to users based on their history of past ratings and user profile has been well-studied for a few decades now. Some of these approaches take advantage of historical ratings and are referred to as "Collaborative filtering" methods [38, 16, 30, 37]. While the other that make use of the user-profile attributes are called "Content-based filtering" techniques [35, 32]. There are several approaches that combine these techniques and are referred to as "Hybrid" [8, 32]. There are many survey articles [33, 1] that discuss a variety of these approaches. The recommendation problem can be mapped to a standard classification setting, hence latent factor models [27, 17] and dimensionality reduction techniques are also applied. As these problems can be treated as matrix completion problems, matrix factorization [27] based models are also quite widely used.

There are several recent related works that discuss the importance of understanding the changing user interests over time [39, 26, 6, 11, 29, 24]. Most of these penalize the objective or use a corrective scheme for accommodating the changing preferences, rather than explicitly modeling them. Many temporal models for recommendation were designed to detect drifts in users interests and altered their algorithms accordingly [6, 26]. Other methods, have used seasonality and trends [3] as additional context for segmenting the user ratings. There are also tensor factorization [9] approaches, that extend the matrix factorization [41] techniques to include the temporal component.

There has also been some research on implicit feedback data sets [18, 3]. However, most of these works do not explicitly model the user behavioral states which is essential, as shown in this work, to estimate the user revisit time for an item. Understanding future preferences is not specific to recommender systems, and have received much interest in several other fields, such as consumer research. The relationship between repetition of a stimulus (such as food, drinks, commodity items etc.) and its attractiveness has been modeled using an inverted-U shaped function. This relationship was used by McAlister to propose the dynamics attribute satiation model of consumer choice applied to soft drink consumption behavior [31]. More general consumer choice models were later introduced which accommodated either a short term loyalty for the last purchased brand or a devaluation of the last purchased brand [4, 14, 19]. There are also some recent progress on dynamic content consumption analysis [2]. However, most of these approaches do not model the explicit user behavioral states in estimating the time-sensitive future preferences. Furthermore, several of these consumer research approaches are based on questionnaires and surveys.

2. TEMPORAL CONTENT CONSUMPTION

We identify two types of temporal dependencies in the consumption of items:

1. *Reinforcing response*: Systematic exploitation of our recent choices aids our future decision making. As a result, we find ourselves sticking to items such as listening to the same music bands again and again, watching the same kinds of movies and frequenting the same types of restaurant etc. Consumer research scientists have identified this effect as inertia or a short term loyalty for the last purchased brand [20].

2. *Devaluing response*: Psychologists have associated repetitive exposures to stimuli with satiation and repulsion [15]. Stimulus satiation often produce shifts in interests and other variety and novelty seeking behavior [20]. Satiation is identified as a temporary phenomenon which diminishes with time due to forgetting [15].

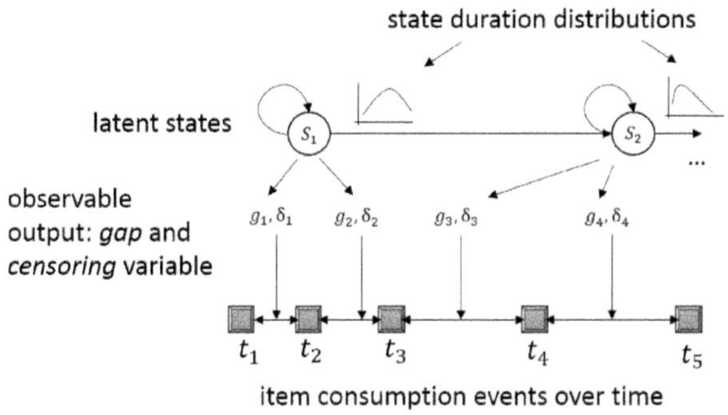

Figure 1: Using observed gap sequence and censoring variable for training a latent state model for item consumption.

The reinforcing and devaluing response is closely associated to a user's content consumption behavior in activity streams [21]. In this work, we model these two response characteristics with psychological preference states of *sensitization* and *boredom*. An item in the sensitization state is consumed rapidly with *small* gaps between its successive consumptions. A *longer* time gap characterizes temporary boredom with the item followed by forgetting. In other words, these states characterize an overall *likeness* for each item. An item with high likeness score takes longer to devalue and recur earlier than an item with relatively low likeness score.

We *explicitly model* these psychological states in this work. We also characterize user's preference for an item as a function of these psychological states using hazard functions which we will discuss a bit later.

2.1 A Semi-Markov Model

The gaps between successive consumptions of an item help us characterize the psychological preference states of the users. We propose a latent state dynamic model for item consumption to infer user preference states. We specifically use a hidden semi-Markov model (HSMM) because of it's ability to model both the consumption gaps (emission distribution) and the time spend by an item in a particular state (state duration distribution).

Let us consider an item i consumed by the user u at times t_1^{ui}, $t_2^{ui} \dots t_n^{ui}$, where t_n^{ui} is the last consumption event for the item in the observation period. The gap observations g_1^{ui}, $g_2^{ui} \dots g_n^{ui}$ denote the time gap between the consumption events, such that $g_x^{ui} = t_{x+1}^{ui} - t_x^{ui}$, for $x = 1 \dots (n-1)$ and $g_n^{ui} = T - t_n^{ui}$, where T is time of the end of the observation period. The last gap length observation is incomplete as we haven't observed the next return for that item yet. Such observations whose values are only known to be larger than a certain value are said to be right censored and are handled using a special status variable (δ_t^{ui}). The status variable is set to 0 for censored observations and and is set to 1 otherwise. It is important to handle censored observations while modeling duration data to prevent a bias towards smaller durations [22]. The $\{g, \delta\}_{1 \dots n}^{ui}$ constitute the observable output from the model. This is shown in Figure 1. For simplicity, we drop the superscript ui and it is assumed, unless otherwise stated, that variables are always defined with respect to a particular user and item.

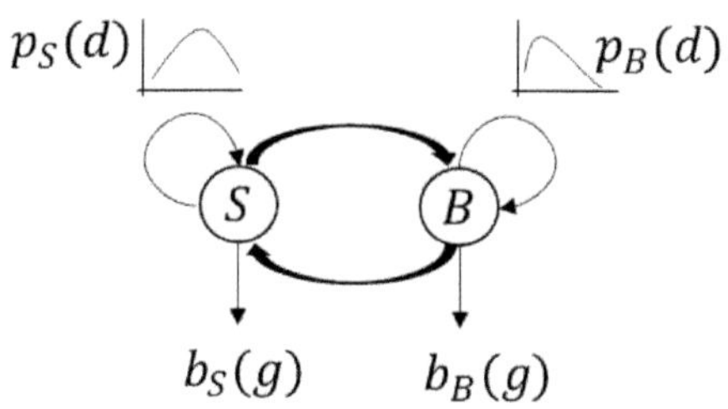

Figure 2: The hidden semi-markov model for gap length sequence.

We include two latent psychological states in the model to capture the states of *Sensitization* (S) and *Boredom* (B). Each state is further associated with an emission density distribution b_m (and a cumulative distribution B_m) for the next gap length g for $m \in \{S, B\}$. More formally, $b_m(g) = P(G = g|m)$, where $P(.)$ is a state-conditioned distribution on gap-length random variable (G). The likelihood of an observed output $\{g, \delta\}$ for a state m can be computed as: $P(\{g, \delta\}|m) = (1 - \delta) * b_m(g) + \delta * (1 - B_m(g))$. Here, the likelihood for a data which is not censored is the probability density function $b_m(g)$, while the likelihood of a censored data is equal to the probability of $P(G > g) = (1 - B_m(g))$.

The semi-markov model allows us to explicitly model state durations, which is the time an item spends in a particular state before transitioning to another state. We denote the duration density distribution by $p_m(D = d)$, where D is the duration random variable. Figure 2 displays the discussed parameters of our model. We model $\log(G)$ (rather than G) to include non-linearity in the perception of time [40]. A parametric form is assumed for the emission and the state duration distributions: $b_m(\log(g)) = \text{Log-logistic}(\mu_m, \sigma_m))$ and $p_m(d) = \text{Gamma}(\alpha_m, \beta_m)$. Our choice of parametric form allows us to capture time dependence characteristics of our data discussed further in section 3.3. The complete set of model parameters include $\lambda = (A, \pi, b_m(g), p_m(d))$, where π denotes the initial state probability distribution over m latent states and A denotes the transition probability matrix between those states. For our model with two latent states $A(m, n) = 1$ for $m \neq n$ and 0 otherwise.

2.2 Prediction

Given the model parameters, and the observed gap sequence, we an use the HSMM model to track the past preference states of the user and make predictions about her future behavior. A good reference for the estimation and inference methodologies for HSMM can be found here [43, 42]. In this subsection, we briefly describe the prediction procedures relevant for our discussion.

At any point let $t_1 \dots t_n$ denote the observed consumption events for an item, $g_{1 \dots (n-1)}$ denote the corresponding gap length observations. The model parameters (λ) are estimated via maximum likelihood estimation using the forward-backward algorithm [43]. Using inference, we can compute a distribution for the latent states variables $s_{1 \dots (n-1)}$, corresponding to the gap observations, using the entire observed gap sequence, i.e. $P(s_i | g_{1 \dots (n-1)}, \lambda)$ for $i = 1 \dots (n-1)$ using the forward-backward algorithm. A one-step lookahead using the forward algorithm allows us to also predict the distribution for the next latent state s_n of the item.

For brevity, we denote this distribution as $\mathfrak{s}_n$ such that $\mathfrak{s}_n(m) = P(s_n = m|g_{1...(n-1)}, \lambda)$. Since we have only two states, $\mathfrak{s}_n(S) = 1 - \mathfrak{s}_n(B)$.

We compute the expected gap till the next consumption of the item ($\mathbb{E}(G_n|g_{1...(n-1)}, \lambda)$) using the state conditioned emission distributions as follows. The expectation of the state emission distribution provides us the expected gap length conditioned on the item state and model parameters ($\mathbb{E}(G|m, \lambda)$). We then marginalize out the future state variable using the next state distribution ($\mathfrak{s}_n$) to compute the expectation for the next gap length;

$$\mathbb{E}(G_n|g_{1...(n-1)}, \lambda) = \mathfrak{s}_n(S) * \mathbb{E}(G|S, \lambda) + \mathfrak{s}_n(B) * \mathbb{E}(G|B, \lambda) . \tag{1}$$

We further obtain a dynamic measure of item consumption rate using techniques from survival analysis. Survival analysis [23, 13] is a field of statistics which deals with duration data, such as the time of occurrence of an event, referred to as *death*. A hazard function is used to compute a temporal measurement of the event rate conditioned on survival until or beyond a certain time computed as follows:

$$h(t) = P(T = t|T >= t) = \frac{f(t)}{1 - F(t)}, \tag{2}$$

where, f and F are the probability density and cumulative distributions. We use the hazard function for the gap length variable to capture the instantaneous rate of an item's consumption given the time since it's last consumption $(t - t_n)$; i.e. $P(G_n = (t - t_n)|G_n >= (t - t_n)|g_{1...(n-1)}, \lambda)$. The hazard function can be directly associated with a user's preference for the item, which provides us a unique mechanism for quantifying user's dynamic preference (DP).

However, here again, we have direct access to the state condition gap distribution, rather than the gap distribution. Hence, the state conditioned dynamic preference score for some time $t > t_n$ is computed as,

$$DP(t|m, \lambda) = \frac{b_m(t - t_n)}{1 - B_m(t - t_n)}, \tag{3}$$

Furthermore, marginalizing over the predicted state distribution for the future state ($\mathfrak{s}_n$) provides us the dynamic preference score for time t given model parameters and the observed gap sequence as follows:

$$DP(t|g_{1...(n-1)}, \lambda) = \frac{\mathfrak{s}_n(S) * b_S(t - t_n) + \mathfrak{s}_n(B) * b_B(t - t_n)}{\mathfrak{s}_n(S) * (1 - B_S(t - t_n)) + \mathfrak{s}_n(B) * (1 - B_B(t - t_n))} . \tag{4}$$

3. EXPERIMENT SETUP

We apply our HSMM model of item consumption to music listening data. The domain of music is particularly well suited for our analysis, with repetition naturally occurring even at the song level. For other types of domains (e.g. movies, books, clothes, holiday destinations), repetitive behavior emerges at a higher level of abstraction such as by defining similarity clusters on the attributes of the items (genre, trend, categories etc.).

3.1 Data

We use a public dataset from the popular music service Last.fm [7] that contains the complete music listening histories of around 1000 users as recorded until May, 2009. This is also the only publically available dataset, to our knowledge, that provides the comprehensive listing of users choices during a period of time. The dataset contains the song name, the artist name and the timestamp for the different songs the user listened to during this period.

We construct our dataset using a subset of the data comprising the first four months of listening activities for each user. Of this dataset, the first 3 months is used for training and the fourth month is used for testing purposes. During this period a user is seen to listen to multiple songs over time. Her listening activity is further broken down into sessions where a session is defined as a continuous stream of listening activity interrupted by only *small* pauses. Based on visual examination and with the intention of accommodating most of the listening activity of a day in one session, we use 6 hours as the threshold on the gap between two songs for terminating the session. We use these sessions as the unit of time throughout our discussion. Hence, an item consumption at time t for a user corresponds to her listening to the corresponding song in the t-th session.

For each user a set of familiar (I^u) is identified and includes those which have been consumed at least three times during the training period. The training and test data is filtered to remove all users which have less than 10 familiar items. Table 1 summarizes the basic statistics for the final training and testing dataset used for our experiments.

Training Data	No of users	687
	Mean no of familiar items per user	224
	Mean number of sessions per user	68
Test Data	No of users	593
	Mean number of sessions per user	25
	Mean number of familiar items consumed per session	14

Table 1: Dataset statistics.

3.2 Clustering

In Figure 3, we show the cumulative distribution of the number of repeat consumptions of an item in the training period. More than 90% of user-items have fewer than 10 repetitions making it difficult to obtain a statistical estimate of a separate HSMM model for each user-item pair. Instead, we cluster the user-item pairs and train a separate HSMM model for each cluster. The average rate of consumption or *likeness* score f, as defined below, is used for clustering.

$$f = \frac{n^t}{t_{n^t} - t_1 + \epsilon}, \tag{5}$$

where, n^t is the total number of item consumptions during the training period, t_1 and t_{n^t} is the time of the first and last item consumption during the training period. The constant ϵ is the minimum time period over which the average consumption rate is computed.

We consider two approaches for clustering user-item pairs based on the *likeness* score - equal interval binning and k-means clustering. We further consider different number of clusters for partitioning the data. A large number of clusters result in noisy and sparse clusters. On the other hand, too few clusters overgeneralize the model. We set

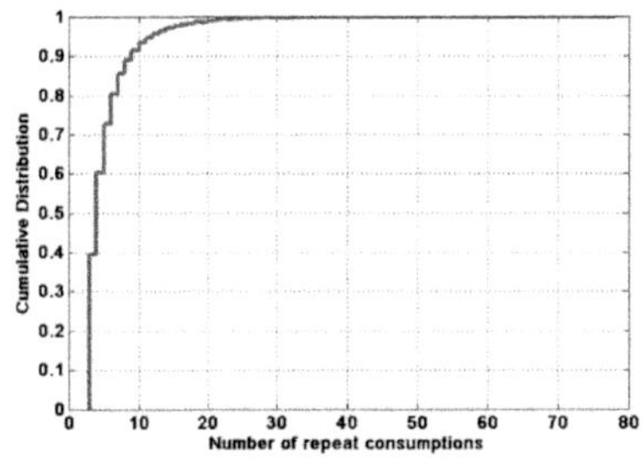

Figure 3: Cumulative distribution of the number of repeatitions of an item for the training data.

aside a validation dataset by removing a 30% random sample from the training data, and use this to evaluate the clustering schemes and the number of clusters. The models are trained on the remaining training data. The performance of a clustering scheme is measured using Root Mean Squared Error (RMSE) between the predicted and observed log-transformed gap length sequences in the validation dataset. The k-means clustering algorithm with 25 clusters is found to perform the best. Our analysis going forward is based on these user-item clusters, and the corresponding estimates of model parameters λ_c.

3.3 Model Parameters

We now analyze the model parameters trained on our dataset and discuss their relationships to the latent psychological states. We also show the existence of sensitization and boredom states through our analysis.

Emission probability distributions Figures 4 (a) and (b) show the emission probability distributions $b_m(\log(g))$ for the two latent states S and B, respectively. The probability distributions are plotted corresponding to each clusters. The log-gap lengths are marked along the x-axis while the y-axis indicates the index for the clusters which are organized in increasing order of likeness scores. The value of the probability distributions (log transformed to highlight the differences between the clusters) for a particular clusters and gap length is indicated by a color. First we note that the for the same cluster, the emission distribution is spread across longer gap lengths for state B than state S. This justifies the nomenclature for the states as we expected items in the sensitization states to be consumed faster than items in the boredom state. Secondly, we find that items which have a higher likeness score have shorter return cycles than items with lower likeness score.

The hazard functions for the two states show significant differences (Figure 4 (c) and (d)). As before, the hazard functions are plotted for log-gap lengths along the x-axis for each cluster, and the different clusters are organized along the y-axis in increasing order of likeness score. For the state S, items have declining hazard function which indicates that the event rate decreases with log-time. On the other hand, the hazard function for the state B gradually increases and then declines. Such a uni-modal shape of the hazard function indicates a peak rate of occurrence at a particular log-time and fits well with our boredom hypothesis. This is the main reason for our choice of log-logistic distribution that fits well both a declining and a uni-modal hazard function.

State duration distributions Figure 5 shows the state duration distributions and the hazard functions for the state duration for the latent states S and B. The state duration length is marked on the x-axis, while the y-axis indicates the clusters. The color is used to denote the magnitude of the log-transformed probability distribution and the hazard functions. First, we find that clusters with lower likeness scores have a shorter dwell time in the sensitization state and longer dwell time in the boredom state than clusters with higher likeness scores. Secondly, the hazard has an increasing shape for both the states which indicates that the rate of moving out of the state increases with time spent in the state. This indicates that items in the sensitization state eventually devalue while those in the boredom state eventually return to the sensitization states when user preferences recover. The gamma distribution allows an increasing/declining hazard function and provides an adequate fit for the temporal dynamics of the state transitions.

3.4 Relaxing Modeling Assumptions

We now consider several relaxations of our model (HSMM) for item consumption and evaluate them at predicting the gap sequences for the items in the dataset. The following relaxations are considered:

1. **HMM** We use a Hidden Markov Model (HMM) to model the timing of item consumption. As before, we consider two latent states S and B and model the emission distributions for each state using a Log-logistic distribution on the log-transformed gap length. The HMM model assumes that the state durations are geometrically distributed and are independent of the time spent in the state. A transition matrix captures the probability of transitioning between states. The complete set of model parameters include $\lambda = (A, \pi, b_m(g))$.
2. **Loglogistic** We do not model the temporal order in the gap sequence. Instead gap lengths between item consumptions are assumed to follow a Log-logistic distribution. Such a model picks up the predominant recency based dynamics in the data producing a declining hazard function for the consumption event. The complete set of model parameters include $\lambda = (\mu, \sigma)$.
3. **Exponential** Consumption events are modeled to occur at a constant rate using an exponential distribution. The model parameters include $\lambda = (\mu)$.

All models are learnt using the training data for the same frequency-based user-item clusters as described earlier, and evaluated on the test data. The performance is measured using the prediction error on the log-transformed gap length sequences in the test data using RMSE. The results are summarized in Table 2. Our HSMM model performs significantly better (p-value$<10^{-5}$) than all the other models which illustrates the value achieved by the different components of our model.

4. STiC RECOMMENDER

A temporal recommendation algorithm based on our item consumption model is proposed and evaluated.

4.1 Design

Our HSMM model, as mentioned earlier, predicts the time when an item would be consumed next based on the psychological state of the user. Further state and time based preference score for the item can be computed using (4). This

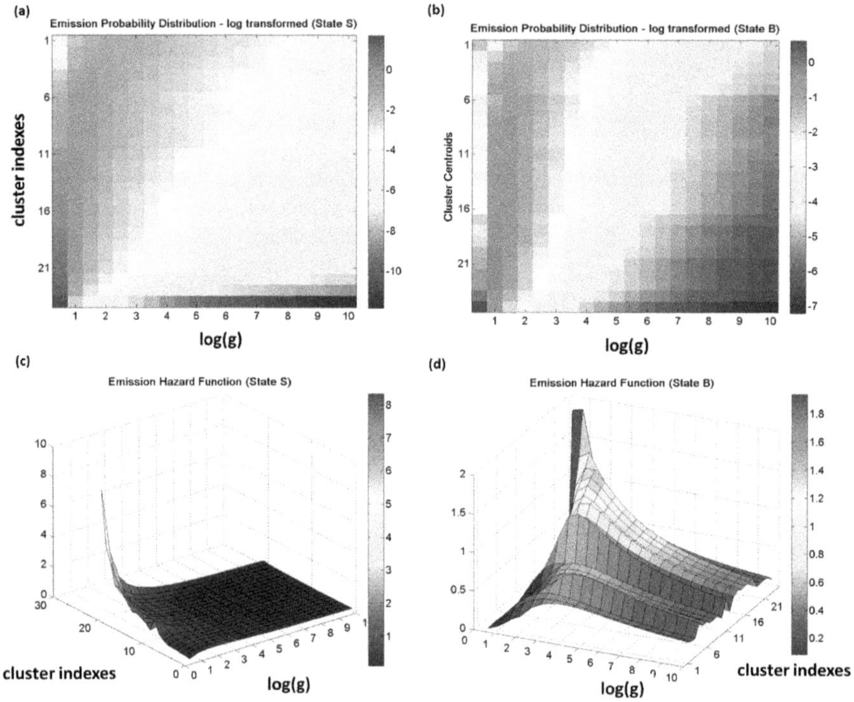

Figure 4: Emission probability and hazard function distributions. The cluster indxes are labeled in increasing order of likeness score. (To be viewed in color)

Model	RMSE on the Test Data
HSMM	0.9791
HMM	1.0691
Loglogistic	1.1943
Exponential	1.1860

Table 2: RMSE scores on the log-transformed gap length sequence

provides us valuable information for making time sensitive recommendations to the users. We now propose the (**STiC**) recommender which uses **S**tate and **Ti**me **C**onditioned preference scores for dynamically ranking items. The scores are computed in an online manner for the next user session using her past consumption history and the cluster level model parameters learnt from the training period (λ_c).

4.2 Evaluation

There are certain challenges in evaluating a time-sensitive recommendation based on the dynamic preferences of users. Firstly, a direct assessment of an user's temporal preference is hard to obtain. For example, even when abundant explicit feedback in terms of ratings for items are available, a user rarely rates the same item repeatedly nor does the rating correspond to the consumption preference at that time (as the user may rate the item after arbitrary long time). As a result, we base our model evaluation on actual consumption choices resulting from an activity stream, as it reflects the real-time interests of a user.

We compare our model against various popular static and temporal recommendation methods. Both the training and the test data is transformed into a per user choice matrix (C^u) such that $C^u(i,t) = 1$, if the item i is consumed during the session t, 0 for all the items that are not consumed during that session.

4.2.1 Metrics:

The standard RMSE metric meant for explicit rating data is not applicable to our setup. We consider the following metrics, well suited to implicit datasets [3, 18, 34], for evaluating our model and the comparison baselines. The metrics have been modified to make the evaluation sensitive to time.

1. **T-Precision, T-Recall and T-F_1 measures** Improvements in RMSE scores provide little information on the impact on user experience. Furthermore, since users are generally only recommended a list of top K items, more recently evaluation based on precision, recall and F_1 have become popular [10]. We compare the top-10 recommendation list generated by the model for a user sessions against the actual items consumed by the user in the sessions and compute the precision, recall and F_1. These scores are then averaged across all user sessions in the test period.

2. **T-AUC** The AUC scores measure the likelihood of the recommender to rank preferred items over the not-preferred items. We compute the average AUC score across user sessions in the test period.

3. **T-Rank** The rank metric was recently proposed to evaluate recommenders in the presence of implicit feedback [18]. The metric computes the expected percentile rank of an item selected during the test period

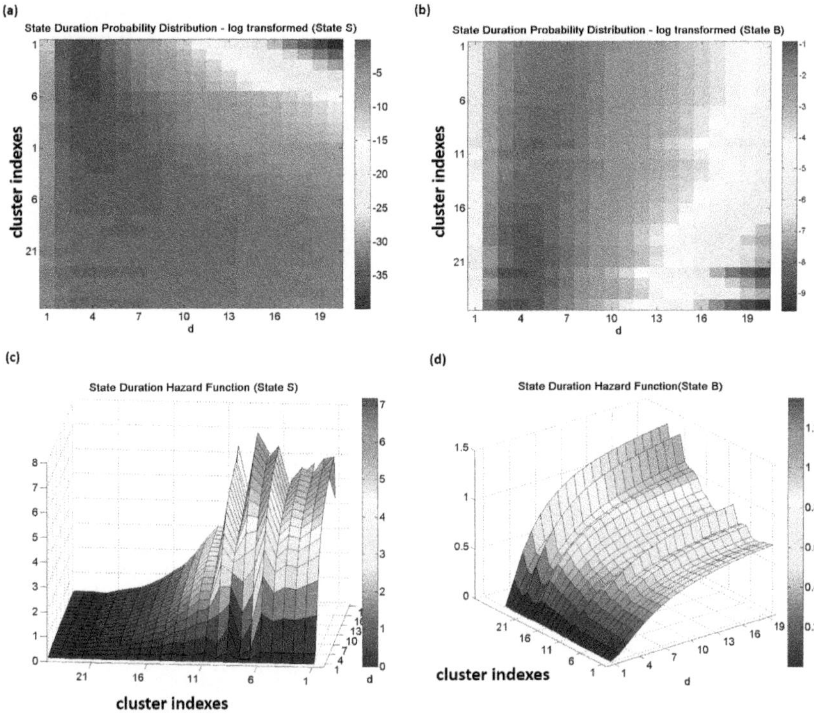

Figure 5: State duration probability and hazard function distributions. The cluster indxes are labeled in increasing order of likeness score. (To be viewed in color)

in the recommender's ranking list. For a temporal setting, session specific rank scores are computed and averaged across all users and session in the test period:

$$\text{T-Rank} = \frac{\sum_{u,i,t} C^u(i,t) * \text{rank}^{ui}(t)}{\sum_{u,i,t} C^u(i,t)}, \tag{6}$$

where $\text{rank}^{ui}(t)$ denotes the percentile rank of item i in the ranked list of items generated for the user u for the session t.

It should be noted that for a recommender, higher values of T-Precision, T-Recall, T-F_1, and T-AUC scores and low values of T-Rank scores are preferred.

4.2.2 Baselines:

We compare the STiC recommender against several state-of-the-art static and temporal recommendation approaches. Some of the approaches have been modified to work with implicit activity data. We further use the validation dataset to obtain the optimal parameters for the baselines.

1. **Static** The model computes a preference score vector by computing the average number of time each item was consumed per user session during the training period. By definition this model is time-insensitive.

2. **SVD++** Matrix factorization based approaches such as Singular Value Decomposition (SVD) are known to perform well when an explicit user-item ratings matrix is known and prediction accuracy is evaluated using RMSE on the user ratings [5]. The SVD++ model is shown to perform better at top-K recommendations than basic SVD and is used for comparison. The implicit data is converted into an explicit rating using the complementary cumulative distribution of a user's item consumptions [3]. Items in the top 80-100% of the distribution are given a rating of 5, those in the 60-80% are given a rating of 4 and so on.

3. **Restricted Boltzmann machines (RBM)** Another time-insensitive baseline includes RBM's, a two-layer undirected graphical models used for collaborative filtering process [36]. In this approach, a conditional multinomial is used to model the columns of the observed rating matrix and a conditional Bernoulli distribution is used for hidden user features. The rating matrix used was same as the SVD++ baseline.

4. **Time-Weighted** Previous research [11] have found that incorporating time by time weighting user ratings (usually using an exponential decay) such that recent ratings are weighted more than old ratings leads to performance improvements. Hence, we compare our model against a time-weighted recommender that computes a temporal preference score vector over the items using an exponential moving average: $P^u(t) = \lambda^u * P^u(t-1) + (1-\lambda^u) * C^u(t-1)$; $P(1) = C(1)$. Here λ^u is the decay weight vector which is learnt from the training dataset using stochastic gradient descent.

5. **TSVD++** The TSVD++ model extends matrix factorization models to incorporates temporal drifts in user interests [26]. Changes in preference factors with time are captured using a linear function. The TSVD++ model is trained using the user choice matrices.

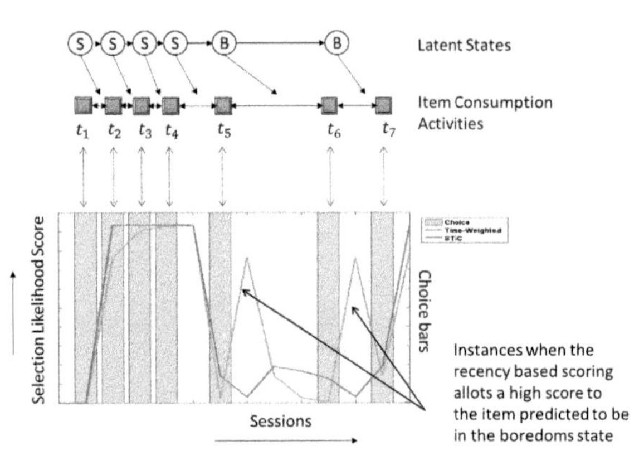

Figure 6: STiC model predictions compared against that of time-weighted model. The top part of the figure shows the STiC model's state predictions for the item. The bottom part displays how the same item is scored by the two models. The item is scored high by the time-weighted model even after the user state has changed (the item has become boring). Instead, the STiC model gives a low score to the item at those instances.

6. **Tensor Factorization (Tensor)** Tensor factorization allows us to further generalize matrix factorization to include time. The binary rating (or activity) matrix along with the time dimension is considered as a three dimensional tensor. A low rank factorization is performed on the tensor by minimizing the total squared error on the observed ratings. Alternating least squares is used to approximate the user, item and time factors. The factors are then combined to reconstruct the complete rating matrix. The implementation details are described in [9].

4.3 Results

The evaluation results are summarized in Table 3. Incorporating time is generally found to improve the performance over non-temporal counterparts [27, 26, 9], as seen from the better performance of temporal models with latent factors, such as *TSVD++* and *Tensor* over *SVD++* and *RBM*. Similarly the *time-weighted* (non-latent temporal) model, performs better compared to its *static* counterpart. Our approach *STiC* outperforms all the baselines, including the latent factor temporal models, as it explicitly models the user behavioral states.

While all of our baseline latent factor models perform well in terms of low RMSE scores (shown in brackets) on the training choice matrix (RBM (0.788227), SVD++ (1.28967), TSVD++ (0.198687), Tensor(0.176084)), they did not perform well in the temporal choice prediction task. Instead, the static and time-weighted models which are trained per user fair much better. Such findings can be explained on two grounds. Firstly, the latent factor model are optimized to minimize the squared error of the predicted to the observed values rather than their ability to rank items based on users preferences. Secondly, they are primarily intended to identify similarities between users and items to discover new items for them. Instead, for our task, we are more interested in predicting the temporal characteristics of user choices for a restricted set of familiar items. This further demonstrates the importance of using gap measurements in predicting the next expected visit of the user to a item. Our STiC model is a hybrid approach that combines the individual likeness scores with a cluster based model for preference dynamics, and is superior to the rest of the models.

We investigate the differences between our STiC Model and the popular time-weighted model (our best performing baseline) in further detail. Our other baselines (which perform significantly worse) are not further considered due to space limitations. A major difference between the time-weighted and the STiC models stems from the fact that the time-weighted model assumes user preferences to be predominantly recency based, while the STiC model captures different user states of sensitization and boredom and allows for both recency and diversity driven behaviors based on the user state. As we discussed in Section 1, this impacts quality of user experience in two important ways: (1) *not recommending* the items that are *boring* or user has lost interest and (2) *recommending* items where the user has restored recent interest. We illustrate below the importance of these two factors through more detailed experiments.

(A) Not recommending items which are boring: We examine the one-step lookahead state predictions made by the STiC model ($\mathfrak{s}_n$) for an item and corresponding observed gap lengths (Figure 6) (a)). For the same item Figure 6 (b) displays the selection likelihood scores, scaled to the same range, as generated by both the models. We find that the time-weighted model continues to score the item based on recency even when the user's preference state for the item, as predicted by the STiC model, has changed. Hence, items which a user is bored of, are scored high by the time-weighted model but not by the STiC model.

In order to generalize our findings across users we allot a time-sensitive boredom score to items;

$$\text{Boredom-Score}(t) = \text{Time till next consumption at time 't'}. \quad (7)$$

We borrow the concept of *future lifetime* [13] from survival analysis to compute the boredom score using our STiC model. The future lifetime is defined for an event as the remaining time till death given survival until a specified time. Given the cumulative distribution (F) over the time of the occurrence of the event and some maximum threshold for time (t_s), the expected future lifetime at t_0 can be computed as:

$$E(T|T > t_0) = \frac{1}{1 - F(t_0)} \sum_{t=t_0}^{t_s} 1 - F(t) \quad (8)$$

For our scenario, the boredom score directly maps to the expected future lifetime for item consumptions. We denote the future gap as random variable G_f and the next future gap as random variable G_{fn}. At some time 't', the gap since the last consumption of the item is $t - t_n$, and the expected next future gap is defined as $\mathbb{E}(G_{fn}|G_n > (t - t_n), g_{1\dots(n-1)}, \lambda)$. We first compute the state conditioned expected future gap using the state emission distributions:

$$\mathbb{E}(G_f|G > (t - t_n), m, \lambda) = \frac{1}{1 - B_m(t - t_n)} \sum_{s=(t-t_n)}^{t_s} 1 - B_m(s) \, . \quad (9)$$

Model	T-Precision	T-Recall	T-F_1	T-AUC	T-Rank
Static	0.108	0.1229	0.115	0.5986	0.3827
Time-Weighted	0.133	0.1842	0.1545	0.6542	0.3682
SVD++	0.072	0.1312	0.093	0.5175	0.4766
RBM	0.0862	0.1298	0.1036	0.5436	0.4276
TSVD++	0.0772	0.1001	0.0872	0.571	0.4212
Tensor	0.1031	0.1195	0.1107	0.545	0.3982
STiC	**0.1641**	**0.2148**	**0.1861**	**0.692**	**0.3254**

Table 3: Comparing the STiC model with popular static and temporal recommendation models on a variety of temporal evaluation metrics. The STiC model is found superior to all baselines on all evaluation metrics.

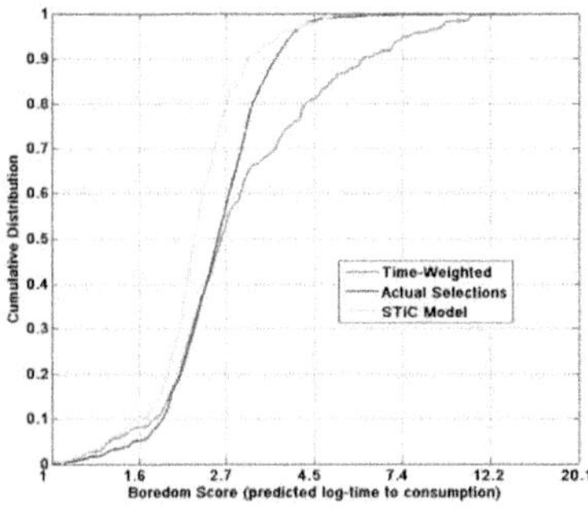

Figure 7: The cumulative distribution for the recommendation likelihood for the time-weighted and the STiC model given boredom scores. Time-weighted model recommends more item with higher boredom scores, while STiC is more conservative than the actual user.

We then marginalizing over the the future state predictions ($\mathfrak{s}_n$) to compute the boredom score:

$$\begin{aligned}\text{Boredom-Score}(t) =& \mathbb{E}(G_{fn}|G_n > (t-t_n), g_{1\ldots(n-1)}, \lambda) \\ =& \mathfrak{s}_n(S) * \mathbb{E}(G_f|G > (t-t_n), S, \lambda) \\ &+ \mathfrak{s}_n(B) * \mathbb{E}(G_f|G > (t-t_n), B, \lambda) \ . \end{aligned} \tag{10}$$

We now map the cumulative distribution of the likelihood to occur in the top-10 recommendation list for the two models; Time-weighted and STiC, against the boredom scores predicted by the STiC model (Figure 7). The threshold t_s is set to 60 (a reasonable high value) sessions. For reference, the actual consumption likelihood of the user is also plotted in the same figure. We find that the time-weighted model recommends more item with higher boredom scores than the STiC model and those actually consumed by the user. The STiC model on the other hand is found to be slightly more conservative than the actual user.

(B) Recommending restored items in addition to sensitized items: The STiC model further allows partitioning the items consumed in a future sessions into two sets: Sensitized and Restored items. If $P(S|g_{1\ldots(n-1)}, \lambda) > P(B|g_{1\ldots(n-1)}, \lambda)$, then the item is allocated to sensitized set. Otherwise the item is added to the restored set.

We use our classification scheme to further compare the recommendation performance on specifically the restored items. Empirically, users were found to consume sensitized items only around 23% of the times. For the rest of the times they consumed items from the restored sets. This suggests that the ability to recommend the restored items is crucial for improving recommendation performance. The Table 4 summarizes the performance scores for the models separated based on the item set. We find that both the time-weighted and the STiC model are extremely good at recommending sensitized items. The time-weighted model, is particular bad at recommending restored items while the STiC model continues to work well.

5. CONCLUSIONS

Understanding the changing user preferences is very important in the context of recommendation. Most of the changing user interests are available in the form of activity streams, where each activity (such as listening to a song or viewing an shopping item) represents the user's interest to a specific item. In this paper, we proposed a behavior-based model for understanding changing user's interests using a hidden semi-Markov model. We used latent psychological states, sensitization and boredom, to represent the user's behavior in this model. We showed that existing state-of-the-art temporal models fails to predict the time of next expected visit of an user to an item as compared to our model. We attribute two main causes for this: (1) not recommending the bored items and (2) recommending the items where an user has restored her interests. In our experiments, we performed several analysis to justify these two reasons, in addition to overall superior performance of our model.

6. ACKNOWLEDGMENTS

We gratefully acknowledge the University of Minnesota Doctoral Dissertation Fellowship, SOBACO grant, the NSF EAGER grant number 00032116 and the DARPA grant number W911NF-12-C-0028 for sponsoring this work.

7. REFERENCES

[1] Gediminas Adomavicius and Alexander Tuzhilin. Toward the next generation of recommender systems: A survey of the state-of-the-art and possible extensions. *Knowledge and Data Engineering, IEEE Transactions on*, 17(6):734–749, 2005.

[2] Ashton Anderson, Ravi Kumar, Andrew Tomkins, and Sergei Vassilvitskii. The dynamics of repeat consumption. In *Proceedings of the 23rd international conference on World wide web*, pages 419–430. International World Wide Web Conferences Steering Committee, 2014.

[3] Linas Baltrunas and Xavier Amatriain. Towards time-dependant recommendation based on implicit feedback. In *Workshop on context-aware recommender systems (CARS̈09)*, 2009.

[4] Kapil Bawa. Modeling inertia and variety seeking tendencies in brand choice behavior. *Marketing Science*, 9(3):263–278, 1990.

[5] James Bennett and Stan Lanning. The netflix prize. In *Proceedings of KDD cup and workshop*, volume 2007, page 35, 2007.

[6] Huanhuan Cao, Enhong Chen, Jie Yang, and Hui Xiong. Enhancing recommender systems under volatile userinterest

Item set	Model	T-Precision	T-Recall	T-FMeasure	T-Rank
Sensitized items	Time-Weighted	0.1853	0.4752	0.2666	0.0245
	STiC	**0.1956**	**0.4785**	**0.2777**	**0.0189**
Restored items	Time-Weighted	0.0223	0.0634	0.033	0.4428
	STiC	**0.0511**	**0.109**	**0.0696**	**0.3847**

Table 4: Recommendation performance of the STiC and the time-weighted recommender for different item sets. Both the time-weighted and STiC model perform well on sensitized items while, time-weighted is particular bad at recommending restored items compared to STiC.

drifts. In *Proceedings of the 18th ACM conference on Information and knowledge management*, pages 1257–1266. ACM, 2009.

[7] O. Celma. Music recommendation datasets for research. 2010.

[8] Mark Claypool, Anuja Gokhale, Tim Miranda, Pavel Murnikov, Dmitry Netes, and Matthew Sartin. Combining content-based and collaborative filters in an online newspaper. In *Proceedings of ACM SIGIR workshop on recommender systems*, volume 60. Citeseer, 1999.

[9] Pierre Comon, Xavier Luciani, and André LF De Almeida. Tensor decompositions, alternating least squares and other tales. *Journal of Chemometrics*, 23(7-8):393–405, 2009.

[10] Paolo Cremonesi, Yehuda Koren, and Roberto Turrin. Performance of recommender algorithms on top-n recommendation tasks. In *Proceedings of the fourth ACM conference on Recommender systems*, pages 39–46. ACM, 2010.

[11] Yi Ding and Xue Li. Time weight collaborative filtering. In *Proceedings of the 14th ACM international conference on Information and knowledge management*, pages 485–492. ACM, 2005.

[12] John D Eastwood, Alexandra Frischen, Mark J Fenske, and Daniel Smilek. The unengaged mind defining boredom in terms of attention. *Perspectives on Psychological Science*, 7(5):482–495, 2012.

[13] Regina C Elandt-Johnson. *Survival models and data analysis*, volume 110. John Wiley & Sons, 1980.

[14] Moshe Givon. Variety seeking through brand switching. *Marketing Science*, 3(1):1–22, 1984.

[15] Murray Glanzer. Curiosity, exploratory drive, and stimulus satiation. *Psychological Bulletin*, 55(5):302, 1958.

[16] Jonathan L Herlocker, Joseph A Konstan, Al Borchers, and John Riedl. An algorithmic framework for performing collaborative filtering. In *Proceedings of the 22nd annual international ACM SIGIR conference on Research and development in information retrieval*, pages 230–237. ACM, 1999.

[17] Thomas Hofmann. Latent semantic models for collaborative filtering. *ACM Transactions on Information Systems (TOIS)*, 22(1):89–115, 2004.

[18] Yifan Hu, Yehuda Koren, and Chris Volinsky. Collaborative filtering for implicit feedback datasets. In *Data Mining, 2008. ICDM'08. Eighth IEEE International Conference on*, pages 263–272. IEEE, 2008.

[19] Barbara E Kahn, Manohar U Kalwani, and Donald G Morrison. Measuring variety-seeking and reinforcement behaviors using panel data. *Journal of Marketing Research*, pages 89–100, 1986.

[20] B.E. Kahn, M.U. Kalwani, and D.G. Morrison. Measuring variety-seeking and reinforcement behaviors using panel data. *Journal of Marketing Research*, pages 89–100, 1986.

[21] Komal Kapoor, Nisheeth Srivastava, Jaideep Srivastava, and Paul Schrater. Measuring spontaneous devaluations in user preferences. In *Proceedings of the 19th ACM SIGKDD international conference on Knowledge discovery and data mining*, pages 1061–1069. ACM, 2013.

[22] Nicholas M Kiefer. Economic duration data and hazard functions. *Journal of economic literature*, pages 646–679, 1988.

[23] David G Kleinbaum and Mitchel Klein. *Survival analysis*. Springer, 1996.

[24] Noam Koenigstein, Gideon Dror, and Yehuda Koren. Yahoo! music recommendations: modeling music ratings with temporal dynamics and item taxonomy. In *Proceedings of the fifth ACM conference on Recommender systems*, pages 165–172. ACM, 2011.

[25] Yehuda Koren. Factorization meets the neighborhood: a multifaceted collaborative filtering model. In *Proceedings of the 14th ACM SIGKDD international conference on Knowledge discovery and data mining*, pages 426–434. ACM, 2008.

[26] Yehuda Koren. Collaborative filtering with temporal dynamics. *Communications of the ACM*, 53(4):89–97, 2010.

[27] Yehuda Koren, Robert Bell, and Chris Volinsky. Matrix factorization techniques for recommender systems. *Computer*, 42(8):30–37, 2009.

[28] Ravi Kumar, Prabhakar Raghavan, Sridhar Rajagopalan, and Andrew Tomkins. Recommendation systems: A probabilistic analysis. In *Foundations of Computer Science, 1998. Proceedings. 39th Annual Symposium on*, pages 664–673. IEEE, 1998.

[29] Tong Queue Lee, Young Park, and Yong-Tae Park. A time-based approach to effective recommender systems using implicit feedback. *Expert systems with applications*, 34(4):3055–3062, 2008.

[30] Greg Linden, Brent Smith, and Jeremy York. Amazon. com recommendations: Item-to-item collaborative filtering. *Internet Computing, IEEE*, 7(1):76–80, 2003.

[31] Leigh McAlister. A dynamic attribute satiation model of variety-seeking behavior. *Journal of Consumer Research*, pages 141–150, 1982.

[32] Prem Melville, Raymond J Mooney, and Ramadass Nagarajan. Content-boosted collaborative filtering for improved recommendations. In *AAAI/IAAI*, pages 187–192, 2002.

[33] Prem Melville and Vikas Sindhwani. Recommender systems. In *Encyclopedia of machine learning*, pages 829–838. Springer, 2010.

[34] Douglas W Oard, Jinmook Kim, et al. Implicit feedback for recommender systems. In *Proceedings of the AAAI workshop on recommender systems*, pages 81–83. Wollongong, 1998.

[35] Michael J Pazzani. A framework for collaborative, content-based and demographic filtering. *Artificial Intelligence Review*, 13(5-6):393–408, 1999.

[36] Ruslan Salakhutdinov, Andriy Mnih, and Geoffrey Hinton. Restricted boltzmann machines for collaborative filtering. In *Proceedings of the 24th international conference on Machine learning*, pages 791–798. ACM, 2007.

[37] Badrul Sarwar, George Karypis, Joseph Konstan, and John Riedl. Item-based collaborative filtering recommendation algorithms. In *Proceedings of the 10th international conference on World Wide Web*, pages 285–295. ACM, 2001.

[38] Xiaoyuan Su and Taghi M Khoshgoftaar. A survey of collaborative filtering techniques. *Advances in artificial intelligence*, page 4, 2009.

[39] John Z Sun, Kush R Varshney, and Karthik Subbian. Dynamic matrix factorization: A state space approach. In *Acoustics, Speech and Signal Processing (ICASSP), 2012 IEEE International Conference on*, pages 1897–1900. IEEE, 2012.

[40] Taiki Takahashi. Loss of self-control in intertemporal choice may be attributable to logarithmic time-perception. *Medical hypotheses*, 65(4):691–693, 2005.

[41] Hsiang-Fu Yu, Cho-Jui Hsieh, Si Si, and Inderjit S Dhillon. Scalable coordinate descent approaches to parallel matrix factorization for recommender systems. In *ICDM*, pages 765–774, 2012.

[42] Shun-Zheng Yu. Hidden semi-markov models. *Artificial Intelligence*, 174(2):215–243, 2010.

[43] Shun-Zheng Yu and Hisashi Kobayashi. An efficient forward-backward algorithm for an explicit-duration hidden markov model. *Signal Processing Letters, IEEE*, 10(1):11–14, 2003.

Leveraging In-Batch Annotation Bias for Crowdsourced Active Learning

Honglei Zhuang
LinkedIn Corporation
University of Illinois at Urbana-Champaign
hzhuang3@illinois.edu

Joel Young
LinkedIn Corporation
joyoung@linkedin.com

ABSTRACT

Data annotation bias is found in many situations. Often it can be ignored as just another component of the noise floor. However, it is especially prevalent in crowdsourcing tasks and must be actively managed. Annotation bias on single data items has been studied with regard to data difficulty, annotator bias, etc., while annotation bias on batches of multiple data items simultaneously presented to annotators has not been studied. In this paper, we verify the existence of "in-batch annotation bias" between data items in the same batch. We propose a factor graph based batch annotation model to quantitatively capture the in-batch annotation bias, and measure the bias during a crowdsourcing annotation process of inappropriate comments in LinkedIn. We discover that annotators tend to make polarized annotations for the entire batch of data items in our task. We further leverage the batch annotation model to propose a novel batch active learning algorithm. We test the algorithm on a real crowdsourcing platform and find that it outperforms in-batch bias naïve algorithms.

Categories and Subject Descriptors

H.2.8 [**Database Applications**]: Data mining; J.4 [**Social and Behavioral Sciences**]: Psychology

Keywords

Crowdsourcing; active learning; annotation bias

1. INTRODUCTION

Online crowdsourcing platforms leverage Internet users across the world to provide a scalable method for annotating data sets for various machine learning tasks. There are several systems providing online crowdsourcing services, *e.g.* Amazon Mechanical Turk [1] and CrowdFlower [2]. Although far cheaper than employing and training expert annotators, crowdsourcing can still be expensive as building high-performance classifiers often requires large sets of annotated data with multiple annotations for each data item. To minimize these costs, we turn to active learning, a technique for selecting particular unlabeled data instances for labeling to (hopefully) best improve classifier performance. Unfortunately, traditional active learning methods assume reliable annotators—this assumption is not feasible with crowdsourcing. A number of studies [12, 24, 26, 29] have discussed the topic of overcoming the annotation errors of crowds on single data items in active learning.

In addition to each individual annotator's annotation bias, we find interference between data items simultaneously presented for annotation through crowdsourcing. There are many situations in which batches of multiple data items are judged by crowds at the same time. A typical example is when evaluating results of a search engine given a certain query, the retrieved web pages are judged by crowds (either by explicit labeling or implicit click through rate) in batches. Other examples include object recognition [22] and clustering [8]. Batch active learning is particularly vulnerable as multiple data items are submitted simultaneously for annotation both to reduce annotation costs and to minimize classifier retraining cycles.

Although the annotation bias of individual annotators on single data items is well explored [15, 16, 28], there is little published research on annotation bias introduced by presenting data items in batches to crowd annotators. Scholer *et al.* [18] explored factors such as time intervals between two judgments that may affect the quality of annotation in a TREC data set, but without explicitly modeling the annotation bias.

In this paper, we study in-batch annotation bias; that is, the annotation interference between items in small sets of data items. As a motivating example, consider Table 1 showing annotation results from a crowdsourced task to identify inappropriate comments on LinkedIn posts. Batch 1 (left column) and Batch 2 (right column) capture two batches submitted separately for crowd annotation as to which comments are inappropriate. Both batches are sampled from comments on the same post. The *Label* columns show the crowdsourced annotation results. Although the final comment in each batch is identical, they were annotated differently. In Batch 1, it is labeled as an acceptable comment, probably because it is presented to the crowds along with all the other comments containing URLs. However, in Batch 2, it is labeled as inappropriate, perhaps as it is the only com-

[1] `https://www.mturk.com/`
[2] `http://www.crowdflower.com/`

WSDM'15, February 2–6, 2015, Shanghai, China.
ACM 978-1-4503-3317-7/15/02.
http://dx.doi.org/10.1145/2684822.2685301.

Table 1: Motivating example. The left column and the right column are two batches of data items sent to crowdsourcing for annotation of inappropriate comments. All data items are from comments on the same post. A "Yes" in the *Label* column indicates the comment is labeled as inappropriate by the crowds, while a "No" means the comment is acceptable. The last comments of both batches are the same comment yet are assigned different labels by the crowds. Annotations were generated by majority voting by annotators with greater than 70 percent accuracy on co-mingled quiz batches.

Batch 1		Batch 2	
Label	Comment content	*Label*	Comment content
Yes	`www.youtube.com/watch?v=BKorP55Aqvg`	No	Even after doing all this, sometimes it still doesn't work I might add. It is part of the job.
No	something related: `https://www.youtube.com/watch?v=BKorP55Aqvg`	No	Chernobyl nuclear power plant was probably engineered using "quality (sic !), speed and cost"...
No	`https://www.youtube.com/watch?v=BKorP55Aqvg` Its tough to be an engineer!	No	I think a culture where folks can air grievances can be very productive as long as they can be accumulated to identify themes and trends. Otherwise, ... *[Omitted]*
Yes	`http://youtu.be/BKorP55Aqvg`	No	Brian, my favorite saying as an engineer is: "I told you so 100 times." You should put that at the top of your list :)
No	Now from the perspective of the engineer: `https://www.youtube.com/watch?v=BKorP55Aqvg`	**Yes**	Now from the perspective of the engineer: `https://www.youtube.com/watch?v=BKorP55Aqvg`

ment in this batch containing a URL. Although both batches are given to the crowds with exactly the same instructions, the crowds can still make incoherent judgments. We focus on the case of small batch (*e.g.* size $k \leq 5$), as annotators are unlikely to see a large batch of data items at the same time. We leave the case of larger batches to future study.

There are three major questions to address: Do annotations of data items in the same batch interfere with each other? If we find in-batch annotation bias, can we quantitatively measure the bias? Regarding the impact of in-batch annotation bias, how can we design a batch active learning algorithm that is still effective? We present the following contributions exploring these questions:

1. *Verifying and modeling in-batch annotation bias.* We conduct preliminary studies exploring the existence of in-batch annotation bias. We then propose a factor graph model to capture the annotating behaviors of crowd annotators of data items in batches.

2. *Proposing active learning algorithms with in-batch annotation bias.* Based on the proposed annotating model, we propose a novel batch active learning algorithm, leveraging the in-batch annotation bias to help improve the classifier performance, and prevent it from being hurt by biased annotation.

3. *Real-world experiments on a crowdsourcing platform.* We conduct experiments on an online crowdsourcing platform to actively build a classifier for inappropriate comments identification on LinkedIn data set.

The rest of this paper is organized as follows: Section 2 briefly introduces the background and the data set used, defines the research problem, and presents preliminary experiments on verifying in-batch annotation bias; Section 3 proposes a factor graph based annotation model; Section 4 proposes a novel batch active learning algorithm with in-batch annotation bias; Section 5 shows the experimental results; Section 6 introduces related work and Section 7 concludes.

2. PRELIMINARIES

In this section, we briefly introduce the problem space, the data set used, and refine the particular active learning problem we are trying to solve. We then refine our definition of "in-batch annotation bias" referring to the interference between annotations of different data items presented together to the annotators. From this foundation we present a series of studies to verify the existence of in-batch annotation bias, and how the data items in a batch may interfere with the annotation of each other.

2.1 Background and Data Set

LinkedIn is the world's largest professional network service operator, with more than 300 million members in over 200 countries and territories [3]. LinkedIn allows users to comment on posts published by both companies and LinkedIn influencers [4]. Unfortunately, a certain portion of the comments might be spams, offensive, or otherwise inappropriate to display. To maintain a high-quality member experience, it is critical to identify and prevent these comments from being displayed.

We employ a supervised classifier (*e.g.* logistic regression) trained offline, which requires a sufficiently large set of annotated data. In order to collect training data, we use CrowdFlower for data annotation. Annotators are provided an annotation codebook with definitions of inappropriate comments, as well as several examples of both inappropriate and acceptable comments. In this task, we define inappropriate comments as promotional, profane, blatant soliciting, random greeting comments, as well as comments with *only* web links and contact information. Comments on the same post are grouped together and divided into batches, where each batch consists of up to five comments. All comments in a batch are displayed simultaneously to the annotators.

We sample a data set of 431,525 comments on 89,355 posts of companies and influencers in LinkedIn. 128,587 of them are comments on "company updates", 48,207 of them are on "influencer updates" and 254,731 are on "influencer articles". In order to track the performance of crowd annotators, we construct a ground truth data set with 2,835 comments. The ground truth data set is annotated by 9 trained LinkedIn employees (experts) using the same codebook and interface as used for the crowdsourcing experiments. Each comment is classified as either *inappropriate* or *acceptable*. The average Cohen's kappa for all annotator pairs is 0.7881.

[3]`http://press.linkedin.com/about`

[4]LinkedIn influencers are a selected set of industry and thought leaders.

2.2 Batch Active Learning

Active learning algorithms iteratively choose unlabeled data items for labeling by an external oracle (*e.g.* expert human annotators) and then fold the new labeled data back into the training data set. A model is retrained on the updated training set. When more than one data item is chosen in an iteration it is called *batch* active learning. More precisely, suppose the unlabeled data set is U, labeled set is L, and the labels of L are in y_L. A typical active learning algorithm chooses a subset $A \subset U$ with a given size k and obtains their labels y_A from an oracle. The selected data is then moved from U and added to L with their labels y_A concatenated to y_L.

Existing active learning algorithms often assume the annotation provided by the oracle is reliable. However, this assumption is rarely true, especially when crowds are employed as the oracle. Let A be some subset of data items and y'_A (different from y_A, which is the ground truth labeling) is their annotations drawn from some round of crowdsourcing. Then, treating crowdsourcing as a random process, we regard y'_A as a random variable described by distribution $q(y'_A|A)$. In this light, our objective is now to design an active learning algorithm which leverages $q(y'_A|A)$ while choosing unlabeled data items in each iteration. More formally,

Problem 1. **Batch active learning from biased crowds.** Let L be a data set with known labels y_L, and U be an unlabeled data set where each item i in L and U is described by feature vector X_i. For a set of data A consisting of k items, a crowd provides a (biased) annotation drawn from distribution $q(y'|A)$. The objective is to choose the best subset $A^* \subset U$ satisfying $|A| = k$, so that after adding A and the annotation given by the biased oracle y'_A into L and y_L, the performance of classifier trained on the new labeled data is optimized.

Before we develop the active learning algorithm, we need to first understand the crowds' annotation behavior, and model their annotating distribution $q(y'|A)$.

2.3 In-Batch Annotation Bias

Annotation bias has been observed in multiple fields, including machine translation [4], image labeling [27], and information retrieval [18]. Most studies focus on annotation bias on a single data item, resulted from variance across annotators. This bias can often be corrected either by collecting data from multiple annotators or carefully choosing annotators.

However, due to limits of time and cost, or the nature of data, data items are also often organized into small batches, and presented to the annotators at the same time. This particular way of presenting data items can introduce additional annotation bias, which cannot be fixed using multiple annotators. Suppose the batch is represented by a set of data items $b = \{b_i\}$. If the annotation from the crowd annotators on a certain data item b_i in the batch, represented by y'_i, follows a different distribution from the annotation on the same data item but displayed alone, or from the distribution when it is assembled with different other data items in batch b', then there is a certain kind of annotation bias introduced by the way we display data items. For example, in our inappropriate comment identification task, if an acceptable comment is presented along with a whole batch of inappropriate comments, it might be more likely to be mistakenly chosen as inappropriate; it could also be more likely to be correctly labeled, if other comments in the same batch happened to provide some examples as *reminders* of some subtle rules of inappropriate comments (*e.g.* the comment containing URL in Table 1). In contrast, if a comment is presented alone, annotators are more likely to make relatively independent judgments, but also lose the possibility to be implicitly taught by other comments in the same batch. We refer to this potential annotation bias as "in-batch annotation bias".

Verifying in-batch annotation bias. Based on the ground truth data for inappropriate comment identification task, we conduct experiments verifying different factors that may result in in-batch annotation bias.

We first study how the batch size can affect annotating behavior of crowds. Each time we take a comment as a *data item of interest*, then sample uniformly at random from the other comments of the same post, to construct two batches of data items, with sizes $k_1 < t_k$ and $k_2 \geq t_k$ respectively, where t_k is the batch size threshold which defines the treatment. The comment in the batch of size k_1 is *untreated*, and is put into the control group, while the comment in the batch of size k_2 is *treated*, and is placed into the test group.

Another factor to be explored is the number of positives (*i.e.* inappropriate comments in our settings) in the batch. We take the same *data item of interest* as above then randomly sample $\pi_1 < t_\pi$ and $\pi_2 \geq t_\pi$ items from all the inappropriate comments in the same post, joined with $k - \pi_1 - 1$ and $k - \pi_2 - 1$ acceptable comments, also randomly sampled from the same post to form two batches in the control and test group respectively. Here k is fixed to be five, and $0 \leq t_\pi \leq k - 1$ is a given threshold.

We mix batches in both groups together and collect their annotations from CrowdFlower with the tasks structured to prevent the same annotators from labeling a particular data item multiple times. We compare the probability of each data item of interest being annotated as inappropriate in both the control and test groups. As we already know the ground truth of each comment, we separately study data items with different ground truth labels. Specifically, for a positive data item of interest, we compare its true positive rate in the control group TPR_1 and in the test group TPR_2 by calculating the ratio TPR_2/TPR_1; for a negative data item of interests we compare its false positive rate in control and test groups by FPR_2/FPR_1.

Observation results. In Figure 1 and 2 we plot the ratios of true positive and false positive rates TPR_2/TPR_1 and FPR_2/FPR_1 for each treatment with thresholds t_k and t_π respectively. In Figure 1(a), we do not observe significant [5] bias under treatments of different batch size thresholds, which means the true positive rate is not likely to be influenced by the batch size. On the other hand, in Figure 1(b), we see that presenting data items with other data items can reduce the false positive rate as compared to presenting only a single data item. This indicates that annotation bias exists when data items are organized into batches.

Moreover, Figure 2(a) shows TPR_2/TPR_1 is significantly less than one, when the treatment is set to "having one or more other positive data items in the same batch", which

[5] By "significant", we mean the ratio 1.0 is not within the 95% confidence interval for the observed results.

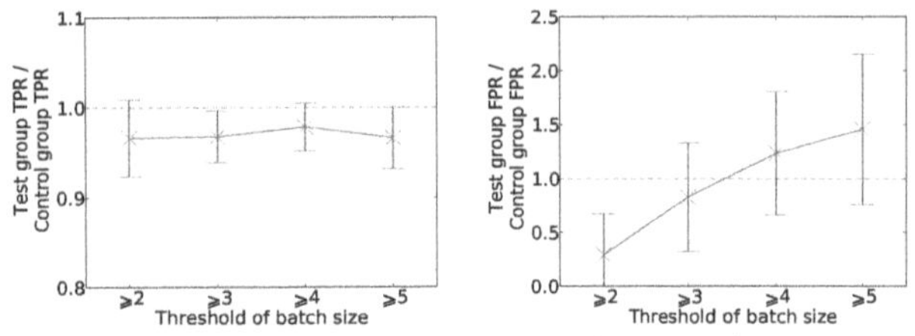

(a) TPR_2/TPR_1 (b) FPR_2/FPR_1

Figure 1: Comparing ratios of true positive rates (TPR) and false positive rates (FPR) when annotating with different thresholds t_k on the batch sizes.

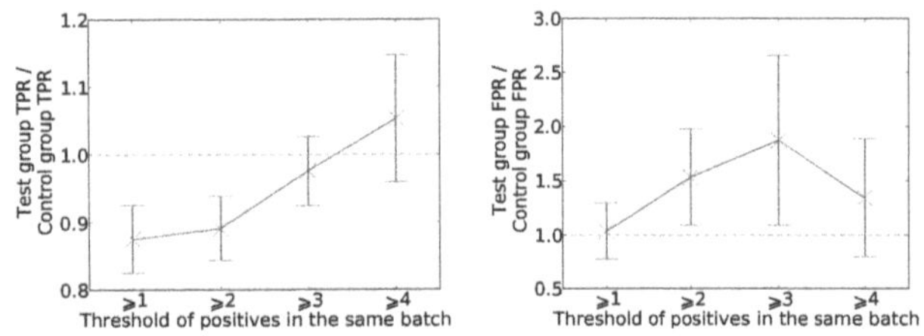

(a) TPR_2/TPR_1 (b) FPR_2/FPR_1

Figure 2: Comparing ratios of true positive rates (TPR) and false positive rates (FPR) when annotating with different thresholds t_π on the number of positives.

means that positive data items are less likely to be identified correctly when there are other positive data items in the same batch. This conclusion is still significant when t_π is increased to two; however there is not sufficient evidence to support this when t_π is greater than two. On the other hand, Figure 2(b) shows that FPR_2/FPR_1 is significantly larger than one, when t_π is set to either two or three. This suggests that negative data items appearing along with a number of other positive data items can also influence crowd annotation. The observational results verify that annotation towards data items in the same batch can influence each other. In certain scenarios, the in-batch annotation bias can adversely impact annotation quality.

3. A FACTOR GRAPH MODEL FOR BATCH ANNOTATION

An intuitive explanation to the phenomenon illustrated in Figure 2 is that when an annotator works on a batch of data items, she may have a prior distribution of counts of different labels in a batch. That is, for a batch of comments, an annotator may be reluctant to mark many comments as inappropriate due to a prior belief that inappropriate comments are rare. Although the prior could be overcome when the labels are certain, this "inertial thinking" can overwhelm the annotation of difficult or uncertain data items. Based on this intuition, we introduce a factor graph model to describe the annotating distribution with in-batch annotation bias. We then use the model to characterize the bias in actual crowd-annotated data.

Model description. We represent a set of data items by d-dimensional feature vectors $X = \{x_i\}$, where $x_i \in \mathbb{R}^d$. The data items are organized into batches $B = \{b_j\}$ of size k, where each batch is a list of data items $b_j = [b_j^{(1)}, \cdots, b_j^{(k)}]$ with size k. Without loss of generality, we suppose each batch b_j receives one annotation represented by $y'_j = [y_j'^{(1)}, \cdots, y_j'^{(k)}]$, where $y_j'^{(i)} \in \mathcal{Y}$, and $\mathcal{Y}$ is the set of possible labels. If each batch can receive multiple annotations, we can produce multiple batch-annotation pairs with the same batch data associated with different annotations. The set of annotations is denoted as $Y' = \{y'_j\}$. Notice that we are modeling the annotation $y_j'^{(i)}$ of data item $b_j^{(i)}$, which is different from the ground truth label $y_{b_j^{(i)}}$.

In the graphical representation of the proposed batch annotation model shown in Figure 3, each annotation of a single data item $y_j'^{(i)}$ is represented by a random variable (clear circles), and the feature vector $x_{b_j^{(i)}}$ is represented by k observed variables (shaded circles). For simplicity, we only draw the model for a single batch b_j with a fixed size k, and assuming $b_j = [1, 2, \cdots, k]$.

In addition, there are k factor functions $\phi\left(x_i, y_j'^{(i)}\right)$, modeling the correlation between human annotation and data item features:

$$\phi(x_i, y_j'^{(i)}) = \exp\left[\alpha^\top f(x_i, y_j'^{(i)})\right] \tag{1}$$

where α is a vector of weighting parameters; $f(x_i, y_j'^{(i)})$ maps the feature vector according to $y_j'^{(i)}$, which in the binary classification case can simply be $f(x_i, y_j'^{(i)}) = y_j'^{(i)} x_i$.

To further consider the in-batch annotation bias, an additional factor function $\gamma\left(y'_j\right)$, defined as:

$$\gamma\left(y'_j\right) = \exp\left[\beta^\top g(y'_j)\right] \tag{2}$$

where in this model, we simply consider the count of different labels appearing in this annotation. Thus $g(y'_j)$ can be an indicator function, where each element corresponds to a possible distribution over counts of different labels within a size-k batch. For example, in a binary classification task, $g(y'_j)$ can be a $(k+1)$-dimensional vector, where the (k_1+1)-th element is 1 when $|y'_j| = k_1$, leaving all the other elements as 0. β is a vector of weighting parameters.

The likelihood function can be written as:

$$\begin{aligned}\mathcal{L} &= \prod_j \frac{1}{Z_j} \prod_{i=1}^{k} \phi(x_{b_j^{(i)}}, y_j'^{(i)}) \cdot \gamma\left(y'_j\right) \\ &= \prod_j \frac{1}{Z_j} \exp\left[\sum_{i=1}^{k} \alpha^\top f(x_{b_j^{(i)}}, y_j'^{(i)}) + \beta^\top g(y'_j)\right]\end{aligned} \tag{3}$$

where $Z_j = \sum_{y'} \exp\left[\sum_{i=1}^{k} \alpha^\top f(x_{b_j^{(i)}}, y'^{(i)}) + \beta^\top g(y')\right]$ is the normalizing factor for each annotation of a batch.

Model learning. We learn the model through gradient descent. By defining $\theta = \left[\alpha^\top \ \beta^\top\right]^\top$ and $h(b_j, y'_j) = \left[\sum_{i=1}^{k} f(x_{b_j^{(i)}}, y_j'^{(i)})^\top \ g(y'_j)^\top\right]^\top$, our learning objective is to find the best θ^* to optimize the log-likelihood.

The simplified expression of log-likelihood is:

$$\log \mathcal{L} = \sum_j \left[\theta^\top h(b_j, y'_j) - \log Z_j\right]$$

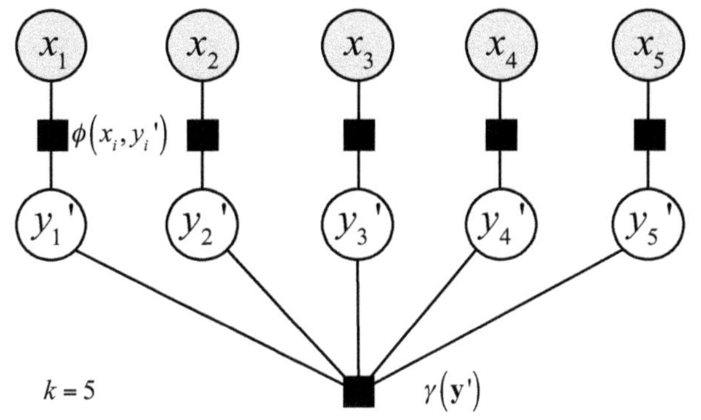

Figure 3: A graphical representation of the batch annotation model ($k = 5$).

And the gradient can be calculated by

$$\frac{\partial \log \mathcal{L}}{\partial \theta^{(m)}} = \sum_j \left[h^{(m)}(b_j, y'_j) - \sum_{y'} \frac{\exp\left(\theta^\top h(b_j, y')\right)}{Z_j} h^{(m)}(b_j, y') \right]$$
$$= \sum_j \left[h^{(m)}(b_j, y'_j) - \mathbb{E}_{y'} \left[h^{(m)}(b_j, y') \right] \right]$$

Calculation of the gradient is exponential to the batch size k. This isn't problematic, however, as at least for our tasks, k is small—typically $k \leq 5$. Thus, the computational cost is acceptable.

Parameter analysis. We learn the model based on annotations from crowds on the task of inappropriate comment identification. There are 6,121 annotations on 1,000 batches of size $k = 5$. Each batch of comments was constructed randomly without replacement. We encode the annotation by the label set $\mathcal{Y} = \{0, 1\}$, where 1 (positive) represents "inappropriate comment", and 0 (negative) represents "acceptable comments". Figure 4(b) presents the log-likelihood curve during the training process, which clearly shows that the model converges within 200 iterations.

Figure 4(a) shows the parameter β of the learned model, where $\beta(k_1)$ is the weight for annotation y' satisfying $||y'||_1 = k_1$ (i.e. the $(k_1 + 1)$-th element of vector β). The greater $\beta(k_1)$ is, the more likely annotators are to produce an annotation with k_1 positive labels among all the k data items. This suggests that annotators for this task tend to make polarized annotations, namely either none or all of the data items are positive. A possible reason is when an annotator already sees four of the data items in a batch are positive (negative), she may unjustly annotate the other data items also as positive (negative) without carefully checking the item itself.

Time complexity analysis. We provide a time complexity analysis of training the batch annotation model. Suppose the size of training data set is n. The dimension of parameter α is $d \times (|\mathcal{Y}| - 1)$, while the dimension of parameter β is $\binom{k+1}{|\mathcal{Y}|-1}$. For each batch-annotation pair, calculating the gradient requires $O(|\mathcal{Y}|^k)$ steps. Thus the time complexity for an iteration of model training is $O(n|\mathcal{Y}|^k + d|\mathcal{Y}| + \binom{k+1}{|\mathcal{Y}|-1})$. As both k and $|\mathcal{Y}|$ are small (effectively constant), the model training is computable, and will only increase linearly with regard to the feature number d.

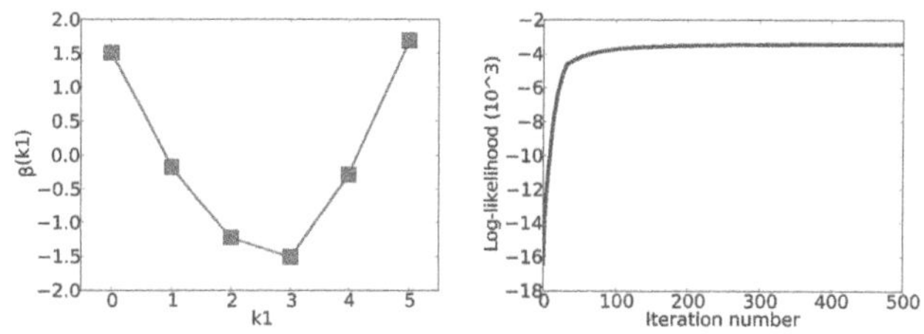

(a) Parameter analysis (b) Convergence analysis

Figure 4: Factor graph model parameter and convergence results when trained to characterize in-batch bias in crowdsourced annotation.

4. ACTIVE LEARNING WITH IN-BATCH ANNOTATION BIAS

In this section, we propose an active learning algorithm taking advantage of in-batch annotation bias. For all the possible annotations on a subset of data items, we calculate the utility of each annotation weighted by its probability, where the utility is measured by the training likelihood on labeled data and the entropy of the unlabeled data based on the classifier updated by the subset. Then we optimistically choose the largest weighted utility as the quality function for this subset of data items. The active learning algorithm presented below is summarized in Algorithm 1.

Suppose the predictive probability of data item i is represented by $p(y|x_i; w_L)$, where w_L is the parameter for a classifier trained on data set L with labels y_L. Denote the annotating probability of a batch of data items as $q(y'_A|x)$, where y'_A contains the annotation of all the data items in A. An intuitive objective is to find a subset $A \subset U$ satisfying $|A| = k$, to optimize the expected utility of the classifier over the annotation distribution:

$$A^* = \arg\max_A \sum_{y'_A \in \mathcal{Y}^k} q(y'_A|x_A) F(L \cup A, y_L \cup y'_A, U \setminus A)$$

where $F(L \cup A, y_L \cup y'_A, U \setminus A)$ measures both the likelihood of labeled data and the uncertainty of all the unlabeled data based on the classifier trained on the labeled set extended by A and its annotation y'_A:

$$F(L \cup A, y_L \cup y'_A, U \setminus A) = \left[(1 - \lambda) \sum_{l \in L \cup A} \log p(y_l|x_l; w') \right.$$
$$\left. + \lambda \sum_{u \in U \setminus A} \sum_{y_u \in \mathcal{Y}} p(y_u|x_u; w') \log p(y_u|x_u; w') \right]$$

where λ is a given constant between 0 and 1, and w' is the classifier parameters trained on $L \cup A$, where A is annotated by y'_A.

By employing the factor graph model to estimate the annotating probability q, we have:

$$q(y'_A|x_A) = \frac{1}{Z_A} \exp\left[\sum_{a \in A} \alpha^\top f(x_a, y'_a) + \beta^\top g(y'_A) \right]$$

where Z_A is the normalizing factor.

However, directly optimizing this objective function is computationally difficult. Instead, we optimize the following objective:

$$\max_{A, y' \in \mathcal{Y}^k} q(y'|x_A) \left[F(L \cup A, y_L \cup y', U \setminus A) - F(L, y_L, U) \right]$$

which optimistically evaluates a subset A by the maximum product of the possible gain given a certain annotation y', and the probability that this annotation happens. A similar strategy is employed in [9]. Note that we are taking the increment of the F function by adding A instead of directly taking its value. Because given a subset A, if there exists an annotation y' that causes a drop of F function, then it should be penalized more as the probability of this annotation increases. In contrast, if annotating A with y' increases the F function, we favor y' as its probability increases.

Optimizing this objective function is still NP-hard as one has to enumerate all the possible subsets of U. Instead, we represent the chosen set A and their labels y'_A by a continuous matrix $S \in \mathbb{R}^{|U|\times|\mathcal{Y}|}$ where each row corresponds to an unlabeled data item in U, and a $|\mathcal{Y}|$-dimensional vector ν, where each element ν_y indicates the count of chosen data items that are annotated with label y. Without loss of generality, we assume all the unlabeled data items in U are indexed by $1, \ldots, |U|$. The following constraints must be satisfied for S and ν to be valid:

1. $0 \le S \le 1$;
2. $\forall y \in \mathcal{Y}, \sum_i S_{i,y} = 1$;
3. $\sum_y \nu_y = k$, so that the total size of chosen set is k;
4. $\forall i, \sum_y \nu_y S_{i,y} \le 1$, to make sure each data item can only be chosen once.

Thereby the y-th column of S is a vector indicating which data item will be chosen and annotated as y, and $\sum_y \nu_y S_{i,y}$ for each i represents how likely i will be chosen in A. We denote the set of all the S that satisfying all the above constraints with regard to a given ν as Φ_ν.

By representing A and y'_A by S and ν, we further relax the q function with regard to S and ν by:

$$\hat{q}(S,\nu|X) = \frac{1}{Z_{S,\nu}} \exp\left[\sum_{i,y} S_{i,y}\nu_y \alpha^\top f(x_i,y) + \beta^\top \hat{g}(\nu)\right] \quad (4)$$

where the output of $\hat{g}(\nu)$ is equal to $g(y')$ for any y' with exactly the same count of different labels as ν indicates. And the normalizing factor can be estimated by:

$$Z_{S,\nu} = \sum_{\mu} \exp\left[\sum_i \sum_{y,\tilde{y}} S_{i,y}\mu_{\tilde{y},y}\alpha^\top f(x_i,\tilde{y}) + \beta^\top \hat{g}(\mu^\top \mathbf{1})\right] \quad (5)$$

where $\mathbf{1}$ is an all-1 vector with $|\mathcal{Y}|$ dimensions, and μ is a $|\mathcal{Y}|$-by-$|\mathcal{Y}|$ matrix, with each element as a non-negative integer, satisfying $\mu\mathbf{1} = \nu$. Although calculating the normalizing factor needs to enumerate all the possible μ, it is still computationally feasible as both the label space size $|\mathcal{Y}|$ and batch size k are usually small.

Similarly, we can relax the F function with regard to L and U. For simplicity, we omit the variable L, y_L, U as they do not change during our optimization:

$$\begin{aligned}\hat{F}(S,\nu) = \Big[&(1-\lambda)\sum_{l\in L} \log p(y_l|x_l;w') \\ &+ (1-\lambda)\sum_{i,y} S_{i,y}\nu_y \log p(y|x_i;w') \\ &+ \lambda \sum_{i,y} S_{i,y}(1-\nu^\top \mathbf{1})p(y|x_i;w')\log p(y|x_i;w')\Big]\end{aligned} \quad (6)$$

Input: Initial labeled set L, unlabeled set U, batch size k, iteration number N, step length η, λ, Trained annotation model θ

for $n \leftarrow 1, \ldots, N$ **do**
  Train classifier based on L;
  $\mathcal{O}^* \leftarrow -\infty$;
  // Enumerate ν
  forall ν **do**
    Initialize S;
    // Optimize by S
    repeat
      Calculate $\nabla_S \mathcal{O}$ according to Eq. (8);
      $Z \leftarrow S + \eta\nabla_S O$;
      $S \leftarrow \arg\min_{S'\in\Phi_\nu} \frac{1}{2}||S' - Z||_F^2$;
      Update classifier w' w.r.t. S, ν;
    until *converged*;
    if $\mathcal{O}(S,\nu) > \mathcal{O}^*$ **then**
      $\mathcal{O}^* \leftarrow \mathcal{O}(S,\nu)$;
      $S^* \leftarrow S$;
  Extract A from S^*;
  Acquire labels of A from crowds;
  Add A and their labels into L and remove A from U;

Algorithm 1: Active learning with in-batch annotation bias.

Now we can optimize

$$\mathcal{O}(S,\nu) = \hat{q}(S,\nu|X)\left[\hat{F}(S,\nu) - F(L,y_L,U)\right] \quad (7)$$

where w' is the classifier parameter trained on the union of L and a weighted data set which assumes the unlabeled data are labeled as indicated by S and weighted by corresponding $\nu_y S_{i,y}$.

The proposed objective function can be optimized by enumerating all the possible ν, and optimizing S given ν, as both the batch size k and label space size $|\mathcal{Y}|$ is not large. Fixing ν, the optimization problem may be solved by gradient descent. It can still be challenging to calculate the gradient, as w' is a function of S. However, as our adjustment of S is subtle, we can assume w' to be fixed for the gradient, but update w' by retraining the model after S is adjusted. The gradient can be calculated as:

$$\begin{aligned}\frac{\partial \mathcal{O}(S,\nu)}{\partial S_{i,y}} = &\frac{\partial \hat{q}(S,\nu|X)}{\partial S_{i,y}}\left[\hat{F}(S,\nu) - F(L,U)\right] \\ &+ \hat{q}(S,\nu|X)\frac{\partial \hat{F}(S,\nu)}{\partial S_{i,y}}\end{aligned} \quad (8)$$

where $\partial\hat{q}/\partial S_{i,y}$ and $\partial\hat{F}/\partial S_{i,y}$ can be obtained from Equation (4), (5) and (6). In order to take care of all the constraints of S, since the feasible set is the intersection of multiple linear inequalities, we can project the updated (possibly not feasible) Z into the feasible set after each update, by finding the closest point S in the feasible set Φ_ν, which is a quadratic optimization problem minimizing the Frobenius norm $||S - Z||_F$ with constraints.

Once the solution S^* and ν^* that optimize the objective function above is obtained, we can choose set A accordingly. One way is to calculate the vector $\sigma = S^*\nu^*$ and take the top-k data items i with the top σ_i values in σ vector, as subset A. Another way is, for each $y \in \mathcal{Y}$, take the top-ν^*_y data items i with maximal $S_{i,y}$ values. We selected the second method as we find it more comfortable with our intuitions regarding the underlying processes.

Time complexity analysis. To be general, we assume the training complexity of the classifier is $O(\tau(|L|))$. At each iteration, we need to enumerate all the possibie ν, which is $\binom{k+1}{|\mathcal{Y}|^2-1}$. Optimizing S needs to calculate $\nabla_S \mathcal{O}$, which takes $O(|U||\mathcal{Y}| + |\mathcal{Y}|^k)$. Updating the classifier with regard to S takes $O(\tau(|L| + |\mathcal{Y}||U|))$. Assuming the total iterations to run before S converge is T. Extracting A from S^* is $O(|U|)$. Thus, at each iteration, the time complexity of selecting a batch of data items with size k, is $O\left(\tau(|L|) + \binom{k+1}{|\mathcal{Y}|^2-1}T\left(|U||\mathcal{Y}| + |\mathcal{Y}|^k + \tau(|L| + |\mathcal{Y}||U|)\right)\right)$. Notice that k and $|\mathcal{Y}|$ are very small in most cases. For example, in our inappropriate comment identification task, $|\mathcal{Y}| = 2$ and $k = 5$, both $k^{|\mathcal{Y}|}$ and $|\mathcal{Y}|^k$ is less than 10^2.

5. EXPERIMENTAL RESULTS

We test the effectiveness of our proposed active learning algorithm by conducting real experiments with a crowdsourcing service platform, on live LinkedIn data.

Data set. We sample a subset of 7,012 comments from a collection of posts with more than 5 comments, as the pool of data items for active learning. Among which, 30 comments are labeled by LinkedIn employees, serving as the initial labeled data set L for active learning, while the others (U) are left unlabeled. An additional subset of 1,715 comments are sampled from the ground truth data set labeled by LinkedIn employees (Cf. Section 2), where 1,372 of them become the test data set for evaluating the classifier performance and the other 343 comments form a validation data set.

Comparing method. We compare the performance of our proposed method with random selection and two of the existing algorithms:

- *Random (RND) Baseline.* Data items are picked at random. In particular, posts are selected uniformly at random without replacement. For each selected post, comments are again selected uniformly at random without replacement.

- *Maximum Uncertainty (MU).* Selects those data items for which the current classifier is most uncertain where uncertainty is measured by entropy and calculated as follows:

$$A^* = \arg\max_{A \in U} \sum_{a \in A} \sum_{y \in \mathcal{Y}} -p(y|x_a, w_L) \log p(y|x_a, w_L)$$

  where $|A|$ is our batch size k.

- *Discriminative Active Learning (DA).* This method uses a similar objective function as the proposed method (WDA) but without weighting F with annotating probability q. It is equivalent to the discriminative active learning algorithm proposed in [9].

* *Weighted Discriminative Active Learning (WDA).* This is our proposed method discussed in Section 4.

Experimental setup. For each of the above algorithms, we run for 20 iterations, starting from the same initial training set L consisting of 30 annotated data items drawn from the expert labeled ground truth. The base classifier used is logistic regression with L2 regularization as implemented in Weka [6]. In our task we only display comments (data items) on a common post in a particular batch. This is implemented for the above algorithms as follows: at each iteration for each algorithm we restrict the chosen set A_p to be a subset of comments on some post p. This is repeated for every post with more than k (set to 5 for all experiments) comments left in the unlabeled data set U. After all the batches (A_p) are generated, they are ranked by the active learning objective function and the top 50 batches are sent to the crowdsourcing platform for annotation. After the data items are annotated, they are added into the training data set and removed from the unlabeled data set. The classifier is then retrained on the new training data set.

We utilize CrowdFlower as our crowdsourcing platform. As discussed in Section 2, the codebook definitions for inappropriate comments and examples of both inappropriate and acceptable comments is presented to the annotators at each iteration. Each annotator is first evaluated with ten "test questions", *i.e.* batches of data items with known annotation, for the crowdsourcing system to assess their "trust". Only annotators who can correctly answer at least 70% of the test questions can proceed to the actual annotation task. Each batch of data items must be labeled by at least five annotators before it is returned from CrowdFlower. We determine the final label for each data item with majority voting of the returned annotations.

Evaluation. We evaluate the performance of each classifier at each iteration with the following metrics calculated against the test set:

- *Area under ROC (AUC).*

- *$F_{0.5}$-score ($F_{0.5}$).* Calculated with $F_{0.5} = \frac{(1+0.5^2)\times precision \times recall}{0.5^2 \times precision + recall}$ as we value precision more than recall.

- *Optimized F_1-score (F_1^*).* As the data distribution can be extremely imbalanced in our task, we optimize each classifier's threshold in terms of F_1-score with the validation set, instead of using the default of 0.5. We then test the classifier's F_1 performance with that threshold.

- *Optimized $F_{0.5}$-score ($F_{0.5}^*$).* Similarly, we can optimize the $F_{0.5}$-score based on the validation set and evaluate on the test data set.

- *Recall @ Precision (R@P).* We find the recall at a minimum precision by adjusting the classifier threshold and reporting the highest recall with precision greater than a certain value. In these experiments, we use Recall@0.95 and Recall@0.90.

We also evaluate each algorithm by its average classifier performance across all iterations. For optimized F-score, the classifier threshold is recalculated at each iteration.

Performance comparison. Table 2 shows the average classifier performance for each of our evaluated algorithms. All of the active learning algorithms outperform the random baseline. Among all the active learning algorithms, WDA outperforms the other baseline methods for both optimized F-measures as well as recall at a fixed precision. It also achieves a performance close to maximum uncertainty in terms of $F_{0.5}$-score, without optimizing the threshold. Especially in terms of R@.95, WDA achieves an

[6] `http://www.cs.waikato.ac.nz/~ml/weka/`

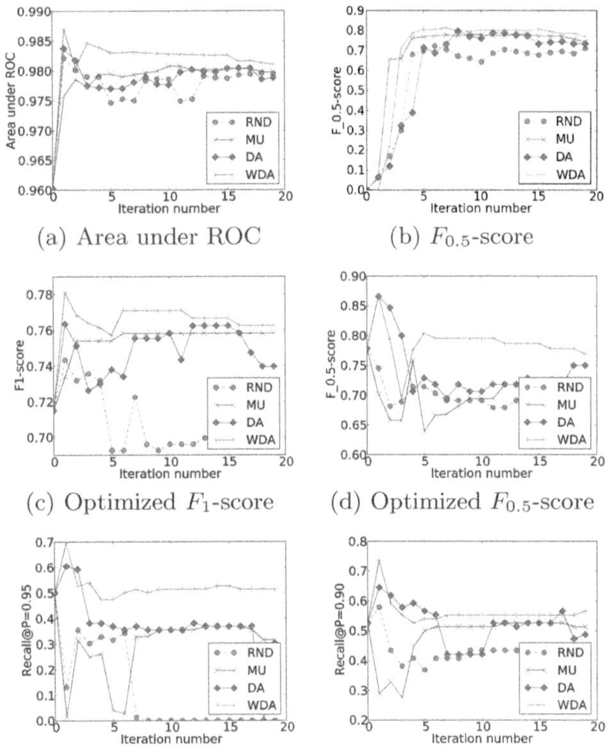

(a) Area under ROC (b) $F_{0.5}$-score

(c) Optimized F_1-score (d) Optimized $F_{0.5}$-score

(e) Recall@Precision=0.95 (f) Recall@Precision=0.90

Figure 5: Comparing learning curves of different active learning algorithms.

Table 2: Performance of active learning algorithms. All results are shown as percents.

Method	AUC	$F_{0.5}$	F_1^*	$F_{0.5}^*$	R@.95	R@.90
RND	97.73	57.74	70.75	69.95	11.45	43.49
MU	97.86	**68.58**	75.40	69.83	29.74	48.16
DA	97.82	60.84	74.80	73.98	37.50	52.17
WDA	**98.17**	68.39	**76.45**	**78.69**	**51.97**	**56.05**

average performance of 51.97%, while maximum uncertainty does not reach 30%. Most interestingly, it outperforms DA on all measures giving further evidence that our factor graph model is indeed learning and leveraging the in-batch annotation bias. Learning curves of different measures are also shown in Figure 5. After iteration seven, RND's performance on F_1 and R@.95 plummets. We suspect this is due to noisy annotation. Simultaneously, the recall for WDA at 95% precision converges to a stable value much higher than the other methods.

Case study. To better understand what is happening with the annotations, we performed a case study comparing the WDA and non-WDA annotations. We compare several pairs of batches constructed by WDA and other baselines having at least one comment in common but annotated differently. Some examples are shown in Table 3. In the first pair, WDA selected five comments predicted to be identically annotated as inappropriate while RND, picking at random, chose a mix with three actually inappropriate comments (the last three). The comment in common is correctly annotated as inappropriate in the WDA constructed batch but not in the randomly constructed batch. The third comment in the random batch is actually also inappropriate according to our codebook yet was mislabeled by a majority of the crowd annotators. WDA tends to construct batches where the biased annotation probability and the classifier predicted probability are relatively coherent, which in turn helps crowds perform more correct annotation.

The second example compares WDA to DA. The fifth comment in the WDA constructed batch is actually a blatant solicitation. It starts with "I am Madame Clarisse..." but ends with advertising loan services. For DA, on the other hand, this same comment is not identified as inappropriate. We notice that there is another inappropriate comments in the same batch, which is correctly identified. As we observed in Figure 4(a), annotators are more reluctant to label two inappropriate comments than only one in a batch.

6. RELATED WORK

Annotation bias. A number of studies have been conducted on evaluating data quality collected from crowds, and modeling annotator behaviors to optimize the data quality. Snow *et al.* [21] explored the performance with non-expert annotators in several NLP tasks. Raykar *et al.* [14, 15, 16] studied how to learn a model with noisy labeling. Specifically, they employ a logistic regression classifier, and insert hidden variables indicating whether an annotator tells the truth. Whitehill *et al.* [28] modeled the annotator ability, data item difficulty, and inferred the true label from the crowds in a unified model. Venanzi *et al.* [23] proposed a community-based label aggregation model to identify different types of workers, and correct their labels correspondingly. However, they do not study the case when data items are grouped into batches. Das *et al.* [5] addressed the interactions of opinions between people connected by networks. Demeester *et al.* [6] discussed the disagreement between different users on assessment of web search results. Their studies also focus on understanding annotator behavior, but none of them consider the case when multiple data items are organized into a batch.

Scholer *et al.* [17, 18] studied the annotation disagreements in a relevance assessment data set. They discovered the correlation between annotations of similar data items. They also explored "threshold priming" in annotation, where the annotators tend to make similar judgments or apply similar standard on consecutive data items they review. However, their studies focus more on qualitative conclusions, without a quantitative model to characterize and measure the discovered factors. Carterette *et al.* [2] provided several assessor models for the TREC data set. Mozer *et al.* [13] studied the similar "relativity of judgments" phenomenon on sequential tasks instead of small batches. Also, they focused more on debiasing not active learning.

Batch active learning. Active learning has been extensively studied. Settles *et al.* [19] summarized a number of active learning strategies. Batch active learning, in contrast to traditional active learning settings, aims to choose a set of data items to query, which proposes some unique challenges. Some strategies focus on optimizing the helpfulness of a data batch. Hoi *et al.* [11, 10] utilized Fisher information matrix to choose the data items that are likely to change the classifier parameters most. Brinker *et al.* [1] studied batch active learning for SVM and aimed to max-

Table 3: Case study results. The left column shows the batches constructed by WDA method, while the right column shows the batches constructed by different baselines. y_i' gives the crowdsourced annotation with "Yes" marking inappropriate comments and "No" for acceptable comments. Comments whose label is bolded are common to both batches.

WDA		RND	
y_i'	Comment content	y_i'	Comment content
Yes	please check my profile. harvindersinghlongowal@yahoo.com	No	when fresher will get experience until they don't give opportunity.
Yes	Dear sir, I am interested, please check up my profile	No	only experience no fresher .... very baddddddddddddddd
Yes	Dear sir I interest your job. please check my details.	No	review my stats and kindly notify for further proceedings
Yes	Interested. Please see my profile.	Yes	please check my profile, mobile number is. 09559186335
Yes	Hello Sir, Please check my profile. I am ready to work in any part of world. Thank you,	**No**	Hello Sir, Please check my profile. I am ready to work in any part of world. Thank you,

WDA		DA	
y_i'	Comment content	y_i'	Comment content
No	What we need*	No	Exactly, what I needed to read today. It really is almost like scary when you get a gift like this read. ... *[Omitted]*
No	Thank You... sounds familiar...Seen 3 recession...been last person in company (28 years old) before company bancrupty, giving 260 people notice before that, part of the job was to sold the assets, basically buried the company... Never get fired after that...:-) But i can relax now only in different atmosphere...vacation..summer house without phone...:-)	Yes	Good day, My Name is Peter Williams, am a supplier We suppliers all kind of metals and plastic and scrap, If you are interested in any product kindly send me email and the materials you want so i could send you our quotation okay. If you are interested in any of materials, Kindly revert back to me via "infocuixin.sl@gmail.com" Thanks
No	That was the message I needed. I will not dwell...I love my job!	No	Thanks for the article, Sallie. I like your secret #3 above-responsibility to those who have helped you before. ... *[Omitted]*
No	I don't relax well either, why do that when I could go for a walk?	No	Yes, we do!! Please tell her to check us out at EllevateNetwork.com
Yes	I am Madame Clarisse Sweet, ... *[Omitted]* I'd like to know if you have found an investor to assist you in realizing your projects otherwise the jeans Jeanne couple can help you if this is the couple who helped me find my loan of 75,000 € It I can help you as you who is in need he can be reached at the following email: naillejvalane@gmail.com	**No**	I am Madame Clarisse Sweet, ... *[Omitted]* I'd like to know if you have found an investor to assist you in realizing your projects otherwise the jeans Jeanne couple can help you if this is the couple who helped me find my loan of 75,000 € It I can help you as you who is in need he can be reached at the following email: naillejvalane@gmail.com

imize the diversity within the selected set of data samples. Guo *et al.* [9] proposed discriminative active learning strategy by formulating the problem as an optimization problem. A number of strategies also aim at choosing the most representative data batch with regard to the unlabeled data set. Yu *et al.* [30] proposed a transductive experimental design, which prioritizes the data samples that represent the hard-to-predict data. Chattopadhyay et al. [3] tried to choose the data batch to minimize Maximum Mean Discrepancy (MMD) to measure the difference in distribution between the labeled and unlabeled data. There are studies addressing both intuitions. Wang *et al.* [25] designed a framework to minimize the upper bound of empirical risk, which aims to find a batch of data items that are both discriminative and representative. However, all of the above studies assume reliable oracles—which never are in multiple-annotator scenarios such as crowdsourcing.

Active learning with crowds. Crowdsourcing serves as a potentially ideal oracle for active learning. Two perspectives have been explored; first is how to select data items to query when the oracles are noisy. Sheng *et al.* [20] provided an empirical study on the performance of repeated labeling and developed an active learning strategy addressing both the "label uncertainty" and "model uncertainty". Second is how to select annotators for crowdsourcing. Donmez *et al.* [7] studied this problem, by modeling the querying problem as a multi-armed bandit problem. Each annotator is regarded as as a bandit, and a binary reward function is defined based on whether the oracle provides a correct label. Yan *et al.* [29] explore both the problem of selecting query samples and selecting oracles, in context of a logistic regression classifier. Kajino *et al.* [12] proposed a convex optimization function for active learning in crowds. However, none of them leverages in-batch bias for active learning.

7. CONCLUSION

In this paper, we study the in-batch data annotation bias from crowds, which occurs when data items are organized into small batches. Our experimental results on a crowdsourcing platform suggest that the annotation of data items is impacted by other data items presented in the same batch. We propose a factor graph based batch annotation model, to capture the in-batch annotation bias of crowds. Based on the annotation model, we propose a novel active learning algorithm, which takes advantage of our batch annotation model to construct batches of unlabeled data items that reduce annotation error and improve classifier performance.

It may not be the case that the particular bias we found in our task generalizes to other tasks—this requires more experimentation. Regardless, it is reasonable to expect *some* form of in-batch bias. Our factor graph model can be trained on a preliminary annotation to detect whatever in-batch bias is present and then our proposed active learning algorithm can leverage that model to improve performance.

The proposed annotation model has broad application as strict independence between annotations of different data items can not be achieved in many annotation tasks. Without much training, crowd annotators are more likely to be steered by in-batch bias into making unnecessary mistakes. Although the batch annotation model is learned from the annotations of inappropriate comments in online social networks, we argue that the conclusion drawn from the model is not task-specific and should be applicable to most crowdsourcing labeling tasks. For example, it would be interesting to use the model to explore in-batch bias in conference paper reviewing. This paper has focused on one annotation task. A next step is to evaluate the proposed algorithms on other tasks. It is also interesting to evaluate if the model parameters can be directly transferred between tasks without retraining.

8. REFERENCES

[1] K. Brinker. Incorporating diversity in active learning with support vector machines. In *ICML*, volume 3, pages 59–66, 2003.

[2] B. Carterette and I. Soboroff. The effect of assessor error on ir system evaluation. In *SIGIR*, pages 539–546. ACM, 2010.

[3] R. Chattopadhyay, Z. Wang, W. Fan, I. Davidson, S. Panchanathan, and J. Ye. Batch mode active sampling based on marginal probability distribution matching. In *KDD*, pages 741–749. ACM, 2012.

[4] T. Cohn and L. Specia. Modelling annotator bias with multi-task gaussian processes: An application to machine translation quality estimation. In *ACL*, pages 32–42, 2013.

[5] A. Das, S. Gollapudi, R. Panigrahy, and M. Salek. Debiasing social wisdom. In *KDD*, pages 500–508. ACM, 2013.

[6] T. Demeester, R. Aly, D. Hiemstra, D. Nguyen, D. Trieschnigg, and C. Develder. Exploiting user disagreement for web search evaluation: an experimental approach. In *WSDM*, pages 33–42. ACM, 2014.

[7] P. Donmez, J. G. Carbonell, and J. Schneider. Efficiently learning the accuracy of labeling sources for selective sampling. In *KDD*, pages 259–268. ACM, 2009.

[8] R. G. Gomes, P. Welinder, A. Krause, and P. Perona. Crowdclustering. In *NIPS*, pages 558–566, 2011.

[9] Y. Guo and D. Schuurmans. Discriminative batch mode active learning. In *NIPS*, pages 593–600, 2008.

[10] S. C. Hoi, R. Jin, and M. R. Lyu. Large-scale text categorization by batch mode active learning. In *WWW*, pages 633–642, 2006.

[11] S. C. Hoi, R. Jin, J. Zhu, and M. R. Lyu. Batch mode active learning and its application to medical image classification. In *ICML*, pages 417–424. ACM, 2006.

[12] H. Kajino, Y. Tsuboi, and H. Kashima. A convex formulation for learning from crowds. In *AAAI*, 2012.

[13] M. C. Mozer, H. Pashler, M. Wilder, R. V. Lindsey, M. C. Jones, and M. N. Jones. Decontaminating human judgments by removing sequential dependencies. *NIPS*, 23, 2010.

[14] V. C. Raykar and S. Yu. Ranking annotators for crowdsourced labeling tasks. In *NIPS*, pages 1809–1817, 2011.

[15] V. C. Raykar, S. Yu, L. H. Zhao, A. Jerebko, C. Florin, G. H. Valadez, L. Bogoni, and L. Moy. Supervised learning from multiple experts: whom to trust when everyone lies a bit. In *ICML*, pages 889–896. ACM, 2009.

[16] V. C. Raykar, S. Yu, L. H. Zhao, G. H. Valadez, C. Florin, L. Bogoni, and L. Moy. Learning from crowds. *JMLR*, 11:1297–1322, 2010.

[17] F. Scholer, D. Kelly, W.-C. Wu, H. S. Lee, and W. Webber. The effect of threshold priming and need for cognition on relevance calibration and assessment. In *SIGIR*, pages 623–632. ACM, 2013.

[18] F. Scholer, A. Turpin, and M. Sanderson. Quantifying test collection quality based on the consistency of relevance judgements. In *SIGIR*, pages 1063–1072. ACM, 2011.

[19] B. Settles. Active learning literature survey. *University of Wisconsin, Madison*, 52:55–66, 2010.

[20] V. S. Sheng, F. Provost, and P. G. Ipeirotis. Get another label? improving data quality and data mining using multiple, noisy labelers. In *KDD*, pages 614–622. ACM, 2008.

[21] R. Snow, B. O'Connor, D. Jurafsky, and A. Y. Ng. Cheap and fast—but is it good?: evaluating non-expert annotations for natural language tasks. In *EMNLP*, pages 254–263, 2008.

[22] H. Su, J. Deng, and L. Fei-Fei. Crowdsourcing annotations for visual object detection. In *Human Computation Workshops at AAAI*, 2012.

[23] M. Venanzi, J. Guiver, G. Kazai, P. Kohli, and M. Shokouhi. Community-based bayesian aggregation models for crowdsourcing. In *WWW*, pages 155–164, 2014.

[24] S. Vijayanarasimhan and K. Grauman. Large-scale live active learning: Training object detectors with crawled data and crowds. In *CVPR*, pages 1449–1456. IEEE, 2011.

[25] Z. Wang and J. Ye. Querying discriminative and representative samples for batch mode active learning. In *KDD*, pages 158–166. ACM, 2013.

[26] F. L. Wauthier and M. I. Jordan. Bayesian bias mitigation for crowdsourcing. In *NIPS*, pages 1800–1808, 2011.

[27] P. Welinder, S. Branson, P. Perona, and S. J. Belongie. The multidimensional wisdom of crowds. In *NIPS*, pages 2424–2432, 2010.

[28] J. Whitehill, T.-f. Wu, J. Bergsma, J. R. Movellan, and P. L. Ruvolo. Whose vote should count more: Optimal integration of labels from labelers of unknown expertise. In *NIPS*, pages 2035–2043, 2009.

[29] Y. Yan, G. M. Fung, R. Rosales, and J. G. Dy. Active learning from crowds. In *ICML*, pages 1161–1168, 2011.

[30] K. Yu, J. Bi, and V. Tresp. Active learning via transductive experimental design. In *ICML*, pages 1081–1088. ACM, 2006.

Listwise Approach for Rank Aggregation in Crowdsourcing

Shuzi Niu[†], Yanyan Lan[‡], Jiafeng Guo[‡], Xueqi Cheng[‡], Lei Yu[†] and Guoping Long[†]
[†]Institute of Software, Chinese Academy of Sciences, Beijing, P. R. China
[‡]Institute of Computing Technology, Chinese Academy of Sciences, Beijing, P. R. China
{shuzi,yulei,guoping}@iscas.ac.cn, {lanyanyan,guojiafeng,cxq}@ict.ac.cn

ABSTRACT

Inferring a gold-standard ranking over a set of objects, such as documents or images, is a key task to build test collections for various applications like Web search and recommender systems. Crowdsourcing services provide an efficient and inexpensive way to collect judgments via labeling by sets of annotators. We thus study the problem of finding a consensus ranking from crowdsourced judgments. In contrast to conventional rank aggregation methods which minimize the distance between predicted ranking and input judgments from either pointwise or pairwise perspective, we argue that it is critical to consider the distance in a listwise way to emphasize the position importance in ranking. Therefore, we introduce a new listwise approach in this paper, where ranking measure based objective functions are utilized for optimization. In addition, we also incorporate the annotator quality into our model since the reliability of annotators can vary significantly in crowdsourcing. For optimization, we transform the optimization problem to the Linear Sum Assignment Problem, and then solve it by a very efficient algorithm named CrowdAgg guaranteeing the optimal solution. Experimental results on two benchmark data sets from different crowdsourcing tasks show that our algorithm is much more effective, efficient and robust than traditional methods.

Categories and Subject Descriptors

H.3.3 [**Information Search and Retrieval**]: Relevance Feedback

General Terms

Algorithms

Keywords

Crowdsourced Labeling; Rank Aggregation; Evaluation Measures

WSDM'15, February 2–6, 2015, Shanghai, China.
Copyright 2015 ACM 978-1-4503-3317-7/15/02 ...$15.00.
http://dx.doi.org/10.1145/2684822.2685308 .

1. INTRODUCTION

Inferring ranking over a set of objects is a critical task for building gold-standard test collections in many ranking-based real applications, such as information retrieval and recommender systems. Recently, crowdsourcing services have attracted much attention since it provides an inexpensive and efficient means to obtain judgments over the objects. Typically, there are two kinds of judgments widely adopted in crowdsourcing, i.e. ratings and preferences. For example in a query-document relevance labeling task, annotators are asked to present the rating for each document such as binary or graded relevance judgments with absolute labeling strategy [13], while they are asked to present preferences for each document pair with relative labeling strategy [3].

In literature, many rank aggregation methods have been proposed to find a consensus ranking over these judgments. They all fall into the framework of minimizing a distance between predicted ranking and input judgments. According to different distances used for optimization, they can be mainly divided into three categories: pointwise, pairwise and listwise approaches. Pointwise rank aggregation methods like MedianRank [7] utilize Footrule Distance as the objective function, which aims to well predict the rank of each object from annotators' judgments on that object. Pairwise methods such as Bradley-Terry [23], MPM [26] and CrowdBT[4] measure the distances in a pairwise way, and pairs are viewed as independent. We can see that both pointwise and pairwise approach define the distance from a local perspective. Therefore, they all ignore the position importance in ranking, which is nevertheless critical for rank aggregation. Traditional listwise rank aggregation methods such as Cranking [16] and Plackett-Luce [10] are infeasible for most crowdsourced labeling tasks, such as crowdsourced pairwise labeling task.

Therefore we propose a novel listwise approach to tackle this problem. The key idea is that in order to take position importance into account, it is better to define the distance in a listwise way. Inspired by the fact that IR measures such as NDCG and RBP are designed for this purpose, and usually used for evaluation in rank aggregation, we propose to directly utilize these measures for distance definition. However, the characteristics of crowdsourcing poses two challenges to this approach: (1) Annotators usually provide ratings or preferences over a subset of objects in crowdsourcing, which make the computation of ranking measures impossible since the ranking information cannot be induced from the incomplete input information; (2) Annotator quality should be considered in the objective function since the reliability of annotators can vary significantly in crowdsourcing.

To address these challenges, we propose to map the judgments (ratings or preferences) to input ranking, and incorporate annotator quality in this process. Specifically, the rank of an object is viewed as a random variable and defined in the form of pairwise contests. The distribution of the random variable is then derived iteratively based on the pairwise probability, which can be estimated through pairwise preference relationships conveyed in judgments. Meanwhile, annotator quality is modeled as the probability that one agrees with the (unknown) true pairwise preference relationships, which is estimated in an iterative way based on the intermediate aggregation results. By incorporating annotator quality into the definition of the pairwise probability, we obtain the final form of rank distribution of each object. Based on this listwise mapping, we define the new objective functions for rank aggregation as the expectation of IR measures (i.e. NDCG and RBP) over the rank distribution, called expected measures. Note that the ground-truth label of an object in the expected measure is derived from its rank using a mapping function as in [19].

Due to the property of ranking measures [15], we find that expected ranking measures have a general formulation as a sum of utility functions on ranks in both the induced ranking inputs and the output permutations. Therefore, the goal of the optimization approach is to find a ground-truth permutation which maximize the sum of utility functions. As a sequence, it is natural to transform the rank aggregation problem to the Linear Sum Assignment Problem (LSAP for short), where the profit for each assignment is defined by taking the sum of utility functions over all the induced ranking inputs. As the utility functions are represented as a product of two functions, the optimal solution of the optimization problem can be directly obtained through sorting as shown by Rearrangement Inequality. We refer this optimization algorithm as CrowdAgg.

Finally we conduct extensive experiments on two benchmark data sets from different crowdsourcing tasks, i.e. query-document relevance labeling and music similarity labeling. One is collected based on graded judgments, and the other is based on pairwise preferences. Experimental results show that CrowdAgg is much more effective, efficient and robust than traditional rank aggregation methods in both data sets.

In summary, the main contributions of our proposed approach are listed as follows:

- we introduce expected measures as the new objective functions for rank aggregation to consider position importance, by utilizing rating and preference judgments in a listwise way;
- We incorporate annotator quality into the expected measures to well cope with the reliability of annotators in crowdsourcing;
- We propose an efficient algorithm by formalizing the aggregation problem as LSAP and obtaining an optimal solution with Rearrangement Inequality.

2. BACKGROUNDS

In this section, we first give a problem formalization of rank aggregation in crowdsourcing. We then review some related works of traditional pointwise and pairwise rank aggregation methods. Finally, we give a brief introduction to some major evaluation measures used in rank aggregation.

2.1 Rank Aggregation in CrowdSourcing

Assume that we are given a set of n objects denoted as $D = \{x_1, x_2, \ldots, x_n\}$ and a set of m annotators in a crowdsourcing task. Each annotator i provides a set of labels τ_i over these objects, which are often unreliable and incomplete. Typically, each τ_i can be represented in two forms: ratings or preferences.

(1) With absolute labeling strategy, annotators are asked to present the relevance rating of each object. Usually, the ratings are incomplete, which means that annotators may only rate a subset of all the objects. We denote this subset labeled by annotator i as D_i. In this case, τ_i can be represented as $(\tau_i(x_1), \cdots, \tau_i(x_n))$, where

$$\tau_i(x_j) = \begin{cases} z_j^{(i)} \in \{0, 1, \cdots, C-1\}, & \text{if } x_j \in D_i; \\ Null, & \text{if } x_j \notin D_i. \end{cases}$$

(2) With relative labeling strategy, annotator are asked to present the relative relevance between any two objects. Usually, the preferences are also incomplete, which means that annotators may only provide preferences over a subset of all the possible object pairs. We denote this subset labeled by annotator i as P_i. In this case, τ_i can be represented as $(\tau_i(x_1, x_2), \cdots, \tau_i(x_{n-1}, x_n))$, where $\tau_i(x_s, x_t)$ is defined as follows, and $z_j^{(i)} = 1$ means x_s is more relevant than x_t in terms of annotator i; otherwise $z_j^{(i)} = 0$.

$$\tau_i(x_s, x_t) = \begin{cases} z_j^{(i)} \in \{0, 1\}, & \text{if } (x_s, x_t) \in P_i; \\ Null, & \text{if } (x_s, x_t) \notin P_i. \end{cases}$$

The goal of rank aggregation in crowdsourcing is then to find a consensus ranking π over these n objects which best represents the ranking relations conveyed in multiple sets of labels $\{\tau_1, \ldots, \tau_m\}$ in the form of ratings or preferences, where π is a permutation and $\pi(x_i)$ stands for the position of object x_i in the final consensus ranking π. To this end, most aggregation algorithms try to optimize a distance measure M between the inputs $\tau_1, \cdots, \tau_m$ and the final ranking π, which can be formulated as follows.

$$\max_{\pi \in \Pi} \sum_{i=1}^{m} M(\pi, \tau_i). \tag{1}$$

2.2 Rank Aggregation Methods

Here we briefly review some of the traditional rank aggregation methods in unsupervised scenario. According to different kinds of distance measures used for optimization, they can be mainly divided into three categories: pointwise, pairwise and listwise methods.

2.2.1 *Pointwise Rank Aggregation Methods*

Pointwise rank aggregation methods utilize the label information per object from all the inputs to define the ranking function or objective function. The distance measure between the consensus ranking and the input ranking for Borda Count [1] and Median Rank [7] is decomposed into position difference per object. Borda Count [1] minimizes the average Spearman Rank Coefficient and obtains the optimal ranking by the mean position of each object. Median

Rank [7] optimizes the average Spearman Footrule Distance between the consensus ranking and each ranking input, and obtains the optimal solution by sorting objects according to their median rank in ascending order.

2.2.2 *Pairwise Rank Aggregation Methods*

Pairwise rank aggregation methods organize their ranking inputs in a pairwise way whether for ranking functions or optimization objective functions.

Graph based Method. Condorcet Fuse [18] constructs the Condorcet Graph with n items and its arc representing the pairwise comparison results between two items by majority voting, and a Hamiltonian path is obtained from this graph by QuickSort. With all the aggregated pairwise preferences summarized in a tournament, GreedyOrder [5] minimizes the pairwise disagreement cost in this tournament to obtain the consensus ranking.

Pairwise Preference Matrix Based Methods. With all the inputs summarized in a pairwise preference matrix, SVP (Singular Vector Projection) [9] minimized nuclear norm of this pairwise preference matrix by rank-2 factorization.

Pairwise Probabilistic Approach. Probabilistic approaches define the generative probability of pairwise preferences and optimize the likelihood function by a gradient based approach [23, 26, 4]. Bradley-Terry [23] defines the pairwise probability based on the Bradley-Terry model [22]. In crowdsourcing, annotator accuracy should be incorporated. MPM (Multinomial Preference Model) [26] models both the power of rank difference and the deviation from the consensus ranking per annotator in the pairwise generative probability. Crowd-BT [4] extends the Bradley-Terry model by explicitly incorporating the labeling qualities of different annotators. The key preprocess in EloRating [2, 27] is to estimate pairwise probabilities and annotator qualities through EM algorithm, then obtain the relevance score from the remaining preferences with the estimated information through Elo-Rating system.

2.2.3 *Listwise Rank Aggregation Methods*

Listwise rank aggregation methods take the position importance into consideration and treat ranking inputs in a listwise way whether for ranking functions or optimization objective functions. Plackett-Luce [10] and Cranking [16] define the similarity measure to be the generative probability of each ranking list with Plackett-Luce model [22] and Mallow's model [22] respectively, and optimize this similarity function by a maximum likelihood procedure. Although the annotator quality can be incorporated into the optimization objective function, these listwise methods do not work when these inputs are in the form of pairwise preferences. St.Agg [20], one of state-of-the-art methods in traditional rank aggregation tasks like metasearch, can solve this problem by deriving one item's rank position from its pairwise preferences with other items, but it is not fit for the crowdsourced setting. So these listwise approaches are not used as baselines in our experiments.

2.3 Evaluation Measure

Given a set of objects $D = \{x_1, \cdots, x_n\}$, and the ground-truth labels $Y = (y_1, \cdots, y_n)$, which are usually based on multi-grade ratings. Let π be the consensus ranking list over D by some rank aggregation method. Evaluation measures such as NDCG [12], Precision [6] and RBP [17] defined as follows are often employed to evaluate the performance of this aggregation method.

$$\text{NDCG@}k(\pi, Y) = \frac{\sum_{j=1}^{n} g(y_j) D(r_j^{\pi}) I(r_j^{\pi} \leq k)}{\text{DCG}_{\max}(n)}, \quad (2)$$

where r_j^{π} stands for the rank of x_j in the ranking list π, $g(y_j)$ is the gain function with $g(y_j) = 2^{y_j} - 1$, $D(r_j^{\pi})$ is the discount function with $D(r_j^{\pi}) = \frac{1}{\log(1+r_j^{\pi})}$, $I(\cdot)$ is an indicator function with $I(A) = 1$ if A is true and $I(A) = 0$ otherwise.

$$\text{Precision@}k(\pi, Y) = \sum_{j=1}^{n} \frac{y_j}{k} I(r_j^{\pi} \leq k), \quad (3)$$

$$\text{RBP}(\pi, Y) = (1-p) \sum_{j=1}^{n} y_j p^{r_j^{\pi} - 1} \quad (4)$$

where $p \in [0, 1]$ is a constant value. y_j in Eq.(3) and Eq.(4) takes a binary value from 0 and 1, which can be transformed from multi-level ratings like LETOR[1].

3. MOTIVATION

For the aggregation task in crowdsourcing, pointwise and pairwise rank aggregation methods will be unsuitable, because both the position importance and annotator quality, which are two main characteristics of crowdsourced data, are not incorporated in these aggregation methods.

First, both the traditional pointwise and pairwise methods define the distance from a local perspective. For example, the Spearman Rank Correlation used in Borda Count [1] treats each object equal, and measures the distance between two ranking lists π and τ as $\sum_{j=1}^{n} (\pi(x_j) - \tau(x_j))^2$, where $\pi(x_j)$ and $\tau(x_j)$ means the position of x_j in the ranking list π and τ respectively. The distances used in pairwise methods treat each object pair as equal, and do not distinguish the different impact of pairs from different positions. Therefore, both pointwise and pairwise methods ignore the position importance in ranking, which is nevertheless critical for rank aggregation. Specifically, one usually cares more about objects ranked high in the output ranking list, and thus objects with different positions as well as pairs constructed from different positions should have different impact on the distance measure.

Second, the reliability of judgments obtained at low cost from crowdsourcing services varies significantly, which is the major difference from traditional aggregation task. Experimental results in [26] shows that the aggregation methods taking annotator quality into consideration, such as MPM [26] always achieve better performances than those without annotator quality factor, such as Borda Count [1] minimizing $\sum_{i=1}^{m} \sum_{j=1}^{n} (\pi(x_j) - \tau_i(x_j))^2$. So it is reasonable to satisfy the majority for some cases while put emphasis on a small subset for the other cases, which can be adjusted by weighting judgments from various sources differently.

To tackle these challenges, we propose to define the distance in a listwise way which taking both position importance and annotator quality into consideration, namely listwise rank aggregation approach.

4. LISTWISE RANK AGGREGATION

Inspired by the fact that position importance is considered in IR evaluation measure such as NDCG and RBP, we

[1] http://research.microsoft.com/en-us/um/beijing/projects/letor/

propose to directly utilize these measures as the distance to optimize. Specifically, the output ranking list is viewed as (unknown) ground-truth, and the input judgments from annotator i can be viewed as some observations of the ground-truth waiting for evaluation. When defining the specific distance based on these evaluation measures, however, we find the characteristics of crowdsourcing pose great challenges to this approach.

Firstly, the incompleteness and labeling form (ratings or preferences) make the computation of these measures impossible. As we described above, the annotators usually only select a subset of data for labeling, thus the labeled data are incomplete. Furthermore, labels from annotators either in ratings or preferences, are quite different from the required full-order ranking input in the computation of evaluation measures. Therefore, the direct computation of evaluation measures based on these kinds of data is not available.

Secondly, the annotator quality is not included in these evaluation measures. As we know, the reliability of annotators can vary significantly in crowdsourcing, which make annotator quality an important factor to consider in rank aggregation. However, it is not easy to include this factor in the computation of these evaluation measures.

To address these challenges, we propose to map the judgments (ratings or preferences) to input ranking, and incorporate annotator quality during this process. In the following subsection, we will introduce how we conduct the mapping and incorporation process.

4.1 Listwise Mapping

We cannot induce a ranking list directly by sorting based on ratings or pairwise comparisons mainly due to their incompleteness. In order to make the computation of evaluation measures possible with the input judgments (ratings or preferences), we propose a mapping function from the judgments to input rankings. By analyzing these evaluation measures, we find that the rank of an object is actually needed in the computation. Therefore, we turn to the problem how to map the judgments to obtain the rank of each object. However, since the provided judgments are often incomplete, we incorporate uncertainty into the mapping process. Specifically, we view the pairwise contest as a random variable, then the rank of each object can be defined based on all the results of pairwise contests. Furthermore, the annotator quality can be incorporated in the derivation of the rank distribution.

4.1.1 Randomized Pairwise Comparisons

A pairwise contest between x_s and x_t refers to deciding which one is ranked higher in terms of annotator i. We view each pairwise contest as a Bernoulli trial, so that the result that x_s wins the contest denoted as X_{st} follows the Bernoulli distribution, $X_{st}^{\tau_i} \sim Binomial(1, P(x_s \prec_{\tau_i} x_t))$, where pairwise probability $P(X_{st}^{\tau_i} = 1) = P(x_s \prec_{\tau_i} x_t)$ means the probability that x_s is ranked higher than x_t, denoted as $p_{st}^{\tau_i}$.

To estimate the pairwise probability $p_{st}^{\tau_i}$ when the input judgments are ratings, we first transform the rating data to preference data so that we can treat both types of judgements in a unified way.

$$\tau_i(x_s, x_t) = \begin{cases} 1, & \text{if } \tau_i(x_s) > \tau_i(x_t), \\ 0, & \text{if } \tau_i(x_s) < \tau_i(x_t), \\ Null, & \text{otherwise.} \end{cases} \qquad (5)$$

According to previous studies [8, 20], the pairwise probability that one document x_s is more relevant than x_t is dependent on the relative rank position difference between two documents. The basic idea is to estimate this probability by leveraging all pairwise preference relationships conveyed in judgments from an annotator. On the basis of the preference data (either directly provided in preference judgments or generated from ratings as above), we give the estimation of the pairwise probability $p_{st}^{\tau_i}$ as shown in Eq.(6).

$$p_{st}^{\tau_i} = \begin{cases} \frac{N_i(x_s) - N_i(x_t)}{n}, & N_i(x_s) > N_i(x_t), \\ 1 - \frac{N_i(x_t) - N_i(x_s)}{n}, & N_i(x_s) < N_i(x_t), \\ 0.5, & N_i(x_s) = N_i(x_t) \text{ or } \tau_i(x_s, x_t) = Null, \end{cases} \qquad (6)$$

where $N_i(x_j)$ denotes the number of pairwise contests that x_j wins in τ_i, which is determined by the known pairwise preferences in Eq.(7),

$$N_i(x_j) = \sum_{l=1, l \neq j, \tau_i(x_j, x_l) \neq Null}^{n} \tau_i(x_j, x_l). \qquad (7)$$

4.1.2 Incorporating Annotator Quality

To incorporate annotator quality into the distance, we propose to introduce a parameter η_i to stand for the quality of annotator i. It is natural that we define the parameter as the degree the judgments by annotator i agrees with the (unknown) ground-truth. Since we have turned both types of input judgements into preference data above, we define the degree based on preferences in a unified way. That is the ratio of the number of preference pairs appear in both the judgments of annotator i and ground-truth against the number of all the preference pairs in ground-truth. The formal definition of the quality of annotator i is represented as follows.

$$\eta_i = \frac{\sum_{s,t} I(\tau^*(x_s, x_t) = 1 \&\& \tau_i(x_s, x_t) = 1)}{\sum_{s,t} I(\tau_i(x_s, x_t) = 1)}, \qquad (8)$$

where τ^* denotes the ground-truth and $I(\cdot)$ is the indicator function. We can see that when annotator i is perfect, we have $\eta_i \approx 1$; if he/she is a random spammer, we have $\eta_i \approx 0.5$; if he/she is a malicious (i.e. poorly informed) spammer, we have $\eta_i \approx 0$. Note that in estimation of the annotator quality, the ground-truth τ^* is actually unknown. Instead, we estimate the annotator quality in an iterative way by taking the aggregated ranking in previous step as the approximation of the ground-truth. Please refer to section 5.3 for detailed machinery to parameter estimation.

With the annotator quality defined above, we modify the pairwise probability $p_{st}^{\tau_i}$ by incorporating this quality factor as follows

$$\eta_i p_{st}^{\tau_i} + (1 - \eta_i)(1 - p_{st}^{\tau_i}). \qquad (9)$$

4.1.3 From Pairwise Contests to Rank Distribution

We now derive the rank of an object. When the results of pairwise contests are deterministic and the data is complete, the rank of an object x_j provided by annotator i is determined by the number of objects being beaten in Eq.(11).

$$r_j^{\tau_i} = \sum_{l=1, l \neq j}^{n} I(x_j \prec_{\tau_i} x_l) \qquad (11)$$

Algorithm 1 Iterative Procedure for Rank Distribution of x_j in τ_i.

Input: (1)An item set D with n items; (2)Pairwise preferences from input τ_i with Eq.(5); (3)Annotator quality η_i;
Output: A rank distribution of item x_j on n positions.
Compute $\{p_{jl}^{\tau_i}\}_{l=1,l\neq j}^{n}$ using Eq.(9);
initialize the distribution:$[P^{(0)}(r_j^{\tau_i}=0), P^{(0)}(r_j^{\tau_i}=1)] = [1,0]$;
$t = 1$;
for each $x_l \in D - x_j$ **do**

$$\begin{aligned}&[P^{(t)}(r_j^{\tau_i}=0),\ldots,P^{(t)}(r_j^{\tau_i}=t+1)]\\&=[P^{(t-1)}(r_j^{\tau_i}=0),\ldots,P^{(t-1)}(r_j^{\tau_i}=t)]*[p_{jl}^{\tau_i},1-p_{jl}^{\tau_i}];\end{aligned} \quad (10)$$

$t++$;

end for
return $[P^{(n-1)}(r_j^{\tau}=0),\ldots,P^{(n-1)}(r_j^{\tau}=n-1)]$.

Algorithm 2 Divide-and-Conquer Algorithm for Rank Distribution of x_j in τ_i.

Input: (1)An item set D with n items; (2)Pairwise preferences from input τ_i with Eq.(5); (3)Annotator quality η_i;
Output: A rank distribution of item x_j on n positions $[P(r_j^{\tau_i}=0),\ldots,P(r_j^{\tau_i}=n-1)]$.
Compute $\{p_{jl}^{\tau_i}\}_{l=1,l\neq j}^{n}$ using Eq.(9) and $p_{jj}=1$;
return DC-RankDistribution($\{p_{jl}^{\tau_i}\}_{l=1}^{n}$,1,$n$).

DC-RankDistribution($\{p_{sl}\}_{l=1}^{n}$,a,b):
if $a+1 == b$ **then**,
    return $[p_{sa},1-p_{sa}]*[p_{sb},1-p_{sb}]$;
else if $a == b$ **then**,
    return $[p_{sa},1-p_{sa}]$;
end if
mid=(a+b)/2;
return DC-RankDistribution($\{p_{sl}\}_{l=1}^{n}$,a,mid)*DC-RankDistribution($\{p_{sl}\}_{l=1}^{n}$,mid + 1,b);

When the pairwise contests are random experiments like Bernoulli trials, the rank of object x_j provided by annotator i is a random variable, which means the number of successes of the $n-1$ independent Bernoulli trials defined in Eq.(12).

$$r_j^{\tau_i} = \sum_{l=1,l\neq j}^{n} X_{jl}^{\tau_i} \quad (12)$$

The distribution of $r_j^{\tau_i}$ is the convolution of the individual probability density distributions [21]. This yields an iterative computation of the rank distribution with complexity $O(n^2)$, as shown in Alg. 1. The operator $*$ in Alg. 1 stands for the convolution operation. Specifically, the distribution of $r_j^{\tau_i}$ is initialized ($t=0$) by the indicator function with the probability at the top position is 1 and 0 otherwise. When a new object x_l comes, the rank distribution of x_j is updated by the convolution between its current rank distribution and the pairwise contest distribution denoted as $[p_{jl}^{\tau_i}, 1-p_{jl}^{\tau_i}]$ estimated by annotator τ_i. For the iteration t, the running time of this convolution computation between the rank distribution (a sequence with length $t+2$) and pairwise contest distribution (a sequence with length 2) is $O(2t)$. The final distribution ($t=n-1$) of $r_j^{\tau_i}$ involves such $n-1$ convolutions, so the time complexity for computing rank distribution of x_j is $\sum_{t=0}^{n-1} 2t = \mathcal{O}(n^2)$.

The time complexity of the Alg. 1 can be improved with divide-and-conquer strategy. The main idea comes from the fact that the required rank distribution can be divided into convolutions of two parts: the first part is convolutions of the first $\frac{n}{2}$ objects, and the second part is convolution of the rest $\frac{n}{2}$ objects. For each convolution, the divide-and-conquer process continues. Therefore, we can change the original sequential computation process to the following divide-and-conquer process as shown in Alg. 2. Suppose the distribution of pairwise contest between x_j and x_j is denoted as $[1,0]$, then the rank distribution of x_j by annotator τ_i can be computed as the convolution of n sequences with each sequence represented as a pairwise contest distribution $[p_{jl}^{\tau_i}, 1-p_{jl}^{\tau_i}]$. For the first iteration ($T=1$), there are $\frac{n}{2}$ convolution computations between any two sequences with length 2, thus $\frac{n}{2}$ sequences with length 3 will be obtained; for the T-th iteration, there are $\frac{n}{2^T}$ convolutions between any two sequences with length $2^{T-1}+1$, and thus $\frac{n}{2^T}$ sequences with length 2^T+1 will be obtained by FFT (Fast Fourier Transform). Finally, the rank distribution of x_j will be derived after $\log_2 n$ iterations, and the time complexity for this efficient algorithm is $\sum_{T=1}^{\log_2 n} \frac{n}{2^T}(2^T+1)\log_2(2^T+1) = O(n \log_2^2 n)$.

4.2 Expected Ranking Measures

Through listwise mapping described above, all the judgments (ratings or preferences) provided by each annotator can be transformed to the listwise information, described as ranks of all the objects in D with estimated rank distributions. Therefore, the input data has become the form of ranking lists.

Recall that we view the output consensus ranking as the ground-truth, and the input ranking lists from each annotator as observations waiting for evaluation. In this sense, the computation of traditional evaluation measures is still infeasible in application, since the ground-truth is in the form of a ranking list. Inspired by using extended evaluation measures such as κ-NDCG and κ-RBP for ranking based ground-truth as in [19], where a mapping function $\kappa: \kappa(r_j^{\pi}) = \frac{n-r_j^{\pi}}{n}$ is utilized to map the rank r_j^{π} to ground-truth label, we propose to define the listwise distance on the basis of these measures as follows.

$$\begin{aligned}\kappa\text{-NDCG}(\pi,\tau_i) &= \sum_{j=1}^{n} \frac{g(\kappa(r_j^{\pi}))D(r_j^{\tau_i})}{\text{DCG}_{\max}(n)},\\ \kappa\text{-RBP}(\pi,\tau_i) &= \sum_{j=1}^{n} \kappa(r_j^{\pi})p^{r_j^{\tau_i}-1}.\end{aligned}$$

Obviously they can be represented as the following general form $Ev(\pi,\tau_i) = \sum_{j=1}^{n} v(r_j^{\pi}, r_j^{\tau_i})$, where Ev stands for any evaluation measures.

The above measures represent a distance between the output consensus ranking π and the input ranking with respect to τ_i. Since the input ranking with respect to τ_i is stochastic according to section 4.1.3, we propose to use expectation as the distance. As a consequence, the expectation over the rank distribution is conducted, and we obtain the expected measures defined as follows as the final listwise distance.

$$Ev_s(\pi,\tau_i) = \sum_{j=1}^{n}\sum_{r=0}^{n-1} v(r_j^{\pi}, r_j^{\tau_i})P(r_j^{\tau_i}=r) \quad (13)$$

5. OPTIMIZATION ALGORITHMS

In this section, we investigate optimization algorithms to solve the problem maximizing these expected measures, such as κ-NDCG$_s$ and κ-RBP$_s$. Firstly, we find that these expected measures can be represented as a summation of the utility function for each item at a certain position, and obtain the final objective function $\mathcal{L}(\eta, \pi)$ parameterized by annotator quality $\eta = (\eta_1, \cdots, \eta_m)$ and the aggregated ranking π. Then given the annotator quality η, the optimization problem can be easily interpreted as the assignment problem with a cost function in the form of linear sum, called the Linear Sum Assignment Problem (LSAP for short). Therefore we can transform the optimization problem to the LSAP. With each utility function expressed as a special product form in expected measures, the optimal ranking can be directly obtained by Rearrangement Inequality. After the optimal ranking is obtained, we update the annotator quality η with its definition formula, and repeat the above optimization process until the obtained ranking list keeps unchanged. In this way, we obtain an alternating approach to optimize $\mathcal{L}(\eta, \pi)$, referred to as CrowdAgg.

5.1 General Form of Expected Measures

As shown in Eq. (13), these expected ranking measures can be formulated into a general form as the sum of utility functions. Each utility function measures the utility that an object with ranking information encoded in its rank distributions, is placed at some position in the output permutation, denoted as u_s in this paper. As a consequence, the original expected measures can be rewritten as follows:

$$Ev_s(\pi, \tau_i) = \sum_{j=1}^{n} u_s(r_j^\pi), \text{where } u_s(r_j^\pi) = \sum_{r=0}^{n-1} v(r_j^\pi, r) P(r_j^\tau = r).$$

The optimization objective is to find a permutation which maximizes the sum of utility functions in Eq. (14).

$$\max_{\pi \in \Pi, \eta \in [0,1]^m} \mathcal{L}(\eta, \pi) = \sum_{i=1}^{m} Ev_s(\pi, \tau_i) = \sum_{j=1}^{n}\sum_{i=1}^{m} u_s(r_j^\pi) \tag{14}$$

5.2 Optimization with fixed Parameter η

Through the representation as the sum of utility functions in the above section, we can easily interpret this optimization problem with fixed annotator quality η as to find the optimal assignment of positions for each object according to inputs $(\tau_1, \cdots, \tau_m)$. Moreover, each utility function is a function on an individual object and its output position. Therefore, the optimization problem in our listwise rank aggregation is intrinsically a Linear Sum Assignment Problem (LSAP), which is formalized as follows.

The object set is denoted as $D = \{x_1, \ldots, x_n\}$ and the possible position set is represented as $R = \{1, \ldots, n\}$. For any object x_j, the permutation π can be viewed as the assignment of object $x_j, j = 1, \ldots, n$ to the position r_j^π, which brings about the utility denoted by $w(r_j^\pi, j) = \sum_{i=1}^m u_s(r_j^\pi) = \sum_{i=1}^m \sum_{r=0}^{n-1} v(r_j^\pi, r) P(r_j^{\tau_i} = r)$.

To find the optimal permutation, we need to optimize the following function in Eq. (15).

$$\max_{\pi \in \Pi} \sum_{j=1}^{n} w(r_j^\pi, j) \tag{15}$$

Many classical algorithms such as Hungarian method [14] have been proposed to solve this LSAP. For a LSAP with size n, the running time of Hungarian algorithm is $O(n^4)$. The high time complexity motivates us to further probe the optimization problem. In light of the factorization in $v(\cdot, \cdot)$ [15], we find that the utility function $u_s(\cdot, \cdot)$ for most expected measures can be factorized as a product of two functions. One is on positions in output permutation denoted as $h(\cdot)$, and the other is the function of position per object in the estimated ranking input denoted as $f(\cdot)$. The mathematical form is shown as below.

Table 1: Factorizations of Expected Ranking Measures

measures	$f(\cdot)$	$h(\cdot)$
κ-NDCG$_s$	$\frac{1}{\text{DCG}_{max}(n)} \sum_{r=0}^{n-1} \frac{P(r_j^{\tau_i}=r)}{\log(1+r)}$	$g(\kappa(r_j^\pi))$
κ-RBP$_s$	$(1-p) \sum_{r=0}^{n-1} p^{r-1} P(r_j^{\tau_i} = r)$	$\kappa(r_j^\pi)$

$$u_s(r_j^\pi, r_j^{\tau_i}) = h(r_j^\pi) f(r_j^{\tau_i}) \tag{16}$$

For example, κ-NDCG$_s$ and κ-RBP$_s$ can both be represented in this way. Specifically, two different kinds of definition of $f(\cdot)$ and $h(\cdot)$ with regard to these expected measures are listed in Table 1.

According to the definition of $w(r_j^\pi, j)$ and the factorization of utility function $u_s(\cdot, \cdot)$ in Eq. (16), $w(r_j^\pi, j) = \sum_{i=1}^m h(r_j^\pi) f(r_j^{\tau_i}) = h(r_j^\pi)(\sum_{i=1}^m f(r_j^{\tau_i}))$.

Let $u_j = h(r_j^\pi)$ and $v_j = \sum_{i=1}^m f(r_j^{\tau_i})$, the infimum and supremum of the objective function in Eq. (14) will be directly obtained by the Rearrangement Inequality [11] as shown in Lemma 1.

LEMMA 1. *Let $0 \le u_1 \le \ldots \le u_n$ and $0 \le v_1 \le \ldots \le v_n$. Then for any permutation ϕ*

$$\sum_{i=1}^{n} u_i v_{n+1-i} \le \sum_{i=1}^{n} u_i v_{\phi(i)} \le \sum_{i=1}^{n} u_i v_i.$$

Specifically, we can see that $u_j = h(r_j^\pi)$ and $v_j = \sum_{i=1}^m f(r_j^{\tau_i})$ satisfies the non-negative conditions since $f(\cdot)$ and $h(\cdot)$ are both positive. Sorting $x_1, \ldots, x_n$ according to v_j in descending order, we obtain the optimal permutation π_G with the supremum of the objective function based on Lemma 1. As a consequence, we obtain a simple algorithm which can efficiently find the optimal solution for the optimization problem with fixed η by sorting based on v_j. The details of algorithm are shown in Alg. 3.

Algorithm 3 Maximize $\mathcal{L}(\eta, \pi)$ with fixed η

Input: An item set D and a collection of ranking inputs $\{\tau_1, \ldots, \tau_m\}$ over D;
Output: An aggregated ranking π.
1: Compute $F(x_j) = \sum_{i=1}^m f(r_j^{\tau_i})$, where f is defined for different measures in Table 1;
2: Obtain the permutation π by sorting $F(x_j)$ in descending order;
3: **return** π.

5.3 Estimating Parameter η with Fixed π

Recall that η is defined as the degree the judgments by annotator i agrees with the unknown ground-truth. We propose an iterative way to estimate η by taking the currently aggregated ranking list π as the approximation of the ground-truth. Therefore, η can be estimated, where each η_i is calculated as the pairwise agreement between π and the input τ_i.

$$\eta_i = \frac{\sum_{s,t} I(\pi(x_s, x_t) = 1 \&\& \tau_i(x_s, x_t) = 1)}{\sum_{s,t} I(\tau_i(x_s, x_t) = 1)} \tag{17}$$

5.4 CrowdAgg

As described above, a natural optimization strategy to maximize the objective $\mathcal{L}(\eta, \pi)$ is the alternating approach: (1) initialize $\eta = 1$; (2) fix η and optimize over π by LSAP as described in Alg. 3; (3) fix π and estimate the η as described in Eq. (17); (4) repeat step (2) and (3) until the obtained permutations keep stable. This alternating approach for optimizing $\mathcal{L}(\eta, \pi)$ is referred to as CrowdAgg.

6. EXPERIMENTS

In this section we present our experimental results. Firstly, we introduce the experimental setting, including data sets, baseline methods and evaluation measures. Then we present ranking performance comparison between our proposed CrowdAgg and the baseline methods. In addition, we empirically study the annotator accuracy and the robustness of these rank aggregation methods with respect to two kinds of noisy annotators, such as spammers and malicious annotators [4]. Finally, we compare the running time of the proposed CrowdAgg with the state-of-the-art rank aggregation algorithms.

6.1 Experimental Setting

Here we implement our listwise rank aggregation methods CrowdAgg where Alg. 2 is used to compute rank distributions. We denote the algorithm optimizing expected measures κ-NDCG and κ-RBP as CrowdAgg$_{\text{NDCG}}$ and CrowdAgg$_{\text{RBP}}$, respectively.

Data Sets. To evaluate the performance of our proposed method, we use two data sets from two different kinds of crowdsourcing tasks as described below. Conventional rank aggregation data sets like Million Query data sets from meta-search application may not simulate the crowdsourced setting well, so we utilize such two benchmark data sets directly from crowdsourced labeling tasks.

(1) *Graded Judgment Data from Crowdsourced Relevance Labeling Task. CS-TREC2011* data set is a collection of topic-document pairs labeled as relevant or non-relevant by Mechanical Turks. Therefore, the judgments are provided in the form of ratings. There are 100 topics with 190 documents per topic, and the number of annotators is varied with topics, about 43 on average. Each annotator rates less than 10 documents on average.

(2) *Preference Judgment Data from Crowdsourced Similarity Labeling Task. MIREX2005* data set is a collection of music form Symbolic Melodic Similarity task in Music Information Retrieval Evaluation eXchange (MIREX) in 2005. This task aims to find a ranking list of musical pieces according to the similarity to certain piece of music, which acts as a query in information retrieval. There are 11 pieces of music as queries. Pairwise preference labels are collected from Mechanical Turks in [25]. The ground-truth is in the form of 5-grade judgements [24].

Baseline Methods. Since pointwise methods and listwise methods can only be applied to graded judgment data[2], we use pairwise rank aggregation methods as our baselines to obtain a comprehensive comparison on both data sets. According to whether annotator quality is considered in the model, traditional pairwise rank aggregation methods fall into two categories: (1) Methods without annotator quality, such as CondorcetFuse [18], GreedyOrder [5], BradleyTerry [23]; (2) Methods with annotator quality, such as MPM [26], Crowd-BT [4] and EMEloRating [2, 27]. Here we describe some parameter settings in these methods: the learning rates used in gradient methods for BradleyTerry (0.1 for both data sets), MPM (0.1 for MusicCrowd and 0.0001 for TREC2011) and Crowd-BT (0.01 for both data sets) were chosen according to the best performance in terms of NDCG@10, and the parameter setting in EMEloRating is the same as in [2].

Evaluation Methods. There are several routines to evaluate these unsupervised rank aggregation methods. One of the leading methods is to use traditional IR evaluation measures with ground-truth labels given for evaluation. In this paper we use NDCG@$\{3, 5, 7, 9, 10\}$, RBP, Precision@$\{3, 5, 7, 9, 10\}$ and MAP for evaluation. Routinely the constant value p in RBP is 0.95. In MIREX2005, the transformation of five-grade relevance labels to binary values is mentioned in the background for RBP.

6.2 Ranking Accuracy Analysis

The ranking performance comparison results on both CS-TREC2011 and MIREX2005 are shown in Table 2. It is clear that our proposed methods CrowdAgg outperform the baseline methods on both data sets in most cases.

In terms of NDCG@10, CrowdAgg$_{\text{NDCG}}$ achieves 1.5% improvement with respect to the best pairwise rank aggregation method, i.e. GreedyOrder on CS-TREC2011, and 6.2% improvement with respect to the best pairwise method, i.e. MPM on MIREX2005. In terms of RBP, the improvement of CrowdAgg$_{\text{RBP}}$ is 5.6% with respect to the best pairwise method, i.e. GreedyOrder on CS-TREC2011, and 5.4% with respect to the best pairwise method.

The improvements can be explained as follows: (1) Compared with the first kind of pairwise rank aggregation methods (without annotator quality), CrowdAgg are superior by distinguishing the reliability of preference judgments by the annotator quality; (2) Compared with the second kind of pairwise rank aggregation methods, CrowdAgg obtain better ranking performance by treating the judgments per annotator in a listwise way and taking into consideration of position importance in optimization. Besides, more precise estimation of annotator quality η can be obtained from better aggregated ranking and enhance each other in an alternating way in CrowdAgg.

6.3 Annotator Quality Analysis

In this section, we empirically study the influence of annotator quality. Firstly, we validate the hypothesis that annotator quality will impact much to the results and thus should be taken into consideration in the rank aggregation method. Secondly, we compare the quality distribution among different methods as conducted in [4].

6.3.1 *Impact of Annotator Quality*

To validate the hypothesis that annotator quality is important for rank aggregation, we propose to verify whether the aggregation methods with annotator quality will perform better than that without annotator quality. Therefore, we consider the methods with annotator quality, such as MPM, Crowd-BT, EMEloRating and our proposed CrowdAgg$_{\text{NDCG}}$. These methods can be easily reduced to the version without annotator quality by treating each annotator equally. Specifically, we set these annotator quality parameters $\eta = 1$ as in MPM, Crowd-BT and CrowdAgg$_{\text{NDCG}}$, and denote the new corresponding version as MPM-eq, Crowd-BT-eq,

[2]St.Agg [20] does not incorporate the annotator quality.

Table 2: Ranking Performance Comparison of Preference Aggregation Methods on two data sets (CS-TREC2011 and MIREX2005). For each specific metric, the result with bold type is significantly better than the other corresponding results through one-tailed and paired t-tests (p-value< 0.05).

(a) CS-TREC2011

Methods	P@3	P@5	P@7	P@9	P@10	MAP	N@3	N@5	N@7	N@9	N@10	RBP
CondorcetFuse	0.597	0.604	0.621	0.626	0.621	0.560	0.591	0.597	0.609	0.613	0.611	0.564
GreedyOrder	0.710	**0.698**	0.674	0.661	0.657	0.604	0.713	**0.704**	0.688	0.679	0.676	0.621
BradleyTerry	0.373	0.370	0.386	0.378	0.377	0.326	0.377	0.375	0.384	0.379	0.379	0.345
MPM	0.690	0.690	0.671	0.663	0.657	0.570	0.687	0.687	0.676	0.671	0.667	0.580
Crowd-BT	0.403	0.416	0.416	0.422	0.417	0.534	0.404	0.412	0.413	0.417	0.414	0.473
EMEloRating	0.690	0.666	0.673	0.654	0.649	0.588	0.691	0.676	0.679	0.667	0.663	0.602
$\text{CrowdAgg}_{\text{NDCG}}$	**0.713**	0.694	0.680	0.673	0.673	0.635	**0.715**	0.702	**0.692**	**0.687**	**0.686**	0.657
$\text{CrowdAgg}_{\text{RBP}}$	0.680	0.684	**0.686**	**0.679**	**0.674**	**0.636**	0.683	0.686	0.686	0.682	0.679	**0.658**

(b) MIREX2005

Methods	P@3	P@5	P@7	P@9	P@10	MAP	N@3	N@5	N@7	N@9	N@10	RBP
CondorcetFuse	0.364	0.455	0.468	0.434	0.418	0.472	0.523	0.596	0.514	0.478	0.414	0.170
GreedyOrder	0.273	0.418	0.455	0.424	0.409	0.459	0.444	0.525	0.490	0.462	0.399	0.171
BradleyTerry	0.242	0.400	0.429	0.424	0.499	0.441	0.412	0.496	0.460	0.447	0.385	0.170
MPM	0.485	0.509	0.494	0.475	0.446	0.516	0.695	0.693	0.612	0.576	0.501	0.179
Crowd-BT	0.576	0.564	0.507	0.465	0.446	0.608	0.814	0.801	0.640	0.578	0.496	0.200
EMEloRating	0.364	0.436	0.455	0.424	0.409	0.495	0.606	0.629	0.568	0.511	0.436	0.203
$\text{CrowdAgg}_{\text{NDCG}}$	**0.697**	**0.600**	**0.546**	**0.485**	**0.455**	0.712	**0.955**	**0.880**	**0.703**	**0.621**	**0.532**	0.214
$\text{CrowdAgg}_{\text{RBP}}$	0.697	0.600	0.546	0.485	0.455	**0.713**	0.955	0.879	0.702	0.620	0.531	0.**215**

$\text{CrowdAgg}_{\text{NDCG}}$-eq. While for EMEloRating, we simply take all the pairwise preferences as output to the Elo rating system without filtering by annotator quality, denoted as EMEloRating-eq.

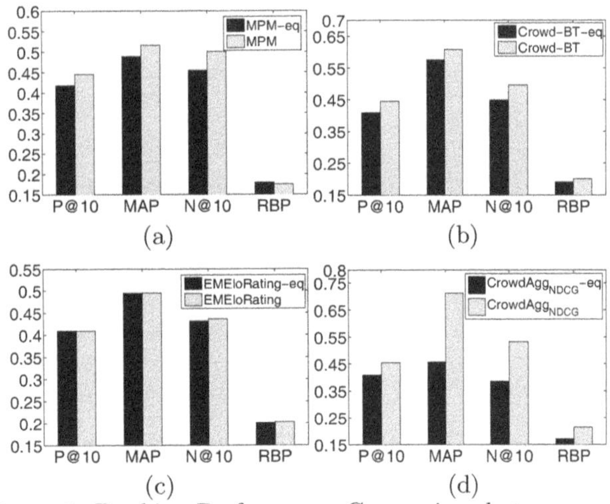

Figure 1: Ranking Performance Comparison between models without and with annotator quality on MIREX2005 (The comparison results are significant through paired t-tests with p-value< 0.05.)

We conduct experiments on MIREX2005 with the two groups of aggregation methods, as mentioned above. The ranking performances are compared between the original one and the corresponding reduced version in terms of P@10, MAP, NDCG@10 and RBP. The comparison results are shown in Fig. 1. Obviously the method with annotator quality can significantly outperform the corresponding method without annotator quality. For example, the improvement of Crowd-BT is 10.3% with the consideration of annotator quality in terms of NDCG@10. The largest performance difference between $\text{CrowdAgg}_{\text{NDCG}}$ and $\text{CrowdAgg}_{\text{NDCG}}$-eq is 56% with respect to MAP, while the smallest performance difference is 11.1% in terms of P@10. Note that the performance difference between EMEloRating and EMEloRating-eq is relatively small. Through our analysis, we find the major reason lies in the EM process of the EMEloRating-eq method, which also takes the annotator quality into consideration in essence. In other words, EMEloRating-eq is not a true reduced version without annotator quality.

6.3.2 *Accuracy for Different Distributions of Annotator Quality*

Here we study the difference between the estimated annotator quality distribution and the ground-truth quality distribution. We say the estimated annotator quality is more accurate if the difference is small. There are various definition of annotator quality for different aggregation methods, such as adherence parameter in MPM [26], pairwise preference accuracy ACC in Crowd-BT [4] (known as the accuracy based on Wilcoxon-Mann-Whitney statistics employed in [26]), and confusion matrix C in EMEloRating. In this paper, we conduct a similar empirical study as in [4], and thus employ pairwise preference accuracy ACC to compute the annotator quality.

$$ACC = \frac{\sum_{s,t} I(y_s > y_t) I(\pi(x_s, x_t))}{\sum_{s,t} I(y_s > y_t)}, \tag{18}$$

where y_s is the ground-truth label for each item $x_s \in D$.

Specifically, we conduct experiments on MIREX2005 with 11 topics to evaluate the quality distribution of annotators for each topic. We calculate the KL-divergence between the estimated quality distribution and the ground-truth distribution. The average divergence score is for $\text{CrowdAgg}_{\text{NDCG}}$, Crowd-BT, EMEloRating and MPM is 1.43, 2.86, 2.14,1.93, respectively. Obviously, $\text{CrowdAgg}_{\text{NDCG}}$ achieves the smallest divergence. It indicates that our proposed CrowdAgg can make better estimation on the annotator quality than the baseline methods. We randomly selected 9 topics from MIREX2005 and plot the quality distributions of different methods and groud-truth in Fig. 2 for illustration. Each sub figure is corresponding to one topic. From Fig. 2 we can also find that the distribution estimated from $\text{CrowdAgg}_{\text{NDCG}}$ (i.e. blue curve) in each sub figure is more similar to the real distribution (i.e. black histogram) than other methods.

6.4 Robustness Analysis

In this section we investigate the robustness of aggregation algorithms to spammers. Similar to [4], we mainly care

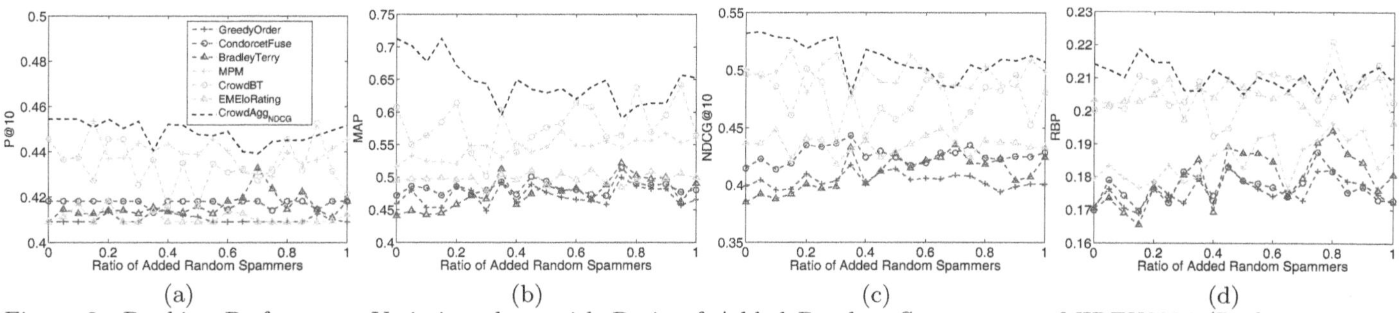

Figure 3: Ranking Performance Variation along with Ratio of Added Random Spammers on MIREX2005 (Performance variation results for various aggregation methods are significantly different through paired t-tests with p-value< 0.05.)

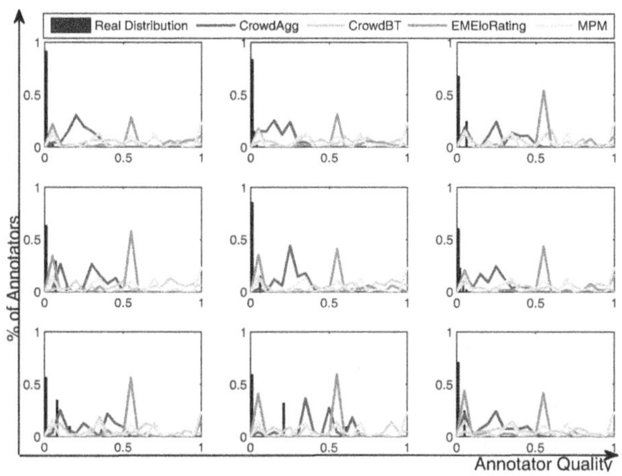

Figure 2: Quality Distribution of Annotators computed from the ground-truth labels (Real Distribution) and Estimated in aggregation methods on randomly sampled 9 topics of MIREX2005

about two kinds of spammers, random spammers and malicious (i.e. poorly informed) spammers. The random spammers assign the label randomly, while the malicious spammers assign the wrong label most of time. We investigate the robustness of all these aggregation methods to two kinds of spammers respectively, and the experimental results are shown only on MIREX2005 for space limitation. Similar results can be also obtained on CS-TREC2011.

6.4.1 Random Spammers

To simulate the labeling behavior of spammers, we define the decision function on the labels of the pairwise objects between x_i and x_j. For random spammer, the decision function τ_{RandSpam} as follows is proposed, where $y(x_i, x_j)$ is the preference label inferred from the ground-truth relevance labels in MIREX2005.

$$\tau_{\mathrm{RandSpam}}(x_i, x_j) = \begin{cases} 1 - y(x_i, x_j) \text{ with probability } 0.5 \\ y(x_i, x_j) \text{ with probability } 0.5 \end{cases}$$

Here we consider the robustness of aggregation methods with the addition of random spammers. Since the number of annotators m is different for different topics, we consider the number of random spammers to be added is in proportion to m, and refer the proportion as *Ratio of Added Random Spammers*. We vary the ratio from 0 to 1 with a step of 0.05, and obtain 20 different data sets for each given ratio. The performance is then averaged over the 20 data sets for each ratio. The ranking performance comparisons over different algorithms in terms of P@10, MAP, NDCG@10 and RBP are shown in Fig. 3.

To quantitatively compare the robustness of different methods, we use the coefficient of variation of performance[3], which is a widely used measure for variance comparison. From the results, we find that our proposed CrowdAgg$_{\mathrm{NDCG}}$ achieve the best coefficient of variation in terms of RBP among methods from top to bottom in the legend (0.0227, 0.0245, 0.0436, 0.0330, 0.0312, 0.0191, 0.0185), and is the third best in terms of NDCG@10 among methods from top to bottom in the legend (0.0147, 0.0174, 0.3347, 0.0228, 0.0406, 0.3238, 0.0216). Furthermore, we can see that with the increase of the ratio of added random spammers, CrowdAgg$_{\mathrm{NDCG}}$ can almost always outperform all the other methods. Therefore, we conclude that our proposed CrowdAgg is robust to random spammers.

6.4.2 Malicious Spammers

To simulate the labeling behavior of malicious spammers, we define the decision function $\tau_{\mathrm{MaliSpam}} = 1 - y(x_i, x_j)$, where $y(x_i, x_j)$ is the preference label inferred from the ground-truth relevance labels in MIREX2005.

Here we consider the robustness of aggregation algorithms with the addition of malicious spammers. We introduce *Ratio of Added Malicious Spammers* and conduct experiments with different ratios as in the above section. The performance comparison results are depicted in Fig. 4.

Similarly, we also compare the robustness of different methods in terms of coefficient of variation of performance. From the results, we find that our proposed CrowdAgg$_{\mathrm{NDCG}}$ achieve the best coefficient of variation in terms of both NDCG@10 and RBP among methods from top to bottom in the legend (NDCG@10:0.0100, 0.0122, 0.0112, 0.0186, 0.0498, 0.0175, 0.0099; RBP:0.0118, 0.0174, 0.0218, 0.0407, 0.0382, 0.0275, 0.0116). Meanwhile, we can also see that with the increase of the ratio of added malicious spammers, CrowdAgg$_{\mathrm{NDCG}}$ can almost always outperform all the other methods. Therefore, CrowdAgg is also robust to malicious spammers on MIREX2005.

In summary, our proposed CrowdAgg is robust to both random spammers and malicious spammers. Each random spammer always provides half useful information to derive the ground truth ranking, so there is no reason for the performance decline in Fig. 3. Each malicious spammer always provides harmful information to derive the ground truth

[3]Coefficient of variation is defined as the the ratio of the standard deviation to the mean

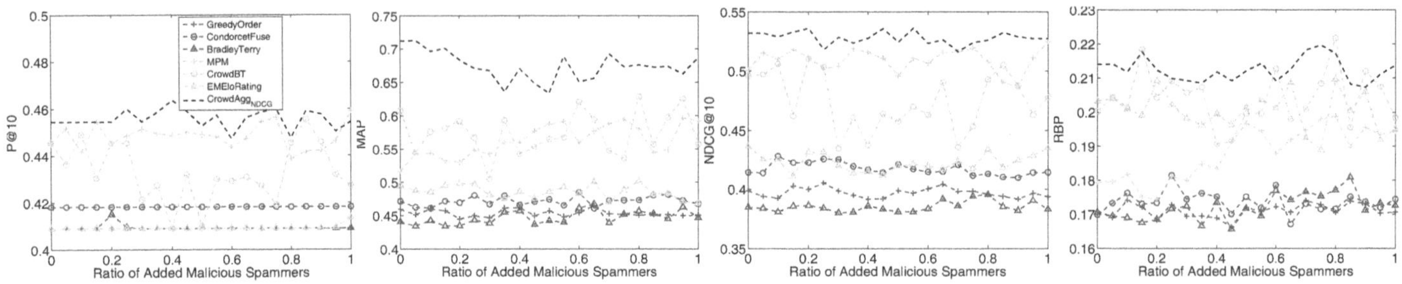

(a) (b) (c) (d)

Figure 4: Ranking Performance Variation along with Ratio of Added Malicious Spammers on MIREX2005 (Performance variation results for various aggregation methods are significantly different through paired t-tests with p-value< 0.05.)

ranking, so the performance decline in Fig. 4 is deemed to appear when the ratio achieves some threshold. In terms of different spammers, CrowdAgg is more robust to the malicious spammers than the random spammer, which is promising in real application.

7. CONCLUSION

In this paper, we propose a listwise rank aggregation method in crowdsourcing. The main idea is to adopt IR measures as objective function to take position importance into consideration, as compared with traditional pointwise or pairwise rank aggregation methods. To solve the challenges introduced by the characteristics of crowdsourcing, we propose to map the judgments (ratings or preferences) to input ranking and incorporate annotator quality in this process. So we define the new expected measures, and use them as objective functions. For optimization, we propose a novel alternative optimization algorithm named CrowdAgg based on LSAP and the iterative estimation of annotator quality. Finally, our experimental results on benchmark data sets shows the effectiveness and robustness of our proposed CrowdAgg.

For future work, we will investigate how to adapt our listwise rank aggregation method to an active learning setting, which is suitable to be blended to crowdsourcing.

Acknowledgments

This research work was funded by the 973 Program of China under Grants No. 2012CB316303, No. 2014CB340401, the 863 Program of China under Grants No. 2012AA011003, the National Natural Science of China under Grant No. 61472401, No. 61203298, No. 61100072, and the National Key Technology R&D Program of China under Grants No. 2012BAH39B02, No. 2012BAH46B04.

8. REFERENCES

[1] J. A. Aslam and M. Montague. Models for metasearch. SIGIR2001, pages 276–284.

[2] M. Bashir, J. Anderton, J. Wu, P. B. Golbus, V. Pavlu, and J. A. Aslam. A document rating system for preference judgements. SIGIR '13, pages 909–912.

[3] B. Carterette, P. N. Bennett, D. M. Chickering, and S. T. Dumais. Here or there: Preference judgments for relevance. ECIR'08, pages 16–27, 2008.

[4] X. Chen, P. N. Bennett, K. Collins-Thompson, and E. Horvitz. Pairwise ranking aggregation in a crowdsourced setting. WSDM '13, pages 193–202.

[5] W. W. Cohen, R. E. Schapire, and Y. Singer. Learning to order things. *JAIR1999*, 10(1):243–270, May.

[6] C. D. Manning, P. Raghavan, and H. Schĺźtze. *Introduction to Information Retrieval*. Cambridge University Press, 2008.

[7] R. Fagin, R. Kumar, and D. Sivakumar. Efficient similarity search and classification via rank aggregation. pages 301–312.

[8] M. Farah and D. Vanderpooten. An outranking approach for rank aggregation in information retrieval. SIGIR2007, pages 591–598.

[9] D. F. Gleich and L.-h. Lim. Rank aggregation via nuclear norm minimization. KDD2011, pages 60–68.

[10] J. Guiver and E. Snelson. Bayesian inference for plackett-luce ranking models. ICML2009, pages 377–384.

[11] G. H. Hardy, J. E. Littlewood, and G. Pĺőlya. *Inequalities*. Cambridge University Press, 1952.

[12] K. Järvelin and J. Kekäläinen. Cumulated gain-based evaluation of ir techniques. *ACM TOIS2002*, 20(4):422–446.

[13] J. Kekäläinen. Binary and graded relevance in ir evaluations-comparison of the effects on ranking of ir systems. *IPM*, 41(5):1019–1033, Sept. 2005.

[14] H. W. Kuhn. The hungarian method for the assignment problem. *Naval Research Logistics*, 2(1-2):83–97, 1955.

[15] Q. Le and A. Smola. Direct optimization of ranking measures. *arXiv Preprint arXiv: 0704.3359*, 2007.

[16] G. Lebanon and J. D. Lafferty. Cranking: Combining rankings using conditional probability models on permutations. ICML2002, pages 363–370.

[17] A. Moffat and J. Zobel. Rank-biased precision for measurement of retrieval effectiveness. *ACM TOIS2008*, 27(1):2:1–2:27, Dec.

[18] M. Montague and J. A. Aslam. Condorcet fusion for improved retrieval. pages 538–548.

[19] S. Niu, J. Guo, Y. Lan, and X. Cheng. Top-k learning to rank: labeling, ranking and evaluation. SIGIR '12, pages 751–760.

[20] S. Niu, Y. Lan, J. Guo, and X. Cheng. Stochastic rank aggregation. UAI2013, pages 478–487.

[21] A. Papoulis. *Random Variables and Stochastic Processes*. McGraw-Hill, 1991.

[22] P. R.L. The analysis of permutations. *Applied Statistics*, 24(2):193–202, 1974.

[23] L. L. Thurstone. The method of paired comparisons for social values. *The Journal of Abnormal and Social Psychology*, 21(4):384, 1927.

[24] R. Typke, M. den Hoed, J. de Nooijer, F. Wiering, and R. C. Veltkamp. A ground truth for half a million musical incipits. *JDIM*, 3(1):34–38, 2005.

[25] J. Urbano, J. Morato, M. Marrero, and D. Martín. Crowdsourcing preference judgments for evaluation of music similarity tasks. In *SIGIR CSE*, pages 9–16.

[26] M. N. Volkovs and R. S. Zemel. A flexible generative model for preference aggregation. WWW2012, pages 479–488.

[27] J. Wu. Applying em to compute document relevance from crowdsourced pair preferences. Master's thesis, Northeastern University, 2013.

WorkerRank: Using Employer Implicit Judgements To Infer Worker Reputation

Maria Daltayanni
UC Santa Cruz
mariadal@cs.ucsc.edu

Luca de Alfaro
UC Santa Cruz
luca@ucsc.edu

Panagiotis Papadimitriou
Elance-oDesk
papadimitriou@elance-odesk.com

ABSTRACT

In online labor marketplaces two parties are involved; employers and workers. An employer posts a job in the marketplace to receive applications from interested workers. After evaluating the match to the job, the employer hires one (or more workers) to accomplish the job via an online contract. At the end of the contract, the employer can provide his worker with some rating that becomes visible in the worker online profile. This form of explicit feedback guides future hiring decisions, since it is indicative of worker true ability. In this paper, first we discuss some of the shortcomings of the existing reputation systems that are based on the end-of-contract ratings. Then we propose a new reputation mechanism that uses Bayesian updates to combine employer implicit feedback signals in a link-analysis approach. The new system addresses the shortcomings of existing approaches, while yielding better signal for the worker quality towards hiring decision.

Categories and Subject Descriptors

H.4.4.3.4 [**Information Systems**]: World Wide Web—*Web applications, Crowdsourcing, Reputation Systems*

General Terms

Algorithms, Design, Experimentation, Performance

Keywords

Online Markets, Reputation, Link Analysis, Crowdsourcing

1. INTRODUCTION

In online labor marketplaces, such as Elance-oDesk [1] and Freelancer [2], two parties are involved; employers and workers. Employers post job openings and candidate workers apply to them, based on their qualifications, skills and interests. The employers review the applicants' online resumes, and interview few applicants to decide hiring. The worker explicit reputation, i.e., the ratings that the worker has received in his past jobs in the platform, is one of the most important considerations for the employer hiring decision, since it reveals how other employers evaluate the worker true ability in real job scenarios. Although the reputation information is a useful signal, reputation scores are usually *skewed* towards high ratings [19], because employers care about the impact of their feedbacks on the workers' future opportunities for jobs in the marketplace. The skewed distribution of ratings makes them less helpful in identifying very competent workers.

The reputation signal is also very *sparse*, since a worker needs to apply, get hired and complete few jobs to obtain a representative reputation score. Usually, an unknown rating implies that we have no explicit information about the employer's preference for the worker. In that case we need to build a model to predict the unknown information, or, alternatively make inferences from the employer's behavior[4].

To address the limitations of the existing reputation systems in labor marketplaces, we present *WorkerRank*, a new reputation system that leverages employers' implicit judgements at the application evaluation moment, rather than the employers' explicit feedback at the job completion moment. Although the implicit judgements are more noisy than the explicit ones, they are more broadly available, since the number of applications is usually one to two orders of magnitudes higher than the number of hires. Moreover, the implicit actions of the employers are not revealed and, consequently, the employers do not bias their judgements towards high ratings (as happens when they aim to avoid the negative impact on the workers). As a result, the obtained ratings are not skewed.

We consider an employer decision to hire worker A, thus ranking A above some other candidate B, as an input that "A won over B" in a match. The employer decisions can thus be interpreted as a set of match outcomes. There are many algorithms ([16], [17], [18], [31]) that can be used to aggregate match outcomes. Our reputation system builds upon the Elo ratings system[16] that is widely used to evaluate chess players. In particular, we assign each worker an initial rating and we treat the applicants to a job opening as the participants in a chess tournament. Applicants that get hired get their scores increased and those who are rejected get their scores decreased. The extent of the increase or the decrease depends upon the ratings of the other applicants, i.e., the better the rejected applicants are, the more the rating of the hired worker increases. Similarly, the worse the hired applicants are, the more the ratings of the rejected applicants decrease.

To deal with the noise of implicit judgements, we assign each employer a score that quantifies the agreement of his decisions with the observed quality of the workers. We then use the obtained scores to weigh the employer judgements. For example, if an employer tends to take decisions that are very different from the rest

[1] http://www.elance-odesk.com
[2] http://www.freelancer.com

WSDM'15, February 2–6, 2015, Shanghai, China.

ACM 978-1-4503-3317-7/15/02 ...$15.00.
http://dx.doi.org/10.1145/2684822.2685286.

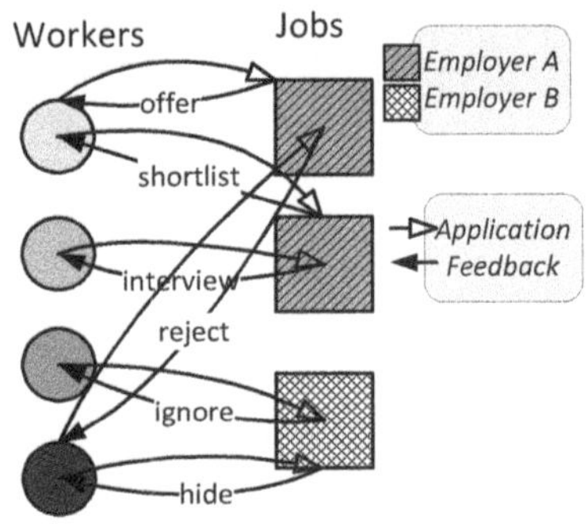

Figure 1: Bipartite graph between workers and jobs posted by employers

of the employers, his score will be low and his hiring decisions will have a small impact on the worker ratings. The rest of the paper is organized as follows. In Section 2 we present some notation and in Section 3 we introduce WorkerRank, the new proposed reputation system. We evaluate the new reputation approach on a real-world dataset from oDesk in Section 4. Our results show that the new reputation system not only provides information for far more workers in the marketplace, but it also serves as a better discriminatory signal for hiring decisions. In Section 5 we discuss some related work and we conclude in Section 6.

2. NOTATION

We represent the labor marketplace data with a directed bipartite graph $G = (U, V, A)$ (Figure 1); U is the set of jobs posted by employers within a specific time period; V is the set of workers who applied to the posted jobs (see Figure 1). Edge $(v, u) \in A$ represents the application of worker $v \in V$ to job $u \in U$. Edge $(u, v) \in A$ represents the employer action on the the worker's application. We consider the following six employer actions:

- *hire*, the employer hires the worker;
- *interview*, the employer contacts the worker to obtain a better understanding of his skills, but the worker is not hired;
- *shortlist*, the employer shortlists the worker for future consideration, but the worker is not invited for interview;
- *ignore*, the employer reviews the worker online resume, but he takes no action on it;
- *hide*, the employer reviews the worker resume and he "hides" the applicant without notifying him; and
- *reject*, the employer reviews the worker resume and notifies him that he will not be considered for the job.

Note that if an employer is never presented with a worker's info, no action is logged in our dataset. Among the six actions, we consider the first three as positive indications of the worker ability, and the last three as negative. We also assume that the employer actions indicate a ranking on the applicant perceived ability to accomplish the job in the following decreasing order: hire > interview > shortlist > ignore > hide > reject. For example, a worker that is selected to be interviewed, is considered to be a better fit for the job than a worker who is ignored. The goal of this paper is to compute a score $r(v)$ for each worker v that is informative of his ability to accomplish the jobs that he applies to. Score $r(v)$ is considered informative if the relative difference between $r(v)$, $r(v')$ for workers v and v' is predictive for the relative ranking of v, v' in the future jobs that they apply.

3. PROPOSED REPUTATION SYSTEM

In this section we describe a reputation system that builds upon the employer decisions on the worker applications. In Section 3.1 we provide our generic approach and in Section 3.2 we show how we can improve our scores by leveraging job specific information. Finally, in Section 3.3 we discuss how we can combine our reputation system scores with the end-of-contract ratings to obtain a hybrid reputation system.

3.1 WorkerRank

The WorkerRank reputation system assigns *reputation* scores $r(v)$ to each worker $v \in V$. Along with reputation scores, WorkerRank also computes an *importance* score $b(u)$ for each opening $u \in U$ that reflects how a job is important in terms of how objective its employer is when judging candidates. The scores are computed via a reputation calculation process on the application graph G, using the Elo constants for t_{elo}, K, as shown in Algorithm 1.

Comparing Performances: The intuition of simulating jobs by tournaments, and looking at the worker performances at each job in pairwise manner, offers a dynamic way for comparison; first, higher label workers clearly win lower label opponents (for example, hire wins over interview, shortlist wins over hide). Also, draws in positive label workers provide useful information about how their qualities compare. While a draw between two hired workers is an instance of equality between their qualities, the same does not necessarily hold in the case of draws between negative label workers (such as two rejected candidates). That is because in certain cases, rejecting or hiding a candidate may reflect the fact that the employer had offered only a limited number of positions hence he had to reject some good quality candidates. Other similar exceptions may apply too. Hence in our algorithm we exclude draws among negative label workers.

Algorithm: In step 1 we initialize reputation $r(v)$ of each worker v to 1.0 and importance $b(u)$ of each opening to 1.0. Then, in steps 3 - 13 we consider each job as a tournament and in steps 5 - 13 we update the worker scores by considering every pair (v, v') of worker applications at a job u to be a game in the job tournament with possible outcome of matches:

$$t(v, v', u) = \begin{cases} 0, & \text{if } v \text{ lost against } v' \text{ at job } u \\ 0.5, & \text{if } v \text{ came to draw with } v' \text{ at job } u \\ 1, & \text{if } v \text{ won against } v' \text{ at job } u \end{cases} \quad (1)$$

At step 3 we initialize the outcome variables $T_{v,u}, X_{v,u}$ to 0 for each candidate v who applied to job u. At step 5, we compute $T_{v,u}$ as the sum of the actual points that v scored in job u against the other opponent candidates. At step 6, we compute $X^i_{v,u}$ as the sum of expected points that v would earn at time i against each opponent candidate $v' \neq v$ at job u, according to Elo's formula[16]:

$$t^i_{elo}(v, v', u) = \frac{1}{1 + 10^{(r^i(v') - r^i(v))/400}}, \forall v' : (v', u) \in A \quad (2)$$

For example, consider workers v_1, v_2, v_3 and v_4 who applied to a job; v_1 gets an offer, v_2 is interviewed but never hired and v_3 and v_4 are rejected without interview. Each applicant participates in 3 games versus the other applicants. Worker v_1 wins all three games versus v_2, v_3 and v_4, since he received an offer which is the most positive employer judgement. Worker v_2 loses against v_1 but wins

Algorithm 1 WorkerRank: Compute Workers Reputation Scores and Jobs Importance Scores

Input: Graph $G = (U, V, A)$

Output: Reputation scores $r(v)$ for workers $v \in V$, importance scores $b(u)$ for jobs $u \in U$

1: Initialize $i = 0$; $r^0(v) = 1, \forall v \in V$; $b^0(u) = 1, \forall u \in U$
2: **for** $u \in U$ **do** ▷ for each job tournament
3: $\quad T_{v,u} = 0, X^i_{v,u} = 0, \forall v : \exists(v,u) \in A$
4: $\quad$ **for** $v, v' : (v,u) \in A, (v',u) \in A, v \neq v'$ **do**
5: $\quad\quad T_{v,u} \mathrel{+}= t(v,v',u)$, and $T_{v',u} \mathrel{+}= t(v',v,u)$
6: $\quad\quad X^i_{v,u} \mathrel{+}= t^i_{elo}(v,v',u)$, and $X^i_{v',u} \mathrel{+}= t^i_{elo}(v',v,u)$
7: $\quad$ **end for** ▷ for each worker pair game
8: $\quad i \leftarrow i+1$
9: $\quad \delta^i(v,u) \leftarrow b^{i-1}(u)\cdot(T_{v,u} - X^{i-1}_{v,u})$
10: $\quad \delta^i(v',u) \leftarrow b^{i-1}(u)\cdot(T_{v',u} - X^{i-1}_{v',u})$
11: $\quad r^i(v) \leftarrow r^{i-1}(v) + \frac{K}{\binom{n}{2}}\cdot\delta^i(v,u)$ ▷ Update reputation
12: $\quad r^i(v') \leftarrow r^{i-1}(v') + \frac{K}{\binom{n}{2}}\cdot\delta^i(v',u)$
13: $\quad b^i(u) \leftarrow \dfrac{n^i_c(e) - n^i_w(e)}{n^i_c(e) + n^i_w(e)}$ ▷ Update job importance
14: **end for**

over v_3 and v_4. Finally, each of the workers v_3 and v_4 loses in the games against v_1 and v_2 but they draw when they face each other. The worker points in this job are 3 for v_1, 2 for v_2 and 0.5 for either of v_3 and v_4. At step 9, the rating update $\delta^i(v,u)$ of worker v due to his application to job u at the i-th time step is calculated as follows:

$$\delta^i(v,u) = b^{i-1}(u)(T_{v,u} - X^{i-1}_{v,u}) \tag{3}$$

where $b^{i-1}(u)$ is the importance score of job u from the $i-1$-th step, $T_{v,u}$ is the sum of the actual points that v scored in job u and $X^{i-1}_{v,u}$ is the sum of points he was expected to score based on his rating and the ratings of the other applicants from the previous step. Time steps advance at each new job occurrence. Note that the score update is multiplied by the importance of the job, $b(u)$, so that employer bias is taken into account, as shown in Equation 5. Also note that the more the applicants in an opening, the more the expected points, since the update includes a summation term for each applicant. What is more, the higher the difference between the rating of worker v and the ratings of the other applicants of job u, the more the points that v is expected to score. This is particularly useful since application success of an applicant is not independent from the application success of the remaining candidates at a particular job. Finally, to obtain the rating of worker v at the i-th time step, at step 11, we add the average of his partial rating updates (Equation 3) to his rating from the previous time step, $r^{(i-1)}(v)$:

$$r^i(v) = r^{i-1}(v) + \frac{K}{n-1}\cdot\delta^i(v,u) \tag{4}$$

The K-factor which represents the maximum possible adjustment per game is set to 32, and is normalized by dividing over $n-1$, where n is the number of the job applicants. Normalization is completed by the summation over all pairs of candidates. Normalization is important, since without it, we would have dramatic inflation/deflation of scores at jobs with high application rate. Popular jobs usually require generic skills, hence inflated scores would not necessarily imply that the quality of their hired workers is higher. A worker's reputation is updated according to the average win/loss score incurred in comparisons with other applicants to each job. This average ensures that applicants gain according to their relative position in the applicant ranking, rather than the number of applicants. Note that since δ can also be negative, applicants to many jobs being rejected by many employers is not necessarily a good strategy. After calculating the worker ratings, at step 13 we compute the importance scores of jobs $b(u)$. The intuition in Formula 5 is to give more credence to rating updates (Equation 4) that come from jobs posted by unbiased employers. The importance score is high for employers who make decisions that respect the worker ratings and it is low for employers who do not. Notice that after the occurrence of a small amount of job tournaments, the worker ratings is an outcome taken out of the aggregation of all employers judgements (step 11). At the same time, Elo scoring is based on a self-correcting rating system[1]. Hence the following formula reflects importance of a job as a measure of judgement deviation between the job's respective employer and the rest employers:

$$b^i(u) = \frac{n^i_c(e,u) - n^i_w(e,u)}{n^i_c(e,u) + n^i_w(e,u)} \tag{5}$$

$e \in E$ denotes employer (in the set of employers E) who posted job $u \in U$, $n_c(e,u)$ denotes the number of applicant pairs that were "correctly" ranked by employer e in job u and $n_w(e,u)$ denotes the number of applicant pairs that were "wrongly" ranked. We regard a pair of applicants as correctly ranked if the employer prioritizes the applicant with the highest reputation score. For example, if applicants v and v' have ratings $r(v) = 1$ and $r(v') = 2$ and employer e hires v' and rejects v, then the pair is considered to be correctly ranked.

3.2 Skill WorkerRank

The approach described in Section 3.1 predicts a reputation score for each worker based on application data. That score is computed in a global scope over all jobs where workers have applied. Although global scores provide a signal for the quality of workers, they may not be as powerful to discriminate among similar score workers and guide hiring with accuracy. For example, consider candidates v_1, v_2 in the example of Figure 2. The skills listed under each job reflect the skill-set required for the job. Also assume that v_2 is better in java than v_1, however v_1 is better overall than v_2, which can be due to the fact that v_1 has applied to more jobs where he received offers. At this point our reputation system would prioritize v_1 in the candidates list, missing the fact that v_2 is better in java.

Our goal is to achieve higher accuracy at predicting worker quality and prioritize candidates appropriate for the particular job. As mentioned above, besides the information regarding which worker applied to which job, there is further information regarding what skills each job requires and what skills each worker claims in their profile description. Given this information, we use WorkerRank to derive scores for candidates in a skill-wise fashion, such that eventually we learn how good each worker is at each particular skill. Then, if a job requires a skill, we may rank candidates according to their reputation scores at that particular skill and suggest the top ranked ones for getting hired. In the used example, workers v_1, v_2 who both claim to be experts in java (and they apply to job u_2 which requires java) will obtain a java score that will show their quality in that skill. The expectation is that ranking v_2 on top will lead to successful hiring decision.

Skill-wise reputation algorithm: We consider set of skills S, where $S_u \subseteq S$ denotes the skills required for job $u \in U$ and $S_v \subseteq S$ denotes the skills claimed by worker $v \in V$. Also, we consider bipartite graph $G_S = (U \times S, V \times S, A_S)$ similar to the definition in Section 3.1, where:

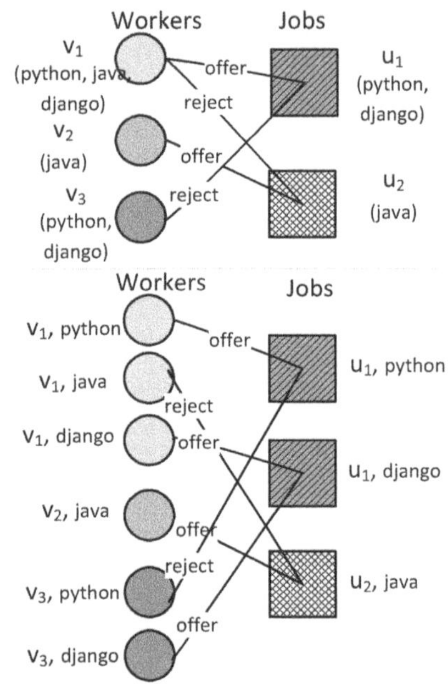

Figure 2: Skill-wise bipartite graph

- each worker node v is replaced by set of pair (worker, skill) nodes (v, s), one node for each skill claimed by the worker
- each job node u is replaced by set of pair (job, skill) nodes (u, s), one node for each skill required for the job
- each (worker, job) edge (v, u) is replaced by set of pair ({worker, skill}, {job, skill}) edges, $(\{v, s\}, \{u, s\})$, one edge for each skill that the worker claims and the job requires.

Then we run Algorithm 1 on G_S. The reputation and importance scores are derived skill-wise, such that we obtain a set of reputation scores $r(v, s)$, where$(v, s) \in V \times S$ and a set of importance scores $b(u, s)$, where$(u, s) \in U \times S$. Obtaining reputation scores for each $\{$worker, skill$\}$ pair provides information about the performance of the worker at the particular skill. Figure 2 describes an example for graphs G and G_S, with candidates v_1, v_2, v_3 applying to jobs u_1, u_2. Workers v_1, v_3 apply to job u_1 (v_1 receives an offer) and v_1, v_2 apply to job u_2 (v_2 receives an offer). The skills required for job u_1 are $\{$python, django$\}$ and the skills required for job u_2 are $\{$java$\}$. Worker v_1 claims to have skills $\{$python, java django$\}$, v_2 claims $\{$java$\}$, and worker v_3 claims $\{$python, django$\}$.

Correlation between skills and hires: Looking at the application data (enriched with skills information) we observe that in most cases jobs require more than one skills. In that case, we need to decide a ranking for candidates based on the intersection of their scores on a set of different skills. That ranking will reflect their suitability for the multi-skill requiring job. In our example where job u_1 requires python and django, we need to rank candidates according to their quality in python and their quality in django. However, the python-score may be more informative about hiring than the django-score. For example, it may more beneficial to hire a candidate with a high python-score than hire one with a high django-score. Hence it is important to measure how each skill contributes towards hiring, before we rank candidates according to skills.

In order to combine a set of scores for each worker across the set of skills required for a job, we allow for a weighted average over the worker's skill-wise scores. We use logistic regression to compute coefficients for skills as features, where we use the binary outcome of the application (hire/no-hire) as the response variable. Coefficients for skill scores will eventually show how informative each skill is about the quality of the worker, measured by the worker's potential of getting hired.

In Algorithm 2 we aggregate skill-wise scores into a single reputation/importance score for each worker/job respectively. The input of the new algorithm is the set of scores derived by Algorithm 1 for the sets of $\{$worker, skill$\}$, $\{$job, skill$\}$ pairs. The output of Algorithm 2 is the final reputation score for each worker and importance score for each job, after examining workers' quality across their skill-set and tuning it according to the significance of each skill.

Algorithm 2 Combine Skill-wise Scores into Reputation

Input: Set of skill-wise scores $r(v, s)$, $b(u, s)$, where $(v, s) \in V \times S$, $(u, s) \in U \times S$

Output: Reputation scores $r(v)$ for workers $v \in V$, Importance scores $b(u)$ for jobs $u \in U$

1: Consider feature variables $f(s) \leftarrow r(\cdot, s)$, $\forall s \in S$, and set of feature variables $F \leftarrow \cup_{s \in S} f(s)$
2: Consider response variable $y \leftarrow$ hiring outcome, where $y \in \{hire, no\text{-}hire\}$
3: Learn coefficients $w(f) \leftarrow LR(F, R), \forall f \in F$
4: **for** $v \in V$ and $u \in U$ **do**
5: $\quad r(v) \leftarrow \dfrac{\sum_{s \in S} r(v, s) \cdot w(s)}{\sum_{s \in S} w(s)}$
6: $\quad b(u) \leftarrow \dfrac{\sum_{s \in S} b(u, s) \cdot w(s)}{\sum_{s \in S} w(s)}$
7: **end for**

In step 1 we consider the set of features F, where one's reputation score $r(\cdot, s)$ at a particular skill $s \in S$ is regarded as a feature. We use $f(s) = r(\cdot, s)$ to denote feature regarding reputation score at skill s. For example, if $s =$ python, then any (denoted by '$\cdot$') worker's score in python, $r(\cdot, \text{python})$, is a feature. Recall that the coefficients pertain to how each skill score of a worker contributes towards his getting hired. In step 2 we consider response variable y to be the binary hiring outcome $y \in \{hire, no\text{-}hire\}$. Then in step 3 we run logistic regression (LR) on the set of features F with response variable y and we obtain coefficients $w(f)$ for each skill-score variable $f \in F$. Finally, in steps 5 - 6 we aggregate the input skill-wise scores using weights across skills learned at step 3. The output of the algorithm is a single reputation score for each worker (step 5) and a single importance score for each job of the application data (step 6).

3.3 Hybrid Model

While it is interesting to compare implicit judgements against explicit judgements in order to infer a quality measurement for workers, we expect that a hybrid model which combines both, shall yield better results. In this section we use rank aggregation to combine WorkerRank ranking with feedback ranking into an optimal listing of workers such that we predict true ranking (as specified by employer judgements) with higher accuracy.

In particular, we use the weighted rank aggregation method described in [29]. In this approach the function performs rank aggregation via a Cross-Entropy Monte Carlo algorithm. The algorithm searches for a desired list which is as close to the provided ordered lists as possible. In our implementation we use the Spearman distance to measure the correlation of the ordered lists of implicit and explicit reputation rankings. The convergence criterion used is the repetition of the same minimum value of the objective function in a number of consecutive iterations.

4. EXPERIMENTAL RESULTS

To evaluate the proposed reputation system, we compare WorkerRank with baseline schemes in terms of a) the sparsity of the signal in the marketplace, b) the time needed to obtain a signal for new workers, and c) discriminatory power for hiring decisions. During the evaluation, WorkerRank is compared against a baseline collaborative filtering approach which uses data of *implicit* reputation to rank workers (as a reminder, WorkerRank also runs on implicit reputation data). In addition, we compare WorkerRank against the current ranking approach that is based on *explicit* reputation data.

4.1 Setting

Dataset: We use a sample of real-world application data, along with explicit reputation scores provided by oDesk[27]. The oDesk dataset spans the time period of 53 weeks between January 2013 through January 2014 and it contains approximately 10M applications submitted by 0.5M workers to 1.1M job openings posted by 0.2M employers. Note that we do not account for unseen applications (case where employer has taken no action). In table 1 we provide some statistics regarding the dataset. In the experiments we use a sample of the applications submitted during the testing period. Tables 2 and 3 show a real job posting example. This example includes information about the job title, category, description, required skills, candidate applicants along with their declared skills, hire decision, reputation scores learned via WorkerRank and via skill-based WorkerRank. We observe overlapping skills among the job required skills and the skill-sets declared by the candidates. In Figure 4 we show the distribution of the ratings data. As studied in [19], we encounter skewness towards the high rating values. Note that in addition to the entire labels range, we also ran our model on binary hire/no-hire data and we obtained similar results. This confirms that our model can be run in any platform where hiring information is available, which is the case in most labor marketplace platforms.

Baseline - Explicit Data (Feedback): A baseline approach currently used in the marketplace is to represent the quality of workers based on *explicit* data; in particular, it collects the explicit star ratings assigned to each worker by the employers according to their performance on accomplished jobs, and aggregates them in an average ratings score. Then the workers quality is estimated according to the average employers feedback. The average employers rating $q(e, v)$ is used to rank candidate workers $v \in V$ who apply at a new job posting of employer $e \in E$, as follows:

$$q(e,v) = \frac{1}{N} \sum_{e':(v,u')\in A} \sum_{u'\in U_{e'}} q(e',v) \qquad (6)$$

where $(v, u') \in A$ denotes application of worker v to job u' posted by employer e', $U_{e'}$ is the set of jobs posted by e', $q(e', v)$ is the explicit ratings score in $[1, 5]$ assigned to v by e', and $N = \sum_{e'} |U_{e'}|$ is the number of accomplished jobs, posted by employers e'. Note that employers provide explicit reviews only to workers who have accepted their offer and upon completion of the job.

Baseline - Implicit Data (CF): In certain cases, reputation systems are used to provide ratings in recommendation problems. We view WorkerRank as a CF approach based on implicit data represented on a hiring actions bipartite graph, and we use a collaborative filtering (CF) scheme as one of the baseline approaches, as follows. We consider employers e, e' similarity $sim(e, e')$ and we collect the sets of jobs at which workers received an offer within the study training period. Then for each employer we count the total number of offers assigned to each worker by similar employers in the training set and we estimate worker quality score according to their hire rate, weighed by employer similarity. For employer e who posts a new job u, we compute recommended score for candidates v as the hire rate in jobs posted by employers e', neighbors of e, weighed by their similarity, $sim(e, e')$. Denoting employer implicit actions (offer, interview, reject, and more) by $q_{im}(e', v)$, we consider the following baseline implicit reputation score:

$$q_{im}(e,v) = \frac{1}{\sum_{e'} |sim(e,e')|} \sum_{e':(v,u)\in A} \sum_{u\in U_{e'}} sim(e,e') q_{im}(e',v) \qquad (7)$$

where $q_{im}(e', v)$ takes values in $\{0 \text{ if } v \text{ was not hired}, 1 \text{ else}\}$. *Similarity* between employer e and neighbor e', $sim(e, e')$, is defined by their cosine similarity based on their ratings on workers that e and e' have co-rated. Then e receives recommendations from the neighbor e' judgements [4].

In the testing phase we rank candidates by collaborative implicit hire rates and by explicit ratings reputation to recommend the top ranked workers for the new job openings. Then we compare the two baseline performances with WorkerRank performance.

Table 1: Dataset Statistics

	Training	Testing
Application dates	03/01/2013 – 03/01/2014	03/02/2014 – 18/02/2014
#Jobs	1,151,859	1,446
#Workers	477,464	21,642
#Employers	232,014	1,405
#Applications	9,214,557	34,054
Avg # cands / job	24.1	22.5
Min # cands / job	11	11
Max # cands / job	50	50
Median # cands / job	23	20

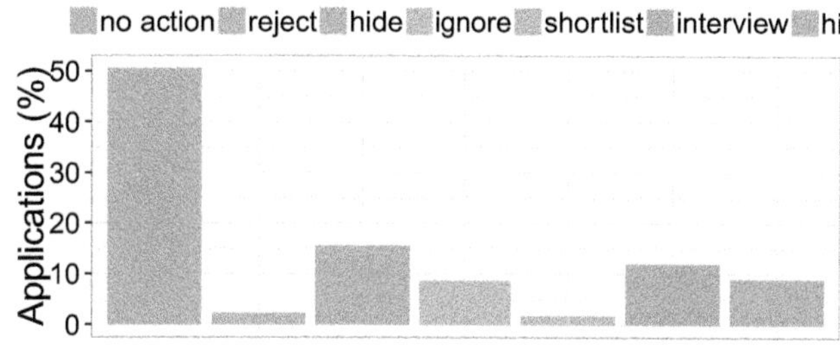

Figure 3: Histogram of application success label rates

Table 2: Job Posting Example (Applicants shown in table 3)

Title	*Wordpress Developer*
Category	*Web Development*
Required Skills	*wordpress, css, php*
Description	*1.Need Wordpress theme developed. Slider, logo, left sidebar menu, copyright.* *2.Must be experienced Wordpress developer.* *3.Must know CSS, php, Wordpress, html.* *4.Will provide visual design guide.*

Table 3: Skill-based reputation versus global reputation scores

Candidate	App.Success	Skill 1	Skill 2	Skill 3	Skill 4	Skill5	reputation	skill-reputation
v_1	offer	css3	php	wordpress	html	css	2.54	2.28
v_2	**offer**	css3	php	wordpress	html5	css	1.42	**4.67**
v_3	offer	web dev	sofw dev	–	–	–	1.39	2.05
v_4	**reject**	css3	php	wordpress	html5	ajax	**4.82**	3.40
v_5	reject	gr.design	visual-c++	wordpress	web design	illustration	1.38	1.06
v_6	reject	css3	php	javascript	html	jquery	1.05	2.45

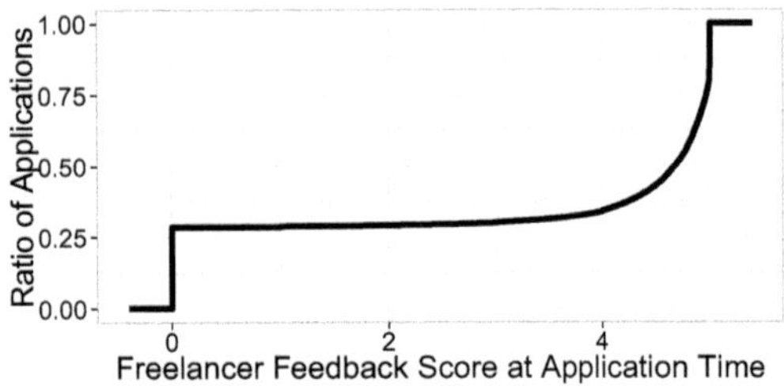

Figure 4: Data Skewness

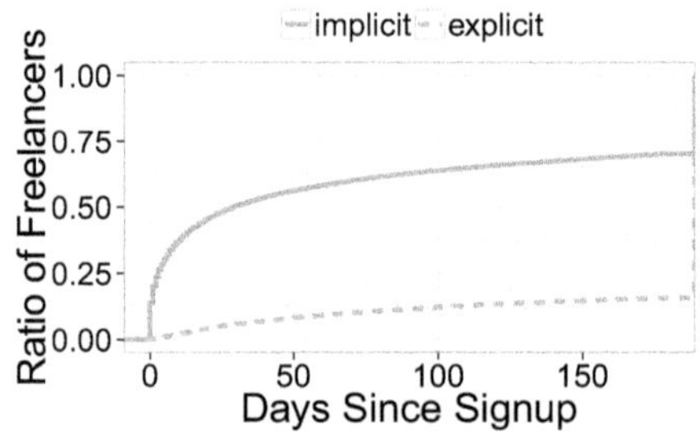

Figure 5: Cold Start: WorkerRank vs Explicit Feedback

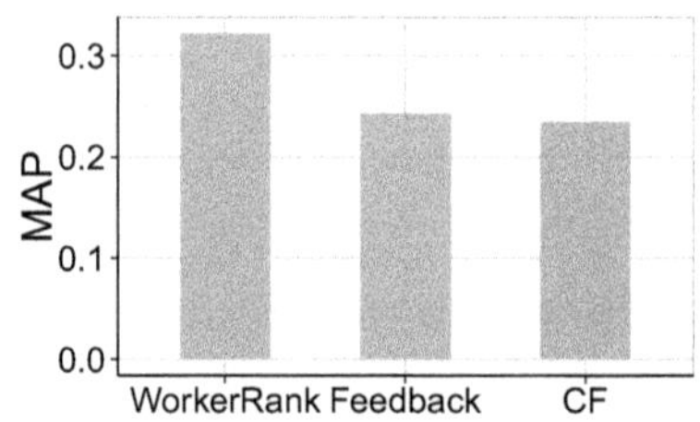

Figure 6: MAP in predicting the hiring outcome

4.2 Coverage

First, we show that since WorkerRank's results become available at the time of application, the coverage of workers for whom we obtain reputation signal is higher compared to the coverage obtained from explicit feedback. In particular, we run WorkerRank over the applications of the first 52 weeks of the dataset. During this time period we also keep track of the feedback ratings that the workers receive after the job is completed. Then we report the number of applications of the 53-rd week for which there is a WorkerRank score versus the applications for which there is an employer feedback score. Our results show that out of 88, 294 applications in the 53-rd week, we have WorkerRank scores for 79, 083 (89.6%), while we have feedback scores only for 52, 471 (59.4%). The increase in the marketplace application coverage is +50.8%. We present these results in table 5. Note that the above measurements account for both active and inactive applications.

4.3 Cold Start

Second, we show that WorkerRank is faster in acquiring signal for new workers joining the system, compared to the explicit feedback approach. Since the online marketplaces grow fast, the identification of new competent workers is very significant for their healthy development. For all workers who joined the platform during the last 3 months of our study period, we calculate the percentage of workers for whom we obtain reputation signals within X days. X is varying from 1 to 120 days. As presented in Figure 5, the WorkerRank scores are available for more than 60% of the new workers within 3 months of their joining the platform and the percentage ratio grows to 75% after another 4 months. On the contrary, there are less than 10% of new workers who received feedback at the end of their first 3 months in the platform and this percentage does not exceed 18% at the end of the additional 4-month period.

4.4 Ranking Precision

Third, we show that WorkerRank outperforms baseline approaches accuracy in ranking workers by quality, thus yielding a more reliable system for ranking candidates in new job openings.

WorkerRank vs Implicit vs Explicit Baselines:

MAP: We use Mean Average Precision (MAP) to evaluate rankings produced by the baseline and WorkerRank scores. The truth rankings to compare against, are specified by employer true scores that they implicitly assigned to candidates through their hiring actions in past jobs. As shown in Figure 6, by using WorkerRank, employers encounter approximately 1 good worker for every 3 workers in the ranked list. That performance is compared against 1 good worker for every 5 (or, 4 respectively) workers that the employer encounters by using the baseline CF ranking (or, explicit feedback, respectively). Overall, the new algorithm improves the chances of identifying good workers in the top results by 39.1% (33.3%, respectively). Also note that WorkerRank proposes an advanced approach that builds on the truth data, and outperforms basic learning to rank methods that would use the truth implicit data to rank (such as running one single-tournament Elo over the entire data-set).

Lift: To compare WorkerRank against the explicit feedback scores as signals for taking hiring decisions, first we rank all of the applications by the WorkerRank scores of the applicants. Then we calculate the hiring *lift* in the top x percent of the applications as follows:

$$lift(x) = \frac{\text{hiring probability in the top-}x\%\text{ applicants}}{\text{hiring probability across all applicants}} \quad (8)$$

Lift shows the performance of the examined methods versus that of a random scoring of applicants. We present the results in the bar-

Table 4: Performance Improvement: WorkerRank vs Baselines

	Explicit Feedback	Implicit Reputation		% Improvement	
	Ratings Based (RB)	Collab Filtering (CF)	WorkerRank (WR)	WR vs CF	WR vs RB
MAP	0.24	0.23	0.32	**+39.1%**	**+33.3%**
AUC	0.59	0.52	0.65	**+25.0%**	**+10.1%**
% Covered applications	59.4%	–	80.8%	–	**+50.8%**

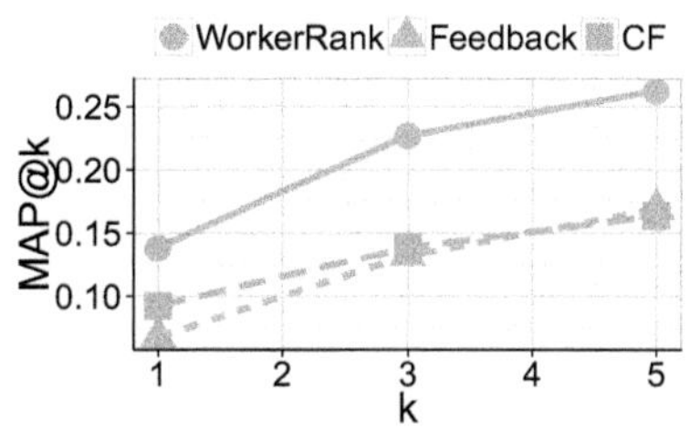

Figure 7: MAP@k in predicting the hiring outcome

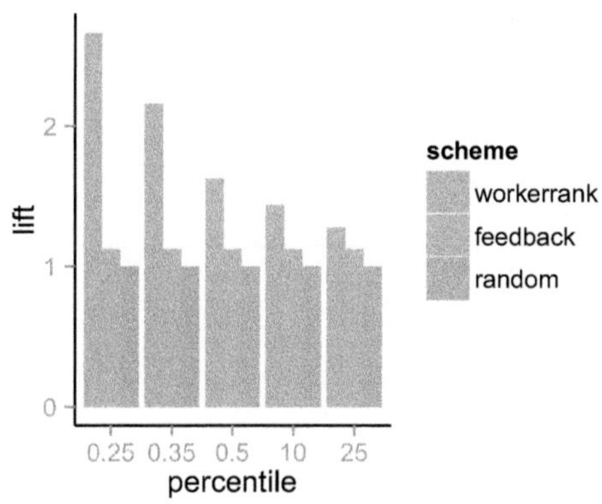

Figure 8: Lift in predicting the hiring outcome

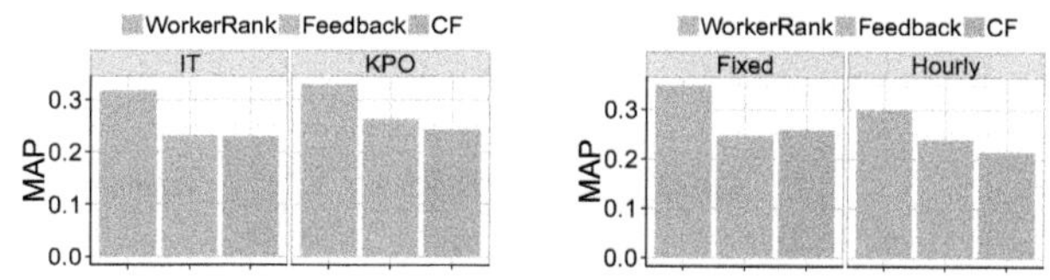

Figure 9: MAP across different job segments and types

plot of Figure 8. The plot has five triplets of bars and each triplet looks at a different percentage value of the top ranked workers, $x \in \{0.25, 0.35, 0.5, 10, 25\}$. Left bars look at the ratings obtained by WorkerRank, center bars look at the explicit feedback ratings, while right bars reflect random worker ranking. The height of each bar shows the lift value for the corresponding scheme, for the corresponding x value. For example, the first left bar from the left shows that the top-0.25% of applicants as ranked by WorkerRank are 2.66 times more likely to be hired than a random applicant. We observe that the lift of the explicit feedback scores is flat at 1.1 for all x values, since the top 25% of the applications correspond to workers with perfect 5-score rating. This shows that the existing reputation system does not provide a sufficient signal to discriminate high quality workers. On the other hand, WorkerRank ratings yield an increasing lift as we limit the percentage of the top-x% applications that we consider. The Elo lift is higher than the feedback lift for $x = 25\%$ and it exceeds 2.5 as we limit x to the top 0.25% of the applications. Note that for an average of 36 applications per job, that percentage implies that the top 9 candidates are 2.66 times more likely to be hired than any random candidate, as opposed to the almost equal likelihood that explicit feedback yields (1.1 times more likely than random).

Performance across Job Types: We also illustrate how WorkerRank outperforms the baseline approaches when studied in category subsets of the datasets. Figure 9(a) shows how the algorithms perform when applied on the different segments of jobs, Knowledge Processing Outsourcing (KPO) and Information Technology (IT). Figure 9(b) shows how the algorithms perform when applied on different type jobs (fixed-price (fp) versus hourly-rate (hr)). An interesting illustration is that of Figure 4.4, which shows how the different approaches behave on different job categories. For example, employers in software engineering jobs appear to provide more precise feedback about the quality of workers they have collaborated with, whereas in sales and marketing feedback ratings do not reflect the overall quality of workers as accurately.

Hybrid: WorkerRank and Explicit Feedback: In Figures 11(a) and 11(b) we show how the hybrid approach performs at MAP and MAP@k: for $k \in [1, 5]$, compared to the two approaches it combines; WorkerRank and explicit reputation. The hybrid model appears to slightly improve WorkerRank, the best of two approaches, although the improvement is not as high as it was in the comparison between implicit versus explicit reputation in Figures 6 and 7. It is interesting to mention that in all cases the hybrid model improves WorkerRank and explicit feedback, except for the hourly rate jobs and the Web Development category, where WorkerRank marginally outperforms the hybrid model and significantly outperforms the explicit reputation model.

Finally, during rank aggregation which derives the hybrid model, we tested a few weighting combinations to prioritize the influence of one of the two rankings (WorkerRank or explicit). Equal weights on the two rankings appears to be the best combination that makes the hybrid model behave optimally. The Figures shown for the hybrid model performance assume equal weight on the two lists.

Skill-wise WorkerRank vs WorkerRank: In Figure 12 we show how skill-wise WorkerRank performs at MAP compared to the plain WorkerRank approach. Since skills are available for approximately 65% of the jobs, we use a subset of the dataset in this experiment. As mentioned earlier, skill-wise WorkerRank produces specialized scores for workers, pertaining specifically to the skills that potential jobs require. The results show that ranking workers by skill-wise scores is more accurate than ranking them based on the WorkerRank scores. In particular, the improvement shown in the MAP Figure provides a better system to rank workers. However in certain cases skill-wise scores do not appear experimentally to differ from WorkerRank scores. That is because for several jobs a sin-

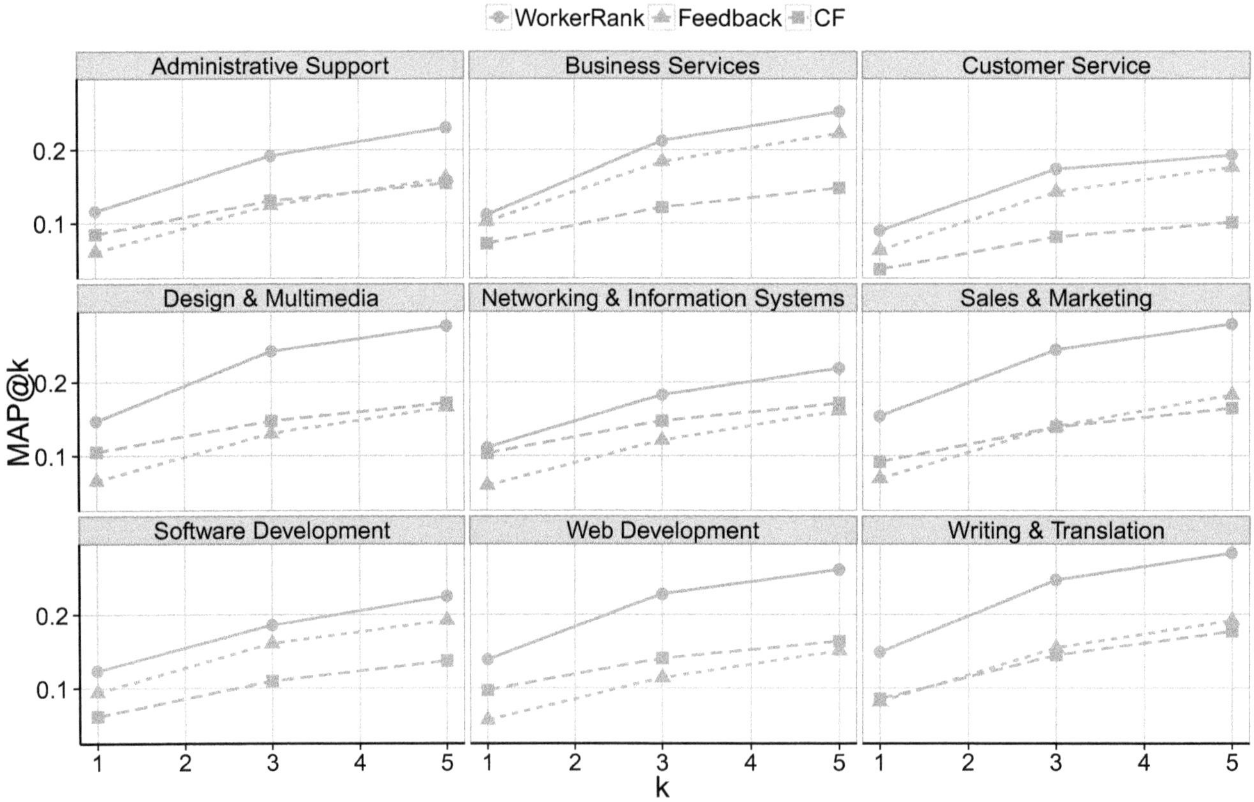

Figure 10: MAP across different job categories

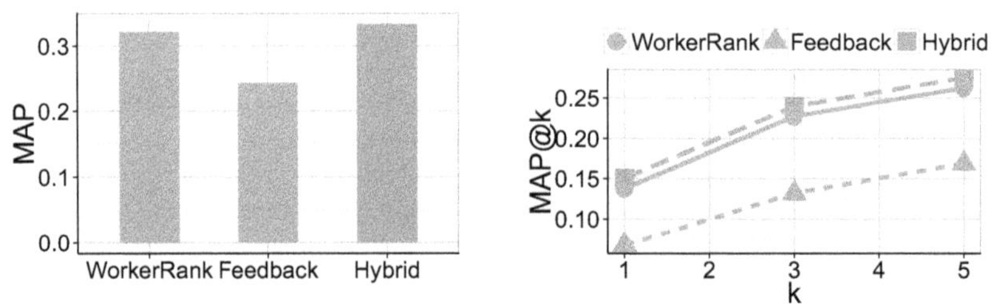

Figure 11: (a) MAP@Inf, (b) MAP@k for hybrid model in predicting the hiring outcome

Table 5: Performance Improvement: Hybrid vs WorkerRank

	WorkerRank	Hybrid	% Improvement
	WR	HB	HB vs WR
MAP@1	0.14	0.15	**+9.1%**
MAP@3	0.23	0.24	**+5.6%**
MAP@5	0.26	0.27	**+4.8%**
MAP@Inf	0.32	0.35	**+3.5%**

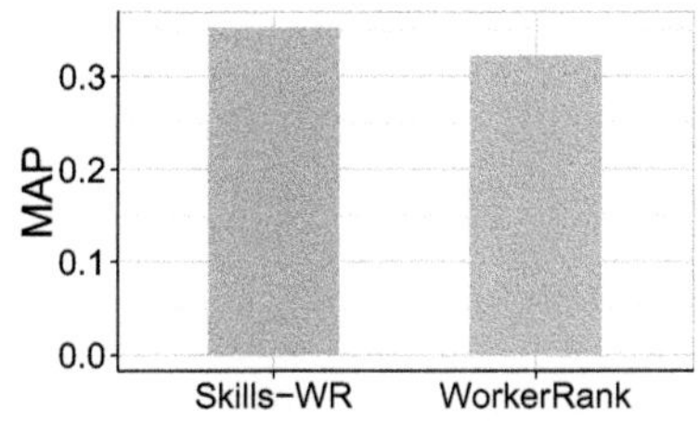

Figure 12: MAP in skill-wise WorkerRank

gle skill is specified instead of a set of skills. This is one of the reasons why skill scores do not add significant knowledge to our estimations about workers quality. We apply logistic regression to combine skill-wise scores in a weighted fashion such that the intersection of our knowledge about the ability of the workers on multiple scores is incorporated.

5. RELATED WORK

The problem tackled in this paper overlaps with four research fields; graph link analysis, building online reputation systems, game competition match analysis and predicting high-quality response in query-answering.

Graph link analysis research is related to our work, since we represent our data using a bipartite graph and we perform link analysis to examine the job applications of workers along with the respective employer feedback (edge weight). Several approaches have been proposed about ranking graph nodes in a network, such as PageRank [28], [10] and HITS [21], while Donato et. al. extend the study of HITS in [9] and Zhang et. al. in [36] study how PageRank and HITS perform when applied on the Java forum domain. Finally, Mishra et.al. [26], and Lescovec et. al. in [25] and [24] , present their node scoring methods with the presence of both positive and negative edge weights. Note that in our approach we also implicitly make use of negative information about applications, such as the "ignore", "hire" and "reject" feedback responses by the employer. However we only account for the relativity among different feedback labels, that is, who won over whom, hence we do not face restrictions of edge positivity.

Research on online reputation systems is directly related to our work, as we build a reputation system for workers in the labor marketplace, and we derive additional heuristic de-bias scores for employers. In [3] and [2] Adler et.al. tackle the problem of measuring the quality of contributions in Wikipedia, while Tan et.al. expand on this problem in [33]. Kokkodis et.al. in [22] discuss how to address data sparseness in building labor marketplace reputation systems. In [15], Dellarocas summarizes online reputation mechanisms and challenges they face in terms of usage and evaluation. What is more, Archack in [7] discusses how reputation challenges strategic behavior of contestants in the TopCoder marketplace, while Chen in [12] describes their de-biasing mechanism for building a reputation system in a comments rating environment. TwitterRank [35] is another reputation system which aims to build reputation scores such that they incorporate a measure of influence for the Twitter users. Finally, in our past approaches in [14] and [13], we discuss the usage of link analysis using weighting schemes in order to build reputation systems.

It is interesting to reference a few game competition works such as the Elo method [16] that we are using in our current approach in order to predict the expected hire probability of each worker given our prior knowledge about their opponent's performance and their own performance. Elo is using a Bayesian update scheme to score chess game players based on past matches activity and update their scores by their expected performance in future tournaments. Glickman in [17] presents an improved approach, which keeps updating the mean and variance of the player scores such that confidence information is also carried along with the player's quality estimation. Methods tackling further improvement of match updates are proposed, such as TrueSkill [18] which tackles multi-player and multi-team challenges, while Nikolenko et.al. further improve TrueSkill's challenges of multiway ties and variable team size. Finally, Sismanis in [31] proposes a re-visit on the Elo method which incorporates tournament recency and other parameters in the tournament analysis in order to avoid over-fitting of the player ratings.

Moreover, query answering methods are referenced since they tackle the challenge of predicting quality of a response content such as question answers and social media content; that challenge is similar to our work's goal of predicting worker quality scores. Several approaches have been proposed aiming to identify quality in social media content such as Agichtein et. al. [5] and Bian et. al. [8]. Shah et.al. [30], Suryanto et.al. [32], Jurczyk et. al. [20] and Anderson et. al. [6] study quality of answers in question answering, while Tsaparas et.al. [34], study quality of online review systems, such as in Yelp or Epinions. Finally, Chen et. al. [11] study de-biasing approaches to set votes more informative in question-answering systems towards higher quality in answer and expert ranking.

Finally, Kokkodis et al. [23] formulate the problem of hiring in work marketplaces as a binary classification problem, where the target variable is the hiring decision. An informative reputation mechanism like the one we present in this paper can be a very predictive signal in such classifiers.

6. CONCLUSIONS

The results of our experiments show that WorkerRank improves ranking of candidates compared to baseline approaches, since its reputation scores reflect worker quality more accurately. What is more, WorkerRank solves the basic problems encountered in explicit reputation systems (unreliable employer ratings, limited coverage of worker scores, cold start problem for new workers with no history information). Our future work includes research on weighting schemes as discussed in[14] and modeling implicit actions on the marketplace website.

7. REFERENCES

[1] Elo rating system - Wikipedia, the free encyclopedia.

[2] B. T. Adler and L. de Alfaro. A content-driven reputation system for the wikipedia. In *Proceedings of the 16th International Conference on World Wide Web*, WWW '07, pages 261–270, New York, NY, USA, 2007. ACM.

[3] B. T. Adler, L. de Alfaro, I. Pye, and V. Raman. Measuring author contributions to the wikipedia. In *Proceedings of the 4th International Symposium on Wikis*, WikiSym '08, pages 15:1–15:10, New York, NY, USA, 2008. ACM.

[4] G. Adomavicius and A. Tuzhilin. Toward the next generation of recommender systems: A survey of the state-of-the-art and possible extensions. *IEEE Trans. on Knowl. and Data Eng.*, 17(6):734–749, June 2005.

[5] E. Agichtein, C. Castillo, D. Donato, A. Gionis, and G. Mishne. Finding high-quality content in social media. In *Proceedings of the 2008 International Conference on Web Search and Data Mining*, WSDM '08, pages 183–194, New York, NY, USA, 2008. ACM.

[6] A. Anderson, D. Huttenlocher, J. Kleinberg, and J. Leskovec. Discovering value from community activity on focused question answering sites: A case study of stack overflow. In *Proceedings of the 18th ACM SIGKDD International Conference on Knowledge Discovery and Data Mining*, KDD '12, pages 850–858, New York, NY, USA, 2012. ACM.

[7] N. Archak. Money, glory and cheap talk: Analyzing strategic behavior of contestants in simultaneous crowdsourcing contests on topcoder.com. In *Proceedings of the 19th International Conference on World Wide Web*, WWW '10, pages 21–30, New York, NY, USA, 2010. ACM.

[8] J. Bian, Y. Liu, D. Zhou, E. Agichtein, and H. Zha. Learning to recognize reliable users and content in social media with coupled mutual reinforcement. In *Proceedings of the 18th International Conference on World Wide Web*, WWW '09, pages 51–60, New York, NY, USA, 2009. ACM.

[9] A. Borodin, G. O. Roberts, J. S. Rosenthal, and P. Tsaparas. Link analysis ranking: algorithms, theory, and experiments. *ACM Transactions on Internet Technology (TOIT)*, 5(1):231–297, 2005.

[10] S. Brin and L. Page. The anatomy of a large-scale hypertextual web search engine. In *Proceedings of the Seventh International Conference on World Wide Web 7*, WWW7, pages 107–117, Amsterdam, The Netherlands, The Netherlands, 1998. Elsevier Science Publishers B. V.

[11] B.-C. Chen, A. Dasgupta, X. Wang, and J. Yang. Vote calibration in community question-answering systems. In *Proceedings of the 35th International ACM SIGIR Conference on Research and Development in Information Retrieval*, SIGIR '12, pages 781–790, New York, NY, USA, 2012. ACM.

[12] B.-C. Chen, J. Guo, B. Tseng, and J. Yang. User reputation in a comment rating environment. In *Proceedings of the 17th ACM SIGKDD International Conference on Knowledge Discovery and Data Mining*, KDD '11, pages 159–167, New York, NY, USA, 2011. ACM.

[13] M. Daltayanni and L. de Alfaro. Recommending workers in the labor marketplace. *In Workshop: Data Design for Personalization: Current Challenges and Emerging Opportunities. In conjunction with WSDM 2014.*

[14] M. Daltayanni, L. de Alfaro, P. Papadimitriou, and P. Tsaparas. On assigning implicit reputation scores in an online labor marketplace. In *EDBT*, pages 724–725, 2014.

[15] C. Dellarocas. The digitization of word of mouth: Promise and challenges of online feedback mechanisms. *Manage. Sci.*, 49(10):1407–1424, Oct. 2003.

[16] A. E. Elo. *The rating of chessplayers, past and present.* Arco Pub., New York, 1978.

[17] M. E. Glickman. The glicko system. 1995.

[18] R. Herbrich, T. Minka, and T. Graepel. Trueskilltm: A bayesian skill rating system. In B. Schoelkopf, J. Platt, and T. Hoffman, editors, *NIPS*, pages 569–576. MIT Press, 2006.

[19] N. Hu, J. Zhang, and P. A. Pavlou. Overcoming the j-shaped distribution of product reviews. *Commun. ACM*, 52(10):144–147, Oct. 2009.

[20] P. Jurczyk and E. Agichtein. Discovering authorities in question answer communities by using link analysis. In *Proceedings of the Sixteenth ACM Conference on Conference on Information and Knowledge Management*, CIKM '07, pages 919–922, New York, NY, USA, 2007. ACM.

[21] J. M. Kleinberg. Authoritative sources in a hyperlinked environment. *J. ACM*, 46(5):604–632, Sept. 1999.

[22] M. Kokkodis and P. G. Ipeirotis. Have you done anything like that?: predicting performance using inter-category reputation. In S. Leonardi, A. Panconesi, P. Ferragina, and A. Gionis, editors, *WSDM*, pages 435–444. ACM, 2013.

[23] M. Kokkodis, P. Papadimitriou, and I. Panagiotis. On hiring decisions in online labor markets. In *WSDM*, 2015.

[24] J. Leskovec, D. Huttenlocher, and J. Kleinberg. Predicting positive and negative links in online social networks. In *Proceedings of the 19th international conference on World wide web*, WWW '10, pages 641–650, New York, NY, USA, 2010. ACM.

[25] J. Leskovec, D. Huttenlocher, and J. Kleinberg. Signed networks in social media. In *Proceedings of the SIGCHI Conference on Human Factors in Computing Systems*, CHI '10, pages 1361–1370, New York, NY, USA, 2010. ACM.

[26] A. Mishra and A. Bhattacharya. Finding the bias and prestige of nodes in networks based on trust scores. In *Proceedings of the 20th international conference on World wide web*, WWW '11, pages 567–576, New York, NY, USA, 2011. ACM.

[27] oDesk. https://www.odesk.com.

[28] L. Page, S. Brin, R. Motwani, and T. Winograd. The pagerank citation ranking: Bringing order to the web, 1999.

[29] V. Pihur, S. Datta, and S. Datta. Weighted rank aggregation of cluster validation measures. *Bioinformatics*, 23(13):1607–1615, July 2007.

[30] C. Shah and J. Pomerantz. Evaluating and predicting answer quality in community qa. In *Proceedings of the 33rd International ACM SIGIR Conference on Research and Development in Information Retrieval*, SIGIR '10, pages 411–418, New York, NY, USA, 2010. ACM.

[31] Y. Sismanis. How i won the "chess ratings - elo vs the rest of the world" competition. *CoRR*, abs/1012.4571, 2010.

[32] M. A. Suryanto, E. P. Lim, A. Sun, and R. H. L. Chiang. Quality-aware collaborative question answering: Methods and evaluation. In *Proceedings of the Second ACM International Conference on Web Search and Data Mining*, WSDM '09, pages 142–151, New York, NY, USA, 2009. ACM.

[33] C. H. Tan, E. Agichtein, P. Ipeirotis, and E. Gabrilovich. Trust, but verify: Predicting contribution quality for knowledge base construction and curation. In *WSDM*, 2014.

[34] P. Tsaparas, A. Ntoulas, and E. Terzi. Selecting a comprehensive set of reviews. In *Proceedings of the 17th ACM SIGKDD International Conference on Knowledge Discovery and Data Mining*, KDD '11, pages 168–176, New York, NY, USA, 2011. ACM.

[35] J. Weng, E.-P. Lim, J. Jiang, and Q. He. Twitterrank: Finding topic-sensitive influential twitterers. In *Proceedings of the Third ACM International Conference on Web Search and Data Mining*, WSDM '10, pages 261–270, New York, NY, USA, 2010. ACM.

[36] J. Zhang, M. S. Ackerman, and L. Adamic. Expertise networks in online communities: Structure and algorithms. In *Proceedings of the 16th International Conference on World Wide Web*, WWW '07, pages 221–230, New York, NY, USA, 2007. ACM.

The Information Life of Social Networks

Lada A. Adamic
Facebook
Menlo Park, CA 94025
USA
ladamic@fb.com

ABSTRACT
Vast amounts of information are propagated in online social networks such as Facebook. This talk will describe several studies characterizing how information diffuses over social ties, from the growth of individual cascades [1] to the predictability of their eventual size [2]. It will also characterize the diffusion of specific kinds of information, including rumors [3], memes [4], and social movements.

Categories and Subject Descriptors
H.2.8 [Database Management]: Database applications—Data mining

Keywords
Social networks; information diffusion

WSDM'15, February 2–6, 2015, Shanghai, China.
ACM 978-1-4503-3317-7/15/02.
http://dx.doi.org/10.1145/2684822.2685325

REFERENCES
[1] Dow, P. A., Adamic, L.A. and Friggeri. A. 2013. The Anatomy of Large Facebook Cascades." *ICWSM*'13, Boston, MA, USA.

[2] Cheng, J. Adamic, L.A. Dow, P. A., Kleinberg, J.M and Leskovec, J. 2014. Can cascades be predicted?. WWW '14. ACM, New York, NY, USA, 925-936. DOI=http://doi.acm.org/10.1145/2566486.2567997.

[3] Friggeri, A., Adamic, L. A., Eckles, D., & Cheng, J. 2014. Rumor Cascades, *ICWSM'14*, Ann Arbor, MI, USA.

[4] Adamic, L. A., Lento, T. M., Adar, E., and Ng, P. C. 2014. Information Evolution in Social Networks, Technical Report. http://arxiv.org/pdf/1402.6792.pdf

User Modeling for a Personal Assistant

Ramanathan Guha* Vineet Gupta Vivek Raghunathan Ramakrishnan Srikant

Google
Mountain View, CA, USA
{guha,vineet,vraghunathan,srikant}@google.com

ABSTRACT

We present a user modeling system that serves as the foundation of a personal assistant. The system ingests web search history for signed-in users, and identifies coherent contexts that correspond to tasks, interests, and habits. Unlike past work which focused on either in-session tasks or tasks over a few days, we look at several months of history in order to identify not just short-term tasks, but also long-term interests and habits. The features we use for identifying coherent contexts yield substantially higher precision and recall than past work. We also present an algorithm for identifying contexts that is 8 to 30 times faster than previous algorithms. The user modeling system has been deployed in production. It runs over hundreds of millions of users, and updates the models with a 10-minute latency. The contexts identified by the system serve as the foundation for generating recommendations in Google Now.

1. INTRODUCTION

During the last two decades, web search has become the most widely used method for answering information needs. Over this period, search engines have become increasingly sophisticated at finding and ranking search results. While this model for answering information needs has been extremely successful, there are some limitations:

- Mobile device usage has exploded in the last five years. Typing a search query on a smartphone is very slow compared to a desktop. A system that automatically shows the right information at the right time would provide a dramatically better user experience on the phone.
- For topics the user is interested in, the user needs to repeatedly query the search engine to determine whether there is interesting fresh content. If such content appears only occasionally, the user is destined to either be disappointed with most searches not returning anything new, or miss interesting fresh content with high probability.
- Search engines are only mildly personalized. Interactions with search engines are often reminiscent of the movie "50 First Dates", in that the search engine appears to have forgotten all past interactions.

The last three years have seen the introduction of a new category of mobile personal assistants, including Google Now [1] and Cortana [2]. These assistants share the goal of showing the user the right information at the right time, without the user querying for information. The primary motivation of this paper is to enable such personal assistants to address the problems discussed above:

- **Contextual assistance**: The personal assistant should be able to detect a change in the user context, and make useful recommendations for that context. For example, if a user is in a city away from home, the assistant might show a personalized list of nearby restaurants and their reviews, without the user ever typing a query.
- **Interest updates**: Users are often interested in certain topics, like a particular sports team, a celebrity, or a favorite TV show. Personal assistants save users the trouble of finding new information by automatically alerting the user to any new piece of information about their favorite topics.
- **Fully personalized**: The personal assistant utilizes the user model to fully personalize the experience. For example, when suggesting restaurants, in addition to the spatio-temporal context, the assistant personalizes the suggestions based on the user's cuisine preferences and price sensitivity.

We emphasize that such personal assistants (or discovery engines) complement traditional search engines, and while they may substantially reduce the need to use search engines on a smartphone, are not replacements for a search engine.

The foundation for such a personal assistant is a user modeling system that, given a sequence of user actions, identifies coherent **contexts**. A context is a set of user actions corresponding to a single information need. Contexts include:

- **Tasks**: Tasks typically have a beginning and an end, e.g., buying a camera or planning a trip to Paris. Tasks can span multiple sessions, and some long-running tasks, such as planning a wedding, may span weeks or months.

*Authors are listed alphabetically.

WSDM'15, February 2–6, 2015, Shanghai, China.

http://dx.doi.org/10.1145/2684822.2685309.

- **Interests**: Interests may span months or years, and often do not have an end. Examples include following sports teams, celebrities, or TV shows.
- **Habits**: These are actions that users take on a regular basis, e.g., reading a favorite blog or news site, checking stock prices, or checking traffic in the daily commute.

These contexts are annotated with context types, entities, and names.

We have built a system, called **Taba**, comprised of two parts:

1. An user modeling system that builds the user model described above. The system scales to hundreds of millions of users, and updates the user model within 10 minutes of a new user action.
2. A content recommendation system that does collaborative filtering over contexts and users, and also predicts how interested the user will be in recommendations for the context.

In this paper, we focus on the user modeling system, and motivate the user model by describing how the recommendation system uses the contexts. Both these systems have been deployed as part of Google Now, serving tens of millions of recommendations daily.

Paper Outline.

We discuss related work in Section 2. In Section 3, we describe the features and algorithms for identifying tasks, interests and habits from a user's history. We evaluate our user model in Section 4. In Section 5, we describe how the user model serves as the foundation for prediction and recommendation systems in Google Now. We conclude in Section 6.

2. RELATED WORK

Early work on grouping search queries (e.g., [21]) focused on sessions, defined purely by the temporal gap between queries. Spink et al. [22] found that a large majority of multiple-query sessions included multiple topics. Jones et al. [12] showed that using query reformulation and query words to identify topics yielded substantially higher accuracy than only using timeouts.

Subsequent work in this area can be split into two groups: papers that focus on in-session tasks, and those that identify cross-session tasks.

2.1 In-Session Tasks

Lucchese et al. [17] proposed techniques for identifying "task-based sessions": sets of possibly non-contiguous queries within a session that correspond to a user task. They recognized that standard clustering algorithms are too expensive, and proposed a new clustering algorithm QC_{HTC}, which avoids computing the full similarity graph by just considering a cluster to be represented by the first and the last queries in the session.

Li et al. [16] also consider in-session tasks. They use query words, query co-occurrence, and the temporal sequence of queries as their main signals. Their learning algorithm is quadratic, but they have a linear approximation which works well in practice. Hua et al. [10] showed the importance of semantic features for in-session task identification.

User behavior within a session (typically 30 minutes) is quite different from user behavior across months of history. In-session tasks tend to be uniform and small, while long-term tasks and interests tend to be diverse and large. Hence intuitions that work well for in-session tasks do not always scale to identifying coherent contexts across months of history. For example, representing contexts by the first and last queries is reasonable for in-session tasks, but cannot capture a context with hundreds of queries.

2.2 Cross-Session Tasks

Several papers have recently addressed the considerably more challenging problem of identifying longer range tasks across sessions. Kotov et al. [14] formulate the problem of identifying cross-session tasks as follows: given a query, identify all related queries from previous sessions that are part of the same task. Their main focus is trying to predict if the task will be continued later, so they restrict themselves to primarily syntactic features such as number of words the queries have in common, edit distance between queries and the time between queries. The authors continued their research on task continuation in Agichtein et al. [3], and added semantic features such as ODP categories, and demonstrated that automated systems can significantly outperform human raters on predicting task continuation.

Lucchese et al. [18, 19] have extended their work above to cluster their already computed in-session tasks by using clustering algorithms which produce a specified number of clusters. They use average pairwise similarity to determine the similarity between tasks. Their primary focus is clustering in-session tasks across users, but they do use their algorithm to produce cross-session task clusters for individual users.

Wang et al. [23] propose an algorithm for identifying cross-session search tasks using a variety of signals. They built a training set by completely annotating 5 days of query logs for 1436 users, and learned a latent structural SVM classifier to compute the similarity between pairs of queries. Then they use a bestlink clustering algorithm [11] to cluster queries — each query is clustered with the most similar query that occurred before it, as long as their similarity exceeded a threshold.

2.3 Our Contributions

There are three main differences between our work and prior work on in-session and cross-session tasks.

- We focus on user history over many months, often with thousands of queries and clicks. This lets us identify long-term interests and habits in addition to identifying short-term tasks — identifying such contexts over many months (versus short time spans) is critical for the user model to be useful in a personal assistant (see Section 5).
- We present a set of features that yield better precision/recall than past work [23] while simultaneously being much faster to compute.
- Working over longer time spans means that $O(n^2)$ algorithms do not scale. We present a near-linear segmentation algorithm that is much faster than prior work.

Finally, this is a production system running continuously over hundreds of millions of users with a 10-minute turnaround time for incorporating new user actions into the model. This has implications for the design of features and algorithms, as we will see in the rest of the paper.

3. USER MODELING

3.1 Problem Statement

The input to the user modeling system is a **sequence of observations** from a single user. In this paper, an *observation* is a query together with its associated web results and clicks. Conceptually, an observation could also be a video watch, or a URL visited in a browser.

The output is a **set of contexts**, where a context is a sequence of observations that constitutes a single information need.

In general, the definition of a single information need is ambiguous, and in fact it can differ among users as well. For a researcher in information retrieval, the queries "graph clustering algorithms" and "synonyms in web search ranking" may be part of different contexts about different papers. For a beginning undergraduate, they would be part of the same context, "Information Retrieval Course".

To determine whether two observations are part of the same information need, we asked human raters: "Are these part of the same task or interest?" We pick a random sample of pairs of observations from a random sample of users, and the ratings on this sample serve as the ground truth. The goal of our algorithm is to partition the sequence of observations into a set of contexts, and we evaluate the precision and recall of the algorithm against the sampled ratings.

We break the context inference problem into two subproblems:

1. Given two candidate contexts, should we merge them into a single context? We formulated this as supervised classification, with the additional requirement that the score returned by the classifier should also serve as a similarity score (Section 3.2).

2. Using the classifier to make decisions, we wish to segment the set of input observations into coherent contexts (Section 3.5).

This approach is similar to supervised clustering, e.g., [9].

Once we have identified contexts, we add semantic annotations like context types and attribute entities (Section 3.6).

3.2 Classification

Given two contexts C_1 and C_2, we need a similarity function that lets us decide whether these two contexts should be merged into a single context. In addition, we would like the function to return a score that reflects the degree of similarity between the contexts.

Compared to prior work, there are three differences in our similarity computation:

1. Given two contexts with m and n observations respectively, we compute the similarity score in $O(m+n)$ time, i.e., linear in the size of the contexts. A straightforward pair-wise similarity computation would need $O(mn)$ time, which would be too slow for our application.

2. Instead of weighting features by inverse document frequency or inverse query frequency, we weight based on the probability that two observations with that feature are merged into the same context (Section 3.3).

3. We incorporate the degree of confidence in a feature into the similarity calculation (Section 3.4).

3.2.1 Classifier

We use the term **feature dimension** to denote a set of homogeneous features, e.g., the set of query words is a feature dimension, or the set of Freebase entities is a feature dimension. Each word or entity will then be called a **feature**. Similarity metrics such as cosine similarity make sense within a feature dimension, but not across feature dimensions, as features are not comparable across dimensions.

We use a linear classifier for our similarity function:

$$\text{Similarity}(C_1, C_2) = w_0 + \sum_{i=1}^{n} w_i v_i(C_1, C_2) \qquad (1)$$

where w_i is the weight of the ith feature dimension, and $v_i(C_1, C_2) \in [-1, 1]$ is the score (value of the similarity metric) of the ith feature dimension for the contexts C_1 and C_2. We consider two contexts to be similar if their similarity score is greater than zero, hence w_0 serves as an (optional) offset. Given a training dataset consisting of pairs of contexts, with the scores of each feature dimension, we use an off-the-shelf SVM classifier to learn the weights w_i.

3.2.2 Feature Dimensions

Figure 1 summarizes the feature dimensions that we used, along with their similarity metrics. Note that all of these are applicable to pairs of contexts, not just pairs of observations.

The Location and Temporal dimensions require custom similarity functions (discussed below). The other feature dimensions all use one of the following similarity metrics:

- *Cosine* is the standard cosine similarity, used when the feature dimension is a weighted vector of features.

- *ScaledCosine* is a variant of cosine similarity that takes into account missing features (e.g., some queries or clicks may not map to any entities), or low confidence in inferred features. ScaledCosine is discussed in Section 3.4.

- *MaxFraction* computes for each context the fraction of observations that satisfy some property (e.g., matching an observation in the other context). It then takes the maximum of these two fractions as the similarity.

- *NormIntersection* is a symmetric version of Jaccard containment [4]. NormIntersection is defined for a pair of sets A, B as

  $$\text{NormIntersection}(A, B) = \frac{|A \cap B|}{\min(|A|, |B|)}$$

  This function does not satisfy $\text{NormIntersection}(A, B) = 1 \Rightarrow A = B$, but we prefer it to Jaccard similarity as $A \subseteq B \Rightarrow \text{NormIntersection}(A, B) = 1$, so we would merge A, B as expected.

We typically use ScaledCosine for feature dimensions where we expect missing features or variance in the confidence in features. For feature dimensions where each feature is approximately equally predictive of similarity (like query or URL), we treat the features as a set and use NormIntersection or MaxFraction for similarity.

Feature Dimension	Similarity Function	Inputs to the similarity function
QueryWords	Cosine	Stemmed query words in each context, weighted by frequency and PVFW
QueryRefinements	ScaledCosine	Stemmed words in the refinements of queries in each context
SameWebResults	NormIntersection	Set of top 10 web results for the queries in each context
SameQuery	NormIntersection	Set of queries in each context
Spelling	MaxFraction	Fraction of queries in C_1 that are mis-spellings of queries in C_2, and vice versa
SubQuery	MaxFraction	Fraction of queries in C_1 that are sub-queries of queries in C_2, and vice versa
ClickWords	Cosine	Stemmed words in the titles of clicked URL in each context
QueryClickWords	Cosine	Stemmed query words of C_1 with stemmed click title words C_2, and vice versa
SameClick	NormIntersection	Set of clicked URLs in each context
URLDomain	ScaledCosine	URL domains (for clicks and web results), weighted by frequency and PVFW
ContextType	ScaledCosine	Context types (see Section 3.6.1) with weights
Category	ScaledCosine	Categories for each context (using an off-the-shelf classifier), with weights
Forums	ScaledCosine	Forum results for queries in each context, weighted by frequency
Entity	ScaledCosine.	Weighted vector of Freebase entities extracted from queries and clicks
Location	See Section 3.2.2	Locations referenced in queries and clicks
Session	MaxFraction	Fraction of queries in C_1 in the same session as a query in C_2, and vice versa
Temporal	See Section 3.2.2	Temporal distance between contexts

Figure 1: Features

Query refinements are other queries that frequently co-occur with the given query in search sessions of many users. The other feature dimensions based on queries and clicks are self-explanatory.

The next two feature dimensions, *ContextType* and *Category*, map queries and clicks into taxonomies. *Category* uses an off-the-shelf classifier with around 1500 categories. However, there are many cases where observations that map to different categories would be considered part of the same context, while observations that map to the same category would be considered part of different contexts. *ContextType* is described in more detail in Section 3.6.1, and has the property that if two observations map to different context types, they will not be considered part of the same context. The third taxonomy-like feature is *Forums*, which uses the set of forums that we get when search results for the query are restricted to forums. Forums are especially helpful for tail queries, where they capture fine-grained user interests.

For the *Entity* feature dimension, we identify and score freebase entities for each query and URL. We start with off-the-shelf query-to-entity and document-to-entity extractors. We then do additional disambiguation by using click entities (and if present, knowledge panel entities) to disambiguate query entities, and query entities to disambiguate click entities.

For each observation, we normalize the weight of the features within a feature dimension to be at most 1 + the number of clicks. Intuitively, we give the query and each click equal weight, and an observation that has more clicks has more weight. We aggregate the features from observations to contexts using either set union or by adding the feature vectors. For each feature dimension, we can compute similarity of two contexts with m and n observations respectively in $O(m+n)$ time.

For *Session* and *Temporal*, we compute, for each observation, the time gap to the closest observation in the other context in $O(m \log n + n \log m)$ time. For *Session*, we then use the fraction of observations that occur in the same session as an observation in the other context. For *Temporal*, we compute the average, over all observations, of the number of days to the closest observation in the other context.

Finally, *Location* is the only feature where we do use $O(mn)$ time. We compute the fraction of locations in the context that are close to some location in the other context. (Computing the average lat-long is not very meaningful, *e.g.*, consider a context whose locations include San Francisco and California.) Fortunately the number of locations is much smaller than other features, hence the overall execution time continues to be linear in the size of contexts.

3.3 Predictive Value Feature Weighting (PVFW)

A standard approach in information retrieval is to weight features by inverse document frequency or inverse query frequency. We found that such weighting was useful for very popular words, entities or domains, but not useful beyond the head. For example, consider the queries "Ecco shoes" and "Rockport shoes". "Shoes" is a common word with a small IDF, while "Ecco" and "Rockport" have large IDFs, so the cosine similarity of the query words weighted by IDF is small. However, the word "shoes" is a good indicator that these queries are part of the same context, so we would like "shoes" to have the higher weight, not the brands.

In order to accomplish this, we directly measure the predictive value of a feature. Let O_i, O_j be a random pair of observations for a random user. Then we define the predictive value weight w_f for a feature f as:

$$\begin{aligned} w_f &= \Pr(O_i, O_j \text{ in same context} \mid O_i, O_j \text{ have feature } f) \\ &= \frac{\sum_{u \in U} |P_{fc}(u)|}{\sum_{u \in U} |P_f(u)|} \end{aligned}$$

where U is the set of users, and for a user u, $P_f(u)$ is the set of all pairs of observations that have the feature f, and $P_{fc}(u)$ the set of all pairs of observations that both have the feature f and are in the same context at the end of segmentation.

The intuition is similar to co-training [5, 7]: we leverage information from all the other features to determine the usefulness of this feature. There is a circularity here, that the segmenter uses the classifier that in turn uses the segmenter to determine the feature weights. In practice, we built the initial version of the segmenter without feature weights. Once we had contexts for all users, we computed feature weights, re-ran the segmenter, and continue to update the feature weights periodically.

3.4 Incorporating Confidence: ScaledCosine

We motivate ScaledCosine with the following examples:

- When we infer entities from queries or URLs, we often get entities with low confidence. For the query "WSDM 2015", the only entity is "Web Services Distributed Management", with low confidence. Simply computing the cosine similarity between the set of entities in this query and a different query will not capture that this is a low confidence inference.
- For a click on a Wikipedia article, the PVFW weight we compute for the domain `wikipedia.org` is less than 0.1, i.e., the probability that two wikipedia clicks end up in the same context is less than 10%. `insideevs.com` is however a very specialized website, and gets a score of 0.83. But a simple cosine similarity cannot distinguish between a pair of clicks to `wikipedia.org` and a pair of clicks to `insideevs.com`: both of these pairs will get a cosine similarity of 1.

Given a pair of contexts, let

- c be the cosine similarity,
- s_1 (s_2) be the sum of the weights of the features in the first (second) context, and
- m_1 (m_2) be the maximum possible value of s_1 (s_2).

A natural approach would be to try multiplying c by $\frac{s_1}{m_1} \times \frac{s_2}{m_2}$, so that the similarity is low when we have less confidence. However, this conflates two very different cases:

- The similarity value is low because the contexts are very dissimilar.
- The similarity value is low because we do not have much data for this feature dimension.

Hence we first determine a **neutral point** t, so that contexts with cosine similarity $c \ll t$ are considered similar, while contexts with cosine similarity $c \gg t$ are considered dissimilar.[1] We define ScaledCosine for a feature dimension as:

$$\textbf{ScaledCosine} = (c - t) \times \frac{s_1}{m_1} \times \frac{s_2}{m_2}$$

Intuitively, if there is no uncertainty or missing features, $s_1 \approx m_1$, $s_2 \approx m_2$, and the ScaledCosine is simply $c - t$. Since the threshold t is offset in the classifier, the ScaledCosine behaves exactly like the cosine similarity.

If there is very little data for one or both contexts, the ScaledCosine will be close to zero because we scale $c - t$. If the contexts are dissimilar and there is sufficient data, the ScaledCosine will be negative, thus distinguishing the two cases discussed above.

If there is sufficient data and $c \approx t$, the ScaledCosine will be close to zero. However, conflating this case with that of missing data is not a problem because, in both cases, there is no strong signal from this feature dimension as to whether or not the two contexts should be merged.

[1] We can determine t by training a SVM for a feature dimension. Then $t = -w_0$.

1. Initialize each observation as a candidate context.
2. While Similarity(closest pair of candidates) > 0:
   a. Merge the two candidate contexts that are most similar.
   b. Recompute similarity score between the new context and all other candidates.

Figure 2: Hierarchical Agglomerative Clustering

1. Initialize each observation as a candidate context.
2. Within each session, use HAC to merge contexts.
3. For threshold $t_i \in [t_1, t_2, ..., t_k]$:
   a. Find all pairs of candidate contexts that share a feature, together with a light-weight similarity score.
   b. Sort candidate pairs by the light-weight similarity score.
   c. For each candidate pair (c_p, c_q):
      If c_p was already merged into a context c_r, $c_p := c_r$.
      If c_q was already merged into a context c_s, $c_q := c_s$.
      If $c_p = c_q$, skip this pair. Else:
         Compute Similarity(c_p, c_q), and merge if score $> t_i$.
         If the last N candidate pairs had scores $< t_i$, break.

Figure 3: Near-Linear Agglomerative Clustering (NLAC)

3.5 Segmentation

Prior work in user modeling used best-link or average-link, both of which are $O(n^2)$, where n is the number of observations for the user. Conceptually, we would argue that hierarchical agglomerative clustering (HAC) is a good fit, on the grounds that by merging the most similar contexts first, we defer the ambiguous cases to when we have more data. We summarize the HAC algorithm in Figure 2. However, a straightforward implementation of HAC is $O(n^2 \log n)$, which is not scalable when we wish to identify long-term interests that span months.

We now describe a near-linear approximation to HAC that gives us similar clustering quality for our domain. The key insights are to prune the search space, and use lightweight similarity scores to identify candidate pairs with high similarity. Figure 3 sketches our NLAC algorithm.

- In Step 2, we run HAC on the set of observations in each search session. Since sessions are typically small (and we split large sessions), this allows the algorithm to quickly reduce the number of contexts. While useful, this step is not critical to performance.
- In Step 3a, we compute an approximation to the similarity function, similar to canopy clustering [20]. We build an inverted index over the features, and use that to compute, in near linear time, all pairs of contexts that share a feature, as well as a light-weight similarity score for each pair of contexts. (This is similar to using LSH [13], except that we hash each feature.) Figure 4 shows the algorithm to compute cosine similarity for one feature dimension.[2] We repeat this algorithm for

[2] Note that line 6 in Figure 4 can lead to quadratic execution time for features that occur in many contexts. Hence, we sample the set of pairs if the list is long. If two contexts are indeed similar, we expect that some other (more specific) feature will result in them being added to the candidate pairs. In addition, even for high-frequency features, the lists get shorter in later passes as we merge contexts.

For each context c_i: (1)
  Compute L, the L_2-norm for feature dimension F. (2)
  For each feature term $f_j \in F$ with weight w_j in c_i: (3)
    Add $(c_i, w_j/L)$ to inverted index list for f_j. (4)

For each feature term $f_j \in F$ in the inverted index: (5)
  For each pair of values (c_k, w_k) and (c_m, w_m): (6)
    $W(c_k, c_m) := W(c_k, c_m) + w_k w_m$ (7)

// Now $W(c_k, c_m) = \text{cosine}(c_k, c_m)$ for feature dimension
// F for every pair of contexts c_k, c_m.

Figure 4: Computing Candidate Pairs and Cosine Similarity (for one feature dimension)

each feature dimension, and then, take the weighted sum of the cosines (Equation 1) to get the light-weight similarity score.

- Steps 3b and 3c are critical to performance. Sorting by the light-weight similarity score and using early termination at the end of step 3c allows us to limit the number of full similarity computations.
- In Step 3, we set $t_1 > t_2 > ... > t_k$. The intuition is that while the lightweight scores serve as a reasonable proxy for the full score, they do diverge, especially when c_p and c_q have been merged into other contexts. The descending thresholds t_i ensure that, like HAC, we do the high confidence merges first, and defer the borderline cases. For our dataset, we found that $k = 3$ gave us the same quality as higher values of k.

3.6 Semantic annotations

Once we have contexts, we annotate them with structured metadata. We describe some of these annotations here.

3.6.1 Context Types

Context types are a classification of contexts into popular user information needs at a coarse level, for example, *Travel*, *Soccer* or *Health*. Context types serve several purposes:

- We prune out contexts that map to types like *Health* or other sensitive subjects.
- We identify key attributes based on the context type, e.g., hotels and attractions for *Travel*, or teams and players for *Soccer*.
- Context types let us customize the experience for specific types, e.g., travel.
- Context types are also used by the classifier as a signal.

We bootstrap the context type classifier with a set of hand-built matchers:

- Category nodes from an off-the-shelf classifier with around 1500 categories, for both queries and URLs.
- Types of the freebase entities in the queries and URLs.
- Words in the query or URL title.
- URL patterns.

For popular (head) context types, the above matchers give us sufficient precision and recall. As we expand the set of types, we plan to use matchers to bootstrap the classifier, and use co-training [5, 7] to increase recall.

3.6.2 Attribute Entities

Attributes are freebase types that are especially appropriate for a given context type, e.g., for *Travel*, attributes include location, hotels and restaurants. Attribute entities are the entities in the context whose freebase type matches the attribute.

The primary benefit of using attribute entities rather than all the entities in the context is that attribute entities are usually much higher quality. Hence many of the use cases in Section 5 rely on attribute entities. These entities are also used in context type classification, e.g., in order to label a context with context type Books, we require the identification of an entity of type author or book title.

3.7 Scaling it up

Even with fast clustering algorithms, deploying a user modeling system for a personal assistant in production involves significant scaling challenges. The first observation is that computing features like categories, forums and entities on-the-fly as we process queries and clicks is prohibitively expensive. Hence we pre-compute such expensive features for a few billion frequent clicks and queries, and look these up at runtime. For tail queries and clicks, we fall back to cheaper features such as query words and click titles.

Consider a batch implementation that partitions input data by user and parallelizes computation using Mapreduce [8]. If we wish to run over a hundred million users, with around 5 seconds per user (Section 4.3.4), that works out to 6000 days of CPU time for just segmentation — without counting the load on the back-end for feature lookups. An obvious optimization is to skip over users with no new data since the last run. However, active users tend to have many more observations than inactive users, and hence this optimization (while helpful) does not result in a huge drop in computation time. Clearly, any system that relies on repeated batch runs will result in large latency between new observations coming in and user model updates.

We rely on two solutions to scale our system. First, we have an incremental version of the segmentation algorithm. Given a new observation, the incremental algorithm uses a subset of features to pick the top few candidates from among the existing contexts. The algorithm looks up all the features for those contexts, and for any observations in the same session as the new observation. It then computes the similarity between the current observation and each of the chosen contexts and observations to determine the best match.[3] If the score for the best match is above the threshold, the observation is either merged into an existing context, or can merge with a recent observation to start a new context.

Second, we have built a streaming infrastructure to determine when to run the incremental update versus rerunning segmentation on all the user's data. Given a new observation, the decision is a function of metadata such as the number of new input observations, sessions, and time since the last full model update. This function lets us measure and tune the trade-off between the slight drop in precision and recall for the incremental algorithm (compared to the full version), versus the resource savings.

[3] While Wang et al. [23] can be considered an incremental algorithm, the resource savings in our incremental algorithm come from not having to look up features for all the observations in the user's history.

The streaming infrastructure also enforces privacy requirements that if a user partially or completely deletes their data, there is a hard deadline by which the deletes are reflected in any contexts inferred for that user.

The result of this architecture is a system that has a soft deadline of 10 minutes by when a new observation is incorporated into the user model, and precision and recall very close to the full segmenter, while requiring dramatically fewer resources.

4. USER MODEL EVALUATION

We first describe how we generated the evaluation dataset. We then discuss the evaluation methodology, followed by experimental results.

4.1 Dataset

4.1.1 *Can we annotate the complete user history?*

In previous work [23, 16], researchers often had human raters completely annotate search histories for a small number of users, and used that as training data. There are two reasons why this was not an option for us.

- Fully annotating the history into contexts is feasible when the number of queries per user is small (e.g., 15 queries per user in [23]), or when identifying in-session tasks (since the number of queries in a session is small and they are more homogeneous). For our sample of users, we had an average of 1425 queries per user. From personal experience trying to do this on our own search history, fully partitioning thousands of queries into contexts is next to impossible, especially since there is often not a single "right" way to partition queries into contexts, e.g., should San Francisco and Palo Alto restaurants be in two separate contexts, or in a single context?
- For privacy reasons, raters are not allowed to see a user's full search history. In our evaluation, each rater saw only a single pair of observations from a user.

Hence, instead of fully annotating the user history, we pick pairs of observations from a sample of users.

4.1.2 *Can we select pairs of observations at random?*

We initially tried picking pairs of observations at random to send to raters, but found that only 1% of the pairs were positive, 59% were negative, and the raters did not agree on the remaining 40%. So we instead picked pairs of observations that shared at least one feature. The implication is that the true recall may be slightly lower than the recall on the dataset. However, since a pair of observations with zero common features are very unlikely to be rated part of the same context, we do not expect this difference to be significant.

4.1.3 *Can we trust the ratings?*

We sent each pair of observations to three raters. Each rater is asked whether

- the pair of observations is part of the same task, interest or habit (*Yes*);
- the observations are related, but may not be part of the same task or interest (*Maybe*); or
- the observations are not related (*No*).

We found that when all three raters agreed, the resulting dataset was very high quality. However, when there was disagreement, either the example was ambiguous, or (in our opinion) some of the raters were wrong — and it was not always the majority that was right. Hence we restricted our dataset to those pairs where all three raters agreed.

4.1.4 *Dataset Description*

We picked a random sample of 500 users, biased towards users with more queries. Users with more queries are much more likely to see recommendations both because they are more active and because we have more data to generate recommendations. Hence skewing towards active users gives us a more representative sample of our user base.

We picked 50 pairs of observations for each user, over a period of 6 months, for a total of 25,000 pairs of observations. We then used the subset of the data where all the raters unanimously voted either *Yes* or *No*: 48.7% of pairs were in this subset, yielding 12,181 examples. Out of these, 10.5% were *Yes* and the remaining 89.5% were *No*.

4.2 Methodology

The User Modeling algorithm has three key components:

1. The features used to compare pairs of contexts.
2. The classifier that determines whether two contexts should be merged.
3. The segmentation algorithm which uses the classifier to identify contexts from the sequence of observations.

The three components are somewhat independent, but not completely so. In particular, [23] fixed the segmentation algorithm to be BestLink, and used a latent structural SVM to learn the classifier in order to minimize errors in the final segmentation. They found that this yielded slightly better results (3% gain in precision, 2% gain in recall) compared to learning the classifier over pairs of observations (the "AdaptClu" algorithm in [23]).

Since we do not have fully annotated user histories, we did not use a latent structural SVM to train the classifier based on segmentation results. However, we did tune the precision-recall trade-off of the classifier based on segmentation results. We found that such tuning captures some of the gains of training the classifier using segmentation results.

In the rest of this section, we focus on the features and segmentation algorithms. We used an off-the-shelf SVM classification library [6] for the second component. The first and third components are agnostic to the choice of classifier, and using a more sophisticated classifier should help improve the segmentation quality further.

4.3 Experimental Results

Our primary point of comparison is with Wang et al. [23], the most recent work on finding cross-session search tasks. For segmentation algorithms, we also compare against HAC and canopy clustering [20].

All experiments were run using 10-fold cross-validation for the classifier, and 5-fold cross-validation for the segmenter. We measure precision, recall, and F_1 (the harmonic mean of precision and recall).

4.3.1 *Predictive Value Feature Weighting and Scaled-Cosine*

To our surprise, Predictive Value Feature Weighting (PVFW) and ScaledCosine did not matter for the classifier:

	Precision	Recall	F_1
Base	0.938	0.862	0.898
PVFW	0.960	0.854	0.904
PVFW+ScaledCosine	0.963	0.830	0.892

However, for the segmenter, PVFW + ScaledCosine does better than the base algorithm, and the difference is statistically significant.

	Precision	Recall	F_1
Base	0.807	0.907	0.854
PVFW	0.844	0.899	0.871
PVFW+ScaledCosine	0.894	0.878	0.886

For the classifier, when looking at a single pair of observations, the variance in confidence is only across feature dimensions, e.g., the inferred entities may be low confidence while the categories are high confidence. For the segmenter, when looking at a pair of contexts, there is variance in confidence both across feature dimensions and across observations within a single feature dimension, e.g., within a context the inferred entities may be high confidence for some observations and low confidence for other observations. Hence PVFW+ScaledCosine has much more scope to improve precision and recall in the segmenter than in the classifier.

4.3.2 *Taba vs Wang Features*

We also compared our features with those used by Wang et al. [23]. We found that our features dramatically outperformed the Wang features. Combining both set of features yielded a small improvement over the Taba features.

Features	Precision	Recall	F_1
Wang	0.949	0.719	0.818
Taba	0.963	0.830	0.892
Taba+Wang	0.968	0.848	0.904

4.3.3 *The Top Feature Dimensions*

To determine which feature dimensions were most important for the classifier, we used forward selection. We started with no feature dimensions, and picked the feature dimension with the highest F_1 (Query Words). We then added the feature dimension that improved F_1 the most (Category). Repeating this process yielded the results below:

Features	Precision	Recall	F_1
Query Words	0.940	0.682	0.790
+ Category	0.933	0.792	0.857
+ Entity	0.938	0.802	0.865
+ Forum	0.937	0.810	0.869

Interestingly, the model with just two dimensions (Query Words and Category) outperforms Wang, even though Wang has both of these features (and many more). PVFW+Scaled-Cosine may not matter for classification when we have all the Taba features (due to redundancy between features), but does matter when we have only a few features.

4.3.4 *NLAC is very fast, and just as accurate.*

We compared HAC, NLAC and BestLink, using the Taba features:

Segmenter	Precision	Recall	F_1	Time/User (s)
NLAC	0.894	0.878	0.886	4.26
Canopy	0.896	0.867	0.881	34.97
BestLink	0.901	0.812	0.855	53.58
HAC	0.892	0.879	0.885	122.96

NLAC was 30 times faster than HAC, and around 8 to 12 times faster than BestLink and Canopy clustering [20]. While Canopy and NLAC are motivated by similar intuitions, the details matter. Canopy runs HAC within each canopy. For our dataset, we often have large canopies, and that slows down the Canopy algorithm. In contrast, NLAC only re-computes similarity when deciding whether to merge two candidates, and is thus substantially faster. By making several passes, starting with a high threshold, NLAC is able to maintain accuracy while requiring substantially fewer full similarity computations than Canopy.

With respect to quality, NLAC, HAC and Canopy were very similar. Since both NLAC and Canopy are approximations to HAC, this says that both NLAC does not sacrifice quality for the performance gains. (While NLAC has the highest F_1, the difference from HAC or Canopy is not statistically significant.) BestLink did worse on F_1 than the other three algorithms, and the difference was statistically significant.[4]

We wished to experiment with Wang+BestLink, but found that it was more than 1000 times slower than Taba+NLAC. Computing the Wang features for a pair of observations was more than 100 times slower than computing the Taba features, and BestLink computes similarity for many more pairs than NLAC.[5] Hence we were unable to compare the Wang and Taba features for segmentation.

4.3.5 *Context Distributions*

Finally, we looked at the distribution of time spans of the contexts. While this sample is biased towards more active users, it is still noteworthy that half the queries were in contexts that spanned more than a month.

	Contexts per User	Queries per Context	% of Queries
Multi-query	171	7.5	90
Multi-session	91	11.3	72
Multi-day	75	12.7	67
Span > 1 week	59	14.7	61
Span > 1 month	36	19.7	50

[4]In our initial set of experiments, where we trained on 60 users and tested on 40 users, the gap between BestLink and the other algorithms was much larger. This suggests that BestLink is more sensitive to the amount of training data and the quality of the classifier.

[5]The slowest Wang feature is edit distance — for every pair of observations, we need to compute the minimum and average edit distance between their sets of web results. For a user with 2000 queries and 10 web results per query, the Wang+BestLink algorithm would need to compute the edit distance between 200 million pairs of URLs.

5. USE CASES IN A PERSONAL ASSISTANT

The primary goal for a personal assistant system is to determine the most relevant information for a user at a given point in time. We now describe, by walking through some real world (deployed) examples, how the user model defined in Section 3 serves as the foundation for building a personal assistant. We can group these examples into two classes, based on the source of the content:

- The content is a feed of public data extrinsic to the user contexts, and the primary problem is to match contexts against the content.
- The observations and contexts are the source of the information, and collaborative filtering is used to generate recommendations.

5.1 Matching public data feeds against the user model

This class includes many use cases that are highly rated by users. Examples include:

- Sports score updates for teams that the user follows. The content is a licensed third party feed of sports scores, where the sports teams have been reconciled against Freebase. The attributes (Section 3.6.2) from contexts with the appropriate context type tell the personal assistant which teams the user follows.
- Entity reminders personalized to a user. The entities are those identified as attributes of the appropriate type. Examples include reminders when
  - an artist a user is interested in is performing nearby,
  - a band a user likes releases an album,
  - an author a user follows releases a new book.

At first glance, it may appear that we do not need contexts for these examples: couldn't we simply count entities referenced in the user's query stream? While counting entities will work reasonably well, using contexts can yield significantly better results. For example, merging queries that are about different players in a football team together with queries directly referencing the football team gives a more accurate estimate of the level of interest in a football team.

The second takeaway is that most of these use cases will not work if we have only a few days of data. For example, there is typically a long gap between when the user searches for an artist and when that artist is performing nearby. Similarly, recall for sports teams would be very poor with just one week of data. Being able to scale context identification to many months of data is critical for these use cases.

5.2 Collaborative filtering

Matching public data feeds against the user model works well when such feeds are available. For the huge number of use cases where there are no public data feeds, the observations and contexts serve as the source of recommendations.

5.2.1 *Interest Updates*

We show personalized content recommendations for the user's long term interests, using collaborative filtering. Our system consists of the following components:

- **Fresh Aggregates**: For each entity (or query) that occurs in a sufficiently large number of contexts, we get the set of users who have that entity (query) in any of their contexts. We then aggregate what those users have read recently.[6] Thus for a given entity, we have aggregate statistics on what fresh content would be interesting for users with that entity.
- **Context Relevance Score**: We use a number of signals computed from the context to decide whether the user will be interested in updates for this context. The signals include a "fresh intent" score (a combination of how often the user looked at fresh content in this context, and how often other users looked at fresh content in similar contexts), the recency of the context, and the temporal distribution of activity in the context. This is similar in spirit to the work by Agichtein et. al. [3] on predicting search task continuation. Computing these signals over the context is more accurate than looking at an entity or query in isolation. For example, a user may not have looked at a player recently, but if she has recently looked at articles about the player's team, that is indirect evidence of continued interest in the player.
- **Recommendation Ranking**: Given a context with a high context relevance score, we look up the fresh aggregates for each entity and query in the context. Each aggregate gives us the articles users interested in that entity or query have read recently, and combining these lists gives us a candidate set of recommendations. These recommendations are filtered for quality, and then scored for timeliness (to get new content) and relevance to the context.

5.2.2 *Task Recommendations*

The goal is to assist users with longer tasks, e.g., trip planning or buying a camera, by leveraging the experience of users with similar tasks. The approach is similar to the system for interest updates, though the details are quite different:

- We use **context aggregates** instead of fresh aggregates. For each URL, entity or query that occurs in a sufficiently large number of contexts, we compute aggregate statistics over the set of contexts in which that URL (or entity or query) appears. For example, given an URL, the aggregates tell us what other URLs, entities and queries users looked at later in that context. We also compute meta-data, such as the fraction of clicks in those contexts that are on news or videos.
- The context relevance score function is tuned differently, e.g., with much tighter bounds on how recently the last activity in that context occurred. For long-term interests, people are usually interested in fresh content even without recent activity. However, recommendations for tasks are only useful when the user is actively involved in the task.
- The scoring functions for recommendations are different, e.g., diversity matters more, and freshness matters less.

[6]For privacy reasons, the algorithm only retains articles that have been read by a sufficiently large number of users.

6. CONCLUSION

We presented a user modeling system that, given web search history for opted-in users, identifies coherent contexts not just within sessions or over a few days, but across months of data. Looking at these long time spans allows the system to identify long-term tasks, interests and habits, in addition to identifying short-term tasks.

Our work includes three main technical contributions. First, we showed that intuitions and algorithms that work well over small time periods often do not scale to large time spans — this opens up a very interesting (and high impact) area for future research. Second, we have identified a set of features that yield much higher precision/recall than prior work, and whose computation requires only a small fraction of the CPU time (compared to prior work). Finally, we presented a new segmentation algorithm, NLAC, that uses indexing and lightweight scoring to provide similar precision and recall to HAC while being 30 times faster.

The last two contributions were critical, since our user modeling system is deployed in production for hundreds of millions of users, as part of Google Now. The contexts identified by the system are used both for recommending content from public data feeds, as well as serving as input to a collaborative filtering system for generating interest updates and task recommendations.

There are many promising directions for future work. We highlight three areas. First, while our set of features outperform prior work, we think there is plenty of scope for doing even better. In particular, it would be interesting to see if embedding query words (as well as other feature dimensions) in a vector space (e.g., [15]) and computing similarity between words in that vector space will yield better results than the bag of words approach. Second, modeling relationships between contexts (sub-contexts, related contexts) will yield a much richer user model. Finally, the incremental version of our algorithm has not yet been able to match the quality (precision/recall) of the non-incremental version. Developing an incremental algorithm that yields similar quality, or even just being able to predict when an incremental algorithm would do poorly, are challenging problems.

Acknowledgments

We thank Carolyn Au, Aparna Chennapragada, Andrew Dai, Elena Erbiceanu, Surabhi Gupta, Mahesh Keralapura, Karthik Lakshminarayanan, Carl Lischeske, David Martin, Kiran Panesar, Kelvin So, Shen Wang, Chenjun Wu, and Matt Wytock, who worked with us to design, build and launch the Taba system. We thank Andrew Kirmse, Baris Gultekin, Pablo Bellver, German Cheung, Jan-Willem Maarse, Anand Pillai, Jie Shao, Phil Verghese, Randy Wilson and Benyu Zhang for their help in launching Taba as part of Google Now. We thank Anurag Vyas for help in analyzing the evaluation data.

7. REFERENCES

[1] Google Now, `http://www.google.com/landing/now/`.

[2] Microsoft Cortana, `http://www.windowsphone.com/en-us/how-to/wp8/cortana/meet-cortana`.

[3] E. Agichtein, R. W. White, S. T. Dumais, and P. N. Bennet. Search, interrupted: Understanding and predicting search task continuation. In *SIGIR*, 2012.

[4] P. Agrawal, A. Arasu, and R. Kaushik. On indexing error-tolerant set containment. In *SIGMOD*, 2010.

[5] A. Blum and T. Mitchell. Combining labeled and unlabeled data with co-training. In *Proc. of the Conf. on Computational Learning Theory*, 1998.

[6] C.-C. Chang and C.-J. Lin. LIBSVM: A library for support vector machines. *ACM Transactions on Intelligent Systems and Technology*, 2:27:1–27:27, 2011.

[7] M. Collins and Y. Singer. Unsupervised models for named entity classification. In *Joint SIGDAT Conf. on Empirical Methods in NLP and Very Large Corpora*, 1999.

[8] J. Dean and S. Ghemawat. Mapreduce: Simplified data processing on large clusters. *CACM*, 51(1), Jan. 2008.

[9] T. Finley and T. Joachims. Supervised clustering with support vector machines. In *ICML*, 2005.

[10] W. Hua, Y. Song, H. Wang, and X. Zhou. Identifying users' topical tasks in web search. In *WSDM*, 2013.

[11] A. K. Jain, M. N. Murty, and P. J. Flynn. Data clustering: A review. *ACM Comput. Surv.*, 31(3):264–323, Sept. 1999.

[12] R. Jones and K. L. Klinkner. Beyond the session timeout: Automatic hierarchical segmentation of search topics in query logs. In *CIKM*, 2008.

[13] H. Koga, T. Ishibashi, and T. Watanabe. Fast agglomerative hierarchical clustering algorithm using locality-sensitive hashing. *Knowl. Inf. Syst.*, 12(1):25–53, May 2007.

[14] A. Kotov, P. N. Bennett, R. W. White, S. T. Dumais, and J. Teevan. Modeling and analysis of cross-session search tasks. In *SIGIR*, 2011.

[15] Q. V. Le and T. Mikolov. Distributed representations of sentences and documents. In *ICML*, 2014.

[16] L. Li, H. Deng, A. Dong, Y. Chang, and H. Zha. Identifying and labeling search tasks via query-based Hawkes processes. In *SIGKDD*, 2014.

[17] C. Lucchese, S. Orlando, R. Perego, F. Silvestri, and G. Tolomei. Identifying task-based sessions in search engine query logs. In *WSDM*, 2011.

[18] C. Lucchese, S. Orlando, R. Perego, F. Silvestri, and G. Tolomei. Discovering tasks from search engine query logs. *ACM Trans. Inf. Syst.*, 31(3), Aug. 2013.

[19] C. Lucchese, S. Orlando, R. Perego, F. Silvestri, and G. Tolomei. Modeling and predicting the task-by-task behavior of search engine users. In *OAIR*, 2013.

[20] A. McCallum, K. Nigam, and L. H. Ungar. Efficient clustering of high-dimensional data sets with application to reference matching. In *SIGKDD*, 2000.

[21] C. Silverstein, H. Marais, M. Henzinger, and M. Moricz. Analysis of a very large web search engine query log. *SIGIR Forum*, 33, 1999.

[22] A. Spink, M. Park, B. J. Jansen, and J. Pedersen. Multitasking during web search sessions. *Inf. Process. Manage.*, 42(1), Jan. 2006.

[23] H. Wang, Y. Song, M.-W. Chang, X. He, R. W. White, and W. Chu. Learning to extract cross-session search tasks. In *WWW*, 2013.

Predicting The Next App That You Are Going To Use

Ricardo Baeza-Yates
Yahoo Labs
Barcelona, Spain
rbaeza@acm.org

Di Jiang*
CS and Eng. Dept.
HKUST, Hong Kong, China
dijiang@cse.ust.hk

Fabrizio Silvestri
Yahoo Labs
Barcelona, Spain
silvestr@yahoo-inc.com

Beverly Harrison
Yahoo Labs
Sunnyvale, US
beverlyh@yahoo-inc.com

ABSTRACT

Given the large number of installed apps and the limited screen size of mobile devices, it is often tedious for users to search for the app they want to use. Although some mobile OSs provide categorization schemes that enhance the visibility of useful apps among those installed, the emerging category of homescreen apps aims to take one step further by automatically organizing the installed apps in a more intelligent and personalized way. In this paper, we study how to improve homescreen apps' usage experience through a prediction mechanism that allows to show to users which app she is going to use in the immediate future. The prediction technique is based on a set of features representing the real-time spatiotemporal contexts sensed by the homescreen app. We model the prediction of the next app as a classification problem and propose an effective personalized method to solve it that takes full advantage of human-engineered features and automatically derived features. Furthermore, we study how to solve the two naturally associated cold-start problems: app cold-start and user cold-start. We conduct large-scale experiments on log data obtained from Yahoo Aviate, showing that our approach can accurately predict the next app that a person is going to use.

Categories and Subject Descriptors

J.0 [**Computer Applications**]: GENERAL.

General Terms

Design, Experimentation, Performance.

Keywords

Aviate, Prediction, Mobile App, Machine Learning.

*This work was done while the author was an intern at Yahoo Labs, Barcelona, Spain

WSDM'15, February 2–6, 2015, Shanghai, China.
Copyright 2015 ACM 978-1-4503-3317-7/15/02 ...$15.00.
http://dx.doi.org/10.1145/2684822.2685302.

1. INTRODUCTION

Mobile devices (smartphones and tables) are ubiquitous in today's lives. This high popularity also corresponds to a huge growth in the availability and usage of mobile applications (commonly referred to as apps). Mobile applications are very easy to install and this usually correspond to having mobile phones with a very large number of apps installed. An empirical study conducted by Yahoo Aviate team shows that on average there are 96 apps installed on each mobile device. This large number of apps installed calls for the design of new paradigms aimed to manage the installed apps. In particular, one of the major issues associated with the high number of apps installed on a smartphone is that of their visibility. When a user needs a particular app it is not always available immediately and the search through the large number of installed apps might take lots of time. This is the reason why homescreen apps are becoming more and more popular. Homescreen apps act as an intelligent layer between the underlying mobile operating system and the user interface. They manage the installed apps in a highly personalized manner rather than simply relying on manual (or trivial) categorization schemes.

The basic building block that we consider at the heart of an effective personalized management of apps is a personalized app prediction mechanism. In other words, the most important feature of our homescreen app is that of anticipating the user needs even before the user would click on the relative icon on his/her mobile phone. Ideally, once the predictor has made its guess the homescreen app should show the application already opened as the user picks up the phone and unlocks it. Even if this scenario might sound futuristic, we show here that to predict which app a user is going to open, is actually feasible. Our solution leverages the sequence of real-time spatiotemporal contexts that are continuously sensed by the homescreen app (in this case, the Yahoo Aviate application).

App Prediction Problem is formally defined as follows: *Given a list of installed apps $\{a_{u1}, a_{u2}, ..., a_{un}\}$ by a user u on his/her phone and the user's spatiotemporal context C, the problem of app usage prediction is to find an app a_{ui} that has the largest probability of being used under C. Specifically, we aim to solve the problem:*

$$\max_{a_{ui}} P(a_{ui}|C, u), \forall i, 1 \leq i \leq n;$$

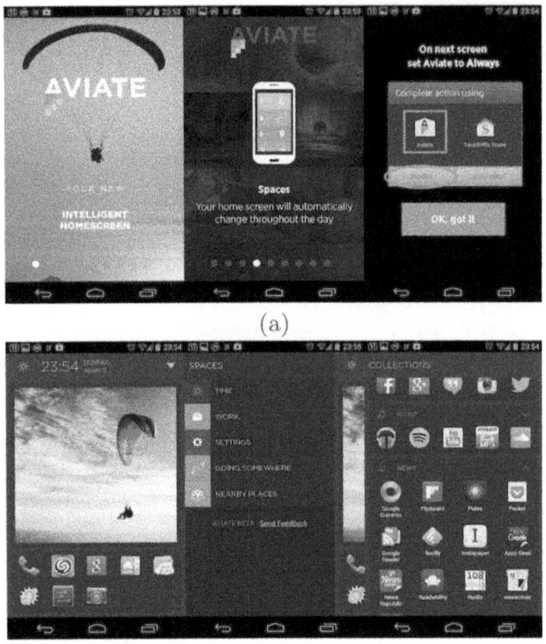

(a)

(b)

Figure 1: Screenshot of Homescreen App Aviate.

We model the problem of app usage prediction as a supervised classification problem. Through a comprehensive study of the log data obtained from Aviate (see Figure 1), we propose several features from two different perspectives: basic features (i.e., signals) obtained from the mobile phone's sensors and the session features capturing sequential patterns of app usage. Based on these features, we design highly scalable algorithms to train the prediction models.

In addition, the application prediction functionality in Aviate (or in a homescreen app in general) suffers from two inherent cold-start problems: app cold-start and item cold-start. The first one deals with the problem of not knowing anything about past usages of that app by the mobile phone user. The latter deals with the problem of generating predictions when the user first install Aviate. In this paper we also propose several techniques to alleviate the effects of cold start. Conducting extensive experiments on Aviate log data, our experimental results show that the user's app usage is predictable based on the user's usage history and the wisdom of the crowd.

The contributions of this paper are summarized as follows:

- We conduct a large scale comprehensive study of mobile app usage.
- We propose several domain-specific features for app usage prediction. We studied how to conduct efficient app usage prediction and we conduct a preliminary study on how to handle the app cold-start and user cold-start problems.
- We conduct extensive and large scale experiments based on usage information recorded into a log from Aviate. We show that our method outperforms existing ones.

The remainder of this paper is organized as follows. In Section 2, we review the related work. In Section 3, we describe the empirical study of app usage. In Section 4, we describe the methods for app prediction. In Section 5, we discuss how to handle the cold start problem. Finally, we present experimental evaluations in Section 6 and conclude the paper in Section 7.

2. RELATED WORK

The problem of predicting app usage has been already proposed by other researchers in the past. In particular, Tan *et al.* [16] proposed a prediction algorithm for predicting mobile application usage patterns. They conducted experiments on the Nokia MDC dataset which contains a small group of 38 users and their experiments show promising results. Huang *et al.* [6] studied the problem of pre-loading the right apps in memory for faster execution or can pop the desired app up to the mobile's home screen. Similarly to our work, Huang *et al.* [6] exploit contextual information such as time, location, and the user profile, to predict the user's app usage using the Nokia MDC dataset already mentioned. Yan *et al.* [18] designed a app preloading method by using contexts such as user location and temporal access patterns to predict app launches with 34 volunteers. Pan *et al.* [13] proposed a different prediction problem: finding the most likely mobile application that a user will install. They exploited social information coming from friends of the user in a social networks. Parate *et al.* [14] designed an app prediction algorithm that predicts which app will be used next without sensor context. Zou *et al.* [20] proposed some light-weighted Bayesian methods to predict the next app based on the app usage history. Krishnaswamy *et al.* [8] developed a general-purpose service that runs on the phone and discovers frequent co-occurrence patterns indicating which context events frequently occur together. Liao *et al.* [9] designed a widget that is able to predict users' app usage by constructing temporal profiles which identify the relation between apps and their usage times.

Our work is also related to app analytics and app recommendation. Kai *et al.* [17] proposed a framework called App Developer Inspector, which aims to effectively profile app developers in aspects of their expertise and reputation in developing apps. Jiang *et al.* [7] presented a framework to provide independent search results for Android apps with semantic awareness. Yin *et al.* [19] proposed an Actual-Tempting model that captures such factors in the decision process of mobile app adoption. Henze *et al.* [5] reported on five experiments that were conducted by publishing apps in the Android Market. Based on these outcomes, the authors identified factors that account for the success of experiments using mobile application stores. Lin *et al.* [11] presented a framework that incorporates features from version descriptions into app recommendation. Lin *et al.* [10] described a method that accounts for nascent information culled from Twitter to provide relevant recommendation in such cold-start situations.

Our work differs from the previously proposed methods in several ways:

1. To the best of our knowledge, this work is the largest scale of evaluation for app usage. In existing work, the scale of user study is usually limited to less than 40 users, while our study is four orders of magnitude larger;

Table 1: Examples of Aviate Log Data (the user ID is anonymized to ensure privacy).

User ID	App Action
xx8ae648c10	{"ts":"2014-01-10 12:27:39","et":"App_Opened"} ["com.skype.raider"]
xx8ae648c10	{"ts":"2014-01-10 12:36:09","et":"App_Opened"} ["com.android.dialer"]
xx8ae648c10	{"ts":"2014-01-10 12:47:41","et":"Location_Update"} ["37.393093","-122.079788","20.000000","0.000000"]
xx8ae648c10	{"ts":"2014-01-10 12:57:42","et":"Context_Triggered"} ["Work"]

2. We achieve the highest precision for app prediction. The precision of the state-of-the-art is usually far below 90%;

3. Besides achieving high precision, our method is highly scalable for big data;

4. We study the cold start problems that are still open in app usage prediction and we study both perspectives of cold start: users and apps.

3. APP USAGE CHARACTERIZATION

As this is the first time that such a large scale analysis is performed, we present here some basic statistics of the Aviate sample log data. The log sample contains more than 60 million records with about 200K anonymized users that have a total of more than 70K unique apps by January 2014. An example of the events recorded in the log are shown in Table 1. For example, the first log entry indicates that "Skype" (the app) *com.skype.raider* was opened by user *xx8ae648c10* at *2014-01-10 12:47:39*. The third entry shows that the user's location is moved to the GPS location *(37.393093, -122.079788)*. The fourth entry tells us that Aviate's working mode is switched to *Work*.

Aviate records 10 types of actions in total. The distribution of those actions is depicted in Figure 2. As expected, *App Open* represents a large fraction of app actions. This actually confirms that the app prediction problem could impact significantly on Aviate by improving its user experience. Furthermore, we observe that the fraction of *App Installed* event is relatively low but is non-negligible (around 250K times in our dataset). Just to put this into perspective every ten times a user changes location he or she installs an app. For this reason the app cold-start problem is an important one that needs a particular attention.

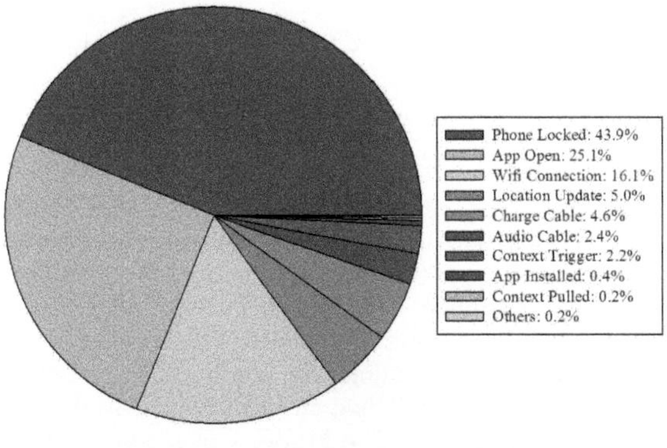

Figure 2: Distribution of Actions.

4. APP USAGE PREDICTION

In this section we discuss the problem of predicting the next app that a given user is going to open as she will pick up her mobile phone. We start by presenting a naive prediction strategy based on apps popularity in 4.1. We discuss our set of features, namely *basic* and *session* features in Sections 4.2 and 4.3, respectively. Then we discuss how to train the prediction model and how to generate predictions in Section 4.4.

4.1 Predictions by Popularity

At first sight the app prediction problem might seem to be straightforwardly solvable by always predicting the most popular app. While it is obvious that a popularity score computed globally among all the users is not going to work in practice, it might seem reasonable to consider a *per-user* popularity score. We discuss two kinds of popularity-based features: *Global Frequency* and *Timeslot Frequency*. *Global Frequency* represents the number of times that an app has been opened by a particular user. *Timeslot Frequency*, instead, is the number of times that an app has been opened within a specific timeslot of the day (e.g. at Noon). We consider timeslots of granularity ranging from 1 day to 1 second and based on the two kinds of frequencies we predict the next app by selecting the one with the highest (global or timeslot-based) popularity. We run a test to evaluate the effectiveness of popularity-based approaches. We extract popularity statistics on 80% of the log data and we test the methods on the remaining 20%. Results show that using *Global Frequency* we can achieve an average precision of up to 16.7%. We observe similar results also when we consider timeslot-based statistics. Results of predictions using various timeslot granularities are shown in Figure 3. Using 1 day based timeslots we reach a precision of 16.3%. Reducing the timeslot to 1 hour the prediction precision decreases to 15.2% and the precision further decreases to 12.6% when the timeslot size is 1 second. Results shown in Figure 3 demonstrate that differently from what the intuition suggests, solely relying on timeslots is not effective to find any useful pattern in real-life app usage scenarios. We further investigate the prediction performance of considering a week as a cycle. We calculate the frequencies of each app at each day in a week and using the most frequent one at the corresponding date. The prediction precision is 10.5% showing that app usage does not have very strong periodic phenomenon in terms of week.

In order to understand why popularity-based prediction might fail, we study the distribution of the *activeness* of the apps, in other words how an app is used. The activeness of an app a is denoted as Δ_a, which is formally defined as follows:

$$\Delta_a = \frac{\sum_{i=1}^{S} \frac{F_{ai}}{F_i}}{S},$$

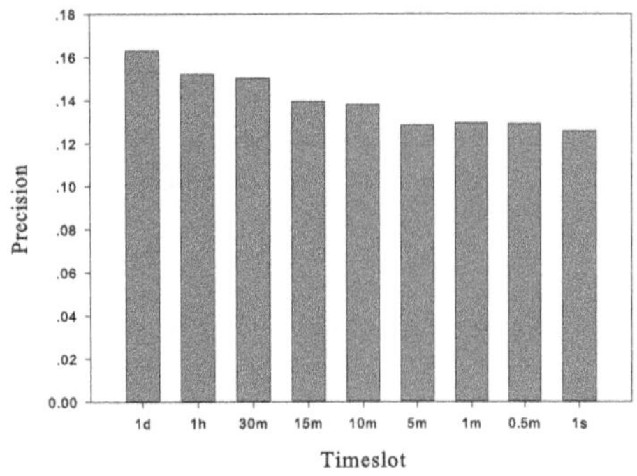

Figure 3: App Usage Prediction by Timeslot Frequency.

where S is the number of timeslots, F_{ai} is the frequency of a in timeslot i and F_i is the frequency of all apps in the i-th timeslot. Δ_a reflects a's activeness across different timeslots in each day. We show app activeness with its activeness rank (in decreasing order of activeness) for the 30 most popular apps in Figure 4. In the plot each line corresponds to a different timeslot granularity. We find that the activeness of the apps on mobile device follows a power-law distribution. A small fraction of dominant apps take a large proportion of the whole activeness. Most of these dominant apps are related to basic services like browser, phone and communication. These dominant apps are frequently used in each timeslot, making the other apps hard to predict if only the frequencies are considered. Hence, we need to look for more effective features to approach the problem.

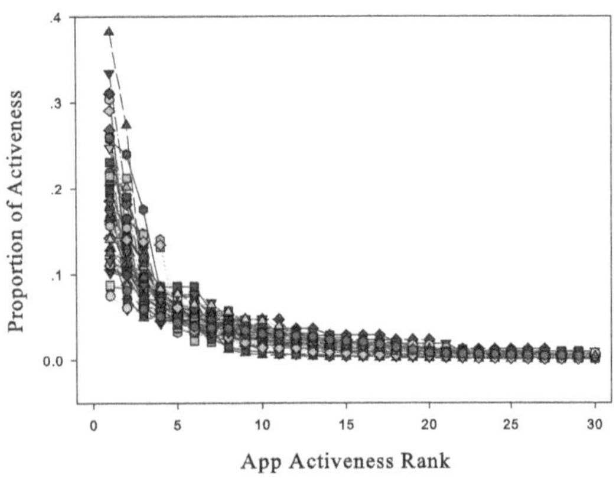

Figure 4: Activeness Proportion v.s. Activeness Rank

4.2 Basic Features

Since app usage is strongly related to the user's spatiotemporal context, we discuss some basic features that can be directly obtained from the sensors of mobile devices. These basic features defining the user's spatiotemporal contexts are the following: *Time, Latitude, Longitude, Speed, GPS Accuracy, Context Trigger Context Pulled, Charge Cable, Audio Cable*. The first five features are self-explanatory. *Charge Cable* and *Audio Cable* indicate whether the corresponding cable is plugged into the mobile device. *Context Trigger Context Pulled* indicate whether the corresponding Aviate user has switched the ambient in which he operates (e.g., "work", "home", etc). Among these features, only *context trigger* and *context pulled* are peculiar of Aviate whereas the other features are obtained from the OS. These features help to represent the spatiotemporal context of actions related to the app open event. The feature *Time* is normalized between 00:00:00-23:59:59, in order to capture daily app usage patterns. As a side note, we have also tried to add the App Activeness feature to our set of basic features. The contribution of avtiveness has not been significant therefore we have removed it and we are not going to consider it in the experiments we show next.

4.3 Session Features

Basic features do not capture latent relations between app actions. Intuitively, and as also reported by Huang *et al.* [6], the correlation between sequentially used apps may have a strong contribution to the accuracy of app prediction. In this section we propose a method to extract session features by considering the sequential relationships existing among app actions.

We exploit the ideas presented in *word2vec* [12]. In word2vec documents are modeled as sequences of terms and a context of a term is defined to be the k immediately preceding and following terms in the document. Likewise, we model documents with sequences of app events but we cannot simply choose the preceding and following actions as the context of an app given that they may be associated with events happened a long time back in the past (or ahead in the future). Based on this observation, we propose a Gaussian based method to identify the context of each app action. The context is defined as the set of other actions that are conducted before or after the current one within a time period whose duration is obtained by sampling from an empirically defined Gaussian distribution. For example, in Table 1 we show a context relative to *App Open:com.android.dialer* formed by the following two app actions: *App Open:com.skype.raider*, and *Location Update:(37.393093, -122.079788, 20.000000, 0.000000)*.

Our objective is to find distributed representations of these features that are useful for predicting the surrounding actions of the current context. More formally, given an app action τ and its context C_τ, the objective is to maximize the average log probability:

$$\frac{1}{T}\sum_{t=1}^{T}\sum_{\tau'\in C_t}\log p(\tau'|\tau_t), \tag{1}$$

where C_t is the context of τ_t and T is the number of app actions. The probability $p(\tau'|\tau_t)$ is calculated as follows:

$$p(\tau'|\tau_t) = \frac{e^{V_{\tau'}\cdot V_{\tau_t}}}{\sum_{t=1}^{T} e^{V_{\tau'}\cdot V_{\tau_t}}} \tag{2}$$

where $V_{\tau'}$ is the distributed representation of τ' and V_{τ_t} is the distributed representation of τ_t.

In order to enhance the efficiency, the full softmax in the above formula is approximated by the hierarchical softmax [12]. In order to efficiently compute the distributed representations, we parallelize the training procedure using a MapReduce paradigm. The Mapper and Reducer are presented in Algorithms 1 and 2. The MapReduce procedure iterates for a predefined number of times and the output vectors are the session features for mobile apps.

Algorithm 1 Mapper of Distributed Representation

```
load the vectors of app actions from the previous iteration;
initialize the Huffman tree based on the loaded vectors;
for each app action a do
    draw a temporal gap g1 from Gaussian distribution G;
    draw a temporal gap g2 from Gaussian distribution G;
    consider the actions between g1 and g2 as the context C_a;
    train a based on C_a;
end for
for each app action action a do
    emit(key=ID_a,value=Vector_a);
end for
```

Algorithm 2 Reducer of Distributed Representation

```
for each app action a do
    calculate average and normalize the corresponding vectors;
end for
flush updated vectors to HDFS;
```

Based on Algorithms 1, and 2, we define distributed representations of the following six app actions: *Last App Open, Last Location Update, Last Charge Cable, Last Audio Cable, Last Context Trigger, Last Context Pulled.* The corresponding distributed representations of the six actions are in turns considered as the session features for the app prediction method we use.

4.4 Building Prediction Models

By merging basic and session features for each *App Open* event, we obtain the training instances for the prediction model. In order to achieve a balance between effectiveness and efficiency, we propose the Parallel Tree Augmented Naive Bayesian Network (PTAN) as the prediction model. PTAN is a parallel version of the Tree Augmented Naive Bayes (TAN) [3], which has been proposed in order to remove the strong assumptions of independence in native Bayes and exploit the correlations among attributes. This model captures the latent correlations between different features and can be easily deployed on parallel computing frameworks such as Hadoop. The training procedure of PTAN can be divided into two phases: (1) parallel structure training and (2) parallel parameters estimation. The first phase is to learn the structure of the Bayesian network. The procedure of constructing the PTAN bayesian network from data is as follows:

1. Based on the training data from all users, we compute the conditional mutual information between any two attributes $\mathbf{f_x}$ and $\mathbf{f_y}$ given the app a. Conditional mutual information is defined as follows:

$$I_p(\mathbf{f_x}, \mathbf{f_y}|a) = \sum_{\mathbf{f_x}, \mathbf{f_y}, a} P(f_x, f_y, a) \log \frac{P(f_x, f_y|a)}{P(f_x|a)P(f_y|a)}.$$

2. Build a complete undirected graph in which the vertices are the features. Annotate the weight of an edge connecting feature $\mathbf{f_x}$ and $\mathbf{f_y}$ by $I_p(\mathbf{f_x}, \mathbf{f_y}|a)$.

3. Build a maximum weighted spanning tree for the complete undirected graph. The maximum spanning tree problem can be transformed to the minimum spanning tree problem simply by negating edge weights [2]. Kruskal's algorithm [4] is used to solve the minimum spanning tree problem.

4. Transform the resulting undirected tree to a directed one by choosing a root variable and setting the direction of all edges to be outward from it. Construct a Bayesian network by adding a vertex labeled by app variable a and adding an arc from a to each feature vertex.

The highest computational cost is associated with the first and the third step in the above algorithm. If we assume there exist m training instances and each instance has n features then the first step has complexity of $O(n^2 m)$. The third step has a complexity of $O(n^2 \log n)$. Since $m \gg \log n$, the first step is the bottleneck of building the Bayesian network structure. Hence, in PTAN, we parallelize the first step again using MapReduce. The Mapper for parallelizing the first step is presented in Algorithm 3 and the Reducer can be straightforwardly developed by aggregating the values based on the keys.

Algorithm 3 TAN Structure Learning Mapper

```
for each app action entry {u, a, f1, f2, f3, ..., fn} do
    for each feature pair (fi, fj) do
        emit(key={fi, fj, a},value=1);
        emit(key={fi, a},value=1);
        emit(key={fj, a},value=1);
    end for
end for
```

After learning the structure of PTAN, we estimate a set of parameters for each individual user, in order to achieve the personalization effect. The conditional probability is estimated as follows:

$$P(f_i = k|pa(f_i) = j) = \frac{N_{ijk} + N'_{ijk}}{N_{ij} + N'_{ij}}, \tag{3}$$

where f_i is a feature, $pa(f_i)$ is the set of the parents of f_i, N_{ij} is the number of times $pa(f_i) = j$, N_{ijk} is the number of times $f_i = k$ given $pa(f_i) = j$ in the training set, and N'_{ij} and N'_{ijk} are the smoothing parameters that we set both to 0.5 by default. Smoothing is fundamental for the prediction performance when some user contains very few training instances for an app. Furthermore, parameters estimation for each user is also parallelized. The Mapper is presented in Algorithm 4 and the Reducer can be straightforwardly developed by aggregating the values based on the keys. When the parameters for the Bayesian network have been estimated we compute the probability that a user u is going to use mobile app a_{ui} when it finds herself within the context $C = \{f_1, f_2, ..., f_n\}$ as follows:

$$\begin{aligned} &P(a_{ui}|f_1, f_2, ..., f_n) \\ &\propto P(a_{ui})P(f_1, f_2, ..., f_n|a_{ui}) \\ &= P(a_{ui}) \prod_{i=1}^{n} P(f_i|pa(f_i)) \end{aligned} \tag{4}$$

Based on this equation we consider the app that has the highest probability as the prediction result. It is straightforward to transform this prediction algorithm into a top-k recommendation one just by sorting apps according to the computed probability scores.

Algorithm 4 TAN Parameter Learning Mapper

```
for each action long entry {u, c, a_1, a_2, a_3, ..., a_n} do
    for each pair (a_i, pa(a_i)) do
        emit(key=a_i, pa(a_i), value=1);
        emit(key=pa(a_i), value=1);
    end for
end for
```

5. COLD START PROBLEMS

In this section, we discuss how to handle two of the main challenges we face when homescreen apps that are deployed in real-life environments. The first problem is the *App Cold Start*, which happens when a user installs a new app on her device. The second problem is the *User Cold Start* that arises when a user installs and open the homescreen app for the first time. User cold start is more severe than the first one given that in order to reduce the risk of app abandonment it is important to provide high quality personalized predictions already from the first interactions with the homescreen app. We discuss how to tackle these two cold start problems in Sections 5.1 and 5.2.

5.1 App Cold Start

For a newly installed app a_i, we have no user-specific information available on the app. In particular the probability of opening an app for a given user u, $P(a_{ui})$, is unavailable. On the other hand, $P(f_i|pa(f_i))$, the prior probability for a given feature, can be obtained from information on other users. Therefore, for newly installed apps, how to estimate its $P(a_{ui})$ is critical. We present the app activeness for newly installed apps in Figures 5 (Daily) and 6 (Hourly). We can see that a significant fraction of the newly installed apps is very active within the first few hours. After this period of time the newly installed apps are used significantly less. In contrast, some apps are used frequently and for a long time after their installation. Hence, in order to better estimate $P(a_i)$, we categorize apps as *short-term apps* and *long-term apps* depending on their activeness longevity.

In order to capture the temporal prominence of each app we fit app usage data into a Beta(α, β) variable and to differentiate apps by their temporal significance we use the excess kurtosis [15] to evaluate the temporal peakedness of each app. The excess kurtosis ϱ of a Beta(α, β) distribution is defined as follows:

$$\varrho = \frac{6[\alpha^3 - \alpha^2(\alpha\beta - 1) + \beta^2(\beta + 1) - 2\alpha\beta(\beta + 2)]}{\alpha\beta(\alpha + \beta + 2)(\alpha + \beta + 3)}. \quad (5)$$

An app with a high ϱ value indicates that it is likely to be a short-term app while an app with a low ϱ value is likely to be a long-term app. Through using ϱ, we can categorize the apps into short-term apps and long-term app. Table 2 shows some examples after categorization. As an example, we can observe that while communication apps are usually long-term game apps tend to have a shorter life span.

Short-term App. We assign to short-term apps a $P(a_{ui})$ value of $\overline{P}(a_i)$, which is the average opening frequency obtained from other users' historical information. After a fixed time period (two hours, for example) we can replace $\overline{P}(a_i)$ with the actual app's usage information for that particular user, namely $P(a_{ui})$.

Long-term App. For long-term apps, we exploit the well-known concept of "wisdom of the crowd". When an app has been opened very few times its $P(a_i)$ should approximate the average value coming from other users. As the number of open events grow we can switch to the actual $P(a_{ui})$. Hence, we used Bayesian average [1] to effectively blend actual usage information with that coming from other users' history. The equation for calculating $P(a_{ui})$ is therefore given by:

$$P(a_{ui}) = \frac{C \cdot \Omega_{a_i} + O_{a_{ui}}}{C + O_u}, \quad (6)$$

where $O_{a_{ui}}$ is the number of openings of the app a_i by the current user U, O_u is the sum of all app openings by u, and Ω_{a_i} is the average opening probability of a_i by all other users. C is a constant whose value is set to match the expected variation between data sets containing the history from different users. The value of $P(a_{ui})$ for an app with a small number of open events tends to be closer to the average opening probability of that same app by all other users. The more openings an app has received by the current user, the more accurate the probability estimation is.

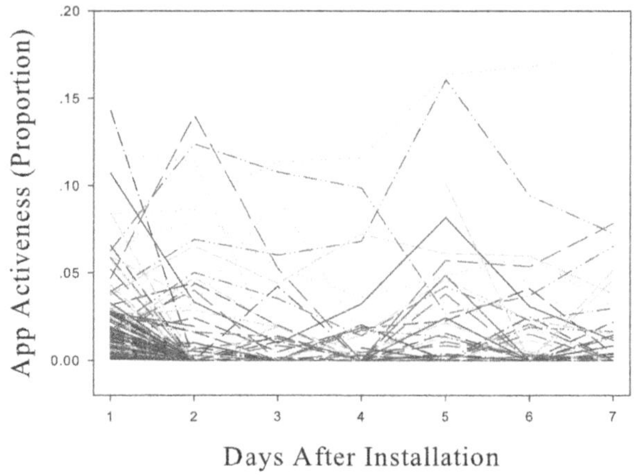

Figure 5: Daily App Activeness (Proportion) After Installation.

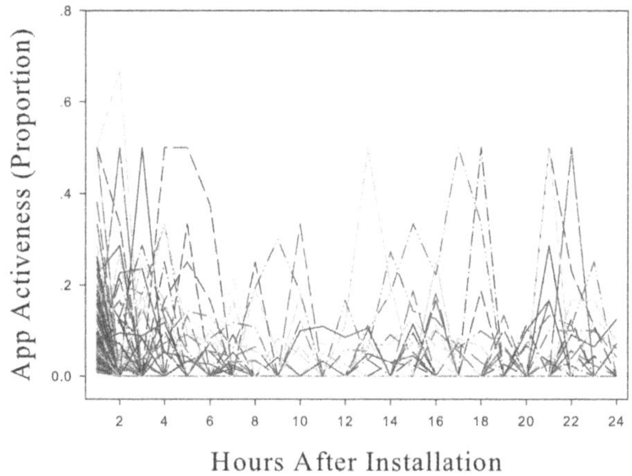

Figure 6: Hourly App Activeness (Proportion) After Installation.

Table 2: Examples of Short-term and Long-term Apps.

Short-term Apps
jp.gree.jackpot
com.rockstargames.gtasa
com.sq.dragonsworld
com.cocoapps.elbomberman
com.zhan_dui.animetaste
com.sweettracker.smartparcel
com.mobie.catholiclife
com.partyplay.xxl
com.king.candycrushsaga
com.battlelancer.seriesguide
Long-term Apps
com.quixey.android
com.google.android.talk
com.whatsapp
mobi.mgeek.TunnyBrowser
com.fitbit.FitbitMobile
com.spotify.mobile.android.ui
com.google.android.apps.authenticator2
com.facebook.katana
com.myfitnesspal.android
com.google.android.gm

On the other hand, when an app has received just a small number of openings, its estimated $P(a_{ui})$ value is close to its unweighted average opening probability computed on all the other users.

5.2 User Cold Start

In this subsection, we discuss two different strategies to tackle the user cold start problem. In Section 5.2.1 we discuss the *Most Similar User Strategy* essentially based on collaborative filtering. In Section 5.2.2 we discuss the *Pseudo User Strategy* that is designed to synthesize an appropriate pseudo-history for the new user so that the PTAN model can be effectively trained on this surrogate usage data.

5.2.1 Most Similar User Strategy

When a new user installs homescreen apps such as Aviate, it is not true that we do not know anything about her. In particular, we know her apps inventory and using this information we can identify the most similar user from the set of known users by using metrics such as, for instance, Jaccard similarity between the new user and the known ones.

After the most similar user has been found, we can use this user's model to predict the behavior of the new user. We name this strategy as the *Most Similar User Strategy*. In fact, the most similar user may have an app inventory that is very different from that of the user under consideration. In some extreme cases the app inventory can be totally different from those installed by known users and the most similar user strategy would not have any sensitive advantage over a purely random strategy. Of course we can resort to put a threshold on the minimum acceptable similarity. While this strategy improves the average accuracy of the method it also limits the coverage, i.e., the number of users for which recommendations can be generated.

5.2.2 Pseudo User Strategy

In order to solve the problem of the strategy presented above we propose the *Pseudo User* strategy, which consists in generating a "pseudo history" used in place of the actual one to train the PTAN model for the new user. Let us assume there are k users $U = \{u_1, u_2, u_3, ..., u_k\}$ and let us further assume that each user u has an app inventory I_u. When a new user with app inventory I_{new} installs the homescreen app, we obtain I'_u for each u by only keeping the apps in I_{new}. We want to find a subset of users U' satisfying the following conditions:

$$\min \sum_{u \in U'} |c(u)|$$

$$\text{subject to} \quad \bigcup_{u \in U'} I'_u = I_{new} \ .$$

The cost of an user $c(u)$ is defined as the inverse of its similarity to the current user, i.e., $c(u) = 1/J(I_{new}, I_u)$. The idea is to find a small amount of similar users whose app inventories cover all the apps in the inventory of the new user. It is straightforward to prove that the problem is NP-hard (it is essentially a weighted set-covering problem) and the $O(\log |I_{new}|)$-approximation algorithm we use to generate the pseudo user is presented in Algorithm 5. After obtaining U' we aggregate log entries for each user in U' and we filter out the *App Open* events for those apps that are not in I_{new}. What it is left is considered to be the *Pseudo User* data used in PTAN training.

Algorithm 5 Building Pseudo User

1: $U' \leftarrow \emptyset$
2: $I \leftarrow \emptyset$
3: **repeat**
4: choose $u \in \mathcal{U}$ minimizing $\frac{c(u)}{|I \cup I_u - I|}$
5: let $U' \leftarrow U' \cup u$
6: let $I \leftarrow I \cup I'_u$
7: **until** $I = I_{new}$

6. EXPERIMENTS

In this section we measure the performance of the proposed method. Experiments are conducted on Aviate log data collected from October 2013 to April 2014. We randomly choose 480 active Aviate users for our experiments. For each user, we use 80 percent of the data as training data and the remaining 20 percent as testing data. For all the methods we extract features (both basic and session) using events within a sliding window of 12 hours, as we assume that any event only influence future events that happen within 12 hours. In Section 6.1 we measure the performance of the propose app prediction algorithm. In Sections 6.2 and 6.3, we evaluate the performance of our solution to the app and user cold start problems, respectively.

6.1 App Usage Prediction

As we have stated in the previous sections, we modeled the app prediction problem as a classification problem and we opted for a parallelized version of the Tree Augmented Naive Bayes (TAN) algorithm to build the classifier. In order to assess the effectiveness of PTAN we compare it with the best ML algorithms that are suitable for this problem, namely Naive Bayes, SVM, C4.5, and Softmax Regression (i.e., Multinomial Logistic Regression). In the experiments we report the score for precision, that is the percentage of correctly predicted opened apps over the total number of app opened by users in the test data.

Figure 7 shows the performance of different methods in the case of a model trained when the context is made up of only the basic features. In this case, C4.5 achieves the highest precision of 34.9%. We investigated the reasons why C4.5 results is the best method for basic features and we conjecture that is due to that some apps have a very clear fingerprint in terms of sensor usage that a classification tree is able to surface. For example, by analyzing the decision tree, we found that when the charge cable is plugged in, the predicted apps were some video games or using bluetooth. Intuitively, game apps or file transmission apps usually consume more battery energy, therefore when you plug your charge cable (and you do not wait too much time before taking an action), it is very likely you are going to use one of the two classes of applications mentioned above.

We then evaluate the hypothesis we made that sequence-based patterns are useful for building more effective classifiers. For methods such as Naive Bayes, C4.5, PTAN and Softmax Regression, the session features are effective to boost the performance. Therefore, these results confirm the assumption that the sequential correlations between app actions are critical for app usage prediction. Combining basic features and session features is an effective strategy for Bayes methods. With both types of features, Naive Bayes achieves a precision of 76.3% and *PTAN achieves the highest precision of 90.2%.* We also studied the impact of dominant apps (i.e, the most frequent apps) in app prediction. By filtering the top five dominant apps for each user, we reevaluate the performance of the five methods. The performance of Naive Bayes with basic and session features is heavily influenced, giving a precision of 39.3%. Among the five methods, PTAN still achieves the highest precision of 85.7% with all the features. Therefore, we can conclude that while dominant apps are easy to predict using even just a Naive Bayes classifier, when they are removed a strong signal can still be obtained by opportunely combining the other features we have designed (in particular features about event sequences).

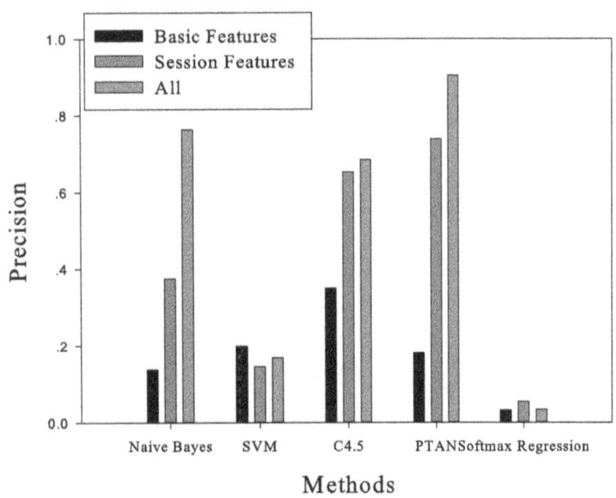

Figure 7: App Usage Prediction (All Apps).

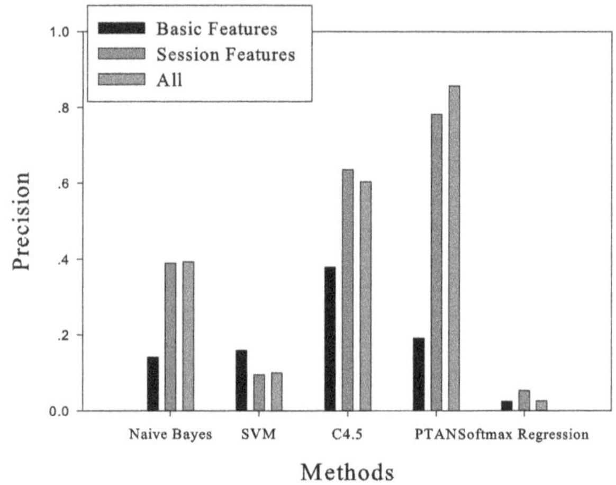

Figure 8: App Usage Prediction (Dominant Apps Filtered).

In order to comprehensively measure the performance of the proposed method, we compare it with the state-of-the-art counterparts. Although some methods described in Section 2 are related to our work, some of them are not comparable with PTAN because they use some additional information. We select EWMA [16], CPD [16], LU-2 [20], LUT [20], and BN [20] as comparison baselines as they can be used on our dataset. We evaluate these baselines by varying the different values of the parameters that characterize those methods. Figure 9 shows the performance of EWMA and CPD on the full set of apps (including dominant ones) and Figure 10 shows the performance of EWMA and CPD when dominant apps have been filtered out from the dataset. With the full set of apps EWMA achieved the highest precision of 16.7%. When dominant apps were filtered out, instead, CPD has a precision of 19.5%, which is the highest in this case. We further observe that EWMA performs better with all apps while CPD performs better when the dominant apps are filtered. Figure 11 shows the performance of LU-2, LUT and BN. LU-2 shows the best performance with all apps, achieving a precision of 15.7% while BN achieves the highest precision of 10.1%.

From the various results shown we can conclude that PTAN significantly outperforms the five baselines we consider by a large margin. We remark that the experiments done using the techniques presented in the papers describing the baselines were done on a much smaller dataset containing usage data on 38 users in total. Our user set is one order of magnitude larger while the dataset is several order of magnitude larger. Nevertheless the performance reported for papers on the baselines methods are consistent with the ones we report here.

6.2 App Cold Start

We now assess the performance of the method discussed in Section 5.1 and we evaluate its effectiveness in alleviating the app cold start problem. For each app installment, we process the original dataset by splitting it into two subsets: one subset containing all the events referred to the period before the app installment and one subset containing the remaining events. We then build a model for predicting app opening events contained in the second file by using events

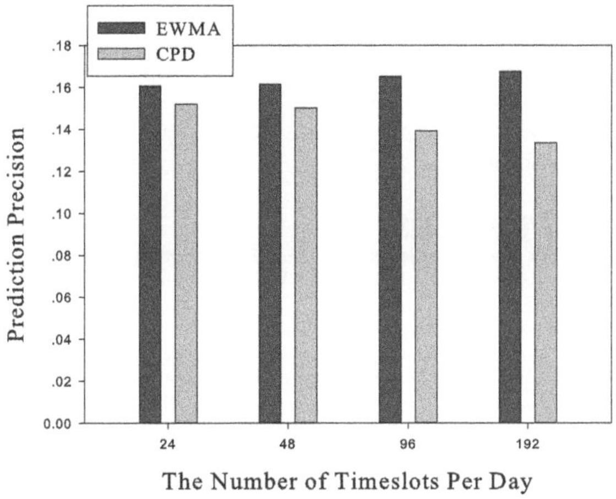

Figure 9: App Usage Prediction of Baselines (All Apps).

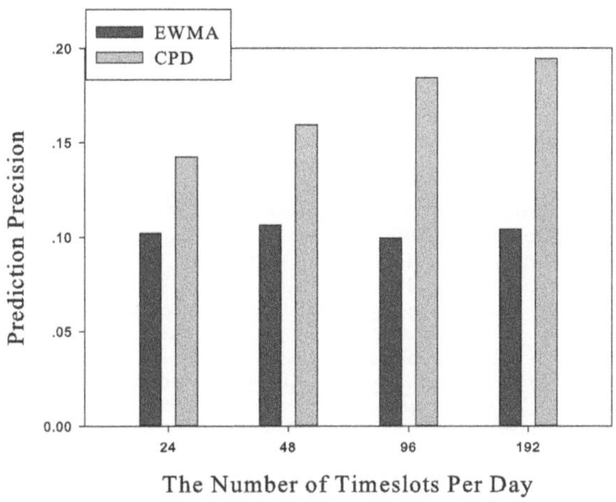

Figure 10: App Usage Prediction of Baselines (Dominant Apps Filtered).

in the first file. For short-term apps (those that are heavily used in the moments immediately following their installation), the precision of app prediction improves from 86.3%[1] to 87.1% after applying the strategy described in Section 5.1. In particular the precision for new apps is about 91.3% and for existing apps is about 86.25%. The prediction quality for existing apps is thus not heavily hurt. The results confirm that in the case of short-term apps we usually observe opening events during the first day after they are installed. The number of opening events steadily decreases afterwards. Therefore, assigning a relatively high probability for these apps is useful for improving the performance. Note that the increase in precision is significant since users open many apps each day and the opening of the newly installed apps may only happen in a relatively small fraction of the cases. Indeed, the percentage of newly installed apps in the test data is only 1.42%.

The precision we measure in the case of long-term apps is 89.3% when we use the general method, but no newly

[1]Precision percentages are different from the previous section as we are reporting results on a different partitioning of the dataset created to test cold start methods.

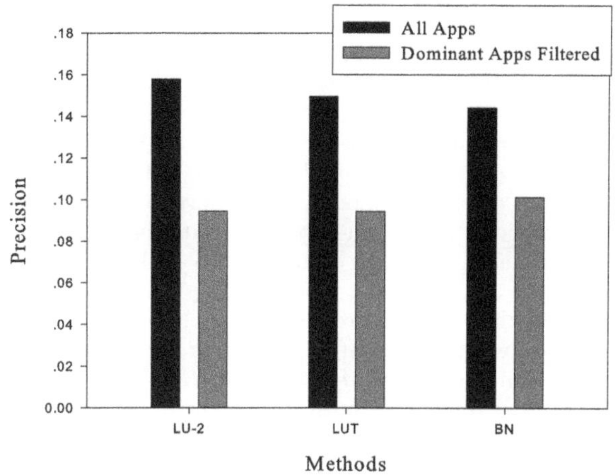

Figure 11: App Usage Prediction of Baselines.

installed app is correctly predicted in this case. By applying the proposed cold-start strategy the precision measured increases up to 90.3% on average. More accurately the precision is 91.1% for new apps and 89.26% for existing apps, also confirming that in this case the precision on existing apps is not heavily hurt.

6.3 User Cold Start

Experimental results show that the *Most Similar User Strategy* achieves an average precision of 32.7%. We present the correlation between app inventory similarity and app prediction precision in Figure 12. We observe that the app inventory is useful yet not very effective. There are two main reasons that may explain this result. First, it is not easy to find a user with highly similar inventory. In our dataset, the Jaccard similarity between two different app inventories is typically low. We found an average value of 0.121465 ($\pm$0.038955) and a median of 0.117647. Second, even when the similarity is high the corresponding precision increase is not always satisfactory. In many cases, we observe that the precision is almost zero even when similarity of the two app inventories is relatively high.

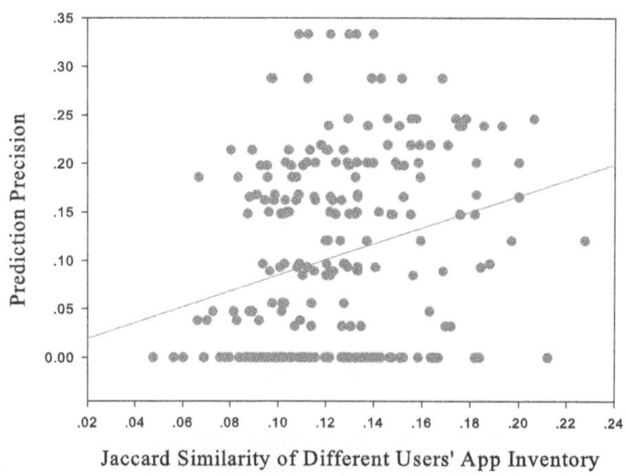

Figure 12: App Prediction By Similar User.

On the other hand, the average precision of the *Pseudo User Strategy* is 45.7%. Therefore we confirm that estimating usage data about apps in a new user inventory using this strategy is effective to boost the performance of the prediction model.

Besides reporting the effectiveness of the two proposed user cold start strategies we also studied after how many days the app prediction model can achieve acceptable prediction precision. The result is presented in Figure 13 where we show that even after just one single day of data about the user has been collected the prediction's precision increases up to more than 56%. Precision further increases up to 81.5% when two days of historical data are considered.

We can conclude that *Most Similar User Strategy* and *Pseudo User Strategy* are both useful but only in the very same day the homescreen app has been installed. After that, for a typical user, high-precision prediction models can be trained using the real (i.e., collected) usage data from that user.

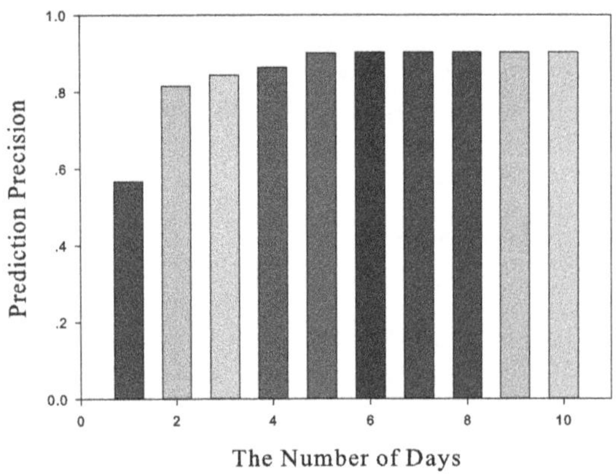

Figure 13: App Prediction Precision v.s. Number of Days.

7. CONCLUSIONS

In this paper we have proposed a new methodology to predict what is the next mobile app that a user is going to open. We conducted a comprehensive analysis on a very large scale mobile log containing events recorded by Aviate, the Yahoo's homescreen app. We proposed a set of basic and session features that are designed to capture the sequential correlation between different actions involving mobile apps; e.g., plugging the charging cable. Based on these features, we built a Parallel TAN model to efficiently solve our app prediction problem. We further studied how to alleviate the app cold start problem and the user cold start problem. We conducted a wide spectrum of experiments to study the parameter sensitivity and effectiveness of the proposed method. Experimental results demonstrated that app usage is predictable even though a naive strategy based on popularity features fail to achieve high effectiveness. The proposed method outperformed the state of the art by a large margin.

In the future we plan to further improve the prediction performance at cold start. In particular the problem to improve the performance of user cold start app prediction remains open. Regarding app cold start it is an open problem that of optimizing the performance of the predictor in the presence of a mix of cold and non-cold apps. Finally, it is related the problem of finding the top-k applications that a user would open instead of the next one. The problem, then, could be cast into a learning to rank rather than into a classification one.

8. REFERENCES

[1] George EP Box and George C Tiao, *Bayesian inference in statistical analysis*, vol. 40, John Wiley & Sons, 2011.

[2] David Eppstein, *Spanning trees and spanners*, Handbook of computational geometry (1999), 425–461.

[3] Nir Friedman, Dan Geiger, and Moises Goldszmidt, *Bayesian network classifiers*, Machine learning **29** (1997), no. 2-3.

[4] John C Gower and GJS Ross, *Minimum spanning trees and single linkage cluster analysis*, Applied statistics (1969), 54–64.

[5] Niels Henze, Martin Pielot, Benjamin Poppinga, Torben Schinke, and Susanne Boll, *My app is an experiment: Experience from user studies in mobile app stores*, International Journal of Mobile Human Computer Interaction (IJMHCI) **3** (2011), no. 4, 71–91.

[6] Ke Huang, Chunhui Zhang, Xiaoxiao Ma, and Guanling Chen, *Predicting mobile application usage using contextual information*, Proceedings of the 2012 ACM Conference on Ubiquitous Computing, ACM, 2012, pp. 1059–1065.

[7] Di Jiang, Jan Vosecky, Kenneth Wai-Ting Leung, and Wilfred Ng, *Panorama: A semantic-aware application search framework*, Proceedings of the 16th International Conference on Extending Database Technology, ACM, 2013, pp. 371–382.

[8] Shonali Krishnaswamy, Joao Gama, and Mohamed Medhat Gaber, *Mobile data stream mining: from algorithms to applications*, Mobile Data Management (MDM), 2012 IEEE 13th International Conference on, IEEE, 2012, pp. 360–363.

[9] Zhung-Xun Liao, Po-Ruey Lei, Tsu-Jou Shen, Shou-Chung Li, and Wen-Chih Peng, *Mining temporal profiles of mobile applications for usage prediction*, Data Mining Workshops (ICDMW), IEEE 12th International Conference on.

[10] Jovian Lin, Kazunari Sugiyama, Min-Yen Kan, and Tat-Seng Chua, *Addressing cold-start in app recommendation: latent user models constructed from twitter followers*, Proceedings of the 36th international ACM SIGIR conference on Research and development in information retrieval, ACM, 2013, pp. 283–292.

[11] ———, *New and improved: modeling versions to improve app recommendation*, Proceedings of the 37th international ACM SIGIR conference on Research & development in information retrieval, ACM, 2014, pp. 647–656.

[12] Tomas Mikolov, Ilya Sutskever, Kai Chen, Greg S Corrado, and Jeff Dean, *Distributed representations of words and phrases and their compositionality*, Advances in Neural Information Processing Systems, 2013, pp. 3111–3119.

[13] Wei Pan, Nadav Aharony, and Alex Pentland, *Composite social network for predicting mobile apps installation.*, AAAI, 2011.

[14] Abhinav Parate, Matthias Böhmer, David Chu, Deepak Ganesan, and Benjamin M Marlin, *Practical prediction and prefetch for faster access to applications on mobile phones*, Proceedings of the 2013 ACM international joint conference on Pervasive and ubiquitous computing, ACM, 2013, pp. 275–284.

[15] Gamini Premaratne and Anil Bera, *Modeling asymmetry and excess kurtosis in stock return data*, Illinois Research & Reference Working Paper No. 00-123 (2000).

[16] Chang Tan, Qi Liu, Enhong Chen, and Hui Xiong, *Prediction for mobile application usage patterns*, Nokia MDC Workshop, vol. 12, 2012.

[17] Kai Xing, Di Jiang, Wilfred Ng, and Xiaotian Hao, *Adi: Towards a framework of app developer inspection*, Database Systems for Advanced Applications.

[18] Tingxin Yan, David Chu, Deepak Ganesan, Aman Kansal, and Jie Liu, *Fast app launching for mobile devices using predictive user context*, Proceedings of the 10th international conference on Mobile systems, applications, and services, ACM, 2012.

[19] Peifeng Yin, Ping Luo, Wang-Chien Lee, and Min Wang, *App recommendation: a contest between satisfaction and temptation*, Proceedings of the sixth ACM international conference on Web search and data mining.

[20] Xun Zou, Wangsheng Zhang, Shijian Li, and Gang Pan, *Prophet: what app you wish to use next*, Proceedings of the 2013 ACM conference on Pervasive and ubiquitous computing adjunct publication, ACM, 2013, pp. 167–170.

You Are Where You Go: Inferring Demographic Attributes from Location Check-ins

Yuan Zhong[†‡], Nicholas Jing Yuan[†], Wen Zhong[†⋆], Fuzheng Zhang[§†], Xing Xie[†]
[†]Microsoft Research
[‡]Northeastern University, Boston, MA, USA
[⋆]Stony Brook University, Stony Brook, NY, USA
[§] University of Science and Technology of China, Hefei, China
{nicholas.yuan, xingx} at microsoft.com, zhong.yu at husky.neu.edu, wen.zhong at stonybrook.edu, zhfzh at mail.ustc.edu.cn

ABSTRACT

User profiling is crucial to many online services. Several recent studies suggest that demographic attributes are predictable from different online behavioral data, such as users' "Likes" on Facebook, friendship relations, and the linguistic characteristics of tweets. But location check-ins, as a bridge of users' offline and online lives, have by and large been overlooked in inferring user profiles.

In this paper, we investigate the predictive power of location check-ins for inferring users' demographics and propose a simple yet general *location to profile (L2P)* framework. More specifically, we extract rich semantics of users' check-ins in terms of *spatiality*, *temporality*, and *location knowledge*, where the location knowledge is enriched with semantics mined from heterogeneous domains including both online customer review sites and social networks. Additionally, tensor factorization is employed to draw out low dimensional representations of users' intrinsic check-in preferences considering the above factors. Meanwhile, the extracted features are used to train predictive models for inferring various demographic attributes.

We collect a large dataset consisting of profiles of 159, 530 verified users from an online social network. Extensive experimental results based upon this dataset validate that: 1) Location check-ins are diagnostic representations of a variety of demographic attributes, such as gender, age, education background, and marital status; 2) The proposed framework substantially outperforms compared models for profile inference in terms of various evaluation metrics, such as precision, recall, F-measure, and AUC.

Categories and Subject Descriptors

H.2.8 [**Database Applications**]: Data mining; D.4.8 [**Performance**]: Modeling and prediction; J.4 [**Social and Behavioral Science**]: Sociology

General Terms

Algorithms, Performance, Measurement

WSDM'15, February 2–6, 2015, Shanghai, China.

http://dx.doi.org/10.1145/2684822.2685287.

Keywords

Demographics; spatiality; temporality; location knowledge; tensor facotorization; prediction

1. INTRODUCTION

Long conceived as a significant research area, the inference of demographic attributes has been extensively studied in linguistics [14, 26], psychology [8], and sociology [17]. Before the rise of social networks, a host of different works have looked into data sources from a myriad of domains, such as Internet browsing behaviors [18], written texts [11], telephone conversations [5], real-world mobile network communication records (CALL and SMS) [10] and answers to specific psychological tests [8] to predict various profile attributes like gender, age, income, and personality.

The recent explosive growth of online social media and social networking websites has allowed billions of users around the world to create and view friendship connections, self-expressions, newsfeeds, etc., and lifted the role of profile attributes to an even higher position. Social networks like Facebook[1], Sina Weibo[2], and Renren[3] treat certain profiles (gender, birthday, residence, etc.) as mandatory information for registration. With these attributes, users are served with a personalized experience. Existing works have examined diverse data sources on social networks, validating that communication behaviors (replying/retweeting [23]/"Likes" [13]), linguistic characteristics of tweets [20], group memberships [16] and friendships [33] are useful for profile inference.

However, *human mobility*, as a very informative and fundamental user behavior, has been overlooked by most previous works for profile inference. In fact, users' demographic attributes are of great importance in terms of at least two conspicuous aspects: 1) commerce: the profile contributes significantly to link prediction, item recommendation, and targeted advertising, which are crucial for most companies; 2) uses: the profile is directive for content sharing, membership attachment, and trust establishment, which are pervasive for various personalized services.

In this paper, we look into demographics inference through one of the most popular human mobility data, location check-ins from online social networks. In particular, we uncover three distinct aspects embodied in the check-in data that are potentially correlated with users' profiles, namely *temporality*, *spatiality* and *location knowledge*.

[1]`http://www.facebook.com`
[2]`http://www.weibo.com/signup/signup.php`
[3]`http://www.renren.com`

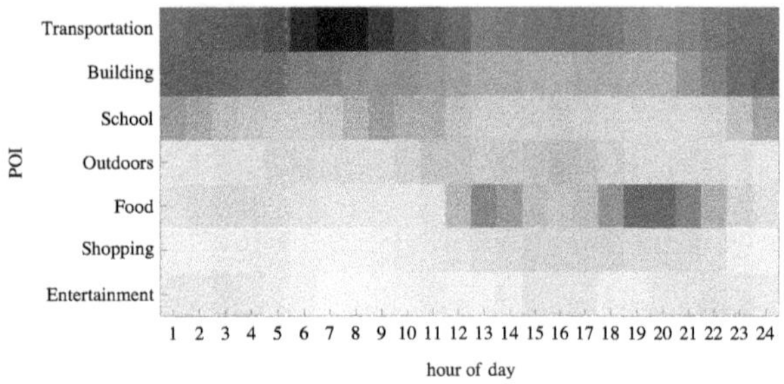

Figure 1: Hourly density distribution of check-ins w.r.t different categories of POIs

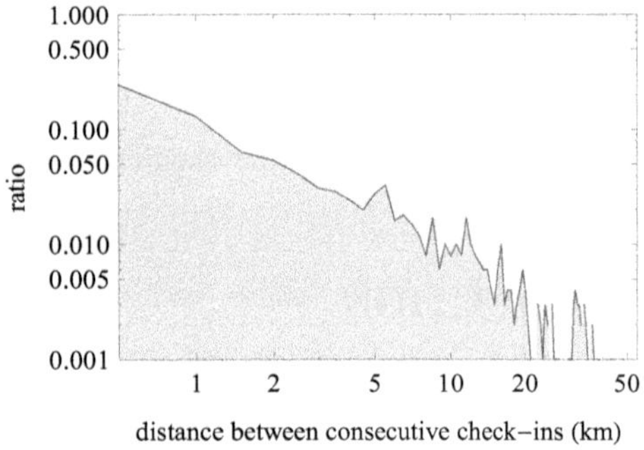

Figure 2: Distance between consecutive check-ins

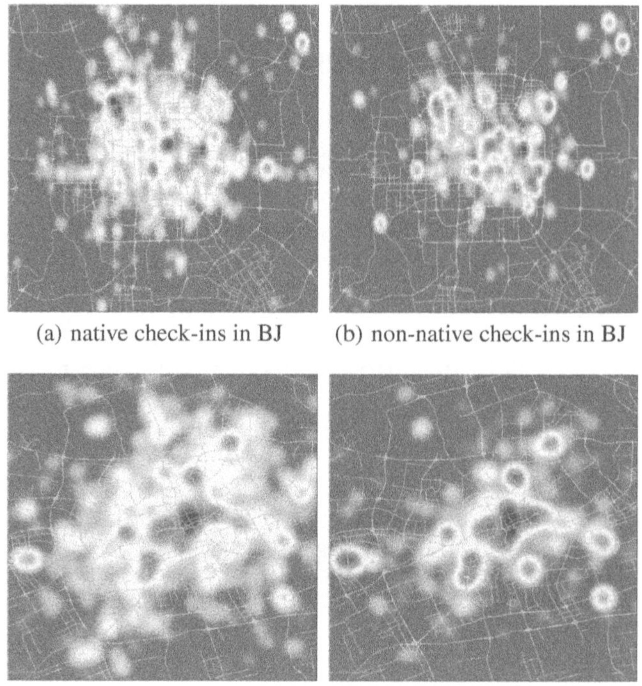

(a) native check-ins in BJ (b) non-native check-ins in BJ

(c) native check-ins in SH (d) non-native check-ins in SH

Figure 3: Density distribution of native and nonnative check-ins in Beijing (BJ) and Shanghai (SH)

• **Temporality**: Human mobility is imbued with ample temporal patterns at different granularities, e.g., day of the week and time of day. For example, office staff commute from home to their company every weekday morning. It's common to see a retired person shopping in the supermarket on a weekday afternoon and a taxi driver working at midnight during holidays. Recent studies have also found that human mobility follows a high degree of regularity [12]. As an example, Figure 1 shows the hourly density distribution of different types of check-ins from Sina Weibo (China's Twitter) based on 10,000 randomly sampled users' check-in histories, which clearly indicates different patterns for various categories of POIs, e.g., the concentration of "food" related check-ins mostly occur at noon and dinner time, while most transportation related check-ins occur in the early morning.

• **Spatiality**: Human mobility is the manifestation of spatial variation. More specifically, the spacial scale is restricted by transportation conditions. For instance, one cannot check in at Stanford University if he has just checked in at Northeastern University only half an hour before. This makes mobility distinctive from unrestrained behaviors such as "Liking", following, replying and retweeting on social networks. For example, Figure 2 presents the distance between consecutive check-ins of 100,000 randomly sampled users, in which we find that a large proportion of the distance is less than 20 kilometers. As another example, we plot the density distributions of check-ins by natives and non-natives in Beijing and Shanghai. As is shown in Figure 3, natives' check-ins (Figure 3(a) and Figure 3(c)) are more diverse in terms of geo-spatial distribution while the non-natives check-ins (Figure 3(b) and Figure 3(d)) are skewed to certain scenic areas and hot spots.

• **Location knowledge**: Human mobility strongly correlates to the functionality of locations which motivates people to travel between different places. Apt instances are: students go to school because they acquire knowledge there; businessmen go to a city's central business district because they conduct commercial affairs there; people go to restaurant districts because they have lunch or dinner there. A check-in is typically associated with a Point of Interest (POI), which belongs to a certain category, e.g., teaching building or shopping mall. Furthermore, the semantics of a location sometimes contain far more information than just the category, e.g., the atmosphere and price range of a restaurant, or the quality of a college.TThese semantics can be enriched with "human knowledge" which are revealed from customer review sites (such as Yelp[4] and Dianping[5]) and online social networks (when users mention these locations).

Based on these factors, we propose a location to profile *(L2P)* framework for inferring demographic attributes of online users including gender, age, education background, sexual orientation, marital status, blood type and zodiac sign. To the best of our knowledge, this is the first work focusing on inference of demographic attributes through location check-ins. On the whole, this paper offers the followings contributions:

• We exploit the semantics of user location check-ins from three points of views, i.e. *spatiality*, *temporality* and *location knowledge*. In particular, we conflate Points of Interest (POIs) of Sina Weibo with Dianping (a review site known as China's Yelp) and explicitly learn the location knowledge of a POI from various aspects such as *categories*, *reviews* and *keywords*.

• We propose an *L2P* framework, incorporating *spatiality*, *temporality*, *location knowledge* features with a tensor model so as to in-

[4] http://www.yelp.com
[5] http://www.dianping.com

Table 1: Demographic Attributes and Corresponding Categories

Attribute	Completion Rate	Categories
gender	94.0193%	male, female
age	33.1588%	the specific age number
education background	36.7228%	university, non-university
sexual orientation	2.5549%	heterosexuality, bisexuality, male homosexuality, female homosexuality
marital status	2.6396%	single, courtship (seeking a relationship), in love, married
blood type	1.6376%	O, A, B, AB
zodiac sign	58.1649%	twelve zodiac signs

fer various demographics (e.g. sexual orientation, education background and marital status) for a particular user based on check-in records.

• Based on a large dataset collected from Sina Weibo, we have conducted extensive experiments to validate the effectiveness of the proposed feature and framework. The results show that our approach significantly outperforms baseline models in terms of multiple metrics such as precision, recall, F-measure and area under curve (AUC).

The rest of this paper is structured as follows: Section 2 introduces the experimental dataset and demographic attributes. The *L2P* framework is proposed in Section 3. Experimental results based on a large-scale dataset are presented in Section 4. Related work is reviewed in Section 5 and the paper is concluded in Section 6 with a brief discussion of limitations and directions of future research.

Table 2: Demographics Distribution

(a) Marital Status

Status Type	Fraction
single	59.31%
courtship	17.07%
in love	12.74%
married	10.87%

(b) Blood Type

Blood Type	Fraction
O	34.97%
A	25.36%
B	25.66%
AB	14.00%

(c) Sexual Orientation

Orientation Type	Fraction
heterosexuality	86.26%
male homosexuality	2.66%
female homosexuality	1.68%
bisexuality	9.40%

2. DATASET AND DEMOGRAPHICS

In this section, we introduce the collected dataset of user profiles and location check-ins, and devise a method for generating ground truth data that is used to train and validate the performance of our inference model.

2.1 Dataset

In order to investigate and evaluate the performance of our inference framework, we crawled 3,354,918 users' profiles on Sina Weibo whose residential cities are provided as "Beijing" or "Shanghai" (two metropolitan cities in China) from Sina Weibo using the LifeSpec data platform [32]. The profile information also contains user ID, nickname, number of followers and followees, gender, birthday, education background, sexual orientation, marital status, blood type, zodiac, etc.

Additionally, we crawled $81,781,544$ location check-ins of these users in the two cities through Sina Weibo API[6]. Check-in records include check-in time, identity of the checked-in POI, and information of the POI (e.g. POI name, latitude, longitude, province, city and category, where the category follows a taxonomy [7]).

We note that all data we collected (including profile attributes and check-ins) is either through Open API or publicly available on Sina Weibo, i.e., no private data is used in the experiment.

2.2 Ground Truth Construction

To build a standard ground truth for our dataset, we are faced with several challenges. For one, out of privacy and safety concerns, some people tend to provide incomplete or even misleading profile information like gender and birthday. For another, nowadays, online social networks have many latent commercial zombie users with fake profiles. In order to address the above problems, we only consider verified accounts, since Sina corporation conducts manual verifications of these users (users are asked to submit officially authenticated materials such as copies of their ID cards and employment certificates) so as to make sure that these accounts provide real and authentic profile information.

Two matters should be noted: 1) verified users consist of a portion of celebrities, e.g. famous singer Taylor Swift and tech entrepreneur Bill Gates. 2) Sina corporation cannot inspect two subjective attributes, i.e. sexual orientation and marital status. For the former issue, we implement an auxiliary filter on the measurement of the number of followers of each user. Based on our finding, this approach effectively excludes celebrities, making our dataset more representative. For the latter issue, it is convinced that most normal users have the freedom not to offer these subjective attributes, but actually have no incentive to provide fake information.

As a result, we obtain $159,530$ verified users ($117,413$ Beijing users and $42,117$ Shanghai users) with both their profiles and check-in histories. Compared to many existing manually labeled experimental datasets [20, 23, 16], our approach generates a larger scale and more reliable dataset.

2.3 Demographics Description

Table 1 presents the completion rate (ratio of effective users) as well as the categories of different demographic attributes for the collected users. As is shown, most users provide their gender information, and a large portion of the users provide age, educational background and zodiac sign. Here, the raw educational attribute is provided as the name of universities or schools. For the sake

[6]`http://bit.ly/1rgzRch`
[7]`http://bit.ly/1nnFztU`

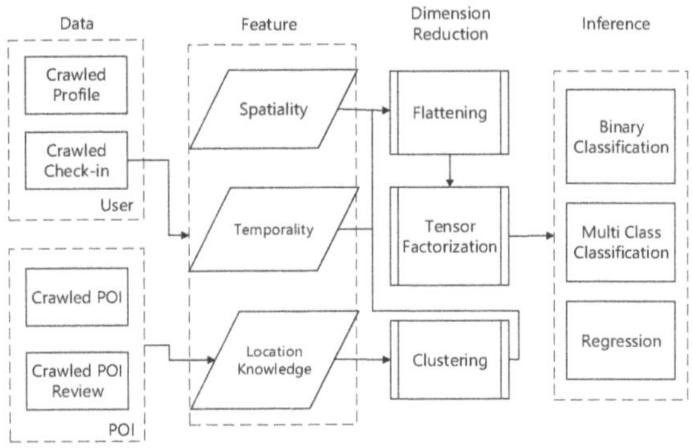

Figure 4: The Location to Profile (*L2P*) framework

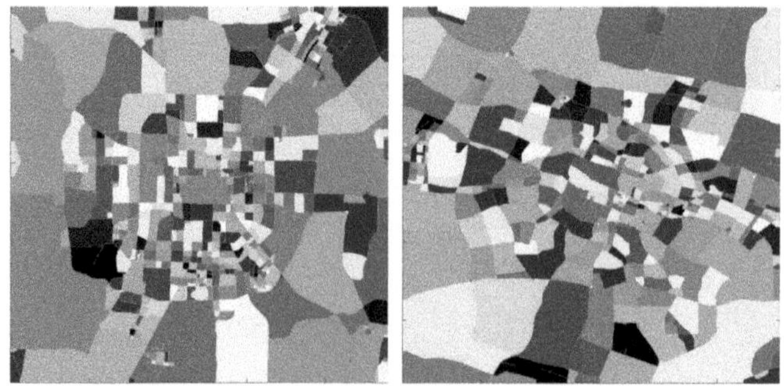

(a) Beijing (b) Shanghai

Figure 5: Region segmentation for spatiality

of simplicity, we categorize it into two types: university and non-university for users who provide educational attributes. For marital status, we consider four statuses that have a dominant number of users in our dataset, while the others like divorced, widowed, separated, engaged etc. are excluded. Within the users who provide gender attributes, 45.81% are males, and 54.19% are females. Table 2 offers more statistics with respect to other attributes such as marital status, blood type, and sexual orientation.

3. LOCATION TO PROFILE *(L2P)*

In this section, we describe the *location to profile (L2P)* framework, which aims to predict a given users' demographic attributes based on his/her location check-ins. As illustrated in Figure 4, our proposed framework consists of four modules:

• The *data crawling module* accumulates user profiles and location check-ins with corresponding POI information on Sina Weibo and crawl customer reviews from Dianping.

• The *feature extraction module* extracts rich features from location check-ins of a given user in terms of spatiality, temporality and location knowledge, where the location knowledge is enriched with signals from both online review sites and social media, as detailed later in Section 3.1 and Section 3.2.

• The *dimension reduction module* incorporates the extracted features of users with a tensor model and performs tensor factorization to reduce the dimensionality of features, as demonstrated in Section 3.3.1.

• The *inference module* reduces the profile inference task to various classification and regression tasks and provides the final inference result, as detailed in Section 3.3.2.

3.1 Spatiality and Temporality

3.1.1 Spatiality

As indicated in Section 1, location check-ins are not uniformly distributed in the geo-spatial space. For a common person, his/her range of movement is mostly concentrated on several hubs like home, workplace, relatives' homes, etc. In addition, some businesses tend to be located in some concentrated areas, e.g., financial districts, high-tech districts and restaurant streets. Hence, people who frequently appear in these areas may exhibit similar demographic attributes.

To capture the spatial distributions of users' check-ins, we segment a city into disjointed regions. Each check-in of a user is assigned to the region that the check-in occurs in. Nevertheless, instead of using a uniform segmentation (grids) for a city, we adopt a morphological segmentation of urban spaces [31], where the regions are segmented using high level roads in a road network. Since transportation in urban areas is usually restricted by networks, such segmentation preserves the semantics of users' movements and the topology of road networks. Figures 5(a) and Figure 5(b) visualize the segmentation results of Beijing and Shanghai, where the segmented regions are indicated with different colors.

3.1.2 Temporality

Human location check-ins change over time during a day and a week. The underlying principle is that most people follow regular, predictable and stable patterns during their everyday lives, in spite of leading a host of different kinds of lifestyles.

Weekday and weekend patterns cover most people and nearly all kinds of jobs. Here, we split a week into two parts: weekdays and weekends. For both of them, we split a day into hourly time bins. Thus, we have a total of 24×2 time bins for the expression of temporal patterns. Similar to spatiality, we discretize the timestamps and assign the corresponding time bins for each check-in of a user.

3.2 Location Knowledge Enrichment

Here, we converge on the methodology of enriching the knowledge of a user's check-in location. Originally, a checked-in POI is associated with some basic information, e.g., the category. However, in order to predict user profiles, we need to extract more semantic and latent information for a POI. As a result, the enriched location knowledge of a given POI can be represented by a set of semantic features, such as the followings:

• Category feature. This feature shows the types and characteristics of location check-ins. All POIs follow a hierarchical taxonomy defined by Sina Weibo, and each POI is associated with a code, which is a 1-1 mapping to a certain category in the taxonomy.

• Review feature. Delivering users' interests and opinions on a POI, this feature is represented by scores of multi-aspects, e.g., when evaluating a restaurant, users are usually concerned with the atmosphere, service, taste and overall rating. We note that for different categories of POIs, the concerned aspects may vary.

• Keyword feature. Manifesting users' viewpoints toward a POI, this feature is a distribution over characteristic keywords (such as luxury, vintage, etc.) of a check-in location.

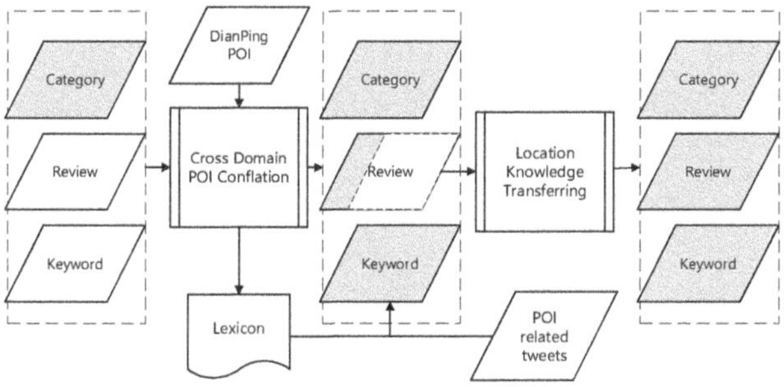

Figure 6: Location Knowledge Enrichment

Figure 6 sketches the location knowledge enrichment process. For the category feature, it is automatically attached to POI information in the crawled location check-in dataset. For learning the review and keyword features, we devise an incremental enrichment process. As is shown in Figure 6, the "location knowledge" of the POIs (indicated by the red part) grows as the process runs step by step. Specifically, we first conflate the POIs between Sina Weibo and Dianping, which is the largest user-generated review site in China. Later, we enrich the matched POIs with review features from Dianping. Next, we create a high utility keyword lexicon that contains relevant keywords for certain types of POIs (e.g., "delicious" is a high utility keyword for restaurants). Then, the keyword feature of all POIs can be derived from POI-related tweets on Sina Weibo based on the created lexicon. Finally, we train classifiers and regression models to transfer the review features from the matched POIs to the remaining unmatched POIs .

We note that in the above process, we utilize user generated data such as public reviews and related tweets of a POI, however, such side information is not directly related to an individual's check-ins, which are used as input for inferring users' profiles.

3.2.1 Cross domain POI conflation

Dianping and Sina Weibo are heterogeneous social networks facilitating users' different needs where Dianping is a specialized user review website while Sina Weibo is a social networking site. After crawling $2,699,822$ POIs with the corresponding $29,326,863$ reviews on Dianping, we devise a cross-domain POI conflation approach to link Dianping POIs with Sina Weibo POIs. Specifically, we extract the *name*, *address*, *telephone number*, *longitude* and *latitude* for POIs collected from both Dianping and Sina Weibo. As shown in Algorithm 1, for a pair of POIs $p_S^{(i)}$ (on Sina Weibo) and $p_D^{(j)}$ (on Dianping), we calculate Jaccard distance (1-Jaccard similarity) for name $d_N(p_S^{(i)}, p_D^{(j)})$ and address $d_A(p_S^{(i)}, p_D^{(j)})$, Hamming distance for telephone number $d_T(p_S^{(i)}, p_D^{(j)})$, and compute the geo-distance $d_G(p_S^{(i)}, p_D^{(j)})$ based on their latitudes and longitudes. As shown in Algorithm 1 lines 3-6, for each Sina Weibo POI $p_S^{(i)}$, we search for the POIs that are with the minimum distances in terms of different attributes (names, addresses, telephone numbers, geo-distances) from Dianping, and verify whether these POIs are matched to $p_S^{(i)}$ according to several fuzzy matching rules.

By applying the fuzzy matching algorithm, 35.26% POIs on Sina Weibo were matched to POIs on Dianping. In our practice, the thresholds in Algorithm 1 are chosen as follows: $\theta_A = \theta_N = 0.1$, $\theta_G = 50m$. To inspect the performance of the matching algorithm, we randomly sample 200 matched POIs, and manually check the correctness of the results, which achieve an accuracy of 99.5%.

Algorithm 1: Fuzzy POI Matching

Input: Sina Weibo POIs: $P_S = \{p_S^{(i)}\}_{i=1}^q$,
DianPing POIs: $P_D = \{p_D^{(j)}\}_{j=1}^m$
Output: $\{k_i\}_{i=1}^q$, where $p_S^{(i)}$ is matched to $p_D^{(k_i)}$ when $k_i > 0$, and $k_i = 0$ indicates no POI is matched to $p_S^{(i)}$

1 $J \leftarrow \{1, 2, \ldots, m\}$;
2 **for** $i = 1 : q$ **do**
3 $\quad j_T \leftarrow \arg\min_{j \in J} d_T(p_S^{(i)}, p_D^{(j)})$;
4 $\quad j_N \leftarrow \arg\min_{j \in J} d_N(p_S^{(i)}, p_D^{(j)})$;
5 $\quad j_A \leftarrow \arg\min_{j \in J} d_A(p_S^{(i)}, p_D^{(j)})$;
6 $\quad j_G \leftarrow \arg\min_{j \in J} d_G(p_S^{(i)}, p_D^{(j)})$;
7 $\quad$ **if** $d_T(p_S^{(i)}, p_D^{(j_T)}) = 0$ **then** /* identical phone number */
8 $\quad k_i \leftarrow j_T, J \leftarrow J - \{j_T\}$;
9 $\quad$;
10 $\quad$ **else if** $d_G(p_S^{(i)}, p_D^{(j_N)}) \leq \theta_G$ **and** $d_A(p_S^{(i)}, p_D^{(j_N)}) \leq \theta_A$ **then**
$\qquad$ /* most similar name, close, and similar address */
11 $\qquad k_i \leftarrow j_N, J \leftarrow J - \{j_N\}$;
12 $\quad$ **else if** $d_N(p_S^{(i)}, p_D^{(j_G)}) \leq \theta_N$ **and** $d_A(p_S^{(i)}, p_D^{(j_G)}) \leq \theta_A$ **then**
$\qquad$ /* most close, similar name and address */
13 $\qquad k_i \leftarrow j_G, J \leftarrow J - \{j_G\}$;
14 $\quad$ **else if** $d_N(p_S^{(i)}, p_D^{(j_A)}) \leq \theta_N$ **and** $d_G(p_S^{(i)}, p_D^{(j_A)}) \leq \theta_G$ **then**
$\qquad$ /* most similar address, similar name and close */
15 $\qquad k_i \leftarrow j_A, J \leftarrow J - \{j_A\}$;
16 $\quad$ **else**
17 $\qquad k_i \leftarrow 0$;
18 **return** $\{k_i\}_{i=1}^q$

3.2.2 Lexicon creation

After the conflation of Dianping and Weibo POI, part of the Sina Weibo POIs are associated with corresponding reviews and users' aggregated scores for multi-aspects (like environment, taste, price etc.). Thus the review features for the matched POIs are already attained (as shown in Figure 6 where the review feature in the second phase is partially filled with red). The goal of this step is to create a high utility lexicon from users' review contents on Dianping. Specifically, we conduct Chinese word segmentation to segment each review to a set of words and eliminate the stop words. Since high utility keywords for different categories of POIs may vary (e.g., "delicious" is often used when talking about food in a restaurant, while "king-size" is usually used when talking about bed size in a hotel room), we categorize all POIs into several divisions as follows: *travel & accommodation*, *buildings & institutions*, *campus life*, *restaurant & delicacy*, *shopping & service*, *life & entertainment*, *park & outdoors*, *company* and *others*. Then for each division, we choose the top-n important words as the keywords (n is set to 200 in our implementation). Here, the importance of a term is defined by term frequency with a logarithmic factor which is widely used in information retrieval, given by:

$$tf_k = 1 + \log(f_k), \tag{1}$$

where f_k is the raw frequency of a keyword k in the reviews of a certain POI. As a result, we obtain a set of keywords for each category division, and the lexicon is merged by the keywords of all sets.

Meanwhile, we collect POI-related tweets for all crawled POIs on Sina Weibo using the open API [8]. Next, for each POI (matched or unmatched), we generate the keyword features by computing the distribution over the keywords in the created lexicon using the POI-related tweets (pre-processed with Chinese word segmentation and

[8] http://bit.ly/1rQQZXe

stop words filtering). Hence, we obtain the keyword features for all POIs.

3.2.3 Location knowledge transferring

As indicated in Section 3.2.1, only a fraction (35.26%) of Weibo POIs have been matched, not to mention that actually some unpopular matching POIs have vacant review scores for different aspects. Since users' review keywords fully embody their ratings, transferring the knowledge of review keywords as ratings is intuitive. In order to obtain the review features for all collected POIs, we develop a supervised learning approach to "transfer" the review features of matched POIs that have multi-aspect review scores to the remaining POIs.

Specifically, given the keyword feature of a POI F_K, the score of a certain aspect is considered a function of the keyword features, i.e., $r_i = r_i(F_K)$, where $i = 1, 2, \ldots, M$ is the index of all review aspects (merged from different category divisions) and $r_{all} = r_{all}(F_K)$ is the overall rating of a POI. The key insight behind this is that the multi-aspect scores provided by users are typically reflected from their reviews. Thus, we utilize the matched POIs that have multi-aspect review scores as the training data to learn the mapping functions $\{r_i\}_{i=1}^{M}$ as well as the overall rating r_{all}, where the review score is deemed as the label and the keyword feature of a POI is considered as the input feature.

We note that the score for a single review aspect is a categorical variable $(1, 2, \ldots, 5)$ indicated by "stars" and the overall rating of a POI is a continuous valued rating. Thus, we train linear kernel SVM classifiers for individual review aspects and logistic regression to learn the overall rating of a POI. We conduct a 10-fold cross-validation on the POIs using the trained classiers and regression models. Then, we apply the trained models to infer the aspect scores and overall ratings for the remaining POIs that have no review features. As a result, for each POI, we obtain the review feature $F_R = (r_1, r_2, \ldots, r_M, r_{all})$.

3.3 Dimension Reduction and Profile Inference

3.3.1 Dimension reduction

After feature extraction from *spatiality*, *temporality* and *location knowledge* aspects, we obtain a large scale feature set for users' check-ins. To reduce the dimensionality of the features and mine intrinsic representation of users, we feed the features into a three-way tensor T and conduct tensor factorization.

As shown in Figure 7, the three-ways of $T \in \mathbb{R}^{I_1 \times I_2 \times I_3}$ represent users, location knowledge features and contextual features respectively, where I_1 is the number of users, I_2 is the dimensionality of location knowledge features and I_3 is the dimensionality of the contextual features including both spatiality and temporality.

Here, in order to construct the three-way tensor, Cartesian production is implemented over feature spaces within context dimension and location knowledge dimension severally. More specifically, for context dimension, given a check-in corresponding to region α and time bin β, the index is determined by $\alpha \times N_T + \beta$, in which N_T is the number of time bins. For the dimension of location knowledge, we first cluster check-ins according to review features and keyword features separately (we employ k-means clustering in our practice while other clustering methods can generally be applied), resulting in N_R review-based clusters and N_K keyword-based clusters respectively. Then we flatten category, review, and keyword features using an approach similar to the context dimension. For example, assuming a user's check-in c is associated with a POI that belongs to category α_1, cluster α_2 of the N_R review-based clusters, and cluster α_3 of the N_K keyword-based clusters respectively, the final coordinate of c in the location knowledge dimension is given by $\alpha_1 \times N_R \times N_K + \alpha_2 \times N_K + \alpha_3$.

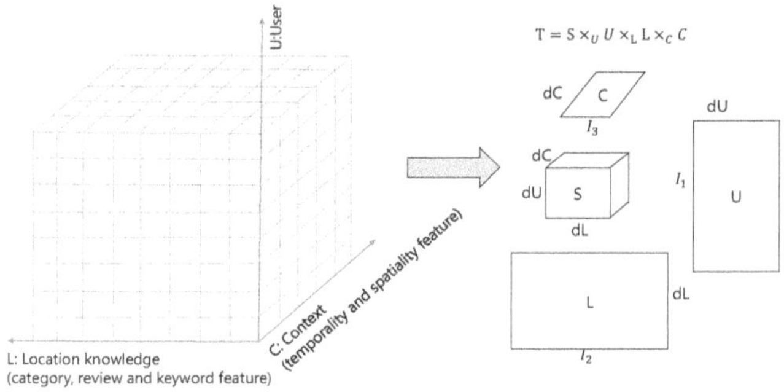

Figure 7: Tensor decomposition model

Later, we employ the Tucker Decomposition technique which decomposes T by:

$$T = S \times_U \mathrm{U} \times_L \mathrm{L} \times_C \mathrm{C},$$

where $S \in \mathbb{R}^{dU \times dL \times dC}$ is the core tensor indicating interactions between user, context and location knowledge. $U \in \mathbb{R}^{I_1 \times dU}$, $L \in \mathbb{R}^{I_2 \times dL}$ and $C \in \mathbb{R}^{I_3 \times dC}$ are the factor matrices considering the low dimensional representation of users, locations and contexts (spatiality and temporality) respectively.

The tensor model offers several advantages for dimension reduction compared to other approaches, e.g., the tensor model intrinsically captures interactions between different features within various domains similar to matrix factorization. However, compared to matrix factorization, the tensor model is more suitable for high dimensional data.

3.3.2 Profile inference

Let U be the factorized user intrinsic matrix generated using the method described in Section 3.3.1, which already incorporates users' similar patterns in terms of spatiality, temporality, and location knowledge. By considering each row of U as the feature vector of a user and the actual demographic attribute as the label, we transform the profile inference task to several classification or regression tasks as follows.

- Gender. A binary classification task classifying users' gender: *male* and *female*.
- Age: A regression task inferring the specific age, where age is a continuous valued attribute.
- Education Background. A binary classification task distinguishing users' education level: *university* and *non-university*.
- Sexual Orientation. A multi-class classification task differentiating four kinds of sexual orientation: *heterosexuality*, *bisexuality*, *male homosexuality* and *female homosexuality*.
- Marital Status. A multi-class classification task predicting four kinds of marital status: *single*, *courtship*, *in love* and *married*.
- Blood Type. A multi-class classification task identifying four common blood types: *O*, *A*, *B* and *AB*.
- Zodiac: A multi-class classification task demarcating twelve zodiac signs.

Over the last several decades, various algorithms have been proposed for learning classification and regression functions. We evaluate a number of well-adopted learning algorithms to learn the models separately and examine their performance in the experiments. Specifically, for binary classification tasks, we compare logistic regression, SVM, and LambdaMART [28]; for regression tasks, we try models such as linear regression, Poisson regression, and boosted tree regression [9]; for multi-class classification, we evaluate multi-class logistic regression, multi-class neuron networks [19], and a parallel ensemble method [24] (refer to Section 4 for the results).

4. EXPERIMENTS

4.1 Settings

4.1.1 Preliminary

Our experiments are guided by the following considerations: 1) Whether location check-ins have predictive power for demographic attributes; 2) Whether all the proposed features (spatiality, temporality and location knowledge) contribute to the performance of inferring demographic attributes; and 3) How well the proposed *L2P* framework applies to different demographic attributes.

With the purpose of testing the generality and robustness of our L2P framwork, we perform experiments on Beijing and Shanghai separately. For each city, we conducted a 10-fold cross validation for inferring each demographic attribute. For the profile inference procedure (introduced in Section 3.3.2), we used 6 parts for training, 2 parts for validation, and the remaining 2 parts for testing if not specified elsewhere (we also study the effect of varying the ratio of training data in the experiments). The validation set was used to tune the hyper-parameters of the learning algorithms, such as the number of trees in LambdaMART, and then we fixed the parameters to train the models using the training set. The test set was used to evaluate the performance of the trained models. Note that all the reported results are the average performances over the 10 trials.

For the parameters, we set $n = 200$ for choosing the top-n keywords in lexicon creation (Section 3.2.2). In the procedure of location knowledge transferring (Section 3.2.3), N_R and N_K are set to 100 by default, and dU is set to 200 by default if not specified elsewhere in Section 4.2. The effect of different N_R, N_K, and dU are studied later in the experiments.

4.1.2 Baselines

To the best of our knowledge, there exists no model directly predicting user demographics from human location check-ins. We then compare our method with the following baselines. Here, by analogizing a POI as a "Like", we compare our approach against a recently famous profile inference method proposed by Kosinski et al. [13], which extracts principle components from the User-POI matrix and performs logistic/linear regression based on the derived user feature vector. We refer to this baseline as the POI-based method (shortened as **POI** method). We term our approach that comprehensively considers spatiality, temporality, and location knowledge as the **STL** method, and further evaluate the following baselines for comparison.

- Spatiality-based method (**S**), which only considers the spatial information in the tensor (degenerated as a matrix), and performs profile inference using extracted user features similar to the STL method.

- Spatiality and Temporality-based method (**ST**), which goes one step further than S, leveraging both the spatial and temporal features in the tensor for prediction.

- Spatiality, Temporality, and Category-based method (**STC**), which adopts spatial, temporal and category features in the tensor for prediction, i.e., without location knowledge enrichment as in the STL method.

4.1.3 Criteria

We evaluate the results using the following measurements in terms of different inference tasks. Effective and common metrics for binary classification such as precision, recall, F-measure and Area Under the ROC Curve (AUC) are all evaluated. For multi-class classification, average precision (over different classes), average recall, and average F-measure are employed. We use RMSE (Root-Mean-Square Error) for examining the performance of regression models.

4.2 Results

4.2.1 Gender

Table 3 presents the results of gender inference for users in Beijing and Shanghai. As is shown in Table 3(a), the STL method achieves the best performance in terms of all measurements, where the F1 score is above 0.8 for both Beijing and Shanghai users, which significantly outperforms competing methods. In particular, the STL method, which considers the complement set of location knowledge features, gains more than 0.05 improvement over the STC method and 0.1 improvement over the POI method in terms of AUC for both Beijing and Shanghai users. This indicates that the location semantics, particularly, the review and keyword features learned from different domains, contribute a lot to the predictive power of the STL method.

We further study the performance of different learning algorithms (Section 3.3.2) for gender inference, and the dimensions of user intrinsic matrix dU in tensor factorization (Section 3.3.1) for the STL method. Figure 8 illustrates the AUC for SVM (linear kernel), LR and LambdaMart classifiers. As is shown, the LambdaMART classifier performs the best over other classifiers. As the number of dimensions dU increases from 50 to 200, the results of all classifiers improve and tend to be stable when $dU = 300$, then decrease when dU further increases.

Table 3: Performance of Gender Inference

(a) Beijing

	Precision	**Recall**	**F1**	**AUC**
POI	0.7102	0.7055	0.7078	0.7502
S	0.6921	0.6899	0.6910	0.7321
ST	0.7321	0.7429	0.7375	0.7746
STC	0.7727	0.7631	0.7679	0.8027
STL	**0.8211**	**0.8059**	**0.8134**	**0.8548**

(b) Shanghai

	Precision	**Recall**	**F1**	**AUC**
POI	0.7362	0.7434	0.7398	0.7463
S	0.7197	0.7218	0.7207	0.7266
ST	0.7528	0.7596	0.7562	0.7682
STC	0.7819	0.7704	0.7761	0.8151
STL	**0.8368**	**0.8127**	**0.8246**	**0.8654**

4.2.2 Age

Age inference is considered a regression task. Figure 9 plots the RMSE of all compared methods when changing the ratio of training data. As is shown, the STL method and POI method perform better than other methods for age inference, but STL still outperforms the POI method. For example, when we use only 15% data for training, the RMSE of the STL method is less than 5, which is a significant improvement over the POI method. Table 4 gives the results of different regression models for STL, where the boosted tree regression model achieves the best performance.

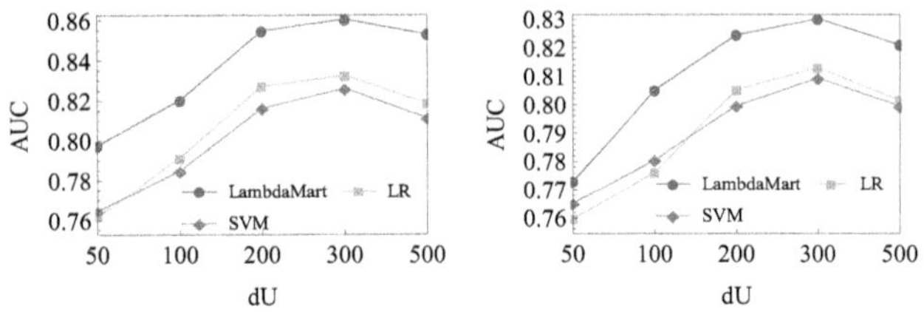

(a) Beijing (b) Shanghai

Figure 8: Performance of different classifiers for STL changing over dU

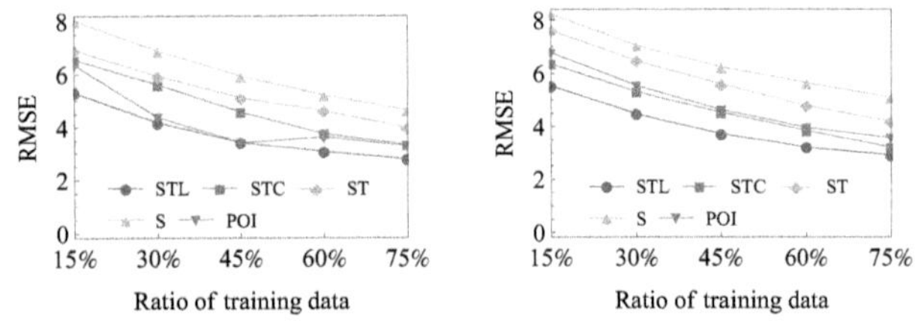

(a) Beijing (b) Shanghai

Figure 9: RMSE w.r.t. ratio of training data

Table 4: RMSE of Different Regression Models for STL

	Beijing	Shanghai
Poisson	3.463	3.602
Linear	3.312	3.399
Boosted Tree	**3.067**	**3.204**

4.2.3 *Education background*

The results of education background inference are presented in Table 5. Surprisingly, the inference results of all methods are remarkably higher than gender and age, which indicate that users' education levels are highly predictable from their physical movements. For example, the AUC of STL method for Beijing users is higher than 0.9. Meanwhile, we study the effect of N_K (number of keyword-based clusters) and N_R (number of review-based clusters) for dimension reduction in location knowledge enrichment. As shown in Table 6, the performance is comparatively stable for different settings of N_R and N_K.

4.2.4 *Sexual orientation and marital status*

Table 7 presents the evaluation results for inferring sexual orientation and marital status. Here, due to space limit, we report the overall results for Beijing and Shanghai users, and based on the best-performed parallel ensemble classifier. We note that for both sexual orientation and marital status, the inference problem is reduced as a 4-class classification task. Although the performance is not as strong as the gender/education inference, the STL method still outperforms other methods in terms of all measurements, and for all compared methods the results of sexual orientation inference are better than marital status.

4.2.5 *Blood type and zodiac sign*

We note that for blood type and zodiac inference, which have rarely been considered in existing literatures our work is rather initiatory and purely driven by curiosity. As is shown in Table 8, the location check-ins show weak predictive power for these attributes.

Remark: From the above inference results, we can discover that gender and education attributes achieve the best results because they are highly predictable from check-in records and the binary classification is relatively easy. Considering the identification of sexual orientation and marital status, since they are multi-class classification tasks and the attribute completion rate is very low, the prediction is not as good as gender and education. Careful scrutiny reaveals that sexual orientation inference is better than that of marital status, because sexual orientation (such as bisexuality and homosexuality) is more distinctive than marital status (such as single and courtship). The performances of blood type and zodiac sign are the weakest among all the demographics, indicating that they are merely predictable from human location check-in records. However, we should note that our model still perfoms much better than random guess. As is shown in the above prediction tasks, an ascending order of the predictive power for the compared methods are S, POI, ST, STC and STL. Spatial feature, which is extracted based on road networks in coarse granularity, leads to weaker performance than POI. On the basis of spatiality (S), we iteratively add tempo-

Table 5: Performance of Education Background Inference

(a) Beijing

	Precision	Recall	F1	AUC
POI	0.7564	0.7702	0.7632	0.7992
S	0.7385	0.7294	0.7339	0.7723
ST	0.7655	0.7702	0.7678	0.8150
STC	0.8073	0.7921	0.7996	0.8413
STL	**0.8774**	**0.8829**	**0.8801**	**0.9021**

(b) Shanghai

	Precision	Recall	F1	AUC
POI	0.7759	0.7817	0.7788	0.8205
S	0.7394	0.7191	0.7291	0.7659
ST	0.7804	0.7631	0.7717	0.8041
STC	0.8115	0.8058	0.8086	0.8503
STL	**0.8823**	**0.8726**	**0.8774**	**0.8957**

Table 6: Performance w.r.t. Number of Clusters in Dimension Reduction

	Beijing		Shanghai	
	F1	AUC	F1	AUC
$N_R = 100, N_K = 100$	0.8801	0.9021	0.8774	0.8957
$N_R = 100, N_K = 200$	0.8812	**0.9100**	0.8762	0.8946
$N_R = 200, N_K = 100$	0.8792	0.8977	**0.8801**	0.8896
$N_R = 200, N_K = 200$	**0.8867**	0.9017	0.8792	**0.9051**

Table 7: Sexual Orientation and Marital Status Inference

	Sexual Orientation			Marital Status		
	Precision	Recall	F1	Precision	Recall	F1
POI	0.4637	0.4586	0.4611	0.3257	0.3302	0.3279
S	0.4496	0.4503	0.4499	0.3291	0.3287	0.3289
ST	0.4613	0.4599	0.4606	0.3451	0.3502	0.3476
STC	0.4826	0.4855	0.4840	0.3683	0.3677	0.3680
STL	**0.5235**	**0.5122**	**0.5178**	**0.3855**	**0.3789**	**0.3822**

Table 8: Blood Type and Zodiac Inference

	Blood Type			Zodiac		
	Precision	Recall	F1	Precision	Recall	F1
POI	0.2801	0.2729	0.2765	0.1203	0.1236	0.1219
S	0.2744	0.2738	0.2741	0.1103	0.1052	0.1077
ST	0.2775	0.2742	0.2758	0.1256	0.1260	0.1258
STC	0.2894	0.2901	0.2897	0.1286	0.1243	0.1264
STL	**0.3012**	**0.3103**	**0.3057**	**0.1303**	**0.1275**	**0.1289**

raility (ST), category (STC), and location knowledge (STL), making the feature more sophisticated step by step. ST and STC baselines, which convey temporal patterns, result in enhanced achievements over spatiality-based methods (S and POI), where the STC method partially considers location knowledge from the category information of a POI. The STL method, which incorporates more location knowledge transfered from review sites, gains the most remarkable improvement against all other baselines.

5. RELATED WORK

5.1 Inferences of Demographic Attributes

Demographics inference has been studied in academia for more than fifty years. Several early stage works have researched author identification [17] and gender discrimination [14, 26]. In 1992, Costa Jr and McCrae [8] predicted demographic attributes and personalities through people's answers to a specific psychometric test. [11] adopted psychological approach and analyzed testers' written words to classify their personality type.

The proliferation of digital communication and Internet brought a brand new opportunity for inferring demographic attributes. With a concentration on differences in gender sociolinguistics, Boulis and Ostendorf [5] studied users' telephone conversation data and predicted gender attributes using machine learning techniques. Murray and Durrell [18] adopted LSA to analyze users' browsing behavior for demographic attributes classification. Back et al. [3] predicted personality, i.e. neuroticism, openness, agreeableness, conscientiousness, narcissism, and extroversion solely from email addresses.

In recent years, the fast development of online social networks and mobile computing technologies have provided researchers with a convenient way to infer people's demographic attributes. Kosinski et al. [13] employed Facebook "Likes" data, SVD dimension reduction technique and logistic regression to predict private traits and attributes. Pennacchiotti and Popescu [20] put forward a machine learning framework to detect users' political affiliation, ethnicity identification, and business affinity. Brdar et al. [6] proposed a multi-level classification model to predict people's attributes like gender, age, marital status, and job type, among others.

Our work differs from existing approaches in that we focus on users' location check-in data from online social networks for demographic inference, which has rarely been explored before.

5.2 Location Understanding

Existing approaches on enriching location knowledge can be categorized in terms of different data sources: *GPS trace*, *Web* and *location-based social networks (LBSN), and Volunteered Geographic Information (VGI)*.

• GPS trace: A myriad of scholars have carefully researched into location knowledge extraction from GPS traces [7, 15]. They employed and devised different methods for mining and extracting semantically important locations.

• Web: An early location semantics study [21] addressed the deficiency of traditional physical/geographical location presentation by linking location to an unambiguous "web-like" URI. Focusing on location extraction from web contextual information, Qin et al. [22] proposed a detection ranking framework and addressed challenges in location name detection and location entity disambiguation. Wang et al. [27] proposed a generative model to learn latent aspect ratings from online reviews, demonstrating the effectiveness of the proposed model using data from a hotel review site.

• LBSN and VGI: Recently, several works have been proposed on location knowledge mining in LBSN and VGI. Ye et al. [30] developed techniques for location semantic annotation by extracting features of places from *explicit patterns (EP)* and *implicit relatedness* and learning SVM to support multi-label classification. [21] and [29] respectively presented methodologies to analyze spatial and temporal dimension semantics of POI from LBSN and VGI.

Our location knowledge enrichment is distinctive from existing works in the following ways: 1) We enrich the understanding of a POI by transferring location knowledge from heterogeneous domains, after conflating POIs between an online customer review site and an online social network; 2) We explicitly model three types of location knowledge, namely category features, review features, and keyword features, where review features and keyword features are learned from heterogeneous user generated data (online reviews and POI-related tweets).

5.3 Tensor factorization

Tensor factorization is widely applied in a variety of areas. The first application in data mining is [1] in 2005, focusing on chat room tensor construction and factorization techniques performance comparisons. Later in text analysis, Bader et al. [4] developed nonnegative tensor factorization to extract discussions from email communications and proved the superiority of nonnegative matrix factorization. The application of tensor factorization on recommendation and prediction is also carefully studied in several works [2, 25] where Acar et al. [2] explored matrix and tensor factorization models in temporal link prediction and Symeonidis et al. [25] proposed a unified framework modeling 3-order tensor, user, item and tag.

To the best of our knowledge, our work is the first to apply tensor factorization for profile inference in real world online social networks where features are organized in a three-way tensor, which consists of user, context (spatiality and temporality) and location knowledge.

6. CONCLUSION AND DISCUSSIONS

In this paper, we have addressed the problem of demographics inference from location check-ins, and developed a comprehensive *L2P* framework to capture temporality, spatiality and location knowledge at the same time. Extensive experiments based on our large-scale Sina Weibo dataset have validated the effectiveness of the proposed methods for inferring a variety of demographic attributes.

Although this is, to our best knowledge, the first work that explores demographic inference from location check-ins, the proposed methodology is far from perfect and may suffer from several limitations. For example, our experiments are based on a dataset with users who use online social networks and post check-ins, which may not be a representative sample set of the whole targeted population. Another issue is the profiles of users who live in metropolitan cities (Beijing and Shanghai in our dataset) may create bias in the inference result. However, we believe that the proposed *L2P* framework is general enough to be applied on other forms of human mobility data with a finer granularity and larger coverage, e.g., GPS traces collected from phones.

There are many directions that can be further explored to improve the current *L2P* framework. For one thing, location check-ins may suffer from data sparsity for representing human mobility, given that few people are willing to post locations all the time. One possible solution may come from extracting POI-level locations from a large quantity of normal tweets, like "I am shopping with my daughter at Walmart in L.A.!". It is also possible that other signals could be integrated into the *L2P* framework, e.g., the current model has not exploited users' friendship relations on social networks, which might affect users' check-in behaviors.

References

[1] E. Acar, S. A. Camtepe, M. S. Krishnamoorthy, and B. Yener. Modeling and multiway analysis of chatroom tensors. In *Intelligence and Security Informatics*, pages 256–268. Springer, 2005.

[2] E. Acar, D. M. Dunlavy, and T. G. Kolda. Link prediction on evolving data using matrix and tensor factorizations. In *Data Mining Workshops, 2009. ICDMW'09. IEEE International Conference on*, pages 262–269. IEEE, 2009.

[3] M. D. Back, S. C. Schmukle, and B. Egloff. How extraverted is honey. bunny77@ hotmail. de? inferring personality from e-mail addresses. *Journal of Research in Personality*, 42(4): 1116–1122, 2008.

[4] B. W. Bader, M. W. Berry, and M. Browne. Discussion tracking in enron email using parafac. In *Survey of Text Mining II*, pages 147–163. Springer, 2008.

[5] C. Boulis and M. Ostendorf. A quantitative analysis of lexical differences between genders in telephone conversations. In *Proceedings of the 43rd Annual Meeting on Association for Computational Linguistics*, pages 435–442. Association for Computational Linguistics, 2005.

[6] S. Brdar, D. Culibrk, and V. Crnojevic. Demographic attributes prediction on the real-world mobile data. In *Proc. Mobile Data Challenge by Nokia Workshop, in Conjunction with Int. Conf. on Pervasive Computing, Newcastle, UK*, 2012.

[7] X. Cao, G. Cong, and C. S. Jensen. Mining significant semantic locations from gps data. *Proceedings of the VLDB Endowment*, 3(1-2):1009–1020, 2010.

[8] P. T. Costa Jr and R. R. McCrae. Reply to ben-porath and waller. *Psychological Assessment*, 4(1):20–22, 1992.

[9] G. De'Ath. Boosted trees for ecological modeling and prediction. *Ecology*, 88(1):243–251, 2007.

[10] Y. Dong, Y. Yang, J. Tang, and N. V. Chawla. Inferring user demographics and social strategies in mobile social networks. 2014.

[11] L. A. Fast and D. C. Funder. Personality as manifest in word use: correlations with self-report, acquaintance report, and behavior. *Journal of personality and social psychology*, 94 (2):334, 2008.

[12] M. C. Gonzalez, C. A. Hidalgo, and A.-L. Barabasi. Understanding individual human mobility patterns. *Nature*, 453(7196):779–782, 2008.

[13] M. Kosinski, D. Stillwell, and T. Graepel. Private traits and attributes are predictable from digital records of human behavior. *Proceedings of the National Academy of Sciences*, 110(15):5802–5805, 2013.

[14] W. Labov. *The social stratification of English in New York City.* PhD thesis, Columbia university., 1964.

[15] J. Liu, O. Wolfson, and H. Yin. Extracting semantic location from outdoor positioning systems. In *MDM*, page 73, 2006.

[16] A. Mislove, B. Viswanath, K. P. Gummadi, and P. Druschel. You are who you know: inferring user profiles in online social networks. In *Proceedings of the third ACM international conference on Web search and data mining*, pages 251–260. ACM, 2010.

[17] F. Mosteller and D. L. Wallace. Inference in an authorship problem: A comparative study of discrimination methods applied to the authorship of the disputed federalist papers. *Journal of the American Statistical Association*, 58(302): 275–309, 1963.

[18] D. Murray and K. Durrell. Inferring demographic attributes of anonymous internet users. In *Web Usage Analysis and User Profiling*, pages 7–20. Springer, 2000.

[19] G. Ou and Y. L. Murphey. Multi-class pattern classification using neural networks. *Pattern Recognition*, 40(1):4–18, 2007.

[20] M. Pennacchiotti and A.-M. Popescu. Democrats, republicans and starbucks afficionados: user classification in twitter. In *Proceedings of the 17th ACM SIGKDD international conference on Knowledge discovery and data mining*, pages 430–438. ACM, 2011.

[21] S. Pradhan. Semantic location. *Personal Technologies*, 4(4): 213–216, 2000.

[22] T. Qin, R. Xiao, L. Fang, X. Xie, and L. Zhang. An efficient location extraction algorithm by leveraging web contextual information. In *proceedings of the 18th SIGSPATIAL international conference on advances in geographic information systems*, pages 53–60. ACM, 2010.

[23] D. Rao, D. Yarowsky, A. Shreevats, and M. Gupta. Classifying latent user attributes in twitter. In *Proceedings of the 2nd international workshop on Search and mining user-generated contents*, pages 37–44. ACM, 2010.

[24] L. Rokach. Ensemble-based classifiers. *Artificial Intelligence Review*, 33(1-2):1–39, 2010.

[25] P. Symeonidis, A. Nanopoulos, and Y. Manolopoulos. A unified framework for providing recommendations in social tagging systems based on ternary semantic analysis. *Knowledge and Data Engineering, IEEE Transactions on*, 22 (2):179–192, 2010.

[26] P. Trudgill. *The social differentiation of English in Norwich*, volume 13. CUP Archive, 1974.

[27] H. Wang, Y. Lu, and C. Zhai. Latent aspect rating analysis without aspect keyword supervision. In *Proceedings of the 17th ACM SIGKDD international conference on Knowledge discovery and data mining*, pages 618–626. ACM, 2011.

[28] Q. Wu, C. J. Burges, K. M. Svore, and J. Gao. Adapting boosting for information retrieval measures. *Information Retrieval*, 13(3):254–270, 2010.

[29] M. Ye, K. Janowicz, C. Mülligann, and W.-C. Lee. What you are is when you are: the temporal dimension of feature types in location-based social networks. In *Proceedings of the 19th ACM SIGSPATIAL International Conference on Advances in Geographic Information Systems*, pages 102–111. ACM, 2011.

[30] M. Ye, D. Shou, W.-C. Lee, P. Yin, and K. Janowicz. On the semantic annotation of places in location-based social networks. In *Proceedings of the 17th ACM SIGKDD international conference on Knowledge discovery and data mining*, pages 520–528. ACM, 2011.

[31] J. Yuan, Y. Zheng, and X. Xie. Discovering regions of different functions in a city using human mobility and pois. In *Proceedings of the 18th ACM SIGKDD international conference on Knowledge discovery and data mining*, pages 186–194. ACM, 2012.

[32] N. J. Yuan, F. Zhang, D. Lian, K. Zheng, S. Yu, and X. Xie. We know how you live: exploring the spectrum of urban lifestyles. In *Proceedings of the first ACM conference on Online social networks*, pages 3–14. ACM, 2013.

[33] E. Zheleva and L. Getoor. To join or not to join: the illusion of privacy in social networks with mixed public and private user profiles. In *Proceedings of the 18th international conference on World wide web*, pages 531–540. ACM, 2009.

SimApp: A Framework for Detecting Similar Mobile Applications by Online Kernel Learning

Ning Chen, Steven C. H. Hoi†, Shaohua Li, Xiaokui Xiao
Nanyang Technological University, Singapore, †Singapore Management University, Singapore
{nchen1,lishaohua,xkxiao}@ntu.edu.sg,†chhoi@smu.edu.sg

ABSTRACT

With the popularity of smart phones and mobile devices, the number of mobile applications (a.k.a. "apps") has been growing rapidly. Detecting semantically similar apps from a large pool of apps is a basic and important problem, as it is beneficial for various applications, such as app recommendation, app search, etc. However, there is no systematic and comprehensive work so far that focuses on addressing this problem. In order to fill this gap, in this paper, we explore multi-modal heterogeneous data in app markets (e.g., description text, images, user reviews, etc.), and present "SimApp" – a novel framework for detecting similar apps using machine learning. Specifically, it consists of two stages: (i) a variety of kernel functions are constructed to measure app similarity for each modality of data; and (ii) an online kernel learning algorithm is proposed to learn the optimal combination of similarity functions of multiple modalities. We conduct an extensive set of experiments on a real-world dataset crawled from Google Play to evaluate SimApp, from which the encouraging results demonstrate that SimApp is effective and promising.

Categories and Subject Descriptors

I.2.6 [**Artificial Intelligence**]: Learning; H.4 [**Information Systems Applications**]: Miscellaneous

General Terms

Algorithm and Experimentation

Keywords

Mobile applications; similarity function; multi-modal data; multiple kernels; online kernel learning

1. INTRODUCTION

The proliferation of smart phones in recent years has led to a huge and rapid growth of mobile applications ("apps"). According to a recent report [1], as of June 2014, there were over 1.5 million apps available on Google Play (one of the largest app markets), and the number of apps grew by around 60% between July 2013 and June 2014. With such a large amount of apps, if a specific app is given as a query, it is very difficult to find all other apps that are *similar* to the query app. In this paper, two apps are considered to be *similar* to each other if they implement related semantic (high-level) requirements.

The problem of knowing the semantic similarity between apps is very important because it has many benefits for different stakeholders in the mobile app ecosystem. For example, it can help app platform providers improve the performance of their app recommendation systems and enhance the user experience of app search engines. For app developers, detecting similar apps can be useful for various purposes, such as identifying direct competing apps, assessing reusability (if open source) and many more. The potential application value of this problem motivates our work.

Detecting similar apps is a nontrivial and difficult problem, as our goal is to find apps that share the same high-level concept. In this paper, we try to solve this problem by exploiting multi-modal heterogeneous data in app markets, such as Google Play, Apple App Store, etc. Generally, app markets contain rich contents associated with apps, e.g., description text, screenshot images, user reviews, etc. Such information usually describes conceptual characteristics of apps, and thus is helpful in addressing our problem.

One of the key challenges is how to explore and combine different modalities of data in app markets to measure the similarity between apps in a principled way. Previous studies [24, 2] provided simple solutions in their app recommendation systems, which were based on app description, title and user reviews. However, these methods are far from comprehensive and systematic, since other kinds of rich metadata have not been well exploited. To fill this gap, in this paper, we present a novel framework named "SimApp" for modeling app similarity by leveraging multi-modal heterogeneous data in app markets via an online kernel learning approach. Figure 1 depicts the overview of the SimApp framework. First of all, we measure the pairwise app similarity by defining a variety of kernel (similarity) functions on different modalities. Second, we assume the target app similarity function is a linear combination of the multiple kernels, and then employ online learning techniques [17] to learn the optimal combination weights from streams of training data. Finally, the learned app similarity function can facilitate a number of applications. In particular, we conduct an extensive set of experiments to evaluate the efficacy of SimApp based on a

WSDM'15, February 2–6, 2015, Shanghai, China.
Copyright 2015 ACM 978-1-4503-3317-7/15/02 ...$15.00.
http://dx.doi.org/10.1145/2684822.2685305.

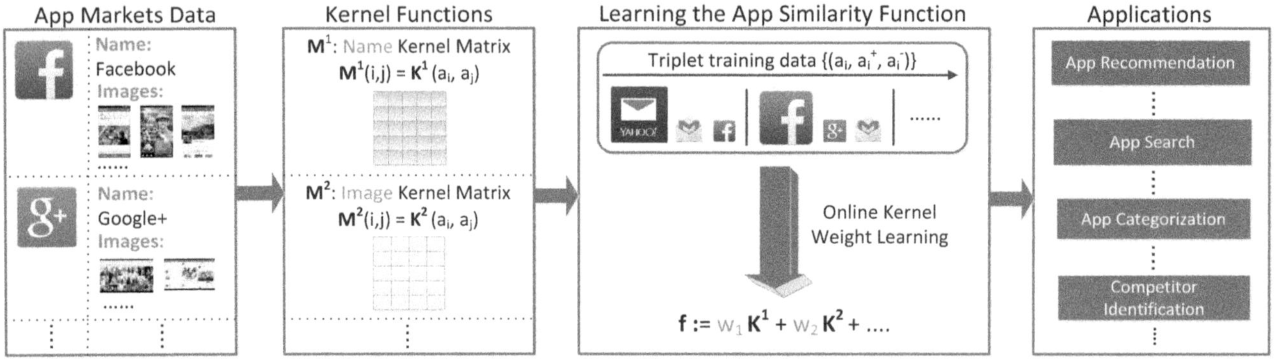

Figure 1: Overview of our proposed SimApp framework. The first block shows the data associated with apps. Only two modalities, i.e., *Name* and *Images*, are presented for illustration. In the second block, we define two kernel functions K^1 and K^2 to measure the pairwise app similarity in modalities of *Name* and *Images*, respectively. In the third block, we learn the optimal combination weights (w_1, w_2, ...) by using our proposed Online Kernel Weight Learning (OKWL) algorithm. The learned app similarity function f can be applied to a variety of applications presented in the last block.

similar app recommendation task. Preliminary empirical results have validated the effectiveness of SimApp in modeling app similarity. Supplementary materials (including datasets, code, etc.) are publicly available at[1].

In summary, this paper makes the following contributions:

- We study the problem of modeling high-level mobile app similarity. To the best of our knowledge, this is the first systematic and comprehensive work that focuses on this problem;
- We present SimApp as a novel framework to tackle this problem, which fuses multi-modal data in app markets by learning the optimal combination weights from streams of training data;
- We conduct an extensive set of experiments to evaluate the performance of SimApp on a real-world dataset.

The rest of the paper is organized as follows: Section 2 discusses related work; Section 3 gives the problem formulation; Section 4 presents SimApp; Section 5 shows the empirical results; finally Section 6 concludes this paper.

2. RELATED WORK

Our work relates to various studies in multiple important research areas, ranging from data mining, machine learning, software engineering to security. In this section, we group related studies into four categories, and survey the literature of each category in detail.

2.1 High-level Software Similarity

Our work **closely** relates to studies on detecting semantically similar software applications. To our best knowledge, there are two lines of related work in this direction.

In [26], Zhu et al. explored the mobile app classification problem, however we aim to address a different problem, i.e., deriving a function to measure the high-level similarity between apps. Thus far, little work has been done on this problem. Two recent studies, which focused on app recommendation, presented simple methods to measure the similarity between apps by using meta-information in app markets [24, 2]. Specifically, Yin et al. [24] treated the description of an app as a document and applied LDA [3] to learn its latent topic distribution. In this way, each app is represented as a fixed length vector. Then, the similarity between two apps is computed as the cosine similarity of their vectors. Similarly, Bhandari et al. [2] linked the title, description and user reviews of an app as one document, and then built the vector using the *tf-idf* weighting scheme. They also used cosine similarity to calculate the pairwise similarity. In contrast, we exploit more types of metadata (e.g., images, numerics, etc.) in app markets, and propose a principled way to combine such multi-modal heterogeneous data to measure the high-level similarity between apps.

Another line of related work is to categorize or detect semantically similar traditional software applications by using low-level data, e.g., source code, byte code, etc [19, 15]. For example, McMillan et al. [15] proposed an approach called CLAN to detect similar Java applications using API calls. Compared with this line of work, our work differs in that we focus on using high-level (not implementation-level) data in app markets to measure the similarity between apps, and propose a very different solution.

2.2 Low-level Software Similarity

Our work is also related to studies on modeling low-level software similarity, e.g., code clone detection [16]. Fragments of code (low-level implementation) are identified as code clones if they are exactly the same as or similar to each other [16]. Many techniques have been developed to detect code clones for traditional software applications [10, 12]. For example, Liu et al. [12] proposed a tool named GPLAG, which applies subgraph isomorphism comparison to Program Dependence Graphs (PDGs) to detect plagiarized (similar) code. Recently, there are some studies focusing on detecting mobile app clones via analyzing byte codes or opcodes [25, 5]. For example, Zhou et al. [25] presented an app similarity measurement system named *DroidMOSS* based on fuzzy hashing technique to detect app clones.

In general, our work differs from works in this area in two aspects. First and foremost, the goal of our problem is different. Our problem aims to find apps that implement similar semantic requirements. Whether two apps are similar or not is determined by the high-level functionalities they perform rather than their low-level implementations. Second, to

[1] https://sites.google.com/site/appsimilarity/

achieve our goal, we explore a very different data source, i.e., app markets, and present a new framework using very different techniques.

2.3 Data Mining with App Markets Data

Our work is in general related to the emerging studies on mining app markets data to facilitate various applications [11, 7, 27, 6, 20]. For example, Lin et al. [11] proposed a framework to incorporate version histories into app recommendation systems. Zhu et al. [27] presented a ranking fraud detection system for apps, which is based on mining apps' historical ranking and rating records.

Although the nature of data studied in the above works is similar to ours, the techniques used and research goals are totally different. Our work aims to use the knowledge discovered from app markets data to detect similar apps.

2.4 Online Learning

In this paper, we explore online learning techniques [9, 17] to learn the best combination weights of various modalities from streams of training data in the form of triplets.

Compared with batch learning, online learning has several advantages, e.g., fast and simple, thus making it applicable to applications in a variety of domains [14, 4, 22, 23, 21]. For example, Chechik el al. [4] proposed an online learning algorithm named OASIS to incrementally learn a better distance metric from image data for retrieval. Compared with the above studies, our work differs in two points. First, we formulate and solve a challenging problem in a completely different domain with its distinct features. Second, the goal of our proposed technique is different, i.e., learning a kernel function from multi-modal heterogeneous data.

Our work is also related to recent work on Online Multiple Kernel Learning (OMKL) [8]. In general, our work differs from studies in this area in two aspects. First, we focus on a more specific problem, i.e., detecting similar apps, and present the SimApp framework to solve it. Second, the OMKL technique aims to learn the optimal weights of multiple kernels for classification tasks, while the goal of our proposed online learning algorithm in SimApp is to learn the app similarity function from streams of triplets.

3. PROBLEM FORMULATION

In this section, we formally formulate the problem of mobile app similarity modeling using app markets data.

DEFINITION 1 (MOBILE APP SIMILARITY MODELING). Given a collection of mobile apps $\mathcal{A}$, the objective of mobile app similarity modeling problem is to learn a function $f : \mathcal{A} \times \mathcal{A} \rightarrow \mathbb{R}_+$, such that $f(a_i, a_j)$ measures the semantic similarity between app a_i and app a_j.

In our problem, two apps are considered to be similar to each other if they implement related semantic requirements. An intuitive example is shown in Figure 2 to better understand our problem. Figure 2 presents the names and logos of four popular apps. Obviously, "Facebook" and "Google+" are both social networking apps, so they are considered to be similar to each other in our problem. In the same way, "Dropbox" is similar to "Google Drive" as both apps are used to store and share files. "Facebook" is not similar to "Dropbox" as they perform very different functionalities. The goal of our problem is to learn a function f, which assigns higher scores to pairs of more similar apps, e.g., f ("Facebook", "Google+") $>$ f ("Facebook", "Dropbox").

Figure 2: Four popular mobile apps.

In Definition 1, a key element is a mobile app $a_i \in \mathcal{A}$, which is defined as follows.

DEFINITION 2 (MOBILE APP). Each mobile app $a_i \in \mathcal{A}$ is modeled as a k-dimensional tuple $a_i = [m_{i1}, m_{i2}, ..., m_{ik}]$, where each $m_{ij} (1 \leq j \leq k)$ is a modality (attribute) of mobile app a_i.

In this work, we explore the multi-modal heterogeneous data in app markets to model apps. Specifically, we use the modalities shown in Table 1 to represent an app, since they are supported by most mainstream app markets. The "Modality" column of Table 1 shows the names of the modalities, and the "Description" column briefly describes these modalities. Figure 3 shows an example of the multi-modal information associated with the "Facebook" app on Google Play. From Table 1 and Figure 3, we can see that, these multi-modal data in general describe high-level characteristics of apps, and thus is suitable for solving the problem presented in Definition 1.

Table 1: The modality set of mobile apps.

ID	Modality	Description
1	Name	The title of the app.
2	Category	The category label of the app.
3	Developer	The developer of the app.
4	Description	The description text of the app.
5	Update	The latest changes to the app.
6	Permissions	The permissions required by the app.
7	Images	The screenshots of the app.
8	Content Rating	The content level of the app.
9	Size	The storage space needed for the app.
10	Reviews	The comments posted by users.

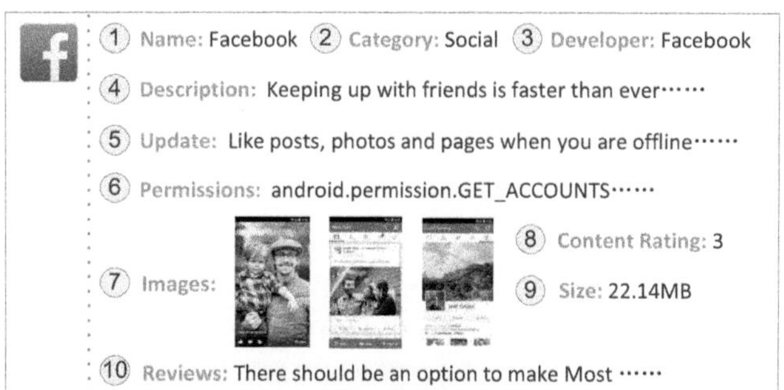

Figure 3: Example of the multi-modal information associated with the "Facebook" app on Google Play. The circled numbers correspond to the IDs shown in Table 1.

4. APP SIMILARITY MODELING

In this section, we propose the SimApp framework for mobile app similarity modeling. As shown in Figure 1, SimApp consists of two stages. First, we define a series of 10 kernel (similarity) functions in different modalities (as shown in Table 1) for measuring the similarity between apps (see Section 4.1). Second, we assume the target app similarity function f is a linear combination of the multiple kernels, and present a novel Online Kernel Weight Learning (OKWL) algorithm to learn the optimal combination weights of these 10 kernels from streams of training triplets (see Section 4.2).

4.1 Kernels for Measuring App Similarity

In machine learning, kernel is essentially a mapping function that transforms a given low-dimensional space into some higher-dimensional (possibly infinite) space. A kernel function can be thought of as a pairwise similarity function. In this subsection, we build a variety of kernel functions, denoted as $K^k(1 \leq k \leq 10)$, to measure app similarity for each modality shown in Table 1. Without loss of generality, all kernel values are within the range of $[0, 1]$.

4.1.1 App Similarity using Name

Each mobile app has a *name* (title), which is given by its developer. Since app name is the first thing potential users see when they browse the app markets, it is often descriptive, explicit, and stating what the app can do for users. When two app names share many common words, it is reasonable to infer that these two apps perform similar functionalities. As app name is essentially a short string of characters, we employ the well-known string kernel [13] to measure the app similarity in this modality. Let s_i and s_j denote the names of app a_i and app a_j, respectively. Then, we have,

$$K^1(a_i, a_j) = \sum_{u \in \Sigma^*} \phi_u(s_i)\phi_u(s_j)$$

where Σ^* denotes the set of all subsequences, u denotes a subsequence, and ϕ is a feature mapping function. For space limitation, please refer to [13] for more details about string kernel. In particular, we set the max length of subsequences equal to 3, and the decay factor equal to 0.5.

4.1.2 App Similarity using Category

To make it more easier for users to browse and discover apps, app markets usually define a list of *categories* to organize apps. In general, apps belong to the same category are more related to each other than apps in other categories. Therefore, we can use such category information to measure the similarity between apps. Let c_i and c_j denote the category labels of app a_i and app a_j, respectively, thus,

$$K^2(a_i, a_j) = \begin{cases} \alpha & \text{if} \quad c_i == c_j \\ 0 & \text{if} \quad c_i \neq c_j \end{cases}$$

where α is a pre-defined parameter. For simplicity, we set α equal to 1.0 in this work.

4.1.3 App Similarity using Developer

Every app is created by one *developer*, who is either an individual or a company. A developer usually maintains a list of apps that belong to different categories in the app market. We collect all the category labels in the app market and build a category dictionary with size d_c. Then, the developer of an app can be converted into a feature vector $\mathbf{d} \in \mathbb{R}^{d_c}$ using the *tf-idf* weighting scheme. Here, *tf* is the number of the developer's apps that belong to a category, and *idf* is the total number of apps in that category. Let $\mathbf{d}_i$ and $\mathbf{d}_j$ represent the developers of app a_i and app a_j, respectively. We measure the app similarity in this modality by using the RBF (radial basis function) kernel, which is usually a reasonable first choice,

$$K^3(a_i, a_j) = exp\left(-\frac{\|\mathbf{d}_i - \mathbf{d}_j\|^2}{2\sigma^2}\right)$$

where σ is the bandwidth parameter. If not specified, we set σ as the average Euclidean distance in this work.

4.1.4 App Similarity using Description

The *description* text of an app usually describes its main functionalities provided for users. If two app descriptions are related to each other, probably there are some function overlaps between these two apps. We collect all the descriptions and treat them as documents. Then, we apply LDA [3] to learn the latent topic distribution for each of them. In this way, the description of an app is represented as a fixed length vector $\mathbf{t} \in \mathbb{R}^{d_t}$, where d_t is the number of discovered topics (we set $d_t = 1000$). The i-th dimension of this vector is the distribution over the i-th topic. Let $\mathbf{t}_i$ and $\mathbf{t}_j$ denote the descriptions of app a_i and app a_j, respectively. We use the normalized liner kernel, which is widely used for text classification, for measuring the app similarity in this modality, formally,

$$K^4(a_i, a_j) = \frac{\mathbf{t}_i^T \mathbf{t}_j}{\|\mathbf{t}_i\| \, \|\mathbf{t}_j\|}$$

Remark. K^4 is exactly the same as the method used in [24] to measure the app similarity. Our purpose in doing so is to make more fair comparisons in our experiments (see Section 5.4). Without loss of generality, the scheme used in K^4 is also employed for other text data in this work.

4.1.5 App Similarity using Update

The *update* text is provided by developers to keep users informed about changes made to the latest version of apps. Following the same scheme used for *description* text, each update of an app is converted into a fixed length vector $\mathbf{u} \in \mathbb{R}^{d_u}$, where d_u is the number of latent topics (we set $d_u = 1000$). Let $\mathbf{u}_i$ and $\mathbf{u}_j$ denote the updates of app a_i and app a_j, respectively. Then, we measure the app similarity in this modality by using the normalized liner kernel,

$$K^5(a_i, a_j) = \frac{\mathbf{u}_i^T \mathbf{u}_j}{\|\mathbf{u}_i\| \, \|\mathbf{u}_j\|}$$

4.1.6 App Similarity using Permissions

Each app has a list of *permissions* that it needs to access specific functionalities or information on users' smart phones. To represent the permissions of an app, we use the well-known bag-of-word (BoW) model. First, we collect all the permissions and compile a permission dictionary with size d_p. Then, the permissions of an app are transformed into a feature vector in $\mathbb{R}^{d_p}$ using the *tf-idf* weighting scheme. In such a way, an app a_i can be represented by a feature vector $\mathbf{p}_i \in \mathbb{R}^{d_p}$. We also use the RBF kernel to measure the app similarity in the permission space, formally,

$$K^6(a_i, a_j) = exp\left(-\frac{\|\mathbf{p}_i - \mathbf{p}_j\|^2}{2\sigma^2}\right)$$

4.1.7 App Similarity using Images

In app markets, app developers can upload some screenshot images to show their apps' features and functionalities. We use the bag-of-(visual) word model for visual feature representation. Specifically, we first compute the SIFT descriptors for each screenshot image. Then, we apply the K-means algorithm over all the SIFT descriptors, and obtain d_i (we set $d_i = 2000$) clusters as the visual words. Finally, each given image is represented as a histogram of visual words, i.e., a fixed length feature vector $\mathbf{i} \in \mathbb{R}^{d_i}$. Since an app a usually has more than one screenshot image, we use the centroid of all images belong to app a to represent it in the visual space, formally,

$$\bar{\mathbf{a}} = \sum_m \frac{\mathbf{i}_m}{|a|}$$

where $\mathbf{i}_m$ denotes one image of app a, and $|a|$ is the total number of images that belong to app a. We measure the visual similarity between two apps a_i and a_j using the RBF kernel, formally,

$$K^7(a_i, a_j) = exp\left(-\frac{\|\bar{\mathbf{a}}_i - \bar{\mathbf{a}}_j\|^2}{2\sigma^2}\right)$$

4.1.8 App Similarity using Content Rating

The *content rating* of an app provides users concise and impartial information about the content and age appropriateness of this app. Let cr_i and cr_j denote the content ratings of app a_i and app a_j, respectively. The similarity between a_i and a_j in this modality is given by,

$$K^8(a_i, a_j) = \begin{cases} \beta^{|cr_i - cr_j|} & \text{if} \quad |cr_i - cr_j| < cr_{max} - cr_{min} \\ 0 & \text{if} \quad |cr_i - cr_j| == cr_{max} - cr_{min} \end{cases}$$

where cr_{max} and cr_{min} are the maximum rating and minimum rating, respectively, in the target app market content rating system. β is a decay paratemer which we set equal to 1/3 in this work.

4.1.9 App Similarity using Size

The *size* information indicates the storage space required by the apps. Two apps have large difference in size tend to be not similar to each other. Let s_i and s_j denote the size of app a_i and app a_j, respectively. We measure the similarity between a_i and a_j in this modality as follows,

$$K^9(a_i, a_j) = exp\left(-\frac{|s_i - s_j|}{\gamma}\right)$$

where we set γ as the median size (unit: MB) of all apps in our data collection.

4.1.10 App Similarity using Reviews

User review is a crucial component of app markets. Each app usually has a list of reviews posted by different users. These user reviews contain rich information on various aspects of apps (such as functionality, quality, performance, etc.), thus could be useful for measuring app similarity. To represent the reviews of an app, we concatenate all the reviews of one app together as a document. Then, following the same scheme employed for *description* and *update* text, for each app a_i, we denote $\mathbf{r}_i \in \mathbb{R}^{d_r}$ as its review topics distribution, where d_r is the number of discovered topics (we set $d_r = 1000$). Finally, we employ the normalized liner kernel to quantify the app similarity in this modality,

$$K^{10}(a_i, a_j) = \frac{\mathbf{r}_i^T \mathbf{r}_j}{\|\mathbf{r}_i\| \, \|\mathbf{r}_j\|}$$

4.2 Learning Optimal Weights for Kernels

In the previous subsection, we introduce various kernel functions ($K^1 \sim K^{10}$) to measure the similarity between apps in different modalities. The next challenge is how to find the best way to combine these kernels. In this work, we assume the target app similarity function f is a linear combination of the multiple kernels, i.e.,

$$K(a_i, a_j; \mathbf{w}) = \sum_{k=1}^{n} w_k K^k(a_i, a_j) \tag{1}$$

where a_i and a_j are the i-th and j-th app, respectively. $K(a_i, a_j; \mathbf{w})$ represents the target app similarity function f. K^k is the kernel defined under the k-th view (modality) of apps, n is the total number of kernels, and $\mathbf{w} \in \mathbb{R}^n$ is the weight vector with each element w_k represents the weight of the k-th kernel.

One simple way is to let humans assign the weights of different kernels. However, such strategy depends too much on domain knowledge and often cannot find the best combination. Therefore, in this work, we explore online learning techniques to learn the optimum combination weights $\mathbf{w}$ from streams of triplets. The reasons we choose the online learning scheme are that (i) it can avoid the expensive re-training cost when new training data arrives; and (ii) it is highly efficient and scalable for large scale applications.

4.2.1 Relative Similarity Learning

In the training phase, we assume a collection of training instances is given sequentially in the form of triplet [4], i.e.,

$$\mathcal{T} = \{(a_i, a_i^+, a_i^-), i = 1, ..., m\}$$

where each triplet (a_i, a_i^+, a_i^-) indicates that app a_i is more semantically similar to app a_i^+ than a_i^-. Here m is the total number of triplets in the training data. We aim to learn the target app similarity function $K(a_i, a_j; \mathbf{w})$ in Equation (1), which assigns higher similarity scores to pairs of more relevant apps, i.e.,

$$K(a_i, a_i^+) > K(a_i, a_i^-), (a_i, a_i^+, a_i^-); \forall i$$

In such a triplet setting, we only need to give the relative order of similarity rather than an exact measure of similarity, thus is more feasible in practice. Such triplet instances can be generated in practice as follows. Let $\mathcal{A}$ denote a set of training apps. In the 1st step, for each app $a_i \in \mathcal{A}$, we need to create a list of apps that are relevant to a_i, denoted as $L(a_i)$. This can be achieved through various ways. For example, we can use existing app search engines to find apps that share the same query. In the 2nd step, in order to build a training triplet (a_i, a_i^+, a_i^-), we can first uniformly sample an app a_i from $\mathcal{A}$; then uniformly sample an app a_i^+ from $L(a_i)$; and finally uniformly sample an app a_i^- from $\mathcal{A} - L(a_i)$.

4.2.2 Online Kernel Weight Learning Algorithm

We propose an online kernel learning algorithm which is an application of the stochastic sub-gradient method [18]. The algorithm learns from side information in the form of triplet as described above. Our goal is to learn a similarity function $K(a_i, a_j; \mathbf{w})$, for all triplets in $\mathcal{T}$ satisfying,

$$K(a_i, a_i^+) > K(a_i, a_i^-) + \epsilon$$

where ϵ is a margin factor (should be positive) which is set equal to 1.0 in our experiments. For each triplet (a_i, a_i^+, a_i^-), we define the following hinge loss,

$$\begin{aligned} l(a_i, a_i^+, a_i^-) &= max\{0, \epsilon - K(a_i, a_i^+) + K(a_i, a_i^-)\} \\ &= max\{0, \epsilon - \mathbf{w} \cdot \mathbf{s}_i^+ + \mathbf{w} \cdot \mathbf{s}_i^-\} \end{aligned}$$

where $\mathbf{s}_i^+ = [K^1(a_i, a_i^+), ..., K^k(a_i, a_i^+), ..., K^n(a_i, a_i^+)]^T$ and $\mathbf{s}_i^- = [K^1(a_i, a_i^-), ..., K^k(a_i, a_i^-), ..., K^n(a_i, a_i^-)]^T$.

Our goal is to find the minimizer of the object function,

$$\min_{\mathbf{w}} \frac{\lambda}{2} \|\mathbf{w}\|^2 + \frac{1}{m} \sum_{i=1}^{m} l(a_i, a_i^+, a_i^-) \tag{2}$$

where λ is a regulization parameter.

Algorithm 1: Online Kernel Weight Learning

Input: $\mathcal{T}$, λ, T, η_0

1 Initialize weights: $w_{1,k} = 1/n, \forall k = 1, ..., n$

2 **for** $t = 1, 2, ..., T$ **do**

3   Set $\eta_t = \eta_0/(1 + \lambda\eta_0 t)$.

4   Receive one triplet $(a_{i_t}, a_{i_t}^+, a_{i_t}^-)$ from $\mathcal{T}$.

5   Compute $\mathbf{s}_{i_t}^+$ and $\mathbf{s}_{i_t}^-$.

6   **if** $w_t \cdot s_{i_t}^+ - w_t \cdot s_{i_t}^- \geqslant \epsilon$ **then**

7   update $\mathbf{w}_{t+1} \leftarrow (1 - \eta_t\lambda)\mathbf{w}_t$

8   **end**

9   **else if** $w_t \cdot s_{i_t}^+ - w_t \cdot s_{i_t}^- < \epsilon$ **then**

10   update $\mathbf{w}_{t+1} \leftarrow (1 - \eta_t\lambda)\mathbf{w}_t + \eta_t(\mathbf{s}_{i_t}^+ - \mathbf{s}_{i_t}^-)$

11   **end**

12 **end**

Output: $\mathbf{w}_{T+1}$

Next, we describe the core procedure of our proposed Online Kernel Weight Learning (OKWL) algorithm for solving the optimization problem given in Equation (2) in detail.

Algorithm 1 shows the pseudo-code of the OKWL algorithm. The inputs include (i) a set of training triplets $\mathcal{T}$; (ii) a regulization parameter λ; (iii) a learning rate constant η_0; and (iv) the number of iterations T. Among them, the proper η_0 can be determined experimentally by using a sample of training triplets. Initially, we set $\mathbf{w}_1 = [w_{1,1}, ..., w_{1,k}, ..., w_{1,n}]^T$, where $w_{1,k} = 1/n, \forall k = 1, ..., n$, n is the number of kernels, so each kernel is assigned the same weight (Line 1). For each training iteration t, we first set the learning rate $\eta_t = \eta_0/(1+\lambda\eta_0 t)$ (Line 3). Then, for a triplet $(a_{i_t}, a_{i_t}^+, a_{i_t}^-)$ received from $\mathcal{T}$ (Line 4), we compute $\mathbf{s}_{i_t}^+$ and $\mathbf{s}_{i_t}^-$, respectively (Line 5). The objective function based on this triplet is:

$$\mathcal{L}(\mathbf{w}; i_t) = \frac{\lambda}{2} \|\mathbf{w}\|^2 + l(\mathbf{w}; (a_{i_t}, a_{i_t}^+, a_{i_t}^-)) \tag{3}$$

Then, the sub-gradient of $\mathcal{L}(\mathbf{w}; i_t)$ with respect to $\mathbf{w}$ is given by:

$$\nabla_t = \frac{\partial \mathcal{L}(\mathbf{w}; i_t)}{\partial \mathbf{w}} = \begin{cases} \lambda \mathbf{w}_t & \text{if } \mathbf{w}_t \cdot (\mathbf{s}_{i_t}^+ - \mathbf{s}_{i_t}^-) \geqslant \epsilon \\ \lambda \mathbf{w}_t + \mathbf{s}_{i_t}^- - \mathbf{s}_{i_t}^+ & \text{if } \mathbf{w}_t \cdot (\mathbf{s}_{i_t}^+ - \mathbf{s}_{i_t}^-) < \epsilon \end{cases}$$

We then update $\mathbf{w}_{t+1} \leftarrow \mathbf{w}_t - \eta_t \nabla_t$ (Line 6-11), formally:

$$\mathbf{w}_{t+1} = \begin{cases} (1 - \eta_t\lambda)\mathbf{w}_t & \text{if } \mathbf{w}_t \cdot (\mathbf{s}_{i_t}^+ - \mathbf{s}_{i_t}^-) \geqslant \epsilon \\ (1 - \eta_t\lambda)\mathbf{w}_t + \eta_t(\mathbf{s}_{i_t}^+ - \mathbf{s}_{i_t}^-) & \text{if } \mathbf{w}_t \cdot (\mathbf{s}_{i_t}^+ - \mathbf{s}_{i_t}^-) < \epsilon \end{cases}$$

Finally, after the predefined T iterations, we output the learned weight vector $\mathbf{w}_{T+1}$ as the optimal combination of different kernels.

5. EMPIRICAL EVALUATION

In this section, we report the results of an extensive set of experiments based on a similar app recommendation task.

5.1 Dataset

Our empirical evaluation is based on a real-world dataset crawled from Google Play. For each app, we collected all the data (associated with it) available on Google Play, including app name, description, screenshots, user reviews, etc. Note that, each kernel function defined in Section 4.1 corresponds to a specific kind of data we have collected. This yielded a dataset that consists of 21,624 apps from 42 different categories. We think such a scale is enough to work with to draw solid conclusions. The "Total" column of Table 2 shows some statistics of the whole dataset. To facilitate our empirical studies, we further split the whole dataset into a training set and a test set (see "Training" and "Test" columns in Table 2). Specifically, from each of the 42 categories, we randomly choose about 80% of the apps in the category as the training data and the remaining as the test data.

Table 2: Some statistics of the Google Play dataset. The notation "#" represents the number of some object.

Set	Training	Test	Total
# Apps	16,955	4,669	21,624
# Permissions	153,639	42,869	196,508
# Reviews	16,872,290	5,037,246	21,909,536
# Images	136,792	37,601	174,393

5.2 Evaluation Measures

We introduce the evaluation metrics used in our empirical studies. For each query app, all other apps are ranked according to their similarities to the query app. Thus, we adopt two rank-based metrics, i.e., Precision@K and mean Average Precision (mAP), which are presented below,

- **Precision@K:** For each query app, we compute the proportion of similar apps in the top-K results. When averaged across all query apps, this yields the Precision@K measure.

- **mean Average Precision:** mAP for a set of app queries is the mean of the average precision scores for each app query, i.e.,

$$mAP = \frac{\sum_{q=1}^{Q} AveP(q)}{Q}$$

where Q is the number of app queries, and $AveP(q)$ is the average precision for an app query q. Average precision for each app query is the average value of all the precision values from the rank positions that have a similar app.

Table 3: The base kernels and the optimal weights learned by OKWL ($\eta_0 = 0.01, \lambda = 10^{-4}, T = 100K$). The largest weight is in blue color, and the lowest weight is in red color.

Kernel	K^1	K^2	K^3	K^4	K^5	K^6	K^7	K^8	K^9	K^{10}
Modality	Name	Category	Developer	Description	Update	Permissions	Images	Content Rating	Size	Reviews
Weight	0.1679	0.1676	0.0827	0.1288	0.0455	0.0027	0.0960	0.0394	0.0353	0.2338

5.3 Experimental Setup

5.3.1 Build an App-App Relevance Matrix

To quantitatively evaluate SimApp, we need to create an app-app relevance matrix $\mathbf{R}_{AA}$ as our ground truth labels. Google Play has a *"Similar"* functionality, which recommends users a list of similar apps for each app. We collected a set of m such lists $L = \{l_1, l_2, ..., l_m\}$ from the web portal of Google Play, where $l_k (1 \leq k \leq m)$ is the k-th list. Given two apps a_i and a_j, let $freq(a_i, a_j)$ denote the number of lists they both appear in. We consider a_i and a_j are similar to each other if and only if $freq(a_i, a_j)$ exceeds a threshold θ (which is used to reduce noise), formally,

$$\mathbf{R}_{AA}(a_i, a_j) = \begin{cases} 1 & if \quad freq(a_i, a_j) \geq \theta \\ 0 & if \quad freq(a_i, a_j) < \theta \end{cases}$$

For the training set and the test set shown in Table 2, we build two matrices $\mathbf{R}_{AA}^{train}$ and $\mathbf{R}_{AA}^{test}$, respectively, where we use the threshold $\theta = 2$.

5.3.2 Training Triplets Sampling

We use $\mathbf{R}_{AA}^{train}$ to sample training triplets $\mathcal{T}' = \{(a_i, a_i^+, a_i^-), i = 1, ..., m\}$ as follows. Let $\mathcal{A}$ be all the apps in the training set. First of all, we randomly sample an app a_i from $\mathcal{A}$. Then we uniformly sample an app a_i^+ from the set of apps which are similar to a_i ($\mathbf{R}_{AA}^{train}(a_i, a_i^+) = 1$). Finally, we uniformly sample an app a_i^- from the set of apps which are not similar to a_i ($\mathbf{R}_{AA}^{train}(a_i, a_i^-) = 0$). In such a way, we generate a set of 100K training triplets $\mathcal{T}'$ which is used to train OKWL in our experiments.

5.3.3 Choose the Learning Rate Constant

The learning rate constant η_0 is a key parameter of the OKWL algorithm, which is determined experimentally as follows. Given the training triplets $\mathcal{T}'$, we fix $\lambda = 10^{-4}$, $T = 30K$, and then run OKWL with different values of $\eta_0 \in [0.0001, 0.1]$. Figure 4 traces the training error over the training triplets as it progresses during learning. From the results shown in Figure 4, we can see that, larger values of η_0 (i.e., 0.1 and 0.01) are more attractive, because OKWL (i) achieves better asymptotic performance; and (ii) converges much faster. Between 0.1 and 0.01, to make OKWL more robust, we choose $\eta_0 = 0.01$ as its training error curve shown in Figure 4 is more smooth.

5.3.4 Compared Methods

We compared the following methods in our experiments:

- Single: A single kernel defined in Section 4.1. We examine $K^1 \sim K^{10}$ one by one.
- Uniform: $K^1 \sim K^{10}$ are uniformly combined with each kernel assigned the same weight.
- SimApp: We use the proposed OKWL algorithm for combining $K^1 \sim K^{10}$. Specifically, we run OKWL with $\eta_0 = 0.01, \lambda = 10^{-4}$ and $T = 100K$, the learned weights of kernels $K^1 \sim K^{10}$ are presented in Table 3.

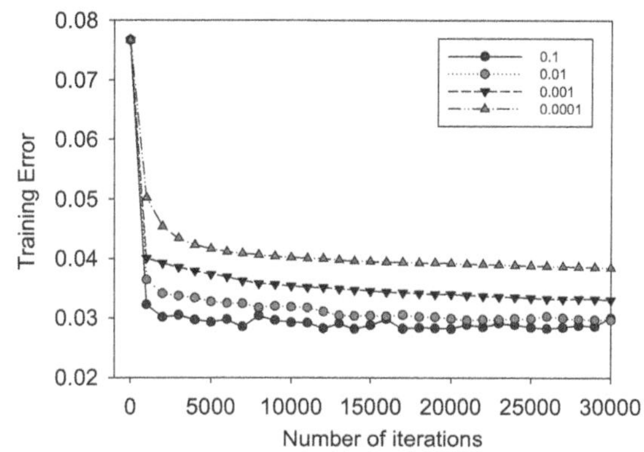

Figure 4: Training error of OKWL as a function of the number of iterations. $\eta_0 \in \{0.1, 0.01, 0.001, 0.0001\}$.

5.4 Quantitative Results

We evaluate the efficacy of SimApp by measuring the similar app recommendation accuracy. Specifically, for each query app in the test set shown in Table 2, we rank all other test apps according to their similarities to the query app, and extract top ones as recommended apps.

In the **first** experiment, we evaluate and compare all the methods listed in Section 5.3.4 in terms of Precision@K ($1 \leq K \leq 5$). We use $\mathbf{R}_{AA}^{test}$ (described in Section 5.3.1) as the ground truth. Since the largest K value in this experiment is 5, we only use test apps that have at least 5 similar apps as query apps, thus resulting in a total of 1910 query apps. Figure 5 shows the top-K app recommendation results, from which we can draw some observations.

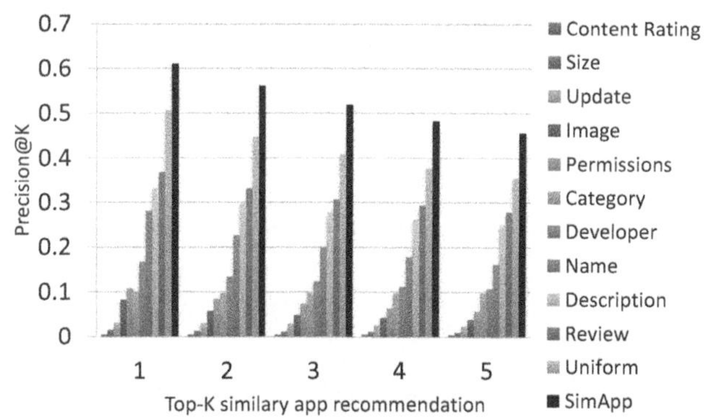

Figure 5: The average precision of top-K similar app recommendation (better viewed in color).

First of all, with K varying from 1 to 5, SimApp always achieves the best performance among all the evaluated methods. By looking into the results, we find that (i) compared with *Uniform* combination, SimApp improves the precision scores by more than 20%; and (ii) the top-1 and top-5 precision scores achieved by SimApp are 0.610 and 0.455, respectively. Such fair results indicate that SimApp is able to model the app similarity.

Second, the *Uniform* combination performs better than all the single kernels ($K^1 \sim K^{10}$), and reports the second best results. This fact indicates that the idea of combining different modalities is helpful in measuring app similarity. However, such kind of naive combination cannot yield the best results, thus learning the weights of different modalities in an effective way is needed.

Third, the *Reviews* kernel (K^{10}) reports the best performance among all the single kernels. Its relatively good results indicate that user review is the most informative modality when measuring app similarity. Two possible reasons are: (i) users often discuss functionalities of apps in the reviews; (ii) users tend to compare apps with their similar competitors in their reviews.

Fourth, the *Description* kernel (K^4) attains the second best results among all the single kernels. Note that, K^4 is used in [24] as a part of their app recommendation system. From Figure 5, we can see that, SimApp performs much better than K^4. For example, SimApp achieves 0.610 while K^4 only achieves 0.331 in terms of Precision@1. This fact indicates that SimApp can improve the overall performance of the app recommendation system proposed in [24].

Finally, the *Content Rating* kernel (K^8) and the *Size* kernel (K^9) report the worst performance among the 10 single kernels. For K from 1 to 5, their precision scores are most zero consistently. Such results indicate that *Content Rating* and *Size* are the least useful modalities.

In the **second** experiment, we evaluate and compare all the methods listed in Section 5.3.4 in terms of mAP. We also use $\mathbf{R}_{AA}^{test}$ as the ground truth and all the apps (that have at least one similar app) in the test set shown in Table 2 as query apps. The mAP results are presented in Figure 6, from which we can draw two observations.

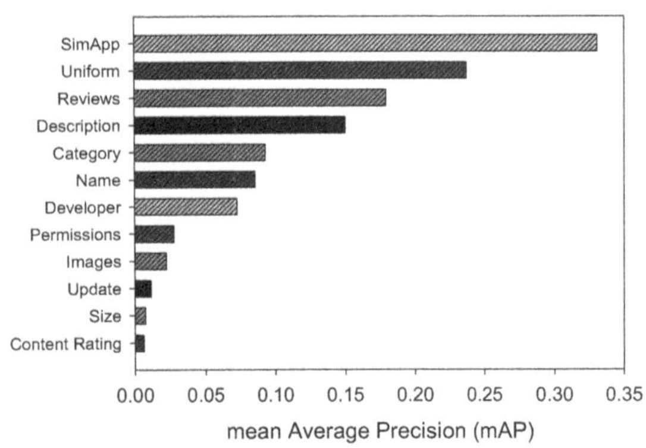

Figure 6: Evaluation of the mAP performance.

First of all, SimApp again performs the best among all the evaluated methods, which further validates its efficacy in app similarity modeling.

Second, the mAP results attained by all the methods are not high, e.g., 0.331 achieved by SimApp. This could be the result of several reasons. Most importantly, our labels that measure the pairwise app similarity (i.e., $\mathbf{R}_{AA}^{test}$) may be partial. This means that some pairs of apps that are similar to each other are not labeled as such; while some pairs of apps that are not similar to each other are labeled as such. The partial labels would lead to an underestimate of the performance of SimApp (in terms of both mAP and Precision@K). To obtain a more accurate estimate of the real power of SimApp, we conduct a human evaluation experiment which is presented in the next subsection.

5.5 Human Evaluation Experiment

5.5.1 Setup

We choose a subset of test apps as query apps used in this experiment as follows. For each test app in the test set, we retrieve its top-10 similar apps as determined by Google Play's (web portal) *"Similar"* functionality ("Google Play" in short). If all these 10 similar apps exist in our whole dataset shown in Table 2, we select this test app as a candidate query app. In such a way, we get a set of candidate query apps covering 32 different categories. Then, for each of the 32 categories, we randomly select one query app from the candidates, thus obtaining a total number of 32 query apps.

For each query app, apart from the top-10 similar apps as ranked by Google Play (verified on July 9th, 2014), we also retrieved its top-10 similar apps (from the whole dataset) as determined by SimApp (using the weights shown in Table 3). All 32 query apps were presented to two human annotators (the first and the third authors), asking them to label which of the 20 retrieved apps are semantically similar to the query app. The two annotators made the first round of labeling independently, then had a discussion on those inconsistent cases, and finally reached an agreement. We collected the final labeling results and calculated Precision@K values.

5.5.2 Results

Table 4 shows the average precisions across all 32 query apps. From the results shown in Table 4, we can draw the following observations. First, SimApp consistently achieves better results than Google Play throughout the full range of K evaluated. Second, SimApp attains 0.875 and 0.819 in terms of Precision@1 and Precision@5, respectively, which are much higher than the values calculated using $\mathbf{R}_{AA}^{test}$ as shown in Figure 5. Such good results indicate that SimApp is effective in modeling app similarity, and potentially valuable for stakeholders in the mobile app ecosystem (even for those who have built some app similarity functions).

Table 4: Precision@1, @5, @10 of Google Play and SimApp.

	Precision@1	Precision@5	Precision@10
Google Play	0.688	0.725	0.663
SimApp	**0.875**	**0.819**	**0.769**

Threats to Validity. Despite the encouraging results, this study has three threats to validity. First, Google Play's *"Similar"* function is a "black box" to us, it may consider more factors (e.g., popularity) than just similarity measure, thus may influence the comparison results. Second, our dataset is relatively small, which makes it difficult for SimApp to retrieve similar apps for some query apps, thus lowering SimApp's performance. Third, the limited number of query apps and subjectivity (due to expensive cost of labeling) may affect the accuracy of the results. We plan to examine these threats in great efforts in our future work.

Next, in Figure 7, we show two successful (failure) cases of SimApp (Google Play). The first column of Figure 7 shows two query apps, i.e., "AntiVirus Security - FREE" (antivirus app) and "Subway Surfers" (parkour game). For each query app, we list two lines of top-10 results, where the upper line is ranked by Google Play, and the lower line is ranked by

Figure 7: Two examples of top-10 recommended similar apps (better viewed in color).

SimApp. The name of each app is shown beneath the app logo. One app is similar (not similar) to the query app if its name is in black (red) color.

The **first** example presents the query app "AntiVirus Security - FREE". The top-10 results ranked by Google Play are bad, since only "Lookout Security & Antivirus" (5th) and "Free Antivirus & Security" (10th) are similar to the query app, and the rest 8 apps bear no semantic similarity as they are either communication tools or web browsers. In contrast, SimApp achieves much better results. All 10 apps ranked high provide antivirus functionalities, and thus are similar to the query app. In the following, we illustrate the behaviour of SimApp and explain why it performs well in this example via the results shown in Table 5.

Table 5 presents the similarity scores between the query app "AntiVirus Security - FREE" (denoted as q) and a list of apps computed by SimApp. The "Apps" row of Table 5 lists 10 apps, where apps $a_1 \sim a_5$ and $a_6 \sim a_{10}$ are the top-5 apps ranked by SimApp and Google Play, respectively (shown in Figure 7). Every cell (a_i, K^j) $(i, j \in [1, 10])$ in Table 5 represents the kernel value $K^j(a_i, q)$, which measures the similarity between a_i and q in the j-th modality. The "Total" row shows the overall similarity scores computed by using the kernel weights shown in Table 3. The "Rank" row presents the rank positions given by SimApp.

Some observations can be drawn from the results shown in Table 5. First, app a_1 "AntiVirus PRO Android Security" is reasonably ranked 1st by SimApp, since most kernel values $K^j(a_1, q)(j \in [1, 10])$ are high. Second, app a_6 "WhatsApp Messenger" (not similar to q), which is ranked 1st by Google Play, is reasonably ranked much lower by SimApp (401st). The reason is that, although $K^2(a_6, q) = 1.00$, other kernel (especially kernel with large weight) values are low, e.g., $K^{10}(a_6, q) = 0.07$. Similarly, for apps a_7, a_8, a_9 (all are not similar to q), which are ranked high by Google Play, SimApp also correctly assigns them low ranking positions.

The **second** example shown in Figure 7 presents the query app "Subway Surfers", which is a popular parkour game. The top-10 results ranked by Google Play are also not very good. Half of top-10 results are not semantically similar to the query app as they are not parkour games. For example, the ranked 1st game "Fruit Ninja Free" is a popular juicy action game. SimApp again attains much better results than Google Play. All top-10 results share the same concept with the query app, i.e., "running".

6. CONCLUSION AND FUTURE WORK

This paper presents SimApp, a novel framework for finding similar mobile apps. We found encouraging results from a set of experiments, which not only validate the efficacy but also show the potential application prospect of our technique. In the future, we plan to (i) explore more modalities of apps; and (ii) apply our technique to solve other challenging tasks, e.g., finer-granularity app categorization.

7. ACKNOWLEDGMENTS

This work was supported by a grant (ARC19/14) from MOE, Singapore and a gift from Microsoft Research Asia. Steven HOI's work is funded through a research grant 14-C220-SMU-016 from MOE's AcRF Tier 1 funding support through Singapore Management University. We thank the anonymous reviewers for their greatly helpful comments.

8. REFERENCES

[1] App Annie Special Report: A Look at the Growth of Google Play. `http://blog.appannie.com/google-io-special-report-launch-2014/`.

[2] U. Bhandari, K. Sugiyama, A. Datta, and R. Jindal. Serendipitous recommendation for mobile apps using item-item similarity graph. In *AIRS*, pages 440–451, 2013.

[3] D. M. Blei, A. Y. Ng, and M. I. Jordan. Latent dirichlet allocation. *JMLR*, 3:993–1022, Mar. 2003.

[4] G. Chechik, V. Sharma, U. Shalit, and S. Bengio. Large scale online learning of image similarity through ranking. *JMLR*, 11:1109–1135, Mar. 2010.

[5] K. Chen, P. Liu, and Y. Zhang. Achieving accuracy and scalability simultaneously in detecting application clones on android markets. In *ICSE*, pages 175–186, 2014.

Table 5: Similarity scores (computed by SimApp) between the query app "AntiVirus Security - FREE" and a list of apps. $K^1 \sim K^{10}$ are defined in Section 4.1. Kernel values larger than 0.5 are in bold blue. "AntiVirus PRO", "Tablet AntiVirus" and "Lookout" are short for "AntiVirus PRO Android Security", "Tablet AntiVirus Security FREE" and "Lookout Security & Antivirus", respectively.

	Top-5 apps ranked by SimApp					Top-5 apps ranked by Google Play				
Apps	AntiVirus PRO (a_1)	Tablet AntiVirus (a_2)	Anti-Virus (a_3)	Antivirus for Android (a_4)	360 Security (a_5)	WhatsApp Messenger (a_6)	LINE (a_7)	Skype (a_8)	Viber (a_9)	Lookout (a_{10})
K^1 (Name)	0.43	0.68	0.18	0.20	0.50	0.03	0.02	0.04	0.06	0.13
K^2 (Category)	1.00	0.00	1.00	1.00	0.00	1.00	1.00	1.00	1.00	0.00
K^3 (Developer)	1.00	1.00	0.56	0.37	0.81	0.44	0.62	0.40	0.15	0.40
K^4 (Desc.)	0.95	0.93	0.83	0.72	0.80	0.03	0.17	0.10	0.05	0.75
K^5 (Update)	0.80	0.29	0.43	0.37	0.52	0.32	0.46	0.55	0.37	0.51
K^6 (Perm.)	1.00	0.99	0.53	0.29	0.65	0.43	0.45	0.51	0.56	0.59
K^7 (Images)	0.62	0.72	0.48	0.41	0.37	0.26	0.39	0.31	0.33	0.58
K^8 (Content)	1.00	1.00	1.00	0.33	1.00	0.33	0.33	0.33	0.33	1.00
K^9 (Size)	0.99	0.83	0.41	0.38	0.96	0.44	0.16	0.27	0.18	0.63
K^{10} (Reviews)	0.84	0.97	0.68	0.90	0.83	0.07	0.04	0.02	0.02	0.49
Total	0.81	0.70	0.63	0.62	0.58	0.30	0.33	0.31	0.27	0.41
Rank	1	2	3	4	5	401	137	311	615	57

[6] N. Chen, J. Lin, S. C. H. Hoi, X. Xiao, and B. Zhang. Ar-miner: Mining informative reviews for developers from mobile app marketplace. In *ICSE*, pages 767–778, 2014.

[7] Y. Chen, H. Xu, Y. Zhou, and S. Zhu. Is this app safe for children?: A comparison study of maturity ratings on android and ios applications. In *WWW*, pages 201–212, 2013.

[8] S. C. Hoi, R. Jin, P. Zhao, and T. Yang. Online multiple kernel classification. *Mach. Learn.*, 90(2):289–316, Feb. 2013.

[9] S. C. Hoi, J. Wang, and P. Zhao. Libol: A library for online learning algorithms. *JMLR*, 15:495–499, 2014.

[10] Z. Li, S. Lu, S. Myagmar, and Y. Zhou. Cp-miner: Finding copy-paste and related bugs in large-scale software code. *IEEE Trans. Softw. Eng.*, 32(3):176–192, 2006.

[11] J. Lin, K. Sugiyama, M.-Y. Kan, and T.-S. Chua. New and improved: Modeling versions to improve app recommendation. In *SIGIR*, pages 647–656, 2014.

[12] C. Liu, C. Chen, J. Han, and P. S. Yu. Gplag: Detection of software plagiarism by program dependence graph analysis. In *KDD*, pages 872–881, 2006.

[13] H. Lodhi, C. Saunders, J. Shawe-Taylor, N. Cristianini, and C. Watkins. Text classification using string kernels. *JMLR*, 2:419–444, Mar. 2002.

[14] J. Ma, L. K. Saul, S. Savage, and G. M. Voelker. Identifying suspicious urls: An application of large-scale online learning. In *ICML*, pages 681–688, 2009.

[15] C. McMillan, M. Grechanik, and D. Poshyvanyk. Detecting similar software applications. In *ICSE*, pages 364–374, 2012.

[16] C. K. Roy and J. R. Cordy. A survey on software clone detection research. *SCHOOL OF COMPUTING TR 2007-541, QUEEN'S UNIVERSITY*, 115, 2007.

[17] S. Shalev-Shwartz. Online learning and online convex optimization. *Found. Trends Mach. Learn.*, 4(2):107–194, Feb. 2012.

[18] J. C. Spall. *Introduction to Stochastic Search and Optimization*. John Wiley & Sons, Inc., New York, NY, USA, 1 edition, 2003.

[19] S. Ugurel, R. Krovetz, and C. L. Giles. What's the code?: Automatic classification of source code archives. In *KDD*, pages 632–638, 2002.

[20] N. Viennot, E. Garcia, and J. Nieh. A measurement study of google play. In *SIGMETRICS*, pages 221–233, 2014.

[21] P. Wu, S. C. H. Hoi, H. Xia, P. Zhao, D. Wang, and C. Miao. Online multimodal deep similarity learning with application to image retrieval. In *MM*, pages 153–162, 2013.

[22] H. Xia, S. C. H. Hoi, R. Jin, and P. Zhao. Online multiple kernel similarity learning for visual search. *IEEE Trans. Pattern Anal. Mach. Intell.*, 36(3):536–549, 2014.

[23] H. Xia, P. Wu, and S. C. H. Hoi. Online multi-modal distance learning for scalable multimedia retrieval. In *WSDM*, pages 455–464, 2013.

[24] P. Yin, P. Luo, W.-C. Lee, and M. Wang. App recommendation: A contest between satisfaction and temptation. In *WSDM*, pages 395–404, 2013.

[25] W. Zhou, Y. Zhou, X. Jiang, and P. Ning. Detecting repackaged smartphone applications in third-party android marketplaces. In *CODASPY*, pages 317–326, 2012.

[26] H. Zhu, H. Cao, E. Chen, H. Xiong, and J. Tian. Mobile app classification with enriched contextual information. *TMC*, 2013.

[27] H. Zhu, H. Xiong, Y. Ge, and E. Chen. Ranking fraud detection for mobile apps: A holistic view. In *CIKM*, pages 619–628, 2013.

Personalized Mobile App Recommendation: Reconciling App Functionality and User Privacy Preference

Bin Liu*
Rutgers University
binben.liu@rutgers.edu

Deguang Kong
Samsung Research America
deguang.k@samsung.com

Lei Cen
Purdue University
lcen@purdue.edu

Neil Zhenqiang Gong
UC Berkeley
neilz.gong@berkeley.edu

Hongxia Jin
Samsung Research America
hongxia@acm.org

Hui Xiong
Rutgers University
hxiong@rutgers.edu

ABSTRACT

Recent years have witnessed a rapid adoption of mobile devices and a dramatic proliferation of mobile applications (Apps for brevity). However, the large number of mobile Apps makes it difficult for users to locate relevant Apps. Therefore, recommending Apps becomes an urgent task. Traditional recommendation approaches focus on learning the *interest* of a user and the *functionality* of an item (*e.g.*, an App) from a set of user-item ratings, and they recommend an item to a user if the item's functionality well matches the user's interest. However, Apps could have privileges to access a user's sensitive resources (*e.g.*, contact, message, and location). As a result, a user chooses an App not only because of its functionality, but also because it respects the user's *privacy preference*.

To the best of our knowledge, this paper presents the *first* systematic study on incorporating both interest-functionality interactions and users' privacy preferences to perform personalized App recommendations. Specifically, we first construct a new model to capture the trade-off between functionality and user privacy preference. Then we crawled a real-world dataset (16, 344 users, 6, 157 Apps, and 263, 054 ratings) from Google Play and use it to comprehensively evaluate our model and previous methods. We find that our method consistently and substantially outperforms the state-of-the-art approaches, which implies the importance of user privacy preference on personalized App recommendations. Moreover, we explore the impact of different levels of privacy information on the performances of our method, which gives us insights on what resources are more likely to be treated as private by users and influence users' behaviors at selecting Apps.

*This work was done during an internship at Samsung Research America, San Jose, CA.

WSDM'15, February 2–6, 2015, Shanghai, China.

http://dx.doi.org/10.1145/2684822.2685322.

Categories and Subject Descriptors

H.2.8 [**Database Management**]: Database Applications—*Data mining*

General Terms

Algorithms, Experimentation

Keywords

Recommender Systems; Mobile Apps; Privacy and Security

1. INTRODUCTION

Mobile devices are becoming more and more popular in the past few years. For instance, it was reported that the smartphone market was bigger than the PC market in 2011 for the first time in history [28]. Thereafter, the smartphone market has continued to increase dramatically, *e.g.*, the smartphones shipped in the third quarter of 2013 increased 44% year-on-year [27]. One of the reasons lies in the fact that users are able to augment the mobile devices' functions via taking advantage of various feature-rich third-party *applications* (or Apps for brevity), which can be easily obtained from centralized markets such as Google Play and App Store. However, the number of Apps has recently increased dramatically, which makes it hard for a user to locate relevant Apps. For instance, as of July 2013, Google Play had over 1 million Apps with over 50 billion cumulative downloads, and the number of Apps has reached over 1.2 million in June 2014 [12]; as the beginning of June 2014, App Store had 1.2 million Apps and a cumulative of 75 billion downloads [4]. Therefore, it is urgent to develop effective *personalized* App recommendation systems.

Conventional recommender systems [1, 18, 25, 19, 8, 13] essentially aim to learn the *interest* of each user and the *functionality* of each item (*e.g.*, an App in our problem), given the list of items used or rated by each user. Then, an item is recommended to a user if the item's functionality matches the user's interest. For instance, matrix-factorization-based approaches [18, 25] model a user's interest as a latent vector and an item's functionality as another latent vector; and an item is recommended to a user if the item's functionality vector is close to the user's interest vector in the latent space. Such *interest-functionality* driven recommendation systems have been successfully used to recommend products in e-commence (*e.g.*, Amazon) [21], movies (*e.g.*, Netflix) [5], musics [3], point-of-interests [29, 22], and used for link prediction and attribute inference [10].

However, these approaches are not appropriate for App recommendations. Specifically, unlike items such as music, movies, and point-of-interests, Apps could have privileges to access the user's personal information such as locations, contacts, and messages. Moreover, users might have different *privacy preferences*, *e.g.*, user A tends to not share contacts with the App while user B tends to not allow the App to access her/his locations. Although an App's functionality may matches a user's interest well, the user could still choose to not install it or dislike it if it does not respect the user's privacy preference. Indeed, according to a recent report [7], 54% of surveyed users have decided not to install Apps that want to access their sensitive personal information and 30% of users have uninstalled at least one App after they realized that the App was collecting unexpected personal information. Therefore, whether a user selects/likes an App is a result of the trade-off between two factors:

(1) the degree of match between the user's interest and the App's functionality, which we call *functionality match*;

(2) the degree to which the App respects the user's privacy preference, which we call *privacy respect*.

However, conventional recommendation approaches do not capture this trade-off, which limits their performances on recommending Apps.

Our work: In this paper, we aim to bridge this gap via incorporating both interest-functionality interactions and users' privacy preferences. Specifically, we first construct a new latent factorization model to capture the trade-off between functionality and user privacy preference. Different users might have different definitions on *private data* and could have different privacy concerns on different operations (*e.g.*, read or write) on the private data. Thus, in our model, we consider three levels of privacy information to characterize users' privacy preferences. Moreover, our model takes the sparse user-app rating matrix and the set of privacy-sensitive privileges (*e.g.*, App's permissions) of each App at a given privacy level as an input, and it automatically learns the interest and privacy preference of each user, and the functionality of each App in the latent space, which are further used to predict users' preferences for new Apps. Then, we crawled a real-world dataset which consists of $16,344$ users, $6,157$ Apps, and $263,054$ rating observations from Google play, and we use the dataset to comprehensively evaluate our method and previous approaches. We find that our method consistently and substantially outperforms the state-of-the-art approaches. Furthermore, we explore the impact of different privacy levels on the performance of our method, and we observe that treating different operations with different privacy concerns achieves better recommendation performances.

Our key contributions are summarized as follows:

- We provide the *first* systematic study on leveraging both interest-functionality expectation and user privacy preference to provide personalized App recommendations.
- We propose a new model to capture the trade-off between functionality and user privacy preference.
- We crawled a real-world dataset from Google Play, and we use it to comprehensively evaluate our approach and state-of-the-art methods and explore the impact of privacy levels on the performance of our method. We find that our method consistently and substantially outperforms state-of-the-art approaches.

Table 1: Six dangerous permissions. They manipulate sensitive information *locations*, *contacts*, and *messages*, respectively.

Permission	Description
ACCESS_FINE_LOCATION	allow App to access precise (*e.g.*, GPS) location
ACCESS_COARSE_LOCATION	allow App to access approximate (*e.g.*, cell towers, Wi-Fi) location
READ_CONTACTS	allow App to read contacts info
WRITE_CONTACTS	allow App to write contacts info
READ_SMS	allow App to read SMS messages
WRITE_SMS	allow App to write SMS messages
SEND_SMS	allow App to send SMS messages

2. PROBLEM FORMALIZATION

We first identify that whether a user adopts an App is a result of the trade-off between the App's functionality and the user's privacy preference. Second, we introduce our defined hierarchy of user privacy concerns. Third, we formally define our *privacy-respect App recommendation* problem.

2.1 Trade-off between Functionality and Privacy

We focus on Android Apps, though our approach is also applicable to other types of Apps. Android system is a permission-based framework. A permission is related to a critical resource (*e.g.*, Internet, contact, and message) on the mobile device, and granting a permission to an App allows the App to either read or write the corresponding resource. Table 1 shows some permission examples and their corresponding descriptions. For instance, giving the permission READ_CONTACTS to an App makes it capable to read the user's contact data.

We identify that whether a user adopts an App is a result of the trade-off between the App's functionality and the user's privacy preference. To achieve the functionality desired by the user, the App might need to manipulate the user's certain type of private data through requesting the corresponding sensitive permissions. For instance, Google Map, a navigation App, requires the user's GPS location data and thus needs the ACCESS_FINE_LOCATION permission. Moreover, the App could also request other sensitive permissions intentionally [26] or unintentionally [9] for non-functionality purposes such as advertisements. For instance, Shekhar *et al.* [26] found that around 25% of Android Apps access users' location data only for advertisements; Felt *et al.* [9] found that around 30% of Android Apps request sensitive permissions that are not used by them at all. A user with low privacy concerns with the requested permissions/resources might sacrifice its privacy for the App's functionality, while a user with high privacy concerns might sacrifice the App's functionality for privacy or might transfer to another App that provides the same functionality but uses less private resources.

2.2 User Privacy Levels

Different users could have different definitions on *private resources* and could have different privacy concerns to different operations (*e.g.*, read or write) on the resources. We define three privacy levels, each of which consists of a set of resources and corresponding operations. A user's privacy

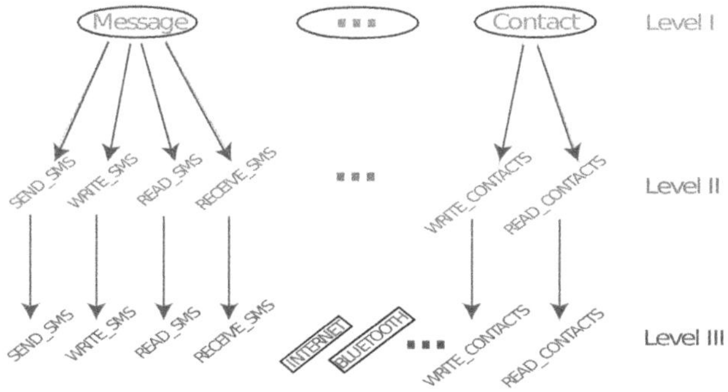

Figure 1: Illustration of the three privacy levels. Level I corresponds to *privacy-sensitive resources*; Level II corresponds to *privacy-sensitive permissions* (refer to Table 2); Level III is a superset of Level II.

preference essentially characterizes the concerns for the operations on the private resources in a given privacy level. Figure 1 illustrates the hierarchy of the three privacy levels.

- **Level I:** This level considers 10 resources (*e.g.*, contact, message, and location) as private. The 10 resources are listed in the first column of Table 2. However, this level does not distinguish the operations that can be applied to the private resources. Thus, this privacy level is represented as a binary vector of the 10 resources. If a user does not concern a certain private resource such as message, the user would accept an App to read, write, or even send messages.

- **Level II:** This level considers the same 10 resources in Level I as private. However, this level explicitly distinguishes different operations that can be applied to the resources. In this level, a user could have a low privacy concerns on reading messages but a high privacy concern on writing messages. This level of privacy can be expressed by the set of Android permissions that are related to the 10 resources. In total, there are 23 such permissions. Level II is more fine-gained than level I, and Table 2 described mappings between level I and level II.

- **Level III:** This level considers all critical resources including the 10 resources in the Level I and II and other resources (*e.g.*, Internet and bluetooth) on a mobile device as private, and it also distinguishes different operations. This level is more complete and more fine-grained than the Level II, and it can be expressed as a binary vector of all dangerous Android permissions. In total, we identified 72 such permissions, which are a superset of level II permissions.

For the same App, users with different privacy levels could behave differently at whether adopting the App or not. In our experiments, we will explore the impact of the three privacy levels on the performance of our method.

2.3 Privacy-respect App Recommendation

We use M and N to denote the number of users and the number of apps, respectively; we denote by the set of users as $U = \{u_1, u_2, \cdots, u_M\}$ and the set of Apps as $V = \{v_1, v_2, ..., v_N\}$. Let S be the set of privacy-sensitive operations or resources at a given privacy level. Depending on the privacy level, S can be the 10 private resources (Level I), the 23 sensitive Android permissions (Level II), or all dangerous Android permissions (Level III). For each App j, we have its privacy-sensitive operations/resources Π_j at a given privacy level, where $\Pi_j \subseteq S$. Π_j can be obtained by App code analysis.

Table 2: *Privacy-sensitive resources* (Level I) vs. corresponding *privacy-sensitive permissions* (Level II).

Privacy-sensitive Resources	Privacy-sensitive Permissions
Contact	READ_CONTACTS WRITE_CONTACTS
Message	READ_SMS WRITE_SMS SEND_SMS RECEIVE_SMS RECEIVE_MMS SEND_RESPOND_VIA_MESSAGE
Location	ACCESS_FINE_LOCATION ACCESS_COARSE_LOCATION
Phone_state	MODIFY_PHONE_STATE READ_PHONE_STATE
Phone_call	CALL_PHONE CALL_PRIVILEGED
Calendar	READ_CALENDAR WRITE_CALENDAR
Call_log	READ_CALL_LOG WRITE_CALL_LOG
Browser_history	READ_HISTORY_BOOKMARKS WRITE_HISTORY_BOOKMARKS
Camera	CAMERA
Audio	RECORD_AUDIO MODIFY_AUDIO_SETTINGS

Suppose we are given a sparse matrix of user-App response records (*e.g.*, ratings or likes) and the set of privacy-sensitive operations/resources of each App at a given privacy level, our goal is to recommend most relevant Apps for each user by learning both interest and privacy preference of each user and functionality of each App.

3. PROPOSED METHOD

This section presents our proposed user privacy-respect App recommendation model.

3.1 General Idea

We aim to quantify the trade-off between App's functionality and user privacy preference. Suppose $g_{\text{func},i,j}$ is the *functionality match score* of the interest of user i and functionality of App j and $g_{\text{privacy},i,j}$ is the *privacy respect score* of the privacy preference of user i and the privacy information used by App j.

Modeling functionality match: Following the latent factor models in standard recommendation systems [18, 25], we model a user i's interest as a user latent vector $\mathbf{u}_i^{\text{interest}} \in \mathbb{R}^K$ and an App j's functionality as an App latent vector $\mathbf{v}_j \in \mathbb{R}^K$, where K is the number of latent dimensions of user interests and App functionalities. More specifically, each

Table 3: Mathematical Notations

Symbol	Size	Description
$\mathbf{U}$	$K \times M$	user latent factor
$\mathbf{V}$	$K \times N$	App latent factor
$\mathbf{P}$	$K \times S$	privacy information latent factor
Π_j	$\Pi_j \in S$	privacy information set for App j
y_{ij}	$\mathbb{R}$	user i's rating for App j

element $u_{ik} \in \mathbf{u}_i^{\text{interest}}$ encodes the preference of user i to "preference aspect" k, and each element $v_{ik} \in \mathbf{v}_j$ reflects the aspect affinity of App j to aspect k, where $k = 1, 2, \cdots, K$. Then the functionality match score $g_{\text{func},i,j}$ is modeled as:

$$g_{\text{func,i,j}} = f\left(\mathbf{u}_i^{\text{interest}}, \mathbf{v}_j; \Theta_1\right).$$

Modeling privacy respect: We also adopt a latent factor model to describe user privacy preference and App's private information. This latent factor model assumes that it is possible to group users by a relatively small number of privacy profiles. Specifically, we denote a user i's privacy preference as a latent factor $\mathbf{u}_i^{\text{privacy}} \in \mathbb{R}^K$. Accordingly, we model each privacy information (*i.e.*, a privacy-sensitive resource or permission) in the set of privacy information S at a given privacy level as a privacy latent factor $\mathbf{p}_s \in \mathbb{R}^K$. Note that although different number of latent dimensions can be applied to model functionality factors and privacy factors, we assume they are the same for simplicity. Therefore, we model the privacy respect score as:

$$g_{\text{privacy}} = f\left(\mathbf{u}_i^{\text{privacy}}, \sum_{s \in \Pi_j} \mathbf{p}_s; \Theta_2\right),$$

where Π_j is the set of privacy information associated with the App j.

Trade-off between functionality and privacy: We model a user i's overall preference (denoted as $g_{i,j}$) for an App j as a weighted sum of the functionality match score and the privacy respect score. Specifically, we have:

$$g_{i,j} = g_{\text{func},i,j} + \lambda g_{\text{privacy},i,j}, \tag{1}$$

where λ is used to balance App functionality and user privacy preference.

3.2 Model Specifications

Here we present a detailed model specification. Instead of separately representing user interest and user privacy preference with two latent factors, we amalgamate user interest latent vector and user privacy latent vector as one user profile latent factor $\mathbf{u}_i \in \mathbb{R}^K$, which is a K-dimension vector. This amalgamation can reduce parameters to learn and thus improve computational efficiency.

Each App j is modeled by a functionality latent factor and a privacy latent factor as $\mathbf{v}_j + \lambda \sum_{s \in \Pi_j} \mathbf{p}_s$, where Π_j is the privacy information set for App j. For example, if App j requests three permissions `ACCESS_FINE_LOCATION` (index: 2), `READ_CONTACTS` (index: 4), and `INTERNET` (index: 7), then $\Pi_j = \{2, 4, 7\}$ at the privacy level Level III. The cardinality of the set Π_j is the number of elements in Π_j, i.e., $|\Pi_j| = 3$ in our example. Privacy latent factor representation $\sum_{s \in \Pi_j} \mathbf{p}_s$ provides flexibility for Apps with different number of privacy information.

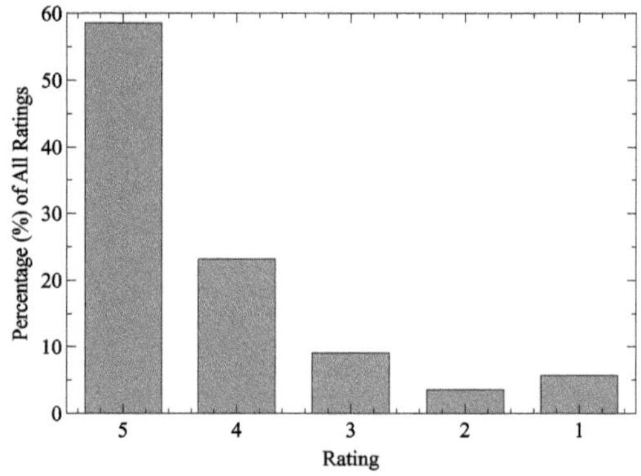

Figure 2: Rating distribution.

Then a user i's preference score for an App j can be represented as

$$x_{ij} = \mathbf{u}_i^T \left(\mathbf{v}_j + \lambda \frac{1}{|\Pi_j|} \sum_{s \in \Pi_j} \mathbf{p}_s\right) \tag{2}$$

where $\frac{1}{|\Pi_j|}$ is placed for each App to adjust the unbalanced number of privacy informations.

To model user profile and App profile, it is practical to formulate the user-App preference score x_{ij} to follow some probability distribution $\Pr(y_{ij}|x_{ij}, \Theta)$, then we can infer the latent factors $\mathbf{u}_i$, $\mathbf{v}_j$, and $\mathbf{p}_s$ through statistical inference methods. One most used probabilistic model, as used in probabilistic matrix factorization (PMF) [25], is to assume $\Pr(y_{ij}|x_{ij}, \Theta)$ as a Gaussian distribution. However, the rating distribution in an App dataset is polarized as shown in Figure 2, which indicates that Gaussian distribution would not be a good choice for our problem. Therefore, instead of using a Gaussian distribution, we adopt a Poisson distribution:

$$y_{ij} \sim \text{Poisson}(x_{ij})$$
$$\Pr(y_{ij}|x_{ij}) = (x_{ij})^{y_{ij}} \frac{\exp\{-x_{ij}\}}{y_{ij}!}. \tag{3}$$

As noticed by [13, 8, 23], Poisson distribution is a better choice for modeling discrete user-item responses. Firstly, it better captures real user-item response data. By setting non-negative constrains on latent factors, Poisson latent factor model force response variables to be in a wider range than the rating based response. As a result, it can better capture preference order. Secondly, due to the form of Poisson distribution, only the observed part of user-item matrix needs to be iterated during modeling, which provides advantage for the sparsity of user-item matrix in recommendation problems. Therefore, we model user-App preference as:

$$\Pr(y_{ij}|u_i, v_i, p_s) = (x_{ij})^{y_{ij}} \frac{\exp\{-x_{ij}\}}{y_{ij}!}, \tag{4}$$

where $x_{ij} = \mathbf{u}_i^T \left(\mathbf{v}_j + \lambda \frac{1}{|\Pi_j|} \sum_{s \in \Pi_j} \mathbf{p}_s\right)$. Further, u_{ik}, v_{ik}, and p_{sk} can be given Gamma distributions as empirical priors, *i.e.*, the user-App preferences can be modeled as a generative process:

1. For each user i, generate user latent factor:
$$u_{ik} \sim \text{Gamma}(\alpha_U, \beta_U), \tag{5}$$
2. For each App j, generate App functionality latent factor:
$$v_{jk} \sim \text{Gamma}(\alpha_V, \beta_V), \tag{6}$$

3. For each privacy information s, generate privacy latent factor:
$$p_{sk} \sim \text{Gamma}(\alpha_P, \beta_P), \quad (7)$$
4. For each user-App pair $\langle i, j\rangle$, generate Poisson response:
$$\Pr(y_{ij}|u_i, v_i, p_s) = (x_{ij})^{y_{ij}} \frac{\exp\{-x_{ij}\}}{y_{ij}!},$$

where $\Theta = \{\mathbf{U}, \mathbf{V}, \mathbf{P}\}$ are parameters to be estimated, and $\Phi = \{\alpha_U, \beta_U, \alpha_V, \beta_V, \alpha_P, \beta_P\}$ are model hyperparameters.

3.3 Model Estimation

Let $\Pr(\mathbf{U}, \mathbf{V}, \mathbf{P}|\mathbf{Y}, \Phi)$ be the posteriori probability of generation of $\mathbf{U}, \mathbf{V}, \mathbf{P}$, given observations of $\mathbf{Y}$ and prior distribution Φ, according to the maximum a posteriori (MAP) rule, we need to maximize:
$$\max_{\mathbf{U},\mathbf{V},\mathbf{P}} \Pr(\mathbf{U}, \mathbf{V}, \mathbf{P}|\mathbf{Y}, \Phi)$$
$$\propto \max_{\mathbf{U},\mathbf{V},\mathbf{P}} \Pr(\mathbf{Y}|\mathbf{U}, \mathbf{V}, \mathbf{P})\Pr(\mathbf{U}, \mathbf{V}, \mathbf{P}|\Phi) \quad (8)$$
where $\Pr(\mathbf{u}_i, \mathbf{v}_j, \mathbf{p}_s|\alpha_u, \beta_u, \alpha_v, \beta_v, \alpha_s, \beta_s)$ are the prior distributions for $\mathbf{U}$, $\mathbf{V}$, $\mathbf{P}$ generated from Eqs.(5, 6, 7), and $\Pr(y_{ij}|\boldsymbol{u}_i, \boldsymbol{v}_j, \mathbf{p}_s)$ can be computed using Eq.(4).

Following the likelihood principle, we can determine the optimal solution for $\mathbf{U}, \mathbf{V}, \mathbf{P}$ to Eq.(8) by Maximum a Posteriori (MAP) estimation. Specifically, we have:
$$\begin{aligned}
\Pr(\mathbf{Y}|\mathbf{U}, \mathbf{V}, \mathbf{P}) &= \prod_{i=1}^{M}\prod_{j=1}^{N} (x_{ij})^{y_{ij}} \exp\{-x_{ij}\}/y_{ij}! \\
\Pr(\mathbf{U}|\alpha_U, \beta_U) &= \prod_{i=1}^{M}\prod_{k=1}^{K} \frac{u_{ik}^{\alpha_U-1}\exp(-u_{ik}/\beta_U)}{\beta_U^{\alpha_U}\Gamma(\alpha_U)} \\
\Pr(\mathbf{V}|\alpha_V, \beta_V) &= \prod_{j=1}^{N}\prod_{k=1}^{K} \frac{v_{jk}^{\alpha_V-1}\exp(-v_{jk}/\beta_V)}{\beta_V^{\alpha_V}\Gamma(\alpha_V)} \\
\Pr(\mathbf{P}|\alpha_P, \beta_P) &= \prod_{s=1}^{S}\prod_{k=1}^{K} \frac{p_{sk}^{\alpha_P-1}\exp(-p_{sk}/\beta_P)}{\beta_P^{\alpha_P}\Gamma(\alpha_P)},
\end{aligned} \quad (9)$$
where
$$x_{ij} = \boldsymbol{u}_i^\top \left(\boldsymbol{v}_j + \lambda\frac{1}{|\Pi_j|}\sum_{s\in\Pi_j} \boldsymbol{p}_s\right)$$
Then the log-likelihood of Eq.(8) is given by
$$\begin{aligned}
\mathcal{L} &= \log \Pr(\mathbf{U}, \mathbf{V}, \mathbf{P}, \mathbf{F}|\mathbf{Y}, \Phi) \\
&= \sum_{i=1}^{M}\sum_{k=1}^{K}\Big((\alpha_U - 1)\ln u_{ik} - u_{ik}/\beta_U\Big) \\
&+ \sum_{j=1}^{N}\sum_{k=1}^{K}\Big((\alpha_V - 1)\ln v_{jk} - v_{jk}/\beta_V\Big) \\
&+ \sum_{s=1}^{S}\sum_{k=1}^{K}\Big((\alpha_P - 1)\ln p_{sk} - p_{sk}/\beta_P\Big) \\
&+ \sum_{i=1}^{M}\sum_{j=1}^{N}(y_{ij}\ln x_{ij} - x_{ij}) + \text{const}.
\end{aligned} \quad (10)$$
Thus maximization of Eq.(8) w.r.t $\mathbf{U}, \mathbf{V}, \mathbf{P}$ is equivalent to maximization of Eq.(10). To control the model complexity, we further add a penalty term, then the objective function becomes
$$\mathcal{Q} = \mathcal{L} - \frac{\eta}{2}\left(||\mathbf{U}||_F^2 + ||\mathbf{V}||_F^2 + ||\mathbf{F}||_F^2\right) \quad (11)$$

Taking derivatives on $\mathcal{Q}$ with respect to u_{ik}, v_{jk}, and p_{sk}, we have
$$\begin{aligned}
\frac{\partial \mathcal{Q}}{\partial u_{ik}} &= \frac{\alpha_U - 1}{u_{ik}} - \frac{1}{\beta_U} - \eta \times u_{ik} \\
&+ \sum_{j=1}^{N}\left(\frac{y_{ij}}{x_{ij}} - 1\right)\left(v_{jk} + \frac{\lambda}{|\Pi_j|}\sum_{s\in\Pi_j} p_{sk}\right) \\
\frac{\partial \mathcal{Q}}{\partial v_{jk}} &= \frac{\alpha_V - 1}{v_{jk}} - \frac{1}{\beta_V} - \eta \times v_{jk} + \sum_{i=1}^{M}\left(\frac{y_{ij}}{x_{ij}} - 1\right)u_{ik} \quad (12) \\
\frac{\partial \mathcal{Q}}{\partial p_{sk}} &= \frac{\alpha_P - 1}{p_{sk}} - \frac{1}{\beta_P} - \eta \times p_{sk} \\
&+ \sum_{i=1}^{M}\sum_{j=1}^{N}\left(\frac{y_{ij}}{x_{ij}} - 1\right)\lambda u_{ik}\frac{\mathbb{I}(s \in \Pi_j)}{|\Pi_j|}
\end{aligned}$$
We adopt the ascending gradient method [6] to infer the latent factors. Specifically, parameters θ are updated by the following equation:
$$\theta \leftarrow \theta + \epsilon \times \frac{\partial \mathcal{Q}}{\partial \theta}, \quad (13)$$
where θ is an element in $\{\mathbf{U}, \mathbf{V}, \mathbf{P}\}$, $\frac{\partial \mathcal{Q}}{\partial \theta}$ is the derivatives according to Equation (12), and ϵ is the learning rate. The algorithms iterate over $\{\mathbf{U}, \mathbf{V}, \mathbf{P}\}$ until one of the following termination conditions is reached (a) the value of objection function $\mathcal{Q}$ in Equation (11) keeps stable, or (b) the maximum number of iterations is reached.

4. EXPERIMENTS

4.1 Experimental setup

We aim to answer the following two questions:

- **Question 1**: Whether, and to what extent, our privacy-respect App recommendation model improves upon previous recommendation approaches that do not consider user privacy preferences?
- **Question 2**: How privacy levels (as introduced in Section 2.2) influence the performance of our approach?

Towards this goal, we first crawled a user-app rating dataset from Google Play via reverse engineering the service protocol. Then, using the crawled dataset, we compare our method with state-of-the-art latent factor based recommendation models and explore the impact of the three privacy levels on the performance of our approach.

4.2 Data Collection

We collected our dataset from Google Play. On Google Play, a user's ratings about Apps he/she used are publicly available. Once we obtain the Google ID of a user, we can locate all Apps the user has rated. Therefore, we first obtain a list of Google user IDs from Gong et al. [11] and write a crawler to retrieve all rated Apps of these users. Moreover, for each retrieved App, we crawled its permissions from Google Play. Our crawls were performed during June and July of 2014.

We remove unpopular Apps and users with too few rated Apps from our collected dataset to avoid *cold start* problem. Specifically, we first remove Apps with less than 5 users and then exclude users with less than 10 Apps. After this preprocessing step, our dataset has 16,344 users, 6,157 Apps,

Table 4: Data Description

users	Apps	ratings	sparsity	avg ratings
16,344	6,157	263,054	99.74%	16.09

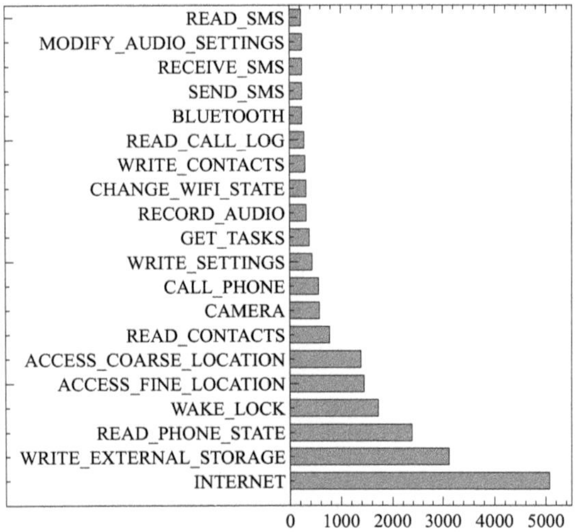

Figure 3: The top 20 most frequently used permissions and the number of Apps (out of the 6,157 Apps in our dataset) that require those permissions.

and 263,054 rating observations. The user App rating matrix has a sparsity as high as 99.74%. Each user rated 16.09 Apps on average, which is a very small fraction of all the Apps. Table 4 shows some basic statistics of our preprocessed dataset.

Figure 3 shows the top 20 most frequently used permissions and the number of Apps that require those permissions. While permissions such as `INTERNET` might not lead to privacy concerns for most users, some permissions (*e.g.*, `READ_CONTACTS`, `ACCESS_FINE_LOCATION`, and `CALL_PHONE`) could raise serious privacy concerns depending on how they are used by the Apps.

4.3 Compared Approaches

We compare our proposed model with the following latent factor based recommendation models:

- Singular Value Decomposition (SVD) [18]: SVD is a low dimension decomposition based recommendation method.
- Probabilistic Matrix Factorization (PMF) [25]: PMF extends SVD to a probabilistic framework.
- Non-negative Matrix Factorization (NMF) [19]: Similar to SVD, but NMF requires the latent vectors to be non-negative.
- Poisson Factor Model (Poi-FM) [13, 8]: Poisson factor model provides an alternative for latent factor model for different applications, and previous work [13] shows that Poisson factor model outperforms Gaussian based PMF.

Besides comparing to previous methods that do not consider user privacy preferences, we also investigate how different privacy levels impact the performance of our method. Specifically, we compare the following three variants of our method:

- **Privacy_Res.**: Privacy-respect App recommendation with Level I as the privacy level. Recall that this level considers the 10 resources listed in Table 2 as private data and do not distinguish different operations. Thus, each App's permissions are transformed to a 10-dimensional binary vector, which represents the private resources used by the App.
- **Sensitive_Perm.**: Privacy-respect App recommendation with Level II as the privacy level. Level II considers the 23 dangerous permissions that are related to the 10 sensitive resources. Therefore, we have a 23-dimensional binary vector to represent the private resources used by an App.
- **All_Danger_Perm.**: Privacy-respect App recommendation with Level III as the privacy level. Level III considers all critical resources (corresponding to 72 dangerour Android permissions) on a mobile device as private. Therefore, we have a 72-dimensional binary vector to represent the private resources used by an App.

Training and testing: We sample 80% of rated Apps of each user uniformly at random as training data, and we use the remaining rated Apps for testing. All the latent factor models are implemented with stochastic gradient ascent/descent optimization method with an annealing procedure to discount learning rate ϵ at iteration nIter with $\epsilon^{\text{nIter}} = \epsilon\frac{\nu}{\nu+\text{nIter}-1}$ by setting $\nu = 50$. For SVD, PMF, and NMF, learning rates are set as $1e^{-3}$; learning rates for Poisson based methods are empirically set as $1e^{-4}$. For Poisson based latent factor models including both baseline Poi-FM and our proposed model, we set $\alpha_U = \alpha_V = \alpha_P = 20$ and $\beta_U = \beta_V = \beta_P = 0.5$; penalty weight η is set as $1e^{-5}$; functionality-privacy trade-off weight λ is empirically set as 1.

4.4 Evaluation Metrics

In App recommendation, we present to the user a list of recommendations, thus we evaluate the models in terms of ranking. Specifically, we present each user with N Apps that have the highest predicted values but are not rated by the user in the training phase, and we evaluate different approaches based on which of these Apps were actually adopted by the user in the test phase.

Precision and Recall: Given a top-N recommendation list $C_{N,\text{rec}}$, precision and recall are defined as

$$\begin{aligned} \text{Precision@}N &= \frac{|C_{N,\text{rec}} \bigcap C_{\text{adopted}}|}{N} \\ \text{Recall@}N &= \frac{|C_{N,\text{rec}} \bigcap C_{\text{adopted}}|}{|C_{\text{adopted}}|}, \end{aligned} \tag{14}$$

where C_{adopted} are the Apps that a user has adopted in the test data. The precision and recall for the entire recommender system are computed by averaging the precision and recall over all the users, respectively.

F-measure: F-measure balances between precision and recall. We consider the F_β metric, which is defined as

$$F_\beta = (1+\beta^2)\cdot\frac{\text{Precision}\times\text{Recall}}{\beta^2\cdot\text{Precision}+\text{Recall}}. \tag{15}$$

The F_β metric with $\beta < 1$ indicates more emphasis on precision than recall. In our experiments, we use F_β metric with $\beta = 0.5$.

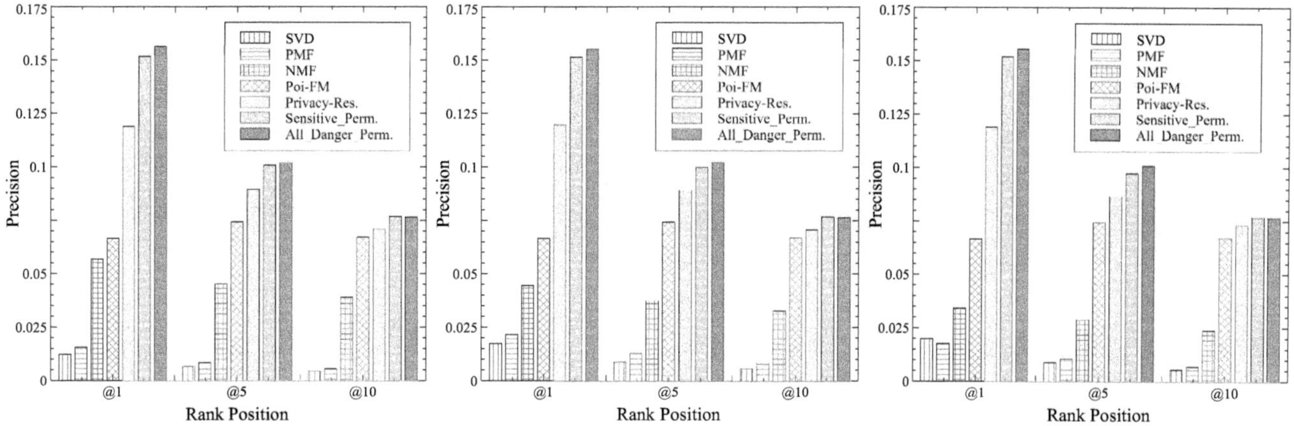

(a) $K = 20$ (b) $K = 30$ (c) $K = 50$

Figure 4: Precision @N with different latent dimensions K.

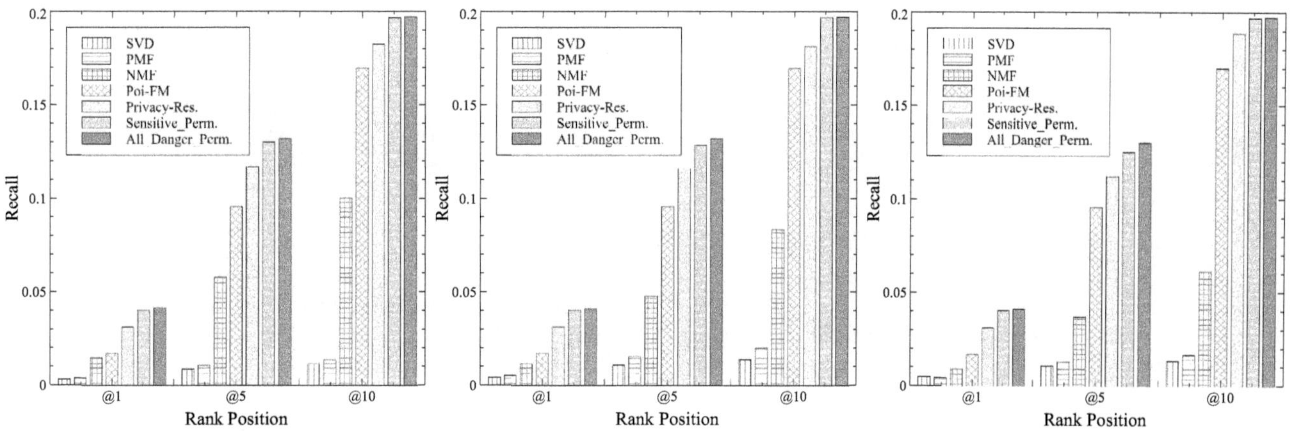

(a) $K = 20$ (b) $K = 30$ (c) $K = 50$

Figure 5: Recall @N with different latent dimensions K.

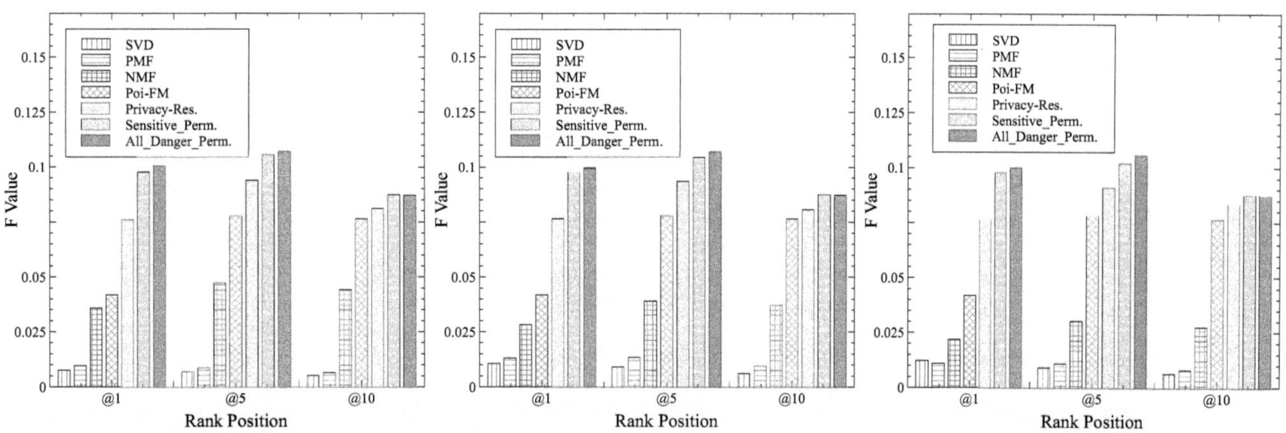

(a) $K = 20$ (b) $K = 30$ (c) $K = 50$

Figure 6: F_β @N with different latent dimensions K ($\beta = 0.5$).

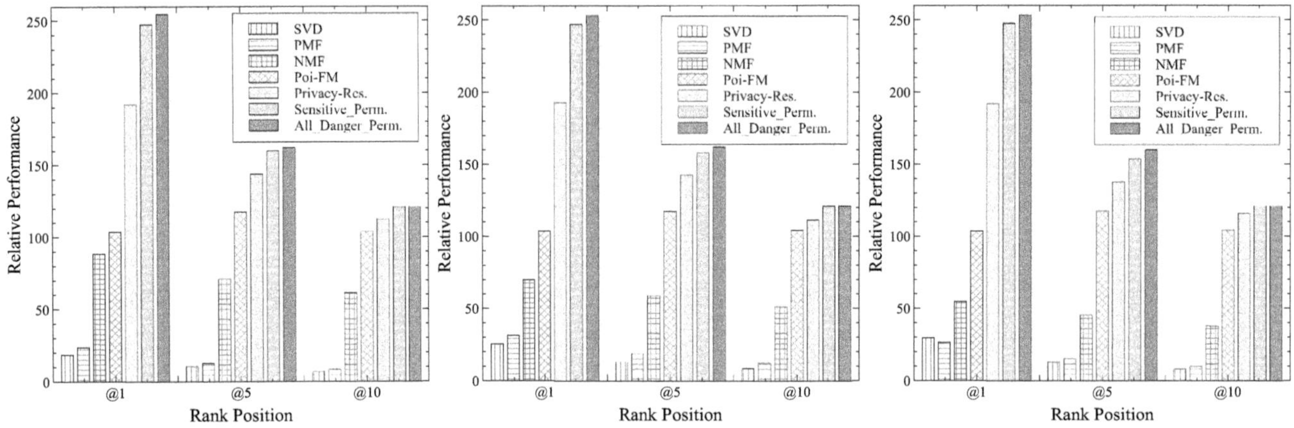

(a) $K = 20$ (b) $K = 30$ (c) $K = 50$

Figure 7: Relative performance @N with different latent dimensions K.

r-Recall and r-Precision: Similar to Yin et al. [30], we also compare the different models in terms of relative precision and recall. Let C denote the candidate Apps, the precision and recall in a top-N list of a random recommender system are $\frac{|C_{\text{adopted}}|}{|C|}$ and $\frac{N}{|C|}$, respectively. Then, the relative precision and recall [30] are defined as

$$\text{rPrecision@}N = \frac{\text{Precision@}N}{|C_{\text{adopted}}|/|C|} = \frac{|C_{N,\text{rec}} \bigcap C_{\text{adopted}}| \cdot |C|}{|C_{\text{adopted}}| \cdot N}$$
$$\text{rRecall@}N = \frac{\text{Recall@}N}{N/|C|} = \frac{|C_{N,\text{rec}} \bigcap C_{\text{adopted}}| \cdot |C|}{|C_{\text{adopted}}| \cdot N} \quad (16)$$

Note that the relative precision and recall have the same value. Therefore, we only show one of them and we name it as the relative performance, which measures the improvement upon a random recommendation method.

4.5 Comparison Results

Figure 4, Figure 5, Figure 6, and Figure 7 respectively show the precision@N, recall@N, F_β@N, and relative performance@N of all compared approaches on our dataset, where $N = 1, 5, 10$. For each approach, we explore 3 latent dimension settings, *i.e.*, $K = 20$, $K = 30$, and $K = 50$.

4.5.1 Comparing Our Method with Previous Approaches

We find that our approach consistently outperforms previous methods for different N and different K. Specifically, we observe that NMF outperforms both SVD and PMF, and that Poisson based factor model Poi-FM can further improve upon NMF with all the three considered number of latent dimensions. Moreover, our privacy-respect App recommendation methods with the three privacy levels all further improve upon Poi-FM with significant margins for all the four evaluation metrics. To better demonstrate the improvements, Table 5 shows the absolute improvements of our proposed method, with different privacy levels, as compared to the best baseline method Poi-FM when $K = 30$ and $N = 1$. We can see significant improvement margins. While precision and recall may change with different N, F-measure provides a stable comparisons as it is the harmonic mean of precision and recall. In terms of F-measure, we can observe

Table 5: Absolute improvements of our proposed method with different privacy levels as compared to the best baseline method Poi-FM ($K = 30$, $N = 1$).

metric	Privacy_Res.	Sensitive_Perm.	All_Danger_perm.
F-measure	**3.46% ↑**	**5.56% ↑**	**5.80% ↑**
precision	5.31% ↑	8.49% ↑	8.86% ↑
recall	1.45% ↑	2.33% ↑	2.43% ↑
relative	89.16 ↑	143.45 ↑	149.39 ↑

a 3.46% improvement for **Privacy_Res.**, a 5.56% improvement for **Sensitive_Perm.**, and a 5.80% improvement for **All_Danger_perm.**.

Our results show that once we consider user privacy preference, performance of App recommendation gets improved no matter what privacy level is used.

4.5.2 Impact of Privacy Levels

We find that our method with Level II privacy information (*i.e.*, **Sensitive_Perm.**) can improve upon our method with Level I privacy information (*i.e.*, **Privacy_Res.**) with notable margins. This implies that users treat different operations (*e.g.*, read and write) on the 10 private resources with different privacy concerns. However, **Sensitive_Perm.** and **All_Danger_Perm.** have very close performances consistently for all settings we considered. Figure 8 shows a zoom in comparisons of the three levels. Our observations indicate that users probably do not treat resources (*e.g.*, Internet, Bluetooth) other than the 10 resources in the privacy level Level I and Level II as private resources, and thus accessing those resources would not influence whether a user likes/adopts an App.

4.5.3 Summary

We find that our privacy-respect App recommendation method significantly outperforms previous approaches that do not consider user privacy preference. Moreover, we find that users are more likely to treat the 10 resources in Level I and Level II as private resources and they treat different operations (*e.g.*, read and write) on these resources with different privacy concerns.

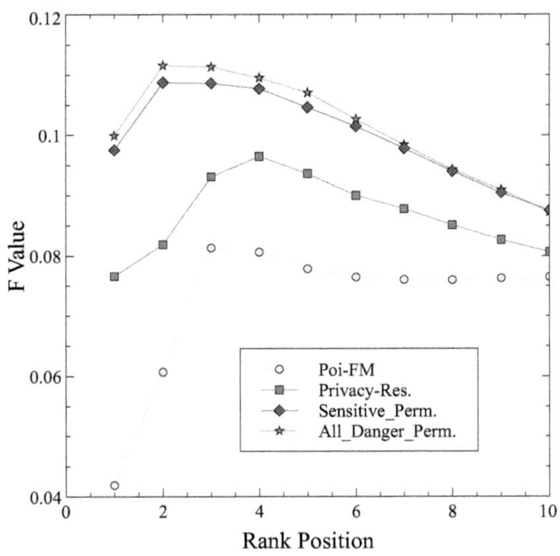

Figure 8: Zoom in comparisons between our methods with the three privacy levels (i.e., Privacy_Res., Sensitive_Perm., and All_Danger_perm.) and the best baseline method (i.e., Poi-FM) for $K = 30$.

5. RELATED WORK

Most of related works come from two research fields: personalized recommendation methodologies especially latent factor model based recommendation models, and mobile App rankings and recommendations.

Personalized Recommendation: Latent factor models have become popular and been widely used in recommendation systems. These work include matrix factorization [18], Probabilistic Matrix Factorization (PMF) [25] and its Bayesian version [24], and their other variants [17, 2, 16]. In our case and many cases alike, the recommendation system needs to infer user preferences from user feedbacks. Latent factor models, which are suitable for better capturing preference order are preferred and followed in our approach. One option in designing latent factor model is to set non-negative constrains on latent factors to force response variables to be in a wider range than the rating based response, which is normally limited to a certain range of integers. As a result, non-negative matrix factorization based methods are widely used [19, 31, 14] due to this advantage.

Furthermore, most of these latent factors based studies along this line of research assume that the user response follows Gaussian distribution with expectation from the product of user and item latent factors. However, some recent work [13, 8, 23] have pointed out that Poisson distribution could be a better choice for modeling user response. Firstly, it better captures real consumption data; secondly, due to the form of Poisson distribution, only the observed part of user-item matrix need to be iterated during modeling. This is a big advantage considering the usually extreme sparsity of user-item matrix in recommendation problems, providing better scalability.

This paper follows the state-of-the-art latent factor model to propose a novel model that is more suitable for App recommendation task by introducing users' privacy preference information. Experimental evidence shows advantage of our approach against above state-of-the-art models.

Mobile App Ranking and Recommendation: There have been a few previous works on App recommendation, but these works only focused on recommending the most relevant Apps to a user without considering *user privacy preference*. Work from [15] provides a context-aware recommendation using tensor factorization by including context information such as location, moving status and time. To address the cold-start problem for App recommendation, [20] proposed to incorporate side information from Twitter. Information of followers of the App's official Twitter account is collected and utilized to model the App, providing an estimation about which users may like the App, even when the App still has no official rating yet. Yin *et al.* [30] considered a trade-off between satisfaction and temptation for App recommendation with a special focus on the case that a user would like to replace an old App with a new one. An interesting dataset is collected via an App from users, revealing users' process of choosing a new App after comparing it with those already obtained ones. And the satisfaction and temptation of an App is evaluated and used to facilitate the recommendation algorithm.

More recently, Zhu *et al.* [32] proposed a mobile App recommendation (more precisely, *ranking*) system by considering both the App's popularity and security risks. They provide an identical global ranking of Apps to every user, and thus their work is not *personalized* App recommendation.

As described above, different from all previous work on App recommendation (personalized or unpersonalized), this paper, to the best of our knowledge, is the first one that proposes to incorporate user privacy preference into mobile App recommendation. Experiments on real-life data show affirmative results for the contribution of privacy information in App recommendation.

6. CONCLUSION AND FUTURE WORK

In this paper, we present the *first* systematic study on leveraging the trade-off between a user's interest-functionality expectation and her/his privacy preference to perform personalized privacy-respect App recommendations. Specifically, we first propose a new model to capture the trade-off between functionality and user privacy preference. Our model is flexible to incorporate three levels of privacy information. Moreover, we crawled a real-world dataset from Google Play and use it evaluate our method. Our results demonstrate that our method achieves consistent and substantial performance improvement over previous approaches. This implies that it is important to consider user privacy preference on personalized App recommendations. Furthermore, we explore the impact of different levels of privacy information on the performances of our method. We find that treating different operations with different privacy concerns achieves better recommendation performances.

A few interesting future directions include measuring users' different privacy preferences in the three privacy levels in the wild and constructing a more fine-grained model to capture the trade-off between functionality expectation and privacy preference.

7. REFERENCES

[1] G. Adomavicius and A. Tuzhilin. Toward the next generation of recommender systems: A survey of the state-of-the-art and possible extensions. *Knowledge and Data Engineering, IEEE Transactions on*, 17(6):734–749, 2005.

[2] D. Agarwal and B.-C. Chen. Regression-based latent factor models. In *Proc. of the 15th ACM SIGKDD Int'l Conf. on Knowledge Discovery and Data Mining*, KDD '09, pages 19–28, 2009.

[3] N. Aizenberg, Y. Koren, and O. Somekh. Build your own music recommender by modeling internet radio streams. In *Proc. of the 21st int'l conf. on World Wide Web*, pages 1–10, 2012.

[4] App Store Statistics. `http://en.wikipedia.org/wiki/App_Store_(iOS)`.

[5] R. M. Bell and Y. Koren. Lessons from the netflix prize challenge. *SIGKDD Explor. Newsl.*, 9(2):75–79, Dec. 2007.

[6] D. P. Bertsekas. *Nonlinear programming*. Athena Scientific, 1999.

[7] J. L. Boyles, A. Smith, and M. Madden. Privacy and data management on mobile devices. *Pew Internet & American Life Project*, 2012.

[8] J. Canny. Gap: A factor model for discrete data. In *Proc. of the 27th ACM SIGIR Conf. on Research and Development in Information Retrieval*, SIGIR '04, pages 122–129, 2004.

[9] A. P. Felt, E. Chin, S. Hanna, D. Song, and D. Wagner. Android permissions demystified. In *CCS*, 2011.

[10] N. Z. Gong, A. Talwalkar, L. Mackey, L. Huang, E. C. R. Shin, E. Stefanov, E. R. Shi, and D. Song. Joint link prediction and attribute inference using a social-attribute network. *ACM Transactions on Intelligent Systems and Technology (TIST)*, 5(2):27, 2014.

[11] N. Z. Gong, W. Xu, L. Huang, P. Mittal, E. Stefanov, V. Sekar, and D. Song. Evolution of social-attribute networks: measurements, modeling, and implications using google+. In *Proceedings of the 2012 ACM conference on Internet measurement conference*, pages 131–144. ACM, 2012.

[12] Google Play Statistics. `http://en.wikipedia.org/wiki/Google_Play`.

[13] P. Gopalan, J. M. Hofman, and D. M. Blei. Scalable recommendation with poisson factorization. *CoRR*, abs/1311.1704, 2013.

[14] Q. Gu, J. Zhou, and C. H. Ding. Collaborative filtering: Weighted nonnegative matrix factorization incorporating user and item graphs. In *SDM*, pages 199–210, 2010.

[15] A. Karatzoglou, L. Baltrunas, K. Church, and M. Böhmer. Climbing the app wall: Enabling mobile app discovery through context-aware recommendations. In *Proc of the 21st ACM Int'l Conf. on Information and Knowledge Management*, CIKM '12, pages 2527–2530, 2012.

[16] D. Kong, M. Zhang, and C. H. Q. Ding. Minimal shrinkage for noisy data recovery using schatten-p norm objective. In *ECML/PKDD 2013*, pages 177–193, 2013.

[17] Y. Koren. Factorization meets the neighborhood: a multifaceted collaborative filtering model. In *Proc. of the 14th ACM SIGKDD Int'l Conf. on Knowledge Discovery and Data Mining*, KDD '08, pages 426–434, 2008.

[18] Y. Koren, R. Bell, and C. Volinsky. Matrix factorization techniques for recommender systems. *Computer*, 42(8):30–37, Aug. 2009.

[19] D. D. Lee and H. S. Seung. Algorithms for non-negative matrix factorization. In *NIPS*, pages 556–562, 2000.

[20] J. Lin, K. Sugiyama, M.-Y. Kan, and T.-S. Chua. Addressing cold-start in app recommendation: latent user models constructed from twitter followers. In *Proc. of the 36th int'l ACM SIGIR conf. on Research and development in information retrieval*, SIGIR '13, pages 283–292, 2013.

[21] G. Linden, B. Smith, and J. York. Amazon.com recommendations: Item-to-item collaborative filtering. *IEEE Internet Computing*, 7(1):76–80, Jan. 2003.

[22] B. Liu, Y. Fu, Z. Yao, and H. Xiong. Learning geographical preferences for point-of-interest recommendation. In *Proc. of the 19th ACM SIGKDD Int'l Conf. on Knowledge Discovery and Data Mining*, KDD '13, pages 1043–1051, 2013.

[23] B. Liu, H. Xiong, S. Papadimitriou, Y. Fu, and Z. Yao. A general geographical probabilistic factor model for point of interest recommendation. *Knowledge and Data Engineering, IEEE Transactions on*, PP(99), 2015.

[24] R. Salakhutdinov and A. Mnih. Bayesian probabilistic matrix factorization using markov chain monte carlo. ICML '08, pages 880–887, 2008.

[25] R. Salakhutdinov and A. Mnih. Probabilistic matrix factorization. In *NIPS*, volume 20, 2008.

[26] S. Shekhar, M. Dietz, and D. S. Wallach. Adsplit: Separating smartphone advertising from applications. In *Usenix Security*, 2012.

[27] Smartphone Sales in the Third Quarter of 2013. `http://www.finfacts.ie/irishfinancenews/article_1026800.shtml`.

[28] The Smartphone Market is Bigger Than the PC Market. `http://www.businessinsider.com/smartphone-bigger-than-pc-market-2011-2`.

[29] M. Ye, P. Yin, W.-C. Lee, and D.-L. Lee. Exploiting geographical influence for collaborative point-of-interest recommendation. In *Proc of the 34th Int'l ACM SIGIR Conf on Research and Development in Information Retrieval*, SIGIR '11, pages 325–334, 2011.

[30] P. Yin, P. Luo, W.-C. Lee, and M. Wang. App recommendation: a contest between satisfaction and temptation. WSDM '13, pages 395–404, 2013.

[31] S. Zhang, W. Wang, J. Ford, and F. Makedon. Learning from incomplete ratings using non-negative matrix factorization. In *SDM'06*, 2006.

[32] H. Zhu, H. Xiong, Y. Ge, and E. Chen. Mobile app recommendation with security and privacy awareness. In *Proc. of the 20th ACM Int'l Conf. on Knowledge Discovery and Data Mining*, KDD '14, 2014.

Inferring Movement Trajectories from GPS Snippets

Mu Li
Carnegie Mellon University
muli@cs.cmu.edu

Amr Ahmed
Google Strategic Technologies
amra@google.com

Alexander J. Smola
Carnegie Mellon University
Google Strategic Technologies
alex@smola.org

ABSTRACT

Inferring movement trajectories can be a challenging task, in particular when detailed tracking information is not available due to privacy and data collection constraints. In this paper we present a complete and computationally tractable model for estimating and predicting trajectories based on sparsely sampled, anonymous GPS land-marks that we call GPS snippets. To combat data sparsity we use mapping data as side information to constrain the inference process. We show the efficacy of our approach on a set of prediction tasks over data collected from different cities in the US.

Keywords

GPS; Movement trajectories; Motion modeling

1. INTRODUCTION

Smart mobile devices are becoming ubiquitous due to ready availability of bandwidth and low entry cost. By now most mobile phones and many tablets carry a Global Positioning System (GPS) or equivalent sensor that can be used to locate the devices in high accuracy, even without using the mobile network. This allows app-designers and website developers to provide hyper-localized services, e.g. for shopping, restaurant recommendation (Yelp, Urban Spoon, ...), context-aware assistance (Square, Siri), device location (Find My Friends, Foursquare), and contextual metadata for user generated content (Twitter, Facebook).

Unfortunately, continuous logging of location data is very costly in terms of energy, hence it is inadvisable to use GPS location information beyond need, especially on devices that are as energy-constrained as mobile phones. As a result, GPS location records are only available in the form of *GPS trajectory snippets* and sporadically, e.g. when a navigation software is activated (e.g. Bing Maps, Apple Maps, Mapquest), or whenever there is abundant power (e.g. while plugged into a car charger). While this data is obviously biased, it provides us with valuable observations regarding travel times, and it allows us to infer properties of individual road segments at a spatial resolution exceeding that offered by the GPS itself.

WSDM 2015, February 02 - 06 2015, Shanghai, China

http://dx.doi.org/10.1145/2684822.2685313.

Modeling trajectories is a highly desirable task since it allows one to improve the prediction of future locations, that is, to *extrapolate future behavior*. This is crucial for saving battery on mobile phones, and to establish geofences that can be exploited by location based services (Square, Remember the Milk). Moreover, it allows us to fill in the blanks between intermittent observations, that is, to *interpolate between past actions*. Note that the second task is considerably easier since we know both approximate start and endpoints of the trajectory. Both of these tools are important to assess the popularity of places and to establish the preferred trajectory between two locations. Numerous challenges arise when working with such GPS snippet data:

- The data collected is sampled non-uniformly, based on a number of decisions influenced by power constraints, business logic, and context.
- The data available to such algorithms needs to respect appropriate privacy policies to retain the trust of the users of the location based service. This may affect e.g. distribution, length, accuracy, location, identity and quantity.
- The data is often noisy, in particular when recording it in cities, where urban canyons may bias the inferred locations generated by the GPS.
- People are not always rational in their path planning. That is, given a GPS snippet of observed locations, they do not always follow the shortest or quickest path between them for numerous reasons. At a minimum, the latent motivations of leisure, convenience, bounded knowledge are poorly understood and unobserved.
- The travel speeds are highly variable, depending on time, roads, driving style, and context. Moreover, waiting times on road intersections also fluctuate widely.
- The inference framework needs to be scalable to large collections of trajectories, many locations, and many GPS snippets. It helps if the problem decomposes hierarchically and if there is only a need to share parameters locally (i.e. for adjacent observations), besides a succinct set of global parameters.

Outline: We begin by a description of the model in Section 2 and details on an efficient inference algorithm in Section 3. We then give experimental results in Section 6 and a summary. Finally we give an overview of related work in Section 7 and contrast those approaches to ours and then conclude in Section 8.

2. MODEL

Modeling movement trajectories requires a rather delicate compromise between computational efficiency and fidelity of the model. On one hand, a fair amount of details is required for the model to be truthful. On the other hand, this can lead to considerable expense in the dynamic programs executed for inference. In the following we describe a model that, as we believe, offers a balanced compromise between these two aims.

2.1 Trajectory Data

Observations are in the form of sets of sequences of GPS location snippets with an approximate level of accuracy and a timestamp added to each such observation. The diagram below depicts the relationship between reported locations o_i, also referred-to as observations, true device locations, s_i, and possible paths ξ taken between the latter. We assume that the paths are constrained by roads, i.e. the GPS snippet will only follow paths that are considered fit for this purpose.

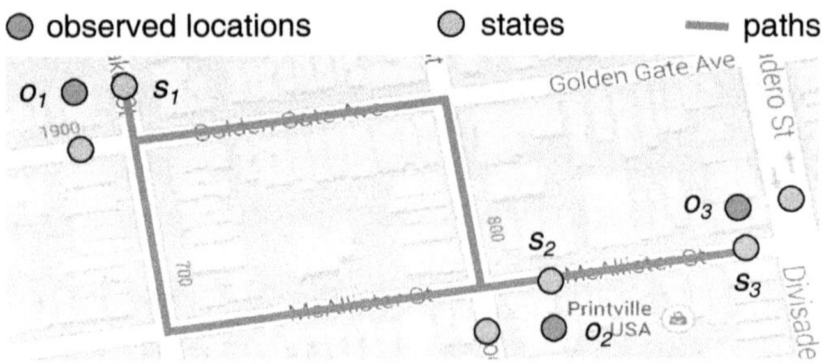

We assume that the data have the following structure:

- A GPS observation o consists of a (latitude, longitude) pair, a direction heading, and a timestamp.
- We denote by $O = (o_1, \ldots, o_n)$ a GPS snippet of a given length n
- $\mathcal{O} = \{O_1, O_2, \ldots\}$ contains all GPS snippets.
- The state s is a location on a road segment. Its position can be determined by which segment it lies in and the offset to the segment beginning. A state shares properties of the road segment, such as direction heading, and also properties of the observation it maps to, such as the timestamp.
- $S = (s_1, \ldots, s_n)$ denotes a sequence of states.
- The index variables i, j usually indicate road segments.
- The index variable k is an indicator for points in a trajectory and segments in a path.
- The variable ξ denotes a path between locations s_i, s_{i+1} that the GPS snippet might have taken. Note that ξ is typically the composition of several road segments.

Denote by θ the parameters, then $p(O, S|\theta)$ is the probability of mapping a observed trajectory snippet O into a sequence of states S. Our goal is to maximize the following log-likelihood

$$\log p(\mathcal{O}|\theta) = \sum_{O \in \mathcal{O}} \log \sum_{S} p(O, S|\theta), \qquad (1)$$

where the summations are over all available trajectory snippets and all possible state sequences, respectively.

We make a first order Markov assumption to simplify the inference. More specifically, we assume that $p(O, S|\theta)$ is a product of observation models and motion models, each of which only depends on the previous observation.

$$p(O, S|\theta) = \prod_{k=1}^{n} p(o_k|s_k, \theta) p(s_{k+1}|s_k, \theta) \qquad (2)$$

where $p(s_{n+1}|s_n, \theta) = 1$ for the virtual state s_{n+1}.

Given this data our goal is to map the observations to an actual path that a GPS snippet might have taken and to infer future propensities of following a given path. This will allow us to infer actual travel times on road segments. In other words, we aim to infer a distribution over paths ξ that is consistent with the locations, timings and direction headings observed via a sequence of GPS records.

2.2 Observation Model

We assume that observed locations and directions are drawn independently. This is reasonable, when taking into account that direction inference on the device may involve not only past locations but also additional observables such as acceleration and magnetic field.

Observed locations are assumed to be normally distributed around the true locations. Moreover, since directions are constrained to $[0, 2\pi]$ we cannot model directional data as explicitly Gaussian. However, we assume that the log-likelihood is a quadratic function of the deviation between observed and true heading. As a result, the observation model is given by

$$p(o|s) \propto \exp\left(-\frac{1}{2\sigma_d^2}\left\|o^{\text{loc}} - s^{\text{loc}}\right\|^2 - \frac{1}{2\sigma_l^2}\left\|o^{\text{dir}} - s^{\text{dir}}\right\|^2\right), (3)$$

where $\left\|o^{\text{dir}} - s^{\text{dir}}\right\|$ is meant to denote the angle on the ring $[0, 2\pi]$, i.e. we assume that we have an approximately Gaussian distribution over relative headings.

To ground observations we assume that true locations and true directions are predominantly constrained by the directions and locations of the underlying road network. For this to be feasible, we assume that we have access to underlying mapping data. In other words, our aim is also to supplement the mapping data with GPS snippet data, as inferred from GPS traces.

2.3 Motion Model

The key to our analysis is a detailed motion model. We will discuss the numerous challenges posed by an efficient inference algorithm for it. It incorporates travel times and corresponding distributions over alternative paths that a GPS snippet might have taken to reach a destination. Moreover, it incorporates the aggregate probability of certain trajectories by explicitly modeling the distribution over turns at intersections.

Intuitively we capture the joint distribution as follows: a given trajectory follows a sequence of turns at any given time. Each of the associated road segments and intersections take some time t to traverse. Moreover, segments need to be consecutive in order to constitute a valid path. This yields the following likelihood model for a sequence of observations O and locations S:

$$\begin{aligned} p(O, S|\theta) &= \prod_k p(o_k|s_k, \theta) p(s_{k+1}|s_k, \theta) \\ &= \prod_k p(o_k|s_k, \theta) \sum_{\xi} p(\xi|s_k, \theta) p(s_{k+1}|s_k, \xi, \theta) \quad (4) \end{aligned}$$

In other words, we need to sum over all paths ξ that could have led from s_k to s_{k+1}. The propensity of taking a certain path ξ will depend on s_k, simply via direction heading, location, speed and other context.

Furthermore, the state s_{k+1} is only reachable from s_k via ξ. This is encoded as follows: Let $\pi(i, j)$ be the turning probability from road segments i into j, where i and j are adjacent. Assume that the path ξ consists of n sequential road segments $(i_1, \ldots, i_n)$. If ξ starts with s_k, then

$$p(\xi|s_k, \theta) = \prod_{\iota=1}^{n} \pi(i_\iota, i_{\iota+1}), \tag{5}$$

and it will be 0 otherwise.

Note that our model uses a first order Markov assumption, namely that $s_{k+1}|\text{past}$ follows $s_{k+1}|s_k$. A more advanced model could incorporate longer sequence histories, albeit at the expense of a significantly more expensive dynamic program. In fact, a longer history would only be solvable by means of sampling, hence we focus on the more directly accessible first order Markov assumption in the present paper.

2.4 The Inverse Gaussian Distribution

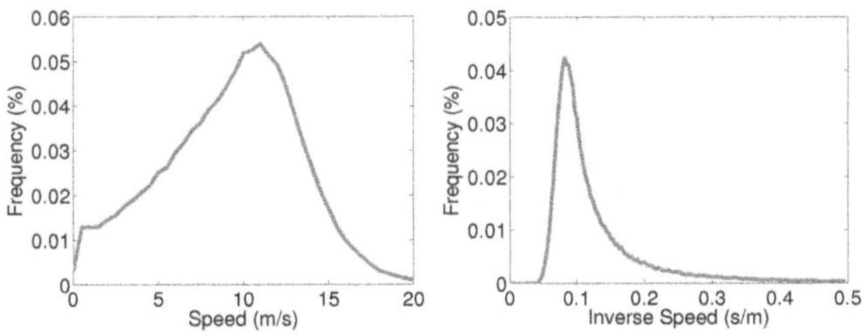

Figure 1: Left: histogram of speeds reported by GPS records; right: distribution of inverse speeds. Note that the time distribution is distinctively non-Gaussian.

Besides requiring spatially contiguous trajectories we also need to ensure that the travel occurs within the constraints of available travel times. This means that the GPS snippet needs to start and finish near well-defined locations at a well-defined point in time.

At first glance, this would suggest that the time to travel from s to s' would follow a Normal distribution. However, when analyzing road segments we do not condition on the distance traveled but rather on the start and stop location. Correspondingly, the distribution is over travel times which are inversely related to speed. An empirical inspection of speed distributions on a segment, as in Figure 1 confirms that a Normal distribution would be a terrible fit for the observed data. Under the assumption that the *velocities* follow a Normal distribution this means that the *travel times* follow an *inverse Gaussian distribution.* Before going into specifics on how this is used, we briefly review its properties here.

The inverse Gaussian distribution $\mathrm{IG}(\mu, \lambda)$ is a member of the exponential family. Hence parameter inference is straightforward and can be solved as a convex minimization problem. Its probability density is given by

$$p(x; \mu, \lambda) = \left(\frac{\lambda}{2\pi x^3}\right)^{\frac{1}{2}} \exp \frac{-\lambda(x-\mu)^2}{2\mu^2 x}, \tag{6}$$

with $\mu, \lambda > 0$. It has mean μ and variance $\frac{\mu^3}{\lambda}$. From its definition we can see that it has reference measure $x^{-\frac{3}{2}}$ and sufficient statistics $\phi(x) = (x, x^{-1})$. Its normalization can be computed efficiently by a variable transform which yields a Gaussian integral. It captures the first passage time of a Brownian random walk, hence it is quite appropriate for modeling the time to reach a given location.

2.5 Modeling Travel Times

We now discuss how to model the travel times between observations. In the following we assume that the path ξ contains road segments $i_1, \ldots, i_n$. The k-th segment has length ℓ_{i_k} and is traversed at speed v_{i_k} with variance in travel time δ_{i_k}.

A straightforward way is to model the travel time on each road segment as an inverse Gaussian distribution. However, this is not suitable for our purpose. The issue is that we have a sum over many segments and the inverse Gaussian distribution is not closed under addition. This complicates inference and leads to a potentially less faithful model.

Instead, we now make the following simplified assumption: the average speed along a path ξ is given by a length-weighted average of speeds over road segments. Moreover, we assume that likewise, the variance is a linear combination of per-segment variances:

$$v_\xi = \frac{1}{\ell_\xi} \sum_{k=1}^{n} \ell_{i_k} v_{i_k} \text{ and } \delta_\xi = \frac{1}{\ell_\xi} \sum_{k=1}^{n} \ell_{i_k} \delta_{i_k} \tag{7}$$

where $\ell_\xi = \sum_{k=1}^{n} \ell_{i_k}$ is the total length of the path.

The advantage of this approach is that we can now model both time and variance as functions that are given by linear combinations of per-segment attributes. An equivalent view would be that we construct a Reproducing Kernel Hilbert Space into which we map all segments and perform estimation in this space [ ].

Therefore the expected time to traverse the segment is given by $t_\xi = \ell_\xi / v_\xi$. Note that we need to scale the variance with the total length of the segment, since it is reasonable to assume that it should scale $O(\ell_\xi)$ with longer intervals. The travel time of this path is then modeled as

$$T(\ell_\xi) \sim \mathrm{IG}\left(v_\xi^{-1} \ell_\xi, (\delta_\xi \ell_\xi)^2\right) \tag{8}$$

As per the properties of the inverse Gaussian distribution this amounts to a mean travel time of $v_\xi^{-1} \ell_\xi$ and a variance of $v_\xi^{-3} \delta_\xi^{-2} \ell_\xi$. This allows us to measure the probability of reaching s_{k+1} if traveling from s_k along ξ within a given travel time, which is obtained by from the GPS timestamps of the observations that adjacent steps map into.

2.6 Covariates

Both travel speed and variance of different segments are correlated. For example, nearby road segments often share similar values, so do roads in the same city, roads of the same type, or traffic at different times of the day. This challenge can be addressed by building a hierarchical model with a broad range of covariates governing the relationship between these parameters. We use the following attributes in our model:

- Information regarding the type of road (e.g. highway, major road, or residential) is highly indicative of the travel time on a given segment.
- The number of lanes and information regarding traffic signs convey information about travel speeds.

Algorithm 1 Inference Algorithm

repeat
  Randomly sample a set of trajectories $\mathcal{O}$
  For each trajectory in $\mathcal{O}$ do dynamic programming discussed in Section 3.2.
  Update transition probability π by (13)
  Update inverse Gaussian distribution parameters ω and γ by (15) and (16)
until converged

- Information about usage type (bicycle, number of lanes, pedestrians, speed limit).
- Location (street name, city, state, country, ZIP code).
- Traffic is highly time-varying, e.g. the time of rush-hours may differ between days of the week and weekend traffic patterns may be different yet. Hence it is worth incorporating temporal information (time, week day, holiday) into the traffic estimates.
- We control for endogenous effects.

The dataset used in the experiments is anonymous. This means that we have no information as to whether two snippets are generated by the same user. Recall that we made the somewhat simplified assumption that speed v and dispersion δ are linear combinations of the per-path contributions. In this case, we define the feature vector for segment ξ by the linear combination of per-segment features:

$$\phi_\xi := \frac{1}{\ell_\xi} \sum_{k=1}^{n} \ell_{i_k} \phi_{i_k}. \tag{9}$$

Then the average speed and variance of this segment, which are defined in (7), can be rewritten as

$$v_\xi = \langle \phi_\xi, \omega \rangle \quad \text{and} \quad \delta_\xi = \langle \phi_\xi, \gamma \rangle , \tag{10}$$

where both ω and γ are parameters will be learned.

Lastly, for computational convenience, we treat intersections as road segments with a fixed virtual length. This allows us incorporate all parts into a common inference framework without specific per-segment accounting.

3. INFERENCE

Our goal is to find a suitable set of parameters $\theta = \{\omega, \gamma, \pi\}$ that allow us to capture both the distribution over road segments, the probability of turns, and the variance of travel times. One possible way is to maximize the log-likelihood defined in (1). That is, we aim to solve the nonconvex optimization problem

$$\underset{\omega,\gamma,\pi}{\text{maximize}} \; \log p(\mathcal{O}|\omega, \gamma, \pi) \tag{11}$$

subject to the positive speeds and variances constraints:

$$\langle \omega, \phi_i \rangle > 0 \text{ and } \langle \gamma, \phi_i \rangle > 0 \text{ for all segments } i.$$

Algorithm 1 summarizes the sketch of the inference. Specifically, on each iteration, we first randomly sample a set of GPS snippets, and then sequentially update the parameters according to their subgradients. The constraints can be easily achieved by nonnegativity constraints on ω and γ, given that ϕ_i has only nonnegative entries.

The key challenge is on calculating the gradients. We first introduce auxiliary results on deriving partial derivatives, next we explain how to calculate the conditional probabilities via dynamic programming, and finally we present how to update the parameters.

3.1 Subgradients

We have a number of observed (GPS locations) and hidden (true locations, paths, intersection times) variables and joint inference is a nonconvex problem. Let us briefly consider the general problem of computing gradients of a probability distribution $p(x, y; \theta)$ that consists of observed x and unobserved y random variables. Moreover, assume that p factorizes into terms

$$p(x, y; \theta) = \prod_{c \in C} \psi_c(x_c, y_c; \theta)$$

where x_c and y_c denote the corresponding (typically overlapping) subsets of (x, y) that are involved in the function ψ_c. This holds for the likelihood of the sequence of observations. In this case we have [ ]:

$$\partial_\theta \log p(x; \theta) = \sum_{c \in C} \mathbf{E}_{y_c|x} \left[\partial_\theta \log \psi_c \left(x_c, y_c; \theta \right) \right] . \tag{12}$$

This can be seen via

$$\begin{aligned} &\partial_\theta \log p(x; \theta) \\ &= \frac{1}{p(x;\theta)} \sum_{c \in C} \int dy \prod_{c' \neq c} \psi_{c'}(x_{c'}, y_{c'}; \theta) \partial_\theta \psi_c(x_c, y_c; \theta) \\ &= \frac{1}{p(x;\theta)} \sum_{c \in C} \int dy p(x, y; \theta) \frac{\partial_\theta \psi_c(x_c, y_c; \theta)}{\psi_c(x_c, y_c; \theta)} \\ &= \sum_{c \in C} \int dy p(y|x; \theta) \partial_\theta \log \psi_c(x_c, y_c; \theta) \end{aligned}$$

The claim follows from integrating out all hidden variables except for y_c. The advantage of this strategy is that it suffices to compute expectations with respect to subsets y_c of variables at a time. For instance, in our case this involves only variables for adjacent road segments and transition probabilities.

3.2 Dynamic Programming

The key in computing the gradients is the ability to compute the expectation in (12), which is essentially calculating the conditional probabilities over the latent variables s_k and ξ. However, this task is potentially quite expensive. For instance, naively we would have to take all paths from s_k to s_{k+1} into account, regardless of how improbable and far they may be. Moreover, a naive application of $p(o_k|s_k)$ equally yields a near infinite number of possible latent states that could have led to the observation o_k, assuming an improbably inaccurate GPS measurement. In practice, these eventualities need to be ignored to keep the algorithm feasible.

We do so by imposing a hard constraint on the distance between o_k and s_k. Since there are typically only a relatively modest number of streets, this limits the number of possible locations s_k to tens rather than millions. Likewise, while we allow for arbitrarily slow movement, we limit the maximum speed in which the trajectory will neither violate the laws of physics nor violate the laws of traffic substantially.

Denote by $\text{Paths}(s_k, s_{k+1})$ the set of admissible paths. The transition probability between states is then given by

$$p(s_{k+1}|s_k, \theta) = \sum_{\xi \in \text{Paths}(s_k, s_{k+1})} p(\xi_k|s_k, \theta) p(s_{k+1}|\xi_k, s_k, \theta).$$

Note that dynamic programming would be more appropriate if we had a substantially larger set of Paths(s_k, s_{k+1}). However, it was computationally more efficient to perform the above computation in a brute-force fashion in our case, since there are relatively few admissible paths between adjacent states.

Next consider the trajectory of a path, as observed by O. Here we need to resort to the forward-backward algorithm to compute the likelihoods along the trellis of admissible states.

$$\alpha(s_k) = \sum_{s_{k-1}} p(o_{k-1}|s_{k-1})p(s_k|s_{k-1}, \theta)\alpha(s_{k-1})$$

$$\beta(s_k) = \sum_{s_{k+1}} p(o_k|s_k)p(s_{k+1}|s_k, \theta)\beta(s_{k+1})$$

where we define $\alpha(s_1) = 1$ and $\beta(s_n) = p(o_n|s_n, \theta)$. Hence marginals and pairwise probabilities are given by

$$p(s_k|O) \propto \alpha(s_k)\beta(s_k)$$
$$p(s_k, s_{k+1}|O) \propto \alpha(s_k)p(s_{k+1}|s_k, \theta)p(o_{k+1}|s_{k+1}, \theta)\beta(s_{k+1}).$$

Using these probabilities we can compute the expectation over latent variables s_k, ξ as required for the gradients. Note that the algorithm is $O(m)$ due to the simple recursion in the dynamic program, where m is the number of observations.

3.3 Updating Parameters

Recall that the objective (1) is given by a sum over trace likelihoods $\log \sum_S p(O, S|\theta)$ for all available GPS snippets. Moreover, note that $p(O, S|\theta)$ can be expanded via (4). In turn, $p(\xi|s, \theta)$ can be expanded further via (5). Putting everything together we obtain the objective:

$$\log p(\mathcal{O}|\omega, \gamma, \pi) = \sum_{O \in \mathcal{O}} \log \sum_S p(O, S|\theta)$$
$$= \sum_{O \in \mathcal{O}} \log \sum_S \left\{ \prod_k p(o_k|s_k, \theta)p(s_{k+1}|s_k, \theta) \right\}$$
$$= \sum_{O \in \mathcal{O}} \log \sum_S \left\{ \prod_k p(o_k|s_k, \theta) \left[\sum_\xi p(\xi|s_k, \theta)p(s_{k+1}|s_k, \xi, \theta) \right] \right\}$$
$$= \sum_{O \in \mathcal{O}} \log \sum_S \left\{ \prod_k p(o_k|s_k, \theta) \right.$$
$$\left. \times \left[\sum_\xi \left(\prod_{\iota=1}^{n} \pi(i_\iota, i_{\iota+1}) \right) p(s_{k+1}|s_k, \xi, \theta) \right] \right\}$$

Updating Transition Probability π

Note that $\pi(a, b) \neq 0$ only if the locations (a, b) are adjacent to another since otherwise there is quite a noticeable difference between the speeds and heading cannot be any transition between them. This simplifies computing expectations greatly. The gradient with respect to π can be computed by taking the expectation over adjacent states

$$\psi(a, b) := \sum_{O \in \mathcal{O}} \sum_{o_i \in O} \mathbf{E}_{\xi|O} \left[\sum_{k=1}^{n_\xi} \{(i_k, i_{k+1}) = (a, b)\} \right]$$

using dynamic programming. Here the sum over the sequence is due to the fact that we assumed that $\pi(a, b)$ is stationary and by subsequent application of the product rule for differentiation. Consequently we can update π to

$$\pi(a, b) = \psi(a, b) / \sum_a \psi(a, b). \tag{13}$$

The normalization by $\psi(a, b)$ is needed to ensure that π encodes proper conditional probabilities. An analogous result holds if we make $\pi(a, b)$ dependent on additional covariates, such as time. Moreover, $\psi(a, b)$ can be modified easily using a conjugate prior.

Updating Inverse Gaussian Distribution Parameters γ, ω

To update the associated parameters recall the probability density (6) and moreover that we model the parameters via $\mu = \ell_\xi / v_\xi$ and $\lambda = \ell_\xi^2 \delta_\xi^2$. Plugging this into the appropriate time distribution we obtain

$$-\log p(t|v_\xi, \delta_\xi, \ell_\xi) = \frac{1}{2} \log 2\pi + \frac{3}{2} \log t - \log \delta_\xi - \log \ell_\xi$$
$$+ \frac{t}{2} \delta_\xi^2 v_\xi^2 - \ell_\xi \delta_\xi^2 v_\xi + \frac{1}{2t} \ell_\xi^2 \delta_\xi^2 \tag{14}$$

Note that due to our specific choice of parametrization, the problem is nonconvex in v_ξ and δ_ξ. Nonetheless, it has a unique minimum. We have

$$-\partial_\gamma \log p(t|v_\xi, \delta_\xi, l_\xi) = \phi_\xi \left[\frac{\delta_\xi}{t} (tv_\xi - \ell_x)^2 - \frac{1}{\delta_\xi} \right]$$
$$-\partial_\omega \log p(t|v_\xi, \delta_\xi, l_\xi) = \phi_\xi \left[\delta_\xi^2 (tv_\xi - \ell_\xi) \right]$$

Since the times are defined via the distance between observations o_k and o_{k+1}, it suffices if we are able to take the expectation over segments $\xi|o_k, o_{k+1}$ and aggregate over all observation pairs (o_k, o_{k+1}) to obtain proper gradients. Finally, note that $p(\xi|s_k, \theta)$ only depends on s_k insofar as segments that start too far from s_k or that result in discontiguous paths are omitted. Hence we need not concern ourselves with any explicit parameters inherent to $p(\xi|s_k, \theta)$.

Finally, to ensure nonnegativity of the velocity and dispersion, and to exploit the fact the features are typically very sparse, we use nonnegative feature maps ϕ_ξ and multiplicative updates, i.e. exponentiated gradient [ ]. That is, we perform coordinate-wise updates

$$\omega^{(t+1)} = \omega^{(t)} .* \exp\left(\eta t^{-\frac{1}{2}} \partial_\omega \log p(\mathcal{O}|\theta)\right) \tag{15}$$

$$\gamma^{(t+1)} = \gamma^{(t)} .* \exp\left(\eta t^{-\frac{1}{2}} \partial_\gamma \log p(\mathcal{O}|\theta)\right) \tag{16}$$

where η is the learning rate, t is an iteration counter, and both $.*$ and exp are carried out element by element.

4. EVALUATION TASKS

Two tasks are designed to evaluate the proposed algorithm. We test how well the model fits the data by estimating a past location or travel time to reach an internal point on a given trajectory (interpolation task). The second task tests how well the model generalizes to future events by estimating either the GPS snippet location in the future at a given time or the time needed to reach a future location. Future prediction is a challenging task considering that the GPS snippet could take various paths in the future, thus the quality of the prediction depends on how well the model estimates the transition probabilities and how well the model estimates the speed of each road segment.

4.1 Inferring the Past

In this task, we are interested in predicting a point, s, within a trajectory. Let s_- and s_+ be the previous and next observed points of s respectively in the trajectory, and let t be the travel time between s_- and s_+. Two tasks can be performed.

Time inference. Assume the location of s is given, and the goal is to estimate the travel time from s_- to s. Denote by ξ is the most likely path from s_- to s_+ passing through s, and by ξ_- the path section from s_- to s. Then we estimate the travel time by interpolation $t_- = \frac{|\xi_-|}{|\xi|}t$, where $|\xi|$ is the length of path ξ.

Location inference. The goal is to estimate the location given the travel time t_- from $s-$ to s. Let ξ be the most likely path from s_- to s_+. We make an assumption that s lies in ξ and denote by ξ_- the sub-path. Then ξ_- is determined by the interpolation $|s_-| = \frac{t_-}{t}|\xi|$.

4.2 Predicting the Future

In this section we focus on predicting a future event beyond the boundaries of the observed trajectory. Again, let s be the point of interest in the future, and s_- be the last observed point in a given trajectory. Unlike the case in Section 4.1, s_+ is unknown here, so that s can not obtained by interpolation. Instead, we will use the learned *motion model*. As in Section 4.1, we consider two tasks: predicting the travel time, given a future location and predicting the future location after a given time period.

Predicting travel time t. Since the location of s is known, we could find all possible paths between s_- and s. Let ξ be one of them. By the inverse Gaussian model, the expected time reaching s via ξ is $v_\xi^{-1}\ell_\xi$. Then we sum over all possible paths from s_- to s to predict the travel time t:

$$\left(\sum_\xi p(s|s_-,\xi)\right)^{-1} \sum_\xi p(s|s_-,\xi)\frac{\ell_\xi}{v_\xi}, \quad (17)$$

where $p(s|s_-,\xi)$ contains both transition probability of path ξ and the probability to arrive at location s after time given by t_ξ.

Predicting future location s. Now we describe how to predict the future location s given the travel time t. To accomplish this, we first find all possible paths starting from s_-. Let ξ be one of such paths. Then we predict the most likely future location after traveling along this path for time t. We let the travel speed be v_ξ and the time variance of this speed is σ_ξ. Thus, the most likely traveled distance ℓ is

$$t = \underset{x}{\mathrm{argmax}}\ p(x; v_\xi^{-1}\ell, \delta_\xi^2\ell^2). \quad (18)$$

where p is the probability density of the inverse Gaussian distribution defined in (6). This equation has a closed form solution, usually called the mode and is given by:

$$t = \frac{\ell_\xi}{v_\xi}\left[\left(1 + \frac{3}{2}\frac{1}{\ell_\xi v_\xi \sigma_\xi^2}\right)^{\frac{1}{2}} - \frac{3}{2}\frac{1}{\ell_\xi v_\xi \sigma_\xi^2}\right]. \quad (19)$$

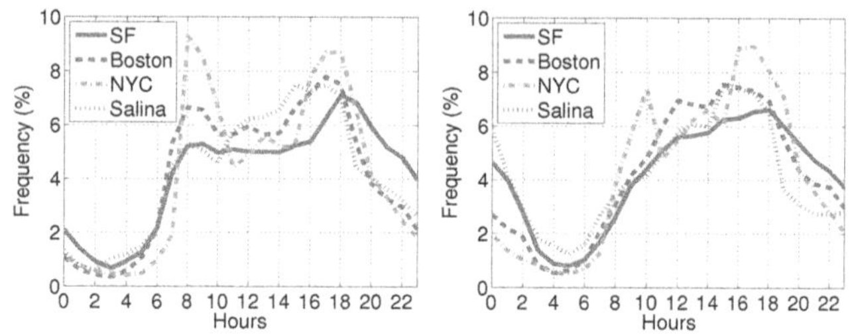

Figure 2: Histogram of traffic frequency. Left: weekdays, right: weekends. Note the rather pronounced double rush hour in NYC and Boston.

Substituting (19) back into (18) we obtain the solution:

$$\ell = t_g v_\xi \left(1 + 3/tv_\xi^2\delta_\xi^2\right)^{\frac{1}{2}}, \quad (20)$$

This solution comprises two terms, the first is the distance traveled with speed v_ξ and time t. The second term takes into account the variance of the speed.

5. DATASETS

To demonstrate the efficacy of our approach we sampled GPS trajectory data in 2013 from four US cities: San Francisco (CA), New York City (NY), Boston (MA) and Salina (KS) and corresponding map data. The resulting dataset comprises around 20 million trajectories, 50,000 road segments and 100,000 intersections.

	SF	Boston	NYC	Salina
segments	17,602	6,639	17,409	9,041
intersections	34,989	9,902	29,453	23,622
trajectories	8.1M	6.8M	3.8M	3.3M

Figure 2 shows temporal patterns of these trajectories. There are clear peaks corresponding to rush hours at 8am and 6pm during weekdays. As expected, there is a temporal shift and smoothing on weekends when rush hours are not quite as prominent.

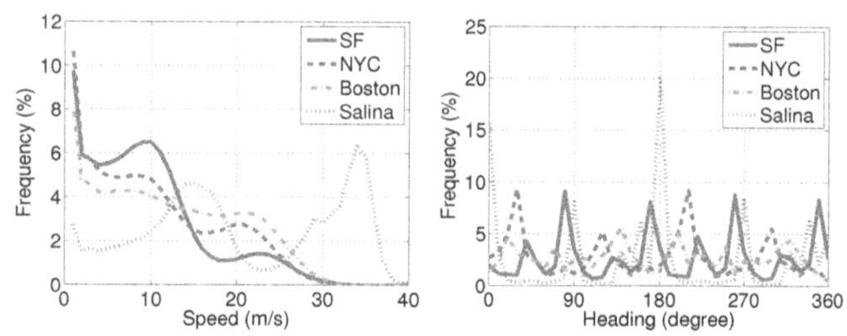

Figure 3: Left: histogram of travel speeds. Right: distribution over heading directions.

There is quite a noticeable difference between the speeds and heading directions in different cities, as can be seen in Figure 3. More specifically, traffic in San Francisco is much slower than in New York and Boston. Moreover, note the pronounced bimodality for Salina. This is likely due to the fact that one of the highways is a major thoroughfare for interstate transport. Also note the strong directionality of traffic in all cities with the exception of Boston. This arises from a grid-layout of the roads.

Figure 4: Road Segments and Intersections

The road segments and intersections are obtained from mapping data, as represented in Figure 4. Both segments and intersections are directional.

6. EXPERIMENTS

We present the experimental results of the two challenge tasks described in Section 4 : inferring the past and predicting the future. However, we first present the features used to learn the speed of road segments.

6.1 Feature Sets for Learning Speeds

We constructed a set of binary features, ϕ for each road segment to learn the speed of road segments as detailed in Section 2.6. Note that ϕ denotes the features of a road segment instances, i.e. the appearance of a road segment within a given trajectory at a given time. These features can be categorized into three sets:

Road features. These features capture several facets of the road attributes such as road type "major road", "high way", etc.

Temporal features. We sliced time into workday and weekend hours to obtain 48 features. A given road segment instance was assigned to an hour based on the time of the majority of GPS points that fell into it.

Individual Speed. We used trajectory ID as the feature to model individual speed preference along the trajectory. This produced tens of millions of unique features.

We combined road and time features to obtain cross-features. In other words, a feature from the road feature group was paired with a feature from the time feature group to form a new feature. This new feature has value 1 if and only if the former two are both equal to 1. This allows us to model non-linear interactions between features since we employ a linear model as described in Section 2.6. This feature combination is also equivalent to a hierarchical model. Due to the large size of the trajectory feature group, we did not combine it with other features.

6.2 Models Compared

To our best knowledge, most of the work in the literature (as we will discuss in Section 7) focuses on on personalized long term trajectory prediction with *continuous* GPS recording [16, 17]. In contrast, our data consists of a large number of anonymous snippets without user IDs. Hence their algorithm does not apply directly. Instead, we compared the proposed algorithm against several variants to understand the contribution of each component in our model.

`Full-Model`. This model used the full set of features, and parameters were learned by Algorithm 1.

`GPS-Speed`. The recorded GPS speeds was directly used without learning ω. In other words, we modeled the speed of a trajectory by the average of its recorded speeds from GPS points. The remaining components were the same as `Full-Model`. Probability π were modeled as usual.

`Common`. The individual speed feature group was removed compared to `Full-Model`. In this model, the speed and time variance only depend on the location and time.

`Shortest-Path`. Only the shortest path between two states was considered, the remaining components were the same as in `Full-Model`. This variant has a computational advantage compared to other variants above. However, it restricts the allowed behavior by assuming people always choose the shortest path to the destination.

6.3 Experimental Setup

To carry out the tasks described above we randomly chose 30% of the trajectories as the test set. We held out a randomly selected internal GPS point of each trajectory in this set to accomplish the task of inferring the past. To predict the future, we elided the last point in the trajectory. To use these removed points for evaluation, their true location, which is required in estimating the travel time, is chosen to be the nearest point in a road segment.

We trained a single model on all trajectories from the four cities. We ran the optimization algorithm for a set of iterations until convergence. In each iteration, we randomly sampled 1,000 trajectories from a random zip code area for processing. The search diameter, namely the maximal distance from possible true locations (states) to observed locations, was limited by 50 meters. For computing expectations over hidden paths ξ, we also limited ourselves to paths containing at most 15 road segments, which was roughly 1.5 kilometer long. Those paths were computed by the breadth-first search algorithm and stored at the beginning before optimization starts. Hence all possible paths between two locations could be fetched during training. The running time of the training procedure took several hours on a single machine with a parallel implementation. In other words, the dynamic program on each trajectory was parallelized.

We fixed $\delta_d = 100$ and $\delta_l = \frac{\pi}{4}$ for the motion model. The learning rates were chosen from the interval $[1, 0.01]$ by examining the convergence rate. Empirically we found that the features constructed from the trajectory IDs (in the Individual speed group) are much sparser than the other two feature groups. This imbalance slows the convergence of the stochastic gradient descent. Instead of performing feature normalization, we placed different learning rates η_1 and η_2 of these two kinds of features respectively. In addition, we only tune η_1 by fixing $\eta_2 = 10\eta_1$. Lastly, we used the top 5 candidate paths when predicting future locations.

Table 1: Average errors of estimating past locations and travel times.

	time error (sec.)				location error (m)				heading direction error (·°)			
	SF	NYC	Boston	Salina	SF	NYC	Boston	Salina	SF	NYC	Boston	Salina
`Full-Model`	2.27	3.23	1.21	0.82	26.9	40.1	16.0	19.2	20.8	19.3	12.6	16.8
`common`	2.38	3.36	1.43	0.80	25.9	38.0	17.0	18.3	17.6	16.6	11.0	15.2
`GPS-speed`	2.99	4.51	1.85	0.98	31.5	50.3	22.3	21.7	17.2	19.1	12.4	14.1
`Shortest-path`	2.28	3.27	1.25	0.81	26.1	39.7	16.2	19.2	21.8	20.0	12.9	18.3

Table 2: Average error of predicting a future location and the travel time. The top 5 locations candidates are considered.

	time error (sec.)				location error (m)				heading direction error (·°)			
	SF	NYC	Boston	Salina	SF	NYC	Boston	Salina	SF	NYC	Boston	Salina
`Full-Model`	3.56	4.83	2.41	1.19	57.8	70.5	44.4	33.5	20.1	19.3	12.9	16.3
`common`	3.95	5.20	2.81	1.27	67.1	77.6	50.9	36.3	17.4	16.2	11.2	15.5
`GPS-speed`	4.71	6.62	3.41	1.42	59.8	77.8	50.7	31.2	19.8	19.4	12.9	17.0
`Shortest-path`	4.40	6.03	2.73	1.46	68.7	83.4	49.2	40.6	22.1	21.5	12.9	19.3

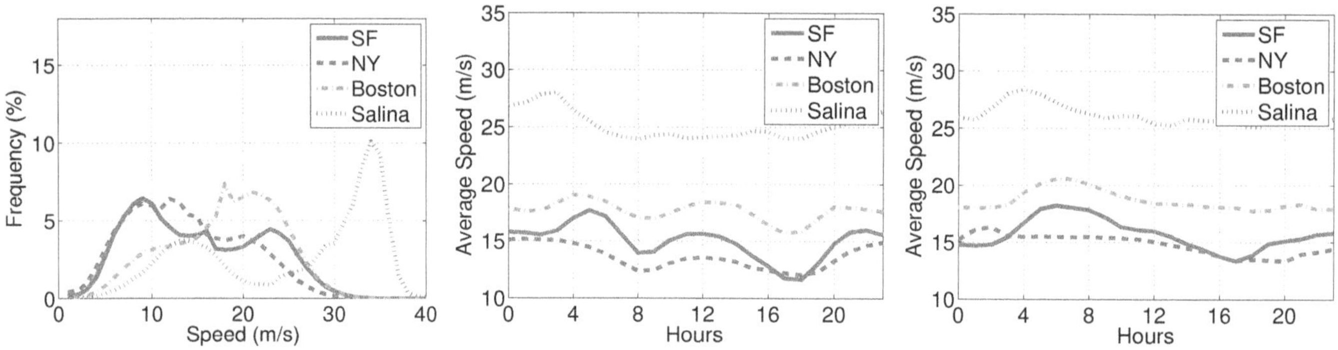

Figure 5: Left: histogram of learned travel speeds. There is a reduction of low speeds portion comparing to the recorded GPS speeds in Figure 3. Middle and right: travel speed as a function of the time of day on weekdays and weekend. As before, the effect of rush hours are quite visible in their reduction of travel speeds.

6.4 Learned Travel Speeds

The learned travel speeds are demonstrated in Figure 5. The positions of the modes in the histogram of the learned speeds are similar to the ones from GPS which were shown in Figure 3. However, a noticeable differences is the significant reduction of low speeds (less than $10m/s$). These speeds might have happened near a red traffic light or a stop sign. The proposed model has a smoothing effect because it uses a smoothed constant speed between two locations and thus misses these range of speeds.

There is a strong pattern of the fall and rise of the traveling speed along time as shown in Figure 5. As expected, the traveling speed decreases during the two rush hours in weekdays in all cities. However this effect is less obvious in Salina, whose traffic is mainly on the interstate highways.

6.5 Time and Location Prediction

We first present the results of estimating past locations and travel times. The average test errors are summarized in Table 1. The average test errors of travel time, location, and heading direction are below 5 seconds, 50 meters, and 20 degrees, respectively. Several reasons contributed to the errors, such as the complexity of city roads, e.g. frequent turning and waiting, and the degradation of data precision due to urban canyons. We believe that our models fit the data reasonably well.

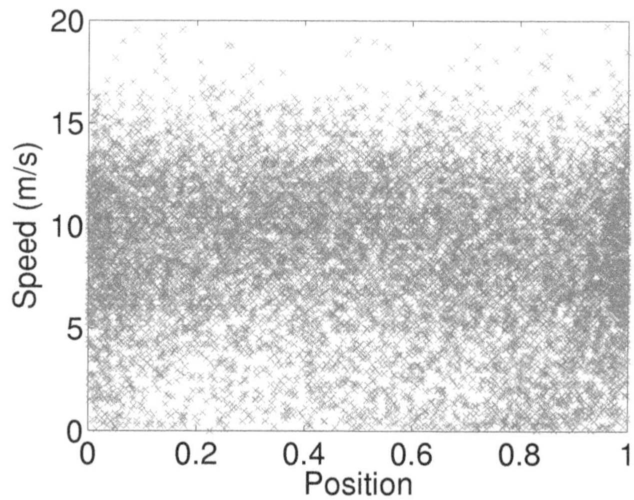

Figure 6: Recorded speeds in different positions of a road segment during the time between 7pm and 9pm.

The estimation errors differ among cities, which can be better observed in the top of Figure 7. As expected, the existence of major arterial highways in Boston and Salina makes the estimation problem easier than in SF and NYC because the speed has lest variation in highways than local

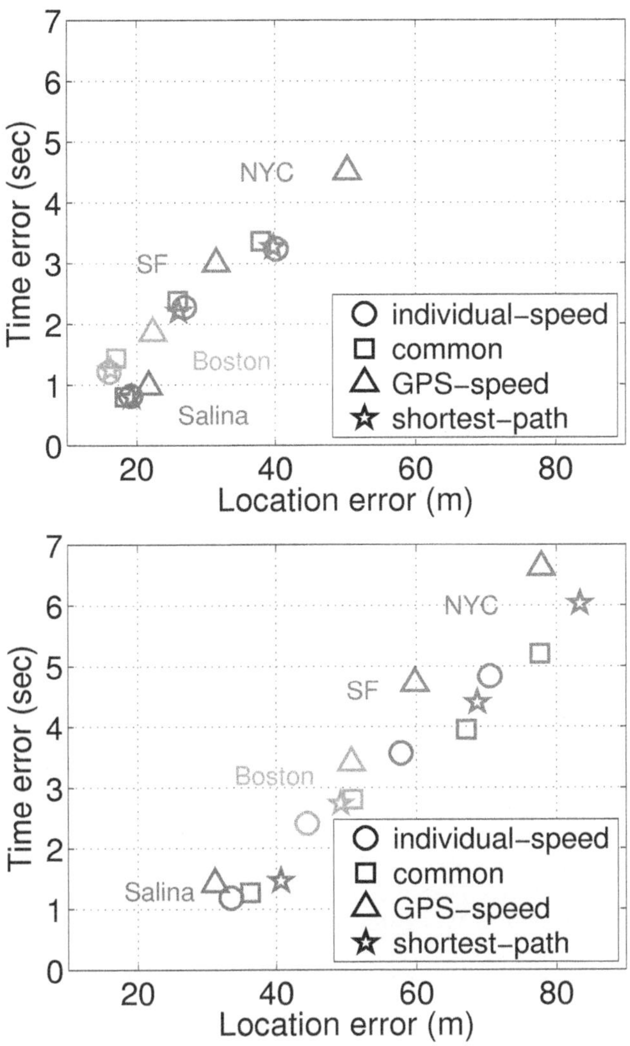

Figure 7: Top: location and time error for different cities when performing interpolation. Bottom: corresponding extrapolation errors.

city roads. Moreover, Manhattan has a higher density of roads and people than the San Francisco area. As expected it has larger estimation error than the latter.

Next we turn to comparing the different variants of the models. The best (statistically significant) results are highlighted via underlines in Table 1, which are also visualized in Figure 7. As can be seen, the model `GPS-speed` performs worse than the other models. We believe this happens because the infrequently sampled GPS points induce highly variable recorded speeds which in turn increases the estimation errors. To see this point, refer to to Figure 6 which shows the recorded speeds at a particular road segment have a large variation. In addition, the gap between `GPS-speed` and the best two other models increase from Salina to NYC (left to right in Figure 7), where the traffic environment becomes more complex.

Finally we show the results of predicting future locations and travel time in Table 2 and also in the bottom of Figure 7. Comparing to the result obtained when inferring past locations, there is an increase on both location error and time error as expected (since we have less constraints). However, the errors are still within reasonable ranges. The increase of errors in time, location and heading directions are less than 2 second, 40 meters, and almost 0, respectively.

The same conclusion observed from estimating past locations are still applicable when estimating future locations. In addition, the model `Full-Model` with all functionality performs better than the slightly simplified model `common` and then the model that only takes shortest paths into consideration. There are two reasons for this. First, the assumption that people always choose the shortest path may be too restrictive. People take a longer path for several possible reasons: easier to drive, personal preference, or even due to turning mistakes. Taking into account a few more possible paths take into considerations this variation better. Second, the travel time and location are predicted by the motion model while in the previous task (predicting the past) we simply interpolate the values. Hence a better motion model like `Full-Model` that takes into consideration individual preference, is more likely to have better individual motion models and therefore gives better results in the future-prediction task.

7. RELATED WORK

There is increasing interest in estimating and predicting travel times as the GPS devices become more available on recent years. There are mainly two research directions. The first is mapping an observed noisy GPS location to a real location, and recovering the trajectory from temporal data. There is a rich of work in this topic, such as [11, 9, 3]. [8] models the whole trajectory path by taking account of the road speed constraint while [10] adopts a HMM model. A related topic is inference the map from the GPS trajectories [6].

The second direction of research is more focused on measuring and predicting the travel time. Most of the work in the literature is focused on high frequency, long sequence of GPS data [14] or highway traffic estimation [15]. [4] presented a probabilistic model of travel time in arterial network based on taxi GPS data. The travel time of each road segment is modeled independently as a Normal and log-normal distribution. A lower-bound of the log-likelihood is solved by an EM-like algorithm to avoid the computational intractable integrals. [13] used a similar model but from a Bayesian approach with an MCMC algorithm for inference. Very recently, [12] used a tensor decomposition method on Beijing taxi GPS data.

By observing that travel times are usually correlated between adjacent roads, [5] proposed modeling the travel times by general features which are related to the road and temporal information. However, their work assume the true position and paths are available. [16, 17] also used general features to modeling taxi driver preference from the inverse reinforcement learning approach.

Our work is different on several aspects. First our model can not only map trajectories to real locations but also modeling road speed and variance, and predicting future travel time and position. Second, we focus on noisy and sparsely sampled anonymous GPS sequences, while most of the work in the literature focus on long, personalized and densely sampled GPS sequences or high precision high-wag data. Third, we model the travel speeds and variance as a function of road, time and personal preference and we consider non-linear models. Fourth, the travel time is modeled as an inverse Gaussian distribution with the path speeds and variance as parameters. During inference the gradient can be computed in a simple close form. Thus this gives a more faithful approximation of the data as we shown in Figure 1 and is more computationally efficient due to the existence of a closed form solution. Fifth, we perform a joint inference over mapping observations to true locations, discovering possible paths, and inferring travel times. We achieved this by a probabilistic model that considers all possible mapping sequences, potentially paths between two locations, and road transition probabilities. Finally, most importantly, we use millions of trajectories from different cities to demonstrate the scalability of the proposed algorithm. This data is an order of magnitude larger than previous work.

8. CONCLUSION

Nowadays there are new challenges to the task of inferring movement from GPS data. The data may be short and anonymous due to increasing demand of privacy control. The limited power capacity of mobile devices places extra constraints on the sampling frequency of locations, inducing temporal sparse GPS recordings. The spatial coverage and volume of these GPS snippets is quite high due to increasing availability of smart phones and other mobile GPS devices.

In this paper we presented an efficient probabilistic model to analyze this challenging GPS snippet data to perform the following three tasks simultaneously: location mapping, path discovery and travel time estimation. We give an efficient scalable inference algorithm and demonstrated its efficiency by using tens of millions of GPS trajectories snippets from four different cities. The experimental results showed that this algorithm performed well on both estimating past and predicting future locations and travel times.

9. REFERENCES

[1] Christopher Bishop. *Pattern Recognition and Machine Learning.* Springer, 2006.

[2] T. Gärtner, P. A. Flach, A. Kowalczyk, and A. J. Smola. Multi-instance kernels. In *Proceedings of the International Conference on Machine Learning*, pages 179–186. Morgan Kaufmann Publishers Inc., 2002.

[3] Timothy Hunter, Pieter Abbeel, and Alexandre M Bayen. The path inference filter: model-based low-latency map matching of probe vehicle data. In *Algorithmic Foundations of Robotics*, pages 591–607. Springer, 2013.

[4] Timothy Hunter, Ryan Herring, Pieter Abbeel, and Alexandre Bayen. Path and travel time inference from gps probe vehicle data. *NIPS Analyzing Networks and Learning with Graphs*, 2009.

[5] Erik Jenelius and Haris N Koutsopoulos. Travel time estimation for urban road networks using low frequency probe vehicle data. *Transportation Research Part B: Methodological*, 53:64–81, 2013.

[6] J. Kivinen and M. K. Warmuth. Additive versus exponentiated gradient updates for linear prediction. In *Proc. 27th Annual ACM Symposium on Theory of Computing*, pages 209–218. ACM Press, New York, NY, 1995.

[7] Xuemei Liu, James Biagioni, Jakob Eriksson, Yin Wang, George Forman, and Yanmin Zhu. Mining large-scale, sparse gps traces for map inference: comparison of approaches. In *Proceedings of the 18th ACM SIGKDD international conference on Knowledge discovery and data mining*, pages 669–677. ACM, 2012.

[8] Yin Lou, Chengyang Zhang, Yu Zheng, Xing Xie, Wei Wang, and Yan Huang. Map-matching for low-sampling-rate gps trajectories. In *Proceedings of the 17th ACM SIGSPATIAL International Conference on Advances in Geographic Information Systems*, pages 352–361. ACM, 2009.

[9] Tomio Miwa, Daisuke Kiuchi, Toshiyuki Yamamoto, and Takayuki Morikawa. Development of map matching algorithm for low frequency probe data. *Transportation Research Part C: Emerging Technologies*, 22:132–145, 2012.

[10] Paul Newson and John Krumm. Hidden markov map matching through noise and sparseness. In *Proceedings of the 17th ACM SIGSPATIAL International Conference on Advances in Geographic Information Systems*, pages 336–343. ACM, 2009.

[11] Mahmood Rahmani and Haris N Koutsopoulos. Path inference of low-frequency gps probes for urban networks. In *IEEE Conference on Intelligent Transportation Systems (ITSC)*, pages 1698–1701. IEEE, 2012.

[12] Yilun Wang, Yu Zheng, and Yexiang Xue. Travel time estimation of a path using sparse trajectories. In *Proceeding of the 20th SIGKDD conference on Knowledge Discovery and Data Mining*, 2014.

[13] Bradford S Westgate, Dawn B Woodard, David S Matteson, and Shane G Henderson. Travel time estimation for ambulances using bayesian data augmentation. *Annals of Applied Statistics*, 2013.

[14] Daniel B Work, O-P Tossavainen, Sébastien Blandin, Alexandre M Bayen, Toch Iwuchukwu, and Ken Tracton. An ensemble kalman filtering approach to highway traffic estimation using gps enabled mobile devices. In *IEEE CDC*, pages 5062–5068. IEEE, 2008.

[15] Yufei Yuan, JWC Van Lint, R Eddie Wilson, Femke van Wageningen-Kessels, and Serge P Hoogendoorn. Real-time lagrangian traffic state estimator for freeways. *IEEE Trasaction on Intelligent Transportation Systems*, 13(1):59–70, 2012.

[16] Brian D Ziebart, Andrew L Maas, J Andrew Bagnell, and Anind K Dey. Maximum entropy inverse reinforcement learning. In *AAAI*, pages 1433–1438, 2008.

[17] Brian D Ziebart, Andrew L Maas, Anind K Dey, and J Andrew Bagnell. Navigate like a cabbie: Probabilistic reasoning from observed context-aware behavior. In *Ubiquitous Computing*, pages 322–331. ACM, 2008.

Regressing Towards Simpler Prediction Systems

Tushar Chandra
Google, Inc.
tushar@google.com

Abstract

This talk will focus on our experience in managing the complexity of Sibyl, a large scale machine learning system that is widely used within Google. We believe that a large fraction of the challenges faced by Sibyl are inherent to large scale production machine learning and that other production systems are likely to encounter them as well[1]. Thus, these challenges present interesting opportunities for future research.

The Sibyl system is complex for a number of reasons. We have learnt that a complete end-to-end machine learning solution has to have subsystems to address a variety of different needs: data ingestion, data analysis, data verification, experimentation, model analysis, model serving, configuration, data transformations, support for different kinds of loss functions and modeling, machine learning algorithm implementations, etc. Machine learning algorithms themselves constitute a relatively small fraction of the overall system.

Each subsystem consists of a number of distinct components to support the variety of product needs. For example, Sibyl supports more than 5 different model serving systems, each with its own idiosyncrasies and challenges. In addition, Sibyl configuration contains more lines of code than the core Sibyl learner itself. Finally existing solutions for some of the challenges don't feel adequate and we believe these challenges present opportunities for future research.

Though the overall system is complex, our users need to be able to deploy solutions quickly. This is because a machine learning deployment is typically an iterative process of model improvements. At each iteration, our users experiment with new features, find those that improve the model's prediction capability, and then "launch" a new model with those improved features. A user may go through 10 or more such productive launches. Not only is speed of iteration crucial to our users, but they are often willing to sacrifice the improved prediction quality of a high quality but cumbersome system for the speed of iteration of a lower quality but nimble system.

In this talk I will give an example of how simplification drives systems design and sometimes the design of novel algorithms.

Categories and Subject Descriptors
I.2.6 Computing Methodologies, ARTIFICIAL INTELLIGENCE, Learning: Parameter learning

Keyword
Machine Learning

REFERENCE

[1] D. Sculley, G. Holt, D. Golovin, E. Davydov, T. Phillips, D. Ebner, V. Chaudhary, and M. Young. Machine learning: The high interest credit card of technical debt. In SE4ML: Software Engineering for Machine Learning (NIPS 2014 Workshop), 2014.

WSDM'15, February 2–6, 2015, Shanghai, China.
ACM 978-1-4503-3317-7/15/02.
http://dx.doi.org/10.1145/2684822.2697048

Global Optimization for Display Ad

Rong Ji
Alibaba
jinrong.jr@alibaba-inc.com

Abstract
Online display advertisement has been examined by numerous studies. Most online display ad systems take the greedy approach, namely they display, for each user, the set of ads that match best with the user's interests. One shortcoming of the greedy approach is that it does not take into account the budget limitation of each advertiser. As a result, we often observed that some ads are popular and match with the interests of millions of users; but due to the budget restriction, these ads can only be presented by a limited times, leading to a suboptimal performance.

To make our point clear, let's consider a simple case where we only have two advertisers (i.e. A and B), and two users (i.e. a and b). We assume that both advertisers have only a budget of one display. We further assume that user a is interested in both ads even though he is more interested in ad A, while user b is only interested in ad A. Now, if we take the greedy approach, we will always present ad A to user a; as a result, if user a comes before user b, we will have no appropriate ad to be displayed for user b. On the other hand, if we can take into account the budget limitation of both advertisers, a better approach is to present ad B to user a and ad A to user b. This simple example motivates us to develop the global optimization approach for online display advertisement that explicitly take into account the budget limitation of advertisers when deciding the ad presentation for individual users.

The key idea of the proposed approach is to compute a user-ad assignment matrix that maximizes the number of clicks under the constraint of ad budgets from individual advertisers. The main computational challenge is the size of variable to be optimized: since the number of users and advertisements involved in our system are 1 billion and ten thousands, respectively, we need to estimate a matrix of billions times ten thousands. We address this challenge by converting the original optimization problem into its dual problem, in which the number of variables is reduced to only ten thousands. A distributed computing algorithm, based on the Nesterov's method and map-reduce framework, was developed to efficiently solve the related optimization problem. We have observed that, the proposed algorithm significantly improves the effectiveness of ad presentation compared to the greedy algorithm.

Categories and Subject Descriptors
H.4.0 Information Systems, INFORMATION SYSTEMS APPLICATIONS: General

Keyword: online advertisement

WSDM'15, February 2–6, 2015, Shanghai, China.
ACM 978-1-4503-3317-7/15/02.
http://dx.doi.org/10.1145/2684822.2697048

Back to the Past: Supporting Interpretations of Forgotten Stories by Time-aware Re-Contextualization

Nam Khanh Tran, Andrea Ceroni, Nattiya Kanhabua, and Claudia Niederée

L3S Research Center / Leibniz Universität Hannover, Germany

{ntran, ceroni, kanhabua, niederee}@L3S.de

ABSTRACT

Fully understanding an older news article requires context knowledge from the time of article creation. Finding information about such context is a tedious and time-consuming task, which distracts the reader. Simple contextualization via Wikification is not sufficient here. The retrieved context information has to be time-aware, concise (not full Wiki pages) and focused on the coherence of the article topic. In this paper, we present an approach for time-aware re-contextualization, which takes those requirements into account in order to improve reading experience. For this purpose, we propose (1) different query formulation methods for retrieving contextualization candidates and (2) ranking methods taking into account topical and temporal relevance as well as complementarity with respect to the original text. We evaluate our proposed approaches through extensive experiments using real-world datasets and ground-truth consisting of over 9,400 article/context pairs. To this end, our experimental results show that our approaches retrieve contextualization information for older articles from the New York Times Archive with high precision and outperform baselines significantly.

Categories and Subject Descriptors H.3.3 [Information Storage and Retrieval]: Information Search and Retrieval
General Terms Algorithms; Experimentation
Keywords Time-aware re-contextualization; Temporal context; Complementarity; News; Interpretation; Wikipedia

1. INTRODUCTION

If we see the 1950's advertisement shown in Figure 1, we might find trouble in understanding the point it makes, or we are outraged about the (not so) implicit message given that women are too weak or too stupid to open a ketchup bottle. At first glance, it seems difficult to imagine how this can be used for advertising a household product. However, if we look into the context information on the right side of the figure, we might understand that the advertisement follows the gender stereotype of a housewife at that time.

WSDM'15, February 2–6, 2015, Shanghai, China.
Copyright 2015 ACM 978-1-4503-3317-7/15/02 ...$15.00.
http://dx.doi.org/10.1145/2684822.2685315.

Figure 1: Ketchup advertisement (1953) and its context.

The research challenge addressed in this paper is how such context can be computed for helping in the interpretation of past or forgotten stories, e.g., from a news archive. We call this process *time-aware re-contextualization* [6] or contextualization, for short. The process automatically provides complementing information to a textual document, which reflects required but not expressed context for fully understanding it. Although contextualization might also be necessary due to differences in cultural background or domain expertise, we focus on supporting time-aware interpretation, where a large time-gap between creation and reading time has to be bridged.

The need for dealing with content from the past is not restricted to expert users, such as, journalists, historians or researchers. Due to the growing age of the Web, general Web users are increasingly confronted with the content of different age assuming knowledge of the context at the respective time for its interpretation.

Just adding information, which is related to the entities and concepts mentioned in the text, as it is done in Wikification approaches, for example, [28, 29] or for a domain specific case [17], is not sufficient for many reasons. First, we require a kind of a virtual time-travel, in which - by the information about the past - we are mentally transported into the time of content creation, in our example the US of the 50s. Second, the context information should be digestible in a short time with minimal disruption from the main reading. Therefore, we aim for a contextualization unit granularity, which is considerably smaller than a full Wikipedia page. Finally, contextualization has to coherently consider the specific aspects about entities, concepts or terms, which are relevant in the text under consideration.

Therefore, time-aware re-contextualization, which aims to associate an information item d (such as, a paragraph in a text) with time-aware, concise and coherent context information c for easing its understanding, is a challenging task. Several subgoals of the information search process have to be combined with each other [6]: (1) c has to be relevant for d, (2) c has to complement the information already available in d and the surrounding document, (3) c has to consider the time of creation (or reference) of d, and (4) the context information should be concise to avoid overloading the user.

In [6], we focused on defining the problem and providing a simple proof-of-concept implementation, which relies on manual work for query formulation. The work presented in this paper automates the process of time-aware re-contextualization and provides advanced approaches for retrieval of contextualization candidates and ranking them by taking into consideration complementarity. In more detail, we follow a two-step process. In the first step, we identify contextualization candidates based on contextualization hooks, i.e., the parts of document that require contextualization.[1] For this purpose, we explore and analyze different methods for formulating (generating) queries, which are used for retrieving adequate contextualization candidates from an underlying knowledge source. In the second step, we rank the candidates. Similarly to diversification approaches, (e.g., [38]), this requires balancing two goals: high content-based and temporal relevance for the text to be contextualized, on one hand, and complementarity for providing information that cannot already be found in the text, on the other hand. For our contextualization approach, we use Wikipedia as the knowledge source (because of its world-wide topical and temporal coverage) for contextualizing old stories from news articles.

Our main contributions in this paper can be summarized as follows:

1. We propose effective query formulation methods that take into account the contextualization hooks as well as recall-oriented query performance prediction using a set of novel features for adaptivity to the difficulty of the documents to be contextualized.
2. We present a time-aware ranking method based on learning-to-rank techniques using a novel feature set, and we propose a complementarity computation, which exploits ideas from search result diversification in ranking.
3. Using real-world datasets, we conduct extensive experiments to evaluate our time-aware re-contextualization approach, which achieves high precision and gains considerable improvement over the baselines. For fostering further research on this challenging task, a manually annotated ground-truth is made available.

We start the rest of the paper with a discussion of related work in Section 2. We outline our approach overview in Section 3, and we describe our proposed methods for query formulation and ranking contextualization candidates in Sections 4 and 5, respectively. In Section 6, we describe the experimental settings, followed by a discussion of experimental results in Section 7. Section 8 concludes our paper and presents directions for future work.

[1]Possible contextualization hooks are, for example, entity or concept mentions, and other phrases.

2. RELATED WORK

Basic forms of contextualization have already been suggested in early works (such as [28, 29]). The Wikify! system [28], for example, enables an automated linkage of entity and concept mentions with Wikipedia pages. Meanwhile, a lot of progress has been made in further developing the entity disambiguation step (see e.g. [19]), which is crucial for robust linking of entity mentions to Wikipedia entity pages or entity representations in other knowledge bases, such as, Yago, DBPedia or Freebase. Entity linking, or Entity Disambiguation, detects entity name mentions within text and links them to the corresponding entities in a knowledge base. In contrast to our approach, both Wikification and entity linkage approaches lack two ingredients of time-aware contextualization, (a) they do not take into account the temporal aspect of the text to be enriched and (b) the additional information provided is rather general (e.g., Wikipedia articles about an entity) and not focused to the topical information need resulting from the text under consideration.

In the area of time-aware information retrieval (IR), it has been shown that explicitly modeling the time dimension in ranking can improve the retrieval effectiveness for time-sensitive queries. Basically, there are two types of temporal information particularly useful for time-aware information retrieval: (1) the publication or creation time of a document [20, 22], and (2) temporal expressions mentioned in a document or a query [2]. Aforementioned works address one of two main aspects for temporal relevance, namely, recency ranking [10, 11] or time-dependent ranking [2, 22]. The first aspect takes into account the freshness of web documents, whereas the second aspect considers temporal information needs and the temporal profiles of documents.

Retrieving and processing external information to be added to documents gain increasing interest in the recent years. In [21], for example, news articles are enriched with related predictions – sentences containing temporal references to the future – retrieved from other documents in the same collection. Other works [13, 33, 35] exploit social media (e.g., Twitter) as external sources when processing news articles. In [35], the most *interesting* tweets regarding a given news are selected by formulating the tweet selection as an optimization problem. The objective function, representing how much a tweet set is interesting with respect to a news, takes into account diversity, popularity, authority, and opinions of tweets within the set.

The work in [33] discovers social media utterances that discuss a given news article. Multiple query models are generated from a news article by considering its internal structure, term selection strategies, as well as utterances which explicitly contain links to the article. The different resulting ranked list are then merged through data-fusion techniques. In [13], the authors present a topic modeling approach which jointly exploits news articles and Twitter for event summarization. In order to generate a representative but not redundant summary of an event, complementarity between tweets and news article sentences is assessed by considering both their similarity and their difference. In contrast to those approaches, our work adds the time dimension to the contextualization task. Moreover, we are not looking for more information on the current context, but we try to re-construct the original context of a document.

The contextualization task is also related to the diversification problem in IR [7, 38, 39]. In [38], different metrics

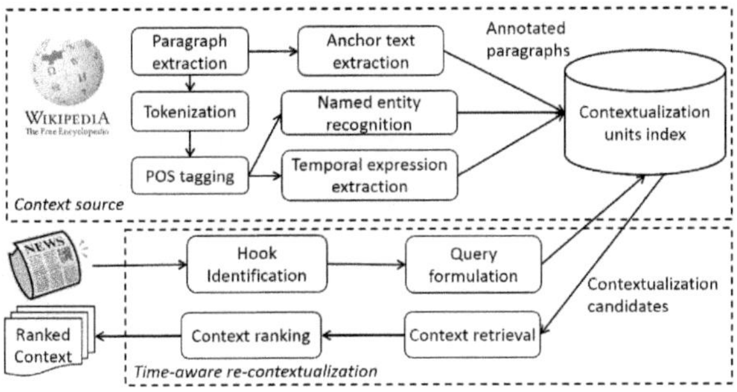

Figure 2: Time-aware re-contextualization approach.

are proposed to measure redundancy in order to investigate the novelty and redundancy of relevant documents in filtering systems. In [7], Clarke et. al. presented a framework for evaluation that systematically rewards novelty and diversity, whereas Zhu et. al. [39] addressed diversification as a learning problem and proposed a novel relational learning-to-rank approach to formulate the task.

In contrast to these studies on analyzing the relation between results to select diverse outcomes for a given query, we mainly focus on the relation between queries (documents in our case) and results (contexts) for finding the ones that are not only topical and temporal relevant, but also complement information already available in the documents.

Automatically formulating queries from text [18] can be done by using tf–idf, mutual information, natural language processing, or machine learning [34, 36, 37]. Assuming the presence of basic metadata and structure for documents, as in [33], some of methods in our paper build queries by exploiting the title and lead paragraph of documents. Similarly to [14], we also explore approaches that assume the availability of manual annotations as seeds for query formulation. The advantage of having such additional information is that the information needs of the users are made explicit, possibly driving to more effective queries. We formulate queries by combining annotations via Query Performance Prediction (QPP) [9], using both pre–retrieval [15] and post–retrieval [5] features. The formers are based only on the query and corpus-based statistics, while the latter also analyze the retrieved list of results. In line with the previous work on time–aware performance predictor [23], we investigate novel features for QPP that explicitly take the temporal dimension into account. Differently from the previously mentioned approaches, which focus on precision metrics, we consider the performances of queries in terms of recall, which have been recently remarked and considered in different information retrieval scenarios [8, 25].

3. APPROACH OVERVIEW

In the general contextualization model underlying our approach we distinguish the information items d to be contextualized and the context source, where the information for the contextualization comes from. Within d a contextualization hook h is an aspect or part of d that requires further information for its time-aware interpretation. The context source is organized into contextualization units cu. In our approach, we have pre-processed a Wikipedia dump as the context source resulting in annotated and indexed Wikipedia paragraphs as contextualization units (see Figure 2). For information items d to be contextualized, we use articles from the New York Times Archive[2] with manually annotated contextualization hooks, i.e., we assume that a reader has marked the places he/she finds difficult to understand.

Starting from the contextualization hooks, the next process is to retrieve a ranked list of contextualization units from the context source. In time-aware re-contextualization the time gap between the creation and reading time of d imposes additional challenges. In our approach, the contextualization process consists of two main steps: (1) formulating queries that are able to retrieve contextualization units, which are good candidates for contextualization; (2) retrieving and ranking the candidates from the context source using the queries from step (1). For step (1) we explore document-based and hook-based query formulation methods and present a procedure that selects good queries based on recall-oriented query performance prediction. For step (2), we employ a retrieval method based on language modeling and re-rank the retrieved contextualization candidates based on a variety of features and a learning to rank approach for ensuring complementarity. The methods developed for steps (1) and (2) are described in more detail in Sections 4 and 5, respectively.

4. QUERY FORMULATION

The goal of the query formulation phase consists of generating a set of queries Q_d for a given document d to retrieve contextualization candidates as input for re-ranking. We explore two families of query formulation methods, one using the document to be contextualized itself as a "generator" of queries (Section 4.1), and the other using contextualization hooks as generators (Sections 4.2 and 4.3). Since some of these methods can generate more than one query from an input document, we will discuss two procedures to merge the ranked result lists in Section 5.1.

4.1 Document-based Query Formulation

The first family of query formulation methods exploits the document content and structure. Similarly to [33], we use three methods to formulate queries from documents: *title*, *lead*, and *title+lead*. *Title* formulates a query consisting of the document title, which is indicative of the main topic of the article. *Lead* uses the lead paragraph of a document, representing a concise summary of the article and including its main actors. *Title+lead*, as a combination of the previous two methods, formulates a query consisting of both the title and the lead paragraph of the document.

Before being performed, all the queries are pre–processed by tokenization, stop-word removal, and stemming. We did not investigate further information extraction approaches for query formulation, since it has been already proven in [33] that the methods described above perform better than more complex information extraction techniques, e.g., keyphrase extraction.

4.2 Basic Hook-based Query Formulation

As already introduced in Section 3, documents in our model are assumed to contain a set of hooks explicitly representing the information needs of the reader or, more precisely, what requires contextualization to be understood and interpreted. The analysis done in [6] showed that contextu-

[2] http://catalog.ldc.upenn.edu/LDC2008T19

alization hooks are not only entity mentions, concept mentions, but also general terms and even short phrases.

We consider two basic hook–based query formulation methods: *all_hooks* and *each_hook*. *All_hooks* includes all the hooks for a document in a single query, representing a tailored perspective of the user's combined information needs for the document. *Each_hook* queries each hook separately, focusing on specific information about single actors, aspects, or sub–topics of the document. The queries generated by these methods are augmented with the title of the document, under the assumption that it is a good representative of the document's topic.

We also experimented with more advanced methods based on identifying hook relationships, for instance considering their co–occurrence in a document collection. However, since these approaches did not perform better than the *all_hooks* method described before, we will not discuss them further.

4.3 Learning to Select Hook-based Queries

Different methods based on ranking and selection of query terms from an initial query might be employed [1, 24, 27], considering the entire set of hooks for a document as the initial query. We explore an adaptive method which formulates queries based on the characteristics of the input document and hooks. Our approach consists of predicting the performances of candidate queries representing subsets of hooks for a given document, ranking them according to the predicted performance, and selecting the top-m of them to be actually performed for the document. The value of m is identified through experiments. In contrast to previous works in query performance prediction, the prediction model is trained on *recall* instead of *precision*. Furthermore, we define novel features for query performance prediction that explicitly take the temporal dimension into account. Finally, our method assesses performances of subsets of query terms (hooks) and can generate more than one query (subsets of hooks).

4.3.1 Candidate Queries

Given a document d and the set of its hooks H_d, we compute its power set $\mathcal{P}(H_d)$ and we create a candidate query for each set of hooks $p \in \mathcal{P}(H_d)$. Again, candidate queries are augmented with the title of the document.

The effort of the computation of features for each element in the power set is not critical in our scenario for two reasons. First, working with short text like news articles limits the number of hooks within the text. Second, the features employed to predict the query performances (Section 4.3.2) are either pre-retrieval measures, which can be computed off–line, or do not require heavy post-retrieval computation.

4.3.2 Features

We measure the performances of each candidate query in terms of its recall because, as already explained, at retrieval phase we are interested in retrieving as much contextualization candidates as possible. In this work we predict query performances with a regression model learned via Support Vector Regression (SVR) [12]. In this model, each learning sample $s = (\boldsymbol{f}_q, r_q)$ consists in a feature vector $\boldsymbol{f}_q$ describing query q (as well as the document it refers to) and its recall r_q, i.e., the label to be predicted. Note that different numbers of top–l results can be used to compute the recall, i.e., the labels, and the choice is discussed in Section 7.

The feature set that we use to represent queries and the document it belongs to are described in the rest of this section. It is composed of novel temporal features for query performance prediction, along with more standard features [4, 16, 30].

Linguistic Features. We compute a family of linguistic features [30] for a query by considering its text and the document it refers to. This results in a set of features both at query and document level: the length of the query, in words; the number of duplicate terms in the query; the number of entities (people, locations, organization, artifacts) in the query; the number of nouns in the query; the number of verbs in the query; the number of hooks in the query; the length of the document's title; the length of the document's lead paragraph; the number of entities in the document (title and lead paragraph); the number of nouns in the documents; the number of verbs in the document; the number of hooks for the document; the number of duplicates in the document.

Document Frequency. The Document Frequency of a hook h represents the percentage of contextualization units in the corpus containing h and it is computed as:

$$df(h) = \log \frac{N_h}{N} \quad (1)$$

where N_h is the number of contextualization units in the corpus containing h and N is the size of the corpus. At document level, we compute the document frequency for every hook of the document the query belongs to, i.e., $df(h)\ \forall h \in H_d$, and then we derive aggregate statistics like average, standard deviation, maximum value, minimum value. Similarly, at query level, we compute $df(h)$ for every hook in the query and we derive the same aggregate statistics as before. In the following, we will refer to average, standard deviation, maximum value, and minimum value simply as *aggregate statistics*.

Temporal Document Frequency. In order to restrict the popularity of a term to a particular time period $T = [t_0 - w; t_0 + w]$, we compute Eq. 1 only for those contextualization units having at least one temporal reference contained in T. This can be done efficiently since contextualization units in our corpus have been annotated with the temporal references mentioned in them. The time period we are interested in is centered around the publication date of the document, i.e., $t_0 = p_d$, and the parameter w determines the width of the interval. After experimenting different values of w, we set $w = 2years$ for our study.

Scope. The scope of a query has been defined in [16] as the percentage of documents (contextualization units in our case) in the corpus that contain at least one query term. Besides the scope of the query itself, we also compute the scope of the document title and the scope of the document hooks H_d when queried together.

Temporal Scope. We define the temporal scope of a query as the percentage of contextualization units in the corpus that contain at least one query term and at least one temporal expression within a given time period. The time period that we consider is the same as the one considered for the computation of temporal document frequency, i.e., a period centered around the publication date of the document and with a temporal window equal to w. Again, we experimented different values of w and we set $w = 2years$.

Relevance. For a given query q, we retrieve the top-k contextualization units and we compute aggregated statistics of their relevance scores given by the underlying retrieval model. The value of k has been empirically set to 100 after experimenting different candidate values. We also computed relevance features at document level, using both document's title and document's hooks as queries.

Temporal Similarity. For a given query q generated from a document d and every retrieved contextualization unit c in its top-k result set (again, $k = 100$), we compute the temporal similarity between q and c and we derive aggregated statistics over the elements in the result set. Temporal similarity between time points t_1 and t_2 is computed through the time-decay function [22]:

$$TSU(t_1, t_2) = \alpha^{\lambda \frac{|t_1 - t_2|}{\mu}} \tag{2}$$

where α and λ are constants, $0 < \alpha < 1$ and $\lambda > 0$, and μ is a unit of time distance. The temporal similarity between a query q and a result c is computed as $\max_{t \in T_c}\{TSU(t, p_d)\}$, where T_c is the set of temporal references mentioned in c and p_d is the publication date of the document where q refers to. This can be done efficiently since temporal references mentioned in contextualization units have been extracted and stored at indexing time.

We also computed temporal similarity features at document level, using both document's title and document's hooks as queries. The computation of the features is the same as the one described above.

5. CONTEXT RANKING

In this section, we describe the methods used in addressing the second part of the contextualization process outlined in Section 3: retrieving and re-ranking context. For the retrieval step, given the queries generated from different query formulation methods described in previous section, we use a retrieval model based on language modeling to create a ranked list of contextualization candidates. Later, learning to select relevant context items is applied to this ranked list.

5.1 Retrieval Model

For the retrieval step, we use query-likelihood language modeling [31] to determine the similarity of a query with the context. In particular, given a query q generated by using one of the methods described in Section 4 for the document d, we compute the likelihood of generating the query q from a language model estimated from a context c with the assumption that query terms are independent.

$$P(c|q) \propto P(c) \prod_{w \in q} P(w|c)^{n(w,q)} \tag{3}$$

where w is a query term in q, $n(w, q)$ is the term frequency of w in q, and $P(w|c)$ is the probability of w estimated using Dirichlet smoothing:

$$P(w|c) = \frac{n(w, c) + \mu P(w)}{\mu + \sum_{w'} n(w', c)} \tag{4}$$

where μ is the smoothing parameter, $P(w)$ is the probability of each term w in the collection.

To combine the rankings produced by each query of a document, we exploited two combining methods namely round-robin, which chooses one result from each ranked list, skipping any result if it has occurred before, and CombSUM, which sums up a result's scores from all ranked lists where it was retrieved. In the experiment, we observed that round-robin method achieves better performance than CombSUM especially in terms of recall, which also reported in [33]. Therefore, we decided to use round-robin method for combining different ranked lists.

5.2 Learning to Rank Context

Once we have obtained a ranked list of contextualization candidates for each document, we turn to context selection (re-ranking) where we need to decide which of the context items are most viable. Our ranking algorithm needs to balance two goals, i.e., high topical and temporal relevance for the document, as well as complementarity for providing additional information. In this work, we use supervised machine learning, that takes as input a set of labeled examples (context to document mappings) and various complementarity features of these examples similar to diversity features [38].

Topic Diversity. This class of features is aimed to compare the dissimilarity between document d and context c on a higher level by representing them using topics. We use latent Dirichlet allocation (LDA) [3] to model a set of implicit topics distribution of the document and context. We define this feature as follows.

$$R_1(c, d) = \sqrt{\sum_{k=1}^{m} (p(z_k|d) - p(z_k|c))^2}$$

where m is the number of topics and z_k is the topic index.

Text Difference. In this case, we represent the document and context as a set of words. The novelty of context c is measured by the number of new words in the smoothed set representation of c. If a word w occurred frequently in context c but less frequently in document d, it is likely that new information not covered by d is covered by c. For computation, a document and its context are represented by a set of informative words (removing stop words and stemming) denoted by $Set(d)$ and $Set(c)$, respectively. We compute the text difference feature as follows.

$$R_2(c, d) = \|Set(c) \cap \overline{Set(d)}\|$$

Entity Difference. The way of computing entity difference is similar to the one for text difference, with the difference that a document and its context are represented by a set of entities. The feature is denoted as $R_3(c, d)$.

Anchor Text Difference. Anchor texts can be regarded as a short summary (i.e., a few words) of the target document and captures what the document is about. This feature can be computed similarly as text and entity features, which is denoted as $R_4(c, d)$. We extract anchor texts using WikiMiner [29] with a confidence threshold γ.

Distributional Similarity. The next feature we use is distribution similarity, which is denoted as $R_5(c, d)$.

$$R_5(c, d) = -KL(\theta_c, \theta_d) = -\sum_{w_i} P(w_i|\theta_c) \log \frac{P(w_i|\theta_d))}{P(w_i|\theta_c)}$$

where θ_d and θ_c are the language models for a document d and its context c, respectively, and are multinomial distributions. We compute θ_d (and similarly for θ_c) using maximum likelihood estimation (MLE) given as:

$$P(w_i|d) = \frac{tf(w_i, d)}{\sum_{w_j} tf(w_j, d)}$$

The problem with using MLE is that if a word never occurs in the document d, the probability $P(w_i|d)$ will be zero; $P(w_i|d) = 0$. Thus, a word in the context c but not in the document d will make $KL(\theta_c|\theta_d) = \infty$. In order to solve this problem, we make use of the Dirichlet smoothing method.

$$P_\lambda(w_i|d) = \frac{tf(w_i, d) + \lambda p(w_i)}{\sum_{w_j}(tf(w_j, d) + \lambda p(w_j))}$$

Geometric Distance. There are several ways to compute geometric distance measure, such as, Manhattan distance and Cosine distance. We leverage Cosine distance because of its robustness to document length.

$$R_6(c, d) = \cos(c, d) = \frac{\sum_{k=1}^{n} w_k(c) w_k(d)}{\|d\| \; \|c\|}$$

In our experiment, we used each unique word as one dimension and the *tf.idf* score as the weight of each dimension.

Relevance and temporal features. In order to retrieve high topical and temporal relevant contextualization candidates for the document, we consider also relevance and temporal features. For the former one, we exploit the retrieval scores of context returned by our retrieval model. For the later one, we apply temporal similarity measurement, i.e., TSU which is described in the previous section.

6. EXPERIMENTAL SETUP

Document Collections. In our experiments, we used the New York Times Annotated Corpus, which contains 1.8 million documents from January 1987 to June 2007, as the document collection to be contextualized. For context source, we employed Wikipedia because it is considered the largest and most up-to-date online encyclopedia covering a wide temporal range of general and specific knowledge. We obtained the Wikipedia dump of February 4, 2013 and considered *paragraphs* as contextualization units. In this particular snapshot, we obtain 4,414,920 Wikipedia articles that contain 25,708,539 paragraphs. For each paragraph, we used Stanford CoreNLP [26] for tokenization, entity annotation and temporal expression extraction. In addition, *anchor* texts found in the paragraph hyperlinks are also extracted. We used Apache Solr[3] to index the annotated paragraphs.

Ground-truth Dataset. In order to obtain ground-truth dataset (both for training and evaluation), we manually selected a set of 51 articles that spanned a wide range of topics (business, technology, education, science, politics, and sports) focusing on the older ones (29 articles published in 1987, 2 articles in 1988, 6 articles in 1990, 7 articles in 1991, and 7 articles in 1992) and recruited six human annotators to manually annotate those articles. The annotators were presented with an annotation interface with which they can evaluate article/context pairs (relevant or non-relevant). The annotation guidelines specified that the annotators should assign relevance to the context that contains *additional information* which complements the information in the article and does provide a good answer to (at least) one of the questions they think up when reading the article. For each article, we retrieved up to 20 contextualization candidates with each query formulation method and removed duplicates afterwards. In total, our annotation dataset consists of 9,464 article/context pairs, where the annotators evaluated 26.9 relevant context per article on average. To foster further research on this challenging task, our ground-truth dataset is publicly available.[4] We measured the inter-annotator agreement using Cohen's kappa statistic. We averaged the pairwise kappa values of all possible combinations of annotators that had overlapping candidates they had annotated and we obtained a fair agreement of $\kappa_c = 0.37$ given the high complexity of this contextualization task, which includes objectivity and subjectivity.

Parameter Settings. For query performance prediction, the regression model described in Section 4.3.2 was built by using the Support Vector Regression implementation of LibSVM[5]. In particular, we trained a n-SVR model with Gaussian Kernel through 10–fold cross validation. The open parameters were tuned via grid search to $C = 3$, $\gamma = 0.5$ and $\nu = 0.75$. Linguistic features were extracted using Stanford CoreNLP [26].

For re-ranking context, we performed 5-fold cross validation at document level. We reported scores averaged over all testing folds. We conducted experiments using several machine learning algorithms to confirm the robustness of our approach, i.e., it does not depend on any specific algorithm. In this paper, we employed Random forests (RF), RankBoost (RB) and AdaRank that are implemented in RankLib.[6] In order to compute topic-based feature, we employed the topic modeling tool Mallet[7] by specifying the number of topics to 100, for this task. In addition, we set the confidence threshold to $\gamma = 0.3$ for extracting anchor texts using WikiMiner. For smoothing, we set $\mu = 2000$ and $\lambda p(w_i) = 0.5$.

For computing temporal similarity feature, we set $\lambda = 0.25$, $\alpha = 0.5$, and $\mu = 2years$ in our experiments. We also observed that changing those parameters did not affect the correlation capabilities of the feature.

Evaluation Metrics. The evaluation metrics, we considered precision at rank 1, 3, 10 (P@1, P@3, P@10 respectively), recall, and mean average precision (MAP). These measures provide a short summary of quality of the retrieved context. In our experiment, a context is considered relevant if it is marked as relevance by an annotator, otherwise we consider it as non-relevance. We used the top-20 returned context for evaluation because it is not expected that readers consider more than 20 contextualization units. Statistical significance was performed using a two-tailed paired t-test and is marked as $^\blacktriangle$ and $^\vartriangle$ for a significant improvement (with $p < 0.01$ and $p < 0.05$, respectively), and significant decrease with $^\blacktriangledown$ and $^\triangledown$ (for $p < 0.01$ and $p < 0.05$, respectively).

Baselines. For comparing to our approach, we considered three following competitive baselines.

Milne and Witten (M&W). The method proposed by Milne and Witten [29] which represents the state-of-the-art in automatic linking approaches. We use the algorithm and best-performing settings as described in [29]. In order to apply this method for our task, we consider all paragraphs of all linked pages as a candidate set.

Language Model (LM). The standard query-likelihood language model is used for the initial retrieval as described in Section 5 which provides the top retrieved documents as a candidate set for the contextualization task.

[3] https://lucene.apache.org/solr/

[4] http://www.l3s.de/~ntran/contextualization/

[5] http://www.csie.ntu.edu.tw/~cjlin/libsvm/

[6] http://sourceforge.net/p/lemur/wiki/RankLib/

[7] http://mallet.cs.umass.edu/topics.php

Time-aware Language Model (LM-T). Since we aimed at adding context to past stories, the temporal dimension is important. We selected a state-of-the-art time-aware ranking method, which has been shown very effective for answering temporal queries, as our third baseline. It assumes the textual and temporal part of the document d are generated independently from the corresponding parts of the context c, yielding

$$P(d|c) = P(d_{text}|c_{text}) \times P(d_{time}|c_{time}) \quad (5)$$

where d_{time} is the document's publication date, c_{time} is the set of temporal expressions in the context c.

The first factor $P(d_{text}|c_{text})$ can be computed by Eq. 3 and Eq. 4. The second factor in (5) is estimated, based on a simplified variant of [2], as

$$P(d_{time}|c_{time}) = \frac{1}{| c_{time} |} \sum_{t \in c_{time}} P(d_{time}|t) \quad (6)$$

If the document has zero probability of being generated from the context, Jelinek-Mercer smoothing is employed, and we estimate probability of generating the document's publication date from context c as

$$P(d_{time}|c_{time}) = (1 - \lambda)\frac{1}{| C_{time} |} \sum_{t \in C_{time}} P(d_{time}|t) + \lambda\frac{1}{| c_{time} |} \sum_{t \in c_{time}} P(d_{time}|t) \quad (7)$$

where $\lambda \in [0, 1]$ is a tunable mixing parameter which is set to $\lambda = 0.5$ in our experiment (changing this parameter does not affect our results), and C_{time} refers the temporal part of the context collection treated as a single context and $P(d_{time}|t)$ is estimated by using time-decay function, i.e., TSU computed as in Eq. 2.

7. RESULTS AND DISCUSSION

7.1 Query Formulation

We evaluate and compare the performances of the different query formulation methods described in Section 4, focusing on recall metric. The results reported in the rest of this section are averaged over the 51 documents in our dataset.

In order to fairly evaluate and compare the recall capabilities of the different methods, which can generate different numbers of queries, we allow each method to retrieve the same number of results k. The choice of the method that we used to create a single result set of k elements from different ranked lists have been discussed in Section 5.1.

7.1.1 Prediction Performances

The query formulation method described in Section 4.3 is based on predicting the performances (recall in our case) of candidate queries, ranking them according to the prediction, and then using the top-m queries to retrieve results. Thus, the quality of the query performance prediction itself has to be evaluated before assessing and comparing the performances of the whole query formulation method.

The regression model has been trained via 10–fold cross validation, and the results reported hereafter have been averaged over the 10 folds. The Correlation Coefficient is equal to 0.973, the Root Mean Squared Error equals to 0.056, and the Mean Absolute Error equals to 0.037. The low error

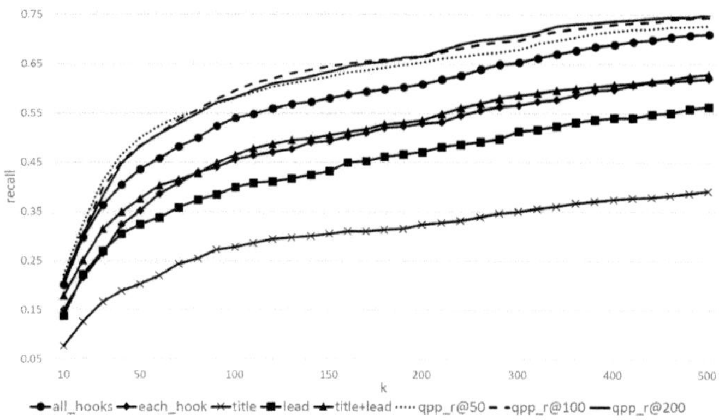

Figure 3: Recall curves of document-based and hook-based methods.

values and high correlation value, if compared with the performances in predicting query precision reported in previous works (e.g. [5, 32]), show that the recall of queries in our task can be predicted quite accurately by using the features described in Section 4.3.2.

Feature Analysis. In order to analyze which are the most important features in our model, we identified the top–10 features according to their absolute correlation coefficient. Referring to Section 4.3.2, these are: *max query relevance, number of hooks in document, min document's hooks df, max document's hooks temporal df, document's hooks scope, avg query temporal similarity, document's title temporal scope, std query relevance, avg document's title temporal similarity*, and *std query temporal similarity*. The presence of temporal document frequency, temporal similarity, and temporal scope shows that the temporal features that we defined play an important role in the model. We can also note that both query–level and document–level features are important, since the set is made of 4 features from the former and 6 features from the latter class. Finally, there is only one linguistic feature in the set, namely the number of hooks in the document, confirming that this class of features alone does not correlate well with query performances [4].

7.1.2 Comparison of Query Formulation Methods

In this section, we compare recall values for the document–based methods (*title, lead, title+lead*), the basic hook–based methods (*each_hook, all_hooks*), as well as the method based on query performance prediction, hereafter called *qpp*. For the latter method, we report the performances achieved when using prediction models trained with different labels: we experimented with different l values, namely $l = 50, 100$ and 200, for the computation of the recall at l to be used as label. These three methods will be called *qpp_r@50, qpp_r@100* and *qpp_r@200*, respectively, in the rest of the experiments. Note that each *qpp* method considered here uses the top-2 queries, according to their predicted performances, to retrieve the results. The choice of selecting $m = 2$ queries will be explained in more detail in Section 7.1.3.

The recall curves of the different methods, for different values of top–k results, are shown in Figure 3. The curves of *title* and *lead* are the lowest ones, while their combination (*title + lead*) becomes comparable with *each_hook*. Querying using all the hooks of a document together, i.e., *all_hooks*, exposes higher recall values than all the aforementioned methods, showing that performing hook–based

	R@50		R@100		R@200	
	qpp	*all_hooks*	*qpp*	*all_hooks*	*qpp*	*all_hooks*
easy	0.6208	0.5666	0.7361	0.6969	0.7951	0.7686
hard	0.3837	0.3094	0.4606	0.3892	0.5391	0.4550

Table 1: Recall of *all_hooks* and *qpp* methods over different classes of documents grouped by their retrieval difficulty.

queries does lead to better performances in terms of recall with respect to document–based methods. The difference in performances between *each_hook* and *all_hooks* is due to the fact that querying all the hooks together prefers contextualization candidates that contain many hooks. These are potentially more relevant, as they refer to different aspects (hooks) of the same document. Regarding the *qpp* methods, for $k > 20 - 30$, the recall values achieved are between 3% and 7% higher than the ones obtained by *all_hooks*. For larger values of k, e.g. $k > 400$, the difference between the *qpp* methods and *all_hooks* reduces because the prediction models used by the *qpp* methods have been optimized for lower values of k (recall that $l = 50, 100, 200$). This means that, if the number of k results to be retrieved for the re-ranking phase is known and fixed in advance, this information can be exploited early in the training of the query performance prediction model by setting $l = k$, leading to higher recall values for that particular k.

Another comparative analysis between *qpp* methods and *all_hooks* can be done by categorizing the documents according to their *difficulty*, which we define in terms of the amount of relevant context that can be retrieved for a given document. This means that difficult documents are those for which few relevant context can be retrieved, before the re-ranking phase. We categorize documents in *easy* and *hard* with respect to the *all_hooks* method, since it represents a baseline in this comparative analysis with *qpp* methods.

The splitting of the documents in easy and hard was performed by considering the recall at $k = 200$ achieved by *all_hooks* for the different documents. Since the recall values associated to the different documents exhibited a uniform distribution, we split the document set in two equal parts, one representing easy documents and the other representing hard documents.

Table 1 shows the performances of *qpp_r*@50, *qpp_r*@100, and *qpp_r*@200 compared to the ones of *all_hooks* for the different categories of difficulty. The comparison between each *qpp* method and *all_hooks* is done considering the recall at those k values used to train the prediction model (i.e. $k = l$, $l = 50, 100, 200$). Besides *qpp_r*@50, *qpp_r*@100, and *qpp_r*@200 are on average better than *all_hooks* both for easy and hard documents, their improvements are greater for hard documents. In case of *qpp_r*@100, for instance, the relative improvement with respect to the recall value achieved by *all_hooks* is 5.6% for easy documents and 18.3% for hard documents. We believe that the capability of getting higher recall improvements for documents whose relevant context units are difficult to retrieve is a considerable characteristic for the *qpp* methods.

As a conclusion, in this section we proved that exploiting hooks in query formulation is more effective, in terms of recall, than document–based query formulation methods. Moreover, we showed that learning to select candidate hook-based queries can be better, again in terms of recall, than the basic hook–based query formulation methods.

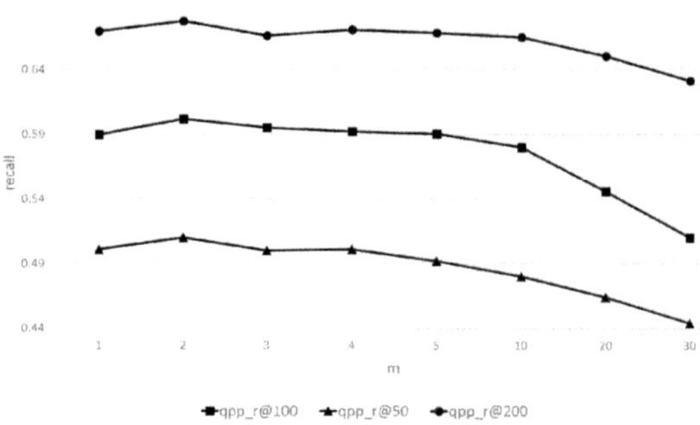

Figure 4: Recall values of *qpp_r*@50, *qpp_r*@100, and *qpp_r*@200 by varying the number of top–m queries.

7.1.3 Number of Queries

The number of top ranked queries that *qpp* methods perform is an open parameter, which we tuned via an empirical analysis observing the recall performances when selecting different numbers of top–m ranked queries. Recall that, for sake of fair comparison, we allow each method to pick the same number of results k from the result lists retrieved by the queries that it generated for a given document. This means that increasing the number of queries to be selected and performed does not necessarily lead to higher recall.

Figure 4 shows the recall values achieved by *qpp_r*@50, *qpp_r*@100 and *qpp_r*@200 (computed at top–50, top–100 and top–200 results, respectively) for different numbers of top–m selected queries. A common trend over the different curves can be observed that they stay quite stable for small values of m, exhibiting a little peak for $m = 2$, and then they decrease for increasing values of m. After observing this behavior, we decided to fix the number of performed queries to $m = 2$.

7.2 Context Ranking

In this subsection, we report the retrieval performances of different query formulation methods and analyze the effectiveness of our context ranking methods trained by using different machine learning algorithms. Firstly, we investigate the performance of the standard, well-known Wikification technique, i.e., the M&W method, in retrieving contextualization candidates. Our experiment considers all paragraphs of all linked pages as candidates. This method achieves the low recall value of 0.229, which indicates that current semantic linking approaches are not appropriate for the contextualization task.

Table 2 shows the results of different query formulation methods. The first group (top) reports results for candidate retrieval based on document-based query models in which the best performing model is *title + lead* that uses content from the article's title and lead paragraph. Turning into models derived from contextualization hooks, Table 2 shows that the *qpp_r@100* model performs the best among all hook-based query models and significantly improves over *title + lead* on all metrics.

Similar to the previous experiment, Table 3 reports the results of *all_hooks* and *qpp_@100* retrieval baselines on a subset of difficult documents (here recall is computed on top-20 candidates). On this subset, *qpp_r@100* also shows

	P@1	P@3	P@10	MAP	Recall
Document-based query models					
title	0.2156	0.1895	0.1745	0.2446	0.1211
lead	0.4902$^\blacktriangle$	0.4641$^\blacktriangle$	0.3333$^\blacktriangle$	0.4908$^\blacktriangle$	0.2603$^\blacktriangle$
title + lead	0.5294$^\blacktriangle$	0.4705$^\blacktriangle$	0.3901$^\blacktriangle$	0.5161$^\blacktriangle$	0.2723$^\blacktriangle$
Basic hook-based query models					
each_hook	0.3333	0.3464	0.2745	0.4003	0.1969
all_hooks	0.5490	0.5098	0.4137	0.5640	0.2979
Query performance prediction model					
qpp_r@100	**0.5882**	**0.5490**$^\blacktriangle$	**0.4529**$^\blacktriangle$	**0.5802**$^\blacktriangle$	**0.3097**$^\blacktriangle$

Table 2: Retrieval performance of document-based and hook-based query models. The significance test is compared with Row 1 (within the first group) and Row 3 (for the second and third groups).

	P@1	P@3	P@10	MAP	Recall
all_hooks	0.5000	0.3462	0.2885	0.4487	0.2217
qpp_r@100	0.5000	**0.4743**$^\triangle$	**0.3730**$^\triangle$	**0.5048**$^\triangle$	**0.2357**

Table 3: Retrieval performance of *all_hooks* and *qpp_@100* on a set of difficult documents.

significant improvement over *all_hooks* in terms of precision. In short, the results on different query formulation methods indicate that using hook-based approaches outperforms the document-based approach that based on merely article internal structure. Using the query performance prediction method obtains the highest performance on all metrics, followed by *all_hooks*.

We now present the results of our re-ranking approach when using a set of innovative complementarity features to further improve performances of the context ranking step, especially in terms of precision. We select *title + lead* for the document-based approach and *all_hooks, qpp_r@100* for the hook-based approach.

	P@1	P@3	P@10	MAP	Recall
title + lead					
LM	0.5294	0.4705	0.3901	0.5161	0.2723
RF	**0.7672**$^\blacktriangle$	0.5757$^\triangle$	**0.4909**$^\blacktriangle$	**0.6170**$^\blacktriangle$	**0.3522**$^\blacktriangle$
RB	0.6036	**0.5945**$^\triangle$	0.4694$^\blacktriangle$	0.5945	0.3417$^\blacktriangle$
AdaRank	0.6254	0.5406	0.4143	0.5457	0.3249
all_hooks					
LM	0.5490	0.5098	0.4137	0.5640	0.2979
RF	**0.8272**$^\blacktriangle$	**0.6630**$^\blacktriangle$	**0.5014**$^\blacktriangle$	**0.6427**$^\triangle$	0.3611$^\blacktriangle$
RB	0.7855$^\blacktriangle$	0.6593$^\blacktriangle$	0.5009$^\blacktriangle$	0.6475$^\triangle$	**0.3637**$^\blacktriangle$
AdaRank	0.6472	0.5836	0.4687	0.6034	0.3372$^\triangle$
qpp_r@100					
LM	0.5882	0.5490	0.4529	0.5802	0.3097
RF	**0.8054**$^\blacktriangle$	**0.6993**$^\blacktriangle$	0.5140$^\blacktriangle$	0.6498$^\blacktriangle$	**0.3951**$^\blacktriangle$
RB	0.7218	0.6915$^\blacktriangle$	**0.5300**$^\blacktriangle$	**0.6632**$^\blacktriangle$	0.3792$^\blacktriangle$
AdaRank	0.6072	0.6139	0.4895	0.6109	0.3479$^\blacktriangle$

Table 4: Retrieval performance of different machine-learned ranking methods compared to the best performing retrieval baselines.

The first (top) group in Table 4 shows the results when applying machine learning to *title + lead* retrieval baseline. All three algorithms are able to improve precision at rank k, MAP and Recall. Random forest (RF) and RankBoost (RB) obtain significant improvement where RF achieves the highest scores on most metrics, except precision at rank 3 where RB is the best. The second (middle) group reports the results of *all_hooks* retrieval baseline, augmented by the re-ranking step. In this case, RF and RB are again able to significantly improve over *all_hooks* on all metrics while AdaRank is also performing significantly better than *all_hooks* in terms of recall. Among three algorithms, RF achieves the highest results, except for recall. Similarly, all three machine learning algorithms perform significantly better than the *qpp_@100* retrieval baseline. Again, in this case RF obtain the highest performances, closely followed by RB.

In order to compare our approach to time-aware language model which takes into account temporal information, we use the queries derived from query performance prediction method, i.e., *qpp_@100* that obtain the highest results among our query formulation methods. Table 5 shows that using time-aware language models is not efficient in our case. This is possibly due to that lots of relevant context (paragraphs in our case) do not have any temporal information as shown in Figure 5. Consequently, these candidates are ranked low (e.g., higher than 20) in the ranked list returned by LM-T. This result indicates that purely using the time dimension in context retrieval is not sufficient in the contextualization task. It also confirms the importance of complementarity that is used in our re-ranking step.

qpp_@100	P@1	P@3	P@10	MAP	Recall
LM-T	0.5882	0.4967	0.4176	0.5446	0.2796
LM	0.5882	0.5490	0.4529	0.5802	0.3097$^\triangle$
RF	**0.8054**$^\triangle$	**0.6993**$^\blacktriangle$	**0.5140**$^\blacktriangle$	**0.6498**$^\blacktriangle$	**0.3951**$^\blacktriangle$

Table 5: Retrieval performance of our proposed ranking method and the state-of-the-art time-aware language modeling approach. The significance test is compared against LM-T.

8. CONCLUSIONS

In this paper we have presented an approach for the novel and challenging task of time-aware re-contextualization of content with a gap between creation and reading time. We have shown that our approach can compute relevant and complementing contextualization information with high precision. In the experiments, hook-based query formulation methods have outperformed document-based ones supporting the validity of our contextualization model, and the predominance of query formulation methods relying on several hooks shows the importance of comprehensive contextualization approaches that go beyond the consideration of individual hooks. Furthermore, our experiments have confirmed that complementarity, which is used in the re-ranking step, plays an important role in contextualization.

Although the results achieved in this paper are promising, the task of time-aware re-contextualization still requires further investigation. As a future work, we have planned to further improve our methods and to investigate into strategies for automatic hook identification. Furthermore, we are planning to combine our re-ranking approach with a diver-

News article - *Maj. Gen. Richard V. Secord, a main organizer of the Iran arms sales and the contra supply operation, testified today that he had been told that President Reagan had been informed that proceeds from the sales to Iran had been diverted to the Nicaraguan rebels.*

Context - *Speaking of the Iran-Contra affair, a Reagan administration scandal that involved the diverting of funds being shipped to Iran to the contras in Nicaragua, Reagan says, "None of the arms we'd shipped to Iran had gone to the terrorists who had kidnapped our citizens." Of the scandal, Reagan writes, " and, I presume, knew how deeply I felt about the need for the contras' survival as a democratic resistance force in Nicaragua. Perhaps that knowledge... led them to support the contras secretly and saw no reason to report this to me." He also says of himself, "As president, I was at the helm, so I am the one who is ultimately responsible."*

Figure 5: Example of contextualization candidate for a given document with no explicit temporal information.

sification approach, such that we can compile the retrieved contextualization information into concise contextualization sets with little overlap between the items. Finally, we also plan to look into the personalization of contextualization approaches taking into account individual differences in contextualization needs.

Acknowledgments The work was partially funded by the European Commission for the FP7 project ForgetIT under grant No. 600826 and the German Federal Ministry of Education and Research (BMBF) for the project *"Gute Arbeit" nach dem Boom (Re-SozIT)* (01UG1249C).

9. REFERENCES

[1] M. Bendersky and W. B. Croft. Discovering key concepts in verbose queries. In *SIGIR '08*, 2008.

[2] K. Berberich, S. J. Bedathur, O. Alonso, and G. Weikum. A language modeling approach for temporal information needs. In *ECIR '10*, 2010.

[3] D. M. Blei, A. Y. Ng, and M. I. Jordan. Latent dirichlet allocation. *J. Mach. Learn. Res.*, 2003.

[4] D. Carmel and O. Kurland. Query performance prediction for ir. In *SIGIR '12*, 2012.

[5] D. Carmel and E. Yom-Tov. Estimating the query difficulty for information retrieval. In *SIGIR '10*, 2010.

[6] A. Ceroni, N. K. Tran, N. Kanhabua, and C. Niederée. Bridging temporal context gaps using time-aware re-contextualization. In *SIGIR '14*, 2014.

[7] C. L. Clarke, M. Kolla, G. V. Cormack, O. Vechtomova, A. Ashkan, S. Büttcher, and I. MacKinnon. Novelty and diversity in information retrieval evaluation. In *SIGIR '08*, 2008.

[8] G. V. Cormack and M. R. Grossman. Evaluation of machine-learning protocols for technology-assisted review in electronic discovery. In *SIGIR '14*, 2014.

[9] S. Cronen-Townsend, Y. Zhou, and W. B. Croft. Predicting query performance. In *SIGIR '02*, 2002.

[10] N. Dai, M. Shokouhi, and B. D. Davison. Learning to rank for freshness and relevance. In *SIGIR '11*, 2011.

[11] A. Dong, Y. Chang, Z. Zheng, G. Mishne, J. Bai, R. Zhang, K. Buchner, C. Liao, and F. Diaz. Towards recency ranking in web search. In *WSDM '10*, 2010.

[12] H. Drucker, C. J. C. Burges, L. Kaufman, A. J. Smola, and V. Vapnik. Support vector regression machines. In *NIPS '97*, 1997.

[13] W. Gao, P. Li, and K. Darwish. Joint topic modeling for event summarization across news and social media streams. In *CIKM '12*, 2012.

[14] G. Golovchinsky, M. N. Price, and B. N. Schilit. From reading to retrieval: Freeform ink annotations as queries. In *SIGIR '99*, 1999.

[15] C. Hauff, D. Hiemstra, and F. de Jong. A survey of pre-retrieval query performance predictors. In *CIKM '08*, 2008.

[16] B. He and I. Ounis. Inferring query performance using pre-retrieval predictors. In *SPIRE '04*, 2004.

[17] J. He, M. de Rijke, M. Sevenster, R. van Ommering, and Y. Qian. Generating links to background knowledge: a case study using narrative radiology reports. In *CIKM '11*, 2011.

[18] M. Henzinger, B.-W. Chang, B. Milch, and S. Brin. Query-free news search. In *WWW '03*, 2003.

[19] J. Hoffart, M. A. Yosef, I. Bordino, H. Fürstenau, M. Pinkal, M. Spaniol, B. Taneva, S. Thater, and G. Weikum. Robust disambiguation of named entities in text. In *EMNLP '11*, 2011.

[20] R. Jones and F. Diaz. Temporal profiles of queries. *ACM Trans. Inf. Syst.*, 2007.

[21] N. Kanhabua, R. Blanco, and M. Matthews. Ranking related news predictions. In *SIGIR 11*, 2011.

[22] N. Kanhabua and K. Nørvåg. Determining time of queries for re-ranking search results. In *ECDL '10*, 2010.

[23] N. Kanhabua and K. Nørvåg. Time-based query performance predictors. In *SIGIR '11*, 2011.

[24] C.-J. Lee, R.-C. Chen, S.-H. Kao, and P.-J. Cheng. A term dependency-based approach for query terms ranking. In *CIKM '09*, 2009.

[25] C. Li, Y. Wang, P. Resnick, and Q. Mei. Req-rec: High recall retrieval with query pooling and interactive classification. In *SIGIR '14*, 2014.

[26] C. D. Manning, M. Surdeanu, J. Bauer, J. Finkel, S. J. Bethard, and D. McClosky. The Stanford CoreNLP natural language processing toolkit. In *ACL '14*, 2014.

[27] K. T. Maxwell and W. B. Croft. Compact query term selection using topically related text. In *SIGIR '13*, 2013.

[28] R. Mihalcea and A. Csomai. Wikify!: linking documents to encyclopedic knowledge. In *CIKM '07*, 2007.

[29] D. Milne and I. H. Witten. Learning to link with wikipedia. In *CIKM '08*, 2008.

[30] J. Mothe and L. Tanguy. Linguistic features to predict query difficulty. In *SIGIR '05*, 2005.

[31] J. M. Ponte and W. B. Croft. A language modeling approach to information retrieval. In *SIGIR '98*, 1998.

[32] F. Raiber and O. Kurland. Query-performance prediction: Setting the expectations straight. In *SIGIR '14*, 2014.

[33] M. Tsagkias, M. de Rijke, and W. Weerkamp. Linking online news and social media. In *WSDM '11*, 2011.

[34] P. D. Turney. Learning algorithms for keyphrase extraction. *Inf. Retr.*, 2000.

[35] T. Štajner, B. Thomee, A.-M. Popescu, M. Pennacchiotti, and A. Jaimes. Automatic selection of social media responses to news. In *KDD '13*, 2013.

[36] I. H. Witten, G. W. Paynter, E. Frank, C. Gutwin, and C. G. Nevill-Manning. Kea: Practical automatic keyphrase extraction. In *DL '99*, 1999.

[37] Y. Yang, N. Bansal, W. Dakka, P. Ipeirotis, N. Koudas, and D. Papadias. Query by document. In *WSDM '09*, 2009.

[38] Y. Zhang, J. Callan, and T. Minka. Novelty and redundancy detection in adaptive filtering. In *SIGIR '02*, 2002.

[39] Y. Zhu, Y. Lan, J. Guo, X. Cheng, and S. Niu. Learning for search result diversification. In *SIGIR '14*, 2014.

Diluted Treatment Effect Estimation for Trigger Analysis in Online Controlled Experiments

Alex Deng
Microsoft
One Microsoft Way
Redmond, WA 98052
alexdeng@microsoft.com

Victor Hu
Microsoft
One Microsoft Way
Redmond, WA 98052
vihu@microsoft.com

ABSTRACT

Online controlled experiments, also called A/B testing, is playing a central role in many data-driven web-facing companies. It is well known and intuitively obvious to many practitioners that when testing a feature with low coverage, analyzing all data collected without zooming into the part that could be affected by the treatment often leads to under-powered hypothesis testing. A common practice is to use triggered analysis. To estimate the overall treatment effect, certain dilution formula is then applied to translate the estimated effect in triggered analysis back to the original all up population. In this paper, we discuss two different types of trigger analyses. We derive correct dilution formulas and show for a set of widely used metrics, namely ratio metrics, correctly deriving and applying those dilution formulas are not trivial. We observe many practitioners in this industry are often applying approximate formulas or even wrong formulas when doing effect dilution calculation. To deal with that, instead of estimating trigger treatment effect followed by effect translation using dilution formula, we aim at combining these two steps into one streamlined analysis, producing more accurate estimation of overall treatment effect together with even higher statistical power than a triggered analysis. The approach we propose in this paper is intuitive, easy to apply and general enough for all types of triggered analyses and all types of metrics.

Categories and Subject Descriptors

G.3 [**Probability and Statistics**]: Experiment Design

General Terms

Measurement; Experimentation; Design; Theory

Keywords

Controlled experiment; A/B testing; Feature Coverage; Variance reduction; Dilution; Metric

WSDM'15, February 2–6, 2015, Shanghai, China.
Copyright 2015 ACM 978-1-4503-3317-7/15/02 ...$15.00.
http://dx.doi.org/10.1145/2684822.2685307 .

1. INTRODUCTION

In the recent decade, online controlled experiment, also known as A/B testing, has become a must for most of data driven web facing companies. The strength of A/B testing lies in the ability to establish causal relationship between the treatment tested and the effect using simple data collection mechanism that can be implemented as embedded components into existing web services (2). Unlike other statistical methods for causal inference which typically rely on strong assumptions that cannot be verified and therefore tend to produce more false assertions than expected (4), A/B testing makes few assumptions. It is also intuitively easy for non-statisticians to understand. In A/B testing, experimentation units, usually users, are randomly split into control group and treatment group. Traffic in the two groups are then exposed to two different versions of the web service. After collecting data from the two groups over a period of time, we analyze the data at the end of the experiment to compare the two groups, see Figure 1[1]. Because of the random traffic splitting, the two groups are the same by design except for exposure to different versions of the web service. Any true difference between the two must come from the difference of the two versions. In the language of Rubin Causal Model, randomization makes sure that the treatment assignment is *ignorable* (5).

In online controlled experiment, we typically use standard statistical inference methods. There are often two goals:

1. Hypothesis testing: Test the hypothesis that there is no difference between the treatment and the control. If the hypothesis is rejected, we know the treatment has an effect. The confidence level is typically controlled at 5% false positive(claiming an effect by mistake).
2. Point estimation: Estimate the treatment effect. The result is usually presented in a form of 95% confidence interval.

These two goals are deeply connected. In fact knowing confidence interval gives an alternative hypothesis testing method by checking whether 0 is in the 95% confidence interval. In this connection, point estimation goes beyond the simple Boolean claim on whether there is a treatment effect by also providing a possible range for the treatment effect and is therefore more preferable. However, in some cases pure hypothesis testing is much easier to conduct than providing confidence intervals. When testing a feature with low coverage, hypothesis testing of the treatment effect can

[1]Although the name A/B testing might suggests there is only one treatment and one control, it can be extend to multiple treatments and that is very common in practice.

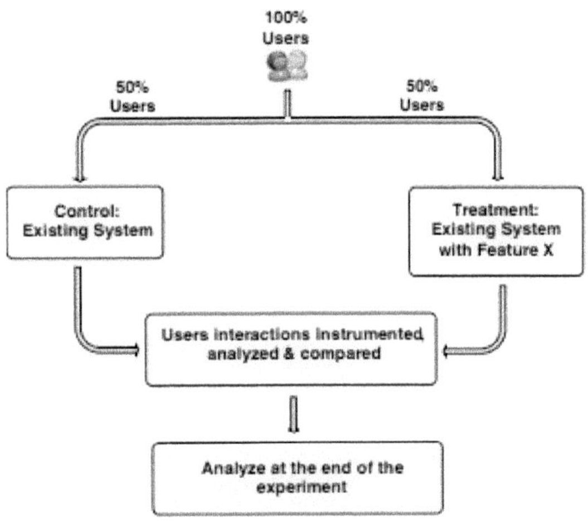

Figure 1: Illustration of Online A/B testing as in (2). Experimentation unit here is user but can be changed to other units such as page-views or visits.

be more efficiently conducted using trigger analysis focusing only on "subset of the data that could be impacted by the treatment"(we will give definition to what this means in Section 2). This is intuitively obvious because by focusing on the triggered subset, the treatment effect is more concentrated and hence stronger. Put it in the other direction, keeping a subset of the data that couldn't be impacted by the treatment is like adding extra noise and will dilute the treatment effect. Analyzing on triggered population is called trigger analysis, in contrast with all up analysis on the original all up or overall population. Hypothesis testing in trigger analysis is also a testing procedure for all up analysis. This is because if there is a treatment effect for triggered subset, there must be a treatment effect for the overall population. Trigger analysis also can provide point estimation for the treatment effect on the triggered population. To provide a point estimation for the overall treatment effect on the all up population, we need to translate our estimate of triggered effect back to the overall effect. This translation is also called dilution because the overall treatment effect is the triggered treatment effect diluted by untriggered complement. Because of this, we also call this overall treatment effect estimation after translation *diluted treatment effect*. The translation step seems straightforward to many people at first glance, and indeed it is for some metrics. But as we will show in Section 2 and Section 3, it turns out to be difficult for a large set of common metrics such as session success rate per user(SSR). Session success rate per user is defined as the average over all users' observed session success rate. Note that at each experiment unit level (user in this case), session success rate is a ratio of the number of successful sessions to the number of sessions, hence the name ratio metrics. These kind of metrics are widely used in search engine evaluation. They are also called double averaging metrics because each user's session success rate is by itself an average. It is different from session success rate (per session) which is defined as the ratio of total successful sessions to the total number of sessions. The double averaged ratio metrics has the advantage of being more robust against outliers as users are treated equally instead of allowing a few super heavy users dominate the metrics with high weightings. Ratio metrics are very common in online A/B testing especially when giving each experiment unit equal weight is preferred. The goal of this paper is to show how to do point estimation for overall treatment effect for all metrics including ratio metrics. We will get it right and get it in an elegant way.

Traditionally majority of interest has been focused on the hypothesis testing side. This is because for many applications of A/B testing, people just need to tell whether or not there is a treatment effect and more importantly, if there is any, whether treatment is better or worse. We call this type of A/B testing *action centric A/B testing*. In recent years, experienced by both authors working in Microsoft, there is a growing demand in what we called *value centric A/B testing*, in which we are also interested in estimating the overall treatment effect of a feature. There are several reasons behind this trend. First is for ROI(return of investment) calibration. Knowing the value of a feature and cost of a feature allows us to know the ROI. If we need to make choices between two or more features with different cost, ROI could help us make final decision. Also in a lot of cases not all treatments with positive effect are worth shipping. New features almost always come with maintenance cost and we should only ship features that are *practically significant*, not just statistically significant. Second reason is for team commitment and performance evaluation. In a data driven culture, part of team performance should be evaluated using objective measurement such as total contribution of features shipped measured by some metrics. A team would often commit to improve certain metric, their OEC(overall evaluation criteria) by x%. This is a crucial step and in some sense a manifesto of a truly data driven culture. For this to be possible, point estimation of overall treatment effect needs to be reported and recorded for each feature shipped. Triggered treatment effect is of little use here because it is often much easier to achieve a large movement (3), and we need to measure impact on the overall population for fair comparison across different teams.

The paper is organized as follows. Section 2 introduces two common types of trigger analyses used in search engine evaluation. We also show why translation from triggered effect to diluted effect is only straightforward for additive metrics like sessions per user and queries per user, and could be involved for ratio metrics such as Session Success Rate per user. We derive exact dilution formula in Section 3 with mild assumptions. The heart of this paper is Section 4 where we introduce a unified approach for all treatment effect dilution problems from a different angle by realizing the whole purpose of trigger analysis with effect dilution is nothing but trying to provide an unbiased estimator for the overall treatment effect with smaller variance. Therefore, instead of tackling the effect dilution problem, we directly tackle the problem of estimating overall treatment effect with extra information of feature triggering. This new approach always provides unbiased point estimation and confidence interval for the overall treatment effect. Moreover, it also quantifies the benefit of using triggering information from a variance reduction perspective. Section 5 provides empirical results from applying this approach on real experimentation data, followed by conclusion in Section 6. In addition, we put a

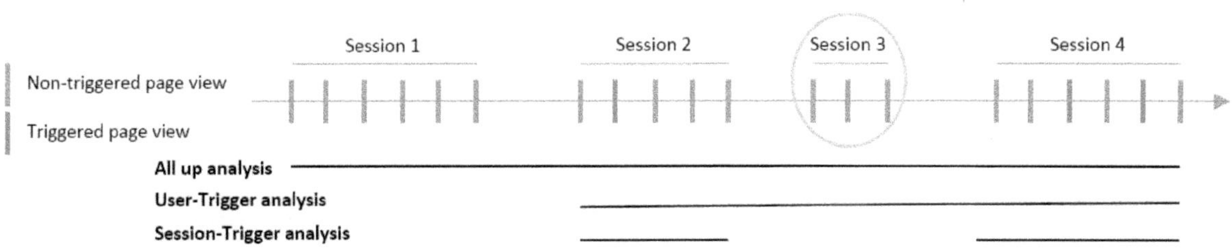

Figure 2: Different types of triggering analysis. User-trigger analysis will analyze from session 2 to session 4. Session-trigger analysis will remove session 1 and session 3. The yellow circled session 3 is a session that is included in user-trigger analysis but not in session-trigger analysis

toy example in Appendix to illustrate the steps of different methods.

Our contribution in this paper includes:

1. We show common mistakes of applying dilution formula to ratio metrics.

2. We derive the exact dilution formula for both additive metrics and ratio metrics. The derivation uses a novel method that we believe is worthy of sharing.

3. The unified overall treatment effect estimation approach is a fresh look of the dilution problem. It applies to all metrics. Comparing to dilution formula, it is easier to implement, requires less assumptions and also less error prone.

2. TRIGGER ANALYSIS

Many online services, especially a complex technology such as search, has many features that only affects a small proportion of traffic. Feature coverage is the proportion of traffics that trigger the feature. For example, a better search result for weather prediction only triggers when user search something related to weather. Some low coverage features trigger for less than 0.1% traffics.

For a low coverage feature, straightforwardly perform hypothesis testing on all up data can suffer from low statistical power. Unless the treatment effect on those triggered traffic is very large, overall effect after diluted by those traffic without feature triggering could be extremely small. In search engine feature experiment in Bing, overall effect for low coverage feature is typically smaller than 0.1%. Also see Rule #2 in (3). Even if all up analysis does show statistically significant result, the accuracy of this estimation could be much lower than the triggered treatment effect. For a feature with coverage less than 20%, we require team to also provide trigger analysis.

Definition of triggering at each impression level (e.g.page-view or query-view) is conceptually easy. We know exactly whether a feature triggered or not in treatment, and with proper counterfactual logging, we should be able to tell whether a feature *would be triggered if it were in treatment* for control group. However, many metrics are only defined at experiment unit level, typically user in online A/B testing. To define many metrics properly, we cannot simply filter out triggered impressions for trigger analysis. To see that, a session is defined as a set of consecutive impressions from a user and we define a successful session if we believe user completed his or her "task" successfully in the session[2]. And if we filter down to triggered impressions, we might only get a subset of impressions for each sessions of a user. Without the holistic view of the whole session we cannot properly define session success. Another example is that sometimes a feature is triggered to help user complete their task easier in follow on impressions within the same session. For instance, speller correction suggestion is triggered when we detect a potential misspelling. A user can click the suggestion and get better results if that is what they really want to query and achieve task completion on that next corrected query(see Figure 3). Although we draw heuristics from search evaluation, we believe similar arguments apply to other domain of online A/B testing.[3]

Figure 3: Speller correction for query "sttle".

Due to the reason aforementioned, in search engine evaluation and many other web services, we need to keep session intact when doing trigger analysis. This leads to the concept of session-trigger analysis, in which we take the subset of sessions with at least one triggering event. In particular, users who never trigger the feature will be excluded from the analysis. See Figure 2 for an illustration. However, some feature might have long lasting effects that will not only affect the current session but also affect subsequent sessions. In this case, similar to the logic that we want to maintain the whole session structure when doing trigger analysis, we might also want to keep all sessions after the first triggering event of a user. We can remove sessions before the first triggering event for obvious reason that a feature cannot impact anything before the first exposure. This leads us to the second type of trigger analysis. We call it user-trigger analysis. In Figure 2, we illustrate the difference between all up analysis, session-trigger and user-trigger analysis. The first trigger event is in session 2, so session 1 will be excluded from the analysis. Session 3 is included in user-trigger analysis but not in the session-trigger analysis.

[2]Detailed definition of session and success is out of the scope of this paper.

[3]In other web services, a session normally represent a visit.

SS	Number of Sessions
SatSS	Number of Satisfied/Success Sessions
Tr	Subscript or prefix for triggered
UnTr	Subscript or prefix for untriggered
Overall	Subscript for all up analysis and effect
N	Number of experiment units, typically users
Denom	Denominator

Table 1: Common notations used in formula derivation and variance reduction models.

In practice, user-trigger analysis is more widely used because it applies to general scenarios without assuming the treatment effect only last within the same session the treatment triggered. Using user trigger analysis also make other user based metrics such as sessions per user and queries per user available. If users are very satisfied with a new feature, he or she would return more often to perform more tasks. Those treatment effect impacted sessions might or might not trigger the feature again. In session-trigger analysis, the metric sessions per user merely counts sessions that trigger the feature and therefore loses its meaning of measuring general user engagement. The advantage of using session-trigger is more sensitive by further zooming into the feature impacted subset. Session-trigger analysis supports all session based metrics such as session success rate per user, session time to success per user, as well as all page based metrics such as click through rate, conversion rate, and other ratio metrics. In Section 5 we show for low coverage features, session-trigger analysis can outperform user-trigger analysis. Of course it is important to keep in mind that for session-trigger analysis we assume the treatment has no impact on sessions without triggering. This is also an assumption that we can verify by doing trigger-complement analysis, in which we analyze the complement data of session-trigger analysis and test whether there is indeed no evidence of any impact.

2.1 Effect Dilution

In the context of trigger analysis, assume we have an estimate of the treatment effect in terms of a delta $\Delta_{Tr}(X)$, calculated as the difference of a metric X between treatment group and control group. Here the subscript "Tr" stands for "trigger" and we will use "Tr" and "UnTr" as shorthand for "trigger" and "untrigger". We will use these shorthand that should make sense with contexts. See Table 1 for a complete reference. If Δ_{Tr} is an unbiased estimator for the treatment effect on triggered population(triggered user or triggered sessions), how can we translate it into an unbiased estimator for the treatment effect on the overall population?

A formula that is frequently used for user-trigger analysis is:

$$\Delta_{overall} = \Delta_{Tr} \times \frac{N_{Tr}}{N}, \qquad (1)$$

where N_{Tr} and N are user counts in the trigger analysis and all up analysis respectively and for session-trigger N_{Tr}/N is an estimate of the user-trigger rate or feature user coverage. A similar formula for ratio metrics in a session-trigger analysis takes a similar form:

$$\Delta_{overall} = \Delta_{Tr} \times \frac{N_{Tr}}{N} \times \overline{\left(\frac{\text{TrDenominator}}{\text{Denominator}}\right)} \qquad (2)$$

where "Denominator" is the denominator of the ratio metrics such as sessions or pages. For session success rate per user, the additional multiplier $\overline{(\frac{TrSS}{SS})}$ is the average session trigger rate for triggered users. For click through rate per user, that would be the average page trigger rate for triggered users where the triggering is defined at the whole session level, i.e. all page views in a triggered session counted as triggered.

There are simple heuristics behind formula (1). For user-trigger analysis, if the treatment effect estimated on the triggered population is Δ_{Tr} and this population is just N_{Tr}/N of the total population, and if the treatment effect on untriggered population is 0, then the overall treatment effect has to be the triggered treatment effect Δ_{Tr} diluted by the trigger rate. For ratio metric in a session-trigger analysis, the same user dilution first need to be applied. Then within triggered users, we still need to dilute by the fact not all sessions are triggered. An intuitive choice seems to be using the average trigger rate of the ratio metric's denominator.

A closer look at this argument above begs more explanation, especially for the session-trigger formula (2). In fact these two formulas are both problematic in general for ratio metrics like session success rate per user, as exemplified by the following using session time to success per user (TTS). Time to success is measuring how fast users get to a satisfied result.[4]:

1. User 1: 1 session-triggered session saving 100(msec), 1 non-session-triggered session, so no savings. User level average TTS saving is -50(msec).
2. User 2: 1 session-triggered session saving 20(msec), 9 non-sesssion-triggered sessions, so no savings. User level average TTS saving is therefore -2(msec)

Taking average of the two users, $\Delta_{Overall} = -26$(msec). However, using formula (2), we first compute $\Delta_{Tr} = -(100+20)/2 = -60$(msec), and then diluted it into $-60 \times 1 \times (1/2+1/10)/2 = -18$(msec). We get very different estimates. In fact, we observed some cases that when we applied diluted formula and compare the result $\Delta_{Overall}$ to the 95% confidence interval we got straight from all up analysis, the formula estimate did not even fall into the interval!

This example exposed the intuition why the formula could fail. When we reason about diluted the average triggered effect by $\overline{(\frac{\text{TrDenominator}}{\text{Denominator}})}$, we are implicitly making a lot of assumptions. Roughly speaking because the treatment effect is itself an average, the dilution by the triggered rate of the denominator should be applied to each individual user level treatment effect first before the average is taken. This could be different from the formula, if there is some correlation between the treatment effect and the trigger rate of the denominator; See Section 3.3.

In the next section, we will derive a rigorous universal formula by using potential outcome framework(5). This framework will enable us to see through the problem in a crystal clear lens. We will suggest how to implement the formula. In Section 4 we argue that variance reduction framework provides a much general implementation that will supersede the formula. Nevertheless the discussion in the next section paves the way for a deeper understanding.

[4]The original example was contributed by our colleague Aron Inger and Ron Kohavi and we made some minor modification.

3. EXACT DILUTION FORMULA

3.1 Rubin's potential outcome framework

Rubin potential outcome framework, also known as Rubin causal model(RCM)(5) is an approach to analyze causal effect based on a conceptual potential outcome pair. For each subject, say user, if there is a causal effect caused by certain treatment, we model this by a pair (X_T, X_C). X_T and X_C is the measurement if the subject is given treatment or not, respectively. And the difference $X_T - X_C$ is the causal effect of the treatment. Note that both X_T and X_C could be nondeterministic and $X_T - X_C$ could be random. The goal of the causal inference is therefore to estimate the *average treatment effect*(ATE) over a population. ATE is

$$\mu = \mathbb{E}(X_T - X_C).$$

In reality, there is no way we can observe the pair. If a subject is exposed to treatment, we observe X_T and not X_C, and vice versa. The missing part is called *counterfactual*.

In online A/B testing, we can estimate $\mathbb{E}X_T$ and $\mathbb{E}X_C$ seperately using sample average in each group. This is because both groups are sampled from the same population. Using $\mathbb{E}(X_T - X_C) = \mathbb{E}X_T - \mathbb{E}X_C$, we see that $\Delta = \overline{X_T} - \overline{X_C}$ is an unbiased estimator for the ATE.

The procedure above is an example of the following rule of thumb:

> To estimate causal effect, we can always transform an unbiased estimator based on potential outcome pairs into an unbiased estimator using observations from treatment group and control group in a randomized experiment.

The advantage of deriving a formula under the potential outcome framework is that we reduce the problem of having two groups of subjects into only one group. This simplification makes the derivation a lot easier and lucid.

3.2 Additive Metrics

Metrics like Queries per user or sessions per user satisfy the following additivity property. For any user, if X is the metric in all up analysis, TrX is that in triggered analysis and UnTrX for trigger-complement analysis, then $X = TrX + UnTrX$. Metrics like session success rate per user or click through rate per user does not have this property since the numerator and denominator are both additive but the ratio is not.

This property is very crucial for a simple formula like (1) to work. To see that, under the potential outcome framework, each user has a potential pair $(X_{iT}, X_{iC}), i = 1, \ldots, N$ and the estimated treatment effect is defined as $\Delta_{overall}(X) = \sum(X_{iT} - X_{iC})/N$.

$$\begin{aligned}
N \times \Delta_{overall}(X) &= \sum(X_{iT} - X_{iC}) \\
&= \sum_{UTr}(X_{iT} - X_{iC}) + \sum_{Tr}(X_{iT} - X_{iC}) \\
&= \sum_{UTr}(X_{iT} - X_{iC}) + \\
&\sum_{Tr}(TrX_{iT} - TrX_{iC}) + \sum_{Tr}(UnTrX_{iT} - UnTrX_{iC}) \\
&= \sum_{Tr}(TrX_{iT} - TrX_{iC}),
\end{aligned}$$

where Tr and $UnTr$ in the subscript of the sum indicate triggered users and untriggered users. The third equation uses the additivity and the last equation uses the fact that there is no treatment effect for untriggered users and even for triggered users, there is no effect on trigger complement.

Divide both side by N and we get the formula (1)

$$\begin{aligned}
\Delta_{overall}(X) &= \frac{\sum_{Tr}(TrX_{iT} - TrX_{iC})}{N_{Tr}} \times \frac{N_{Tr}}{N} \\
&= \Delta_{Tr}(X) \times \frac{N_{Tr}}{N}.
\end{aligned}$$

We make the remark that this formula is correct for both user-trigger analysis and session-trigger analysis, provided that the metric satisfies the additivity property.

3.3 Ratio Metrics

A Ratio metric has a form $X_i = Num_i/Denom_i$ where we use "num" and "denom" as shorthands for numerator and denominator. Both Num and Denom are additive, i.e., $Num = TrNum + UnTrNum$ and $Denom = TrDenom + UnTrDenom$. The complete potential outcome pair is

$$(Num_{iT}, Denom_{iT}, Num_{iC}, Denom_{iC}).$$

In the following discussion, we will assume $Denom_{iT} = Denom_{iC} = Denom_i$, i.e., there is no treatment effect on the denominator. This is an assumption that we need to provide a clean formula. We will discuss its rationale why it is a reasonable assumption. In fact in the next section, we will see in a unified framework we don't even need this assumption. Another key assumption is that there is no treatment effect on untriggered components, i.e. $UnTrX_{iT} - UnTrX_{iC} = 0$. Now we derive the formula for general ratio metrics. Readers are welcome to think about session success rate or click through rate. For session success rate, Num is successful session count and $Denom$ is session count. For click through rate, Num is click count and $Denom$ is page-view count. The following derivation also works for both user-trigger analysis and session-trigger analysis.

$$\begin{aligned}
N \times \Delta_{overall}(X) &= \sum(X_{iT} - X_{iC}) \\
&= \sum_{UTr}(X_{iT} - X_{iC}) + \sum_{Tr}(X_{iT} - X_{iC}) \\
&= \sum_{Tr}(X_{iT} - X_{iC}) \quad \text{no effect on untriggered users} \\
&= \sum_{Tr} \frac{Num_{iT} - Num_{iC}}{Denom_i} \quad \text{common denominator} \\
&= \sum_{Tr} \frac{TrDenom_i}{Denom_i} \times (TrX_{iT} - TrX_{iC}).
\end{aligned}$$

The last equation is from $Num_{iT} - Num_{iC} = TrNum_{iT} - TrNum_{iC} = TrDenom_i \times (TrX_{iT} - TrX_{iC})$.

$TrDenom_i/Denom_i$ is the trigger rate (TR) of the denominator. For session success rate, this is the session trigger rate for a triggered user. Divide both side by N we get the formula

$$\Delta_{Overall}(X) = \frac{1}{N} \sum_{Tr} TR_i \times (TrX_{iT} - TrX_{iC}) \qquad (3)$$

If this trigger rate TR and the user level treatment effect $TrX_{iT} - TrX_{iC}$ are independent, the r.h.s. can be simplified to[5]

$$1/N \times N_{Tr} \times \overline{TR} \times \overline{TrX_{iT} - TrX_{iC}}$$
$$= 1/N \times N_{Tr} \times \overline{TR} \times \Delta_{Tr}(X).$$

Therefore

$$\Delta_{Overall}(X) = \Delta_{Tr}(X) \times \frac{N_{Tr}}{N} \times \overline{TR}.$$

This is formula (2).

From this derivation, it is clear that formula (2) relies on the independence assumption which is normally not guaranteed. The counterexample we gave in the last section is a case where user 1 has both larger treatment effect and higher trigger rate, demonstrating a positive correlation between the two. In practice, there are many cases where a treatment will impact heavy user and light user differently and at the same time heavy user could also have higher or lower different trigger rate for a low coverage feature. The dependency between trigger rate and the treatment effect is very common. Therefore formula (2) is only an approximation that could be off when the aforementioned correlation is high.

3.4 Discussion: Implementation and Assumption Checking

Formula (3) cannot be simplified further into a direct translation from Δ_{Tr} to $\Delta_{Overall}$. For most cases, the trigger rate TR only has finite possibilities. If we first group all users by trigger rate,

$$\Delta_{Overall}(X) = \frac{1}{N}\sum_r r \times \sum_{TR=r}(TrX_{iT} - TrX_{iC})$$
$$= \frac{N_{Tr}}{N} \times \frac{1}{N_{Tr}} \times \sum_r r \times N_{TR=r} \times \Delta(TrX|TR=r) =$$
$$\frac{N_{Tr}}{N}\left(\frac{1}{N_{Tr}} \times \sum_r r \times N_{TR=r} \times \Delta(TrX|TR=r)\right).$$

The first term is still the user trigger rate. The rest in the parenthesis can be calculated by first grouping users by trigger rate TR, and then calculating the delta of the metric in each sub group, multiplied by trigger rate r. Those group level values are then averaged using the weight $N_{TR=r}/N_{Tr}$. Note that $N_{Tr} = \sum_r N_{TR=r}$ so these weights sum up to 1 and this last step is a weighted average.

In practice it is usually hard to match for all values of TR, we can resort to some discretization to reduce the number of sub groups. This also means we are sacrificing accuracy.

We do not recommend the approach above for all these practical concerns. The following is an alternative that is much easier to implement. Re-arrange r.h.s. of Formula (3) as

$$\frac{1}{N}\sum_{Tr}(TR_i \times TrX_{iT}) - \frac{1}{N}\sum_{Tr}(TR_i \times TrX_{iC}). \quad (4)$$

We see that to estimate the overall treatment effect of a metric X, instead of estimating its value in both treatment and control by taking sample average, we can conceive of a derived metric $Y_i = TR_i \times TrX_i$ and calculate sample average $\overline{Y}$ in treatment and control. Note that for untriggered users, $TR_i = 0$ and hence $Y_i = 0$.

$$\Delta_{Overall} = \overline{Y_{iT}} - \overline{Y_{iC}}.$$

This suggests that we only need to compute the Δ for this new dummy metrics to get an unbiased estimator for the overall treatment effect. This is considerably easier to implement than the trigger rate grouping method. In the next section we will further extend and improve this.

The assumption that there should be no difference for the trigger complement set is a more fundamental assumption that justifies using session-trigger analysis. If there is effect carried on from triggered session to untriggered session, then user-trigger analysis would be preferred. One way to check this assumption is to test this assumption by doing trigger-complement analysis, similar to how we test treatment effect in the trigger analysis. If there is no statistically significant movement, based on Occam's Razor principle, we'll happily accept this assumption.

Another assumption is that there is no effect on the denominator. This is also something we can test with statistical test. When this test fails, the idea of using this ratio metric is at stake. What does it mean if click through rate decreased but number of page-view increased? A feature can clearly make user happier to try our service more for harder tasks with lower success rate or conversion rate. For this reason, when we look at a ratio metric, it is fair to assume the denominator does not move. Otherwise we should avoid using this metric.

4. A UNIFIED FRAMEWORK: DILUTION AS VARIANCE REDUCTION

Formulas like (1) for additive metrics and (3) for ratio metrics leave a lot to be desired. First it feels redundant that we need different formulas for different type of metrics. What if we have another type of metrics that are not covered by either additive metrics or ratio metrics? The novel derivation method we displayed using potential outcome framework can be used on new types of metrics. But it won't guarantee the result can be simple enough to have an clean implementation. As we have already seen, implementating Formula (3) involves nontrivial investigation and we were lucky to have one.

Fortunately, there is a unified framework that solves this whole dilution problem in a more elegant way. The idea was laid out in *Improving the sensitivity of online controlled experiments by utilizing pre-experiment data* (1). The dilution problem has seemingly no relationship with pre-experiment data and yet the method is general enough to cast the dilution problem as a special case.

4.1 Dilution and Variance Reduction

The ultimate purpose of dilution is to more accurately estimate the overall treatment effect. If we also want to maintain unbiasedness of the estimator, by variance-bias tradeoff, reducing variance is the only way. The whole purpose of using trigger analysis and then applying correct dilution formula to translate the estimated effect back to overall population should be evaluated by two criteria. 1) Is the new estimator unbiased? 2) Is the variance of the estimator reduced?

[5]Rigorously, this is not exact equality. But they are both unbiased estimators for the same quantity under the independence assumption.

This line of thoughts lead us to a new approach. Why do we need to separate the job into two steps and try to derive the correct dilution formula? Can we tackle this problem as a whole and focus on reducing variance?

In Deng et al. (1), the authors provided a practical, almost assumption-less and intuitive approach to reduce variance of treatment effect estimator. The key step is to find other metrics that are not supposed to be affected by the treatment effect. These metrics are called covariates and are used to adjust the estimator similar to linear regression without all the burdens of linearity and normal assumptions of linear regression. Also see Yang and Tsiatis (7) and Tsiatis (6) for alternative approaches and general theory of semiparametric methods.

4.2 Variance Reduction Framework

Suppose X is the metric of interest and we wish to estimate the treatment effect

$$\mu = EX_T - EX_C.$$

The naive estimator is $\Delta(X) = \overline{X_T} - \overline{X_C}$. If we have another metric Y which is not affected by the treatment effect. Then

$$EY_T - EY_C = 0,$$

and therefore

$$\Delta^* = (\overline{X_T} - \overline{X_C}) - \theta \times (\overline{Y_T} - \overline{Y_C}) = \Delta(X) - \theta\Delta(Y) \quad (5)$$

remains to be an unbiased estimator for the same treatment effect μ for arbitrary choice of θ. Recall our goal is to reduce variance of the estimator. Minimizing the variance of Δ^* we get the optimal θ

$$\theta^* = \frac{\text{Cov}(\Delta(X), \Delta(Y))}{\text{Var}(\Delta(Y))} = \frac{\text{Cov}(\overline{X_T}, \overline{Y_T}) + \text{Cov}(\overline{X_C}, \overline{Y_C})}{\text{Var}(\overline{Y_T}) + \text{Var}(\overline{Y_C})}$$

where the second equality is due to the fact treatment and control are two independent groups of subjects. In practice since we don't need to use the exact optimal θ, we can simply use control group alone

$$\theta^* = \frac{\text{Cov}(\overline{X_C}, \overline{Y_C})}{\text{Var}(\overline{Y_C})} = \frac{\text{Cov}(X_C, Y_C)}{\text{Var}(Y_C)}$$

or similarly use treatment data, or form the average of both. When treatment effect is not huge, these difference choices do not make big difference. Under null hypothesis when there is no treatment effect, all those choices all converge to the same value. Also, as pointed out in Deng et al. (1), although it seems that we need to estimate θ^* from the data and hence a concern about accuracy of this estimation, it is really not an issue at all. This is because Δ^* is unbiased for any chosen θ and even if we don't accurately estimate the optimal θ^*, we still get most of the variance reduction from using a close enough estimate.

We can also see the optimal variance reduced from this approach.

$$\text{Var}(\Delta^*) = (1 - \rho^2)\text{Var}(\Delta),$$

where $\rho = Corr(X_C, Y_C) = Corr(X_T, Y_T)$. That is, the higher the correlation between X and Y the larger the variance reduced[6].

[6]In practice we don't use this formula to estimate the variance of Δ^*. Instead we directly work out the variance of (5) with estimated covariances and θ^* plugged in.

This method can apply to multiple covariates. When $\mathbf{Y}$ is multi-variate, θ^* is also a vector and the variance reduction is $1-R^2$ where R^2 is the variance explained by the covariates, similar to R^2 in multiple linear regression.

Deng et al. (1) showed that for online A/B testing, covariates Y are abundant. The authors recommended using the same metric of interest calculated using pre-experiment data. In their empirical study, these pre-experiment covariates can reduce variance for metrics like queries per user by 40% to 50%. The method was also called *CUPED* from initials in *Controlled experiments by Utilizing Pre-Experiment Data.*

4.3 Unified Dilution

In Section 3 we've derived different formulas for additive metrics and ratio metrics. From variance reduction perspective, we can unify all these into one step without differentiating additive and ratio metrics, and potentially support all different types of metrics. The implementation is also significantly cleaner and easier.

To apply variance reduction, we only need to propose covariates that are highly correlated to the metric of interest and not affected by treatment. The intuition behind the trigger analysis is that trigger complement data is not affected by the treatment effect and therefore only add noises. This makes it a perfect covariate! Note that we make no assumption on the form of metric X, be it additive or ratio or other functional forms.

Some other covariates available include trigger rate and other pre-experiment metric values. Pre-experiment metrics are the topics of Deng et al. (1) and we treat them as orthogonal to our focus in this paper. We propose the following variance reduction formula:

$$X \sim UnTrX + TR + (IsTR = 1), \quad (6)$$

where the r.h.s. lists covariates and the '+' means additional covariates. $UnTrX$ represents the same metric calculated from trigger complement data. For user with 100% trigger rate, there is no trigger-complement data so $UnTrX$ is not well defined. To deal with that, we add one additional binary covariate ($IsTR = 1$) that indicates whether there is no trigger complement data. When this is true, we define $UnTrX$ to be 0 or arbitrarily. See more discussion of this implementation detail in Deng et al. (1, Section 4.2).

In the last section we also showed for ratio metrics, sample average of a dummy metric $Y = TR \times TrX$ can be used to estimate overall treatment effect for a metric X. We can extend this by further applying variance reduction on top of it:

$$Y := (TR \times TrX) \sim UnTrX + TR + (IsTR = 1) \quad (7)$$

This is similar to Model (6) except the l.h.s. is replaced by dummy metric Y. The theory of variance reduction gurantees that this can produce another unbiased estimator for $EY_T - EY_C$, which is the same as $EX_T - EX_C$ based on Formula (3).

4.4 Connection to Dilution Formula

There is a deep connection between dilution with variance reduction framework and simple dilution formula. To see that, we use additive metrics as an example for simplicity and apply the VR formula $X \sim UnTrX$.

To apply variance reduction on additive metrics, since $X = TrX + UnTrX$, we get

$$\theta^* = \frac{\text{Cov}(X, UnTrX)}{\text{Var}(UnTrX)} = \frac{\text{Cov}(TrX, UnTrX) + \text{Cov}(UnTrX, UnTrX)}{\text{Var}(UnTrX)} = 1 + \frac{\text{Cov}(TrX, UnTrX)}{\text{Var}(UnTrX)}$$

If we ignore the second term and $\theta^* = 1$, then the variance reduction formula (5) reduces to

$$\Delta^* = \Delta(X) - \Delta(UnTrX) = \frac{N_{Tr}}{N} \times \Delta_{Tr}(X)$$

since $X = TrX + UnTrX$ and $X = UnTrX$ for untriggered users and $\Delta_{Tr}(X) = \Delta_{Tr}(TrX)$.

The ignored second part of θ^* is trying to achieve additional variance reduction by exploiting the correlation between TrX and $UnTrX$. In other words, the dilution formula (1) is a special case with suboptimal choice of θ^* under the variance reduction framework, and can be superseded by variance reduction.

5. RESULTS AND DISCUSSION

We evaluate the performance of the unified dilution framework in two phases. High quality labeled A/B experiments were selected. Different models were applied to each metric and their variance reduction rates were compared. We further compared the two main trigger analysis methods: user-trigger analysis and session-trigger analysis.

5.1 Data and Metrics

Three A/B experiments that have different trigger rates are selected. The experiments were labeled positive or negative with high confidence. In each experiment, millions of users and queries are included with the rich click information. The scale of the data set is 1000 times more than what usually is affordable for human judgment data.

The evaluation is done for three methods: the formula approach that computes the delta for $TR \times TrSSR$ (implementation of Formula (3) in the form of (4) and we call it the Exact Formula), using $TR_i \times TrSSR_i$ as response (model (7)) and using SSR as response directly (model (6)) for the variance reduction framework. For all three methods, we can also compare user-trigger and session-trigger approaches. Among the three, only model (6) is generic and can be easily modified and applied to other types of metrics. Using $TR_i \times TrSSR_i$ either directly or as the response in model (7) are extensions of Formula (3) and can only be applied to ratio metrics.

For performance measures, we mainly focus on the variance reduction rate. The advantage of variance reduction rate is that it can be directly translated to the accuracy of the point estimation for the overall treatment effect, because higher variance reduction corresponds to better accuracy or narrower confidence interval of the estimate. Quite often, improvement of variance reduction also leads to a difference between whether the statistical test is significant or not. Variance reduction also translates to traffic or sample size saving. A $x\%$ variance reduction is equivalent to being able to reach to the same statistical power with $x\%$ less traffic/sample size.

Experiments	Trigger Rate	
	%Triggered Users	%Triggered Sessions
ExpA	5.26%	1.27%
ExpB	33.46%	20.83%
ExpC	65.17%	60.35%

Table 2: Trigger User and Trigger Session Ratios.

Experiments	User Trigger		
	Exact Formula	Mod. (7)	Mod. (6)
	VR rate	VR rate	VR rate
ExpA	88.60%	**98.42%**	95.60%
ExpB	-17.14%	**84.80%**	78.57%
ExpC	-49.47%	**61.45%**	36.03%

Table 3: User Trigger Three Models Variance Reduction comparison.

5.2 Variance Reduction Rate

We first characterize the trigger rate for 3 experiments **ExpA**, **ExpB**, **ExpC**. **ExpA** considers changing in positions in the Related Search blocks, **ExpB** focuses on video answer in task panes, while **ExpC** looks at creating dynamic sizing for results. Table 2 shows the percent of users and sessions funneled into user-trigger and session-trigger analysis for 3 example experiments. ExpA, for instance, have only 5.26% users exposed to the treatment and only 1.27% overall sessions have treatments in them.

We have carried out another set of 3 experiments with triggering rates close to **ExpA**, **ExpB**, **ExpC** respectively. The results for both sets are similar. For pair of flights with very different treatments, when trigger rate is similar, the resulting variance reduction rate is similar. we have done analysis for dozens of experiments with other trigger rate values. As expected, trigger rate is the key factor that affects the variance reduction rate while the particular feature changes do not matter much.

ExpA, **ExpB**, **ExpC** are also different types of flights in themselves. **ExpA** considers changing in positions in the Related Search blocks, **ExpB** focuses on video answer in task panes, while **ExpC** looks at creating dynamic sizing for results. The trigger rates for the 3 experiments are illustrated in the Trigger Rate Table. The number of total users ranges from 28 million to 40 million for the 3 experiments.

Table 3 shows the results on the 3 experiments for user-trigger models using Exact Formula (4), variance reduction method using model (7) and model (6). VR method using model (7) yields the largest variance reduction rate in all three experiments. It is surprising that using the exact formula directly without VR can lead to increased variance for high coverage features as shown in ExpB and ExpC. Turned out this is due to additional variance contributed by the multiplication factor TR. For high coverage feature where TR can be large for some user but low for others, the variance in TR can generate extra variance. To get most out of the exact formula, we need to group users by their trigger rate TR to remove variance contributed by TR. This is done implicitly by adding TR as one of the covariates in model (7), which eventually leads to the largest variance reduction. However, even without any cue from the exact formula (4), using the generic variance reduction model (6) also performs quite well.

Experiments	Session Trigger		
	Exact Formula	Mod. (7)	Mod. (6)
	VR rate	VR rate	VR rate
ExpA	97.12%	**99.44%**	98.25%
ExpB	28.12%	**89.85%**	85.99%
ExpC	-31.32%	**69.10%**	53.97%

Table 4: Session Trigger Three Models Variance Reduction Comparison.

Experiments	User Trigger	Session Trigger
	Variance	Variance
ExpA	4.40%	1.75%
ExpB	21.43%	14.01%
ExpC	63.97%	46.03%

Table 5: Variance Using Mod. (6): User Trigger, Session Trigger. Variance is measured as percentage of the variance from all up analysis.

Table 4 compares the three models using session-trigger covariates for the two VR methods. Similar to user-trigger scenario, VR method using $TR \times TrSSR$ (model (7)) has the highest variance reduction rate in all 3 experiments even if directly using $TR \times TrSSR$ can increase variance as in ExpC.

We now compare the variance reduction rate for user-trigger and session-trigger methods. We use VR method with SSR (model (6)) in the example because this is a generic method not depending on any theoretically derived formula. Table 5 shows the variance using Model (6) measured as percentage of corresponding original all up analyses' variances. Session-trigger method consistently leads to smaller varaince. Note that although the varaince reduction rate in previous tables might not be quite different for low coverage experiment as in ExpA, the true variance difference is huge. To see that, for ExpA, the variance after reduction is 4.4% (user-trigger) compared to 1.75% (session-trigger). Session-trigger with VR model (6) produced a variance that is only 40% of the variance from user-trigger with the same VR model. This also clearly translates to the sensitivity improvement that reflects in the p value.

For all 3 experiments, the change from using user-trigger to session-trigger leads to the improvement for making correct data-driven decisions. In both ExpB and ExpC, user-trigger analysis are boarder line significant, which makes it hard to draw a clear decision by itself. Session-trigger analysis, however, confirms the movement and lifts the confidence of the decision, a clean data-driven decision can be drawn directly.

5.3 Impact on Hypothesis Testing

If we are not concerned about the "value centric" estimation for relative delta, but rather only focus on the "action centric" hypothesis testing, then it is possible to do A/B experiments only based on user-triggered sessions or session-triggered sessions, i.e., the analysis methods shown in Figure 2, also known as trigger analysis. Table 6 compares the t-statistics for using generic VR method model (6) to using trigger analysis. They both gave statistically significant results in the 3 experiments. VR methods won on ExpA and the trigger analysis won for ExpB. Note that t-statistics

Experiments	VR Using SSR	Trigger Analysis
	Session Triggered	Session Triggered
	t stats	t stats
ExpA	6.72	3.32
ExpB	3.97	5.26
ExpC	3.50	3.39

Table 6: Sensitivity comparison for VR model using SSR and trigger analysis.

Session Trigger Complement			
Experiments	ExpA	ExpB	ExpC
P value	0.23	0.38	0.55

Table 7: P value for A/B testing on the session trigger complement.

are random numbers influenced by the estimated delta. In connection to the discussion in Section 4.4, we believe in general VR metric would be slightly more powerful than trigger analysis due to its extra variance reduction. But the main advantage of using VR method is the direct estimation of overall treatment effect, not just the treatment effect on triggered population.

5.4 Assumption Checking and Final Remarks

Results in this section suggest that we can use the variance reduction model directly for estimating overall treatment effect without the two steps approach involving a trigger analysis and a dilution step. For a general metric X, we recommend model (6) which can be easily implemented. For ratio metrics, model (7) is a strong alternative. However it does rely on extra assumption such as no treatment effect on the denominator of the ratio metrics which is used to prove formula (3). This makes it less reliable and applicable.

Another assumption for doing session-trigger analysis is that the treatment effects are contained completely in triggered sessions. One way to verify this assumption is to do hypothesis testing for the metric of interest on session-trigger complement sets. Table 7 shows that all the resulting p values are not statistically significant for the three experiments. Therefore, we don't see evidence there are any treatment effects in session-trigger complement sets in these three examples[7].

6. CONCLUSIONS

In this work we looked at the dilution problem for estimating the overall treatment effect in online controlled experiments. We showed the right way for doing this is not obvious for a large set of widely used metrics, the ratio metrics. We first theoretically derived the dilution formula, based on Rubin's potential outcome framework. Furthermore, we discovered the connection between the variance reduction framework and the dilution problem and successfully reformulated the problem as a special case of variance reduction. We presented empirical results for the unified dilution appro-

[7]Note that we can never prove there is no effect in session-trigger complement, unlike user-trigger compliment. And any statistical test have false negatives. We call out Occam's Razor in this case that we choose to believe a simpler model(no effect in session-trigger compliment) given no evidence against it.

ach and demonstrated that it yields significant improvement in the accuracy for the overall treatment effect estimation. We compared two different trigger analyses, session-trigger analysis and user-trigger analysis in detail. We are not aware of other literature on the same topic. We believe the work here is a novel application of the variance reduction framework in "value centric" online controlled experiments and greatly improves the accuracy of treatment effect estimation for low coverage features.

7. ACKNOWLEDGMENTS

We wish to thank Ron Kohavi, Aron Inger, Toby Walker, Brian Frasca and others from Microsoft Analysis and Experimentation Platform, Georg Buscher, Aidan Crook, Siamak Faridani, Widad Machmochi, Anand Oka from Bing Measurement group and Jan Pedersen from Bing Search Relevance for providing the problem, motivation, suggestions, comments and support on this work. We also wish to thank Yu Guo, Xiaolin Shi, Roger Longbotham for reading early draft and giving thoughtful feedbacks. Last but not the least, we thank all 4 reviewers who gave valuable suggestions to help us improved this paper.

APPENDIX

Illustrative Toy Example

In this section we give detailed steps of 2 methods we compared in Section 5: (1) the formula approach that computes the delta for $TR \times TrX$ (Formula (4)), (2) using X as response directly (model (6)). Model 7 is very similar to Model 6 so we leave it as an exercise to readers. As in Section 5 we chose the metric X to be SSR. Note that the framework in this paper assumes enough sample size for central limit theorem to be applicable. Small sample toy example like this is only for illustration.

Group	User	S1	S2	S3	S4	S5	X	TR	TrX	UnTrX	TR=1
T	A	1	***0***	0	0	1	2/5	1/5	0	1/2	0
T	B	***1***	***1***	***0***	***1***		3/4	1	3/4	0	1
T	C	***1***	0	0			1/3	1/3	1	0	0
T	D	0	0	0			0	0	0	0	0
C	E	0	1	***0***	1	1	3/5	1/5	0	3/4	0
C	F	***1***	***1***	***1***			1	1	1	0	1
C	G	0	0	1			1/3	0	0	1/3	0
C	H	0	***1***	0	0		1/4	1/4	1	0	0

We use the toy example listed in the table above throughout this section. 8 users in this example are split into treatment and control with up to 5 sessions observed. Each entry in the table indicates success or not, and triggered sessions are emphasized as bold and italic.

The first step is to calculate the metric value X, the trigger rate TR and the trigger-complement metric value $UnTrX$. In our toy example of SSR, X is simply the average of each data row, and trigger rate TR is the number of bold and italic entry divided by the number of non-empty entries. $UnTrX$ is the SSR calculated using plain entries(not bold and italic). Two special cases are user B and F, who have all sessions triggered. Hence there is no trigger-complement sessions and we define $UnTrX$ as 0 and also mark $TR = 1$ as 1.

Exact Formula 4. Formula 4 is straightforward to apply. We just take delta of $TR \times TrX$ calculated in treatment group and control group.

$$\mathrm{T}: (1/5 \times 0 + 1 \times 3/4 + 1/3 \times 1 + 0)/4 = 0.271$$
$$\mathrm{C}: (1/5 \times 0 + 1 \times 1 + 0 \times 1/3 + 1/4 \times 1)/4 = 0.313$$
$$\text{Overall Effect}: 0.271 - 0.313 = -0.042$$

For test, we calculated variance of $TR \times TrX$ for the two groups to be 0.127 and 0.224. And the variance of the delta is estimated to be $0.127/4 + 0.224/4 = 0.088$. Finally we get our z-score of $-0.042/\sqrt{0.088} = -0.142$.

VR: Formula 6. To apply Formula 6 the gist is to estimate θ^*. Note that $\theta^* = \mathrm{Var}(Y)^{-1} \times \mathrm{Cov}(X, Y)$ where Y is the vector $(UnTrX, TR, IsTR = 1)$ and Var and Cov here are matrices. For the control group, θ^* is

$$\begin{pmatrix} 0.127 & -0.081 & -0.090 \\ -0.081 & 0.192 & 0.213 \\ -0.090 & .213 & 0.250 \end{pmatrix}^{-1} \times \begin{pmatrix} -0.010 \\ 0.130 \\ 0.151 \end{pmatrix} = \begin{pmatrix} 0.488 \\ 0.317 \\ 0.512 \end{pmatrix}.$$

For illustration we'll just take this $\theta*$. In practice, one can use a weighted average of θ^* estimated from control and treatment. Using this θ^*,

$$\begin{aligned} \Delta_{VR} &= \Delta(X) - 0.488 \times \Delta(UnTrX) \\ &- 0.317 \times \Delta(TR) - 0.512 \times \Delta(IsTR = 1) \\ &= -0.175 - 0.488 \times (-0.145) - 0.317 \times 0.021 - 0.512 \times 0 \\ &= -0.111 \end{aligned}$$

To get z-score, we also need to calculate the variance. which is

$$\begin{aligned} &\mathrm{Var}(\overline{X}_T) + \mathrm{Var}(\overline{X}_C) + (\theta^*)^T \left(\mathrm{Cov}(\overline{Y}_T) + \mathrm{Cov}(\overline{Y}_C)\right) \theta^* \\ &- 2 \times (\theta^*)^T \left(\mathrm{Cov}(\overline{X}, \overline{Y}_T) + \mathrm{Cov}(\overline{X}, \overline{Y}_C)\right) \\ &= 0.00435 \end{aligned}$$

The variance reduction rate hence is $1 - 0.00435/0.086 = 95.0\%$. Z-score is then $-0.111/\sqrt{0.00434} = -1.685$.

References

[1] Alex Deng, Ya Xu, Ron Kohavi, and Toby Walker. Improving the sensitivity of online controlled experiments by utilizing pre-experiment data. In *Proceedings of the sixth ACM international conference on Web search and data mining*, pages 123–132. ACM, 2013.

[2] Ron Kohavi, Roger Longbotham, Dan Sommerfield, and Randal M. Henne. Controlled experiments on the web: survey and practical guide. *Data Mining Knowledge Discovery*, 18:140–181, 2009.

[3] Ron Kohavi, Alex Deng, Roger Longbotham, and Ya Xu. Seven rules of thumb for web site experimenters. 2014.

[4] Jim Manzi. *Uncontrolled: The Surprising Payoff of Trial-and-Error for Business, Politics, and Society.* Basic Books, 2012.

[5] Paul R Rosenbaum and Donald B Rubin. The central role of the propensity score in observational studies for causal effects. *Biometrika*, 70(1):41–55, 1983.

[6] Anastasios Tsiatis. *Semiparametric Theory and Missing Data.* Springer-Verlag, 2006.

[7] Li Yang and Anastasios A. Tsiatis. Efficiency study of estimators for a treatment effect in a pretest-posttest trial. *The American Statistician*, 55, 2001.

Inverting a Steady-State

Ravi Kumar Andrew Tomkins Sergei Vassilvitskii Erik Vee
Google
Mountain View, CA
{ravi.k53, atomkins, sergeiv, erikvee}@gmail.com

ABSTRACT

We consider the problem of inferring choices made by users based only on aggregate data containing the relative popularity of each item. We propose a framework that models the problem as that of inferring a Markov chain given a stationary distribution. Formally, we are given a graph and a target steady-state distribution on its nodes. We are also give a mapping from per-node scores to a transition matrix, from a broad family of such mappings. The goal is to set the scores of each node such that the resulting transition matrix induces the desired steady state. We prove sufficient conditions under which this problem is feasible and, for the feasible instances, obtain a simple algorithm for a generic version of the problem. This iterative algorithm provably finds the unique solution to this problem and has a polynomial rate of convergence; in practice we find that the algorithm converges after fewer than ten iterations. We then apply this framework to choice problems in online settings and show that our algorithm is able to explain the observed data and predict the user choices much better than other competing baselines across a variety of diverse datasets.

1. INTRODUCTION

The theory of Markov chains provides a beautiful algebraic formulation of the conditions under which a steady state exists for a random walk, and the nature of that steady state. Given a transition matrix of the Markov chain, one may then determine whether it meets the conditions, and compute the steady state if it exists.

In practice, however, it may be easier to observe the steady state than the underlying transitions. Consider for example a video sharing website that recommends a number of follow-on videos to the viewer of a particular video, and also displays the number of times each video has been viewed. The popularity of each video is directly proportional to the steady state distribution in the random walk defined by the follow-on videos, but an outside observer does not know which edges have been traversed to attain this steady state.

WSDM'15, February 2–6, 2015, Shanghai, China.
Copyright 2015 ACM 978-1-4503-3317-7/15/02 ...$15.00.
http://dx.doi.org/10.1145/2684822.2685310 .

Thus, rather than determining the steady state from the matrix, we are often faced with the inverse problem:

> Given the steady state, can we recover some properties of the underlying process?

Such a problem is highly under-constrained, as there are numerous ways to set potentially quadratically-many transition probabilities so as to produce the desired steady state. Our main result is a solution to this problem under a natural set of constraints.

We will assume first that the graph of the Markov chain is known. This is tantamount to assuming that certain transitions are known to be zero, or equivalently, from any state, there is a known set of available alternatives from which the user must choose. In many situations, these alternatives are present explicitly as a set of "related items" on a page: related videos on `youtube.com`, related restaurants on `yelp.com`, various types of related products on `amazon.com`, and so forth.

So far, the assumption is quite weak. We now introduce a stronger axiom about the transition matrix, which somewhat surprisingly will in general result in a *unique* Markov chain that produces the given steady state. Our axiom can be described as follows.

First, we assume that each state i of the Markov process has an unknown *score* s_i, and there is a known mapping from the the scores to the full transition matrix. We require further that this mapping is *continuous, monotonic, and unbounded.* That is, all else held constant, an increase in the score of i will always increase the transition probability of an edge to i (monotonicity), and as the score becomes sufficiently high, this transition probability will become arbitrarily close to 1 (unboundedness). Note that the most natural mapping satisfying this condition makes the probability of transition from a node to its neighbor be proportional to the neighbor's score. To the best of our knowledge, this kind of inverse problem has not been considered in the literature before; see Section 2.

Our main result states that in this setting, if a natural condition on the graph of the Markov process holds with respect to the given steady-state distribution, then:

1. For any desired steady state, there is an assignment of scores to the nodes that attains this steady state.

2. The scores yielding a particular steady state are unique up to scalar multiplication.

3. An efficient algorithm exists to find these scores.

Let us give a couple of examples to develop the intuition for this model. First, consider a music recommendation site that allows users to navigate from one song to any of a set of related songs. We model that user's likelihood of transitioning from song A to B as proportional to similarity$(A, B) \cdot$ score(B), which is monotonic and unbounded, as long as the similarity scores are positive. If we know the overall visit popularity of the songs, we can therefore learn the scores that attain these visit popularities. As another example, consider a user of a recommendation site. The user picks a next object to consider from among a known slate of candidates with probability proportional to some (increasing and unbounded) function of the candidate object's overall score. The increasing function may be postulated or identified empirically from data. Our techniques may then be applied to learn the score of each item.

We apply our framework to four diverse choice settings, from choosing which link to follow in a Wikipedia article to reach a particular webpage, to natural restaurant selection problems, to deciding which comedy clip is funnier. We show that by only considering the *structure* of the graph and ignoring the metadata, the model can explain the data and predict the individual user choices 10 to 40% better than strong baselines based on popularity, pagerank, or maximum entropy approaches (see below for a broader discussion of related work).

2. RELATED WORK

To the best of our knowledge, the problem of inverting a steady-state distribution has not been considered in the literature before. Tomlin proposed a notion of *Temperature Rank* [31], which is related to our work. In his model, we are given the link structure on the web pages along with the steady-state traffic on all the web pages and the goal is to identify the transition probabilities on the edges by enforcing flow conservation of the traffic. Since the optimization problem is under-constrained, the idea is to use maximum-entropy regularization and a practical heuristic based on iterative matrix scaling [29] to compute the probabilities. Importantly, the transition probabilities do not depend on the neighborhood of a node but depend only on the endpoints of an edge. Even though at the end the method produces a score for each node in the graph, it is a simple heuristic with no provable guarantees. Our model, on the other hand, is based on a concrete transition probability model that takes the neighborhood of a node into account and does not need any form of regularization since the number of parameters is exactly the number of nodes. Furthermore, our algorithm is provably correct and has many additional desirable properties including uniqueness and a polynomial rate of convergence. We will use Temperature Rank as one of our baselines.

Markov chains have been studied in the literature for over a century; see the books by Kemeny and Snell [17] and Levin, Perese, and Wilmer [21]. Typical problems in Markov chains include studying the stationary distribution and mixing times. As we mentioned earlier, as far as we know, the problem of steady-state inversion has not been directly addressed in the Markov chain literature.

PageRank [7, 28] popularized Markov chains in the web search and data mining communities. PageRank postulates a random surfer model in which a uniform random walk is conducted on the link structure of the web graph, after making it ergodic by adding a random teleportation step. The stationary distribution of this random walk yields a score, called PageRank, for each node in the graph. Our method also yields a score for each node, but both our model and goals are different from PageRank. In PageRank, the random walk (modulo the teleportation) is uniform on the neighborhood of a source node, whereas in our case, the walk is weighted by the score of a destination node. Hence, the "normalization" factor for the random walk in PageRank is proportional to the size of the out-neighborhood of a source node whereas in our case, it is the sum of the scores of all nodes in the out-neighborhood of the source node. We will in fact use PageRank as one of our baselines and show that the more general score-based method better explains the data. There have been several papers on PageRank computation (e.g., [8, 13, 15, 16, 20, 22, 25]) and other link analysis methods (e.g, [1, 5, 18, 27, 30]). For a detailed introduction to PageRank and its related methods, see the surveys by Berkhin [4], and Langville and Meyer [19].

Another work that is related in spirit to ours is the classical Metropolis–Hastings method [12, 26]. In this method, we are given a graph and a desired stationary distribution on the nodes of the graph and the goal is to design a random walk (Markov chain) such that the stationary distribution of this random walk is exactly the desired stationary distribution. This is achieved by carefully adjusting the transition probabilities in the walk. Unlike our problem, the main goal in Metropolis–Hastings is to compute the probabilities on the edges to achieve the desired node probabilities. Even though Metropolis–Hastings has been studied for more than half a century, very little is known about it from a formal point of view, especially, its mixing time and rate of convergence. For more details, see the nice survey by Chib and Greenberg [9]. In general, the problem of designing transition probabilities (or more generally, edge weights) to achieve a global objective has been studied in the optimization community. For example, Ghosh, Boyd, and Saberi [10] considered the global objective of minimizing the total effective resistance and Boyd, Diaconis, and Xiao [6] considered the objective of minimizing the mixing time. These problems are typically cast as convex optimization problems and solved directly instead of trying to define a score for each node.

Discrete choice theory is a classic topic in statistics and behavioral economics and is the closest body of work to our objective. The goal of the theory to explain and predict choices between two or more discrete alternatives. Discrete choice models are characterized by the nature of the set of alternatives (choice set), the process by which the choice probabilities are defined, and the utility derived by making a particular choice. See the books by Ben-Akiva and Lerman [3] and by Hensher, Rose, and Greene [14]. There is a variety of discrete choice models depending on what we assume about the alternatives. Our choice of choice probabilities (no recursion intended!) is loosely motivated by the axioms formulated by Duncan Luce [23, 24], which state that a user's likelihood to select one object over another is unaffected by the nature of the other alternatives. Our framework is reminiscent of multinomial choice models: the choice set is given by the neighborhood of a node in the graph, the choice probabilities are defined according to the score of the nodes, and the implicit utility is to match the given steady-state distribution. However, our framework is more general than choice models. First, it does not need to know which item was chosen, rather, it relies on aiming to match a desired steady-state distribution. Second, it does not assume that the random variables follow given distributions, a very common assumption in the statistical modeling of choice. Third, it has provable convergence guarantees, which are hard to obtain for many heuristic and optimization methods used in discrete choice theory. Last, it works with weighted graphs and also for a broad family of functions that can be applied to the scores of a neighborhood. As we will show formally, the unweighted case of the steady-state inversion problem is related to the choice model.

3. PRELIMINARIES

Let $G = (V, E)$ be a weighted directed graph where $V = \{1, \ldots, n\}$ and $w_{ij} > 0$ is the *weight* of an edge $(i, j) \in E$. For a directed edge $(i, j) \in E$, we call j the out-neighbor of i and i the in-neighbor of j. Let $\Gamma_{\text{out}}(i)$ denote the set of out-neighbors of i and let $\Gamma_{\text{in}}(i)$ denote the set of in-neighbors of i. For a set $S \subseteq V$ let $\Gamma_{\text{in}}(S) = \cup_{v \in S} \Gamma_{\text{in}}(v)$ and $\Gamma_{\text{out}}(S) = \cup_{v \in S} \Gamma_{\text{out}}(v)$. Let G be strongly connected, i.e., any node is reachable from every node.

Let $s : V \to \mathbb{R}^{>0}$ be a *score* function on the nodes V. Such a score function naturally defines a Markov chain on V given by the following transition probability from i to j:

$$T_{G,s}(i, j) = \frac{w_{ij} s_j}{\sum_{j' \in \Gamma_{\text{out}}(i)} w_{ij'} s_{j'}}.$$

Note that the strong-connectedness of G guarantees that the Markov chain is recurrent. If the Markov chain is also aperiodic then the stationary distribution is unique. Given a score function s, let $\pi_{G,s}$ denote the stationary distribution of the Markov chain.

Let $p : V \to (0, 1]$ be a given probability distribution over the nodes of G so that $\sum_{i \in V} p_i = 1$. By removing each node i where $p_i = 0$, we will assume without loss of generality that $p_i > 0$ for all $i \in V$.

PROBLEM 1 (STEADY-STATE INVERSION). *Given a strongly connected weighted graph $G = (V, E)$, and a distribution p on V, find a score function $s : V \to \mathbb{R}^{>0}$ such that $\pi_{G,s} = p$.*

Note that a priori it is unclear if such a score function always exists or if it is unique.

4. FEASIBILITY AND SOLVABILITY

In this section we study the necessary and sufficient conditions for the feasibility of the steady-state inversion problem and show how to find the scores in polynomial time if the problem is feasible.

We first illustrate a simple example to show that a solution to the steady-state inversion problem may not always exist. Let G be the directed three node cycle $A \to B \to C \to A$, with an additional self loop on A. For any score function s, it is easy to see that the stationary distributions on B and C must be equal. If not, the the steady-state inversion problem on this graph is infeasible.

4.1 Reduction to the bipartite case

To study the conditions under which a solution exists and to find a solution, we convert the steady-state inversion problem on general graphs to a related problem on directed weighted bipartite graphs.

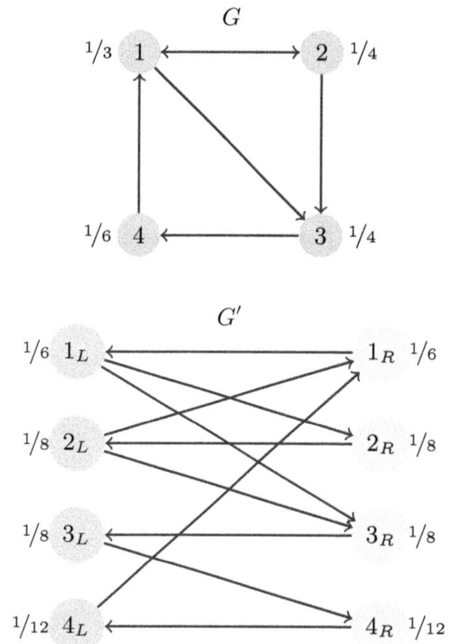

Figure 1: Reduction to the bipartite case: original graph G and the given steady-state distribution p and the bipartite form G' and the new distribution p'.

Let $G = (L, R, E)$ be a directed weighted bipartite graph. Let $T'_{G,s} : L \times R \to [0, 1]$ be a submatrix of the transition matrix defined as $T'_{G,s}(i_L, j_R) = T_{G,s}(i_L, j_R)$ for $i_L \in L$ and $j_R \in R$. Note that since G is bipartite, $T'_{G,s}$ is itself a transition matrix. Let p be a probability distribution on the nodes $L \cup R$. Let p_L (resp. p_R) be the conditional distribution on the nodes in L (resp. R). We define the following problem.

PROBLEM 2 (BIPARTITE STEADY-STATE INVERSION). *Given a directed bipartite graph $G = (L, R, E)$, and probability distributions p_L on L and p_R on R, find a score function $s : R \to \mathbb{R}^{>0}$ such that $p_R = p_L \cdot T'_{G,s}$.*

We now show how to reduce the steady-state inversion problem on graphs to bipartite steady-state inversion. Let $G = (V, E)$ be the given instance of the steady-state inversion problem and let p be the given distribution on V.

Let $G' = (L, R, E')$ be a bipartite graph derived from G in the following manner. For each node $i \in V$, create two nodes i_L and i_R: $L = \{i_L \mid i \in V\}$ and $R = \{i_R \mid i \in V\}$. For each edge $(i, j) \in E$ with weight w_{ij}, add an edge (i_L, j_R) with weight w_{ij} to E'. For each node $i \in V$, add a back edge (i_R, i_L) of weight 1 to E'. Let p' be a distribution on $L \cup R$ given by $p'(i_L) = p'(i_R) = p(i)/2$. We give an example of the reduction in Figure 1.

LEMMA 3. *Let s' be the solution to the bipartite steady-state inversion problem on G' and p'. Then, s defined by $s(i) = s'(i_R)$ is a solution to the steady-state inversion problem on G.*

PROOF. By construction, we have $p'(i_R) = p(i)/2 = p'(i_L)$. Also, by the construction of G' from G and the definition of

s from s', we have $T'_{G',s'} = T_{G,s}$ and hence,

$$p(i) = 2p'(i_R) = 2p'(i_L) \cdot T'_{G',s'} = p(i) \cdot T_{G,s},$$

where the second equality follows since s' is a solution to the bipartite steady-state inversion problem. Therefore, s is a solution to the steady-state inversion problem on G and p. □

4.2 Algorithm for bipartite graphs

Let $G = (L, R, E)$ be a bipartite graph and let p be a distribution on $L \cup R$. We define a notion of graph consistency and show that the steady-state inversion problem is feasible if and only if the bipartite graph is consistent.

DEFINITION 4 (CONSISTENCY). *A directed bipartite graph $G = (L, R, E)$ is* consistent *with a distribution p on $L \cup R$ if*

$$\sum_{i \in L} p_i = \frac{1}{2} = \sum_{j \in R} p_j,$$

and there exist values $\alpha_{ij} \geq 0$ for all $(i, j) \in E$ so that for every node $i \in L$,

$$p_i = \sum_{j \in \Gamma_{\text{out}}(i)} \alpha_{ij},$$

and for every node $j \in R$,

$$p_j = \sum_{i \in \Gamma_{\text{in}}(j)} \alpha_{ij}.$$

The consistency condition is equivalent to saying that the stationary distribution p is a result of specific choices (namely the α_{ij}'s) made by each node. Consistency is a condition that is ensured in many natural settings. For example, a bipartite graph obtained (according to the reduction in Section 4.1) from a strongly connected directed graph with self-loops at all nodes, is consistent with any distribution. Another example of a bipartite graph that is consistent with any distribution is one in which for any subset $L' \subseteq L$, we have $\sum_{i \in L'} p_i \leq \sum_{j \in R'} p_j$, where $R' = \cup_{i \in L'} \Gamma_{\text{out}}(i)$; this is related to the Hall's theorem condition [11] for the existence of a perfect matching in bipartite graphs. Observe that the three node cycle example above is consistent only when the stationary distribution on nodes B and C is the same. Clearly if the consistency condition is not met, there is no way to satisfy the steady-state equations in the original graph. However, surprisingly, the converse is also true: if the consistency condition is met, then the node scores can be set so as to realize the target steady state.

This is our main result, which we now state and prove.

THEOREM 5. *Let $G = (L, R, E)$ be a weighted bipartite graph and p be a distribution on $L \cup R$ that is consistent with G. Then for any $\epsilon > 0$, there exists a score function s such that*

$$(1 - \epsilon) p_R \leq p_L \cdot T'_{G,s} \leq (1 + \epsilon) p_R;$$

moreover, s can be computed in polynomial time.

We prove this Theorem by giving an algorithm to find the desired scores s. The algorithm will begin with some assignment of the scores, and then increase the scores for the nodes whose realized probability is far below the desired probability. To state the algorithm, for a node $j \in R$, let

$$q_j(s) = (p_L \cdot T'_{G,s})_j,$$

be the probability mass at node j after one step of the random walk from P_L, based on the scores s.

Let $\epsilon > \delta > 0$ and consider the following algorithm, which obtains a sequence of approximations to the score function. (For simplicity of exposition, we have separated the roles of δ and ϵ; later in Theorem 10, we will set $\delta = \epsilon/2$.)

Algorithm 1 Bipartite steady-state inversion

$t \leftarrow 0$
for $j \in R$ **do**
  Initialize $s_j^t = p_j$
end for
repeat
  $t \leftarrow t + 1$
  for $j \in R$ **do**
    if $q_j(s^{t-1}) \geq p_j(1 - \epsilon)$ **then**
      $s_j^t \leftarrow s_j^{t-1}$ {Leave score unchanged}
    else
      Solve the following for x:
      $q_j(s_1^{t-1}, \ldots, s_{j-1}^{t-1}, x, s_{j+1}^{t-1}, \ldots, s_n^{t-1}) = p_j(1 - \delta)$
      $s_j^t \leftarrow x$ {Increase score}
    end if
  end for
until $\forall j \in R, \quad s_j^t = s_j^{t-1}$

4.3 Algorithm Analysis

LEMMA 6. *Algorithm 1 is well defined, i.e., s_j^{t+1} exists as defined for every t. Furthermore, the algorithm produces a sequence of score functions $s^0, s^1, \ldots$ that is increasing in each coordinate, i.e., for all $j \in R$, $s_j^0 \leq s_j^1 \leq \cdots$.*

PROOF. To see that s_j^t exists for all t and j, first note that when $q_j(s^{t-1}) \geq p_j(1 - \epsilon)$, it follows trivially. So consider the case that $q_j(s^{t-1}) < p_j(1 - \epsilon)$. We need to show that the equation

$$q_j(s_1^{t-1}, \ldots, s_{j-1}^{t-1}, x, s_{j+1}^{t-1}, \ldots, s_n^{t-1}) = p_j(1 - \delta)$$

has a solution. For convenience, let

$$Q_j(x) = q_j(s_1^{t-1}, \ldots, s_{j-1}^{t-1}, x, s_{j+1}^{t-1}, \ldots, s_n^{t-1}).$$

Notice that

$$\lim_{x \to \infty} Q_j(x) = \sum_{i \in \Gamma_{\text{in}}(j)} p_i.$$

Since p is consistent with G, this sum either surpasses p_j or approaches p_j in the limit. Since $Q_j(s_j^{t-1}) < p_j(1 - \epsilon)$, and Q_j is increasing in x and continuous, there is some $x \geq s_j^{t-1}$ for which $Q_j(x) = p_j(1 - \delta)$, as desired. Note that this also shows that the sequence is non-decreasing. □

Thus, we have a sequence of score functions that is non-decreasing in each coordinate. We will show that each coordinate is upper bounded. At a high level, the proof argues that any node whose score increases beyond bound must already be taking almost all of the probability mass from its in-neighbors (by unboundedness), but that these neighbors must among them have enough probability mass (by consistency), thus reaching a contradiction.

LEMMA 7. *For all $j \in R$ there is an upper bound u_j such that $s_j^t \leq u_j$ for all $t \geq 0$.*

PROOF. Let $Z \subseteq R$ be the set of nodes for which the upper bound exists. We will show that $Z = R$. We begin by showing that Z is always non-empty.

Fix a time t, and let Z' be the set of nodes for which $q_j(s^t) > p_j$. Note that if $q_j(s^t) \leq (1-\epsilon)p_j$ for some $t = t_0$, then $q_j(s^t) \leq (1-\delta)p_j$ for all $t \geq t_0$. This follows from the fact that $Q_j(x)$ is non-increasing for all coordinates $k \neq j$. Thus if Z' is empty, then the total probability mass on the nodes in R is:

$$\sum_{j \in R} q_j(s^t) \leq \sum_{j \in R} (1-\delta)p_j < 1,$$

a contradiction. Therefore Z' and $Z \supseteq Z'$ are non-empty.

Since Z is non-empty, consider what happens when $Z \neq R$. Intuitively, since the scores for these nodes are increasing, it must be the case that their probability mass is below the target. We will again show that not all of the nodes can have their probability mass below the target simultaneously.

Assume without loss of generality that $\min w_{ij} = 1$, and let $W = \max w_{ij}$. Let $s_{\max} = \max_{j \in Z} s_j$ be the maximum score for any node in Z, and denote by

$$M = \frac{s_{\max} n^2 W}{\epsilon p_{\min}},$$

where $p_{\min} = \min_{j \in R} p_j$. Consider the time t when the scores for all nodes in $R \setminus Z$ are at least M. Note that since scores in $R \setminus Z$ tend to infinity such a time must exist.

We partition the nodes in L into three sets, those that are not connected to any node in Z,

$$A = \{v_i \in L \mid \Gamma_{\text{out}}(v_i) \cap Z = \emptyset\};$$

those connected to nodes in Z and in $R \setminus Z$,

$$B = \{v_i \in L \mid \Gamma_{\text{out}}(v_i) \cap Z \neq \emptyset, \Gamma_{\text{out}}(v_i) \cap R \setminus Z \neq \emptyset\};$$

and those connected only to Z,

$$C = \{v_i \in L \mid \Gamma_{\text{out}}(v_i) \subseteq Z\}.$$

Since the nodes in $R \setminus Z$ have scores that are increasing, it must be the case that:

$$\sum_{j \in R\setminus Z} q_j(s^t) < (1-\epsilon) \sum_{j \in R \setminus Z} p_j. \tag{1}$$

Now consider the total probability mass for nodes in $R \setminus Z$

$$\begin{aligned}
\sum_{j \in R\setminus Z} q_j(s^t) &= \sum_{i \in A \cup B} p_i \frac{\sum_{j \in \Gamma_{\text{out}}(v_i) \cap R \setminus Z} w_{ij} s_j}{\sum_{j \in \Gamma_{\text{out}}(v_i)} w_{ij} s_j} \\
&= \sum_{i \in A} p_i + \sum_{i \in B} p_i \left(1 - \frac{\sum_{j \in \Gamma_{\text{out}}(v_i) \cap Z} w_{ij} s_j}{\sum_{j \in \Gamma_{\text{out}}(v_i)} w_{ij} s_j}\right) \\
&> \sum_{i \in A} p_i + \sum_{i \in B} p_i \left(1 - \frac{\sum_{j \in \Gamma_{\text{out}}(v_i) \cap Z} W s_{\max}}{M}\right) \\
&\geq \sum_{i \in A} p_i + \sum_{i \in B} p_i \left(1 - nW s_{\max} \cdot \frac{\epsilon p_{\min}}{n^2 W s_{\max}}\right) \\
&\geq \sum_{i \in A \cup B} p_i - \epsilon p_{\min}.
\end{aligned} \tag{2}$$

Finally, consider the total probability mass for nodes in Z. Intuitively the nodes in Z inherit all of the probability mass in from nodes in C, and some of the probability mass from those in B; formally, since p is consistent with G, we have

$$\sum_{j \in Z} p_j \geq \sum_{i \in C} p_i. \tag{3}$$

Combining (1) and (2), we have

$$(1-\epsilon) \sum_{j \in R \setminus Z} p_j > \sum_{i \in A \cup B} p_i - \epsilon p_{\min}.$$

Since by consistency

$$\sum_{j \in R} p_j = \sum_{i \in A \cup B \cup C} p_i = \frac{1}{2},$$

this is equivalent to

$$\left(\frac{1}{2} - \sum_{j \in Z} p_j\right) - \epsilon \sum_{j \in R \setminus Z} p_j > \left(\frac{1}{2} - \sum_{i \in C} p_i\right) - \epsilon p_{\min}.$$

Rewriting, we obtain

$$\sum_{i \in C} p_i + \epsilon \left(p_{\min} - \sum_{j \in R \setminus Z} p_j\right) > \sum_{j \in Z} p_j.$$

Since $R \setminus Z$ is non-empty, this implies

$$\sum_{i \in C} p_i > \sum_{j \in Z} p_j,$$

which directly contradicts (3). □

4.4 Rate of convergence

In order to analyze the convergence time of the algorithm we give an explicit upper bound on the value of the scores, and then give a lower bound on the amount by which the scores increase in every iteration.

LEMMA 8. *Let s^t and s^{t+1} be the score functions at time t and $t+1$ respectively. Then for each $j \in R$ either $s_j^t = s_j^{t+1}$ or*

$$\frac{s_j^{t+1}}{s_j^t} \geq \frac{1-\delta}{1-\epsilon} > 1.$$

PROOF. If s_j^t increases from time t to $t+1$, then we know that

$$\sum_{i \in \Gamma_{\text{in}}(j)} p_i \frac{s_j^t w_{ij}}{\sum_{j' \in \Gamma_{\text{out}}(i)} s_{j'}^t w_{ij'}} = Q_j(s_j^t) < (1-\epsilon)p_j,$$

and

$$\sum_{i \in \Gamma_{\text{in}}(j)} p_i \frac{s_j^{t+1} w_{ij}}{\sum_{j' \in \Gamma_{\text{out}}(i)} s_{j'}^{t+1} w_{ij'}} = Q_j(s_j^{t+1}) = (1-\delta)p_j,$$

i.e.,

$$\frac{Q_j(s_j^{t+1})}{Q_j(s_j^t)} \geq \frac{1-\delta}{1-\epsilon}.$$

By an averaging argument, there exists an $i \in \Gamma_{\text{in}}(j)$ such that

$$\left(\frac{s_j^t w_{ij}}{\sum_{j' \in \Gamma_{\text{out}}(i)} s_{j'}^t w_{ij'}} \bigg/ \frac{s_j^{t+1} w_{ij}}{\sum_{j' \in \Gamma_{\text{out}}(i)} s_{j'}^{t+1} w_{ij'}}\right) \geq \frac{1-\delta}{1-\epsilon}.$$

We will focus on this i. Note that $j \in \Gamma_{\text{out}}(i)$. Hence, the above expression can be written as

$$\left(\frac{s_j^t}{s_j^t + Z} \Big/ \frac{s_j^{t+1}}{s_j^{t+1} + Z} \right) \geq \frac{1-\delta}{1-\epsilon},$$

where $Z = (1/w_{ij}) \cdot \sum_{j' \in \Gamma_{\text{out}}(i) \setminus \{j\}} s_{j'}^t w_{ij'} \geq 0$ and we used the fact that $s_{j'}^{t+1} = s_{j'}^t$ for $j' \in \Gamma_{\text{out}}(i) \setminus \{j\}$. We now claim the following: for $z \geq 0$ and $\rho > 1$,

$$\frac{a}{a+z} \Big/ \frac{b}{b+z} \geq \rho \Longrightarrow \frac{a}{b} \geq \rho.$$

Given this claim, the proof is complete by setting $z = Z, a = s_j^t, b = s_j^{t+1}$, and $\rho = (1-\delta)/(1-\epsilon)$.

The claim is easy to see: indeed, after algebraic manipulations, it is equivalent to

$$az \geq \rho bz + ab(\rho - 1).$$

Using $\rho > 1$ and $z \geq 0$, we see that $a \geq \rho b$ and the claim is hence proved. □

For the explicit upper bound, let $M_1 = 1$ and for $i > 1$, $M_k = \left(\frac{n^2 W}{\epsilon p_{\min}}\right)^{k-1}$. We will show that any point of the algorithm at most $n - k$ nodes can have value of M_k.

Lemma 9. *At any time t, for all $k \in \{1, \ldots, n\}$ and all nodes $j \in R$:*

$$|\{s_j \geq M_k\}| \leq n - k.$$

Proof. We prove the lemma by induction. The scores are initialized so that $s_i = p_i$. As we saw in the proof of Lemma 6 at least one of the initial scores is such that $Q_j(s_i) \geq (1-\epsilon)p_i$ and it never increases. Since $p_i < 1$ the statement holds.

Now suppose the statement holds for all $k^* < k$. Let Z be the set of nodes with scores less than M_{k-1}. Lemma 6 states that not all of the scores in $R \setminus Z$ can be larger than $M_{k-1} \cdot \frac{n^2 W}{\epsilon p_{\min}}$. Therefore at least one of the nodes in $R \setminus Z$ will have a score bounded by $M_{k-1} \cdot \frac{n^2 W}{\epsilon p_{\min}} = M_k$, and the proof follows. □

Theorem 10. *Let $\delta = \epsilon/2$. Then the algorithm terminates after at most*

$$O\left(\frac{n^2}{\epsilon} \log \frac{nW}{\epsilon p_{\min}}\right)$$

iterations.

Proof. From Lemma 8, in every iteration at least one score increases by a factor of

$$\frac{1-\delta}{1-\epsilon} \geq 1 + \frac{\epsilon}{2}.$$

Since each score is bounded by M_n, the number of times each score can increase is bounded by:

$$\log_{1+\epsilon/2} M_n = O\left(n \log_{1+\epsilon/2}\left(\frac{n^2 W}{\epsilon p_{\min}}\right)\right) = O\left(\frac{n}{\epsilon} \log \frac{nW}{\epsilon p_{\min}}\right).$$

Summing over all nodes completes the proof. □

4.5 Uniqueness

We show that the solution to the steady-state inversion problem is unique up to normalization. More formally,

Theorem 11. *For any two solutions s and s' to the steady-state inversion problem, there exists a constant $c > 0$ such that $s = c \cdot s'$ element-wise.*

Proof. Consider the solution s' and normalize it so that s and s' agree on some node v. Let $Z = \{i \mid s_i' > s_i\}$. Without loss of generality $Z \neq \emptyset$, since otherwise we can swap the roles of s and s'.

Consider the nodes in $A = \Gamma_{\text{in}}(Z) \setminus Z$. Note that $A \neq \emptyset$ since the graph is strongly connected and $v \notin Z$. Then,

$$\begin{aligned}\sum_{i \in Z} p_i &= \sum_{j \in A} p_j \frac{s_i w_{ji}}{\sum_{i' \in \Gamma_{\text{out}}(j)} s_{i'} w_{ji'}} \\ &> \sum_{i \in A} p_j \frac{s_i' w_{ji}}{\sum_{i' \in \Gamma_{\text{out}}(j)} s_{i'}' w_{ji'}} \\ &= \sum_{i \in Z} p_i.\end{aligned}$$

Here the inequality follows from the fact that $\frac{x}{x+y}$ is increasing in x and decreasing in y, and the last equality follows from s' being a solution. □

4.6 Generalizations

We now state a generalization of our result on the steady-state inversion problem. As before, let $G = (V, E)$ be an instance of the steady-state inversion problem and let $f : \mathbb{R}^2 \to \mathbb{R}$ be a function. We can define the transition matrix $T_{G,s}^f$ with respect to f and a score function s as

$$T_{G,s}^f(i,j) = \frac{f(w_{ij}, s_j)}{\sum_{j' \in \Gamma_{\text{out}}(i)} f(w_{ij'}, s_{j'})},$$

i.e., f is applied to the edge weight and the score function. Let $\pi_{G,s}^f$ be the stationary distribution of the Markov chain. Note that the problem considered in Section 4.1 corresponds to $f(x, y) = x \cdot y$.

We now state the sufficient conditions on f for the feasibility of the corresponding steady-state inversion problem, i.e., given p, does there exist a score function s such that $\pi_{G,s}^f = p$. We state the result for the bipartite case as in Section 4.2.

Theorem 12. *Given a graph G and a probability distribution p, and a function f, the steady-state inversion problem with f is feasible if p is consistent with G and f satisfies the following two properties: (i) $f(x, y)$ is continuous and increasing in y and (ii) $\lim_{y \to \infty} f(\cdot, y) = \infty$.*

We omit the details of this proof in this version.

4.7 Connections to choice theory

The steady-state inversion problem is somewhat related to the classical discrete choice problem. We recall the *Choice Axiom* formulated by Luce in his seminal work [23, 24]. The axiom states that when faced with a choice between two objects, the relative probability of selecting one object over another is independent of the presence of other alternatives. An equivalent formulation states that each object has a latent score s_i and objects are selected with probability proportional to their score.

Let U be the universe of objects. An instance of the choice problem is of a collection of m observations, $O_1, \ldots, O_m$ where each observation O_i is a tuple containing a set $S_i \subseteq U$ of objects a user was choosing between as well as the object $\text{sel}(S_i) \in S_i$ that was selected. The goal is then to find scores that maximize the likelihood of the data, where the likelihood of the data is:

$$\mathcal{L} = \prod_{i \in m} \frac{s_{\text{sel}(S_i)}}{\sum_{u_k \in S_j} s_k}.$$

We can model this as an instance of the bipartite steady-state inversion problem. Create one node v_i for each observation O_i, and one node u_j for each item in the universe U. Let $V = \cup\{v_i\}$. We create a bipartite graph $G = (V, U, E)$ with the following each edges. For each observation O_i, set $\Gamma_{\text{out}}(v_i) = S_i$. Finally, for each node $u_j \in U$, set

$$p_j = \frac{1}{m} \cdot |\{i \mid \text{sel}(S_i) = u_j\}|,$$

i.e., the number of times item u_j was selected, scaled appropriately.

THEOREM 13. *The solution to the steady-state inversion problem defined above maximizes the likelihood in the choice problem.*

PROOF. First observe that the instance of the bipartite steady-state inversion problem is consistent. For each observation O_i, let $\alpha_{ij} = 1/m$ if $j = \text{sel}(S_i)$ and 0 otherwise. By construction this setting of α's satisfies the consistency property.

Let s^* be the solution to the steady-state inversion problem. For every item $u_j \in U$ we have:

$$\frac{1}{m} \cdot |\{i \mid \text{sel}(S_i) = u_j\}| = \sum_{i: u_j \in S_i} \frac{1}{m} \cdot \frac{s_j}{\sum_{u_k \in S_j} s_k}. \quad (4)$$

On the other hand, the log-likelihood of the data in the choice problem is:

$$\log \mathcal{L} = \sum_{i=1}^{m} \left(\log s_{\text{sel}(S_i)} - \log \sum_{u_k \in S_i} s_k \right).$$

Optimality conditions imply that for any element u_j:

$$\begin{aligned} 0 &= \frac{\partial \log \mathcal{L}}{\partial s_j} \\ &= \sum_{i|\text{sel}(S_i)=s_j} \frac{1}{s_j} - \sum_{i|u_j \in S_i} \frac{1}{\sum_{u_k \in S_i} s_k} \\ &= |\{i \mid \text{sel}(s_i) = u_j\}| - \sum_{i|u_j \in S_i} \frac{s_j}{\sum_{u_k \in S_i} s_k}, \end{aligned}$$

which is exactly the condition in (4). Since we know the solution to the steady-state inversion problem is unique (Theorem 11), the proof follows. □

The connection to choice theory also explains the consistency condition (Definition 4) required for the feasibility of the bipartite steady-state inversion problem. Below we show that the consistency condition is satisfied if and only if there exists a set of individual choices that lead to the observed stationary distribution.

THEOREM 14. *Let $G = (L, R, E)$ and a distribution p be an instance of the bipartite steady-state inversion problem. Then p is consistent with G if and only if there is an equivalent discrete choice problem. Moreover, such a discrete choice problem can be found in polynomial time.*

PROOF. Suppose that p is consistent with G. Let α_{ij} be the rational weights on the edges that satisfy consistency. Let

$$N = \left(\prod_{(i,j) \in E} \alpha_{ij} \right)^{-1}.$$

We will create a discrete choice problem with N observations. For each node $i \in L$ create $1/p_i$ observations, each with the identical choice set of$\Gamma_{\text{out}}(i)$. For each $j \in \Gamma_{\text{out}}(i)$, designate u_j as selected $1/\alpha_{ij}$ times. Note that by the choice of N all of these are integer quantities. It is easy to see that this choice problem is equivalent to the steady-state inversion problem.

If G and p are consistent, then one can find the α_{ij} with a single round of maximum flow. Given the bipartite graph G create a source node s, connected to each node $v_i \in L$ with an edge of capacity p_i. In addition, create a sink node t, connected to each node $v_j \in R$ with an edge of capacity p_j. Compute the maximum flow on the resulting graph. If the value of the max flow is below $1/2$ then p is not consistent for G. If the value of the flow is $1/2$, then setting α_{ij} to the flow on each edge (i, j) will satisfy the consistency constraints. □

5. EXPERIMENTS

The solution to the steady-state inversion problem together with the modeling assumptions made by choice theory allow us to predict the number of times each particular choice was made by observing only the final outcomes of the decision process. For example, given the relative popularity of web pages, we can infer the number of times users followed each particular link. Our main experiment will show that by only considering the *structure* of the graph, that is the underlying choice sets, we can reduce the error by almost a factor of 2 compared to raw popularity based predictions. In all of the experiments we set $\epsilon = 10^{-5}$; we will refer to this setting of the scores as Steady-State Inversion. We also study the performance of this algorithm, especially its convergence and running time properties.

5.1 Data

We consider the following four datasets for our evaluation. The datasets span different genres and cover different online user experiences. Three of the datasets are publicly available for repeatability purposes.

Wikipedia paths.

WIKI is is a set of navigation paths through Wikipedia, collected as part of the Wikispeedia human computation game [32, 33]. In the game subjects were asked to navigate from a starting Wikipedia page to a particular target only by following links in the documents. The dataset consists of 51,318 (source, destination) paths which we then decompose into 199,945 transition pairs. The dataset is publicly available from `snap.stanford.edu/data/wikispeedia.html`.

We let the subgraph induced by the transition pairs denote the choice sets available at each web page, and set the desired stationary distribution probability to be proportional to the number of times the node appears in the dataset. Our goal is then to predict the number of transitions along every link in the graph.

Restaurant choice.

REST captures the decisions made by a user as a result of a broad restaurant search query issued to Google. For each query we look at the restaurants offered in the search results and note which of the choices was first clicked. Each result displays some metadata about the restaurant such as the star rating, type of cuisine etc. It is important to note that unlike traditional search results, the UI treatment displays all of the options in a horizontal panel, thereby reducing position effects.

We take a random sample of 100,000 queries, which had 66,464 unique selection choices. Our goal is to predict the restaurant that will be clicked by the user in each of the queries.

Entree recommendations.

ENTREE is a public log of the interactions with the Entree Chicago restaurant recommendation system (available at `kdd.ics.uci.edu/databases/entree/entree.html` as part of the UCI repository [2]). The data consists of 50,672 user sessions, with each session consisting of restaurants explored and the final restaurant chosen by the user (the End point). We treat the explored restaurants as a choice set and the final restaurant as the action. There are 27,668 unique choice sets, and 1,066 total restaurants selected.

Comedy.

COMEDY is the result of YouTube Comedy Slam, a video discovery experiment (available at `archive.ics.uci.edu/ml/datasets/YouTube+Comedy+Slam+Preference+Data`, also from [2]) that ran on YouTube in 2011 and 2012. In the experiment users were shown a pair of videos in random order and were asked to vote for the video that was funnier. We use this as a binary choice dataset, with 225,593 total choices over 75,447 unique choice sets.

5.2 Baselines and metrics

We compare our algorithm to the following four baselines. Each of these baselines will compute a score for each node in the graph.

- Uniform: The score of each node is identical, simulating a uniform random walk on the graph.
- Popularity: The score of each node is set to the popularity of the node. This captures the notion that popular items should have higher scores, but is agnostic to the structure of the graph, and thus cannot differentiate between an item being popular because it is present in many choice sets (and thus has many chances of being selected), or popular because it has very high quality (and thus is selected almost every time it is present).
- PageRank: The score of each node is set to the PageRank [7] of the node.
- Temperature Rank: The score of each node is set to the Temperature Rank [31] of the node.

We will use two metrics to explore our results. The first is the RMSE of predicting the number of transitions along each link. The second is the log-likelihood of the data using the particular set of scores under the choice model. To be able to interpret the numbers across the four datasets, we scale them so that the numbers for Popularity are always unit.

5.3 Predicting the transitions

We show the RMSE of the transition prediction tasks for both datasets in Table 1, where we normalize the results to have the Popularity RMSE = 1.0. Note that lower values mean better prediction.

For all datasets our algorithm outperforms the four baselines, reducing the error by 10–30% over the best available baseline. Note that on the WIKI dataset all of the other baselines outperform the Popularity baseline. Nonetheless, the Steady-State Inversion solution is better still. On the other hand, for restaurant choice, Popularity is the strongest baseline, but Steady-State Inversion beats it by an additional 10%. Note again that in all of the prediction tasks we do not take *any* metadata into account; these predictions are based solely on the structure of the graph.

A trend nearly identical to that in Table 1 is obtained for the log-likelihood metric as well. For sake of brevity, we do not repeat the numbers.

5.4 Rate of convergence

The algorithm we presented is guaranteed to converge to the optimal set of scores. Below we show that the upper bound on the convergence derived in Theorem 10 is incredibly pessimistic and in practice, the algorithm reaches a good solution after fewer than ten iterations, and converges soon after.

In Figures 2 and 3 we plot the log-likelihood as well as the RMSE as the function of the number of iterations on the WIKI and REST datasets. Again we normalize the likelihood so that it is -1 for the Popularity baseline. By design, the algorithm begins with the popularity baseline. It is evident that the biggest gains in RMSE and likelihood occur during the first few iterations, after that the algorithm quickly hits diminishing returns and terminates after 32 iterations for WIKI and 9 iterations for REST. Similar trends are observed for the other two datasets and we do not repeat the corresponding plots.

6. CONCLUSIONS

In this paper, we studied the following setting. Users navigate between states according to a Markov process. We are able to observe the steady state of this process, and we wish to learn the transition matrix. Even though this problem is underconstrained in general (as the steady state has linear number of variables, while the matrix can have quadratically many variables), we used a specific form of the transition matrix: each state of the Markov process has an unknown score and the probability of transition from a source state to a destination state is dependent on the score of the destination state. We showed a natural sufficient condition on the feasibility of the problem. For the instances that are feasible we gave a simple iterative algorithm to solve this inverse problem; we also showed the polynomial rate of convergence of this algorithm, and proved the solution unique. We then applied this algorithm to a few natural settings and showed

	Popularity	Uniform	PageRank	Temperature Rank	Steady-State Inversion
WIKI	1.0	0.65	0.83	0.65	**0.57**
REST	1.0	1.17	1.39	1.21	**0.89**
ENTREE	1.0	0.69	1.01	0.56	**0.42**
COMEDY	1.0	0.65	0.90	0.78	**0.36**

Table 1: The RMSE of the transition prediction task normalized by the RMSE obtained by the Popularity baseline.

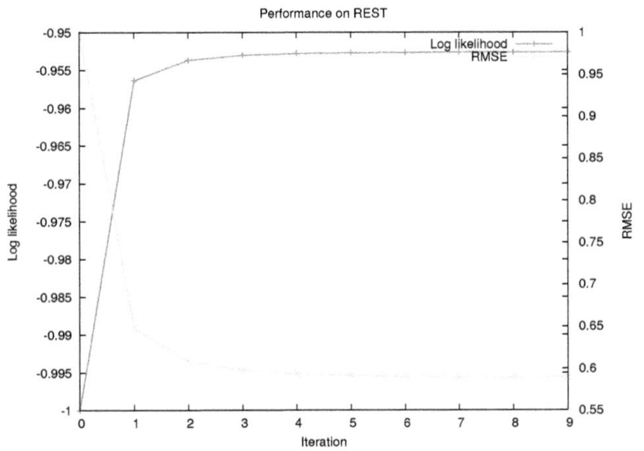

Figure 3: The log-likelihood and RMSE as a function of the number of iterations on the REST dataset.

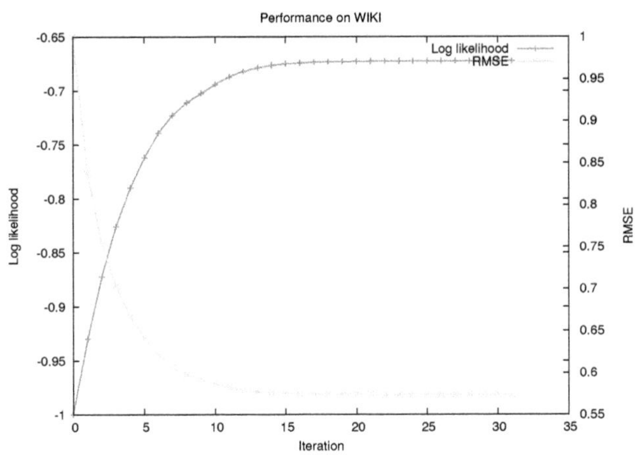

Figure 2: The log-likelihood and RMSE as a function of the number of iterations on the WIKI dataset.

that this algorithm has a better likelihood of predicting transitions in user behavior than other strong baselines.

Our work throws open a number of research questions. Even though our algorithm admits an obvious parallelization and is reasonably efficient in practice, making it scale to hundreds of millions of nodes would be very useful. It will also be interesting to study our model with a random teleportation component, as in PageRank. Finally, using our framework for other application domains including opinion ratings seems fruitful.

Acknowledgments

We thank Bill Heavlin and the reviewers for many useful pointers and suggestions.

7. REFERENCES

[1] K. Avrachenkov, D. Nemirovsky, and K. S. Pham. A survey on distributed approaches to graph based reputation measures. In *Performance Evaluation Methodologies and Tools*, pages 1–9, 2007.

[2] K. Bache and M. Lichman. UCI Machine Learning Repository, 2013.

[3] M. Ben-Akiva and S. Lerman. *Discrete Choice Analysis: Theory and Application to Travel Demand.* MIT Press, 1985.

[4] P. Berkhin. A survey on PageRank computing. *Internet Mathematics*, 2(1):73–120, 2005.

[5] A. Borodin, G. O. Roberts, J. S. Rosenthal, and P. Tsaparas. Link analysis ranking: Algorithms, theory, and experiments. *ACM Trans. Internet Technol.*, 5(1):231–297, 2005.

[6] S. Boyd, P. Diaconis, and L. Xiao. Fastest mixing Markov chain on a graph. *SIAM Review*, 46:667–689, 2004.

[7] S. Brin and L. Page. The anatomy of a large-scale hypertextual Web search engine. *Computer Networks*, 56(18):3825–3833, 2012.

[8] Y.-Y. Chen, Q. Gan, and T. Suel. Local methods for estimating PageRank values. In *CIKM*, pages 381–389, 2004.

[9] S. Chib and E. Greenberg. Understanding the Metropolis–Hastings algorithm. *American Statistician*, 49(4):327–335, 1995.

[10] A. Ghosh, S. Boyd, and A. Saberi. Minimizing effective resistance of a graph. *SIAM Review*, 50:37–66, 2008.

[11] P. Hall. On representatives of subsets. *J. London Math. Soc.*, 10(1):26–30, 1935.

[12] W. K. Hastings. Monte Carlo sampling methods using Markov chains and their applications. *Biometrika*, 57(1):97–109, 1970.

[13] T. H. Haveliwala. Topic-sensitive PageRank. In *WWW*, pages 517–526, 2002.

[14] D. Hensher, J. Rose, and W. Greene. *Applied Choice Analysis: A Primer.* Cambridge University Press, 2005.

[15] S. Kamvar, T. Haveliwala, and G. Golub. Adaptive methods for the computation of PageRank. *Linear Algebra and its Applications*, pages 51–65, 2004.

[16] S. D. Kamvar, T. H. Haveliwala, C. D. Manning, and G. H. Golub. Extrapolation methods for accelerating PageRank computations. In *WWW*, pages 261–270, 2003.

[17] J. G. Kemeny and J. L. Snell. *Finite Markov Chains (with a New Appendix "Generalization of a Fundamental Matrix")*. Springer, 1983.

[18] J. M. Kleinberg. Authoritative sources in a hyperlinked environment. *J. ACM*, 46(5):604–632, 1999.

[19] A. N. Langville and C. D. Meyer. Deeper inside PageRank. *Internet Mathematics*, 1(3):335–380, 2004.

[20] A. N. Langville and C. D. Meyer. Updating PageRank with iterative aggregation. In *WWW (Posters)*, pages 392–393, 2004.

[21] D. A. Levin, Y. Peres, and E. L. Wilmer. *Markov Chains and Mixing Times*. American Mathematical Society, 2008.

[22] N. Litvak, W. R. W. Scheinhardt, and Y. Volkovich. In-degree and PageRank: Why do they follow similar power laws? *Internet Math.*, 4(2-3):175–198, 2007.

[23] R. D. Luce. *Individual Choice Behavior: A Theoretical Analysis*. Wiley, 1959.

[24] R. D. Luce. The choice axiom after twenty years. *Journal of Mathematical Psychology*, 15(3):215–233, 1977.

[25] F. McSherry. A uniform approach to accelerated PageRank computation. In *WWW*, pages 575–582, 2005.

[26] N. Metropolis, A. W. Rosenbluth, M. N. Rosenbluth, A. H. Teller, and E. Teller. Equations of state calculations by fast computing machines. *Journal of Chemical Physics*, 21(6):1087–1092, 1953.

[27] A. Y. Ng, A. X. Zheng, and M. I. Jordan. Stable algorithms for link analysis. In *SIGIR*, pages 258–266, 2001.

[28] L. Page, S. Brin, R. Motwani, and T. Winograd. The PageRank citation ranking: Bringing order to the Web. Technical report, InfoLab, Stanford University, 1999.

[29] R. B. Potts and R. M. Oliver. *Flows in Transportation Networks*. Academic Press, 1972.

[30] D. Rafiei and A. O. Mendelzon. What is this page known for? Computing Web page reputations. In *WWW*, pages 823–835, 2000.

[31] J. A. Tomlin. A new paradigm for ranking pages on the world wide Web. In *WWW*, pages 350–355, 2003.

[32] R. West and J. Leskovec. Human wayfinding in information networks. In *WWW*, pages 619–628, 2012.

[33] R. West, J. Pineau, and D. Precup. Wikispeedia: An online game for inferring semantic distances between concepts. In *IJCAI*, pages 1598–1603, 2009.

Automatic Gloss Finding for a Knowledge Base using Ontological Constraints

Bhavana Dalvi
Carnegie Mellon University
Pittsburgh, PA 15213
bbd@cs.cmu.edu

Einat Minkov
University of Haifa
Haifa, Israel, 31905
einatm@is.haifa.ac.il

Partha P. Talukdar
Indian Institute of Science
Bangalore, India 560012
ppt@serc.iisc.in

William W. Cohen
Carnegie Mellon University
Pittsburgh, PA 15213
wcohen@cs.cmu.edu

ABSTRACT

While there has been much research on automatically constructing structured Knowledge Bases (KBs), most of it has focused on generating facts to populate a KB. However, a useful KB must go beyond facts. For example, glosses (short natural language definitions) have been found to be very useful in tasks such as Word Sense Disambiguation. However, the important problem of Automatic Gloss Finding, i.e., assigning glosses to entities in an initially gloss-free KB, is relatively unexplored. We address that gap in this paper. In particular, we propose GLOFIN, a hierarchical semi-supervised learning algorithm for this problem which makes effective use of limited amounts of supervision and available ontological constraints. To the best of our knowledge, GLOFIN is the first system for this task.

Through extensive experiments on real-world datasets, we demonstrate GLOFIN's effectiveness. It is encouraging to see that GLOFIN outperforms other state-of-the-art SSL algorithms, especially in low supervision settings. We also demonstrate GLOFIN's robustness to noise through experiments on a wide variety of KBs, ranging from user contributed (e.g., Freebase) to automatically constructed (e.g., NELL). To facilitate further research in this area, we have made the datasets and code used in this paper publicly available.

Categories and Subject Descriptors: I.2.6[Artificial Intelligence]: Learning - Knowledge acquisition

Keywords: Gloss Finding; Hierarchical Learning; Web Mining.

1. INTRODUCTION

Automatic construction of knowledge bases (KBs) has attracted much attention over the past years. Knowledge bases provide a structured representation of entities and the relationships between them, which is key in semantic processing tasks such as concept tagging, disambiguation and normalization. Freebase [6] and DBPedia [28] are well-known examples of KBs that represent broad-domain world knowledge, which are constructed and maintained collaboratively. Much work has been done on development of information extraction systems to produce such KBs: e.g., the Never-Ending-Language-Learning (NELL) [7], TextRunner [45], and PROSPERA [33] are targeted at extracting facts at Web scale.

While facts are obviously essential for a KB, a useful KB must contain more than facts. Many widely-used KBs, including Freebase and WordNet, also include *glosses*—i.e., natural language definitions of the entities in the KB. A large KB may contain glosses for each of the many entities it contains. In manually-constructed KBs like WordNet [29], glosses are typically provided when the KBs are constructed by human experts; however, in many automatically generated KBs, like NELL [30] or YAGO [39], there are no glosses, or only a few. For instance, YAGO supports glosses, but only a small fraction of entities (68.9K out of 10M) have glosses assigned to them. Since manually adding definitions for a large number of entities is infeasible, glosses must be added automatically. In this paper, we focus on the problem of augmenting an existing KB with gloss information. To the best of our knowledge, this is the first attempt of enriching automatically-constructed KBs with glosses.

To illustrate the problem, Figure 1 (top part) describes the structure of the NELL KB, as an example. As shown, the entities represented in NELL are organized in a hierarchy, in which nodes are linked with *is-a* (subset) relations. General semantic categories, like *Fruit* and *Company*, are represented by nodes that are linked to higher level categories in the hierarchy–*Food* and *Organization*, respectively. Concrete entity nodes, such as *Microsoft* and *Google*, are linked to their category–*Company*. In addition, entities are associated in NELL with their lexical aliases; e.g., 'Microsoft' and 'MS' are both aliases of *Microsoft*. Notably, lexical aliases are often ambiguous, e.g., the name 'Apple' refers to either *Fruit:Apple* or *Company:Apple*. While this representation of NELL KB provides valuable structured semantic knowledge, it does not contain glosses. Ideally, we would like to associate glosses to each entity node. E.g., *Company:Apple* may be described as "Apple, formerly Apple Inc, is an American company headquartered in Cupertino...".

In addition to helping users understand the semantics (or intended semantics) of an entity, glosses are used in many technical tasks. In information retrieval, several recent approaches to query expansion make use of glosses [10, 13] to improve the performance of ad-hoc information retrieval, based on a semantic, entity-rich representation of queries and documents. More generally, in the *entity linking* (EL) task [21, 8], named entity mentions in text are mapped onto canonicalized nodes in the KB, thus disambiguating the named entity mentions. Classical approaches to EL make heavy

WSDM'15, February 2–6, 2015, Shanghai, China.

http://dx.doi.org/10.1145/2684822.2685288.

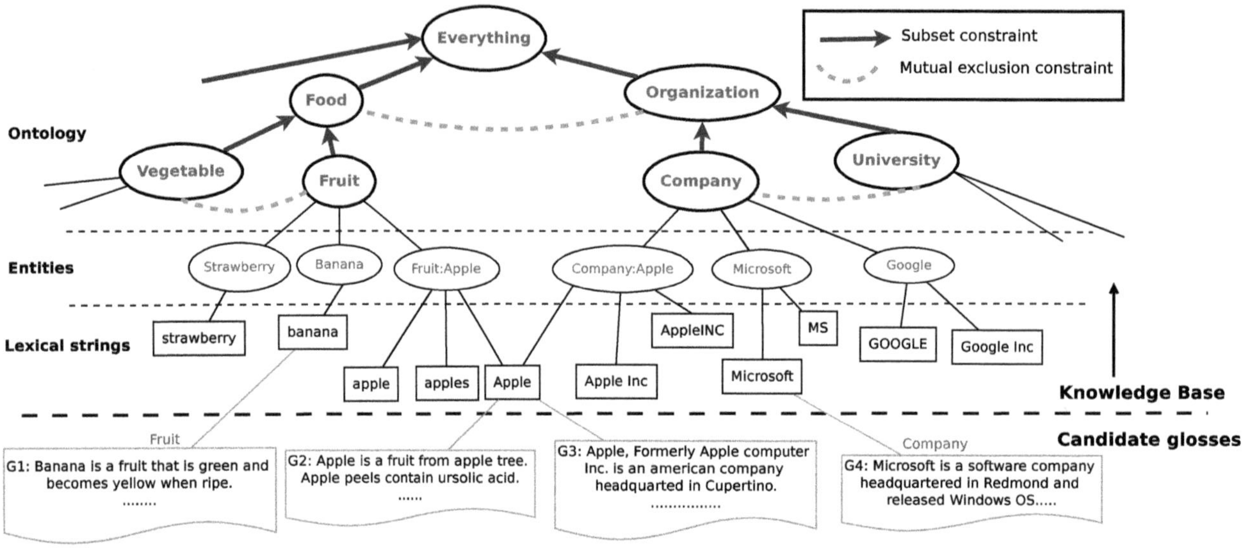

Figure 1: Graph constructed by GLOFIN for the gloss finding problem using lexical matches and ontological constraints (e.g., mutual exclusion, subsumption etc).

use of glosses: typically, an entity mention and surrounding context are treated as a query against a repository of glosses, with cosine similarity or word overlap [24] between the query and the node descriptions used for scoring, and the highest-scoring gloss being used to indicate the matching entity. For example, given a mention of 'Apple' in the context of 'Cupertino', a better match is to be expected against the gloss of *Company:Apple* (Fig. 1), compared with the alternative, *Fruit:Apple*. Having glosses for KB entities can also provide a basis for enriching entities with additional structured knowledge i.e. in asserting or refuting uncertain relations.

One potential way of producing glosses might be to construct sentences out of the facts already stored in the KB: e.g., if the entity node *Michael Jordan* is linked to the category node *Professor* and related to the entity *UC/Berkeley* via the relationship *employedBy*, then it is possible to create a gloss that contains the sentence "Michael Jordan is a professor working at UC/Berkeley". However, many KB entities have few known relationships, resulting in short and uninformative descriptions. Hence, rather than treating the task as a natural-language generation task, we consider an alternative method: we collect large numbers of definitional sentences, and attempt to match these existing sentences to KB entities. While the experiments described in this paper focus on definitions collected from DBPedia, our approach is general, and could be applied to definitions harvested from any dictionary or glossary.

In short, the gloss finding task addressed in this paper corresponds to matching potential glosses with the respective KB nodes. While some matches are obvious, many are ambiguous. While ambiguous matches are a problem in many other alignment tasks (e.g., the EL task described above)[1], this task is unusual in that it is an *asymmetric* resource alignment, where a collection of lexical glosses, which contain no structure information, is aligned against a structural KB, which contains no textual descriptions.

We define and address this task using semi-supervised learning (SSL) techniques. We rely on several simple intuitions. First, it has already been observed [39, 34] that entity ambiguity is often resolved given its semantic category. Hence, rather than solve a named entity linking problem, we solve an entity categorization problem and map glosses to entity categories. Second, we use the unambiguous glosses as labeled data for this entity categorization task. However, such labeled data is limited and noisy. We therefore propose **Gloss Finder (GLOFIN)**, a semi-supervised Expectation Maximization (EM) method that learns effective classifiers given little labeled data and large amount of unlabeled data. GLOFIN uses constrained optimization, taking into account the hierarchy of semantic categories present in the knowledge base. Specifically, GLOFIN incorporates known constraints between the given semantic classes, including subset relationships (e.g., "Mammal" is subset of class "Animal"), and mutual exclusion constraints (e.g., "Mammal" is mutually exclusive with "Automobile").

Contributions of this paper

- We formulate an approach to the important problem of Automatic Gloss Finding for Knowledge Bases (KB), i.e., automatically identifying glosses (short definitional sentences) for entities in a KB. Even though glosses have been found to be very useful in other related areas (e.g., Word Sense Disambiguation), the task of adding glosses to entities in a gloss-free KB is relatively unexplored – we address that gap in this paper.
- We propose GLOFIN for the gloss finding problem. To the best of our knowledge, this is the first such system for this task. GLOFIN is a semi-supervised algorithm which also makes use of available ontological constraints. Through extensive experiments on real-world datasets, we demonstrate GLOFIN's effectiveness. In particular, it is encouraging to find that GLOFIN outperforms even other state-of-the-art semi-supervised baselines, especially in limited supervision settings.
- We demonstrate GLOFIN's robustness to KB quality through experiments on KBs, ranging from hand-curated KBs (e.g., Freebase) to automatically constructed ones (e.g., NELL).
- To facilitate further research on this topic, we have made the gloss finding datasets and GLOFIN code publicly available[2].

[1]Some methods for semantic enrichment of text map ambiguous words to multiple concepts, rather than perform alignment [18]

[2]Dataset and code available to download at `http://rtw.ml.cmu.edu/wk/WebSets/glossFinding_wsdm_2015_online/index.html`

Outline

The rest of the paper is organized as follows. We describe the related work in Section 2. We then present our proposed gloss finding algorithms in Section 3. Datasets and experimental methodology are presented in Section 4. Experimental results are presented in Section 5, followed by the conclusions and future work.

2. RELATED WORK

Glosses are an important resource for word meanings, which have been used by word sense disambiguation (WSD) [35] algorithms for decades. For example, the popular Lesk method [24] and its variants [22, 3] infer a word's sense by measuring the overlap between available context words and the glosses of candidate senses. Traditionally, WordNet [17] has been used as the main resource of word senses and respective glosses. Several recent works have investigated the problem of automatic gloss extraction, so as to improve coverage in specific knowledge domains. Duan and Yates [14] constructed sense descriptions for selected keywords given unlabeled documents in the biomedical domain, and used these descriptions to perform WSD. Others [16, 5] constructed domain-specific glossaries using definitional sentences extracted from the Web, and successfully used these glossaries for domain specific WSD. We share their motivation for obtaining glosses, however rather than generate these glosses, our goal is to associate available glosses with an existing KB.

In this work we match glosses against the respective entity nodes in the KB. This task is closely related to Entity Linking (EL), an entity-focused variant of the WSD problem [31], where named entity mentions in a given text are linked with the respective nodes in a KB. Advanced EL methods consider multiple entity mentions in a document collectively in order to enrich the contextual information that is modeled per entity [19, 42]. Such methods are ineffective for short text fragments, like search queries, or glosses. In fact, we face a 'chicken and egg' problem, as most EL methods assume that KB entities have glosses, whereas we do not [20, 25]. Here, we are instead interested in enriching a KB with glosses, so as to support entity linking and other downstream applications, such as ad-hoc information retrieval [10].

Various works have addressed the problem of resource alignment, but considered different settings. The Yago ontology [39], for example, unifies Wikipedia and WordNet using heuristics that consider the structure of both resources. Ponzetto and Navigli [38] mapped Wikipedia articles onto WordNet synsets, using the textual descriptions of entity pairs. We rather consider an asymmetric setting, where the KB includes a semantic structure but lacks textual descriptions, and the aligned glosses are not assumed to be organized in any fashion. Similarly, a recent work [37] addressed the alignment of an arbitrary pair of lexical resources, including machine-readable dictionaries with no structure. They proposed to induce a network structure for dictionary resources; however textual similarity remains an important component in their approach. Importantly, having enriched a given KB with glosses using our proposed framework will facilitate its alignment and integration with other KBs [9].

In this work, we address the gloss finding problem using a semi-supervised framework. In particular, we consider label propagation (LP), where gloss nodes are associated with candidate entity nodes based on their relatedness in a joint graph. Talukdar [41] discuss the use of weakly supervised label propagation methods in information extraction and integration. Previous work applied LP to perform WSD [46], and the graph modeled words in parallel documents in two languages, where word ambiguity in one language was resolved based on graph relatedness to their candidate translation in the other language, and vice versa. The use of graph-based methods is highly prevalent in WSD. In particular, random walks over a semantic graph, like WordNet, have been shown to yield state-of-the-art results [38, 1]. Notably, linking nodes in the WordNet graph based on lexical gloss overlaps has been shown to contribute significantly to the performance of graph-based WSD [1].

The GOLFIN algorithm that is proposed in this paper is inspired by the EM framework that has been employed by Dalvi et al. [12, 11] for the task of exploratory learning (semisupervised learning in the presence of unanticipated classes) and hierarchical semi-supervised learning. The methods proposed in this paper are different in the sense that we incorporate a class hierarchy into the model. Further, the divide and conquer method proposed by Dalvi et al. [11] was limited to tree structured class hierarchy, whereas we propose a mixed integer programming based optimization method that can deal with any class hierarchy defined by sets of subset and mutual exclusion constraints. Interestingly, another recent work has used mixed integer linear programming techniques to encode ontological constraints [34]–they assign multiple plausible KB categories to 'emerging' entities, which are not yet represented in the KB, and consider mutual exclusion constraints as a post-processing step, so as to output a consistent set of category assignments. In contrast, we apply subset as well as mutual exclusion constraints, within an iterative EM algorithm, using semi-supervised learning. Finally, while the application of earlier variants of the EM-based framework focused on the named entity categorization task, we use the proposed methods for addressing the novel task of generating glosses for an existing KB.

3. AUTOMATIC GLOSS FINDING

In this section, we first go through the background information, and then describe approaches to the Gloss Finding problem, including GLOFIN, our proposed method. Before getting into the details of methods, in Section 3.2, we first describe an entity-gloss candidate generation stage whose output is used by all the methods considered in the paper. After that, in Section 3.3 we propose our first attempt at the gloss finding problem, using Label Propagation (LP). However, through experiments on real datasets as we will see in Section 5, we find that such LP-based methods are not always effective on the gloss finding problem. To overcome this limitation, in Section 3.4 we present our proposed method GLOFIN.

3.1 Preliminaries

Here we briefly present the relevant terminologies and the problem statement for the gloss finding task.

3.1.1 Knowledge Base (KB)

In this paper, we consider a KB as a directed graph consisting of the following three types of nodes and relations among them. Part of a KB is shown in the top half of Figure 1.

- **Category nodes**: Each category node corresponds to a semantic type. For example, in Figure 1, *University* and *Vegetable* are examples of category nodes. Category nodes are inter-linked through the *subCategoryOf* relation, resulting in the overall ontology (category hierarchy). Additionally, two categories may be connected through a *mutuallyExclusive* relationship (shown using red dotted lines). For example, in Figure 1, *Fruit-subCategoryOf-Food* and *Food-mutuallyExclusive-Organization*.
- **Entity nodes**: Entities are instances of categories. An entity node is connected to its most specific category node though an *isA* edge. In Figure 1, *Banana-isA-Fruit*.

- **Lexical string nodes**: Lexical string nodes correspond to text fragments (usually noun phrases) used to express entities in free text. For example, the lexical strings *Apple* or *Apple Inc.* may be used to refer to the entity *Company:Apple*. Please note an *ambiguous* lexical string may be connected to multiple entities: *Apple* in Figure 1 is connected to both *Company:Apple* and *Fruit:Apple*.

Note that even though a KB may contain additional types of relations among its nodes (e.g., *Microsoft-competesWith-Google*), we omit them here as they are not relevant for the rest of the paper.

3.1.2 Glosses

Glosses are natural language definitions of entities in the KB. For example, *"Platinum is a chemical element with the chemical symbol Pt and an atomic number of 78"* is a valid gloss for *Platinum*, whereas *"Platinum deposits are present in the state of Tamil Nadu, India."* is not a gloss. In this paper, we consider DBPedia abstracts as a repository of glosses. However, our methods are generic, and applicable to any set of definitional sentences as candidate glosses.

3.1.3 The Gloss Finding Problem

Given a KB (e.g., NELL or Freebase) and a repository of candidate glosses (e.g., DBPedia abstracts), the Gloss Finding Problem requires to identify for each entity in the KB the correct gloss(es) from the candidate gloss pool. For example in Figure 1, we would like to infer that for entity *Fruit:Apple*, *"Apple is a fruit from apple tree ..."* is the only correct gloss. Sometimes it is possible that for certain entities in the KB, there exists no correct gloss in the given candidate gloss pool (e.g., *Strawberry* in Figure 1).

3.2 Candidate Entity-Gloss Generation

In this step, for each gloss in the candidate pool of glosses given as input, we first identify the noun phrase that is being defined by the gloss. We refer to this noun phrase as *head-NP* in this paper. For DBPedia abstracts this step is trivial in the sense that DBPedia dataset gives us the head-NP for each short abstract. However, we can easily apply existing syntactic taggers, e.g., the Stanford tagger [26], and detect the *head-NP* in the definitional sentence(s). After this, the head NP of each gloss is lexically matched against the entities in the KB. Even though simple string matching is used for the experiments in this paper, more sophisticated string matchers may also be used.

At the end of this stage, we end up with a set of candidate entity-gloss matchings. Note that this relationship may be many-many and thereby ambiguous as one entity may be connected to multiple glosses, and a single gloss may be assigned multiple entities. Such ambiguity are resolved using the techniques described below.

3.3 First approach: Label Propagation

In order to remove uncertainties from the candidate matchings generated in Section 3.2, we first use Modified Adsorption (MAD) [40], a representative graph-based semi-supervised learning (SSL) algorithm. This choice was prompted by the fact that such Label Propagation (LP) techniques have achieved considerable success in various weakly-supervised NLP tasks, and that they could potentially exploit the graph structure of the current problem.

In order to apply MAD to this Gloss Finding problem, we first create an augmented version of the graph in Figure 1 by connecting each gloss to the content words which passed a TF-IDF based filtering. Mutual exclusion constraints were not used in this augmented graph as MAD is not capable of handling such relations. We then inject each entity node with its own node-specific label. This self-labeling approach was also used in [44], although for an entirely different problem. Starting with this augmented graph and self-injected seed labels, the MAD algorithm is used to classify the rest of the nodes in the graph. At the end of the algorithm, MAD assigns each candidate gloss a set of labels, where each label corresponds to an entity since the labels were entity-specific self-injections.

This distribution of entities on a candidate gloss node is intersected with the candidate entities generated in Section 3.2, and the resulting entities are sorted based on the assignment score generated by MAD. The top entity in this ranked list is then chosen as the inferred entity match for the candidate gloss. In experiments below, LP-based approach is only effective in some settings. To address this shortcoming, we propose a new method, GLOFIN.

Algorithm 1 GLOFIN

Input: X_l labeled glosses; Y_l category labels of X_l; X_u unlabeled glosses; O class constraints (subclass-superclass or mutual-exclusion kind). $N = |X|$ and K is the number of classes.
Output: Y_u labels for X_u
Initialize parameters θ_j^0 for each C_j using seeds provided for C_j.
for t = 1 ... till convergence **do**
  for i=1 to $|X|$ **do**
    {E step: Assign a bit vector of categories to each gloss}
    Find $P(C_j|x_i;\theta_j^{t-1})$ for all classes C_j
    Y_i^t = find consistent assignment by solving MIP($P(C_j|x_i)$, O).
  end for
  {M step: Recompute model parameters.}
  Recompute θ_j^t based on current class assignments Y^t.
end for
return

3.4 Proposed Approach: Gloss Finder (GLOFIN)

We propose Gloss Finder (GLOFIN), a hierarchical semi-supervised Expectation Maximization (EM) algorithm for the Gloss Finding problem. GLOFIN uses automatically acquired labeled data (the unambiguous candidate glosses) and large amount of unlabeled data (the rest of the candidate glosses) in an iterative EM framework to learn a model for this task. The GLOFIN algorithm is presented in Algorithm 1. Before presenting the details of the algorithm, let us define the following notations.

Let $X = \{x_1, \ldots x_N\}$ be the candidate glosses, and $\{C_1, \ldots C_K\}$ be the KB categories. Let $y_{ji} \in \{0, 1\}$ be an indicator variable specifying whether candidate gloss x_i belongs to category C_j. Using the model parameters θ_j for class C_j, we can estimate $P(C_j|x_i)$, the probability of gloss x_i belonging to category C_j. GLOFIN aims to find optimal values of label assignments y_{ji} and cluster models θ_j, so as to maximize the overall data likelihood. Let *Subset* be the set of all subset or inclusion constraints, and *Mutex* be the set of all mutual exclusion constraints. In other words, *Subset* = $\{\langle i, k\rangle : C_i \subseteq C_k\}$ and *Mutex* = $\{(i, k) : C_i \cap C_k = \phi\}$.

GLOFIN takes in as input the set of glosses X, out of which X_l is the labeled subset with category labels in Y_l, and the remaining X_u is unlabeled. Additionally, it takes as input a set of ontological constraints, O. In the E step of this algorithm, each candidate gloss X_i is assigned a bit vector of labels $Y_i = [y_{1i}, \ldots y_{Ki}]$. The class hierarchy is incorporated as constraints on bits in this bit vector. For example, if for a gloss with head NP *Cat*, a bit corresponding to KB category *Mammal* is set then the bit corresponding to category *Animal* should also be set due to the subset constraint: *Mammal* $\subseteq$ *Animal*, and for the same gloss the bit corresponding to category *Reptile* should not be set due to the mutual exclusion constraint: Mammal $\cap$ Reptile = ϕ. The M step recomputes the model parameters for each KB category using the label assignments done in the E step.

The E step of GLOFIN (Algorithm 1) may be broken down into two stages, which we describe in greater detail below.

Assigning Entities to Candidate Glosses (Algorithm 1: Line 6)

This step computes probabilities $P(C_j|x_i;\theta_j)$, where θ_j is the current estimate of model parameters for category C_j. A variety of techniques may be used for this estimation, and we briefly describe one such choice here: the semi-supervised version of multinomial Naive Bayes [36]. In this model $P(C_j|x_i) \propto P(x_i|C_j) * P(C_j)$, for each unlabeled gloss x_i. The probability $P(x_i|C_j)$ is estimated by treating each feature in x_i as an independent draw from a class-specific multinomial. In this task, the features are word occurrences in the candidate glosses, and the number of outcomes of the multinomial is the vocabulary size. We shall refer to this version of GLOFIN as **GLOFIN-NB**. Additional variants using other learning algorithms, along with features used by our methods are discussed in Section 4.

Entity Assignment Refinement using Ontological Constraints (Algorithm 1: Line 7)

Given the category memberships probabilities $\{P(C_j|x_i)\}$ estimated above, this step computes the category membership variables $\{y_{ji}, \forall\ 1 \le i \le N,\ 1 \le j \le K\}$. GLOFIN solves a Mixed-Integer Program (MIP) to estimate these variables. One such problem is solved for each gloss. This MIP takes the scores $\{P(C_j|x_i)\}$, and class constraints O as input and produces a bit vector of labels as output, each bit representing whether the gloss belongs to that particular category.

The MIP formulation for gloss x_i is presented in Equation 1. For each gloss, this method tries to maximize the sum of scores of selected labels, after penalizing for violation of class constraints. Let ζ_{jk} are slack variables for *Subset* constraints, and δ_{jk} are slack variables for *Mutex* constraints.

$$\underset{\{y_{ji}\},\zeta_{jk},\delta_{jk}}{\text{maximize}} \left(\sum_{\mathrm{j}} \mathrm{y_{ji}} * \mathrm{P(C_j|x_i)} - \sum_{\langle \mathrm{i,k}\rangle \in \mathrm{Subset}} \zeta_{\mathrm{ik}} - \sum_{\langle \mathrm{i,k}\rangle \in \mathrm{Mutex}} \delta_{\mathrm{ik}} \right)$$

$$\text{subject to,} \quad \begin{aligned} & y_{ji} \ge y_{ki} - \zeta_{jk}, \quad \forall \langle j,k\rangle \in \textit{Subset} \\ & y_{ji} + y_{ki} \le 1 + \delta_{jk}, \quad \forall \langle j,k\rangle \in \textit{Mutex} \\ & \zeta_{jk}, \delta_{jk} \ge 0,\ y_i \in \{0,1\}, \quad \forall j,k \end{aligned} \tag{1}$$

3.5 Scaling GLOFIN

The MIP formulation presented in Equation 1 adds a constraint for each subset or mutual exclusion constraints in the KB ontology. Further, in the E step of every iteration, we solve a MIP for each gloss. We make the method more scalable and efficient in following ways:

- We discard redundant mutex constraints - i.e., the ones that can be inferred using remaining subset and mutex constraints.
- We reduce the number of classes considered per gloss, by keeping only top-Q classes relevant to the gloss, as detailed below.
- Since the MIP for each gloss is independent from other MIPs, we parallelize the E step of every iteration, and consolidate results in the M-step.

Reducing the MIP size per gloss: We keep only a small number of categories in the optimization problem that is being solved for each gloss. We tried following ways of limiting candidate classes:

- Diameter of the class graph: The class graph is an undirected graph of ontology classes, where nodes are classes and edges represent either subset or mutual exclusion constraints. In this approximation, we rank all classes by the scores $P(C_j|x_i)$ for a datapoint x_i, and choose the top Q classes, where Q is the diameter of the category graph. Since the class assignments are hierarchical, we also include all ancestors of these top-Q classes in the optimization.
- Square-root of number of classes: Here, we select $Q = \sqrt{K}$, where K is the total number of classes in the ontology. Similar to diameter based method, we include all ancestors of these top-Q classes in the optimization.
- Thresholding: If the score $P(C_j|x_i)$ is greater than a predefined threshold then we consider the category. Note that the threshold is set for the entire dataset, but for each datapoint might result in different number of categories.

4. DATASETS AND EXPERIMENTAL METHODOLOGY

In our experiments, we enrich two existing knowledge bases with available glosses, namely NELL and Freebase. NELL is a machine generated knowledge base that does not have existing glosses, whereas most Freebase entities have glosses we can compare against. Our resource of glosses is DBPedia, a database of factual descriptions extracted from Wikipedia. DBPedia contains a large set of Wikipedia titles and short abstracts. We do not use any structure information from DBPedia to make sure that our methods are generic, and applicable to any set of definitional sentences as candidate glosses. E.g., we can replace DBPedia abstracts with definitions from online glossaries like Wiktionary or WordNet without any need to change the GLOFIN method.

A DBPedia short abstract is essentially the first paragraph (up to 500 characters) on the Wikipedia page of that entity. Some sample entity titles and their corresponding DBPedia abstracts are given in Table 1. We consider two experimental datasets that were labeled for evaluation purposes. We have made both these gloss finding datasets available[3] for research community to help the future research in this field.

Entity Title	Definition (DBPedia short abstract)
Platinum	Platinum is a chemical element with the chemical symbol Pt and an atomic number of 78. ...
Britwell	Britwell is a residential housing estate and civil parish in the north west of Slough Berkshire in the south of England. ...

Table 1: Sample candidate glosses

4.1 Freebase dataset

Freebase is a huge tuple database used to structure general human knowledge. The data in Freebase is collaboratively created, structured, and maintained. Public read/write access to Freebase is allowed through an HTTP-based graph-query API using the Metaweb Query Language (MQL) as a data query and manipulation language. Currently Freebase consists of over 44M topics and 2613M facts about entities, their relationships and attributes. We use the Freebase entity snapshot provided by ERD'14 challenge [8] as a gold standard mapping of Freebase to DBPedia abstracts. Thus

[3]The dataset can be downloaded from `http://rtw.ml.cmu.edu/wk/WebSets/glossFinding_wsdm_2015_online/index.html`

we get a good quality training and test data for our semisupervised methods on the task of finding glosses for Freebase.

Table 2 includes detailed statistics of the Freebase dataset. Overall, Freebase entities in this dataset belong to 46 Freebase classes. Having considered their parent types, the dataset includes a set of 66 classes. There are 5.5M Freebase entities in total that belong to these 66 classes. In order to obtain the underlying subset and mutual exclusion constraints, we built a co-occurrence matrix of entities belonging to each pair of classes. Based on this matrix, we inferred 46 subset and 1,455 mutual exclusion constraints.

Statistic	Dataset	
	Freebase	NELL
#Classes	66	275
#Subset class constraints	46	313
#Mutex class constraints	1455	18.1K
Diameter of class graph	4	10
$\sqrt{\#classes}$	9	17
#DBPedia abstracts	284.5K	246.7K
#Words	496.8K	472.4K
#(abstract, word) edges	5.7M	7.1M
#Unambiguous DBPedia abstracts	257.3K	195.8K
#Ambiguous DBPedia abstracts	32.8K	50.0K
#Ambiguous abstracts with ground-truth KB mappings	12.4K	383

Table 2: Statistics about the datasets. (Sections 4.1, and 4.2)

4.2 NELL dataset

The NELL knowledge base is created by a machine learning system named Never Ending Language Learning [30]. NELL is composed of various information extraction components [7, 43, 23] that independently extract facts from text and semi-structured information on the Web. Our version of the NELL KB consists of 275 categories and 1.67M instances belonging to these categories. Though the facts in NELL are extracted by a computer system, it takes as input a human created ontology containing categories, plus subset and mutual exclusion constraints between them.

We constructed a dataset using the NELL KB and DBPedia abstracts. Statistics about the NELL dataset are included in Table 2. Unlike Freebase, NELL entities do not have glosses associated with them, so we do not have ground truth gloss data for NELL. Further, since this KB is automatically generated by a computer system it contains many noisy facts, hence the training data used by our methods is noisy.

Next we present results of two manual evaluation experiments for the NELL dataset. We do our first evaluation to understand the quality of automatically acquired seeds and predicted entity labels for ambiguous DBPedia abstracts. This will later help us to make claims about robustness of our proposed methods towards noisy training data. Further, we do not have a gold standard set of mappings from DBPedia abstracts to NELL entities, which are needed to evaluate our systems. Hence, we manually constructed a gold standard set of mappings by labeling 383 ambiguous DBPedia abstracts to the correct NELL entities. Also note that these gold standard mappings are used only as a test set, and our methods use only automatically generated training data for learning.

Quality of automatically acquired seeds

Our methods use unambiguous mappings of DBPedia abstract onto NELL entity as labeled data. Since these mappings are determined automatically for the NELL dataset, we performed manual evaluation in order to assess the quality of the unambiguous alignments, inspecting 100 randomly sampled unambiguous DBPedia-NELL matches. For each abstract in this sample, we evaluate whether the assigned class is *precise*, *correct*, and whether a higher level category is correct. We illustrate these measures using examples. If a DBPedia abstract about "Shively Field (public airport)" was mapped to the category "airport", then the mapping is considered to be precise, correct, and the higher level category is correct as well. Mapping between another DBPedia abstract about "Christopher McFarland (baseball player)" to the category "person-north-america", is judged as correct, but not precise, as there exists more concrete "athlete" category in NELL. Finally, a mapping between "Jonathan Andersson (hockey player)" and "director" is incorrect and not precise. The higher level category in this case is correct however, since "director" is a descendant of "person", which is correct.

Statistic	Value
#unambiguous abstracts evaluated	100
#abstracts s.t. assigned category was correct	81
#abstracts s.t. assigned category was most precise	72
#abstracts s.t. assigned higher level category was correct	94

Table 3: Evaluating quality of unambiguous mappings of DBPedia abstracts to NELL entities/categories. (Section 4.2)

Table 3 shows the results of this evaluation. We found that out of 100 unambiguous mappings between abstracts and NELL categories, 72% were precise and 81% were correct. The higher level category was correct in 94% of the considered examples. While these alignments are imperfect, the experimental results described below will show that our techniques make effective use of this automatically labeled data.

Manually creating gold-standard mappings from DBPedia abstracts to NELL entities

As we have already stated, NELL does not have glosses for its entities and unlike Freebase there is no gold-standard mapping available from DBPedia abstracts to NELL entities. Hence we randomly sampled 383 DBPedia abstracts for which multiple candidate NELL entities and categories were found. For each abstract, we manually checked whether one of the candidate NELL entities and categories was a correct match. We also checked whether the most precise entity is present in the NELL KB. For some DBPedia abstracts, the most precise (entity, category) combination was not present in NELL, but the most precise category was present. The statistics of our evaluation are listed in Table 4.

Statistic	Value
#abstracts evaluated	383
%abstracts $\exists$ at least 1 NELL entity, category match	79%
%abstracts $\exists$ most precise entity candidate in KB	68%
%abstracts $\exists$ most precise category candidate in KB	98%

Table 4: NELL Dataset: Manual evaluation of ambiguous glosses. Please refer Section 4.2 for more details.

From Table 4 we can say that 79% DBPedia abstracts have at least one correct entity match in the candidate entity set. E.g., a DBPedia abstract about "Michael Jordan" as Basketball player, can be matched to the NELL entity "Michael Jordan:Person", however most precise entity will be "Michael Jordan:Athlete". We consider "Michael Jordan:Person" as a correct candidate entity, however "Michael Jordan:Athlete' is the most precise entity, and "Athlete" is the most precise category.

4.3 Methods

We experimented with the following eight methods for the gloss finding task. First two methods are existing baseline methods.

- **SVM:** This is a traditional supervised linear SVM algorithm applied for the task of classifying head-NPs from candidate glosses into KB categories. We learnt a separate binary classifier for each KB category. For this purpose, we used the publicly available LibLinear package [15] with varying values of parameter 'C' that controls penalty on slack variables. A similar method was used by Martinez et al. [27] which trains a decision list classifier on monosemous (unambiguous) words for the word sense disambiguation task; we choose a more widely used supervised learning method, SVM.
- **Label propagation:** This is a representative graph-based semi-supervised learning (SSL) algorithm, called Modified Adsorption (MAD) [40], as described in Section 3.3.

The next three methods are variants of our proposed GLOFIN algorithm (Section 3.4) using different document representations.

- **GLOFIN-NB:** As already described in Section 3.4, this is a semi-supervised version of multinomial Naive Bayes [36].
- **GLOFIN-KM:** Here we use the seeded spherical K-Means algorithm proposed by Basu and Mooney [4] as another variant of semi-supervised EM.
- **GLOFIN-VMF:** Banerjee et al. [2] proposed a generative mixture model approach to clustering datapoints based on von Mises-Fisher distribution, defined for data distributed on the unit hypersphere (L_2 norm equals 1). We use a seeded version of this algorithm, similar to Dalvi et al. [12] who used it for the task of exploratory learning.

To evaluate the benefits of incorporating hierarchy, we also consider flat versions of semisupervised Naive Bayes, seeded spherical K-Means and seeded von-Mises Fisher. For each flat method, the E step (Algorithm 1: Line 6) computes $P(C_j|x_i)$ for all leaf classes C_j in the ontology and picks the one with maximum probability, skipping the mixed integer programming step (Algorithm 1: Line 7). M step does not change. These methods are referred to as GLOFIN-flat-NB, GLOFIN-flat-KM and GLOFIN-flat-VMF.

4.4 Features

Each gloss can be represented by the term frequency (TF) of words that occurred in it. We can also collect inverse document frequency (IDF) of each word in the vocabulary from the entire gloss corpus. This gives us a choice of using either TF (mere term frequencies) or TFIDF (multiplication of TF and IDF values) feature representations. We use the TFIDF values to threshold the words used for each gloss. For all the experiments presented here, we keep only those words per gloss that exceed a TFIDF threshold of 1E-3, thereby discarding stop-words.

For each method, we performed experiments with both TF and TFIDF based feature representations (considering only those words that pass TFIDF threshold). In our experiments we found that SVM and Label-propagation methods give better performance for TFIDF based feature representation, whereas all semisupervised EM methods (GLOFIN variants) work best with a TF based feature representation. Henceforth, we present all results using these feature representations.

Since feature engineering is not the focus of this paper, we use a standard bag of words features for all our experiments. Any additional features can be incorporated easily in our algorithm and are complementary to the techniques introduced in this paper.

5. EXPERIMENTAL RESULTS

5.1 Gloss Finding Results

In this section we present experimental results on the gloss finding task. For the first set of results we use all unambiguous glosses (glosses with only one candidate entity mapping to the KB) as training data. The next set of experiments make use of only 10% of unambiguous matches as training data, to test the robustness of the methods for more ambiguous data. We compare all eight methods that we presented in Section 3: SVM, label propagation, the hierarchical and flat variants of GLOFIN.

For the SVM method, we tried different values of 'C' for the LibLinear package. We observed the change in performance varying the values of 'C' in the range [1E-24, 100] for both datasets (plots omitted due to space constraints). We found that best performance is achieved for 'C' in the range [1E-6, 0.01]. Results presented here are with C = 1E-6 (results for C = 0.01 are very similar).

From the experiments presented here, we try to answer the following research questions:

- How does our proposed GLOFIN-NB method compare with SVM and label propagation on the task of assigning glosses for NELL and Freebase datasets?
- How do the Naive Bayes, K-Means and von Mises-Fisher variants of GLOFIN compare?
- Does the use of ontological constraints always improve results for GLOFIN?
- What is the effect of the different strategies of limiting the set of considered classes per gloss on scalability (and performance) of GLOFIN?

5.1.1 *Comparing GLOFIN-NB against SVM and label propagation*

Method	Performance on Ambiguous Glosses					
	NELL			Freebase		
	P	R	F1	P	R	F1
SVM	59.3	21.3	31.3	87.8	13.0	22.7
Label Propagation	42.8	54.0	47.8	89.8	**89.1**	**89.4**
GLOFIN-NB	**70.4**	**65.4**	**67.8**	**94.6**	74.2	83.2

Table 5: Comparison of gloss finding methods using all unambiguous glosses as training data and ambiguous glosses as test data. Best values in each column are bold-faced. GLOFIN-NB method is robust to noisy training data for the NELL dataset. Please refer Section 5.1.1 for more details.

Here we compare our proposed GLOFIN-NB method against supervised SVM and semi-supervised label propagation methods. We compare them in two settings: first using all unambiguous glosses as training data and second, by simulating a harder problem i.e. using only 10% of the unambiguous glosses for training.

Using all unambiguous glosses for training: Table 5 shows the summary of results while using all unambiguous glosses as training data and ambiguous glosses for evaluation.

We can see that, supervised SVM classification performs worst on both datasets. Label propagation gives the best F1 score for Freebase, however it performs poorly on the NELL dataset, whereas GLOFIN-NB works well on both NELL and Freebase datasets. On the Freebase dataset, GLOFIN-NB has higher precision, lower recall, and hence slightly lower, but comparable F1 than the label propagation method.

Method	NELL Dataset						Freebase Dataset					
	Ambiguous glosses			All glosses			Ambiguous glosses			All glosses		
	Precision	Recall	F1	Precision	Recall	F1	Precision	Recall	F1	Precision	Recall	F1
SVM	64.2	17.3	27.3	99.9	27.9	43.7	87.8	11.3	20.1	97.9	71.1	82.5
Label Propagation	55.0	12.3	20.1	99.7	5.2	9.8	84.6	27.5	41.5	99.7	88.1	**93.6**
GLOFIN-NB	71.7	62.0	**66.5**	99.9	62.0	**76.5**	95.1	72.0	**82.0**	97.6	79.6	87.6

Table 6: Comparison of gloss finding methods with 10% of the unambiguous abstracts used as training data. GLOFIN-NB always gives best or near-best F1 scores. Please refer Section 5.1.1 for more details.

Both label propagation and GLOFIN-NB perform better on the Freebase dataset than the NELL dataset. This can be explained by the the difference in quality of the automatically acquired seeds for the two datasets. Note that the unambiguous glosses used for the Freebase dataset are very accurate, whereas for the NELL dataset our evaluation in Table 3 shows that only 81% of the seed gloss mappings were accurate. Hence the results in Table 5 indicate that our proposed GLOFIN-NB method is relatively robust to noise compared to the label propagation method.

We also investigated why the supervised SVM method performs poorly even though 80% of the total data is used as training. We found that there is a huge skew in the class frequencies. For the Freebase dataset with 45 leaf classes, the average number of training instances per class are 2.27K with a standard deviation of 10.8K; e.g., "/location/location" category has 72.6K training examples, whereas "/education/university" category has just 10 training examples. We hypothesize that the small amount of training data for many KB categories is the reason why the SVM method performs poorly.

Note that in Table 5, the number of unambiguous glosses used as training data covered a large part of the overall dataset (80% for NELL and 90% for Freebase). However, in real life scenarios, the amount of training data can be much smaller. The Freebase dataset is artificially created using ERD'14 data and a subset of Freebase KB categories. NELL populates its KB by bootstrapping against many different categories simultaneously, beginning with a small set of hand-chosen seeds. It may be the case that this learning process tends to favor entity names that can be confidently assigned to a single category (i.e., that are not highly ambiguous); to support this conjecture, we note that an alternative instance of NELL which used a larger set of automatically generated low-quality seeds required modifications to suppress the use of ambiguous entities in bootstrapping [32]. This suggests that other real-world KBs may have a lower proportion of unambiguous entities. Next, we conduct experiments which simulates this setting, by using only 10% of the available unambiguous matches as seeds.

Using 10% unambiguous glosses for training: Table 6 shows detailed results of GLOFIN-NB compared to SVM and label propagation methods when only 10% of the unambiguous glosses are used as training data. Since we are using only a fraction of unambiguous glosses as training data, the rest of them can be used as test data. Additionally, all gold-standard mappings of ambiguous glosses are always part of test data. We generate 10 random train/test partitions and average results on these 10 runs. Performance on ambiguous glosses is particularly interesting hence is listed separately. Note that "All glosses" include ambiguous as well as unambiguous glosses.

We can see that with less training data the performance of all methods degrades, to varying degrees. Also, all methods give higher performance on "all glosses" compared to the harder task of matching ambiguous glosses. In terms of F1 scores on ambiguous glosses, SVM results in the worst performance and GLOFIN-NB method gives the best performance. In terms of F1 score on "all glosses", Comparing GLOFIN-NB vs. label propagation we can see that GLOFIN-NB performs better in all cases, except Freebase dataset "all glosses" case where GLOFIN-NB has comparable precision and lower recall, and hence lower F1 score compared to label propagation.

To summarize, GLOFIN performs best on the harder task of matching ambiguous glosses when the amount of training data is small.

Discussion: Comparing the results across Tables 5 and 6, we can hypothesize that, with large fraction (90% for Freebase dataset) of the glosses being unambiguous in our artificially created dataset, it is very easy to get high values for F1 score using label propagation (Table 5), because the rest of the 10% nodes might get high quality labels from its nearest neighbors. However when the amount of training data is smaller, generative models like GLOFIN-NB work better (Table 6) as they generalize better.

One more advantage of GLOFIN lies in its generative nature. Label propagation is a transductive approach, whereas GLOFIN is a generative approach, I.e., EM models learnt by GLOFIN on a set of datapoints can be applied to an unseen datapoint having similar vocabulary. In other words, they can predict labels for an unseen datapoint. However label propagation just predicts labels for the datapoints in the set being used while learning.

Method	Performance on Ambiguous Glosses					
	NELL			Freebase		
	P	R	F1	P	R	F1
GLOFIN-flat-KM	74.8	36.5	49.1	97.6	61.0	75.1
GLOFIN-KM	65.2	49.8+	56.5+	96.1	71.8+	82.2+
GLOFIN-flat-VMF	73.6	44.5	55.5	96.3	56.0	70.8
GLOFIN-VMF	77.2+	59.5+	67.2+	95.7	59.3+	73.2+
GLOFIN-flat-NB	70.3	59.1	64.3	95.9	71.1	81.7
GLOFIN-NB	70.4+	65.4+	**67.8+**	94.6	74.2+	**83.2+**

Table 7: Comparison of GLOFIN variants using all unambiguous glosses as training data and ambiguous glosses as test data. Best values of F1 for each dataset is bold-faced. '+' in front of a hierarchical method score indicates that the score improved over its flat version. (a) All hierarchical methods perform better than their flat counterparts. (Section 5.1.2) (b) GLOFIN-NB method performs the best (Section 5.1.3)

5.1.2 *Effect of using ontological constraints*

From Table 7, we can also see that all hierarchical semisupervised EM methods are better than their flat counterparts. Hence we conclude that using ontological constraints improves the gloss finding performance. Note that relative improvements of the hierarchical methods are higher for the NELL dataset (upto 21% relative improvement in F1 scores). The reason traces back to evaluation of NELL seeds in Section 4.2, Table 3. We saw that 81% leaf category seed labels were correct, whereas 94% of higher level category labels were correct. Thus learning separate model parameters for higher level categories in the ontology and using ontological constraints to resolve ambiguity employed by hierarchical GLOFIN proves beneficial. Since Freebase seed labels are more accurate, and hierarchy contains just 2 levels, hierarchical models do not have the much added advantage over flat models as for the NELL dataset, resulting in only 9% relative improvement in F1 scores.

5.1.3 Comparing variants of GLOFIN

Table 7 shows detailed results of our proposed methods (GLOFIN-NB, GLOFIN-KM and GLOFIN-VMF) w.r.t their flat counterparts (GLOFIN-flat-NB, GLOFIN-flat-KM and GLOFIN-flat-VMF). GLOFIN-NB method works the best on both NELL and Freebase datasets.

GLOFIN-NB outperforms GLOFIN-KM in the experiments. Importantly, GLOFIN-NB models class priors (as discussed in Section 5.1.1)). As mentioned before, the class frequencies in our datasets are very skewed; hence modeling class priors is highly useful. In contrast, GLOFIN-KM merely computes cosine similarity of a datapoint with respect to a cluster centroid, hence its inferior performance. The GLOFIN-VMF method provides the second-best performance to GLOFIN-NB on the ambiguous gloss. Although GLOFIN-VMF is cluster-based, it also models class priors.

5.1.4 Comparing different ways of scaling GLOFIN

We tried various approximations to reduce runtime of GLOFIN(Please refer to Section 3.5 for details). The summary is presented in Table 8. We found that setting Q, the number of classes considered in a MIP (Equation 1), as the diameter of the class graph gives huge time savings and does not harm the performance in terms of F1 score on ambiguous entities. Hence we use this approximation for all runs of GLOFIN in this paper. In addition to this, we also use 12 parallel threads in the E step to compute label assignments of all datapoints in parallel.

Note that for NELL dataset these approximations are crucial. Otherwise, run time on a PC machine (with 30GB memory) exceeds 64 hours. Due to large processing requirements, we do not have F1 scores for this case. Besides, results in Table 6 are averaged over 10 random train/test partitions for both NELL and Freebase. However, due to large processing times for some variants, results in Table 8 are averaged over 3 and 9 train/test partitions for the NELL and Freebase respectively.

Approximations	Performance on Ambiguous Glosses			
	NELL		Freebase	
	F1	Time	F1	Time
keep all classes	-	>230.4K	80.4	15.2K
Q = diameter	68.1	5.2K	81.8	5.7K
$Q = \sqrt{K}$	65.5	14.5K	83.1	3.6K
score threshold= 1E-5	64.5	22.9K	71.4	9.3K

Table 8: Comparison of different approximations to scale our GLOFIN-NB method using 10% of the unambiguous glosses as training and ambiguous glosses as test data. Time measurements are in seconds. Refer to Section 5.1.4 for more details.

5.2 Evaluating NELL to Freebase mappings via common glosses

Aligning two KBs to the same set of glosses gives information about how the categories in those two KBs should be aligned. To evaluate the value of this information, we took the output of GLOFIN-NB and randomly sampled 100 glosses that were assigned to entities from both NELL and FreeBase. Then we did a manual evaluation whether the entities from NELL and Freebase correspond to each other, and whether the categories they belong to in the respective KBs are semantically similar.

Eval Type	Statistic	Value
#Abstracts	Evaluated	100
	Assigned entities are correct, corresponding categories are semantically related	93
	Assigned NELL category is precise	92
	Assigned Freebase category is precise	38
#Category pairs	Found in 100 abstracts evaluated	39
	NELL category = Freebase category	6
	NELL category $\subset$ Freebase category	23
	Freebase category $\subset$ NELL category	1

Table 9: Evaluating quality of NELL to Freebase mappings via common DBPedia abstracts. (Please refer to Section 5.2.)

From Table 9, we can see that out of 110 abstracts that were evaluated, 93 of them had correct NELL and Freebase entities assigned to them, and their corresponding categories were semantically related. For 92 of those abstracts, the NELL category was precise and correct, while for 38 of them the Freebase category was precise. This is due to the fact that the Freebase categories we use to build our dataset are more general categories like "/organization/organization", "/location/location", and more precise categories like "/location/city" and "/organization/biotech-company" are missing. NELL has all these categories at finer granularity, hence it can classify DBPedia abstracts into more fine-grained categories. For instance, a DBPedia abstract about "Biotronik" is classified into "biotechcompany" category from NELL, and "/organization /organization" category from Freebase. We evaluated whether the entities from the two KBs are correct, and whether the corresponding categories are semantically related.

We also evaluated whether we can come up with a relationship between the categories corresponding to NELL and Freebase mappings. From 100 abstracts, we found 39 category pairs, which we manually evaluated. We found 6 category pairs that can be considered as equivalent. E.g., We marked the category "geopoliticallocation" from NELL to be equivalent to category "/location/location" from Freebase. In 23 category pairs, we found that the NELL category was strict subset of Freebase category. E.g., the "actor" category from NELL is strict subset of "/person/person" category from Freebase. Only one category in Freebase "/broadcast/broadcast" was found to be strict subset of a NELL category "company". For 9 category pairs we could not define a equality or subset relation between them. They include either semantically unrelated class pairs like "visualartist" and "/location/location" corresponding to incorrect entity matches, and semantically related categories like "drug" and "/business/brand". There are many drugs like Donnatal, Excedrin that are classified as "drugs" in NELL and as "/business/brand" in Freebase. Though these categories are related to each other we can not easily classify them into equivalence or subset relations. We have also provided some sample outputs of our methods at the following URL `http://rtw.ml.cmu.edu/wk/WebSets/glossFinding_wsdm_2015_online/index.html`.

Acknowledgments:

This work is supported in part by the Google PhD fellowship in Information Extraction, a Google research grant and BSF grant No. 2010090. The views and conclusions contained herein are those of the authors and should not be interpreted as necessarily representing the official policies or endorsements, either expressed or implied, of Google, or BSF.

6. CONCLUSION

In this paper, we proposed GLOFIN, a method for the important but relatively unexplored problem of Automatic Gloss Identification, i.e., automatically generating glosses (short definitional sentences) for an initially gloss-free knowledge base (KB) by matching candidate glosses to entities in the KB. To the best of our knowledge, this is the first such system for this task. GLOFIN employs hierarchical clustering algorithm that internally uses unambiguous DBPedia abstracts as seeds and the KB ontology as constraints to match an ambiguous candidate gloss to the right entity from KB. GLOFIN uses mixed integer programming formulation to assign the most likely set of labels for each gloss, while following the class constraints posed by the KB ontology.

We present experiments using NELL and Freebase as KBs and DBPedia abstracts as candidate glosses. Our quantitative and qualitative evaluations show that GLOFIN is effective and that it outperforms other state-of-the-art algorithms like label propagation and Support Vector Machines (SVM). We also demonstrate GLOFIN's robustness to noise through experiments on a wide variety of KBs, ranging from user contributed (e.g., Freebase) to automatically constructed (e.g., NELL). To facilitate further research in this area, we have made the datasets and code used in this paper publicly available. In future, we would like to extend GLOFIN to discover new entities and new categories to further enrich the knowledge bases. We are also working on extracting a large set of definitional sentences from a web scale text corpus, that can enable us to improve the coverage of glosses and entities in the KB beyond those that are part of existing online glossaries like Wikipedia.

7. REFERENCES

[1] E. Agirre, O. L. de Lacalle, and A. Soroa. Random walks for knowledge-based word sense disambiguation. *Computational Linguistics*, 2014.

[2] A. Banerjee, I. S. Dhillon, J. Ghosh, and S. Sra. Clustering on the unit hypersphere using von mises-fisher distributions. In *JMLR*, 2005.

[3] S. Banerjee and T. Pedersen. Extended gloss overlaps as a measure of semantic relatedness. In *IJCAI*, 2003.

[4] S. Basu, A. Banerjee, and R. Mooney. Semi-supervised clustering by seeding. In *ICML*, 2002.

[5] F. D. Benedictis, S. Faralli, and R. Navigli. Glossboot: Bootstrapping multilingual domain glossaries from the web. In *ACL*, 2013.

[6] K. Bollacker, C. Evans, P. Paritosh, T. Sturge, and J. Taylor. Freebase: a collaboratively created graph database for structuring human knowledge. In *SIGMOD*, 2008.

[7] A. Carlson, J. Betteridge, B. Kisiel, B. Settles, E. R. H. Jr., and T. M. Mitchell. Toward an architecture for never-ending language learning. In *AAAI*, 2010.

[8] D. Carmel, M.-W. Chang, E. Gabrilovich, B.-J. P. Hsu, and K. Wang. ERD 2014: Entity recognition and disambiguation challenge. *SIGIR Forum*, 2014.

[9] N. Choi, I.-Y. Song, and H. Han. A survey on ontology mapping. *SIGMOD*, 2006.

[10] J. Dalton, L. Dietz, and J. Allan. Entity query feature expansion using knowledge base links. In *SIGIR*, 2014.

[11] B. Dalvi, W. W. Cohen, and J. Callan. Classifying entities into an incomplete ontology. In *AKBC*, 2013.

[12] B. Dalvi, W. W. Cohen, and J. Callan. Exploratory learning. In *ECML*, 2013.

[13] B. Dalvi, C. Xiong, and J. Callan. A language modeling approach to entity recognition and disambiguation for search queries. In *ERD, Entity Recognition and Disambiguation Challenge at SIGIR*, 2014.

[14] W. Duan and A. Yates. Extracting glosses to disambiguate word senses. In *NAACL HLT*, 2010.

[15] R.-E. Fan, K.-W. Chang, C.-J. Hsieh, X.-R. Wang, and C.-J. Lin. Liblinear: A library for large linear classification. *JMLR*, 2008.

[16] S. Faralli and R. Navigli. A new minimally-supervised framework for domain word sense disambiguation. In *EMNLP-CONLL*, 2012.

[17] C. Fellbaum. *WordNet: An Electronic Lexical Database*. MIT Press, 1998.

[18] E. Gabrilovich and S. Markovitch. Computing semantic relatedness using wikipedia-based explicit semantic analysis. In *IJCAI*, 2007.

[19] H. Hajishirzi, L. Zilles, D. S. Weld, and L. Zettlemoyer. Joint coreference resolution and named-entity linking with multi-pass sieves. In *EMNLP*, 2010.

[20] X. Han, L. Sun, and J. Zhao. Collective entity linking in web text: a graph-based method. In *SIGIR*, 2011.

[21] H. Ji, R. Grishman, and H. T. Dang. Overview of the TAC 2011 knowledge base population track. In *TAC*, 2011.

[22] A. Kilgarriff and J. Rosenzweig. English senseval:report and results. In *LREC*, 2000.

[23] J. Krishnamurthy and T. M. Mitchell. Which noun phrases denote which concepts? In *NAACL HLT*, 2011.

[24] M. Lesk. Automatic sense disambiguation using machine readable dictionaries: how to tell a pine cone from an ice cream cone. In *International conference on Systems documentation*, 1986.

[25] T. Lin, O. Etzioni, et al. Entity linking at web scale. In *AKBC*, 2012.

[26] C. D. Manning, M. Surdeanu, J. Bauer, J. Finkel, S. J. Bethard, and D. McClosky. The Stanford CoreNLP natural language processing toolkit. In *ACL demo*, 2014.

[27] D. Martinez, O. L. de Lacalle, and E. Agirre. On the use of automatically acquired examples for all-nouns word sense disambiguation. *JAIR*, 2008.

[28] P. N. Mendes, M. Jakob, and C. Bizer. Dbpedia: A multilingual cross-domain knowledge base. In *LREC*, 2012.

[29] G. A. Miller. Wordnet: a lexical database for english. *Communications of the ACM*, 1995.

[30] T. Mitchell. Nell: Never-ending language learning. *http://rtw.ml.cmu.edu/rtw/*.

[31] A. Moro, A. Raganato, and R. Navigli. Entity linking meets word sense disambiguation: a unified approach. *TACL*, 2014.

[32] D. Movshovitz-Attias and W. W. Cohen. Alignment-hmm-based extraction of abbreviations from biomedical text. In *BioNLP workshop*. NAACL, 2012.

[33] N. Nakashole, M. Theobald, and G. Weikum. Scalable knowledge harvesting with high precision and high recall. In *WSDM*, 2011.

[34] N. Nakashole, T. Tylenda, and G. Weikum. Fine-grained semantic typing of emerging entities. *ACL*, 2013.

[35] R. Navigli. Word sense disambiguation: A survey. *ACM Computing Surveys*, 41(2), 2009.

[36] K. Nigam, A. McCallum, S. Thrun, and T. Mitchell. Text classification from labeled and unlabeled documents using EM. *Machine learning*, 2000.

[37] M. T. Pilehvar and R. Navigli. A robust approach to aligning heterogeneous lexical resources. In *ACL*, 2014.

[38] S. P. Ponzetto and R. Navigli. Knowledge-rich word sense disambiguation rivaling supervised systems. In *ACL*, 2010.

[39] F. M. Suchanek, G. Kasneci, and G. Weikum. Yago: a core of semantic knowledge. In *WWW*, 2007.

[40] P. Talukdar and K. Crammer. New regularized algorithms for transductive learning. In *ECML-PKDD*. 2009.

[41] P. P. Talukdar. Graph-based weakly-supervised methods for information extraction & integration. 2010.

[42] C. Wang, K. Chakrabarti, T. Cheng, and S. Chaudhuri. Targeted disambiguation of ad-hoc, homogeneous sets of named entities. In *WWW*, 2012.

[43] R. C. Wang and W. W. Cohen. Character-level analysis of semi-structured documents for set expansion. In *EMNLP*, 2009.

[44] D. Wijaya, P. P. Talukdar, and T. Mitchell. Pidgin: ontology alignment using web text as interlingua. In *CIKM*, 2013.

[45] A. Yates, M. Cafarella, M. Banko, O. Etzioni, M. Broadhead, and S. Soderland. Textrunner: open information extraction on the web. In *NAACL HLT demo*, 2007.

[46] M. Yu, S. Wang, C. Zhu, and T. Zhao. Semi-supervised learning for word sense disambiguation using parallel corpora. In *FSKD*, 2011.

Finding Subgraphs with Maximum Total Density and Limited Overlap

Oana Denisa Balalau*
Institut Mines Telecom,
Telecom Paristech, CNRS
oana.balalau@telecom-paristech.fr

Francesco Bonchi
Yahoo Labs
Barcelona, Spain
bonchi@yahoo-inc.com

T-H. Hubert Chan†
Dept. of Computer Science
The University of Hong Kong
hubert@cs.hku.hk

Francesco Gullo
Yahoo Labs
Barcelona, Spain
gullo@yahoo-inc.com

Mauro Sozio‡
Institut Mines Telecom,
Telecom Paristech, CNRS
sozio@telecom-paristech.fr

ABSTRACT

Finding dense subgraphs in large graphs is a key primitive in a variety of real-world application domains, encompassing social network analytics, event detection, biology, and finance. In most such applications, one typically aims at finding several (possibly overlapping) dense subgraphs which might correspond to communities in social networks or interesting events. While a large amount of work is devoted to finding a single densest subgraph, perhaps surprisingly, the problem of finding several dense subgraphs with limited overlap has not been studied in a principled way, to the best of our knowledge. In this work we define and study a natural generalization of the densest subgraph problem, where the main goal is to find at most k subgraphs with maximum total aggregate density, while satisfying an upper bound on the pairwise Jaccard coefficient between the sets of nodes of the subgraphs. After showing that such a problem is NP-Hard, we devise an efficient algorithm that comes with provable guarantees in some cases of interest, as well as, an efficient practical heuristic. Our extensive evaluation on large real-world graphs confirms the efficiency and effectiveness of our algorithms.

1. INTRODUCTION

Finding dense subgraphs in large graphs has emerged as a key primitive in a variety of real-world application domains [19], ranging from biology [13, 18] to finance [12]. In the Web domain, Gibson *et al.* [14] have observed that dense subgraphs might correspond to thematic group of pages or spam link farms. In the context of social networks, finding dense subgraphs has been employed for organizing social events and community detection [21], as well as for expert team formation [23, 8]. Angel *et al.* [2] have shown how finding dense subgraphs in the entity co-occurrence graph constructed from micro-blogging streams can be used to automatically detect important events.

Many of the aforementioned applications ask for finding several (possibly overlapping) dense subgraphs, which might correspond to communities in social networks or important events. Perhaps surprisingly, such a problem has not been studied in a principled way to the best of our knowledge. In this work we aim at filling this gap.

In a first attempt to give a formal definition for such a problem, one could aim at finding at most k subgraphs with maximum aggregate total density. However, it turns out that such a formulation might lead to find several subgraphs being very similar between each other and in particular sharing a large fraction of nodes of a relatively dense subgraph. Such a solution is not really interesting as the dense subgraphs to be found should ideally exhibit some appreciable degree of diversity among each other. Therefore, we enforce an upper bound on the pairwise Jaccard coefficient between the sets of nodes of the subgraphs.

Several definitions of density have been studied in the literature, among which the *average degree* density stands outs as a natural and widely used definition. Subgraphs with maximum average degree density are usually referred to as *densest subgraphs*. One appealing feature of such a definition is that densest subgraphs can be found in polynomial time using the linear programming (LP) algorithm presented in [9] or the maximum flow algorithm in [15], while there are efficient algorithms which come with provable approximation guarantees [9]. In our work we focus on the average degree density.

A natural heuristic for our main problem is the following one: Greedily find one densest subgraph in the current graph, remove all its vertices and edges, and iterate until k subgraphs are found or the current graph is empty (see e.g., [23]). This heuristic, although reasonable, might potentially deliver arbitrarily bad solutions in terms of our objective function, as we show in the remainder. Another observation is that such an approach would produce subgraphs which are pairwise disjoint. By allowing some limited amount of overlap, one could find more interesting (i.e., denser) solutions,

*Partially funded by a Google Faculty Research Award.
†Partially funded by France/HK Grant: F-HK31/11T and Hong Kong RGC HKU17200214E.
‡Partially funded by a Google Faculty Research Award and the France/HK PHC Procore 2012 grant 26893QA.

WSDM'15, February 2–6, 2015, Shanghai, China.
Copyright 2015 ACM 978-1-4503-3317-7/15/02 ...$15.00.
http://dx.doi.org/10.1145/2684822.2685298.

while maintaining enough diversity among the subgraphs extracted. Another drawback of the previous heuristic is that algorithms for finding densest subgraphs (based on linear programming and maximum flow) cannot cope with large graphs containing millions of edges.

In our work we present an efficient algorithm for our problem which comes with provable guarantees in some cases of interest. We introduce the concept of minimality of a densest subgraph, (roughly speaking a densest subgraph is minimal if it does not contain any other densest subgraph) and develop efficient algorithms for finding minimal densest subgraphs, which will be pivotal in solving our main problem. Our algorithm for finding minimal densest subgraphs turns out to be the fastest known algorithm for the exact computation of a densest subgraph as it can handle large graphs containing up to 10 million edges, as shown by our experimental evaluation. We finally devise an efficient heuristic so to find subgraphs with limited overlap on even larger input graphs.

More in detail, the contributions of this paper are summarized as follows:

- We define the (k, α)-DENSE SUBGRAPH WITH LIMITED OVERLAP problem ((k, α)-DSLO): given an integer $k > 0$ as well as a real number $\alpha \in [0, 1]$, find at most k subgraphs that maximize the total aggregate density, i.e., the sum of the average degree of each subgraph, under the constraint that the the maximum pairwise Jaccard coefficient between the set of nodes in the subgraphs be at most α. We prove that (k, α)–DSLO is NP-hard even when $\alpha = 0$ (disjoint subgraphs).

- We improve the LP-based approach by Charikar [9], thus achieving the fastest known exact algorithm for the densest subgraph problem. Our algorithm has the desirable property of producing *minimal* densest subgraphs and use our fast LP solver as a subroutine. In particular, we prove that the number of calls to an LP-solver is logarithmic in the number of nodes with high probability. This allows us to deal with large real-world graphs.

- We devise an algorithm (MINANDREMOVE) for the (k, α)-DSLO problem. We prove that, in the case the input graph contains k disjoint densest subgraphs, our algorithm is guaranteed to find an optimum solution for (k, α)-DSLO. In the general case, we show empirically that our algorithm can find solutions that are very close to an optimum solution of our problem.

- We present a fast heuristic (FASTDSLO) for (k, α)-DSLO which, albeit less accurate than MINANDREMOVE, is able to find dense subgraphs with limited overlap on even larger graphs (containing up to 100 million edges).

In Section 2 we discuss the related work, while in Section 3 we define our main problem formally and prove its NP-hardness. All our algorithms are presented in Section 4, while Section 5 contains an experimental evaluation on large real-world graphs. Finally, in Section 6 we draw our conclusions and discuss interesting directions for future work.

2. RELATED WORK

Finding a single densest subgraph. The problem of finding a dense subgraph from a large input graph has been widely studied [19]. Generally speaking, such a problem aims at finding a subgraph of a given input graph that maximizes some notion of density. A density notion widely employed in the literature is the average degree. Due to its popularity, the corresponding problem of finding a subgraph that maximizes the average degree has been commonly referred to as the *densest-subgraph* problem. The densest subgraph can be identified in polynomial time by solving a parametric maximum-flow problem [15]. Charikar [9] introduces a linear-programming formulation of the problem, while also showing that the greedy algorithm proposed by Asashiro *et al.* [5] produces a $\frac{1}{2}$-approximation in linear time. The densest-subgraph problem has also been studied in a streaming context [6].

A more difficult variant of the densest-subgraph problem is the so-called *DkS* problem, which consists of finding a densest subgraph of k vertices. Such a problem is known to be NP-hard [4], while an algorithm with approximation guarantee of $\mathcal{O}(n^{\frac{1}{4}})$ has been presented in [7]. It is also well known that there cannot be any PTAS for the *DkS* problem under reasonable complexity assumptions [16]. Some variants of the *DkS* problem are introduced by Andersen and Chellapilla [1] and further investigated in [17].

A number of works depart from the classic average-degree maximization problem and focus on extracting a subgraph maximizing other notions of density. Tsourakakis *et al.* [23] resort to the notion of quasi-clique to define an alternative measure of density, while Wang *et al.* [25] focus on a density based on triangle counting. Sozio *et al.* [21] focus on minimum degree density while enforcing so-called *monotone* constraints.

Finding multiple densest subgraphs. Unlike its single-subgraph counterpart, the problem of finding a set of k dense subgraphs has received considerably less attention. Few authors [24, 23] have discussed it, without providing any rigorous formulation of the problem. Instead they consider the most obvious heuristic that iteratively finds and removes the densest subgraph until k subgraphs have been found. In our work, we precisely formulate and characterize the problem of finding at most k disjoint subgraphs that maximize the sum of densities, while also showing, both theoretically and empirically, that the aforementioned simple heuristic is not well-suited for such a problem.

Apart from that, existing research has considered tangentially related problems, such as finding *nested* subgraphs containing a set of query nodes and exhibiting non-increasing densities [22], discovering overlapping dense subgraphs containing a query node [11], or extracting all *large-enough* dense bipartite subgraphs in massive graphs [14]. Furthermore, Angel *et al.* [3] focus on maintaining the set of all (possibly overlapping) subgraphs exceeding a density threshold under streaming edge weight updates. Chen and Saad [10] instead propose a matrix-blocking model to identify dense subgraphs that best cover the input graph. Particularly, the latter problem differs from ours as it aims at finding a set of dense subgraphs that cover most of the input graph, while discarding outlier (i.e., non-dense) graph zones, but it does not attempt at maximizing the sum of the densities of k subgraphs.

3. DEFINITION AND COMPLEXITY

In this section, we define our problem formally and we study its computational complexity.

Given an undirected graph $G = (V, E)$, we define its density $\rho(G)$ to be $\frac{|E|}{|V|}$, which corresponds to half the average degree of the nodes in G. For a set of vertices $S \subseteq V$, we denote the subgraph of G induced by S as $G(S) = (S, E(S))$, where $E(S) = \{\{u, v\} \in E | u, v \in S\}$).

In a first attempt to give a formal definition for our problem, one could aim at finding at most k subgraphs with maximum aggregate total density. However, it turns out that such a formulation might lead to find several subgraphs being very similar between each other and in particular sharing a large fraction of nodes of a relatively dense subgraph. Such a solution is not really interesting as the dense subgraphs to be found should ideally exhibit some appreciable degree of diversity among each other. Therefore, we enforce an upper bound $\alpha \in [0, 1]$ on the pairwise Jaccard coefficient between the sets of nodes of the subgraphs, with one indicating that the two subgraphs contain exactly the same nodes and zero indicating that they are disjoint. Our problem can then be formalized as follows.

Definition 3.1 ((k, α)-DSLO) *Given an undirected graph $G = (V, E)$, an integer $k > 0$, as well as a rational number $\alpha \in [0, 1]$, find a set of sets of vertices $\mathcal{S} = \{S_1, \ldots, S_{\bar{k}}\}$ with $\bar{k} \leq k$, and $S_i \subseteq V, \forall S_i \in \mathcal{S}$, such that*

$$\sum_{i=1}^{\bar{k}} \rho(G(S_i))) \quad \textit{is maximum, and}$$

$$\frac{|S_i \cap S_j|}{|S_i \cup S_j|} \leq \alpha \quad \forall S_i, S_j \in \mathcal{S}. \tag{1}$$

Theorem 3.1 *(k, α)-DSLO is NP-hard.*

We prove NP-hardness by reducing the well-known maximum independent set problem to a special case of (k, α)-DSLO i.e., to case where $\alpha = 0$. Particularly, we show that given a graph G and a positive integer k, it is NP-hard to find k disjoint subsets $S_1, S_2, \ldots, S_k$ of nodes such that the sum of densities $\sum_{i=1}^{k} \rho(S_i)$ is maximized. In particular, we consider a decisional version of the problem, in which we are given a target τ, and the problem is to decide if there are k disjoint subsets whose sum of densities is at least τ.

Our hardness proof reduces from the NP-hardness of maximum independent set on degree bounded graphs [20]. In particular, for any fixed $\Delta \geq 3$, given a graph G with maximum degree at most Δ and an integer k, it is NP-hard to decide if G contains an independent set with size k.

Reduction Construction. Given an instance $G = (V, E)$ of the maximum independent set problem with maximum degree at most Δ, we construct a graph $\widehat{G}$ and select a threshold τ such that G has an independent set of size k *iff* $\widehat{G}$ contains k disjoint subsets whose sum of densities is at least τ.

Node Gadget. We choose some $N = n^4$, where $n = |V|$. Given a node u, we create a gadget graph G_u as follows. Let C_u be a set of N independent nodes, which forms the *core* of G_u. Let A_u be a set Δ independent nodes, which are the *arms* of G_u. The graph G_u is a complete bipartite graph between C_u and A_u, and so contains $N\Delta$ edges.

Interaction between Node Gadgets. For distinct nodes u and v in V, the cores C_u and C_v are disjoint. If $\{u, v\} \notin E$, then A_u and A_v are disjoint; but if $\{u, v\} \in E$, then $|A_u \cap A_v| = 1$, i.e., the two gadgets G_u and G_v share exactly one arm. Moreover, each arm node can be shared by at most 2 gadget graphs. Since G has degree at most Δ, each arm of a gadget graph can be potentially used to connect with another gadget according to G. This completes the description of graph $\widehat{G}$.

Before we state our threshold τ, we consider the densities of subgraphs in $\widehat{G}$.

Lemma 3.1 *The density of any subset of nodes in $\widehat{G}$ is at most Δ. Moreover, if the density of a subset S is at least $\Delta - \frac{1}{2}$, then S must contain all the arms A_u of some u.*

PROOF. The result follows from the following statement. Suppose S is a subset of nodes in $\widehat{G}$ that intersects the cores of some r gadgets. Suppose for some $D > 0$, for each $i \in [r]$, S contains d_i arm nodes of gadget graph G_i, where $d_i \leq D$. (Observe that each arm node can belong to more than one gadget graph G_i.) Then, we show that the density of S is at most D.

For $i \in [r]$, suppose S contains n_i nodes from the core C_i of gadget graph G_i. The total number of edges induced by S is $\sum_{i\in[r]} n_i d_i$. If none of the G_i's share an arm, the number of nodes in S is $\sum_{i\in[r]}(n_i + d_i)$. Observe that for each pair of G_i's that share an arm, the number of nodes decreases by 1. Since each G_i can share arms with at most d_i other gadgets, the maximum number of pairs that can share an arm is $\frac{\sum_{i\in[r]} d_i}{2}$.

Hence, $|S| \geq \sum_{i\in[r]}(n_i + d_i) - \frac{\sum_{i\in[r]} d_i}{2} = \sum_{i\in[r]}(n_i + \frac{d_i}{2})$. Therefore, the density of S is at most $\frac{\sum_{i\in[r]} n_i d_i}{\sum_{i\in[r]}(n_i + \frac{d_i}{2})} \leq \max_{i\in[r]} \frac{n_i d_i}{n_i + \frac{d_i}{2}} \leq \frac{ND}{N + \frac{D}{2}}$, where the last inequality follows because the expression $\frac{n_i d_i}{n_i + \frac{d_i}{2}}$ is increasing in both n_i and d_i.

Finally, observing that $\frac{ND}{N + \frac{D}{2}} \leq D$, we finish the proof of the statement. □

The following lemma completes the reduction proof.

Lemma 3.2 *The graph G (with maximum degree at most Δ) contains an independent set of size k iff the graph $\widehat{G}$ contains k disjoint subsets whose sum of densities is at least $\tau = k\Delta - \frac{1}{n}$.*

PROOF. The forward direction is easy because each point in the independent set corresponds to a disjoint gadget graph, which has density $\frac{\Delta N}{N+\Delta} \geq \Delta - \frac{1}{n^2}$, because $\Delta < n$ and $N = n^4$. Hence, the sum of the densities of the k disjoint gadget graphs is at least $k\Delta - \frac{1}{n}$.

For the backward direction, observe that each of the k disjoint subsets S_i's in $\widehat{G}$ must have density at least $\Delta - \frac{1}{2}$. Otherwise, there exists $k - 1$ disjoint subsets whose sum of densities is at least $(k - 1)\Delta + \frac{1}{2} - \frac{1}{n} > (k - 1)\Delta$. This implies that there exists a subset in $\widehat{G}$ with density strictly larger than Δ, which is impossible by Lemma 3.1.

Hence, we conclude that each of k disjoint subsets S_i's must have density at least $\Delta - \frac{1}{2}$, which implies by Lemma 3.1 that each S_i must contain all the arms of some core A_u for some $u \in V$. This means the k subsets S_i's correspond to k independent nodes in G. □

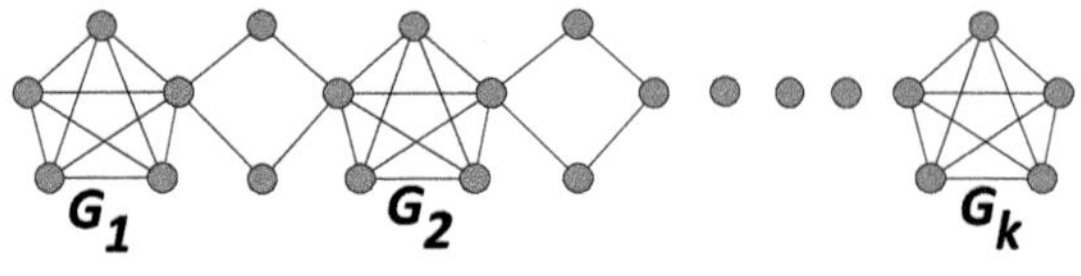

Figure 1: A graph G where Naive gives poor results. Notice that G is a non-minimal densest subgraph.

4. ALGORITHMS

As (k, α)-DSLO is NP-Hard, we devise heuristics that work well in practice while also exhibiting provable guarantees in some cases of interest. We start by considering one natural heuristic for the disjoint case ($\alpha = 0$): at each step, we compute the densest subgraph in the current graph (using for example the approach in [9]), we remove all its nodes and edges from the current graph, iterating until we find exactly k subgraphs or until the current graph contains no edges. We hereinafter refer to this heuristic as NAIVE.

This simple heuristic gives unfortunately very poor results in the worst case, as illustrated in Figure 1.

In that example the density $\rho(G)$ of the graph is 2 (there are $10k + 4(k-1)$ edges and $5k + 2(k-1)$ nodes), like every subgraph G_i of G. NAIVE would find the whole graph G and then would stop giving a solution with total density equal to 2, while an optimum solution to our problem is composed of the disjoint subgraphs $G_1, \ldots, G_k$ with total density equal to $2k$. This highlights one of the limitations of NAIVE and paves the way to the definition of minimal dense graphs.

Definition 4.1 *(Minimal dense graphs) An undirected graph G with density $\rho(G)$ is a* minimal dense graph *if for any proper subgraph H of G, $\rho(H) < \rho(G)$. Moreover, we say that G is a minimal densest subgraph if it is minimal and has maximum density.*

Notice that the graph G in Figure 1 is a non-minimal densest subgraph.

Finding minimal dense graphs plays an important role in solving our problem, as illustrated by the following variant of NAIVE. At each step we compute a *minimal* densest subgraph, we remove its nodes and edges from the current graph, and we iterate until k subgraphs are found or there are no edges left in the current graph. Including at each step a minimal dense subgraph H, rather than a supergraph G of H, would not decrease the total density of our solution (as H is as dense as G) and might actually increase it, as fewer edges are removed from the current graph after including H in the solution. It turns out that this simple variant of NAIVE, finds k disjoint densest subgraphs, if they exist. This is proved in Section 4.2. In Section 4.1, we show how to efficiently compute minimal densest subgraphs.

Drawing inspiration from the techniques developed for computing minimal densest subgraphs, we then address the (k, α)-DSLO problem. The main challenge here is to take full advantage of the overlap between subgraphs so to maximize our objective function. Computing minimal subgraphs is desirable also in this case, in order to minimize the number of edges that are removed at each step. This is discussed in Section 4.2. In Section 5, we perform an extensive evaluation of our algorithms showing the effectiveness of our heuristics for (k, α)-DSLO on large real-world graphs and that minimal densest subgraphs can be computed efficiently on large graphs containing millions of edges.

4.1 Finding Minimal Densest Subgraphs

Our algorithm for computing minimal densest subgraphs is inspired by the linear programming (LP)-based algorithm for the densest subgraph developed by Charikar [9]. In order to have some provable guarantees for our problem, we need to dive deeper into the structure of the solutions of the LP. We start by recalling the algorithm in [9].

Given a graph $G = (V, E)$, Charikar [9] proposed the following LP formulation for the densest subgraph problem. For each edge $ij \in E$ we introduce a variable x_{ij} taking values in $[0, 1]$, while for each node v we introduce variable x_v (taking values in $[0, 1]$). We have the following linear program:

$$\max \sum_{ij \in E} x_{ij} \qquad \text{(BasicLP)}$$

$$\text{s.t.} \quad x_{ij} \leq y_i \qquad \forall ij \in E \qquad (2)$$

$$x_{ij} \leq y_j \qquad \forall ij \in E \qquad (3)$$

$$\sum_{i \in V} y_i \leq 1 \qquad (4)$$

$$x_{ij}, y_i \geq 0 \qquad \forall i, j. \qquad (5)$$

To gain an intuition about the above LP, consider a densest subgraph $H = (S, E(S))$, $S \subseteq V$. We can then define a feasible solution $z^S = (x^S, y^S)$ for BasicLP as follows:

$$x_{ij}^S = \begin{cases} \frac{1}{|S|} & \text{if both } i, j \in S \\ 0 & \text{otherwise.} \end{cases}$$

$$y_i^S = \begin{cases} \frac{1}{|S|} & \text{if } i \in S \\ 0 & \text{otherwise.} \end{cases}$$

Recall that the density of the subgraph $H = (S, E(S))$ is defined as $\rho(H) = \rho(S) = \frac{|E(S)|}{|S|}$. Observe that z^S is feasible for the basic LP, and has objective value $\rho(S)$. Vice versa, given an optimum solution $z^S = (x^S, y^S)$ for BasicLP, one can construct an optimum solution for the densest subgraph problem using the *rounding* algorithm described in [9]: We first order the y_i^S's by non-increasing order. Let $y_1, \ldots, y_n$ be the variables so ordered. We then find the prefix $y_1, \ldots, y_k$ in such ordering whose corresponding induced subgraph H achieves maximum density, for any value of k in $[2, n]$. It can be proved that H is a densest subgraph.

One can then solve BasicLP using efficient LP solvers such as Gurobi or CPLEX and then compute the densest subgraph by running the algorithm described above. In the rest of this section, we present a more efficient algorithm for computing the densest subgraph, which allows us to deal with large real-world graphs containing millions of edges. The latter algorithm uses the following fact.

Lemma 4.1 *Each optimal solution of BasicLP is a convex combination of points in $\{z^S : S \subseteq V,\ S \text{ is densest subgraph}\}$.*

PROOF. Suppose $z^* = (x^*, y^*)$ is an optimal solution. Then, since the objective value to be maximized is the sum of all x_{ij}'s, it follows that if z^* is optimal, it must be the case that $\sum_{i \in V} y_i^* = 1$, and for all $ij \in E$, $x_{ij}^* = \min\{y_i^*, y_j^*\}$.

We prove the result by induction on the number k of non-zero coordinates of y^*. If E contains at least one edge, it follows that $k \geq 2$. For the base case $k = 2$, suppose $\{i, j\}$ is the support of y^*. Since $x_{ij}^* = \min\{y_i^*, y_j^*\}$ is maximized when $y_i^* = y_j^* = \frac{1}{2}$, the result follows.

For the inductive step, suppose y^* has $k > 2$ non-zero coordinates corresponding to some subset $S \subseteq V$, where $k = |S|$. If all the non-zero y_i^*'s are the same for $i \in S$, then it follows that $z^* = z^S$, and the result follows; otherwise, let $\alpha := \min\{y_i^* : i \in S\}$. Observe that $k\alpha \leq 1$.

Define $\widehat{z} = (\widehat{x}, \widehat{y})$ as follows.

$$\widehat{x}_{ij} = \begin{cases} \frac{x_{ij}^* - \alpha}{1 - k\alpha} & \text{if both } i, j \in S \\ 0 & \text{otherwise.} \end{cases}$$

$$\widehat{y}_i = \begin{cases} \frac{y_i^* - \alpha}{1 - k\alpha} & \text{if } i \in S \\ 0 & \text{otherwise.} \end{cases}$$

Hence, $z^* = k\alpha \cdot z^S + (1 - k\alpha)\widehat{z}$, and the number of non-zero coordinates of $\widehat{y}$ is strictly less than k. Hence, to complete the inductive step, it suffices to show that $\widehat{z}$ is an optimal solution to the basic LP.

Observe that since the objective function is linear, $p(z^*) = k\alpha \cdot p(z^S) + (1 - k\alpha)p(\widehat{z})$, it is enough to show that $\widehat{z}$ is feasible, because if $p(\widehat{z}) < p(z^*)$, it must be the case that $p(z^S) > p(z^*)$, which violates the optimality of z^*.

To check the feasibility of $\widehat{z}$, we have for $ij \in E(S)$, $\widehat{x}_{ij} = \frac{x_{ij}^* - \alpha}{1 - k\alpha} = \frac{\min\{y_i^*, y_j^*\} - \alpha}{1 - k\alpha} = \min\{\widehat{y}_i, \widehat{y}_j\}$.

Moreover, $\sum_{i \in V} \widehat{y}_i = \sum_{i \in S} \frac{y_i^* - \alpha}{1 - k\alpha} = \frac{\sum_{i \in S} y_i^* - k\alpha}{1 - k\alpha} = 1$, because $\sum_{i \in S} y_i^* = 1$. Therefore, $\widehat{z}$ is feasible and this completes the inductive step. □

The following corollary follows from Lemma 4.1.

Corollary 4.1 *Suppose S_1, S_2 both induce densest subgraphs in V. Then, both $S_1 \cap S_2$ and $S_1 \cup S_2$ induce densest subgraphs in V.*

Another interesting consequence of Lemma 4.1 is that we can find a densest subgraph by first solving BasicLP, and then returning the subgraph consisting of all nodes whose corresponding variables have values strictly larger than zero in our solution.

We now focus on computing a minimal densest subgraph H of a graph G given in input. We recall that any (proper) subgraph of H must have density strictly smaller than H.

As we shall use an LP-based approach to find a densest subgraphs, we start by showing how to speed up the LP-based algorithm presented in [9]. As proved in Lemma 4.1, the subgraph induced by variables with maximum value in an optimum solution for BasicLP is a densest subgraph. Starting from a solution for BasicLP we can then derive a densest subgraph in $O(n)$, in contrast with the rounding algorithm described in [9], which requires $\Omega(n \log n + m)$ operations, where n, m are the number of nodes and edges in G, respectively. To the best of our knowledge, this fact was not known before. We shall refer to this more efficient algorithm for the densest subgraph as FASTLP.

Our algorithm for finding minimal dense subgraphs employs two subroutines: TRYREMOVE and TRYENHANCE. The former one takes as input a graph G and a node u and checks whether u can be removed from G without decreasing its density. This is done by computing a densest subgraph in the input graph $(V \setminus \{u\}, E)$ and checking whether the density drops. If this is not the case, u can be removed from G. A pseudocode for TRYREMOVE is shown in Algorithm 1.

Algorithm 1 TRYREMOVE(u, G)

Input: A graph $G = (V, E)$ and a node u to be removed.
Output: Returns a densest subgraph in G not containing u, or *null* if every densest subgraph in G must contain u.
Solve the BasicLP with input $(V \setminus \{u\}, E)$ and run FASTLP to find a densest subgraph H in $(V \setminus \{u\}, E)$.
if $\rho(H) \geq \rho(G)$ **then**
    return H
else
    return null
end if

We could then compute H by iterating through all nodes and checking for each such a node whether it can be removed or not. This algorithm would not be efficient, in that, it requires to solve $\Theta(n)$ LPs, one for each node of G. Therefore, we devise a much more efficient algorithm which requires to solve $O(\log n)$ LPs, with high probability. Such an algorithm employs the subroutine TRYENHANCE, which receives in input a graph G, a node u, as well as density $\rho_{\max}$ of a densest subgraph in G. It returns a densest subgraph in G which contains u while having smallest number of nodes (or null in case there is no densest subgraph containing u).

This is achieved by solving a carefully defined LP whose objective is to maximize y_u subject to the constraint that the density is equal to $\rho_{\max}$. The main intuition is that for each densest subgraph in G with S nodes there is a solution to the LP where variables have all values $\frac{1}{|S|}$. Therefore, by maximizing y_u we can find a densest subgraph containing u with smallest number of nodes. This is proved in Lemma 4.2 and follows partially from Lemma 4.1. See Algorithm 2 for a pseudocode of TRYENHANCE.

Algorithm 2 TRYENHANCE$(u, G, \rho_{\max})$

Input: a graph $G = (V, E)$, a node $u \in V$, the density $\rho_{\max}$ of the densest subgraph in G.
Output: Returns a densest subgraph in G containing u with minimum cardinality or *null* if there is no densest subgraph containing u.
Modify the basic LP by adding the constraint $\sum_{ij \in E} x_{ij} = \rho_{\max}$, maximizing the objective function y_u; solve the modified LP by running FASTLP.
If there is no feasible solution to the modified LP **then** return *null*.
Run FASTLP to find a densest subgraph $H = (\bar{V}, \bar{E})$ starting from the LP solution.
return H

Lemma 4.2 *Given a graph $G = (V, E)$ and a node $u \in V$, the subroutine* TRYENHANCE *returns a densest subgraph in G containing u with the smallest number of nodes.*

PROOF. The smallest densest subgraph containing u is unique, because by Corollary 4.1, the intersection of all densest subgraphs containing u is also a densest subgraph.

Consider the optimal solution $z = (x, y)$ computed from the modified LP in the subroutine TRYENHANCE$(u, G, \rho_{\max})$. By Lemma 4.1, z is a convex combination of z^{S_i}'s, where each S_i induces a densest subgraph in G. Since the objective is to maximize y_u, and z^S is a feasible solution, it follows that y_u is positive, which means that at least one of the S_i's must contain u. Since for each S_i containing u, $y_u^{S_i} = \frac{1}{|S_i|}$, it follows that if z is a convex combination of more than one S_i's, the value y_u could be strictly improved by $z^{\overline{S}}$, where $\overline{S}$ is the intersection of all S_i's containing u.

Hence, it follows that $z = z^{\overline{S}}$ for some densest subgraph induced by $\overline{S}$, which has to be the smallest densest subset containing u. □

The main steps for finding efficiently a minimal densest subgraph are the following ones. At each iteration: 1) we pick one node u from our current graph, uniformly at random; 2) we execute the subroutines TRYREMOVE and TRYENHANCE with input u and our current graph; 3) our current graph is then set to be the smallest subgraph among the ones returned by the previous subroutines. It turns out that $2\log_{\frac{4}{3}} n$ iterations suffice to find a minimal densest subgraph, with high probability. This is proved in Corollary 4.3, while Lemma 4.3 proves that our algorithm finds a minimal densest subgraph.

In order to speed up even further our algorithm, we include a preprocessing phase where we remove nodes not belonging to any densest subgraph. This is done as follows. We first run the linear-time greedy algorithm presented by Charikar in [9] so to find a 2-approximation solution to the densest subgraph. Let ρ_{apx} be the density of the graphs so found. As noted in [17], no nodes with degree smaller than the density of the densest subgraph belongs to any densest subgraph. Therefore, we can safely remove all nodes with degree smaller than ρ_{apx} from the input graph. A pseudocode of our algorithm is shown in Algorithm 3.

Algorithm 3 FINDMINIMAL(G)

```
Input: A graph G = (V, E) with n nodes.
Output: A minimal densest subgraph in G.
Run the greedy algorithm to find a 2-approximation solution for the densest subgraph. Let ρ_apx be the density of such a subgraph.
Remove iteratively nodes with degree smaller than ρ_apx and let Ḡ be the graphs so obtained.
Find a densest subgraph H = (V̄, Ē) in Ḡ by running FASTLP. Let ρ_max be its density.
while (true) do
    let u be a node picked uniformly at random from V̄
    let H1 := TRYREMOVE(u, H)
    let H2 := TRYENHANCE(u, H, ρ_max)
    IF H1 is null return H2
    let Ĥ be the subgraph with minimum number of nodes between H1 and H2, breaking ties arbitrarily
    H := Ĥ
end while
return H
```

Lemma 4.3 FINDMINIMAL(G) *returns a minimal densest subgraph of* G.

PROOF. Algorithm 3 always terminates. After each iteration of the *while* loop, either TRYREMOVE(u, H) returns *null* and therefore the algorithm terminates or the node u is removed from the current graph. Hence, at each iteration the number of nodes of the current graph decreases by at least one. Observe that the graph H is always a densest subgraph, throughout the execution of the algorithm. When the algorithm terminates, it must be the case that TRYREMOVE(u, H) returns *null*, for some node u in H. This means that every densest subgraph of H must contain u. By Lemma 4.2, TRYENHANCE($u, H, \rho_{\max}$) returns the smallest densest subgraph containing u, and so it must be minimal. □

We prove that $O(\log n)$ iterations of the *while* loop of FINDMINIMAL(G) suffice to find a minimal densest subgraph in G. To this end, we show that at each iteration the number of nodes in the current subgraph decreases by a constant fraction with constant probability. A standard measure concentration argument concludes the proof. Let $H = (\bar{V}, \bar{E})$ be a densest subgraph of G. For a node $u \in \bar{V}$, $\epsilon > 0$, we say that u is ϵ-bad in $H = (\bar{V}, \bar{E})$ if both $H_1 :=$ TRYREMOVE(u, H) and $H_2 :=$ TRYENHANCE($u, H, \rho_{\max}$) contain more than $(1-\epsilon)|\bar{V}|$ nodes, and neither of them is *null*.

Lemma 4.4 *Given a graph* $H = (\bar{V}, \bar{E})$ *with maximum density* $\rho_{\max}$, *the fraction of* ϵ*-bad nodes in* $\bar{V}$ *is at most* 2ϵ, *for any* $\epsilon > 0$.

PROOF. For contradiction's sake, suppose the set B of ϵ-bad nodes has size more than $2\epsilon|\bar{V}|$. For each $u \in B$, define $A_u := \bar{V} \setminus$ TRYREMOVE(u, H). Observe that $u \in A_u$, and by the definition of ϵ-bad, $|A_u| < \epsilon|\bar{V}|$.

Consider an arbitrary order of $B := \{u_1, u_2, \ldots, \}$. Since B contains more than $2\epsilon|\bar{V}|$ points, and each $|A_u| < \epsilon|\bar{v}|$, there exists a smallest i such that $\epsilon|\bar{V}| \leq |\cup_{j=1}^{i} A_{u_j}| < 2\epsilon|\bar{V}|$.

Observe that there exists $\widehat{u} \in B \setminus (\cup_{j=1}^{i} A_{u_j})$. Since for each j, TRYREMOVE(u_j, H) is a densest subgraph, then by Lemma 4.1, $\cap_{j=1}^{i}$TRYREMOVE$(u_j, H) = \bar{V} \setminus (\cup_{j=1}^{i} A_{u_j})$ induces a densest subgraph that contains $\widehat{u}$ and has size at most $(1-\epsilon)|\bar{V}|$. Therefore, it follows that the algorithm TRYENHANCE($\widehat{u}, H, \rho\max$) will return a densest subgraph that has size at most $(1-\epsilon)|\bar{V}|$, thereby contradicting that $\widehat{u}$ is ϵ-bad. □

By taking $\epsilon = \frac{1}{4}$ in Lemma 4.4, we have the following corollary.

Corollary 4.2 *At each iteration of* FINDMINIMAL(G), *the algorithm either terminates with a minimal densest subgraph, or with probability at least* $\frac{1}{2}$, *the number of nodes in* $\widehat{H}$ *is at most* $\frac{3}{4} \cdot |\bar{V}|$.

Corollary 4.3 *By standard Chernoff bound, the number of iterations in* FINDMINIMAL(G) *is at most a constant times its mean, which is at most* $2\log_{\frac{4}{3}} n$, *where* n *is the number of nodes in* G.

Our algorithm FINDMINIMAL(G) allows us to compute minimal densest subgraphs in graphs containing millions of edges. In particular, the pruning step and the fact that we can bound the number of iterations by a logarithmic function allows us to save several order of magnitudes in terms of running time.

4.1.1 Finding All Minimal Densest Subgraphs

Armed with an efficient algorithm for finding minimal densest subgraphs, we now present an algorithm that computes all such graphs. Our algorithm computes at each step a minimal densest subgraph by running Algorithm 3, it removes all its nodes and edges from the current graph and

Algorithm 4 FINDALLMINIMAL(V)

Input: Graph $G = (V, E)$.
Output: Returns a list L of all minimal densest subgraphs.
$L := \emptyset$
while (true) **do**
  $\widehat{H}$ = FINDMINIMAL(G)
  IF $\widehat{H}$ is not a densest subgraph **break**;
  $L := L \cup \{\widehat{H}\}$
  remove all nodes and edges incident to $\widehat{H}$ from G
end while
return L

iterates until no densest subgraph can be found. A pseudocode is shown in Algorithm 4.

Minimal densest subgraphs must be disjoint, for otherwise, their intersection would be a densest subgraph (from Corollary 4.1), which would contradict the fact that they are minimal. Lemma 4.5 then follows.

Lemma 4.5 *Given an undirected graph $G = (V, E)$, our algorithm* FINDALLMINIMAL(V) *finds all minimal densest subgraphs in G.*

4.2 Main Algorithms

Drawing inspiration from the theory and the techniques developed in the previous section for finding minimal densest subgraphs, we devise one algorithm for our main problem (k, α)-DSLO. In this case, we face the additional challenge of taking full advantage of the overlap between the subgraphs.

Our algorithm is inspired by FINDMINIMAL and proceeds as follows. At each step i, we compute a minimal densest subgraph $G_i = (V_i, E_i)$ of our current graph $G = (V, E)$ and we remove $\lceil(1-\alpha)|V_i|\rceil$ nodes (and their edges) from V. We remove those nodes that are not well connected with nodes outside G_i, as they will contribute less to the total density in the next steps of the algorithm. Formally, for any node v in V_i let $\Delta_G(v)$ be the set of neighbors of v in G. We remove the $\lceil(1-\alpha)\rceil|V_i|$ nodes (and their edges) with minimum value $|\Delta_G(v) \setminus V_i|$. We iterate until k subgraphs are found or the current graph becomes empty. Observe that the constraint on the Jaccard coefficient is not violated. A pseudocode of our algorithm is shown in Algorithm 5.

We can prove an interesting property of MINANDREMOVE. Observe that if there are k disjoint densest subgraphs in G then MINANDREMOVE would return the same solution of FINDALLMINIMAL. Then, our main theorem follows from Lemma 4.5.

Theorem 4.1 *If there are k disjoint densest subgraphs in the input graph G, then* MINANDREMOVE *computes an optimum solution for (k, α)-DSLO, for any $\alpha \geq 0$.*

Although, we cannot give any guarantee for the general case of (k, α)-DSLO (i.e. for any $\alpha \geq 0$) we show the effectiveness of our main algorithm in our experimental evaluation. In particular, we are able to derive an upper bound on any optimum solution for (k, α)-DSLO and show that MINANDREMOVE is very close to such an upper bound in our experiments (up to a factor of 0.9).

Finally, we present a fast heuristic FASTDSLO for finding dense subgraphs with limited overlap. Our heuristic computes at each step i a 2-approximation solution G_i to the densest subgraph problem using the greedy algorithm presented in [9]. Then, similarly to MINANDREMOVE $\lceil(1-\alpha)\rceil|V_i|$ nodes are removed from the current graph so to satisfy the requirement on the pairwise Jaccard coefficient. A pseudocode is shown in Algorithm 6. Our experimental evaluation shows that although our heuristic is less accurate than MINANDREMOVE, it is still not too far from an optimum solution while it can handle graphs with more than 100 million edges within a few hours.

Algorithm 5 MINANDREMOVE(G, k, α)

Input: A graph $G = (V, E)$, an integer $k > 0$, $\alpha \in [0, 1]$
Output: A list L of at most k subgraphs of G, $G_i = (V_i, E_i)$, s.t. the constraint on the pairwise Jaccard coefficient on the V_i's is not violated (Equation (1)).
$L := \emptyset$
while $< k$ subgraphs are found and G is not empty **do**
  Find a minimal densest subgraph $G_i = (V_i, E_i)$ of G by running Algorithm 3
  $L := L \cup \{G_i\}$
  For each node v in V_i, let $\Delta_G(v)$ be the set of neighbors of v in G.
  Remove the $\lceil(1-\alpha)|V_i|\rceil$ nodes with minimum value $|\Delta_H(v) \setminus V_i|$ and all their edges from G.
end while
return L

Algorithm 6 FASTDSLO(G, k, α)

Input: A graph $G = (V, E)$, an integer $k > 0$, $\alpha \in [0, 1]$
Output: A list L of at most k subgraphs of G, $G_i = (V_i, E_i)$, s.t. the constraint on the pairwise Jaccard coefficient on the V_i's is not violated (Equation (1)).
$L := \emptyset$
while $< k$ subgraphs are found and G is not empty **do**
  Find a 2-approximation solution $G_i = (V_i, E_i)$ to the densest subgraph problem by running the greedy algorithm in [9].
  $L := L \cup \{G_i\}$
  For each node v in V_i, let $\Delta_G(v)$ be the set of neighbors of v in G.
  Remove the $\lceil(1-\alpha)|V_i|\rceil$ nodes with minimum value $|\Delta_H(v) \setminus V_i|$ and all their edges from G.
end while
return L

5. EXPERIMENTS

We perform our experimental evaluation on a Linux server with Intel Xeon E7-4870 at 2.40GHz, while limiting the total amount of main memory available to 64 GB. We solve linear programs with the Gurobi Optimizer version 5.6.3. All our algorithms are implemented in Java.

We consider 8 datasets in total grouped according to their size[1]. We ignore the direction of the edges in the directed graphs, as it is irrelevant to our purposes. Most of our experiments are conducted on the datasets that contain up to 11 million edges, as illustrated in Table 1. We refer to this set of datasets as *large* datasets.

Name	Nodes	Edges	Description
web-Stanford	281K	1.9M	Hyperlink network
com-Youtube	1.1M	3M	Social network
web-Google	875K	4.3M	Hyperlink network
Youtube-growth	3.2M	9.3M	Social network
As-Skitter	1.69M	11M	Internet topology

Table 1: Large real-world datasets.

The second group of datasets consists of *very large* datasets containing up to more than 100 million edges where we evaluate our fast heuristic. In Table 2 we specify all the details for this group of datasets. We refer to this set of datasets as *very large* datasets.

Name	Nodes	Edges	Description
Live Journal	4.8M	43M	Social network
Hollywood-2009	1.1M	57M	Social network
Orkut	3M	117M	Social network

Table 2: Very large real-world datasets.

We evaluate our algorithm MinAndRemove against two variants of the Naive algorithm. In the first variant we compute at each step a densest subgraph with the LP-based approach proposed in [9], we remove all its nodes and edges from the graph, and we iterate until k subgraphs have been found or the graph has become empty. We refer to this algorithm as NaiveDensest. In the second variant we compute at each step the $\frac{1}{2}$-approximation algorithm proposed in [9] instead of a densest subgraph. We refer to this algorithm as NaiveGreedy. The reason to consider also this second variant is that the $\frac{1}{2}$-approximation algorithm is much faster than the LP-based optimal approach.

We tested NaiveDensest on the large datasets and it did not terminate after 16 hours of computation on any dataset. We also evaluated the maximum flow algorithm proposed in [15], which turned out to be even slower. Therefore, in the rest of the experimental evaluation we focus on evaluating MinAndRemove against NaiveGreedy.

We start by measuring the total density when $k = 10$, while varying α between 0.1 and 0.5. Let $\rho_{\max}$ be the density of a densest subgraph in the input graph. Observe that $k \cdot \rho_{\max}$ gives us an upper bound on the value of any optimum solution for (k, α)-DSLO, for any value of α. Therefore, we can use such an upper bound to give an idea of how close our results are to an optimum solution. Given that we use only an upper bound, clearly, our results might be even closer to the actual optimum solution.

In Table 3, we measure the ratio between the total density computed by our main algorithm and our upper bound, when $k = 10$. We can see that in all cases our algorithm yields a solution that is at least within a factor of 0.44 of the value of an optimum solution, while in many cases it yields an approximation factor of 0.8 (meaning that it reaches the 80% of the upper bound on the optimum objective-function value). We can also see that the quality of the solution increases as a function of α showing that our algorithm takes full advantage of the overlap between the subgraphs. This is not the case for one dataset only ($web - Google$), however, we observe that the results are already very good for this dataset when $\alpha = 0.1$, making it harder to improve upon such a solution. We also recall that our upper bound might be loose and that we might have computed an optimum solution for such a dataset.

Next, we evaluate our algorithm MinAndRemove against NaiveGreedy, when $k = 10$. Table 4 shows the ratio between the total density of the subgraphs found by our algorithm and those of NaiveGreedy. We can see that in most cases MinAndRemove yields a solution that is a factor of 1.5 larger than that of MinAndRemove, and always at least 10% denser. We expect that the advantage of MinAndRemove against NaiveGreedy would be even more remarkable for larger values of k. Table 5 shows the total running time of our algorithm, which is always at most 3.2 hours, while in many cases is as less as 30 mins. We recall that instead the basic LP-based approach by Charikar [9] could not terminate after 16 hours of computation on any of the selected datasets. On the other hand, as expected, NaiveGreedy is faster than our method. However, NaiveGreedy does not ensure optimality in finding the densest subgraph at each step, and this results in consistently less dense solutions.

In Table 6, we set $\alpha = 0.3$ and we measure the ratio between the density of MinAndRemove and an upper bound to any optimum solution as a function of k. We can see that when k is at most 4 our solution is very close to an optimum solution for (k, α)-DSLO (up to a factor of 0.9). For larger values of k, our solution is still within a factor of 1/2 of an optimum solution or better. This might depend on the fact that our upper bound becomes loose when k is large.

We then evaluate the impact of computing at each step minimal densest subgraphs in MinAndRemove, as opposed to computing densest subgraphs. We perform the following experiment. Starting from the input graph, we remove at each step minimal densest subgraphs until the current graph is left with no edges. We then perform a similar experiment where at each step (possibly non-minimal) densest subgraphs are removed from the current graph. Our experiments show (which are omitted for lack of space) that in the former case we gain a factor of 1% (on average) in the total density, which is significant given that MinAndRemove might deliver near-optimal solutions. We also observe that all our datasets contain at most one densest subgraph. This fact could not be verified prior to our work.

Our experimental evaluation shows that MinAndRemove can handle large graphs containing up to more than 10 million edges within 3 hours or less, while delivering near-optimal solutions for our problem. For even larger graphs we resort to our fast heuristic which is evaluated on graphs

[1]Sources: snap.stanford.edu , konect.uni-koblenz.de, law.di.unimi.it/datasets.php

$k = 10$	$\alpha = 0.1$	$\alpha = 0.2$	$\alpha = 0.3$	$\alpha = 0.4$	$\alpha = 0.5$
web-Stanford	.717	.738	.767	.790	.816
com-Youtube	.480	.521	.518	.613	.623
web-Google	.808	.808	.808	.808	.808
Youtube-growth	.440	.467	.538	.593	.579
As-Skitter	.585	.597	.599	.625	.647

Table 3: Ratio between the density of MinAndRemove and our upper bound

$k = 10$	$\alpha = 0.1$	$\alpha = 0.2$	$\alpha = 0.3$	$\alpha = 0.4$	$\alpha = 0.5$
web-Stanford	1.469	1.512	1.570	1.617	1.671
com-Youtube	1.192	1.293	1.287	1.522	1.547
web-Google	1.595	1.595	1.595	1.595	1.595
Youtube-growth	1.2	1.271	1.467	1.617	1.578
As-Skitter	1.125	1.147	1.151	1.202	1.244

Table 4: Ratio between the density of MinAndRemove and NaiveGreedy

$k = 10$	$\alpha = 0.1$	$\alpha = 0.2$	$\alpha = 0.3$	$\alpha = 0.4$	$\alpha = 0.5$
web-Stanford	0.3h	0.21h	0.21h	0.23h	0.21h
com-Youtube	0.54h	0.54h	0.63h	0.55h	0.47h
web-Google	2.15h	2.31h	2.31h	2.12h	2.73h
Youtube-growth	1.5h	1.74h	2.19h	1.8h	3.13h
As-Skitter	1.29h	1.47h	2.85h	2.53h	1.78h

Table 5: Running time when varying α for MinAndRemove

$\alpha = 0.3$	$k = 2$	$k = 4$	$k = 6$	$k = 8$	$k = 10$
web-Stanford	.991	.914	.858	.808	.767
com-Youtube	.840	.744	.638	.570	.518
web-Google	.991	.915	.863	.836	.808
Youtube-growth	.845	.738	.664	.593	.538
As-Skitter	.914	.783	.693	.641	.599

Table 6: Ratio between the density of MinAndRemove and our upper bound

containing up to more than 100 million edges. Similarly to the previous case, we can derive an upper bound on the optimum solution as a function of the densest subgraph found by our heuristic. Namely, let ρ_A be the density of the densest subgraph found by FASTDSLO (which we recall is a 2-approximation for the densest subgraph problem). Then, $2k \cdot \rho_A$ gives an upper bound to any optimum solution for (k, α)-DSLO.

In Table 7, we set $k = 10$ while we measure the ratio between the density of FASTDSLO and an upper bound to any optimum solution, as a function of α. Although our heuristic turns out to be less accurate than MINANDREMOVE it delivers solutions with an approximation factor of around 0.2 or more, while it can handle very large graphs with more than 100 million edges within a few hours. We also observe that our upper bound might be even looser in this case, as it is based on an approximation of the density of a densest subgraph. Table 8 show the running time of FASTDSLO when $k = 10$ and α varies between 0.1 and 0.5. We can observe that the running time is around half an hour for the smaller datasets and does not exceed 2.3 hours on the largest dataset (Orkut).

6. CONCLUSIONS

This paper studies the problem of finding at most k subgraphs from a large graph given in input such that the total density be maximized, while satisfying a constraint on the pairwise Jaccard coefficient between the subgraphs. Although very natural, this variant of the densest subgraph problem has been surprisingly neglected so far.

After showing the NP-hardness of this problem (even when the subgraphs are disjoint), we develop an algorithm that computes an optimum solution for our problem in the case when there are k disjoint densest subgraphs in the input graph. Moreover, our experimental evaluation on large real-world graphs shows that our algorithm delivers near-optimal solutions, in that, they are very close to an upper bound on any optimum solution.

We introduce the concept of minimality of densest subgraphs and develop efficient algorithms for finding minimal densest subgraphs, which play an important role in solving our main problem. It turns out that our algorithm for finding minimal densest subgraphs is the fastest known algorithm for the exact computation of a densest subgraph, as shown by our experimental evaluation. We presented an efficient heuristic for our problem which, albeit less accurate, can handle graphs containing up to 100 million edges.

We will devote our future investigation to devise even more scalable algorithms and to adapt our algorithm into a dynamic environment, where edges might be added to the current graph or removed. Another interesting direction is to determine whether finding minimal densest subgraphs can

$k = 10$	$\alpha = 0.1$	$\alpha = 0.2$	$\alpha = 0.3$	$\alpha = 0.4$	$\alpha = 0.5$
LiveJournal	.244	.245	.251	.285	.276
Hollywood-2009	.187	.190	.199	.210	.231
Orkut	.187	.200	.218	.249	.271

Table 7: Ratio between the density of FastDSLO and our upper bound

$k = 10$	$\alpha = 0.1$	$\alpha = 0.2$	$\alpha = 0.3$	$\alpha = 0.4$	$\alpha = 0.5$
LiveJournal	0.56h	0.52h	0.63h	0.54h	0.54h
Hollywood-2009	0.34h	0.3h	0.33h	0.37h	0.34h
Orkut	1.97h	2.15h	1.2h	2.16h	2.26h

Table 8: Running time of FastDSLO on very large datasets as a function of α

be a valuable tool in finding interesting patterns in social networks and other real-world graphs.

7. REFERENCES

[1] R. Andersen and K. Chellapilla. Finding dense subgraphs with size bounds. In *WAW*, 2009.

[2] A. Angel, N. Sarkas, N. Koudas, and D. Srivastava. Dense subgraph maintenance under streaming edge weight updates for real-time story identification. *PVLDB*, 5(6), 2012.

[3] A. Angel, N. Sarkas, N. Koudas, and D. Srivastava. Dense subgraph maintenance under streaming edge weight updates for real-time story identification. *PVLDB*, 5(6), 2012.

[4] Y. Asahiro, R. Hassin, and K. Iwama. Complexity of finding dense subgraphs. *Discr. Ap. Math.*, 121(1-3), 2002.

[5] Y. Asahiro, K. Iwama, H. Tamaki, and T. Tokuyama. Greedily finding a dense subgraph. *J. Algorithms*, 34(2), 2000.

[6] B. Bahmani, R. Kumar, and S. Vassilvitskii. Densest subgraph in streaming and mapreduce. *PVLDB*, 5(5), 2012.

[7] A. Bhaskara, M. Charikar, E. Chlamtac, U. Feige, and A. Vijayaraghavan. Detecting high log-densities: an $O(n^{1/4})$ approximation for densest k-subgraph. In *STOC*, pages 201–210, 2010.

[8] F. Bonchi, F. Gullo, A. Kaltenbrunner, and Y. Volkovich. Core decomposition of uncertain graphs. In *KDD*, 2014.

[9] M. Charikar. Greedy approximation algorithms for finding dense components in a graph. In K. Jansen and S. Khuller, editors, *APPROX*. Springer, 2000.

[10] J. Chen and Y. Saad. Dense subgraph extraction with application to community detection. *TKDE*, 24(7), 2012.

[11] W. Cui, Y. Xiao, H. Wang, Y. Lu, and W. Wang. Online search of overlapping communities. In *SIGMOD*, 2013.

[12] X. Du, R. Jin, L. Ding, V. E. Lee, and J. H. Thornton, Jr. Migration motif: a spatial - temporal pattern mining approach for financial markets. In *KDD*, 2009.

[13] E. Fratkin, B. T. Naughton, D. L. Brutlag, and S. Batzoglou. MotifCut: regulatory motifs finding with maximum density subgraphs. In *ISMB*, 2006.

[14] D. Gibson, R. Kumar, and A. Tomkins. Discovering large dense subgraphs in massive graphs. In *VLDB*, 2005.

[15] A. V. Goldberg. Finding a maximum density subgraph. Technical report, University of California at Berkeley, 1984.

[16] S. Khot. Ruling out PTAS for graph min-bisection, dense k-subgraph, and bipartite clique. *J. Computing*, 36(4), 2006.

[17] S. Khuller and B. Saha. On finding dense subgraphs. In *ICALP*, 2009.

[18] M. A. Langston and et al. A combinatorial approach to the analysis of differential gene expression data: The use of graph algorithms for disease prediction and screening. In *Methods of Microarray Data Analysis IV*. 2005.

[19] V. E. Lee, N. Ruan, R. Jin, and C. C. Aggarwal. A survey of algorithms for dense subgraph discovery. In *Managing and Mining Graph Data*. 2010.

[20] C. H. Papadimitriou and M. Yannakakis. Optimization, approximation, and complexity classes. *J. Comput. Syst. Sci.*, 43(3), 1991.

[21] M. Sozio and A. Gionis. The community-search problem and how to plan a successful cocktail party. In *KDD*, pages 939–948, 2010.

[22] N. Tatti and A. Gionis. Discovering nested communities. In *ECML/PKDD (2)*, 2013.

[23] C. Tsourakakis, F. Bonchi, A. Gionis, F. Gullo, and M. Tsiarli. Denser than the densest subgraph: Extracting optimal quasi-cliques with quality guarantees. In *KDD*, 2013.

[24] E. Valari, M. Kontaki, and A. N. Papadopoulos. Discovery of top-k dense subgraphs in dynamic graph collections. In *SSDBM*, 2012.

[25] N. Wang, J. Zhang, K.-L. Tan, and A. K. H. Tung. On triangulation-based dense neighborhood graph discovery. *PVLDB*, 4(2), 2010.

Modeling Website Popularity Competition in the Attention-Activity Marketplace

Bruno Ribeiro
Carnegie Mellon University
School of Computer Science
Pittsburgh, PA, USA.
ribeiro@cs.cmu.edu

Christos Faloutsos
Carnegie Mellon University
School of Computer Science
Pittsburgh, PA, USA.
christos@cs.cmu.edu

ABSTRACT

How does a new startup drive the popularity of competing websites into oblivion like Facebook famously did to MySpace? This question is of great interest to academics, technologists, and financial investors alike. In this work we exploit the singular way in which Facebook wiped out the popularity of MySpace, Hi5, Friendster, and Multiply to guide the design of a new popularity competition model. Our model provides new insights into what Nobel Laureate Herbert A. Simon called the "marketplace of attention," which we recast as the *attention-activity marketplace*. Our model design is further substantiated by user-level activity of 250,000 MySpace users obtained between 2004 and 2009. The resulting model not only accurately fits the observed Daily Active Users (DAU) of Facebook and its competitors but also predicts their fate four years into the future.

Categories and Subject Descriptors

G.3 [**Probability and Statistics**]: Time series analysis; G.1.7 [**Ordinary Differential Equations**]: Convergence and stability

Keywords

Online Social Network Competition Forecast; Market of Attention; Non-equilibrium Statistical Physics

1. INTRODUCTION

Membership-based websites such as Facebook are a proven success in what the late Nobel Laureate Herbert A. Simon called "the marketplace of attention." In a 1969 lecture [41] Simon observed that many information systems were designed as if information was scarce, when the problem is just the opposite: "[...] in an information-rich world, the wealth of information means a dearth of something else: a scarcity of whatever it is that information consumes. What information consumes is rather obvious: it consumes the attention of its recipients." In this context, Facebook, its competitors, and other analogous membership-based websites can be understood as Simon's *information processing systems* that speak more than they help us listen (digest information) [41].

By casting the website popularity competition (e.g. Facebook v.s. MySpace) into Simon's framework, note that some websites have an added complexity: user attention is converted into content through user activity, which in turn consumes the attention of other users, in what we will call an *attention-activity marketplace*. This observation inspires the following set of questions:

- Can the attention-activity marketplace help explain the death of MySpace, Hi5, Friendster and Multiply[1]?
- Was Facebook the likely reason why MySpace, Hi5, Friendster, and Multiply popularity dwindled or did they die of "natural causes", e.g., "users were bored"?
- More broadly, is it possible to model the dynamics of user attention and activity as to capture the phenomenon that drives down the popularity of well established websites (e.g. MySpace)?
- Is it possible to learn the parameters of such model using widely available Daily Active Users (DAU) time series?

Model

In this work we take a positive step toward answering the above questions. We use the puzzling way by which Facebook has interfered with the popularity of its competitors on July 2008 to put forth a set of desired model properties. One of the key desired properties is modeling user attention as a scarce resource that must be consumed by websites or other online user activities. With the captured share of attention a website engages a user in content creation (activity), which in turn captures the attention of other users. Users also have other online interests aside from the website and these interests also compete for attention (a competing website or other online activities). The popularity competition ensues when two websites fight for the attention of their concurrent users (the *concurrent adopters* of both websites). Media, marketing, and word-of-mouth adoptions complement the model as the driving forces behind membership growth.

The resulting model is a compartmental reaction-diffusion population-level model that provides DAU popularity forecasts and offers a compelling hypothesis for the popular-

[1]Section 2 provides a brief history of the Facebook, MySpace, Hi5, Friendster and Multiply websites.

WSDM'15, February 2–6, 2015, Shanghai, China.

ACM 978-1-4503-3317-7/15/02 ...$15.00.
http://dx.doi.org/10.1145/2684822.2685312.

ity competition of membership-based websites such as Facebook, MySpace, Hi5, Friendster, and Multiply. Our model is an attention-activity market generalization of our previous single website model in Ribeiro [37]. The resulting code of the algorithm is available online[2].

Agreement with Observed Data

Our modeling framework reveals interesting traits in our data. Websites almost universally have low barriers of adoption, as opposed to adoptions in consumer products such as smartphones and laptop computers that have a steep barrier to adopting multiple products. Signing up for Facebook and the like is free and reasonably effortless. The main resource consumed by these websites is our time. Not coincidentally *time* is H.A. Simon's choice of attention metric [41]. As long as we see value in spending our time at these websites – rather than somewhere else – Facebook, MySpace, Hi5, Friendster, and Multiply can co-exist without interfering with each other.

Conversely, a website that suddenly increases its attention consumption may prey on the attention of its competitors, driving them to their (popularity) death; website death can happen as a result of a negative attention-activity feedback loop (less attention→less content→less attention) that is a function of the size of the concurrent adopter population and the amount of attention (time) left to the competitor. This observation helps explain how a Facebook website change may have suddenly (July 2008) interfered with the popularity of its competitors after a long period of non-interfering co-existence (see Figure 1). The July 2008 Facebook user behavior change is documented in Viswanath et al. [47]. Section 2 offers more details about this event.

Last, and perhaps almost as importantly, our model showcases the possibility of predicting popularity trends of competing websites using the widely available DAU time series. Using training data that includes a few months-worth of DAU data after the competition for attention starts to show a clear signal in the DAU time series, our model is able to accurately forecast the popularity of two competing websites nearly five years into the future. We also show that our model principles are consistent with detailed user-level activity of 250,000 MySpace users measured between 2004 and 2009.

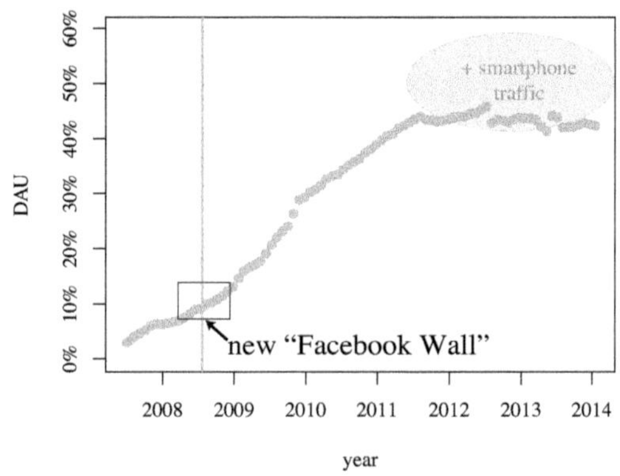

(a) Facebook DAU time series showing insignificant DAU bump near July 20, 2008.

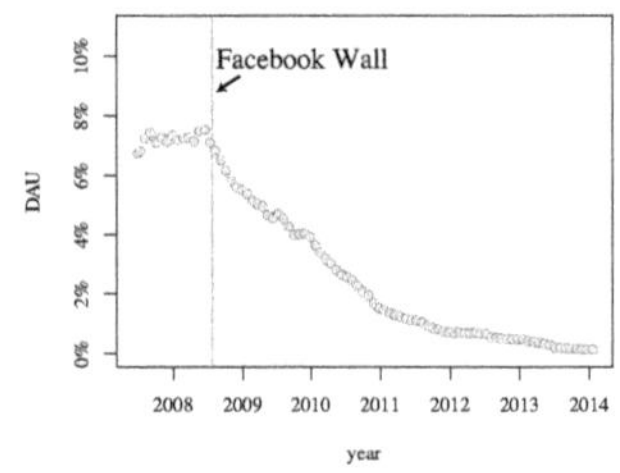

(b) MySpace DAU.

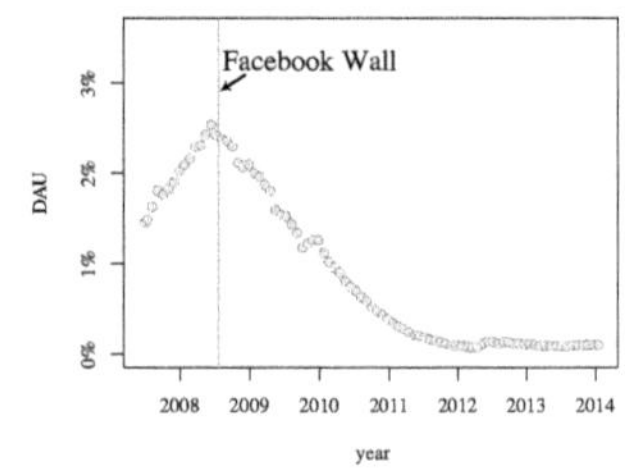

(c) Hi5 DAU.

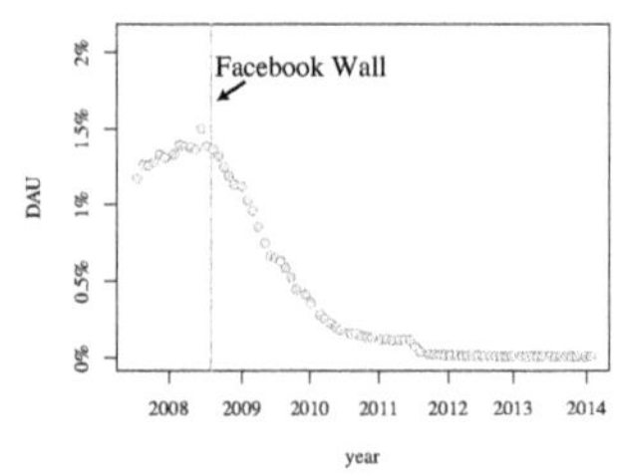

(d) Friendster DAU.

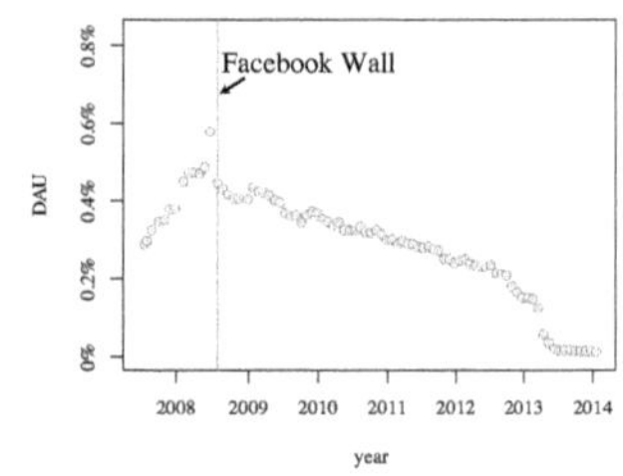

(e) Multiply DAU.

Figure 1: (Facebook's Popularity Competition) DAU/AIP of Facebook, MySpace, Hi5, Friendester, and Multiply websites from June 2007 to February 2014. Gray vertical lines show the time of the introduction of the "new Facebook".

Outline

The outline of this work is as follows. Section 2 introduces the websites and datasets used in this study and presents key DAU patterns in the Facebook, MySpace, Hi5, Friendster and Multiply DAU data. These patterns are used to inform a set of desired model properties that are used to guide the development of our model. Section 3 presents an overview of the related work. Section 4 introduces our model. Section 6 fits the model parameters to the data and uses the fitted model to predict the DAU years into the future. Finally, Section 7 presents our conclusions and future work.

2. DESIRED MODEL PROPERTIES

In what follows we draw key findings from our datasets and the existing literature to inform our model design through a set of required model properties. The next section, Section 3, contrasts the existing literature through the lenses of these desired model properties.

2.1 Datasets

In this work we use two complementary sources of data. The first datasets are provided by Amazon's Alexa web analytics company totaling 32 years of DAU data. The DAU time series is measured from June 2007 to January 2014 as a fraction of the total Active Internet Population (AIP) of each day. We note in passing that Alexa's DAU/AIP measurements of Facebook and other websites may have a **strong U.S. and Canada bias**. A good argument for using the DAU/AIP instead of the raw DAU value is that the DAU/AIP ameliorates seasonal effects such as school breaks and holidays. But in order to simplify our notation, throughout this work we use DAU to refer to the quantity DAU/AIP. As standard practice we smooth out the DAU outliers using a moving median with a 31-day DAU interval

[2] http://www.cs.cmu.edu/~ribeiro/Ribeiro_F_AttComp.zip

centered around each day. Our second dataset records the activity of 250,000 MySpace subscribers from 2004 to early 2009, collected by Ribeiro et al. [38].

Figure 1 shows the DAU time series of Facebook, MySpace, Hi5, Friendester, and Multiply. It is important to note that Alexa's datasets do not include smartphone traffic. Even without Facebook's smartphone data its usage reaches an impressive 45% of the AIP. According to Facebook's own (unverifiable) records, adding smartphone-only users takes the DAU to 60% of the U.S. and Canada AIP [14], an extra 15% DAU of what is reported by Alexa. Facebook's 60% DAU is reported to have remained stable in the last couple of years [14]. We are interested in the first years of the competition between Facebook, MySpace, Hi5, Friendester, and Multiply, a time when smartphone-only usage was likely small. *Thus, the DAU omission of smartphone traffic should not affect our analysis.* However, as a reference for our predictions, we include a circle in Figure 1(a) to represent the uncertainty that Facebook's smartphone-only DAU adds to our data. In what follows we provide a brief overview of the websites analyzed in this work:

- **myspace.com:** MySpace was founded in 2003 and from 2005 until early 2008 MySpace was the most visited social networking website in the world. In June 2006 MySpace surpassed Google as the most visited website in the United States. But by April 2008 Facebook usage overtook MySpace [13].
- **facebook.com:** Facebook was founded on February 4, 2004. It was initially limited to students at various other universities but soon it was opened to any individual older than 13. Facebook is the largest online social network in the world today. Recently its IPO raised $16 billion, making it the third largest in U.S. history [13].
- **hi5.com:** Founded in 2003, Hi5 is an online social network where users can share photos and play games. Today, social games, virtual goods, and other premium content monetizes the website [13].
- **friendster.com:** Friendster launched in 2002 as one of the first social networking sites. The service allowed users to communicate with other members, share online content and media, discover new events, brands, and hobbies. The site, at its peak, reached tens of millions of registered users according to CrunchBase [13].
- **multiply.com:** Multiply is a mix between an e-commerce platform and a social networking website, offering sellers a combination of e-commerce and social communications tools. The website ceased operations in May, 2013 [13].

2.2 Desired Model Properties

In what follows we use our data together with other measurements reported in the literature to suggest key properties that we use as guiding principles of our model of website popularity competition.

2.2.1 Attention-Activity Feedback Mechanism

Attention is a scarce resource that must be consumed by websites. With the captured share of attention a website engages users into content creation, which in turn further captures the attention of other users. Users also have other interests apart from the website that also compete for their attention. Our previous success in modeling the DAU times series through the attention-seeking interaction between users of successful and unsuccessful membership-based websites in Ribeiro [37] showcases the value of this property in popularity models. And indeed, recent results coming out of Facebook [2] indicate that the activity of our friends on Facebook incites us to login and become active which, in turn, incites our friends to either become active or stay active.

The attention-activity feedback mechanism may also come about due to the marginal increase in website utility as it gains more active users, an effect known as *network effect* or *network externality* discussed at length in Farrell and Klemperer [15]. There are many types of network effect, but the most widely used effect in its purest form can be described in the following *path-dependent cumulative return* rule (see Arthur [1] for more details): higher DAU → more advertisement revenue → better website features → less inactive users (increased DAU).

Extrapolating the above observations to all online social interactions (email, chat, OSN, blog activity) informs the first requirement of our model:

> *The popularity of a website should be modeled by an attention-activity feedback mechanism between all user activities, both inside and outside the website of interest.*

2.2.2 Concurrent Adoptions

A key factor in modeling popularity competition lies in the interactions of concurrent adopters, users that have accounts in both competing websites. The size of concurrent adopter population may be affected by factors that prevent concurrent adoptions, as follows: Once an individual joins website a she will be less interested in joining other competing websites, either due to the *network effect* (e.g., her friends are all in a), adoption cost (e.g., her "things" are all in a), or because her "product needs" are already fulfilled by a (e.g., why join two RSS news aggregators?). Henceforth, we refer to this effect as the *inertia* effect, a force that (at least initially) opposes concurrent adoptions. The *inertia* effect is one of the main arguments in favor of network effect [4,15,17,21,25,30,33,34,42,43,50] and threshold [20,40] adoption models.

However, as it is often the case in social studies, the *opposite* explanation seems as plausible: website adopters – specially the ones that do not adopt the "leading" website as with Hi5 and Google+ adopters – are more likely to be "technology enthusiasts" than the average Internet user and, thus, also more likely to join multiple websites. The case exists for the existence of concurrent adoptions in the wild, as documented by Goga et al. [19]. We refer to this effect as the *momentum* effect, where a user adopting a website signals a higher-than-average likelihood of her adopting its competitor.

In real world scenarios the above opposing forces likely co-exist in a population-level sense through distinct users.

> *A model of popularity competition should include a tunable parameter that covers a large spectrum of net population-level effects of concurrent adoptions, from strong inertia to strong momentum.*

Model	Model Properties				
	Competition	Attention-Activity Feedback	Attention Sharing	Concurrent Adoptions	Disjoint Interfering Adopters
Proposed Model	✓	✓	✓	✓	✓
Ribeiro [37]	-	✓	-	-	-
Beutel et al. [6]	✓	-	-	✓	-
Viswanath et al. [47]	✓	-	-	✓	-
Cauwels and Sornette [8]	-	-	-	-	-
Network Effect Adoptions	✓	-	-	-	-
Diffusion of Innovation	✓	-	-	✓	-
Threshold Adoption	✓	-	-	-	-

Table 1: Model properties matrix

2.2.3 Non-interfering to Sudden DAU Interference

In Figure 1 we observe a sudden synchronous drop in the popularity of MySpace, Hi5, Friendster, and Multiply by July 2008. The date coincides with the observation of a significant change in Facebook's user behavior [47]. Analyzing the activity of 60,000 Facebook users between September 2006 and January 2009, Viswanath et al. [47] observed only one significant Facebook user activity change starting in July 20th of 2008, which Viswanath et al. points out that coincides with the time that Facebook introduced the beta-test of its "new Facebook" design [47].

Indeed, in July 20, 2008 Facebook introduced the "new Facebook Wall" with a radically different content-pushing (*news feed*) interface, offered only to "selected users" [32]. By September 2008 these "selected users" already amounted to 30 million [23]. The sudden appearance of this new feature – which could have been disproportionally adopted by "tech enthusiasts" concurrent adopters – only marginally affects Facebook's DAU (the inset in Figure 1(a) shows an insignificant DAU bump) while it shows a noticeable and seemly lasting impact on MySpace, Hi5, Friendster, and Multiply DAU time series.

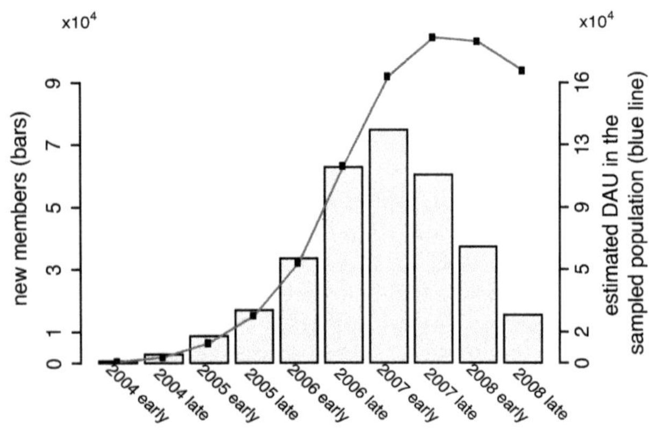

Figure 2: MySpace growth × activity. Number of observed new users (bars) and active users (line) per semester from 2004 to 2008. Note the bell shape in the green bars, a characteristic of adoption saturations (see Rogers [39]).

The attention-activity marketplace provides an easy way to assess such sudden changes. Facebook's growth is accompanied by a growing number of MySpace, Hi5, Friendster, and Multiply adopters that become concurrent adopters. Figure 1 shows that the growing concurrent adopter base does not interfere with MySpace, Hi5, Friendster, and Multiply DAU time series. This happens because Facebook's attention share does not interfere with concurrent adopter attention to its competitors. After July 2008 concurrent adopters find themselves spending more time on Facebook, time now taken out of the budget of attention of Facebook's competitors. A significant enough reduction in attention from concurrent adopters creates a critical mass that affects content creation on these competitors, reducing the attention and content creation (activity) of other users, which in turn further reduces the attention level of concurrent adopters; if this negative attention-activity feedback crosses a particular threshold, the negative feedback loop drives the website to its death. The above observation prompts the following model property:

> *Below a given attention budget, a website may consume extra attention from its concurrent adopters without interfering with its competitors. Further attention gains come at the expense of its competitors.*

2.2.4 Disjoint Interfering Adopters

Recent reports indicate that today Facebook user base (penetration) reaches 69% of the U.S. Internet population [49]. In contrast, MySpace, even without Facebook's competition, would in all likelihood never have reached this success. By mid 2007 – when Facebook's DAU was at a mere 3% – MySpace's DAU was already stable and new adoptions in clear decline showing signs of saturation (for MySpace adoptions see green bars in Figure 2; for the characteristics of adoption saturation see Rogers [39]).

This saturation is unlikely to be due to MySpace's competition for users with Facebook. The 2007 "drop-out" (hazard) rates of MySpace's new adopters were identical to that of 2006 as shown by the Kepler-Meier hazard rate estimates in Figure 3. The use of the Kepler-Meier estimator is needed as our MySpace user activity data is right censored (collection stopped by January 2009). It is only by 2008 that new adopters show different hazard rates for MySpace users signifying that these adopters were in average more committed to MySpace than 2006 and 2007 new adopters. Thus,

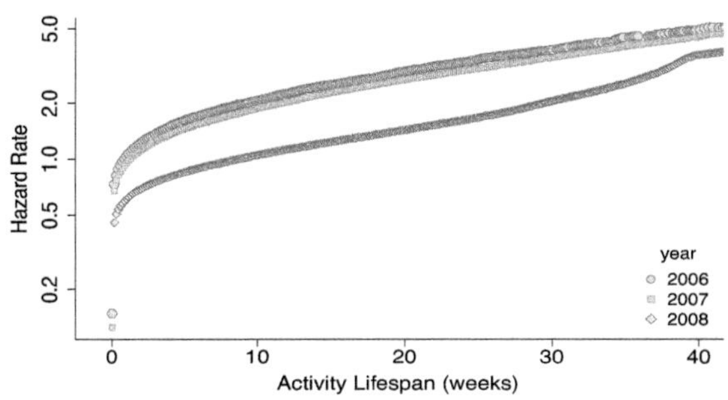

Figure 3: MySpace hazard rate estimates for new subscribers starting in 2006, 2007 and 2008, respectively. Estimates from their first year of activity.

it is unlikely that even if MySpace was allowed to take its course without any competition it would not have reached Facebook's 69% U.S. penetration. The same probably can be said about Hi5, Friendster, and Multiply although we do not have user-level data for these websites. The reason behind the opposition to adopt a website – whether by principle, lack of features of broad appeal, or other factors – are transparent to the model. It is only important to model that such opposition exists.

It is as important, however, to note that a user only interested in one website (say, Facebook) may still indirectly affect the DAU of that website's competitors (say, MySpace and Hi5). To illustrate, consider Facebook users that are "opposed" to joining MySpace. The activity of these users help create content on Facebook, which in turn attracts the attention of concurrent adopters. Thus, the activity of "Facebook-only" users can indirectly affect the activity of "MySpace" users.

> *Hence, a model of popularity competition should include disjoint populations of adopters that, however, affect each other through the attention and activity of concurrent adopters.*

3. RELATED WORK

Adoption models describe phenomena as diverse individuals deciding to adopt a new technology [5, 15, 16, 18, 25, 30, 36, 37] or individuals adopting a new health habit [9, 10]. These models have deeply influenced the study of online social network growth [3, 9, 22, 24, 27, 28, 44]. In the literature the work that is closest to ours is that of Prakash et al. [36]. Prakash et al. models the popularity of two competing products (e.g., smartphones) using a generalization of the diffusion of innovation model (detailed below). The model in Prakash et al. does not capture users finite attention or their inertia/momentum in concurrent adoptions. Moreover, the model in Prakash et al. does not consider disjoint interfering adopters. Beutel et al. [6] extends the model of Prakash et al. to include interfering adopters. Table 1 compares the models in the literature against the desired model properties specified in Section 2.

Our model is a generalization of the our previous single-website model in Ribeiro [37], where the popularity of membership-based websites is modeled using a population-level reaction-diffusion-decay model. Our new model significantly generalizes that model by explicitly modeling user's attention, attention sharing, website competition, and disjoint adoptions in a marketplace where users must share their finite attention. Note that in our generalization we make do without the spontaneous exponential decay required in Ribeiro [37] by modeling the attention grabbing influence of other online activities.

Another work closely related to ours is that of Cauwels and Sornette [8] which focuses on describing the evolution of the Facebook DAU. Cauwels and Sornette, however, is incomplete in the sense that its time-series analysis is tailored towards Facebook's success and, thus, cannot capture DAU decays. The work of Liu et al. [31] models the popularity of applications inside online social networks such as Facebook. More generally, regarding product adoptions can be classified as: (a) Network effect adoption models (a.k.a. network externality models) [4,15,17,21,25,30,33,34,42,43,50], where individual rationality and adoption costs and utilities are modeled in a game-theoretic framework; (b) Threshold adoption models [20, 40], where an individual adopts if enough of his or her friends are adopters; (c) Diffusion of innovation models [5, 16, 18, 36], where adopters influence others to adopt through word-of-mouth; In the absence of fine-grained individual-level data these models provide demand forecasting at the aggregate (population) level; and finally (d) Adoption models from influence and network structure [3, 9, 22, 24, 26–28, 44], where an individual adoptions depends not only on whether his or her friends adopt but also on how these friends are connected among themselves. A variety of works also consider the relationship between community growth inside an online social network (OSN) websites and their network structure [3,24,27]. These studies, however, focus on (i) the growth of communities inside the OSN (not the growth of the OSN itself) and (ii) the role of network structure disregarding whether the community is alive (active) or dead (inactive). A more thorough review can be found in Ribeiro [37].

4. MODEL

Compartmental models of interacting populations have been successfully applied in mathematical biology [35] and social systems [11, 12]. Our model considers a large segmented user population that interact through catalytic reactions and media & marketing diffusions. Reaction and diffusion processes find applications in chemistry, physics, and applied mathematics [11, 12, 35, 45, 46]. *We choose to avoid stochastic models (which would allow us to give confidence intervals to our predictions) because very little is known about the stochastic behavior of the dynamics between inactive and active members of websites and between the latter and non-members.*

Our model can be described as follows. The user state is a tuple $(W_a, W_b) \in \{\emptyset U, A, I\}^2$, where W_a and W_b represent the state of the user with respect to competing websites a and b, respectively. For each website a user can be in one of four states: $\emptyset$ is a permanent state signifying that the user will never adopt the website; all remaining three states are likely transient: U: the user is willing to join but she is still unaware of the website; A: the user is an active member of the website, and finally I: the user is an inactive member of the website.

4.1 Catalytic Reactions & Marketing Diffusion

We use the following notation to mark interactions between users in distinct populations. Let $S_{(W_a,W_b)}(t) \in (0,1)$ be the fraction of the active Internet population at state $(W_a, W_b) \in \{\emptyset U, A, I\}^2$ at time t. We use the notation

$$S_{(W_a,W_b)} \xrightarrow{\upsilon \times S_{(W'_a,W'_b)}} S_{(W^\dagger_a,W^\dagger_b)}$$

to denote a population of users in state (W'_a, W'_b) acting as catalysts of users in state (W_a, W_b), inciting them to state $(W^\dagger_a, W^\dagger_b)$ in the next dt time step, with probability υdt, $\upsilon \in \mathbb{R}^+$. The above notation directly translates into the differential equations:

$$\frac{dS_{(W^\dagger_a,W^\dagger_b)}(t)}{dt} = \cdots + \upsilon S_{(W'_a,W'_b)}(t) S_{(W_a,W_b)}(t)\,,$$
$$\frac{dS_{(W_a,W_b)}(t)}{dt} = \cdots - \upsilon S_{(W'_a,W'_b)}(t) S_{(W_a,W_b)}(t)\,,$$

where "..." represents the contributions of other reactions and diffusions that flow into the same state. We also use other two important definitions: $(W_a, \star)$ represents users with state W_a on website a and any state on website b. We also use $\overline{S}_{(W_a,W_b)}(t)$ to denote the fraction of the Internet population that is not in state (W_a, W_b) at time t. **The DAU of website a is given by**

$$S_{(A,\star)}(t) = \sum_{k \in \{\emptyset,U,A,I\}} S_{(A,k)}(t)$$

and website's b DAU is

$$S_{(\star,A)}(t) = \sum_{k \in \{\emptyset,U,A,I\}} S_{(k,A)}(t).$$

4.1.1 *Disjoint Population Dynamics*

The equations describing the dynamics of users of website a that will never join website b are as follows (a symmetric set of equations model website b users that will never join website a). The first **reaction**

$$S_{(U,\emptyset)} \xrightarrow{\gamma_a S_{(A,\star)}} S_{(A,\emptyset)} \quad \{\textsf{word-of-mouth}\}$$

describes the catalytic reaction at rate $\gamma_a S_{(A,\star)}$ that happens when an active member of website a influences a unaware users $(U, \emptyset)$ to join website a, which can happen either through word-of-mouth or because of increased utility (e.g., *network effects*), two widely known phenomena in the specialized literature [5, 15, 39]. Unaware users can also join website a through media & marketing campaign **diffusions**

$$S_{(U,\emptyset)} \xrightarrow{\lambda_a} S_{(A,\emptyset)} \quad \{\textsf{marketing}\}\,.$$

The remaining catalytic **reactions** are

$$S_{(I,\emptyset)} \xrightarrow{\alpha_a S_{(A,\star)}} S_{(A,\emptyset)} \quad \{\textsf{website activity}\}\,,$$

describing the population-level influence that the content created by active users of website a exert on a's inactive users, prodding them into activity (for more details on these dynamics see Ribeiro [37]); and finally

$$S_{(A,\emptyset)} \xrightarrow{\beta_a \overline{S}_{(A,\star)}} S_{(I,\emptyset)} \quad \{\textsf{external activity}\}\,,$$

modeling the influence of people doing things other than spending time on website a exert on website a users to also do something else.

4.1.2 *Joint Unaware Population Dynamics*

We now apply the same mechanisms used above to describe the dynamics of website a users that are willing to join website b but are still unaware of website b. In what follows we only present website a's equations; the symmetric corresponding set of equations should be used to describe the dynamics from website's b point of view. Users unaware of website a join through word-of-mouth and media & marketing **diffusions**:

$$S_{(U,U)} \xrightarrow{\lambda_a} S_{(A,U)} \quad \{\textsf{marketing}\}\,,$$
$$S_{(U,U)} \xrightarrow{\gamma_a S_{(A,\star)}} S_{(A,U)} \quad \{\textsf{word-of-mouth}\}\,.$$

The forces that users on website a and people outside website a exert on each other manifest in the following catalytic **reactions**:

$$S_{(I,U)} \xrightarrow{\alpha_a S_{(A,\star)}} S_{(A,U)} \quad \{\textsf{website activity}\}\,,$$
$$S_{(A,U)} \xrightarrow{\beta_a \overline{S}_{(A,\star)}} S_{(I,U)} \quad \{\textsf{external activity}\}\,.$$

Up until now websites a and b do not interfere with each other. In what follows we consider the dynamic of concurrent adopters. But first users must become concurrent adopters. A user of website a becomes a concurrent adopter of website b through the following catalytic **reactions** and **diffusions**:

$$S_{(A,U)} \xrightarrow{\zeta_a \lambda_b} S_{(A,A)} \quad \{\textsf{marketing+inertia|momentum}\}\,,$$
$$S_{(A,U)} \xrightarrow{\zeta_a \gamma_b S_{(\star,A)}} S_{(A,A)} \; \{\textsf{word-of-mouth+inertia|momentum}\}\,,$$
$$S_{(I,U)} \xrightarrow{\zeta_a \lambda_b} S_{(I,A)} \quad \{\textsf{marketing+inertia|momentum}\}\,,$$
$$S_{(I,U)} \xrightarrow{\zeta_a \gamma_b S_{(\star,A)}} S_{(I,A)} \; \{\textsf{word-of-mouth+inertia|momentum}\}\,,$$

where $\zeta_a \in \mathbb{R}^+$ is a parameter that covers the spectrum of net population-level effects from **inertia** for $\zeta_a < 1$ to **momentum** for $\zeta_a > 1$. In order to reduce the model complexity and also model the relative interest generated by the websites over time, we can further reduce the parameter space of our model $\zeta_a(t) = \zeta S_{(A,\star)}(t)/(S_{(A,\star)}(t) + S_{(\star,A)}(t))$ and $\zeta_b = \zeta S_{(\star,A)}(t)/(S_{(A,\star)}(t)+S_{(\star,A)}(t))$, where $\zeta \in \mathbb{R}^+$. In what follows we cover the dynamics of concurrent adopters.

4.1.3 *Concurrent Adopters Dynamics*

In our current attention-activity marketplace model concurrent adopters do not interfere with each other's inactive→active dynamics. This is because spending more time (attention) on website a is assumed not to make the activity of other users (say, on website b) seem less interesting. Using the fact that Facebook suffered nearly no lasting DAU effect around the July 2008 website redesign as a guiding principle (as shown by the tiny DAU bump in the inset of Figure 1(a)), we will assume that the extra time spent on website a does not increase the user activity (attention-grabbing activity) rate α_a, that is, α_a remains unchanged in the following catalytic **reactions**:

$$S_{(I,A)} \xrightarrow{\alpha_a S_{(A,\star)}} S_{(A,A)} \quad \{\text{website } a \text{ activity}\},$$

$$S_{(A,I)} \xrightarrow{\alpha_b S_{(\star,A)}} S_{(A,A)} \quad \{\text{website } b \text{ activity}\},$$

$$S_{(I,I)} \xrightarrow{\alpha_a S_{(A,\star)}} S_{(A,I)} \quad \{\text{website } a \text{ activity}\},$$

$$S_{(I,I)} \xrightarrow{\alpha_b S_{(\star,A)}} S_{(I,A)} \quad \{\text{website } b \text{ activity}\}.$$

Interestingly, according to our framework an increase in α_a happens only when a new "user activity" feature is added, which our model predicts will cause an abrupt permanent change in the DAU slope. For instance, in February 2009 Facebook introduced the "Like" feature [48] and, indeed, in Figure 1(a) we observe a small but sustainable sharp jump in the DAU time series. Similarly, in September 2009 Facebook introduced the "tagging" feature [48] and, again, we observe another DAU sustainable sharp jump followed by a slope change. In these scenarios α_a becomes $\alpha_a(t)$, a right-continuous step function that sharply changes after a new "user activity" feature is added. In order to keep model complexity down in our experiments and because these unpredictable changes are not of interest to out forecast, we consider α_a as a constant in the results presented in Section 6.

Attention Sharing of Concurrent Adopters.

In what follows we model the attention sharing behavior of users. In the attention-activity marketplace the concurrent adopters are responsible for driving otherwise self-sustaining websites (see Ribeiro [37] for a precise definition of website self-sustainability) to their "unnatural" death. In our model the average time a user spends on the website is latent, as we are modeling the DAU. However, we can model its effect on the parameters of our model. Let B be the average time budget of time that a user is willing to spend at online social interactions. Let B_a, B_b, and B_o be the times that the user spends at websites a, b, and at other activities o s.t. $B_o = B - B_a - B_b$. If at time t_0 B_a sharply increases byΔ_a and B_o sharply decreases byΔ_a then B_b remains constant. In this scenario the DAU of website b remains unchanged and websites a and b do not interfere with each other.

However, if the sharp increase in B_a byΔ_a is met with a decreaseΔ_b in B_b, i.e., users are not willing to further compromise B_o, then β_b also abruptly changes to follow the abrupt change in B_b as $\beta_b(1+\Delta_b/B_b)$. Define $\eta_b' := \Delta_b/B_b$; using the Heaviside step function, $H(t_0)$, at time t_0 yields the catalytic **reactions** that model the attention sharing behavior of concurrent adopters:

$$S_{(A,A)} \xrightarrow{\beta_a \overline{S}_{(A,\star)}} S_{(I,A)} \quad \{\text{external activity}\},$$

$$S_{(A,I)} \xrightarrow{\beta_a \overline{S}_{(A,\star)}} S_{(I,I)} \quad \{\text{external activity}\},$$

$$S_{(A,A)} \xrightarrow{(1+H(t_0)\eta_b)\beta_b \overline{S}_{(\star,A)}} S_{(A,I)} \quad \{\text{external activity}\},$$

$$S_{(I,A)} \xrightarrow{(1+H(t_0)\eta_b)\beta_b \overline{S}_{(A,\star)}} S_{(I,I)} \quad \{\text{external activity}\}.$$

5. DAU MODEL FIT

In this section we briefly introduce the challenges of learning the parameters of our model from the DAU data. The DAU time series only provides information about $S_{(A,\star)}$ and $S_{(\star,A)}$. The parameters introduced in Section 4.1 need to be estimated together with the population compartment fractions. The latter is what mathematical biologists call the *carrying capacity* of each of our four compartments, represented by the population fractions: (1) users "opposed" to both websites a and b: $C_{00} := S_{(\emptyset,\emptyset)}$; (2) the users opposed to website b: $C_{10} := \sum_{k\in\{U,A,I\}} S_{(k,\emptyset)}$; (3) users opposed to website a: $C_{01} := \sum_{k\in\{U,A,I\}} S_{(\emptyset,k)}$; and (4) the fraction of concurrent adopters

$$C_{11} := \sum_{k_a\in\{U,A,I\}} \sum_{k_b\in\{U,A,I\}} S_{(k_a,k_b)},$$

such that $C_{00} + C_{10} + C_{01} + C_{11} = 1$.

Note that because the DAU time series starts June 18, 2007 and not when the websites were created, we also need to parametrize the unobservable quantities $S_{(I,\star)}(t_{-1})$ and $S_{(\star,I)}(t_{-1})$, where t_{-1} ="June 18, 2007". For the remaining quantities that need to be initialized with values greater than zero due to the t_{-1} start, e.g., $S_{(A,A)}(t_{-1})$, we use independence assumptions, e.g., $S_{(A,A)}(t_{-1}) = S_{(A,\star)}(t_{-1})S_{(\star,A)}(t_{-1})$. We fit the model parameters to the DAU data using the Levenberg-Marquardt algorithm [29]. Our results in Section 6 show the model fit using the first two years of DAU data to train the model, the following four months for model selection, and the remaining years as holdout data to evaluate the model predictions.

The Levenberg-Marquardt algorithm only finds a locally optimal solution starting from an initial parameter guess. Hence, the initial guess may significantly influence the output of the algorithm. Due to the large number of parameters of our model we run the Levenberg-Marquardt algorithm with multiple initial parameter guesses, choosing the fitted parameters that best fit our model selection data. In order further reduce the number of parameters to be learned, we tried the options of learning C_{11} or setting $C_{11} = \min(C_{10}, C_{01})$. While these two options give similar results, the option C_{11} requires at least ten times the number of initializations and, in the end, $C_{11} = \min(C_{10}, C_{01})$ in all examples we tried. Therefore, in the scenarios presented in Section 6 we set $C_{11} = \min(C_{10}, C_{01})$ to speed up computations.

6. RESULTS

In this section we briefly introduce our results. In all of our results an extra four months of DAU data is used to select the best parameter fit that does not overfit the data (model selection phase). The fitted models and their predictions show great agreement with the data. But the learned parameter should be interpreted carefully given that most differential equations in our model are quadratic (the ones with ζ are cubic) and the model has a multitude of parameters and latent variables. The only observable quantities (the DAUs) are the aggregates $S_{(A,\star)}$ and $S_{(\star,A)}$, the DAU data is left-censored (our DAU time series starts mid 2007 when, for instance, MySpace was already four years old), only two years of DAU data are used to fit the model, and the maximum DAU of Facebook in the training set is 20%.

Nevertheless, the learned parameter seem to offer interesting insights into the popularity growth of Facebook and the death of its competitors. As expected, the model predicts *momentum* in concurrent adoptions for all websites, that is, users of MySpace, Hi5, Friendster, and Multiply were more likely than the average user to adopt Facebook.

Facebook v.s. MySpace.

Figure 4 shows the results of the model fit using the first two years (24 months) of the DAU time series of the competition between Facebook and MySpace. These 28 months (24 months for training and 4 months for the model selection phase) are shown as blue points in the plot. The gray vertical line separates the training & model selection data from the remaining 50 months (4.1 years) of DAU data used to test our predictions, shown in the plot as gray points. The model shows great agreement with the data, both in the training (blue line) and prediction (red line) phases. The inset in Figure 4 gives a closer look at the MySpace results.

The model – which was trained with Facebook's peaking at only 20% DAU – estimates the total (unaware + active + inactive) Facebook population at $C_{10} + C_{11} = 77\%$ and MySpace's population at $C_{01} + C_{11} = 22\%$; the model also estimates that Facebook user base grew largely due to word-of-mouth and that the July 20, 2008 change in Facebook reduced the average time spent on MySpace by 88%. The model fit also estimates $\zeta = 4$, that is, by 2008 MySpace users were about twice as likely to join Facebook than the average Facebook adopter (recall that $\zeta_a(t) = \zeta S_{(\star,A)}(t)/(S_{(\star,A)}(t) + S_{(A,\star)})(t))$.

In light of our findings, it seems that MySpace's documented "white flight" and "teen disengagement" in 2007 [7] – often anecdotally cited by the lay press as the primary reason of MySpace's death – may have had only a marginal role in MySpace's demise. While in hindsight many social causes could explain MySpace's demise, they would not explain why Hi5, Friendster, and Multiply simultaneously suffered the same effect. Moreover, by 2007 MySpace's DAU was stable – and our model predicts it would have remained stable in the absence of Facebook's change –, thus, making the "white flight" and "teen disengagement" 2007 hypothesis rather unlikely as the main cause of MySpace's death.

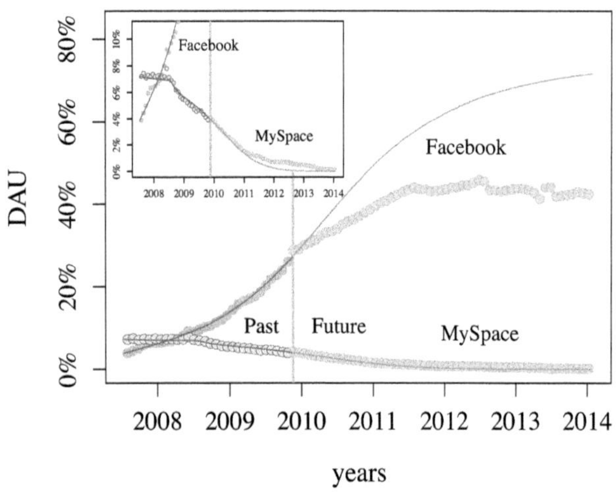

Figure 4: Model fit and predictions for the competition Facebook v.s. MySpace.

Facebook v.s. Multiply.

Figure 5 shows the results of the model fit using the first two and a half years (31 months) of the DAU time series in the competition between Facebook and Multiply. The larger training data was required to achieve a better quality fit of the parameters (harder to learn on Multiply). Unlike MySpace, Hi5, and Friendster, the model now predicts that Multiply survives Facebook's "attention raid". The model fit shows great agreement with the data up until May, 2013 when Multiply officially closed operations. The model estimates the total (unaware + active + inactive) Facebook population at $C_{10}+C_{11} = 64\%$ and Multiply's population at $C_{01} + C_{11} = 0.9\%$; the model estimates that both Facebook and Multiply user base grew largely due to word-of-mouth. The model also estimates that immediately after the July 20, 2008 event the average time spent on Multiply decreases "only" by 24%, which is why Multiply is projected to survive. The model fit also estimates $\zeta = 7.5$, that is, Multiply users were over seven times as likely to join Facebook than the average Facebook adopter.

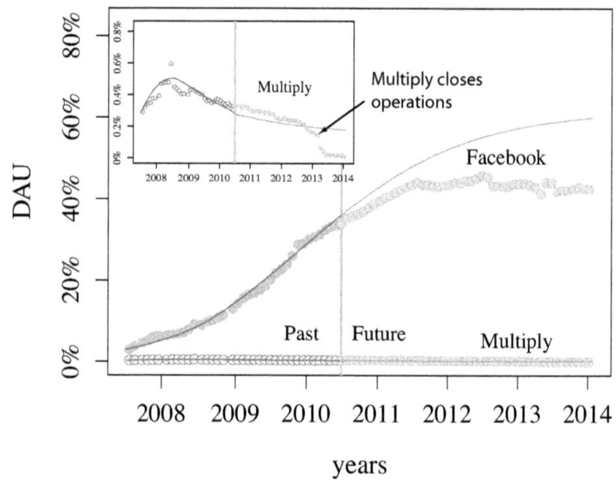

Figure 5: Model fit and predictions for the competition Facebook v.s. Multiply.

Facebook v.s. Hi5.

Figure 6 shows the results of the model fit using the first two years (24 months) of the DAU time series in the competition between Facebook and Hi5. The model fit shows great agreement with the data, blue line shows the model fit and red line shows its prediction. The model was able to capture the sharp elbow near July 20, 2008. Here the model estimates the total (unaware + active + inactive) Facebook population at $C_{10} + C_{11} = 59\%$ and Hi5's population at $C_{01} + C_{11} = 5\%$; the model estimates that Hi5 user base grew largely due to media & marketing campaigns and that Facebook's growth was through word-of-mouth; the July 20, 2008 event largely reduced the average time spent on Hi5 by 95%. The model fit also estimates $\zeta = 3.7$, that is, by 2008 Hi5 users were almost four times as likely to join Facebook than the average Facebook adopter.

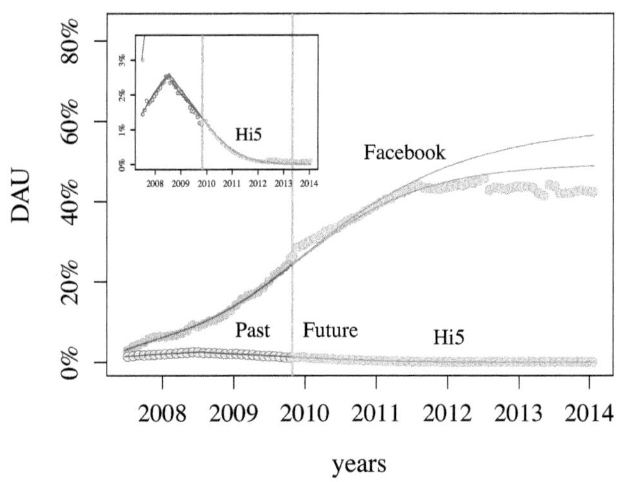

Figure 6: Model fit and predictions for the competition Facebook v.s. Hi5.

Facebook v.s. Friendster.

Figure 7 shows the results of the model fit using the first two years (24 months) of the DAU time series in the competition between Facebook and Multiply. The model shows good agreement with the data both in the fitting phase (blue line) and the prediction phase (red line). The model estimates the total (unaware + active + inactive) Facebook population at $C_{10} + C_{11} = 59\%$ and Multiply's population at $C_{01} + C_{11} = 3.6\%$; the model estimates that both Facebook and Friendster user base grew largely due to word-of-mouth. Immediately after the July 20, 2008 event the average time spent on Friendster is estimated to have decreased by nearly 99%. The model fit also estimates $\zeta = 1.8$ showing that Friendster users were almost twice as likely to join Facebook than the average Facebook adopter.

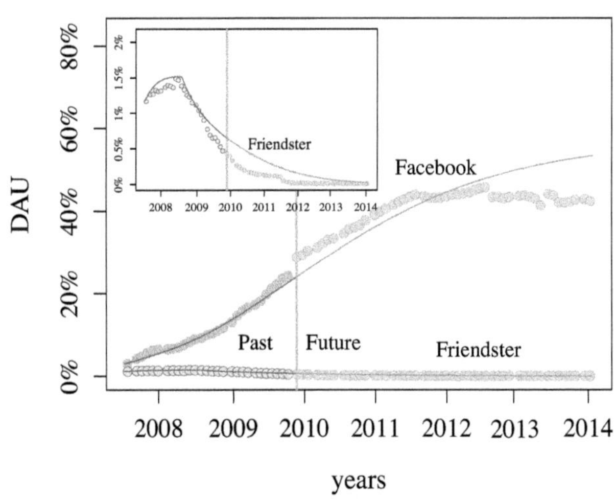

Figure 7: Model fit and predictions for the competition Facebook v.s. Friendster.

7. CONCLUSIONS

Our study sheds light onto the role of the attention-activity marketplace in the popularity (DAU time series) of membership-based websites. Making use of the unique way by which Facebook affected its competitors in July, 2008, we derive a set of modeling principles that inform our proposed attention-activity model design. Through a series of catalytic reactions that model user attention and activity interactions, together with media & market diffusions, we propose a model that well captures the popularity competition between websites. We fit the model parameters to real-world DAU time series data and show that our model not only fits well the DAU data but can also predict its future evolution.

In a 1969 lecture Herbert A. Simon warned us that information systems that help us generate more content than they help us reduce our time consuming such content would exacerbate the scarcity of attention [41]. Our work takes a positive step towards modeling such phenomenon in Internet companies, providing insights into the connections between website popularity and user attention. The model shows that two competing websites can co-exist without interfering with each other as long as users have enough attention to spare; this agrees with our data showing that before its new attention-demanding "Wall" feature Facebook did not seem to interfere with the popularity of MySpace, Hi5, Friendster, or Multiply. Conversely, the model shows that websites fiercely compete when they share a sizable population of attention-starved users, and that such population can play a central role into the negative attention feedback loop that leads to the death of a website. The model shows, for instance, that the popularity of a website with a large user base of tech savvy users – or novelty-driven teen users – can be easily preyed upon by a competing website, thus reducing the long-term viability of such websites.

Our hope is that further research in this direction will provide a better picture of the attention-activity marketplace, helping the design of information systems that do not need to overload the finite attention capacity of its users in order to survive.

8. ACKNOWLEDGMENTS

This work was supported by NSF grant CNS-1065133 and ARL Cooperative Agreement W911NF-09-2-0053. The views and conclusions contained in this document are those of the author and should not be interpreted as representing the official policies, either expressed or implied of the NSF, ARL, or the U.S. Government. The U.S. Government is authorized to reproduce and distribute reprints for Government purposes notwithstanding any copyright notation hereon.

9. REFERENCES

[1] W. B. Arthur. *Increasing Returns and Path Dependence in the Economy.* U. Michigan Press, 1994.

[2] Lars Backstrom, Eytan Bakshy, Jon M Kleinberg, Thomas M Lento, and Itamar Rosenn. Center of attention: How facebook users allocate attention across friends. *ICWSM*, 2011.

[3] Lars Backstrom, Dan Huttenlocher, Jon Kleinberg, and Xiangyang Lan. Group formation in large social networks: membership, growth, and evolution. In *SIGKDD*, pages 44–54, 2006.

[4] Venkatesh Bala and Sanjeev Goyal. A Noncooperative Model of Network Formation. *Econometrica*, 68(5):1181–1229, September 2000.

[5] Frank Bass. Comments on "A New Product Growth for Model Consumer Durables The Bass Model". *Management science*, 50(12 supplement):1833–1840, 2004.

[6] Alex Beutel, B Aditya Prakash, Roni Rosenfeld, and Christos Faloutsos. Interacting viruses in networks: can both survive? In *SIGKDD*, 2012.

[7] Danah Boyd. White flight in networked publics? how race and class shaped american teen engagement with myspace and facebook. In Lisa Nakamura, Peter Chow-White, and Alondra Nelson, editors, *Race After the Internet*, pages 203–222. Routledge, 2011.

[8] Peter Cauwels and Didier Sornette. Quis pendit ipsa pretia: Facebook valuation and diagnostic of a bubble based on nonlinear demographic dynamics. *The Journal of Portfolio Management*, 38(2):56–66, 2012.

[9] Damon Centola. The spread of behavior in an online social network experiment. *Science*, 329(5996):1194–1197, 2010.

[10] Nicholas Christakis and James Fowler. The Spread of Obesity in a Large Social Network over 32 Years. *New England Journal of Medicine*, 357(4):370–379, July 2007.

[11] Vittoria Colizza, Romualdo Pastor-Satorras, and Alessandro Vespignani. Reaction–diffusion processes and metapopulation models in heterogeneous networks. *Nature Physics*, 3(4):276–282, March 2007.

[12] Vittoria Colizza and Alessandro Vespignani. Epidemic modeling in metapopulation systems with heterogeneous coupling pattern: Theory and simulations. *Journal of Theoretical Biology*, 251(3):450–467, April 2008.

[13] Crunchbase. `http://www.crunchbase.com`.

[14] Mike Develin. Facebook engagement data `http://goo.gl/7Yk6KQ`.

[15] Joseph Farrell and Paul Klemperer. Coordination and lock-in: Competition with switching costs and network effects. *Handbook of industrial organization*, 3:1967–2072, 2007.

[16] John C. Fisher and Robert H. Pry. A simple substitution model of technological change. *Technological forecasting and social change*, 3:75–88, 1972.

[17] David Garcia, Pavlin Mavrodiev, and Frank Schweitzer. Social Resilience in Online Communities: The Autopsy of Friendster. In *COSN*, pages 39–50, 2013.

[18] Paul Geroski. Models of technology diffusion. *Research policy*, 29(4):603–625, 2000.

[19] O. Goga, H. Lei, SHK. Parthasarathi, G. Friedland, R. Sommer, and R. Teixeira. Exploiting innocuous activity for correlating users across sites. In *WWW*, 2013.

[20] Mark Granovetter. Threshold models of collective behavior. *American journal of sociology*, pages 1420–1443, 1978.

[21] Matthew O. Jackson. A survey of network formation models: stability and efficiency. *Group formation in economics: networks, clubs and coalitions. Cambridge University Press, Cambridge*, pages 11–57, 2005.

[22] Emily Jin, Michelle Girvan, and M Newman. Structure of growing social networks. *Physical Review E*, 64(4):046132, September 2001.

[23] Facebook Inc. Josh Elman. The new profile: Full rollout is coming: `http://goo.gl/wqFwlD`.

[24] Sanjay Ram Kairam, Dan J Wang, and Jure Leskovec. The life and death of online groups: Predicting group growth and longevity. In *WSDM*, pages 673–682, 2012.

[25] Michael Katz and Carl Shapiro. Network externalities, competition, and compatibility. *The American economic review*, 75(3):424–440, 1985.

[26] Ravi Kumar, Jasmine Novak, and Andrew Tomkins. Structure and Evolution of Online Social Networks. In *link.springer.com*, pages 337–357. Springer New York, New York, NY, August 2010.

[27] Jure Leskovec, Lars Backstrom, Ravi Kumar, and Andrew Tomkins. Microscopic evolution of social networks. In *SIGKDD*, pages 462–470, 2008.

[28] Jure Leskovec, Jon Kleinberg, and Christos Faloutsos. Graph evolution: Densification and shrinking diameters. *TKDD*, 1(1):2, 2007.

[29] Kenneth Levenberg. A method for the solution of certain non-linear problems in least squares. *Quarterly Journal of Applied Mathmatics*, II(2):164–168, 1944.

[30] Stan J Liebowitz and Stephen E Margolis. Network externality: An uncommon tragedy. *The Journal of Economic Perspectives*, 8(2):133–150, 1994.

[31] Han Liu, Atif Nazir, Jinoo Joung, and Chen-Nee Chuah. Modeling/predicting the evolution trend of osn-based applications. In *WWW*, 2013.

[32] Facebook Inc. Mark Slee. Check out the new facebook: `https://www.facebook.com/notes/facebook/check-out-the-new-facebook/23612952130`.

[33] M. Marsili. The rise and fall of a networked society: A formal model. *PNAS*, 101(6):1439–1442, January 2004.

[34] A. Montanari and A. Saberi. The spread of innovations in social networks. *PNAS*, 107(47):20196–20201, November 2010.

[35] James Dickson Murray. *Mathematical biology*, volume 2. springer, 2002.

[36] B Aditya Prakash, Alex Beutel, Roni Rosenfeld, and Christos Faloutsos. Winner takes all: competing viruses or ideas on fair-play networks. In *WWW*, pages 1037–1046. ACM Press, 2012.

[37] Bruno Ribeiro. Modeling and predicting the growth and death of membership-based websites. In *WWW*, 2014.

[38] Bruno Ribeiro, William Gauvin, Benyuan Liu, and Don Towsley. On myspace account spans and double pareto-like distribution of friends. In *INFOCOM NetSciCom*, pages 1–6, 2010.

[39] M. Rogers Everett. *Diffusion of innovations*. Free Press, 5th edition, 2003.

[40] Thomas C. Schelling. *Micromotives and macrobehavior*. WW Norton & Company, 2006.

[41] Herbert A. Simon. Designing Organizations for an Information-Rich World. In *H.A. Simon Lectures*, pages 37–72. Carnegie Mellon Library, 1969.

[42] Brian Skyrms and Robin Pemantle. A Dynamic Model of Social Network Formation. In *scholar.google.com*, pages 231–251. Springer Berlin Heidelberg, Berlin, Heidelberg, July 2009.

[43] Tom A B Snijders. Stochastic actorâĂŘoriented models for network change. *The Journal of Mathematical Sociology*, 21(1-2):149–172, April 1996.

[44] Johan Ugander, Lars Backstrom, Cameron Marlow, and Jon Kleinberg. Structural diversity in social contagion. *PNAS*, 109(16):5962–5966, 2012.

[45] N. G. van Kampen. Stochastic processes in physics and chemistry. *North-Holland*, 1, 1981.

[46] F. van Wijland, K. Oerding, and H. J. Hilhorst. Wilson renormalization of a reaction–diffusion process. *Physica A: Statistical Mechanics and its Applications*, 251(1-2):179–201, March 1998.

[47] Bimal Viswanath, Alan Mislove, Meeyoung Cha, and Krishna P Gummadi. On the evolution of user interaction in Facebook. In *the 2nd ACM workshop*, page 37, 2009.

[48] Wikipedia. Facebook features: `http://en.wikipedia.org/wiki/Facebook_features`.

[49] Wikipedia. Facebook: `http://en.wikipedia.org/wiki/Facebook`.

[50] H. Young. The dynamics of social innovation. *PNAS*, 108(4):21285–21291, December 2011.

Exploring the Space of Topic Coherence Measures

Michael Röder
Leipzig University
R&D, Unister GmbH
Leipzig, Germany
roeder@informatik.uni-leipzig.de

Andreas Both
R&D, Unister GmbH
Leipzig, Germany
andreas.both@unister.de

Alexander Hinneburg
Martin-Luther-University
Halle-Wittenberg, Germany
hinneburg@informatik.uni-halle.de

ABSTRACT

Quantifying the coherence of a set of statements is a long standing problem with many potential applications that has attracted researchers from different sciences. The special case of measuring coherence of topics has been recently studied to remedy the problem that topic models give no guaranty on the interpretablity of their output. Several benchmark datasets were produced that record human judgements of the interpretability of topics. We are the first to propose a framework that allows to construct existing word based coherence measures as well as new ones by combining elementary components. We conduct a systematic search of the space of coherence measures using all publicly available topic relevance data for the evaluation. Our results show that new combinations of components outperform existing measures with respect to correlation to human ratings. Finally, we outline how our results can be transferred to further applications in the context of text mining, information retrieval and the world wide web.

Categories and Subject Descriptors

[**Document representation**]: Document topic models

General Terms

Measurement

Keywords

topic evaluation; topic coherence; topic model

1. INTRODUCTION

A set of statements or facts is said to be coherent, if they support each other. Thus, a coherent fact set can be interpreted in a context that covers all or most of the facts. An example of a coherent fact set is "the game is a team sport", "the game is played with a ball", "the game demands great physical efforts". A long standing open question is how to quantify the coherence of a fact set [5]. Approaches proposed in scientific philosophy have formalized such measures as functions of joint and marginal probabilities associated with the facts. Bovens and Hartmann [5] discuss many examples that lead to a demanding set of complex properties such a measure needs to fulfill. An example is the non-monotonic behavior of coherence in case of growing fact sets. The coherence of the two fact sets "the animal is a bird" and "the animal cannot fly" can be increased by adding the fact "the animal is a penguin". The non-monotonicity becomes apparent when the coherence is lowered again by adding non-related facts [5]. The discussion of coherence measures in that community deals mainly with schemes that estimate the hanging and fitting together of the individual facts of a larger set. Examples of such schemes are (i) to compare each fact against the rest of all other fact, (ii) compare all pairs against each other, and (iii) compare disjoints subsets of facts against each other. Such theoretical work on coherence from scientific philosophy—see [7] for an overview— has potential to be adapted in computer science, e.g., coherence of word sets.

Interest into coherence measures has arisen in text mining, as unsupervised learning methods like topic models give no guarantees on the interpreteability of their output. Topic models learn topics—typically represented as sets of important words—automatically from unlabeled documents in an unsupervised way. This is an attractive method to bring structure to otherwise unstructured text data. The seminal work of [13] proposed automatic coherence measures that rate topics regarding to their understandability. The proposed measures treat words as facts. This important restriction will apply to all analyses presented in this paper. An example of such set is {*game, sport, ball, team*}, which we will use throughout the paper to illustrate the methods. Furthermore, [13] restricts coherence to be always based on comparing word pairs. Our analyses will go beyond this point.

Evaluations in [13] based on human generated topic rankings showed that measures based on word co-occurrence statistics estimated on Wikipedia outperform measures based on WordNet and similar semantic resources. Subsequent empirical works on topic coherence [12, 18, 10] proposed a number of measures based on word statistics that differ in several details: definition, normalization and aggregation of word statistics and reference corpus. In addition, a new method based on word context vectors has been proposed recently [1].

WSDM'15, February 2–6, 2015, Shanghai, China.

ACM 978-1-4503-3317-7/15/02 ...$15.00.
http://dx.doi.org/10.1145/2684822.2685324.

Looking at the two lines of research on coherence, scientific philosophy and topic modelling, we note that the contributions are mainly complementary. While the former proposed a good number of schemes for comparing facts or words, the latter proposed useful methods for estimating word probabilities and normalizing numeric comparisons. However, a systematic, empirical evaluation of the methods of both worlds and their yet unexplored combinations is still missing.

Human topic rankings serve as the gold standard for coherence evaluation. However, they are expensive to produce. There are three publicly available sources of such rankings: first, Chang et al. [6] that have been prepared by Lau et al. [10] for topic coherence evaluation, second, Aletras and Stevenson [1] and third, Rosner et al. [16]. A systematic, empirical evaluation should take all these sources into account. For this reason, we choose the concept of a framework providing an objective platform for comparing the different approaches. Following our research agenda, this will lead to completely new insights of the behavior of different algorithms with regard to the available benchmarks. Hence, it will be possible to finally evaluate the reasons for specific behavior of topic coherences on a comparable basis.

Our contributions are these: First, we propose a unifying framework that spans a configuration space of coherence definitions. Second, we exhaustively search this space for the coherence definition with the best overall correlation with respect to all available human topic ranking data. This search empirically evaluates published coherence measures as well as unpublished ones based on combinations of known approaches. Our results reveal a coherence measure based on a new combination of known approaches that approximates human ratings better than the state of the art.[1] Finally, we note that coherence measures are useful beyond topic modelling. We discuss applications to search, advertising and automatic translation.

The rest of the paper is structured as follows: In section 2, we briefly review related work. Our unifying framework is introduced in section 3. Section 4 describes data preparation and evaluation results and section 5 discusses our findings. In section 6 the runtimes of the measures ar analyzed. Section 7 explains how coherence measures can be applied beyond topic modelling. Our conclusions are stated in section 8.

2. RELATED WORK

The evaluation of topic models needs next to holdout perplexity an additional measure that can rate topics with respect to understandability and interpretability by humans [6]. Measures based on evaluation of topic model distributions can produce useful results [2, 11]. However, they are difficult to link with human generated gold standards.

Newman et al. [13] represented topics by sets of top words and asked humans to rate these sets as good, neutral or bad. Several automatic topic ranking methods that measure topic coherence are evaluated by comparison to these human ratings. The evaluated topic coherence measures take the set of N top words of a topic and sum a confirmation measure over all word pairs. A confirmation measure depends on a single pair of top words. Several confirmation measures were evaluated. The coherence based on *pointwise mutual information* (PMI) gave largest correlations with human ratings. *UCI coherence* is calculated by[2]:

$$C_{\mathrm{UCI}} = \frac{2}{N \cdot (N-1)} \sum_{i=1}^{N-1} \sum_{j=i+1}^{N} \mathrm{PMI}(w_i, w_j) \quad (1)$$

$$\mathrm{PMI}(w_i, w_j) = \log \frac{P(w_i, w_j) + \epsilon}{P(w_i) \cdot P(w_j)} \quad (2)$$

Probabilities are estimated based on word co-occurrence counts. Those counts are derived from documents that are constructed by a sliding window that moves over the Wikipedia, which is used as external reference corpus. Each window position defines such a document. For our example topic from section 1 we would calculate:

$$\begin{aligned} C_{\mathrm{UCI}} = \frac{1}{6} \cdot \big(&\mathrm{PMI}(\textit{game}, \textit{sport}) + \mathrm{PMI}(\textit{game}, \textit{ball}) \\ &+ \mathrm{PMI}(\textit{game}, \textit{team}) + \mathrm{PMI}(\textit{sport}, \textit{ball}) \\ &+ \mathrm{PMI}(\textit{sport}, \textit{team}) + \mathrm{PMI}(\textit{ball}, \textit{team})\big) \end{aligned} \quad (3)$$

Mimno et al. [12] proposed to use an asymmetrical confirmation measure between top word pairs (smoothed conditional probability). The summation of *UMass coherence* accounts for the ordering among the top words of a topic.[2]

$$C_{\mathrm{UMass}} = \frac{2}{N \cdot (N-1)} \sum_{i=2}^{N} \sum_{j=1}^{i-1} \log \frac{P(w_i, w_j) + \epsilon}{P(w_j)} \quad (4)$$

Word probabilities are estimated based on document frequencies of the original documents used for learning the topics. The calculation for our example would be:

$$\begin{aligned} C_{\mathrm{UMass}} = \frac{1}{6} \Big(&\log(P(\textit{sport}|\textit{game})) + \log(P(\textit{ball}|\textit{game})) \\ &+ \log(P(\textit{ball}|\textit{sport})) + \log(P(\textit{team}|\textit{game})) \\ &+ \log(P(\textit{team}|\textit{sport})) + \log(P(\textit{team}|\textit{ball}))\Big) \end{aligned} \quad (5)$$

Stevens et al. [18] found that both—UCI and UMass coherence—perform better if parameter ϵ is chosen to be rather small instead of $\epsilon = 1$ as in respective original publications.

Aletras and Stevenson [1] introduced topic coherence based on context vectors for every topic top word. A context vector of a word w is created using word co-occurrence counts determined using context windows that contain all words located ± 5 tokens around the ocurrences of the word w. Largest correlation to human topic coherence ratings were found when defining the elements of these vectors as *normalized PMI* (NPMI) [4]. Additionally, they showed that restricting the word co-occurrences to those words that are part of the same topic performs best (*top word space*). Thus, the j-th element of the context vector $\vec{v_i}$ of word w_i has NPMI:

$$v_{ij} = \mathrm{NPMI}(w_i, w_j)^{\gamma} = \left(\frac{\log \frac{P(w_i, w_j) + \epsilon}{P(w_i) \cdot P(w_j)}}{-\log(P(w_i, w_j) + \epsilon)} \right)^{\gamma} \quad (6)$$

[1]Data and tools for replicating our coherence calculations are available at `https://github.com/AKSW/Palmetto` .

[2]ϵ is added to avoid logarithm of zero.
C_{UCI} as well as C_{UMass} can be used with the arithmetic mean or only with the sum of the single elements, because the mean calculation doesn't influence the order of evaluated topics that have the same number of top words.

For our example topic, the vector of its top word *game* would be calculated as:

$$\vec{v}_{game} = \{\text{NPMI}(game, game)^{\gamma}, \text{NPMI}(game, sport)^{\gamma}, \text{NPMI}(game, ball)^{\gamma}, \text{NPMI}(game, team)^{\gamma}\} \tag{7}$$

An increase of γ gives higher NPMI values more weight. Confirmation measures between pairs of context vectors are vector similarities like cosine, Dice or Jaccard that are averaged over all pairs of a topics top words like in [13].

$$C_{cos} = \frac{1}{6} \cdot \big(cos(\vec{v}_{game}, \vec{v}_{sport}) + cos(\vec{v}_{game}, \vec{v}_{ball}) + cos(\vec{v}_{game}, \vec{v}_{team}) + cos(\vec{v}_{sport}, \vec{v}_{ball}) + cos(\vec{v}_{sport}, \vec{v}_{team}) + cos(\vec{v}_{ball}, \vec{v}_{team})\big) \tag{8}$$

Alternatively, topic coherence is computed as average similarity between top word context vectors and their centroid $\vec{v}_c$.

$$\vec{v}_c = \vec{v}_{game} + \vec{v}_{sport} + \vec{v}_{ball} + \vec{v}_{team} \tag{9}$$

$$C_{cen} = \frac{1}{4} \cdot \big(cos(\vec{v}_{game}, \vec{v}_c) + cos(\vec{v}_{sport}, \vec{v}_c) + cos(\vec{v}_{ball}, \vec{v}_c) + cos(\vec{v}_{team}, \vec{v}_c)\big) \tag{10}$$

Additionally, [1] showed that the UCI coherence performs better if the PMI is replaced by the NPMI.

Lau et al. [10] structured the topic evaluation in two different tasks—word intrusion and observed coherence. In the first task, an intruder word has to be identified among the top words of a topic. For the second task, topics have to be rated regarding their coherence, while ratings are compared to human ratings. Both tasks can be done for single topics or the whole topic model. [10] confirmed that the UCI coherence performs better with the NPMI.

Theoretical work on coherence of sets of statements in a broader sense are reviewed in [7]. We follow their notation but adapt presentation of measures to word coherence. Shogenji's [17] and Olsson's [14] coherences are defined as:

$$C_S = \frac{P(w_1, \ldots, w_N)}{\prod_{i=1}^{N} P(w_i)} \tag{11}$$

$$C_O = \frac{P(w_1, \ldots, w_N)}{P(w_1 \vee \ldots \vee w_N)} \tag{12}$$

The usage of these coherences for our example is straight forward:

$$C_S = \frac{P(game, sport, ball, team)}{P(game) \cdot P(sport) \cdot P(ball) \cdot P(team)} \tag{13}$$

$$C_O = \frac{P(game, sport, ball, team)}{P(game \vee sport \vee ball \vee team)} \tag{14}$$

Fitelson [8] evaluated a single word in the context of all subsets that can be constructed from the remaining words. The set of all subsets without word w_i is denoted by $S(i)$. Fitelson's coherence is defined by comparing the probability of the i-th word with every single set in $S(i)$:

$$C_F = \frac{\sum_{i=1}^{N} \sum_{j=1}^{2^{N-1}-1} m_f(w_i, S(i)_j)}{N \cdot (2^{N-1} - 1)} \tag{15}$$

$$m_f(w_i, S(i)_j) = \frac{P(W_i|S(i)_j) - P(W_i|\neg S(i)_j)}{P(W_i|S(i)_j) + P(W_i|\neg S(i)_j)} \tag{16}$$

Note that this approach takes relationships between word sets into account and goes beyond averaging confirmations between word pairs.[3]

Douven and Meijs [7] took this approach further by creating pairs of word subsets $S_i = (W', W^*)$. These pairs are tested whether the existence of the subset W^* supports the occurrence of the subset W'. This is done using several confirmation measures and has been adapted to the evaluation of topics by Rosner et al. [16]. The authors found that using larger subsets W' and W^* can lead to better performing coherence measures.

3. FRAMEWORK OF COHERENCE MEASURES

Our new unifying framework represents a coherence measure as composition of parts that can be freely combined. Hence, existing measures as well as yet unexplored measures can be constructed. The parts are grouped into dimensions that span the configuration space of coherence measures. Each dimension is characterized by a set of exchangeable components.

Coherence of a set of words measures the hanging and fitting together of single words or subsets of them. Thus, the first dimension is the kind of segmentation that is used to divide a word set into smaller pieces. These pieces are compared against each other, e.g., segmentation into word pairs. The set of different kinds of segmentation is $\mathcal{S}$. The second dimension is the confirmation measure that scores the agreement of a given pair, e.g., NPMI of two words. The set of confirmation measures is $\mathcal{M}$. Confirmation measures use word probabilities that can be computed in different ways, which forms the third dimension of the configuration space. The set of methods to estimate word probabilities is $\boldsymbol{\mathcal{P}}$. Last, the methods of how to aggregate scalar values computed by the confirmation measure forms the fourth dimension. The set of aggregation functions is Σ.

The workflow of our framework as shown in figure 1 comprises four steps. First, the word set t is segmentated into a set of pairs of word subsets S. Second, word probabilities P are computed based on a given reference corpus. Both, the set of word subsets S as well as the computed probabilities P are consumed by the confirmation measure to calculate the agreements φ of pairs of S. Last, those values are aggregated to a single coherence value c.

In summary, the framework defines a configurations space that is the cross product of the four sets $\mathcal{C} = \mathcal{S} \times \mathcal{M} \times \boldsymbol{\mathcal{P}} \times \Sigma$. In the following subsections, these four dimensions are explained in more detail.

3.1 Segmentation of word subsets

Following [7], coherence of a word set measures the degree that a subset is supported by another subset. The result of the segmentation of a given word set W is a set of pairs of subsets of W. The definition of a subset pair consists of two parts that are differently used by the following confirmation mearsures. The first part of a pair is the subset for which the support by the second part of the pair is determined. Most proposed coherence measures for topic evaluation compare pairs of single words, e.g., the UCI coherence. Every single

[3] In section 3.1, we will give an example for S_{any}^{one} which is the equivalent to the $(w_i, S(i)_j)$ pairs of Fitelson's coherence.

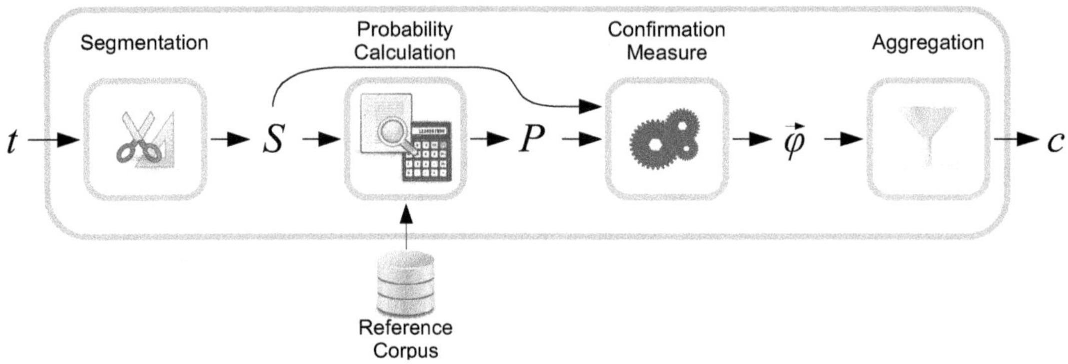

Figure 1: Overview over the unifying coherence framework—its four parts and their intermediate results.

word is paired with every other single word. Those segementations are called *one-one* and are defined as follows:

$$S^{one}_{one} = \Big\{(W', W^*)|W' = \{w_i\}; \\ W^* = \{w_j\}; w_i, w_j \in W; i \neq j\Big\} \quad (17)$$

$$S^{one}_{pre} = \Big\{(W', W^*)|W' = \{w_i\}; \\ W^* = \{w_j\}; w_i, w_j \in W; i > j\Big\} \quad (18)$$

$$S^{one}_{suc} = \Big\{(W', W^*)|W' = \{w_i\}; \\ W^* = \{w_j\}; w_i, w_j \in W; i < j\Big\} \quad (19)$$

The latter two are variations of the first one that require an ordered word set. They compare a word only to the preceding and succeeding words respectively, as done by the UMass coherence.

Douven and Meijs [7] proposed several other segmentations that have been adapted to topic evaluation by [16]. These definitions allow one or both subsets to contain more than one single word.

$$S^{one}_{all} = \Big\{(W', W^*)|W' = \{w_i\}; \\ w_i \in W; W^* = W \setminus \{w_i\}\Big\} \quad (20)$$

$$S^{one}_{any} = \Big\{(W', W^*)|W' = \{w_i\}; \\ w_i \in W; W^* \subseteq W \setminus \{w_i\}\Big\} \quad (21)$$

$$S^{any}_{any} = \Big\{(W', W^*)|W', W^* \subset W; W' \cap W^* = \emptyset\Big\} \quad (22)$$

S^{one}_{all} compares every single word to all other words of the word set. S^{one}_{any} extends S^{one}_{all} by using every subset as condition. S^{any}_{any} is another extension that compares every subset with every other disjoint subset. Figure 2 shows the different sets of subset pairs produced by applying the different segmentations to the running example.

The approach in [1] compares words to the total word set W using words context vectors. Therefore, we define another segmentation

$$S^{one}_{set} = \Big\{(W', W^*)|W' = \{w_i\}; w_i \in W; W^* = W\Big\} \quad (23)$$

Note that this segmentation does not obey the requirement $W' \cap W^* = \emptyset$ stated in [7]. Therefore, it is only used together with coherence measures based on the ideas in [1].

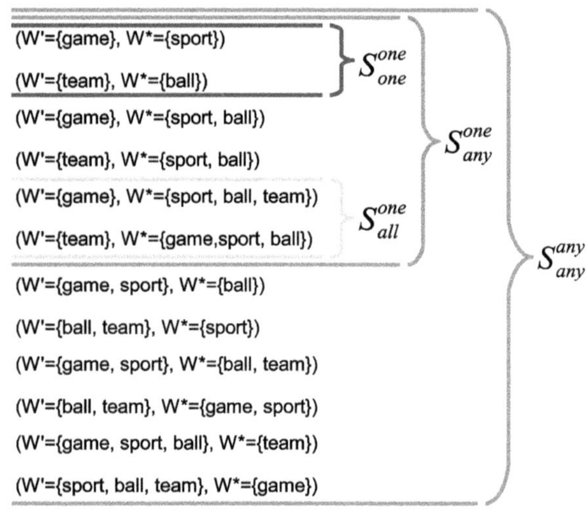

Figure 2: S^{one}_{one}, S^{one}_{all}, S^{one}_{any} and S^{any}_{any} segmentations of the word set {game, ball, sport, team} and their hierarchy.

3.2 Probability Estimation

The method of probability estimation defines the way how the probabilities are derived from the underlying data source. *Boolean document* ($\mathcal{P}_{bd}$) estimates the probability of a single word as the number of documents in which the word occurs divided by the total number of documents. In the same way, the joint probability of two words is estimated by the number of documents containing both words divided by the total number of documents. This estimation method is called boolean as the number of occurrences of words in a single document as well as distances between the occurrences are not considered. UMass coherence is based on an equivalent kind of estimation [12]. Text documents with some formatting allow simple variations, namely the *boolean paragraph* ($\mathcal{P}_{bp}$) and *boolean sentence* ($\mathcal{P}_{bs}$). These estimation methods are similar to *boolean document* except instead of documents paragraphs or sentences are used respectively.

Boolean sliding window ($\mathcal{P}_{sw}$) determines word counts using a sliding window.[4] The window moves over the documents one word token per step. Each step defines a new virtual document by copying the window content. *Boolean document* is applied to these virtual documents to compute

[4]The window size is added to the name, e.g., $\mathcal{P}_{sw(10)}$ for a sliding window of size $s = 10$.

word probabilities. Note that *boolean sliding window* captures to some degree proximity between word tokens.

3.3 Confirmation Measure

A confirmation measure takes a single pair $S_i = (W', W^*)$ of words or word subsets as well as the corresponding probabilities to compute how strong the conditioning word set W^* supports W'. This could be done either directly as proposed in [7, 12, 13] or indirectly as done in [1].

3.3.1 Direct confirmation measures

Measures to directly compute the confirmation of a single pair S_i of words or word subsets are:

$$m_d(S_i) = P(W'|W^*) - P(W') \quad (24)$$

$$m_r(S_i) = \frac{P(W', W^*)}{P(W') * P(W^*)} \quad (25)$$

$$m_{lr}(S_i) = \log \frac{P(W', W^*) + \epsilon}{P(W') * P(W^*)} \quad (26)$$

$$m_{nlr}(S_i) = \frac{m_{lr}(S_i)}{-\log(P(W', W^*) + \epsilon)} \quad (27)$$

$$m_l(S_i) = \frac{P(W'|W^*)}{P(W'|\neg W^*) + \epsilon} \quad (28)$$

$$m_{ll}(S_i) = \log \frac{P(W'|W^*) + \epsilon}{P(W'|\neg W^*) + \epsilon} \quad (29)$$

$$m_c(S_i) = \frac{P(W', W^*)}{P(W^*)} \quad (30)$$

$$m_{lc}(S_i) = \log \frac{P(W', W^*) + \epsilon}{P(W^*)} \quad (31)$$

$$m_j(S_i) = \frac{P(W', W^*)}{P(W' \vee W^*)} \quad (32)$$

$$m_{lj}(S_i) = \log \frac{P(W', W^*) + \epsilon}{P(W' \vee W^*)} \quad (33)$$

In [7], the confirmation measures m_d, m_r and m_l are called difference-, ratio- and likelihood-measure. There, log-likelihood (m_{ll}) and log-ratio measure (m_{lr}) are also defined—the last is the PMI, the central element of the UCI coherence. Normalized log-ratio measure (m_{nlr}) is the NPMI. The log-conditional-probability measure (m_{lc}) is equivalent to the calculation used by UMass coherence [12]. The last two confirmation measures are the Jaccard and log-Jaccard measures.

A small constant ϵ is added to prevent logarithm of zero. Following [18], we set it to a small value ($\epsilon = 10^{-12}$).[5] Olsson's and Fitelson's coherences as well as a logarithmic variant of Shogenji's coherence (formulas 12, 16 and 11) are denoted by m_o, m_f and m_{ls}.

3.3.2 Indirect confirmation measures

Instead of directly computing the confirmation of $S_i = (W', W^*)$, indirect computation of confirmation assumes that given some word of W, direct confirmations of words in W' are close to direct confirmations of words in W^* with respect to this given word. Thus, indirect confirmation computes similarity of words in W' and W^* with respect to direct confirmations to all words.

[5]Additionally ϵ is used in m_l and m_{ll} for preventing division by 0.

Why is this an advantage? For example, assume word x semantically supports word z but they do not appear frequently together in the reference corpus and have therefore low joint probability. Thus, their direct confirmation would be low as well. However, the confirmations of x and z correlate with respect to many other words y in W. An example is that x and z are both competing brands of cars, which semantically support each other. However, both brands are seldom mentioned together in documents in the reference corpus. But their confirmations to other words like "road" or "speed" do strongly correlate. This would be reflected by an indirect confirmation measure. Thus, indirect confirmation measures may capture semantic support that direct measures would miss.

This idea can be formalized by representing the word sets W' and W^* as vectors with dimension of the total size of the word set W. Such vector can be computed with respect to any direct confirmation measure m. In case W' and W^* consist of single words, the vector elements are just the direct confirmations as suggested in [1]. In case W' and W^* are sets of more than one word, the vector elements are the sum of the direct confirmations of the single words. Following [1], the vector elements can be non-linearly distorted.

$$\vec{v}_{m,\gamma}(W') = \left\{ \sum_{w_i \in W'} m(w_i, w_j)^{\gamma} \right\}_{j=1,\dots,|W|} \quad (34)$$

Given context vectors $\vec{u} = \vec{v}(W')$ and $\vec{w} = \vec{v}(W^*)$ for the word sets of a pair $S_i = (W', W^*)$, indirect confirmation is computed as vector similarity. Following [1], we equip our framework with the vector similarities cosine, dice and jaccard:

$$s_{cos}(\vec{u}, \vec{w}) = \frac{\sum_{i=1}^{|W|} u_i \cdot w_i}{\|\vec{u}\|_2 \cdot \|\vec{w}\|_2} \quad (35)$$

$$s_{dice}(\vec{u}, \vec{w}) = \frac{\sum_{i=1}^{|W|} \min(u_i, w_i)}{\sum_{i=1}^{|W|} v_i + w_i} \quad (36)$$

$$s_{jac}(\vec{u}, \vec{w}) = \frac{\sum_{i=1}^{|W|} \min(u_i, w_i)}{\sum_{i=1}^{|W|} \max(u_i, w_i)} \quad (37)$$

Thus, given a similarity measure sim, a direct confirmation measure m and a value for γ, an indirect confirmation measure $\tilde{m}$ is

$$\tilde{m}_{sim(m,\gamma)}(W', W^*) = s_{sim}(\vec{v}_{m,\gamma}(W'), \vec{v}_{m,\gamma}(W^*)) \quad (38)$$

3.4 Aggregation

Finally, all confirmations $\vec{\varphi} = \{\varphi_1, \dots \varphi_{|S|}\}$ of all subset pairs S_i are aggregated to a single coherence score. Arithmetic mean (σ_a) and median (σ_m) have been used in the literature. Additionally, we evaluate geometric mean (σ_g), harmonic mean (σ_h), quadratic mean (σ_q), minimum (σ_n) and maximum (σ_x).

3.5 Representation of existing measures

Now we are ready to describe all coherence measures from section 2 as instances within the new framework. The coherences of [12, 13, 1] can be written as:

$$C_{\text{UMass}} = (\mathcal{P}_{bd}, S_{pre}^{one}, m_{lc}, \sigma_a) \quad (39)$$

$$C_{\text{UCI}} = (\mathcal{P}_{sw(10)}, S_{one}^{one}, m_{lr}, \sigma_a) \quad (40)$$

$$C_{\text{NPMI}} = (\mathcal{P}_{sw(10)}, S_{one}^{one}, m_{nlr}, \sigma_a) \quad (41)$$

Name	20NG	Genomics	NYT	RTL-NYT	RTL-Wiki	Movie
Topics	100	100	100	1095	1096	100
Top words	10	10	10	5	5	5
Documents	19 952	29 833	—	—	7 838	108 952
Paragraphs	155 429	2 678 088	—	—	319 859	2 136 811
Sentences	341 583	9 744 966	—	—	1 035 265	6 583 202
Tokens	2 785 319	114 065 923	—	—	13 679 052	86 256 415
Vocabulary	109 610	1 640 456	—	—	591 957	1 625 124

Table 1: Datasets used for evaluation.

The coherences defined in [7] and transformed in [16] can be written as:

$$C_{\text{one-all}} = (\mathcal{P}_{bd}, S_{all}^{one}, m_d, \sigma_a) \quad (42)$$

$$C_{\text{one-any}} = (\mathcal{P}_{bd}, S_{any}^{one}, m_d, \sigma_a) \quad (43)$$

$$C_{\text{any-any}} = (\mathcal{P}_{bd}, S_{any}^{any}, m_d, \sigma_a) \quad (44)$$

Shogenji's [17], Olsson's [14] and Fitelson's [8] coherences do not define how the probabilities are computed. Therefore, these measure definitions can be combined with every method of probability estimation[6]:

$$C_S = \left(\cdot, S_{one}^{all}, m_{ls}, \sigma_a\right) \quad (45)$$

$$C_O = \left(\cdot, S_{set}^{set}, m_o, \sigma_i\right) \quad (46)$$

$$C_F = \left(\cdot, S_{any}^{one}, m_f, \sigma_a\right) \quad (47)$$

Using the context-window-based probability estimation $\mathcal{P}_{cw}$ described in section 2, we are able to formulate the context-vector-based coherences defined in [1] within our framework[7]:

$$C_{\text{cos}} = \left(\mathcal{P}_{cw(5)}, S_{one}^{one}, \tilde{m}_{cos(nlr,\gamma)}, \sigma_a\right) \quad (48)$$

$$C_{\text{dice}} = \left(\mathcal{P}_{cw(5)}, S_{one}^{one}, \tilde{m}_{dice(nlr,\gamma)}, \sigma_a\right) \quad (49)$$

$$C_{\text{jac}} = \left(\mathcal{P}_{cw(5)}, S_{one}^{one}, \tilde{m}_{jac(nlr,\gamma)}, \sigma_a\right) \quad (50)$$

$$C_{\text{cen}} = \left(\mathcal{P}_{cw(5)}, S_{set}^{one}, \tilde{m}_{cos(nlr,\gamma)}, \sigma_a\right) \quad (51)$$

This shows that the framework can cover all existing measures. However, it allows to construct new measures that combine the ideas of existing measures.

4. EVALUATION AND DATA SETS

The evaluation follows a common scheme that has already been used in [1, 10, 13, 16]. Coherence measures are computed for topics given as word sets that have been rated by humans with respect to understandability. Each measure produces a ranking of the topics that is compared to the ranking induced by human ratings. Following [10], both rankings are correlated using Pearson's r. Thus, good quality of a coherence measure is indicated by a large correlation to human ratings.

Word counts and probabilities are derived from Wikipedia. In case the corpus, which was used as training data for topic learning, was available, we computed coherence measures a second time using counts derived from that corpus.

During evaluation, we tested a wide range of different parameter settings. Window sizes varied between $[10, 300]$ for the sliding and $[5, 150]$ for the context window. The parameter γ varied in $\{1, 2, 3\}$. Overall, our evaluation comprises a total of 237 912 different coherences and parameterizations.

In literature, other evaluation methods has been used as well, e.g., humans were asked to classify word sets using different given error types [12]. However, since the data is not freely available, we can not use such methods for our evaluation.

A dataset comprises a corpus, topics and human ratings. Topics had been computed using the corpus and are given by word sets consisting of the topics top words. Human ratings for topics had been created by presenting these word sets to human raters. Topics are rated regarding interpretability and understandability using three categories—good, neutral or bad [13].

The generation of such a dataset is expensive due to the necessary manual work to create human topic ratings. Recently, several datasets have been published [1, 6, 10, 16]. Additionally, the creation of such a dataset is separated from the topic model used to compute the topics, since the humans rate just plain word sets without any information about the topic model [1, 6, 10, 15, 16]. This opens the possibility to reuse them for evaluation.

The *20NG* dataset contains the well known 20 Newsgroups corpus that consists of Usenet messages of 20 different groups. The *Genomics* corpus comprises scientific articles of 49 MEDLINE journals and is part of the TREC-Genomics Track[8]. Aletras and Stevenson [1] published 100 rated topics for both dataset, each represented by a set of 10 top words. Further, they published 100 rated topics that have been computed using 47 229 New York Times articles (*NYT*). Unfortunately, this corpus is not available to us.

Chang et al. [6] used two corpora, one comprising New York Times articles (*RTL-NYT*) and the other is a Wikipedia subset (*RTL-Wiki*). A number of 900 topics were created for each of these corpora. [10] published human ratings for these topics. Human raters evaluated word subsets of size five randomly selected from the top words of each topic. We aggregated the ratings for each word set. Word sets with

[6] S_{one}^{all} is used to formulate Shogenji's coherence and is defined like S_{all}^{one} but with W' and W^* swapped. $S_{set}^{set} = \{(W', W^*)|W', W^* = W\}$ is used for Olsson's coherence. Note that S_{set}^{set} contains only one single pair. Therefore, the aggregation function is the identity function σ_i. These special segmentation schemas are used only for these two coherences.

[7] We added window size to the model name, e.g., $\mathcal{P}_{cw(5)}$ for the window size $s = \pm 5$. The context window is only used for indirect coherence measures. For represent all measures mentioned in [1] instead of m_{nlr} the measures m_{lr} or $m_P = P(W', W^*)$ could be used respectively.

[8] `http://ir.ohsu.edu/genomics`

		Name	C_V	C_P	C_{UMass}	$C_{\text{one-any}}$	C_{UCI}	C_{NPMI}	C_A
coherences		$\mathcal{S}$	$\mathcal{S}_{set}^{one}$	$\mathcal{S}_{pre}^{one}$	$\mathcal{S}_{pre}^{one}$	$\mathcal{S}_{any}^{one}$	$\mathcal{S}_{one}^{one}$	$\mathcal{S}_{one}^{one}$	$\mathcal{S}_{one}^{one}$
		$\mathcal{P}$	$\mathcal{P}_{sw(110)}$	$\mathcal{P}_{sw(70)}$	$\mathcal{P}_{bd}$	$\mathcal{P}_{bd}$	$\mathcal{P}_{sw(10)}$	$\mathcal{P}_{sw(10)}$	$\mathcal{P}_{cw(5)}$
		$\mathcal{M}$	$\tilde{m}_{cos(nlr,1)}$	m_f	m_{lc}	m_d	m_{lr}	m_{nlr}	$\tilde{m}_{cos(nlr,1)}$
		Σ	σ_a	σ_a	σ_a	σ_a	σ_a	σ_a	σ_a
using corpus		20NG	0.665	0.756	0.395	0.563	0.312	0.486	0.563
		Genomics	0.671	0.652	0.514	0.549	0.624	0.630	0.632
		RTL-Wiki	0.627	0.615	0.272	0.545	0.527	0.573	0.542
		Movie	0.548	0.549	0.093	0.453	0.473	0.438	0.431
		average	0.628	0.643	0.319	0.528	0.484	0.532	0.542
using the Wikipedia	$N = 10$	20NG	0.859	0.825	0.562	0.822	0.696	0.780	0.739
		Genomics	0.773	0.721	0.442	0.452	0.478	0.594	0.530
		NYT	0.803	0.757	0.543	0.612	0.783	0.806	0.747
		average	0.812	0.768	0.516	0.629	0.652	0.727	0.672
	$N = 5$	RTL-NYT	0.728	0.720	0.106	0.438	0.631	0.678	0.687
		RTL-Wiki	0.679	0.645	0.350	0.499	0.558	0.606	0.602
		Movie	0.544	0.533	0.143	0.454	0.447	0.452	0.465
		average	0.650	0.633	0.200	0.464	0.545	0.579	0.585
		average	**0.731**	0.700	0.358	0.546	0.599	0.653	0.628

Table 2: Coherence measures with strongest correlations with human ratings.

less than three ratings or words with encoding errors are removed.[9]

The RTL-Wiki corpus is published in bag-of-words format that is unsuitable for paragraph-, sentence- or window-based probability estimations. Therefore, we have retrieved the articles in version of May 2009 from Wikipedia history records. Not all articles of the original corpus were available anymore. Therefore, the recreated corpus is slightly smaller than the original one.

Rosner et al. [16] published the *Movie* corpus—a Wikipedia subset—and 100 rated topics. Topics are given as sets of five top words. Like the RTL-Wiki corpus this corpus was recreated and is slightly smaller than the original one.

Table 1 shows an overview of sizes of the different datasets used for evaluation. All corpora as well as the complete Wikipedia used as reference corpus are preprocessed using lemmatization and stop word removal. Additionally, we removed portal and category articles, redirection and disambiguation pages as well as articles about single years.

5. RESULTS AND DISCUSSION

Table 2 shows the best performing coherence measures with respect to the different datasets.[10]

The largest correlations for all datasets (except for the Movie dataset) were reached, when the coherence measures relied on probabilities derived from the Wikipedia instead of the corpus used for topic learning. We focus our discussion on these calculations.

Most correlations computed for topics with 10 top words are higher than those of topics with 5 top words. Thus,

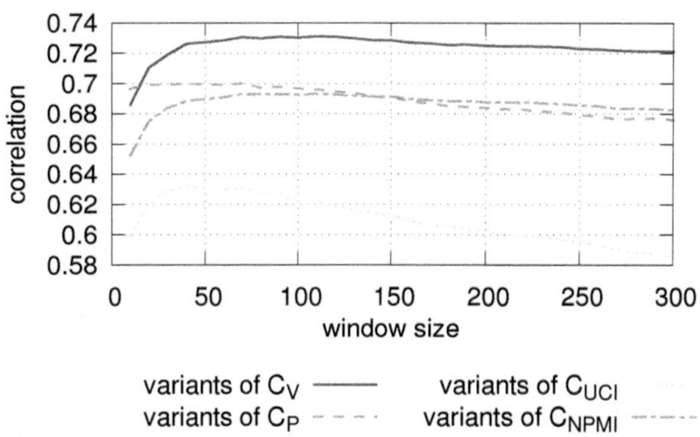

Figure 3: The influence of the sliding window's size on the correlation of variants of different coherences and human ratings.

evaluation of the topic quality is harder, if the number of top words N is small.

Looking at already proposed coherence measures (five most right columns of table 2), our results confirm that on average UCI coherence performs better with NPMI. Among already proposed coherence measures, the NPMI showed best overall performance. Slightly lower correlations are obtained by the best performing vector-based coherence of those proposed in [1]. UMass coherence has lower correlations—especially in cases of small word sets. Shogenji's (0.034) and Olsson's (0.218) coherences (not shown in table 2) have low correlations, while Fitelson's coherence (0.541) is comparable to $C_{one-any}$ proposed in [16].

The best performing coherence measure (the most left column) is a new combination found by systematic study of the configuration space of coherence measures. This measure (C_V) combines the indirect cosine measure with the NPMI and the boolean sliding window. This combination has been overlooked so far in the literature. Also, the best direct coherence measure (C_P) found by our study is a new combination. It combines Fitelson's confirmation measure

[9] The RTL-Wiki dataset contains 23 word sets with 6 words and more than 3 ratings that were removed as well to ensure comparability of ratings

[10] Further results can be found in the supplementary material. Results differing to Aletras and Stevenson [1] might be caused by a different preprocessing and different versions of the Wikipedia.

Name	direct	indirect
$\mathcal{P}_{bd}$	0.648	0.664
$\mathcal{P}_{bp}$	0.679	0.698
$\mathcal{P}_{bs}$	0.664	0.691
$\mathcal{P}_{sw(70)}$	0.700	0.731
$\mathcal{P}_{sw(110)}$	0.668	0.731
$\mathcal{P}_{cw(50)}$	—	0.695
S_{any}^{any}	0.617	0.730
S_{all}^{one}	0.456	0.728
S_{any}^{one}	0.648	0.730
S_{one}^{one}	0.699	0.711
S_{pre}^{one}	0.700	0.711
S_{suc}^{one}	0.695	0.711
S_{set}^{one}	—	0.731
σ_a	0.700	0.731
σ_g	0.468	0.606
σ_h	0.457	0.590
σ_m	0.659	0.730
σ_n	0.482	0.573
σ_q	0.648	0.716
σ_x	0.513	0.670

Table 3: Best correlations for the probability estimations, segmentations and aggregations if they were combined with a direct or indirect confirmation measure.

with the boolean sliding window. This one is still better than published measures.

Among probability estimation methods, the boolean paragraph, boolean sentence and context window methods performed better than the boolean document (see table 3). The boolean sliding window performed best, but the window size should be larger than proposed in [13]. Figure 3 shows the correlation to human ratings achieved by variants of C_V, C_P, UCI and NPMI with different window sizes. It shows that only the C_P coherence has a very high correlation with a small window ($s = 10$). The correlation of C_V and NPMI remains on a high level, when the window size is larger than 50. The UCI coherence benefits from a larger window size, too, and reaches its best correlation at $s = 70$. An explanation for the good performance of the boolean sliding window is that it implicitly represents distances between word tokens within large documents. Further, large documents that are known to have good quality in Wikipedia, are implicitly up weighted because they contain more windows than smaller documents.

Among the segmentation methods, if a direct confirmation measure is used the single-word-based segmentation methods (S_{one}^{one}, S_{pre}^{one} and S_{suc}^{one}) have the highest and S_{all}^{one} has the worst correlations. This changes when an indirect confirmation measure is used. While all segmentation methods reach a very high correlation, the single-word-based segmentations have slightly lower correlations than those that take larger subsets into account (S_{any}^{any}, S_{any}^{one}, S_{all}^{one}, S_{set}^{one}).

The arithmetic mean is the aggregation with the highest correlations. Combined with indirect confirmation measures the median and the quadratic mean created high correlations, too.

Among the direct confirmation measures, only m_f, m_{nlr}, m_{lr} and m_d reach higher correlations (see table 4). The last

Name	direct	indirect $\tilde{m}_{cos}$	indirect $\tilde{m}_{dice}$	indirect $\tilde{m}_{jac}$
m_c	0.581	0.619	0.628	0.626
m_d	0.623	0.675	0.676	0.664
m_f	0.700	0.685	0.453	0.539
m_j	0.478	0.582	0.592	0.576
m_l	0.381	0.388	0.380	0.380
m_{lc}	0.493	0.374	0.238	0.238
m_{lj}	0.574	0.249	0.210	0.205
m_{ll}	0.582	0.563	0.472	0.507
m_{lr}	0.632	0.714	0.672	0.670
m_{ls}	0.172	0.714	0.672	0.670
m_{nlr}	0.693	0.731	0.689	0.691
m_o	0.478	0.582	0.592	0.576
m_P	—	0.575	0.605	0.590
m_r	0.378	0.605	0.577	0.557

Table 4: Best correlations for the confirmation measures used directly or combined with an inderect confirmation measure.

corpus left out	coherence $\mathcal{P}$ $\mathcal{S}$ $\mathcal{M}$ Σ	average correlation
20NG	$(\mathcal{P}_{sw110}, S_{any}^{any}, \tilde{m}_{cos(nlr,1)}, \sigma_m)$	0.708
Genomics	$(\mathcal{P}_{sw70}, S_{set}^{one}, \tilde{m}_{cos(nlr,1)}, \sigma_a)$	0.724
NYT	$(\mathcal{P}_{sw110}, S_{set}^{one}, \tilde{m}_{cos(nlr,1)}, \sigma_a)$	0.717
RTL-NYT	$(\mathcal{P}_{sw110}, S_{set}^{one}, \tilde{m}_{cos(nlr,1)}, \sigma_a)$	0.732
RTL-Wiki	$(\mathcal{P}_{sw110}, S_{set}^{one}, \tilde{m}_{cos(nlr,1)}, \sigma_a)$	0.741
Movie	$(\mathcal{P}_{sw70}, S_{set}^{one}, \tilde{m}_{cos(nlr,1)}, \sigma_a)$	0.769

Table 5: Coherence measures with the highest average correlations if one dataset has been left out.

three benefit from a combination with an indirect measure, while the correlation of m_f drops.

The small differences in correlation of coherences with a) different window sizes and b) segmenation methods that are very similar to each other, leads to a large number of coherences having a high average correlation that is only slightly lower than the best performing coherence C_V. Thus, there are many variants of C_V that are performing very good as long as they use

- a sliding window with a window size $s \geq 50$,
- a segmentation method that takes larger subsets into account and
- σ_a or σ_m as summarization method.

We confirm this by generating *leave one out averages* by calculating the average using only five of the six datasets. Table 5 shows that independently from the dataset left out, C_V or one of its variants fullfilling the points above achieves the highest average correlation. For every coherence in table 2, figure 4 shows the six averages. It can be seen that the set of averages of C_V only overlap with the averages of C_P and are clearly higher than those of the other coherences.

6. RUNTIMES

Next to the quality it is important to know the costs of a certain coherence measure. Therefore, we have analyzed the runtimes of all coherence measures. For this experiment, we used the 100 topics of the NYT dataset and the Wikipedia

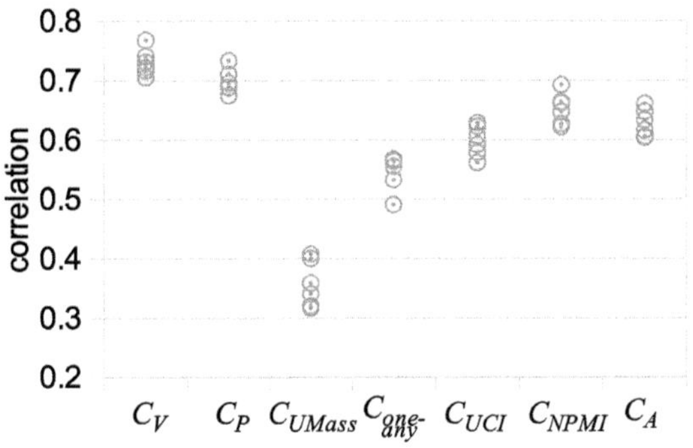

Figure 4: The leave one out averages of the coherence measures.

Name	runtime in s
C_V	315.2
C_P	317.7
C_{UMass}	13.7
$C_{\text{one-any}}$	13.7
C_{UCI}	356.1
C_{NPMI}	356.1
C_A	301.8

Table 6: Runtimes on the NYT dataset and the Wikipedia as reference corpus.

as reference corpus. Table 6 shows the overall runtimes of the coherence measures to compute the results presented in table 2.

For the runtime of a coherence measure, the most important component is the probability estimation. The fastest one is the boolean document that needed only 13.7s to retrieve all neccessary probabilities. The boolean paragraph and the boolean sentence based estimation methods needed 34.4s and 138.8s. Both suffer from the fact that there are much more paragraphs and sentences than single documents. But they are still faster than the window based approaches since the reference corpus can be divided into paragraphs or sentences while preprocessing the corpus. In contrast, both window based estimation methods had the highest runtimes. This is caused by the need of retrieving the single positions of the words inside the documents to check whether these positions are inside the same window. As parameters for the runtime of all probability calculation we can identify a) the number of topics, b) the number of top words per topic (N) and c) the size of the reference corpus. On the other hand, the size of the window does not have an influence on the runtimes.

Another important component is the segmentation. While the segmentation of a specific topic is very fast, it controls the number of confirmation values that have to be calculated. Thus, it has a high impact on the time needed by the confirmation measure and the aggregation component. Table 7 shows the number of subset pairs S_i that the different segmentations create and two examples of the influence of this number on the runtime of confirmation measures and aggregations. It can be seen that S_{any}^{one} and S_{any}^{any} have an exponential complexity.

7. APPLICATIONS

Coherence measures can be applied to automatically rate quality of topics computed by topic models. This can be

Name	$\lvert S \rvert$	runtimes in s	
		$m_{cos(m_{nlr},1)}$	σ_m
S_{all}^{one}	N	0.002	<0.001
S_{set}^{one}	N	0.002	—
S_{pre}^{one}	$\frac{N\cdot(N-1)}{2}$	0.002	<0.001
S_{suc}^{one}	$\frac{N\cdot(N-1)}{2}$	0.002	<0.001
S_{one}^{one}	$N\cdot(N-1)$	0.002	0.001
S_{any}^{one}	$N\cdot(2^{(N-1)}-1)$	0.140	0.023
S_{any}^{any}	$\sum_{i=1}^{N-1}\left(\binom{N}{i}\cdot(2^i-1)\right)$	1.436	0.322

Table 7: Different segmentation schemes, the number of subset pairs S_i they contain ($\lvert S \rvert$) and examples of their influence on runtimes of confirmation measures and aggregations.

used in data exploration systems like TopicExplorer[11] [9] that use word representations of topics to show the user an overview of large document collections. Topics that cannot be interpreted are filtered out using coherence measures. Thus, usability of the system is increased by hiding topics that would confuse users.

As example table 8 shows the five topics with highest and lowest coherence respectively of a total of 200 topics that are computed by Latent Dirichlet Allocation [3] using English Wikipedia. It clearly shows the difference between the quality of the topic representations as best topics allow to guess a general topic while the worst topics are not interpretable.

However, coherence measures have applications beyond topic models. First, precision of key word search in document collections can profit by filtering out documents that contain the query key words in some proximity but the words are located in nearby but thematically different passages. The approach would extract a word set for each document that covers the query words as well as the main words of the documents passage that contains the query words. Low quality hits for the query are filtered out by setting a minimum threshold for the coherence of the extracted word set.

Second, coherence can be used to select advertising links that fits a web page. The approach is similar as above. A word set is extracted from a web page that contains the most describing words of the pages content. Advertising links are selected that maximize coherence of the union of the web page's word set with descriptive words of the respective ad.

Third, coherence can be used to improve automatic translations of web pages. When using a dictionary to translate a sentence from a web page into another language, usually ambiguous translations of single words remain. Coherence measures can be used select the most coherent combination among the ambiguous translations.

8. CONCLUSION

We proposed a unifying framework that span the space of all known coherence measures and allows to combine all main ideas in the context of coherence quantification. We evaluated 237 912 coherence measures on six different benchmarks for topic coherence—to the best of our knowledge, this is the largest number of benchmarks used for topic coherences so far. We introduced coherence measures from

[11] `http://topicexplorer.informatik.uni-halle.de`

coherence	topic
0.94	company sell corporation own acquire purchase buy business sale owner
0.91	age population household female family census live average median income
0.86	jewish israel jew israeli jerusalem rabbi hebrew palestinian palestine holocaust
0.85	ship navy naval fleet sail vessel crew sink sea submarine
0.83	guitar album track bass drum vocal vocals release personnel list
...	
0.35	number code type section key table block set example oth
0.34	group official website member site base oth form consist profile
0.34	part form become history change present create merge forme separate
0.29	know call name several refer oth hunter hunt thompson include
0.27	mark paul heart take read harrison follow become know include

Table 8: The five Wikipedia topics with highest and lowest coherences using best preforming measure C_V.

scientific philosophy that have been not used in the area of topic evaluation and—in the case of Fitelson's coherence—showed a good performance. Using our framework, we identified measures that clearly outperform all coherences proposed so far.

In the future, a next step will be a more detailed investigation on the sliding window and could bring up new probability estimation methods. Future work will include transfer of coherence to other applications beyond topic models, which can be done in a systematic way using the new unifying framework. Hence, our research agenda may lead to completely new insights of the behavior of topic models. Finally, our open framework enables researchers to measure the impact on a comparable basis for fields of application like text mining, information retrieval and the world wide web. Additionally, it will be possible to finally evaluate the reasons for specific behavior of statistics-driven models and uncover distinguishing properties of benchmarks.

9. ACKNOWLEDGMENTS

We want to thank Jey Han Lau and Jordan Boyd-Graber for making their data available. A special thanks goes to Nikos Aletras for publishing his data and several discussions about his approach. The work of the first author has been supported by the ESF and the Free State of Saxony. The work of the last author has been partially supported by the Klaus Tschira Foundation.

10. REFERENCES

[1] N. Aletras and M. Stevenson. Evaluating topic coherence using distributional semantics. In *Proc. of the 10th Int. Conf. on Computational Semantics (IWCS'13)*, pages 13–22, 2013.

[2] L. Alsumait, D. Barbará, J. Gentle, and C. Domeniconi. Topic significance ranking of lda generative models. In *Proc. of the Europ. Conf. on Machine Learning and Knowledge Disc. in Databases: Part I*, ECML PKDD '09, pages 67–82, 2009.

[3] D. M. Blei, A. Y. Ng, and M. I. Jordan. Latent dirichlet allocation. *Journal of Machine Learning Research*, 3:993–1022, 2003.

[4] G. Bouma. Normalized (pointwise) mutual information in collocation extraction. In *From Form to Meaning: Processing Texts Automatically, Proc. of the Biennial GSCL Conference 2009*, pages 31–40, Tübingen, 2009.

[5] L. Bovens and S. Hartmann. *Bayesian Epistemology.* Oxford University Press, 2003.

[6] J. Chang, S. Gerrish, C. Wang, J. L. Boyd-graber, and D. M. Blei. Reading tea leaves: How humans interpret topic models. In *Advances in Neural Information Processing Systems 22*, pages 288–296. 2009.

[7] I. Douven and W. Meijs. Measuring coherence. *Synthese*, 156(3):405–425, 2007.

[8] B. Fitelson. A probabilistic theory of coherence. *Analysis*, 63(279):194–199, 2003.

[9] A. Hinneburg, R. Preiss, and R. Schröder. Topicexplorer: Exploring document collections with topic models. In *ECML/PKDD (2)*, pages 838–841, 2012.

[10] J. H. Lau, D. Newman, and T. Baldwin. Machine reading tea leaves: Automatically evaluating topic coherence and topic model quality. In *Proc. of the Europ. Chap. of the Assoc. for Comp. Ling.*, 2014.

[11] D. Mimno and D. Blei. Bayesian checking for topic models. In *Proc. of the Conf. on Empirical Methods in Natural Language Processing*, pages 227–237. 2011.

[12] D. Mimno, H. M. Wallach, E. Talley, M. Leenders, and A. McCallum. Optimizing semantic coherence in topic models. In *Proc. of the Conf. on Empirical Methods in Natural Language Processing*, pages 262–272. 2011.

[13] D. Newman, J. H. Lau, K. Grieser, and T. Baldwin. Automatic evaluation of topic coherence. In *Human Language Technologies: The 2010 Annual Conference of the North American Chapter of the Association for Computational Linguistics*, pages 100–108. 2010.

[14] E. Olsson. What is the problem of coherence and truth? *The Jour. of Philosophy*, 99(5):246–272, 2002.

[15] M. Röder, M. Speicher, and R. Usbeck. Investigating quality raters' performance using interface evaluation methods. In *Informatik 2013*, pages 137–139. GI, 2013.

[16] F. Rosner, A. Hinneburg, M. Röder, M. Nettling, and A. Both. Evaluating topic coherence measures. *CoRR*, abs/1403.6397, 2014.

[17] T. Shogenji. Is coherence truth conducive? *Analysis*, 59(264):338–345, 1999.

[18] K. Stevens, P. Kegelmeyer, D. Andrzejewski, and D. Buttler. Exploring topic coherence over many models and many topics. In *Proc. of the 2012 Joint Conf. on Empirical Methods in Natural Language Processing and Computational Natural Language Learning*, EMNLP-CoNLL '12, pages 952–961, 2012.

Dynamic Information Retrieval Modeling

Hui Yang
Georgetown University
huiyang@cs.georgetown.edu

Marc Sloan
University College London
m.sloan@cs.ucl.ac.uk

Jun Wang
University College London
junwang@cs.ucl.ac.uk

Categories and Subject Descriptors

H.3.3 [**Information Search and Retrieval**]: Retrieval models; Relevance feedback; Search process

Keywords

Dynamic Information Retrieval Modeling; Probabilistic Relevance Model; Reinforcement Learning

ABSTRACT

In Dynamic Information Retrieval modeling we model dynamic systems which change or adapt over time or a sequence of events using a range of techniques from artificial intelligence and reinforcement learning. Many of the open problems in current IR research can be described as dynamic systems, for instance, session search or computational advertising. State of the art research provides solutions to these problems that are responsive to a changing environment, learn from past interactions and predict future utility. Advances in IR interface, personalization and ad display demand models that can react to users in real time and in an intelligent, contextual way.

The objective of this half-day tutorial is to provide a comprehensive and up-to-date introduction to Dynamic Information Retrieval Modeling. We motivate a conceptual model linking static, interactive and dynamic retrieval and use this to define *dynamics* within the context of IR. We then cover a number of algorithms and techniques from the artificial intelligence (AI) and online learning literature such as Markov Decision Processes (MDP) [1], their partially observable variation (POMDP) [5] and multi-armed bandits [7].

Following this we describe how to identify dynamics in an IR problem and demonstrate how to model them using the described techniques. The remainder of the tutorial will then cover an array of state-of-the-art research on dynamic systems in IR and how they can be modeled using using dynamic IR [2, 6]. We use research on session search [3], multi-page search [4] and online advertising [8] as in-depth examples of such work.

This tutorial is of relevance to IR practitioners and researchers, where we will present the merits of dynamic information retrieval modeling and introduce the relevant techniques. The content will be of particular interest to researchers working in the areas of statistical modeling, personalization and recommendation, and is also relevant to practitioners in Web search, online advertising and anyone who works with big data.

After this tutorial, attendees will:

- Be able to identify the dynamics in an IR system
- Be able to model these dynamics using techniques from AI and reinforcement learning
- Have knowledge of the state-of-the-art research in dynamic information retrieval modeling

WSDM'15, February 2–6, 2015, Shanghai, China.
ACM 978-1-4503-3317-7/15/02.
http://dx.doi.org/10.1145/2684822.2697038.

1. SPEAKERS

Grace Hui Yang is an Assistant Professor in the Department of Computer Science at Georgetown University. Grace obtained her PhD from School of Computer Science, Carnegie Mellon University. Grace's current research interests include session search, search engine evaluation, privacy-preserving information retrieval, and information organization. Prior to this, she conducted research on question answering, ontology construction, near-duplicate detection, multimedia information retrieval and opinion and sentiment detection. The results of her research have been published in SIGIR, CIKM, ACL, TREC, ECIR, and WWW since 2002. Grace serves on the Editorial Board for Information Retrieval Journal. She also served as an area chair/senior program committee member for SIGIR 2014 and co-chaired the SIGIR 2013 and SIGIR 2014 Doctoral Consortium. She is a program committee member in SIGIR, ACL, EMNLP, CIKM, WSDM, and KDD. Home page: `http://www.cs.georgetown.edu/~huiyang`

Marc Sloan is a senior graduate student completing his PhD thesis in University College London. He has interned at Microsoft Research working on contextual, session based search result blending. His background is in information retrieval, machine learning and financial computing and his thesis is on dynamic IR. His research interests in information retrieval include applying reinforcement learning techniques such as multi-armed bandits and POMDPs to IR learning systems over time, contextual session search and query suggestion. Marc has published and presented reinforcement learning in IR research at top-tier conferences and workshops such as SIGIR, WWW, WSCD and the Large-scale Online Learning and Decision Making Workshop. Homepage: `http://mediafutures.cs.ucl.ac.uk/people/MarcSloan/`

Jun Wang is Senior Lecturer (Associate Professor) in Computer Science, University College London and the Founding Director of the MSc/MRes Web Science & Big Data Analytics programme. His main research interests are statistical modelling of information retrieval, collaborative filtering and computational advertising. He was a recipient of the SIGIR Doctoral Consortium Award in 2006, the Microsoft Beyond Search award in 2007 and won the Best Paper Prizes in ECIR09 and ECIR12. JunâĂŹs recent service includes (Senior) PCs for SIGIR, CIKM, WSDM, and RecSys, and presenting an ECIR2011 tutorial on Risk Management in Information Retrieval, a CIKM2011 tutorial on statistical IR modeling and a CIKM2013 tutorial on Computational Advertising. Home page: `http://www.cs.ucl.ac.uk/staff/J.Wang/`

2. GUEST SPEAKER

Maarten de Rijke is full professor of Information Processing and Internet in the Informatics Institute at the University of Amsterdam. De Rijke leads the Information and Language Processing Systems group, one of the world's leading academic research groups in information retrieval. During the most recent computer science research assessment exercise, the group achieved maximal scores on all dimensions. His research focus is on intelligent information access, with projects on self-learning search engines, semantic search, and social media analytics. A Pionier personal innovational research incentives grant laureate (comparable to an advanced ERC grant), De Rijke has generated over 35MEuro in project funding. With an h-index of 50 he has published over 600 papers, published or edited over a dozen books, is the Editor-in-Chief of ACM Transactions on Information Systems and of Springer's Information Retrieval book series, (associate) editor for various journals and book series, and a current and former coordinator of retrieval evaluation tracks at TREC, CLEF and INEX. He was co-chair for SIGIR 2013, general chair for ECIR 2014 and will be program co-chair for information retrieval for CIKM 2015 and short paper co-chair for SIGIR 2015. He is the director of the University of Amsterdam's Intelligent Systems Lab (ISLA), of the Center for Creation, Content and Technology (CCCT), of the Ad de Jonge Center for Intelligence and Security Studies, and of the Amsterdam Data Science research center. The retrieval and language technology developed by his research group is being used by organizations around the Netherlands and beyond, and has given rise to various spin-off initiatives. Homepage: `https://staff.fnwi.uva.nl/m.derijke/`

3. REFERENCES

[1] BELLMAN, R. A markovian decision process. *Indiana University Mathematics Journal 6* (1957), 679–684.

[2] FETTERLY, D., MANASSE, M., NAJORK, M., AND WIENER, J. A large-scale study of the evolution of web pages. In *WWW '03*, pp. 669–678.

[3] GUAN, D., ZHANG, S., AND YANG, H. Utilizing query change for session search. In *SIGIR '13*, pp. 453–462.

[4] JIN, X., SLOAN, M., AND WANG, J. Interactive exploratory search for multi page search results. In *WWW '13*, pp. 655–666.

[5] KAELBLING, L. P., LITTMAN, M. L., AND CASSANDRA, A. R. Planning and acting in partially observable stochastic domains. *Artificial intelligence 101*, 1 (1998), 99–134.

[6] LESKOVEC, J., BACKSTROM, L., AND KLEINBERG, J. Meme-tracking and the dynamics of the news cycle. In *KDD '09*, pp. 497–506.

[7] ROBBINS, H. Some aspects of the sequential design of experiments. *Bulletin of the American Mathematical Society 58*, 5 (Sep 1952), 527–535.

[8] YUAN, S., AND WANG, J. Sequential selection of correlated ads by pomdps. In *CIKM '12*, pp. 515–524.

Scalability and Efficiency Challenges in Large-Scale Web Search Engines

B. Barla Cambazoglu
Yahoo Labs
Barcelona, Spain
barla@yahoo-inc.com

Ricardo Baeza-Yates
Yahoo Labs
Barcelona, Spain
rbaeza@acm.org

ABSTRACT

Commercial web search engines need to process thousands of queries every second and provide responses to user queries within a few hundred milliseconds. As a consequence of these tight performance constraints, search engines construct and maintain very large computing infrastructures for crawling the Web, indexing discovered pages, and processing user queries. The scalability and efficiency of these infrastructures require careful performance optimizations in every major component of the search engine.

This tutorial aims to provide a fairly comprehensive overview of the scalability and efficiency challenges in large-scale web search engines. In particular, the tutorial provides an in-depth architectural overview of a web search engine, mainly focusing on the web crawling, indexing, and query processing components. The scalability and efficiency issues encountered in the above-mentioned components are presented at four different granularities: at the level of a single computer, a cluster of computers, a single data center, and a multi-center search engine. The tutorial also points at the open research problems and provides recommendations to researchers who are new to the field.

Categories and Subject Descriptors

H.3.3 [**Information Storage and Retrieval**]: Information Search and Retrieval

Keywords

Web search engines; crawling; indexing; query processing; caching; efficiency; scalability.

1. OUTLINE

The tutorial is composed of four sections. The first section provides the main concepts. Each of the remaining sections covers a particular architectural component in a web search engine.

WSDM'15, February 2–6, 2015, Shanghai, China.
ACM 978-1-4503-3317-7/15/02.
http://dx.doi.org/10.1145/2684822.2697039.

1.1 Main Concepts

In this section, we provide the necessary background for the following sections. First, we explain the main challenges posed by the Web and its characteristics. Second, we present the main components of a search engine and possible software/hardware architectures. Finally, we summarize the interactions among the three main components: crawler, indexer, and query processor.

1.2 Web Crawling

The web crawler is responsible for discovering new web pages and downloading their content while refreshing the content of previously downloaded pages [6]. The main performance objective for a crawler is to achieve high page download rates. The efficiency of a sequential web crawler is mainly determined by the selection and implementation of proper data structures. Scalability is commonly achieved through multi-threading and parallelization. In addition to such standard techniques, our tutorial covers geographically distributed web crawling, which emerges as a promising option for further scalability, and discusses the web partitioning and crawler placement problems.

1.3 Indexing

The indexing process involves various parsing, extraction, and classification tasks, through which certain features are extracted and the textual content of downloaded pages are converted into an inverted index [7]. The main performance metrics for an indexer are the length of deployment cycles, compactness, and the speed of index updates. So far, most algorithmic improvements are concentrated on index compression. At the architectural level, the efficiency and scalability are tried to be improved via index partitioning, pruning, and replication. In addition, our tutorial covers the indexing strategies for geographically distributed web search engines.

1.4 Query Processing

Query processing involves generating the set of best-matching results for a given user query [2]. The success of a query processor is mainly assessed by its throughput and average response latency. A large body of research work assume relatively standard processing techniques using an inverted index while large-scale search engines rely on more sophisticated techniques. In addition to the state-of-the-art ranking techniques employed in web search engines, our tutorial covers a variety of problems including query processing on multi-core architectures, early exit optimizations, pipelined query processing, query forwarding, and distributed web search engines.

This section will also cover caching in web search engines. The idea behind caching is to speed up query response times by storing precomputed query results, also reducing the computational workload of backend search systems. Caching happens at different architectural layers in a web search engine. The tutorial covers common challenges in caching, such as admission, eviction, and prefetching. It also focuses on the freshness problem, which recently attracted much research attention.

2. LEARNING OBJECTIVES

The following are the main objectives of the tutorial.

- To provide an in-depth background on the architectural components of a web search engine.
- To present the fundamental scalability and efficiency issues which have been often addressed in the information retrieval literature.
- To shed some light into the techniques used in large-scale commercial search engines and bridge the gap between the industry and academia.
- To identify open research problems in the context of web search engine scalability and efficiency, promoting further research on the topic.

3. PREVIOUS OFFERINGS

The structure of the tutorial is based on a book chapter published by the presenters [3]. Earlier versions of the tutorial were presented in SIGIR'13 [4], WWW'14 [1], and SIGIR'14 [5]. The tutorial was also given in two summer schools: in the 2nd COST 804 Training School on Energy Efficiency in Large Scale Distributed Systems, and more recently, in the 3rd MUMIA Training School on Information Retrieval and Interactive Information Access. The latest version of the tutorial slides is available online.[1]

4. SHORT BIOGRAPHIES

Berkant Barla Cambazoglu received his BS, MS, and PhD degrees, all in computer engineering, from the Computer Engineering Department of Bilkent University in 1997, 2000, and 2006, respectively. He has then worked as a postdoctoral researcher in the Biomedical Informatics Department of the Ohio State University. He is currently employed as a senior researcher in Yahoo Labs, where he is heading the web retrieval group. He has many papers published in prestigious journals including IEEE TPDS, JPDC, Inf. Syst., ACM TWEB, and IP&M, as well as top-tier conferences, such as SIGIR, CIKM, WSDM, WWW, and KDD.

Ricardo Baeza-Yates is VP of Yahoo Labs for Europe and Latin America, leading the labs at Barcelona, Spain and Santiago, Chile. Until 2005, he was the director of the Center for Web Research at the Department of Computer Science of the Engineering School of the University of Chile, and ICREA Professor at the Dept. of Information and Communication Technologies of University Pompeu Fabra in Barcelona, Spain. He is co-author of the bestseller textbook Modern Information Retrieval by Addison-Wesley, first published in 1999 with a second edition in 2011, as well as co-author of the second edition of the Handbook of Algorithms and Data Structures, Addison-Wesley, 1991; and co-editor of Information Retrieval: Algorithms and Data Structures, Prentice-Hall, 1992, among more than 400 other publications. He has been PC-Chair of the most important conferences in the field of Web Search and Web Mining. He has given tutorials in most major conferences many times, including SIGIR, WWW and VLDB. He has won several awards and is, both, ACM and IEEE Fellow.

5. REFERENCES

[1] R. Baeza-Yates and B. B. Cambazoglu. Scalability and efficiency challenges in large-scale web search engines. In *Proceedings of the Companion Publication of the 23rd International Conference on World Wide Web Companion*, pages 185–186, 2014.

[2] R. Baeza-Yates and B. Ribeiro-Neto. *Modern Information Retrieval*. Addison-Wesley Publishing Company, USA, 2nd edition, 2011.

[3] B. B. Cambazoglu and R. Baeza-Yates. Scalability challenges in web search engines. In M. Melucci, R. Baeza-Yates, and W. B. Croft, editors, *Advanced Topics in Information Retrieval*, volume 33 of *The Information Retrieval Series*, pages 27–50. Springer Berlin Heidelberg, 2011.

[4] B. B. Cambazoglu and R. Baeza-Yates. Scalability and efficiency challenges in commercial web search engines. In *Proceedings of the 36th International ACM SIGIR Conference on Research and Development in Information Retrieval*, page 1124, 2013.

[5] B. B. Cambazoglu and R. Baeza-Yates. Scalability and efficiency challenges in large-scale web search engines. In *Proceedings of the 37th International ACM SIGIR Conference on Research and Development in Information Retrieval*, page 1285, 2014.

[6] C. Olston and M. Najork. Web crawling. *Foundations and Trends in Information Retrieval*, 4(3):175–246, 2010.

[7] J. Zobel and A. Moffat. Inverted files for text search engines. *ACM Computing Surveys*, 38(2), 2006.

[1] `http://labs.yahoo.com/presentation/scalability-and-efficiency-challenges-in-large-scale-web-search-engines/`

Offline Evaluation and Optimization for Interactive Systems

Tutorial Abstract

Lihong Li
Microsoft Research
One Microsoft Way
Redmond, WA 98052
lihongli@microsoft.com

Categories and Subject Descriptors

H.3.3 [**Information Systems**]: Information Storage and Retrieval—*Information Search and Retrieval*; I.2.6 [**Artificial Intelligence**]: Learning

General Terms

Experimentation; Performance

Keywords

Offline evaluation; counterfactual analysis; advertising; information retrieval; Web search; recommender systems; interactive systems; contextual bandits

ABSTRACT

Evaluating and optimizing an **interactive** system (like search engines, recommender and advertising systems) from historical data against a predefined **online** metric is challenging, especially when that metric is computed from user feedback such as clicks and payments. The key challenge is **counterfactual** in nature: we only observe a user's feedback for actions taken by the system, but we do not know what that user would *have* reacted to a different action. The golden standard to evaluate such metrics of a user-interacting system is online A/B experiments (a.k.a. randomized controlled experiments), which can be expensive in terms of both time and engineering resources. *Offline* evaluation/optimization (sometimes referred to as off-policy learning in the literature) thus becomes critical, aiming to evaluate the same metrics *without* running (many) expensive A/B experiments on live users.

One approach to offline evaluation is to build a user model that simulates user behavior (clicks, purchases, etc.) under various contexts, and then evaluate metrics of a system with this simulator. While being straightforward and common in practice, the reliability of such model-based approaches relies heavily on how well the user model is built. Furthermore, it is often difficult to know *a priori* whether a user model is good enough to be trustable.

Recent years have seen a growing interest in another solution to the offline evaluation problem. Using statistical techniques like importance sampling and doubly robust estimation, the approach can give unbiased estimates of metrics for a wide range of problems. It enjoys other benefits as well. For example, it often allows data scientists to obtain a confidence interval for the estimate to quantify the amount of uncertainty; it does not require building user models, so is more robust and easier to apply. All these benefits make the approach particularly attractive to a wide range of problems. Successful applications have been reported in the last few years by some of the industrial leaders.

This tutorial gives a review of the basic theory and representative techniques. Applications of these techniques are illustrated through several case studies done at Microsoft and Yahoo!.

PRESENTER'S BIO

Lihong Li is a Researcher in the Machine Learning Department at Microsoft Research-Redmond. Prior to joining Microsoft, he was a Research Scientist in the Machine Learning Group at Yahoo! Research in Silicon Valley. He obtained a PhD degree from Rutgers University in Computer Science. His main research interests are machine learning with interaction, including reinforcement learning, multi-armed bandits, online learning, active learning, and their numerous applications on the Web like recommender systems, search, and advertising. He has published over 50 research papers, and is the winner of an ICML Best Student Paper Award, a WSDM Best Paper Award, an AISTATS Notable Paper Award, and a Yahoo! Superstar Team Award. He has served as area chair or senior program committee member at ICML, NIPS, and IJCAI. **URL**: `http://research.microsoft.com/en-us/people/lihongli`.

WSDM'15, February 2–6, 2015, Shanghai, China.
ACM ACM 978-1-4503-3317-7/15/02.
http://dx.doi.org/10.1145/2684822.2697040

Real-Time Bidding: A New Frontier of Computational Advertising Research

Tutorial Abstract

Jun Wang and Shuai Yuan
Department of Computer Science, University College London
{j.wang, s.yuan}@cs.ucl.ac.uk

Categories and Subject Descriptors

H.3.5 [**Information Storage and Retrieval**]: Online Information Services—*Commercial services*

General Terms

Algorithms, Measurement, Economics

Keywords

Computational advertising; Real-time bidding; Bidding algorithms; Revenue optimisation; Datasets

ABSTRACT

In display and mobile advertising, the most significant development in recent years is the Real-Time Bidding (RTB), which allows selling and buying in real-time one ad impression at a time. Since then, RTB has fundamentally changed the landscape of the digital marketing by scaling the buying process across a large number of available inventories. The demand for automation, integration and optimisation in RTB brings new research opportunities in the IR/DM/ML fields. However, despite its rapid growth and huge potential, many aspects of RTB remain unknown to the research community for many reasons. In this tutorial, together with invited distinguished speakers from online advertising industry, we aim to bring the insightful knowledge from the real-world systems to bridge the gaps and provide an overview of the fundamental infrastructure, algorithms, and technical and research challenges of this new frontier of computational advertising. We will also introduce to researchers the datasets, tools, and platforms which are publicly available thus they can get hands-on quickly.

Presenter's Bios

Dr. Jun Wang is a Senior Lecturer (Associate Professor) in University College London. He has published over 70 research papers in leading journals and conference proceedings including ACM Trans. on Information Systems, IEEE Trans. on Multimedia, ACM Multimedia System Journal, WWW, CIKM, ACM SIGIR, SIGMM. He received the Best Doctoral Consortium award in ACM SIGIR06 for his work on collaborative filtering, the Best Paper Prize in ECIR09 for his work on applying Modern Portfolio Theory of Finance (Mean-variance Analysis) to document ranking in Information Retrieval, and the Best Paper Prize in ECIR12 for top-k retrieval modelling. He has extensive experiences in giving tutorials on top conferences: his recent tutorials about risk management and portfolio theory of information retrieval were given in CIKM2011 and ECIR2011. Dr. Jun Wang has also delivered the following tutorials:

- ECIR 2011, Risk Management in Information Retrieval.
- CIKM 2011, Statistical Information Retrieval Modelling: From Probability Ranking Principle to recent advances in diversity, Portfolio Theory, and beyond.
- SIGIR 2013, Dynamic IR Modelling.

URL: `http://web4.cs.ucl.ac.uk/staff/jun.wang`

Shuai Yuan is completing his Ph.D. in University College London. He has been working on mathematical models of online advertising with a number of companies such as MediaGamma, AppNexus, Advance International Media, Bright, Dot.tk, and Miaozhen. He has the background of information retrieval, data mining, machine learning, and economic theories; his research interests on computational advertising have focused on supply side optimisation in RTB, bidding algorithms, and statistical arbitrage. Shuai Yuan has published several papers in top-tier venues including CIKM, SIGKDD, and ADKDD. Among them, he published the first empirical study on RTB auctions. He and his colleagues won the 3rd season of iPinyou Global Bidding Algorithm Competition in 2013, and the Best Paper Award of ADKDD 2014. He also contributes to an open advertising dataset project.

URL: `http://www.yuan-shuai.info`

WSDM'15, February 2–6, 2015, Shanghai, China.
Copyright 2015 ACM 978-1-4503-3317-7/15/02 ...$15.00.
http://dx.doi.org/10.1145/2684822.2697041.

Learning About Health and Medicine from Internet Data

Elad Yom-Tov
Microsoft Research Israel
13 Shenkar st.
Herzeliya 46733, Israel
eladyt@microsoft.com

Ingemar Johansson Cox
University College London
Gower st.
London WC1E 6BT, U.K.
ingemar.cox@di.ku.dk

Vasileios Lampos
University College London
Gower st.
London WC1E 6BT, U.K.
v.lampos@ucl.ac.uk

ABSTRACT

Surveys show that around 70% of US Internet users consult the Internet when they require medical information. People seek this information using both traditional search engines and via social media. The information created using the search process offers an unprecedented opportunity for applications to monitor and improve the quality of life of people with a variety of medical conditions. In recent years, research in this area has addressed public-health questions such as the effect of media on development of anorexia, developed tools for measuring influenza rates and assessing drug safety, and examined the effects of health information on individual wellbeing. This tutorial will show how Internet data can facilitate medical research, providing an overview of the state-of-the-art in this area. During the tutorial we will discuss the information which can be gleaned from a variety of Internet data sources, including social media, search engines, and specialized medical websites. We will provide an overview of analysis methods used in recent literature, and show how results can be evaluated using publicly-available health information and online experimentation. Finally, we will discuss ethical and privacy issues and possible technological solutions. This tutorial is intended for researchers of user generated content who are interested in applying their knowledge to improve health and medicine.

Categories and Subject Descriptors

H.3 [**Information Search and Retrieval**]: Search process; I.2 [**Applications and Expert Systems**]: Medicine and science

Keywords

Medicine, Information Retrieval, Machine Learning, User-Generated Data

WSDM'15, February 2–6, 2015, Shanghai, China.
ACM 978-1-4503-3317-7/15/02.
http://dx.doi.org/10.1145/2684822.2697042

1. OVERVIEW

Pew surveys recently found that more than 70% of US Internet users consult the Internet when they require medical information [3]. The data created by people who thus seek information offers an unprecedented opportunity for applications to monitor and improve the quality of life of people with a variety of medical conditions.

For the past decade, such data has been used in a variety of ways to the betterment of medical research and practice. Internet data has proven useful over traditional tools in several areas: First, it is a more sensitive sensor than that afforded by medical records in diseases where only a minority of infected people seek medical attention [9]. Thus, tracking the rates of influenza-like illness through Internet searches [2, 4, 8] and social media [5, 1, 6] has been the focus of significant research.

Second, Internet data can provide information where the its collection in the physical world would be difficult, if not impossible. For example, the mental state of cancer patients in the first few days following diagnosis has been analyzed using web searches [7], and changes in mood prior to the appearance of abnormal mental states detected [13].

A third area where Internet data is advantageous is where traditional data gathering is dependent on people making associations between different events, which are not always easy to link. Thus, the identification of adverse drug reactions is dependent on the realization of a causal link between taking a drug and the appearance of an adverse reaction. Internet query logs have been used to form this association without the need for voluntary reporting, consequently discovering previously unknown adverse reactions [12].

Finally, Internet data is useful when the activity of interest is primarily web-driven. This includes the actual search for medical information, as well as when studying patient groups. Here, studies have shown the effect of information on users learning about health topics [10] and demonstrated the detrimental effect of well-intentioned interventions for anorexia patients [11].

This tutorial will show how Internet data can facilitate medical research, providing an overview of the state-of-the-art in this area. The tutorial will be roughly divided into three main parts. The first part will discuss areas where Internet data is useful for medical research, and show examples representing the state of the art in the field. The second part will give researchers tools to address medical questions using Internet data. The third part will discuss ethical questions and privacy issues associated with this type of research, and possible technological solutions to the latter.

During the tutorial we will discuss the information which can be gleaned from a variety of Internet data sources, including social media, search engines, and specialized medical websites. We will provide an overview of analysis methods used in recent literature, and show how results can be evaluated using publicly-available health information and online experimentation. Finally, we will discuss ethical and privacy issues and possible technological solutions. This tutorial is intended for researchers of user generated content who are interested in applying their knowledge to improve health and medicine.

Our goal is to familiarize participants with the state of the art of the field, to show common approaches and tools used to address health questions with Internet data, to demonstrate where Internet data is useful (and where it is not) and to discuss open questions in the field.

2. INSTRUCTORS

Elad Yom-Tov is a Senior Researcher at Microsoft Research. Before joining Microsoft he was with Yahoo Research, IBM Research, and Rafael. Dr. Yom-Tov studied at Tel-Aviv University and the Technion, Israel. He has published three books, over 80 papers (of which 3 were awarded prizes), and filed more than 30 patents (19 of which have been granted so far). He is a Senior Member of IEEE and held the title of Master Inventor while at IBM. He has published several papers demonstrating the use of Internet data for learning about medicine, including the detection of side effect of drugs from query logs, the effects of media on the development of anorexia, and the information needs of cancer patients, among others.
URL: `http://www.yom-tov.info`

Ingemar J. Cox is a professor in the Computer Science departments at the University of Copenhagen and University College London (UCL). He is a Fellow of the ACM and IEEE. He is an inventor or co-inventor on 37 patents. Currently his primary research interests are in information retrieval and the application of data mining methods to online resources for medical purposes. He is presently part of a large UK EPSRC Interdisciplinary Research Centre on Early Warning Sensing Systems for Infectious Diseases ("i-Sense"), where he leads research targeting influenza.
URL: `http://mediafutures.cs.ucl.ac.uk/people/IngemarCox`

Vasileios Lampos is a Research Associate at the Computer Science department of UCL and a visiting researcher at Google. Before joining UCL, Dr. Lampos has worked as a Research Associate in the Natural Language Processing (NLP) group at the University of Sheffield. He was awarded his Ph.D. from the University of Bristol under the supervision of Prof. Nello Cristianini. His research interests span from Statistical NLP applications to Computational Social Science; he has published several papers on case studies of Social Media analysis, including the theme of influenza-like illness rates modelling from Twitter data. Currently, he participates in the interdisciplinary EPSRC project "i-Sense", with the general aim to develop a variety of sensing systems for the timely diagnosis and prevention of infectious diseases.
URL: `http://www.lampos.net`

3. REFERENCES

[1] A. Culotta. Towards detecting influenza epidemics by analyzing Twitter messages. In *Proceedings of the First Workshop on Social Media Analytics - SOMA '10*, pages 115–122. ACM Press, 2010.

[2] G. Eysenbach. Infodemiology: Tracking flu-related searches on the web for syndromic surveillance. In *AMIA 2006 Symposium Proceedings*, pages 244–248, 2006.

[3] S. Fox and M. Duggan. Health online 2013. *Health*, 2013.

[4] J. Ginsberg, M. Mohebbi, R. Patel, L. Brammer, M. Smolinski, and L. Brilliant. Detecting influenza epidemics using search engine query data. *Nature*, 457(7232):1012–1014, 2009.

[5] V. Lampos and N. Cristianini. Tracking the flu pandemic by monitoring the social web. In *Cognitive Information Processing (CIP), 2010 2nd International Workshop on*, pages 411–416. IEEE, 2010.

[6] V. Lampos and N. Cristianini. Nowcasting Events from the Social Web with Statistical Learning. *ACM Transactions on Intelligent Systems and Technology (TIST)*, 3(4):1–22, 2012.

[7] Y. Ofran, O. Paltiel, D. Pelleg, J. M. Rowe, and E. Yom-Tov. Patterns of information-seeking for cancer on the internet: an analysis of real world data. *PloS one*, 7(9):e45921, 2012.

[8] P. M. Polgreen, Y. Chen, D. M. Pennock, and F. D. Nelson. Using internet searches for influenza surveillance. *Clinical Infectious Diseases*, 47:1443Ű8, 2008.

[9] E. Yom-Tov, D. Borsa, I. J. Cox, and R. A. McKendry. Detecting disease outbreaks in mass gatherings using internet data. *Journal of medical Internet research*, 16(6), 2014.

[10] E. Yom-Tov and L. Fernandez-Luque. Information is in the eye of the beholder: Seeking information on the MMR vaccine through an internet search engine. In *Proceedings of the 2014 conference of the American Medical Informatics Association*, 2014.

[11] E. Yom-Tov, L. Fernandez-Luque, I. Weber, and P. S. Crain. Pro-anorexia and pro-recovery photo sharing: A tale of two warring tribes. *J Med Internet Res*, 14(6):e151, Nov 2012.

[12] E. Yom-Tov and E. Gabrilovich. Postmarket drug surveillance without trial costs: discovery of adverse drug reactions through large-scale analysis of web search queries. *Journal of medical Internet research*, 15(6), 2013.

[13] E. Yom-Tov, R. W. White, and E. Horvitz. Seeking insights about cycling mood disorders via anonymized search logs. *Journal of medical Internet research*, 16(2), 2014.

Distributed Graph Algorithmics: Theory and Practice

Silvio Lattanzi
Google Research, New York
silviol@google.com

Vahab Mirrokni
Google Research, New York
mirrokni@google.com

Categories and Subject Descriptors

F.0 [**Theory of Computation**]: General

Keywords

Parallel computing, MapReduce algorithms, Large scale data-mining

ABSTRACT

As a fundamental tool in modeling and analyzing social, and information networks, large-scale graph mining is an important component of any tool set for big data analysis. Processing graphs with hundreds of billions of edges is only possible via developing distributed algorithms under distributed graph mining frameworks such as MapReduce, Pregel, Gigraph, and alike. For these distributed algorithms to work well in practice, we need to take into account several metrics such as the number of rounds of computation and the communication complexity of each round. For example, given the popularity and ease-of-use of MapReduce framework, developing practical algorithms with good theoretical guarantees for basic graph algorithms is a problem of great importance.

In this tutorial, we first discuss how to design and implement algorithms based on traditional MapReduce architecture. In this regard, we discuss various basic graph theoretic problems such as computing connected components, maximum matching, MST, counting triangle and overlapping or balanced clustering. We discuss a computation model for MapReduce and describe the sampling, filtering, local random walk, and core-set techniques to develop efficient algorithms in this framework. At the end, we explore the possibility of employing other distributed graph processing frameworks. In particular, we study the effect of augmenting MapReduce with a distributed hash table (DHT) service and also discuss the use of a new graph processing framework called ASYMP based on asynchronous message-passing method. In particular, we will show that using ASyMP, one can improve the CPU usage, and achieve significantly improved running time.

WSDM'15, February 2–6, 2015, Shanghai, China.
ACM 978-1-4503-3317-7/15/02.
http://dx.doi.org/10.1145/2684822.2697043.

1. SHORT BIOGRAPHIES OF THE TUTORS

Silvio Lattanzi

Silvio Lattanzi is a Senior Research Scientist at Google Research New York. He received his Phd from University La Sapienza of Rome. During his PhD he interned twice at Google Research Mountain View and once at Yahoo! Research Santa Clara, he also spent a semester visiting University of Texas Austin. His main research interests are in large-scale graph mining, information retrieval and probabilistic algorithms. Silvio has published several papers in top tier conferences in information retrieval, social network analysis and algorithms. He also served as program committee or senior program committee for several conferences including WWW, WSDM and KDD. Recently, he serves as a tech lead for the large-scale graph mining project at Google Research New York.

Vahab Mirrokni

Vahab Mirrokni is leading the algorithms research group at Google Research New York where he is a Senior Staff Research Scientist. He joined Google after research appointments at Microsoft Research, MIT, and Amazon.com. He received a B.Sc. from Sharif University in 2001 and a Ph.D from MIT in 2005. He has published more than 100 papers in journals and conferences and has filed more than 30 patents in these areas. He has been the co-winner of the SODA 2005 best student paper award, and the ACM EC 2008 outstanding paper award. Vahab's main research interests are algorithms design, large-scale graph mining, and the Internet Economics. He has served as a PC, and Senior PC member of several top conferences in these areas including EC, WWW, KDD, WSDM, and SODA. Previously, he has presented tutorials at ICML, WWW, ACM EC, and SIGMETRICS conferences. At Google, he leads several efforts in optimization for online advertising and large-scale graph mining. Vahab is now the tech lead manager for the large-scale graph mining project at Google Research New York.

DL-WSDM'15: Workshop on Deep Learning for Web Search and Data Mining

Bin Gao
Microsoft Research
13F, Bldg 2, No. 5, Danling St
Beijing, 100080, P. R. China
bingao@microsoft.com

Jiang Bian
Microsoft Research
13F, Bldg 2, No. 5, Danling St
Beijing, 100080, P. R. China
jibian@microsoft.com

ABSTRACT

In recent years, deep learning has been a very hot topic in the machine learning community. It has brought break-through results in image classification and speech recognition. Most recently, researchers have also got many promising results in natural language processing using deep learning techniques. As machine learning techniques are widely used in the Web search and data mining applications, many researchers and practitioners are studying the possibility of applying the recently-developed deep learning techniques into these applications. Some of them have made very promising progress, and thus it is a good time to hold a workshop to discuss and share the problems and progress in using deep learning techniques to improve Web search and data mining tasks.

Categories and Subject Descriptors

I.2.6 [**Computing Methodologies**]: Artificial Intelligence - Learning

Keywords

Machine learning; deep learning; information retrieval; data mining.

1. DESCRIPTION

The main objective and goal of this workshop is to bring together researchers and practitioners that are applying machine learning (especially deep learning) techniques in Web search and data mining tasks, and enable them to share their latest research results, to express their opinions, and to discuss future directions.

The algorithms and applications discussed in this workshop are in the scope of Web search and data mining tasks.

We expect that the WSDM audience get more familiar with the progress of deep learning and get more willing to try deep learning techniques in their research or application problems.

WSDM'15, February 2–6, 2015, Shanghai, China.
ACM 978-1-4503-3317-7/15/02.
http://dx.doi.org/10.1145/2684822.2697028.

2. TOPICS AND THEMES

The topics and themes in this workshop are highly related to WSDM. They include but not limited to:

1. Deep learning algorithms and models for search and data mining
2. Unsupervised feature learning models for search and mining applications
3. Inference and optimization algorithms in deep learning for search and data mining
4. Semi-supervised learning and transfer learning algorithms
5. Deep learning implementation issues, parallelization, software platforms, and tools

3. ORGANIZERS

Bin Gao is a lead researcher in Internet Economics and Computational Advertising Group (IECA), Microsoft Research. His research interests include machine learning, data mining, information retrieval, and computational advertising. He has authored two book chapters, 30 papers in top conferences and journals, and over 20 granted or pending patents. He co-authored the best student paper at SIGIR (2008). He serves as PC for SIGIR (2009 2014), WWW (2011 2013), and senior PC for CIKM (2011). He is a reviewer for TKDE, TIST, PRL, IRJ, etc. He is a tutorial speaker at WWW (2011) and SIGIR (2012). He is a workshop organizer at ICDM (2012), SIGIR (2013), KDD (2013), and ICML (2014).

Jiang Bian is a researcher in Microsoft Research, and his current research focuses on machine learning, data mining, and computational advertising. Before joining Microsoft, he worked at Yahoo! Labs and did many studies on content optimization and personalization for Yahoo!'s key content modules as well as local content search and recommendation for Yahoo!'s local services. Jiang received his B.S. from Peking University (2006) and Ph.D. from Georgia Institute of Technology (2010), both in Computer Science. He authored tens of academic research papers receiving hundreds of citations, filed a couple of U.S. patents, and served as PC member for a few international conferences, such as WWW, KDD, SIGIR, AAAI, IJCAI, CIKM, etc. He played as local co-chair for CIKM 2013. And, he also served as peer reviewer for a few journals, including TOIS, TIST, TKDE, JMLR, etc.

HIA'15: Heterogeneous Information Access Workshop at WSDM 2015

Ke Zhou
Yahoo Labs
London, U.K.
kezhou@yahoo-inc.com

Roger Jie Luo
Yahoo Labs
Sunnyvale, USA
luojie@yahoo-inc.com

Djoerd Hiemstra
Department of Computer Science
University of Twente
hiemstra@cs.utwente.nl

Joemon M. Jose
School of Computing Science
University of Glasgow
Joemon.Jose@glasgow.ac.uk

ABSTRACT

The HIA'15 workshop aims to bring together information retrieval practitioners from industry and academic researchers concerned with heterogeneous information access and search federation. We would like to create a forum to encourage discussion and exchange of ideas on heterogeneous information access in different contexts. To facilitate the discussion, we encourage submissions on ideas and results from different aspects of heterogeneous information access including aggregated search, composite retrieval, personal search, structured search, etc. Another objective of the workshop is to encourage submissions with novel ideas (e.g. new applications) on heterogeneous information access and potential future directions of this area.

Categories and Subject Descriptors

H.3.3 [**Information Systems**]: Information Search and Retrieval

Keywords

federated search, aggregated search, composite retrieval

1. INTRODUCTION

Information access is becoming increasingly heterogeneous. Especially when the user's information need is for exploratory purpose, federating a set of diverse results from different resources [6] could benefit the user. For example, when a user is planning a trip to China, retrieving and showing results from vertical search engines like travel, flight information, map and Q2A sites could satisfy the user's rich and diverse information need. It is also common that users search their own desktop (e.g. Splotlight) to re-find or browse different types of files (source codes, documents, emails, etc.) when aiming to fulfill a given work task. This heterogeneous search paradigm is useful in many contexts and brings many new challenges.

Aggregated search [1] and composite retrieval [3] are two instances of this new search paradigm that aims to be suitable for such information needs. Federation could also be useful in several other scenarios: a user aims to re-find comprehensive information about his query in his personal search [4]; or a user searches and gathers different nugget information (e.g. an entity) from a set of RDF Web datasets [2] (e.g., DBpedia, IMDB, etc.); or a user searches a set of different files in a peer-to-peer online file sharing systems [5]. This is an emerging area as different services provided are becoming more heterogeneous and complex. Therefore, there are a number of directions that might be interesting for both the research and industrial community. How to select the most relevant resources and present them concisely in order to best satisfy the user? How to model the complex user behavior in this search scenario? How can we evaluate the performance of these systems? Those are a few key interesting research questions to study for heterogeneous information access. The main objective of the workshop is to draw researchers' attention to this rising field as well as to inspire them to discuss and collaborate in order to further define new directions for heterogeneous information access.

2. WORKSHOP TOPICS

The workshop topics are within the context of heterogeneous information access. They include but are not limited to:

- User Modelling for Heterogeneous Information Access
  - Short and Long-term User Modelling
  - Personalization
  - Diversification
  - Coherence
- Metrics and Measurements
  - Metrics based on test collection

WSDM'15, February 2–6, 2015, Shanghai, China.
ACM 978-1-4503-3317-7/15/02.
http://dx.doi.org/10.1145/2684822.2697029.

- Controlled laboratory study
- Online metrics
- Test Collection

- Optimization
  - Resource/Vertical Selection
  - Result Presentation Visualization Strategies
  - Presentation Optimization
  - Result Diversification
- Applications
  - Aggregated/Federated Search
  - Composite Retrieval
  - Personal Search
  - Structured/Semantic Search
  - Peer-to-peer information retrieval

3. WORKSHOP ORGANIZERS

- **Ke Zhou** is a research scientist working in Yahoo Labs London. He was previously a research associate in Language Technology Group in University of Edinburgh working on text mining and information retrieval. He has conducted his PhD research on evaluation of aggregated search at the Information Retrieval Group in University of Glasgow. He has published in reputable conferences and journals (SIGIR, WWW, CIKM, TOIS) and served as PC member for SIGIR, CIKM, ECIR and AIRS. He also served as a co-organizer for NTCIR-11/12 IMine task and TREC FedWeb 2014 task.

- **Roger Jie Luo** is a Research Scientist and an engineering & science lead at Yahoo Labs. At Yahoo, he lead the efforts to improve the ranking of aggregated search results on the Yahoo! search result page and on understanding the users' intents given a query. He obtained his PhD in computer science on machine learning from Swiss Federal Institute of Technology in Lausanne (EPFL), Switzerland.

- **Djoerd Hiemstra** is an associate professor of search engine and database technology at the University of Twente. He wrote an often cited PhD thesis on the use of statistical language models for information retrieval. His research interests include information retrieval, natural language processing and probabilistic graphical models. He co-authored over 200 research papers. Djoerd co-organized several workshops and conferences including ACM SIGIR 2007, several editions of the Dutch-Belgian Information Retrieval Workshop (DIR), the SIGIR 2010 workshop on Accessible search and the ECIR 2013 workshop on Group membership and search.

- **Joemon M. Jose** is a full Professor at the School of Computing Science, University of Glasgow. He is a fellow of the BCS, IET and a chartered information technology professional (CITP), member of the ACM and IEEE. He has a well-established reputation in research on multimedia information retrieval, developing advanced retrieval models, studying the role of emotion in search, personalization and adaptive retrieval. He has published over 150 journal and conference articles and leads a team of 9 PhD students and 2 post-doctoral researchers. He successfully, as local coordinator, completed 4 major EU funded projects on multimedia retrieval and multi-modal interaction (SALERO, MIAUCE, SEMEDIA, K-SPACE) and now participates in the LiMOSiNe project. He has organized number of information retrieval related events like ICMR 2014, ECDL 2010, workshops at previous SIGIR conferences, IR Fest in Glasgow 2005 etc. He has been senior PC member of the SIGIR, CIKM, ECIR conferences.

4. WORKSHOP PROGRAM

4.1 Invited Speakers

- Yiqun Liu, Associate Professor, Tsinghua University
- Maarten de Rijke, Professor, University of Amsterdam
- Milad Shokouhi, Senior Applied Science Lead, Microsoft Research Cambridge
- Gui-rong Xue, Senior Director, Aliyun.com; Associate Professor, Shanghai Jiao-Tong University

4.2 Program Committee

- Jaime Arguello (University of North Carolina at Chapel Hill, USA)
- Roi Blanco (Yahoo! Lab Barcelona, Spain)
- Mohand Boughanem (University of Toulouse, France)
- Jamie Callan (Carnegie Mellon University, USA)
- Zhicheng Dou (Microsoft Research Asia, China)
- Jin Young Kim (Microsoft Bing, USA)
- Yiqun Liu (Tsinghua University, China)
- Ilya Markov (University of Amsterdam, Netherlands)
- Maarten de Rijke (University of Amsterdam, Netherlands)
- Pavel Serdyukov (Yandex Moscow, Russia)
- Milad Shokouhi, (Microsoft Research Cambridge, U.K.)
- Paul Thomas (CSIRO, Australia)
- Arjen P. de Vries (CWI, Netherlands)
- Hengshuai Yao (Yahoo Labs Sunnyvale, USA)
- Qian You (Amazon, USA)

5. REFERENCES

[1] J. Arguello, F. Diaz, J. Callan, and J.-F. Crespo. Sources of evidence for vertical selection. In *SIGIR '09*, pages 315–322, New York, NY, USA, 2009. ACM.

[2] D. Herzig, and T. Thanh. Heterogeneous web data search using relevance-based on the fly data integration. In *WWW '12*, pages 141–150, New York, NY, USA, 2012. ACM.

[3] H. Bota, K. Zhou, J. M. Jose, and M. Lalmas. Composite retrieval of heterogeneous web search. In *WWW'14*, pages 119–130, International World Wide Web Conferences 2014.

[4] K. Jinyoung, and W. B. Croft. Ranking using multiple document types in desktop search. In *SIGIR'10*, pages 50–57, Proceedings of the 33rd international ACM SIGIR conference on Research and development in information retrieval. ACM, 2010.

[5] T. Almer S., D. Hiemstra, and D. Trieschnigg. Peer-to-peer information retrieval: An overview. In *TOIS 2012*. ACM Transactions on Information Systems (TOIS) 30.2 (2012): 9.

[6] M. Shokouhi and S. Luo. Federated search. In *FTIIR*. Foundations and Trends in Information Retrieval 5.1 (2011): 1-102.

WSDM'15 Workshop Summary / Scalable Data Analytics: Theory and Applications

Kaizhu Huang
Dept. of Electronic and Electric Engineering
Xi'an Jiaotong-Liverpool University
Ren'ai Road 111
Higher Education Town, SIP
Suzhou, Jiangsu, China
kaizhu.huang@xjtlu.edu.cn

Haiqin Yang[1,2], Irwin King[1,2], Michael R. Lyu[1,2]
[1] Shenzhen Key Laboratory of Rich Media Big Data Analytics and Application
SZRI, Chinese University of Hong Kong
[2] Dept. of Computer Science & Engineering
Chinese University of Hong Kong, Hong Kong
{hqyang,king, lyu}@cse.cuhk.edu.hk

ABSTRACT

The SDA workshop at WSDM 2015 is the fifth International Workshop on Scalable Data Analytics, following the previous four workshops of SDA respectively held at IEEE Big Data 2013, PAKDD 2014, IEEE Big Data 2014, and IEEE ICDM 2014. This series of workshops aims to provide professionals, researchers, and technologists with a single forum where they can discuss and share the state-of-the-art theories and applications of scalable data analytics technologies. In particular, in the era of information explosion, the scientific, biomedical, and engineering research communities are undergoing a profound transformation where discoveries and innovations increasingly rely on massive amounts of data. The characteristics of volume, velocity, variety and veracity originated in the massive big data then bring challenges to current data analytics techniques. The focus of the fifth SDA is to discuss how we can scale up data analytics techniques for modeling and analyzing big data from various domains.

Categories and Subject Descriptors

I.2.6 [**ARTIFICIAL INTELLIGENCE**]: Learning—*Knowledge acquisition* ; H.m [**Information Systems**]: MISCELLANEOUS

Keywords

Big Data, Scalable, Data Analytics

1. INTRODUCTION

With the fast evolving technology for data collection, data transmission, and data analysis, the scientific, biomedical, and engineering research communities are undergoing a profound transformation where discoveries and innovations increasingly rely on massive amounts of data. New prediction techniques, including novel statistical, mathematical, and modeling techniques are enabling a paradigm shift in scientific and biomedical investigation. Data become the fourth pillar of science and engineering, offering complementary insights in addition to theory, experiments, and computer simulation. Advances in machine learning, data mining, and visualization are enabling new ways of extracting useful information from massive data sets. The characteristics of volume, velocity, variety and veracity bring challenges to current data analytics techniques. It is desirable to scale up data analytics techniques for modeling and analyzing big data from various domains.

This series of workshop features the following topics of interest, but not limited to:

- Distributed data analytics architectures
- Theory and algorithms for scalable descriptive statistical modeling
- Theory and algorithms of scalable predictive statistical modeling
- Scalable analytics techniques for temporal and spatial data
- Scalable data analytics algorithms in large graphs
- Novel applications of scalable machine learning

Following the previous four workshops, the fifth International Workshop on SDA aims to provide professionals, researchers, and technologists with a single forum where they can discuss and share the state-of-the-art theories and applications of scalable data analytics technologies. The specific focus of the fifth SDA will be described in the next section.

2. WORKSHOP FOCUS

This fifth International Workshop on SDA focuses on scalable extensions of many famous machine learning algorithms as well as their interesting applications in big data. In particular, the workshop discusses distributed and scalable versions of metric learning algorithms, scalable and discriminative feature generation algorithms, scalable text clustering and document representation, fast and multilevel co-clustering algorithms, scalable non-negative matrix factorization, and scalable point-of-interest recommendation. Applications of these scalable extensions in social networks,

WSDM'15, February 2–6, 2015, Shanghai, China.
ACM 978-1-4503-3317-7/15/02.
http://dx.doi.org/10.1145/2684822.2697030.

document classification, pattern recognition are also the focus of this year's workshop. Expert researchers in the above mentioned fields submitted position papers in the fifth SDA workshop and they exchange ideas specifically in the following aspects:

- Retweet scale prediction model
- Efficient influence maximization algorithm in social networks
- Scalable text clustering and fast multilevel co-clustering for social network data
- Fast and hybrid deep belief network for document representation
- Distributed non-negative matrix factorization
- Accelerated information-theoretic metric learning
- Heterogeneous information network based ranking and clustering of mobile apps
- Scalable and discriminative random nonlinear features from data
- Scalable point-of-interest recommendation for social networks
- Other fundamental and theoretic analysis in big data

3. CONCLUSION

Following the previous successful four SDA workshops respectively at IEEE Big Data 2013, PAKDD 2014, IEEE Big Data 2014, and IEEE ICDM 2014, the fifth International Workshop on Scalable Data Analytics aims to provide professionals, researchers, and technologists with a single forum where they can discuss and share the state-of-the-art theories and applications of scalable data analytics technologies. More specifically, this workshop accepts position papers that investigate scalable extensions of many famous machine learning algorithms (e.g., scalable metric learning, scalable non-negative matrix factorization, scalable feature extraction, and scalable and fast text clustering algorithms) as well as their interesting applications in massive data (e.g. social networks, document classification, and large-scale pattern recognition). New research trends in Scalable Data Analytics will be also extensively discussed in the workshop.

Acknowledgments

The workshop was partly supported by the National Basic Research Program of China (2014CB340401, 2014CB340405, and 2012CB316301), National Science Foundation of China (NSFC 61473236), the Research Grants Council of the Hong Kong Special Administrative Region, China (Project No. CUHK 413212 and CUHK 415113), Microsoft Research Asia Regional Seed Fund in Big Data Research (Grant No. FY13-RES-SPONSOR-036), and Jiangsu University Natural Science Research Programme (14KJB520037).

The 2nd workshop on Vertical Search Relevance at WSDM 2015

Dawei Yin
Yahoo Labs
daweiy@yahoo-inc.com

Chih-Chieh Hung
Rakuten Inc.
smalloshin@gmail.com

Rui Li, Yi Chang
Yahoo Labs
{ruililab,yichang}@yahoo-inc.com

It is our great pleasure to welcome you to the VSR 2015, the second International Workshop on Vertical Search Relevance, held as part of the WSDM 2015 conference in Shanghai, China.

Background: As the popularity of search engines has grown, the information needs of end users continue being refined. One of the emerging trends is using vertical search intent. For example, a user may want to find a restaurant near her current location; another user may want to follow the recent development of a breaking event such as the earthquake in Japan. Some recent studies show that at least 20% of Web queries have some local intent [3]. As a result, vertical search engines start attracting more and more attention. For example, many search engines provide specialized vertical search results for local search[1]and for real-time search [2]. Furthermore, vertical search results are often slotted into general Web search results [1, 2]. Thus, designing effective ranking functions for vertical search has become practically important to improve users' search experience.

A natural way to build a vertical search engine is to apply the existing ranking techniques on a vertical. In the TREC conference, several specialized tracks such as blog and chemical tracks have been introduced to provide a test bed to study retrieval tasks on these special text collections. The main focus of these tracks is on content-based relevance and most participants extend traditional IR techniques to consider a few task-specific ranking signals. Recently, learning to rank approaches have been studied extensively and shown to be effective to combine many useful signals into a ranking function. To adapt such a technique on a vertical, an intuitive approach is to construct a training data set by collecting a set of queries and documents which belong to the vertical and asking human editors to give a single relevance label between a query and a document. A ranking function thus can be learned for the vertical.

[1]Google Local. http://local.google.com/.
[2]Cinicalkey. https://www.clinicalkey.com/

WSDM'15, February 2–6, 2015, Shanghai, China.
ACM 978-1-4503-3317-7/15/02.
http://dx.doi.org/10.1145/2684822.2697031.

However, we observed that in many verticals, the meaning of relevance is domain-specific and usually consists of multiple well-defined aspects. Blindly applying the conventional learning to rank approaches by ignoring vertical-specific domain knowledge may not be effective. Thus, we have identified a list of challenging research issues in the field of relevance for vertical search, which mainly fall into two categories. First category includes how to learn an effective ranking model considering multi-facets relevance: (1) Since there are several pertinent aspects in a vertical, human editors naturally need to consider and tradeoff the relevance from different aspects before making the overall relevance judgment. Thus assessing aspect relevance is a necessary step. (2) Trading off multiple aspects is not trivial since such a tradeoff can vary for different queries or in different contexts. (3) For different verticals, different aspects are involved and the tradeoff among aspects is vertical-dependent. Collecting training data with overall relevance for a new vertical requires human editors learn how to appropriately tradeoff different aspects. Second category focuses on building effective business model in the context of specific vertical search systems.

Objectives: This workshop is dedicated to presentations and discussions on relevance for vertical search. For the workshop, we aim to bring together researchers from IR, ML, NLP, and other areas of computer and information science who are working on or interested in this area, and provide a forum for them to identify the issues and the challenges, to share their latest research results, to express a diverse range of opinions about this topic, and to discuss future directions.

Review Process: The call for papers solicited submissions in the area of vertical search. Themes of interests were diverse and spanned technologies and applications, models, algorithms, and evaluation methods. Each submission was reviewed by at least two Program Committee members and final decisions were made by the workshop chairs. PC members are listed below and include many experts in the field. We are grateful to all of them for their thorough and insightful reviews.

Program: In this year's workshop, we are delighted to have several invited talks in both academic and industrial tracks as part of the workshop. Min Zhang from Tsinghua University, Jun Xu from Chinese Academy of Sciences, Ya Zhang from Shanghai Jiaotong University will give the invited talks in the academic track. Toru Shimizu from Yahoo Japan, Hao Ma from Microsoft Research, Tzu-Chiang Liou from Yahoo Taiwan and Jie Luo from Yahoo Labs will give invited talks in the industrial track.

We hope that you will find this workshop interesting and thought-provoking and that the workshop will provide you with a valuable opportunity to share ideas with other researchers and practitioners from institutions around the world.

1. REFERENCES

[1] J. Arguello, F. Diaz, J. Callan, and J.-F. Crespo. Sources of evidence for vertical selection. In *Proceedings of the 32Nd International ACM SIGIR Conference on Research and Development in Information Retrieval*, SIGIR '09, pages 315–322, New York, NY, USA, 2009. ACM.

[2] J. Arguello, F. Diaz, and J.-F. Paiement. Vertical selection in the presence of unlabeled verticals. In *Proceedings of the 33rd International ACM SIGIR Conference on Research and Development in Information Retrieval*, SIGIR '10, pages 691–698, New York, NY, USA, 2010. ACM.

[3] P. Venetis, H. Gonzalez, C. S. Jensen, and A. Halevy. Hyper-local, directions-based ranking of places. *Proc. VLDB Endow.*, 4(5):290–301, Feb. 2011.

An Approach to the Problem of Annotation of Research Publications

Ekaterina Chernyak
National Research University – Higher School of Economics
Moscow, Russia
echernyak@hse.ru

ABSTRACT

An approach to multiple labelling research papers is explored. We develop techniques for annotating/labelling research papers in informatics and computer sciences with key phrases taken from the ACM Computing Classification System. The techniques utilise a phrase-to-text relevance measure so that only those phrases that are most relevant go to the annotation. Three phrase-to-text relevance measures are experimentally compared in this setting. The measures are: (a) cosine relevance score between conventional vector space representations of the texts coded with tf-idf weighting; (b) popular characteristic of probability of term generation BM25; and (c) an in-house characteristic of conditional probability of symbols averaged over matching fragments in suffix trees representing texts and phrases, CPAMF. In an experiment conducted over a set of texts published in journals of the ACM and manually annotated by their authors, CPAMF outperforms both the cosine measure and BM25 by a wide margin.

Categories and Subject Descriptors: I.2.7 Natural Language Processing: Text analysis

Keywords: phrase-to-text relevance; annotated suffix tree; text labelling

1. INTRODUCTION

Automating semantic text analysis is currently one of the most important and demanding issues in informatics and computer science. Many researches currently are engaged in text classification or categorisation problems. Generically, the problem can be stated as follows. Given a collection of text documents and a set of labels represented by a text phrase each, annotate a document with relevant labels. This problem underlies projects in information retrieval [?], text cataloging [?, ?], text annotation [?], etc. Both machine learning approaches, self-learning and supervised learning, have been followed in the literature. Initially, an assumption was that a text document should be annotated by a single category, like in a classifying task. Currently, a more relaxed assumption of using several labels (multi-label classification) is getting prevailed. In our case, the issue is in annotation of research papers, so that a taxonomy of the corresponding domain should be utilized. Specifically, papers in Computer Science can be categorized according to Computing Classification System developed by the international Association for Computing Machinery. CCS is a hierarchical taxonomy in which every topic comprises some finer topics and itself is part of more general topic. For example, according to ACM CCS, "Data mining" is part of "Information systems applications" and it is divided in "Clustering", "Collaborative filtering", "Association rules" and etc. Authors of [?] review and empirically compare supervised methods for multi-label classification, and paper [?] applies some of these methods to ACM CCS.

Self-learning labelling methods so far have received little attention, perhaps because both proper methods and test collections are lacking. In general self-learning methods of text analysis lead to rather poor results in comparison to supervised methods (see, for example [?, ?]). This work presents a study on usage string-to-text relevance measures for self-learning multi-label annotation of research papers. String-to-text relevance measures are widely used in various text analysis tasks [?, ?, ?, ?]. They involve only sequences of characters and their frequencies and disregard syntax, grammar, and semantic features. This makes this approach language independent, thus much universal. On the other hand, loosing natural language features makes it difficult or impossible to exploit important semantic relations, such as synonymy, and of course the sentence structure.

The goal of this paper is to experimentally compare string-to-text relevance measures as tools for self-learning multi-label classification of research papers. We take most popular measures from the vector space [?] and probabilistic models [?]. As to the suffix tree approach [?, ?] we extend it with a relevance measure of our own [?]. Our measure, CPAMF, has a clear operational meaning as a characteristic of conditional probability of symbols averaged over matching fragments of strings and texts .

A very first issue one faces when conducting experiments on text annotation is in finding a reliable test bed. To this end, we use a collection of abstracts of papers published in journals of ACM and manually annotated by the authors of papers with key phrases taken from ACM CCS 2012 taxonomy. We apply several most popular text preprocessing techniques to this collection. To measure the quality of obtained annotations we use two popular measures and a measure of our own.

WSDM'15, February 2–6, 2015, Shanghai, China.

http://dx.doi.org/10.1145/2684822.2697032.

The paper is organised as follows. Section 2 defines relevance measures to be used in the experiments. Section 3 lists the text preprocessing techniques under consideration. Section 4 presents the experimental setup. Section 5 describes three measures to evaluate how good are found annotations. Section 6 presents results of the experimental comparison of text preprocessing techniques and relevance measures. Section 7 gives a conclusion. The work was partly supported by the group project "Methods for text analysis and visualization" funded by the NRU HSE Academic Fund in 2013-2014 and supervised by prof. Boris Mirkin.

2. RELEVANCE MEASURES

Consider three models of text representation: vector space model (VSM), probabilistic model (PM) and annotated suffix trees (AST) and corresponding phrase-to-text relevance measures. The relevance measures are used to annotate research papers. Each paper is represented by its abstract and a set of taxonomy topics (index terms), manually assigned by the authors of the paper. The better the computational annotations match those manual, the better the labelling algorithm.

2.1 Vector space model

According to [?], a text document is represented as a set of words (or any other document constituents). Each word corresponds to a dimension in the vector space. A vector component is usually the tf-idf weight, which stands for the frequency of the word in the document divided by the logarithm of the relative number of documents containing the word [?]. The phrase-to-text relevance is defined in the following way: represent both the phrase and the text as vectors in the same vector space. Then the relevance value is computed as the similarity between the vectors.

Let us consider the abstract of a research paper and the ACM CCS taxonomy topic as two sets of terms, where the term is either a word as it occurs in the text or a preprocessed word. The tf-idf weight of the term is $w_{ia} = tf \times idf = tf_{ia} * \log \frac{|A|}{n(t_i)+1}$, where tf_{ia} is the frequency of the term t_i in the abstract a, $n(t_i)$ is the number of abstracts, containing the term t_i, $|A|$ is the total number of abstracts.

We construct a corresponding vector in the space of terms for each abstract. The number of dimensions is N, the components are tf-idf weights. In the same way we construct vectors of tf-idf weights for taxonomy topics. We estimate the taxonomy topic-to-abstract relevance as the cosine between corresponding vectors. Let w_{ia}, w_{iq} be the tf-idf weights of the t_i for the abstract $a \in A$ and taxonomy topic q. The cosine relevance measure is as follows:

$$relevance(topic, abstract) = \cos \vec{q}\vec{a} = \frac{\vec{a} \times \vec{q}}{||\vec{a}|| \times ||\vec{q}||} = \\ = \frac{\sum_{i=1}^{N} w_{ia} \times w_{iq}}{\sqrt{\sum_{i=1}^{N} w_{ia}} \sqrt{\sum_{i=1}^{N} w_{iq}}}$$

2.2 Probabilistic model

The probabilistic model is built under a theoretical assumption that any text under consideration is a mixture of two Poisson distributions. One distribution is responsible for ordinary words, another for so called elite words. The document is in a sense about the concept expressed with elite words [?]. A phrase-to-text relevance measure in this model estimates the probability that the words that occur in the phrase are elite. Let us consider both the abstract and a taxonomy topic as two sets of terms. The BM25 measure is defined as follows:

$$relevance(topic, abstract) = \sum_{i=1}^{N} IDF(t_i) \times \\ \times \frac{k_1 + 1)tf_{ia}}{tf_{ia} + k_1(1 - b + b\frac{|A|}{avgdl})}$$

where $avgdl$ is the average number of words in an abstract, b, k_1 are constant numbers, taken to be equal to 1.5 and 0.75, respectively, according to [?]. The IDF function is used as a normalizing factor:

$$IDF(t_i) = \log \frac{|A| - n(t_i) + 0.5}{n(t_i) + 0.5},$$

where $|A|$ is the total number of annotations and $n(t_i)$ is the number of abstracts containing the term t_i. The IDF function stands for the inverse frequency: the more abstracts contain this term, the less important it is.

2.3 Annotated suffix tree

According to the annotated suffix tree model [?, ?], a text document is not a set of words or terms, but a set of the so-called fragments, the sequences of characters arranged in the same order as they occur in the text. Each fragment is characterized by a float number. The greater the number is, the more important the fragment is for the text. An annotated suffix tree (see Fig. 1) is a data structure used for computing and storing all fragments of the text and their frequencies. It is a rooted tree in which:

- Every node corresponds to one character
- Every node is labeled by the frequency of the text fragment encoded by the path from the root to the node.

To build an AST, we split the text in strings of three words, and apply them consecutively to warrant that the resulting AST has a modest size. Moreover, it is good for matching with taxonomy topics because they are phrases of similar length. Our algorithm for constructing an AST [?] is a light modification of the well-known algorithms for constructing suffix trees [?], [?]. First we build an AST for every abstract. Next we match the taxonomy topics to the AST to estimate the relevance. This is done in several steps:

1. Every taxonomy topic is split in suffixes;
2. Every suffix is matched to the AST. A match is a path from the root of the AST, that coincides with the beginning of the current suffix of the whole suffix. To estimate the match we use scoring function:

$$score(match(suffix, ast)) = \\ = \sum_{node \in match} \phi(\frac{f(node)}{f(parent(node))}),$$

where $f(node)$ is the frequency of the matching node and $f(parent(node))$ is it's parent frequency;

Table 1: Text preprocessing techniques

Name	Description
words	Words
stems	Stems (Porter stemmer in NLTK is used)
coll3	All matches of the taxonomy topic suffixes to the AST built for abstracts. (In this table, the abstracts are split in three word strings.)
coll3.5	Terms from coll3 set consisting of 5 or more characters

3. Then the relevance is estimated by averaging the score of a symbol:

$$relevance(topic, abstract) = SCORE(topic, ast) = = \frac{\sum_{suffix} score(match(suffix, ast))/|suffix|}{|string|},$$

where $|suffix|$ and $|string|$ are the lengths of the suffix and the string.

Note, that "score" is a scaling function, that converts a match score into a relevance estimation. We consider three types of the scaling functions, according to [?], where the AST method was used to categorize e-mails:

- Linear function: $\phi(x) = x$
- Logit function:

$$\phi(x) = \log \frac{x}{1-x} = \log x - \log(1-x)$$

- Root function $\phi(x) = \sqrt{x}$

Of them, only the linear scaling function has an obvious meaning: it stands for the conditional probability of characters averaged over matching fragments (CPAMF).

Big ASTs may suffer from the noise produced by the first levels in the tree. The nodes on these levels have approximately the same frequencies, which are rather high, and equally influence scores of any match. The first level in the AST is responsible for single characters, the second level for pairs of characters and so on. We assume that such short fragments of texts hardly can be meaningful. To check whether these nodes really produce noise in the relevance estimates or not, we compute relevance estimates at which a few initial levels of the AST are not taken into account. We denote by $\phi.X$ such a scaling function ϕ that accounts only those nodes that start from the level $X = 1, 2, \ldots$.

On the whole we use three classes of AST relevance score functions with different scaling functions and noise removal options. The method outputs the list of taxonomy topics in the descending order of their relevance scores.

3. TEXT PREPROCESSING

Vector space model and probabilistic model require a text to be represented as a set of terms. A term is an unmodified word or a word after preprocessing. With AST text model, we use the AST matches to taxonomy topics as terms. These matches may include rather long fragments, quite capable to capture the word order. Table 1 enumerates all preprocessing techniques used in our experiments.

Table 2: Relevance measures used in the experiment

Name	Description
cosine	Cosine relevance measure
BM25	BM25 relevance measure
ast.linear	Linear scaled CPAMF
ast.logit	Logit scaled CPAMF
ast.root	Root scaled CPAMF

4. EXPERIMENTAL SETUP

To computationally compare different relevance measures for annotating research papers one needs: an input dataset, methods for measuring relevance and measures to evaluate computational results Let us describe the experimental setup in more detail.

4.1 Input dataset

We adopt the set of research paper abstracts from the ACM Digital Library. Every abstract is already annotated by the authors with so called index terms that are taxonomy topics from the ACM Computing Classification System 2012. Our task is to obtain relevant taxonomy topics and evaluate how well they match the index terms assigned to the paper. Hence the input dataset is threefold:

1. A collection of 244 abstracts of papers published from January 2007 to March 2013 in the following ACM Journals: ACM Transactions on Knowledge Discovery from Data (TKDD), ACM Transactions on Internet Technology (TOIT) and ACM Transactions on Speech and Language Processing (TSLP)
2. The ACM CCS 2012 taxonomy which comprises 2074 taxonomy topics. There are 6 levels the first of which has 13 major divisions.
3. Index terms that are labels assigned to each of the papers by the author(s).

4.2 Relevance measures

We use the three popular relevance measures defined above to estimate the taxonomy topic-to-text relevance: cosine, BM25 and CPAMF with the three scaling functions defined above.

5. RESULT EVALUATION MEASURES

Index terms are used to check, whether an algorithm has obtained a correct annotation by using this or that relevance measure. We use two popular evaluation measures MAP (Mean Average Precision) and $nDCG$ (normalized Discounted Cumulative Gain) [?]. They are widely used for assessment of sets of ordered (ranged) items that appear, for example, in a recommender system [?] or a news extraction system [?]. Learning to rank [?, ?] appears to be another application of the measures as learning criteria. MAP and $nDCG$ suit our purpose quite well, as using any relevance measure results in an ordered list of taxonomy topics. To apply any of MAP and $nDCG$, several steps are required:

- Taxonomy topics are listed in the descending order of the utilized relevance measure
- First k (top k) taxonomy topics are taken into account disregarding the rest

- The evaluation measure is applied to the top k taxonomy topics

MAP is computed as follows:

$$AveP = \frac{\sum_{k=1}^{n} P(k) \times rel(k)}{|relevant\_topics|}$$

$$MAP = \frac{\sum_{a \in abstracts} AveP(a)}{abstracts},$$

where $P(k)$ is precision at k [11], $rel(k)$ is 1 if kth taxonomy topic is the index term and 0 otherwise, $|relevant\_topics|$, is the number of index terms, n is the number of taxonomy topic under consideration. $AveP$ stands for average precision. This feature is computed for every research paper after which MAP is used to aggregate $AveP$.

$nDCG$ is the proportion of the real discounted cumulative gain (DCG) in the ideal gain DCG: $nDCG_k = \frac{DCG_k}{IDCG_k}$, where $DCG_k = rel(1) + \sum_{i=2}^{k} \frac{rel(i)}{\log_2 i}$ is the number of index terms among top k taxonomy topics, normalized by their rank. $IDCG_k = rel(1) + \sum_{i=2}^{irrelevant\_topics} \frac{1}{\log_2 i}$ is the ideal DCG. Of course $nDCG$ can be averaged [?]. Therefore, we compute the average $nDCG$ value for all the 244 abstracts. We take $k = 15$ to be obviously larger than the number of manually assigned index terms.

Also, we propose our own evaluation measure, I_k, which we call $Intersection@k$. For every abstract a we set $i(a) = 1$ if there is an index term among top k taxonomy topics in the corresponding ordering and 0, otherwise. Then $I_k = \sum_{a \in abstracts} i(a)$ This measure has two main advantages. It allows to separate "good" research papers, that are annotated well by the authors, from those "complex" ones, that are not; and to set an optimal k for every research paper.

In fact, MAP and $nDCG$ can be also exploited to set the threshold k, but they are not as intuitive as the I_k.

6. RESULTS

There are four measures to evaluate the quality of the ordered lists of taxonomy topics: intersect I_k at k where $k = 5, 15$; MAP and $nDCG$ at $k = 15$. These measures are used to compare both a) relevance measures and b) preprocessing techniques.

Comparing the values of the relevance measures in Table ??, one can note, that:

- The best results for cosine relevance measure are achieved after using the coll3 preprocessing techniques, since MAP_{15} and $nDCG_{15}$ as well as I_{15} are maximal. However using unmodified words and stems preprocessing techniques leads comparable results.
- For BM25 relevance measure the stemming technique is the winner, as I_5 shows, but at $k = 15$ the unmodified words technique seems to be a better option.
- I_k values provide clear evidence that in general the BM25 relevance measure is not as precise as cosine relevance measure.
- The non-scaling linear CPAMF function provides the highest values according to all three quality measures I_k, MAP_{15} and $nDCG_{15}$.
- The root scaling function achieves a similar accuracy of the labels in contrast to the logit scaling function.

Table 3: Results of using three relevance measures on texts preprocessed with different techniques

Preprocessing technique	I_k		MAP_{15}	$nDCG_{15}$
	I_5	I_{15}		
Cosine relevance measure				
words	44	73	0.0748	0.0245
stems	37	77	0.0788	0.0250
coll3	41	76	0.0911	0.0278
coll3.5	31	71	0.0642	0.0237
BM25 relevance measure				
words	14	52	0.0631	0.0279
stems	21	36	0.0869	0.0259
coll3	15	46	0.0524	0.0224
coll3.5	16	46	0.0577	0.0228
CPAMF relevance measure				
linear.0	75	102	0.3588	0.1124
linear.1	77	105	0.3550	0.1133
linear.2	75	103	0.3486	0.1120
root.0	75	102	0.3657	0.1125
root.1	77	104	0.3561	0.1122
root.2	77	106	0.3497	0.1126
logit.0	36	57	0.1214	0.0450
logit.1	18	33	0.0521	0.0216
logit.2	29	56	0.0780	0.0335

Among the three measures of relevance the linear CPAMF is the most accurate. For example, when CPAMF is used, 7577 index terms are placed among the top five taxonomy topics, whereas the cosine measure and BM25 lead to just 44 and 21 index terms, respectively. The MAP_{15} and $nDCG_{15}$ values for the linear CPAMF are almost four or five times higher than for the cosine measure or BM25. Our hypothesis of the noise coming from the second and third levels of the ASTs is not supported by the experimental results. Clearing only of the very first level, one letter frequencies, is reasonable.

Another way to compare I_k values for different relevance measures is to draw the hit curves, which are piecewise linear curves on the (k, I_k) plane. A hit curve connects I_k values at different k. The higher the hit curve, the more accurate is the relevance measure. If a hit curve for relevance measure A is higher than that for the relevance measure B, one can safely conclude that A is more accurate than B.

The comparison of hit curves on Figure ?? proves that no matter what parameters of relevance measures are, the ast.linear and ast.root relevance measures outperform the cosine and the BM25. Between these two popular relevance measures, cosine and BM25, the former is better than the latter.

7. CONCLUSION

This work explores the issue of computationally annotating/labelling research publications using topics taken from a taxonomy of the research domain under consideration. A specific of this issue is that it concerns mental rather than real objects. Hence the issue of validity of empirical data becomes of great importance. It is not always obvious how to annotate a paper with topics taken from a hierarchical classification system. We suppose that annotations of re-

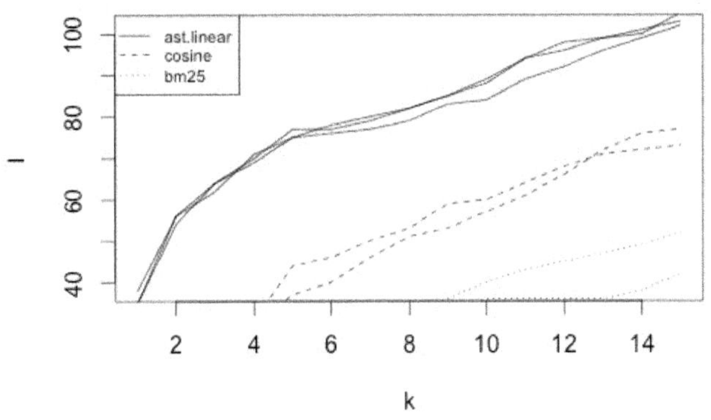

Figure 1: Hit curves of four classes of relevance measures: ast.linear, ast.root, cosine and BM25

search papers made by the authors of research are more adequate than annotations of general documents made by amateurs. Therefore we use research papers published in respected ACM journals and annotated with topics from the ACM CCS 2012. We used string-to-text relevance measure as a main tool for producing self-learning multiple labels. We compared three string-to-text relevance measures: cosine, BM25 and conditional probability of characters averaged over matching fragments in annotated suffix trees (CPAMF).

It appears that the CPAMF outperforms both cosine and BM25 relevance measures in the problem under consideration. Our hypothesis that the first levels of an AST formed by one, two and three letter text fragments give no information for the labelling process proved wrong for the levels 2 and 3, yet correct for the first level. Its removal slightly improves the quality of annotation. Yet in general the match between the automatic annotation and that made by the authors is not quite high, which is not uncommon for self-learning methods in text analysis. Partly this effect is due to differences in the abstracts themselves, but partly this is because the relevance measures take no synonyms into account. Therefore the very first direction to take should be in using synonyms in computing the AST relevance measures. A concept should be represented not by a single string, but by a (fuzzy) set of synonymous topics.

8. REFERENCES

[1] C.D. Manning, P. Raghavan, H. Schutze. *Introduction to information retrieval*, 2008.

[2] F. Sebastiani, Machine learning in automated text categorization. *Journal of ACM Computing Surveys*, 34(1):1-42, 2002.

[3] G. Salton, *Dynamic library and information processing*, 1975.

[4] N. Loukachevitch and B. Dobrov. Large-scale linguistic ontology as a basis for text categorization of legislative documents. *Legal Knowledge and Infromation Systems*, 134:109-134, 2005.

[5] M. Ceci and D. Malerba Classifying web documents in a hierarchy of categories: a comprehensive study. *Journal of Intelligent Information Systems*, 28(1):37-78, 2007.

[6] A.P. Santos and F. Rodrigues. Multi-label hierarchical text vlassification using the ACM taxonomy In *Proceedings of 14th Portuguese Conference on Artificial Intelligence*, pages 553 - 564, Aveiro, Portugal, 2010.

[7] R. Xu, A. Morgan, A. K. Das and A. Garber. Investigation of unsupervised pattern learning techniques for bootstrap construction of a medical treatment lexicon. In *Proceedings of the Workshop on Current Trends in Biomedical Natural Language Processing*, pages 63-70, Stroudsburg, PA, USA, 2009.

[8] J. Grimmer and B. M. Stewart. Text as data: the promise and pittfalls of automatic content analysis methods for political texts. *Political Analysis*, 21(3)267- 297, 2013.

[9] R. Pampapathi, B. Mirkin and M. Levene. A suffix tree approach to anti-spam email filtering. *Machine Learning*, 65(1):309-338, 2008.

[10] B. Mirkin, E. Chernyak and O. Chugunova. Annotated suffix tree method for estimating the string-to-text relevance. *Business-Infromatics*, 21(3):31-41, 2012 (in Russian)

[11] S. Robertson and H. Zaragoza. The probabilistic relevance gramework: BM25 and beyond. *Journal Foundations and Trends in Information Retrieval* 3(4):333-389, 2009

[12] G. Salton and C. Buckley. Term-weighting approaches in automatic text retrieval. *Information Processing and Management*, 25(5):513-523, 1998.

[13] D. Gusfield. *Algorithms on strings, trees and sequences: computer science and computational biology*, 1997.

[14] I. Cantador, A. Bellogin and D. Vallet. Content-based recommendation in social tagging systems. In *Proceedings of the fourth ACM conference on Recommender systems*, pages 237-240, Barcelona, Spain, 2010.

[15] A. Gupta and P. Kumaraguru. Credibility ranking of tweets during high impact events. In *Proceedings of the first Workshop on Privacy and Security in Online Social Media*, pages 2-8, Lyon, France, 2012.

[16] F. Xia, T. Liu, J. Wang, W. Zhang and H. Li. Listwise approach to learning to rank - theory and algorithm. In *Proceedings of the 25th International Conference on Machine Learning*, pages 1192-1199, Helsinki, Finland, 2008.

[17] K. Duh and K. Kirchhoff. Learning to rank with partially-labeled data. In *Proceedings of the 31st Annual International ACM SIGIR Conference*, pages 251-258, Singapore, 2008.

[18] H. Valizadegan, R. Jin, R. Zhang and J. Mao. Learning to rank by optimizing NDCG measure. *Advances in Neural Information Processing Systems*, 22:1883-1191, 2010.

Incorporating Phrase-level Sentiment Analysis on Textual Reviews for Personalized Recommendation

Yongfeng Zhang
State Key Laboratory of Intelligent Technology and Systems
Department of Computer Science and Technology
Tsinghua University, Beijing, 100084, China
zhangyf07@gmail.com

ABSTRACT

Previous research on Recommender Systems (RS), especially the continuously popular approach of Collaborative Filtering (CF), has been mostly focusing on the information resource of explicit user numerical ratings or implicit (still numerical) feedbacks. However, the ever-growing availability of textual user reviews has become an important information resource, where a wealth of explicit product attributes/features and user attitudes/sentiments are expressed therein. This information rich resource of textual reviews have clearly exhibited brand-new approaches to solving many of the important problems that have been perplexing the research community for years, such as the paradox of cold-start, the explanation of recommendation, and the automatic generation of user or item profiles. However, it is only recently that the fundamental importance of textual reviews has gained wide recognition, perhaps mainly because of the difficulty in formatting, structuring and analyzing the free-texts. In this research, we stress the importance of incorporating textual reviews for recommendation through phrase-level sentiment analysis, and further investigate the role that the texts play in various important recommendation tasks.

Categories and Subject Descriptors

H.3.3 [**Information Storage and Retrieval**]: Information Filtering; I.2.7 [**Artificial Intelligence**]: Natural Language Processing; H.3.5 [**Online Information Services**]: Web-based services

Keywords

Personalized Recommendation; Collaborative Filtering; Sentiment Analysis; Text Mining

1. INTRODUCTION

The continuous prospering of various Web2.0 online applications such as e-commerce and social networks has pushed users into the problem of information overwhelming [7]. The difficulty in accessing the desired online items further contributed to the emerging of Personalized Recommender Systems (PRS) [12], which attempt to make personalized and targeted item recommendations to users on various platforms and devices.

The research of personalized recommendation can be generally classified into Content-based [20], Collaborative Filtering (CF)-based [26] and Hybrid approaches [3]. The content-based approach attempts to construct user and item profiles, and thus to make recommendations through some meticulously designed matching strategies [14], while CF-based approaches attempt to learn the preferences of users automatically by considering the historical choices of other users [12]. Hybrid recommender system, on the other hand, aims to combine the advantages of various strategies to make more informed recommendations.

The CF-based approach has gained much attention from the research community, especially since the Netflix grand prize in the year of 2007 through 2009 [2], because the CF-approaches, especially those based on Matrix Factorization (MF) techniques [28, 8] on user-item numerical rating matrices, achieved important success in the task of rating prediction [12], and also exhibited great advantage in many other recommendation tasks [4].

However, the application of CF on numerical ratings has come across many difficulties in face of some key problems like data sparsity [35] and the explainability of numerical ratings [29, 32]. This further leads to some of the most concerned tasks in the research community, such as cold-start recommendation [36, 13], explainability of the recommendations [32], and automatic user/item profile generation.

The continuous growing of online textual user reviews, as another important information resource besides numerical ratings, has shed light on brand new solutions towards these issues. For example, although a user may have only made a single numerical rating towards a product in online shopping websites, she usually expresses more detailed opinions towards various product features/aspects in the corresponding piece of review text [33]. This is exposited in the sampled review in Figure 1, where the user expressed positive

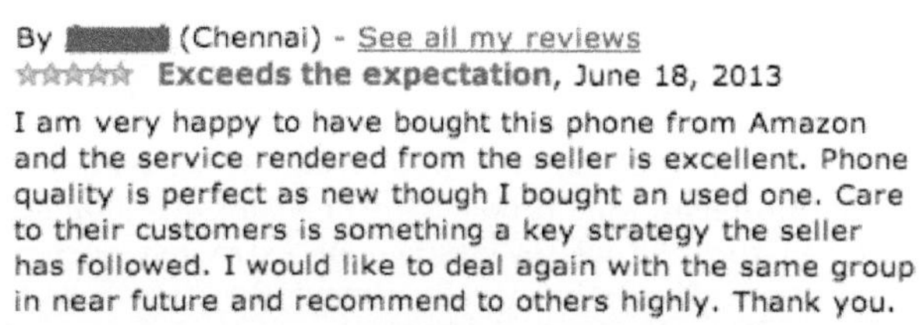

By [redacted] (Chennai) - See all my reviews
Exceeds the expectation, June 18, 2013
I am very happy to have bought this phone from Amazon and the service rendered from the seller is excellent. Phone quality is perfect as new though I bought an used one. Care to their customers is something a key strategy the seller has followed. I would like to deal again with the same group in near future and recommend to others highly. Thank you.

Figure 1: A piece of sampled user review towards the iPhone 5s product extracted from Amazon.com

WSDM'15, February 2–6, 2015, Shanghai, China.

ACM 978-1-4503-3317-7/15/02 ...$15.00.
http://dx.doi.org/10.1145/2684822.2697033.

opinions towards the features *service* and *phone quality* of the product, with the opinion words *excellent* and *perfect*, correspondingly, which composes into his overall numerical rating of five stars.

We see that the textual reviews contain both product-oriented information (i.e. product features) and user-oriented information (i.e. user opinions), and they usually exist in the form of pairs (user takes an opinion word to express his/her attitude towards a product feature). By conducting phrase-level sentiment analysis [15, 10, 5, 31] on the textual reviews, we are able to extract these feature-opinion word pairs, thus to gain more detailed information about the user's overall opinion towards a product (the overall rating), which helps to understand the item characterises and user needs in a wider range of dimension, and to alleviate the problem of data sparsity in the scenario of cold-start recommendation. The extracted features and opinions also help to make explanations about why or why not an item is recommended [32], and to construct user (or item) profiles automatically by estimating their preferences towards the features.

In this research, we aim to stress the importance of making further use of textual reviews in recommender systems. We focus on leveraging phrase-level sentiment analysis on the reviews to better solve the above mentioned cutting-edge research problems. In the following part, we review the related work in Section 2, and exposit some of the research topics, current research progress and the upcoming research plans on each topic in Section 3. Finally, we discuss, conclude and summarize the future directions in Section 4.

2. RELATED WORK

Collaborative Filtering (CF)-based techniques [26] have achieved great success in personalized recommender systems [12] due to their ability to take advantage of the wisdom of crowds, especially in the task of numerical rating prediction. With the remarkable performance on prediction accuracy, the Matrix Factorization (MF) [28] approaches have gained great popularity in both research community and the industry. Some of the commonly used matrix factorization algorithms include Singular Value Decomposition (SVD) [1, 24], Non-negative Matrix Factorization (NMF) [9], Probabilistic Matrix Factorization (PMF) [23, 22] and Max-Margin Matrix Factorization (MMMF) [25, 21].

However, the ratings made by each each is usually far less than the large volume of products in a typical system, which implies that the user-item rating matrices that CF algorithms attempt to tackle with are usually very sparse [35], as exampled in Figure 2, which shows the scattered small communities corresponding to the sparse submatrices on the Yelp rating dataset [35]. Besides, new users and items are continuously added to the online systems, which further worsens the sparsity [34]. All these factors lead to the important cold-start problem in recommender systems, where it is difficult to estimate the preferences or make recombinations to a user who rated only a few of the items [36, 13].

Fortunately, the ever growing availability of textual reviews has shed light on new approaches to alleviate the cold-start problem. The product features and user opinions included in the textual reviews can be extracted, formatted and summarized through Sentiment Analysis [11, 18] techniques. One of the core tasks in sentiment analysis is to determine the sentiment orientations that users express in reviews, sentences or on specific product features, corre-

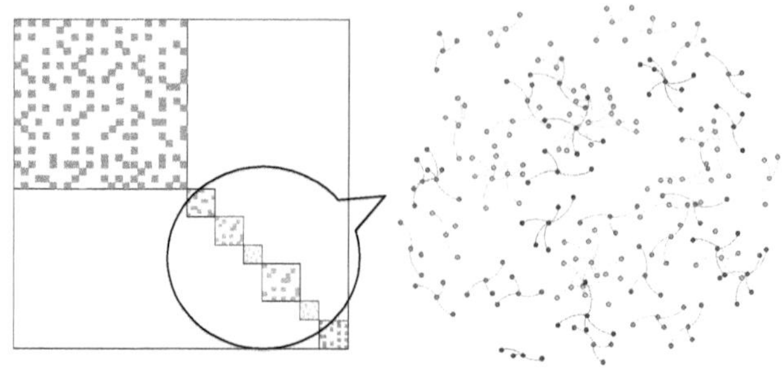

(a) Yelp dataset Matrix (b) Yelp dataset Graph

Figure 2: Structures of Yelp dataset. In the left is the exampled structure of the rating matrix, and in the right is the real structure of the scattered blocks.

sponding to review(document)-level [19], sentence-level [30, 17] and phrase-level [31, 15, 5] sentiment analysis.

Review- and sentence-level sentiment analysis attempt to label a review or sentence as one of some predefined sentiment polarities, which are typically *positive*, *negative* and sometimes *neutral* [11]. Phrase-level sentiment analysis aims to analyze the sentiment expressed by users in a finer-grained granularity. It considers the sentiment expressed on specific product features or aspects [6]. One of the most important tasks in phrase-level sentiment analysis is the construction of Sentiment Lexicon [27, 10, 5, 15], which is to extract feature-opinion word pairs and their corresponding sentiment polarities from these opinion rich user-generated free-texts.

In [16], McAuley et al leveraged topic modelling to help extract the hidden topics from user reviews, thus to help improve the rating prediction accuracy. Textual reviews also help to construct intuitional explanations about why an item is recommended against the others. In [32], Zhang et al proposed a feature-level explainable recommendation strategy where the system persuades a user by telling him about his previously concerned product features in historical reviews.

As an integration of content- and CF-based recommendation strategies, the hybrid recommendation techniques [3] have achieved state-of-the-art performance in real-world applications [12]. However, the manual construction of user and item profiles requires a vast amount of domain knowledge, which is expensive and time consuming [20, 14]. Phrase-level sentiment analysis on textual reviews makes it possible to conduct automatic profile construction, by analyzing and structuring the reviews corresponding to a target user or product. In this work, we exposit the promising potentialities that textual reviews bring into recommender systems, state our current research achievements on the related topics, and pose some of the future research directions.

3. RESEARCH TOPICS

3.1 Cold-Start Recommendation

In CF-based recommendation algorithms, one of the most fundamental causes of cold-start comes from the absence of purchasing or rating information of new users or items. Although various CF techniques attempt to construct meticulously designed algorithms to estimate user preferences from a small number of ratings [13, 36], the performance remains limited as we know little about a user philosophically.

For example, many a user (about 49%) in the commonly used Yelp rating dataset[1] made only a single numerical rating, which makes it difficult to estimate his/her preference in a latent factorization space [36]. However, the corresponding piece of textual review plays a role of the user's explanation towards his/her rating, which may contain the user's opinions towards several features of the product that composes into his final rating. This information source could have been well used to tackle with the cold-start problem.

This procedure is exposited in Figure 4. We first integrate all the textual reviews in a product domain (mobile phone domain in this example) to construct a review corpus. By conducting phrase-level sentiment analysis on this corpus, a sentiment lexicon [27, 10, 5, 15] is constructed, which includes the product feature words (e.g. *screen, battery, price*) extracted from user reviews.

Next, we analyze the review(s) corresponding to each targeted user by extracting the features that he/she concerns. It is important to point out that this procedure can be conducted even though the user made only a single review, because there may also exist a bunch of mentioned features in the review text. Finally, the recommended items can be provided by selecting those products that perform well on those features that the user concerns, and the product performance on each feature can also be estimated from the reviews made by users towards that product.

3.2 Recommendation Explanation

An important problem of traditional CF-based recommendation algorithm in real-world application is the difficulty to explain the recommendation results. This is partially because of the fact that we do not know how a user composed his opinions from the many aspects into a single and simple numerical rating, and that CF algorithms (especially those based on matrix factorization techniques) only attempt to estimate these ratings in a latent (unknown) factorization space. These Latent Factor Models (LFM) makes it even more difficult to make the recommendations explainable, although the algorithm may achieve satisfactory rating prediction accuracies [29].

However, the existence of textual user reviews, as exposited in the previous section, provides a brand new information resource to help understand the user preferences and specific needs. By extracting the frequently mentioned product features from a user's historical reviews, we are able to get to know the product aspects that he/she concerns.

Different users may care about different produce features when making purchasing decisions. For example, a user may choose a mobile phone product given its large screen and good graphics performance, while another may make the same choice while considering its nice product design, although they may well give the same numerical rating of five stars. In many similar cases, the numerical ratings are insufficient to distinguish the preferences of different users, but the textual reviews tell us why a user made such a choice.

Preliminary studies on this research topics have been published in our paper [32], which attempts to improve the rating prediction accuracy and at the same time construct intuitional recommendation explanations. We will further investigate the explanations constructed from textual reviews by considering different explanation forms like product tags and word clouds, etc., as well as the scrutability, effectiveness and efficiency of explanations in recommendation. We will also attempt to bridge up explanations and its application in cold-start recommendation scenarios in the following research tasks.

[1]http://www.yelp.com/dataset_challenge

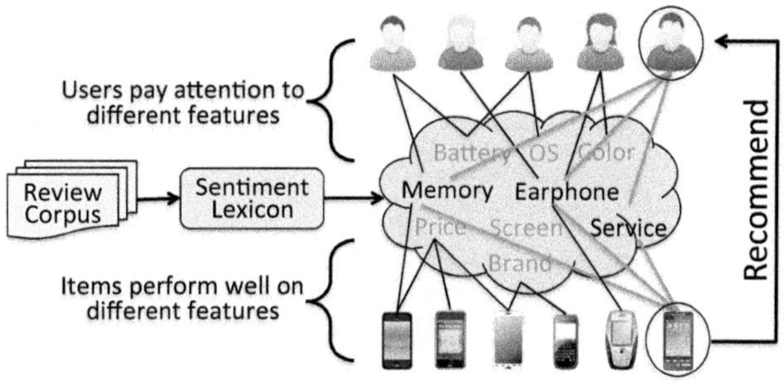

Figure 4: The product feature set of a domain (e.g. mobile phone) is extracted from a review corpus. The preference/profile of a user/item can be constructed by analyzing the corresponding review(s) of the user/item, thus to make cold-start recommendations when the ratings of a user is limited.

3.3 Automatic Profile Generation

The construction of accurate user/item profiles is the key factor in content-based recommendation, and they help to make more informed recommendations in hybrid recommender systems [3]. However, the profile construction process is time consuming, and usually requires the existence of domain knowledge, which is expensive in real-world scenarios.

However, the textual reviews in a specific product domain naturally serve as a kind of domain-dependent information, and it is possible to extract the user-generated domain knowledge with the help of the wisdom of crowds.

This can be intuitionally exposited in Figure 5. We first extract all the matched product features and their accompanying opinion words from each piece of review, and estimate the appropriate score that the user expressed towards each of the features, by considering the sentiment polarities of the opinion words.

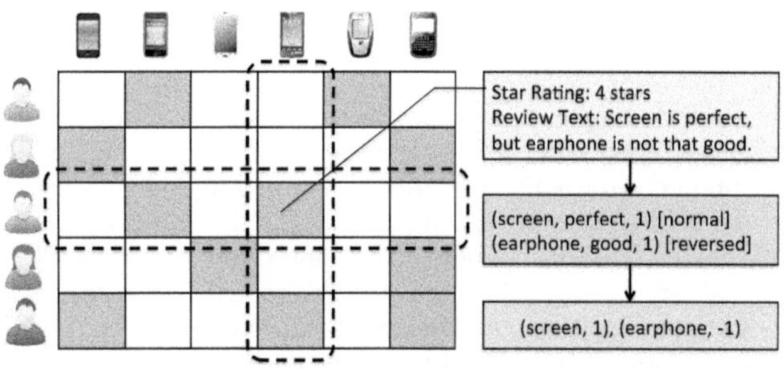

Figure 5: An example of user-item review matrix and automatic profile extraction. Each shaded block is a review made by a user towards an item; the entries included in the review are extracted, and further transformed to feature scores while considering the negation words. The features together with the user opinions extracted from the set of reviews corresponding to a user/item are further aggregated to generate a profile.

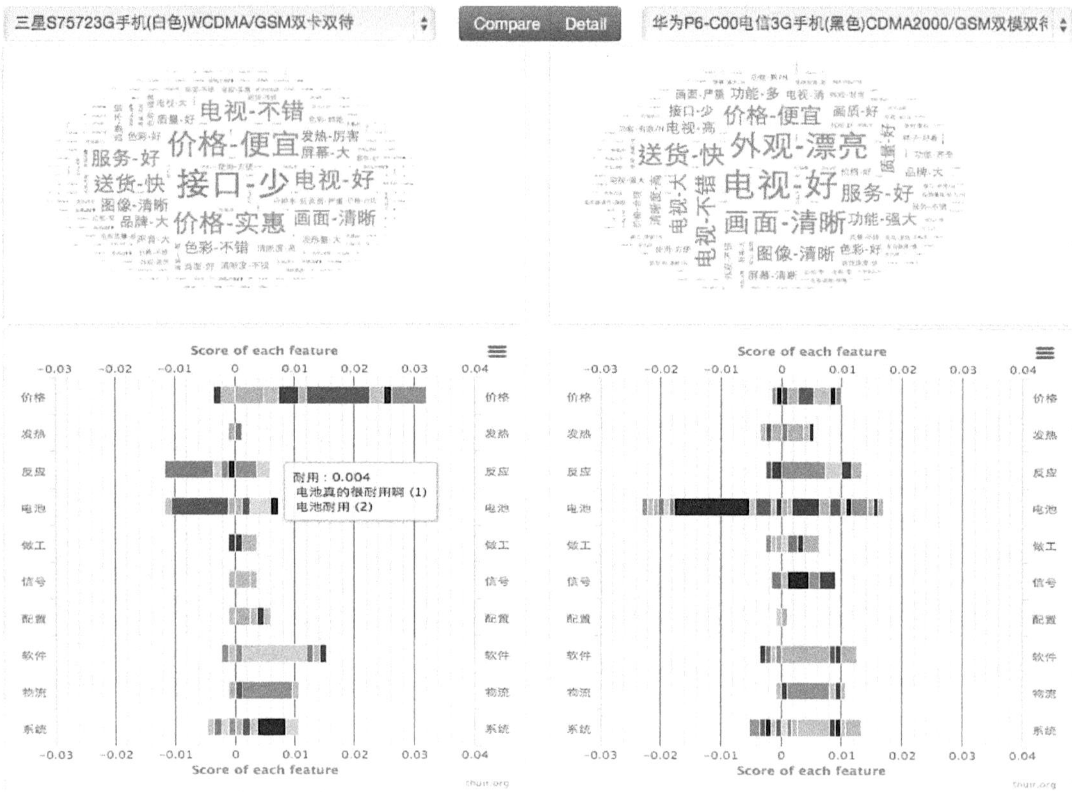

Figure 3: Automatic product profile construction and comparison. The word-cloud based profile displays the Feature-Opinion word pairs extracted from the product's corresponding reviews, where the green ones are positive comments and blue ones are negative, giving an intuitional and first-sight view of the pros and cons of each product. The bar chart based profiles allow the users to examine the detailed scores and reviews on each specific product feature. This demo can be visited at http://mobile.thuir.org.

After that, a simple and direct approach of profile generation for a user is to take all of his/her reviews and calculate the frequency of each feature therein, which intuitionally serve as an indicator of the extent that a user cares about a feature. Symmetrically, we can also consider all the reviews corresponding to a product, and integrate the opinions from different users to estimate its performance on each product feature, thus to construct the product profiles.

The product profiles can be displayed in different forms to help users better understand the pros and cons of a product, or to compare the profiles of two products so as to make more informed purchasing decisions. The reader might refer to our prototype demo systems on smart TV[2] and mobile phone[3] products, and this is also exampled in Figure 3, which displays and compares the profiles of two mobile phones, in the forms of both word cloud and bar charts.

Apart from exhibiting the profiles to users for product comparison, the user and product profiles can also be easily used for content-based or hybrid recommendation, because they model the users and items in the same and intuitional feature space, thus, for example, it would be very easy to calculate the similarity between two users, two products, or even a user and a product. We will further investigate the application of automatic profiling in personalized recommendation in the following work.

[2]http://tv.thuir.org

[3]http://mobile.thuir.org

4. CONCLUSIONS AND RESEARCH PLAN

In this research proposal, we attempt to incorporate textual user reviews to tackle with some of the most cutting-edge topics in the research of personalized recommender systems. We particularly focus on the utilization of phrase-level sentient analysis technique to format, structure and summarize the free-text reviews, so as to take feature-level advantages of this information-rich resource.

We argue that the existence of textual reviews is of fundamental importance to personalized recommendation, even compared with the previously mostly concerned numerical ratings. However, the textual reviews have mostly been ignored for years in the previous research, perhaps due to the tremendous prosperity of collaborative filtering techniques based on user ratings. In the following work, we will continue to investigate the great potential of leveraging textual reviews in solving the problems of cold-start recommendation, recommendation explanation and automatic profile generation for hybrid recommender systems.

5. ACKNOWLEDGEMENT

I would like to sincerely thank my supervisors Prof. Min Zhang, Yiqun Liu, Shaoping Ma and Prof. Yi Zhang from UCSC, as well as Prof. Tat-Seng Chua and Min-Yen Kan from NUS for their continuous mentoring and support during my research career. This work was supported by Tsinghua-Samsung Joint Lab, under the Chinese Natural Science Foundation (61073071) and National High Technology Research and Development (863) Program (2011AA01A205). Part of the work was conducted at the Tsinghua-NUS NExT Search Center supported by the Singapore National Research Foundation & Interactive Digital Media R&D Program Office, MDA under research grant (WBS:R-252-300-001-490).

6. REFERENCES

[1] H. Abdi. Singular value decomposition (svd) and generalized singular value decomposition (gsvd). *Ency. of Measu. and Stat.*, pages 907–912, 2007.

[2] J. Bennett and S. Lanning. The Netflix Prize. *KDD Cup and Workshop*, 2007.

[3] R. Burke. Hybrid Recommender Systems: Survey and Experiments. *User Modeling and User-Adapted Interaction*, 12(4):331–370, 2002.

[4] P. Cremonesi, Y. Koren, and R. Turrin. Performance of recommender algorithms on top-n recommendation tasks. *RecSys*, 2010.

[5] X. Ding, B. Liu, and P. S. Yu. A Holistic Lexicon-Based Approach to Opinion Mining. *WSDM*, pages 231–239, 2008.

[6] M. Hu and B. Liu. Mining and Summarizing Customer Reviews. *KDD*, pages 168–177, 2004.

[7] J. A. Konstan. Introduction to recommender systems: Algorithms and Evaluation. *ACM Transactions on Information Systems (TOIS)*, 22(1):1–4, 2004.

[8] Y. Koren, R. Bell, et al. Matrix factorization techniques for recommender systems. *Computer*, 2009.

[9] D. D. Lee and H. S. Seung. Algorithms for Non-negative Matrix Factorization. *NIPS*, pages 556–562, 2001.

[10] B. Liu, M. Hu, and J. Cheng. Opinion Observer: Analyzing and Comparing Opinions on the Web. *WWW*, pages 342–351, 2005.

[11] B. Liu and L. Zhang. A Survey of Opinion Mining and Sentiment Analysis. *Jour. Mining Text Data*, pages 415–463, 2012.

[12] J. Liu, M. Chen, J. Chen, et al. Recent advances in personal recommender systems. *International Journal of Information and Systems Sciences*, 5(2):230–247, 2009.

[13] N. Liu, X. Meng, and C. Liu. Wisdom of the Better Few: Cold Start Recommendation via Representative based Rating Elicitation. *RecSys*, pages 37–44, 2011.

[14] P. Lops, M. de Gemmis, and G. Semeraro. Content-based recommender systems: State of the art and trends. *Recommender Systems Handbook*, pages 73–105, 2011.

[15] Y. Lu, M. Castellanos, U. Dayal, and C. Zhai. Automatic Construction of a Context-Aware Sentiment Lexicon: An Optimization Approach. *WWW*, pages 347–356, 2011.

[16] J. McAuley and J. Leskovec. Hidden Factors and Hidden Topics: Understanding Rating Dimensions with Review Text. *RecSys*, pages 165–172, 2013.

[17] T. Nakagawa, K. Inui, and S. Kurohashi. Dependency Tree-based Sentiment Classification using CRFs with Hidden Variables. *NAACL*, 2010.

[18] B. Pang and L. Lee. Opinion Mining and Sentiment Analysis. *Foundations and Trends in Information Retrieval*, 2(1-2):1–135, 2008.

[19] B. Pang, L. Lee, and S. Vaithyanathan. Thumbs up? Sentiment Classification using Machine Learning Techniques. *EMNLP*, pages 79–86, 2002.

[20] M. J. Pazzani and D. Billsus. Content-based recommendation systems. *Adaptive Web LNCS*, 2007.

[21] J. Rennie et al. Fast maximum margin matrix factorization for collaborative prediction. *ICML*, 2005.

[22] R. Salakhutdinov and A. Mnih. Bayesian probabilistic matrix factorization using markov chain monte carlo. *ICML*, 2008.

[23] R. Salakhutdinov and A. Mnih. Probabilistic matrix factorization. *NIPS*, 2008.

[24] N. Srebro and T. Jaakkola. Weighted low-rank approximations. *ICML*, 2003.

[25] N. Srebro, J. Rennie, and T. S. Jaakkola. Maximum-margin matrix factorization. *NIPS*, 2005.

[26] X. Su and T. Khoshgoftaar. A survey of collaborative filtering techniques. *Advances in AI.*, 2009.

[27] M. Taboada, J. Brooke, M. Tofiloski, K. Voll, and M. Stede. Lexicon-Based Methods for Sentiment Analysis. *Computational Linguastics*, 37(2), 2011.

[28] G. Takacs, I. Pilaszy, B. Nemeth, and D. Tikk. Investigation of various matrix factorization methods for large recommender systems. *ICDM*, 2008.

[29] N. Tintarev and J. Masthoff. A Survey of Explanations in Recommender Systems. *ICDE*, 2007.

[30] J. Wiebe, T. Wilson, and C. Cardie. Annotating Expressions of Opinions and Emotions in Language. *Language Resources and Evaluation (LREC)*, 2005.

[31] T. Wilson, J. Wiebe, and P. Hoffmann. Recognizing Contextual Polarity in Phrase-Level Sentiment Analysis. *EMNLP*, pages 347–354, 2005.

[32] Y. Zhang, G. Lai, M. Zhang, Y. Zhang, Y. Liu, and S. Ma. Explicit Factor Models for Explainable Recommendation based on Phrase-level Sentiment Analysis. *SIGIR*, pages 83–92, 2014.

[33] Y. Zhang, H. Zhang, M. Zhang, Y. Liu, and S. Ma. Do Users Rate or Review? Boost Phrase-level Sentiment Labeling with Review-level Sentiment Classification. *SIGIR*, 2014.

[34] Y. Zhang, M. Zhang, Y. Liu, S. Ma, and S. Feng. Localized Matrix Factorization for Recommendation based on Matrix Block Diagonal Forms. *WWW*, 2013.

[35] Y. Zhang, M. Zhang, Y. Zhang, Y. Liu, and S. Ma. Understanding the Sparsity: Augmented Matrix Factorization with Sampled Constraints on Unobservables. *CIKM*, 2014.

[36] K. Zhou, S.-H. Yang, and H. Zha. Functional Matrix Factorizations for Cold-Start Recommendation. *SIGIR*, pages 315–324, 2011.

Mining Groups Stability in Ubiquitous and Social Environments: Communities, Classes, Clusters

Mark Kibanov
Knowledge & Data Engineering Group
ITeG Research Center
University of Kassel
Wilhelmshöher Allee 73
34121 Kassel, Germany
kibanov@cs.uni-kassel.de

ABSTRACT

Ubiquitous Computing is an emerging research area of computer science. Similarly, social network analysis and mining became very important in the last years. We aim to combine these two research areas to explore the nature of processes happening around users.

The presented research focuses on exploring and analyzing different groups of persons or entities (communities, clusters and classes), their stability and semantics. An example of ubiquitous social data are social networks captured during scientific conferences using face-to-face RFID proximity tags. Another example of ubiquitous data is crowd-generated environmental sensor data. In this paper we generalize various problems connected to these and further datasets and consider them as a task for measuring group stability. Group stability can be used to improve state-of-the-art methods to analyze data. We also aim to improve the performance of different data mining algorithms, e. g., by better handling of data with a skewed density distribution. We describe significant results some experiments that show how the presented approach can be applied and discuss the planned experiments.

Categories and Subject Descriptors

H.2.8 [**Information Systems**]: Database Applications—*Data Mining*; G.3 [**Mathematics of Computing**]: Probability and Statistics—*Statistical Computing*; J.4 [**Computer Applications**]: Social and Behavioral Science—*Sociology*

General Terms

Algorithms

Keywords

Data Mining, Ubiquitous Systems, Physical Computing

WSDM 2015, February 2–6, 2015, Shanghai, China.

http://dx.doi.org/10.1145/2684822.2697034.

1. INTRODUCTION

Ubiquitous computing as it was described by by Weiser [21] is becoming more real: the technologies become "integral, invisible part of people's lives". Such seamless integration is enabled by different factors: small sensors, affordable smartphones and advanced algorithms. On the other side social networks gained popularity and became an important research topic for different disciplines. The combination of these two areas may create new applications and is an interesting and challenging research topic.

Ubicon (cf., Section 3.1) is an example of a platform which aims to combine both ubiquitous and social computing utilizing RFID-technology, developed by the Sociopatterns initiative[1], and environmental sensors, utilized by EveryAware project[2]. Such applications will need in the future improved data mining techniques and machine learning algorithms to provide more support for the users in their everyday-activities. Furthermore these technologies can be applied in different scenarios – e. g., RFID tags can be used to implement idea of the smart university [4] or in healthcare settings [5].

One of the main data mining principles is finding similar elements in order to generalize knowledge about them. In my ongoing PhD thesis I concentrate on stability of different groups of elements in ubiquitous environments and social networks. We investigate the possibility of improvement of existing algorithms and better predictive analysis. As the social and ubiquitous systems have very diverse data, a group can be defined as community, cluster, class or even a group of nearly placed elements depending on context of data and application type.

The contributions of the presented thesis can be summarized as following:

1. **Definition of groups in social and ubiquitous environments and modeling their stability as a general problem;**
2. **Analysis and evaluation of groups semantics and their stability;**
3. **Application of the groups stability for data mining algorithms and data analysis;**

To the best of the author's knowledge, such analysis has not been addressed before.

[1] `http://www.sociopatterns.org`

[2] `http://www.everyaware.eu`

The rest of the paper is structured as follows. We give basic descriptions and definitions of groups, describe the methodology and give short overview about related work in Section 2. Section 3 provides a description of the datasets which are used for the experiments. The evaluation of the first results and the description of the future experiments is described in Section 4. Finally, Section 5 concludes the paper with a short summary.

2. BACKGROUND AND RELATED WORK

I give a short overview of the different types of the groups considered in the presented PhD thesis and define the task of measuring their stability and finding semantics. Moreover, this section contains key references which are relevant for the presented thesis.

2.1 Community Detection in Graphs

Graph is the most common mathematical representation of the social network. An (undirected) *graph* $G = (V, E)$ is an ordered pair, consisting of a finite set V containing the *vertices/nodes*, and a set E of *edges/connections* between the vertices. A weighted graph is a graph $G = (V, E)$ together with a function $w : E \to \mathbb{R}^+$ that assigns a positive weight to each edge. The larger is the weight of the edge (u, v) the stronger is connection between nodes u and v. The concept of a community intuitively describes a group of vertices out of all nodes of graph $C \subseteq V$ such that members of C are strongly "related" among each other but sparsely "related" to nodes outside of C. We consider non-overlapping communities, where each node belongs to exactly one community, so $C_1 \cup \ldots \cup C_k = V$ and $C_1 \cap \ldots \cap C_k = \{\}$, where $C_1 \ldots C_k$ are the detected communities, are true.

As a community is a concept, without strict definition, there are different algorithms which compute communities in graphs, e. g., *InfoMap* [16]. Fortunato et al. made a comparative analysis of community detection algorithms [9, 10], Papadopoulos et al. considered particularly community detection for social networks [15]. Many authors considered evolution of communities [19, 20].

2.2 Classification Problem

Classification is an important problem for many applications based on the data generated by ubiquitous computing applications because the data collected and used by such applications is often sparse and the lacking information needs to be recovered (predicted with given accuracy or confidence). We define the problem of classification as follows. Each point $p \in P$, from a set of points P, can be assigned to a class $x \in X$, from a finite set of classes X, by a classification function $c : P \to X$. In general, the classification function c is unknown. Thus, given a subset of all classified points $C_{train} \subset C$, the goal is to approximate c by a classification function $\hat{c}$. The most common measures for quality of the classification function (or algorithm) are *Precision*, *Recall* and *F1-Measure* which can be computed for each class x. The *Accuracy* and *AUC* are the measures which can be applied to measure the quality of classifier for the whole dataset.

Naive Bayes, *decision trees* and *k Nearest Neighbor (kNN)* are prominent and well-known families of classification algorithms. *Support Vector Machine* is a newer classification algorithm [7] which gained popularity during the last years. In the proposed PhD thesis I will try to develop methods to improve classification, particularly by changing from kNN algorithm to adaptive kNN algorithm. In this context, e. g., Ougiaroglou et al. [14] and Sun and Huang [18] used variable adaptive k to improve the algorithm.

2.3 Clustering

Clustering is another prominent data mining task. Cluster is a group of similar objects but members of different clusters should be not similar. Given a dataset consisting of different items (objects) D in a metric space. Cluster is a set of objects $Cl \subseteq D$. Similarly to communities (cf. Section 2.1), we consider non-overlapping clusters, each object belongs to exactly one cluster. $Cl_1 \cup \ldots \cup Cl_k = D$ and $Cl_1 \cap \ldots \cap Cl_k = \{\}$, where $Cl_1 \ldots Cl_k$ are the detected clusters, are true.

To determine similarity of two elements, a distance function should be used. The choice of the distance function depends on dataset and task. The most common functions are Euclidean Distance, Manhattan Distance and Max Distance. Unlike in graph, it is usually possible to compute distance between any two elements in a metric space (some nodes in graph are not connected and thus distance between them is not known). In contrast to classification problem, clustering algorithms are not supervised.

Clustering is widely discussed topic in data mining. There are different types of clustering methods: density-based (e. g., DBSCAN [8]), hierarchical (e. g., SLINK [17]), centroid-based (e. g., k-means [13]) and other methods. Xu and II [22] made an overview of different clustering algorithms.

2.4 Groups Stability and Semantic

We define the problem of group stability as follows. Given elements $el \in I$, where I is a set of objects. Each element belongs exactly to one group G_i: $el \in G_i$. The group can be defined, for instance, as cluster, class or community.

We consider two time points t_1 and t_2. The dataset I has a particular group structure at t_1 and t_2: $G_1^{t_1} \ldots G_n^{t_1}$ and $G_1^{t_2} \ldots G_m^{t_2}$. Consider two elements from the dataset which belong to the same group at t_1: $u, v \in G_i^{t_1}$. The group is more stable the larger is the relative frequency that u and v belong to the same group at t_2.

To understand group semantic we consider any feature, set of features or dimension instead of time: e. g., consider multi-layer network. Each layer can be represented as a graph which has the same nodes but different edges. So instead of groups in different time points we consider groups in different graphs $Graph_1$ and $Graph_2$: $G_1^{Graph_1} \ldots G_n^{Graph_1}$ and $G_1^{Graph_2} \ldots G_m^{Graph_2}$. So we can find implications of connections in different layers and thus explore semantics of the networks.

3. DATASETS

As mentioned below, we used the datasets collected using Ubicon-based applications and plan experiments with further datasets. In this section, I shortly introduce the Ubicon platform and describe collected data.

3.1 Ubicon

Ubicon[3] is an open source platform[4] which provides an extensible framework for building and hosting applications targeting both ubiquitous and social environments [2, 3].

[3] `http://ubicon.eu`

[4] `http://code.ubicon.eu`

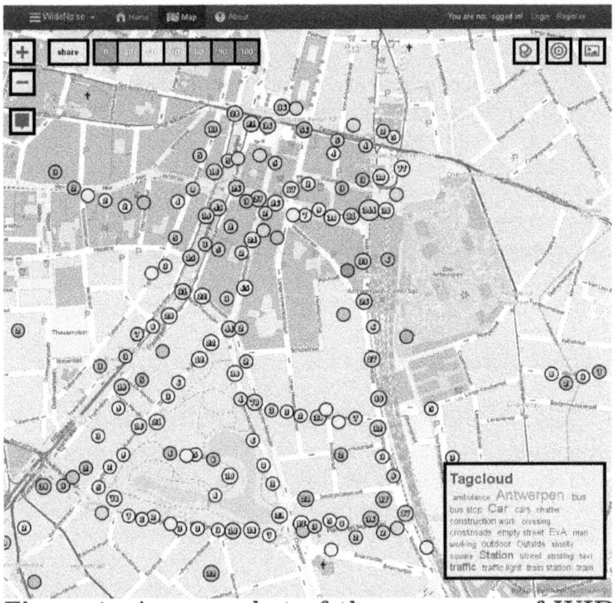

Figure 1: A screenshot of the map page of WIDE-NOISE [3]

From a data-centric view, Ubicon implements a data storage, processing, and serving pipeline. Ubicon hosts different applications, such as MyGroup, Conferator (which utilize RFID proximity tags to support workgroup members or conference participants), WideNoise and AirProbe (which utilize environmental sensors to enable participatory environmental monitoring). The Ubicon platform combines applications which use and collect both ubiquitous and social data. We present data collected using these applications.

3.2 Face-to-face Proximity Networks

We used RFID proximity tags to detect reliable face-to-face contacts. This technology was created by Sociopatterns initiative. The first experiments utilizing this technology were made during the *ESWC 2009* conference [1].

MyGroup and Conferator applications use the described technology to enhance users' experience during conferences and during their everyday workflows in the workgroups.

In our experiments we concentrate on the five datasets collected during the following conferences: LWA 2010, LWA 2011, LWA 2012, Hypertext 2011 and Informatik 2013. We asked participants of these conferences to wear RFID tags during the conferences. All these computer science conferences have different nature (e. g., in terms of size national\international context), so it is especially interesting to compare social interactions during these conferences. We also have been collecting face-to-face contacts data in the "Knowledge and Data Engineering" (*KDE*) research group of the University of Kassel for over two years.

Additional information about conference participants (institute affiliation, gender, country and position) and research group members (publication coauthorship, project cooperations) is available.

3.3 Environmental Sensor Data

Sensor data is another example of ubiquitous data. Using Ubicon-based applications WideNoise and AirProbe, users are able to collect environmental sensor data. The both applications were developed during the EveryAware project. The project created a set of tools for acquisition of sensor and subjective data so that different sensor data can be collected using smartphone embedded and pluggable sensors and subjective data can be input by users [6].

Smartphone application WideNoise Plus lets users to make noise level observations using embedded sensors, tag them, label with subjective perceptions and share these measurements in online social networks. A regular observation is made over 5 seconds with a sampling rate of 0.5 seconds. The location where the measurement was made can be obtained using smartphone GPS module or IP address (if GPS not available). The collected data is available for users online. Till now more than fifty thousand noise measurements were made by users all over the world.

The second EveryAware application – AirProbe – aims measuring air quality, and particularly black carbon concentration in the air. The AirProbe smartphone application and low-cost sensorbox were developed to enable such measurements. The sensorboxes can be connected to the smartphone via bluetooth. These sensorboxes may continuously measure the air quality while the users may tag interesting places or events using the AirProbe application. The majority of data was collected during AirProbe International Challenge case studies in Antwerp, Kassel, London and Turin where users used the tools for two weeks to collect as much data as possible.

The described datasets are examples of the ubiquitous and social networks data. They were collected by Ubicon-based applications. I am planning to use further datasets for the future experiments. The exact list of the datasets is not fix yet, but the group detection algorithms presented in Section 2 should be applicable to these datasets.

4. METHODOLOGY AND EVALUATION

General approach described in Section 2 should be justified for each dataset in order to reach the research goals (cf., Section 1), to improve specific applications and afterwards to generalize the results and make conclusions about groups stability and semantics in ubiquitous environments.

4.1 Community Stability in Face-to-Face Proximity Networks

Community detection is one of the most common approaches of finding groups of densely connected elements in graphs. We applied different community detection algorithms – InfoMap, Label Propagation, Leading Eigenvector, Walktrap, Edge Betweenness and Fast Greedy – to different conferences to determine if the stability of communities is dependent on chosen algorithms or conferences [11, 12].

To analyze the stability of the community structure we define a Community-pair (*c-pair*) as follows: if two nodes u and v belong to the same community, then $cp = (u, v)$ is a *c-pair*. To estimate and compare the stability of communities during different conferences, we compare the *c-pairs* that were formed during different days (e. g., at timepoints t_1 and t_2). Considered community detection algorithms show similar performance with respect to the community stability for these conferences. An interesting observation is that the active communication does not make communities stable – even vice versa. On hypothesis for explaining the negative correlation of community stability and communication is the

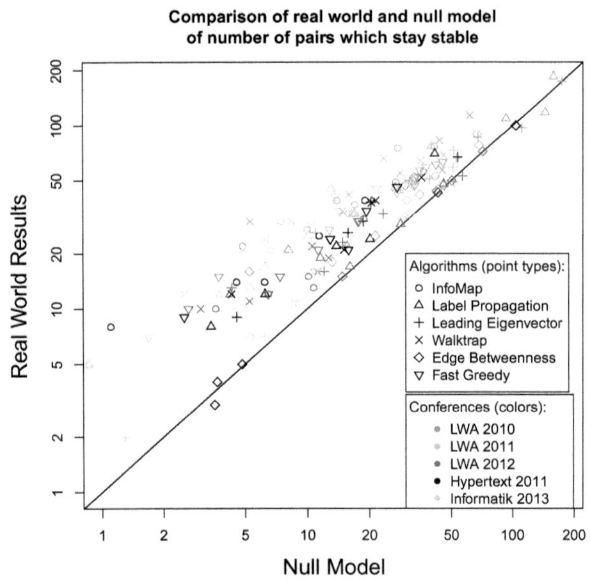

Figure 2: Comparison of the real community stability with the null model of the considered algorithms (marked by the different point types) and conferences (marked by different colors): the x-axis contains the respective null model values, the y-axis contains the respective real values. Both axes are scaled logarithmically.

following: the participants tend to stick to the known persons and tend to have less contacts with new persons that implies both lack of new contacts and stability of the existing communities over the whole conferences.

To clarify the significance of stability, we compared them to a null model and particularly the F1 score of the real data and the null model (cf., Figure 2). The F1 values computed from the real data are almost in every case larger than from the null model. On average, the real world F1 score is twice larger than the obtained null model F1 score.

4.2 Groups in Offline and Online Social Networks

We demonstrated some technical analysis in previous section. Such analysis can give insights about human interactions and improve recommender systems. However, for deep understanding of the nature of the human interactions it is necessary to perform further analysis. Here I give an overview of planned experiments.

Datasets collected using Conferator system show one of the layers of the scientific networks: face-to-face interactions during the conference. However these networks may have more different layers, such as:

- Coauthorship network
- Online professional networks (LinkedIn, ResearchGate)
- Online personal networks (Facebook)
- WWW networks with homepages of the scientists as nodes

An additional information about participants of the experiments is also available (for example, their institutions, conference status, academic status, research area). It is also possible to compute similarity between participants (e. g., based on papers similarity or homepage content similarity).

Comparison of listed layers and properties can be a key for understanding of the nature of human communication and cooperation. Such analysis corresponds with the research goals of the presented PhD thesis: we measure stability of groups, e. g., if the groups (communities) stay the same in different layers of the network; search for semantics of groups (e. g., by comparing which factors have more influence on emerging edges); improve data mining techniques (e. g., by adding additional information to recommender algorithms).

Further interesting topic is the possibility of finding one particular group from the offline world in different online networks (e. g., finding participants of one conference in DBLP coauthorship graph or ResearchGate Network).

4.3 Classification of Noise Measurements

We consider classification problem for sensor data and particularly the task is to improve the performance of datamining algorithms based on group stability. We plan to use item-centered groups for this task: k nearest neighbors are the members of the same group. The task is finding k so that stability of the group in terms of class equality of its members is maximal. Basically, this is an idea of the standard k Nearest Neighbor (kNN) algorithm.

Data collected using ubiquitous applications is crowd- generated and thus has some problems: it is usually almost impossible to control how, where and when the data will be generated. Datasets may be sparse and have skewed density distribution of the data points, thus application of k Nearest Neighbor algorithm may not deliver constant performance. To solve this issue, we try to find an optimal k for the each item to maximize the accuracy of the algorithm.

In the first experiments, the algorithm showed a better performance in terms of accuracy. We are working on improvement of the runtime of the algorithm. We plan to generalize the approach in the future to be able to estimate the group stability based on similarity in general, not only for k Nearest Neighbors algorithm.

4.4 Clustering for origin detection

As described in Section 2.3, the elements of one cluster are elements located near each other in the n-dimensional metric space. Clustering may be useful if a group of similar items needs to be found: for instance, for origin detection of items. I am planning to setup the experiments to explore how the clustering can be used to identify the origin of the item. Considering Widenoise dataset this means finding the user who made current measurement using only features of the measurements (not knowing device ID).

A number of special research questions are connected to this task: *which clustering algorithm fits the best for this purpose? How the features for clustering should be chosen and weighted? What are the best and the worst accuracies of this approach?* These experiments are however not limited to research questions listed above but also lead to general research aims discussed in Section 1: stability of clusters may play a crucial role in accuracy estimation for the algorithm as more stable clusters may deliver more reliable detection of its items origin. Should the approach deliver reliable results, it will show that clusters have semantics: its origin.

The described problem may have a lot of practical applications: restoring of corrupt information, deep analysis of different data, verification of privacy policy. These experiments will be done with different datasets.

5. CONCLUSIONS AND FUTURE WORK

This paper gives a short overview of ongoing PhD thesis which considers mining stability of groups in social and ubiquitous computing. I gave a general motivation for this problem and defined different types of groups (communities, classes, clusters). I described the datasets I used for my experiments. These were collected using Ubicon platform which was shortly overviewed as well. The first experiments and their evaluation were presented in this paper as well.

It is essential for future work to generalize the results and build a unified model for the stability of groups in ubiquitous environments. Also, definition of group can be extended by considering subgroups discovery. Furthermore, I am planning to work with further datasets and to implement further experiments. Moreover I hope to be able to show the proposed general model can be applied to solve different problems.

Acknowledgement

This publication was supported by Kurt-Pauli-Foundation. I appreciate the help of Prof. Dr. Gerd Stumme and Dr. PD Martin Atzmueller who help me to work on my thesis. I appreciate also Martin Becker and Juergen Mueller who assisted me in writing papers and give me important feedback.

6. REFERENCES

[1] H. Alani, M. Szomszor, C. Cattuto, W. Van den Broeck, G. Correndo, and A. Barrat. Live social semantics. In *The Semantic Web - ISWC 2009*, Lecture Notes in Computer Science. Springer Berlin Heidelberg, 2009.

[2] M. Atzmueller, M. Becker, S. Doerfel, M. Kibanov, A. Hotho, B.-E. Macek, F. Mitzlaff, J. Mueller, C. Scholz, and G. Stumme. Ubicon: Observing social and physical activities. In *Proc of CPSCom 2012*, pages 317–324. IEEE Computer Society, Nov. 2012.

[3] M. Atzmueller, M. Becker, M. Kibanov, C. Scholz, S. Doerfel, A. Hotho, B.-E. Macek, F. Mitzlaff, J. Mueller, and G. Stumme. Ubicon and its applications for ubiquitous social computing. *New Rev. of Hyper- and Multimedia*, 20(1), Mar. 2014.

[4] M. Atzmueller, S. Bobek, M. Kibanov, and G. J. Nalepa. Towards the ambient classroom: An environment for enhancing collaborative educational processes. In T. Roth-Berghofer, S. Oussena, and M. Atzmueller, editors, *Proceedings of the Smart University Workshop, SmartUni 2013 – International and Interdisciplinary Conference on Modeling and Using Context, Context 2013, Annecy, Haute-Savoie, France, 28 October, 2013*, 2013.

[5] A. Barrat, C. Cattuto, V. Colizza, L. Isella, C. Rizzo, A. E. Tozzi, and W. Van den Broeck. Wearable sensor networks for measuring face-to-face contact patterns in healthcare settings. In M. Szomszor and P. Kostkova, editors, *Proceedings of the 3rd International ICST Conference on Electronic Healthcare for the 21st century (eHealth 2010)*, 2011.

[6] M. Becker, A. Hotho, J. Mueller, M. Kibanov, M. Atzmueller, and G. Stumme. Subjective vs. objective data: Bridging the gap. CSSWS 2014, Poster, 2014.

[7] C. Cortes and V. Vapnik. Support-vector networks. *Machine Learning*, 20(3):273–297, 1995.

[8] M. Ester, H.-P. Kriegel, J. Sander, and X. Xu. A density-based algorithm for discovering clusters in large spatial databases with noise. In *Proc of KDD 1996*, pages 226–231. AAAI Press, 1996.

[9] S. Fortunato and C. Castellano. Community structure in graphs. In R. A. Meyers, editor, *Encyclopedia of Complexity and Systems Science*, pages 1141–1163. Springer, 2009.

[10] S. Fortunato and A. Lancichinetti. Community detection algorithms: a comparative analysis: invited presentation, extended abstract. In G. Stea, J. Mairesse, and J. Mendes, editors, *VALUETOOLS*, page 27. ACM, 2009.

[11] M. Kibanov, M. Atzmueller, C. Scholz, and G. Stumme. On the evolution of contacts and communities in networks of face-to-face proximity. In *Proc of CPSCom 2013*, pages 993–1000. IEEE Computer Society, 2013.

[12] M. Kibanov, M. Atzmueller, C. Scholz, and G. Stumme. Temporal evolution of contacts and communities in networks of face-to-face human interactions. *Science China Information Sciences*, 57(3), Feb. 2014.

[13] S. P. Lloyd. Least squares quantization in pcm. *IEEE Transactions on Information Theory*, 28(2):129–136, 1982.

[14] S. Ougiaroglou, A. Nanopoulos, A. N. Papadopoulos, Y. Manolopoulos, and T. Welzer-Druzovec. Adaptive k-nearest-neighbor classification using a dynamic number of nearest neighbors. In *Proc of ADBIS 2007*, pages 66–82. Springer, 2007.

[15] S. Papadopoulos, Y. Kompatsiaris, A. Vakali, and P. Spyridonos. Community detection in social media - performance and application considerations. *Data Min. Knowl. Discov.*, 24(3):515–554, 2012.

[16] M. Rosvall, D. Axelsson, and C. T. Bergstrom. The map equation. *The European Physical Journal Special Topics*, 178(1):13–23, 2009.

[17] R. Sibson. Slink: An optimally efficient algorithm for the single-link cluster method. *The Computer Journal*, 16(1):30–34, 1973.

[18] S. Sun and R. Huang. An adaptive k-nearest neighbor algorithm. In *Proc of FSKD 2010*, pages 91–94. IEEE, 2010.

[19] H. Sundaram, Y.-R. Lin, M. De Choudhury, and A. Kelliher. Understanding community dynamics in online social networks: A multidisciplinary review. *Signal Processing Magazine, IEEE*, 29(2):33 –40, Mar. 2012.

[20] M. Toyoda and M. Kitsuregawa. Extracting evolution of web communities from a series of web archives. In *Hypertext 2003*, pages 28–37. ACM, 2003.

[21] M. Weiser. The computer for the 21st century. *Scientific American*, 265:94–104, 1991.

[22] R. Xu and D. C. W. II. Survey of clustering algorithms. *IEEE Transactions on Neural Networks*, 16(3):645–678, 2005.

Sentiment-Specific Representation Learning for Document-Level Sentiment Analysis

Duyu Tang

Research Center for Social Computing and Information Retrieval,
Harbin Institute of Technology, Harbin, China
dytang@ir.hit.edu.cn

ABSTRACT

In this paper, we propose a representation learning research framework for document-level sentiment analysis. Given a document as the input, document-level sentiment analysis aims to automatically classify its sentiment/opinion (such as *thumbs up* or *thumbs down*) based on the textural information. Despite the success of feature engineering in many previous studies, the hand-coded features do not well capture the semantics of texts. In this research, we argue that learning sentiment-specific semantic representations of documents is crucial for document-level sentiment analysis. We decompose the document semantics into four cascaded constitutes: (1) word representation, (2) sentence structure, (3) sentence composition and (4) document composition. Specifically, we learn sentiment-specific word representations, which simultaneously encode the contexts of words and the sentiment supervisions of texts into the continuous representation space. According to the principle of *compositionality*, we learn sentiment-specific sentence structures and sentence-level composition functions to produce the representation of each sentence based on the representations of the words it contains. The semantic representations of documents are obtained through document composition, which leverages the sentiment-sensitive discourse relations and sentence representations.

Categories and Subject Descriptors

I.2.7 [**ARTIFICIAL INTELLIGENCE**]: Natural Language Processing

Keywords

sentiment analysis; deep learning; natural language processing

1. INTRODUCTION

Sentiment analysis (also known as opinion mining [15, 9, 4]) that analyzes people's opinions/sentiments/emotions from texts is an active research field in natural language processing [10]. In this research, we target at the task of document-level sentiment analysis, which is a fundamental and most studied area in sentiment analysis. It aims to classify the sentiment/opinion (suc as *thumbs up* and *thumbs down*) of a document based on the text information.

Most previous studies follow Pang et al. [16] and regard document-level sentiment analysis as a special case of text categorization task. They typically employ machine learning algorithms, such as Supported Vector Machine, to build the sentiment classifier from the texts with accompanying sentiment labels in a supervised learning framework. Under this direction, most studies focus on designing effective features because the performance of a sentiment classifier is heavily dependent on the choice of feature representation of texts [3]. For example, Mohammad et al. [13] build the top-performed system in the Twitter sentiment classification track of SemEval 2013 [14] by using many sentiment lexicons and hand-crafted rules as features.

Despite the success of feature engineering, hand-coded features do not well capture the semantics of texts. Furthermore, it is desirable to discover the semantic representations of texts from the data and make the learning algorithms less dependent on laborious feature engineering. Recently, representation learning (or deep learning [1]) has been shown effective in many natural language processing tasks, such as word-segmentation, pos-tagging, named entity recognition and parsing, etc. However, we find that directly applying these fact-based approaches to document-level sentiment analysis is not effective enough. The reason lies in that they typically fail to capture the sentiment information of texts. Take word embedding[1] as an example, existing context-based learning algorithms [2, 11] only model the contexts of words. As a result, words with similar contexts but opposite polarity, such as *good* and *bad*, are mapped into neighboring vectors. It is meaningful for some tasks such as pos-tagging, but it becomes a disaster for sentiment analysis because they have the opposite sentiment polarity. We therefore focus on developing sentiment-specific representation learning methods for document-level sentiment analysis.

2. THE PROPOSED RESEARCH

In this research, we argue that learning sentiment-specific document semantic is vital for document-level sentiment analysis. According to the principle of *compositionality* that

WSDM'15, February 2-6, 2015, Shanghai, China.
Copyright 2015 ACM 978-1-4503-3317-7/15/02 ...$15.00.
http://dx.doi.org/10.1145/2684822.2697035.

[1]Word embedding is a dense, low-dimensional and real-valued vector for each word.

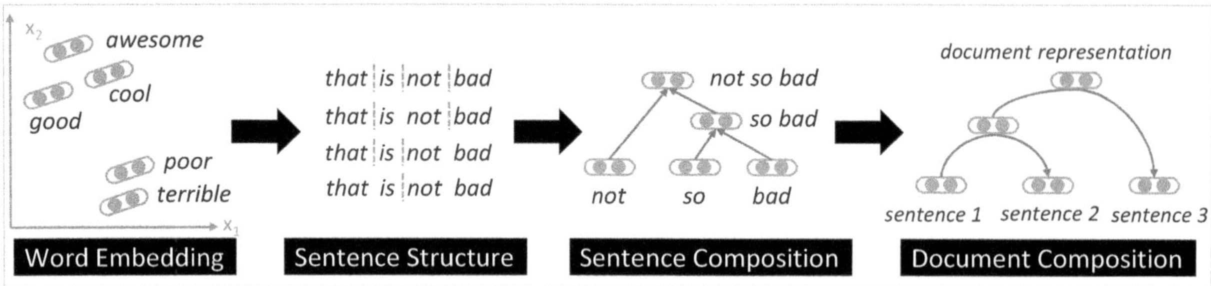

Figure 1: The sentiment-specific representation learning framework for document-level sentiment analysis.

the meaning of a longer expression (a sentence or a document) comes from the meanings of its words and the rules used to combine them [5], we decompose the document semantic into four cascaded constituents: (1) word embedding, (2) sentence structure, (3) sentence composition and (4) document composition. The work-flow of the proposed representation learning framework is illustrated in Figure 1. We learn word embeddings to capture the meanings of words, and then learn sentence structure and sentence composition to produce the representations of sentences based on the word embeddings. Afterwards, we calculate the document representations through document composition based on sentence representations and discourse analysis. We apply the learned document representations as features, and build the document-level sentiment classifier with existing machine learning methods such as SVM. We describe the research question of each constitute in this section.

2.1 Sentiment-Specific Word Embedding

Word embedding is the fundamental component of our representation learning framework because of the principle of *compositionality*. Word embedding is a low-dimensional, dense and real-valued vector for each word. After trained on a corpus, the words with similar grammatical usages and semantic meanings might be mapped into close vectors in the embedding space. Accordingly, the learned word embeddings can be easily utilized as features that capture semantic or clustering information of words for natural language processing tasks [2].

Existing embedding learning algorithms typically only capture the contexts of words but ignore the sentiment information of texts. As a result, words with similar contexts but opposite polarity, such as *good* and *bad*, are mapped into neighboring vectors. It is meaningful for some tasks such as pos-tagging, but it is problematic for sentiment analysis because they have the opposite sentiment polarity. To solve this problem, we propose to learn sentiment-specific word embedding (SSWE) that simultaneously encodes the contexts of words and sentiment information of texts in the continuous representation of words. Thus, the nearest neighbours of SSWE are also semantically similar while it favors words with the same sentiment polarity. We propose two methods based on existing embedding learning algorithms [2, 11] to learn SSWE, which are detailed in Section 3.1.

2.2 Sentiment-Specific Sentence Structure

Handling the complicated expressions delivering people's opinions is one of the most challenging problems in sentiment analysis. Traditional sentiment analysis algorithms typically simply employ bag-of-words to represent a sentence. As a result, they cannot handle the inconsistent sentiment polarity between a phrase and the words it contains, such as "*not bad*" and "*a great deal of*". Bag-of-ngram might cover high-order phrases, however, the use of it will dramatically increase the dimension of feature space.

We argue that learning the structure inherent in a sentence is important to help us understand its meaning. Traditional structure learning algorithms in fact-based NLP tasks (such as trunking and parsing) typically manually design linguistic-driven grammars or learn the patterns from the annotated treebank [10]. However, they cannot well handle the negation, intensification, and contrast phenomenons on the user-generated texts (e.g., reviews, tweets, etc.), which are the major focus of sentiment analysis algorithms. We therefore target at learning the sentiment-specific structures of sentences, which are optimized for sentiment analysis. Our sentiment-specific sentence segmentor [19] is described in Section 3.2.

2.3 Sentence Composition

Sentence representation is a pivot for document-level sentiment analysis because it links the word representations and document representations. Since regarding each sentence as a unique element makes the representation space to be extremely sparse, dominated previous studies investigate sentence composition methods [12] that calculate the representation of a sentence based on the representations of the words it contains. With the revival of interest in deep learning [1], neural network based methods including Recursive Neural Networks [17, 18] and Convolutional Neural Networks [7] have proven effective in sentence-level sentiment classification. However, to our knowledge, whether the compression based methods (such as autoencoder or restricted boltzmann machine) can learn meaningful sentence composition for sentiment analysis still remains unclear [6]. It is desirable to develop a sentiment-tailored composition approach that effectively handle the negation, intensification, and contrast phenomenons in sentiment analysis.

2.4 Document Composition

Learning meaningful and effective document representation is the major focus of the proposed representation learning framework. Given a document and the representation of each sentence it contains, we need to re-visit the principle of *compositionality* and calculate the document representation with document composition. We argue that sentiment-sensitive discourse relation is the key of document composition. A similar idea is given by Zhou et al. [22] that empirically defines a discourse scheme with constraints on sentiment polarity based on Rhetorical Structure Theory (RST). Unlike their method, we want to learn these sentiment-sensitive discourse phenomenons from the data, and make the composition learning algorithm less dependent on feature engineering [8]. After that, the learned document representations will be considered as features for building the sentiment classifier with existing machine learning algorithms.

3. METHODOLOGY

We introduce our algorithms for learning sentiment-specific word embeddings and sentence structures in this part.

3.1 Sentiment-Specific Word Embedding

We extend two state-of-the-art neural network based methods [2, 11] tailored for learning word embeddings, and integrate the sentiment information of sentences (e.g. tweets) to learn the sentiment-specific word embedding (SSWE).

Our **first model** (SSWE$_u$ [21]) is an extension based on the C&W model [2], as illustrated in Figure 2). Collobert and Weston [2] introduce C&W model to learn word embedding based on the contexts of words. Given an ngram such as *"cat chills on a mat"*, C&W replaces the center word with a random word w^r and derives a **corrupted** ngram *"cat chills RANDOM a mat"*. The training objective is that the original ngram is expected to obtain a higher context score than the corrupted ngram by a margin of 1. The ranking objective can be optimized by a hinge loss,

$$loss_{cw}(t, t^r) = max(0; 1 - f^{cw}(t) + f^{cw}(t^r)) \quad (1)$$

where t is the original ngram, t^r is the corrupted ngram, $f^{cw}(\cdot)$ is a one-dimensional scalar representing the context score of the input ngram. During training, the context score $f^{cw}(\cdot)$ is obtained with a feed-forward neural network as shown in Figure 2.

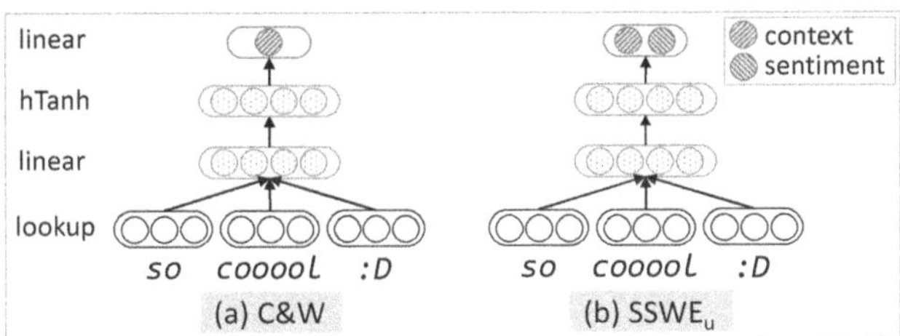

Figure 2: The traditional C&W model and our neural network (SSWE$_u$ [21]) for learning sentiment-specific word embedding.

Formally, $f^{cw}(\cdot)$ is calculated as given in Equation 2, where L is the lookup table of word embedding, w_1, w_2, b_1, b_2 are the parameters of linear layers. The original and corrupted ngrams are treated as inputs of the feed-forward neural network, respectively.

$$f^{cw}(t) = w_2 \cdot a + b_2 \quad (2)$$

$$a = hTanh(w_1 L_t + b_1) \quad (3)$$

We develop a neural network (**SSWE$_u$**) that captures the sentiment information of sentences as well as the contexts of words. Given an original (or corrupted) ngram and the sentiment polarity of a sentence as the input, SSWE$_u$ predicts a two-dimensional vector for each input ngram. The two scalars ($\boldsymbol{f}_0^u$, $\boldsymbol{f}_1^u$) stand for context score and sentiment score of the input ngram, respectively. The training objectives of SSWE$_u$ are that (1) the original ngram should obtain a higher context score $\boldsymbol{f}_0^u(t)$ than the corrupted ngram $\boldsymbol{f}_0^u(t^r)$, and (2) the sentiment score of original ngram $\boldsymbol{f}_1^u(t)$ should be more consistent with the gold polarity annotation of sentence than corrupted ngram $\boldsymbol{f}_1^u(t^r)$. The loss function of SSWE$_u$ is the linear combination of two hinge losses,

$$loss_u(t, t^r) = \alpha \cdot loss_{cw}(t, t^r) + (1 - \alpha) \cdot loss_{us}(t, t^r) \quad (4)$$

where $loss_{cw}(t, t^r)$ is the context loss as given in Equation 1, $loss_{us}(t, t^r)$ is the sentiment loss as described in Equation 5. The hyper-parameter α weighs the two parts.

$$loss_{us}(t, t^r) = max(0, 1 - \delta_s(t)\boldsymbol{f}_1^u(t) + \delta_s(t)\boldsymbol{f}_1^u(t^r)) \quad (5)$$

where $\delta_s(t)$ is an indicator function that reflects the gold sentiment polarity of a sentence,

$$\delta_s(t) = \begin{cases} 1 & \text{if } t \text{ is positive} \\ -1 & \text{if } t \text{ is negative} \end{cases} \quad (6)$$

Our **second model** (SSPE [20]) is an extension based on the context-based method (SkipGram) proposed by Mikolov et al. [11]. Given a word (or phrase) w_i as the input, SkipGram maps it into its embedding representation e_i, and utilizes e_i to predict the context words of w_i, namely w_{i-2}, w_{i-1}, w_{i+1}, w_{i+2}, et al. The training objective of SkipGram is to maximize the average log probability:

$$f_{context} = \frac{1}{T}\sum_{i=1}^{T} \sum_{-c \le j \le c, j \ne 0} log\ p(w_{i+j}|e_i) \quad (7)$$

where T is the occurrence of each phrase in the corpus, c is the window size, e_i is the embedding of the current word w_i, w_{i+j} is the context words of w_i.

We extend SkipGram and develop sentiment-specific phrase embedding (SSPE) to integrate the sentiment information of sentences, as illustrated in Figure 3. Given a triple $\langle w_i, s_j, pol_j \rangle$ as the input, where w_i is a word(or phrase) contained in the sentence s_j whose gold sentiment polarity is pol_j, our training objective is to (1) utilize the embedding of w_i to predict its context words, and (2) use the sentence representation se_j to predict the gold sentiment polarity of s_j, namely pol_j. We simply average the embedding of phrases contained in a sentence as its continuous representation se_j. The objective of the sentiment part is to maximize the average of log sentiment probability:

$$f_{sentiment} = \frac{1}{S}\sum_{j=1}^{S} log\ p(pol_j|se_j) \quad (8)$$

where S is the occurrence of each sentence in the corpus, $\sum_k pol_{jk} = 1$. For binary classification between positive and negative, the distribution of [0,1] is for positive and [1,0] is for negative. The final training objective is to maximize the linear combination of the context and sentiment parts:

$$f_{SSPE} = \alpha \cdot f_{context} + (1 - \alpha) \cdot f_{sentiment} \quad (9)$$

where α is a hyper-parameter that weights the two parts.

We collect massive tweets containing positive and negative emoticons to train the sentiment-specific word embeddings. We regard emoticon signals as the sentiment supervision of

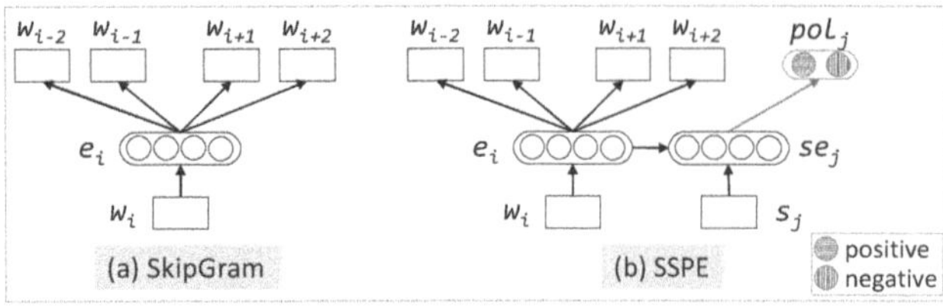

Figure 3: The traditional SkipGram model and our neural network (SSPE [20]) for learning sentiment-specific word embedding.

sentences during training. After using some heuristic filtering rules (detailed in [21, 20]), we collect 10M tweets, selected by 5M tweets with positive emoticons and 5M tweets with negative emoticons, as the training data.

3.2 Sentiment-Specific Sentence Structure

We describe our algorithm for learning sentiment-specific sentence segmentation [19] in this part. We develop a joint segmentation and classification framework, which simultaneously conducts sentence segmentation and sentence-level sentiment classification. The intuitions of the proposed joint model are two-folds:

- The segmentation results have a strong influence on the Sentiment classification performance, since they are the inputs of the sentiment classification model.
- The usefulness of a segmentation can be judged by whether the sentiment classifier can use it to predict the correct sentence polarity.

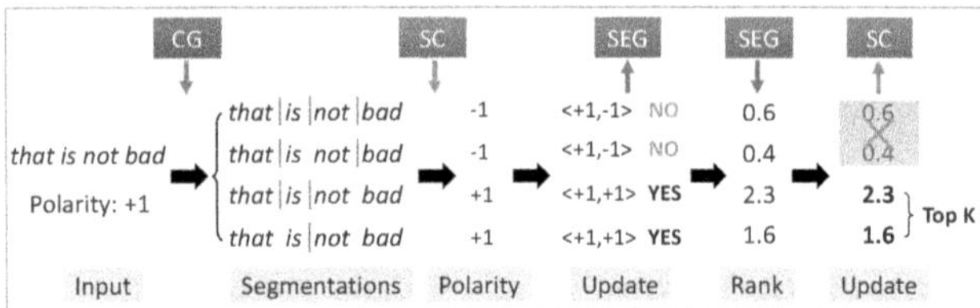

Figure 4: The proposed framework ([19]) for learning sentiment-specific sentence segmentation.

Specifically, we use a log-linear model to score each segmentation candidate, and exploit the phrasal information of top-ranked segmentations as features to build the sentiment classifier. A marginal log-likelihood objective function (as given in Equation 10) is devised for the segmentation model, which is optimized for enhancing the sentiment classification performance.

$$loss = -\sum_{i=1}^{|T|} log(\frac{\sum_{j \in H_i} \phi_{ij}}{\sum_{j' \in A_i} \phi_{ij'}}) + \lambda ||w||_2^2 \qquad (10)$$

where T is the training data; A_i represents all the segmentation candidates of sentence s_i; H_i means the hit candidates of s_i; λ is the weight of the L2-norm regularization factor (detailed in [19]).

4. EMPIRICAL RESULTS

We conducts experiments to evaluate the effectiveness of the proposed algorithms. In this part, we show the empirical results by applying sentiment-specific word embeddings and sentence structures for Twitter sentiment classification.

4.1 Sentiment-Specific Word Embedding

We conduct positive/negative Twitter sentiment classification on the benchmark dataset from SemEval 2013 [14]. In our method ($SSWE_u$), we directly apply the learned SSWE as features for building the sentiment classifier. We compare with the following baseline methods (more baselines are detailed in [21]). Results are given in Table 1.

(1) *DistSuper*: We use the 10 million tweets selected by positive and negative emoticons as training data, and build sentiment classifier with LibLinear based on bag-of-words.

(2) *SVM*: The bag-of-word features and SVM are widely used baseline methods to build sentiment classifiers [16]. We use LibLinear to train the classifier.

(3) *NRC*: NRC-Canada builds the top-performed system in SemEval 2013 Twitter sentiment classification track [13]. They use many lexicons and hand-crafted features.

Method	Macro-F1
DistSuper	61.74
SVM	74.50
NRC (**Top System** in SemEval 2013)	**84.73**
$SSWE_u$	**84.98**
$SSWE_u$+NRC	**86.58**

Table 1: Macro-F1 on positive/negative classification of tweets [21].

Our method ($SSWE_u$) achieves 84.98% by using only $SSWE_u$ as features without using any sentiment lexicons or hand-crafted rules. The results indicate that $SSWE_u$ automatically learns discriminative features from massive tweets and performs comparable with the state-of-the-art manually designed features. After concatenating $SSWE_u$ with the feature sets of *NRC*, the performance is further improved.

We also compare with other word embedding algorithms for Twitter sentiment classification. From Table 2, we find that our sentiment-specific word embeddings ($SSWE_h$, $SSWE_s$, $SSWE_u$) yield better performances.

Embedding	unigram	uni+bi	uni+bi+tri
C&W	74.89	75.24	75.89
Word2vec	73.21	75.07	76.31
ReEmb(C&W)	75.87	–	–
ReEmb(w2v)	75.21	–	–
WVSA	77.04	–	–
$SSWE_h$	81.33	83.16	83.37
$SSWE_r$	80.45	81.52	82.60
$SSWE_u$	**83.70**	**84.70**	**84.98**

Table 2: Macro-F1 on positive/negative classification of tweets with different word embeddings [21].

4.2 Sentiment-Specific Sentence Structure

We evaluate our sentiment-specific sentence segmentor by applying it for Twitter sentiment classification on the benchmark dataset from SemEval 2013. We compare the proposed model (JSC) with two pipelined methods. *Pipeline 1* use the bag-of-word segmentation. *Pipeline 2* use the segmentation with maximum phrase number. The tick *[A, B]* on x-axis means the different features used for classification.

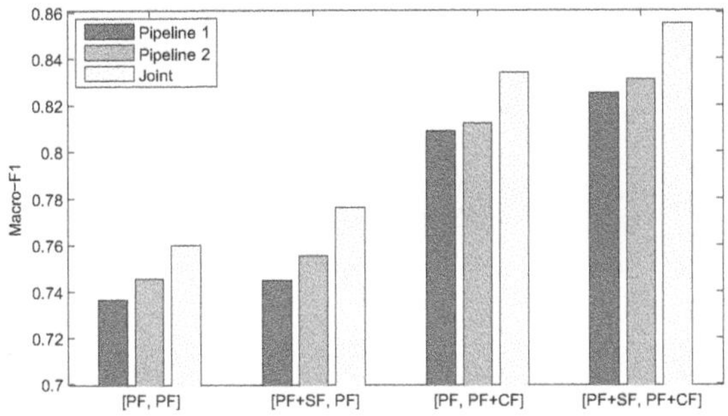

Figure 5: Macro-F1 for positive/negative classification of tweets with joint and pipelined models [19].

From Figure 5, we find that the proposed model consistently outperforms pipelined baseline methods in all feature settings. The reason lies in that our method uses the sentiment information to optimize the sentence segmentor, which in turns produces benefits to the sentiment classifier.

5. RESEARCH ISSUES FOR DISCUSSION

We briefly describe the potential research issues for discussion in this part. For **word embedding**, the issues are which kind of sentiment information (positive/negative or fine-grained sentiment; sentence-level or document-level) might be used, and how to incorporate them for learning better SSWEs. For **sentence structure**, the issue is whether we can manually design a hybrid grammar that integrates both linguistic and sentiment schemes. If not, how can we learn the grammar effectively with minor manually annotations. For **sentence composition**, the issue is how to develop reasonable and effective composition functions to effectively handle the negation, intensification, and contrast phenomenons. For **document composition**, how to carefully define or automatically learn the sentiment-sensitive discourse relations, and then leverage them for document composition are the issues to be solved.

Acknowledgments

This research was partly supported by National Natural Science Foundation of China (No.61133012, No.61273321, No.61300113).

6. REFERENCES

[1] Y. Bengio, A. Courville, and P. Vincent. Representation learning: A review and new perspectives. *IEEE Trans. PAMI*, 2013.

[2] R. Collobert, J. Weston, L. Bottou, M. Karlen, K. Kavukcuoglu, and P. Kuksa. Natural language processing (almost) from scratch. *Journal of Machine Learning Research*, 12:2493–2537, 2011.

[3] P. Domingos. A few useful things to know about machine learning. *Communications of the ACM*, 55(10):78–87, 2012.

[4] R. Feldman. Techniques and applications for sentiment analysis. *Communications of the ACM*, 56(4):82–89, 2013.

[5] G. Frege. On sense and reference. *Ludlow (1997)*, pages 563–584, 1892.

[6] E. Grefenstette, K. M. Hermann, G. Dinu, and P. Blunsom. New directions in vector space models of meaning. In *Proceedings of the ACL: Tutorials*, 2014.

[7] N. Kalchbrenner, E. Grefenstette, and P. Blunsom. A convolutional neural network for modelling sentences. In *Proceedings of ACL*, pages 655–665, 2014.

[8] J. Li, R. Li, and E. Hovy. Recursive deep models for discourse parsing. In *Procedding of EMNLP*. 2014.

[9] B. Liu. Sentiment analysis and opinion mining. *Synthesis Lectures on Human Language Technologies*, 5(1):1–167, 2012.

[10] C. Manning, P. Raghavan, and H. Schutze. *Introduction to information retrieval*, volume 1. Cambridge University Press Cambridge, 2008.

[11] T. Mikolov, K. Chen, G. Corrado, and J. Dean. Efficient estimation of word representations in vector space. *ICLR*, 2013.

[12] J. Mitchell and M. Lapata. Composition in distributional models of semantics. *Cognitive Science*, 34(8):1388–1429, 2010.

[13] S. M. Mohammad, S. Kiritchenko, and X. Zhu. Nrc-canada: Building the state-of-the-art in sentiment analysis of tweets. *Proceedings of SemEval*, 2013.

[14] P. Nakov, S. Rosenthal, Z. Kozareva, V. Stoyanov, A. Ritter, and T. Wilson. Semeval-2013 task 2: Sentiment analysis in twitter. In *SemEval*, 2013.

[15] B. Pang and L. Lee. Opinion mining and sentiment analysis. *Foundations and trends in information retrieval*, 2(1-2):1–135, 2008.

[16] B. Pang, L. Lee, and S. Vaithyanathan. Thumbs up?: sentiment classification using machine learning techniques. In *Proceedings of the EMNLP*, 2002.

[17] R. Socher, J. Pennington, E. Huang, A. Ng, and C. Manning. Semi-supervised recursive autoencoders for predicting sentiment distributions. In *Proceeding of EMNLP*, pages 151–161, 2011.

[18] R. Socher, A. Perelygin, J. Wu, J. Chuang, C. D. Manning, A. Ng, and C. Potts. Recursive deep models for semantic compositionality over a sentiment treebank. In *Proceeding of EMNLP*, 2013.

[19] D. Tang, F. Wei, B. Qin, L. Dong, T. Liu, and M. Zhou. A joint segmentation and classification framework for sentiment analysis. In *Procedding of EMNLP*. 2014.

[20] D. Tang, F. Wei, B. Qin, M. Zhou, and T. Liu. Building large-scale twitter-specific sentiment lexicon: A representation learning approach. In *Proceedings of COLING 2014*, pages 172–182, 2014.

[21] D. Tang, F. Wei, N. Yang, M. Zhou, T. Liu, and B. Qin. Learning sentiment-specific word embedding for twitter sentiment classification. In *Procedding of Annual Meeting of ACL.*, pages 1555–1565. 2014.

[22] L. Zhou, B. Li, W. Gao, Z. Wei, and K.-F. Wong. Unsupervised discovery of discourse relations for eliminating intra-sentence polarity ambiguities. In *Proceeding of EMNLP*, pages 162–171, 2011.

Chronological Scientific Information Recommendation via Supervised Dynamic Topic Modeling

Zhuoren Jiang
College of Transportation Management
Dalian Maritime University
Dalian, China, 116026
jzr_dlmu@hotmail.com

ABSTRACT

Scientific information recommendation is crucial to assist scholars for their researches. Citation recommendation is an important field of scientific recommendation. Traditional approaches ignore the chronological nature of the citation recommendation task. In this study, I propose the "Chronological Citation Recommendation," which assumes initial user information need could shift while they are looking for the papers in different time slices. Specifically, I employed a supervised dynamic topic model to characterize the content "time-varying" dynamics and constructed a novel heterogeneous graph that contains dynamic topic-based information, time-decay citation information and word-based information. I applied different meta-paths for different ranking hypotheses, which carried different types of information for citation recommendation in different time slices along with information need shifting. I plan to generate the final "Chronological Citation Recommendation" rankings by feature integration using Learning to Rank. "Chronological Citation Recommendation" will recommend time-series ranking lists based on initial user textual information need. Preliminary experiments on the ACM corpus show that chronological citation recommendation will significantly improve the citation recommendation performance.

Categories and Subject Descriptors

H.3.3 [**Information Storage and Retrieval**]: Information Search and Retrieval

Keywords

Information Need Shifting, Chronological Citation Recommendation, Heterogeneous Graph

1. INTRODUCTION AND MOTIVATION

As an important research field of scientific recommendation, citation recommendation can help researchers to find and read the potential candidate articles for citation. The past decade has seen the rapid development of citation recommendation in both academic and industrial research. Google Scholar and Microsoft Academic Search have been considered as the indispensable tools for researchers. In order to recommend the high-quality papers, a number of different solutions have be proposed, classic textual information retrieval approaches, topic information of the paper content and citation relationships between papers, have proven to enhance recommendation performance effectively.

However, two important characteristics of citation recommendation are ignored in most previous studies. 1) Unlike other web resource recommendations, citation recommendation is more sensitive to the publication date: scholars read and cite recently published papers for innovative ideas or algorithms, and explore classic models and foundation theories in the papers published in the early stage. 2) A researcher's information need could implicitly shift over different time slices, for instance, given the same query, the scholar might be interested in the publications focusing on *"Latent Semantic Indexing"* or *"Probabilistic Latent Semantic Indexing"* between 1990 and 2000 and *"Word Clustering"* or *"Probability Theory"* studies published before 1990. In this study, I define this phenomenon as **"Information Need Shifting,"** and it challenges most of the existing text or citation based search methods which generate a general ranking list of papers statistically similar to the initial query.

I propose the **"Chronological Citation Recommendation"** in this study, which will 1) provide a time-series candidate citation recommendation result based on the user's textual queries to solve the problem of time preferences of different research tasks; 2) emphasize the dynamic evolution of scientific content, explicitly characterizing scientific information need dynamics to deal with the impact of "Information Need Shifting." One hypothesis is to consider that the additional dynamic content evolvement information could make the scholarly recommendation more accurate and practical. With chronological citation recommendation, researchers can get a set of recommendation paper lists for different time slices (given a textual query), and freely choose the cite paper of their favored time slice. I hope this study can provide researchers a new and distinctive choice for citation recommendation. This study presents two challenges. The first challenge is how to model the "Information Need Shifting." The second challenge is the manner in which to naturally and efficiently combine dynamic content information and the interlinked information.

The contribution of this paper is threefold. First, I propose a novel chronological citation recommendation problem to assist scholars better identify and access the recommendation results and better understand the discipline's development (given a textual query). Chronological citation recommendation, unlike other existing methods, is able to generate multiple lists of ranked papers for a number of time slices. Second, I characterize the information need shifting for citation recommendation by employing time-decayed

WSDM'15, February 2–6, 2015, Shanghai, China.

http://dx.doi.org/10.1145/2684822.2697036.

citation relations between papers/topics, dynamic topic-based information, and word information. All of these indicators are addressed by a number of meta-path plus random walk based features on an innovative heterogeneous graph. Last but not least, I plan to apply learning-to-rank algorithms for graph-based feature integration to generate the final time-series recommendation ranking models. Each ranking model will be utilized to optimize the publication ranking results for a distinct time slice. To the best of my knowledge, few prior studies addressed these problems.

2. BACKGROUND AND RELATED WORK

Scientific Information Recommendation

Scientific information recommendation occurs when a scientific publication, venue, or author is recommended to users based on the similarity between the recommended resource and user profiles or samples of in-progress text. Similar to previous studies in text information retrieval and text mining, a number of studies employed text similarity approaches such as paper/author content matching and unsupervised topic modeling [3, 10].

Scholarly or bibliographic networks are another important approach that have also been used to recommend scientific resources. For instance, Shi, Leskovec and McFarland [13] developed citation projection graphs by investigating citations among publications cited by a given paper. In this study, I employed citation importance decay, which was similar to CiteRank [15], an enhanced ranking algorithm compared to PageRank, which enabled the ranking method to estimate the traffic $T_i(\tau_{dir}, \alpha)$ to a given $paper_i$. For this method, a recent paper was more likely to be selected with a probability that was exponentially discounted according to the age of the paper, τ_{dir}.

However, to the best of my knowledge, few existing studies have investigated the chronological citation recommendation problem. In [6], I used a recursive model "dynamic topic/citation influence model" to address this problem, but the processing time of model is not satisfactory. In this study, I will propose a novel method to address this problem effectively.

Dynamic Topic Modeling

Topic dynamics has been recently investigated. Blei and Lafferty [1] proposed a dynamic topic model (DTM), which explicitly characterized the chronological nature of sequential corpora by utilizing a Markov chain of term distributions over time along with multiple LDA-based topic distributions. Based on [1], Gerrish and Blei proposed the document influence model (DIM) [5], this model respected the ordering of the documents, not only tracked how underlying theme has changed over time, but also captured how past articles exhibit varying influence on future articles. Unfortunately, both DTM and DIM may not be an appropriate solution for this task for three reasons. First, given a textual information need, DTM or DIM alone cannot discover optimized dynamic topic chains in terms of user textual information needs. Second, scientific publications are interlinked by citation, which contains important information. DTM or DIM, however, assumes documents are independent of each other, and the topic number, as other unsupervised LDA approaches, are not given. Liu et al., [10] found that the unsupervised LDA approach is not ideal for scientific publications, and scientific metadata, i.e., author assigned keywords, should be used to enhance the topic modeling performance.

In order to solve this problem, I utilized Labeled-LDA (LLDA) [12], which used corpus metadata, i.e., keywords and categories, to enhance the topic modeling process, constrained topic models by defining a one-to-one correspondence between latent topics and labels which solved the problems of topic number setting and topic interpretability. I proposed my work based on DIM, and added supervised technology into DIM by combining LLDA.

Heterogeneous Graph Mining

The concept of meta-path was first proposed in [14], which could systematically capture the semantic relation between objects in a heterogeneous information network scenario. Different meta-path-based mining tasks were studied including similarity search, relationship prediction, user-guided clustering, and recommendation. It turned out that meta-path served as a very critical feature extraction tool for most of the mining tasks in a heterogeneous information network. In this study, I employed meta-path-based approach as the ranking features, which were extracted from an innovative, dynamic scholarly heterogeneous network. More recently, Lao and Cohen [7] used both supervised and unsupervised methods with the Random Walk with Restart (RWR) algorithm for citation, author, and venue recommendation. Similar approach was also used by [9]. It had been demonstrated that by using the heterogeneous link information in a network, mining functions, such as similarity search, ranking, clustering and classification could be significantly enhanced [14].

3. RESEARCH METHODS

Dynamic Topic Training

As aforementioned, "information need shifting" has a significant impact for citation recommendation, which requires characterization of the "time-varying" content dynamics. This study will model the content dynamics on topic level. Unlike most previous studies that treat topic as a static term-distribution, this model assumes topic can evolve in a historical topic trajectory. I analyze the corpus using a supervised dynamic topic model which is depicted in Figure 1.

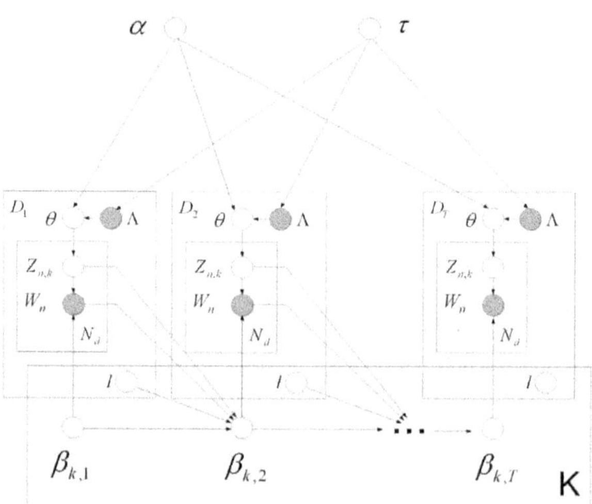

Figure 1: Graphical representation of a supervised dynamic topic model

Here, $\beta_{k,t}$ is considered as the term distribution at time slice t for topic k, $z_{n,k}$ is the indicator that the nth word in document d is assigned to topic k, l is a normally distributed influence score assigned to each article in a specific time slice, N_d represents the word number of document d, θ is a multinomial distribution, represents the topic mixture proportions, α is a Dirichlet prior distribution, Λ is a binary vector of document's labels (keywords metadata), τ represents a labeling prior probability.

This model is based on document influence model (DIM) [5], DIM is a variant of dynamic topic model (DTM) [1], which has been demonstrated as a powerful tool which can explicitly model the dynamics of the underlying topics and an exploratory tool for discovering influential articles. it introduces a Markov chain of term distributions to capture probabilities that drift over time, where the topics associated with slice *t* evolve from the topics associated with slice *t -1*: $\beta_{k,t}|\beta_{k,t-1},(w,l,z)_{t-1,1:D}$ $\sim \mathbb{N}\left(\beta_{k,t-1}+exp\left(-\beta_{k,t-1}\sum_{d}l_{d,k}\sum_{n}w_{d,n}z_{d,n,k},\sigma^{2}I\right)\right)$.

It assumes that the higher the influence, the more the words of the article affect how the topic drifts. While traditional DIM uses LDA [2] to model documents of each time slice, I model them with Labeled LDA (L-LDA) [12], that's only difference between DIM and this model. By combining the supervised technology from L-LDA, I make this model as a supervised dynamic topic model, which overcomes the limitation of traditional DIM: the topics learned from the model are hard to interpret, and the setting of topic number in corpus is arbitrary. L-LDA associates individual words in a document with their most appropriate labels. In this study, the labels come from author-provided metadata such as keywords, and the number of topics in L-LDA is the number of unique labels K in the corpus. The supervised label association is straightforward, I generate the document's labels vector Λ using keyword metadata with the labeling prior probability τ, which can be obtained by observation, then restrict θ to be defined only over the topics that correspond to document's labels. This process will ensure that all the topic assignments are limited to the document's keyword labels. The detailed posterior inference can be found in [5].

By pre-training scholarly corpus using supervised document influence model, I can obtain three time-series distributions in which K is the number of topic in all time slices, T is the number of time slices, time slice T is the latest time slice, time slice 1 is the earliest, and D is the document set. $D=\{D_1,D_2,...D_T\}$, where D_i $(1\leq i\leq T)$ is the candidate documents published in time slice i, and $V=\{w_1,w_2,...,w_{|V|}\}$ represents the vocabulary of corpus:

(1) Time-series document-topic distributions (***TDTD***)

$$\theta=\left\{\quad \theta_{t_1,d^1_{1:D_1},1:K},\quad \theta_{t_2,d^2_{1:D_2},1:K},\quad \cdots\quad \theta_{t_T,d^T_{1:D_T},1:K}\right\}$$

Where, $\theta_{t_i,d^i_m,k}$ is k^{th} topic's $(1\leq k\leq K)$ proportion in $d_m{}^{th}$ document $(1\leq d_m\leq|D_i|)$ published in time slice i $(1\leq i\leq T)$, represents the topic mixture proportions of a document.

(2) Time-series topic-word distributions (***TTWD***)

$$\beta=\left\{\quad \beta_{t_1,w_{1:|V|},1:K},\quad \beta_{t_2,w_{1:|V|},1:K},\quad \cdots\quad \beta_{t_T,w_{1:|V|},1:K}\right\}$$

Where, $\beta_{t_i,w_n,k}$ is the probability of term w_n $(1\leq n\leq|V|)$ for k^{th} topic $(1\leq k\leq K)$ in time slice i $(1\leq i\leq T)$, represents the relevance between term and topic.

(3) Time-series Document-topic influence distributions (***TDTL***)

$$L=\left\{\quad l_{t_1,d^1_{1:D_1},1:K},\quad l_{t_2,d^2_{1:D_2},1:K},\quad \cdots\quad l_{t_{T-1},d^{T-1}_{1:D_{T-1}},1:K}\right\}$$

Where, $l_{t_i,d^i_m,k}$ is the influence of $d_m{}^{th}$ document $(1\leq d_m\leq|D_i|)$ on k^{th} topic $(1\leq k\leq K)$ published in time slice i $(1\leq i\leq T-1)$, represents the document's influence on topic.

These three time-series topic-based distributions will provide the dynamic topic-based information in chronological citation recommendation.

Heterogeneous Graph Construction

In this study, the chronological citation recommendation problem is defined on the sequential scientific publication dataset which can be formatted into a heterogeneous graph. A heterogeneous graph, namely a heterogeneous information network, is a directed graph which contains multiple types of objects and links. In a heterogeneous graph, two different types of vertices can be connected via different paths which always carry different semantic information. A meta-path represents a composite relation over two vertices. For example, $W-T_{time}-P$ denotes a meta-path between a word and a paper connect by a historical topic that has the word and is related to the paper. [14] gives the formal definition of "Heterogeneous information network," "Network schema" and "Meta-path."

I constructed a novel heterogeneous graph (Figure 2) with three kinds of vertices: "Word," W; "Historical Topic," T_{time}; "Paper published in specific time slice," P_{time}. The historical topic is the topic in a specific time slice, that means even the topics share the same label, they are different topics if located in different time slices, i.e. $Language\ model_{(2000-2002)}$ and $Language\ model_{(2006-2007)}$ are two different topics in this study.

Figure 2: Constructed heterogeneous graph

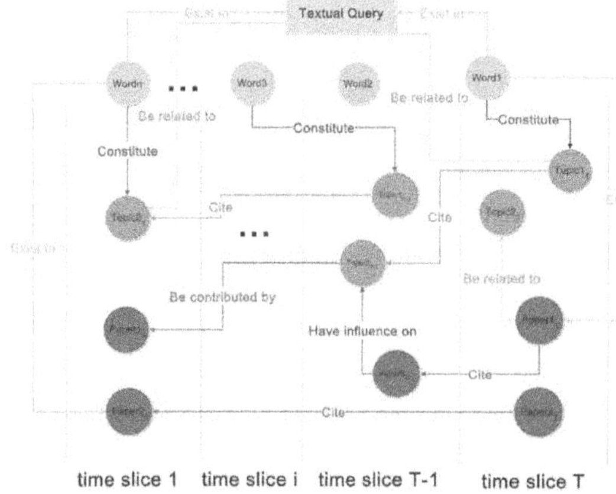

Table 1: Edges in the constructed heterogeneous graph

Edge	Description	Information Carrying
$W\stackrel{e}{\rightarrow}P$	Word exist in paper	Word-based information
$W\stackrel{cons}{\rightarrow}T_{time}$	Word constitute historical topic	Dynamic topic-based information
$T_{time}\stackrel{cite}{\rightarrow}T_{time}$	Historical topic cite historical topic	Time-decay topic citation information
$P_{time}\stackrel{cite}{\rightarrow}P_{time}$	Paper cite paper.	Time-decay paper citation information
$T_{time}\stackrel{cont}{\rightarrow}P_{time}$	Historical topic is contributed by paper	Time-decay paper citation information and dynamic topic-based information
$P_{time}\stackrel{infl}{\rightarrow}T_{time}$	Paper has influence on historical topic	Dynamic topic-based information
$P_{time}\stackrel{r}{\rightarrow}T_{time}$	Paper is related to historical topic	Dynamic topic-based information

Each edge has its own weight. The weight of $W_n\stackrel{e}{\rightarrow}P_i$ is the TF-IDF value of $word_n$ in $paper_i$. The weight of $W_n\stackrel{cons}{\rightarrow}T_k{}^{t_i}$ is the probability $\beta_{t_i,w_n,k}$ from ***TTWD***. The weight of $T_m{}^{t_i}\stackrel{cite}{\rightarrow}T_n{}^{t_j}$ is the time-decay topic citation probability $\frac{1}{out_{T_m{}^{t_i}}}*\varepsilon_{t_i}$, $out_{T_m{}^{t_i}}$ is the number of outlinks of historical topic $T_m{}^{t_i}$, ε_{t_i} is the time decay factor, which can make sure that the citation from historical topic in recent time slice gives more credits, $\varepsilon_{t_i}=\frac{1}{log_2(2+T-i)}$. Similarly, the weight of $P_m{}^{t_i}\stackrel{cite}{\rightarrow}P_n{}^{t_j}$ is the time-decay paper citation probability $\frac{1}{out_{P_m{}^{t_i}}}*\varepsilon_{t_i}$. The weight of $P_m{}^{t_i}\stackrel{infl}{\rightarrow}T_k{}^{t_i}$ is the influence score of $l_{t_i,d^i_m,k}$ from ***TDTL***. The weight of $P_m{}^{t_i}\stackrel{r}{\rightarrow}T_k{}^{t_i}$ is the proportion $\gamma_{t_i,d^i_m,k}$ from ***TDTD***.

In order to estimate the contribution of each paper to a historical topic, I calculated the paper importance given a historical topic $T_n{}^{t_j}$ by using PageRank with Prior algorithm [16]. The normalized topical PageRank authority score is used for the weights of

$T_k{}^{t_j} \overset{cont}{\rightarrow} P_m{}^{t_i}$. For this step, I used classical homogeneous graph that the vertex is a paper. The citation relationship between the vertices is utilized to calculate the PageRank authority scores. Each vertex is also characterized by a topic prior vector which is $\gamma_{t_i,d^i_m,1:K}$ from ***TDTD***. The result of PageRank (with prior) is the historical topic based paper topic authority vector, i.e., for $P_m{}^{t_i}$, the result is a paper authority vector $Authority(P_m{}^{t_i}|T_{1:K}{}^{t_j})$, the authority score of $P_m{}^{t_i}$ given the historical topics $T_{1:K}{}^{t_j}$. Note that $T_k{}^{t_j}$ is contributed by $P_m{}^{t_i}$ ($T_k{}^{t_j} \overset{cont}{\rightarrow} P_m{}^{t_i}$) doesn't necessarily mean $P_m{}^{t_i}$ is related to $T_k{}^{t_j}$ ($P_m{}^{t_i} \overset{r}{\rightarrow} T_k{}^{t_j}$). For example, some "topic modeling" papers published in the year of 2003 can be important for historical topic $Information\ Retrieval_{(2006-2007)}$.

The input of chronological citation recommendation is a piece of text to briefly summarize the information need, i.e., paper abstract or research idea description. I will use starting vertices to represent the user textual query. There are two kinds of starting vertices: W^* and $T_{time}{}^*$. W^* is the word in the query, $T_{time}{}^*$ is the query related historical topics which come from the LDA inference of query [2] for each time slice. The end vertex $P_{time}{}^?$ is the candidate paper in a specific time slice. The output is several lists of ranked candidate papers in different time slices, which could potentially be cited given user's input.

I will use meta-path from starting vertices to candidate paper vertices in the heterogeneous graph as ranking function. In order to quantify the ranking score of candidate vertices relevant to the starting vertices following the meta-path, I propose the simulated random walk based measure to relevance score: $r(v_i^{(1)}, v_j^{(l+1)}) = \sum_{t=v_i^{(1)} \rightsquigarrow v_j^{(l+1)}} RW(t)$. Where t is a tour from $v_i^{(1)}$ to $v_j^{(l+1)}$ following the meta-path, and $RW(t)$ is the simulated random walk probability of the tour t. Suppose $t = (v_{i1}^{(1)}, v_{i2}^{(2)}, \ldots, v_{il+1}^{(l+1)})$, the random walk probability is then $RW(t) = \prod_j w(v_{ij}^{(j)}, v_{i,j+1}^{(j+1)})p(v_{ij}^{(j)})$, $w(v_{ij}^{(j)}, v_{i,j+1}^{(j+1)})$ is the weight of edge $v_{ij}^{(j)} \rightarrow v_{i,j+1}^{(j+1)}$, $p(v_{ij}^{(j)})$ is the vertex prior probability.

Two or more parallel meta-paths leading to the same candidate vertices will be considered. The ranking score of candidate cited paper $P_{time}{}^?$ is the linear combination of the ranking scores for all sub-meta-paths. The meta-paths preliminarily investigated are listed in Table 2.

Modeling Information Need Shifting via Learning to Rank

In this study, I propose various meta-paths to address different ranking hypotheses where each meta-path carries one or more typies of ranking information. It's vital to combine all the information from the meta-paths. Learning-to-rank [8] optimizes ranking performance using machine learning techniques. In the learning-to-rank framework, documents are usually represented by ranking feature vectors. I will use learning-to-rank to combine different meta-path based ranking features, while avoiding manual parameter tuning. Each candidate paper is assigned different ranking scores via various meta-paths. As mentioned in section 1, user information need can vary in different time slices (information need shifting). I will train multi-ranking models, $\{\Phi_1, \Phi_2 ... \Phi_T\}$ (total T time slices), for different time slices, and I assume the importance of different ranking features can be significantly different for different time slices.

I plan to train the ranking models by using a list-wise algorithm (AdaRank [17], Coordinate Ascent [11] or LambdaMART [4]) on the training data. I will use a scientific candidate publication set and a set of testing paper for training and evaluation. The abstracts of testing papers will be used as the experiment query and the (author-provided) reference lists will be employed as the judgment data. The cite time of different cited papers indicates the importance of each cited paper (for nDCG relevance score). N-fold cross-validation will be used in this study.

4. PRELIMINARY EXPERIMENT

Data

I extracted 45,372 publications with 107,691 citation relations from 6,818 journals and 4,455 conference proceedings or workshops on computer science between 1951 and 2011 (from the *ACM digital library*). I used the title and the abstract information to represent the content of the paper. All the selected papers' contents had more than 80 words after removing stop words and stemming each term to its root. The vocabulary size was 6,517. Most frequent 5% and less then 15 times words were removed. Author-provided keywords were used as topic labels. The initial number of labels was 1,082, regardless of time slice, and the total historical topic number was 8,072. To verify and compare different recommendation algorithms, I split the corpus into eight time slices: pre-1990, 1990-1999, 2000-2002, 2003-2005, 2006-2007, 2008-2009, the year 2010, the year 2011. I generated 2,957,476 word exist-in paper relations, 107,691 paper cite paper relations, 2,242,547 historical topic cite historical topic relations.

For citation recommendation evaluation, I used a test collection with 274 papers. The selected papers met the following conditions: (1) the selected papers were excluded from the 45,372 publication candidate citation collection; (2) each selected paper had more than 15 citations from the candidate citation collection, and (3) each paper's abstract had at least 150 words. The abstract was used as a working context to represent information need, and I recommended citations from the candidate citation collection.

Ranking performance comparison

In the experiment, I applied proposed meta-paths for chronological citation recommendation.

I used test paper's original citations as ground truth with the mention times as citation importance. I also split each test paper's citations into eight time slices according cited paper's publication date. Meanwhile, I employed the following baseline feature groups. 1. **PageRank**: Apply classical PagRank algorithm in paper citation network (query independent). 2. **BM25**: BM25 model for test query. 3. **Language Model with Dirichlet prior smoothing (LM-D)**: Language Model with Dirichlet smoothing for test query. 4. **Language Model with Jelinek-Mercer smoothing (LM-JM)**: Language Model with Jelinek-Mercer smoothing for test query. For each baseline feature, I would first generate the whole ranked paper list, then split the list into eight time slices.

As Table 3 shows, experiment result is promising, there are four meta-paths that outperform all the baseline algorithms with averaged MAP indicator, and all of them are significantly better (with t-test $p<0.005$ for averaged MAP in all evaluated time slices). Meanwhile, there are also four meta-paths that outperform all the baseline algorithms with averaged nDCG indicator, three of them (Meta-Path 1, Meta-Ptah 4 and Meta-Path 5) are significantly better (with t-test $p<0.005$ for averaged nDCG in all evaluated time slices).

5. ISSUES FOR DISCUSSION

My study is still preliminary, there are several research issues need to be discussed:

(1) The quality of experiment dataset. After splitting into different time slices, the citations of test corpus is sparse in some time slices, which may cause "bias" for evaluation (this problem is more critical in more recent slices), is there any better solution to solve this problem? (2) I plan to extract more relations, adjust the weight on edges, implement more meta-paths and use them as ranking fea-

Table 2: The meta-path for chronological citation recommendation

No.					Meta-Path	Publication Ranking Hypothesis
1					$W^* \xrightarrow{e} P_{time} \xrightarrow{cite} P_{time}{}^?$	The candidate paper is important, if the candidate paper is cited by the papers have the important words in the query
2					$T_{time}{}^* \xrightarrow{cite} T_{time} \xrightarrow{cont} P_{time}{}^?$	The candidate paper is important, if the candidate paper contributed the historical topics which are cited by the related historical topics of query
3					$W^* \xrightarrow{e} P_{time}{}^? \xrightarrow{r} T_{time}{}^*$	The·candidate paper is important, if the important word in the query is important to the candidate paper, and the candidate paper is also very related to the related historical topics of query
4					$W^* \xrightarrow{e} P_{time} \xrightarrow{cite} P_{time}{}^? \xleftarrow{cont} T_{time}{}^*$	The candidate paper is important, if the candidate paper is cited by the papers which not only have important word in the query but also contribute the related historical topics of query
5					$W^* \xrightarrow{e} P_{time}{}^? \xleftarrow{cite} P_{time} \xrightarrow{r} T_{time}{}^*$	The candidate paper is important, if the candidate paper has important word in the query and is cited by the papers which are related to the related historical topics of query
6					$T_{time}{}^* \xrightarrow{cite} T_{time} \xleftarrow{r} P_{time}{}^? \xrightarrow{infl} T_{time} \xleftarrow{cite} T_{time}{}^*$ $T_{time}{}^* \xrightarrow{cite} T_{time} \overset{cont}{\nearrow} \quad \overset{e}{\nwarrow} W^*$	The candidate paper is important, if the important word in query also is important to the candidate paper or the candidate paper is related to or has influence on or contributes the historical topics which are cited by the related historical topics of query

word information time-decay citation information time-decay topic citation information dynamic topic-based information

Table 3: The Average MAP and nDCG Performance

					MAP10	MAP30	MAP50
				PageRank	0.012500	0.021829	0.028700
				BM25	0.012500	0.015200	0.016114
				LM-D	0.013329	0.015200	0.016129
				LM-JM	0.011229	0.014286	0.015143
				Meta-Path 1	**0.029057***	**0.045514***	**0.055686***
				Meta-Path 2	0.010914	0.019286	0.024671
				Meta-Path 3	0.007071	0.010214	0.011471
				Meta-Path 4	0.026100	0.043857	0.052757
				Meta-Path 5	0.028871	0.038186	0.044429
				Meta-Path 6	0.026886	0.030471	0.032271
					nDCG@10	nDCG@30	nDCG@50
				PageRank	0.022500	0.025900	0.032429
				BM25	0.015129	0.024557	0.025529
				LM-D	0.020229	0.025571	0.027886
				LM-JM	0.019043	0.022557	0.023814
				Meta-Path 1	0.029371	0.037571	0.044329
				Meta-Path 2	0.020243	0.023743	0.031857
				Meta-Path 3	0.024557	0.027471	0.030157
				Meta-Path 4	0.033643	**0.054529***	0.062286
				Meta-Path 5	**0.044486***	0.053257	**0.064800***
				Meta-Path 6	0.040643	0.047643	0.051043

* The best result

tures to apply "Learning to Rank" algorithm to achieve better performance, which model will be suitable for this problem? (3) Is there a better evaluation method to address the chronological citation recommendation problem? (4) Can I explore more sophisticated graph mining methods for chronological citation recommendation?

6. ACKNOWLEDGMENTS

This work is sponsored by the National Natural Science Foundation of China (No. 61202232 and No. 71271034) and China Postdoctoral Science Foundation(2014M551063).

7. REFERENCES

[1] David M Blei and John D Lafferty. Dynamic topic models. In *Proceedings of the 23rd international conference on Machine learning*, pages 113–120. ACM, 2006.

[2] David M Blei, Andrew Y Ng, and Michael I Jordan. Latent dirichlet allocation. *the Journal of machine Learning research*, 3:993–1022, 2003.

[3] Peter Brusilovsky, Oliviero Stock, and Carlo Strapparava. *Adaptive hypermedia and adaptive Web-based systems*. Springer, 2000.

[4] Christopher JC Burges. From ranknet to lambdarank to lambdamart: An overview. *Learning*, 11:23–581, 2010.

[5] Sean Gerrish and David M Blei. A language-based approach to measuring scholarly impact. In *Proceedings of the 27th International Conference on Machine Learning (ICML-10)*, pages 375–382, 2010.

[6] Zhuoren Jiang, Xiaozhong Liu, and Liangcai Gao. Dynamic topic/citation influence modeling for chronological citation recommendation. In *Proceedings of the 5th International Workshop on Web-scale Knowledge Representation Retrieval & Reasoning*, pages 15–18. ACM, 2014.

[7] Ni Lao and William W Cohen. Relational retrieval using a combination of path-constrained random walks. *Machine learning*, 81(1):53–67, 2010.

[8] Tie-Yan Liu. Learning to rank for information retrieval. *Foundations and Trends in Information Retrieval*, 3(3):225–331, 2009.

[9] Xiaozhong Liu, Yingying Yu, Chun Guo, Yizhou Sun, and Liangcai Gao. Full-text based context-rich heterogeneous network mining approach for citation recommendation full-text based context-rich heterogeneous network mining approach for citation recommendation full-text based context-rich heterogeneous network mining approach for citation recommendation. In *Joint Conference on Digital Libraries*, 2014.

[10] Xiaozhong Liu, Jinsong Zhang, and Chun Guo. Full-text citation analysis: A new method to enhance scholarly networks. *Journal of the American Society for Information Science and Technology*, 64(9):1852–1863, 2013.

[11] Donald Metzler and W Bruce Croft. Linear feature-based models for information retrieval. *Information Retrieval*, 10(3):257–274, 2007.

[12] Daniel Ramage, David Hall, Ramesh Nallapati, and Christopher D Manning. Labeled lda: A supervised topic model for credit attribution in multi-labeled corpora. In *Proceedings of the 2009 Conference on Empirical Methods in Natural Language Processing: Volume 1-Volume 1*, pages 248–256. Association for Computational Linguistics, 2009.

[13] Xiaolin Shi, Jure Leskovec, and Daniel A McFarland. Citing for high impact. In *Proceedings of the 10th annual joint conference on Digital libraries*, pages 49–58. ACM, 2010.

[14] Y. Sun, J. Han, X. Yan, P. S. Yu, and T. Wu. PathSim: Meta path-based top-k similarity search in heterogeneous information networks. In *Proc. 2011 Int. Conf. Very Large Data Bases (VLDB'11)*, Seattle, WA, 2011.

[15] Dylan Walker, Huafeng Xie, Koon-Kiu Yan, and Sergei Maslov. Ranking scientific publications using a model of network traffic. *Journal of Statistical Mechanics: Theory and Experiment*, 2007(06):P06010, 2007.

[16] Scott White and Padhraic Smyth. Algorithms for estimating relative importance in networks. In *Proceedings of the ninth ACM SIGKDD international conference on Knowledge discovery and data mining*, pages 266–275. ACM, 2003.

[17] Jun Xu and Hang Li. Adarank: a boosting algorithm for information retrieval. In *Proceedings of the 30th annual international ACM SIGIR conference on Research and development in information retrieval*, pages 391–398. ACM, 2007.

Topics, Tasks & Beyond: Learning Representations for Personalization

Rishabh Mehrotra
Dept of Computer Science,
University College London
London, UK
r.mehrotra@cs.ucl.ac.uk

ABSTRACT

Accurate understanding of a user's interests, preferences and behaviours is possibly one of the most critical research challenges faced while developing personalized systems for behavior targeting and information access. We intend to develop comprehensive latent variable models for web search personalization which jointly models user's topical interests along with user's click based relevance preferences while at the same time taking into account user's intended search tasks along with information about other similar users. We further augment this model by incorporating topic-level relevance parameters, which, to the best of our knowledge, is the first attempt at modeling result ranking preferences at the topic level. Additionally, we intend to explore the possibility of modeling users in terms of the search tasks they perform thereby coupling users' topical interests with their search task behavior to learn user representations. Finally, we wish to evaluate the proposition of extending user representations to hierarchical structures as an alternative to existing flat representations. The evaluation of these alternative approaches for user modeling is based on their performance on a variety of tasks such as collaborative query recommendations, user cohort modeling and search result personalization. This proposal provides the motivation to pursue these research directions, summarizes key research problems being targeted, glances through potential ways of tackling these research challenges and highlights some initial results obtained.

Categories and Subject Descriptors

H.3.3 [**Information Storage And Retrieval**]: Information Search and Retrieval—*User Modelling*

Keywords

User modelling; Personalization; Latent Variable Models; Search Tasks

WSDM'15, February 2–6, 2015, Shanghai, China.

http://dx.doi.org/10.1145/2684822.2697037.

1. INTRODUCTION

Personalization has become an important research topic in machine learning fuelled in part by its major significance in e-commerce and other businesses/services that try to tailor to user-specific needs or preferences. Online products, news, search, media, advertisement, user interfaces, and to a lesser extent healthcare, are several of the areas that have depended on some form of personalization to improve satisfaction or business goals in general. In order to address personalization problems machine learning has long relied on tools such as collaborative filtering (matrix factorization) and models originally developed not necessarily for personalization. However, even though the data available for personalization has grown in richness and size, and the available processing power has also increased, the basic tenet for the methods used has not changed in a major way.

As a consumer of the informational content, different users have distinct preferences of information for decision making; thus accurately understanding their respective information needs and decision preferences is crucial for providing effective decision support. While human behaviours are largely determined by their own goals and preferences, the mined knowledge reveals users' underlying intentions and behaviour patterns, which provide unique signals for human centric optimization and personalization. Web search personalization has recently received a lot of attention by the research community. Personalized search leverages information about an individual to identify the most relevant recommendations for that person. A challenge for personalization is in collecting user profiles that are sufficiently rich to be useful in settings such as result ranking, query recommendations, etc, while balancing privacy concerns.

Accurate understanding of a user's search interests and preferences is arguably one of the most critical research challenges in web search. Existing work on user level personalization has made use of ODP related topical categories or has relied heavily on term based representation of user profiles. There are several challenges with topical analysis of user actions. Most of existing work on analyses user's topical interests and his/her associated click patterns in an isolated manner. We should note that both queries and click-throughs convey useful clues about user's search intent. Capitalizing on both 1) user's topical interests and 2) user's unique result ranking preference should provide a comprehensive understanding of user's search intent. While personalization techniques rely heavily on using ODP-like topic categories, such a method restricts topic-coverage as search logs offer much richer content in terms of the number of topics spanned as well as the granularity level of the topics. Personalization models which learns latent topics in an unsupervised manner from search logs would help capture topical interests embedded in search logs. Efficient user profiles can then be generated by modeling users by a mixture of interests (/topics) and identifying distinct ranking preferences of individual users based on his click patterns.

Furthermore, it should be noted that users interact with search engines to accomplish some task such as *arrange a trip*, *plan a wedding* etc. Such broad requirements prompts the use of multiple queries, sometimes spanning multiple sessions. We define search tasks as the group of queries a user issues to accomplish such overall intended task and advocate the use of such search tasks to build individual user models. We postulate that in a web search setting, a user representation based on the search tasks users' perform would better capture user actions, interests and preferences.

We intend to evaluate the usefulness of deviating from the traditional way of representing users based on a flat d-dimensional representation to user modeling over hierarchies. One possibility is to develop models which learn hierarchical models of user's intended tasks and learn user representations on top of such hierarchies. Overall, we intend to develop comprehensive latent variable models for user modelling and personalization which is able to capture all these goals in a fully unsupervised fashion. We review existing work in Section 2 while the specific research challenges along with possible solutions are discussed in Section 3. Section 4 discusses the results obtained so far while Section 5 highlights key issues for discussion at the consortium.

2. RELATED WORK

Personalizing web search has received a lot of attention by the research community. Prior work has primarily focused on mining general search behaviours but has considerably ignored the importance of identifying individual user's search preferences as well as user variability. A prominent line of prior research uses long-term histories to directly improve retrieval effectiveness. Various authors have considered topic-based representations for personalization [5][6][7] making use of hand-picked ODP topical categories. While such topics are easily specified, much human effort is required in labelling queries for each topic. ODP categories based methods restricts topic coverage in a major way as search logs offer much richer content both in terms of the number of topics involved as well as the granularity level of each topic.

Another line of research in web search personalization has focused on using term based representations for user profiles. Authors in [8] build user interests profiles using terms extracted from user's browsing history following which the term weights are generated using different weighing schemes. While query terms are representative of user interests, they often limit the scope of personalization as different users inherently follow different distributions over words and queries belonging to the same topic/interest might not contain any over-lapping terms. Finding similar users and building user cohorts becomes difficult in such settings.

Finally, very recently, authors in [9] have proposed a generative model which models users as a mixture over latent user groups wherein each group shares a common distribution over queries and a common click preference pattern. While it is tempting to group users into categories, this grouping tends to be rather limited when it comes to large number of users and large amount of behavioural data. An inflation in the number of user clusters decreases the interpretability of these user groups. Also, the proposed model is limiting in the sense that it does not capture the idea that a user might share topical interests with other users in the group but have a different click preferences in terms of what kind of documents the user ideally prefers and clicks.

3. RESEARCH CHALLENGES

Overall, the goal of this research is to develop latent variable models which succinctly represent user information and help in building user profiles for use in personalization based services. We next describe the different research questions we intend to answer with this research.

3.1 Joint model of user interests with click preferences

We intend to propose a latent variable model which captures user's interests in an unsupervised manner wherein a user is characterized by a mixture of interests (/topics) and distinct ranking preferences of individual users are identified based on his click patterns. Our model is able to learn these latent topical interests from search logs by attempting to describe the available data instead of manually fixing the topics beforehand. Such a topical mixture carries considerably more information than user clusters with users sharing topical interests. The click preference of each user is portrayed by the corresponding relative importance of the ranking features, which leads to distinct click patterns over the returned documents. For example, for the same query, some user may want high authority websites (i.e., larger weight on the pagerank score), while the other user may prefer the documents better matched with their queries (e.g., larger weight on the relevance features such as BM25).

Our strategy is thus to describe users as a mixture of topics and to assume that each search task is motivated by choosing a topic of interest first and subsequently a query to describe that search task from the catalogue of words consistent with that particular interest(/topic). Once the query is issues, based on the documents clicked by the user, our model updates the parameters associated with user's click preferences.

3.1.1 *Incorporating Topic-level preference*

As a next step, we augment the framework proposed above by incorporating topic-level click patterns shared by queries belonging to each topic. We postulate that similar to how different users might prefer different ranking features, topics themselves can have an inherent preference over click patterns. Queries belonging to topics like education might warrant documents which better match the query to rank higher while some other topic like News might warrant high authority websites to rank higher than others. We aim to capture this topic-level feature ranking preference by incorporating a parameter β_t for each topic t which would correspond to the relative importance of ranking features for queries arising from the particular topic t.

3.2 Modelling users in terms of search tasks

Existing user modelling methods for web search rely heavily on per user topical interests and hence, fail to differentiate between users which share similar topical interests. We postulate that in web search setting, search logs contain information about various actions that users perform and profiling users based on search tasks would better capture the heterogeneity in user information. Our goal here is to use search log data to create a list of global search tasks. One possible way is to follow the approach of task discovery as proposed in [?] wherein a task is defined as the maximal subsequence of possibly non-consecutive queries in referring to the same latent user need which makes the set of all user tasks a partitioning of the set of all user queries. We formulate the task discovery problem as follows: given a query log QL and a user u, let T_u be the set of user tasks discovered by a query partitioning scheme π; the user task discovery problem can then be described as finding the best query partitioning strategy π^* that approximates the actual set of user tasks Θ such that:

$$\pi^* = argmax_{\pi} \xi(\Theta, T, \pi) \tag{1}$$

where function $\xi(.)$ is an accuracy measure which evaluates how well the query partitioning strategy π approximates the actual user tasks Θ. We use cosine similarity to measure this accuracy. This step is followed by clustering the user tasks identified to obtain universal tasks across all users. The final set of user tasks obtained are represented by a set of query terms and henceforth define the set of tasks used for experiments.

Based on the extracted search tasks, we construct a user-task association matrix which represents the search tasks users have been involved with. For each user u_i, we create a bag-of-queries representation from the list of queries issued by the user and compare each user with each of these search tasks t_j obtained above. For each user-task $<u_i, t_j>$ pair, we populate the corresponding value in the user-task association matrix (R) with the cosine similarity score (r_{ij}) we obtain for the pair. For tasks in which users do not have any matching queries, we assign a score of 0 to the corresponding pair. We model the user-task association in terms of probabilistic matrix factorization problem and learn latent vector representation for each user from the user-task association matrix by fitting a probabilistic model.

We further augment our task based user profiles by incorporating user's topical interest profiles and next describe our tensor based approach for the joint model.

3.3 Coupling Tasks & Topics

Traditional approach to user modelling have heavily relied on building user's topical profiles and developing personalized systems based on the learnt topical profiles. We augment our task based user representation model with user's topical information by coupling the topical interest with task based information in the form of a tensor and learning user profiles based on the decomposition of the $< user, topic, task >$ tensor. We next describe the overall system in detail.

3.3.1 Learning Topical Interest Profiles

Given user's history of search queries, we aim to develop a topic interest model which captures user's interest distribution over different topics. While most of existing techniques rely heavily on using ODP-like topic categories for modeling user's topical interests, such methods severely restrict topic-coverage as search logs offer much richer content in terms of the number of topics spanned as well as the granularity level of the topics - models which learns latent topics in an unsupervised manner from search logs would help capture topical interests embedded in search logs. We make use of the Latent Dirichlet Allocation model to learn the latent set of topics embedded in the search log. We hypothesize that each search query is motivated by choosing a topic of interest first and subsequently a query is issued to describe that search need from the catalogue of words consistent with that particular topic. Based on this intuition, we learn a LDA based topic model and use the learnt model to do topical inference for each user to obtain a topic-distribution for the user over the set of learnt topics. We refer to this distribution as a user's ***topical profile***.

3.3.2 Coupling Topics & Tasks

Our main intuition behind leveraging both the topical profile as well as the search task profile of users is to better differentiate between users who share similar topical profiles. Consider the task of personalizing search results for a query like "building algorithm for user models". This query broadly belongs to the computer science topic and a software engineer would expect a different set of results than a PhD researcher. Indeed, a software engineer performs different search tasks than a researcher and by leveraging their search task information, the user model could help in ranking results accordingly. We formulate this intuition in our model by coupling task information with topical information on a per-user basis. We construct a 3-mode tensor $< user, topic, task >$ to jointly capture user's topical as well as search task based information. Next, we briefly describe the tensor formulation:

3.3.3 Constructing $< user, topic, task >$ Affinity Tensor

To jointly model the user's topical and task preferences, we construct a 3-mode tensor - users, topics and tasks. A third order tensor can be represented as $T \in \Re^{I_1 \times I_2 \times I_3}$ with each element of the tensor denoted as $t_{i,j,k}$ with $i \in (1, I_1)$, $j \in (1, I_2)$ and $k \in (1, I_3)$. The symbol $\circ$ represents the vector outer product. Each element of our tensor ($T \in \Re^{I_1 \times I_2 \times I_3}$), $t_{i,j,k}$ defines user i's combined task based and topical preference - a user's participation in a certain task gets weighted by his topical affinity, thereby coupling his task based and topical affinity. More formally, we define each tensor-component value as follows:

$$t_{i,j,k} = U_{i_{topic_j}} \times U_{i_{task_k}} \tag{2}$$

where $U_{i_{topic_j}}$ is user U_i's topical affinity for topic j obtained from the LDA model learnt before while $U_{i_{task_k}}$ represents the task affinity for user U_i's for search task k obtained in earlier the user-task association phase. I_1, I_2, I_3 are the different dimensions of the different modes of the tensor - in our case, these represent the number of users, number of topics and the number of search tasks extracted respectively. Thus, for each user we construct his coupled task-topic affinity value and populate the corresponding component in the tensor T.

3.3.4 Tensor Decomposition

Tensor decomposition methods are regarded as higher-order equivalents to matrix decompositions. The PARAFAC tensor decomposition [?] allows us to leverage connections between the different users across different topics and different search tasks. By PARAFAC, the input tensors are transformed into Kruskal tensors, a sum of rank-one-tensors. Formally, the tensor $T \in \Re^{I_1 \times I_2 \times I_3}$ is decomposed into com-

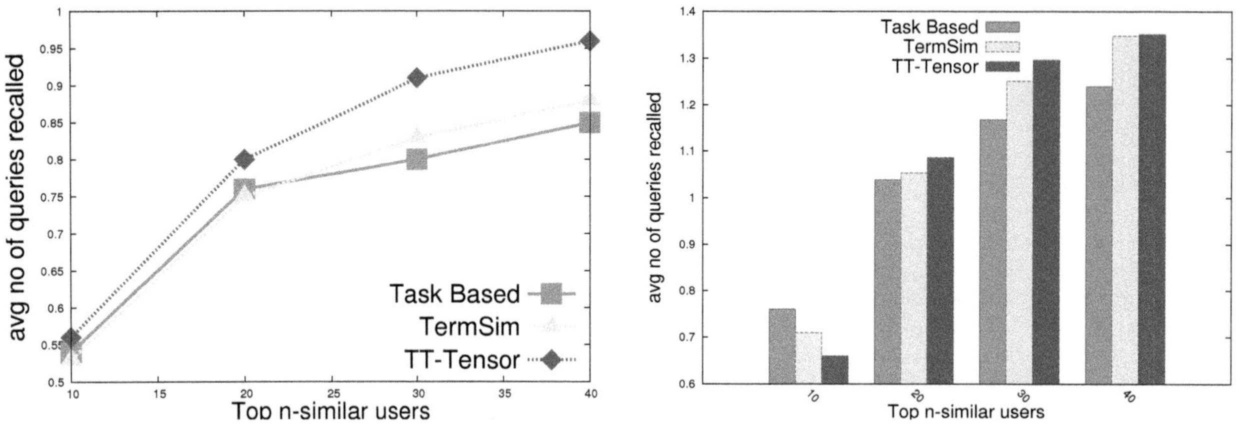

Figure 1: Performance on Collaborative Query Recommendation (left figure: top-10 recommended queries & right figure: top-20 recommended queries). The average number of query matches between the recommended set of queries and user's own test set of (unseen) queries is plotted against the number of similar users considered n where n refers to the number of similar users considered.

ponent matrices $U \in \Re^{I_1 \times d}$, $T \in \Re^{I_2 \times d}$ and $S \in \Re^{I_3 \times d}$ and d principal factors λ_i in descending order. Via these, tensor T can be written as a Kruskal tensor by:

$$T \approx \Sigma_{k=1}^{d} \lambda_k \cdot U^k \circ T^k \circ S^k \quad (3)$$

where λ_k denotes the k-th principal factor. The goal is to compute a decomposition with d-components that best approximates our tensor T, i.e., to find

$$min_{\widetilde{T}} \|T - \widetilde{T}\| \quad (4)$$

such that

$$\widetilde{T} = \Sigma_{k=1}^{d} \lambda_k \cdot U^k \circ T^k \circ S^k \quad (5)$$

We make use of the Alternating Least Squares (ALS) approach to solve the above objective - having fixed all but one matrix, the problem reduces to a linear least-squares problem. In our experiments, we pre-assume a value of $d = 20$ thereby making each user representation a 20-dimensional vector which we use for our experiments.

Overall, the above formulation helps us to couple user's topical interests with their search task associations and learn a user representation based on this coupled tensor. This tensor decomposition based user modelling approach allows us to use multi-modal user information and leverage insights from each of them while learning user representations. An important characteristic of the proposed tensor based approach is that this method is generic enough and allows us to plug-in other sources of user information - click models, data from advertisement responses, etc.

3.4 Extending user representations to hierarchies

The user modeling techniques described above represent users in a flat d-dimensional representation so far. We postulate that hierarchical representations for users would better capture the heterogeneity in user information and aid in personalization. The challenges in moving from a flat representation to a hierarchical are many including coming up with algorithms to find similarity functions which make use of non-flat hierarchical structure based representations. We intend to extend our work to include more structure based user representations and compare them against traditional ways of representing users.

4. PROGRESS SO FAR

The research so far has focused on evaluating the benefits of learning user profiles based on the search tasks users are involved with. We postulate that in a web search setting, a user representation based on the search tasks users' perform would better capture user actions, interests and preferences. Given a search log, we extract search tasks performed by users and find user representations based on these tasks. More specifically, we construct a user-task association matrix and borrow insights from *Collaborative Filtering* to learn a low-dimensional factor model wherein the actions/interests/preferences of a user are determined by a small number of latent factors. By applying probabilistic matrix factorization to the user-task association matrix, we learn *task-based user representations* for each user.

A good user profile for query recommendation should capture a user's specific interests & informational needs. Based on this intuition, we evaluate performance of the the task-based user modeling approach on *Collaborative Query Recommendation* where the goal is to recommend queries to a user based on queries issued by similar users. We calculate the weighted frequency of a candidate query for 10 most similar users of the target user u, and selected the top n queries as recommendation. We make use of the AOL log dataset which consists of ~20M web queries collected over three months and use data for about ~1200 users who have issued more than 550 queries. We run our Task Discovery algorithm on the set of queries for each of these users which results in a total of ~0.12M tasks which we cluster using cosine similarity score to obtain a set of 1529 search tasks using which we create the user-task association matrix. Our baseline(*TermSim*) is a method that only uses bag-of-words based representation for each user where the terms are extracted from user queries & similar users found using cosine similarity between each user's bag-of-word based representations. We consider the test-set of queries in the target user as relevant, and computed average number of relevant queries matched in the recommendation query set as the performance metric.

We plot the average number of query matches between the recommended set of queries and user's own test set of (unseen) queries against the number of similar users considered n where n refers to the top-10 (left) and top-20 (right) query suggestions from n-most similar users. Our initial results [14] (Figure 1) show that the proposed Topic-Task Tensor based user modelling approach(*TT-Tensor*) performs better than *TermSim* as well as *TaskBased* which demonstrates that combining search task information with user's topical interests thus help us better capture different aspects of user profiles and can serve as potent user modelling tools. Since *TermSim* relies strictly on term matching for measuring user similarities, its coverage is limited: it might not capture insights for the users with too few queries or those who shared the same search interest but issued different queries or performed different tasks. Task based user modelling can help in better differentiating between users which have similar topical interests but perform different tasks. The proposed tensor based approach combines the best of both the worlds and hence was able to leverage the topical user profile information with the task aspect.

5. ISSUES FOR DISCUSSION

The major issue for discussion revolves around the fallacies in existing approaches to personalization and understanding realistic expectations from personalization systems. The question of what makes a good personalization system needs to be addressed which would in itself set some basic standards for future personalization systems and help streamline the research in personalization. Another important issue worth deliberation is the role of evaluation in personalization. While industrial researchers have access to a massive user centric data, the amount of research possible from outside the industry in an academic setting is rather limited. How can we negate this factor and ways of coming up with possible remedies is worth discussing. Additionally, while the current research plan is majorly motivated for web search based personalization, an important question is how well these personalization approaches generalize to other domains. Can we come up with domain-agnostic personalization techniques? Would transfer learning play a role in this regard? Should we start looking at cross-domain personalization techniques to harness the rich multi-domain user data we currently have.

6. CONCLUSION

Understanding preferences and informational needs of users is a complex task. In this research, we intend to propose techniques of user modeling aimed at capturing the vast heterogeneity among users thereby helping in developing better personalized systems. The proposed research aims to develop varied user models based on their informational preferences, their topical interests as well as their search task behaviours alongside extending traditional flat representations to richer hierarchies.

7. ACKNOWLEDGEMENTS

This work was supported in part by a Google Faculty Research Award.

8. REFERENCES

1 Andrew Postlewaite. Social norms and social assets. Annual Review of Economics, 3:239-259, 2011.

2 Ehsan Abbasnejad, Scott Sanner, Edwin V. Bonilla, Pascal Poupart: Learning Community-Based Preferences via Dirichlet Process Mixtures of Gaussian Processes. IJCAI 2013.

3 White, R. W., Chu, W., Hassan, A., He, X., Song, Y., Wang, H. (2013, May). Enhancing personalized search by mining and modeling task behavior. In Proceedings of the 22nd international conference on World Wide Web (pp. 1411-1420). International World Wide Web Conferences Steering Committee.

4 Blundell, C., Teh, Y. W. (2013). Bayesian Hierarchical Community Discovery. In Advances in Neural Information Processing Systems (NIPS 2013) (pp. 1601-1609).

5 Kim, Jin Young, Kevyn Collins-Thompson, Paul N. Bennett, and Susan T. Dumais. "Characterizing web content, user interests, and search behavior by reading level and topic." In Proceedings of the fifth ACM international conference on Web search and data mining, pp. 213-222. ACM, 2012.

6 White, Ryen W., Wei Chu, Ahmed Hassan, Xiaodong He, Yang Song, and Hongning Wang. "Enhancing personalized search by mining and modeling task behavior." In Proceedings of the 22nd international conference on World Wide Web, pp. 1411-1420. International World Wide Web Conferences Steering Committee, 2013.

7 Bennett, Paul N., Ryen W. White, Wei Chu, Susan T. Dumais, Peter Bailey, Fedor Borisyuk, and Xiaoyuan Cui. "Modeling the impact of short-and long-term behavior on search personalization." In Proceedings of the 35th international ACM SIGIR conference on Research and development in information retrieval, pp. 185-194. ACM, 2012.

8 Matthijs, Nicolaas, and Filip Radlinski. "Personalizing web search using long term browsing history." In Proceedings of the fourth ACM international conference on Web search and data mining, pp. 25-34. ACM, 2011.

9 Wang, Hongning, ChengXiang Zhai, Feng Liang, Anlei Dong, and Yi Chang. "User Modeling in Search Logs via a Nonparametric Bayesian Approach." (WSDM 2014).

10 Teh, Yee Whye, Michael I. Jordan, Matthew J. Beal, and David M. Blei. "Sharing Clusters among Related Groups: Hierarchical Dirichlet Processes." In NIPS.

11 Wang, Chong, John W. Paisley, and David M. Blei. "Online variational inference for the hierarchical Dirichlet process." In International Conference on Artificial Intelligence and Statistics, (AISTATS 2011) pp. 752-760. 2011.

12 Ahmed, Amr, Yucheng Low, Mohamed Aly, Vanja Josifovski, and Alexander J. Smola. "Scalable distributed inference of dynamic user interests for behavioral targeting." In Proceedings of the 17th ACM SIGKDD international conference on Knowledge discovery and data mining, pp. 114-122. ACM, 2011.

13 D. Blackwell and J. MacQueen. Ferguson distributions via polya urn schemes. The Annals of Statistics, 1973.

14 R. Mehrotra, E. Yilmaz and M. Verma. "Task-Based User Modelling for Personalization via Probabilistic Matrix Factorization." In Proceedings of the 8th ACM Conference on Recommender Systems (RecSys), 2014.

Author Index

www.ingramcontent.com/pod-product-compliance
Ingram Content Group UK Ltd.
Pitfield, Milton Keynes, MK11 3LW, UK
UKHW051413290926
15471UKWH00009B/1589